The philosophical works of Francis Bacon, Baron of Verulam, ... methodized, and made English, from the originals, ... In three volumes. By Peter Shaw, ... Volume 1 of 3

Francis Bacon

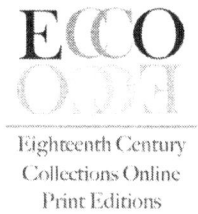

Gale ECCO Print Editions

Relive history with *Eighteenth Century Collections Online*, now available in print for the independent historian and collector. This series includes the most significant English-language and foreign-language works printed in Great Britain during the eighteenth century, and is organized in seven different subject areas including literature and language; medicine, science, and technology; and religion and philosophy. The collection also includes thousands of important works from the Americas.

The eighteenth century has been called "The Age of Enlightenment." It was a period of rapid advance in print culture and publishing, in world exploration, and in the rapid growth of science and technology – all of which had a profound impact on the political and cultural landscape. At the end of the century the American Revolution, French Revolution and Industrial Revolution, perhaps three of the most significant events in modern history, set in motion developments that eventually dominated world political, economic, and social life.

In a groundbreaking effort, Gale initiated a revolution of its own: digitization of epic proportions to preserve these invaluable works in the largest online archive of its kind. Contributions from major world libraries constitute over 175,000 original printed works. Scanned images of the actual pages, rather than transcriptions, recreate the works *as they first appeared.*

Now for the first time, these high-quality digital scans of original works are available via print-on-demand, making them readily accessible to libraries, students, independent scholars, and readers of all ages.

For our initial release we have created seven robust collections to form one the world's most comprehensive catalogs of 18th century works.

Initial Gale ECCO Print Editions collections include:

History and Geography
Rich in titles on English life and social history, this collection spans the world as it was known to eighteenth-century historians and explorers. Titles include a wealth of travel accounts and diaries, histories of nations from throughout the world, and maps and charts of a world that was still being discovered. Students of the War of American Independence will find fascinating accounts from the British side of conflict.

Social Science

Delve into what it was like to live during the eighteenth century by reading the first-hand accounts of everyday people, including city dwellers and farmers, businessmen and bankers, artisans and merchants, artists and their patrons, politicians and their constituents. Original texts make the American, French, and Industrial revolutions vividly contemporary.

Medicine, Science and Technology

Medical theory and practice of the 1700s developed rapidly, as is evidenced by the extensive collection, which includes descriptions of diseases, their conditions, and treatments. Books on science and technology, agriculture, military technology, natural philosophy, even cookbooks, are all contained here.

Literature and Language

Western literary study flows out of eighteenth-century works by Alexander Pope, Daniel Defoe, Henry Fielding, Frances Burney, Denis Diderot, Johann Gottfried Herder, Johann Wolfgang von Goethe, and others. Experience the birth of the modern novel, or compare the development of language using dictionaries and grammar discourses.

Religion and Philosophy

The Age of Enlightenment profoundly enriched religious and philosophical understanding and continues to influence present-day thinking. Works collected here include masterpieces by David Hume, Immanuel Kant, and Jean-Jacques Rousseau, as well as religious sermons and moral debates on the issues of the day, such as the slave trade. The Age of Reason saw conflict between Protestantism and Catholicism transformed into one between faith and logic -- a debate that continues in the twenty-first century.

Law and Reference

This collection reveals the history of English common law and Empire law in a vastly changing world of British expansion. Dominating the legal field is the *Commentaries of the Law of England* by Sir William Blackstone, which first appeared in 1765. Reference works such as almanacs and catalogues continue to educate us by revealing the day-to-day workings of society.

Fine Arts

The eighteenth-century fascination with Greek and Roman antiquity followed the systematic excavation of the ruins at Pompeii and Herculaneum in southern Italy; and after 1750 a neoclassical style dominated all artistic fields. The titles here trace developments in mostly English-language works on painting, sculpture, architecture, music, theater, and other disciplines. Instructional works on musical instruments, catalogs of art objects, comic operas, and more are also included.

The BiblioLife Network

This project was made possible in part by the BiblioLife Network (BLN), a project aimed at addressing some of the huge challenges facing book preservationists around the world. The BLN includes libraries, library networks, archives, subject matter experts, online communities and library service providers. We believe every book ever published should be available as a high-quality print reproduction; printed on-demand anywhere in the world. This insures the ongoing accessibility of the content and helps generate sustainable revenue for the libraries and organizations that work to preserve these important materials.

The following book is in the "public domain" and represents an authentic reproduction of the text as printed by the original publisher. While we have attempted to accurately maintain the integrity of the original work, there are sometimes problems with the original work or the micro-film from which the books were digitized. This can result in minor errors in reproduction. Possible imperfections include missing and blurred pages, poor pictures, markings and other reproduction issues beyond our control. Because this work is culturally important, we have made it available as part of our commitment to protecting, preserving, and promoting the world's literature.

GUIDE TO FOLD-OUTS MAPS and OVERSIZED IMAGES

The book you are reading was digitized from microfilm captured over the past thirty to forty years. Years after the creation of the original microfilm, the book was converted to digital files and made available in an online database.

In an online database, page images do not need to conform to the size restrictions found in a printed book. When converting these images back into a printed bound book, the page sizes are standardized in ways that maintain the detail of the original. For large images, such as fold-out maps, the original page image is split into two or more pages

Guidelines used to determine how to split the page image follows:

• Some images are split vertically; large images require vertical and horizontal splits.
• For horizontal splits, the content is split left to right.
• For vertical splits, the content is split from top to bottom.
• For both vertical and horizontal splits, the image is processed from top left to bottom right.

2436 97 16

THE

PHILOSOPHICAL WORKS

OF

FRANCIS BACON,

Baron of *Verulam,* Viscount *St. Albans,*

and LORD HIGH-CHANCELLOR of *England;*

Methodized, and made *English,* from the ORIGINALS,

WITH

OCCASIONAL NOTES, to EXPLAIN what is Obscure,

And shew how far the several PLANS of the AUTHOR,
for the Advancement of all the Parts of Knowledge,
have been executed to the present Time.

In THREE VOLUMES.

By *PETER SHAW,* M. D.

LONDON:

Printed for J. J. and P KNAPTON, D. MIDWINTER and A WARD,
A. BETTESWORTH and C HITCH, J. PEMBERTON, J. OSBORN
and T. LONGMAN, C. RIVINGTON, F. CLAY, J. BATLEY,
R. HETT, and T. HATCHETT. M.DCC.XXXIII.

THE

PHILOSOPHICAL WORKS

OF

FRANCIS BACON,

Baron of VERULAM, Viscount St. ALBANS,

AND

Lord High-Chancellor of *England;*

Methodized, and made *English*, from the ORIGINALS.

WITH

OCCASIONAL NOTES,

To explain what is obscure, and shew how far the several PLANS of the AUTHOR, for the Advancement of all the Parts of Knowledge, have been executed to the Present Time.

In THREE VOLUMES.

By *PETER SHAW*, M. D.

VOL. I.

Moniti Meliora.

LONDON

Printed for J. J. and P. KNAPTON, D. MIDWINTER and A WARD; A BETTESWORTH and C. HITCH; J PEMBERTON; J OSBORN and T. LONGMAN; C RIVINGTON; F. CLAY; J. BATLEY, R. HETT; and T. HATCHETT.

M DCC.XXXIII

T O

THE RIGHT HONOURABLE

HORATIO WALPOLE *Esq*;

One of his M A J E S T Y ' S Moſt
Honourable Privy-Council, *&c.*

S I R,

THE Philoſophical Works of the
Lord *Bacon*, here laid before You,
contain the nobleſt Scheme that, poſſibly, was ever advanced for the Good
of Mankind: tho' it has the misfortune
to remain unexecuted in moſt of its Articles.

[*A 2]   Whether

Whether this proceeds from any Fault in the Thing itſelf; or rather from a Want of being ſufficiently underſtood and regarded; muſt be left to Perſons of your approved Capacity and Judgment.

To render the whole Plan more eaſily intelligible, is the Deſign of the preſent *Edition*; and to procure it a proper Regard, the End of the preſent Addreſs.

The Labour I have beſtowed upon the Work, is humbly ſubmitted to your Cenſure. And, if I might ſpeak for my Author; he likewiſe wou'd be pleaſed with a Judge, who reſembles him ſo much in extenſive Knowledge, and great Application to Buſineſs.

Might I alſo ſpeak for the wiſer and better Part of the Nation; they wou'd
unani-

unanimoufly wifh this great Scheme under the Confideration of fo able a Perfon; who has already improved and executed very important Defigns for the Publick Good.   I am

S I R,

Your moft Obedient,

Humble Servant,

PETER SHAW.

GENERAL PREFACE.

THE *Lord* Bacon's *Philosophical Works were, by the Author, all intended to be in* Latin *accordingly he wrote most of them originally in that Language* [a], *and others, first wrote in* English, *he afterwards put into* Latin [b], *as he designed to have done the rest* [c], *with considerable Improvements and Corrections. So that those Philosophical Pieces of his, which he left only in* English, *are not to be looked upon as perfect, or as having received the degree of Perfection he purposed to give them*

This Observation may help to remove a light Prejudice in those, who, from having read the Lord Bacon's English *Pieces, conceive that he was not the Philosopher he is represented by the Learned; and especially by Foreigners, who appear to extol him in a superlative manner For, such a difference in Opinion seems principally owing to this, that one side has read only the* English, *and the other, only the* Latin *Works of the Author*

It is true indeed, that some of his best Pieces have been translated into English, *by other hands.* Dr. Wats *has given a Translation of the* de Augmentis Scientiarum [d]; *an anonymous Gentleman has given an Extract out of the* Novum Organum [e], *another*

A 2

Gentle-

---

[a] *Vz* the *Novum Organum,* the *History of Winds,* the *History of Life and Death,* the *History of Condensation and Rarifaction,* the *Piece de Sapientia Veterum,* the *Animated Astronomy,* the *Censure of Authors,* &c

[b] As the *Advancement of Learning,* and the *Essays*

[c] Such as the *New Atlantis, Sylva Sylvarum,* &c

[d] The *Advancement and Proficiency of Learning or the Partitions of Sciences Nine Books Written in Latin by the Lord Viscount St Albans,* &c Interpreted by *Gilbert Wats, London,* 1674

[e] The *Novum Organum* of the Lord Viscount *St Albans* epitomized, for the clearer understanding of his *Natural History* Translated, and taken out of the *Latin,* by *M D B D London,* 1676

Gentleman has given a Translation of the History of Winds[a], *another, with the Assistance of Dr.* Rawley, *a Translation of the* History *of* Life and Death[b], *after a much worse had been given before;* Sir Arthur Gorges *gave a Translation of the Piece* de Sapientia Veterum[c]; *and Dr* Willymott *a Translation of the* Essays[d] *and hence it might be hoped, that* English *Readers, as well as the* Learned, *and* Natives, *as well as* Foreigners, *should have formed a true Judgment of the Lord* Bacon's Philosophical Works *But here the Fate of the Author, and the* English *Reader, may deserve to be pitied - for among the several Translations above enumerated, there are but few that tolerably express the Sense and Meaning of the Author, and none, that acquaint the Reader with the whole of his Designs. Dr* Wats's *Translation of the* de Augmentis Scientiarum, *is by the Learned accounted low, flat, and incongruous, so as no way to give the Spirit, Vivacity, and Mind of the Author, or shew his Views in a tolerable Light. Whence, it were not easy to imagine that the Original should be so excellent, whilst the Copy was so wretched The Defects of this Performance having been observed long since, Dr* Rawley, *the Author's Chaplain, was importuned to give a better* English *Version of that noble Work, and rescue the Honour of his Patron[e]*

The English Extract, *or* Epitome, *of the* Novum Organum, *affords but a very faint, imperfect, and disadvantageous Idea of the* Plan, Design, *and* Discoveries, *of that extraordinary Piece, yet the Epitomizer seems, by his Preface, acquainted with the Author's general Views in that Work, and has given a short Account*

count

---

[a] The *Natural and Experimental History of Winds*, &c Translated into *English* by R G Gent London, 16-1

[b] *History, Natural and Experimental, of Life and Death* or of the *Prolongation of Life* Written by the Lord Viscount *St Albans* London, 1677

[c] The *Wisdom of the Ancients*, &c Done into *English* by Sir *Arthur Gorges*, Knt London, 1680

[d] *Lord Bacon's Essays* or *Counsels Moral and Civil* Translated from the *Latin* by *William Willymott*, LL D Fellow of *King's College* in *Cambridge*, and Master of a private School at *Isleworth* in *Middlesex* In two Volumes 8vo London, 1720

[e] " I is our humble Suit to you, and we do earnestly sollicit you, to give yourself the " trouble to correct the too much defective Translation of the *de Augmentis Scientiarum*, " which Dr *Wats* hath set forth It is a thousand pities, that so worthy a Piece should " lose its Grace and Credit by an ill Expositor, since those Persons who read that Trans- " lation, taking it for genuine, and upon that Presumption not regarding the *Latin* Edi- " tion, are hereby robbed of the Benefit, wh ch (if you would please to undertake the " Business they might receive This tendeth to the Dishonour of that Noble Lord, and " the Hindrance of the *Advancement of Learning*" Dr *Tenison's* Account of the Lord *Bacon's* Works, p 26, 27

count of them [a] . *but when he comes to translate and epitomize, he strangely mangles the sense, and defaces the whole; so that it cannot easily be known, or tolerably understood   Indeed the Design was imperfect; for the* Novum Organum *being entirely aphoristical, its Nature will not admit of epitomizing to any advantage; but, as the Epitomizer himself observed, rather requires a Comment.*

These

[a] " I need not recommend this useful Treatise, seeing that it proceeds from such a Genius, whose most trivial Conceptions have obtained the Esteem of his Age, not inferior in Learning to any of the former   He was a Person of a sound Judgment, sharp Wit, vast Comprehension, and of extraordinary Abilities, both natural and acquired   But I need not run over the Praises of a Person so well known amongst us, to gain a kind Reception and favourable Interpretation of this obscure, but useful Book   for the things therein contained are so excellent in themselves, and so well designed, that we may be inclinable of our own accord to embrace and peruse them

" The Author's Purpose is, to censure the Limitations of Sciences to the Bounds prescribed to us by the shallow Pates of some of former Ages, to discover the Mistakes of our Understandings, to point at the Sources from whence they proceed, to rectify the common Errors of Men, back'd by ill-grounded Axioms, to direct us to a right Interpretation of Nature's Mysteries, and to oblige us to settle our Judgments upon better and surer Principles than ordinary   his Purpose is to open us a Gate to a greater Proficiency and Improvement in all kinds of Learning, to pull down the Walls of Partition, and remove the *non plus ultra*, that we might sail to those *Indies* full of Gold and Jewels, I mean, the Sciences not yet discover'd to our World, and fetch from thence all the Rarities, the Knowledge, and Inventions, that may pleasure and benefit our human Life   For that purpose, he adviseth us not to take Things and Notions too much upon trust, but to ground our Belief upon Practice, and well-order'd Experience   He lays down several Principles, which may seem strange and new, but if they be rightly examined, we shall find them naturally proceeding from the Nature of Things

" I confess, the most excellent Conceptions are wrapped up in obscure Terms, and in such new-contrived Expressions, that King *James*, at the first perusal, judged this *Novum Organum* to be past all Mens Understanding   But we may consider, that a new Method, and new Things and Principles, deserve new Expressions, and that our learned Author speaks not to the Vulgar, but the Learned, to whom he discovers other Lands never found out before, and adviseth them to adventure to seek, and to proceed on, without minding the Discouragements and Prohibitions of our Predecessors in Learning

" This Treatise, therefore, was look'd upon as a seasonable Addition to his *Natural History*, but because the whole would have made it too voluminous, I have been desired to gather out such Observations and Directions, as might be answerable to that Subject   I must needs confess, after a serious Perusal, I did scarce know what was to be set aside   for all the Things therein contained, are so material and seasonable, that I have wonder'd that our *English Curiosi* have not had the desire to study and understand the Directions that are there given, to undeceive their mistaken Judgments.   In such a case, that this *Novum Organum* might be the better intelligible, a meer Interpretation is not sufficient, in regard of the Author's difficult and new-found Expressions, a *Comment* would be required   which if it were well and judiciously composed, according to the Author's true Meaning and Intent, I am persuaded every one would be of my Judgment, that it is the best and most useful Treatise of our Days, for the Purpose designed   I am persuaded it might be of singular use to such *Virtuosi* amongst us, as

" are

These two Pieces, therefore, being fundamental, and leading to all the rest, if they have not hitherto been tolerably translated, the English Reader could have no tolerable notion of what the Author designed, and executed, in the rest of his Philosophical Works, which entirely depend upon these and thus, tho' the History of Winds, *the* History of Life and Death, &c *had been better translated than they are, yet the Readers thereof, having never been let into the Scheme of the* GRAND INSTAURATION, *or the general Design of the Author's Philosophical Works, these subsequent Pieces could not be seen in their true light, nor indeed be rightly understood whence it is certain, that they have to many appeared strange and disorderly Things*

It may here be added, that the Latin *Works themselves were not originally published in their true Order, but in Parts, at different times, according as they happened to be wrote, or as the Author judged them suitable to promote his general End, procure Assistance, or the like, but chiefly to prevent Accident, or Disaster, and put at least some Portions of his general Scheme out of the danger of perishing And hence, the natural Order of his Works being often inverted, it was not easy to form a true Judgment of the Whole, or to perceive the Connection and Dependance of the several Parts*

The Author had several Reasons for publishing his Works in Latin *For as his Designs were extensive, and regarded the Benefit of Mankind in general. he thought it best to deliver them in the most general Language, that they might be read by the Men of all Nations Again, they have a more particular regard to Posterity, and* Latin *seems the most suitable Language for conveying things safe and unaltered to After-Ages This also is the Language of the Learned, and the Author's Desire was to have the Learned for his first Readers, as supposing their Minds already open'd, and prepared to receive, and improve, what he delivers But he was more particularly desirous of having the learned Men of foreign Countries amongst his early Readers, that he might by this means anticipate, or have some fore-taste of the Judgment of Posterity. For Distance of Place has here a similar Effect with Distance of Time And lastly, he was desirous of being read, after some Years were*

passed,

---

are not perfectly acquainted with the *Latin* Tongue, and yet employ their Time and Studies in the Improvement of their Abilities, and finding out Inventions useful to the Life of Man for would supply them with such Principles, as their Leisure and Convenience might wonderfully improve in new Discoveries, &c ' Pref to the Epit of the Nov Organ

paffed, *by the Body of his own Countrymen. How prudently this Scheme was laid, and how far he put it in the way of execution, the thing itfelf muft fpeak*

The Defign of thefe Volumes, *is to give a* Methodical *English* Edition *of his* Philofophical Works, *fitted for a commodious and ready Perufal, fomewhat in the fame manner as the* Philofophical Works *of* Mr. Boyle *were, a few Years fince, fitted, in three* Quarto *Volumes* [a].

All the Author's Pieces that were originally written in Latin, *or by himfelf tranflated into* Latin, *are here new done from thofe* Originals; *with care all along to collate his own* English *with the* Latin, *where the Pieces were extant in both Languages.*

The Method obferved in thus rendring them into English, *is not that of a direct Tranflation, (which might have left them more obfcure than they are, and no way fuited this Defign,) but a kind of* open Verfion, *which endeavours to exprefs, in modern* English, *the Senfe of the Author, clear, full, and ftrong, tho' without deviating from him, and, if poffible, without lofing of his Spirit, Force, or Energy. And tho' this Attempt may feem vain, or bold, it was doubtlefs better to have had the View, than willingly to have aimed at fecond Prizes.*

The Liberty fometimes taken, not of abridging, (for juft and perfect Writings are incapable of Abridgment,) but of dropping, or leaving out, fome Parts of the Author's Writings, may require greater Excufe But this was done in order to fhorten the Works, whofe Length has proved one Difcouragement to their being read. And regard has been had to omit none of the Philofophical Matter, *but only certain perfonal Addreffes, Compliments, Exordiums, and the like for as the Reafons and Ends, for which thefe were originally made, fubfift no longer; it was thought fuperfluous to continue fuch Particularities, in a Work of this general nature.*

The philofophical Matter thus feparated, is difpofed into that which appear'd to be the moft natural Order, or fuch as is indicated by the Author; and would, perhaps, have been, in great meafure, obferved by himfelf, had he given an Edition *of all his Works No Merit, therefore, can be claimed in this, fince the Order was pointed out by the Author; who not only had the right to marfhal his own Works; but was concerned to place them in fuch a manner, as beft fuited the Defign.*

After

[a] Printed at *London, Ann* 1725

After the general Difpofal of the feparate Pieces, fo as to follow one another in the jufteft Order, the proper Divifions, or Sections of each particular Piece, come to be confider'd And here, the Method obferved has been fuch, as might preferve an Uniformity in the Whole, and fit thefe Writings for general Ufe. Accordingly the feveral Pieces are divided, and broke, into diftinct Sections, and Paragraphs, this Contrivance having been found to help the Underftanding, affift the Memory, and eafe the Reader.

To render the Work ftill more familiar, and to put it in the way of being farther improved, particular Prefaces, *and* Notes, *are added to explain, or illuftrate, the more obfcure Pieces, Paffages, and Expreffions, fhew where the Author's Schemes have been executed; and refer the Reader from one part of the Work to another, where the fame Subject is treated, fo as in fome measure, to make the whole a Comment upon itfelf And the better to fecure this End, there is added, at the beginning of the firft Volume, a fmall* Gloffary, *or Explanation, of the more uncommon* Philofophical Terms, *made ufe of by the Author, large explicit* Tables of Contents *to each Volume,* Appendixes *to imperfect Works, and an Alphabetical* Index *to the Whole.*

This Edition *was not undertaken of a fudden, but intended many Years fince The principal Inducement to it was, the Service it might poffibly be of in promoting Knowledge, and exciting Philofophers to endeavour the farther Difcovery and Improvement of Arts For there fcarce feems to be any natural Means more powerful to promote this End, than a general fpreading of the Lord* Bacon's Philofophical Writings *The Defign was delay'd, for fome time, in expectation of a compleat* Edition *of all the Author's original Pieces; which was lately publifhed, from* Dr Mead's Collection, *in four* Folio Volumes, by Mr Blackbourne *of which* Edition, *confiderable Ufe has here been made And if too little Time, and too flender Abilities, have not been employ'd in methodizing, tranflating, and illuftrating thefe Writings, fome farther Improvement of the Sciences might be juftly expected from the prefent Labour At leaft, fomething of the kind was thought neceffary, and the Whole is propofed but as an Attempt towards a more ferviceable* Englifh *of the Lord* Bacon's Philofophical Works.

What thefe Works are, is not eafy to exprefs; and their real Character, tho' not fufficiently known, need not be here dwelt on, as they now lie open to an eafy Perufal The principal Obftacle

to

to their Currency appears to be this, that some modern Philoso-phers, and Men of Letters, tho' they allow the Lord Bacon to have been a Great Man, for his Time, yet imagine that his Phi-losophy is now almost superseded by later Improvements, and Dis-coveries.

This, upon a careful Examination, will perhaps be found a fatal Mistake, that keeps some of the most serviceable Philosophical Wri-tings hitherto extant, from being duly studied and improved For it appears impossible that the Lord Bacon's Discoveries should grow out of date, unless the Frame of Things was to alter· since he con-stantly endeavours to copy Nature, which is always the same; so that his distinguishing Merit lies in this, and in having every where open'd the Springs of Knowledge and Practice.

As to the modern Discoveries and Improvements, however great and numerous they may be, yet they are, in general, no more than a part of what this Author foresaw in his Mind; and taught the ways of bringing to light. adding withal such farther Directions, that if Men are not wanting to themselves, they may obtain still greater Things. For he has shewn us the Art of inventing Arts; which many of the Ancients seem'd to despair of; and which the Moderns, perhaps, are not hitherto sufficiently versed in. So that till no more Discoveries remain to be made in Nature, it should seem that this Author's Philosophical Writings cannot be super-seded.

If there are any other Objections lying against the Author, in his Philosophical Capacity, it is probable they may arise from a want of thoroughly understanding his Works, and will therefore vanish, upon becoming better acquainted with him: For his best Defence is that of being well understood.

And in order thereto, he may, in some places, require a careful Reader, or one that has been a little broke, and practised in a sci-entifical doubting of himself, and a prudent Suspension of the Judg-ment: otherwise we shall be sometimes apt, through Haste, Inad-vertence, or an Opinion of the common Methods of Thinking, and Reasoning, to attribute those Faults to the Author, that might be more justly placed.

Perhaps, a sure Rule to know whether his Works are rightly understood is this; that he who understands them, will usually find them the Result of deep Thought, and well weigh'd Experience; so as to prove not only strong and just, but, in an extraordinary manner, useful; teaching more than they directly express; and leading both the Mind and Hand to new Arts, and farther Discoveries. This certainly is the Purport of his Writings; and unless the Reader, by conversing with them, shall be instructed, some way or other, to improve Philosophy, or the general State of Knowledge; he may be assured that he does not fully understand the Author, who professes himself to have done nothing, unless he has taught Posterity to do more.

29 MR 64

CON-

CONTENTS

OF THE

FIRST VOLUME.

The ARRANGEMENT and GENERAL SURVEY of
KNOWLEDGE, &c.

PRELIMINARIES.

SECT. I.

Containing a Plan for the Rectification of Knowledge in general.

SECT.

Aspiring

The CONTENTS.

SECT. IV.
The publick Obstacles to Learning considered.

The Distribution of KNOWLEDGE into particular SCIENCES.

SECT. I
Of HISTORY.

Inductive

The CONTENTS.

SECT II
Of POETRY.

Sets

The CONTENTS.

The CONTENTS.

SOPHISM

(4.) Whe-

The CONTENTS.

APHO-

APHO-

The

SECT.

The CONTENTS.

The CONTENTS.

SECT. XXVII

The Doctrine of Inspired Theology, or Divinity.

The

The CONTENTS.

A

GENERAL SUPPLEMENT

TO THE

De Augmentis Scientiarum.

Supplement I. *The* New Atlantis; *or, A Plan of a Society for the Promotion of Knowledge.*

Delivered in the Way of FICTION.

who

Their

The CONTENTS.

Supplement II. *The Beginning of a History of Great Britain.*

Supplement III. *Containing the Lives, or Civil Characters, of* Julius Cæsar, Augustus Cæsar, *King* Henry VII. *and Queen* Elizabeth.

I

A Civil Character of *Julius Cæsar.*

Supplement IV. Select Speeches on particular Occasions, Civil, Judicial and Moral.

SECT. I.
SPEECHES on Civil Occasions.

SPEECH I.

SPEECH II

SPEECH III.

SPEECH IV

The CONTENTS.

Supplement

Supplement V. *Select Letters upon various Occasions.*

The CONTENTS.

The CONTENTS.

The CONTENTS.

Supplement VI. *A Collection of Apophthegms,* 511

Car-

Supplement.

Their

End of the Contents.

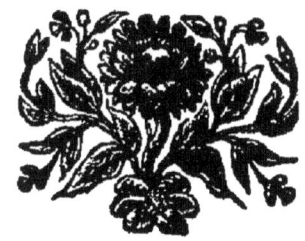

ERRATA in VOL I

In the General Preface, pag viii lin 38 after *English* insert *Edition*

Pag. 15 lin penult for *Fourth* read *Fifth*
18 lin ult for Sect XVII. read Sect XVIII
31 lin 10 for *non appearance* read *appearance*
35 lin 34 for *Aexander* read *Alexander*
65 lin 16 in the Margin, for *sensible* read *feasible*
70 lin. 22 for *Acausticks* read *Acousticks*
72 lin 45 for *Newyntt* read *Nieuentyt*
75 lin 7 for *Acceden s* read *Accidents*
87 l.n 9 after *Metaphysicks* insert or
158 lin 39 after *would* d-le *only*
175 Ln 21 for *to Secrets,* read *to the Secret*
193 lin 6 for *case* read *cases*
199 lin 17 instead of *so are the four latter,* read *so the four latter are.*
ibid lin 38 for *Wesenfelds* read *Wesenfeld*
200 lin 3 dele the first *to*
259 lin 35 for *turning* read *tuning*
295 lin 34. for *Insolations* read *Insolations*
303 lin ult for *Supplement* V Sect I read *Supplement* V Sect II
331 l.n 11 read *studied, full, strong, and definitive*
414. lin. ult for *eighteen,* read *sixteen*
509 l.n 35 for *Jesuit,* read *Friar*
563 l.n 2 for V read IV and alter the following Numbers accordingly
586 lin 30 for VIII read VII.
600 lin. ult dele *that*   29 MR 64

A

SUMMARY VIEW

OF THE

AUTHOR's LIFE.

A

SUMMARY VIEW

OF THE

AUTHOR's LIFE.

FRANCIS BACON was born at *London*, in *York-house* in the *Strand*; *January* 22, 1560. His Father was Sir *Nicholas Bacon*, a Counsellor of State to Queen *Elizabeth*, and Lord Keeper of the Great Seal of *England*: and his Mother, a Daughter of Sir *Anthony Cook*, of *Giddy-Hall* in *Essex*, who had been Governor to King *Edward* VI[a].

Being thus descended, he was early initiated in a Court Life; and, as himself expresses it[b], both by Family and Education, tinged with Civil Affairs, and biass'd by Opinions During his Childhood, he was taken notice of at Court for a more than ordinary Capacity; whence the Queen delighted to talk with him; and would often, for his Gravity, term him the *Young Lord-Keeper*.

He was early [c] sent to *Trinity-College* in *Cambridge*, where he studied under Dr *Whitgift*, afterwards Archbishop of *Canterbury*. His Genius shew'd itself at the University, by the uncommon Progress he made in the Arts and Sciences so that, what seems almost incredible, he not only understood *Aristotle's* Philosophy at about the Age

of

[a] Dr *Rawley's* Life of the Author, *p.* 1. and *Dugdale's* Baronage, *p* 437
[b] See the *Scripta*, published by *Gruter; de Interpretatione Naturæ, Prooemium*, in init.
[c] He was matriculated, *June* 10 *An.* 1573

of Sixteen, but was even then come to a Diflike thereof, upon finding it rather contentious than useful[a]

His Father called him from the Univerfity, at this early Age,
to attend the Ambaffador, Sir *Amyas Pawlet*, into *France*, who
foon after charged him with fome particular Commiffion from
thence to the Queen in which Commiffion, he acquitted himfelf
with great Approbation, and returned to *France* again, in order to
continue there for fome time[b]

During his Stay in *France* his Father died[c], without making any
feparate Provifion, as he had intended, for him fo that being the
younger Brother of Five, he received no more than a fifth Share of a
fmall perfonal Eftate, and therefore ftruggled with Difficulties, in
point of Fortune, for fome Part of his Life.

Upon returning from abroad, he applied himfelf to the Study of the
Common Law, in the way of a Profeffion, and for that purpofe
feated himfelf in *Gray's-Inn*, where he foon became fo eminent, as
at the age of Twenty eight, to be chofe by that honourable Society
for their Lent-Reader[d], and afterwards for their double Reader.

And having always thought himfelf peculiarly indebted to his
Country, he now bent his Endeavours to obtain fome honourable
Poft in the Government, with a View, as himfelf declares[e], to procure the greater affiftance to his Capacity and Induftry, in perfecting
his philofophical Defigns And being already acquainted with the
Civil Arts, he recommended himfelf to fuch Friends, as he knew
were able to ferve him[f]

But his Advancement in the Queen's Time was flow, and not very
confiderable for he had fome potent Enemies at Court, who did
their utmoft to keep him under[g] He was, however, made one of
the Clerks of the Council, and fworn of the Council learned, extraordinary, to her Majefty but could not in her Reign obtain the
Place of Sollicitor-General, for which he earneftly ftrove, even by
the Interceffion of his noble Patron the Earl of *Effex*[h]

Being now arrived at full maturity, whilft, as himfelf obferves[i], his
Thoughts were bent upon Ambition, an ill State of Health admonifhed

[a] See *Rawley's* Life of the Author p 5 See alfo *Tenifon's Baconiana*, p 10
[b] It fhould feem that during his Continuance abroad he made the Tour of *Italy*, and vifited *Rome* See Vol II p 127
[c] See Vol III p 232
[d] Dr *Rawley's* Life of the Author, p 5, 6 and *Dugdale's* Baronage, p 437, 438.
[e] See the Scripta in Proem de Interpretatione *Naturæ*
[f] See his Letters, Vol I p 413——459
[g] See Vol I p 418, 424
[h] See Vol I 432
[i] In Proem de Interpret *Naturæ*

nished him that his Endeavours were unprosperous. whence frequently considering that he was not performing his Duty, whilst he left those Studies unprosecuted by which he might do service to Mankind, and followed those that depended upon the Will of others, he, for a time, broke off all further Thoughts of rising in Life, and more vigorously prosecuted the Design of his *Instauration* [a]

But upon the Death of Queen *Elizabeth*, and the coming in of King *James*, his former Views return'd, and he now made great Advances in Dignity and Preferment. being first knighted, then created Baron of *Verulam*, and lastly Viscount *St. Albans* His Places were, Council learned extraordinary to the King, as he had before been to the Queen, Sollicitor-General, Attorney-General, Counsellor of State, Lord Keeper of the Great Seal, and Lord High Chancellor of *England*

He was knighted by the King in person at *Whitehall*, in the Year 1603, he was sworn Sollicitor General in 1607, made Attorney-General in 1613; appointed Lord Keeper, and chose of the Privy-Council in 1716, made Lord High Chancellor in 1618, created Baron of *Verulam* the same Year; and Viscount *St Albans* in 1620.

Towards the beginning of these Promotions he married a Daughter of *Benedict Barnham*, Alderman of *London*; but died without Issue.

He did not obtain his Posts of Honour and Preferment without labour they were generally the effect of his own Schemes, contrived and executed with great Application and Address [b].

His Behaviour in the several Posts he passed through, was such, as (notwithstanding the Efforts of some powerful Enemies) procured him an almost universal Esteem for Learning, Parts, and Probity, till at length he was accused of Bribery and Corruption in the Execution of his highest Office, that of Lord Chancellor.

Instead of defending himself against this Accusation, he made a full and ingenuous Confession [c] to the House of Peers; who, upon the 3d of *May*, 1621, gave Judgment against him, " That he should " be fined 40,000 *l* and remain Prisoner in the Tower during the " King's Pleasure, that he should for ever be incapable of any Office, " Place, or Employment, in the State or Commonwealth, and that " he should never sit in Parliament, or come within the Verge of the " Court " After

[a] See the Place last cited
[b] See his Letters, *Sect* I *passim Vol* I *p* 413, *&c*
[c] See *Vol* I This Confession has been construed a Weakness by some, who did not reflect, that it is noble in an Offender to confess, and that generous Minds are the aptest to accuse themselves

After this, he retired from Civil Affairs, and for five Years gave himself wholly up to Philosophy and Writing; so that, during this Time, he executed several Portions of his grand *Instauration:* but did not live to finish the whole, so far as he had hoped to do.

He died *April* 9, 1626 at the Earl of *Arundel's* House at *Highgate,* of a Fever, attended with a Defluxion upon his Breast.

He lies buried in St *Michael's* Church at *St Albans;* a Monument being there erected for him, (with his full Portrait, in the posture of studying,) by Sir *Thomas Meautys,* once his Secretary, and afterwards Clerk of the Council; with a *Latin* Inscription, by Sir *Henry Wotton,* to this effect

FRANCIS BACON, *Baron of* Verulam, *and Viscount* St. Albans;
or, in more eminent Titles,
The Light of the Sciences, and the Law of Eloquence,
sate thus.
Who, when he had explained all the Secrets of civil and natural
Knowledge, fulfilled that Decree of Nature; let Compounds
be Separated; in the Tear of our Lord 1626.
Aged 66.
This Monument was erected, to the Memory of so great a Man,
by Thomas Meautys, *who revered him when alive,*
and admires him now dead.

To give a full Character of the Lord *Bacon,* requires a more than ordinary Skill, the following are but some faint Touches.

The Faculties of his Mind were great, and happily united for his Imagination, Memory, and Reason were all extraordinary. He knew what was in Books, but had a Knowledge superior to them He was indefatigable in Study, and found himself better turned for that, than for any thing else; as having a Mind quick and ready to perceive the Correspondencies of things; fix'd and intent to discover their nicer Differences, and this joined with a Love of Enquiry, a Patience of Doubting; a Pleasure in Contemplation, a Backwardness in Asserting; a Readiness in acknowledging an Error; and a scrupulous Exactness in Disposing and Methodizing at the same time neither affecting Novelty, nor adoring Antiquity, but hating all kinds of Imposture and Delusion [a]

To consider him in his Philosophical Capacity, History scarce affords us a fit Philosopher wherewith to compare him. *Plato* and *Aristotle*
were

---

[a] See *Pr...m de Interpret. Nat.* See also *Vol.* II *p* 332—335.

were Men of a different Caſt they paid not ſo great a regard to Truth and Utility ; nor inſtructed Mankind ſo juſtly, nor open'd the hidden Veins of Science ſo ſuccefsfully, nor taught the Art of philoſophical Invention, ſo happily as the Lord *Bacon*.

He excelled no lefs in particular Sciences than in general Philoſophy. The Law was his Profeſſion, whereof he was ſo great a Maſter, as to ſtand in competition with the celebrated Lord *Coke* tho' ſome good Judges are of opinion, that the Compariſon does too much honour to the latter [a]

He was a great Maſter in all matters relating to the State [b], and as acceptable in the Houſe of Commons, as in the Council [c]

His Failings were chiefly of the moral or oeconomical kind, and ſeem owing to an Exceſs of certain Virtues, *viz* Generoſity bordering upon Profuſeneſs, and Good-nature approaching to Facility. For in his Poſts of Profit, he laid up nothing, but was over-indulgent to his Servants, and ſuffer'd them to make their own Advantages. And from no fouler an Origin ſeems to have proceeded the Bribery and Corruption of which he was guilty [d] The Gifts he took being commonly by the Hands of his Servants, for interlocutory Orders; whilſt all his Decrees were ſo equitable, that not one of them was ever reverſed as unjuſt [e] More might be ſaid to extenuate his Crime, if a Crime of ſuch a nature could be extenuated · The Corruption of the Times; the Inveteracy of his Enemies, and the King's withdrawing of his Favour, all conſpired to make him a Sacrifice [f]

Some have thought that he was reduced to extreme Poverty, and ſhew'd an abject Spirit, after his Fall, particularly in the ſupplicating Letters he wrote to the King but let his whole Behaviour, his Penſions, his Eſtate, and thoſe Letters be well conſider'd, and the Caſe will appear much otherwiſe [g] 'Tis certain, that he had his **Errors** and his **Frailties**; and without them would have appear'd more than human but to take him as he was; we muſt acknowledge him one of the greateſt Men that the World has known

[a] See Mr *Locker's* Character of the *Lord Bacon*, in Mr *Blackbourn's* Edition Vol I p 178
[b] See his Speeches, Letters, &c See alſo *Osborn's* Advice to a Son, *page* 150
[c] See *Rawley's* Life, p 12 and Vol I p
[d] See *Ruſhworth's* Collections, Vol I and *Teniſon's Baconiana*, p 254
[e] See *Baconiana*, p 255
[f] See *Buſhel's* Extract, p 19 and *Teniſon's Baconiana*, p 16
[g] See *Teniſon's Baconiana*, pag 254, 255 See alſo *Rawley's* Life, pag 6, 7

A SMALL

GLOSSARY,

OR

EXPLANATION,

OF

Certain PHILOSOPHICAL TERMS, either Invented, or Ufed in a New Senfe, by the AUTHOR.

ABSTRACTION.

THIS Word the Author frequently ufes, to exprefs the man- ABSTRAC-
ner of *forming Notions*, that is, not fimple Ideas, or Senfa- TION, *of No-*
tions, which require no Action or Operation of the Mind *tions.*
befides bare Perception, but the Manner of deducing, taking, or
abftracting juft Notions from Things, after a due confideration of all
the Particulars that fhould go to conftitute fuch Notions.

Thus *Notions haftily abftracted from Things* are faulty, flight, *Notions haftily*
fuperficial and imperfect Notions, derived from confidering only a *abftracted*
few obvious Particulars, as the common Notion of *Moifture* is haftily
abftracted or taken from confidering only Water whereas fuch a
Philofophical Notion of Moifture fhould be formed, and introduced,

as

as might agree with all *Instances*, *viz.* to Quickſilver, which is moiſt in reſpect of Gold, to Oil, which is moiſt, in reſpect of Leather, &c

The due Abstraction, therefore, or Formation of Notions, is a particular Operation, or Work, of the Underſtanding, that requires the uſe of *Induction*, in the Author's Senſe thereof, which ſee, under the Word *Induction*. And in this Operation of the Mind, the Perfection of Thought, Language, and all Philoſophy principally conſiſts

ADVENTITIOUS

By *Adventitious*, or *Transcendental Conditions of Things*, the Author underſtands the Exiſtence of Things in a determinate, or certain Quantity, under certain invariable Differences, or, to expreſs it otherwiſe, the Laws, or neceſſary Cauſes in Nature, whereby ſome Things exiſt, and others do not, why there are ſuch large Quantities of ſome Things, and leſs of others, why ſome Things are poſſible, others impoſſible, and the like Thus to enquire into the phyſical, (not final) Cauſes, why there is more Iron than Gold in the World; more Marble than Diamond, why it is impoſſible for Men to preſerve their own Bodies in a ſound State for ever, and the like, is enquiring into the Adventitious, or Tranſcendental Conditions of Things, and a neglected part of *Primary Philoſophy* : which ſee.

ANTICIPATION

By *Anticipation*, the Author, in a particular Senſe, underſtands the common Method of Reaſoning, and judging of Things with a kind of natural Impatience, Precipitancy, blind Fury, and head-ſtrong Appetite, without a due regard to the real Merits of the Caſe, or without a proper Regulation and Government of the Mind, by the uſe of his new Machine, or Logick So that the Method of Anticipation is directly oppoſite to his Method of Induction, or *Interpretation of Nature*, which ſee

APHORISMS.

The Author takes *Aphoriſms* in a ſomewhat ſtricter ſenſe than the common, and means by them, not looſe and ſcatter'd Obſervations thrown together in a Heap, but matter of well-weigh'd Obſervation and Experience, thoroughly digeſted in the Mind, and afterwards clearly and methodically ſet down in Writing, with a ſteady View to ſome uſeful End without admitting any foreign Ornament, Superfluity, or Exaggeration, but keeping cloſe to the Truth of Nature, and Reality

AP·

APPROXIMATIONS.

By *Approximations* the Author underſtands ſuch Particulars as approach, or, in ſome degree, come up to *Optatives*, or the *Deſiderata* in Arts and Sciences · ſo as, when thoſe Optatives, or Deſiderata, are, for the preſent, impoſſible to be obtained; we may ſtill have ſomething of the ſame kind, within our power, tho' of an inferior degree. See *Optatives* APPROXIMA-
TIONS

ART OF INVENTING

By *the Art of Inventing Arts* is meant the Uſe of a well-regulated and perfect *Induction*, applied to Phyſicks, being an Art, or actual *Demonſtration*, as juſtly ſuited to this purpoſe, as *Algebra* in Mathematicks and may diſcover Arts with as much Certainty, as that can form Equations See *Induction, Interpretation of Nature*, and *Inveſtigation of Forms*. See alſo *Inductive Hiſtory*, and *Learned Experience*. ART OF IN-
VENTING
ARTS *or the*
Art of Enqui-
ry, Indication,
or Direction

ASSEMBLAGES.

By *greater Aſſemblages, or Colleges, of Matter* are underſtood the *four Elements*, as they are commonly called, *viz*. Fire, Air, Water, and Earth and by the *ſmaller Aſſemblages*, all the other natural Bodies, as Animals; Plants and Foſſils. ASSEMBLAGES
of Matter.

ATTRACTION. See *Sympathy*

AXIOMS.

By *Axioms* the Author does not mean *Mathematical Axioms*, or ſelf-evident Propoſitions, but a very different Thing . *viz*. ſolid Portions of Truth, duly raiſed from Enquiries conducted in the inductive Method, or drawn, as rich Corollaries, from particular Hiſtories of Nature and Art, ſo as to be pregnant with the Matter of a juſt Theory, and ſure Directions for Practice. And theſe Axioms can be no otherwiſe formed, than by a careful and accurate *Induction*. In other Words, a perfect *Axiom* is a ſummary Expreſſion of the *Form, Law, Nature*, or *Eſſence* of a Thing diſcover'd after a due Excluſion and Rejection of every Nature, or Property, that is not eſſential ; ſo that the *Diſcovery of Forms*, and the raiſing of *perfect Axioms* are reciprocal, or one and the ſame thing. See *Forms*. But beſides theſe *perfect Axioms*, there are others of an inferior Nature, tending to raiſe up the more perfect by degrees. AXIOMS, *how*
formed

2 CANONS.

CANONS

CANON.

Canons, in the Author's particular Senfe of the Word, are the fame as *Axioms*, unlefs we except that they more particularly regard Practice, as *Axioms*, if we make the difference, regard Theory. The Word *Canons* is alfo fometimes ufed for ufeful Obfervations of a general nature, or large extent

CIVIL HISTORY.

C. -H.-
STORY.

By *Civil Hiftory* is meant an Account of the Works and Acts of Men, as *Natural Hiftory* is an Account of the Works and Acts of Nature

CONFUTATION

CONFUTA-
TIO, of D-
monftra- Ex-
Pl. .ded as
and th- Na
tur.l Peafon

This Word is ufed, not fo much in a new Senfe, as applied in a new Manner, or to a new Purpofe, *viz.* the *Confutation of De-monftrations;* the *Confutation of Philofophies*, and the *Confutation of the natural Reafon*, which may feem harfh and ftrange Expreffions but, as Sophifms are confuted in the vulgar Logic, fo the Author confutes the vulgar Demonftrations, the vulgar Philofophies, and the common method of Reafoning, by fhewing them all to be unfit for promoting the Sciences, which requires the ufe of perfect *Induction*

COSMICAL

Co. cal
3. u a -d
Q-al. i

Cofmical Motions, and *Cofmical Qualities*, are thofe Motions and Qualities which Things have, as they are Parts of the Univerfe, or general Syftem of Nature, and would not have the fame, if they were not Parts of one great Whole

ELECTIONS.

ELECTION,
A-T -u

By *Elections*, with regard to a found and ferviceable *Aftrology*, is meant the choice of proper Times, or Seafons, for performing certain Actions or Operations, fo as to procure the affiftance of the Celeftial Influences, when thefe may be ferviceable *Elections*, therefore, are one principal Ufe of Aftrology, and *Predictions* another

EXCLUSION.

EXCLU O ,
and Fe, T -

By the Method of *Exclufion*, or *Rejection*, is meant the throwing out of an Enquiry all the Subjects that have not the Nature fought, and belongs particularly to genuine *Induction*, or the Art of *Invefti-gating Forms* where it conftantly makes a *Table* by itfelf, called

l

the

the *Table of Declination, Abfence* in *Approach, Exclufion,* or *Re-jection.*

The Expreffion has alfo a lower, or more obvious Signification, denoting the refufal, or non-admittance, of dubious and uncertain Particulars, or Matters of flight Obfervation and Experience, into an Enquiry, or any particular Hiftory of Nature or Art, as alfo the weeding of fuch Hiftories, and throwing out fuch Particulars

FORMS.

By *Forms,* the Author underftands *thofe real Appetites, Powers,* FORMS *philo-* Motions, or active Laws of Nature, by which all Things exift, and *fophical* have their Effects. And to the Difcovery of thefe Laws, his principal Endeavours are directed, as to a Thing that alone will conftitute a juft and univerfal Theory, and direct to an extenfive Practice. So that his *Inftauration,* or Scheme for rebuilding Arts and Sciences, and bringing them to their Perfection, depends upon the *Difcovery of Forms ;* or the finding of Natures convertible with any Natures affigned, that fhall limit, and reftrain, and conftitute the former   Thus by difcovering the *Form of Gold,* we fhould learn what conftitutes that Metal, or gives it the fpecific Differences which diftinguifh it from all other Things ; and, at the fame time, obtain a Rule for introducing that *Form,* or the Nature of Gold, into Silver, or any other Body fufceptible thereof   But thefe *Forms* are not yet difcover'd, and can be inveftigated no other way than by the Ufe and Application of the Art of *Induction* ; which, itfelf is not hitherto extant in all its Parts   See *Induction.*

Befides this eminent Senfe of the Word, it is alfo ufed, in a *Forms com-* more common Acceptation, for the Figure, Shape, Fafhion, or Man- *mon* ner of Things.

GENERATIONS.

Generations are the ordinary Productions of Nature, as diftin- GENERA- guifhed from the extraordinary, or monftrous, which the Author TIONS calls *Pretergenerations.*

GEORGICKS

This Expreffion of *Georgicks* is transferr'd from Agriculture into GEORGICKS, *of* Ethicks ; fo as to denote the Art of cultivating, or improving the *the Mind* Mind in Moral Virtue

HISTORY.

By pure *Hiftory,* the Author means a Collection, or faithful and HISTORY exact Defcription of the Works, Facts, or Appearances of Nature, without meddling with their Caufes, which is a Province that belongs to the *Interpreter of Nature.*   *Nar-*

Narrative *Narrative Hiſtory* is diſtinguiſhed from *Inductive Hiſtory*, the
Hiſtory former containing Deſcriptions, or relating the Facts and Works of
Nature, with no view to the founding a juſt Philoſophy, which is
the Deſign of *Inductive Hiſtory* See *Inductive* and *Natural Hiſtory*

I D O L S.

Idols, of the By *Idols of the Mind* are denoted the various kinds of falſe Repre-
Mind ſentations, Imaginations, Figments, and wrong Notions, which Men
receive from Education, Party, particular Studies, *&c.* ſo as to diſtinguiſh theſe from true Notions, which are duly abſtracted, and repreſent Things as they are See *Abſtraction.*

I N D U C T I O N.

Induction This Word is uſed, not in the common, but a much more noble
Senſe, by the Author, to ſignify an *Art*, of which he was the Inventor. This Art has a great reſemblance with Algebra, and is to
the Inveſtigation of Forms, what that is with regard to the forming
of Equations. It conſiſts of ſeveral Parts, and is extremely well
ſuited to natural Enquiries, and the Diſcovery of new Arts, and
Works ſo that it may well be called a *Philoſophical Algebra,* or
the Art of Inventing Arts; a conſiderable Branch whereof, is deliver'd in the Author's Piece called *Novum Organum.* See *Art of Inventing Arts.*

I N D U C T I V E   H I S T O R Y

Inductive *Inductive, Primary,* or *Mother-Hiſtory,* is a Natural and Expe-
Hiſtory rimental Hiſtory, collected, not in the ordinary way of Natural Hiſtories, for Amuſement, Delight, or the ſake of the direct Matters
themſelves, but with a View to the building up a ſolid and ſerviceable
Philoſophy *Inductive Hiſtory,* therefore, was a Thing entirely
wanting, till the Author ſet ſome Examples of it in his Hiſtory of
Winds, Life and Death, &c wherein he uſes his own *Art of Induction* See *Induction*

I N D U C T I V E   M E T H O D

Inductive *Inductive Method,* is the Method laid down by the *Art of Induc-
Method.* *tion* See *Induction,* and *Forms.*

I N S T A N C E S.

Inſtances By *Inſtances,* the Author underſtands Particulars, Facts, Obſervations, Experiments, Natural Bodies, Inſtruments, or any thing fitted
to afford Light and Information in Enquiries. But as it were endleſs

to purfue the Infinity of Things in particular Enquiries, the Author, under the Doctrine of Inftances, has fhewn which are *Prerogative*, that is, which are of fuch a nature as that a few of them may do the Office of many, and thus greatly fhorten the Bufinefs of Enquiry. *Prerogative Inftances*

INSTAURATION.

The *Inftauration* is the Author's general Scheme or Plan, which he lays down for the improvement of Knowledge This Scheme confifts of fix Parts, *viz.* (1.) A Survey of the prefent Stock of Knowledge, with an account of its Deficiencies, and the ways of fupplying them (2) A new Art of Induction, Philofophical Algebra, Machine, or particular Logick, for difcovering Arts, and interpreting Nature. (3) The Materials for Inductive Hiftory. (4) The Inductive Hiftory itfelf (5.) The beft Philofophy that the Author could raife without the affiftance of *Induction* And (6.) a genuine and found Philofophy raifed by the *Art of Induction*. *INSTAURA- TION*

INTERPRETATION.

What the Author properly means by the *Interpretation of Nature*, is the Exercife of the laft Part of his Art of *Induction*, when the *Interpreter* having all his *Tables*; and the requifite Materials and Helps before him, examines what is the Refult of any particular Enquiry, fo as at length to difcover the *Form* of the Nature fought, find the Caufes of Effects, and draw out the *Axioms* that direct new Experiments and Works It is therefore the Bufinefs of the *Natural* or rather *Inductive Hiftorian*, to collect the Matter or *Inftances* of an Enquiry; range them into regular *Tables*, &c and the Bufinefs of the *Interpreter of Nature* to examine and compare the whole, with a View to the Inveftigation of *Forms*, the Difcovery of *Caufes*, and the raifing of *Axioms*. *INTERPRETA- TION of Na- ture* *Interpreter of Nature*

But befides this limited Senfe of the Term *Interpretation* of Nature, it has another, more general, and denotes the fober, artificial, juft and regular Procedure of the Mind in the Difcovery of Truth, according to the patient and laborious Method of *Induction*: in which light it is oppofed to the vulgar *Method of Anticipation*, which, when foberly confider'd, appears a kind of frantick, deform'd and unruly Thing.

LEARNED EXPERIENCE.

By *Learned Experience* the Author underftands the *Art of Experimenting*, or the proper Method of making and conducting Experiments *LEARNED EX- PERIENCE* riments, so as that they shall afford Light, or lead to some certain Discoveries, and not remain casual, fluctuating Things, tried in the way of Amusement, or fruitless Curiosity.

LITERARY HISTORY

LITERARY
HISTORY

By *Literary History* is meant the History of Matters any way relating to Learning, thro' all the Ages and over all the Countries of the World

MACHINE

MACHINE for
the Mind

What this is, see explained under the Term *Novum Organum.*

MAGICK

MAGICK

The Word *Magick* is used by the Author in its ancient honourable Sense, or rather in one still more sublime and noble, for that practical Doctrine, or Science, which, from a *Discovery of Forms,* may produce very great Works and Effects, in the way of over-ruling, or commanding the general Laws of Nature. But as *Forms* are not hitherto discovered, *Natural Magick,* which depends thereon, has at present no place among the Sciences. Otherwise, as Mechanicks is to Physicks, so is Magick to Metaphysicks, or the Discovery of Forms

Persian Magick

The *Persian Magick* is a sublime kind of Wisdom, or Science, depending upon the Discovery of the natural Relations betwixt the Parts of the Universe, and more particularly as applied to find out what Relations and Conformities Civil States, or the Art of Government, should bear to the Regulation and Government of the World.

MATHEMATICKS.

MATHEMA-
TICKS

Mathematicks, in the strict Sense, is that part of *Metaphysicks* (in the Author's acceptation) which considers Quantity; but is more advantageously made an Appendage, or auxiliary Branch of Science, subservient to *Physicks, Metaphysicks, Mechanicks,* and *Magick.*

MECHANICKS.

MECHANICKS.

Mechanicks is of two kinds, *empirical* and *rational.* By *empirical Mechanicks* the Author understands that general Method of operating in Arts, which has no Dependance upon *Physicks,* and proceeds without any Knowledge of Causes. And by rational *Mechanicks* he understands that Method of operating, which is accompanied with a Knowledge of physical Causes.

META-

METAPHYSICKS.

This Word is ufed in a particular Senfe by the Author, to denote that contemplative Part of Natural Philofophy, which difcovers *Forms,* and *final Caufes,* fo as to fhorten the Way to Knowledge, fet the human Power at liberty; and find out the true ultimate Caufes of Things See *Phyficks.* _{METAPHY-SICKS}

NATURAL HISTORY.

By *Natural Hiftory* the Author underftands a Defcription of Generations, Prætergenerations, and Arts; or all the Productions of Nature, as well the ordinary as extraordinary and monftrous, and alfo of Experience, or human Arts, and Inventions. See *Hiftory.* _{NATURAL HISTORY}

NATURAL THEOLOGY See *Divine Philofophy,* under *Philofophy.*

NATURES.

The Author makes frequent ufe of the word *Nature* or *Natures,* to exprefs what we often mean by Properties, but the Term is ftill of greater extent, and more generally ufeful Thus (1) Natures are the fame as Things, (2) the *Nature enquired into,* is the Subject fought, or the Object of Enquiry, but (3) to *introduce a given Nature,* is to introduce the *Form,* or *effential Properties,* of one thing into another; fo as to convert the one into the other And (4.) *Nature united,* or *fummed up,* is the Difcovery of the general Law, Uniformity, or Unity of Action, employ'd by Nature, or rather, the Author of Nature, in the production of all natural Works and Effects

NOVUM ORGANUM.

Novum Organum is not only the Title of that Piece wherein the Author defcribes his *New Logick, Art of Induction, Philofophical Algebra,* or new *Machine* for working with the Underftanding upon all Subjects, to the greateft Advantage; but alfo denotes the Art itfelf, whereby, as by an *Engine* or *artificial Help for the Mind,* Men may perform incomparably more than by their own natural Powers; and ordinary Capacities be thus enabled to profecute Enquiries, and promote general Knowledge, as effectually as Men of Genius the Method of working with this Help being like the Method of working with *Algebra;* or rather with a general Engine, or Inftrument, proportion'd to the Strength, and fitted to the Ufe of all Men.

OPTATIVES.

By *Optatives* the Author underſtands *Deſiderata*, or ſuch Particulars as might be wiſhed for, in order to the Accommodation of Life, and the Enlargement of Arts, as for Example, Power over the Weather, the Longitude at Sea, new mechanical Motions, &c.

PERCEPTION.

By *Perception*, applied to inanimate Bodies, we are to underſtand the ſame Paſſion, or Suffering, as happens in animate Bodies; excepting only the Difference that depends upon the Spirit in Animals, or a want of the Senſes

PHILOSOPHY

By *Philoſophy* in general, the Author underſtands all Knowledge, except Revelation, or inſpired Theology; ſo that Arts and Sciences are but other Words for *Philoſophy*.

Primary Philoſophy, in the general Senſe, denotes a kind of *common Science*, or Collection of neutral *Axioms*, belonging indifferently to all the Sciences, together with the Doctrine of Adventitious or Tranſcendental Conditions. See *Adventitious Conditions*

By *Natural Philoſophy* the Author underſtands Philoſophy applied to the Things of Nature (as diſtinguiſhed from the Doctrine of the Deity, and the Doctrine of Man) ſo as to diſcover Cauſes, and produce Effects. See *Phyſicks* and *Metaphyſicks*

Divine Philoſophy, or *Natural Theology*, is a Science formed in the Mind of Man, by means of the Light of Nature, and the Contemplation of the Works of God, and tends to confute Atheiſm, and determine the Laws of Nature, but not to eſtabliſh any Religion.

Philoſophia Prima, has the ſame ſignification with Primary Philoſophy, but in a more particular Senſe, denotes the Author's intended *imperfect Philoſophy*, to be raiſed in the beſt manner poſſible, without the Aſſiſtance of the *Art of Induction*, as his *Philoſophia Secunda* was to have been a pure and perfect axiomatical or univerſal Philoſophy, raiſed by the *Art of Induction*

PHYSICKS.

By *Phyſicks* the Author underſtands that contemplative Part of *Natural Philoſophy*, which diſcovers the efficient Cauſes, and the Compoſition, Matter, and Structure of Things, as *Metaphyſicks* diſcover

cover their *Forms* and *Ends*.   *Physicks* therefore, and *Metaphysicks*, are the two contemplative, or theoretical Parts of Natural Philosophy, to which answer the two practical ones of *Mechanicks* and *Magick*.

By *Physicks of Creatures*, or *Concrete Physicks*, we are to under-*Physicks of* stand that Part of *Physicks*, which exhibits the Varieties and lesser *Creatures* Assemblages, or Collections of Things, pursued in the Concretes or Bodies themselves.   And this Part borders upon Natural History.

Physicks of Natures, or *abstract Physicks*, is the same Part pur-*Physicks of* sued, not in Concretes, or Individuals, but in their Accidents or *Natures.* Qualities, so as to approach the Nature of Metaphysicks

PNEUMATICAL BODIES.

By *Pneumatical Bodies* the Author means such as make no sen-*Pneumati-* sible Resistance to the Touch, or are not perceived, or found ponde-*cal Bodies* rous upon the Balance in the open Air.

PRÆTERGENERATIONS.
For the Meaning of this Word, see *Generations:*

PRÆTERGE-
NERATIONS.

PRIMARY HISTORY.   See *Inductive History*

PRIMARY PHILOSOPHY.   See *Philosophy.*

PROFESSORIAL.
By *Professorial Learning, and Professorial Arts and Sciences*, the *Professo* Author understands the Arts and Sciences, as taught in the common *RIAL, Learn-* Schools, and Universities, where he judges the Arts are not much *ing, Arts and Sciences.* improved, but only retailed out in a sophistical manner, or dressed, adorned, and fashioned into Systems, that are apt to deceive by their beautiful Appearance

PROMPTUARY.
By *Promptuary Method* is meant the procuring a Fund of Matter *Promptuary* for Discourse, by laying up, for use, Arguments ready composed, with *Method.* regard to such Subjects as frequently occur.

REASON.
By *Reason* the Author frequently understands the rash, and impru-*Reason* dent, use of the rational Faculty, in philosophical Subjects, so as presently to come at some erroneous Conclusion, and proceed upon it as if it were true, without inuring this Faculty to the same laborious
Search,

Search, Sufpenfion, and Scrupuloufnefs in Philofophy, as is practifed in Mathematical Demonftrations. See *Confutation.*

REDUCTION.

REDUCT.   By *Reduction* the Author underftands a proper Contrivance, or
artificial Means, for bringing thofe Things under the Judgment of
the Senfes which naturally efcape them. or Means of ftrengthening,
affifting, and improving the Senfes, as by Telefcopes, Microfcopes,
Speaking-Trumpets, Ear-Trumpets, &c.

REJECTION. See *Exclufion*

SCALA INTELLECTUS.

SCALA INTEL-
LECTUS   By *Scala Intellectus* the Author underftands the proper Application of the Art of *Induction,* to the more interefting and important
Subjects of Philofophy, fo as duly to profecute a Set of capital Enquiries, that fhall lead, by degrees, to the moft fublime, noble, and
general Axioms, pregnant with Doctrine and Directions for forming
a juft Theory of Nature, and the perfecting of Arts

SPIRIT

SPIRIT   By the Spirit in Bodies the Author means a more fubtile and rarified Matter, of the fame Nature with the Bodies themfelves, refiding
in all their tangible Parts, multiplying itfelf, or, as it were, feeding
upon them; but, unlefs hindred, continually flying off into the Air,
fo as in time to wafte, exhauft, and confume the Bodies.

SUBSTITUTION.

SUBSTITU-
TION   By *Subftitution* we are to underftand the Means of fubftituting, or
ufing, one Object for another, where the Senfes fail us, and where Inftruments for helping, or improving the Senfes, are of no fervice Thus,
tho' we cannot directly examine Flame, we may fometimes advantageoufly fubftitute its *Pabulum,* or the Matter whereof it confifts,
viz. Oil, or Spirit of Wine; &c.

SYLVA SYLVARUM.

SYLVA SYL-
VARU   By *Sylva Sylvarum,* is underftood, as its Name implies, a *Wood*
of Experiments and Obfervations, or a Collection of Materials,
ready procured, and laid up for forming particular Hiftories of Nature
and Art, in the Author's inductive manner.

SYMPATHY.

By *Sympathy, Confent, Attraction,* &c we are to underftand, SYMPATHY not any imaginary Powers, but real Appetites, or Laws of Motion, or Nature, found in certain Things, whereby they have a Tendency towards, or operate upon, one another at a diftance.

TABLES.

By *Tables* we are to underftand Sets of Papers, containing each TABLE. its feparate Matter, or particular *Inftances*, Experiments, Obferva- tions, &c. for filling up the Heads of any Enquiry, and working upon any Subject, in the Method of Induction, fo as no way to truft or burthen the Memory, or confound the Underftanding; but proceed as in Algebraical Operations, or as with a certain Machine, or well- adapted mechanical Contrivance for the purpofe. See the Article *Novum Organum.*

TOPICAL INVENTION.

By *Topical Invention* we are to underftand a new Method, de- TOPICAL IN- pending upon a Mixture of Logic and Philofophy, of fetting down VENTION the principal Heads, or leading Particulars, of an Enquiry; fo as that the whole may be profecuted to the beft Advantage, both with regard to the Operation of the Mind, and the Difcovery of the Thing fought.

TRADITIVE

By *Traditive Doctrine*, we are to underftand all the Arts re- TRADITIVE lating to Words and Difcourfe; as Grammar, Hieroglyphicks, Wri- DOCTRINE ting, Cypher, &c

By *Traditive Lamp*, the Author denotes a new Method of Teach- TRADITIVE ing; or a fcientifical, initiative, leading, and improveable manner LAMP of delivering down the Sciences to Pofterity; inftead of the Doctrinal or Dogmatical Method in ufe.

By *Traditive Prudence*, the Author underftands the Doctrine of TRAD TIVE Method in Speech. PRUDENCE

TRANSCENDENTAL. See *Adventitious Conditions.*

UNION AND UNITY OF NATURE. See *Nature*

WORKS.

By *Works* the Author underftands confiderable Acts of the Human WORKS Power, or Mafteries over Nature; fo as by folid, and rational Means,

to

to fubdue and bend her to the more ufeful Purpofes; as in lengthening the common Period of Life, making the Wind do the Office
of animal Strength, governing the Weather with all other Things
of the like ufeful kind, in refpect to the Accommodation of Life.

N B The Defign of this *Gloffary* is not to give exact Definitions of
the Author's Philofophical Terms, but only fome general Notions of them, to prevent any Mifconftruction, and facilitate
the underftanding of his Works. In which View, it might
not be amifs for thofe unacquainted with the Author, to
go over the *Gloffary* once or twice, before the whole Work
is begun to be read   For as he had different Views, with regard to the Improvement of Philofophy, from any of his Predeceffors, he was under a neceffity of coining new Terms, where
none were extant to exprefs his Meaning   But when Words had
already been applied, in a Senfe approaching to that he intended, he
ufes them in a guarded manner, fo as to exprefs no other than Actions, Facts, Phænomena, or Realities, as they are found in Nature   And under this Reftriction we are to underftand the Words
*Antipathy, Attraction, Fuga Vacui, Motion of Connexion, Sym-
pathy,* &c

29 MR 64

I N-

INSTAURATION

PART I.

h

PREFACE.

THE *Design of this first Part of the* INSTAURATION, *is to give a summary Account of that Stock of Knowledge whereof Mankind are possessed; to lay this Knowledge down under such natural Branches, or scientifical Divisions, as may most commodiously admit of its farther Improvement, to point out its Deficiences, or* Desiderata, *and, lastly, to shew, by Examples, the direct Ways of supplying these Deficiences*

In the Execution of this Plan, the Author ranges all human Knowledge under the several Arts *and* Sciences, *in the order of Nature, so as to shew how these are formed from the general Mass, and how they may be improved   Whence he is often obliged to depart from the received* Divisions *of the* Sciences, *tho without absolutely disapproving the Use of those* Divisions *on other Occasions. For the Nature of his Design laid him under a double necessity of altering them,* first, *because to class and sort Matters as they are related in Nature, is a quite different End and Intention from that of throwing them together in a Heap for use   Thus, a Secretary of State sorts and distributes his Papers in his general Office, so as to lay those of like kind together,* viz. *Treaties along with Treaties, Instructions along with Instructions, Foreign Letters, Domestic Letters,* &c. *each in their separate Cells, tho' in some particular Cabinet he may lay such together, as, however different in kind, are likely to be used together   After the same manner the Author, in* this *general* Repository *of Learning, was necessitated to make his Divisions according to the Natures, not according to the common Uses of Things · whereas, had he been to treat any particular Science, he would perhaps have followed the Divisions that are better accommodated to Use and Practice*

h 2

His

His second *Reason for altering the received Divisions is, that as he every where sets down the* Desiderata *in the Sciences; and works up these* Desiderata *into one Body with the rest, he was, on this account also, obliged to alter, and enlarge the former Division, to make room for new Arts, and new Branches of Science*

With regard to the Matter, or Things delivered in the following Piece, the Author foresaw that the principal Objections would lie against those set down as deficient, those he proposes to be effected, and those of an inferior, or secondary Consideration

For, the Deficiences here pointed out, may be imagined already supplied by some one or other of the Ancients or Moderns. But in this Particular, great Diligence and Attention are required, to perceive, in a strong and pure Light, the several Designs and Schemes of the Author, in their full Latitude, Scope, and Tendency · and, on the other hand, a sober Examination of such supposed Ancients and Moderns must be undertaken, to shew whether this be more than a light Suspicion, or whether they have, in reality, had any such Views for the perfecting of Arts and Sciences [a].

As to the several great Things pointed out to be performed; if they appear too difficult, or unsuitable to human Abilities, the Author desires to be understood in this Light, that all those Things are to be esteemed possible, and performable, which may be effected, (1) by certain Persons, tho' not by every one, (2.) by many in conjunction, tho' not by any sole Hand, (3) by a Succession of Ages, tho' not in a single Age, and (4) by publick Care, and a publick Expence, tho' not by private Industry, and a private Purse

But for those who had rather abide by that Saying of Solomon, *there is a* Lion *in the* Way; *than that of* Virgil, possunt quia posse videntur [b], *the Author is content they should esteem his Labours only as Wishes, provided they be Wishes of the better sort because, as it requires some Skill to ask a proper Question; so it requires some Knowledge to make a reasonable Wish*

But as there are some Particulars in the following Work, which may appear too great, there are others, that may be thought too minute and trivial To this the Author answers, that his Design was to make a general Map of the Sciences; without omitting the lesser, or more remote Islands yet, not so as to exhibit an ostentatious Muster-Roll of Arts and Sciences, but to give, in a concise, and
lively

---

[a] See the first Part of the *Novum Organum*, passim.
[b] To think Things possible, will make them so

lively manner, the Marrow, or Kernels of the Sciences, selected from a large Mass of Matter. For tho' it be a common Practice with those who seek a Character for general Learning, to deal in Terms, and make a specious Shew of the Outsides of Arts; thus raising the Wonder of the Ignorant, but rendring themselves ridiculous to the Masters in Science, the Author hopes, on the contrary, that chiefly the Persons best skilled in the several Arts and Sciences he endeavours to improve, will here find the most Exercise for their Judgments; and those not so well versed therein, less proportionably.

Again, he would have it remembred, that as many private Gentlemen are eminent, and distinguished at their Country-Seats, but appear less considerable, when they come to the Metropolis: so the secondary, or smaller Arts, lose of their Dignity, when placed in the same Work among the nobler; tho' they still appear great, and excellent, to such as have bestowed their principal Time and Pains upon them. We are also required to remember, that the Author every where prefers Utility, and Advantage, to Beauty, Elegance, and Grandeur

This leads us to observe his general manner of Procedure, as it differs from that of ordinary Writers. For, instead of practising the common Artifices of Writing, so as to raise a Reputation by answering, or confuting, the Doctrines and Opinions of others, and setting his own in the strongest Blaze, by borrowed Ornaments, he is content to use the less pompous Arts, and deliver sound and serviceable Matter in a clear Method, and easy Expression. He no way affects to differ from others; nor innovates without necessity; or for the sake of some considerable Advantage, being firmly persuaded, that if what he delivers be just and useful, the Voice of Nature will answer to it, tho' the Voice of Men should cry it down. And, in this Sense, he applies to himself that Verse in Virgil, Non canimus surdis, respondent omnia Sylvæ[a].

In the same manner, he often compares his own Procedure in intellectual Matters, to that Expedition of the French against Naples; whereof Alexander Borgia used to say, that they came not with Sword, but Chalk, in hand, to mark out their Lodgings, rather than to fight for so the Author's Design is to gain a peaceable Entrance for Truth, into those Minds that are capable of lodging so great a Guest, by singling, and marking out such Minds, as it were with Chalk, and not forcing a Way for Truth by Controversy, Confutation, and Contention

To

[a] Our Lays are heard, the Woods approve them all.

PREFACE.

To the same purpose he adds, that he should be considered as a Herald whose Office is not to fight, but to be, as Homer *expresses it, a Messenger of Gods and Men, and therefore, that it is against the Law of Arms, to attack or wound such a Herald, especially as he sounds not the Alarm to Battle, or Altercation, but rather a Surcease, that Men being at Peace among themselves, may turn their united Forces against Nature, break down her strong Holds, and, as far as the Author of Nature allows, enlarge the Empire of Man*

In this gentle manner of Procedure, therefore, the principal Arts employed by the Author are Order, Metaphor, and, where the Subject would allow it, Perspicuity of Style. For when much new Matter is to be delivered, new Expressions, or a new use of the old ones must be introduced And this latter Expedient, to avoid Opposition and too sudden an Innovation, is frequently practised by the Author

There was a particular Reason for the use of Metaphor, and a figurative Style, in the following Piece, being written at a Time when Men s Minds were under a strong Prejudice, from the Doctrine of Aristotle *and the Schools For it must be carefully observed, that the only effectual way of conquering Prejudices, and delivering new Doctrines to advantage, is artfully to steal into the Mind under the Cover of Metaphor and Allusion And hence it is, that the Style of the following Piece is designedly more figurative than in other Parts of the* Instauration

Upon the whole, it appears that the Original of this Work has been greatly laboured, not only with regard to the Matter, but also to the Method, and the Style. so that it may admit of a Question, whether a more useful, more exact, and perfect Philosophical Writing can be any where found This is mentioned the rather, that the Errors, and Insufficiency of the Translator, may not be laid at the door of the Author.

And as so much pains has been taken on the side of the Author, some also is doubtless required on the side of the Reader ; in order fully to enter into the Sense and Energy of the Piece so that, at length, it may be generally understood, as it deserves, the Directions it delivers be more effectually pursued, and Arts and Sciences no longer remain those imperfect Things they are.

We must particularly remember, that the Examples of Works, here left us by the Author, are but Examples, that shew the way of improving the Sciences, and should, by no means, be esteemed just Treatises the utmost he intended them for, being to serve as Specimens,

a See n either pag 148 and *Novum Organum*, Part I passim

mens, Patterns, or Sketches, from which some Judgment might be formed, or a just Expectation conceived, of the respective Pieces when they should be finished

To sum up all, the Reader has here a Work fundamental to the Improvement of the Sciences, that strongly endeavours to enlarge the present Stock of human Knowledge, and raise it to the highest Pitch whereof it is capable. What a Pitch that is, must not be judged of from the mere natural Abilities of Men; but as they may be assisted by Art, or by a new Method of Working with the Mind, which is delivered in the Novum Organum, or second Part of the INSTAURATION

29 MR 64

A N

AN
ANALYTICAL VIEW
OF THE
SCHEME
OF THE

DE AUGMENTIS SCIENTIARUM;

OR,

The Divifion of KNOWLEDGE into proper Branches;
in order to its farther Improvement.

PRELIMINARIES.

I

The Difcredits of Learning.

THE Objections to Learning confider'd, under (1) the Objections of *Divines*, (2) the Objections of *Politicians*, and (3) the Objections to the Fortune, Behaviour, and Studies of *Learned Men.*

1 *Divines* alledge, (1) that the Defire of Knowledge was the Original Sin, (2) that it is infinite and anxious, and (3) that it caufes Herefies and Atheifm

2 *Politicians* alledge, (1) that Learning unfits Men for Arms, (2) incapacitates them for Civil Affairs, and (3) proves dangerous to States.

3 *Learned Men* objected to, (1) as apt to neglect their private Affairs, and impoverifh themfelves, (2) as not properly applying to Perfons in Power, (3) as failing in point of Behaviour, and (4) fometimes, as giving into grofs Flattery.

II.

The Diseases of Learning.

viz

1 A Fondness for Style, or Words, rather than Matter.
2. Idle Disputes, and Cavils.
3. Credulity and Imposture.

III

The Peccant Humours of Learning.

viz.

1. Affectation of Antiquity, or Novelty.
2 Diffidence of the Possibility of new Discoveries.
3 Strong Prepossession that the best Opinions and Philosophies have always prevailed
4 An unseasonable and hasty Reducing of Knowledge to Methods and Systems
5 The Neglect of general Philosophy ; as a thing superior to the common Arts and Sciences.
6. Admiration of the contemplative Powers of the Understanding , and an untimely Desertion of Observation and Experience.
7 The tinging, infecting, or corrupting of *General Philosophy* with particular Arts and Studies.
8 Impatience of Doubting ; or the want of a proper Suspension of the Judgment.
9 A dogmatical and imperious manner of Teaching and Delivering the Sciences
10. Narrow Views in Learned Men , regarding not the Advancement of the Sciences, but inferior Considerations
11 A Mistaking of the true End of Knowledge, and turning aside to Curiosity, Amusement, Lucre, Promotion, &c.

IV.

The Dignity of Learning argued from Divine Authority.

(1) The Wisdom, or Knowledge of the Creator. (2) The Knowledge of Angels (3) The Production of Light (4) The Employment in Paradise. (5) The Life of *Cain* and *Abel* (6) Inventors before the Flood. (7) The Confusion of Tongues (8) The Learning of *Moses*. (9) *Job* (10) *Solomon* (11) The Procedure of *Christ*, in subduing Ignorance, working Miracles, and sending the Gift of Tongues. (12) The Learning of St. *Paul* (13) The Learning of many Fathers of the Church (14) Learning raises the Mind to glorify God. And, (15) is the Preservative against Error and Infidelity.

V
The Dignity of Learning shewn from Human Testimony.

(1) Inventors of Arts deified among the Heathens   (2) Civil Policy regulated, and States advanced, by Learning   (3) Learned Princes the best Governours   (4) Learning has a great Influence upon military Virtue.

VI
The Dignity of Learning argued from the Influence it has upon Moral Virtue.

(1) That Learning is sovereign in curing the Diforders of the Mind   (2) Has a greater Dominion than any Temporal Power, as ruling over Reafon and Belief   (3) Advances Private Men   (4) Affords great Delight to the Mind   (5) Gives Perpetuity and Fame, and may remain after Death.

VII
The Public Means of promoting Learning.
viz

In *general*, (1) Ample Rewards ; (2) Prudent Direction, and, (3) United Labours

In *particular* ; (1) Select Places for Study, (2) Proper Books, and, (3) Suitable Teachers

The Places must have four Requifites, viz (1) Convenient Buildings, (2) Anfwerable Endowments, (3) Certain Privileges, and, (4) Laws of Difcipline.

Books must have two Requifites, viz. Libraries ; and good Editions.

Teachers to be of two forts, viz   Readers in the prefent Arts and Sciences, and Enquirers after new ones

Under thefe Acts for advancing the Sciences, are found fix Defects, viz (1) The Want of a Foundation for Arts, and Philofophy at large   (2) The Want of competent Salaries for Readers and Profeffors   (3) The Want of a Stock to defray the Charge of Experiments   (4) A Want of Infpecting the Univerfities, to fee what Cuftoms, Readings, and Exercifes fhould be repealed or alter'd, as Time alters, or Learning improves.   (5) Want of mutual Correfpondence, and Intelligence, among the different Univerfities of *Europe*.   And, (6) the Want of a public Inftitution for enquiring into the Arts hitherto undifcover'd.

THE DISTRIBUTION OF KNOWLEDGE.

KNOWLEDGE divided, with regard to the intellectual Faculties of (1) the Memory, (2) the Imagination, and (3) the Reafon, into I. *Hiftory*, II. *Poetry*, and III *Philofophy*

I

HISTORY divided into (1) *Natural*, and (2) *Civil*

(1)

(1) *Natural Hiftory* divided, with regard to the Subject, into three Parts, treating (1) of Generations, (2) of Prætergenerations, and (3) of Arts

Natural Hiftory again divided, with regard to its Ufes, into *Narrative* and *Inductive*

(2) *Civil Hiftory*, in the general, divided into three particular kinds; *viz* (1) *Literary*, (2) *Civil*, and (3) *Sacred*

1 *Literary Hiftory* relates (1) what kinds of Learning and Arts flourifhed in what Ages, and Parts of the World, (2) their Antiquities and Progrefs on the Globe, &c

2 *Particular Civil Hiftory* divided into three kinds; *viz.* the *unfinifhed*, the *finifhed*, and *defaced*, and accordingly found in *Memoirs, juft Hiftory*, and *Antiquities*

Juft Civil Hiftory divided into three kinds, with regard to its three Objects; *viz* a Portion of Time, a memorable Perfon, or an illuftrious Action, and accordingly found under the Form of *Annals*, or *Chronicles*, *Lives*, and *Narratives*, or *Relations*

Hiftory of Times divided into general and particular, or as it relates the Tranfactions of the whole World, or only of a particular Nation.

Hiftory of Times is likewife divided into *Annals* and *Journals*, the former to contain the Matters of greater, and the other the Matters of leffer confequence to a State

Particular Civil Hiftory is alfo divifible into *pure* and *mixed* and of this *mixed Hiftory* there are two eminent kinds, the one principally *civil*, the other principally *natural*

Cofmographical Hiftory is alfo a *mixt Hiftory*

3 *Sacred* or *Ecclefiaftical Hiftory* in general, divided into (1) the general Hiftory of the Church, (2) the Hiftory of Prophecy, and (3) the Hiftory of Providence

The general Hiftory of the Church has three Parts, and defcribes (1) the Perfecution, (2) the Migration, and (3) the Peace of the Church

The Hiftory of Prophecy has two Parts, *viz* (1) the Prophecies themfelves, and (2) their Accomplifhments.

The Hiftory of Providence regards, (1) the revealed, and (2) the fecret Will of God, fo as to fhew the Agreement there fometimes is betwixt them.

Hiftory has three *Appendages*; *viz Speeches, Letters*, and *Apophthegms.*

II

POETRY divided into (1) *Narrative*, or *Heroical*; (2) *Dramatical*, and (3) *Allegorical.*

III

PHILOSOPHY divided into three Branches, *viz* (1) Divine, (2) Natural, and (3) Human.

But the *Trunk* is a *Primary* or *General* Science, containing (1) the Axioms of all Sciences, capable of fupplying the Branches, and, (2) the Adventitious or Tranfcendental Conditions of Things.

(1) *Divine Philosophy*, or Natural Theology, has two Parts; the one relating to the Being and Attributes of God, the other, to the Nature of Spirits and Angels

(2) *Natural Philosophy* divided into *Speculative* and *Practical*

Speculative Philosophy divided into *Physicks* and *Metaphysicks*.

Physicks divided into (1) *The Doctrine of Principles*, (2) *The Doctrine of the Structure of the Universe*, and, (3) *The Doctrine of the Variety of Things*

The Doctrine of the Variety of Things divided into *Concrete Physicks*, and *Abstract Physicks*, or Physicks of Creatures, and Physicks of Natures.

Concrete Physicks divided as *Natural History*

Abstract Physicks divided into (1) the Doctrine of the Schemes of Matter, and (2) the Doctrine of Appetites and Motions

To *Physicks* belong three *Appendages*, viz (1) the Measure of Motions, (2) Natural Problems; and, (3) the Opinions of the ancient Philosophers.

Metaphysick divided into (1) the Investigation of Forms, and (2) the Enquiry after *Final Causes*

Practical Philosophy divided conformably to the Theoretical, viz into *Mechanicks* and *Magick*.

To Practical Philosophy belong two Appendages, viz (1) an Inventory of human Knowledge, and, (2) a Calendar of Leading Experiments

Mathematicks makes an Appendage to Physicks, Metaphysicks, Mechanicks, and Magicks, and is divided into *pure* and *mixed*.

Pure Mathematicks divided into *Geometry* and *Arithmetick*.

Mixed Mathematicks divided into *Perspective*, *Musick*, *Astronomy*, *Cosmography*, *Architecture*, *Mechanicks*, &c

(3) *Human Philosophy* has two general Parts, viz. *Human*, and *Civil Doctrine*

Human Doctrine divided into the Doctrine of the human *Body*, and of the human *Soul*

But here is interposed a *general Science* of the Nature and State of Man, wherein both Body and Soul participate.

This *general Science* is divided (1) into the *Doctrine of the human Person*, and (2) the *Doctrine of Union*

(1) The *Doctrine of the human Person* has two Parts, and considers (1) the Miseries, and (2) the Prerogatives, or Excellencies of Mankind.

(2) The *Doctrine of Union* has two Parts, relating how the Soul and Body mutually act upon each other, (1) by *Notices*, or Indication, and, (2) by Impression

The *Doctrine of Notices* regards Physiognomy, and the Interpetation of Dreams

The *Doctrine of Impression* considers (1) how far the Body may affect the Soul; and (2) how, and to what degree, the Passions of the Soul may affect the Body

The Doctrine of the Human Body divided into four Parts, viz (1) *Medicine*; (2) *Cosmeticks*, (3) *Gymnasticks*, and, (4) the *Art of Elegance*.

1. *Medicine* divided into three Parts, viz (1) the Preservation of Health, (2) the Cure of Diseases, and, (3) the Prolongation of Life ·

2 The *Art of Cosmeticks* divided into *civil* and *effeminate*

3 *Gymnasticks* divided into the *Arts of Activity*, and the *Arts of Endurance* or *Suffering*.

4. The *Art of Elegance* divided with regard to the *Eye* and the *Ear*, or into *Painting*, *Musick*, &c.

The DOCTRINE OF THE HUMAN SOUL divided into (1) the *Doctrine of the inspired Substance*; and (2) the *Doctrine of the sensitive Soul.*

Two *Appendages* to this *Doctrine of the Soul*; viz *Divination* and *Fascination*

The *Doctrine of the sensitive Soul* divided into (1) the *Doctrine of voluntary Motion*, and (2) the *Doctrine of Sense and Sensibility*.

The DOCTRINE OF THE MENTAL FACULTIES divided into (1) Lo-GICKS, and (2) ETHICKS

The *Logical*, or *Rational*, *Arts*, are four, viz (1) the *Art of Enquiry or Invention*, (2) the *Art of Examination*, or *Judging*, (3) the *Art of Custody*, or *Memory*, and (4) the *Art of Elocution*, or *Delivery*.

[1] The Art of *Enquiry*, or *Invention*, relates either to the discovery of *Arts*, or *Arguments*,

The Art of Discovery divided into two Parts; as it proceeds (1) from Experiment to Experiment, which is *Learned Experience*, or (2) from Experiments to Axioms, which is the Art of Induction

The *Art of discovering Arguments* divided into (1) the *Topical*; and (2) the *Promptuary Method.*

Topical Invention divided into *general* and *particular*

[2] The *Art of Examination*, or *Judging*, divided into *corrupt* and *genuine*; or *Syllogism* and *Induction*

The *Art of Judging* again divided into *Analyticks*, and the *Doctrine of Confutations.*

The *Doctrine of Confutations* divided (1) into the Confutation of Sophisms; (2) the Confutation of Interpretation, and (3) the Confutation of *Idols*, or false Notions

The Doctrine of *Idols* divided (1) into *Idols of the Tribe*; (2) *Idols of the Den*, and (3) *Idols of the Market.*

Appendix to the Art of Judging, shewing what kind of Demonstration should be applied to each Subject

[3] The *Art of Custody*, or *Memory*, divided (1) into the Doctrine of *Helps for the Memory*, and (2) the Doctrine of the Memory itself.

Artificial Memory, or the Doctrine of Helps for the Memory, has two Parts, viz. *Prænotion* and *Emblem*

[4] The *Art of Elocution*, or *Doctrine of Delivery*, divided into (1) *Grammar*, (2) *Method*, and (3) *Ornament of Speech*

1. *Grammar*, divided into (1) the *Art of Speaking*, and (2) the *Art of Writing.*

A *Traditive Doctrine* has more Descendants besides *Words* and *Letters*, and may be divided into (1) Hieroglyphicks and Gestures, and (2) Real Characters.

Grammar

Grammar again divided into *Literary* and *Philosophical*, or with regard to Words and Things

The *Art of Speaking* regards the Accidents of Words; viz. (1) Sound, (2) Measure, and (3) Accent.

The *Art of Writing* has two Parts, with regard (1) to *Alphabet*, and (2) *Cypher*

The *Art of Cypher* has two Parts, viz *Cyphering* and *Decyphering*

2 The *Method of Speech*, or *Doctrine of Traditive Prudence*, distinguish'd (1) into *Doctrinal* and *Initiative*, (2) into *open* and *concealed*, (3) into *Aphoristical* and *Regular*, (4) into *Question* and *Answer*, and (5) the *Method* of *conquering Prejudice*

The two Parts of *Method*; viz *general* and *particular*. the one regarding a Whole, the other its Parts

3 The *Doctrine of Ornament in Speech*, under which comes *Rhetorick*, or *Oratory*

Three *Appendages* to this Doctrine, viz (1) *a Collection of Sophisms*, (2) *a Collection of studied Antithets*, and (3) *a Collection of lesser Forms of Speech*.

Two general *Appendages to the Doctrine* of Delivery, viz. (1) the *Art of Criticism*, and (2) *School-Learning*

Criticism divided with regard (1) to the giving *Editions of Authors*, (2) the *Illustrating of Authors* by Notes, &c. and (3) the *Judging* or *Censuring of Authors*

School-Learning consider'd under the Heads of (1) publick *Schools* and *Colleges*, (2) of preparing the *Genius*, (3) of *suiting the Study to the Genius*; (4) the Use of *Academical Exercises*; and (5) the Action of the Stage, consider'd as a Part of Discipline in Schools

ETHICKS, or *Morality*, divided into (1) the *Doctrine of the Image of Good*, and (2) the *Cultivation*, or *Georgicks*, of the Mind

The Doctrine of the *Image of Good* divided into *Simple* and *Compound*

Good divided (1) into *Individual* or *Self Good*, and (2) *Good of Communion*

Individual Good divided into *Active* and *Passive*

Passive Good divided into *Perfective* and *Conservative*

The *Good of Communion*, or *Duties*, with regard to Society, divided (1) into the *Duties of Man in common*, (2) *Respective Duties*, and (3) the *Doctrine of Fraud*

The *Cultivation of the Mind* divided into (1) the Improvement of the Mind, and, (2) the Cure of its Diseases, which regard (1) different Dispositions; (2) Affections, and, 3) Remedies as the Art of Physick regards the Constitution, the Distemper, and the Cure

Appendix to the Cultivation of the Mind; viz. the Relation betwixt the Good of the Mind, and the Good of the Body

CIVIL KNOWLEDGE divided into three kinds of *Doctrine*, or Prudence, viz (1) Prudence in Conversation; (2) Prudence in Business, and, (3) Prudence in Government.

The

The *Doctrine of Bufinefs* divided into (1) the *Doctrine of various Occafions*; and, (2) the *Doctrine of rifing in Life*.

The *Doctrine of Government* divided as it regards (1) the Prefervation, (2) the Happinefs, and (3) the Enlargement of a State.

The *Doctrine of univerfal Juftice*, or Laws, divided (1) as to the Certainty of their Senfe; (2) Juftnefs of Command; (3) Commodioufnefs of Execution, (4) Agreement to the Form of Government, and, (5) as they are productive of Virtue in the Subject.

The *Divifion of Infpired Theology*, or *Divinity*, left to Divines.

Its three *Appendages*; viz (1) The Moderator, or the true Ufe of Human Reafon in Theology, (2) a Difcourfe upon the Degrees of Unity in the City of God, and, (3) the firft Flowings of the Scriptures: or a fhort, found, and judicious Collection of Notes, and Obfervations, upon particular Texts of facred Writ.

D E

AUGMENTIS SCIENTIARUM:

O R, T H E

Arrangement, and General Survey,

O F

K N O W L E D G E ;

W I T H

Its particular DEFECTS; *and the Ways of supplying them, for the Advancement of* ARTS *and* SCIENCES.

THE
ARRANGEMENT,
AND
GENERAL SURVEY,
OF
KNOWLEDGE, &c.

PRELIMINARIES.

SECT. I.

Containing a Plan for the Rectification, and Promotion, of Knowledge in general.

1 **B**Eing convinced, by a careful Obfervation, that the *human Under-* The general *ftanding* perplexes it felf, or makes not a fober and advantageous Defign Ufe of the real *Helps* within its reach ; whence manifold ignorance and inconveniences arife, we are determined to employ our utmoft Endeavours towards reftoring, or cultivating, a juft and legitimate Familiarity betwixt the *Mind* and *Things* [a]

2. But as the *Mind*, haftily, and without choice, imbibes and treafures *Imperfection of* up the firft Notices of Things, from whence all the reft proceed, Errors *the human* muft for ever prevail, and remain uncorrected, either by the natural Powers *Knowledge.* of the Underftanding, or the Affiftance of *Logic.* for the original Notions being vitiated, confufed, and inconfiderately taken from Things, and the fecondary ones form'd no lefs rafhly, *human Knowledge* itfelf, the Thing employ'd in all our Refearches, is not well put together, nor juftly formed, but like a magnificent Structure on a bad Foundation [b]

B 2 3.

[a] That is, as will appear hereafter, the raifing a *new Art*, by joining *Reafon* and *Experiment* together, for the improvement of *Philofophy* See below, 18, 22, and 25

[b] *Human Knowledge* is here confider'd in its common imperfect ftate, not according to what it may be brought to, with the proper Conduct, and Regulation See Sect. II 14

3 And whilst Men agree to admire and magnify the *false Powers of the
Mind*, and neglect or destroy those that might be rendered *true*, there is
no other course left, but with better assistances to begin the *Work* a-new, and
raise or rebuild the *Sciences, Arts*, and all *human Knowledge* from a firm and
solid foundation.

4 This may at first seem an infinite *Scheme*, unequal to human Abilities,
yet it will be found more sound and sober than the Schemes we have already,
as tending to some issue: whereas all hitherto done with regard to the *Sciences*,
is vertiginous, or in the way of perpetual rotation.

5 To tell the truth, Men do not appear to know their own stock and
abilities, but fancy their Possessions greater, and their Faculties less, than they
are: whence either valuing the receiv'd Arts above measure, they look out
no farther, or else despising themselves too much, they exercise their talents
upon lighter matters, without attempting the *capital things* of all.[c] And
hence the Sciences seem to have their *Hercules's Pillars*, which bound the desires and hopes of mankind.

6 But as a false imagination of Plenty comes among the principal causes
of *Want*, and as too great a confidence in things present leads to a neglect
of future assistance, 'tis necessary we should here admonish Mankind that
they do not too highly value and extol either the number or usefulness of
the Things hitherto discovered. For, by closely inspecting the multiplicity
of *Books* upon *Art* and *Science*, we find them to contain numberless repetitions of the same things in point of invention, but differing indeed as to
the manner of treatment: so that the real *Discoveries*, tho' at first blush they
might appear numerous, prove upon examination, but few.[d] And as to
the point of usefulness, the *Philosophy* we principally receiv'd from the *Greeks*,
must be acknowledged puerile, or rather talkative, than generative, as being
fruitful in controversies, but barren of works.[e]

7 And had this not been a lifeless kind of *Philosophy*, 'twere scarce possible it should have made so little progress in so many ages, insomuch that
not only *Positions* now frequently remain *Positions* still, but *Questions* remain
Questions, rather rivetted and cherish'd, than determin'd, by Disputes. Philosophy thus coming down to us in the persons of *Master* and *Scholar*, instead
of *Inventor* and *Improver*.

8

[a] For instance, *theoretical Reasoning*, without a sufficient Ground-work of Fact, and Observation, those being here called *false Powers of the Mind* which lead to Error, and *false Conclusions.* See Sect. III. 42. & *Novum Organum*, Sect. I. 9.

[b] Of the necessity for this, every one is to be convinced from his own observation and experience: but the Reasons for the Undertaking are fully open'd hereafter, especially in the entrance
of the *Novum Organum.* See also below, ib. & Sect II. 14.

[c] Such, for instance, as in moral Philosophy, a command of the Passions, and in natural Philosophy, a command of the Winds, the Weather, &c.

[d] Nor are the Discoveries and Improvements made since this Author wrote, perhaps, so
numerous or so weighty as some imagine: at best they execute but a small part of his general Scheme for the promotion of Knowledge.

[e] And to make a right knowledge both of the *Greek Philosophy*, and of the subtilties of *Nature*,
comes requisite, in order to form this judgment. We are generally so prepossess'd in favour of
this Philosophy, as seldom to see its emptiness. The way of being satisfied is to try its strength
in conquering the difficulties of Nature, and producing *Effects.*

8 In the *Mechanic Arts* the cafe is otherwife, thefe commonly advancing *Mechanic* towards perfection, in a courfe of daily improvement, from a rough unpo- *Arts.* lifh'd ftate, fometimes prejudicial to the firft Inventors, whilft *Philofophy* and the *intellectual Sciences* are, like Statues, celebrated and adored, but never pro- moted　may they fometimes appear moft perfect in the original Author, and afterwards degenerate [a]　For when once men take up with the opinions of others, they no longer improve the *Sciences*, but fervilely beftow their talents in adorning and defending fome particular authors

9 'Tis a fatal miftake to fuppofe that the *Sciences* have gradually arrived at *The Sciences* a ftate of perfection, and then been recorded by fome one Writer or other; *not recorded* and that as nothing better can afterwards be invented, men need but culti- *perfect* vate and fet off what is thus difcovered and compleated　whereas, in reality, this regiftring of the Sciences proceeds only from the affurance of a few, and the floth and ignorance of many　For after the *Sciences*, might thus perhaps, in feveral parts, be carefully cultivated, a man of an undertaking genius rifing up, who by the concifenefs of his method renders himfelf acceptable and famous, he, in appearance, erects an *Art*, but in reality corrupts the labours of his Predeceffors [b]

10. This however is ufually well received by Pofterity, as readily grati- fying their curiofity, and indulging their indolence　But he that refts up- on eftablifh'd Confent, as the judgment approved by Time, trufts to a very fallacious and weak foundation　for we have but an imperfect knowledge of the difcoveries in *Arts* and *Sciences*, made public in different ages and coun- tries, and ftill lefs of what has been done by particular perfons, and tranfact- ed in private　Whence neither the *Births* nor *Mifcarriages of Time* [c] are to be found in our Records

11 Nor is *Confent*, or the continuance thereof, a thing of any great ac- *General Con-* count　for however Governments may vary, there is but *one ftate of the Sci*n- *fent of little* *ces*, and that will for ever be Democratical or popular　But the Doctrines *weight in* of greateft vogue among the people, are either the contentious and quar- *Philofophies.* relfome, or the fhewy and empty, that is, fuch as may either entrap the affent, or lull the mind to reft　whence, of courfe, the greateft Genius's in all ages, have fuffer'd violence, whilft out of regard to their own character, they fubmitted to the *judgment of the Times*, and the Populace [d]　And thus when any more fublime Speculations happen'd to appear, they were commonly tofs'd and extinguifh'd by the breath of popular opinion　Whence Time, like a River, has brought down to us what is light and tumid, but funk what was ponderous and folid [e]

12.

---

[a] As from the time of *Ariftotle* till the revival of Mathematical and Experimental Philofo- phy in *Europe*, particularly by our Author, *Galilæo, Gaffendi*, &c

[b] By wrefting them, fuppofe, and fafhioning them into Methods and Syftems before the time See hereafter Sect III 40

[c] That is, neither the Inventions, nor a Hiftory of the Attempts and Failures, of Antiquity

[d] *Viz* in their affent, and public behaviour, tho' not in their private judgment　The Addrefs of our Author in this particular may deferve to be obferved thro' the whole Work

[e] For inftance, Time has thus brought down the Philofophies of *Plato* and *Ariftotle*, but funk that of *Democritus*, &c　See *Pancirollus de Rebus deperditis, cum Not. Henric Salmuth, & Supplement Mich Watfon*

The Procedure of those who teach the Sciences

12 As to those who have set up for *Teachers of the Sciences*, when they drop their Characters, and at intervals speak their sentiments, they complain of the subtilty of Nature, the concealment of Truth, the obscurity of Things, the entanglement of Causes, and the imperfection of the human Understanding thus rather chusing to accuse the common State of Men and Things, than make confession of themselves. 'Tis also frequent with them to adjudge that impossible in an Art which they find that Art does not effect, by which means they skreen indolence and ignorance from the reproach they merit[a].

The extraordinary Philosopher

13 And even those who by experience propose to enlarge the bounds of the Sciences, scarce ever entirely quit the receiv'd opinions, and go to the fountain-head, but think it enough to add somewhat of their own as prudently considering, that at the time they shew their modesty in *assenting*, they may have a liberty of *adding* But whilst this regard is shewn to Opinions and moral Considerations, the *Sciences* are greatly hurt by such a languid procedure, for 'tis scarce possible at once to admire and excel an author as Water rises no nigher than the Reservoir it falls from. Such men therefore, tho' they improve some things, yet advance the Sciences but little, or rather amend than enlarge them

The innovators character'd

14 There have been also bolder Spirits, and greater Genius's, who thought themselves at liberty to overturn and destroy the *ancient Doctrine*, and make way for themselves and their *own Opinions* but without any great advantage from the disturbance, as they did not effectively enlarge *Philosophy* and *Arts* by practical Works[b], but only endeavour'd to alter men's Notions, and set themselves at the Head of *Opinions*[c].

The ... of ... the Philosophers

15 As for those who, neither wedded to their own nor others Opinions, but continuing friends to liberty, made use of *assistance* in their Enquiries, the success they met with did not answer to expectation, the attempt, tho' laudable, being but feeble for pursuing only the *probable Reasons of things*, they were carried about in a *Circle of Arguments*, and taking a promiscuous liberty, preserv'd not the Rigour of true *Enquirers*, whilst none of them duly convers'd with experience and things themselves

The Mechanical ...

16 Others again, who commit themselves to *mechanical experience*, yet make their experiments at random, without any *method of Enquiry* And the greatest part of these have no considerable Views, but esteem it a great matter if they can make a single Discovery which is both a trifling and unskilful Procedure, as no one can justly, or successfully, discover the nature of any one thing in that thing itself, or without numerous experiments which lead to farther Enquiries[d]

17

---

[a] Nothing is more common than for men to repute Things impossible, or impracticable, for want of a sufficient compass of knowledge to judge of them, and hence several of this Author's Plan have been reputed impracticable particularly that of the *new Atlantis*, for founding a Philosophical College, tho' the *Royal Society* of *London* seems form'd upon that model See *Lord of Verulam's Life* Tom II pag 13 and *Sprat's History of the Royal Society*

[b] See the word *Works* explained in the GLOSSARY

[c] M. *des Cartes* is an eminent Instance of this procedure among the Moderns, tho' the intelligent in Philosophical History find the traces of all his Doctrine among the Ancients

[d] For the proper or *Geometrical Method* of enquiring into Nature, and all Philosophical Subjects, see the *Novum Organum*

17 Laftly, thofe who recommend *Logic* as the beft and fureft Inftrument *The* Logicians. for improving the *Sciences*, very juftly obferve, that the *Underftanding*, left to itfelf, ought always to be fufpected But here the Remedy is neither equal to the Difeafe, nor approved, for tho' the *Logic* in ufe may be properly applied in civil affairs, and the *Arts* that are founded in *Difcourfe* and *Opinion*, yet it by no means reaches the *fubtilty of Nature* and by catching at what it cannot hold, rather ferves to eftablifh Errors, and fix them deeper, than open the *Way to Truth* [a].

18 Upon the whole, Men do not hitherto appear to be happily turned *Infufficiency of* and fitted for the *Sciences*, either by their own induftry, or the authority of *the unaffifted* Authors, efpecially as there is little dependance to be had upon the common *Underftanding* *Demonftrations* and *Experiments* whilft the Structure of the *Univerfe* renders it a *Labyrinth* to the Underftanding, where the *Paths* are not only every where doubtful, but the appearances of things and their figns deceitful; and the *Wreathes* and *Knots* of Nature intricately turn'd and twifted [b]: thro' all which we are only to be conducted by the uncertain Light of the Senfes, that fometimes fhines, and fometimes hides its head, and by *Collections of Experiments* and *particular Facts*; in which no Guides can be trufted, as wanting direction themfelves, and adding to the Errors of the reft In this melancholy ftate of things, one might be apt to defpair both of the *Underftanding* left to itfelf, and of all fortuitous Helps, as of a ftate irremediable by the utmoft efforts of the human Genius, or the often-repeated chance of Trial The only Clue and Method is to begin all a-new, and direct our fteps in a certain order, from the very firft perceptions of the Senfes [c]

19 This, however, is not to be underftood as if nothing had been ef- *The Perfor-* fected by the immenfe Labours of fo many paft Ages· the *Antients* have per- *mance of the* form'd furprizingly in Subjects that required abftract Meditation, and force *Antients* of Genius. But as Navigation was imperfect before the ufe of the *Compafs*, fo will many Secrets of Nature and Art remain undifcovered, without a more perfect knowledge of the Underftanding, its ufes, and ways of working [d].

20. For our own part, from an earneft defire of Truth, we have commit- *The Procedure* ted ourfelves to doubtful, difficult, and folitary ways, and relying on the *of the* Author Divine Affiftance, have fupported our Mind againft the vehemence of *Opinions*, our own internal *Doubts* and *Scruples*, and the Darknefs, and *fantaftic Images* of the Mind that at length we might make more fure and certain Difcoveries for the benefit of Pofterity And if we fhall have effected any thing to the purpofe, what led us to it was a true and genuine humiliation of Mind Thofe who before us applied themfelves to the difcovery of *Arts*, having juft glanced upon Things, Examples, and Experiments, immediately, as if Invention was but a kind of Contemplation, raifed up their own *Spirits*

to.

---

[a] Thofe who would fee this Hiftory of Philofophy more particularly deduced, may confult *Morhof's Polyhiftor* and the other Writers upon *Polymathy* and *Literary Hiftory*

[b] By *Wreathes* and *Knots*, underftand the apparent *complication of Caufes*, and the fuperaddition of Properties not effential to Things, as Light to Heat, Yellownefs to Gold, Pellucidity to Glafs, *&c*

[c] See above, Sect I 3 and the entrance of the *Novum Organum*.

[d] Thefe laft particulars are the Subject of the *Novum Organum*.

to deliver Oracles[a], whereas our method is continually to dwell among things soberly, without abstracting or setting the Understanding farther from them than makes their Images meet which leaves but little work for Genius and mental Abilities[b].

21 And the same humility that we practise in learning, the same we also observe in teaching, without endeavouring to stamp a dignity on any of our Inventions, by the triumphs of Confutation, the citation of Antiquity, the producing of Authorities, or the mask of Obscurity as any one might do, who had rather give lustre to his own Name, than light to the Minds of others We offer no violence, and spread no nets for the judgments of Men, but lead them on to things themselves, and their relations that they may view their own stores, what they have to reason about, and what they may add, or procure, for the common good.

22 And if at any time ourselves have erred, mistook, or broke off too soon, yet as we only propose to exhibit things naked, and open, as they are, our Errors may be the readier observed, and separated, before they considerably infect the *Mass of Knowledge*, and our labours be the easier continued. And thus we hope to establish a true and legitimate Union between the *experimental* and *rational Faculty*, for ever the undue separation whereof, has caused the greatest disturbances in the family of Mankind[c].

23. But as these things are not at our disposal, we here, at the entrance of our *Work*, with the utmost Humility and Fervency, pour forth our Prayers to *God*, that remembring the Miseries of Mankind, and the Pilgrimage of this Life, where we pass but few days and sorrowful, he would vouchsafe, through our hands, and the hands of others, to whom he has given the like Mind, to relieve the human race by a new act of his Bounty We, likewise, humbly beseech him, that what is human may not clash with what is divine, and that when the *ways of the Senses* are open'd, and a greater *natural Light* set up in the mind, nothing of incredulity and blindness towards the *Mysteries* may arise but rather that the Understanding, now clear'd up, and purged of all vanity and superstition, may remain entirely subject to the *divine Oracles*, and yield to *Faith, the things that are Faith's* and lastly, that expelling the *poisonous Knowledge*[d], infused by the Serpent, which puffs up and swells the human Mind, we may neither be wise above measure, nor go beyond the bounds of sobriety, but pursue the Truth in charity

Acts 1. 7 ?
Mankind

24 We now turn ourselves to *Men*, with a few wholesome Admonitions and just Requests And first, we admonish them to continue in a sense of their Duty, as to divine Matters, for the Senses are like the Sun, which displays the face of the Earth, but shuts up that of the Heavens and again, that they run not into the contrary extreme, which they certainly will do,

if

---

[a] That is, run into what we vulgarly call *Theories* and *Speculations*, instead of keeping to *Observations* and *Experiments* See Sect III 42

[b] *abstracting*, and what we commonly call *Metaphysical Reasoning*, any farther than it it conduces to Action in Life is what the Author guards against, as the Bane of Philosophy, or a kind of Infatuation and Delusion See above, Sect I 3 and *Nov Org* Sect I 9, 10

[c] See above, Sect I 1

[d] See hereafter, Sect III 3 —

if they think an *Enquiry into Nature* any way forbid them by Religion [a]
It was not that pure and unfpotted *natural Knowledge*, whereby *Adam* gave
names to things, agreeable to their natures, which caufed his fall, 'tis an
ambitious and authoritative Defire of *moral Knowledge*, to judge of *Good*
and *Evil*, that makes men revolt from God, and obey no laws but thofe of
their own will [b]   But for the *Sciences*, which contemplate Nature, the facred
Philofopher declares, " 'tis the Glory of *God* to conceal a thing, but the
" Glory of the *King* to find it out"   As if the *Divine Being* thus in-
dulgently condefcended to exercife the human Mind by philofophical Enquiries

25   In the next place, we advife all Mankind to think of the true
Ends of Knowledge , and that they endeavour not after it for curiofity, contention, or the fake of defpifing others , nor yet for profit, reputation,
power, or any fuch inferior confideration , but folely for the occafions
and ufes of Life   all along conducting and perfecting it in the *Spirit of
Benevolence*

26   Our Requefts are, (1) That Men would not conceive we here de- *Requefts.*
liver an *Opinion*, but a *Work*, and affure themfelves we attempt not to found
any *Sect*, or particular Doctrine, but to fix an extenfive Bafis for the fervice
of human Nature. (2) That, for their own fakes, they would lay afide the
Zeal and *Prejudices of Opinions*, and endeavour the common Good , and that
being, by our affiftance, freed and kept clear from the Errors and Hindrances
of the way, they would themfelves alfo take part of the Task   (3.) That
they would not defpair, as imagining our Project for a *grand Reftoration*, or
Promotion of all kinds of Knowledge, infinitely beyond the power of Mortals
to execute, whilft in reality, it is the genuine Stop and Prevention of infinite
Error   Indeed, as our ftate is mortal, and human, a full accomplifhment
cannot be expected in a fingle age , and muft therefore be recommended to
pofterity.   Nor could we hope to fucceed, if we arrogantly fearch'd for the
Sciences in the narrow cells of the human Underftanding, and not fub-
miffively in the wider World   (4) In the laft place, to prevent ill effects
from contention, we defire Mankind would confider how far they have a
right of judging our Performance , upon the foundations here laid down :
for we reject all that Knowledge which is too haftily abftracted from
things, as vague, diforderly, and ill-form'd   and we cannot be expected to
abide by a judgement which is itfelf called in queftion [c]

---

[a] See *Glanvil's Philofophia pia*, printed at *London*, in 1671

[b] See hereafter, *Sect* III 3, 4 *&c*

[c] The Author has guarded againft any Mifinterpretation of this laft *Paffage*, which might
otherwife feem fhocking, as if *common Senfe* and *Knowledge* could not judge of his Scheme,
whilft itfelf is no more than *Knowledge* and *common Senfe* at the bottom, though *Knowledge* rectified,
and *common Senfe* improved   See above, 18, 20, 22 and Sect II 7, 8, 9, *&c* After what manner the whole is propofed to be effected, appears in the following Section.

SECT. II.

Exhibiting a short View of the Design and Scope of the INSTAURATION.

This is of the augment of Sciences

I 1 WE divide the whole of the INSTAURATION into *six Parts* · The *first* whereof gives the *Substance*, or *general Description* of the *Knowledge* which Mankind at present possess, as chusing to dwell a little upon things already received, that we may the easier perfect the old, and lead on to new being equally inclin'd to cultivate the Discoveries of Antiquity, as to strike out fresh Paths of Science.

2 In classing the Sciences, we comprehend not only the Things already invented and known, but also those omitted and wanted for the *intellectual Globe*, as well as the terrestrial, has both its Forests and Deserts 'Tis therefore no wonder if we sometimes depart from the common Divisions · For an addition, whilst it alters the Whole, must necessarily alter the Parts, and their Sections whereas the received Divisions are only fitted to the received *Sum of the Sciences*, as it now stands.

3 With regard to the *Things* we shall note as *defective*, 'twill be our Method to give more than the bare *Titles*, or short *Heads* of what we wou'd have done, with particular care, where the Dignity or Difficulty of the Subject requires it, either to lay down the *Rules* for effecting the Work, or make an Attempt of our own, by way of Example, or Pattern, of the whole

The Design of the Novum Organum

II 4 When we have gone thro' the *antient Arts*, we shall instruct the *human Understanding* to discover *new ones*, by a more perfect use of Reason, and the true Helps of the intellectual Faculties; so as to raise and enlarge the Powers of the Mind, and as far as the condition of humanity allows, fit it to conquer the difficulties and obscurities of Nature The thing we mean, is a kind of *Logic*, by us call'd *The Art of interpreting Nature* [a] as differing widely from the common *Logic*, which however pretends to assist and direct the Understanding, and in that they agree But the difference betwixt them consists in three things, *viz* the *End*, the *Order* of demonstrating, and the *Grounds* of Enquiry

Its End

5 The *End* of our *new Logic* is to find, not *Arguments*, but *Arts*, not what agrees with Principles, but *Principles* themselves, not probable *Reasons*, but *Plans* and *Designs of Works* a different intention producing a different effect In one the *Adversary* is conquer'd by *Dispute*, and in the
other

---

[a] The Art of interpreting Nature depends on this Foundation, that Nature has a meaning in all she does whence, as the moral Philosopher, who converses familiarly with Mankind, can interpret their Designs from his Observations, so the *natural Philosopher* interprets the Designs of Nature by the steps he observes her to take

other *Nature* by *Works* And fuitable to this difference of defign, is the nature and order of the Demonftrations. In the *common Logic*, the labour is principally beftowed upon *Syllogifm* whilft the *Logician* fcarce thinks of *Induction*, but touching it flightly, paffes on to the *Forms of Difputation* whereas we reject the *Demonftration by Syllogifm*, as confufed, and letting Nature flip thro' the fingers, whilft we take *Induction* for that *form of Demonftration* which guards the Senfes, preffes Nature clofe, and rules over Works Whence the common *order of Demonftrating* is abfolutely inverted for inftead of flying immediately from the fenfes, and particulars, to generals, as to certain *fix'd Poles*, about which *Difputes* always turn'd, and deriving others from thefe, by intermediates, in a fhort indeed, but precipitate manner, fit for controverfy, but unfit to clofe with nature, we continually raife up *Propofitions* by degrees, and in the laft place, come to the moft *general Axioms*[a] which are not notional, but well defined, and what Nature allows of, as entring the very *effence of things*[b].

6 But the more difficult part of our Task confifts in the *Form of Induc-* **Its manner of** *tion*, and the *Judgment* to be made by it, for that *form* of the *Logicians* which **Demonftra-** proceeds by fimple enumeration, is a childifh thing, concludes unfafely, lies **ting** open to *contradictory Inftances*, and regards only common matters, yet determines nothing whilft the *Sciences* require fuch a *form of Induction*, as can feparate, adjuft and verify *Experience*, and come to a neceffary Determination by proper exclufions and rejections[c].

7. Nor is this all for we likewife lay the foundations of the *Sciences* ftrong- **Its Grounds** er, and clofer, and begin our *Enquiries* deeper, than men have hitherto done, bringing thofe things to the teft, which the *common Logic* has taken upon truft The *Logicians* borrow the *Principles of the Sciences* from the *Sciences* themfelves, venerate the *firft Notions* of the Mind, and acquiefce in the immediate *Informations of the Senfes*, when rightly difpofed but we judge, that every province of the Sciences fhould enter *a real Logic*, with a greater authority than their own principles can give, and that fuch *fuppofed Principles* fhould be examin'd, till they become abfolutely clear and certain. As for *firft notions* of the mind, we fufpect all thofe that the underftanding, left to itfelf, procures, nor ever allow them till approved and authorized by a fecond judgment And as to the *Informations of the Senfes*, we have many ways of examining them· for the Senfes are fallacious, though they difcover their own Errors but thefe lie near, whilft the means of Difcovery are remote

8 The *Senfes* are faulty in two refpects, as they either *fail* or *deceive* us **Endeavour to** For there are many things that efcape the Senfes, tho' ever fo rightly dif- *fupply the im-* pofed, as by the fubtilty of the whole body, or the minutenefs of its parts, **perfections of** the diftance of place, the flownefs or velocity of motion, the commonnefs of **the Senfes**

C 2 the

<hr />

[a] See the *Word* explained in the GLOSSARY

[b] This alludes to the Difcovery of *Forms*, or the real and effential natures of Things, a fubject largely profecuted in the *Novum Organum* But for fuller Information in this Point, fee below, 23 the raifing of a perfect fet of general Axioms in this way, being the completion of the *Philofophia Secunda*

[c] This cannot well be explained in few Words, but is made clear to an attentive Reader of the *Novum Organum*, where the bufinefs of *Experiment* is, by the affiftance of Reafon, reduced to an *Art*, and not left to accident and cafual trial

the object, &c. Neither do the Senses, when they lay hold of a thing, retain it strongly for evidence, and the informations of *Sense*, are in proportion to Man, and not in proportion to the Universe[a]. And 'tis a grand Error to assert that Sense is the measure of Things[b]

9 To remedy this, we have from all quarters brought together, and fitted *Helps for the Senses*, and that rather by *Experiments* than by *Instruments* apt Experiments being much more subtile[c] than the Senses themselves, tho' assisted with the most finished Instruments We, therefore, lay no great stress upon the immediate and natural perceptions of the Senses, but would have the Senses to judge only of *Experiments*, and *Experiments* to judge of *Things*[d] On which foundation, we hope to be patrons of the *Senses*, and interpreters of their oracles

10 And thus we mean to procure the things relating to the *Light of Nature*, and the setting it up in the Mind. which things might of themselves suffice, if the Mind were as white paper But since the minds of men are so strangely disposed, as not to receive the *true images of things*, 'tis necessary also that a Remedy be found for this Evil

And because ... the ... 1. ... 2. ... 11 The *Idols*, or false Notions[e] which possess the Mind, are either *acquired* or *innate* The *acquired* arise either from the Opinions and Sects of Philosophers, or from preposterous Laws of Demonstration but the *innate* cleave to the nature of the *Understanding*, which is found much more prone to error than the *Sense* For however men may amuse themselves, and admire, or almost adore the Mind[f], 'tis certain, that like an irregular Glass, it alters the rays of things, by its figure, and different intersections[g]

12 The two former kinds of *Idols* may be extirpated, tho' with difficulty, but this third is insuperable All that can be done, is to point them out,

and

---

[a] This Position requires an attentive regard, as leading to a Knowledge of the Scantiness of our own Understanding compared to that displayed in the Universe

[b] The Doctrine of the two last Paragraphs may appear contradictory to the Opinion of some Philosophers, who maintain the infallibility of the Senses, as well as of Reason but the Dispute perhaps turns rather upon Words than Things Thus Father *Malbranche* is express, that *the Senses never deceive us, yet are expresly that they should never be trusted*, without being verified charging the Error's arising from self upon *human Liberty* which makes a wrong choice See *Recherche de la Verité*, Lib. I Chap. 6, 7 8 The Difference may arise only from considering the Senses in too common Lights, viz *Physically* or according to common use, and *metaphysically* or *abstractedly* The *Novum Organum* clears the whole See also *Marin Mersennus de la Verité des Sciences*

[c] That is going deeper into the nature of Things, and manifesting their true State to the Sense which, unaided by Experiments, could make very little progress in *natural Philosophy* For *Experiments* are the medium by which we come to a knowledge of Nature's Works, so as to imitate, alter, or improve them by Art

[d] Thus for example the unassisted Senses could never discover the Principles, Contents, and Vertues of mineral Waters, but proper *chemical* and *philosophical Experiments*, exhibit their Principles and Contents to the Senses whence Experiments determine of the Thing, and the Senses of the Experiment and on this footing all *experimental Philosophy* proceeds

[e] The Doctrine of *Idols* is farther touched in the *De Augmentis*, but fully prosecuted and explained in the *Novum Organum*

[f] This is set up Reason, Speculation, and the mental Powers, far above Experience, and the considering of Nature and her Works See hereafter Sect III 42, 43, 44, &c

[g] That is, does not from within itself represent the Works of Nature, as they are in the external World, but imposes on itself false Imaginations for Facts, as is usual in *Theories* and *Speculations*, where Nature and Experience are not consulted.

and mark, and convict that treacherous faculty of the Mind; left when the ancient errors are deftroy'd, new ones fhould fprout out from the ranknefs of the foil and, on the other hand, to eftablifh this for ever, that the Underftanding can make no judgment but by *Induction*, and the juft form thereof Whence *the Doctrine of purging the Underftanding* requires three kinds of *Confutations*, to fit it for the inveftigation of Truth, *viz.* the *Confutation of Philofophies*, the *Confutation of Demonftrations*, and the *Confutation of the natural Reafon* [a] And when this is explain'd, and the real nature of Things, and of the Mind fet forth, we fhall then, by the divine affiftance, have prepared and deck'd the *nuptial Chamber of the Mind and the Univerfe* [b].

III. 13 But as we propofe not only to pave and fhew the way, but alfo to tread in it ourfelves, we fhall next exhibit the *Phænomena of the Univerfe*, that is, fuch *Experience* of all kinds, and fuch a *Natural Hiftory* [c], as may afford a Foundation to Philofophy For as no fine method of Demonftration, or form of explaining Nature, can preferve the mind from error, and fupport it from falling, fo neither can it hence receive any matter of Science Thofe, therefore, who determine not to conjecture and guefs, but to find out and know, not to invent *Fables* and *Romances of Worlds*, but to look into, and diffect the nature of this *real World*, muft confult only things themfelves Nor can any force of Genius, Thought, or Argument, be fubftituted for this labour, fearch and infpection, not even tho' all the wits of men were united this therefore muft either be had, or the bufinefs be deferted for ever

The defign of the Sylva Sylvarum

14. But the conduct of mankind has hitherto been fuch, that 'tis no wonder *Nature* has not open'd herfelf to them For the *information of the Senfes* is treacherous and deceitful, *Obfervation* carelefs, irregular, and accidental, *Tradition* idle, rumorous, and vain, *Practice* narrow, and fervile, *Experience* blind, ftupid, vague and broken; and *natural Hiftory* extremely light and empty wretched materials for the Underftanding to fafhion into Philofophy and Sciences ! Then comes in a prepofterous fubtilty of argumentation, and fifting, as a laft remedy, that mends not the matter one jot, nor feparates the errors [d]. Whence there are abfolutely no hopes of enlarging and promoting the Sciences, without rebuilding them

15 The *firft Materials* for this purpofe muft be taken from a new kind of *Natural Hiftory*, that the Underftanding may have fit fubjects to work upon, as well as real Helps to work with. But our *Hiftory*, no lefs than our *Logic*, differs from the common in many refpects, particularly, (1) in its *end*, or

office,

---

[a] See thefe Terms explained in the GLOSSARY, under *Confutation*

[b] That is have brought mankind to an intimate acquaintance with Nature, or to a ftate of difcovering new Manufactures, Works, and Effects But all this is hereafter more fully and familiarly explained, in the *Short analytical View of the Plan of the* Novum Organum, prefix'd to that Work

[c] Or rather Hiftory of Nature, to diftinguifh it from the common acceptation of *Natural Hiftory*

[d] Unlefs the Reader be verfed in the ways of the *human Mind*, he may be apt to think this naked Defcription a fevere Cenfure It muft, however, be remembred, that this Reprefentation regards the Philofophical ftate of Things a hundred years ago, and not as it is at prefent improved, upon the Scheme laid down by the Author.

ose, (2) its *creation*, (3) its *subtilty*, (4) its *choice*, and (5) its *appointment* for what is to follow

Use.   16 (1) Our *natural History* is not defign'd fo much to pleafe by its variety, or benefit by gainful Experiments, as to give light in the *difcovery of Caufes*, and hold out the *Breaft to Philofophy*[a] for tho' we principally regard *Works*, and the *above parts of the Sciences*, yet we wait for the time of Harveft, and would not reap the Blade for the Ear We are well aware that *Axiom*, rightly framed[b], will draw after them whole fheaves of Works But for that untimely and childifh Defire of feeing fruits of new Works before the feafon, we abfolutely condemn and reject it, as the *golden Apple* that hinders the progrefs

Collection.   17 (2) With regard to its *collection*, we propofe to fhew *Nature* not only in a *free ftate*, as in the Hiftory of *Meteors, Minerals, Plants*, and *Animals*, but more particularly as fhe is bound, and tortur'd, prefs'd, form'd, and turn'd out of her courfe by *Art* and *human Induftry* Hence we would fet down all appofite Experiments of the mechanic and liberal Arts, with many others not yet form'd into Arts for the nature of things is better difcover'd by the torturings of Art, than when they are left to themfelves Nor is it only a Hiftory of Bodies that we would give, but alfo of their *cardinal Virtues*, or fundamental Qualities, as *Denfity, Rarity, Heat, Cold*, &c which fhould be compriz'd in particular Hiftories[c].

Subtilty.   18 (3) The *kind of Experiments* to be procured for our *Hiftory*, are much more *fubtile* and *fimple* than the common abundance of them muft be recovered from darknefs, and are fuch as no one would have enquired after, that was not led by a conftant and certain track to the difcovery of Caufes, as being themfelves of no great ufe, and confequently not fought for their own fake, but with regard to Works like the Letters of the Alphabet with regard to Difcourfe[d]

Choice.   19 (4.) In the *Choice* of our *Narratives* and *Experiments* we hope to have fhewn more care than the other Writers of *Natural Hiftory*, as receiving nothing but upon ocular Demonftration, or the ftricteft fcrutiny of Examination and not heightening what is delivered, to increafe its miraculoufnefs, but thoroughly purging it of fuperftition and fable Befides this, we reject, with a particular mark, all thofe boafted and received falfehoods, which by a ftrange neglect have prevailed for fo many ages, that they may no longer moleft the *Sciences* For as the idle tales of nurfes do really corrupt the minds of children, we cannot too carefully guard the infancy of Philofophy from all vanity and fuperftition And when any new or more curious Experiment is offer'd, tho' it may feem to us certain and well founded, yet we exprefly add the manner wherein it was made, that, after it fhall be underftood how things appear to us, men may beware of any error adhering to them, and fearch after more infallible Proofs We, likewife, all along interpofe

---

[a] That is, afford the firft matter to it

[b] See *Sect. IV*, 23

[c] The Author's particular Hiftories of *Life* and *Death, Winds*, &c are *Inftances* hereof

[d] The want of attending to this Defign of the *Sylva Sylvarum*, has occafion'd it to be much undervalued, to the difadvantage of *Experimental Philofophy*

pofe our Directions, Scruples and Cautions, and religioufly guard againft Phantoms and Illufions [a].

20 (5.) *Laftly*, having well obferved how far *Experiments* and *Hiftory* di-*Its appoint-*ftract the mind, and how difficult it is, efpecially for tender or prejudiced *ments* perfons, to converfe with *Nature* from the beginning, we are continually fub-joining our Obfervations, as fo many firft Glances of *Natural Hiftory* at *Philofophy* and this to give mankind fome Earneft, that they fhall not be kept perpetually floating upon the waves of *Hiftory*, and that when they come to the *Work of the Underftanding*, and the Explanation of Nature, they may find all things in greater readinefs [b]

IV 21   And thus we fhall be prepared to enter upon *Philofophy* itfelf *The Defign of* But in fo difficult a Task, there are certain things to be obferved, as well for *the Enquiries* inftruction as for prefent ufe   The *firft* is to propofe *Examples of Enquiry and into Life and* *Inveftigation*, according to our own method, in certain Subjects of the nobleft *Death, Winds,* kind, but greatly differing from each other, that a Specimen may be had of *Denfity and* every fort   By thefe Examples we mean not illuftrations of Rules and Pre-*Rarity, &c.* cepts, but perfect *Models*, reprefenting, as it were to the eye, the whole progrefs of the Mind, and the continued ftructure and order of Invention, in the moft chofen fubjects · after the fame manner as Globes and Machines facilitate the more abftrufe and fubtile Demonftrations in Mathematicks. Such a Set of *Examples* will, therefore, be a particular application and explana-tion of the *fecond part* of our Work [c]

V 22   The *fifth* Part is only *temporary*, or of ufe but till the reft are *Scope of the* finifhed, whence we look upon it as Intereft till the Principal be paid for *Philofophia* we do not propofe to travel hood winked, fo as to take no notice of what may *prima.* occur of ufe in the way   This part, therefore, will confift of fuch things as we have invented, experienced, or added, by the fame common ufe of the Underftanding that others employ   For as we have greater hopes from our conftant converfation with Nature, than from our force of Genius, the dif-coveries we fhall thus make may ferve as Inns on the road, for the Mind to repofe in, during its progrefs to greater certainties   But this, without being at all difpofed to abide by any thing that is not difcovered, or proved, by the *true form* of Induction   Nor need any one be fhock'd at this fufpenfion of the judgment, in a Doctrine which does not affert that nothing is know-able, but only that things cannot be known except in a certain order and method whilft it allows particular degrees of certainty, for the fake of com-modioufnefs and ufe, 'till the Mind fhall be enter'd into the *explanation of Caufes*

VI

---

[a] The Author mentions in other places the uncommon degree of Pains and Care he be-ftow'd in collecting this Hiftory, affuring us, that the rejection he made of Experiments laid before him was infinite fo that tho' it may have its Errors and Imperfections, efpecially as be-ing publifhed after the Author's death, it muft be allowed a wonderful Performance for a fingle hand, before the Ice of *Experience* was broken

[b] See the Nature and Defign of this *Hiftory* more fully open'd in the *Introduction* to the *Sylva Sylvarum* itfelf

[c] This Part is what the Author elfewhere terms *Scala Intellectus*, or the *Progrefs of the Underftanding*, and was intended to be fupplied by him in the way of *monthly Productions* See his Dedication of the *Hiftory of the Winds* to *Prince Charles*, in the FOURTH SUPPLEMENT to the *de Augmentis Scientiarum*,

VI 23 The 1st Part of our Work, to which all the rest are subservient, is to lay down that Philosophy, which shall flow from the just, pure, and strict Enquiry hitherto proposed But to perfect this, is beyond both our abilities and our hopes yet we shall give the Foundations of it , and recommend the finishing to posterity And what a Work it would then be, is not perhaps easy for men, in the present state of minds and things, to conceive[a] The Point in View is not only the contemplative Happiness, but the whole Fortunes, and Affairs, and Powers, and Works of Men For Man being the Minister and Interpreter of Nature, acts and understands so far as he has observed of the order, the works and mind of Nature , and can proceed no farther for no Power is able to loose or break the Chain of Causes , nor is Nature to be conquer'd but by submission[b] whence those twin Intentions, human Knowledge and human Power, are really coincident , and the greatest hindrance to Works is the ignorance of Causes[c]

24 The capital Precept for the whole conduct is this, that the eye of the mind be never taken off from things themselves , but receive their images truly as they are And God forbid that ever we should offer the *Dreams of Fancy* for a *model of the World* , but rather, thro' the divine favour, write a *Revelation*, and real View of the Stamps and Signatures of the *Creator* upon the *Creatures*[d].

SECT. III.

The Objections against LEARNING *considered.*

I 1 BEfore we come to class and range the *Sciences*, 'tis proper we should sift the *merits of Knowledge* , or clear it of the Disgrace brought upon it by Ignorance, whether disguised (1) in the Zeal of *Divines*, (2.) the Arrogance of *Politicians* , or (3) the Errors of *Men of Letters*

2 Some *Divines* pretend, (1) " that Knowledge is to be received with " great limitation, as the aspiring to it was the original Sin, and the cause of " the Fall , (2) that it has somewhat of the Serpent, and puffeth up, (3) that " Solomon says " *of making books there is no end, much study is weariness of* " *the flesh, for in much wisdom is much grief , and he that increaseth knowledge,* " *increaseth sorrow* " (4) that St *Paul* cautions against " being spoiled ' through vain Philosophy ," (5) " that Experience shews learned men have

---

[a] The Discoveries of Mr *Boyle*, Dr *Hook*, Sir *Isaac Newton*, &c may give us a nearer View of this Work in its physical part , but the *Work itself*, in its full extent, is far from being compleated to this day , and must still be recommended to Posterity

[b] That is by condescending to observe her ways

[c] That human *knowledge* and *human Power* are coincident, will be fully shewn in the *Novum Organum*, where also the nature and uses of this last *Part* are more largely explained

[d] The two foregoing *Sections* being no more than the Out-lines of the *Instauration*, they cannot give a full and distinct View of the Scheme But the Reader will find the whole open to him by degrees , and be enabled at length to perform even an executive part in the *Design*

" have been Hereticks , and learned times inclined to Atheism; and that
" the contemplation of second Caufes takes from our dependance upon God,
" who is the firſt "

3. To this we anſwer, (1) it was not the pure *Knowledge of Nature*, by *Natural Knowledge not the cauſe of the Fall*
the light whereof man gave names to all the creatures in Paradiſe, agree-
able to their natures, that occaſion'd the Fall , but the *proud Knowledge of Good
and Evil*, with an intent in man to give law to himſelf, and depend no more
upon God [a]

4. (2) Nor can any quantity of *natural Knowledge* puff up the Mind , for *Quantity of Knowledge does not inflate.*
nothing fills, much leſs diſtends the Soul, but God Whence as *Solomon* declares,
that the eye is not ſatisfied with ſeeing, nor the ear with hearing , ſo of Knowledge
itſelf, he ſays, *God hath made all things beautiful in their ſeaſons alſo he hath
placed the world in man's heart , yet cannot man find out the work which God
worketh from the beginning to the end* hereby declaring plainly, that God has
framed the Mind like a Glaſs, capable of the image of the Univerſe, and de-
ſirous to receive it, as the eye to receive the Light , and thus it is not only
pleaſed with the variety and viciſſitudes of things, but alſo endeavours to
find out the Laws they obſerve in their changes and alterations And if
ſuch be the extent of the Mind, there is no danger of filling it with any
quantity of Knowledge. But it is merely from its quality, when taken
without the true corrective, that Knowledge has ſomewhat of venom or malignity The corrective which renders it ſovereign, is charity , for accord-
to St *Paul, knowledge puffeth up, but charity buildeth up* [b]

5 (3) For the exceſs of writing and reading books; the anxiety of ſpirit *Three Limita-tions of Know-ledge*
proceeding from Knowledge , and the admonition, that we be not ſeduced
by vain Philoſophy , when theſe paſſages are rightly underſtood, they mark
out the boundaries of human Knowledge , ſo as to comprehend the univerſal
nature of things Theſe limitations are *three* , the *firſt*, that we ſhould not
place our felicity in Knowledge, ſo as to forget mortality , the *ſecond* , that
we uſe Knowledge ſo as to give ourſelves eaſe and content, not diſtaſte and
repining , and the *third*, that we preſume not by the contemplation of *Nature*, to attain to the myſteries of God

6 As to the *firſt, Solomon* excellently ſays, *I ſaw that wiſdom excelleth folly, as
far as light excelleth darkneſs The wiſe man's eyes are in his head, but the fool
walketh in darkneſs and I myſelf perceived alſo that one event happeneth to them
all* And for the *ſecond*, it is certain that no vexation or anxiety of mind re-
ſults from Knowledge, but merely by accident , all Knowledge, and Admiration, which is the ſeed of Knowledge, being pleaſant in itſelf but when we
frame concluſions from our knowledge, apply them to our own particular, and thence miniſter to ourſelves weak fears, or vaſt deſires , then comes
on that anxiety and trouble of mind which is here meant when Knowledge

---

[a] The Reader will eaſily perceive, that the Arguments here employed are *Arguments ad ho-
minem*, or popular Anſwers to the Objections, uſually brought againſt *Learning* by particular
ſets of men , rather than ſuch Inſtances as ſhew the uſefulneſs and advantages of *Philoſophy*, or
the improved ſtate of the mind with intention, that when ſuch *Objections* are anſwered in
their kind, the Author may proceed unmoleſted in his way, to improve the general ſtate of
Knowledge , and ſet it above the reach of future *Objections*.
[b] See *Sect* 1 23 24

is no longer the dry Light of Character, but the drenched one, steeped in the
humours of the affections.

§ 4. The third point deserves to be more dwelt upon. For if any man
should think, by his enquiries after material things, to discover the nature of
God, he is indeed spoiled by vain Philosophy; for the contemplation
of God's works produces Knowledge, tho', with regard to him, not
perfect Knowledge, but Wonder, which is broken Knowledge. It may therefore be properly said, That the Sense resembles the Sun, which shews the earthly Globe, but conceals the celestial. For thus the Sense discovers natural
things, whilst it shuts up divine. And hence some learned men have indeed
been heretical, whilst they sought to seize the secrets of the Deity, born on
the waxen wings of the senses.

§ 5.) As to the point that too much Knowledge should incline to *Atheism*,
and the ignorance of second causes make us more dependant upon *God*, we
ask *Job*'s Question, " *Will ye lye for God, as one man will do for another, to
gratify him.* " For certainly God works nothing in Nature but by second
Causes, and to assert the contrary is mere imposture, as it were in favour of
God, and offering up to the author of truth, the unclean sacrifice of a lye.
And tho' a superficial tincture of Philosophy may incline the mind to Atheism,
yet a farther knowledge brings it back to Religion[a]; for to rest in the entrance of Philosophy, where second causes appear, may induce some oblivion of the highest cause, but when we go deeper, and see the dependance
of causes, and the works of Providence, we shall easily perceive that *the upper
link of nature's chain is fasten'd to Jupiter's throne.* To conclude, let no one
weakly imagine, that men can search too far, or be too well studied in the
Book of God's word, and works, Divinity and Philosophy, but rather let
them endeavour an endless progression in both, only applying all to charity, and not to pride, to use not ostentation, without confounding the two
different streams of Philosophy and Revelation together[b]

II. 9. The Reflections cast upon *Learning* by *Politicians*, are these, (1)" that
" it enervates mens minds, and unfits them for Arms, (2) that it perverts
" their dispositions for Government and Politicks, (3) that it makes them too
" curious and irresolute, by variety of reading, too peremptory or positive
" by strictness of rules, too immoderate and conceited by the greatness of
" instances, too unsociable and unsuitable for the times, by the dissimilitude
" of examples, or at least, (4) that it diverts from action and business, and
" leads to a love of retirement, (5) that it introduces a relaxation in Govern-
" ment, whilst every man is more ready to argue than obey, (6) that *Cato
" be Censor*, when *Carneades* came Embassador to *Rome*, and the young *Ro-
" mans* flock'd about him, allured with his Eloquence, gave counsel in open
" Senate, to grant him his dispatch immediately, lest he should infect the
" minds of the youth, and insensibly occasion an alteration in the State "

---

[a] See more upon this Head in the Author's *Essay on Atheism*, and Mr *Boyle's Essays* upon
the Usefulness of Philosophy

[b] The Dispute betwixt the *rational* and *scriptural Divines* is still on foot; the former are
for reconciling Reason and Philosophy with Faith and Religion, and the latter for keeping them
distinct, as things incompatible, or making Reason and Knowledge subject to Faith and Religion. The Author is clear that they should be kept separate, as will more fully appear hereafter when he comes to treat o Theology. See *de Augm Scient* Sect XXVII

10 (1) But these and the like *Imputations* have rather a shew of gravity, *That Learning* than any just ground   for experience shews that *Learning* and *Arms*, have *and Arms* flourished in the same persons, and ages.   As to persons, there are no better *have flourished in the same* instances than *Alexander* and *Cæsar*, the one *Aristotle's* Scholar in Philosophy, *persons* and the other *Cicero's* rival in eloquence , and again, *Epaminondas* and *Xe-nophon*, the one whereof first abated the power of *Sparta*, and the other first pav'd the way for subverting the *Persian* monarchy.

11   This concurrence of *Learning* and *Arms*, is yet more visible in times *And in the* than in persons, as an age exceeds a man   For in *Ægypt, Assyria, Persia, same Times* *Greece*, and *Rome*, the times most famous for Arms are likewise most admired for Learning , so that the greatest Authors and Philosophers, the greatest Leaders and Governours, have lived in the same ages   Nor can it well be otherwise   for as the fulness of human strength, both in body and mind, comes nearly at an age ; so Arms and Learning, one whereof corresponds to the body, the other to the soul, have a near concurrence in point of time

12. (2) And that Learning should rather prove detrimental than service-*Learning of* able in the Art of Government, seems very improbable . It is wrong to trust *service in Go* the natural body to *Empiricks*, who commonly have a few receipts whereon *vernment* they rely , but know neither the causes of diseases, nor the constitutions of pa-tients, nor the danger of accidents, nor the true methods of cure.   And so it must needs be dangerous to have the civil Body of States managed by empiri-cal Statesmen, unless well mix'd with others who are grounded in Learning.

13   On the contrary, it is almost without instance, that any government was unprosperous under learned Governours   For however common it has been with *Politicians* to discredit learned men, by the name of *Pedants* , yet it appears from History, that the governments of princes in minority have ex-celled the governments of princes in maturity , merely because the manage-ment was in learned hands.   The state of *Rome* for the first five years, so much magnified, during the minority of *Nero*, was in the hands of *Seneca*, a *Pedant*   so it was for ten years, during the minority of *Gordianus* the younger, with great applause in the hands of *Misitheus*, a *Pedant*   and it was as hap py before that, in the minority of *Alexander Severus*, under the rule of wo-men, assisted by *Preceptors*   And to look into the government of the Bishops of *Rome*, particularly that of *Pius*, and *Sextus Quintus*, who were both at their entrance esteemed but pedantical Friars, we shall find that such Popes did greater things, and proceeded upon truer principles of State, than those who rose to the Papacy from an education in civil affairs, and the Courts of Princes   For tho' men bred to Learning are perhaps at a loss in points of convenience, and present accommodations, called *Reasons of State* , yet they are perfect in the plain grounds of religion, justice, honour and moral vir-tue, which if well pursued, there will be as little use of *Reasons of State*, as of Physick in a healthy constitution   Nor can the experience of one man's life, furnish Examples and Precedents for another's   present Occurrences frequently correspond to ancient examples, better than to later   And lastly, the Ge nius of any single man can no more equal Learning, than a private purse hold way with the Exchequer   *How* Learn

14 (3) As to the particular Indispositions of the Mind, for *Politicks* and *ing affects the* *Government*, laid to the charge of *Learning*, if they are allow'd of any force, it *Mind, with*
must *regard to Po- liticks*

muſt be remembred, that *Learning* affords more Remedies, than it breeds Diſea-ſes for if, by a ſecret operation, it renders Men perplexed and irreſolute, on the other hand, by plain precept, it teaches when, and upon what grounds to re-ſolve, and how to carry things in ſuſpence, without prejudice if it makes Men poſitive and ſtiff, it ſhews what things are in their nature demonſtrative, what conjectural, and teaches the uſe of Diſtinctions and Exceptions, as well as the rigidneſs of Principles and Rules If it miſleads, by the unſuitableneſs of Examples, it ſhews the force of Circumſtances, the Errors of Compariſons, and the Cautions of Application, ſo that in all caſes, it rectifies more ef-fectually than it perverts And theſe Remedies it conveys into the Mind much more effectually, by the force and variety of Examples Let a Man look into the Errors of *Clement* the Seventh, ſo livelily deſcribed by *Guic-ciardine*, or into thoſe of *Cicero*, deſcribed by himſelf in his Epiſtles to *At-ticus*, and he will fly from being irreſolute Let him look into the Errors of *Phocion*, and he will beware of Obſtinacy, or Inflexibility Let him read the Fable of *Ixion*, and it will keep him from Conceitedneſs Let him look in-to the Errors of *Cato* the Second, and he will never tread oppoſite to the World

15 (4) For the pretence that *Learning* diſpoſes to Retirement, Privacy, and Sloth, it were ſtrange if what accuſtoms the Mind to perpetual Motion, and Agitation, ſhould induce Indolence, whereas no kind of Men love buſi-neſs, for its own ſake, but the Learned, whilſt others love it for profit, as Hirelings for the Wages; others for honour, others becauſe it bears them up in the eyes of men, and refreſhes their Reputations, which would otherwiſe fade, or becauſe it reminds them of their Fortune, and gives them oppor-tunities of revenging, and obliging, or becauſe it exerciſes ſome faculty, wherein they delight, and ſo keeps them in good-humour with themſelves, &c Whence, as falſe Valour lies in the eyes of the Beholders, ſuch Men's In-duſtry lies in the eyes of others, or is exerciſed with a view to their own De-ſigns, whilſt the Learned love Buſineſs, as an Action according to Nature, and agreeable to the Health of the Mind, as Exerciſe is to that of the Body Whence, of all Men, they are the moſt indefatigable in ſuch buſineſs as may deſervedly fill and employ the Mind And if there are any laborious in Study, yet idle in Buſineſs, this proceeds either from a Weakneſs of Body, or a Softneſs of Diſpoſition, and not from Learning itſelf The Conſciouſ-neſs of ſuch a Diſpoſition may indeed incline a Man to Learning, but Learn-ing does not breed any ſuch Temper in him

16 If it be objected, that *Learning* takes up much time, which might be better employ'd, I anſwer, that the moſt active or buſy Men have many vacant hours, while they expect the tides and returns of Buſineſs, and then the queſtion is, how thoſe Spaces of Leiſure ſhall be fill'd up, whether with Pleaſure, or Study? No fear, therefore, that Learning ſhould diſplace Buſi-neſs, for it rather keeps, and defends the Mind againſt Idleneſs, and Plea-ſure, which might otherwiſe enter, to the prejudice both of Buſineſs and Learning

17 (5) Again, for the Allegation that *Learning* ſhould undermine the Reverence due to Laws and Government, it is a mere Calumny, without ſhadow of Truth. For to ſay, that blind Cuſtom of Obedience ſhould be

a fafer Obligation, than Duty, taught and underftood , is to fay, that a blind Man may tread furer by a Guide, than a Man with his Eyes open can by a Light   And, doubtlefs, *Learning* makes the Mind gentle and pliable to Government , whereas Ignorance renders it churlifh and mutinous and 'tis always found, that the moft barbarous, rude, and ignorant Times, have been moft tumultuous, changeable, and feditious

18 (6.) As to the Judgment of *Cato* the Cenfor, he was punifh'd for his Contempt of *Learning*, in the kind wherein he offended , for when paft threefcore, the humour took him to learn *Greek* which fhews that his former Cenfure of the *Grecian* Learning was rather an affected Gravity, than his inward Senfe   And indeed the *Romans* never arrived at their height of Empire, till they had arrived at their height of Arts   For in the time of the two firft *Cæfars*, when their Government was in its greateft perfection, there lived the beft Poet, *Virgil* , the beft Hiftoriographer, *Livy*, the beft Antiquary, *Varro* , and the beft, or fecond beft Orator, *Cicero*, that the world has known   And let this ferve for an Anfwer to thofe Politicians, who, in a humorous Severity, or affected Gravity, have thrown Imputations upon *Learning* [a]

Cato's Judgment of Learning

III. 19 We come now to that fort of *Difcredit*, which is brought upon Learning by *learned Men* themfelves   And this proceeds either (1) from their *Fortune* , (2) their *Manners* , or (3) the *nature of their Studies*

Learning defended from the Difcredit brought on it by the Learned

(1.) The Difrepute of Learning from the *Fortune*, or Condition of the Learned, regards either their *Indigence*, *Retirement*, or *Meannefs of Employ*

20 As to the point, that *learned Men grow not fo foon rich as others*, becaufe they convert not their Labours to Profit , we might turn it over to the Friars, of whom *Machiavel* faid, " That the Kingdom of the Clergy had " been long fince at an end, if the Reputation and Reverence towards the " Poverty of the *Monks* and *Mendicants* had not born out the Excelles of " *Bifhops* and *Prelates* " For fo the Splendor and Magnificence of the Great had long fince funk into Rudenefs and Barbarifm, if the *Poverty of learned Men* had not kept up Civility and Reputation.   But to drop fuch Advantages, it is worth obferving, how reverend and facred, *Poverty* was efteemed for fome Ages in the *Roman* State , fince, as *Livy* fays, *There never was a Republic greater, more venerable, and more abounding in good Examples, than the* Roman , *nor one that fo long withftood Avarice and Luxury ; or fo much honoured Poverty and Parcimony*   And we fee, when *Rome* degenerated, how *Julius Cæfar*, after his Victory, was counfel'd to begin the Reftoration of the State , by abolifhing the Reputation of Wealth.   And indeed, as we truly fay that Blufhing is the Livery of Virtue, tho' it may fometimes proceed from Guilt , fo it holds true of *Poverty*, that it is the Attendant of *Virtue*, tho' fometimes it may proceed from mifmanagement and accident [b].

The Poverty of the Learned.

21.

[a] Moft of the Exceptions made to *Learning*, may proceed from a mifunderftanding of the word, rather than from any defect in the thing   *Learning* is often taken for a difagreeable, pragmatical, or pedantick Temper and Behaviour, in many of thofe called *learned Men* , but if *Knowledge* were fubftituted for the word *Learning*, moft Difputes of this kind are at an end for who will fay of *Knowledge*, that is of the effential part of acquired *Learning*, that it unfits Men for any Office of Life ? So that if any Objection ftill remains, it fhould rather feem to lie againft the accidental Attendants, or Concomitants, of *Learning*, than *Learning* itfelf

[b] The principal Reafon why Philofophers, and learned Men, fail of raifing Eftates, feems to be

21 As for *Retirement*, it is a Theme so common, to extol a private Life, not mixed with Senfuality and Sloth, for the liberty, the pleafure, and the freedom from Indignity it affords, that every one touches it well, fuch an agreement it has to the Nature and Apprehenfions of Mankind. This may be added, that learned Men, forgotten in States, and not living in the eyes of the world, are like the Images of *Caffius* and *Brutus* at the Funeral of *Junia*, which not being reprefented, as many others were, *Tacitus* faid of them, that *they fo much the more fhined, that they were not feen.*

22 As for their *Manners of Employ*, that moft expofed to contempt, is the Education of Youth, to which they are commonly allotted. But how unjuft this Reflection is, will appear to all who meafure things, not by popular Opinion, but by Reafon. And to fay the truth, how much foever the Lives of Pedants have been ridicul'd upon the Stage, as the Emblem of Tyranny, becaufe the modern Loofenefs, or Negligence, has not duly regarded the choice of proper School-Mafters and Tutors, yet the Wifdom of the ancienteft and beft Times always complain'd, that States were too bufy with Laws, and too remifs in the point of Education. This excellent Part of ancient Difcipline, has, in fome meafure, been revived of late by the *Colleges of Jefuits abroad*, in which particular, they deferve our Imitation.

23 3. The *Manners of Learned Men*, are perfonal, and of all kinds, as well as in other Profeffions, for particular Studies have their particular Influence upon mens minds. But, to view the thing impartially, no Difgrace can be reflected upon Learning from the *Manners of learned Men*, not inherent in them as learned, unlefs it be a fault, that the Times they read of are commonly better than the Times they live in, and the Duties taught, better than the Duties practifed. 'Tis true, they fometimes over-earneftly endeavour to bring things to perfection, and to reduce Morality to Precepts, or Examples of too great height, tho' they have Cautions enow in their Books againft fuch a Procedure.

24 (5) Another *Fault* laid to the charge of learned Men, and arifing from their retired Studies, is, " that *they efteem the Prefervation, Good,* " *and Honour of the Country, before their own Fortunes or Safeties.*" Demofthenes faid well to the *Athenians*, " My Counfels are not fuch, as tend " to aggrandize me, and diminifh you, but fometimes not expedient for " me to give, tho' always expedient for you to follow." So *Seneca*, after concerting the five Years of *Nero's* Minority, to the immortal Glory of learned Governours, held on his honeft courfe of good Counfel, after his Mafter grew extremely corrupt. Nor can this be otherwife, for Learning gives Men a true fenfe of their Frailty, the Cafualty of Fortune, and the Dignity of the Soul and its Office, whence they cannot think any Greatnefs of Fortune a worthy End of their Living, and therefore live fo as to give a clear and acceptable Account to God, and their Superiors; whilft the corrupter fort of Politicians, who are not, by Learning, eftablifhed in a love of Duty, nor ever look abroad into Univerfality, refer all things to themfelves, and thruft

us, have no regard to Univerfality, or a great variety of Particulars, whereas a ftrong attachment and fixednefs to fome one Thing, with a difregard of all others, is the direct way of raifing a Fortune.

* The other Reafon why the Jefuits make fuch excellent Tutors, is perhaps, their being tutored in civil and collegiate Life, fo as to join the *Gentleman* with the *Scholar*.

thrust into the Center of the World, as if all Lines should meet in them and their Fortunes, without regarding, in Storms, what becomes of the Ship of the State, if they can save themselves in the Cockboat of their own Fortune

25 Another Charge brought against learned Men, which may rather be defended than denied, is, " that *they sometimes fail in making court to parti-* " *cular Persons* " This want of application arises from two Causes, the one, the largeness of their Mind, which can hardly submit to dwell in the Examination and Observance of any one Person tho' he who cannot contract the sight of his Mind, as well as dilate it, wants a great Talent in Life The second Cause, is no Inability, but a Rejection upon Choice and Judgment For the honest and just Limits of Observation in one Person upon another, extend no farther than to understand him sufficiently, so as to give him no offence, or be able to counsel him, or to stand upon reasonable guard and caution with respect to one's self But to pry deep into another Man, to learn to work, wind, or govern him, proceeds from a double Heart, which, in Friendship, is want of Integrity, and towards Princes or Superiors, want of Duty The *Eastern* Custom, which forbids Subjects to gaze upon Princes, tho' in the outward Ceremony barbarous, has a good Moral, for Men ought not, by cunning and studied Observations, to penetrate and search into the Hearts of Kings, which the Scripture declares *inscrutable*

Their Failure in point of particular Applications.

26 Another *Fault* noted in learned Men, is, " *that they often fail in point* " *of Discretion and Decency of Behaviour, and commit Errors in ordinary* " *Actions,* whence vulgar Capacities judge of them in greater matters, " by what they find them in small " But this Consequence often deceives. For we may here justly apply the Saying of *Themistocles*, who being asked to touch a Lute, reply'd, " he could not fiddle, but he could make a little " Village a great City " Accordingly many may be well skilled in Government and Policy, who are to seek in little Punctilio's So *Plato* compared his Master *Socrates* to the Shop-Pots of Apothecaries, painted on the outside with Apes and Owls, and Antiques, but contain'd sovereign and precious Remedies

Their Failure in Decency

27 But we have nothing to offer in excuse of those *unworthy Practices,* *whereby some Professors have debased both themselves and Learning* as the *trencher Philosophers,* who, in the decline of the *Roman* State, were but a kind of solemn Parasites *Lucian* makes merry with this kind of *Gentry,* by describing a Philosopher riding in a Coach with a great Lady, who would needs have him carry her Lap-dog, which he doing with an aukward Officiousness, the Page said, " he feared the *Stoick* would turn *Cynick* " But above all, the gross Flattery, wherein many abuse their Wit, by turning *Hecuba* into *Hellena,* and *Faustina* into *Lucretia,* has most diminished the Value and Esteem of Learning. Neither is the modern Practice of *Dedications* commendable for Books should have no Patrons, but Truth and Reason And the ancient Custom was, to dedicate them only to private and equal Friends, or if to Kings and Great Persons, it was to such as the Subject suited These, and the like measures, therefore, deserve rather to be censured than defended Yet the Submission of learned Men to those in power, cannot be condemned *Diogenes,* to one who ask'd him, " how it happen'd that " Philo-

Their Temporizing Flattering, &c

" Philosophers follow'd the Rich, and not the Rich the Philosophers?"
answer'd, ' because the Philosophers know what they want, but the Rich
" do not." And of the like nature was the Answer of *Aristippus*, who having a Petition to *Dionysius*, and no ear given him, fell down at his feet,
whereupon *Dionysius* gave him the hearing, and granted the suit but when
afterwards *Aristippus* was reproved for offering such an Indignity to Philosophy, as to fall at a Tyrant's Feet, he reply'd, " it was not his fault, if
' *Dionysius's* Ears were in his Feet" Nor was it accounted Weakness, but
Discretion in him that would not dispute his best with the Emperor *Adrian*,
excusing himself, " that it was reasonable to yield to one that com-
' manded thirty Legions" These, and the like Condescensions to points
of Necessity and Convenience, cannot be disallow'd for tho' they may have
some shew of external Meanness, yet, in a Judgment truly made, they are
Submissions to the *Occasion*, and not to the *Person* [a]

Errors and Vanities of learned Men.   IV 28 We proceed to the *Errors and Vanities intermixed with the Studies
of learned Men*, wherein the Design is not to countenance such Errors, but,
by a Censure and Separation thereof, to justify what is found and good
For 'tis the manner of Men, especially the evil-minded, to depreciate what
is excellent and virtuous, by taking advantage over what is corrupt and de-

Three principal Vanities of Learning   generate We reckon three principal *Vanities*, for which Learning has been
traduced Those Things are vain, which are either false or frivolous, or de-
ficient in Truth or Use and those Persons are vain, who are either credulous
of Falsities, or curious in things of little use But Curiosity consists either
in *Matter* or *Words*, that is, either in taking pains about vain *Things*, or too
much labour about the *Delicacy of Language* There are therefore in reason,
as well as experience, three *Distempers of Learning*, viz vain *Affectations*,
vain *Disputes*, and vain *Imaginations*, or effeminate *Learning*, contentious
Learning, and fantastical Learning

Luxuriancy of Style   29 The first *Disease*, which consists in a *Luxuriancy of Style*, has been anciently esteemed, at different times, but strangely prevail'd about the time
of *Luther*, who finding how great a Task he had undertaken against the degenerate Traditions of the *Church*, and being unassisted by the Opinions of
his own Age, was forced to awake Antiquity to make a Party for him
Whence the ancient Authors, both in Divinity, and the Humanities, that
had long slept in Libraries, began to be generally read This brought on
a necessity of greater application to the original Languages, wherein those
Authors wrote, for the better understanding, and applying their Works.
Hence also proceeded a delight in their manner of Style, and Phrase, and an
admiration of this kind of Writing, which was much increased by the Enmity now grown up against the School-men, who were generally of the
contrary Party, and whose Writings were in a very different Style and Form
as taking the liberty to coin new and strange Words, to avoid Circumlocu-
tion, and express their Sentiments acutely, without regard to Purity of
Diction, and Justness of Phrase And again, because the great Labour then was
to win and persuade the People; Eloquence and variety of Discourse grew

I

into

---

[a] And hence the Author, in the original of this Piece, and several others used many Apo-
strophes and Compliments to King *James* the First but as neither the *Occasion*, nor the *Person*
subsist any longer, it was thought proper to drop such Digressions in this *Edition*.

into requeft, as moft fuitable for the Pulpit, and beft adapted to the Capacity of the Vulgar, fo that thefe four Caufes concurring, *viz.* (1) Admiration of the Ancients, (2.) Enmity to the School-men, (3) an exact Study of Languages, and (4.) a Defire of powerful Preaching, introduced an affected ftudy of Eloquence, and copioufnefs of Speech, which then began to flourifh This foon grew to excefs, infomuch, that Men ftudy'd more after Words than Matter, more after the choicenefs of Phrafe, and the round and clean Compofition, fweet Cadence of Periods, the ufe of Tropes and Figures, than after Weight of Matter, Dignity of Subject, Soundnefs of Argument, Life of Invention, or Depth of Judgment Then grew into efteem, the flowing and watry Vein of *Oforius*, the *Portugal* Bifhop, then did *Sturmius* beftow fuch infinite Pains upon *Cicero* and *Hermogenes*, then did *Car* and *Afcham*, in their Lectures and Writings, almoft deify *Cicero* and *Demofthenes*, then grew the Learning of the School-men to be utterly defpifed, as barbarous, and the whole bent of thofe Times, was rather upon Fulnefs than Weight

29. Here, therefore, is the firft *Diftemper of Learning*; *when Men ftudy Words, and not Matter* and, though we have given an Example of it from later Times, yet fuch Levities have, and will be found, more or lefs, in all Ages And this muft needs difcredit Learning, even with vulgar Capacities, when they fee learned Men's Works appear like the firft Letter of a Patent, which, tho' finely flourifh'd, is ftill but a Letter *Pygmalion*'s Frenzy feems a good Emblem of this *Vanity* for Words are but the Images of Matter; and unlefs they have Life of Reafon and Invention, to fall in love with them is to fall in love with a Picture.

30 Yet the illuftrating the obfcurities of Philofophy, with fenfible and plaufible Elocution, is not haftily to be condemned For hereof we have eminent examples in *Xenophon*, *Cicero*, *Seneca*, *Plutarch*, and *Plato* [a], and the thing itfelf is of great ufe for altho' it be fome hindrance to the fevere Enquiry after Truth, and the farther progrefs in Philofophy, that it fhould too early prove fatisfactory to the Mind, and quench the defire of farther fearch, before a juft period is made yet when we have occafion for Learning and Knowledge in civil Life, as for conference, counfel, perfuafion, difcourfe, or the like, we find it ready prepared to our hands in the Authors who have wrote in this way But the excefs herein is fo juftly contemptible, that as *Hercules*, when he faw the ftatue of *Adonis*, who was the delight of *Venus*, in the temple, faid with indignation, *there is no divinity in thee*, fo all the followers of *Hercules* in Learning, that is, the more fevere and laborious enquirers after Truth, will defpife thefe delicacies and affectations, as trivial and effeminate

31. This luxuriant *Style* was fucceeded by another, which, tho' more chafte, has ftill its *vanity*, as turning wholly upon pointed expreffions, and fhort periods, fo as to appear concife and round, rather than diffufive, by which contrivance the whole looks more ingenious than it is. *Seneca* ufed this

[a] M *Fontenelle* is an eminent modern Inftance in the fame way thus particularly his *Plurality of Worlds* renders the prefent Syftem of Aftronomy agreeably familiar, as his Hiftory of the *Royal Academy* embellifhes and explains the abftrufe parts of Mathematicks, and Philofophy

kind of Style profusely , but *Tacitus* and *Pliny* with greater moderation   It has also begun to render itself acceptable in our time   But to say the truth, its admirers are only the men of a middle Genius, who think it adds a Dignity to Learning , whilst those of solid judgment justly reject it, as a certain *Disease of Learning*, since it is no more than a jingle, or particular quaint affectation of words[a]   And so much for the *first Disease* of Learning

V 32 The *second Disease* is worse in its nature than the former   *for as the Dignity of matter exceeds the Beauty of words, so Vanity in Matter is worse than Vanity in Words*   whence the Precept of St *Paul* is at all times seasonable   *Avoid prophane and vain babblings, and oppositions of science falsly so called*   He assigns two marks of suspected and falsified science   the one *novelty* and *strangeness* of terms , the other *drastness* of positions , which necessarily induces oppositions, and thence questions and altercations   And indeed, as many solid substances putrefy, and turn into worms , so does sound Knowledge often putrefy into a number of subtle, idle, and vermicular Questions that have a certain quickness of life and spirit, but no strength of matter, or excellence of quality   This kind of *degenerate Learning* chiefly reign'd among the *Schoolmen* , who having subtle and strong Capacities, abundance of leisure, and but small variety of reading, their minds being shut up in a few Authors, as their bodies were in the cells of their monasteries, and thus kept ignorant both of the History of Nature and Times, they, with infinite agitation of wit, spun out of a small quantity of matter, those laborious webs of Learning, which are extant in their books   For the human Mind, if it acts upon matter, and contemplates the nature of Things, and the works of God, operates according to the stuff, and is limited thereby , but if it works upon itself, as the spider does, then it has no end but produces cobwebs of learning, admirable indeed for the fineness of the thread , but of no substance or profit[b]

33 This *unprofitable subtilty* is of two kinds , and appears either in the subject, when that is fruitless speculation or controversy , or in the manner of treating it, which amongst them was this   Upon every particular position they framed objections, and to those objections solutions , which solutions were generally not confutations, but distinctions , whereas the strength of all Sciences, is like the strength of a faggot bound   For the harmony of a Science, when each part supports the other, is the true and short confutation of all the smaller objections , on the contrary, to take out every axiom, as the sticks of the faggot, one by one, you may quarrel with them, and bend them, and break them at pleasure   whence, as it was said of *Seneca*, that he *weakned the weight of things by trivial expression* , we may truly say of the School-men, that *they broke the solidity of the Sciences, by the minuteness of their questions*   For, were it not better to set up one large light in a noble room, than to go about with a small one, to illuminate every corner thereof ?   Yet such is the method of the School-men, that rests not so much

upon

---

[a] Since the establishment of the *French Academy*, a studied plainness, and simplicity of style, begins to prevail in that Nation

[b] For the *Literary History of the Schoolmen*, see *Morhof's Polyhist* Tom II Lib I Cap 14 *Camden's Remains*, &c

[c] This is what the Author endeavours in his *Novum Organum*, which sets up a *general Light* for the improvement of all kinds of Knowledge.

upon the evidence of truth from arguments, authorities and examples, as upon particular confutations and folutions of every fcruple, and objection; which breeds one queftion, as faft as it folves another, juft as in the above example, when the light is carried into one corner, it darkens the reft. Whence the fable of *Scylla* feems a lively image of this kind of Philofophy, who was transformed into a beautiful virgin upwards, *whilft barking monfters furrounded her below* For fo the generalities of the School men are for a while fair and proportionable, but to defcend into their diftinctions and decifions, they end in monftrous altercations, and barking queftions. Whence this kind of knowledge muft neceffarily fall under popular contempt for the people are ever apt to contemn truth, upon account of the controverfies raifed about it, and to think thofe all in the wrong way, who never meet And when they fee fuch Quarrels about fubtilities and matters of no ufe, they ufually give into the judgment of *Dionyfius*, " *That 'tis old men's idle talk* " But if thofe Schoolmen, to their great thirft of truth, and unwearied exercife of wit, had joined variety of reading, and contemplation, they would have proved excellent lights, to the great advancement of all kinds of Arts and Sciences. And thus much for the *fecond Difeafe of Learning*

VI. 34 The *third Difeafe*, which regards *Deceit* or *Falfhood*, is the foulest; as deftroying the effential form of Knowledge, which is nothing but a reprefentation of Truth for the Truth of Exiftence, and the Truth of Knowledge are the fame thing, or differ no more than the direct and reflected ray This vice therefore branches into two, *viz. delight in deceiving*, and *aptnefs to be deceiv'd*, impofture and credulity, which tho' apparently different, the one feeming to proceed from cunning, and the other from fimplicity, yet they generally concur For as an inquifitive man is a pratler, fo a credulous man is a deceiver, for he who eafily believes rumours, will as eafily increafe them

The third Difeafe of Learning, viz Deceit, or Impofture and Credulity

35 This *eafinefs of belief, and admitting things upon weak authority*, is of two kinds, according to the fubject being either a belief of Hiftory, and matter of Fact, or elfe matter of Art and Opinion We fee the inconvenience of the former in *Ecclefiaftical Hiftory*, which has too eafily received and regiftred relations of miracles wrought by martyrs, hermits, monks, &c and their relicks, fhrines, chapels, images, &c So in *Natural Hiftory*, there has not been much judgment employed, as appears from the writings of *Pliny, Cardan, Albertus*, and many of the *Arabians*, which are full of fabulous matters, many of them not only untried, but notorioufly falfe to the great difcredit of *Natural Philofophy*, with grave and fober minds. But the prudence and integrity of *Ariftotle* is here worthy our obfervation, who having compiled an exact *Hiftory of Animals*, dafh'd it very fparingly with fable or fiction, throwing all *ftrange Reports*, which he thought worth recording, into a book by themfelves [a], thus wifely intimating, that matter of Truth, which is the bafis of folid Experience, Philofophy, and the Sciences, fhould not be mix'd with matter of doubtful credit and yet that curiofities

Eafinefs of Belief of two kinds, viz with regard to Hiftory

riofities

---

[a] The fame method was fince obferved by Mr *Boyle*, who collected together fuch Relations of Facts as feem'd lefs credible, under the Title of *Strange Reports*

riofities or prodigies, tho' feemingly incredible, are not to be fuppref's'd, or denied the regiftring

36 Credit, in Arts and Opinions. is likewife of two kinds, *viz* when men give too much belief to Arts themfelves, or to certain Authors in any Art   The Sciences that fway the Imagination more than the Reafon, are principally three, *viz Aftrology, Natural Magick,* and *Alchemy*, the ends or pretenfions whereof, are however noble   For *Aftrology* pretends to difcover the influence of the fuperior upon the inferior Bodies   *Natural Magick* pretends to reduce Natural Philofophy from fpeculation to works   and *Chemiftry* pretends to feparate the diffimilar parts, incorporated in natural mixtures, and to cleanfe fuch bodies as are impure, throw out the heterogeneous parts, and perfect fuch as are immature   But the means fuppofed to produce thefe Effects are, both in theory and practice, full of error and vanity   and befides are feldom delivered with candour, but generally concealed by artifice and enigmatical Expreffions, referring to Traditions, and ufing other Devices to cloak Impofture   Yet *Alchemy* may be compared to the man who told his fons, he had left them Gold buried fomewhere in his vineyard, where they by digging found no Gold, but by turning up the mould about the roots of their vines, procured a plentiful vintage   So the fearch and endeavours to *make Gold,* have brought many ufeful inventions and inftructive experiments to light [a]

Credulity as to Authors 37 *Credulity, in refpect of certain Authors, and making them Dictators* inftead of *Confuls,* is a principal caufe that the Sciences are no farther advanced   For hence, tho' in mechanical Arts, the firft inventor falls fhort, time adds perfection, whilft in the Sciences, the firft Author goes fartheft, and time only abates or corrupts   Thus *Artillery, Sailing, Printing,* &c. were grofsly managed at the firft, but received improvement by time   on the contrary, the *Philofophy* and the *Sciences* of *Ariftotle, Plato, Democritus, Hippocrates, Euclid, Archimedes,* &c flourifh'd moft in the original Authors, and degenerated with Time   The reafon is, that in the *mechanick Arts,* the Capacities and Induftry of many are collected together, whilft in the *Sciences,* the Capacities and Induftry of many have been fpent upon the Invention of fome one man, who has commonly been thereby rather depraved than illuftrated   For as water afcends no higher than the level of the firft fpring, fo knowledge derived from *Ariftotle,* will at moft rife no higher again than the knowledge of *Ariftotle*   And therefore tho' *a fcholar muft have faith in his mafter, yet a man well inftructed muft judge for himfelf* · for Learners owe to their Mafters only a temporary belief, and a fufpenfion of their own judgment, till they are fully inftructed, and not an abfolute refignation, or perpetual captivity.

[a] As among the *Ægyptians,* the *Chinefe,* and the *Arabians,* if their *Hiftories* are to be credited   In later times, they make *Copper* out of *Iron,* to profit, at *Newfohl* in *Germany*   See *Agricola de re Metallica, Morhof, Fr Hoffman,* &c   And thus whilft *Brand* of *Hambrough,* was working upon Urine, in order to find the Philofopher's Stone, he ftumbled upon that called *Kunkel's burning Phofphorus,* in the year 1669   See *Mem de l'Academ Royal des Sciences,* An 1692   And M *Homberg* operating upon *human Excrement,* for an Oil to convert Quickfilver into Silver, accidentally produced that we now call the *Black Phofphorus,* a powder which readily takes fire, and burns like a coal in the open air   See *Mem de l'Acad* An 1711   To give all the Inftances of this kind, were almoft endlefs.

tivity   Let great Authors therefore have their due , but so as not to defraud Time, which is the Author of Authors, and the Parent of Truth.

VII   38 Besides the *three Diseases of Learning* above treated ,   there are *Peccant Humours of Learning, viz an Affectation of Antiquity and Novelty*
some other *peccant Humours*, which falling under popular observation, and reprehension, require to be particularly mentioned   The *first is the affecting of two extremes , Antiquity, and Novelty*   wherein the children of Time seem to imitate their Father , for as he devours his children, so they endeavour to devour each other   whilst *Antiquity* envies new Improvements, and *Novelty* is not content to add, without defacing   The advice of the Prophet is just in this case   *Stand upon the old ways, and see which is the good way, and walk therein.*   For Antiquity deserves that men should stand a while upon it, to view around which is the best way , but when the discovery is well made, they should stand no longer, but proceed with chearfulness.   And to speak the truth, *Antiquity*, as we call it, is the young state of the world , for those times are ancient when the world is ancient; and not those we vulgarly account ancient by computing backwards , so that the present time is the real *Antiquity* [a]

39 Another *Error*, proceeding from the former, is, *a distrust that any thing should be discovered in later times, that was not hit upon before* , as if *Lucian*'s objection against the Gods, lay also against Time   He pleasantly asks why the Gods begot so many children in the first ages, but none in his days; and whether they were grown too old for generation, or were restrained by the *Papian* Law, which prohibited old men from marrying? For thus we seem apprehensive that *Time* is worn out , and become unfit for generation.   And here we have a remarkable instance of the levity and inconstancy of man's humour; which before a thing is effected, thinks it impossible , and as soon as it is done, wonders it was not done before. So the Expedition of *Alexander* into *Asia*, was at first imagin'd a vast and impracticable enterprize , yet *Livy* afterwards makes so light of it, as to say *it was but bravely venturing to despise vain Opinions* [b]   And the case was the same in *Columbus*'s Discovery of the *West Indies*.   But this happens much more frequently in intellectual matters , as we see in most of the Propositions of *Euclid* , which till demonstrated, seem strange , but when demonstrated, the mind receives them by a kind of affinity , as if we had known them before *Distrust of farther Discoveries*

40. Another *Error* of the same nature, is *an Imagination that of all ancient Opinions or Sects, the best has ever prevailed, and suppressed the rest* , so that *That the best Opinions are not the most prevalent.* if a man begins a new search, he must happen upon somewhat formerly rejected , and by rejection, brought into oblivion   as if the multitude, or the wiser sort, to please the multitude, would not often give way to what is light and popular, rather than maintain what is substantial and deep [c].

41. Another different *Error* is *the over-early and peremptory reduction of knowledge into Arts and Methods*, from which time the Sciences are seldom improved *Sudden Reduction of Knowledge into methods.*

L

[a] This is more particularly explained and illustrated in the *Novum Organum*.
[b] *Nihil aliud quam bene ausus est, vana contemnere*
[c] The Author's own conduct in this particular may deserve observation; as turning upon the *artificial use of rational means* to overthrow Prejudice, and establish Truth   See above Sect. I 11. and hereafter in the present Piece, and the *Novum Organum*, passim

improved For as young men rarely grow in stature, after their shape and limbs are fully formed, so Knowledge, whilst it lies in *Aphorisms* and *Observations*, remains in a growing state, but when once fashion'd into Methods, tho' it may be farther polished, illustrated, and fitted for use, it no longer encreases in bulk and substance [a]

Treating of Universal Philosophy

42 Another *Error* is, that after the distribution of particular Arts and Sciences, men generally abandon the Study of Nature, or *universal Philosophy*, which stops all farther progress For as no perfect view of a Country can be taken upon a flat, so it is impossible to discover the remote and deep parts of any Science, by standing upon the level of the same Science, or without ascending to a higher [b]

Too great Reverence to the human Understanding

43 Another *Error* proceeds from too great a reverence, and a kind of adoration paid to the human understanding [c], whence men have withdrawn themselves from the contemplation of nature, and experience, and sported with their own reason and the fictions of Fancy These *Intellectualists*, tho' commonly taken for the most sublime and divine Philosophers [d], are censured by *Heraclitus*, when he says, " *men seek for truth in their own little worlds,* " *and not in the great world without them* " and as they disdain to spell, they can never come to read in the volume of God's works, but on the contrary, by continual thought and agitation of wit, they compel their own *Genius*, to divine, and deliver oracles, whereby they are deservedly deluded [e]

Introducing particular into Philosophy

44 Another *Error* is, that *men often infect their Speculations and Doctrines, with some particular Opinions they happen to be fond of, or the particular Sciences and Arts to they have most applied*, and thence give all other things a tincture that is utterly foreign to them Thus *Plato* mixed Philosophy with Theology, *Aristotle* with Logick, *Proclus* with Mathematicks [f], as these Arts were a kind of elder and favourite children with them So the *Alchemists* have made a Philosophy from a few Experiments of the Furnace, and *Gilbert* another out of the *Load-stone* But of such Authors *Aristotle* says well *Those who take but a few Considerations, may easily pronounce* [g]

Impatience of Doubting and Suspending

45 Another *Error* is *an impatience of doubting, and a blind hurry of asserting without a mature suspension of judgment* For the two ways of contemplation are like the two ways of action, so frequently mention'd by the ancients, the one plain and easy at first, but in the end impassable, the other rough

and

---

[a] Hence Mr *Boyle*, and others, recommend and practise *Essay writing* in *Philosophy*, preferably to the *Systematical Method*

[b] Thus the *Mathematical Philosophy* of our times is not to be measured by mere Mathematicians, but by such as are acquainted with Nature and Universality, as well as *Mathematicks*, so as clearly to discern how far this kind of Philosophy reaches, and where it errs, or falls short It may be proper to consult, upon this occasion, a late Performance, entitled, *Mathematique Universelle*

[c] See above, Sect I 20 & Sect II 11

[d] As *Plato*, for instance among the Ancients, and *des Cartes* among the Moderns

[e] Thus some of the Laws of motion, laid down by *des Cartes*, from *Theory*, are found false in *Experience*

[f] How a universal *Philosophy* is at present disadvantageously wrested into the Channel of Mathematicks, will perhaps be better perceived by Posterity than ourselves See the Author on Mathem. chs hereafter, Sect VII and *Morhof's Polyhist* Tom II pag 149

[g] Hence the principal modern writers of *Literary History* justly recommend *Polymathy*, or a general knowledge of Arts and Sciences, as necessary to those who would thoroughly understand and improve any one in particular See *Morhof, Servius, Stollius,* &c

i

and fatiguing in the entrance, but soon after fair and even · so in contemplation, if we begin with certainties, we shall end in doubts, but if we begin with doubts, and are patient in them, we shall end in certainties [a]

46 Another *Error* lies in the manner of *delivering Knowledge, which is generally magisterial and peremptory, not ingenuous and open, but suited to gain belief without examination* And in compendious Treatises for practice, this form should not be disallowed but in the true delivering of Knowledge both extremes are to be avoided, *viz* that of *Vellerus* the *Epicurean*, " *who feared* " *nothing so much as the non-appearance of doubting,*" and that of *Socrates*, and the Academicks, who ironically doubted of all things but the true way is to propose things candidly, with more or less asseveration, as they stand in a man's own judgment

The magisterial delivering of Knowledge

47 There are other *Errors* in the scope that men propose to themselves for whereas *the more diligent Professors of any Science ought chiefly to endeavour the making some additions or improvements therein, they aspire only to certain second prizes*, as to be a profound commentator, a sharp disputant, a methodical compiler, or abridger, *&c* whence the Returns or Revenues of Knowledge are sometimes increased, but not the Inheritance and Stock [b]

Aspiring but to inferior Qualifications

48 But the greatest *Error* of all, is, *mistaking the ultimate End of Knowledge*, for some Men covet Knowledge, out of a natural Curiosity, and inquisitive Temper, some to entertain the Mind with Variety and Delight, some for Ornament and Reputation, some for Victory and Contention, many for Lucre and a Livelihood, and but few for employing the Divine Gift of Reason, to the use and benefit of Mankind. Thus some appear to seek, in Knowledge, a Couch for a searching Spirit, others, a Walk for a wandring Mind; others, a Tower of State, others, a Fort, or commanding Ground, and others, a Shop for profit, or sale, instead of a Store-house for the Glory of the Creator, and the endowment of human Life But that which must dignify and exalt Knowledge, is the more intimate and strict conjunction of *Contemplation* and *Action* [c], a Conjunction like that of *Saturn*, the Planet of Rest and Contemplation, and *Jupiter*, the Planet of civil Society and Action But here, by *Use* and *Action*, we do not mean the applying of Knowledge to lucre, for that diverts the advancement of Knowledge, as the golden Ball thrown before *Atalanta*, which while she stoops to take up, the race is hindred Nor do we mean, as was said of *Socrates*, to call Philosophy down from Heaven, to converse upon Earth, that is, to leave Natural Philosophy behind, and apply Knowledge only to Morality and Policy. But as both Heaven and Earth contribute to the use and benefit of Man, so the End ought to be, from both Philosophies, to separate and reject vain and empty Speculations, and preserve and increase all that is solid and fruitful. And thus we have opened the chief of those *peccant Humours*, which not only retard

Mistaking the End of Knowledge

[a] *Doubting, in Philosophy*, appears to be the occasional Spring of Examination and Trial, or a principal motive to farther search and experiments, in order to satisfy the Scruples that arise in the Mind To this purpose, see *Glanvil's Scepsis Scientifica*, printed at *London*, 1665, and hereafter under *Physicks*, Sect IV 25
[b] That is, the present System of Knowledge is thus sometimes spread among the Body of a People, but no addition made to its total Sum. And thus the greatest part of Writers are but *Spreaders*, and the original *Inventors* and *Improvers*, a slender Number.
[c] See above, Sect I 1.

retard the *Progress of Learning*, but also occasion it to be traduced[a]. We have been free of our Censures, as not proposing a *Panegyric upon Learning*, or an *Hymn to the Muses*; but, without varnish or amplification, to weigh the Dignity of *Knowledge*, and take its true Estimate by Arguments and Testimonies, *human* and *divine*.

The Dignity of Learning sought from divine Testimony

VIII 49 Next, therefore, let us seek the *Dignity of Knowledge* in its original, that is, in the Attributes and Acts of God, so far as they are revealed to Man, and may be observed with sobriety. But here we are not to seek it by the name of *Learning* for all Learning is Knowledge acquired, but all Knowledge in God is original we must therefore look for it under the name of *Wisdom*, or *Sapience*, as the Scriptures call it.

A difference betwixt Knowledge and Power in the Creation

50 In the work of Creation, we see a double Emanation of Virtue from God, the one relating more properly to *Power*, the other to *Wisdom*, the one express'd in making the Matter, and the other in disposing the Form This being supposed, we may observe, that, for any thing mentioned in the History of the Creation, the confused mass of the Heavens and Earth was made in a moment, whereas the Order and Disposition of it was the work of six days such a mark of difference seems put betwixt the *Works of Power*, and the *Work of Wisdom* whence it is not written that God said, *Let there be Heaven and Earth*, as it is of the subsequent Works, but actually, that *God made Heaven and Earth* the one carrying the style of a Manufacture, the other that of a Law, Decree, or Council

In the celestial Hierarchy

51 To proceed from God to Spirits We find, as far as credit may be given to the celestial Hierarchy, of the supposed *Dionysius*, the *Areopagite*, the first place is given to the *Angels of Love*, termed *Seraphim*, the second, to the Angels of Light, called *Cherubim*, and the third, and following places, to *Thrones*, *Principalities*, and the rest, which are all Angels of Power and Ministry so that the Angels of Knowledge and Illumination, are placed before the Angels of Office and Domination

The Scripture Dispensation

52 To descend from Spirits, and intellectual, to sensible and material Forms We read the first created *Form* was Light, which, in nature and corporeal things, hath a relation and correspondence to Knowledge in Spirits, and things incorporeal · so, in the distribution of Days, we find the Day wherein God rested, and compleated his Works, was blessed above all the Days wherein he wrought them

In Paradise

53 After the *Creation* was finished, it is said, that Man was placed in the Garden to work therein, which Work could only be Work of Contemplation, that is, the end of his Work was but for Exercise and Delight, and not for Necessity · for there being then no Reluctance of the Creature, nor Sweat of the Brow, Man's Employment was consequently matter of Pleasure, not Labour Again, the first Acts which Man performed in *Paradise*, consisted of the two summary parts of Knowledge, a view of the Creatures, and the imposition of Names

54.

---

[a] To this Catalogue of Errors incident to *learned Men*, may be added, the Frauds and Impostures of which they are sometimes guilty, to the scandal of Learning Thus Plagiarism, Pyracy, Falsification, Interpolation, Castration, the publishing of spurious Books, the stealing of Manuscripts out of Libraries, &c. have been frequent, especially among the *Ecclesiastical Writers*, and the *Fratres Falsarii* For instances of this kind, see *Struvius de Doctis Impostoribus*, *Morhof in Polyh* & *de Pseudonymis*, *Anonymis*, &c. *Le Clerc's Ars Critica*, *Cave's Historia Literaria Scriptorum Ecclesiasticorum*, Father *Simon*, *Mabillon*, &c.

54 In the firſt event after the Fall, we find an Image of the two States, *In Cain and* the contemplative and the active, figured out in the perſons of *Abel* and *Cain* ; *Abel).* by the two ſimpleſt and moſt primitive Trades, that of the Shepherd, and that of the Husbandman, where again, the favour of God went to the Shepherd, and not to the Tiller of the Ground.

55 So in the Age before the *Flood*, the ſacred Records mention the name *The Age be-* of the Inventors of Muſick, and Workers in Metal In the Age after the *fore the Flood.* Flood, the firſt great Judgment of God upon the Ambition of Man, was the *Confuſion of Tongues*, whereby the open trade, and intercourſe of Learn- ing and Knowledge, was chiefly obſtructed

56 It is ſaid of *Moſes*, " *That he was ſeen in all the Learning of the* *In Moſes, So-* " *Ægyptians*," which Nation was one of the moſt ancient Schools of the *lomon, &c* World for *Plato* brings in the *Ægyptian* Prieſt ſaying to *Solon*, " *You* Gre- " cians *are ever Children, having no knowledge of Antiquity, nor antiquity of* " *Knowledge*" In the ceremonial Law of *Moſes*, we find, that beſides the prefiguration of *Chriſt*, the mark of the People of God to diſtinguiſh them from the *Gentiles*, the exerciſe of Obedience, and other divine Inſtitutions, the moſt learned of the *Rabbies* have obſerved a natural, and ſome of them a moral Senſe, in many of the Rites and Ceremonies Thus in the Law of the Leproſy, where it is ſaid, " *If the Whiteneſs have overſpread the Fleſh,* " *the Patient may paſs abroad for clean, but if there be any whole Fleſh re-* " *maining, he is to be ſhut up for unclean* " one of them notes a *Principle of* , *Nature*, viz that Putrefaction is more contagious before Maturity, than after Another hereupon obſerves a *Poſition of moral Philoſophy*, or that Men aban- don'd to Vice, do not corrupt the Manners of others, ſo much as thoſe who are but half wicked And in many other places of the *Jewiſh* Law, beſides the Theological Senſe, there are couched many Philoſophical Matters The Book of *Job* is likewiſe pregnant with the deep parts of Na- tural Philoſophy and in the perſon of King *Solomon*, we ſee *Knowledge* pre- ferred to all temporal Felicity

57 Nor did the *Diſpenſation* of God vary in the times after our *Saviour*, *The Goſpel-* who himſelf firſt ſhewed his power to ſubdue Ignorance, by conferring with *Diſpenſation* the Prieſts and Doctors of the Law, before he ſhewed his power to ſubdue Nature by Miracles And the coming of the Holy Spirit was chiefly ex- preſſed in the *Gift of Tongues*, which are but the conveyance of Knowledge

58 So in the election of thoſe Inſtruments it pleaſed God to uſe for plant *In the A-* ing the Faith, tho' at firſt he employ'd Perſons altogether unlearned, *poſtles* otherwiſe than by Inſpiration, the more evidently to declare his immediate working, and to humble all human Wiſdom, or Knowledge, yet, in the next ſucceſſion, he ſent out his divine Truth into the world, attended with other parts of Learning, as with Servants or Handmaids Thus St *Paul*, who was the only learned amongſt the Apoſtles, had his Pen moſt employed in the writings of the New Teſtament

59 Again, we find that many of the ancient Biſhops, and Fathers of the *The Fathers of* Church, were well verſed in all the Learning of the Heathens, inſomuch *the Church* that the Edict of the Emperor *Julian*, prohibiting Chriſtians the Schools, and Exerciſes, was accounted a more pernicious Engine againſt the Faith, than all the ſanguinary Perſecutions of his Predeceſſors Neither could

Clair the First, Bishop of *Rome*, ever obtain the opinion of Devotion, and among the Pious, for designing, tho' otherwise an excellent Person, to extinguish the memory of Heathen Antiquity But it was the *Christian Clergy*, which, amidst the Inundations of the *Scythians* from the Northwest, and the *Saracens* from the East, preserved in her bosom the Relicks even of Heathen Learning, which had otherwise been utterly extinguished And of late years the *Jews*, partly of themselves, and partly provoked by example, have greatly enlivened and strengthened the State of Learning, and contributed to establish the *Roman* See

60 There are, therefore, two principal Services, besides Ornament and Illustration, which *Philosophy* and *human Learning* perform to *Faith* and *Religion*; the one effectually exciting to the exaltation to God's Glory, and the other affording a singular Preservative against Unbelief and Error [a]. Our Saviour says, *Te err, not knowing the Scriptures, nor the power of God*, thus laying before us two Books to study, if we will be secured from Error, viz. the *Scriptures*, which reveal the Will of God, and the *Creation*, which expresses his Power the latter whereof is a key to the former, and not only opens our Understanding, to conceive the true sense of the Scripture, by the general Notions of Reason, and the Rules of Speech, but chiefly opens our Faith, in drawing us to a due consideration of the Omnipotence of God, which is stamped upon his Works And thus much for *divine Testimony*, concerning the *Dignity*, and *Merits of Learning* [b].

IX 61 Next, for *human Proofs* Deification was the highest Honour among the Heathens, that is, to obtain Veneration as a God, was the supreme Respect which Man could pay to Man, especially when given not by a formal Act of State, as it usually was to the *Roman* Emperors, but from a voluntary, internal Assent, and Acknowledgment This Honour being so high, there was also constituted a middle kind for human Honours were inferior to Honours heroical and divine Antiquity observed this difference in their distribution, that whereas Founders of States, Law-Givers, Extirpers of Tyrants, Fathers of the People, and other eminent persons in civil merit, were honoured but with the titles of *Heroes*, or Demi-Gods, such as *Hercules, Theseus, Minos, Romulus*, &c Inventors, and Authors of new Arts, or Discoveries, for the service of human Life, were ever advanced amongst the Gods, as in the case of *Ceres, Bacchus, Mercury, Apollo*, &c And this appears to have been done with great justice and judgment, for the Merits of the former being generally confined within the circle of one Age, or Nation, are but like fruitful Showers, which serve only for a season, and a small extent whilst the others are like the Benefits of the Sun, permanent and universal Again, the former are mixed with Strife and Contention, whilst the latter have the true Character of the divine Presence, as coming in a *gentle Gale*, without noise or tumult.

62,

---

[a] See, upon these Heads, Mr *Boyle's High Veneration that Man's Intellect owes to God*, and his *Christian Virtuoso*

[b] How far the Defence of the *Christian Religion* is owing to Learning, may appear from *Spencer's Edition of Origen against Celsus*, *Grotius de Veritate Religionis Christiana*, *Huet's Demonstratio Evangelica*, &c

62. The Merit of Learning, in remedying the Inconveniences arising from Man to Man, is not much inferior to that of relieving human Necessities. This Merit was livelily described by the Ancients, in the Fiction of *Orpheus*'s Theatre, where all the Beasts and Birds assembled, and forgetting their several Appetites, stood sociably together, listening to the Harp, whose Sound no sooner ceased, or was drown'd by a louder, but they all returned to their respective Natures. For thus Men are full of savage and unreclaimed Desires, which, as long as we hearken to Precepts, Laws, and Religion, sweetly touch'd with Eloquence and Persuasion, so long is Society and Peace maintained but if these Instruments become silent, or Sedition and Tumult drown their Musick, all things fall back to Confusion and Anarchy [a]

The Effects of Learning in Society

63 This appears more manifestly, when Princes, or Governours, are learned. For tho' he might be thought partial to his profession, who said, " *States would then be happy, when either Kings were Philosophers, or Philo-* " *sophers Kings*," yet so much is verified by experience, that the best Times have happen'd under wise and learned Princes For tho' Kings may have their Errors and Vices, like other Men, yet if they are illuminated by Learning, they constantly retain such Notions of Religion, Policy, and Morality, as may preserve them from destructive and irremediable Errors, or Excesses. for these Notions will whisper to them, even whilst Counsellors and Servants stand mute Such Senators likewise as are learned, proceed upon more safe and substantial Principles, than mere Men of experience the former view Dangers afar off, whilst the latter discover them not till they are at hand, and then trust to their Wit to avoid them. This felicity of Times under learned Princes, appears eminent in the age between the death of *Domitian*, and the reign of *Commodus*; comprehending a succession of six Princes, all of them learned, or singular Favourers and Promoters of Learning And this Age, for temporal respects, was the happiest and most flourishing, that ever the *Roman* State enjoyed

64 Nor has *Learning* an influence only over civil Society, and the Arts of Peace, but likewise exerts its power over *military Virtue* as eminently appears in the examples of *Alexander* and *Cæsar* *Alexander* was bred under *Aristotle*, who dedicated several Books of Philosophy to him He was attended by *Callisthenes*, and other learned Persons, in his Camp, and Conquests In what esteem he held Learning, may appear by three particulars, *viz* (1) The Envy he used to express towards *Achilles*, in having so good a Recorder of his Acts as *Homer* · (2) The assignment of that rich Cabinet of *Darius*, to contain *Homer*'s Works (3.) His Letter to *Aristotle*, upon publishing his *Physicks*, expostulating with him for divulging the Secrets of Philosophy, and telling him he esteemed it nobler to excel other Men in Learning and Knowledge, than in Power and Empire

Effects of Learning upon military Virtue

65 The Learning of *Julius Cæsar* need not be argued from his Education, his Company, or his Speeches, as fully declaring itself in his Writings, whereof some are extant, and others unfortunately lost. We have

left

---

[a] This shews the necessity of cultivating Eloquence, or keeping up the Power of Speech, in order to subdue the Passions, inculcate Morality and Religion, and influence civil Society and that the same Art may, in some degree, be used in *Natural Philosophy*, was shewn above, Sect III 31

Left us that excellent *History of his own Wars*, which he barely entitled a *Commentary*, or *Memoir*, wherein all the succeeding times have admired the solid Weight of Matter, and the lively Images of Actions and Persons, expressed in the greatest propriety and perspicuity of Language. That this was not the effect of a natural Gift, but of Learning [a], may appear by that Work of his entitled *de Analogia*, which was a certain *grammatical Philosophy*, wherein he endeavoured to reduce the common use of Speech to Congruity and Correctness, and to suit Words to Things, not by Custom, but Reason [b]

Effect of Learning on private Virtue

66 To proceed from imperial and military, to moral and private Virtue, it is certain, that Learning softens the barbarity and fierceness of men's Minds; but then it must not be superficial, for this rather works a contrary effect. Solid Learning prevents all Levity, Temerity, and Insolence, by suggesting Doubts and Difficulties, and inuring the Mind to ballance the Reasons on both sides, and reject the first offers of Things; or to accept of nothing but what is first examined and tried. It prevents vain Admiration, which is the root of all Weakness; things being admired, either because they are *new*, or because they are *great*. As for *Novelty*, no Man can wade deep in Learning, without discovering *that he knows nothing too rightly*, nor can we wonder at a Puppet-shew, if we look behind the Curtain. With regard to *Greatness*, as *Alexander*, after having been used to great Armies, and the Conquests of large Provinces in *Asia*, when he received accounts of Battles from *Greece*, which were commonly for a pass, a fort, or some walled town, imagined he was but reading *Homer*'s Battle of the Frogs and the Mice: so if a Man considers the universal Frame, the Earth and its Inhabitants will seem to him but as an Ant-hill, where some carry Grain, some their Young, some go empty, and all march but upon a little heap of Dust.

Learning conquers the Fear of Death

67 Learning also conquers, or mitigates, the Fear of Death, and adverse Fortune, which is one of the greatest Impediments to Virtue and Morality. For if a man's Mind be deeply season'd with the consideration of the Mortality and Corruptibility of things, he will be as little affected as *Epictetus*, who, one day, seeing a Woman weeping for her Pitcher that was broken, and the next day, a Woman weeping for her Son that was dead, said calmly, *Yesterday, I saw a brittle Thing broken, and to-day a Mortal die*. And hence *Virgil* excellently joined the *Knowledge of Causes*, and the conquering of *Fears*, together, as Concomitants [c]

Remedies the Diseases of the Mind

68 It were tedious to enumerate the particular Remedies which Learning affords for all the Diseases of the Mind, sometimes by purging the morbific Humours, sometimes by opening Obstructions, helping Digestion, increasing

[a] The diffusive Learning of this extraordinary Personage, may farther appear from *Fabricius's* Account of his Work. See *Jo. Albert Fabricius Bibliotheca Latina*, Vol. I. cap. x.

[b] This Work of *Julius Cæsar*, written in two Books, which out *Ja. Operarius* endeavours to supply in his *Analogia Linguæ Latinæ*, printed at *Paris*, in the year 1698, and at *Amsterdam*, in 1700.

[c] *Felix qui potuit rerum cognoscere causas,*
   Quique metus omnes, & inexorabile fatum,
   Subjecit pedibus, strepitumque Acherontis avari.

creafing the Appetite, and fometimes healing Exulcerations, &c. But, to fum up all, it difpofes the Mind not to fix or fettle in Defects, but to remain ever fufceptible of Improvement and Reformation For the illiterate perfon knows not what it is to defcend into himfelf, or call himfelf to an account, nor the agreeablenefs of that Life, which is daily fenfible of its own Improvement He may, perhaps, learn to fhew, and employ his natural Talents, but not increafe them, he will learn to hide and colour his Faults, but not to amend them like an unfkilful Mower, who continues to mow on without whetting his Scythe The Man of Learning, on the contrary, always joins the Correction and Improvement of his Mind, with the ufe and employment thereof To conclude, *Truth* and *Goodnefs* differ but as the Seal and the Impreffion for Truth imprints Goodnefs, whilft the Storms of Vice and Perturbation break from the Clouds of Error and Falfhood [a]

X 69 From moral Virtue, we proceed to examine *whether any Power be* *Gives great* *equal to that afforded by Knowledge* Dignity of Command is always propor- *power over* *men's Minds* tionable to the Dignity of the Commanded. To have command over Brutes, as a Herdfman, is a mean thing, to have command over Children, as a Schoolmafter, is matter of fmall honour, and to have command over Slaves, is rather a Difgrace than an Honour Nor is the command of a Tyrant much better, over a fervile and degenerate People, whence Honours, in free Monarchies, and Republicks, have ever been more efteemed, than in tyrannical Governments, becaufe to rule a willing People, is more honourable than to compel But the Command of Knowledge, is higher than the Command over a free People, as being a Command over the Reafon, Opinion, and Underftanding of Men, which are the nobleft Faculties of the Mind, that govern the Will itfelf for there is no Power on earth that fets up a Throne in the Spirits of Men, but Knowledge and Learning Whence the deteftable and extreme Pleafure wherewith Arch-hereticks, falfe Prophets, and Impoftors, are tranfported, upon finding they have a dominion in the Faith and Confciences of Men, a pleafure fo great, that if once tafted, fcarce any Torture, or Perfecution, can make them forgo it But as this is what the Apocalypfe calls *the depths of Satan*, fo the juft and lawful Rule over men's Underftanding, by the evidence of Truth, and gentle Perfuafion, is what approaches neareft to the divine Sovereignty [b]

70 With regard to Honours and private Fortune, the benefit of *Learn-* *Raifes private* *ing* is not fo confined to States, as not likewife to reach particular Perfons *Fortunes* For it is an old Obfervation, that *Homer* has given more Men their livings, than *Sylla. Cæfar*, or *Auguftus*, notwithftanding their great Largeffes And it is hard to fay, whether *Arms* or *Learning* have advanced the greater numbers. In point of Sovereignty, if Arms, or Defcent, have obtained the Kingdom, yet Learning has obtained the *Priefthood*, which was ever in competition with *Empire*

71 Again, the pleafure and delight of Knowledge and Learning, fur- *Affords great* pafs all others for if the Pleafures of the Affections exceed the Pleafures *Delight*
of

[a] Moft feem to agree, that *Knowledge* will make Men virtuous; at leaft, that none are truly wife, if they are not virtuous

[b] For the command which *Knowledge* gives Men over the Works of Nature, and over one another, fee Mr. *Boyle's* Effays on the *Ufefulnefs of Experimental Philofophy* Abridg Vol I in *unit*

of the Senses, as much as the obtaining a Defire, or a Victory, exceeds a Song or a Treat, fhall not the Pleafures of the Underftanding exceed the Pleafures of the Affections? In all other pleafures there is a Satiety, and after ufe their Verdure fades, which fhews they are but Deceits and Fallacies, and that it was the Novelty which pleafed, not the Quality whence voluptuous Men frequently turn Friars, and ambitious Princes Melancholicks But of Knowledge there is no Satiety, for here Gratification and Appetite are perpetually interchanging, and confequently this is Good in itfelf, fimply, without fallacy or accident Nor is that a fmall pleafure and fatisfaction to the Mind, which *Lucretius* defcribes to this effect " It is a Scene of Delight to be fafe on fhore, and fee a Ship toffed at " fea, or to be in a Fortification, and fee two Armies join battle upon " a Plain But it is a Pleafure incomparable, for the Mind to be feated by " Learning in the Fortrefs of Truth, and from thence to view the Errors " and Labours of others "

Border Non ...

72 To conclude the Dignity and Excellence of Knowledge and Learning, is what human Nature moft afpires to, for the fecuring of Immortality which is alfo endeavour'd after, by raifing and ennobling of Families, by Buildings, Foundations, and Monuments of Fame, and is, in effect, the bent of all other human Defires But we fee how much more durable the Monuments of Genius and Learning are, than thofe of the Hand The Verfes of *Homer* have continued above five and twenty hundred years, without lofs, in which time, numberlefs Palaces, Temples, Caftles, and Cities, have been demolifhed, and are fallen to ruin It is impoffible to have the true Pictures or Statues of *Cyrus*, *Alexander*, *Cæfar*, or the great Perfonages of much later date, for the Originals cannot laft, and the Copies muft lofe of the Life But the Images of men's Knowledge remain in Books, exempt from the Injuries of Time, and capable of perpetual Renovation Nor are thefe properly called Images, becaufe they generate ftill, and fow their Seed in the minds of others, fo as to caufe infinite Actions and Opinions in fucceeding Ages If, therefore, the Invention of a Ship was thought fo noble, which carries Commodities from place to place, and brings the remoteft Regions acquainted, how much more are Letters to be valued, which, like Ships, pafs thro' the vaft Ocean of Time, and convey Knowledge and Inventions to the remoteft Ages? Nay, fome of the Philofophers, who were moft immerfed in the Senfes, and denied the Immortality of the Soul, yet allowed, that whatever Motions the Spirit of Man could perform without the Organs of the Body, might remain after death, which are only thofe of the Underftanding, and not of the Affections fo immortal and incorruptible a thing did *Knowledge* appear to them[a] And thus having endeavoured to do juftice to the *Caufe of Knowledge*, *divine* and *human*, we fhall leave *Wifdom to be juftified of her Children*[b]

SECT

---

[a] This Section has but occafionally confider'd the *general Merits* of Learning, its *particular* Merits will appear hereafter, when it comes to be branched into the *Sciences* fo that a Judgment cannot juftly be form'd of it from this Examination See below, Sect V VI &c

[b] The Merits of *Learning* have been occafionally fhewn by many, but exprefsly by few Among the later may be reckon'd *Johannes Wouwerius de Polymathia*, *Gulielmus Budæus de Philologia Merit* in his *Polyhiftor* and *Stollius in Introduct in Hiftoriam Literariam* To thefe may be added, Baron *Spanheim*, M *Perault*, Sir *William Temple*, &c

SECT. IV.

The PUBLIC OBSTACLES *to* LEARNING *confider'd.*

1 WE come next to confider what fteps have hitherto been taken, and what farther remains, for the promotion of *Learning.* The Foundation we proceed upon is this, that *all Works are conquer'd,* (1) *by Greatnefs of Reward,* (2) *Juftnefs of Direction,* and (3) *united Labours* The *firft* multiplies Endeavours, the *fecond* prevents Error, and the *third* fupplies the Imperfection of Mankind [a]   But the principal of thefe is *Direction*; for according to the Proverb, *a lame Man in the right way, may beat a Racer in the wrong*   And *Solomon* excellently faid, *If the Iron be blunt, it requireth more ftrength, but Wifdom is that which prevaileth* fignifying that a prudent Choice of the Means, is more effectual than joint Endeavours   But the Acts of great Men rather regard Magnificence and Fame, than Progrefs and Proficiency, and tend more to augment the Mafs of Learning in the multitude of Learned Men, than to rectify or advance the *Sciences* [b].

Publick Endeavours neceffary to advance Learning

2 The *Acts of Merit towards Learning,* regard three Objects, *viz.* (1) the *Places of Learning,* (2) the *Books of Learning,* and (3) the *Perfons of the Learned* For as Water, whether of the Dew of Heaven, or the Springs of the Earth, fcatters, and is loft on the ground, unlefs collected in fome Receptacle, or Ciftern, fo Knowledge, whether from divine Infpiration, or human Senfe, would foon be loft, if it were not preferved in Books, Traditions, Univerfities, Colleges and Schools.

The publick Objects of Learning.

3 The Works regarding the Seats of Learning are four, *viz* (1) *Buildings,* (2) *Endowments,* (3) *Privileges,* (4) *Laws* and *Inftitutions,* all tending to privacy, quiet, and exemption from Cares and Anxieties, like the ftill Stations, defcribed by *Virgil,* for the hiving of Bees

The Works regarding the Seats of Learning

4 The *Works with regard to Books,* are principally two, *viz* (1) *Libraries* [c], which are as Shrines that lodge the Relicks of the ancient Saints, full of Virtue, without Delufion and Impofture, and (2) *new and more correct*

Books

[a] This fundamental Obfervation fhould be kept in mind, throughout the whole *Inftauration,* otherwife many parts of the Author's Scheme will appear impracticable   Thus the particular *Defiderata* of Learning, hereafter fet down, are fome of them too great to be fupplied by a private hand, but require a publick Purfe, an exact Conduct, and united Affiftance, as the *Hiftory of Arts,* the *Literary Hiftory,* the *Philofophical College,* &c   And, doubtlefs fome of the greateft Things that Mankind are capable of performing, remain unattempted, or unaccomplifhed, for want of thefe main Springs of Action

[b] The means of doing which, are pointed out below

[c] For the beft Methods of collecting and difpofing publick *Libraries,* and thofe who have wrote upon the Subject, fee *Morhof* in *Polyhift de Mediis erigendarum Bibliothecarum* Tom I Lib I Cap IV V VI and *Stollii Introduct in Hiftoriam Literariam de Hiftoria Literaria generatim fpectata,* p 78, &c   But particularly M *Naudé's Avis pour dreffer une Bibliotheque,* firft printed at *Paris,* in 1627, and afterwards tranflated into *Latin* by *Schmidius,* with Additions, in 1703. See alfo *Naudé's Catalogus Bibliothecæ Cordejianæ,* printed at *Paris,* in 1643.

true Editions of Authors, with more exact Tranflations, more ufeful Notes, Explanations, &c.

The Works of the Learned
5 The *Works that regard the Perfons of the Learned*, befides the countenancing of them in general, are alfo two viz (1) the Reward and Inftitution of Readers in the Sciences already known, and (2) the Reward and Inftitution of Writers, and Enquirers into the Parts of Learning not hitherto fufficiently profecuted

To provide that the Defects of the Colleges, Arts and Sciences at large
6 Thefe are the Works and Acts wherein the Merits of many Princes, and others, have appeared But, to *look unto that part of the Race which is before us*, we obferve, (1) that, *as there are fo many excellent Foundations of Colleges in Europe, it is ftrange they fhould be all dedicated to certain Profeffions, a few excepted free from Art and Sciences at large* For tho' all Learning fhould be referred to Action, yet we may here eafily fall into the error of fuppofing the Stomach idle, becaufe it neither performs the Office of Motion, as the Limbs, nor of Senfe, as the Head, tho' it digefts and diftributes to all the other Parts in like manner, if a Man thinks Philofophy and Univerfality but idle Studies he does not confider that all Profeffions are from thence fupplied And this feems a principal Caufe of the flow advancement of Learning, as hefe fundamental kinds of Knowledge have been ftudied only in paffage For to make a Tree bear more Fruit, it is not any thing done to the Boughs, but ftirring the Earth, and the putting new Mould about the Roots, that muft effect it' And this dedicating of Foundations to *profeffory Learning*, has not only had a bad effect upon the growth of the Sciences but alfo upon *Governments* For hence Princes generally find a great want of able Men for their fervice, as there is no collegiate Inftitution for Hiftory, modern Languages, Politicks, and the like means of qualifying fuch as are difpofed for the Service of the State[b]

To provide a greater part of the Salary
7 (2 As well as *Founders of Colleges* plant, and *Founders of Lectures* water, we muft next note a defect in *publick Lectures*, whether in Arts or Profeffions viz *the fmallnefs of the Salary generally affigned them* For 'tis neceffary to the progrefs of the Sciences, that *Readers* be of the ableft kind, as men intended for propagating the Sciences to future ages, and not for tranfitory ufe And this cannot be, unlefs the Profits may content the moft Eminent in every Art to appropriate their Lives and Labours to this fole purpofe, who muft therefore have a competency allowed them, proportionable to what might be expected from the practice of a Profeffion For to make the *Sciences* flourifh, *David*'s military Law fhould be obferved, and *thofe who ftay with the Carriage, have equal with thofe who are in the Action,*

---

[a] The thing here intended is a *general College*, fet apart for *fundamental Learning*, or fuch as fhould be preparatory to all Arts Sciences, and Profeffions, that is, for teaching the Principles of *univerfal Philofophy*, or *general Knowledge* For want of fuch a *general Inftitution*, Men are moft eminent in fome one particular Profeffion, are commonly ignorant in all the reft, whereas to make a Man compleat, and eminently ferviceable, 'tis neceffary he fhould be underftand the Principles of *Morality civil Society natural Philofophy*, Law, *Divinity Medicine* &c before he applies himfelf to the Practice and Improvement of any one Art, Science, or Profeffion fuch a Connection all the Parts of Learning have with one another, as together conftituting but one *Corps of Science*

[b] From feeing this ill Effect, perhaps, the *Academy of Politicks* was inftituted by *Lewis* the Fourteenth of *France*, and, lately, a Profeffor of *modern Hiftory* by King *George* the Firft of *England*

Action, or otherwise the Carriages will be ill attended   so *Lecturers in the Sciences*, as being the Guardians of the Stores and Provisions, whence Men in active Life are furnished, ought to share equal Advantages with them   For if the Fathers of the *Sciences* be weak, or ill maintained, the Students will feel the effects of it [a]

8 (3) The next *Defect* may require the assistance of the Chemists, who call upon Scholars to sell their Books, and build Furnaces, quitting *Minerva* and the Muses, as barren Virgins, and relying upon *Vulcan*   And indeed to the deep, fruitful, and operative Study of many Sciences, especially *Natural Philosophy* and *Physick*, Books are not the only Instruments required   and accordingly Spheres, Globes, Maps, &c. have, as well as Books, been provided for the study of *Astronomy* and *Geography*   And some Places destined to *Physick*, have also Gardens for Simples, and the allowance of dead Bodies for Anatomy. *But these are too scanty*   In general, no great proficiency can well be made in the disclosing of Nature, without some PUBLIC ALLOWANCES FOR EXPERIMENTS; whether of the Furnace, Engine, or any other kind and therefore as the Secretaries and Spies of Princes are allowed to bring in *Bills for Intelligence*, so must the Spies and Observers of Nature bring in their *Bills of Charges*, or we shall be ill informed   And if *Alexander* made such a liberal Allowance to *Aristotle*, for Hunters, Fowlers, Fishers, &c in order to a *natural History of Animals*, much better do they deserve it, who labour in the Labyrinths of Art [b].

The third, a want of Apparatus, and publick Allowances for Experiments

9. (4) *Another Defect of great importance*, is a *neglect in Governours of Universities*, with regard to *Consultations*, and *in Princes, of Visitations*; to observe, with diligence, whether the *Readings, Exercises, Disputations*, and other academical Customs, anciently instituted, should be still continued, changed, or reformed. For, as in all Precedents, if the times wherein they began, were dark or ignorant, it derogates from their Authority ; and as most Customs and Orders of Universities began in obscure and ignorant Times, it is the more requisite they should be re-examined   Thus, for instance, Scholars in the Universities begin *Logick* and *Rhetorick* too soon; these being Arts fitter for Graduates, than Children   and when rightly understood, are the gravest of Sciences, and the Arts of Arts, the one for Judgment, the other for Ornament, as affording Rules and Directions for setting out, and disposing of Matter   whence for Minds empty and unfraught to begin with these Arts, the Wisdom whereof is great and universal, renders them contemptible, and sinks them into childish Sophistry, and ridiculous Affectation   Again, the *Exercises of Universities*, make too great a separation between *Invention* and *Memory*, for Speeches are here either premeditated, when nothing is left to Invention, or merely extempory, when little is left to Memory, whereas Business and Action require a mixture of Premeditation and

The fourth, a want of Inspection and Regulation of Universities.

[a] The Salaries allowed by *Lewis* the Fourteenth, procured very able Men for Members of the *Royal Academy of Sciences* at *Paris*, and if that Academy has out-stripp'd most others in Discoveries and Improvements, this may be chiefly owing to the princely Munificence of its Founder, and the Presents extraordinary, wherewith he rewarded such Members as merited it by their Works   See *Fontenelle's History of the Re-establishment*, An 1699
[b] That is, who prosecute the Business of *Experiments*, as in the *Royal Academy of Sciences* at *Paris*, and the *Metallick College* of the King of *Sweden*   but the *Royal Society of London* has no *publick Allowance for Experiments*

Invention Whence the Exercise anſwers not to Practice, nor the Image the Life whereas it is a conſtant rule in Exerciſes, to form them as near as poſſible to Practice, otherwiſe they do not prepare, but pervert the natural Faculties of the Mind, as appears when *Students* come to act in civil Life, for then this want is ſoon perceived by themſelves, and ſooner by others

Trifling a part of Intelligence between the Univerſities of Europe 10 (5.) The next *Defect* goes a little higher for as the *advancement of Learning* greatly depends upon the Orders and Inſtitutions of Univerſities in the ſame Kingdom, it would be ſtill better, *if there were more of mutual Intelligence between the Univerſities* of Europe. There are many Orders and Foundations, which tho' lying under ſeveral Sovereignties, yet take themſelves to have a kind of Society, and Correſpondence, with one another, inſomuch, that they have common Heads and Provincials[a] and, ſurely, as Nature creates Brotherhood in Families, and mechanical Arts make Brotherhood in Communities, as the Divine Unction induces Brotherhood in Kings and Biſhops, and Vows and Rules make Brotherhood in *Orders*, ſo there cannot but be an *illuſtrious Fraternity* in Learning and Illumination, relative to that Paternity attributed to God, the Father of *Lights*[b].

The ſixth a want of publick Writers and Enquirers 11 (6.) The laſt *Defect* is, that there has rarely been any *publick Inſtitution, of Writers, or Enquirers, about ſuch parts of Knowledge as are not already ſufficiently laboured* Whence it were highly proper to examine what parts of Learning have been proſecuted, and what neglected for the opinion of plenty is one cauſe of want, and our great quantity of Books, looks like ſuperfluity, which, however, is not to be remedied by deſtroying thoſe we have already, but by publiſhing more good ones, that, like the Serpent of *Moſes*, might devour the Serpents of the Enchanters.

12 The removal of the five preceding Defects, and even the active part of the ſixth and laſt, *viz.* the Inſtitution of *Writers* and *Enquirers*, are *regal Works*[c]; towards which, the Endeavours of a private Perſon are but as a Statue in a croſs Road, that may point the way it cannot go[d] but the ſpeculative part of the laſt, *viz.* the *Examination of Learning*, may be promoted by private labour We ſhall, therefore, next attempt a general *Survey of Knowledge*, and enquire into what parts thereof lie waſte, or unimproved, in order to furniſh out ſuch a Plan, as may give light to *publick Deſigns*, and excite the *private Endeavours* of others[e]

---

[a] As the *Jeſuits*, for inſtance, and other *religious Orders* abroad

[b] The ill Conſequences of this want of Correſpondence ſtill continue, in ſome degree We in England are but little acquainted with the Tranſactions of foreign *Univerſities*, and thence generally think but contemptibly of them, as particularly of the *Germans*, perhaps for want of knowing them better

[c] And therefore properly laid before *crown'd Heads*, as they were, with great addreſs, by the Author before *King James the Firſt*, tho' without effect But *King Charles* II of *England*, and *Lewis* XIV of *France* entered into the Spirit of his grand Deſign The firſt, upon inſtituting the *Royal Society of London* was ſoon followed by the other, in eſtabliſhing the *Royal Academy of Sciences* at *Paris* And theſe two eminent Examples gave occaſion to the eſtabliſhment of many the like Societies in different parts of *Europe* tho' ſome of an inferiour kind were, before this, formed in *Italy*

[d] Yet private Fortunes may be employ'd to procure theſe publick Advantages, as appears by the noble Inſtitution of *Greſham College*

[e] The Deſign of this *Section* is beautifully exemplified, and deduced, in the *New Atlantis*, or Plan of a *Philoſophical Society*, placed as the FIRST SUPPLEMENT to the preſent *Piece*

THE

THE
DISTRIBUTION
OF
KNOWLEDGE,
Into Particular SCIENCES.

SECT. I.
Of HISTORY.

1. THE *juſteſt Diviſion of Human Learning*, is that derived from the three different Faculties of the *Soul*, the Seat of Learning HISTORY being relative to the *Memory*, POETRY to the *Imagination*, and PHILOSOPHY to the *Reaſon* By *Poetry*, we underſtand no more than *feign'd Hiſtory*, or *Fable* ; without regard, at preſent, to the *poetical Style* *Knowledge, divine and human, ranged under Hiſtory, Poetry and Philoſophy.*

2 HISTORY is properly concerned about *Individuals*, circumſcribed by Time and Place ſo likewiſe is POETRY , with this difference, that its *Individuals* are feign'd, with a reſemblance to true *Hiſtory* , yet, like Painting, ſo as frequently to exceed it. But PHILOSOPHY, dropping *Individuals*, fixes upon *Notions* abſtracted from them ; and is employ'd in compounding and ſeparating theſe *Notions* according to the *Laws of Nature*, and the *Evidence of Things themſelves* Thus HISTORY, POETRY, and PHILOSOPHY flow from the three diſtinct Fountains of the Mind, *viz* the *Memory*, the *Imagination*, and the *Reaſon* , without any poſſibility of increaſing their number For *Hiſtory* and *Experience* are one and the ſame thing , ſo are *Philoſophy* and the *Sciences*

3 Nor does *Divine Learning* require any other *Diviſion :* for tho' *Revelation* and *Senſe* may differ, both in matter and manner , yet the Spirit of Man, and its Cells, are the ſame , and in this caſe receive, as it were, different Liquors thro' different Conduits *Theology*, therefore, conſiſts (1.) of *Sacred Hiſtory* , (2) *Parable*, or *Divine Poeſy* , and (3) of *Holy Doctrine*, or *Precept*,

G 2

as

as its fixed *Philosophy* As for *Prophecy*, which seems a part redundant, 'tis no more than a Species of *History*, *Divine History* having this prerogative over *Human*, that the *Narration* may precede, as well as succeed the *Fact*

History either natural and civil

4 HISTORY is either *natural* or *civil* the *natural* records the Works and Acts of *Nature*, the *civil* the Works and Acts of *Men* Divine Interposition is unquestionably seen in both, particularly in the Affairs of Men, so far as to constitute a different species of *History*, which we call *Sacred*, or *Ecclesiastical* But such is the dignity of *Letters* and *Arts*, that they deserve a separate *History*, which, as well as the *Ecclesiastical*, we comprehend under *Civil History*

Natural History divided into the History of Generations, Præter-generations, and Arts

5 We form our Division of *Natural History* upon the threefold *state* and *condition* of *Nature*, which is (1) either free, and proceeding in her ordinary course, without molestation, or (2) obstructed by some stubborn and less common Matters, and thence put out of her course, as in the production of *Monsters*, or (3) bound and wrought upon by human means, for the production of Things artificial Let all *Natural History*, therefore, be divided into the *History of Generations*, *Præter-generations*, and *Arts*, the *first* to consider *Nature at liberty*, the *second*, *Nature in her errors*, and the *third*, *Nature in constraint*

The History of Arts, why made a species of Natural History

6 The HISTORY OF ARTS should the rather make a Species of *Natural History*, because of that prevalent opinion, as if *Art* were a different thing from *Nature*, and Things natural different from Things artificial, whence many Writers of *Natural History* think they perform notably, if they give us the *History of Animals*, *Plants*, or *Minerals* [a], without a word of the *mechanic Arts* A farther mischief is to have *Art* esteemed no more than an assistant to *Nature*, so as to help her forwards, correct or set her free, and not to bend, change, and radically affect her, whence an untimely Despair has crept upon mankind, who should rather be assured that *artificial Things* differ not from natural in *form* or *essence*, but only in the *efficient* For Man has no power over *Nature* in any thing but Motion, whereby he either puts bodies together, or separates them. And therefore, so far as natural Bodies may be separated or conjoin'd, man may do any thing [b] Nor matters it, if things are put in order for producing effects, whether it be done by human means or otherwise Gold is sometimes purged by the Fire, and sometimes found naturally pure. the Rain-bow is produced after a natural way, in a Cloud above, or made artificially, by the sprinkling of Water below. As *Nature*, therefore, governs all things, by means (1) of her general Course, (2) her Excursion, and (3) by means of human Assistance these three Parts must be received into *Natural History*, as in some measure they are by *Pliny*

7.

---

[a] As *Aristotle*, *Dioscorides*, *Cæsalpinus*, *Cesius*, *Wormius*, *Aldrovandus*, &c

[b] This *fundamental Maxim* will be made great use of in the Course of the Work, and should therefore be well understood and remembred, otherwise we shall easily mistake practicable things for impracticable, when the Author comes to apply so simple a Principle, for producing *uncommon Effects* by *human Means*, or merely by the separation and combination of Matter. Thus a person unacquainted with Distillation and Concentration, would not conceive that Brandy should be separated from *Wine by Fire*, Water from Wine *by Cold*, &c and many more considerable Works be perform'd barely by human *separation* and *combination*, applied in *Mechanics*, *Optics*, *Manufactures* and *Arts*

7 The first of these Parts, the *History of Creatures*, is extant in tolerable perfection[a], but the two others, the *History of Monsters*, and the *History of Arts*, may be noted as deficient. For I find *no competent Collection of the works of Nature digressing from the ordinary course of generations, productions and motions, whether singularities of place and region, or strange events of time and chance; effects of unknown properties, or instances of exceptions to general Rules* We have indeed many books of fabulous Experiments, Secrets and frivolous Impostures, for pleasure and strangeness[b], but a *substantial and well-purged Collection of Heteroclites, or Irregularities of Nature, carefully examined and described, especially with a due rejection of fable and popular error, is wanting*[c] for as things now stand, if false Facts in Nature be once on foot, what thro' neglect of Examination, the countenance of Antiquity, and the use made of them in Discourse, they are scarce ever retracted.

8 The Design of such a Work, of which we have a precedent in *Aristotle*, is not to content curious and vain minds, but (1.) to correct the depravity of *Axioms* and *Opinions*, founded upon common and familiar Examples; and (2) to shew the *Wonders of Nature*, which give the shortest passage to the *Wonders of Art* for by carefully *tracing Nature in her wandrings, we may be enabled to lead or compel her to the same again*[d]. Nor would we in this *History of Wonders* have superstitious Narrations of Sorceries, Witchcrafts, Dreams, Divinations, &c totally excluded, where there is full evidence of the fact. because it is not yet known in what cases, and how far effects attributed to superstition, depend upon natural causes And, therefore, tho' the practice of such things is to be condemned, yet the consideration of them may afford light, not only in the judging of criminals, but in the farther disclosing of Nature Nor should men scruple examining into these things, in order to discover Truth the Sun tho' it passes thro' dirty places, yet remains as pure as before. Those narrations, however, which have a tincture of superstition, should be kept separate, and unmix'd with others, that are merely natural But the Relations of religious prodigies and miracles, as being either false or supernatural, are unfit to enter a *History of Nature*[e]

9. As for the HISTORY OF NATURE WROUGHT OR FORM'D, we have some Collections of *Agriculture* and manual Arts, but commonly with a Rejection

---

[a] By *Aristotle, Dioscorides, Pliny,* and others

[b] As by *Cardan, Paracelsus, Alexis, Baptista Porta,* &c

[c] Nor supplied to this day, tho' many particulars for it may be collected from *Aldrovandus, Weinrichius, Licetus, Bonaventura, Schenkius, Laurentius, Cassanius,* and *Stengelius,* who have all wrote, *de Monstris* To these may be added the *Physica curiosa* of *Schottus, Kircher's Mundus subterraneus,* the *Philosophical Transactions,* the *French Memoirs,* the *Acta Eruditorum,* the *German Ephemerides,* and *Wanley's Wonders of the little World*

[d] Let this *Foundation* for acquiring a Command over Nature be well observed, for many Particulars mention'd hereafter, such as governing the Winds, the Weather, &c would seem impossibilities without it

[e] To this History might perhaps advantageously be added, the *monstrous,* or *anomalous Productions in Arts;* where things happen in an eminent degree, contrary to the expectation of the *Artist.* as the perverting or stopping of vinous Fermentation, by the accidental falling in of a little Soap, the making of solid, or *Loaf Sugar,* from the accidental application of Tobacco-pipe *Clay,* the preventing of Sugar from boiling over, by the accidental dropping in of a Candle, the discharging of *red Ink* by accidentally spitting upon a red Writing, &c Instances of which kind are to be found in the Books of *Chemistry,* and other practical Arts They deserve the rather to be collected, because all such Instances give us the Power of doing the like again, and thus enlarge our command over *Nature.*

jection of familiar and vulgar Experiments, which yet are of more service in the *Interpretation of Nature* than the uncommon ones an Enquiry into mechanical matters being reputed a dishonour to Learning, unless such as appear secrets, rarities and subtilties [a] But the truth is, they are not the highest Instances that give the securest information; for mean and small things often discover great ones, better than great can discover the small and therefore *Aristotle* observes, " *That the nature of every thing is best seen in its smallest portion:* " Whence he seeks the nature of a common-wealth, first in a family. and so the nature of the world, and the policy thereof, must be sought in mean relations and small portions The magnetic virtue of Iron was not first discover'd in Bars, but in Needles

10 But in my judgment the use of *mechanical History* is, of all others, the most fundamental towards such a *Natural Philosophy* as shall not vanish in the fume of subtile, sublime, or pleasing speculations, but be operative to the endowment and benefit of human life as not only suggesting, for the present, many ingenious practices in all trades, by connecting and transferring the observations of one Art to the uses of another, when the Experience of several Arts shall fall under the consideration of one man, but as giving a more true and real illumination with regard to *Causes* and *Axioms*, than has hitherto appeared For as a man's Temper is never well known till he is cross'd, in like manner, the Turns and Changes of Nature cannot appear so fully, when she is left at her liberty, as in the Trials and Tortures of Art

11 We add, that the body of this *Experimental History* should not only be formed from the *mechanic Arts*, but also from the operative and effective part of the *liberal Sciences*, together with numerous practices, not hitherto brought into Arts so that nothing may be omitted which has a tendency to inform the Understanding [b]

12.

---

[a] The History here intended is a thing of vast extent, that requires great abilities, and suitable assistance to execute, and perhaps is the *History of Arts*, which the Royal Academy of Science at Paris have been several years engaged in Such a Work is certainly worthy of that illustrious Society What Particulars the Author would have this History include, may be seen in the Catalogue of *Histories required for interpreting the Works of Nature*, laid down in the *Sylva Sylvarum*, or *third Part of the Instauration*, Sect II The Writings to be consulted for it, are principal, such as *Agricola de re Metallica*, which describes the common methods and ways of working Metals, from the Ore to their saleable state, *Neri's Art of Glass*, with the Notes and Improvements upon it by *Merret* and *Kunckel*, all Mr *Boyle's* Experimental Pieces many of those in the Philosophical Transactions, and foreign Journals, *Pomet* and *Lemery* on Drugs, *Savary's* Dictionary of Commerce, *Stahl* upon Dying, Metallurgy, Fermentation, and other Chemical Arts, *Boerhaave's* Chemistry, *de Lana's Magisterium Naturæ & Artis*, &c But a capital thing wanting to compleat this *History of Arts*, is an Account of the particular *Encheireses*, or secret ways of working which make the mystery of every Art, and are commonly concealed, as lucrative, by Artists These mysteries may, however, be learnt by a right application, and 'tis pity but they were published for the enrichment of *Natural Philosophy*, and the farther improvement of Arts Some Attempts also have been made towards furnishing out this History Dr *Harris's Lexicon Technicum* may pass for a Specimen of the Work, in the Mathematical Part But M *Chambers* has pursued the Design in all its extent A second Edition of his Cyclopædia we presume, may go near to compleat the whole

[b] And therefore no the *History of Sophistications, or Adulterations and Frauds practised in Arts and Trades*, which the learned *Morhof* adds as a fourth part of this *Experimental History* tho'

12 As NATURAL HISTORY has three Parts, fo it has two principal *Two Uſes of* Uſes, and affords, (1) a *Knowledge* of the Things themfelves that are com- *Natural Hi-* mitted to *Hiſtory*; and (2.) the *firſt Matter of Philofophy* But the former, *ſtory* tho' it has its advantages, is of much more inferior confideration than the other, which is a Collection of Materials for a juſt and folid *Induction*, whereon Philofophy is to be grounded. And in this view, we again divide *Natural Hiſtory* into *Narrative* and *Inductive*, the latter whereof is wanting *A pure and* If the *Natural Hiſtory* extant, tho' apparently of great bulk and variety, *general Natu-* were to be carefully weeded of its Fables, Antiquities, Quotations, frivolous *ral Hiſtory* Difputes, Philology, Ornaments, and Table talk, it would fhrink to a flender *wanting* bulk But befides, a *Hiſtory* of this kind is far from what we require, as wanting the two abovemention'd Parts of a *Natural Hiſtory*, viz. *Præter-generations* and *Arts*, on which we lay great ftrefs, and only anfwers one Part in five of the *third*, viz that of *Generations* For the Hiſtory of *Gene-rations* has five fubordinate Parts, viz (1.) The *Celeſtial Bodies*, confidered in their naked *Phænomena*, ſtripp'd of Opinions. (2.) *Meteors*, Comets, and the Regions of the Air (3) The *Earth* and *Sea*, as integral parts of the Univerfe, including Mountains, Rivers, Tides, Sands, Woods, and Iflands, with a view to Natural Enquiries rather than Cofmography (4) The *Elements*, or *greater Affemblages* of matter, as I call them, viz. *Fire, Air, Water*, and *Earth* And (5) The *Species* of Bodies, or more exquifite *Collections of Matter*, by us called the *fmaller Affemblages*, in which alone the induſtry of Writers has appeared, and that too rather in a luxurious than folid manner, as rather abounding in things fuperfluous, viz. the Reprefentations of Plants and Animals, &c. than careful Obfervations, which fhould ever be fubjoined to *Natural Hiſtory*[a] In fine, all the *Natural Hiſtory* we have is abfolutely *Inductive Hi-* unfit for the end we propofe, viz to build *Philofophy* upon, and this both *ſtory wanting* in the manner and the matter thereof, whence we fet down INDUCTIVE HISTORY, as deficient[b]

13 CIVIL HISTORY, in general, may be divided into three particular *Literary Hi-* kinds, viz *Sacred, Civil*, and *Literary*, the latter whereof being wanting, *ſtory wanting* the *Hiſtory of the World* appears like the Statue of *Polypheme*, without its
                                                                      Eye,

---

tho' it may feem fufficiently included under the *Hiſtory of Arts*, as being the fecret part effen-tial to every *Art*, and properly called the *Myſtery*, or Craft thereof Of thefe Impofitions, a large number may be readily collected, and ferve, not only to quicken the underſtanding, and enrich *Experimental Hiſtory*, but alfo contribute to perfect the Science of *Oeconomical Prudence* For contraries illuſtrate each other, and to know the finiſter practices of an *Art* gives light to the *Art itfelf*, as well as puts men upon their guard againſt being deceived See *Morhof's Poly-hiſt* Tom II pag 128

[a] It appears to be the Defign of the *Royal Society*, in their *Philofophical Tranfactions*, to collect Materials for this pure *Natural Hiſtory*, whereto we may add the *French Memoirs*, the *German Ephemerides*, &c And perhaps a judicious Collection from the modern Writings of this kind, wou'd come nearly up to the Thing here intended, and lay the Foundation of an *Inductive Hiſtory*, juſtly noted by the Author as deficient

[b] What the Author underſtands by *Inductive Hiſtory* fully appears in his own *particular Hiſto-ries* of *Life and Death, Winds*, &c which fhew the Way of *inducing* or confequentially dif-covering and drawing out the Defigns and Operations of Nature, by the tabling, or orderly difpofing of Obfervations and Experiments, or managing them fomewhat like *algebraical Equa-tions* This method was obferved with lefs rigour by Mr *Boyle*, whofe Philofophical Pieces are a mixture of *natural* and *inductive Hiſtory* together, but more ſtrictly by Sir *Ifaac Newton* See *Morhof's Polyhiſt* Tom II. p. 127, 128, &c. and the *Novum Organum*, Part II Sect. I &c.

Eve, the part that beft fhews the life and fpirit of the perfon[a] In many particular Sciences indeed, as the *Law, Mathematicks, Rhetoric*, &c there are extant fome fhort Memoirs, and jejune Relations, of Sects, Schools, Books, Authors, and the fucceffions of this kind of Sciences, as well as fome trivial Accounts of the Inventors of Things and Arts but we fay, that A JUST AND UNIVERSAL LITERARY HISTORY has not hitherto been publifhed[b].

D. 5. 14. The *Defign* of this Work fhould be, to relate from the earlieft Accounts of Time, (1) what Particular kinds of *Learning* and *Arts* flourifhed in what Ages, and what Parts of the World, (2) their Antiquities, Progrefs, and Travels on the Globe, (3) their Decline, Difappearance, and Reftoration. In each Art fhould be obferved, (4) its origin and occafion of invention, (5) the manner and form of its delivery, and (6) the means of its introduction, exercife and eftablifhment Add to thefe, (7) the moft famous Sects and Controverfies of learned Men, (8) the Calumnies they fuffer'd, and the Praifes and Honours they receiv'd (9) All along let the beft Authors and Books be noted, with (10.) the Schools, Succeffions, Academies, Societies, Colleges, Orders, and whatever regards the *State of Learning*. But (11) principally let Events be all along coupled with their Caufes, (which is the Soul, as it were, of *Civil Hiftory*,) in relating the Nature of Countries and People, (12.) their difpofition and indifpofition to different kinds of Learning, (13) the accidents of Time, whether favourable or deftructive to the Sciences, (14.) the zeal and mixture of Religion, (15) the feverity and lenity of Laws, (16) the remarkable Patronage, Efforts and Endowments of illuftrious Men, for the promotion of Learning, and the like. All which we would have handled, not in the manner of *Critics*, who barely praife and cenfure, but hiftorically, or in the way of a naked delivery of Facts, with but a fparing ufe of private judgment[c]

15.

---

[a] That is an Account of the Origin, Progrefs, and Fate of Learning, human Inventions and the Sciences over all the Globe, is what gives Light, Life and Spirit to the body of *Civil Hiftory*

[b] Notwithftanding *Gefner's Bibliotheca*, firft printed in the year 1551, and the *Hermes Academicus* of *Mylaus*, firft publifhed in the year 1548

[c] The Defign here fketched out, appears too vaft for any fingle hand, and fhould rather be the work of fome Society or College of learned Men None of the Writers upon *Literary Hiftory* feem to have taken in the whole Plan of the Author Some parts thereof have, however, been attempted, particularly by *Petr Lambecius*, who in the year 1659 publifhed his *Prodromus Hiftoriæ Literariæ*, or *Preliminaries to a general Hiftory of the Rife, Progrefs, Revolutions, and Reftorations of all Languages, Sciences, Faculties, and liberal Arts*, in the order of Time, thro' all Ages with a particular *commemoration of the illuftrious perfons of both Sexes* Printed in Latin, by *Liebezeit* of *Hambourg*, in Folio, and again with Additions by *Jo Albert Fabricius*, in 1710 This Performance, tho' but a Specimen, of an univerfal LITERARY HISTORY, was a Work of immenfe labour and erudition The whole Defign confifted of eight and thirty books, only the firft whereof, and four Chapters of the fecond, ending with the Argonautic Expedition, are here publifhed, with Plans of the thirty two laft Chapters of the fame fecond Book Nor if the whole were executed, would it fully anfwer either to the method, or fill up the Heads, fketched out by the Lord *Bacon* The execution of fuch a grand Defign feems a *Royal Work*, and requires to be executed in Parts See *Morhof Polyhift* Tom I. pag 10 Ed 1714 *&* Stollii *Introductio in* Hiftoriam Literariam, *Ed Jenæ, An* 1728 Many particulars for this *Literary Hiftory* are to be found in the Works of *G J Voffius de Hiftoricis Græcis & Latinis, de Philologia, de Philofophia & Philofophorum Sectis, de Theologia Gentili, Phyfiologia Chriftiana, de Artibus popularibus, de Scientiis Mathematicis* &c This Author in his Book *de Philologia* gives fome directions for the execution He obferves, (1) that *Literary Hiftory fhould contain an account of the learned*

                             Men,

15 For the manner of writing this *History*, we particularly advise that *The manner of writing it* the materials of it be drawn, not only from Histories and Critical Works, but also that the principal Books of every Century be regularly confulted downwards ; fo far we mean, as that a Tafte may be had, or a Judgment formed, of the Subject, Style, and Method thereof , whence the *literary Ge-nius* of every Age, may at pleafure be raifed, as it were from the dead [a]

16. The *ufe and end of this Work* is not to derive honour and pomp to *Its ufe* *Learning*, nor to gratify an eager curiofity, and fondnefs, of knowing and preferving whatever may relate thereto , but chiefly to make learned Men wife, in the prudent and fober exercife and adminiftration of Learning , and by marking out the *Virtues and Vices of intellectual Things*, as well as the motions and perturbations of States, to fhew how the beft Regulation, and Government, may be thence derived for as the works of St *Auftin*, or St *Ambrofe*, will not make fo wife a Divine as a thorough reading of *Ec-clefiaftical Hiftory*, the fame will hold true of learned Men with regard to particular Books, and a *Literary Hiftory* for whoever is not fupported by Examples and the remembrance of Things, muft always be expofed to con-tingencies and precipitancy [b]

Men, and their Writings, the improvement of the Sciences, the Inventors, and the progrefs of Arts (2) That *Xenophon* is faid by *Laertius* and *Suidas*, to be the firft who wrote the *Hiftory or Lives of the Philofophers* , but the Book is loft (3) That the ancient Hiftorians remaining upon this Subject are *Laertius, Philoftratus, Eunapius, Hefychius*, and *Suidas*, among the *Greeks*, and *Cicero, de claris Oratoribus*, and *Suetonius de illuftribus Grammaticis, ac Rhetoribus, & ali-quot Poetis*, among the *Latins* (4) That to this kind belong thofe who have wrote upon the *illuftrious Ecclefiafticks*, as have done St *Jerom, Gennadius Maffilienfis, Ifidorus Hifpalenfis, Hilde-phonfus Toletanus, Sigebertus, Honorius Auguftodunenfis, & Henricus de Gandavo* (5) Among the moderns he reckons *Polydore Virgil, Lilius Gyraldus*, and himfelf, upon the ancient Rheto-ricians, but particularly upon the *Greek* and *Latin* Hiftorians and Poets (6) To thefe he adds many of the Ecclefiaftical Writers and fuch as have given the Lives of eminent Divines, Law-yers and Phyficians See *Voff de Philolog* Ed 1650 pag 71, 72 (7) We may add, *Chrift Nylai Hermes Academicus, feu de Scribenda Univerfitatis Rerum Hiftoria, Conringius de Antiqui-tatibus Academicis, Reineri Reineccii Methodus legendi cognofcendique Hiftoriam, tam facram quam profanam, Pancirollus de Rebus memorabilibus, Georg Pafchius de novis Inventis, quibus facem pratu-lit Antiquitas, Stanley's Lives of the Philofophers, Morhof's Polyhiftor, Struvii Introductio in Noti-tiam Rei Literaria, & Bibliotheca Philofophica, Stollii Introductio in Hiftoriam Literariam*, &c

[a] For the execution of this Defign, *Morhof*, in his *Polyhiftor*, recommends the obfervance of the Direction laid down by M *Naudé* for difpofing a Library, and ranging Books acco-ding to the Subject or Faculties they treat, or rather that propofed by *Lambecius*, for a Philofophical Library See *Morhof's Polyhift* Tom I pag 9—15 Ed 1714 See alfo *Naudai Differtatio de in-ftruenda Bibliotheca*, publifh'd in Latin, with *Additions*, by *Schmidius* An 1703

[b] The ufes of fuch a *Literary Hiftory*, befides the capital one here mention'd, would be great and numerous, for inftance, it would fhew the Origins and Tranfmigrations of Religions, He-refies, Philofophies, Doctrines and Opinions, the Antiquity of Arts, Sciences and Inventions, their introduction and reception in different Countries fuch a Hiftory would perhaps fhew that moft Philofophics, Herefies, Doctrines, and Inventions are originally ancient, and only re-vived or new drefs'd up in later times, and help us to recover the ancient Arts and Secrets now fuppofed to be loft Another principal ufe of it would be to direct our Studies, for ac-quiring a Knowledge of *univerfal Philofophy*, or any particular Branch of it , and lead to Practice and farther Improvement See *Erafmus Bartholinus de Arcanis Scientiarum, Pancirollus de Re-bus deperditis, Alex Taffoni Penfieri diverfi, & Pegelii Thefaurus Rerum felectarum* &c But what we find commonly publifhed under the Title of *Literary Hiftories*, contain little more than an Account of the Editions of Books, with biographical and critical Remarks on the Authors, and are by no means that *univerfal kind of Literary Hiftory* here intended

Particular Civil History 17 CIVIL HISTORY, particularly so called, is of prime dignity and authority among human Writings, as the Examples of Antiquity, the Revolutions of Things, the Foundations of *civil Prudence*, with the names and reputations of Men, are committed to its trust But 'tis attended with no less difficulty than dignity, for it is a Work of great labour and judgment, to throw the mind back upon things passed, and store it with Antiquity, diligently to search into, and with fidelity and freedom relate (1) the *Computations of Time*, (2) the *Characters of Persons*, (3) the *Instability of Counsels*, (4) the *Courses of Actions*, (5) the *Bottoms of Pretences*, (6) the *Secrets of State*, and (7) to set all this to view in proper and suitable language especially as ancient Transactions are uncertain, and late ones exposed to danger Whence such a *Civil History* is attended with numerous Defects, *Its Defects* the greater part of Historians writing little more than empty and vulgar Narrations, and such as are really a disgrace to *History*, while some hastily draw up particular Relations, and trivial Memoirs, some only run over the general heads of Actions, and others descend to the minutest particulars, which have no relation to the principal Actions These in compliance with their Genius, boldly invent many of the things they write, whilst those stamp the image of their own affections upon what they deliver thus preserving fidelity to their party, but not to Things themselves Some are constantly inculcating *Politick*, in which they take most pleasure, and seek all occasions of shewing themselves, thus childishly interrupting the Thread of their *History*, whilst others are too tedious, and shew but little Judgment in the prolixity of their Speeches, Harangues, and Accounts of Actions so that in short, nothing is so seldom found among the Writings of men, as *true and perfect Civil History* [a]

Is of three kinds, viz. 18 This *Civil History* is of three kinds, and bears resemblance to three kinds of *Pictures*, viz the *unfinished*, the *finished*, and the *defaced* Thus *Civil History*, which is the Picture of Times and Things, appears in *Memoirs*, *just History*, and *Antiquities*, but *Memoirs* are *History begun*, or the first Strokes and Materials of it, and *Antiquities*, are *History defaced*, or Remnants that have escaped the Shipwreck of Time

Memoirs of two kinds 19 MEMOIRS, or *Memorials*, are of two kinds, whereof the one may be termed *Commentaries*, the other *Registers* In *Commentaries* are set down naked Events and Actions in sequence, without the Motives, Designs, Counsels, Speeches, Pretexts, Occasions, &c for such is the true nature of a *Commentary*, tho' *Cæsar*, in modesty mix'd with greatness, called the best History in the world a *Commentary*

Registers of two sorts 20 REGISTERS are of two kinds, as either containing the Titles of Things and Persons in order of Time, by way of *Calendar* and *Chronicles*, or else in the way of *Journal*, and preserving the Edicts of Princes, Decrees of Council, judicial Proceedings, Declarations and Letters of State, publick Orations, &c without continuing the thread of the Narration [b]

21

---

[a] Thus perhaps most of the *Histories of Britain* are partial Accounts of the same publick Transactions, differently represented, according to the Principles, or particular Views of the Writer Whence those of *Buchanan, Baker, Clarendon, Kennet, Eachard,* and *Burnet,* are often found partial, whilst that of a Foreigner, M *Thoyras Rapin,* is allow'd the justest general History of our Nation

[b] *Rushworth's Collections* and *Rymer's Fœdera,* are eminent Instances hereof.

I

21 ANTIQUITIES are the *Wrecks of History*, wherein the memory of *And Antiqui-* Things is almost lost, or such Particulars as industrious Persons, with exact *ties.* and scrupulous diligence, can any way collect from Genealogies, Calendars, Titles, Inscriptions, Monuments, Coins, Names, Etymologies, Proverbs, Traditions, Archives, Instruments, Fragments of publick and private History, scatter'd Passages of Books no way historical, &c by which means something is recovered from the Deluge of Time   This is a laborious Work, yet acceptable to Mankind, as carrying with it a kind of reverential awe, and deserves to come in the place of those fabulous and fictitious *Origins of Nations* we abound with tho' it has the less authority, as but few have examined and exercised a liberty of thought about it [a]

22 In these kinds of IMPERFECT HISTORY, no Deficiency need be noted, *Epitomes the* they being of their own nature imperfect but *Epitomes of History* are the *Bane of Civil* Corruption and Moths, that have fretted and corroded many found and ex- *History* cellent bodies of *History*, and reduced them to base and unprofitable Dregs, whence all Men of sound Judgment declare, the use of them ought to be banish'd

23. JUST HISTORY is of three kinds, with regard to the three Objects *Just History of* it designs to represent, which are either a *Portion of Time*, a *memorable Per-* *three kinds,* *son*, or an *illustrious Action*   The first kind we call writing of *Annals*, or *viz Chroni-* *Chronicles*, the second, *Lives*, and the third, *Narratives or Relations*. *Chroni-* *cles.* *nicles* share the greatest Esteem and Reputation, but *Lives* excel in Advantage and Use ; as *Relations* do in Truth and Sincerity. For *Chronicles* represent only grand publick Actions, and external Shews and Appearances to the People, and drop the smaller Passages and Motions of Men and Things. But as the Divine Artificer hangs the greatest Weight upon the smallest Strings, so such *Histories* rather shew the Pomp of Affairs, than their true and inward Springs   And tho' it intersperses Counsel, yet delighting in Grandeur, it attributes more Gravity and Prudence to human Actions, than really appears in them so that *Satyr* might be a truer Picture of human Life, than certain *Histories* of this kind whereas *Lives*, if wrote with care *Lives* and judgment, proposing to represent a Person, in whom Actions, both great and small, publick and private, are blended together, must of necessity give a more genuine, native, and lively Representation, and such as is fitter for imitation [b].

24. PARTICULAR RELATIONS OF ACTIONS, as of the *Peloponnesian War*, *And Rela-* the Expedition of *Cyrus*, &c may, likewise, be made with greater truth and *tions.* exactness, than *Histories of Times*, as their Subject is more level to the Enquiry and Capacity of the Writer whilst they who undertake the *History* of any large portion of Time, must needs meet with Blanks and empty Spaces, which they generally fill up out of their own Invention

H 2   25.

[a] The Subject of *Antiquities* is now found considerably cultivated, by the Labours of *Cambden, Selden Lightfoot, Vossius, Spanheim, Grævius, Gronovius, Dugdale, Van Dale, Pitiscus Struvius, Montfaucon, Potter, Prideaux, Wood*, and many other eminent *Antiquaries* See *Stollii Introductio in Historiam Literariam* Ed Jenæ, An 1728 *De Arte Critica*, pag 152—167 & *Morhof Polyhistor*, Tom 1 lib V. cap 2 *de Scriptoribus Antiquariis*
[b] Eminent Examples whereof we have in *Gassendi's Lives* of *Peiresc, Tycho Brahe, Purbach, Regiomontanus*, and *Copernicus*.

25. This exception, however, must be made to the Sincerity of *Relations*, that if they be wrote near the times of the Actions themselves, they are, in that case, to be greatly suspected of Party or Prejudice. But as 'tis usual for opposite Parties to publish Relations of the same Transactions, they, by this means, open the way to truth, which lies betwixt the two extremes so that after the heat of Contention is allay'd, a good and wise *Historian* may hence be furnished with Matter for a more perfect *History*

26 As to the DEFICIENCIES in these *three kinds of* HISTORY, doubtless many particular Transactions have been left unrecorded, to the great prejudice, in point of Honour and Glory, of those Kingdoms and States where they passed But to omit other Nations, we have particular reason to complain of the Imperfection of the present *History of England*, in the main continuance of it, and the Partiality and Obliquity of that of *Scotland* It would be a very memorable Work, if this Island of *Great Britain*, now joined in Monarchy, were also joined in one *History*, after the manner of the *sacred History*, which draws down the account of the ten Tribes, and of the two Tribes, as twins, together [a]

Biography de-ficient

27 With regard to LIVES, we cannot but wonder that our own Times have so little value for what they enjoy, as not more frequently to write the *Lives* of eminent Men For tho' Kings, Princes, and great Personages are few, yet there are many other excellent Men, who deserve better than vague Reports and barren *Elogies* And altho' many, more mortal in their affections than their bodies, esteem the desire of Fame and Memory but a Vanity, and despise Praise, whilst they do nothing that is praise-worthy, yet this alters not *Solomon*'s Judgment, " *the memory of the Just shall be with praises, but* " *the name of the Wicked shall rot* " the one flourishing, whilst the other consumes, or turns to corruption So in that laudable way of speaking of the dead, " *of happy memory! of pious memory! &c* " we seem to acknowledge, with *Cicero* and *Demosthenes*, " *that a good Name is the proper Inhe-* " *ritance of the deceased* " Which *Inheritance*, as lying waste in our time, deserves to be noted as a *Deficiency* [b]

Relations to be writ more fully

28 In the business of RELATIONS, it is also to be wished that greater diligence were employ'd, for there is no signal Action, but has some good Pen to describe it But very few being qualified to write a *just History*, suitable to its dignity, a thing wherein so many have failed, if memorable Acts were but tolerably related as they pass, this might lay the Foundations, and

---

[a] The Author intended to write such a History himself, and accordingly begun it what was finished of it, stands as the SECOND SUPPLEMENT to this PIECE *de Augmentis Scientiarum* but for the Continuation, we must have recourse to *Drake, Thuanus, Rapin*, &c

[b] It has been so well cultivated since, that a *Library* might be collected of the *Lives of eminent Moderns* Whoever desires to see the necessary Rules for this kind of Writing, the great Utility and more eminent Instances of it, cannot, perhaps, do better than read the learned *Morhof* upon the Subject, in his *Polyhistor*, Tom I lib I cap 19 *de Vitarum Scriptoribus* As for Lives themselves, among the most useful may be reckon'd that extraordinary one of *Peiresc*, written by *Gassend*, that of *Melancthon*, by *Camerarius*, that of *Erasmus*, by M *Le Clerc*, that of Mr *Cowley*, by Bishop *Sprat*, that of the Lord Chief Justice *Hale*, by Bishop *Burnet*, those of Learned Men, by *Thuanus*, in his History, those collected by *Bates*, and those of the Members of the Royal Academy of Sciences at Paris, by M *Fontenelle* See *Struvii Introductio in notitiam Rei Literariæ* Cap VII *de Scriptoribus Vitarum* What the Lord *Bacon* himself perform'd in this way, appears by the THIRD SUPPLEMENT to this PIECE, *de Augmentis Scientiarum.*

and afford Materials for a compleat *History of Times*, when a Writer should arise equal to the Work.

29 HISTORY OF TIMES is either *general* or *particular*, as it relates the Transactions of the whole World, or of a certain Kingdom, or Nation And there have been those, who would seem to give us the *History of the World* from its Origin, but, in reality, offer only a rude Collection of Things, and certain short Narratives instead of a *History* [a] whilst others have nobly, and to good advantage, endeavour'd to describe, as in a *just History*, the *memorable Things*, which in their time happened over all the Globe For human Affairs are not so far divided by *Empires* and *Countries*, but that in many cases they still preserve a connection whence it is proper enough to view, as in one Picture, the *Fates of an Age*. And such a *general History* as this, may frequently contain particular *Relations*, which, tho' of value, might otherwise either be lost, or never again reprinted at least, the heads of such *Accounts* may be thus preserved But upon mature consideration, the Laws of *just History* appear so severe, as scarce to be observed in such a large field of Matter whence the bulkiness of *History* should rather be retrenched, than enlarged · otherwise, he who has such variety of Matter every where to collect, if he preserve not constantly the strictest watch upon his Informations, will be apt to take up with Rumours, and popular Reports, and work such kind of superficial Matter into his *History* And then to retrench the whole, he will be obliged to pass over many things otherwise worthy of relation ; and often to contract and shorten his Style, wherein there lies no small danger of frequently cutting off useful Narrations, in order to oblige Mankind in their favourite way of *Compendium*, whence such Accounts, which might otherwise live of themselves, may come to be utterly lost [b]

30 HISTORY OF TIMES is likewise divisible into ANNALS and JOURNALS, according to the observation of *Tacitus*, where, mentioning the Magnificence of certain Structures, he adds, " 'twas found suitable to the *Roman* " dignity, that illustrious Things should be committed to *Annals*, but such " as *these*, to the *publick Journals of the City*" Thus referring what related to the State of the Commonwealth to *Annals*, and smaller Matters to *Journals* And so there should be a kind of *Heraldry* in regulating the dignities of *Books*, as well as *Persons* for as nothing takes more from the Dignity of a State, than Confusion of Orders and Degrees, so it greatly takes from the Authority of *History*, to intermix Matters of Triumph, Ceremony, and Novelty, with Matters of State And it were to be wish'd that this Distinction prevail'd But in our times, *Journals* are only used at Sea, and in military Expeditions whereas, among the Ancients, 'twas a regal Honour to have

the

Marginal notes:
History of Times, is general or particular.

Divisible into Annals and Journals

---

[a] Some Gentlemen in *England* have lately published Proposals, and a noble Attempt, towards an *Universal History, from the earliest Account of Time, to the present*, wherein the *Plan* appears so justly laid, and what is hitherto executed so exact, that it is greatly to be wished they may meet with suitable Encouragement Among the best *general Histories* wrote of late, are esteemed the following; viz. *Cellarii Historia universalis* Ed Jenæ 1711 *Jo Henric Leoderi Introductio in Historiam universam* Ed Lipsiæ, An 1713 *Johan Clerie Compendium Historiæ universalis* Amstelodami 1697, & Lipsiæ 1713 & *Burchard Gotthelf Struvii Kurtzer Begriff der universal Historie* Jenæ 1726 See *Stollii Introductio in Historiam Literariam*, pag 325, &c
[b] For the *Rules of writing History*, and the *Qualifications of an Historian*, see *Vossius de Arte Historica*, and for the Assistances required in the Work, see *Morhof's Polyhistor*, Tom III lib 2. *de Prudentia Civilis Scriptoribus*, & Tom III lib 4 *de Historiæ Scriptoribus*

the daily Acts of the Palace recorded, as we fee in the cafe of *Ahaſſuerus*, King of *Perſia* And the *Journals* of *Alexander the Great* contained even trivial Matters Yet *Journals* are not deſtined for trivial things alone, as *Annals* are for ſerious ones, but contain all things promiſcuouſly, whether of greater or of leſs concern

Civil Hiſtory, pure and mix'd 31 The laſt Diviſion of CIVIL HISTORY, is into *pure* and *mix'd*. Of the mix'd, there are two eminent kinds, the one principally *civil*, and the other principally *natural* for a kind of Writing has been introduced, that does not give particular Narrations in the continued thread of a *Hiſtory*, but where the Writer collects and culls them, with choice, out of an Author, then reviewing, and, as it were, ruminating upon them, takes occaſion to treat of political Subjects And this kind of *ruminated Hiſtory* we highly eſteem, provided the Writers keep cloſe to it profeſſedly for 'tis both unſeaſonable, and irkſome, to have an Author profeſs he will write a *juſt Hiſtory*, yet be at every turn introducing *Politicks*, and thereby breaking the thread of his Narration All wiſe *Hiſtory* is indeed pregnant with political Rules and Precepts, but the Writer is not to take all opportunities of delivering himſelf of them

Cosmographical Hiſtory 32 COSMOGRAPHICAL HISTORY is alſo *mix'd* many ways, as taking the Deſcriptions of Countries, their Situations and Fruits, from *Natural Hiſtory*, the Accounts of Cities, Governments and Manners, from *Civil Hiſtory*, the Climates, and aſtronomical Phænomena, from *Mathematicks* In which kind of *Hiſtory*, the preſent Age ſeems to excel, as having a full view of the World in this light The Ancients had ſome knowledge of the *Zones* and *Antipodes*, tho' rather by abſtract demonſtration than fact but that little Veſſels, like the celeſtial Bodies, ſhould ſail round the whole Globe, is the happineſs of our Times This great Improvement of *Navigation*, may give us great hopes of extending and improving the SCIENCES, eſpecially as it ſeems agreeable to the Divine Will, that they ſhould be coeval Thus the Prophet *Daniel* foretells, that " *many ſhall go to and fro on the Earth, and* " *Knowledge ſhall be increaſed*," as if the openneſs and thorough paſſage of the World, and the increaſe of Knowledge, were allotted to the ſame Age which indeed we find already true in part; for *the Learning* of theſe Times, ſcarce yields to the former Periods or Returns of Learning, the one among the *Greeks*, and the other among the *Romans*, and in many particulars far exceeds them [a]

Eccleſiaſtical Hiſtory, and its Diviſions Hiſtory of the Church, 33 ECCLESIASTICAL HISTORY, in general, has nearly the ſame Diviſions with *Civil Hiſtory* thus there are *Eccleſiaſtical Chronicles*, *Lives of the Fathers*, *Accounts of Synods*, and other Eccleſiaſtical Matters but in propriety it may be farther divided, (1) into the general *Hiſtory of the Church*, (2) the *Hiſtory of Prophecy*, and (3) the *Hiſtory of Providence* The *firſt* deſcribes the times of the *Church militant*, whether *fluctuating*, as the Ark of *Noah*, unſtable, as the Ark in the Wilderneſs, or *at reſt*, as the Ark in the Temple; that is, in the ſtates of *Perſecution*, *Migration*, and *Peace* And in this part, there is a Redundancy rather than a Deficiency, but it were to be wiſhed the goodneſs and ſincerity of it were equal to the bulk [b]

34

[a] See this farther proſecuted in the *Novum Organum*, Part I.
[b] See *Morhof's Polyhiſtor, de Theologicis Scriptoribus*, Tom III lib 5

34 The *second* part, *viz* the HISTORY OF PROPHECY, confifts of two Relatives; the *Prophecy*, and the *Accomplifhment* whence the nature of it requires, that every *Scripture Prophecy* be compared with the *Event*, thro' all the Ages of the World, for the better confirmation of the *Faith*, and the better information of the *Church*, with regard to the *interpretation of Prophecies not yet fulfilled*　But here we muft allow that Latitude, which is peculiar and familiar to *divine Prophecies*, which have their completion not only at ftated times, but in fucceffion　as participating of the nature of their Author, " *with whom a thoufand years are but as one day*," and therefore are not fulfilled punctually at once, but have a *growing accomplifhment* thro' many Ages　tho' the height or fulnefs of them may refer to a fingle age, or moment　And this is a Work which I find *deficient*　but it fhould either be undertaken with Wifdom, Sobriety, and Reverence, or not at all [a].

The Hiftory of Prophecy, which is wanting

35 The *third* part, the HISTORY OF PROVIDENCE, has been touched by fome pious Pens, but not without a mixture of Party　This *Hiftory* is employ'd in obferving that *divine agreement which there fometimes is betwixt the revealed and fecret Will of God*　For altho' the Councils and Judgments of *God* are fo fecret, as to be abfolutely unfearchable to Man, yet the Divine Goodnefs has fometimes thought fit, for the confirmation of his own People, and the confutation of thofe who are as *without God in the world*, to write them in fuch Capital Letters, *as they who run may read them*　Such are the remarkable Events and Examples of God's Judgments, tho' late and unexpected, fudden and unhoped for Deliverances and Bleffings, Divine Councils dark and doubtful, at length opening and explaining themfelves,[b] *&c*　All which have not only a power to confirm the Minds of the Faithful, but to awaken and convince the Confciences of the Wicked

And the Hiftory of Providence

36 And not only the *Actions* of Mankind, but alfo their SAYINGS ought to be preferved　and may, doubtlefs, be fometimes inferted in *Hiftory*, fo far as they decently ferve to illuftrate the Narrations of Facts　But Books of ORATIONS, EPISTLES, and APOPHTHEGMS, are the *proper Repofitories* of human Difcourfe　The SPEECHES of wife Men, upon matter of Bufinefs, weighty Caufes, or difficult Points, are of great ufe, not only for Eloquence, but for the knowledge of Things themfelves [c]　But the LETTERS of wife Men upon ferious Affairs, are yet more ferviceable in points of *civil Prudence*, as of all human Speech, nothing is more folid or excellent than fuch *Epiftles*　for they contain more of natural Senfe than *Orations*, and more Ripenefs than *occafional Difcourfes*. So LETTERS OF STATE-AFFAIRS,
written

The Appendages of Hiftory

Speeches

Letters.

---

[a] This is attempted by *Grotius*, in his *Commentaries upon the Bible*, by Father *Simon*, in his *Critical Hiftory of the Old and New Teftament*, Dr *Hammond*, *upon the Old and New Teftament*; Dr *Whitby*, *on the New Teftament*, Mr *Whifton*, in his *Accomplifhment of Scripture Prophecies*; M *Le Clerc*, and Bifhop *Sherlock*, in his *Difcourfe of the Ufe and Intent of* Prophecy *in the feveral Ages of the World*

[b] Dr *Hackwell's Apology for Providence*, Dr *Reynolds's God's Revenge againft Murder*, *Beard's Theatre of God's Judgments*, *Fuller's Hiftory of Providence*, *Le Clerc's Defenfe de la Providence*, and *Bayle's Dictionary*, contain many Particulars of this kind

[c] Thus the SPEECHES of the *Author*, which make the FOURTH SUPPLEMENT to this *Work*, and many of thofe preferved in *Rufhworth's Collections*, are highly valuable and inftructive, as opening the Scene of publick Affairs, fhewing the Genius and free Spirit of the *Englifh Nation*, and feeming to contain the Form and Matter of many famous publick Speeches of later Times.

written, in the order of time, by those that manage them, with their Answers, afford the best Materials for *Civil History*[a].

And Apophthegms.

37 Nor do APOPHTHEGMS only serve for Ornament and Delight, but also for Action and *civil Use*, as being the Edge-tools of Speech, which cut and penetrate the Knots of Business and Affairs. For *Occasions have their Revolutions*, and what has once been advantageously used, may be so again, either as an old thing or a new one. Nor can the usefulness of these *Sayings* in Civil Affairs be question'd, when *Cæsar* himself wrote a Book upon the Subject: which we wish were extant, for all those we have yet seen of the kind, appear to be collected with little choice and judgment[b].

SECT. II.

Of POETRY.

Poetry imaginary History.

I 1 POETRY is a kind of Learning generally confined to the measure of Words, but otherwise extremely licentious, and truly belonging to the *Imagination*, which being unrestrained by Laws, may make what unnatural mixtures and separations it pleases. 'Tis taken in two Senses, or with respect to *Words* and *Matter*. The first is but a Character of Style, and a certain form of Speech, not relating to the Subject, for a *true Narration* may be deliver'd in *verse*, and a feign'd one in *prose*[c]; but the second is a capital Part of Learning, and no other than *feign'd History*. And here, as in our Divisions we endeavour to find and trace the true *Sources of Learning*, and this frequently without giving way to Custom, or the established Order, we shall take no particular notice of *Satyr*, *Elegy*, *Epigram*, *Ode*, &c. but turn them over to *Philology*, and the Arts of Speech: and under the name of *Poetry*, treat nothing more than *imaginary History*.

Divided.

2 The justest *Division of Poetry*, except what it shares in common with *History*, (which has its *feign'd Chronicles*, *feign'd Lives*, and *feign'd Relations*)

IS

---

[a] The Advantages to be reaped from *Letters* are largely shewn in *Morhof's Polyhistor*, Tom I Lb I Cap 23 24 25 *de Epistolarum Scriptoribus*, and the judgment here made of them confirmed, and extended to *Philosophical* as well as *Civil* Purposes. Thus, as the *Latin Letters* of Mr *Milton* to foreign States, best shew the Spirit and Conduct of *Oliver Cromwell*, so the private Letters of *des Cartes* and Mr *Locke*, are the best Explanation of the Designs and Views of their *Philosophical Writings*; and therefore as the *Letters* of Ambassadors, and Secretaries of State, give the most authentic and satisfactory Accounts of political Transactions, so the familiar Letters of learned Men disclose their internal Sentiments, and secret Intentions, better than their formal Works which are dress'd out for the *Publick*. And hence the Letters of eminent Men are generally read with great pleasure, and advantage, as those of *Erasmus*, *Grotius*, *Patin*, Sir *William Temple*, Mr *Ray*, and even the supposed *Letters of the Turkish Spy*, the *Spectator*, &c. The select Letters of the *Lord Bacon* therefore, deservedly make the FIFTH SUPPLEMENT to this PIECE of the *de Augmentis Scientiarum*.

[b] And therefore the Author began a new Collection of APOPHTHEGMS, which make the SIXTH SUPPLEMENT to the *de Augmentis Scientiarum*.

[c] Thus *Lucan's Pharsalia*, and *Blackmore's Creation*, are true Histories *in verse*; and *Telemachus*, and the *Travels of Cyrus*, feign'd Histories *in prose*.

is (1) into *Narrative*, (2.) *Dramatic*, and (3) *Allegorical Narrative Poetry* is such an exact imitation of *History*, as to deceive, did it not often carry things beyond probability. *Dramatic Poetry* is a kind of *visible History*, giving the Images of things as if they were present, whilst *History* represents them as past. But *Allegorical Poetry* is *History with its Type*, which represents intellectual Things to the Senses.

3. NARRATIVE POETRY, otherwise called *Heroic Poetry*, seems, with regard to its matter, not the versification, raised upon a noble foundation, as having a principal regard to the dignity of human Nature [a]. For as the active World is inferior to the rational Soul, so *Poetry* gives that to mankind which *History* denies, and in some measure satisfies the Mind with shadows, when it cannot enjoy the substance [b]. For upon a narrow inspection, *Poetry* strongly shews, that a greater grandeur of things, a more perfect order, and a more beautiful variety is pleasing to the Mind, than can any where be found in Nature, after the fall. So that as the Actions and Events, which are the Subjects of true *History*, have not that grandeur which satisfies the Mind, *Poetry* steps in, and feigns more heroical actions. And as *real History* gives us not the success of things, according to the deserts of virtue and vice, *Poetry* corrects it, and presents us with the Fates and Fortunes of persons rewarded or punished according to merit. And as *real History* disgusts us with a familiar and constant similitude of things, *Poetry* relieves us by unexpected turns and changes; and thus not only delights, but inculcates morality and noblenesss of Soul. Whence it may be justly esteemed of a divine nature, as it raises the Mind, by accommodating the Images of things to our Desires, and not, like *History* and *Reason*, subjecting the Mind to Things [c]. And by these its charms, and congruity to the Mind, with the assistance also of Musick, which conveys it the sweeter, it makes its own way, so as to have been in high esteem in the most ignorant ages, and among the most barbarous people, whilst other kinds of *Learning* were utterly excluded [d].

Into Narrative Poetry.

4. DRAMATIC POETRY, which has the *Theatre* for its *World*, would be of excellent use, if it were found: for the *discipline and corruption of the Theatre* is of very great consequence. And the corruptions of this kind are numerous in our times, but the regulation quite neglected [e]. The Action of the Theatre, tho' modern States esteem it but ludicrous, unless it be satyrical and biting, was carefully watch'd by the ancients, that it might improve

Dramatic Poetry.

[a] Upon this Head consult the judicious *French Critic*, *Bossu du Poeme Epique.*

[b] Hence the extreme Pleasure we receive in reading the Origin of the World, the Revolutions and Transactions of Heaven, Earth and Hell, the History and Fate of our first Parents, the Description of Paradise, &c. in *Milton's Paradise lost.*

[c] Which intimates another Species of *Historical Poetry*, viz. the *Physical*, as that of *Lucretius*, which describes the *System of the World*, upon the *Principles of Epicurus*, and that of Sir *Richard Blackmore* upon the footing of the modern *Philosophy.*

[d] Thus in the *Origins of Nations*, we find the first thing studied is generally *Language* and *Poetry*, for the sake, as it should seem, of their great influence in governing the uncultivated minds of men, and the use they are of, in transmitting down History and Antiquities to Posterity.

[e] Mr *Collier* has endeavour'd to shew the immoralities, and rectify the abuses of the *Stage*, by weeding several of our modern Plays. But the due prosecution of this subject, perhaps requires more Knowledge of human Nature, and civil Affairs, than usually comes to one man's share. This subject is also touch'd upon in several of the SPECTATORS.

mankind in virtue   and indeed many wife men and great Philofophers
have thought it to the Mind as the *Bow* to the *Fiddle*[a], and certain it is,
tho' a great Secret in Nature, that *the minds of men in company, are more open
to affections and impreffions, than when alone*

And Allegori-
cal Poetry.   5 But ALLEGORICAL POETRY excels the others, and appears a folemn
facred thing, which Religion itfelf generally makes ufe of, to preferve an
intercourfe between divine and human Things   Yet this alfo is corrupted,
by a levity and indulgence of Genius towards Allegory. Its ufe is ambiguous,
and made to ferve contrary purpofes, for it envelopes as well as illuftrates
the fit ft feeming to endeavour at an *Art of Concealment*, and the other at a

The Ufe of
Method of Inſtruct-
ing in Alle-
gory in
Poet—   *Method of Inſtructing*, much ufed by the Ancients   For when the Difcoveries and Conclufions of Reafon, tho' now common, were new, and firft known,
the human Capacity could fcarce admit them in their fubtile ftate, or till they
were brought nearer to fenfe, by fuch kind of imagery and examples. Whence
ancient times are full of their Fables, their Allegories, and their Similies
Nay, the Apophthegms of the ancient Sages were ufually demonftrated by
Similitudes   And as *Hieroglyphicks preceded Letters, fo Parables preceded
Arguments   And the force of Parables ever was and will be great, as being
clearer than Arguments, and more appofite than real Examples*

6 The other ufe of *Allegorical Poetry* is to envelope things, whofe dignity deferves a Veil, as when the *Secrets* and *Myfteries of Religion, Policy*
and *Philofophy*, are wrapp'd up in *Fables* and *Parables* But tho' fome
may doubt whether there be any myftical Senfe concealed in the *ancient Fables of the Poets*, we cannot but think there is a latent Myftery intended in
fome of them   for we do not therefore judge contemptibly of them, becaufe they are commonly left to *Children* and *Grammarians*, but as *the
Writings that relate thefe Fables, are, next to the facred ones, the moft ancient*,
and the *Fables* themfelves much older ftill, being not delivered as the Inven-

The Philofophy
of Ancient
Fables defeflent
in Poetry.   tions of the Writers, but as things before believed and received, they appear like a *foft whifper from the Traditions of more ancient Nations*, convey'd thro' the Flutes of the *Grecians* But all hitherto attempted towards
the interpretation of thefe *Parables* proving unfatisfactory to us, as having
proceeded from Men of but common-place learning, we fet down the
PHILOSOPHY OF ANCIENT FABLES, as the only DEFICIENCY IN POE-
TRY[b], and fubjoin three *Examples* of the Work, fuch as we defign it,
one in *Natural*, one in *Political*, and one in *Moral Philofophy.*

The.

[a] That is, capable of working upon and influencing the *People*, and hence we have in *England* a variety of *State Plays* and certainly the *Stage* has its ufe in *Government* and *Morality*, as
well as the *Pulpit*, both which may be called the *Schools of a Country*

[b] How far this *Deficiency* is fupplied by the Author, will appear in his Piece *de Sapientia Veterum*, which makes the SEVENTH SUPPLEMENT to the *de Augmentis Scientiarum* and how
far the Defign has fince been carried, may be learnt from the *Opufcula Mythologica*, publifh'd by
Gale, *Voffius de Theologia Gentili*, *Spanheim*, in his Notes upon *Callimachus*, *Boeclerus's Meta-
morphofeis Ovidiana*, *Johan. Conrad Durrius, de recondita Veterum Sapientia in Poetis*, and
Le Clerc's Bibliotheque Univerfelle, where he explains the Hiftories of *Hercules*, *Adonis*, and *Ceres*
See more to this purpofe in *Morhof's Polyhiftor*, under the Chapters de Scriptoribus ad Artem
Poeticam facientibus de Philofophia Moralis Scriptoribus, & de Libris Phyficis fecretioribus   See
alfo *Stollii Introductio in Hiftoriam Literariam*, Cap V de Arte Poetica, & Struvii Bibliotheca.
Philofophica, Cap. III de Scriptoribus Hiftoriæ Philofophicæ, & Cap VI de Scriptoribus Philofophiæ
practicæ.

The FABLE *of* PAN *explained of* NATURAL PHILOSOPHY.

II. 7 THE *Ancients have, with great exactness, delineated* uni- *The Fable of verfal Nature, under the perfon of* Pan. *They leave his* Pan traced. *origin doubtful fome afferting him the fon of* Mercury, *and others the common offspring of all* Penelope's *Suitors* (a). *The latter fuppofition doubtlefs occafion'd fome later Writers to entitle this ancient Fable,* Penelope. *a thing frequently practis'd, when the earlier relations are applied to more modern characters and perfons; tho' fometimes with great abfurdity and ignorance; as in the prefent cafe for* Pan *was one of the* ancienteft *Gods, and long before the time of* Ulyffes *befides,* Penelope *was venerated by antiquity for her matronal chaftity. A third fort will have him the Iffue of* Jupiter *and* Hybris, *that is* Reproach (b) *But whatever his origin was, the* Deftinies *are allowed his* Sifters (c)

8 *He is defcribed by antiquity, with pyramidal horns reaching up to* His Portrait. *heaven* (d), *a rough and fhaggy body* (e), *a very long beard* (f), *of a biform figure, human above, half brute below* (g), *ending in Goats feet* (h) *His arms, or enfigns of power, are, a Pipe in his left hand, compofed of feven Reeds* (i); *in his right a Crook* (k); *and he wore for his mantle a leopard's skin* (l)

9 *His* Attributes *and* Titles, *were, the God of Hunters, Shep-* His Offices. *herds, and all the rural Inhabitants* (m), *Prefident of the Mountains* (n); *and after* Mercury *the next meffenger of the Gods* (o). *He was alfo held the leader and ruler of the* Nymphs, *who continually danced and frisked about him, attended with the* Satyrs, *and their elders the* Sileni (p). *He had alfo the power of ftriking terrors, efpecially fuch as were vain and fuperftitious; whence they came to be call'd* Panic *terrors* (q).

10 *Few actions are recorded of him, only a principal one is,* His Acts. *that he challenged* Cupid *at wreftling, and was worfted* (r). *He alfo catched the Giant* Typhon *in a net, and held him faft* (s). *They relate farther of him, that when* Ceres *growing difconfolate for the Rape of* Proferpine, *hid her felf, and all the Gods took the utmoft pains to find her, by going out different ways for that purpofe,* Pan *only had the good fortune to meet her, as he was hunting, and difcovered her to the reft* (t). *He likewife had the affurance to rival* Apollo *in Mufick; and in the judgment of* Midas *was prefer'd but the Judge had, tho' with great privacy and fecrecy, a pair of Affes Ears faftned on him for his fentence* (u).

I 2   11. *There*

His Amours.   11 *There is very little said of his* Amours; *which may seem strange among such a multitude of Gods, so profusely amorous* (v)   *He is only reported to have been very fond of* Echo, *who was also esteemed his wife* (w), *and one Nymph more called* Syrinx, *with the love of whom* Cupid *inflamed him for his insolent challenge.*

12 *Lastly,* Pan *had no descendant, which also is a wonder, when the male Gods were so extremely prolifick, only he was the* *and Ja-* *reputed father of a servant Girl, called* Iambe, *who used to divert strangers with her ridiculous pratling stories* (x).

The Fable ex- 13 This Fable is perhaps the noblest of all Antiquity, and pregnant
plained in the with the Mysteries and Secrets of Nature   (a) *Pan*, as the name imports,
Origin of Pan represents the *Universe*, about whose origin there are two opinions, viz.
that it either sprung from *Mercury*, that is, the *divine Word*, according to
the Scriptures and Philosophical Divines, or from the *confused seeds of Things*
For they who allow only *one beginning of all things*, either ascribe it to *God*,
or if they suppose a *material beginning*, acknowledge it to be various in its
powers, so that the whole dispute comes to these two points, viz either that
Nature proceeds from *Mercury*, or from *confused mixture*, according to the
Fable [a]

14 (b) The *third origin of Pan* seems borrow'd by the *Greeks* from the
Hebrew Mysteries, either by means of the *Egyptians*, or otherwise, for it relates to the state of the world, not in its first creation, but as made subject
to Death and Corruption after the Fall and in this state it was, and remains
the off-spring of *God* and *Sin*, or *Jupiter* and *Reproach* And therefore these
three several Accounts of *Pan*'s birth may seem true, if duly distinguished
in respect of things and times For this *Pan*, or the *universal Nature of things*,
which we view and contemplate, had its origin from the *divine Word*, and
confused Matter, first created by God himself, with the subsequent Introduction of *Sin*, and consequently *Corruption*

The Desti- 15 (c) The *Destinies*, or the Natures and Fates of things, are justly made
nies being his *Pan*'s Sisters, as the chain of natural Causes links together the rise, dura-
Sister tion, and corruption, the exaltation, degeneration, and workings, the processes, the effects, and changes, of all that can any way happen to Things

His Horns 16 (d) *Horns* are given him, broad at the roots, but narrow and sharp
a-top, because the nature of all things seems *pyramidal* for individuals are
infinite, but being collected into a variety of species, they rise up into *Kinds*,
and these again ascend, and are contracted into *Generals*, till at length Nature may seem collected to a point And no wonder if *Pan*'s *horns* reach
to the *Heavens*, since the *Sublimities of Nature*, or abstract Ideas, reach in a
manner to *Things divine* for there is a short and ready passage from *Meta-*
physicks to *Natural Theology*

17.

---

[a] Namque canebat uti magnum per inana coacta
    Semina terrarumque animæque marisque fuissent,
    Et liquidi simul ignis, & his exordia primis
    Omnia, & ipse tener mundi concreverit orbis.

17 (e) *Pan's* body, or the body of *Nature*, is, with great propriety and *His shaggy body* elegance, painted shaggy and hairy, as representing the *Rays of Things*. for *Rays* are as the *hair*, or *fleece of Nature*, and more or less worn by all bodies. This evidently appears in vision, and in all effects or operations at a distance. for whatever operates thus, may be properly said to emit Rays[a]. (f) But particularly the *beard of Pan* is exceeding long, because *His Beard* the Rays of the celestial bodies penetrate, and act to a prodigious distance. and the Sun himself, when clouded on its upper part, appears to the eye *bearded*.

18. (g) Again, the *Body of Nature* is justly described *biform*, because of the *His biform Body* difference between its superior and inferior parts, as the former, for their beauty, regularity of motion, and influence over the earth, may be properly represented by the *human figure*, and the latter, because of their disorder, irregularity, and subjection to the celestial bodies, are by the *brutal*. This biform figure also represents the participation of one species with another, for there appear to be no *simple Natures*, but all participate or consist of two. thus *Man* has somewhat of the *Brute*, the *Brute* somewhat of the *Plant*, the *Plant* somewhat of the *Mineral*, so that all natural bodies have really two faces, or consist of a superior and an inferior Species.

19 (h) There lies a curious Allegory in the making of *Pan goat-footed*, *His Goat's Feet* on account of the motion of ascent which the terrestrial bodies have towards the air and heavens. for the *Goat* is a clambering creature, that delights in climbing up rocks and precipices. and in the same manner, the matters destined to this lower globe strongly affect to rise upwards, as appears from the Clouds and Meteors.

20 *Pan's Arms*, or the *Ensigns* he bears in his hands, are of two kinds; *His Ensigns, viz. his Pipe.* the one an *Emblem of Harmony*, the other of *Empire*. (i) His Pipe, composed of seven reeds, plainly denotes the consent and harmony, or the concords and discords of things, produced by the motion of the *seven Planets*. (k) His Crook also contains a fine Representation of the *ways of Nature*, which *And Crook* are partly strait, and partly crooked. thus the staff having an extraordinary bend towards the top, denotes, that the Works of *divine Providence* are generally brought about by remote means, or in a circuit, as if somewhat else were intended, rather than the effect produced, as in the sending of *Joseph* into *Egypt*, &c. So likewise in human government, they who sit at the helm, manage and wind the people more successfully, by Pretext and oblique Courses, than they could by such as are direct and strait, so that in effect all *Scepters are crooked a-top*[b].

21 (l) *Pan's Mantle*, or Cloathing, is with great ingenuity made of a *His Mantle* Leopard's Skin, because of the spots it has. for, in like manner, the heavens

vens

[a] This is always supposed the Case in *Vision*, so that the Mathematical Demonstrations in Opticks, proceed upon it. And hence we may the better understand the meaning of the Author, when he mentions, as he frequently does, the *Rays of Things*.

[b] The Reader will find many uncommon Observations of this kind, with regard to *civil Policy*, in the third *Section* of the *Sapientia Veterum*, as if the Author intended to deliver the Secrets of Government, in the least exceptionable way, that of explaining the *political Mythology of the Ancients*. See also the following Fable of *Perseus*, explain'd of *War*.

...vens are fprinkled with Stars, the Sea with Iflands, the Earth with Flowers, and almoft each particular thing, is variegated, or wears a mottled coat.

His Office, as the God of Hunters

22 (m) The *Office of Pan* could not be more livelily expreffed, than by making him the *God of Hunters* for every natural action, every motion and procefs, is no other than a chace thus *Arts* and *Sciences* hunt out their works, and human fchemes and counfels, their feveral ends and all living creatures either hunt out their aliment, purfue their prey, or feek their pleafures, and this in a skilful and fagacious manner[a] He is alfo ftiled the *God of the natu-*

Rural Inhabi-tant

ral Inhabitant, becaufe men in this fituation live more according to Nature, than they do in *Cities* and *Courts*, which corrupt them with effeminate Arts (n) He is likewife particularly ftiled *Prefident of the Mountains*, becaufe in mountains and lofty places, the nature of things lies more open and expofed to the eye and the underftanding[b]

And Meffenger of the Gods

23 (o) In his being called the *meffenger of the Gods*, next after *Mercury*, lies a divine *Allegory*, as, next after the *Word of God*, the image of the World is the herald of the divine power and wifdom, according to the Expreffion of the *Pfalmift* *The Heavens declare the Glory of God, and the Firmament fhew th his hand work.*

Purfuing the Nymphs

24 (p) *Pan* is delighted with the company of the *Nymphs* that is, the *Souls of all living creatures are the delight of the world*, and he is properly called their *Governor*, becaufe each of them follows its *own Nature* as a Leader, and all dance about their own refpective Rings, with infinite variety, and never ceafing motion And with thefe continually join the *Satyrs* and *Silem*, that is, *Youth* and *Age*, for all things have a kind of young, chearful, and dancing time, and again their time of flownefs, tottering, and creeping And whoever, in a true light, confiders the motions and endeavours of both thefe ages, like another *Democritus*, will perhaps find them as odd and ftrange, as the gefticulations and antick motions of the *Satyrs* and *Silem*

His Power of ftriking Ter-rors

25 (q) The *Power* he had of *ftriking terrors*, contains a very fenfible Doctrine, for Nature has implanted *fear* in all living creatures, as well to keep them from rifquing their lives, as to guard againft injuries and violence and yet this *Nature*, or Paffion, keeps not its bounds, but with *juft* and *profitable* fears always mixes fuch as are *vain* and *fenfelefs*, fo that all things, if we could fee their infides, would appear full of *panic terrors*. Thus mankind, particularly the vulgar, labour under a high degree of *Superftition*, which is nothing more than a Panic Dread that principally reigns in unfettled and troublefome Times

His challeng-ing Cupid

26 (r) The *Prefumption of Pan, in challenging* Cupid *to the confliet*, denotes that Matter has an appetite, and tendency to a diffolution of the world, and falling back to its firft *Chaos* again, unlefs this depravity and inclination were reftrained and fubdued by a more powerful concord and agreement of things, properly expreffed by *Love* or *Cupid* 'tis therefore well for mankind,

---

[a] *Torva Leæna Lupum fequitur Lupus ipfe Capellam,*
Florentem Cytifum fequitur lafciva Capella
See hereafter Sect XII of Learned Experience
[b] Particularly the meteors and Cœleftial Bodies, whence Obfervatories for Aftronomy, Meteorology, &c See the Author's NEW ATLANTIS,

mankind, and the state of all things, that *Pan* was thrown, and conquered, in the struggle[a]

27 (s) His *catching and detaining* Typhon *in the net*, receives a similar explanation; for whatever vast and unusual *swells*, which the word *Typhon* signifies, may sometimes be raised in Nature, as in the sea, the clouds, the earth, or the like, yet *Nature* catches, entangles, and holds all such Outrages and Insurrections in her inextricable *Net*, wove as it were of *adamant*. *His catching Typhon in a Net.*

28. (t) That part of the *Fable, which attributes the discovery of lost* Ceres *to* Pan, *whilst he was hunting*, a happiness denied the other Gods, tho' they diligently and expresly sought her, contains an exceeding just and prudent admonition, *viz* that we are not to expect the discovery of things useful in common life, as that of *Corn* denoted by *Ceres*, from *abstract Philosophies*, as if these were the *Gods of the first Order*, no, not tho' we used our utmost Endeavours this way, but only from *Pan*, that is, a *sagacious Experience, and general knowledge of Nature*, which is often found, even by accident, to stumble upon such Discoveries, whilst the Pursuit was directed another way[b] *His finding of Ceres*

29 (u) The Event of *his contending with Apollo in Musick*, affords us an useful Instruction, that may help to humble the human Reason and Judgment, which is too apt to boast, and glory in itself. There seem to be two kinds of *Harmony*, the one of *divine Providence*, the other of *human Reason*. but the government of the world, the administration of its affairs, and the more *secret divine Judgments*, found harsh and dissonant to *human Ears*, or human Judgment, and tho' this ignorance be justly rewarded with *Asses Ears*, yet they are put on and wore, not openly, but with *great secrecy*: nor is the deformity of the thing seen or observed by the vulgar *His contending with Apollo in Musick*

30 (v) We must not find it strange if *no Amours are related of Pan*, besides his marriage with *Echo* for Nature enjoys itself, and in itself all other things he that *loves*, desires enjoyment, but in profusion there is no room for desire and therefore *Pan*, remaining content with himself, has no passion, unless it be for *Discourse*, which is well shadow'd out by *Echo*, or *Talk*, or when it is more *accurate*, by *Syrinx*, or Writing[c] But *Echo* makes a most excellent Wife for *Pan*, as being no other than *genuine Philosophy*, which faithfully repeats his words, or only transcribes exactly as *Nature dictates*, thus representing the true image and reflection of the World, without adding a tittle[d] *His Amours.*

31. (w) It tends also to the support and perfection of *Pan* or *Nature*, to be without offspring, for the *World* generates in its parts, and not in the way of a whole, as wanting a body external to itself, wherewith to generate. *His Offspring.*

32.

[a] These kind of Explanations may appear like forced Accommodations, to hasty and juvenile minds but perhaps will have a greater effect upon sober and philosophical Natures, versed in the Knowledge of *Men* and *Things* It certainly requires a knowledge of History, depth in Philosophy, and a mature Judgment, to discover the Origin, the Intention, and *Use of the ancient Mythology* See the Author's Critique upon the Subject, prefix'd to the *Sapientia Veterum*.

[b] See hereafter Sect XII of *Learned Experience*

[c] Observe that *Syrinx* signifies a *Reed*, or the ancient *Pen*

[d] The Author always endeavours to place himself in this Situation, and accordingly calls himself, and is called by others, the *Secretary of Nature*. See Sir *Henry Wotton's* Letter to the Lord *Bacon*, in the *Reliquiæ Wottonianæ*.

h ...ft's
Days

32 (x) Laftly, for the *fuppofed or fpurious prattling daughter of Pan*, 'tis an excellent addition to the *Fable* , and aptly reprefents the talkative *Philofophies* that have at all times been ftirring, and filled the world with idle *Tales* being ever barren, empty and fervile , tho' fometimes indeed diverting and entertaining , and fometimes again, troublefome and importunate [a].

The Fable *of* Perseus *explained of the Preparation and Conduct neceffary to* War.

The Fable of
Perfeus de-
fcribed

III 33. THE Fable *relates, that* Perfeus *was difpatch'd from the Eaft by* Pallas (a), *to cut off* Medufa's *Head, who had committed great ravage upon the People of the* Weft (b) *For this* Medufa *was fo dire a Monfter, as to turn into ftone all thofe who but looked upon her* (c) *She was a* Gorgon, *and the only mortal one of the three, the other two being invulnerable* (d). Perfeus *therefore preparing himfelf for this grand Enterprize, had Prefents made him from three of the Gods* Mercury *gave him Wings for his Heels,* Pluto, *a Helmet, and* Pallas, *a Shield and a Mirror* (e) *But tho' he was now fo well equipp'd, he pofted not directly to* Medufa, *but firft turned afide to the* Greæ, *who were Half-Sifters to the* Gorgons (f) *Thefe* Greæ *were gray-headed, and like old Women from their birth, having among them all three but one Eye, and one* Tooth, *which, as they had occafion to go out, they each wore by turns, and laid them down again upon coming back* (g) *This Eye and this* Tooth *they lent to* Perfeus (h); *who now judging himfelf fufficiently furnifhed, he, without farther ftop, flies fwiftly away to* Medufa; *and finds her afleep* (i). *But not venturing his Eyes, for fear fhe fhould wake, he turned his head afide, and viewed her in* Pallas's *Mirror* (k) *and thus directing his ftroke, cut off her Head when immediately, from the gufhing Blood, there darted* Pegafus *winged* (l) Perfeus *now inferted* Medufa's *Head into* Pallas's *Shield* (m), *which thence retained the faculty of aftonifhing and benumbing all who look'd on it* (n)

Afford three
Precepts for
War

34 This *Fable* feems invented to fhew the *prudent Method of chufing, undertaking, and conducting a War*, and accordingly lays down three ufeful Precepts about it, as if they were the Precepts of *Pallas* (a)

(1) The firft is, that *no Prince fhould be over-follicitous to fubdue a neighbouring Nation* for the method of enlarging an *Empire*, is very different
from

---

[a] After reading the *Explanation*, it may be proper to read the *Fable* again , which makes the Conformity appear fo great, that one can fcarce help believing, or at leaft wifhing, the Truths drawn out of it by the Author, were originally intended by the Contriver. But of this, in general, fee more in the *Critique* prefix'd to the *Sapientia Veterum*

from that of increasing an *Estate*.   Regard is justly had to Contiguity, or *Explained of*
Adjacency, in private Lands and Possessions, but in the extending of Em- *undertaking a*
pire, the Occasion, the Facility, and Advantage of a War, are to be re- *War that shall be remote*
garded instead of Vicinity   'Tis certain that the *Romans*, at the time they
stretched but little beyond *Liguria* to the *West*, had by their Arms subdued
the Provinces as far as Mount *Taurus* to the *East* (*b*)   And thus *Perseus* readily undertook a very long Expedition, even from the *East* to the extremities of the *West*

   (2) The second Precept is, that *the Cause of the War be just and ho-* *Just*
nourable, for this adds Alacrity both to the Soldiers, and the People who
find the Supplies, procures Aids, Alliances, and numerous other Conveniences   (*c*) Now there is no *Cause of War* more just and laudable, than the
suppressing of *Tyranny*, by which a People are dispirited, benumbed, or
left without Life and Vigour, as at the sight of *Medusa*

   (3) (*d*) Lastly, it is prudently added, that as there were three of the *And sensible*
Gorgons, who represent War, *Perseus* singled her out for his Expedition that
was mortal ·   which affords this *Precept*, that *such kind of Wars should be*
chose, as may be brought to a conclusion, without pursuing vast and infinite
Hopes.

   34 (*e*) Again, *Perseus*'s setting out is extremely well adapted to his Un- *Perseus's set-*
dertaking, and in a manner commands success   he received Dispatch from *ting-out*
Mercury, Secrecy from *Pluto*, and Foresight from *Pallas*.   It also contains
an excellent Allegory, that the Wings given him by *Mercury* were for his
Heels, not for his *Shoulders*, because Expedition is not so much required in
the first Preparations for War, as in the subsequent Matters, that administer
to the first   for there is no Error more frequent in War, than, after brisk
Preparations, to halt for subsidiary Forces, and effective Supplies

   35 The Allegory of *Pluto*'s Helmet, rendering Men invisible and se- *His Helmet,*
cret, is sufficiently evident of itself, but the Mystery of the Shield and the *Shield, and*
Mirror lies deeper   and denotes, that not only a prudent Caution must be *Mirror*
had to defend, like the Shield, but also such an Address and Penetration,
as may discover the Strength, the Motions, the Counsels, and Designs of
the Enemy, like the Mirror of *Pallas*

   36 (*f*) But tho' *Perseus* may now seem extremely well prepared, there *His consulting*
still remains the most important thing of all   before he enters upon the War, *the Greæ*
he must of necessity consult the *Greæ*.   These *Greæ* are *Treasons*, half, but
degenerate Sisters of the *Gorgons*; who are Representatives of *Wars*   for
Wars are generous and noble, but *Treasons* base and vile   (*g*) The *Greæ*
are elegantly described, as hoary-headed, and like old Women from their
birth, on account of the perpetual Cares, Fears, and Trepidations attending
Traitors.   Their force also, before it breaks out into open revolt, consists
either in an *Eye* or a *Tooth*, for all Faction alienated from a State, is both
watchful and *biting*   and this *Eye* and *Tooth* is, as it were, common to all
the disaffected, because whatever they learn and know, is transmitted from
one to another, as by the hands of *Faction*.   And for the *Tooth*, they all
bite with the same, and clamour with one Throat, so that each of them
singly expresses the Multitude.

37 (b) These *Grææ*, therefore, must be prevail'd upon by *Perseus*, to lend him their *Eye* and their *Tooth*, the *Eye* to give him Indications, and make Discoveries, the *Tooth* for sowing Rumours, raising Envy, and stirring up the Minds of the People And when all these things are thus disposed and prepared, then follows the *Action of the War*

38 (1) He finds *Medusa* asleep, for whoever undertakes a War with prudence, generally falls upon the *Enemy unprepared*, and nearly in a state of security, and (x) here is the occasion for *Pallas*'s Mirror for 'tis common enough, before the Danger presents, to see exactly into the state and posture of the Enemy, but the principal use of the Glass is, in the very instant of Danger to discover the manner thereof, and prevent Consternation, which is the thing intended by *Perseus*'s turning his Head aside, and viewing the Enemy in the Glass [a]

39 Two Effects here follow the Conquest (1) (l, The darting forth of *Pegasus*, which evidently denotes *Fame*, that flies abroad, proclaiming the Victory and near 2 *'m* The bearing of *Medusa*'s Head in the Shield, which is the greatest possible Defence and Safeguard for (n) one grand and memorable Enterprize, happily accomplished, bridles all the Motions and Attempts of the Enemy, stupefies Dissaffection, and quells Commotions [b]

The FABLE of DIONYSUS, or BACCHUS, *explained of the* PASSIONS.

IV 40 THE Fable *runs, that Semele, Jupiter's Mistress, having bound him by an inviolable Oath to grant her an un-* known *Request, desired he would embrace her in the same form and manner he used to embrace* Juno *(a) and the Promise being irrevocable [c], she was burnt to death with Lightning in the performance (b). The Embryo, however, was sewed up, and carried in* Jupiter's *Thigh, till the compleat time of its birth but the burthen thus rendering the* Father *lame, and giving him pain, the Child was thence called* Dionysus *(c)[d] When born, he was committed, for some years, to be nursed by* Proserpina, *and when grown up, appeared with such an effeminate Face, that his Sex seemed somewhat doubtful (d). He also died, and was buried for a time, but afterwards revived (e) When a Youth, he first introduced the* culti-

[a] There is the excellence of a *General*, early to discover what turn the Battle is likely to take, and looking prudently behind, as well as before, to pursue a Victory so as not to be unprovided for a Retreat

[b] It may be observed of the Explanation of this *Fable*, and of most of those contained in the *Sapientia Veterum*, that the Author does not explain them in the way of a Recluse, but as a Man who had been conversant in action, and knew the Nature, Secrets, and Springs of publick, as well as private Transactions

[c] The Word has several Significations, according to its different Derivations, but among the rest, it denotes *Danger Pain*

[d] See the Fable of *Jupiter* explained in the *Sapientia Veterum*

*cultivation and dreſſing of Vines; the method of preparing Wine (f);
and taught the uſe thereof whence becoming famous, he ſubdued
the World, even to the utmoſt bounds of the* Indies *(g)   He rode
in a Chariot drawn by Tygers (h)   There danced about him certain deformed* Dæmons *called* Cobali, &c *(i)   The* Muſes *alſo
joined in his Train (k)   He married* Ariadne, *who was deſerted
by* Theſeus *(l).   The Ivy was ſacred to him (m).   He was alſo held
the Inventor and Inſtitutor of religious Rites and Ceremonies, but
ſuch as were wild, frantick, and full of Corruption and Cruelty (n).
He had alſo the power of ſtriking Men with Frenzies (o)   *Pentheus *and* Orpheus *were torn to pieces by the frantick Women at
his* Orgies *the firſt for climbing a Tree, to behold their outrageous
Ceremonies, and the other for the Muſick of his Harp (p).   But
the Acts of this God are much entangled, and confounded, with
thoſe of* Jupiter *(q)*

41 This *Fable* ſeems to contain a little Syſtem of *Morality*, ſo that there is ſcarce any better Invention in all *Ethicks*   (a) Under the Hiſtory of *Bacchus* is drawn the nature of *unlawful Deſire*, or *Affection*, and *Diſorder*, for the appetite and thirſt of apparent Good, is the Mother of all unlawful Deſires, tho' ever ſo deſtructive: and all unlawful Deſires are conceived in un- 'awful Wiſhes, or Requeſts, raſhly indulged, or granted, before they are well underſtood, or conſidered   (b) And when the Affection begins to grow warm, the *Mother* of it, the *Nature of Good*, is deſtroyed and burnt up by the heat   (c) And whilſt an *unlawful Deſire* lies in the *Embryo*, or unripen'd in the Mind, which is its Father, and here repreſented by *Jupiter*, 'tis cheriſh'd and conceal'd, eſpecially in the *inferiour part* of the Mind, correſponding to the *Thigh* of the Body, where Pain twitches and depreſſes the Mind ſo far, as to render its Reſolutions and Actions imperfect and lame. (d) And even after this *Child of the Mind* is confirm'd, and gains ſtrength by conſent and habit, and comes forth into action, it muſt ſtill be nurſed by *Proſerpina*, for a time   that is, it ſkulks and hides its head in a clandeſtine manner, as it were under ground[a], till at length, when the checks of Shame and Fear are removed, and the requiſite Boldneſs acquir'd, it either aſſumes the pretext of ſome Virtue, or openly deſpiſes Infamy   And 'tis juſtly obſerved, that every vehement Paſſion appears of a doubtful Sex, as having the Strength of a *Man* at firſt, but at laſt the Impotence of a *Woman* (e) 'Tis alſo excellently added, that *Bacchus* died, and roſe again, for the Affections ſometimes ſeem to die, and be no more, but there is no truſting them, even tho' they were buried, being always apt and ready to riſe again, whenever the Occaſion, or Object, offers

42 (f) That *Bacchus* ſhould be the *Inventor of Wine*, carries a fine Allegory with it, for every Affection is cunning, and ſubtile, in diſcovering a proper Matter to nouriſh and feed it, and of all things known to Mortals,

Sets forth *the* nature of *unlawful Deſire.*

The Moral of Semele's *Requeſt.*

Bacchus *carried in* Jupiter's *Thigh*

Nurſed by Proſerpina.

His effeminate Face.

His Death and Reſurrection

The Inventor of Wine

K 2   *Wine*

[a] See the *Fable of Proſerpina*, explained in the *Sapientia Veterum*

Wine is the moſt powerful, and effectual, for exciting and inflaming Paſſions of all kinds · being, indeed, like a common fewel to them all

His Conquests   43 (g) 'Tis again, with great elegance, obſerved of *Bacchus*, that he *ſubdued Provinces, and undertook endleſs Expeditions* for the Affections never reſt ſatisfied with what they enjoy, but, with an endleſs and inſatiable Appetite, thirſt after ſomewhat further And (b) *Tygers* are prettily feigned to

His Chariot drawn by Tygers   *draw the Chariot*, for as ſoon as any Affection ſhall, from going on foot, be advanced to ride, it triumphs over Reaſon, and exerts its Cruelty, Fierceneſs, and Strength, againſt all that oppoſe it

The Dæmons about his Chariot   44 (i) 'Tis alſo humorouſly imagined, that *ridiculous Dæmons ſhould dance and friſk about the Chariot*, for every Paſſion produces indecent, diſorderly, interchangeable, and deformed Motions in the Eyes, Countenance, and Geſture, ſo that the Perſon under the impulſe, whether of Anger, Inſult, Love, &c. tho' to himſelf he may ſeem grand, lofty, or obliging, yet in the eyes of others, appears mean, contemptible, or ridiculous

The Muses in his Train   45 (l) The *Muſes* alſo are found in the Train of *Bacchus*, for there is ſcarce any Paſſion without its Art, Science, or Doctrine, to court and flatter it, but in this reſpect, the indulgence of Men of Genius has greatly detracted from the Majeſty of the Muſes, who ought to be the Leaders and Conductors of human Life, and not the Hand-maids of the Paſſions

His Amour with a cast Mistress   46 ( ) The Allegory of *Bacchus*'s falling in love with a *caſt Miſtreſs*, is extremely noble for 'tis certain that the Affections always court and covet what has been rejected upon experience And all thoſe who by ſerving and indulging their Paſſions, immenſely raiſe the value of Enjoyment, ſhould know, that whatever they covet and purſue, whether *Riches, Pleaſure, Glory, Learning*, or any thing elſe, they only purſue thoſe things that have been forſaken, and caſt off with contempt, by great numbers in all ages, after poſſeſſion and experience had of them

The Ivy   47 (m) Nor is it without a myſtery, that the *Ivy was ſacred to* Bacchus, and this for two reaſons firſt, becauſe *Ivy* is an ever-green, or flouriſhes in the Winter, and ſecondly, becauſe it winds and creeps about ſo many things, as Trees, Walls, and Buildings, and raiſes itſelf above them As to the *firſt*, every Paſſion grows freſh, ſtrong, and vigorous, by oppoſition and prohibition, as it were by a kind of Contraſt, or *Antiperiſtaſis*, like the *Ivy*, in the Winter And for the *ſecond*, the predominant Paſſion of the Mind throws itſelf, like the *Ivy*, round all human Actions, entwines all our Reſolutions, and perpetually adheres to, and mixes itſelf in among, or even over-tops them

His frantic Rites   48 (r) And no wonder, that *ſuperſtitious Rites and Ceremonies are attributed to Bacchus*, when almoſt every ungovernable Paſſion grows wanton and luxuriant in corrupt Religions, nor again, that (o) Fury and Frenzy ſhould be ſent and dealt out by him, becauſe every *Paſſion* is a ſhort Frenzy, and if it be vehement, laſting, and take deep root, it terminates in *Madneſs*. (p) And hence the *Allegory of* Pentheus *and* Orpheus *being tore to pieces*, is evident, for every headſtrong Paſſion is extremely bitter, ſevere, inveterate, and revengeful upon all curious Enquiry, wholeſome Admonition, free Counſel and Perſuaſion.

49 (q) Laſtly, the *Confuſion between the Perſons of* Jupiter *and* Bacchus, will juſtly admit of an *Allegory*, becauſe noble and meritorious Actions may ſometimes proceed from Virtue, found Reaſon, and Magnanimity, and ſometimes again from a conceal'd Paſſion, and ſecret deſire of Ill, however, they may be extoll'd and praiſed inſomuch, that 'tis not eaſy to diſtinguiſh betwixt the Acts of *Bacchus* and the Acts of *Jupiter* [a]

The Confuſion of his Story with Jupiter's.

But perhaps we remain too long in the *Theatre*, 'tis time we ſhould advance to the *Palace of the Mind*

SECT. III.

Of PHILOSOPHY.

1 ALL *Knowledge* may be divided into PHILOSOPHY, and INSPIRED THEOLOGY *Philoſophy* has three OBJECTS, viz *God, Nature,* and *Man*, as allo three kinds of *Rays*, for (1) *Nature* ſtrikes the human Intellect with a *direct Ray*, (2) *God*, with a *refracted Ray*, from the Inequality of the Medium betwixt the Creator and the Creatures, and (3) *Man*, as exhibited to himſelf, with a *reflected Ray* Whence 'tis proper to divide Philoſophy into the *Doctrine of the Deity*, *the Doctrine of Nature*, and the *Doctrine of Man*

Philoſophy divided into the Doctrine of the Deity, Nature, and Man

2 But as the DIVISIONS OF THE SCIENCES are not like different Lines that meet in one Angle, but rather like the Branches of Trees that join in one Trunk [b], 'tis firſt neceſſary that we conſtitute an UNIVERSAL SCIENCE, as a *Parent* to the reſt, and making a part of the *common Road to the Sciences*, before the ways ſeparate And *this Knowledge* we call *Philoſophia Prima*, *primitive* or *primary Philoſophy*. It has no other for its oppoſite, and differs from other *Sciences* rather in the limits, whereby 'tis confined, than in the Subject, as treating only the *Summits of Things* And whether this ſhould be noted as wanting, may ſeem doubtful, tho' I rather incline to note it For I find a certain *Rhapſody of Natural Theology, Logicks,* and *Phyſicks*, delivered in a certain ſublimity of Diſcourſe, by ſuch as aim at being admired for ſtanding on the *Pinnacles of the Sciences*, but what we mean is, without ambition, *to deſign ſome* GENERAL SCIENCE, *for the reception of Axioms, not peculiar to any one Science, but common to a number of them.*

Primary Philoſophy, which is deficient.

3.

[a] The Author, in purſuance of his *Deſign of giving Examples and Specimens* of the Works he ſets down as deficient, has thus deprived his Piece *de Sapientia Veterum* of three beautiful Flowers, unleſs the reader ſhall pleaſe to ſupply them in that Performance, by turning hither for them, in the order he will there perceive them indicated by the *Notes*

[b] This Obſervation is the Foundation of Father *Caſtel's* late Piece *de Mathematique univerſelle*, wherein, by the help of ſenſible Repreſentations and Diviſions, he propoſes to teach the *Sciences* readily, and even abſtract Mathematicks, to common Capacities.

3 Axioms of this kind are numerous for example, (1) *If Equals be added to Unequal, the wholes will be unequal* This is a Rule in *Mathematicks*;
which holds also in *Ethicks*, with regard to *attributive Justice* (2) *Things
agreeing to the same third, agree also with one another* This likewise is an
Axiom in Mathematicks, and, at the same time, so serviceable in *Logick*, as to
be the Foundation of *Syllogism* (3) *Nature shews herself best in her smallest
Works* This is a Rule in *Philosophy*, that produced the Atoms of *Democritus*, and was justly employ'd by *Aristotle* in *Politicks*, when he begins the
Consideration of a *Commonwealth* in a *Family* (4) *All things change, but
nothing is lost* This is an *Axiom* in *Physicks*, and holds in *Natural Theology*,
for as the sum of Matter neither diminishes nor increases, so it is equally the
Work of *Omnipotence* to create, or to annihilate it (5) *Things are preserved
from Destruction, by bringing them back to their Principle*. This is an *Axiom
in Physick*, but holds equally in *Politicks*, for the preservation of States, as is
well observed by *Machiavel*, depends upon little more than reforming and
bringing them back to their ancient Customs (6) *A Discord ending immediately in a Concord, sets off the Harmony* This is a Rule in *Musick*, that
also holds true in *Morals* (7) *A trembling Sound in Musick gives the same
relish to the Ear, as the Corrugation of Water, or the sparkling of a Diamond
to the Eye* (8) *The Organs of the Senses resemble the Organs of Reflexion*,
as we see in *Opticks* and *Acousticks*, where a concave *Glass* resembles the *Eye*,
and a *vaulting Cave*, the *Ear* And of these *Axioms* an infinite number
might be collected And thus the celebrated *Persian Magick* was, in effect,
*no more than a notion of the correspondence in the Structure and Fabrick of
Things, natural and civil* Nor let any one understand all this of mere *Similitudes, as they might at first appear*, for they really are one and the same
Footsteps, and Impressions of Nature, made upon different Matters and Subjects And in this light the thing has not hitherto been carefully treated.
A few of these *Axioms* may indeed be found in the Writings of eminent Men,
here and there interspersed occasionally, but a *collected Body of them, which
should have a primitive and summary tendency to the* SCIENCES, *is not hitherto
extant*, tho' a thing of so great moment, as remarkably to shew *Nature to
be one and the same* which is supposed the Office of a *primary Philosophy* [b]

4 There is another part of this PRIMARY PHILOSOPHY, regarding the
alterations or *transcendental Conditions of Things*, as *little, much, like, different, possible, impossible, entity, non-entity*, &c For as these things do not properly come under *Physicks*, and as their *logical Consideration* rather accommo-
dates them to Argumentation, than Existence, 'tis proper that this Point be
not quite deserted, as being of considerable Dignity and Use, so as to have
some place in the *Arrangement of the Sciences* But this should be done in a
manner very different from the common For example, no Writer who
has treated of *much* and *little*, endeavours to assign the cause why some
                          things

---

[a] The Author has given us a *Specimen of his Magick*, which we place as the EIGHTH SUP-
PLEMENT to this PIECE, *de Augmentis Scientiarum*

[b] I am not sensible that any general Collection of this kind has hitherto been published, most
Writers having contented themselves with setting down the Axioms serving to teach the *particular sciences* they treat of Thus many of them are found in Books of *Law, Mathematicks*,
and *Logick* And a capital one of this kind for *Logick*, is that of *Dan Stahl*.

things in nature are so *numerous* and *large*, and others so *rare* and *small*: for, doubtless, 'tis impossible in the *nature of Things*, that there should be as great a quantity of *Gold* as of *Iron*, or *Roses* as plenty as *Grass*, &c so likewise no body that treats of *like* and *different* has sufficiently explained, why betwixt particular Species there are almost constantly interposed some things that partake of both, as *Moss* betwixt *Corruption* and a *Plant*, motionless *Fish* betwixt a *Plant* and an *Animal*, *Bats* betwixt *Birds* and *Quadrupeds*, &c Nor has any one hitherto discovered why *Iron* does not attract *Iron*, as the Loadstone does, and why *Gold* does not attract *Gold*, as *Quicksilver* does, *&c* But of these Particulars we find no mention in the *Discourses of Transcendentals* for *Men have rather pursued the Quirks of Words, than the Subtilties of Things* And therefore we would introduce into *primary Philosophy, a real and solid Enquiry into these Transcendentals, or adventitious Conditions of Beings, according to the Laws of* Nature, *not of* Speech [a] And thus having first *seated the common Parent of the Sciences*, we return to our Division of *Philosophy*, into *divine, natural*, and *human*. For *natural Theology* may be justly called *divine Philosophy*

5 DIVINE PHILOSOPHY is a *Science*, or rather the *Rudiments of a Science*, derivable from *God* by the Light of Nature, and the Contemplation of his Creatures, so that with regard to its Object, 'tis truly *divine*, but with regard to its Acquirement, *natural*. The Bounds of this Knowledge extend to the confutation of Atheism, and the ascertaining the Laws of Nature, but not to the establishing of *Religion* And therefore *God* never wrought a Miracle to convert an Atheist, because the Light of Nature is sufficient to demonstrate a *Deity*, but *Miracles* were designed for the Conversion of the Idolatrous and Superstitious, who acknowledged a *God*, but erred in their worship of him the *Light of Nature* being unable to declare the Will of *God*, or assign the just form of worshipping him. For as the Power and Skill of a Workman are seen in his Works, but not his Person, so the Works of *God* express the Wisdom and Omnipotence of the Creator, without the least representation of his Image And in this particular, the Opinion of the Heathens differ'd from the sacred Verity, as supposing the World to be the Image of God, and Man a little Image of the World The *Scripture* never gives the World that honour, but calls it the Work of his Hands, making only Man the Image of *God* And therefore *the Being of a God, that he Governs the World, that he is All-powerful, Wise, Prescient, Good, a just Rewarder and Punisher, and to be adored, may be shewn and enforced from his Works* and many other wonderful Secrets, with regard

Divine Philosophy, its Nature and Use

to

---

[a] This *Desideratum* is not, that I know of, supplied and as the design is no less than to set down the *Laws of Nature*, by which the Universe and its Parts are govern'd, it can only be derived from Experiment, Observation, and Enquiry, in which light, the modern experimental Philosophy contains many particulars that might be collected together, towards forming a *Body of such philosophical Laws* For not the *final*, but the *physical Causes* of Things, are here required Thus to say, *there is more Iron than Gold in the World, because Iron is the more useful Metal*, or *more Grass than Roses, because Grass feeds more Animals than Roses*, and the like, is only to assign the *final Causes* for which such things were apparently created, and not the *natural Causes*, or by what physical means, or Law of Nature, it happens that *Gold* is not so common as *Iron*, &c, The *Philosophy of Becher*, as explained and illustrated by *Stahl*, gives considerable Light to this *Subject*.

to his Attributes, and much more as to his Dispensation and Government over the Universe, may also be solidly deduced, and made appear, from the same   And this Subject has been usefully treated by several[a]

6 But from the *Contemplation of Nature*, and the *Principles of human Reason*, to dispute or urge any thing with vehemence, as to the *Mysteries of Faith*, or over-curiously to examine and sift them, by prying into the *manner of the Mystery*, is no safe thing   "*Give unto Faith the things that are Faith's*" And the Heathens grant as much, in that excellent and divine *Fable of the Golden Chain*, where "*Men and Gods are represented unable to draw* Jupiter "*to Earth, but* Jupiter *able to draw them up to Heaven*" So that 'tis a vain attempt to draw down the sublime Mysteries of Religion to our Reason, but we should rather raise our Minds to the adorable Throne of heavenly Truth   And in this part of *Natural Theology*, we find rather an excess than any defect   which we have turned a little aside to note, on account of the extreme Prejudice and Danger which both *Religion* and *Philosophy* hence incur, because a mixture of these makes both an *heretical Religion*, and a *fantastical and superstitious Philosophy*[b]

The Doctrine of Spirits   7 'Tis otherwise, as to the *Nature of Spirits and Angels*, this being neither unsearchable nor forbid, but in great part level to the human Mind, on account of their affinity   We are, indeed, forbid in Scripture to worship Angels, or to entertain fantastical Opinions of them, so as to exalt them above the degree of *Creatures*, or to think of them higher than we have reason   but the sober Enquiry about them, which either ascends to a knowledge of their Nature, by the Scale of corporeal Beings, or views them in the Mind, as in a Glass, is by no means forbid   The same is to be understood of *revolted* or *unclean Spirits*   Conversation with them, or using their assistance, is unlawful, and much more in any manner to worship or adore them   but the Contemplation and Knowledge of their Nature, Power, and Illusions, appears from Scripture, Reason, and Experience, to be no small part of *spiritual Wisdom*   And thus 'tis as lawful in *Natural Theology* to investigate the Nature of evil Spirits, as the Nature of Poisons in *Physics*, or the Nature of Vice in *Morality*   But this part of Knowledge relating to Angels and Spirits, which we call the APPENDAGE TO NATURAL THEOLOGY cannot be noted for deficient; as having been handled by many   but we may justly tax no small part of the Writers in this way, either with *Lies*, *Superstition*, or *fruitless Speculation*[c]

Natural Philosophy considered speculative and practical   8 But to leave NATURAL THEOLOGY, and proceed to NATURAL PHILOSOPHY   as it was well said by *Democritus*, that " the Knowledge of " Nature lies concealed in deep Mines and Caves," and by the *Chemists*, that "*Vulcan* is a *second Nature*, imitating concisely what the *first* takes
time

---

[a] And more particularly since, by *Cudworth* in his *Intellectual System of the Universe*, Mr *Boyle*, in his *Christian Virtuoso* &c   Mr *Ray*, in his *Wisdom of the Creation*, Dr *Bentley*, in his Discourse of the Folly and Unreasonableness of Atheism, Dr *Clarke*, in his *Demonstration of the Being and Attributes of God*, Mr *Derham*, in his *Physico Theology*, Mr *Raphson de Deo*, Dr *Newton*, in his *Religious Philosopher*, Mr *Whiston* in his *Astronomical Principles of Religion*, &c

[b] See above, Prelim. Sect. I 8 and hereafter, of *Theology* Sect. ult.

[c] What modern Writers have treated this *Doctrine of Spirits*, and to what purpose, may be seen at one view, in S. *Solan Introd. in Historiam Literariam, Cap III de Pneumatologia*

time and circuit to effect, suppose *Natural Philosophy* were divided, as
it regards the *Mine* and the *Furnace* · thus inftituting two Offices of *Philofophers, Miners,* and *Smelters?* This, indeed, may appear jocular, yet fuch
a kind of Divifion we judge extremely ufeful, when propofed in juft and
familiar terms fo that the *Doctrine of Nature* be divided into *Speculative*
and *Practical,* or the *Search after Caufes,* and the *Production of Effects*
The one *entring into the Bowels of Nature,* and the other *forming her upon
the Anvil* Nor are we infenfible of the ftrict union betwixt *Caufes* and *Effects,* fo that the explanation of them muft, in fome meafure, be coupled
together but as all folid and fruitful *Natural Philofophy* hath both an
afcending, and a defcending Scale of Parts, leading from *Experience to Axioms,* and from *Axioms to new Difcoveries,* it feems moft advifeable here, in
the *Divifion of the Sciences,* to feparate *Speculation* from *Operation,* and treat
them diftinct[a] ·

9 The *fpeculative* or *theoretical Part* of NATURAL PHILOSOPHY, we
divide into PHYSICKS and METAPHYSICKS· taking the word *Metaphyficks*
in a fenfe different from that received And here we muft, once for all, declare, as to our ufe of Words, that tho' our Conceptions and Notions are
new, and different from the common, yet we religioufly retain the *ancient
Forms of Speech* for as we hope that the Method, and clear Explanation,
we endeavour at, will free us from any mifconftruction that might arife
from an ill choice of *Words,* fo in every thing elfe, 'tis our defire, as much
as poffible, without prejudice to Truth and the *Sciences,* not to deviate from
ancient Opinions and Forms of Speech And here I cannot but wonder that
Aristotle fhould proceed in fuch a *fpirit of Contradiction,* as he did to all Antiquity, not only coining new Terms of Science, at pleafure, but endeavouring to abolifh all the Knowledge of the Ancients, fo that he never
mentions any ancient Author but to reprove him, nor Opinion but to confute
it which is the ready way to procure Fame and Followers For certainly it
happens in *philofophical,* as it does in *divine Truth* " *I came in the name of*
" *my Father, and ye received me not; but if one came in his own name, ye*
" *would receive him* " Which *divine Aphorifm,* as applied to *Antichrift,* the
great Deceiver, plainly fhews us that a Man's coming in his own name, without
regard to *Antiquity* or *Paternity,* is no good fign of Truth, tho' joined with
the fortune and fuccefs of *being received* But for fo excellent and fublime a
Genius as *Aristotle,* one would think he catch'd this Ambition from his Scholar, and affected to fubdue all Opinions, as *Alexander* did all Nations and
thus erect himfelf a Monarchy in his own Contemplation Tho' for this,
perhaps, he may not efcape the lafh of fome fevere Pen, no more than his
Pupil, and be called a *fuccefsful Ravager of Learning,* as the other *was of
Countries* But on the other hand, defiring, by all poffible means, to cultivate, and eftablifh, a free *Commerce betwixt ancient and modern Learning,* we
judge it beft, religioufly to fide with *Antiquity,* and therefore to retain the
ancient Terms, tho' we frequently alter their Senfe, according to that mo-

*Speculative
Philofophy di-
vided into
Phyficks and
Metaphyficks*

[a] They are hereafter confider'd together, in the *Novum Organum,* where the Author comes
to apply them in *Bufinefs,* or *practical Philofophy*

derate and laudable ufage in *Politicks*, of *introducing a new ftate of Things, without chaging the popular Terms of Government*

10 Thus then we diftinguifh METAPHYSICKS, as may appear by what was above delivered, from *primary Philofophy* [a], which has hitherto been taken for it, making *this* the common Parent of the Sciences, and *that* a part of *Natural Philofophy* But to affign the proper Office of *Metaphyficks*, as contradiftinguifh'd from *primary Philofophy*, and *natural Theology*, we muft note, that as *Phyfics* regards the things which are wholly immerfed in *Matter*, and no fenfible, fo *Metaphyficks* regards what is more abftracted, and fixed that *Phyfics* fuppofes only Exiftence, Motion, and natural Neceffity, whilft *Metaphyfics* fuppofes alfo *Mind* and *Idea* But to be more exprefs as we have divided *Natural Philofophy* into the Inveftigation of Caufes, and the Production of Effects, and referred the Inveftigation of Caufes to *Theory*, which we again divide into *phyfical* and *metaphyfical*, 'tis neceffary that the real difference of thefe two be drawn from the nature of the Caufes they enquire into and therefore plainly, PHYSICKS enquires into the *Efficient*, and the *Matter*, and METAPHYSICKS into the *Form* and the *End* PHYSICKS, therefore, is vague and inftable, as to *Caufes*, and treats moveable Bodies as its Subjects, without difcovering a *Conftancy of Caufes*, in different Subjects Thus the fame Fire gives hardnefs to *Clay*, and foftnefs to *Wax*, tho' it be no *conftant Caufe* either of hardnefs or foftnefs [b]

SECT. IV.
Of PHYSICKS.

1 WE divide PHYSICKS into three parts, for Nature is either *collected* into one Total, or *diffufed*, and *diftributed* Nature is collected either by reafon of the common Principles of all things, or one integral Fabric of the Univerfe Whence this *union of Nature* produces *two* parts of *Phyfics*, the *one* relating to the *Principles of Things*, and the *other* to the *Structure of the Univerfe* [c], whilft the *third* exhibits all the poffible varieties and leffer collections of Things And this latter is like a firft Glofs, or *Paraphrafe in the Interpretation of Nature* [d] None of the *three* are deficient entirely,

---

[a] Concerning *Primary Philofophy*, fee above, 2, 3, 4

[b] *Phyfics* therefore, may be defined that part of univerfal Philofophy which obferves and confiders the *Procedure of Nature in Bodies*, fo as to difcover her *Laws, Powers*, and *Effects*, and her *material Origin*, and *Caufes* thereof in different Subjects, and thence form Rules for imitating, controlling, or even excelling her Works, in the Inftances it confiders

[c] This Divifion appears, in the judgment of the learned *Morhof*, to have given Mr *Boyle* the occafion of confidering the *Cofmical Qualities* of Things, or thofe Properties of them which refult from their being Parts of the general Frame of *the Univerfe* See Boyle, *Abridgm* Vol I pag 280—296

[d] That is the confideration of Nature's fmaller Works, every where diffufed in the Univerfe, leads to an Interpretation, or unravelling of the general Scheme of Things for in Philofophy we proceed from particulars to generals, as from the reading of paffages to the underftanding of a Book

entircly, but how juſtly and ſolidly they have been treated, is another queſtion

2 This third part we again divide into two others, with regard to *The Doctrine of Variety divided into Phyſicks of Creatures, and Phyſicks of Natures* *Concretes* and *Abſtracts*, or into PHYSICKS OF CREATURES and PHYSICKS OF NATURES the one enquiring into Subſtances, and all the variety of their Accedents, the other into Accidents thro' all the variety of Subſtances. Thus if enquiry be made about a *Lion* or an *Oak*, theſe ſupport many different Accidents: ſo if the enquiry were about *Heat* or *Gravity*, theſe are found in many different Subſtances But as all PHYSICKS lies in the middle, betwixt *Natural Hiſtory* and *Metaphyſicks*, ſo the former part approaches nearer to *Natural Hiſtory*, and the latter to *Metaphyſicks*

3 CONCRETE PHYSICKS has the ſame diviſion with *Natural Hiſtory*, *Concrete Phyſicks divided as Natural Hiſtory* being converſant either about celeſtial Appearances, Meteors, and the terreſtrial Globe or about the larger Aſſemblages of Matter, called the Elements, and the leſſer or particular Bodies as alſo about Prætergenerations and Mechanicks For in all theſe, *Natural Hiſtory* examines and relates the matters of fact, and *Phyſicks* their inſtable, or material and efficient cauſes And among theſe parts of PHYSICKS, *that is abſolutely lame and incompleat, which regards the celeſtial Bodies*, tho' for the dignity of the ſubject it claims the higheſt regard *Aſtronomy*, indeed, is well founded in *Phænomena*; yet 'tis low and far from ſolid But *Aſtrology* is in many things deſtitute of all foundation

4 And to ſay the truth, *Aſtronomy* itſelf ſeems to offer *Prometheus*'s *Phyſical Aſtronomy deficient.* ſacrifice to the Underſtanding, for as he would have impos'd upon *Jupiter* a fair large Hide, ſtuff'd with Straw, and Leaves, and Twigs, inſtead of the Ox itſelf, ſo *Aſtronomy* gives us the number, ſituation, motion, and periods of the Stars, as a beautiful outſide of the Heavens, whilſt the Fleſh and the Entrails are wanting that is, a well-fabricated Syſtem, or the *phyſical Reaſons* and Foundations for a juſt Theory, that ſhould not only ſolve Phænomena, as almoſt any ingenious Theory may do, *but ſhew the ſubſtance, motions and influences of the heavenly Bodies, as they really are* But ſcarce any one has enquired into the phyſical Cauſes of the ſubſtance of the Heavens, ſtellar and interſtellar, the different velocities of the celeſtial Bodies with regard to one another, the different accelerations of motion in the ſame Planet, the ſequences of their motion from Eaſt to Weſt, the progreſſions, ſtations and retrogradations of the Planets, the ſtoppage and accidents of their Motion, by the Perigé and Apogé, the obliquity of their Motions, why the Poles of Rotation are principally in one quarter of the Heavens, why certain Planets keep a fix'd diſtance from the Sun, &c Enquiries of this kind have hitherto been ſcarce touched upon, but the pains has been chiefly beſtowed in *Mathematical Obſervations* and *Demonſtrations* which indeed may ſhew how to account for all theſe things ingeniouſly, but not how they actually are in Nature · how to repreſent the apparent Motions of the heavenly Bodies, and machines of them, made according to particular fancies, but not the real cauſes and truth of things And therefore *Aſtronomy*, as it now ſtands, loſes of its dignity, by being reckon'd among the *Mathematical Arts*, for it ought in juſtice to make the moſt noble

L 2   part

part of *Physics* And whoever despises the imaginary separation between terrestrial and celestial things, and well understands the more general appetites and passions of Matter, which are powerful in both, may receive a clear information of what happens above, from that which happens below and from what passes in the heavens, he may become acquainted with some inferior motions hitherto undiscovered, not as these are governed by those, but as they both have the same common passions We, therefore, report this PHYSICAL PART OF ASTRONOMY *as wanting, under the Title of* ANIMATED ASTRONOMY [a]

A 0025 to be purged

5 But for ASTROLOGY, 'tis so full of superstition, that scarce any thing sound can be discovered in it tho' we judge it should rather be purged than absolutely rejected But if any one shall pretend that this *Science* is founded, not in *Reason* and *physical Contemplations*, but in the direct *Experience* and *Observations* of past ages, and therefore not to be examined by physical Reasons, as the *Chaldeans* boasted, he may at the same time bring back *Divination, Auguries, Sooth-saying*, and give into all kinds of Fables for these also were said to descend from long Experience. But we receive *Astrology* as a part of *Physicks*, without attributing more to it than Reason and the Evidence of things allows, and strip it of its superstition and conceits Thus we banish that empty notion about the horary reign of the Planets, as if each resumed the throne thrice in twenty four hours, so as to leave three hours supernumerary and yet this Fiction produced the *division of the Week*, a thing so ancient and so universally receiv'd Thus likewise we reject, as an idle figment, the doctrine of *Horoscopes*, and the distribution of the *Houses*, tho' these are the darling Inventions of *Astrology*, which have kept Revel, as it were, in the Heavens And we are surprized that some eminent Authors in *Astrology*, should rest upon so slender an argument for erecting them, as because it appears by experience, that the *Solstices*, the *Equinoxes*, the *new and full Moon*, &c have a manifest operation upon natural Bodies, therefore the more curious and subtile positions of the Stars must produce more exquisite and secret effects whereas, laying aside those operations of the Sun, which are owing to manifest heat, and a certain attractive virtue of the Moon, which causes the spring-tides, the other effects of the Planets upon natural bodies, are, so far as experience reaches, exceeding small, weak and latent Therefore the Argument should run thus since these greater revolutions are able to effect so little, those more nice and trifling differences of positions will have no force at all And lastly, for the

Calculation

[a] The Author made an Attempt to supply this *Desideratum*, as may be seen in the NINTH SUPPLEMENT to this Work His Design was to rescue the *Science* from the usurpation of *Mathematics*, and render it more extensive, philosophical and serviceable But he does not appear to have had many followers in this way, few besides *Mathematicians* thinking themselves qualified to improve *Astronomy*; and the Astronomical Mathematicians seldom cultivating more than the *Mathematical or Systematical Part*, as *Galileo, Kepler, Ward, Hevelius* &c except Sir *Isaac Newton* and upon his Foundation, Dr *Gregory*, Dr *Keil*, Mr *Whiston*, &c have introduced more *Natural Philosophy* into *Astronomy* However, the *physical Part* of the Science has not hitherto been sedulously cultivated, and kept clear of *System* and *Hypothesis*, according to the *Direction and Example of the Lord Bacon* See *Morhof's Polyhist Mathemat Stollius de Disciplinis Mathematicis*, and *Wolfii Elementa Matheseos Universæ*

Calculation of Nativities, Fortunes, good or bad Hours of business, and the like *Fatalities,* they are mere levities that have little in them of certainty and solidity, and may be plainly confuted by *physical reasons*

6   And here we judge it proper to lay down some *Rules for the exami-* **Rules for its** *nation of Astrological Matters,* in order to retain what is useful therein, and **amendment.** reject what is insignificant   Thus (1) *Let the greater Revolutions be retain'd, but the lesser of Horoscopes and Houses be rejected,* the former being like Ordnance, which shoot to a great distance, whilst the other are but like small Bows, that do no execution   (2) *The celestial Operations affect not all kinds of bodies, but only the more sensible*   Here we except the operations of the Sun's heat, which may doubtless penetrate Metals, and other subterraneous Bodies   and confine the other Operations chiefly to the Air, the Humours, and the Spirits of things   (3) *All the celestial Operations rather extend to Masses of Things, than to Individuals.* Tho' they may obliquely reach some Individuals also, which are more sensible than the rest   as a pestilent constitution of the air affects those bodies which are least able to resist it. (4) *All the celestial Operations produce not their effects instantaneously, and in a narrow compass, but exert them in large portions of time and space*   Thus Predictions as to the temperature of a year, may hold good, but not with regard to single days.   (5.) *There is no fatal Necessity in the Stars*   And this the more prudent *Astrologers* have constantly allowed.   (6.) We will add one thing more, which, if amended and improved, might make for *Astrology,* viz   that we are certain, *The Celestial Bodies have other Influences besides Heat and Light* [a] ·   but these Influences act not otherwise than by the foregoing **A just Astro-** Rules, tho' they lie so deep in *Physicks,* as to require a fuller explanation **logy** *wanting.* So that, upon the whole, we must register, as defective, an *Astrology wrote in conformity to these Principles,* under the name of ASTROLOGIA SANA [b]

7. This JUST ASTROLOGY should contain, (1) *The Doctrine of the Com-* **How to be sup-** *mixture of Rays,* viz   the Conjunctions, Oppositions and other Situations, or **plied** Aspects of the Planets, with regard to one another, their Transits thro' the Signs of the *Zodiac,* and their Situation in the same Signs   as the situation of Planets in a *Sign,* is a certain conjunction thereof with the Stars of that *Sign.* And as the *Conjunctions,* so likewise should the Oppositions, and other Aspects of the Planets, with regard to the celestial Signs, be remark'd, which has not hitherto been fully done.   The *Commixtures of the Rays* of the fix'd

Stars,

[a] The Author might presume he had a particular Reason for this Observation, more than other Men, as he always fainted when the Moon was eclipsed   Mr *Boyle* offers several Observations for the fuller proof of the *Proposition,* and seems to have taken the occasion of considering the different Effects of Light in different Planets, from this Hint   See *Abridgm of his Philosophical Works,* Vol III pag 34, 35, 36   See also *Placidus de Titis,* in his *Astrologia, Morinus* in his *Astrologia Gallica,* and *Campanella's Astrologicorum* Libri VII *& de Siderali Fato vitando*

[b] This *Work* is not hitherto extant, nor *Physicks* and *Astronomy,* perhaps, improved far enough to afford it compleat   The philosophical Labours of Mr *Boyle,* Dr *Hook,* Dr *Halley,* &c   the Observations of *Hevelius, de la Hire,* Mr *Flamstead,* and many other Members of the *Royal Society* and foreign Academies, with all the Discoveries of Sir *Isaac Newton,* do but afford some Materials for the *Foundation of this Science,* which was solidly begun by the Author in his *Natural History of the Wind*   The great usefulness of the Design in civil and active Life, may require it to be diligently prosecuted   See *Childrey's Indago Astrologica,* printed at *London,* 1652.

Stars, with one another, are of use in contemplating the Fabrick of the World , and the nature of the subjacent Regions · but in no respect for Predictions, because at all times alike. (2) This *Astrology should take in the nearest approache , and the farthest removes of each Planet, to and from the Zenith, according to the Climate* for all the *Planets* have their Summer and Winter , wherein they dart their rays stronger or weaker, according to their perpendicular or oblique direction So we question not but the *Moon* in *Leo*, has, in the same manner as the *Sun*, a greater effect upon natural bodies with us, than when in *Pisces* , by reason of her greater perpendicular elevation, and nearer approach to the larger Stars (3) It should receive the *Apogees* and *Perigees* of the *Planets* , *with a proper Enquiry into what the Vigour of the Parts* may perform of itself , and what thro' their nearness to us for a Planet is more brisk, in its Apogé, but more communicative in its Perigé. (4) *It should include all the other accidents of the Planet's Motions* , their accelerations, retardations, courses, stations, retrogradations, distances from the Sun, increase and diminutions of Light, Eclipses, &c For all these things affect the rays of the Planets, and cause them to act either weaker, stronger, or in a different manner (5) This *Astrology should contain all that can by any means be known or discovered of the nature of the Stars, both erratic and fix'd* , considered in their own essence and activity, viz their magnitude, colour, aspect, sparkling and vibrating of Light , their situation with regard to the Poles or Equinoctial . the Constellations, which thicker set, and which thinner, which higher, which lower , what fix'd Stars are in the *Zodiac*, and what out of it , the different velocities of the Planets , their different latitudes , which of them are retrograde, and which not , their different distances from the Sun , which move swiftest in their Apogé, and which in their Perigé , the irregularities of *Mars*, the excursions of *Venus*, and the extraordinary phases, accidents, and appearances observable in *Venus* and the *Sun*, with other things of this kind (6) *Lastly*, let it contain, from Tradition, the particular natures and alterations of the *Planets* and fix'd *Stars* for as these are delivered with general consent, they are not lightly to be rejected , unless they directly contradict physical reasons And of such Observations let a JUST ASTROLOGY be formed and according to these alone should *Schemes* of the Heavens be made and interpreted [a]

　　Use of Prediction

8 Such an *Astrology* should be used with greater confidence in *Prediction*, but more cautiously in *Election* , and in both cases with due moderation. Thus *Predictions* may be made of *Comets*, and all kinds of Meteors, Inundations, Droughts, Heats, Frosts, Earthquakes, fiery Eruptions, Winds, great Rains, the Seasons of the Year, Plagues, Epidemic Diseases, Plenty, Famine, Wars, Seditions, Sects, Transmigrations of People , and all Commotions

[a] This may shew that the principal use of *Astronomy* is to serve as a Basis for a *just Astrology*, or that *Astronomy* is not so much to be cultivated for its own sake as for laying the Foundations of a more useful *Science*, that of predicting the Changes of the Atmosphere , the Winds, the Weather, the Seasons, and the grand Commotions, and Contingencies on the *Earth* , with a discovery of the ways of preventing or guarding against them See the *Author's History of the Wind*, and Mr *Boyle's* on the new use of *Astronomy*, in his *Memoirs for a general History of the Air*

motions or great Innovations of things Natural and Civil *Predictions* may possibly be made more particular, tho' with less certainty, if when the general tendencies of the Times are found, a good philosophical or political judgment applies them to such things as are most liable to this kind of accidents   For example, from a foreknowledge of the *Seasons* of any year, they might be apprehended more destructive to *Olives* than *Grapes* ; more hurtful in Distempers of the *Lungs* than the *Liver*, more pernicious to the Inhabitants of *Hills* than *Valleys*, and, for want of Provisions, to men of retirement, than *Courtiers* &c. Or if any one, from a knowledge of the Influence which the celestial bodies have upon the spirits of mankind, should find it would affect the people more than their Rulers, learned and inquisitive men more than the military, *&c*   For there are innumerable things of this kind, that require not only a general knowledge, gained from the Stars, which are the *Agents*, but also a particular one of the *passive Subjects*.

9. Nor are *Elections* to be wholly rejected, tho' not so much to be trust- *And Elections* ed as Predictions for we find in Planting, Sowing, and Grafting, Observations of the Moon are not absolutely trifling, and there are many particulars of this kind   But *Elections* are more to be curb'd by our Rules, than Predictions   And this must always be remembred, that *Election* only holds in such cases where the virtue of the heavenly bodies, and the action of the inferior bodies also, is not transient, as in the examples just mentioned for the increases of the Moon and Planets are not sudden things   But Punctuality of time should here be absolutely rejected   And perhaps there are more of these Instances to be found in *Civil Matters*, than some would imagine.

10. There are but four Ways of arriving at this *Science*, viz (1) *by future* *The ways of* *Experiments*, (2) *past Experiments*, (3) *Traditions*, and (4) *Physical Reasons* *arriving at* But (1) 'tis in vain, at present, to think of *future Experiments*, because many *Astrology.* ages are required to procure a competent stock of them   And (2) as for the *past*, 'tis true they are within our reach, but 'tis a work of labour and much time to procure them   Thus *Astrologers* may, if they please, draw from real History all greater accidents, as Inundations, Plagues, Wars, Seditions, Deaths of Kings, &c as also the positions of the Celestial Bodies ; not according to fictitious Horoscopes, but the abovementioned rules of their Revolutions, or such as they really were, at the time, and where the event conspires, erect a probable Rule of Prediction   (3) All *Traditions* should be well sifted, and those thrown out that manifestly clash with *physical Reasons*, leaving such in their full force as comport well therewith.   And (4) those physical Reasons are best suited to this Enquiry, which search into the universal *appetites and passions of Matter*, and the simple genuine motions of the heavenly bodies.   And this we take for the surest *Guide to Astrology* [a].

II.

---

[a] On the Foundations here laid down, Mr *Boyle* makes a defence of *Astrology*, and represents it as one of the most serviceable parts of *Astronomy* See his *Memoirs for a general History of the Air Abridgm* Vol. III pag 33—36   Accordingly, *Astronomy* and *Astrology* were anciently reputed the same Thing   In which Light see also the Author's Specimen of animated or solid *Astronomy*, in the NINTH SUPPLEMENT to this Piece   And for the *History of Astrology*, see *Salmasius de Annis Climactericis, & antiqua Astrologia.*

Celestial Magick, or wild Astrology

11 There remains another piece of *wild Astrology*, tho' usually separated from it, and transferred to *Celestial Magick*, as they call it 'Tis a strange fiction of the human brain, the *receiving the benign Aspect of the Stars upon Seals and Signes of Gems or Metal*, suited to the purpose, so as to detain and fix, as it were, the felicity of that hour which would otherwise be volatile and fugitive Thus to treasure up the *Relicks* of Heaven, in order to revive and preserve the fleeting, and now dead hour, wherein they were taken, is a superstition exceeding that of the *Catholicks* in preserving the *Relicks of Saints.* Let all such Dreams therefore be banish'd Philosophy

Abstract Physics divided, and the Doctrine of the Summes of Matter

12 ABSTRACT PHYSICKS may be justly divided into two parts, the *Doctrine of the Summes of Matter*, and the *Doctrine of Appetites and Motions* The *Summes of Matter* are density, rarity, gravity, levity, heat, cold, tangibility, intangibility, volatile, fixed, determinate, fluid, humid, dry, unctuous, crude, hard, soft, fragile, tensile, porous, united, spirituous, jejune, simple, compound, absolute, imperfectly mix'd, fibrous and veiny, simple position, or equable, similar, dissimilar, specificate, unspecificate, organical, inorganical, animate and inanimate and farther than this we proceed not , for sensible and insensible, rational and irrational, we refer to the *Doctrine of Man*

Appetites and Motions

13 *Appetites and Motions* are of two kinds , as being either *simple Motions*, wherein the spring of all natural Actions is contained, that is, in respect of their Schemes of Matter , or Motions compounded or produced and with these the common Philosophy, which enters but little into the body of Nature, begins But these *compound Motions*, such as Generation, Corruption, &c. should be esteemed certain Results or *Effects of simple Motions*, rather than *primitive Motions* themselves The *simple Motions* are (1) motion of *Resistance*, or preventive of penetration of dimensions , (2.) *motion of Connexion*, preventive of a Vacuum, as 'tis called, (3) motion of Liberty, preventive of preternatural compression, or extension, (4) motion in a new Orb, with regard to rarefaction and condensation, (5) motion of the second Connexion, or preventive of solution of continuity, (6) motion of the greater Congregation, or with regard to masses of connatural Bodies, commonly called natural Motion, (7) motion of the lesser Congregation, vulgarly term'd motion of Sympathy and Antipathy, (8) disponent motion, with regard to the just placing of Parts in the Whole, (9) motion of Assimilation or multiplicative of its own nature upon another body, (10) motion of Excitation, where the nobler agent excites the latent and benumb'd motion in another thing , (11) motion of the Seal, or impression, by an operation without communication of substance, (12) regal motion, or the restraint of other motions by a predominant one, (13) endless motion, or spontaneous rotation, (14) motion of Trepidation, or the motion of systole and diastole, with regard to Bodies placed betwixt things advantageous and hurtful , (15) and lastly, motion couchant, or a dread of motion, which is the cause of many effects. And such are the simple motions that really proceed out of the inward recesses of Nature, and which being complicated, continued, used alternately, moderated, repeated, and variously combined, produce those compound Motions or Results of Motion we call *Generation, Corruption, Increase, Diminution, Alteration, Translation, Mixtion, Separation* and *Conversion.*[a]

14

[a] The Doctrine arising from this *classing of Motions*, is largely explained towards the close of
the

14 The *Measures of Motions* are an *Attendant* on PHYSICKS; as shewing the effects of quantity, distance, or the sphere of activity, intension and remission, short and long continuance, activity, dulness, and incitation. And these are the genuine parts of ABSTRACT PHYSICKS, which wholly consists (1) in *the Schemes of Matter*, (2) Simple Motions, (3) the Results or Sums of Motions, and (4) the Measures of Motions As for voluntary motion in Animals, the motion in the Action of the Senses; the motions of the Imagination, Appetite, and Will, the motion of Mind, the Determination, and other intellectual Faculties; they have their own proper *Doctrines*, under which we range them, confining the whole of PHYSICKS *to Matter* and *Efficient*, and assigning over *Forms* and *Ends* to METAPHYSICKS.

The Measures of Motions an Attendant on Physicks

15. We must annex two *remarkable* APPENDAGES TO PHYSICKS, with regard rather to the manner, than the matter of Enquiry, *viz. Natural Problems*, and the *Opinions of the ancient Philosophers* The first is an *Appendage of Nature at large*, and the other of *Nature united or summed up* both relating to a diligent kind of *doubting*, which is no contemptible part of Knowledge Now, *Problems* contain *particular Doubts*, and *Opinions, general* ones, as to Principles and Structure In the Books of *Aristotle* we have a noble example of *Problems*, deserving not only the Praises, but the Imitation of Posterity since new Doubts are daily arising But the utmost caution is to be used in such an Undertaking. The recording and proposing of *Doubts* has two advantages, the one, as it defends *Philosophy* against Errors, when that which is not clear, is neither judged nor asserted, lest Error thus should multiply Error, but Judgment is suspended upon it, and not made positive the other is, that *Doubts* once register'd, are like so many *Sponges*, which perpetually suck and draw to themselves the increases of Knowledge, whence those things which would have been slightly passed over, unless they had been doubted of before, come now from this very doubting to be more attentively consider'd. But these two advantages will scarce ballance this single Inconvenience, unless well provided against, *viz.* that when a *Doubt* is once admitted for just, and becomes, as it were, authentick, it presently raises up Disputants on both sides, who transmit to Posterity the same liberty of *doubting* still, so that Men seem to apply their Wits rather to nourish the *Doubt* than solve it And of this we every where meet with examples in *Lawyers* and *Scholars*, who, when a Doubt once gains admittance, would have it remain a Doubt for ever, and engage themselves in doubting, as well as asserting whereas the true use of Wit is to render doubtful things certain, and not certain ones doubtful And therefore I set down as wanting A CALENDAR OF DOUBTS, OR PROBLEMS IN NATURE, and recommend it to be undertaken, with care to blot out

Two Appendages to Physicks, viz. (1) natural Problems.

A Calendar whereof is deficient

the *Novum Organum*, tho' it seems to have been little regarded in the modern *mechanical Philosophy*, which accounts for *Phænomena*, without such an exact analysis of Motion, or dividing it into its several species how justly, is another Question Whoever converses with natural and artificial Operations such as *Fermentation, Putrefaction*, and most chemical Processes, will perhaps find the use and necessity of all these different Species, to produce different effects, as they shall be differently combined, and give the true Causes of numerous *Phænomena*, which tho' common, are little attended to

daily, as Knowledge increases, those that are clearly discussed and settled [a]. And this *Calendar* we would have attended with another, of no less utility, for as in every Enquiry there are things plainly true, things doubtful, and things plainly false, 'twere exceeding proper that along with a *Calendar of Doubts*, should go A CALENDAR OF FALSEHOODS AND VULGAR ERRORS, both in natural *History* and *Opinions*, that they may no longer disturb the *Sciences* [b].

16 As to the *Opinions of the ancient Philosophers*, for example those of *Pythagoras*, *Philolaus*, *Xenophanes*, *Anaxagoras*, *Parmenides*, *Leucippus*, *Democritus*, and others, which Men usually pass slightly over, 'tis proper to cast a modest eye upon them   For tho' *Aristotle*, after the *Ottoman* manner, thought he could not reign secure, without putting all his Brethren to death, yet those who do not affect Dominion and Rule, but the Enquiry and Illustration of Truth, will find their account in beholding, at one view, the different Opinions of different Philosophers, as to the Natures of Things But there is no room to expect any pure Truth from these or the like Theories for as the celestial appearances are solved both upon the Suppositions of *Ptolemy* and *Copernicus*, so common experience, and the obvious face of things, may be applied to many different *Theories* whilst a much stricter procedure is required in the right discovery of Truth   For as Children, when they first begin to speak, call every woman Mother, but afterwards learn to distinguish their own   so a childish Experience calls every *Philosophy* its Mother, but when grown up, will easily distinguish its true one In the mean time, 'tis proper to read the *disagreeing Philosophies*, as so many different Glosses of Nature   We could therefore wish there were, with care and judgment, drawn up A WORK OF THE ANCIENT PHILOSOPHIES [c], from the Lives

[a] This *Calendar of Doubts* is not proposed as a temporary, but as a renewable Thing, to be continued down to after-ages, with an Expunction of such Queries as are fully solved, and the insertion of new ones as they arise, till Philosophy is compleated   But I do not find any such *Calendar* extant in form, as it might, perhaps, to advantage, be kept in all *Philosophical Societies*, or Meetings of *learned Men*   Des Cartes made Doubting the first Principle of his *Philosophy*, Mr *Glanvil* wrote his *Scepsis Scientifica* to shew that all dogmatical Doctrine is vain and the Mother of *Ignorance*   The Motto of the *Royal Society* is *Nullius in Verba* many Doubts and Heads of Enquiries are contained in the *Philosophical Transactions*, and the Works of Mr *Boyle*, and Sir *Isaac Newton*, at the End of his *Opticks*, has left a set of Queries of this kind that might be enlarged to *Calendars*, by a judicious *Collection* from various Authors   And with this view may be consulted *Alexander Tassoni Pensieri diversi*, *Arn Seuguerdii Exercitationes Physicæ*, the Works of *La Mothe le Vayer*, M *Bayle*, &c

[b] Dr *Primrose* wrote upon the *vulgar Errors of Physick*, but Dr *Brown*, in his *Pseudodoxia Epidemica*, seems to have expressly intended to supply, in a general and extensive manner, the *Desideratum* here pointed out   To those who would continue the Design, the learned *Morhof* recommends the perusal of *Meric Casaubon's Treatise of Credulity and Incredulity* and adds, that a diligent Enquiry should be made into the *Cause and Origin of Errors*, upon a discovery whereof our Admiration presently ceases, and absurd *Opinions* sink that might otherwise be supported by some imaginary Prodigy   See *Morhof's Polyhistor*, Tom II Lib II. Part I. Cap 1 Sect 9

[c] The Work here proposed is of vast extent, and a fit Undertaking for a *Society* as intended to include all the *ancient and modern Systems of Philosophy*, or the History of *Knowledge* thro' all Ages and Countries   Considerable Progress has, however, been made in it, particularly by *Vossius de Poulosophia*, & *Philosophorum Sectis*, continued with a Supplement by *Russel*, printed at *Jena*, in the year 1705, by *Pancirollus de Rebus Inventis & Perditis*, by *Paschius de Novis Inventis*,

Lives of the old Philosophers, *Plutarch's* Collection of their Opinions, the Citations of *Plato*, the Confutations of *Ariftotle*, and the fcatter'd Relations of other Books, whether ecclefiaftical or heathen , as *Lactantius*, *Philo*, *Philoftratus*, &c For fuch a Work is not yet extant and we would advife it to be done diftinctly, fo that each *Philofophy* be drawn out and continued feparate, and not ranged under Titles and Collections, as *Plutarch* has done For every *Philofophy*, when entire, fupports itfelf, and its Doctrines thus add Light and Strength to each other· which, if feparated, found ftrange and harfh Thus, when we read in *Tacitus*, the Acts of *Nero*, or *Claudius*, clothed with the circumftances of Times, Perfons, and Occafions, every thing feems plaufible, but when the fame are read in *Suetonius*, diftributed under Chapters and Common-places, and not defcribed in the order of Time, they look monftrous, and abfolutely incredible And the cafe is the fame with *Philofophy* propofed entire, and difmember'd, or cut into Articles Nor do we exclude from this *Calendar*, the modern Theories and Opinions, as thofe of *Paracelfus*, elegantly reduced by *Severinus* into a Body and Harmony of *Philofophy*, or of *Telefius*, who, in reftoring the *Philofophy* of *Parmenides*, has turned their own weapons againft the Peripateticks, or of *Gibert*, who revived the Doctrines of *Philolaus*, or of any other, provided he be worthy But as there are whole Volumes of thefe Authors extant, we would only have the Refult drawn out, and joined to the reft [a]. And fo much for Physics, *and its* Appendages.

S E C T. V.

Of METAPHYSICKS.

1. TO METAPHYSICKS we affign the *Enquiry of formal and final Caufes*. But an Opinion has prevailed, as if the *effential Forms* [b], or real Differences *of Things*, were abfolutely undifcoverable by human means granting,

Metaphyficks the Enquiry *after* Forms, *and* final *at* Caufes.

M 2

Inventis, quibus facem pratulit Antiquitas, by *Stanley*, in his *Lives of the Philofophers*, by *Herbelot*, in his *Bibliotheque Univerfelle*, by M *Bayle*, in his *Dictionary*, &c For more *Collections, Hiftories,* and *Writings* to this purpofe, fee *Struvii Bibliotheca Philofophica*, Morhof's *Polyhiftor*, and *Stollii Introductio in Hiftoriam Literariam*

[a] Many, perhaps, may imagine that the Ufefulnefs of fuch a Work would not fufficiently reward the Labour required to compile it but feveral Advantages would attend it Thus, in particular, it might fhew how *Philofophies* have been, through all Ages, borrowed from one another, fo that 'tis almoft impoffible to find or invent one that has not been on foot before, that the modern electic Philofophy, is but the revival of an old one, that even when *notional Philofophy* prevailed, yet Works were performed &c and, in effect, prove to *univerfal Philofophy*, what *literary Hiftory* is to *Hiftory in general*, that is, in the Language of our Author, its Eye

[b] Obferve, that by *Forms* the Author means the fpecifick Differences of Things, whatever they be at the laft, or that which fpecifically diftinguifhes one Thing from another, a Man from a Horfe. Rofemary from Thyme, Cryftal from Diamond, Light from Heat, &c without ufing the Word in the feemingly definitive, but abftrufe Senfe of *Ariftotle* and his Followers, who make a *Form* to be a *Subftance* feen by nobody, but a Thing exifting by itfelf in a fingle point, fo as to be the active Principle, or fole Caufe of all Actions and Operations

at the fame time, that if they could be difcover'd, this, of all the Parts of Knowledge, would be the moft worthy of Enquiry As to the poffibility of the Thing, there are indolent Difcoverers, who feeing nothing but Sea and Sky, abfolutely deny there can be any Land beyond them But 'tis manifeft that *Plato*, a Man of a fublime Genius, who took a view of every thing as from a high Rock, faw in his *Doctrine of Ideas*, that "*Forms were* ' *the true Object of Knowledge*," tho' he loft the advantage of this juft Opinion, by contemplating and grafping at Forms totally abftracted from Matter, and not as determined in it[a] whence he turned afide to Theological Speculations, and therewith infected all his *Natural Philofophy* But if with diligence, ferioufnefs, and fincerity, we turn our eyes to Action and Ufe, we may find, and become acquainted with thofe *Forms*, the knowledge whereof will wonderfully enrich and profper human Affairs

2 The *Forms of Subftance*, indeed, viz the *Species of Creatures*[b], are fo complicated and interwoven, that the Enquiry into them is either vain, or fhould be laid afide for a time, and refumed after the *Forms* of a more fimple nature have been duly fifted and difcover'd For as 'twere neither eafy nor ufeful to difcover the *Form* of a Sound that fhall make a Word, fince Words, b, the Compofition and Tranfpofition of Letters, are infinite, but practicable and eafy to difcover the Form of a Sound expreffing a fingle Letter, or by what Collifion, or Application of the Organs of the Voice it was made, and as thefe *Forms* of Letters being known, we are thence directly led to enquire the *Forms* of Words So, to enquire the *Form* of an Oak, a Lion, Gold, Water, or Air, were at prefent vain, but to enquire the *Form* of Denfity, Rarity, Heat, Cold, Gravity, Levity, and other *Schemes of Matter and Motions*, which, like the Letters of the Alphabet, are few in number, yet make and fupport the *Effences* and *Forms* of all Subftances, is what we would endeavour after, as conftituting and determining that Part of *Metaphyficks* we are now upon

3 Nor does this hinder *Phyficks* from confidering the fame *Natures*, in their fluxile Caufes only Thus, if the *Caufe of Whitenefs* in *Snow*, or *Froth*, were enquired into, 'tis judged to be a fubtile intermixture of Air with Water but this is far from being the *Form of Whitenefs*, fince Air intermix'd with powder'd Glafs, or Cryftal, is alfo judged to produce Whitenefs, no lefs than when mix'd with Water This, therefore, is only the efficient Caufe, and no other than the Vehicle of the *Form*[c]. But if the Enquiry be made in *Metaphyficks*, it will be found that two tranfparent Bodies, intermix'd in their optical portions, and in a fimple order, make Whitenefs. *This part of* METAPHYSICKS *I find defective* and no wonder, becaufe in the method of Enquiry hitherto ufed, the *Forms of Things* can never appear The misfortune lies here, that Men have accuftom'd themfelves to hurry away, and abftract their Thoughts too haftily, and carry them too remote from

Expe-

---

[a] As Mr *Boyle* has excellently fhewn, by a large Induction of *Experiments*, and *Crucial Inftances*, wherewith moft of his *Phyfical Enquiries* are enriched

[b] As Plants, Animals, Minerals, the Elements Fire, Air, Water, Earth, &c

[c] That is the *Form* is contained in it, but the Analyfis not carried far enough, to fhew the *Form* itfelf, or what Whitenefs is, independent of the Thing wherein it refides

Experience and Particulars, and given themselves wholly up to their own Meditations and Arguments [a].

4 The use of this Part of *M taphysicks* is recommended by two princi- *Its Use to* pal Things *first*, as 'tis the Office and Excellence of all *Sciences* to shorten *shorten the* the long turnings and windings of *Experience*, so as to remove the ancient *way to Know-* complaint of the scantiness of Life, and the tediousness of Art; this is best *ledge* perform'd by collecting and uniting the *Axioms of the Sciences* into more general ones, that shall suit the Matter of all *Individuals* For the *Sciences* are like Pyramids, erected upon the single Basis of *History* and *Experience*, and therefore a *History of Nature is* (1) *the Basis of Natural Philosophy*; and (2) the first Stage from the Basis is PHYSICKS, and (3) that nearest the Vertex METAPHYSICKS But (4) for the Vertex itself, " *the* " *Work which God worketh from the beginning to the end*," or the *summary Law of Nature*, we doubt whether human Enquiry can reach it But for the other three, they are the true *Floorings of the Sciences* And as that *Science* is the most excellent, which least burthens the Understanding by its multiplicity, this Property is found in *Metaphysicks*, as it contemplates those *simple Forms of Things*, Density, Rarity, &c which we call *Forms of the first Class*. for tho' these are few, yet, by their Commensurations, and Co-ordinations, they constitute all *Truth* [b]

5 The *second Thing* that ennobles this Part of *Metaphysicks*, relating to *And set free* *Forms*, is, that it releases the human Power, and leads it into an immense *the human* and open Field of Work For *Physicks* directs us thro' narrow rugged *Power*; Paths, in imitation of the crooked ways of ordinary Nature but the ways of Wisdom are every where wide, and abounding in plenty, and variety of means. *Physical Causes*, indeed, by means of new Inventions, afford light and direction in a like case again but *he that understands a* FORM, *knows the ultimate possibility of superinducing that Nature upon all kinds of Matter*, and is therefore the less restrained, or tied down in his working, either as to the Basis of the Matter, or the Condition of the Efficient [c].

6 The *second Part of* METAPHYSICKS, is the *Enquiry of final Causes* · *The second* which we note not as wanting, but as ill-placed these *Causes* being usually *part of Meta-* sought in *Physicks*, not in *Metaphysicks*, to the great prejudice of *Philosophy* *physicks is* *final Causes*.

for

[a] It is easy to observe, that Mr *Boyle's Enquiries into the Origin of Forms and Qualities in Bodies*, endeavour to supply this *Deficiency*, proceed upon the Directions here laid down, and particularly keep close to *Experience* See the *Abridgment* of his Works, *Vol* 1 *pag* 187, to the end of that Volume He seems also to have chose for his *Enquiry* the very Subjects pointed out by the Lord *Bacon*, viz *Heat, Cold, Gravity, Levity, Density, Rarity*, &c as the simplest and fittest to lay the Foundation for discovering the more *complex Forms of Creatures*, particular *Natures*, or *systematical Beings*, as *Plants, Animals*, and *Minerals*, in their *integral Subdivisions* respectively whence we are, for instance, to derive the medicinal Virtues of Herbs, Roots, Flowers, &c For *Physicks*, and *Metaphysicks*, have not obtained their End, till *Forms* are discovered, the Knowledge whereof will enable Mankind to produce Effects, in all possible Cases, equal or superior to those of *Nature*, and give us a great Command of her Works, as more fully appears in the *Novum Organum*

[b] That is, a Knowledge of *simple Forms*, or the *specifick Essences of general Qualities in Matter and Motion*, will, by *Involution* and *Evolution* (to use an algebraical Phrase) constitute and explain all the Truths of *Philosophy*, whose Perfection rests in the Knowledge of *Forms*

[c] That is, a *Knowledge of Forms*, will enable Mankind to effect all physical Possibilities, as is hereafter particularly shewn and illustrated by Examples in the *Novum Organum*.

for the treating of *final Causes* in *Physicks*, has driven out the *Enquiry of phy-sical ones*, and made Men rest in *specious* and *shadowy Causes*, without ever searching in earnest, after such as are *real*, and *truly physical* And this was not only done by *Plato*, who constantly anchors upon this shore, but by *Aristotle*, *Galen*, and others, who frequently introduce such *Causes* as these. " *The Hairs of the Eye-lids are for a Fence to the Sight   The Bones for Pillars* " *and rest to bear the Bodies of Animals   The Leaves of Trees are to defend* " *the Fruit from the Sun and Wind   The Clouds are designed for watering the* " *Earth, &c*" All which are properly alledg'd in *Metaphysicks*, but in *Physicks are* impertinent, and as Remoras to the Ship, that hinder the Sciences from holding on their course of Improvement, and introducing a neglect of searching after *physical Causes* And therefore the Natural Philo-sophies of *Democritus*, and others, who allow no God or Mind in the frame of Things, but attribute the Structure of the Universe to infinite Essays and Trials of Nature, or what they call Fate, or Fortune, and assign'd the Causes of particular things to the necessity of Matter, without any inter-mixture of *final Causes*, seem, so far as we can judge from the Remains of their Philosophy, much more solid, and to have gone deeper into Nature, with regard to *physical Causes*, than the Philosophy of *Aristotle* or *Plato* and this only because they never meddled with final Causes, which the others were perpetually inculcating Tho' in this respect, *Aristotle* is more culpable than *Plato*, as dropping *God*, the Fountain of *Final Causes*, and substi-tuting Nature in his stead, and, at the same, receiving *final Causes* thro' his affection to *Logick*, not *Theology*

Their Office and Use

7 These *final Causes*, however, are not false, or unworthy of Enquiry in *Metaphysick*, but their excursion into the limits of *physical Causes*, hath made a great devastation in that Province, otherwise, when contain'd within their own bounds, they are not repugnant to physical Causes for the Cause, that " *the Hairs of the Eye-lids are to preserve the Sight*," is no way contradictory to this, that " *Pilosity is incident to the Orifices of Moist-* " *ure*," and so of the rest these two kinds of Causes agreeing excellently together, the one expressing the Intention, and the other the Consequence only

8 Nor does this call Divine Providence in question, but rather highly confirms and exalts it for as he is a greater Politician, who can make others the Instruments of his Will, without acquainting them with his Designs, than he who discloses himself to those he employs, so the Wisdom of God appears more wondrous, when Nature intends one thing, and Providence draws out another, than if the Characters of Providence were stamped upon all the Schemes of Matter, and natural Motions So *Aristotle* had no need of a *God*, after having once impregnated Nature with *final Causes*, and laid it down, that " *Nature does nothing in vain*, *always obtains her Ends, when* " *Obstacles are removed, &c*" But *Democritus*, and *Epicurus*, when they advanced their Atoms, were thus far tolerated by some, but when they as-serted the Fabrick of all things to be raised by a fortuitous Concourse of these Atoms, without the help of *Mind*, they became universally ridiculous. So far are *physical Causes* from drawing Men off from *God*, and Providence,

that,

that, on the contrary, the *Philosophers* employ'd in discovering them can find no rest, but by flying to God or Providence at last [a].

SECT. VI.

Of Natural Magick.

1. THE Practical Doctrine of Nature we likewise necessarily divide into *two Parts*, corresponding to those of the *Speculative* [b], for *Physicks*, or the Enquiry of efficient and material Causes, produces Mechanicks, and *Metaphysicks*, the *Enquiry of Forms*, produces Magick [c], whilst the Enquiry of *final Causes* is a barren thing, or as a Virgin consecrated to God. We here understand that *Mechanicks*, which is coupled with physical Causes, for besides the bare *effective* or *empirical Mechanicks*, which has no dependance on *Physicks*, and belongs to *Natural History*, there is another not absolutely *operative*, and yet not strictly *philosophical*. For all Discoveries of Works, either had their rise from accident, and so were handed down from age to age, or else were sought by design: and the latter were either discovered by the *light of Causes and Axioms*, *or acquired by extending, transferring or compounding some former Inventions*. which is a thing more ingenious and sagacious than *philosophical*. But the *Mechanicks* here understood is that treated by *Aristotle* promiscuously, by *Hero* in his *Pneumaticks*, by that very diligent Writer in *Metallicks, George Agricola*, and by numerous others in particular subjects [d]: so that we have no omission to note in this point, only that the *miscellaneous Mechanicks*, after the example of *Aristotle*, should have been more carefully continued by the Moderns, especially with regard to such Contrivances whose Causes are more obscure, or their Effects more noble [e]. whereas the Writers upon these subjects perform very superficially. And it appears to us, that scarce any thing in Nature can be fundamentally discovered, either by accident, experimental attempts, or the light of physical Causes, but only by the *discovery of Forms* [f]. Since, therefore,

The practical Doctrine of Nature divided in correspondence to the theoretical, whence rational Mechanicks.

And Magick, which is defective.

---

[a] This Subject is prosecuted by Mr *Boyle*, in a particular *Treatise*, entitled, *An Enquiry into the final Causes of natural Things*.

[b] See above of *Philosophy*, Sect III 9

[c] In what sense, *Magick* is here understood, see below, § 2

[d] Who describe such *Arts, Experiments,* or *Inventions* as are used in ordinary Life

[e] Instances of this kind are, perhaps, the *artificial Stone* of the ancients, wherewith they built their Amphitheatres and Monuments of perpetuity; the *working the Asbestus into incombustible Cloth*, the making of a soft or *malleable Glass*, &c. See *Pancirollus de Rebus memorabilibus sive deperditis*

[f] The common Method of *Invention*, for want of a Knowledge of *Forms*, proceeds upon a mixture of *physical Reasoning*, and *repeated Trials*, by which means several Discoveries have been made: but if *Forms* were known, that is, what particulars constitute things, or give them their several Natures, nothing would then be left to accident, but Men might proceed directly

therefore we have set down as wanting tha part of *Metaphyficks* which treats of *Fo* , it follows that NATURAL MAGICK, *which is relative to it, muſt ..... be ..... ng*

2 We here underſtand *Magick* in its ancient and honourable ſenſe among the *Perſa* , it ſtood for a ſublimer Wiſdom , or a knowledge of the relations of univerſal Nature and we would have it ſignify *that Science, which leads to the knowledge of hidden Forms, for producing great Effects , and by joining Agents to Patients , ſetting the Capital Works of Nature to view* The common *Natural Magick* found in Books, gives us only ſome childiſh and ſuperſtitious traditions and obſervations of the Sympathies and Antipathies of Things , or occult and ſpecific Properties , which are uſually intermix'd with many trifling *Experiments*, admired rather for their diſguiſe, than for themſelves but as to the truth of Nature, this differs from the *Science* we propoſe, as much as the Romances of *Arthur of Britain, Hugh of Bourdeaux*, or other *imaginary Heroes*, do from the *Commentaries of Cæſar*, in truth of narration *Cæſar* in reality performed greater things, tho' not by *Romantick means*, than ſuch *fabulous Heroes* are feign'd to do This kind of Learning is well repreſented by the *Fable of Ixion* , who thinking to enjoy *Juno*, the Goddeſs of Power, embraced a Cloud , and thence produced *Centaurs* and *Chimæras* for ſo thoſe who, with a hot and impotent deſire, are carried to ſuch things as they ſee only thro' the fumes and clouds of imagination , inſtead of producing *Works*, beget nothing but vain Hopes, and monſtrous Opinions This degenerate *natural Magick* has alſo an effect like certain ſleepy Medicines, which procure pleaſing Dreams · for ſo it firſt lays the Underſtanding aſleep, by introducing ſpecifick properties, and occult virtues, whence men are no longer attentive to the diſcovery of *real Cauſes*, but reſt ſatisfied in ſuch indolent and weak Opinions and thus it inſinuates numberleſs pleaſing Fictions, like ſo many Dreams

3 And here we may properly obſerve that thoſe *Sciences* which depend too much upon *Fancy* and *Faith*, as this *degenerate Magick, Alchemy, Aſtrology*, &c have their *Means* and their *Theory* more monſtrous than their *End* and *Action* The converſion of *Quickſilver* into *Gold* is hard to conceive , tho' it may much more probably be effected by a man acquainted with the nature of gravity, colour, malleability, fixedneſs, volatility, the principles of Metals and Menſtruums, &c than by one who is ignorant of theſe *Natures*, by the bare projection of a few grains of the *Elixir* Underſtand the ſame of the prolongation of Youth, or retarding of old Age , which may more rationally be expected, by obſerving a ſet of Rules, well form'd upon the Art of Medicine, than from a few drops of any precious Liquor or Quinteſſence[a] But men are ſo headſtrong and notional, as not only

a refult from the Knowledge, to the moſt capital *Works*, without intermediate Trials But this anticipating the Doctrine of the *Novum Organum* , tho' with a view to prepare the way to it and if we could ſuppoſe ourſelves Spectators of the Operation that paſſes in the Minds of induſtrious Inventors, ſuch as Mr *Boyle*, or Sir *Iſaac Newton*, for inſtance, ſurely we ſhould perceive ſomething like this *Inveſtigation of Forms*, here meant by the Author, or a train of Thoughts, that after due excluſions and rejections, lead up to the *Invention*

[a] The Author's Enquiry into *Life and Death*, proceeds upon no ſuch weak or ſuperſtitious Hopes, but one ſolid way of phyſical Reaſon, Experiment, Obſervation, laborious Search, and the Inveſtigation of *Forms*

only to promife themfelves Things impoffible, but alfo hope to obtain the moft difficult Ends, without labour or fweat

4 This *Practical Doctrine of Nature* requires two APPENDAGES, of very great confequence The *first* is, that AN INVENTORY BE MADE OF THE STOCK OF MANKIND, containing their whole *Poffeffions* and *Fortunes*, whether proceeding from *Nature* or *Art*, with the addition alfo of things formerly known, but now loft fo that he who goes upon new Difcoveries, may have a knowledge of what has already been done [a] This INVENTORY will be the more artificial and ufeful, if it alfo contain things of every kind, which, according to common Opinion, are *impoffible*; as likewife fuch as feem'd next to impoffible, yet have been effected; the one to whet the human *Invention*, and the other to direct it, fo that from thefe *Optatives* and *Potentials*, *Actives* may the more readily be deduced

5 The *fecond Thing* is that a CALENDAR BE MADE OF SUCH EXPERIMENTS AS ARE MOST EXTENSIVELY USEFUL, AND THAT LEAD TO THE DISCOVERY OF OTHERS For example, the *Experiment of artificial freezing*, by means of *Ice* and *Bay-Salt*, is of infinite extent, and difcovers a fecret Method of Condenfation, of great fervice to mankind [b] *Fire* is ready at hand for rarefaction, but the *means of Condenfation* are wanted. And it would greatly fhorten the way to Difcoveries, to have *a particular Catalogue of thefe* LEADING EXPERIMENTS [c]

Two appendages wanted to the practical Doctrine of Nature viz (1.) An Inventory of Knowledge.

And (2) a Calendar of Leading Experiments.

---

[a] This is another of the *grand Works*, conceived in the Mind of the Author, that requires the united Labours of many to execute The *Literary Hiftory*, the *Hiftory of Arts*, and other *Defiderata*, above fet down, might, if extant, afford great Light and Affiftance in the Collection Among the Books of principal ufe to the Defign, may be reckoned the Natural Hiftories of particular Nations, Travels Voyages, Books of Arts, Books of Inventions, and *Univerfal Dictionaries*, for inftance *Pifo's Hiftories of the Indies*, *Thevenot Tavernier*, *Dampier*, and *Frezier's Voyages*, *Neri's* Art of Glafs the Marquis of *Worcefter's* Scantlings of Inventions, *Parnollu. de Rebus memorabilibus*, *Pegelius's Thefaurus Rerum Selectarum*, *de Lana's Magifterium Natura & Artis*, *Fafchius de Inventis novis & antiquis*, *Becher's Narrifche Weifheit*, but particularly Mr *Chambers's Cyclopadia* See *Morhof's Polyhiftor* Tom I. Cap xx *de Fructu omnis Hiftoria Bibliothecaria*

[b] How far this Experiment has been applied by Mr *Boyle*, appears from his *Hiftory of Cold*, which proceeds almoft wholly upon it tho' it ftill remains capable of infinite applications, as to the *Concentration of Wines*, *Vinegar*, *Spirits*, &c the procuring of *frefh Water at Sea*, the making of *Salt* out of Sea-Water, &c

[c] This *Work*, fo far as I know, remains unattempted, but might be fet about to good advantage, fince the experimental Labours of Mr *Boyle*, Dr *Hook*, and many other eminent Members of the *Royal Society*, and *French Academy* Of what fervice *leading Experiments* are in Philofophy, may appear from the Difcoveries of Mr *Boyle*, and Sir *Ifaac Newton*, which were generally made by their means.

SECT. VII.

Of MATHEMATICKS.

Te Office and
Uſe of Mathe-
maticks
I.

'TWAS well obſerved by *Ariſtotle*, that PHYSICKS and MATHEMA-
TICKS produce PRACTICE, or MECHANICKS therefore, as we have
treated both the *ſpeculative* and *practical* part of the DOCTRINE OF NA-
TURE; we ſhould alſo conſider MATHEMATICKS, as an *auxiliary Science*
to both: which being received into PHILOSOPHY, comes as a *third part*
after PHYSICKS and METAPHYSICKS But upon due recollection, if we deſign'd it as a ſubſtantial and *principal Science*; it were more agreeable to *Method*
and the Nature of the thing, to make it a part of *Metaphyſicks* For *Quan-*
tity, the *Subject of Mathematicks*, applied to *Matter*, is as the *Doſe of Na-*
ture, and productive of numerous Effects in Natural Things, and therefore
ought to be reckon'd among *eſſential Forms*. And ſo much did the power of
Figures and *Numbers* prevail with the ancients, that *Democritus* chiefly placed
the Principles of the Variety of Things in the figures of their Atoms· and
Pythagoras, aſſerted that the nature of things conſiſted of numbers. Thus
much is true, that of *natural Forms*, ſuch as we underſtand them, *Quantity*
is the moſt abſtracted, and ſeparable from Matter· and for this reaſon it
has been more carefully cultivated, and examin'd into, by mankind, than any
other *Forms*, which are all of them more immerſed in Matter. For, as, to
the great diſadvantage of the *Sciences*, 'tis natural for men's minds to delight
more in the open Fields of *Generals*, than in the Incloſures of *Particulars*,
nothing is found more agreeable than *Mathematicks*, which fully gratifies
this appetite of expatiating and ranging at large. But as we regard not only
Truth and Order, but alſo the benefits and advantages of mankind, it ſeems
beſt, ſince *Mathematicks* is of great uſe in *Phyſicks, Metaphyſicks, Mechanicks,*
and *Magicks*, to make it an *Appendage*, or Auxiliary to them all. And this
we are in ſome meaſure obliged to do; from the fondneſs, and towering
notions of *Mathematicians*, who would have their *Science* preſide over *Phy-*
ſicks[a]. 'Tis a ſtrange fatality, that *Mathematicks* and *Logicks*, which ought
to

[a] The learned *Morhof* thus confirms the juſtneſs of this Obſervation, "To ſay the truth,
the modern Philoſophy has ſtill the ſame Defect, for at this day moſt of our *Philoſophical*
Doctrine is made *Mathematical*, ſo as to appear ſubtile in the demonſtration of thoſe Properties which come chiefly under the conſideration of *Mathematicians*, whilſt in diſcovering
the *internal Cauſes of Things*, the *Mathematicians* prove as inſufficient as the Peripateticks, who,
inſtead of *Mathematicks*, make *Logick* preſide over *Phyſicks*. The middle way ſhould be choſe
betwix theſe two extremes, and the ſenſe and meaning of Nature diſcovered" See *Morhof's*
Polybiſt Tom II pag 149 If this Doctrine, ſo fully laid down by the Lord *Bacon*, had been
followed, the Moderns might probably have made many more ſubſtantial Diſcoveries in *Natural*
Philoſophy, Anatomy Chemiſtry, and *Medicine*, than by a raſh application of *Mathematicks*,
which, inſtead of promoting, has prejudiced theſe Sciences.

to be but handmaids to *Phyſicks*, ſhould boaſt their certainty before it, and even exerciſe dominion againſt it But the *place and dignity of this Science* is a ſecondary conſideration, with regard to the thing itſelf

2. *Mathematicks* is either *pure* or *mix'd* To the *pure* belong the *Sciences Divided into pure and mix'd* employ'd about Quantity, wholly abſtracted from Matter and *phyſical Axioms*. This has *two parts*, *Geometry*, and *Arithmetick*, the one regarding *continued*, and the other *diſcrete Quantity* Theſe two *Sciences* have been cultivated with very great ſubtilty and application · but in plain *Geometry* there has nothing conſiderable been added to the Labours of *Euclid*; tho' he lived many ages ſince. The *Doctrine of Solids* has not been proſecuted and extended, equal to its uſe and excellency, neither by the ancients nor the moderns and in *Arithmetick* there is ſtill wanting a ſufficient VARIETY OF SHORT AND COMMODIOUS METHODS OF CALCULATION, eſpecially *The Defects of pure Mathematicks* with regard to *Progreſſions*; whoſe uſe in *Phyſicks* is very conſiderable Neither is *Algebra* brought to perfection As for the *Pythagorical* and *Myſtical Arithmetick*, which began to be recovered from *Proclus*, and certain Remains of *Euclid*, 'tis a *ſpeculative Excurſion* The Mind having this misfortune, that when it proves unequal to ſolid and uſeful things, it ſpends itſelf upon ſuch as are unprofitable [a]

3. *Mix'd Mathematicks* has for its ſubject *Axioms*, and the *Parts of Phyſicks*, and conſiders Quantity ſo far as may be aſſiſting to illuſtrate, demonſtrate, and actuate thoſe, for without the help of *Mathematicks*, many parts of Nature could neither be ſufficiently comprehended, clearly demonſtrated, nor dexterouſly fitted for uſe And of this kind are *Perſpective*, *Muſick*, *Aſtronomy*, *Coſmography*, *Architecture*, *Mechanicks*, &c. In *mix'd Mathematicks* we at preſent find no *entire Parts deficient*, but foretell there will be many found hereafter, if Men are not wanting to themſelves: For if *Phyſicks* be daily improving, and drawing out new *Axioms*, 'twill continually be wanting freſh aſſiſtances from *Mathematicks*, ſo that the *Parts of mix'd Mathematicks*, muſt gradually grow more numerous [b]. *The Defects of mix'd Mathematicks increaſe as Phyſicks improves.*

[a] No part of Learning has perhaps been more cultivated ſince this Author wrote than *Mathematicks*, inſomuch, that every other Science, or the Body of Philoſophy itſelf, ſeems rendered *Mathematical* The Doctrine of *Solids* has been improv'd by ſeveral; the ſhorter ways of *Calculation* here noted as deficient, are in good meaſure ſupplied by exact Tables of *Logarithms*. *Algebra* has been ſo far improved and applied, as to rival, or almoſt prejudice, the *ancient Geometry* Add to this, the new Diſcoveries of the *Method of Fluxions*, the *Method of Tangents*, the *Doctrine of Infinites*, the *Squaring of Curves*, &c For the preſent Syſtem of *Mathematical Learning*, ſee *Wolfii Elementa Matheſeos univerſa*, in two Volumes 4to, printed at *Hall* in the year 1715 or for a more curſory View, Father *Caſtel's Mathematique Univerſelle*, publiſhed this year 1731 But for the *Hiſtory* of Mathematicks, ſee *Voſſius de univerſa Matheſeos Natura & Conſtitutione*, the Almageſt of *Ricciolus*, *Morhof's Polyhiſt Mathemat* and *Wolfius's Commentatio de Scriptis Mathematicis*, at the End of the *ſecond Volume* of his *Elementa Matheſeos univerſa*.

[b] As in effect they are at this day, by the modern improvements in *Opticks, Phonicks, Hydroſtaticks, Pneumaticks, Fortification, Gunnery, Surveying*, &c.

SECT. VIII.

The DOCTRINE OF MAN:
And first, of the HUMAN PERSON.

The subject and use of D...s in the Science

1 HAving gone thro' the *two parts* of PHILOSOPHY that relate to the DEITY, and to NATURE, we come now to the third, or the KNOWLEDGE OF OUR SELVES, which to us is the End of the *Sciences*, tho' but a part of Nature[a] And here we must admonish mankind, that all Divisions of the Sciences are to be understood, and employ'd, so as only to mark out and distinguish, not tear, separate, or make any solution of continuity in their body the contrary practice having render'd particular *Sciences barren*, *empty*, and *erroneous*, whilst they are not fed, supported and kept right, by their *common Parent* Thus we find *Cicero* complaining of *Socrates*, that he first disjoin'd *Philosophy* from *Rhetoric*, which is thence become a frothy, talkative Art So the Art of *Physick*, without the assistance of Natural Philosophy, differs but little from *Empiricism*

The Doctrine of Man divided into human and civil Philosophy

2 The DOCTRINE OF MAN divides itself into *two parts*, or into HUMAN and CIVIL PHILOSOPHY as it considers *Man separate*, *or joined in Society* HUMAN PHILOSOPHY consists in the *Sciences* that regard the *Body*, and those that regard the *Soul of Man*. But before we descend to a more particular distribution, 'tis proper to make one GENERAL SCIENCE, OF THE NATURE AND STATE OF MAN, which certainly deserves to be freed from the rest, and reduced to a *Science* by itself And this will consist of such Things as are common, both to the *Body* and the *Soul*. It may likewise be divided into two parts, *viz* according to the *individual Nature of Man*, and the *Connexion of the Soul and Body* The former we call the DOCTRINE OF THE PERSON OF MAN, and the other the DOCTRINE OF UNION All which being common and mix'd matters, cannot be separately referr'd to the *Sciences* that regard the *Body*, nor to those that regard the *Soul*

The Doctrine of the human Person

3 The DOCTRINE OF THE HUMAN PERSON principally consists in two Things, the Consideration of the miseries of mankind, and its prerogatives or excellencies There are many Writings, both Philosophical and Theological, that elegantly and copiously bewail the human Miseries and it is an agreeable and wholesome topic But the *Prerogatives of mankind* are not hitherto described *Pindar* in his Praise of *Hiero* says, with his usual elegance, that *he crop't the Tops of every Virtue* and methinks it would greatly contribute to the encouragement and honour of mankind, to have these *Tops, or utmost extents of human Nature, collected from faithful History* I mean *the greatest length which human Nature of itself has ever gone, in the several ENDOWMENTS of BODY AND MIND*[b] Thus 'tis said of *Cæsar*, that he could dictate to five amanuenses at once. We read also of the ancient Rhetoricians,

as

---

[a] See above Sect. III 1

[b] The Author himself might surely make an eminent Instance of this kind, as having grasp'd the whole compass of ancient knowledge, and struck out new Methods for improving all the Sciences, and extending the Empire of Man over the Works of Nature

as *Protagoras*, and *Gorgias*, and of the ancient Philosophers, as *Callisthenes*, *Possidonius* and *Carneades*, who could, with eloquence and copiousness, dispute off hand, on either side of an argument which shews the powers of the Mind to advantage. So does also what *Cicero* relates of his master *Archias*, *viz.* that he could make extempore a large number of excellent Verses upon the common transactions of life. 'Tis a great honour to the Memory, that *Cyrus* or *Scipio* could call so many thousands of men by their names   Nor are the victories gain'd in the moral virtues less signal than those of the intellectual faculties   What an example of patience is that of *Anaxarchus*, who when put to the torture, bit off his own tongue, and spit it in the Tyrant's face ? We have many instances of great serenity and composure of mind at the time of Death, as particularly in the Centurion, mention'd by *Tacitus*, who being bid by the Soldier, appointed his executioner, to stretch out his neck strongly, replied, " *I wish you may strike as strongly* " Sir *Thomas More*, the day before his execution, being waited upon by his Barber, to know if he would have his hair off, refus'd it , with this answer, that " *the King and he had a dispute about his* Head, *and till that were ended he would bestow no cost upon it*   And even when he had laid his head upon the block, he raised himself again a little, and gently putting his long beard aside, said, *this surely has not offended the King*   By these examples it will appear that the Miracles of human Nature, and the utmost Powers and Faculties, both of Mind and Body, are what we would have collected into a Volume, that should be a kind of Register of human Triumphs   And with regard to such a Work, we commend the Design of *Valerius Maximus* and *Pliny*, but not their care and choice [a]

4 The Doctrine of Union, *or of the common Tye of Soul and Body*, has two parts   for 's, in all alliances, there is mutual Intelligence, and mutual Offices , so *the Union of the Mind and Body* requires a description of the manner wherein they discover, and act upon, each other, by *Notices*, or *Indication* and *Impression*. The *Description by Indication*, has produced two *Arts of Prediction*, the one honoured with the Enquiry of *Aristotle*, and the other with that of *Hippocrates*   And tho' later Ages have debased these *Arts* with superstitious and fantastical mixtures , yet, when purged, and truly restored, they have a solid foundation in Nature, and use in Life   The *first* of these is *Physiognomy*, which, by the Lineaments of the Body, discovers the Dispositions of the Mind   The *second* is, the *Interpretation of Natural Dreams* , which, from the Agitations of the Mind, discovers the State and Dispositions of the Body   I find the former *deficient in one part* , for tho' *Aristotle* has, with great ingenuity and diligence, treated the Structure of the Body at rest [b], he dropt *the consideration of it in Motion or Gesture*, which is no less subject to the Observations of Art, and more useful than the other   For the Lineaments of the Body shew the general Inclinations and Dispositions of the Mind , whilst the Motions of the Face,

The Doctrine of Union betwixt Soul and Body.

The Doctrine of Gesture deficient

and

---

[a] Mr *Wanly's Wonders of the little World*, was a Work intended to supply, in some measure, this *Desideratum*, as himself intimates in the *Preface*

[b] See his *Physiognomica*, with the *Notes* of *Camillus Baldus*. See also *Baptista Porta's Opus Physiognomicum*.

and the Geftures of the other parts, not only do the fame, but alfo exprefs the prefent Difpofition and Inclination for as the *Tongue* applies to the *Ear*, fo does *Gefture* to the *Eye* And this is well known to many fubtile and defigning Perfons, who watchfully obferve the Countenance and Geftures of others ; and value themfelves for their talent of turning fuch Difcoveries to their own advantage And it muft be acknowledged an excellent way of difcovering Diffimulation in others, and of admonifhing Men to chufe proper times and opportunities for their Addreffes · which is no fmall part of *civil Prudence* A *Work upon this Doctrine of Gefture*, would not only prove ufeful in particular cafes, but ferve as a general Rule, for all Men laugh, weep, blufh, frown, *&c* alike and this holds of nearly all the more fubtile Motions [a] But for *Chiromancy*, 'tis abfolutely a vain thing, and unworthy to be mentioned among thofe we are now treating [b]

Interpretation of Dreams, its best Foundation 5 The INTERPRETATION OF NATURAL DREAMS has been much labour'd, but mix'd with numerous Extravagancies We fhall here only obferve of it, that at prefent it ftands not upon its beft Foundation, which is, that where the fame thing happens from an *internal Caufe*, as alfo ufually happens from an external one, there the external Action paffes into a Dream Thus the Stomach may be oppref's'd by a grofs internal Vapour, as well as by an external Weight whence thofe who have the *Night-mare*, dream that a Weight is laid upon them, with a great concurrence of Circumftances So again, the *Ulcers* being equally toffed by the agitation of the Waves at Sea, as by a collection of Wind in the *Hypochondria*. hence melancholy Perfons frequently dream of failing, and toffing upon the Waters. And Inftances of this kind are numerous [c].

The Doctrine of Impreffion reduced into the Affairs of the Body depend again on the Soul 6 The fecond part of the DOCTRINE OF UNION, which we call IMPRESSION, is not yet reduced to an Art, and but occafionally mentioned by Writers This alfo has *two parts* · as confidering (1) *how, and to what degree, the Humours and Conftitution of the Body may affect the Soul, or act upon it* and (2) *how, and to what degree, the Paffions and Apprehenfions of the Soul may affect and work upon the Body* The firft of thefe we fometimes find touched in *Medicine*, but it has ftrangely infinuated itfelf into *Religion*. Phyficians prefcribe Remedies for the Difeafes of the Mind, *viz* Madnefs, Melancholy, *&c* as alfo to chear the Spirits, ftrengthen the Memory, *&c*. but for Diet, choice of Meats and Drinks, Wafhings, and other Obfervances

relating

---

[a] The learned *Mersc.* obferves, that this *Doctrine of reading the Minds of Men by external Signs* may be many ways ufeful to a *Politician*, and mentions an eminent Inftance thereof, from the *Relation of a certain* Venetian *Ambaffador, concerning the Court of Rome*, who, by this means, difcover'd how the Pope and Cardinals ftood affected to the *State of Venice* He afterwards enumerates the feveral Writers upon this Subject See his *Polyhiftor*, Tom II. Lib. III. *de Artious a materiis & Magia* See alfo an anonymous Treatife of *the different Wills of Men*, printed at *London*, in the year 1669

[b] Of the *Vanity of Chiromancy*, fee *Pafchius de rous Inventis*, p 604, *&c* and for other Authors, who have fhewn the weaknefs of this Art, fee *Stollii Introduct. in Hiftoriam Literariam*, pag 413

[c] Infomuch, that fome will affign the occafions of their Dreams from a recollection of what has paffed in relation to themfelves before-hand, or from the Tranfactions of the preceding Days It were to be wifhed we had a careful *Hiftory* of this kind drawn from Obfervation, and Experience, without any mixture of *Hypothefis* or *Fancy* For we might hence be led into a more rational and philofophical Knowledge of the *Mind* and its *Operations*

relating to the Body, they are found immoderately in the *Sect of the Py-*
thagoreans, the *Manichean Heresy*, and the Law of *Mahomet*. There are
also numerous and strict Ordinances in the *ceremonial Law*, prohibiting the
eating of Blood and Fat, and distinguishing the unclean Animals from the
clean, for Food. Even the *Christian Religion*, tho' it has thrown off the
Veil of Ceremonies, still retains the use of fasting, abstinence, and other
things that regard the subjection and humiliation of the Body; as things not
merely ritual, but advantageous. The root of all these Ordinances, besides the ceremony and exercise of Obedience, is, that the *Soul should sym-*
pathize and suffer with the Body.

7. The other part, which considers the *Operations of the Soul upon the* *And the Ac-*
Body, has likewise been received into *Medicine* for every prudent Physician *tions of the*
regards the *Accidents of the Mind*, as a principal Thing in his Cures, that *Soul upon the*
greatly promotes or hinders the Effects of all other Remedies. But one *Body*
Particular has been hitherto slightly touch'd, or not well examin'd, as its
usefulness and abstruse nature require, *viz how far a fix'd and rivetted Ima-*
gination may alter the Body of the Imaginant for tho' this has a manifest
power to hurt, it does not follow, it has the same to relieve no more than
because an Air may be so pestilent, as suddenly to destroy, another Air
should be so wholesome, as suddenly to recover. This would be an Enquiry of noble use, but it requires a *Delian Diver*; for it is deep plunged[a].

8. But among these DOCTRINES OF UNION, or *Consent of Soul and Body*, *An Enquiry*
there is none more necessary, than *an Enquiry into the proper Seat and Habi-* *after the Seat*
tation of each Faculty of the Soul in the Body, and its Organs. Some, in- *of the Soul re-*
deed, have prosecuted this Subject, but all usually delivered upon it is either *commended.*
controverted, or slightly examin'd, so as to require more pains and accuracy.
The opinion of *Plato*, which seats the *Understanding* in the *Brain, Courage* in
the *Heart*, and *Sensuality* in the *Liver*, should neither be totally rejected,
nor fondly received[b].

[a] The Author has begun this *Enquiry* in his SYLVA SYLVARUM, under the *Article* IMAGINA-
TION, and it has been since prosecuted by many, particularly with a view to the *Cure of Dif-*
eafes See *Pafchius de novis Inventis*, &c Cap VI *de Inventis Medicis*, the Art of curing by,
Expectation, *Medicina Mentis & Corporis Stahlii*, *Cafaubon* of Enthusiasm, *Malbranch's Re-*
ferche de la Verité, and *Morhof's Polyhistor*, Tom II pag 449, *&c.*

[b] This particular Enquiry, seems to have been almost over-look'd by the later *Philofophers*·
what has been done upon it, may, in some measure, appear from *Morhof's Polyhistor*, Tom II.
Part II Lib II Cap 48 *de Homine*, & Cap 29 *de Senfibus Animalium*, *Le Clerc's* Pneumato-
logia, *Struvii Bibliotheca Philofophica*, Cap V Sect. 10, & *Stollii Introduct in Hiftoriam Li-*
terariam, *de Pneumatologia*

SECT. IX.

Of the DOCTRINE *of the* HUMAN BODY.

The Doctrine of the Subject divided according to the four Perfections of the Body.

1. THE DOCTRINE OF THE HUMAN BODY divides itself according to the *Perfections* of the Body whereto it is subservient. These *Perfections* are four, viz (1) *Health*, (2) *Comeliness*, (3) *Strength*, and (4) *Pleasure*; to which correspond as Relatives, (1) the Arts of *Medicine*, (2) *Beauty*, (3) *Gymnastics*, and (4) the Art of *Elegance*. MEDICINE is a noble Art, and honourably descended, according to the *Poets*, who make *Apollo* the Divine God, and his Son *Æsculapius*, whom they also deify, the first *Physician*: the reason for as, in natural Things, the *Sun* is Author and Fountain of Life, so the *Physician*, who preserves Life, seems a Second Original thereof. But Medicine receives far greater honour from the Works of our Saviour, who was Physician both to Soul and Body; and made the latter the standing Subject of his *Miracles*, as the *Soul* was the constant Subject of his *Doctrine*.

Reasons of the Difficulties and Imperfections of this Medicine.

2. Of all the Things that Nature has created, the *human Body* is most capable of *Relief*, tho' this *Relief* be the most liable to Error. For as the subtilty and variety of the Subject affords many opportunities of *Cure*, so likewise a great facility of *Mistake*. And therefore, as the *Art*, especially at present, stands among the most *conjectural ones*, so the Enquiry into it is to be placed among the most subtile and difficult. For of all *natural Bodies*, we find none so variously compounded as the *human*. Vegetables are nourished by *Earth* and *Water*, Brutes by *Herbs* and *Fruits*, but Man feeds upon the Flesh of living Creatures, Herbs, Grain, Fruits, different Juices and Liquors, and these all prepared, preserved, dressed, and mixed in endless variety. Besides, the way of living among other Creatures is more simple, and the Affections that act upon the Body, fewer, and more uniform but *Man* in his Habitation, his Exercises, Passions, &c. undergoes numberless changes. This variable and subtile Composition, and Fabrick of the human Body, makes it, like a kind of curious *musical Instrument*, easily disordered and therefore the *Poets* justly join'd *Musick* and *Medicine* in *Apollo*, because the *Office of Medicine* is to tune the curious Organ of the *human Body*, and reduce it to Harmony.

The means of removing the Difficulties in these respects.

3. The *Subject* being so variable, has render'd the *Art* more *conjectural*; and left the more room for *Imposture*. Other *Arts* and *Sciences* are judged of by their Power and Ability, and not by Success, or Events. The *Lawyer* is judged by the *Ability* of his *Pleading*; not the Issue of the Cause. The *Pilot*, by directing his *Course*, and not by the Fortune of the *Voyage*: whilst the *Physician* has no *particular Act*, that clearly demonstrates his Ability, but is

principally

principally cenfured by the *Event* · which is very unjuft for who can tell if a Patient die or recover, whether it were by *Art*, or by *Accident*? Whence *Impofture* is frequently extoll'd, and *Virtue* decried. Nay, the Weaknefs and Credulity of Men is fuch, that they often prefer a *Mountebank*, or a *Cunning-Woman*, to a learned Phyficin The Poets were clear-fighted in difcerning this Folly, when they made *Æfculapius* and *Circe* Brother and Sifter, and both Children of *Apollo* For in all times, Witches, old Women, and Impoftors, have, in the vulgar opinion, ftood Competitors with Phyficians. And hence Phyficians fay to themfelves, in the words of *Solomon*, *If it befall to me, as befalleth to the Fools, why should I labour to be more wife?* And therefore one cannot greatly blame them, that they commonly ftudy fome other *Art*, or *Science*, more than their Profeffion Hence, we find among them *Poets, Antiquaries, Criticks, Politicians, Divines*, and in each kind more knowing than in Medicine, no doubt, becaufe they find that mediocrity, and excellency in their own *Art*, makes no difference in *Profit* or *Reputation* · for Men's Impatience of Difeafes, the Sollicitations of Friends, the Sweetnefs of Life, and the Inducement of Hope, make them depend upon Phyficians, with all their Defcts. But when this is ferioufly confider'd, it turns rather to the reproach, than the excufe of Phyficians who ought not hence to defpair, but to ufe greater diligence For we fee what a power the Subtilty of the Underftanding has over the variety both of the Matter and Form of Things There is nothing more variable than Men's Faces, yet we can remember infinite Diftinctions of them and a Painter, with a few Colours, the practice of the Hand and Eye, and help of the Imagination, could imitate thoufands, if brought before him As variable as Voices are, yet we can eafily diftinguifh them in different Perfons, and a Mimick will exprefs them to the life. Tho' the Sounds of Words differ fo greatly, yet Men can reduce them to a few fimple Letters. And certainly 'tis not the Infufficiency, or Incapacity of the Mind, but the remotenefs of the Object, that caufes thefe Perplexities and Diftrufts in the *Sciences* for as the *Senfe* is apt to miftake at great diftances, but not near at hand, fo is the *Underftanding* Men commonly take a view of Nature, as from a remote Eminence, and are too much amufed with *Generalities.* whereas, if they would defcend, and approach nearer to Particulars, and more exactly and confiderately examine into things themfelves, they might make more folid and ufeful Difcoveries The Remedy of this Error, therefore, is to quicken or ftrengthen the *Organ*, and thus to approach the Object No doubt, therefore, if *Phyficians*, leaving *Generalities* for a while, and fufpending their Affent, would advance towards Nature, they might be able to *vary their Art as Diftempers vary.* They fhould the rather endeavour this, becaufe the *Philofophies*, whereon *Phyficians*, whether *Methodifts* or *Chemifts*, depend, are trifling, and becaufe *Medicine, not founded on Philofophy, is a weak thing.* Therefore as *too extenfive Generals*, tho' true, do not bring Men home to action, there is more danger in fuch *Generals as are falfe* in themfelves, and feduce, inftead of directing the Mind. *Medicine*, therefore, has been rather *profefs'd*, than *labour'd* and yet more *labour'd* than *advanced*; as the pains

beſtow'd thereon, w re rather *circular* than *progreſſive* for I find great Repe-
t   , and b t l e new Matter, in the Writers of *Phyſick*

Medicine d
vided (1)
 Preſerva-
tion of Health,
2   Cure
of Diſeaſes
and (3) the
Prolongation
of Life.

2 We divide *Medicine* into *three parts*, or Offices, *viz* (1) *the Preſervation of Health*, (2) *the Cure of Diſeaſes*, and (3) *the Prolongation of Life.*
For this laſt part, *Phyſicians* ſeem to think it no capital part of *Medicine,*
but confound it with the other two. as ſuppoſing, that if *Diſeaſes* be prevented,
or cured after invaſion, *long Life* muſt follow of courſe But then they do
not conſider, that *both Preſervation and Cure regard only Diſeaſes, and ſuch
Prolongation of Life a intercepted by them* whence the means of ſpinning
out the full *Thread of Life,* or preventing, for a ſeaſon, that kind of Death
which gradually ſteals upon the Body by *ſimple Reſolution, and the waſting
of Age,* is a Subject that no Phyſician has treated ſuitably to its Merit·
Let none imagine we are here repeating the Decrees of *Fate and Providence,* by
eſtabliſhing a new Office of Medicine, for, doubtleſs, *Providence* alike diſ-
penſes all kinds of Deaths, whether they proceed from Violence, Diſeaſes, or
the courſe and period of Age, yet without excluding the uſe of *Remedies* and
Preparations for them I ſay do not were overruled, but adminiſter to *Nature and Fate*

Preſerva-
tion of Health

3 Many have unſkilfully written upon the PRESERVATION OF HEALTH ,
particularly by attending too much to the *Choice,* and too little to the *Quantity
of Diet.* As to *Quantity,* they, like the *Moral Philoſophers,* highly commend Moderation, whereas, both faſting changed to cuſtom, and full feeding, where a Man is uſed to it, are better *Preſervatives of Health,* than
thoſe Mediocrities they recommend, which commonly diſpirit Nature, and
unfit her to bear exceſs, or want, upon occaſion And for the *ſeveral Exerciſe*, which greatly conduce to the Preſervation of Health, no *Phyſician* has
well diſtinguiſhed, or obſerved them[b], tho' there be ſcarce any tendency to
a Diſeaſe, that may not be corrected by ſome appropriated *Exerciſe* Thus
Bowling is ſuited to the Diſeaſes of the Kidneys, Shooting with the long Bow,
to thoſe of the Lungs, Walking and Riding, to thoſe of the Stomach[c], &c

The Cure of
Diſeaſes im-
perfect
however

6 Great pains have been beſtow'd upon the CURE OF DISEASES, but
to ſmall purpoſe This part comprehends the *Knowledge of the Diſeaſes incident to the human Body,* together with their *Cauſes, Symptoms,* and *Cures*
In this ſecond Office of Medicine, there are many *Deficiencies* And firſt, we
may note the diſcontinuance of that uſeful Method of *Hippocrates, in writing Narratives of PARTICULAR CURES with diligence and exactneſs,* containing the Nature, the Cure, and Event of the *Diſtemper* And this remarkable
Precedent of one accounted the Father of his Art, need not to be backed with
Examples derived from other Arts, as from the prudent practice of the
Lawyers, who religiouſly enter down the more eminent Caſes, and new De-
ciſions, the better to prepare and direct themſelves in future *This Continuation,*
therefore, *of* MEDICINAL REPORTS, we find deficient, eſpecially in form

In Hippo-
cratica Me-
thod of medi-
cinal Reports
deſcribed

of

---

[a] The Author therefore, attempted it, in his *Natural Hiſtory of Life and Death*

[b] For the ancient *Gymnaſticks* ſee *Voſſius de quatuor Artibus popularibus, Hieron Mercurialis
de Arte Gymnaſtica* and *Pancirollus de novis Inventis, quibus facem pretulit Antiquitas*

[c] Dr Fuller has written more upon this Subject, as a *Phyſician* See his *Medicina Gymnaſtica*

of an entire Body, digefted with proper care and judgment[a] But we do not mean, that this Work fhould extend to every common Cafe that happens every day, which were an infinite Labour, and to little purpofe, nor yet to exclude all but Prodigies and Wonders, as feveral have done for many things are new in their manner and circumftances, which are not new in their kind, and he who looks attentively, will find many Particulars worthy of obfervation, in what feems vulgar

7 So in Anatomy, the general parts of the *human Body* are diligently obferved, and even to nicenefs but as to the variety found in different Bodies, here the Diligence of Phyficians fails And therefore tho' *fimple Anatomy* has been fully and clearly handled, yet Comparative Anatomy *is deficient.* For Anatomifts have carefully examin'd into all the Parts, their Confiftencies, Figures, and Situations, *but pafs over the different Figure, and State of thofe Parts in different Perfons*[b] The *Reafon of this Defect,* I take to be, that the former Enquiry may terminate upon feeing two or three Bodies diffected, but the other being comparative, and cafual, requires attentive and ftrict application to many different Diffections. Befides, the firft is a Subject, wherein learned *Anatomifts* may fhew themfelves to their Audience, but the other a rigorous Knowledge, to be acquired only by filent and long Experience. And no doubt but the internal Parts, for variety and proportions, are little inferior to the external, and that *Hearts, Livers,* and *Stomachs* are as different in Men, as *Foreheads, Nofes,* and *Ears* And *in thefe differences of the internal Parts, are often found the immediate Caufes of many Difeafes,* which Phyficians not obferving, fometimes unjuftly accufe the Humours, when the fault lies only in the mechanick Structure of a Part. And in fuch Difeafes, 'tis in vain to ufe *Alteratives,* as the cafe admits not of being alter'd by them, but muft be affected, accommodated, or palliated by a Regimen, and *familiar Medicines.*

(margin: Comparative Anatomy deficient)

8 Again, Comparative Anatomy requires accurate Obfervations upon all the Humours, and the Marks and Impreffions of Difeafes in different Bodies upon Diffection· for the *Humours* are commonly pafs'd over, in *Anatomy,* as loathfome and *excrementitious* things, whereas 'tis highly ufeful and neceffary, to note their nature, and the various kinds that may fometimes be found in the human Body, in what Cavities they principally lodge ; and with what advantage, difadvantage, and the like. So the Marks and Impreffions of Difeafes, and the Changes and Devaftations they bring upon the internal Parts, are to be diligently obferved in different Diffections,

O 2   *viz.*

[a] This *Continuation of the Hiftory of Cafes in Phyfick,* is not hitherto on foot, in the Form here directed, and perhaps no confiderable Foundations are laid for it, by all the numerous *Writers of Obfervations* However, the thing intended feems of late attempted by *Baglivi,* in the way of clofe and attentive *Clinical Obfervation,* in his Treatife *de Praxi Medica ad prifcam Obfervandi rationem revocanda,* and regiftring the *Phænomena of Difeafes* from which, when carried to a due length, and properly ranged for the Underftanding to work upon, a folid Knowledge of the *Nature, Caufes, and Cures of Diftempers* may probably be derived, in the fame manner as other ufeful Difcoveries are made in Arts, and the Syftem of the World, according to the Direction and Example of the Lord *Bacon,* in his *Natural Enquiries,* and particularly his *Hiftory of Life and Death*

[b] One would expect, fo diligently as *Anatomy* has been cultivated fince the Difcovery of the *Circulation,* that this *Part of Medicine* fhould not ftill remain deficient

viz. Impoſthumes, Ulcerations, Solutions of Continuity, Putrefactions, Corroſions, Conſumptions, Contractions, Extenſions, Convulſions, Luxations, Diſlocations, Obſtructions, Repletions, Tumours, and preternatural Excreſcencies, as Stones, Carnoſities, Wens, Worms, &c all which ſhould be very carefully examined, and orderly digeſted in the COMPARATIVE ANATOMY we ſpeak of, and the Experiments of ſeveral Phyſicians be here collected and compared together But this variety of Accidents, is by *Anatomiſts,* either ſlightly touched, or elſe paſſed over in ſilence [a]

The Defect of Anatomy, how to be ſupply'd

9 That *Diſſection* in ANATOMY, owing to its not having been practiſed upon *live Bodies*, needs not be ſpoke to, the thing itſelf being odious, cruel, and juſtly condemned by *Celſus* yet the Obſervation of the Ancients is true, that many ſubtile Pores, Paſſages, and Perforations appear not upon Diſſection, becauſe they are cloſed and concealed in *dead Bodies*, that might be open and manifeſt in *live ones* Wherefore, if we would conſult the Good of Mankind, without being guilty of Cruelty, this *Anatomy of live Creatures* ſhould be entirely deſerted, or left to the *caſual Inſpection of Chirurgeons*, or may be ſufficiently perform'd upon *living Brutes*, notwithſtanding the diſſimilitude between their Parts and thoſe of Men, ſo as to anſwer the Deſign, provided it be done with judgment

A Work wanting upon Incurable Diſeaſes

10 Phyſicians, likewiſe, when they enquire into Diſeaſes, find ſo many which they judge incurable, either from their firſt appearance, or after a certain Period, that the *Proſcriptions of Scylla*, and the *Triumvirate*, were trifling to the *Proſcriptions of the Phyſicians*, by which, with an unjuſt Sentence, they deliver Men over to *Death* numbers whereof, however, eſcape with leſs difficulty, than under the *Roman Proſcriptions* A *Work therefore is wanting upon the* CURES OF REPUTED INCURABLE DISEASES [b], that Phyſicians of Eminence and Reſolution, may be encouraged and excited to purſue this matter, as far as the nature of things will permit ſince to pronounce Diſeaſes incurable, is to eſtabliſh Negligence, and Careleſſneſs, as it were by a Law, and ſcreen Ignorance from Reproach

The Office of a Phyſician to procure eaſy Death

11 And farther, we eſteem it the *Office of a Phyſician, to mitigate the Pains and Tortures of Diſeaſe*, as well as to reſtore Health, and this not only when ſuch a Mitigation, as of a dangerous Symptom, may conduce to Recovery, but alſo, when there being no farther hopes of Recovery, it can only ſerve to make the paſſage out of life more calm and eaſy. For that *complacency in Death*, which *Auguſtus Cæſar* ſo much deſired, is no ſmall Felicity This was alſo obſerved in the Death of *Antoninus Pius*, who ſeemed not ſo much to die, as to fall into a deep and pleaſing Sleep And 'tis deliver'd of *Epicurus*, that he procured himſelf this eaſy Departure; for after his Diſeaſe was judged deſperate, he intoxicated himſelf with Wine, and died in that Condi-

[a] And ſo it continues, in the general, to this day except ſome *extraordinary Caſes*, ſuch as thoſe publiſhed in the *Philoſophical Tranſactions*, and *German Ephemerides*, which, indeed, afford abundance of Inſtances, &c for the *Comparative Anatomy* here ſketch'd out

[b] This *Work* has not, perhaps, hitherto appeared in that extent which the Subject requires, but many Materials may be collected for it from the Writings of Phyſicians, the Hiſtories of extraordinary Cures, by Accident, Nature, Empirical Remedies, Mineral Waters, &c particularly from ſeveral of Sir *Boyle's* Philoſophical Pieces, the *Philoſophical Tranſactions*, the *German Ephemerides*, &c See alſo a ſmall *Treatiſe of Incurable Diſeaſes*, printed at *London*, 1723

Condition But the Physicians of our Times make a scruple of attending the Patient after the Disease is thought past cure, tho', in my judgment, if they were not wanting to their own Profession, and to Humanity itself, they should here give their attendance, to improve their Skill, and make the dying Person depart with greater Ease and Tranquillity *We therefore set down as deficient,* AN ENQUIRY AFTER A METHOD OF CAUSING AN EXTERNAL COMPOSURE IN DYING [a] calling it by the name of *external,* to distinguish it from the *internal Composure,* procured to the Soul in *Death.*

An Enquiry into the Means of procuring Composure in Death deficient

12 Again, we generally find this *Deficiency in the Cures of Diseases,* that tho' the present *Physicians* tolerably pursue the *general Intentions of Cures,* yet they have no PARTICULAR MEDICINES, WHICH, BY A SPECIFICK PROPERTY REGARD PARTICULAR DISEASES for they lose the benefit of Traditions, and approved Experience, by their authoritative Procedure in adding, taking away, and changing the Ingredients of their Receipts at pleasure, after the manner of Apothecaries, substituting one thing for another, and thus haughtily commanding *Medicine,* so that *Medicine* can no longer command the *Disease.* For except *Venice-Treacle, Mithridate, Diascordium,* the *Confection of Alkermes,* and a few more, they commonly tie themselves strictly to no *certain Receipts.* the other saleable Preparations of the Shops being in readiness, rather for general Purposes, than accommodated to any particular Cures, *for they do not principally regard some one Disease,* but have a general Virtue of opening Obstructions, promoting Concoction, *&c* And hence it chiefly proceeds, that *Empiricks,* and *Women, are often more successful in their Cures, than learned Physicians,* because the former keep strictly and invariably to the use of *experienced Medicines,* without altering their Compositions [b]. I remember a famous *Jew Physician* in *England,* would say, " your *European* " Physicians are indeed Men of Learning, but they know nothing of *parti-* " *cular Cures for Diseases* " And he would sometimes jest a little irreverently, and say, " our Physicians were like Bishops, that had the *Keys of binding and* " *loosing,* but no more [c]." To be serious, it might be of great consequence, if

---

[a] Physicians seem to apprehend some Danger, or unfavourable Construction, in pursuing this *Design,* for I have met with nothing upon the Subject and all that they venture to do in Practice, is seldom more than to order *Opiates,* where they have an intention to render Death more calm and placid The *Author* had certainly no design of recommending any Method for this purpose, that should be dangerous, immoral, or contrary to the Rules of Humanity, Decency, and good Sense, as may appear by the several unexceptionable Methods he proposes for lengthening Life, in his *History of Life and Death* If he had been more explicit upon the ways he thought of, for procuring an easy *Death,* perhaps he would not have confined himself to Internals, but have mentioned also some *external Contrivances* for soothing the Mind, lulling the Senses, and introducing Composure, as by *grateful Odours, soft and solemn Musick, pleasing Sights, refreshing Baths,* &c But *Physick* can scarce bear the mention of such things as these and therefore whoever would write an useful *Treatise* on this Subject, should guard it with *Address* and *Judgment*

[b] What the Author here recommends, is a Discovery of *Specifick Medicines,* a Subject nobly treated by Mr *Boyle* and to say the Truth, the Improvement of Medicine principally depends on the Knowledge and Use of *Specificks,* but the *Art of discovering them,* without leaving the Business to Chance and Acciden, seems very little known in our time, tho' the Author, long since, taught and practised it I mean, he taught it in his *Novum Organum,* and practised it in his *History of Life and Death*

[c] Thus Dr *Quincy* comp'a ns, that the standing Medicines of the Shops are left so coarse in the r Composition, that we can do little more than purge or vomit with them, whereas, the removal

if some Physicians, eminent for Learning and Practice, would compile A WORK OF APPROVED AND EXPERIENCED MEDICINES IN PARTICULAR DISEASES For tho' one might speciously pretend, that a learned Physician should rather suit his Medicines occasionally, as the Constitution of the Patient, his Age, Customs the Seasons, &c require, than rest upon any certain Prescriptions, yet this is a fallacious Opinion that under-rates Experience, and over-rates human Judgment And as those Persons in the *Roman* State were the most serviceable, who being either Consuls, favoured the People, or *Tribunes* and inclined to the Senate, so are those the best Physicians, who being either learned, duly value the Traditions of Experience, or Men of eminent Practice, that do not despise Methods, and the general Principles of the Art But if Medicines require, at any time, to be qualified, this may rather be done in the *Vehicles*, than in the Body of the Medicine, where nothing should be alter'd without apparent necessity Therefore *this part* of PHYSICK WHICH TREATS OF AUTHENTICK AND POSITIVE REMEDIES [a], *&c* is a certain but the business of supplying it, is to be undertaken with great judgment, and, as by a COMMITTEE OF PHYSICIANS, *chose for that office*

13 And for the *Imitation of Medicine*, it seems strange, especially as mineral ones have been so celebrated by Chemists, tho' safer for external than internal use, that no body hath hitherto attempted any ARTIFICIAL IMITATIONS OF NATURAL BATHS, AND MEDICINAL SPRINGS, whilst 'tis acknowledged that these receive their virtues from the *mineral Veins* thro' which they pass and especially since human industry can, by certain separations discover with what kind of *Mineral* such Waters are impregnated, as whether by *Copper*, *Vitriol*, *Iron*, &c And if these natural impregnations of Waters are reducible to artificial Compositions, it would then be in the power of Art to make more kinds of them occasionally, and at the same time to regulate their temperature at pleasure *This part*, therefore, of *Medicine*, *concerning the* ARTIFICIAL IMITATION OF NATURAL BATHS AND SPRINGS, we set down as deficient, and recommend as an easy as well as useful undertaking [b]

14.

removal of inveterate Obstructions, and Diseases seated in the habit of the Body, require such Remedies as will preserve their Virtues to the farthest Stages of Circulation, and operate there, without affecting the first Passages See his PHARMACEUTICK LECTURES, and *Mechanical Account of the Operations of* Medicines *on the human Body, in the* APPENDIX to them

[a] Such Medicines, if any where to be found, might, one should think, appear in the publick *Pharmacopœias* of particular *Countries*, or in the most approved, or best authorized *Practices* of every Age, which have usually been made publick by some Writer or other But whoever looks attentively into such Books, will not find what might be expected, or what the nature of Men and Things is certainly capable of affording as if there were some strange Fatality attending the *Art* whereon the Lives and Felicities of Mankind depend Dr *Sydenham*, however, among the *English*, made some practical Improvements in Medicine, and our later *Physician* have gone in on a ready and commodious Method of Practice, which is, in some measure, digested into a Body, for the service of others, under the Title of A NEW PRACTICE OF PHYSICK, the third *Edition* whereof, is the more correct, and somewhat enlarged

[b] And yet it has not been hitherto prosecuted to that length the Subject requires Dr *Lister*, however, and Mr *Boyle*, set in earnest about it, the one writing *de Fontibus Medicatis Angliæ*, and the other *Memoirs for the Natural History of Mineral Waters* the *Royal Academy of Sciences at Paris*, also, thought it an Enquiry worthy of their illustrious Body, as appears from their Memoirs,

14 The laſt *Deficiency* we ſhall mention ſeems to us of great importance, *The Phyſi-cians* CLUE *deficient* viz that the *Methods of Cure in uſe are too ſhort to effect any thing that is difficult, or very conſiderable* For it is rather *vain and flattering, than juſt and rational,* to expect that any *Medicine* ſhould be ſo effectual, or ſo ſuc-ceſsful, as by the ſole uſe thereof to work any great Cure. It muſt be a *pow-erful Diſcourſe,* which tho' often repeated, ſhould correct any deep-rooted and inveterate vice of the Mind. Such Miracles are not to be expected. But the things of greateſt efficacy in Nature, are *Order, Perſeverance,* and an *artificial Change of applications,* which tho' they require exact judgment to preſcribe, and preciſe obſervance to follow, yet this is am-ply recompenced by the great effects they produce To ſee the daily Labours of Phyſicians in their Viſits, Conſultations, and Preſcriptions, one would think that they diligently purſued the Cure, and went di-rectly in a certain beaten Track about it but whoever looks attentively into their Preſcriptions and Directions, will find, that the moſt of what they do is full of uncertainty, wavering, and irreſolution; without any certain View, or Foreknowledge, of the Courſe of the Cure Whereas they ſhould from the firſt, after having fully and perfectly diſcovered the Diſeaſe, chuſe, and reſolve upon, ſome regular *Proceſs* or *Series of Cure,* and not depart from it without ſufficient reaſon Thus Phyſicians ſhould know, for ex-ample, that perhaps three or four Remedies rightly preſcribed in an invete-rate Diſeaſe, and taken in due order, and at due diſtances of time, may perform a Cure, and yet the ſame Remedies taken independently of each other, in an inverted order, or not at ſtated periods, might prove abſo-lutely prejudicial. Tho' we mean not, that every ſcrupulous and ſuperſtitious Method of Cure, ſhould be eſteemed the beſt, but that the Way ſhould be as exact as 'tis confined and difficult. *And this part of Medicine we note as deficient, under the name of* THE PHYSICIANS CLUE OR DIRECTORY [a] And *But princi-pally a* Natu-theſe are the Things wanting in the *Doctrine of Medicine,* for the cure of *ral* Philoſo-Diſeaſes, but there ſtill remains one Thing more, and of greater uſe, than *phy funda-*all the reſt, viz. A GENUINE AND ACTIVE NATURAL PHILOSOPHY, *mental to the* WHEREON TO BUILD THE SCIENCE OF PHYSICK [b] *Art*

15.

Memoirs, and the Sieur *du Clos,* and many others, both in *France, England* and elſewhere, have wrote upon the Subject, but none perhaps to better purpoſe than Dr *Hoffman* who proceed-ing upon direct *Experiment* and *Obſervation* for a ſeries of years, has ſhewn that Medicine may receive very conſiderable improvements in this Way The *ſeveral Pieces* of his upon this ſubject, lately publiſhed, with a few Notes, under the Title of *New Experiments and Obſervations up-on* MINERAL WATERS, may perhaps confirm this to the *Engliſh* Reader

[a] This FILUM MEDICINALE, as the Author terms it, or *Method of preſcribing Medicines in their beſt, exacteſt, and moſt direct order, for effecting a Cure,* is not, that I know of, profeſſedly wrote upon Phyſicians, however, uſually obſerve ſome kind of order in their *Preſcriptions* Thus, for inſtance, they begin the *Cure of inflammatory Diſeaſes* with Bleeding, then proceed to *Emeticks,* next to *Perſpiratives,* or *Sudorificks,* then, near the Criſis, to *Opiates Alteratives,* and *Non-ſignificants,* and conclude with *Purgatives and Stomachicks* But whether this order could not be altered for the better in ſome points, or improved in the whole, may deſerve *Enquiry,* at leaſt the *Phyſical Reaſons* whereon *this Order* depends, have not hitherto been ſatisfactorily ſhewn, ſo that it ſeems rather a Mechanical Proceſs, authorized by Cuſtom, than a rational Method ſcientifically deduced, or the beſt that poſſibly might be diſcovered

[b] The modern Phyſicians have not been wanting in their endeavours to found their Art upon the current Philoſophies of their Times Thus Phyſick, that was lately *Carteſian,* is now becoming *Newtonian.*

The third part of Medicine, or the ways of prolonging Life considered.

15 We make the *third Part of Medicine* regard the *Prolongation of Life* This is a *new Part*, and *deficient*, tho' the moſt noble of all for if it may be ſupplied, Medicine will not then be wholly verſed in ſordid Cures; nor Phyſicians be honoured only for neceſſity, but as Diſpenſers of the greateſt earthly Happineſs, that could well be confer'd on Mortals for tho' the World be but as a wildernefs to a *Chriſtian* travelling thro' it to the *promiſed Land*, yet it would be an Inſtance of the divine Favour, that our clothing, that is, our bodies, ſhould be little worn while we ſojourn here And as this is a *capital part of Phyſick*, and as we note it for *deficient*, we ſhall lay down ſome Directions about it [a]

Authors on the regard had to the prolongation of Life.

16 And *firſt*, no Writer extant upon this Subject has made any great or uſeful diſcovery therein *Ariſtotle* indeed has left us a ſhort Memoir, wherein there are ſome admonitions after his manner, which he ſuppoſes to be all that can be ſaid of the matter, but the moderns have here wrote ſo weakly and ſuperſtitiouſly, that the Subject itſelf, thro' their vanity, is reputed vain and ſenſeleſs (2) The very Intentions of Phyſicians upon this head are of no validity, but rather lead from the point than direct to it For they talk as if *Death* conſiſted in a deſtitution of heat and moiſture, and therefore that natural heat ſhould be comforted, and radical moiſture cheriſhed as if the Work were to be effected by Broths, Lettuce, and Mallows, or again, by Spices, generous Wines, Spirits, or chemical Oils, all which rather do hurt, than good (3) We admoniſh mankind, to ceaſe their Trifling, and not weakly imagine that ſuch a great work as retarding the Courſe of Nature can be effected by a morning's draught, the uſe of any coſtly Medicines, Pearls, or *Aurum Potabile* itſelf, but be aſſured, that the *prolongation of Life* is a laborious work, that requires many kinds of *Remedies*, and a proper continuation and intermixture thereof for it were ſtupidity to expect, that what was never yet done, ſhould be effected, otherwiſe than by means hitherto unattempted (4) Laſtly, we admoniſh them rightly to obſerve and diſtinguiſh betwixt what conduces to Health, and what to a long Life for ſome things, tho' they exhilarate the Spirits, ſtrengthen the Faculties, and prevent Diſeaſes, are yet deſtructive to Life, and, without ſickneſs, bring on a waſting old Age whilſt there are others which prolong Life, and prevent Decay, tho' not to be uſed without danger to Health ſo that when employed for the *prolongation of Life*, ſuch inconveniencies muſt be guarded againſt, as might otherwiſe happen upon uſing them

17

Note But the *Natural Philoſophy* here noted by the Author, as wanting, for this purpoſe, ſhould not be derived from any particular Syſtem, but collected from Nature her ſelf The Experiments and Obſervations of Mr *Boyle*, the *Philoſophical Tranſactions*, and *French Memoirs*, afford many Materials for this Work, which upon the foundation of the modern mechanical Experience, ſeems begun by that excellent Phyſician Dr *Frederick Hoffman*, in his *Medicina Chymical*, and *Pathoſophical Pieces*

[a] The Author had no, at this time, wrote his *Hiſtory of Life and Death*, which proceeds exactly upon the following Directions, and is the Execution of the *Plan* here laid down tho' offered not as a *finiſhed Hiſtory*, but as an *Introduction to farther Enquiry* upon this intereſting Subject, which has not been ſince proſecuted ſuitably to its Merit. See *Morhof's Polyhiſtor*, Tom II Part I Lib II pag 293

17 Things feem to us prefervable either in their *own Subftance*, or by *Repair* in their own Subftance, as a Fly, or an Ant, in *Amber*, a Flower, an *Apple*, &c. in *Conferva* or of Snow, or a Corps in Balfam by Repair, as in *Flame* and without Extremes. He who attempts to *prolong Life*, muft practife both thefe Methods together; for feparate, their force is lefs. The *human Body* muft be preferved as Bodies inanimate are; again, as Flame, and laftly, in fome meafure as Machines are preferved. There are, therefore, three *Intentions for the prolongation of Life*, viz. (1) to hinder wafte, (2) fe-cure a good repair, and (3) to renew what begins to decay. I Wafte is caufed by two depredations, viz. that of the *internal Spirit*, and that of the *external Air*; and both are prevented two ways, viz. by making thefe agents lefs predatory, or the patients, that is, the Juices of the Body, lefs apt to be prey'd on. The Spirit is rendered lefs predatory, if either its fubftance be condenfed, as, (1) by the ufe of Opiates, Preparations of Ni-tre, and in Condift tion, or (2) if it be leffened in Quantity, as by Fafting and Diet, and (3) if it be moderated in its motion, as by reft and quiet. The ambient Air becomes lefs predatory, either when 'tis lefs heated by the Sun, as in the cold countries, caves, hills, or kept from the body, as by clofe skins, the plumage of birds, and the ufe of oil and unguents, with-out fpices. The juices of the body are rendred lefs fubject to be prey'd on, if made more hardy, or more oleaginous, as by a rough aftringent diet, living in the cold, robuft exercifes, the ufe of certain mineral Baths, fweet things, and abftaining from fuch as are falt or acid, but efpecially by means of fuch Drinks as confift of fubtile parts, yet without acrimony or tartnefs. II *Repair* is procured by Nourifhment, and Nourifhment is promoted four ways. (1) by forwarding internal concoction, which drives forth the Nourifh-ment, as by medicines that invigorate the principal Vifcera; (2.) by exciting the external parts to attract the Nourifhment, as by exercife, proper Frictions, Unctions and Baths, (3) by preparing the Aliment itfelf, that it may more eafily infinuate, and require lefs digeftion, as in many artificial ways of preparing meats, drinks, bread, and reducing the Effects of thefe three to one[a]. Again, (4) by the laft act of affimilation, as in feafonable fleep, and ex-ternal applications. III The *Renovation* of parts worn out is perform'd two ways, either by foftening the habit of the body, as with fuppling applica-tions, in the way of Bath, Plaifter, or Unction, of fuch qualities as to infi-nuate into the parts, but extract nothing from them, or by difcharging the old, and fubftituting new moifture, as in feafonable and repeated purg-ing, bleeding, and attenuating Diets, which reftore the bloom of the body.

18 Several *Rules for the conduct of the Work* are derivable from thefe *In-* *dications*, but three of the more principal are the following. And *firft, prolongation of Life is rather to be expected from ftated Diets, than from any com-mon regimen of Food, or the virtues of particular Medicines*; for thofe things that have force enough to turn back the Courfe of Nature, are commonly too violent to be compounded into a Medicine, much more to be mix'd with the ordinary food; and muft therefore be adminiftred orderly, regularly, and

[a] See the Author's *New Atlantis*, Supplement I and the *Sylva Sylvarum*, under the *Articles* Foods and Nourishment.

at set period (2) We next lay it down as a Rule, *that the prolongation of … either … working upon the Spirits, and mollifying the parts, … for the matter of alimentation* For as the human body, and the internal structure thereof, may suffer from three things, viz. the *Spirits*, the *Parts*, and … , the way of prolonging life, by means of alimentation, is tedious indirect and winding , but the ways of working upon the *Spirits* and the *Parts* much shorter for the *Spirits* are suddenly affected, both by Effluvia and the Passions, which may work strangely upon them, and the *Parts* also by Baths, Unguents, or Plaisters, which will likewise have sudden impressions (3) Our last *Precept* is, *that the softening of the external Parts … attempted … such things as are penetrating, astringent, and of … with the body* the latter are readily received and entertained, and properly soften and penetrating things are as vehicles to those that mollify , and more easily convey, and deeply impress the virtue thereof, whilst themselves also, in some measure, operate upon the Parts but Astringers keep in the virtue of them both, and somewhat fix it, and also stop *P… ,* which would otherwise be contrary to mollifying, as sending out the moisture therefore the whole affair is to be effected by these three means used in order and succession, rather than together Observe only, that 'tis not the intention of mollifying to nourish the parts externally , but only to render them more capable of Nourishment for dry things are less disposed to assimilate And so much for the *Prolongation of Life*, which we make the *Third*, or last *Part of Medicine* [a]

19 The *Art of Decoration*, or *Beautifying*, has *two Parts*, civil and effeminate. For cleanliness, and decency of the body, were always allow'd to proceed from moral modesty and reverence , *first*, towards *God*, whose creatures we are , next, towards *Society*, wherein we live , and lastly, towards ourselves, whom we ought to reverence still more than others But false *Decorations*, *Forms* and *Pigments*, deserve the imperfections that constantly attend them , being neither exquisite enough to deceive, nor commodious in application, nor wholesome in their use And 'tis much that this depraved custom of *painting the Face*, should so long escape the penal Laws, both of the church and state, which have been very severe against Luxury in apparel, and effeminate trimming of the hair We read of *Jezabel*, that she painted her Face but not so of *Esther* and *Judith*

20 We take GYMNASTICKS, in a large sense, to signify whatever relates to the habit whereto the human body may be brought, whether of *activity* or *suffering* ACTIVITY has two parts, *Strength* and *Swiftness*, so has ENDURANCE or SUFFERING, viz with regard to natural Wants , and Fortitude under Torture Of all these, we have many remarkable Instances in the Practices of Rope-dancers, the hardy Lives of *Savages*, surprizing Strength

[a] This Part of Medicine continues new still, as not being hitherto received and cultivated by Physicians, as an part of other Profession, tho' perhaps it depends upon more certain Principles in the cure of Diseases and is in its nature, capable of superseding the other Parts of the Profession If the Author's *History of Life and Death* were to be continued, Mr *Graunt's* Natural and Political Observations upon the *Bills of Mortality*, the *Philosophical Transactions*, and the *Germ Ephemerides* are proper Books to consult for the purpose See also *Morhof's Polyhistor* Cap *de Tempore*, and *Paschius de Novis Inventis*, &c. Cap VI *de Inventis Medicis*.

Strength of Lunaticks, and the Conſtancy and Reſolution of many under exquiſite Torments   Any other Faculties that fall not within the former Diviſion, as Diving, or the power of continuing long under water without reſpiration, and the like, we refer them alſo to GYMNASTICKS   And here, tho' the things themſelves are common , yet the Philoſophy and Cauſes thereof are uſually neglected , perhaps becauſe men are perſuaded that ſuch maſteries over Nature, are only obtainable, either from a peculiar and natural diſpoſition in ſome men, which comes not under Rules , or by a conſtant cuſtom from childhood, which is rather impoſed than taught   And tho' this be not altogether true, yet 'tis here of ſmall conſequence to note any *Deficiency*, for the *Olympick Games* are long ſince ceas'd , and a mediocrity in theſe things is ſufficient for uſe , whilſt excellency in them, ſerves commonly but for mercenary ſhew

   21   The ARTS OF ELEGANCE are divided with reſpect to the two Senſes of *Sight* and *Hearing*   *Painting* particularly delights the *Eye* , ſo do numerous other *magnificent Arts*, relating to Buildings, Gardens, Apparel, Veſſels, Gems, &c   *Muſick* pleaſes the Ear, with great variety and apparatus of Sounds, Voices, Strings, and Inſtruments   and anciently *Water-organs* were eſteemed as great Maſter-pieces in this *Art*, tho' now grown into diſuſe. The *Arts* which relate to the *Eye* and *Ear*, are, above the reſt, accounted *liberal* , theſe two Senſes being the more pure , and the *Sciences* thereof more learned, as having *Mathematicks* to attend them   The one alſo has ſome relation to the *Memory* and *Demonſtrations* , the other, to *Manners* and the *Paſſions of the Mind*.   The Pleaſures of the other Senſes, and the *Arts* employ'd about them, are in leſs repute , as approaching nearer to ſenſuality than magnificence   *Unguents*, *Perfumes*, the *Furniture of the Table*, but principally *Incitements to Luſt*, ſhould rather be cenſured than taught.   And it has been well obſerved, that while *States* were in their increaſe, *military Arts* flouriſhed, when at their heights, the *liberal Arts* , but when upon their decline, the *Arts of Luxury*   With the *Arts of Pleaſure*, we join alſo the *jocular Arts* , for the Deception of the Senſes may be reckon'd one of their Delights

The Arts of Elegance divided with relation to the Eye and the Ear

   22   And now, as ſo many things require to be conſidered with relation to the human Body, *viz*   the *Parts*, *Humors*, *Functions*, *Faculties*, *Accidents*, &c ſince we ought to have an *entire Doctrine of the Body of Man*, which ſhould comprehend them all , yet leſt *Arts* ſhould be thus too much multiplied, or their ancient limits too much diſorder'd , we receive into the *Syſtem of Medicine*, the Doctrines of the Parts, Functions, and Humors of the Body ; Reſpiration, Sleep, Generation ; the Fœtus, Geſtation in the Womb , Growth, Puberty, Baldneſs, Fatneſs, and the like , tho' theſe do not properly belong either to the *Preſervation of Health*, *the Cure of Diſeaſes*, *or the Prolongation of Life* , but becauſe the human body is, in every reſpect, the ſubject of Medicine   But for voluntary Motion and Senſe, we refer them to the *Doctrine of the Soul*, as two principal parts thereof   And thus we conclude the *Doctrine of the Body*, which is but as a Tabernacle to the *Soul*.

SECT. X.

Of the DOCTRINE *of the* HUMAN SOUL.

1 WE come to the DOCTRINE OF THE HUMAN SOUL, from whose Tr... es all other *Doctrines* are *derived* It has *two Parts*, the ... of the *rational Soul*, which is divine, the other, of the *ma-* ... ch we have in common with Brutes Two different *Ema* ... manifest in the first *Creation*, the one proceeding from the E ... C..., the other from the *Elements* [a] As to the primitive Emanation of the *rational Soul*, the Scripture says, *God formed Man of the ... the Earth, and breathed into his nostrils the breath of Life* But the Generation of the *irrational and brutal Soul*, was in these words, *Let the ... Let the Earth bring forth* And this *irrational Soul* in Man, is only an instrument to the *rational one*, and has the same origin in us, as in Brutes, ... the *dust of the Earth*, for 'tis not said, *God form'd the body of Man ... of the Earth, but God formed Man*, that is, the whole Man, the Breath of Life excepted, *of the dust of the Earth*. We will therefore stile the *first Part* of the general *Doctrine of the human Soul*, the *Doctrine of the inspired S... ane*, and the other Part, the *Doctrine of the sensitive or produced Soul*. But as we are here treating wholly of *Philosophy*, we would not have borrowed this *Doctrine* from *Divinity*, had it not also agreed with the *Principles of Philosophy*. For there are many excellencies of the *human Soul* above the *Soul of Brutes*, manifest even to those who philosophize only according to ... And wherever so many, and such great excellencies are found, a specifick difference should always be made We do not, therefore, approve that confused and promiscuous manner of the Philosophers, in treating the functions of the Soul, as if the *Soul of Man* differ'd in degree rather than species, from the Soul of Brutes, as the Sun differs from the Stars, or Gold from other Metals There may also be another *Division* of the general *Doctrine of the human Soul*, into the *Doctrine of the Substance and Faculties* of the Soul, and that of the *Use and Objects of the Faculties* And these two *Doctrines* being premised, we come to particulars

2 The *Doctrine of the inspired Substance*, as also of the *Substance of the rational Soul*, comprehends several *Enquiries*, with relation to its nature, as whether the Soul be *native*, or *adventitious*, *separable*, or *inseparable*, *mortal*, or ... now in 'tis subject to the *Laws of Matter*, how far not, and the like B... points of this kind, tho' they might be more thoroughly ... in Philosophy than hitherto they have been, yet in the end they must be turned over to *Religion*, for determination and decision: otherwise they
will

[a] Th... man is divided into three distinct Parts, viz. *Body Soul* and *Spirit*, according to the Doctrine of *Plato*, the opinion of ... and some of the *Moderns* See *Puschius de Novis Inven...* Pag 359 360 S... below § 3.

will be expofed to various Errors, and Illufions of Senfe. For as the *Subflance of the Soul* was not, in its creation, extracted, or deduced from the mafs of Heaven and Earth, but immediately *infpired by God*, and as the Laws of Heaven and Earth are the proper fubjects of Philofophy, no knowledge of the fubftance of the rational Soul can be had from Philofophy, but muft be derived from the fame *divine Infpiration*, whence the Subftance thereof originally proceeded

3 But in the *Doctrine of the fenfitive or produced Soul*, even its fubftance may be juftly enquired into, tho' this Enquiry feems hitherto *wanting*[a] for of what fignificancy are the terms of *Actus Ultimus*, and *Forma Corporis*, and fuch logical trifles, to the knowledge of the Soul's Subftance? The *fenfitive Soul* muft be allow'd a corporeal Subftance, attenuated by heat, and rendered invifible, as a fubtile breath, or *Aura*, of a flamy and airy nature, having the foftnefs of air in receiving impreffions, and the activity of fire in exerting its action, nourifh'd partly by an oily and partly by a watry fubftance, and diffufed thro' the whole body but in perfect creatures, refiding chiefly in the head, and thence running thro' the nerves, being fed and recruited by the fpirituous blood of the Arteries, as *Telefius*, and his Follower *Donatus*, in fome meafure have ufefully fhewn Therefore *let this Doctrine be more diligently enquir'd into*[b], becaufe the ignorance of it has produced fuperftitious and very corrupt opinions, that greatly leffen the dignity of the human Soul, fuch as the *Tranfmigration* and *Luftration* of Souls thro' certain periods of years, and the too near relation, in all refpects, of the human Soul to the Soul of Brutes For this *Soul in Brutes* is a principal Soul, whereof their Body is the Organ, but in Man 'tis itfelf an Organ of the *rational Soul*, and may rather be called by the name *Spirit* than *Soul*

4 The *Faculties of the Soul* are well known, viz the Underftanding, Reafon, Imagination, Memory, Appetite, Will, and all thofe wherewith *Logicks* and *Ethicks* are concern'd In the *Doctrine of the Soul*, the *Origin* of thefe *Faculties* muft be phyfically treated, as they may be innate and adhering to the Soul But their ufes and objects are referr'd to other Arts And in this part nothing extraordinary has hitherto appear'd[c], tho' we do not indeed report it as wanting This *Part of the Faculties of the Soul has alfo two* APPENDAGES, which as they have yet been handled, rather prefent us with fmoak, than any clear flame of truth, one being the doctrine of *natural Divination*, the other of *Fafcination*

The Enquiry of the fenfitive Soul neglected

The Doctrine of the Soul requires an Enquiry into the origin of its Faculties

5

---

[a] See *Cordemoy*, *le Difcernment du Corps & de l'Ame*, *de la Forge*, *Traitte de l'Efprit de l'Homme*, & *Malbranche*, *Refercha de la Verité*

[b] This *Enquiry* lies greatly embroiled by the Moderns, fome feeking the *Soul* all over the *Body*, fome in the Blood, fome in the animal Spirits, fome in the Heart, fome in the Ventricles of the Brain, and fome, with *des Cartes*, in the *Glandula Pinealis* If the Difcovery be poffible, the beft way of making it is perhaps that of the *Author* laid down in the *Novum Organum*, for the *conduct of Enquiries*, and the *invefigation of Forms*, as without fome fuch Method the Mind feems but to fearch in the Dark M *Petit* wrote a curious Piece relating to this fubject, entitled, *de Anima Corpori coextenfa*, printed at *Paris* 1665 See alfo *Stouchenis de Sede Anima in Corpore humano*

[c] See Mr *Locke's Effay upon human Underftanding*, and *Father Malbranche's Refercbe de la Verité*

3

Two A——
degrees of Ar-
tificial Di-
vi——on
——Fasc——
——

5 DIVINATION has been anciently, and properly, *divided into Artificial* and *Natural*. The *artificial* draws its Predictions by reasoning from the indication of signs. But the *natural* predicts from the internal foresight of the mind, without the assistance of signs. *Artificial Divination* is of two kinds, one arguing from Causes, the other only from Experiments, conducted by blind authority. The latter is generally superstitious. Such were the heathen Doctrines about the inspection of Entrails, the flight of Birds, &c. And the formal *Astrology of the Chaldeans* was little better. Both kinds of *Artificial Divination* spread themselves into various *Sciences*. The *Astrologer* has his predictions from the *Aspects of the Stars*. The *Physician* too has his, as to death, recovery, and the subsequent symptoms of diseases, from the *Urine, Pulse, Aspect of the Patient*, &c. The Politician also is not without his predictions, * *O urbem venalem, & cito perituram, si emptorem invenerit.* The Event of which *Prophecy* happened soon after, and was first accomplished in *Sylla*, and again in *Cæsar*. But the Predictions of this kind, being not to our present purpose, we refer them to their proper Arts, and shall here only treat of *natural Divination, proceeding from the internal foresight of the Soul*.

Divi——
——
——
——
——and its
by influx

6 This also is of two kinds, the one *native*, the other by *influx*. The native rests upon this supposition, that the Mind abstracted or collected in itself, and not diffused in the organs of the body, has from the natural power of its own essence, some foreknowledge of future things. And this appears chiefly in sleep, extasies, and the near approach of Death, but more rarely in waking, or when the body is in health and strength. And this state of the mind is commonly procured, or promoted, by abstinence, and principally such things as withdraw the Mind from exercising the functions of the Body, that it may thus enjoy its own nature, without any external interruption. But *Divination by influx*, is grounded upon another supposition, *viz.* that the Mind, as a mirror, may receive a secondary illumination from the foreknowledge of God and Spirits, whereto likewise the above mention'd state and regimen of the Body are conducive. For the same abstraction of the Mind causes it more powerfully to use its own nature, and renders it more susceptive of *divine influxes* only in *Divinations by influx*, the Soul is seized with a kind of rapture, and as it were impatience of the Deity's presence, which the Ancients called by the name of *sacred fury*, whereas in native Divination the Soul is rather at its ease, and free.

Fascination
the effect of
Imagination 7

7 FASCINATION is the Power and artful Act of the Imagination upon the Body of another. And here the School of *Paracelsus*, and the Pretenders to *Natural Magick*, abusively so called, have almost made the force and apprehension of the Imagination equal to the Power of Faith, and capable of working Miracle. Others, keeping nearer to Truth, and attentively considering the secret Energies and Impressions of Things, the Irradiations of the Senses, the Transmissions of Thought from one to another, the Conveyances of magnetick Virtues, &c. are of opinion, that Impressions, Conveyances, and Communications, might be made from Spirit to Spirit, because

* O City set to Sale, whose destruction is at hand, if it find a purchaser!

cauſe *Spirit* is, of all things, the moſt powerful in operation, and eaſieſt to work on   whence many Opinions have ſpread abroad of Maſter-Spirits, of Men ominous, and unlucky, of the Strokes of Love, Envy, and the like   And this is attended with the *Enquiry, how the Imagination may be heighten'd and fortified?*   For if a ſtrong *Imagination* has ſuch power, 'tis worth knowing by what means to exalt and raiſe it [a]

8   But here a Palliative, or *Defence, of a great part of Ceremonial Magick,* would ſlily, and indirectly, inſinuate itſelf, under a ſpecious, tho' dangerous, Pretence, that *Ceremonies, Characters, Charms, Geſticulations, Amulets,* and the like, have not their power from any tacit, or binding, Contract with evil Spirits, but that theſe ſerve only to ſtrengthen and raiſe the Imagination of ſuch as uſe them, in the ſame manner as Images have prevail'd in Religion, for fixing Mens Minds in the Contemplation of Things, and raiſing the Devotion in Prayer   But allowing the Force of Imagination to be great, and that Ceremonies do raiſe and ſtrengthen it, allowing alſo that Ceremonies may be ſincerely uſed to that end, as a phyſical Remedy, without the leaſt deſign of thereby procuring the aſſiſtance of Spirits, yet ought they ſtill to be held unlawful   becauſe they oppoſe, and contradict, that *divine Sentence* paſs'd upon Man for Sin, *In the Sweat of thy Brow thou ſhalt eat thy Bread*   For this kind of Magick offers thoſe excellent Fruits, which God hath ordained ſhould be procured by Labour, at the price of a few eaſy and ſlight Obſervances

Ceremonial Magick not allowable.

9.   There are two other *Doctrines,* which principally regard the Faculties of the *inferior or ſenſitive Soul;* as chiefly communicating with the Organs of the Body; the one is, of *voluntary Motion,* the other, of *Senſe and Senſibility*   The former has been but ſuperficially enquired into, and one entire Part of it is almoſt wholly neglected   The Office and proper Structure of the Nerves, Muſcles, *&c.* requiſite to muſcular Motion, what Parts of the Body reſt while others move, and how the Imagination acts as Director of this Motion, ſo far, that when it drops the Image whereto the Motion tended, the Motion itſelf preſently ceaſes, as in walking, if another ſerious Thought come acroſs our Mind, we preſently ſtand ſtill, with many other ſuch Subtilties, have long ago been obſerved and ſcrutinized   But *how the Compreſſions, Dilatations, and Agitations of the Spirit,* which, doubtleſs, is the Spring of Motion, ſhould guide and rule the corporeal and groſs Maſs of the Parts, has not yet been diligently ſearched into, and treated   And no wonder, ſince the *ſenſitive Soul* itſelf has been hitherto taken for a Principle of Motion, and a Function, rather than a Subſtance   But as 'tis now known to be material, it becomes neceſſary *to enquire, by what Efforts ſo ſubtile and minute a Breath can put ſuch groſs and ſolid Bodies in motion* [b]   Therefore, as this part is deficient, let due Enquiry be made concerning it

Two other Doctrines of the ſenſitive Soul, viz. that of voluntary Motion, and that of Senſe and Senſibility

The Doctrine of muſcular Motion deficient

10

---

[a] The ways of working upon, or with the *Imagination,* are touched by the Author, in his SYLVA SYLVARUM, under the Article *Imagination*   See more to this purpoſe in *Des Cartes* upon the *Paſſions, Caſaubon* upon *Enthuſiaſm,* Father *Malbranche's Reſerche de la Verité,* and the Lord *Shafteſbury's* Letter upon *Enthuſiaſm*

[b] *Muſcular Motion* ſtill remains a kind of Myſtery in Philoſophy, not penetrated to ſatisfaction, even by the modern mechanical and mathematical Learning   The Exiſtence, or Agency of *Animal-*

the SENSE and SENSIBILITY have been much more fully and diligently enquired into, as well in general Treatiles upon the Subject, as in particular ..., viz. *Perspective*, *Musick*, &c. but how justly, is not to the prefent Intention. And therefore we cannot note them as *deficient*: yet there are *two* ... Points ... in ... Doctrine, one, *upon the difference of Perception and Senfe*, and the other, *upon the Form of Light*. In treating of *Senfe and S...*, Philofophers fhould have premis'd the difference between *Perception and Senfe*, as the Foundation of the whole: for we find there is a ... *Power of Perception* in moft natural Bodies, and a kind of appetite to ... what is agreeable, and to avoid what is difagreeable to them. Nor is ... meant of the more fubtile *Perceptions* only, as when the Load-ftone draws Iron, or Flame flies to Petreol, or one drop of Water runs into another, or when the Rays of Light are reflected from a white Object, or when ... Bodies affimilate what is proper for them, and reject what is hurt-ful, or when a Spunge attracts Water, and expels Air, &c. for in all cafes, no one Body applied near to another, can change that other, or be changed by it, unlefs a reciprocal Perception precede the Operation. A Body always perceives the Paffages by which it infinuates, feels the Impulfe of another Body, before it yields thereto, perceives the removal of any Body that ... preffed it, and thereupon recovers itfelf, perceives the Separation of its Continuity, and for a time refifts it, in fine, *Perception is diffufed thro' all Matter*. But it has fuch an acute Perception of *Heat* and *Cold*, as far exceeds the human Touch, which yet paffes for the meafure of Heat and Cold. This *Doctrine*, therefore, has *two Defects*, one, in that Men have gene-rally paffed it over untouch'd, tho' a noble fubject: the other, that they who did attend to it, have gone too far, attributed *Senfe to all Bodies*, and made it almoft a fin to pluck a Twig from a Tree, left the Tree fhould groan, like *Polydorus in Virgil*. But they ought carefully to have fearch'd after the difference betwixt *Perception* and *Senfe*, not only in comparing fen-fible with infenfible Things, in the entire Bodies thereof, as thofe of Plants and Animals, but alfo to have obferved in the fenfible Body itfelf, what fhould

be

... Animal Spirits ..., the introduction of a fubtile elaftick Medium is thought hypothetical, and the Arguments produced for various Hypothefes, in this obfcure Subject, feem inconclufive. Perhaps ... have not proceeded regularly in the *Enquiry*, or patiently obferved and regifter'd all the Phænomena relating to it, but feen a little, prefumed a great deal, and fo jump'd to imperfect and contradictory Conclufions: as will ever be the cafe if this Author, fober and ... our Method of Enquiring or a better, if a better be difcoverable, do not take place in ... See *Borelli de Motu Animalium*, *Boerhaave's Inftitutiones Medicæ*, Sir *Ifaac Newton's* Queries at the end of his *Opticks*, and Dr *Pemberton's Preface to Cowper's Anatomy*.

* This form of Speech may appear fomewhat harfh at firft, becaufe *Perception* is generally ... Perception and the later Philofophers do not attribute a kind of animal *Senfa*tion to Matter, as *Campanella* and *Helmont* did: but the Expreffion means no more, than the general and particular ways wherein Bodies affect each other. Thus the power of *Attraction*, or *Gravity*, as we now ufually call it, is common to all Matter, and may, in a due fenfe, be termed a general *Perception*. And fo refiftance is felt by Bodies upon contact, &c. This Doctrine is more fully explained in the *Novum Organum*, where the feveral kinds of *Motion* are confidered, and require to be duly profecuted for the Improvement of Philofophy: as the Things whereon all the Phænomena and Effects of Nature depend, and comprehending all the ways whereby Bodies affect, alter, and act upon each other: all which ways, may be con-fider'd as fo many *Appetites*, or original Impreffions in Bodies, or, to ufe the modern Phrafe, as fo many *Laws of Nature*.

be the caufe that fo many Actions are performed without any *Senfe* at all. Why the Aliments are digefted and difcharged, the Humours and Juices carried up and down in the Body, why the Heart and Pulfe beat, why the Vifcera act as fo many Work-fhops, and each perform its refpective Office, yet all this, and much more, be done without Senfe   But Men have not yet fufficiently found *of what nature the Action of Senfe is*, and what kind of Body, what Continuance, what Repetitions of the Impreffion are required to caufe Pain or Pleafure   Laftly, they feem totally ignorant of the *diffe-rence between fimple Perception and Senfe*, and how far Perception may be caufed without Senfe   Nor is this a Controverfy about Words, but a Matter of great Importance   Wherefore *let this Doctrine be better examin'd*, as a thing of capital, and very extenfive, Ufe   For the Ignorance of fome ancient Philofophers in this point, fo far obfcured the Light of Reafon, that they thought there was a Soul indifferently infufed into all Bodies; nor did they conceive how *Motion of Election, could be caufed without Senfe, or Senfe exift, without a Soul*

11. That the Form of Light fhould not have been duly enquired into, appears a ftrange over-fight, efpecially as Men have beftow'd fo much pains upon *Perfpective*   for neither has this Art, nor others, afforded any valuable Difcovery in the fubject of Light   Its Radiations, indeed, are treated, but not its Origin   and the ranking of *Perfpective* with *Mathematicks*, has produced this Defect, with others of the like nature, becaufe *Philofophy* is thus deferted too foon.   Again, the *Doctrine of Light*, and the Caufes thereof, have been almoft fuperftitioufly treated in *Phyficks*, as a Subject of a middle nature, betwixt natural and divine, whence certain *Platonifts* would have Light prior to Matter itfelf   for they vainly imagin'd, that Space was firft fill'd with Light, and afterwards with Body   but the Scriptures plainly fay, *that the Mafs of Heaven and Earth was dark, before the Creation of Light.* And as for what is phyfically deliver'd upon this Subject, and according to Senfe, it prefently defcends to *Radiations*, fo that very little *Philofophical Enquiry* is extant about it   And Men ought here to lower their Contemplations a little, and enquire into the Properties common to all *lucid Bodies*; as this relates to the *Form of Light*   how immenfely foever the Bodies concern'd may differ in dignity, as the Sun does from rotten Wood, or putrefied Fifh[a]. We fhould likewife enquire the caufe why fome things take fire, and when heated throw out Light, and others not   Iron, Metals, Stones, Glafs, Wood, Oil, Tallow, by Fire yield either a Flame, or grow red-hot   But *Water* and *Air*, expofed to the moft intenfe Heat they are capable of, afford no Light, nor fo much as fhine   That 'tis not the property of Fire alone to give Light, and that Water and Air are not utter Enemies thereto, appears from the dafhing of Salt-Water in a dark Night, and a hot Seafon; when the fmall Drops of the Water, ftruck off by the motion of the Oars in rowing, feem fparkling and luminous   We have the fame appearance in the agitated Froth of the Sea, called *Sea-lungs*. And, indeed, it fhould be enquired what Affinity Flame and ignited Bodies have with *Glow worms*, the *Luciola*, and the *Indian* Fly, which cafts a Light over a whole Room; the Eyes of certain

The Enquiry into the Origin and Form of Light, deficient

---

[a] Which have a remarkable *luminous Property*

Creatures in the dark, Loaf-Sugar, in fcraping or breaking, the Sweat of a Horfe hard ridden, &c   Men have underftood fo little of this matter, that moft imagine the Sparks ftruck betwixt a *Flint* and *Steel*, to be Air in attrition. But fince the Air ignites not with Heat yet apparently conceives Light, whence Owls, Cats, and many other Creatures fee in the Night, (for there is no Vifion without Light) there muft be a native Light in Air, which, tho' weak and feeble, is proportion'd to the vifual Organs of fuch Creatures, fo as to fuffice them for Sight   The Error, as in moft other cafes, lies here, that Men have not reduced the common Forms of Things from particular Inftances, which is what we make the proper bufinefs of *Metaphyficks*   Therefore let *Enquiry be made into the Form and Origin of Light*, and, in the mean time, we fet it down as *deficient*[a]   And fo much for the *Doctrine of the Subftance of the Soul*, both rational and fenfitive, with its *Faculties*, and the *Appendages of this Doctrine*

SECT. XI.

The DOCTRINE *of the* FACULTIES *of the* HUMAN MIND.

1 THE *Doctrine of the human Underftanding*, and *of the human Will*, are like Twins, for the *Purity of Illumination*, and the *Freedom of Will*, began and fell together · nor is there in the Univerfe fo intimate a Sympathy, as that betwixt *Truth* and *Goodnefs*. The more fhame for Men of Learning, if in Knowledge they are like the winged Angels, but in Affections like the crawling Serpents, having their Minds indeed like a *Mirror*, but a Mirror foully fpotted

2 The *Doctrine of the Ufe and Objects of the mental Faculties*, has *two parts*, well known, and generally received, viz *Logicks* and *Ethicks*. LOGICKS treat of the *Underftanding* and *Reafon*, and ETHICKS of the *Will*, *Appetite*, and *Affections*   the one producing *Refolutions*, the other *Actions*.   The *Imagination*, indeed, on both fides, performs the Office of Agent, or Embaffador, and affifts alike in the judicial and minifterial Capacity   *Senfe* commits all forts of Notions to the *Imagination*, and the *Reafon* afterwards judges of them   In like manner *Reafon* tranfmits felect and approved Notions to the *Imagination*, before the Decree is executed   for *Imagination* always precedes and excites voluntary Motion, and is therefore a common Inftrument both to the *Reafon* and the *Will*   only it has two Faces, that turn'd towards Reafon bearing the *Effigy of Truth*; but that towards Action, the *Effigy of Goodnefs*   yet fo as to appear the Effigies of Sifters

3

---

[a] This Subject has been nobly profecuted, and the Deficiency here noted, in good meafure fupplied by the Labours and Difcoveries of Mr *Boyle* and Sir *Ifaac Newton*   The Author indeed carried the *Enquiry* to a confiderable length himfelf, by means of the *Prifm*, and other Contrivances, as appears by the large *Example* for invefligating the *Form of Light* in the *Novum Organum*, and his *Table of Enquiry* for the particular *Hiftory of Light* and *Splendor*, in the entrance of the *Scala Intellectus*   See Mr. *Boyle of Colours*, and Sir *Ifaac Newton's Opticks*.

3 But the *Imagination* is more than a mere Meſſenger, as being inveſted *The Power of* with, or, at leaſt, uſurping no ſmall Authority, beſides delivering the Meſ- *the* Imagina-ſage. Thus, *Ariſtotle* well obſerves, that the Mind has the ſame command over *ſon.* the Body, as the Maſter over the Slave, but Reaſon over the Imagination, the ſame that a Magiſtrate has over a free Citizen, who may come to rule in his turn For in *Matters of Faith and Religion*, the IMAGINATION *mounts above* REASON Not that divine Illumination is ſeated in the Imagination, but, as in divine Virtues, *Grace* makes uſe of the Motions of the Will, ſo in *Illumination*, it makes uſe of the Motions of the *Imagination* whence *Religion* ſollicits acceſs to the Mind, by Similitudes, Types, Parables, Dreams, and Viſions [a]. Again, the *Imagination* has a conſiderable ſway in *Perſuaſion*, inſinuated by the power of Eloquence for when the Mind is ſooth'd, enraged, or any way drawn aſide by the *artifice of Speech*, all this is done by *raiſing the Imagination* which now growing unruly, not only inſults over, but, in a manner, offers Violence to Reaſon, partly by blinding, partly by incenſing it Yet there appears no cauſe why we ſhould quit our former *Diviſion* for in general, the *Imagination* does not make the *Sciences*, ſince even *Poetry*, which has been always attributed to the *Imagination*, ſhould be eſteem'd rather a Play of Wit, than a *Science*. As for the Power of the *Imagination* in natural things, we have already ranged it under the *Doctrine of the Soul* [b], and for its affinity with *Rhetorick*, we refer it to the Art of *Rhetorick* [c].

4 This part of *human Philoſophy* which regards *Logick*, is diſagreeable to *Whence the* the taſte of many, as appearing to them no other than a Net, and a Snare *diſlike of many* of thorny Subtilty For as Knowledge is juſtly called the Food of the *to* Log ck Mind, ſo in the deſire and choice of this Food, moſt Men have the Appetite of the *Iſraelites* in the Wilderneſs, who, weary of Manna, as a thin, tho' celeſtial Diet, would have gladly return'd to the *Fleſh-pots* thus, generally thoſe *Sciences* reliſh beſt, that participate of ſomewhat more filling, and nearer related to Fleſh and Blood, as *Civil Hiſtory, Morality, Politicks*, whereon Mens Affections, Praiſes, and Fortunes turn, and are employ'd whilſt the other *dry Light* offends, and dries up the ſoft and humid Capacities of moſt Men But if we would rate things according to their real worth, the *rational Sciences* are the Keys to all the reſt, for as the Hand is the *Inſtrument of Inſtruments*, and the Mind the *Form of Forms*, ſo the *rational Sciences* are to be eſteemed the *Arts of Arts* Nor do they direct only, but alſo ſtrengthen and confirm, as the uſe and habit of ſhooting, not only enables one to ſhoot nearer the Mark, but likewiſe to draw a ſtronger Bow

5 The *Logical Arts* are four, being divided according to the Ends they *The four Lo-*lead to for in *rational Knowledge*, Man endeavours (1) *either to find what* *gical Arts* *he ſeeks*, (2) *to judge of what he finds*, (3) *to retain what he has approved*, or (4) *to deliver what he has retained* whence there are as many RATIONAL ARTS, viz (1) the ART OF ENQUIRY, or INVENTION, (2) the ART OF EXAMINATION, or JUDGING, (3) the ART OF CUSTODY, or MEMORY, and (4) the ART OF ELOCUTION, or DELIVERY.

Q 2

6

[a] See hereafter, *Sect* XXVIII *of Inſpired Theology*
[b] See above, *Sect* X
[c] See hereafter, *Sect* XVIII

In enquiry of invention we find re- ... *ing Arguments.*

6 INVENTION is of two very different kinds, the *one of Arts and Sciences*, the other of *Arguments* and *Discourse* The former I set down as *absolutely deficient* And this *Deficiency* appears like that, when in taking the Inventory of an Estate, there is set down, *in Cash, nothing* for as ready Money will purchase all other Commodities, so this *Art*, if extant, would procure all other *Arts* And as the immense Regions of the *West-Indies* had never been discover'd, if the use of the Compass had not first been known, 'tis no wonder, that the Discovery and *Advancement of Arts* hath made no greater progress, when the Art of Inventing, and Discovering, the Sciences remains

The Art of inventing Arts is wanting.

hitherto unknown That this part of Knowledge is wanting, seems clear. for *Logick* professes not, nor pretends, to invent either mechanical or liberal Arts, nor to deduce the Operations of the one, or the Axioms of the other, but only leaves us this Instruction in passage, *to believe every Artist in his own Art* *Celsus* a wise Man, as well as a Physician, speaking of the empirical and dogmatical Sects of Physicians, gravely and ingenuously acknowledges, *that Medicines and Cures were first discover'd, and the Reasons and Causes of them discours'd of afterwards not that Causes, first derived from the nature of things, gave light to the Invention of Cures and Remedies* And *Plato*, more than once, observes, that *Particulars are infinite, that the highest Generalities give no certain Directions, and therefore, that the Marrow of all Sciences, whereby the Artist is distinguished from the unskilful Workman, consists in middle Propositions, which Experience has deliver'd and taught in each particular Science* Hence those who write upon the first *Inventors of Things*, and the *Origins of the Sciences*, rather celebrate *Chance* than *Art*, and bring in Beasts, Birds, Fishes, and Serpents, rather than Men, as the first *Teachers of Arts* No wonder, therefore, as the manner of Antiquity was to consecrate the *Inventors* of useful things, that the *Ægyptians*, an ancient Nation, to which many Arts owe their rise, had their Temples fill'd with the *Images of Brutes*, and but a few *human Idols* amongst them

Most certainly more beholden to Chance than Reason for Inventions.

7 And if we should, according to the Traditions of the *Greeks*, ascribe the first *Invention of Arts to* Men, yet we cannot say that *Prometheus* studied the *Invention of Fire*, or that when he first struck the Flint, he expected Sparks, but that he fell upon it by accident, and, as the Poets say, *stole it from Jupiter* So that as to the *Invention of Arts*, we are rather beholden to the wild Goat for Chirurgery, to the *Nightingal for Musick*, to the *Stork for Glysters*, to the accidental flying off of a Pot's Cover, for *Artillery*; and, in a word, to *Chance*, or any thing else, rather than to *Logick*. Nor does the manner of *Invention*, described by *Virgil*, differ much from the former, *viz* that *Practice and intent Thought* by degrees struck out *various Arts*[a] For this is no other than what Brutes are capable of, and frequently practise, *viz* an intent Sollicitude about some one thing, and a perpetual exercise thereof, which the necessity of their Preservation imposes upon them for *Cicero* truly observed, that *Practice applied wholly to one thing, often conquers both Nature and Art*[b] And therefore, if it may be said, with regard to Men, *that continued Labour and urgent Necessity masters every thing*, so it

may

---

[a] *Ut varias Usus meditando extuderet Artes Paulatim*

[b] *Usus & ... deducet, & ... artem ipse venit.*

may be asked, with regard to Brutes, Who taught them Inftinct? Who taught the *Raven*, in a Drought, to drop Pebbles into a hollow Tree, where fhe chanced to fpy Water, that the Water might rife for her to drink? Who taught the *Bee* to fail thro' the vaft Ocean of Air, to diftant Fields, and find the way back to her Hive? Who taught the *Ant* to gnaw every Grain of Corn that fhe hoards, to prevent its fprouting? And if we obferve in *Virgil*, the word *extundere*, which implies *Difficulty*, and the word *paulatim*, which imports *Slownefs*, this brings us back to the cafe of the *Ægyptian Gods*, fince Men have hitherto made little ufe of their rational Faculties, and none at all of *Art*, in the Inveftigation of Things

8 And this Affertion, if carefully attended to, is proved from the *Form of Logical Induction*, for finding and examining the Principles of the *Sciences* which *Form* being abfolutely defective and infufficient, is fo far from perfecting Nature, that it perverts and diftorts her   For whoever attentively obferves how the *æthereal Dew of the Sciences* is gather'd, (the Sciences being extracted from particular Examples, whether natural, or artificial, as from fo many Flowers,) will find that the Mind of its own natural Motion makes a better *Induction*, than that defcrib'd by *Logicians*   From a bare enumeration of Particulars, in the *logical manner*, where there is no *contradictory Inftance*, follows a falfe Conclufion, nor does fuch an *Induction* infer any thing more than probable conjecture. For who will undertake, when the Particulars of a Man's own Knowledge, or Memory, appear only on one fide; that fomething directly oppofite fhall not lie concealed on the other? as if *Samuel* fhould have taken up with the Sons of *Jeffe* brought before him, and not have fought *David*, who was in the field   And to fay the truth, as this *Form of Induction* is fo grofs and ftupid, it might feem incredible, that fuch acute and fubtile Genius's as have been exercifed this way, could ever have obtruded it upon the World, but that they hafted to *Theories*, and *Opinions*, and, as it were, difdain'd to dwell upon *Particulars* For they have ufed *Examples*, and *particular Inftances*, but as *Whifflers*, to keep the Croud off, and make room for their own *Opinions*, without confulting them from the beginning, fo as to make a juft and mature Judgment of the truth of things   And this Procedure has, indeed, ftruck me with an aweful and religious wonder, to fee Men tread the fame Paths of Error, both in *divine* and *human Enquiries*. For as in receiving *divine Truths*, Men are averfe to become as little Children, fo in the apprehending of *human Truths*, for Men to begin to read, and, like Children, come back again to the firft *Elements of Induction*, is reputed a low and contemptible thing

The Ufe of Induction perverted and neglected.

9. But, allowing the *Principles of the Sciences* might be juftly form'd by the *common Induction*, or by *Senfe* and *Experience*, yet 'tis certain that the *lower Axioms* cannot, in natural things, be with certainty deduced by *Syllogifm* from them   For *Syllogifm* reduces *Propofitions* to *Principles*, by intermediate Propofitions. And this *Form*, whether of *Invention* or *Proof*, has place in the *popular Sciences*, as *Ethicks*, *Politicks*, *Law*, &c. and even in *Divinity*, fince *God* has been pleafed to accommodate himfelf to the human Capacity but in *Phyficks*, where Nature is to be caught by Works, and not the Adverfary, by Arguments, Truth, in this way, flips thro' our Fingers; be-

A genuine and correct Induction to be introduced.

I   caufe

cause the Subtilty of the Operations of Nature, far exceeds the Subtilty of Words. So that *Syllogism* thus failing, there is every where a necessity for employing a *genuine and correct* INDUCTION, as well in the more general Principles, as the inferior Propositions For *Syllogisms* consist of *Propositions*, Propositions of *Words*, but *Words* are the *Signs of Notions*· wherefore if these *Notions*, which are the *Souls of Words*, be unjustly and unsteadily abstracted from things, the whole Structure must fall. Nor can any laborous subsequent Examination of the Consequences of Arguments, or the Truth of Propositions, ever repair the Ruin. for the Error lies in the *first Digestion*, which cannot be rectified by the secondary Functions of Nature [b]

The necessity of genuine Induction, the Cause of Scepticism.

10 It was not, therefore, without cause, that many of the ancient *Philosophers*, and some of them eminent in their way, became *Academicks* and *Scepticks*, who denied all certainty of human Knowledge. and held that the Understanding went no further than *Appearance* and *Probability* 'Tis true, some are of opinion, that *Socrates*, when he declared himself certain of nothing, did it only in the way of *Irony*, and put on the Dissimulation of Knowledge, that by renouncing what he certainly knew, he might be thought to know what he was ignorant of Nor in the later *Academy*, which *Cicero* follow'd, was this Opinion held with much reality but those who excell'd in Eloquence, commonly chose this *Sect*, as the fittest for their purpose, viz acquiring the Reputation of Disputing copiously on both sides of the Question thus leaving the *high Road of Truth*, for *private Walks of Pleasure* Yet 'tis certain there were some few, both in the old and new *Academy*, but more among the *Scepticks*, who held this Principle of doubting in Simplicity and Sincerity of Heart But their chief Error lay in accusing the *Perceptions of the Senses*, and thus pluck'd up the *Sciences by their roots* For tho' the Senses often deceive, or fail us, yet, when industrously assisted, they may suffice for the *Sciences* and this not so much by the help of Instruments, which also have their use, as of such Experiments, as may furnish more subtile Objects, than are perceivable by Sense. But they should rather have charged the Defects of this kind upon the Errors, and Obstinacy of the Mind, which refuses to obey the nature of things, and again, upon corrupt Demonstrations, and wrong ways of arguing and concluding, erroneously infer'd from the Perceptions of Sense And this we say, not to detract from the human Mind, or as if the Work were to be desired, but that proper assistances may be procured, and administer'd to the Understanding, whereby to conquer the Difficulties of Things, and the Obscurities of Nature What we endeavour is, that *the Mind, by the help of Art, may become equal to Things*, and to find a certain *Art of Indication*,

The Art of Indication, or Direction, wanting.

or

[a] This Observation is of the utmost importance insomuch, that it is scarce possible, for want of a Philosophical Language, to express, with *Accuracy* and *Precision*, the Discoveries already made in Nature as may evidently appear in the Writings of that successful Philosopher *Sir Isaac Newton*

[b] To illustrate this Doctrine by an *Example*, we need but consider the general Procedure of Philosophers in their Researches, by means of *Reasoning, Suppositions*, and *uncertain Essays*, instead of a true Observation, careful *Experiment*, and *Confirmation* by repeated Trial Thus the Principles of *Mineral Waters* have long been reason'd about, supposed and guessed at, and but of late begin to be deduced by close *Observation, Experience*, the Method of *Rejection*, and just *Induction* And the same holds true proportionably in *Astronomy, Medicine*, and other Branches of *Physicks*

ol *Direction*, to difclofe, and bring other *Arts* to light, together with their *Axioms* and *Effects* And this *Art* we, upon juft ground, report as *deficient*

11 This ART OF INDICATION has two Parts for *Indication* proceeds (1) from *Experiment* to *Experiment*, or (2) from *Experiments* to *Axioms*, which may again point out new *Experiments* The former we call LEARNED EXPERIENCE, and the latter the INTERPRETATION OF NATURE, *Novum Organum*, or new Machine for the *Mind* The *firft*, indeed, as was formerly intimated, is not properly an *Art*, or any part of *Philofophy*; but a kind of *Sagacity* whence we fometimes call it the *Chafe of Pan*, borrowing the Name from the *Fable* of that God [a] And as there are three ways of walking, *viz.* (1) either by feeling out one's way in the dark, or (2.) when being dim-fighted, another leads one by the hand, and (3) by directing one's Steps by a Light fo when a Man tries all kinds of *Experiments*, without Method, or Order, this is mere groping in the dark, but when he proceeds with fome Direction, and Order, in his Experiments, 'tis as if he were led by the hand; and this we underftand by *learned Experience* but for the *Light* itfelf, which is the third way, it muft be derived from the *Novum Organum* [b]

The two parts of this Art

SECT. XII.

Of LEARNED EXPERIENCE.

1 THE Defign of LEARNED EXPERIENCE, or the Chafe of *Pan* [c], is to fhew the various ways of making *Experiments*. and as we note it for *deficient*, and the thing itfelf is none of the cleareft; we will here give fome fhort Sketch of the *Work*. The *manner of Experimenting* chiefly confifts in the *Variation, Production, Tranflation, Inverfion, Compulfion, Application, Conjunction*, or any other manner of diverfifying, or making *Chance-Experiments* And all this lies without the limits of any *Axiom of Invention* but the *Interpretation of Nature* takes in all the Tranfitions of *Experiments into Axioms*, and of *Axioms into Experiments* [d]

The Defign of Learned Experience.

2 *Experiments are varied firft in the Subject*, as when a known Experiment, having refted in one certain Subftance, is tried in another of the like kind Thus the making of *Paper* is hitherto confin'd to *Linen*, and not applied to Silk, unlefs among the *Chinefe*, nor to Hair-Stuffs and Camblets, nor to Cotton and Skins tho' thefe three feem to be more unfit for the purpofe, and fo fhould be tried in mixture, rather than feparate. Again, *Engrafting* is practifed in Fruit-Trees, but rarely in wild ones, yet an Elm grafted upon an Elm, is faid to produce great Foliage for fhade *Infition* likewife in Flowers, is very rare, tho' now the *Experiment* begins to be made upon Musk-Rofes, which are fuccefsfully inoculated upon common ones We alfo place the *Variations* on the fide of the thing, among the Variations in the

The ways of varying Experiments. (1) in the Subject

I   Matter.

[a] See the *Fable* of PAN explain'd above, *Sect* II of POETRY
[b] *Viz* The *fecond part* of the INSTAURATION
[c] *Viz* The ftarting, hunting, and purfuing of all *natural Things*.
[d] This *Subject* is fully profecuted in the NOVUM ORGANUM

Matter. Thus we see a Scion grafted upon the Trunk of a Tree, thrives better than if fet in Earth: and why should not Onion-feed, fet in a green Onion, grow better, than when fown in the Ground by itfelf, a Root being here fubftituted for the Trunk, fo as to make a kind of Infition in the Root?

3. *An Experiment may be varied in the Efficient.* Thus, as the Sun's Rays are fo contracted by a Burning-glafs, and heighten'd to fuch a degree, as to fire any combuftible Matter: may not the Rays of the Moon, by the fame means, be actuated to fome fmall degree of warmth, fo as to fhew whether all the heavenly Bodies are potentially hot? And as luminous Heats are thus increafed by Glaffes: may not opake Heats, as of Stones and Metals, before ignition, be encreafed likewife? Or is there not fome Proportion of Light here alfo? Amber and Jet, chafed, attract Straws, whence *Quere* if they will not do the fame when warmed at the fire?

4. *An Experiment may be varied in Quantity*, wherein very great care is required, as being fubject to various Errors: For Men imagine, that upon increafing the Quantity, the Virtue fhould increafe proportionably: and thus they commonly poftulate as a *mathematical Certainty*, and yet 'tis utterly falfe. Suppofe a Leaden-Ball, of a pound weight, let fall from a Steeple, reaches the Earth in ten feconds; will a Ball of two pounds, where the Power of natural Motion, as they call it, fhould be double, reach it in five? No, they will fall almoft in equal times, and not be accelerated according to Quantity. Suppofe a Dram of Sulphur would flux half a pound of Steel, will therefore an Ounce of Sulphur flux four Pounds of Steel? 'Tis no confequence; for the Stubbornnefs of the Matter in the Patient is more increafed by Quantity, than the Activity of the Agent. Befides, too much, as well as too little, may fruftrate the Effect: thus in fmelting and refining of Metals, 'tis a common Error to increafe the Heat of the Furnace, or the Quantity of the Flux; but if thefe exceed a due Proportion, they prejudice the Operation: becaufe, by their Force and Corrofivenefs, they turn much of the pure Metal into Fumes, and carry it off, whence there enfues, not only a lofs in the Metal, but the remaining Mafs becomes more fluggifh and intractable. Men fhould therefore remember how *Æfop's* Houfe-wife was deceived, who expected that, by doubling her Feed, her Hen fhould lay two Eggs a day, but the Hen grew fat, and laid none. 'Tis abfolutely unfafe to rely upon any natural *Experiment*, before proof be made of it, both in a lefs and a larger quantity.

5. *An Experiment is produced two ways, viz. by Repetition and Extenfion;* the Experiment being either *repeated*, or *urged* to a more fubtile thing. It may ferve for an *Example of Repetition*, that Spirit of Wine is made of Wine, by one diftillation, and thus becomes much ftronger, and more acrid, than the Wine itfelf: will likewife Spirit of Wine proportionally exceed itfelf in ftrength by another diftillation? But the Repetition alfo of Experiments may deceive; thus here the fecond Exaltation does not equal the Excefs of the firft, and frequently, by repeating an Experiment, after a certain pitch is obtain'd, Nature is fo far from going farther, that fhe rather falls back. Judgment, therefore, muft be ufed in this affair. So Quickfilver put into melted

Lead,

Lead, when it begins to grow cold, will be arrested, and remain no longer fluid but will the same Quickfilver, often ferved fo, become fix'd and malleable?

6 For an *Example of Extenfion* , Water made pendulous above, by means of a long Glafs-ftem, and dipp'd into a mixture of Wine and Water, will feparate the Water from the Wine the Wine gently rifing to the top, and the Water defcending, and fettling at the bottom Now as Wine and Water, being two different Bodies, are feparable by this contrivance , may likewife - the more fubtile parts of Wine, which is an entire Body, be feparated from the more grofs, by this kind of Diftillation, perform'd, as it were, by Gravity , fo as to have floating a-top, a Liquor like Spirit of Wine, or perhaps more fubtile? Again, the *Loadftone* draws Iron in fubftance , but will *Loadftone*, plunged into a folution of Iron, attract the Iron, and cover itfelf with it? So the magnetick Needle applies to the Poles of the World but does it do this after the fame courfe and order that the celeftial Bodies move? Suppofe the Needle held at the South Point, and then let go , would it now turn to the North by the Weft or Eaft? Thus Gold imbibes Quickfilver contiguous to it , but does the Gold do this without increafing its own Bulk, fo as to become a Mafs fpecifically heavier than Gold? Thus Men help their Memories by fetting up Pictures of Perfons in certain places , but would they obtain the fame end, if, neglecting their Faces, they only imagined the Actions or Habits of the Perfons?

(5) By Extenfion

7 An *Experiment may be trai sfer'd three ways*, viz. (1) by Nature, or Chance, into an Art , (2) from one Art, or Practice, to another , and (3) from one part of an Art to another   There are innumerable Examples of the transferring of Experiments from Nature, or Chance, to Arts , as nearly all the mechanical Arts owe their Origins to flender beginnings, afforded by Nature, or Accident   'Tis authoriz'd by a Proverb, that *Grapes among Grapes ripen fooner*   And our Cyder-Makers obferve the rule for they do not ftamp and prefs their Apples, without laying them on heaps, for a time, to ripen by mutual Contact, whereby the Liquor is prevented from being too tart   So the making of artificial Rainbows, by the thick fprinkling of little drops of Water, is an eafy Translation from natural Rainbows made in a rainy Cloud   So the Art of Diftillation might be taken, either from the falling of Rain, and Dew, or that homely Experiment of boiling Water , where Drops adhere to the Cover of the Veffel   Mankind might have been afraid to imitate Thunder and Lightning, by the invention of great Guns, had not the chemical Monk received the firft hint of it by the impetuous Difcharge, and loud Report, of the Cover of his Veffel [a]   But if Mankind were defirous to fearch after ufeful things, they ought attentively, minutely, and on fet purpofe, to view the Workmanfhip and particular Operations of *Nature* , and be continually examining and cafting about, which of them may be transferred to *Arts* [b]   for *Nature is the Mirror of Art*

(6) By Translation, three ways, viz from Nature into an Art.

[a] This Accident is related of *Barth Schwartz*, a Danifh Monk

[b] There are many Inftances of *Arts* copied from Nature in M *Sorell* s Treatife *de la Science univerfelle*

From one Art to another

8 Nor are there fewer *Experiments transferrable from one Art, or Practice, to another*, tho' this be rarely used For *Nature* lies every where obvious to us all tho' particular *Arts* are only known to particular *Artists* *Spectacles* were invented for a help to weak Sights, might not, therefore, an Instrument be discovered, that applied to the Ears, should help the Hearing? *Embalming* preserves dead Bodies, could not therefore something of like kind be transferred to *Medicine*, for the preservation of live ones? So the Practice of sealing in *Wax, Cements*, and *Lead*, is ancient, and paved the way to the printing on Paper, or the *Art of the Press* So in Cookery, *Salt* preserves Meats better in Winter than in Summer might not this be usefully transferred to *Bib*, and the occasional Regulation of their Temperature? So by late experience, *Salt* is found of great efficacy in condensing, by the way of artificial freezing might not this be transferred to the condensing of Metals, since 'tis found that the *Aqua fortes*, compos'd of Salts, dissolve Particles of Gold out of some lighter Metals? So Painting refreshes the Memory by the Image of a thing and is not this transferred in what they call the *Art of Memory*? And let it be observ'd, in general, that nothing is of greater Efficacy in procuring a stock of new and *useful Inventions*, than to have the Experiments of numerous mechanick Arts known to a single Person, or to a few, who might mutually improve each other by Conversation so that by this *Translation of Experiments*, Arts might mutually warm, and light up each other, as it were, by an intermixture of Rays[b] For altho' the *rational way*, by means of a new *Machine for the Mind*, promises much greater things, yet this Sagacity, or *learned Experience*, will, in the mean time, scatter among Mankind many Matters, which, as so many missive Donatives among the Ancients, are near at hand

And from one part of an Art to another

9 The *transferring of Experiments from one part of an Art to another*, differs little *from the transferring one Art to another* But because some Arts are so extensive, as to allow of the Translation of Experiments within themselves, 'tis proper to mention this kind also, especially as 'tis of very great moment in some particular Arts Thus it greatly contributes to enlarge the *Art of Medicine*, to have the Experiments of that part which treats of the *Cures of Disease*, transferred to those parts which relate to the Preservation of Health, and the Prolongation of Life For if any famous Opiate should, in a pestilential Distemper, suppress the violent Inflammation of the Spirits, it might thence seem probable, that something of the same kind, render'd familiar by a due Dose, might, in good measure, check that wasting Inflammation which steals on with Age[c]

10

---

[a] *Kircher* claims the honour of an Invention of this kind, in his *Phonourgia*, tho' perhaps the Ear Trumpet was used in *England* before his time

[b] On this foundation was built that noble *Design* of Mr *Boyle*, for putting out Apprentices to particular Trades, chiefly with a view of having the Knowledge and Practices of such Trades afterwards communicated to himself, or others, whom he should depute for the purpose And whoever would confer a singular Benefit upon Mankind, and improve *Philosophy* in earnest, could not perhaps do better, than by putting such a Design in execution

[c] *Viz.* That kind of Heat, or Inflammation, which dries the *Fibres*, turns the Cartilages and Tendons into bone, and thus stops the Offices and Functions of the Body, whence Decay and Death are naturally brought on by old Age

10. An EXPERIMENT IS INVERTED, *when the contrary of what the Ex-* *(7) The In-* *periment shews, is proved*   for example, *Heat* is increased by Burning-*version of Ex-* Glaffes   but may *Cold* be fo too?   So Heat, in diffufing itfelf, rather mounts *periments.* upwards, but Cold, in diffufing itfelf, rather moves downwards   Thus, if an iron Rod be heated at one end, then erected upon its heated end, and the Hand be applied to the upper part of the Rod, the Hand will prefently be burnt, but if the heated end be placed upwards, and the Hand applied below, it will be burnt much flower   But if the whole Rod were heated, and one end of it wet with Snow, or a Sponge dipp'd in cold Water   would the Cold be fooner propagated downwards, than upwards, if the Sponge were applied below?   Again, the Rays of the Sun are reflected from a white Body, but abforbed by a black one   are Shadows alfo fcatter'd by black, and col-lected by white Bodies?   We fee in a dark place, where Light comes in only at a fmall Hole, the Images of external Objects are received upon white Pa-per, but not upon black

11 An EXPERIMENT IS COMPELL'D, *where 'tis urged or produced to the* *(8) The Com-* *Annihilation or Deftruction of the Power*, the Prey being only catch'd in the *pulfion of Ex-* other *Chafes*, but kill'd in this   Thus the *Loadftone* attracts Iron, urge *periments.* therefore the Iron, or urge the Loadftone, till they attract no longer   for example, if the Loadftone were burnt, or fteep'd in *Aqua fortis*, would it entirely, or only in part, lofe its Virtue?   So if Iron were reduced to a *Crocus*, or made into *prepared Steel*, as they call it, or diffolved in *Aqua fortis*, would the *Loadftone* ftill attract it?   The Magnet draws Iron thro' all known Mediums, Gold, Silver, Glafs, &c.   Urge the Medium, therefore, and, if poffible, find out one that intercepts the Virtue.   Thus make trial of *Quickfilver, Oil, Gums, ignited Gold*, and fuch things as have not yet been tried   Again, *Microfcopes* have been lately introduced, which ftrangely mag-nify minute Objects   urge the ufe of them either by applying them to Ob-jects fo fmall, that their power is loft, or fo large, till 'tis confounded. Thus, for example, can *Microfcopes* clearly difcover thofe things in *Urine*, which are not otherwife perceptible?   Can they difcover any Specks, or Clouds, in Gems that are perfectly clear and bright to appearance?   Can they magnify the Motes of the Sun, which *Democritus* miftook for Atoms, and the Principles of Things?   Will they fhew a mix'd Powder of Vermi-lion and Cerufe in diftinct Grains of Red and White?   Will they magnify larger Objects, as the Face, the Eye, &c   as much as they do a Gnat or a Mite?   Or reprefent a Piece of fine Linen open as a Net?

12. The APPLICATION OF AN EXPERIMENT, *is no more than an inge-* *(9) The Ap-* *nious Tranflation of it to fome other Experiment of ufe*   for example, all Bodies *plication of* have their own Dimenfions and Gravities   *Gold* has more Gravity and lefs *Experiments.* Bulk than *Silver*, and *Water* than *Wine*, hence an ufeful Experiment is derived for difcovering what proportion of *Silver* is mix'd with *Gold*, or of *Water* with *Wine*, from a knowledge of their Meafure and Weight: which was the grand Difcovery of *Archimedes*.   Again, as Flefh putrefies fooner in fome Cellars than in others, 'twere ufeful to transfer this Experiment to the Examination of *Airs*, as to their being more or lefs wholefome to live in,

by

by find ng tl of where it Flesh remains longest unputrified And the same L.... is applic ble to discover the more wholesome or pestilential Sea-fons of the Year Bur Examples of this kind are endlefs, and require that Men fhould have r Lyes continually turn'd one while to the *Nature of* Th g, and not le to human *Ufes*

13 The C ... t on of an EXPERIMENT, to a Conn ction and Chain of A ... ngs which were not uf ful fingle, are made ufeful n C , ... to have Rofes or Fruits come late, the way is to pluck o ... B ..s, or to lay b re th Roots, and expofe them to the open Air, ... the middle of Spring, but 'tis much better to do both togeth r So ... Aver feparate, have a great power of cooling, but much gre ter wh n mix'd together But there may be a Fallacy in this obv s S r, as in cafes where *Axioms* are wanting, if the Con- .. b r .. 1 t gs that oper te by different, and, as it were, con-t ...

14 As to Chance-EXPERIMENTS, thefe are plainly an irrational and ... wild Procedure, when the Mind fuggefts the trial of a thing, not becaufe any K or E perfuades it, but only becaufe nothing of the like kind has been tried before yet even here, perhaps, fome confiderable Myftery lies concealed, provided no ftone in nature were left unturn'd for the capital things of N ture generally lie out of the beaten Paths, fo that even the abfurdnefs of a thing, fometimes proves ufeful But if Reafon alfo be here join'd, fo as to fhew that the like *Experiment* never was attempted, and yet that there is great caufe why it fhould be, then this becomes an excellent Inftrument, and really enters the Bofom of Nature For example, in the Operation of Fire upon natural Bodies, it hath hitherto always happen'd, that either fomething flies off, as Flame and Smoke, in our common Fires, or at leaft, that the parts are locally feparated to fome diftance, as in Diftilla-tion, where the Vapour rifes, and the Fæces are left behind, but no Man hath hitherto tried *clofe Diftillat on* [a] Yet it feems probable, that if the Force of Heat may have its Action confined in the Cavities of a Body, without any poffib lity of lofs or efcape, this *Proteus* of Matter will be manacled, as it were, and forced to undergo numerous Tr nsformations, provided only the Heat be fo moderated and changed, as not to break the containing Vef-fel For this is a kind of *natural Matrix*, where Heat has its Effect without feparating, or throwing off the Parts of a Body In a true *Matrix*, in-deed, there is Nourifhment fupplied, but in point of Tranfmutation, the cafe

---

[a] The Th ng here meant is not, as appears from other Paffages of the Author, the common *clofe Digeftion*, *Diftillation* without the admiffion of Air, or clofe *Sublimation*, as in making Mercury prec p t te per fe, but a new *Digeftion*, practif-d by me ns of the DIGESTOR, or hollow me ta ine Engine, made fo ftrong and firm, as to endure a great Violence of Fire which is an Ope-ra ion that had not perhaps been practifed at the time our Author wrote, but is the reputed Inven on of M *Papin*, and Mr *Boyle*, tho' they nei her of them carried the Difcovery to any great length and even at prefent it feems to reft in the making of Soops, or foftening of ani-mal Bones tho' applicable perhaps, to much nobler Purpofes See more upon this head, in *Morhof's Polyhiftor*, Tom II pag 145

cafe is the fame[a]   And here let none defpair or be confounded, if the Experiments they attempt fhould not anfwer their Expectation   for tho' Succefs be indeed more *pleafing* , yet *Failure*, frequently, is no lefs *informing*   and it muft ever be remembred, that *Experiments of Light* are more to be defired, than *Experiments of Profit*.   And fo much for LEARNED EXPERIENCE, as we call it , which thus appears to be rather a *Sagacity*, or a *fcenting of Nature*, as in hunting, than a direct *Science* [b]

SECT. XIII.

Of the INVENTION *of* ARGUMENTS: *and* TOPICAL INVENTION.

1 THE INVENTION OF ARGUMENTS is not properly an *Invention* , *The Invention* for to *invent*, is to difcover things unknown before , and not to re- *of Arguments,* collect, or admit, fuch as are known already.   The Office and Ufe of this *what* kind of Invention, feems to be no more, than dextroufly to draw out from the Stock of Knowledge laid up in the Mind, fuch things as make to the prefent purpofe   for one who knows little or nothing of a Subject propofed, has no ufe of *Topicks*, or *Places of Invention* , whilft he who is provided of fuitable Matter, will find and produce Arguments, without the help of *Art*, and fuch *Places of Invention* , tho' not fo readily and commodioufly   whence this *kind of Invention*, is rather a bare calling to Memory, or a Suggeftion with Application, than a *real Invention*   But fince the Term is already received, it may ftill be called *Invention* , as the hunting in a Park may be call'd hunting, no lefs than that in the open Field   But not to infift upon the Word, the *Scope and End of the thing itfelf*, *is a quick and ready ufe of our Thoughts, rather than any Enlargement or Increafe of them.*

2 There are *two Methods of procuring a Stock of Matter for Difcourfe* , viz *Two Methods* (1) either by marking out, and indicating the Parts wherein a thing is to be *of procuring* fearch'd after, which is what we call the TOPICAL WAY, or (2) by laying *Matter for* up Arguments for ufe, that were compofed before hand, relating to fuch *Difcourfe, viz.* things as frequently happen, and come in difpute , and this we call the *the* topical *and the* PROMP- *promptuary.*

---

[a] Much Light of Direction for producing uncommon Effects, may be derived from this *Paffage* , as it opens the way for an exact and powerful Imitation of *Nature*, in her *clofe Methods* of operating, in the Formation of Animals in the *Uterus*, and the *Egg*, the Production of Metals and Minerals, in the *clofe Caverns* of the Earth, *&c*   See *Morhof*, in the placea bovequoted , and confult Experience, as to the *clofe Operations* of the *Furnace*

[b] This Section appears to have been little underftood, even by fome eminent Men , who cenfure the Scheme of the Author   and think that *Experiments* muft needs be cafual, and the human Underftanding unable to direct and conduct them to ufeful purpofes, unlefs by accident   The Misfortune feems to lie here, that few converfe fo familiarly with *Nature*, as to judge what may be done in this way, or how the numerous Difcoveries of the Lord *Bacon*, Mr *Boyle*, Dr *Hook*, Sir *Ifaac Newton*, &c   were made   An attentive Perufal of the NOVUM ORGANUM, where this Subject is largely profecuted, will unravel the *Myftery.*

PROMPTUARY WAY but the latter can scarce be called a part of *Science*, as confisting rather in diligence than any artificial Learning. *Aristotle* on this head ingeniously derides the *Sophists* of his time, saying, *they acted like a profeft'd Shoemaker, who did not teach the Art of Shoemaking, but set out a large stock of shoes, of different shapes and sizes*. But it might be replied, that the *Shoemaker* who should have no shoes in his shop, and only make them as they were bespoke, would find few customers. Our *Saviour* speaks far otherwise of *divine Knowledge*, saying, *Therefore every Scribe which is instructed unto the kingdom of heaven, is like unto a man that is an housholder, who bringeth forth out of his treasure things new and old*.

3. We find also that the ancient *Rhetoricians* gave it in precept to the *Orators*, to be always provided of various *Common Places*, ready furnished and illustrated with Arguments on both sides, as for the *intention* of the *Law* against the *words of the Law*, for the truth of Arguments against Testimonies and the like. And *Cicero* himself being taught by long experience, roundly asserts, that a diligent and experienced *Orator* should have such things as come into dispute, ready laboured and prepared, so as that in *Pleading* there should be no necessity of introducing any thing new, or occasional, except new Names, and some particular Circumstances. But as the first *opening* of the *Cause* has a great effect in preparing the minds of the Audience, the exactness of *Demosthenes* judged it proper to compose before-hand, and have in readiness, several Introductions to his Harangues and Speeches: and these Examples, and Authorities, may justly over-rule the opinion of *Aristotle*, who would have us change a *whole Wardrobe for a pair of Sheers*. This *promptuary Method*, therefore, should not be omitted, but as it relates as well to *Rhetorick* as to *Logick*, we shall here touch it but slightly, designing to consider it more fully under *Rhetorick* [a].

4. We divide *topical Invention into general and particular*. The *general* is so copiously and diligently treated in the common *Logicks*, that we need not dwell upon its explanation: we only observe by the way, that this *topical Method* is not only used in Argumentation, and close Conference, but also in *Contemplation*, when we meditate or revolve any thing alone. Nor is its office only confin'd to the suggesting, or admonishing us, of what should be affirmed or asserted, but also what we should examine or question: a prudent questioning being a kind of *half-knowledge*, for, as *Plato* justly observes, *a Searcher must have some general notion of the thing he searches after, otherwise he could never know it when he had found it*, and therefore the more comprehensive and sure our *Anticipation* is, the more direct and short will be the *Investigation*. And hence the same *Topicks* which conduce to the close examining into our own Understandings, and collecting the Notices there treasured up, are likewise assistant in drawing forth our Knowledge. Thus, if a person, skilful in the point under question, were at hand, as we might prudently and advantageously consult him upon it, in like manner, we may usefully select and turn over Authors and Books, to instruct and inform ourselves about those things we are in quest of.

5.

---

[a] See hereafter, Sect. XVIII.

5 But the PARTICULAR TOPICAL INVENTION is much more condu- *The particu-*
cive to the fame purpofes, and to be efteemed a highly fertile thing. Some *lar topical In-*
Writers have lately mentioned it, but 'tis by no means treated according *cient*
to its extent and merit Not to mention the Error and Haughtinefs which
have too long reigned in the *Schools*, and their purfuing with infinite fubtilty,
fuch things as are obvious, without once touching upon thofe that lie remote,
we receive this *Topical Invention* as an extremely ufeful thing that *affords cer-*
tain Heads of Enquiry and Invefligation appropriated to particular Subjects and
Sciences Thefe *Places* are certain mixtures of *Logick*, and the peculiar matter of each Science 'Tis an idle thing, and fhews a narrow mind to think
that the *Art of difcovering the Sciences* may be invented and propofed in perfection from the beginning, fo as to be afterwards only exercifed and
brought into ufe. for men fhould be made fenfible, that the *folid and real*
Arts of Invention grow up and increafe along with Inventions th·mfelves fo
that when any one firft comes to the thorough examination of a *Science*,
he fhould have fome ufeful *Rules of Difcovery*, but after he hath made a
confiderable progrefs in the *Science* itfelf, he may, and ought, to find out new
Rules of Invention, the better to lead him ftill further. The way here is
like walking on a Flat, where after we have gone fome length, we not only
approach nearer the End of our journey, but alfo have a clearer view of
what remains to be gone of it fo in the *Sciences*, every ftep of the way, as
it leaves fome things behind, alfo gives us a nearer profpect of thofe that
remain and as we report this particular topical *Invention deficient*, we think
proper to give an Example of it, in the Subject of *Gravity* and *Levity*

6 (1) *Let Enquiries be made what kind of bodies are fufceptible of the mo-* *An example*
tion of Gravity, what of Levity and if there be any of a middle or neutral *of the parti-*
Nature. *cular topical*
Invention, in
7 (2) *After the fimple Enquiry of Gravity and Levity, proceed to a compa-* *the fubject of*
rative Enquiry, viz which heavy bodies weigh more, and which lefs, in the fame *Gravity and*
dimenfions, and of like ones, which mount upwards the fwifter, and which the *Levity*
flower

8. (3) *Enquire what effect the quantity of the Body has in the motion of Gravi-*
ty This at firft fight may appear a needlefs Enquiry, becaufe Motion may
feem proportionable to Quantity, but the cafe is otherwife. For altho' in
Scales, Quantity is equal to the Gravity, yet where there is a fmall refiftance,
as in the falling of bodies thro' the Air, Quantity has but little force to
quicken the defcent for twenty pounds of lead, and a fingle pound, fall
nearly in the fame time

9 (4.) *Enquire whether the quantity of a Body may be fo increafed, as that*
the Motion of Gravity fhall be entirely loft, as in the Globe of the Earth, which
hangs pendulous without falling Quære, therefore, whether other maffes may be
fo large as to fuftain themfelves For that Bodies fhould move to the centre
of the Earth, is a fiction· and every mafs of matter has an averfion to
local motion, till this be overcome by fome ftronger impulfe [a]

(5)

[a] Hence the famous Law of Motion, that Bodies would for ever continue in that ftate of
Reft or Motion wherein they once are, if fome other Caufe did not put them out of it Hence
the

10 5, *Enquire into the Effects and Nature of resisting Mediums, as to their affecting the Motion of Gravity*, for a falling body either penetrates and cuts thro' the body it meets in its way, or else is stopped by it. If it pass through, there is a penetration, either with a small resistance, as in Air, or with a greater, as in Water. If it be stop'd, 'tis stop'd by an unequal resistance where there is a preponderancy, as when Wood is laid upon Wax, or by an equal resistance, as when Water is laid upon Water, or Wood upon Wood of the same kind; which is what the Schools pretend, when they idly imagine that bodies do not gravitate in their own places. And all these circumstances alter the motion of Gravity, for heavy bodies move after one way in the ballance, and after another in falling; and, which may seem strange, after one way in a ballance suspended in the Air, and after another in a ballance plunged in Water, after one way in falling thro' Water, and after another when floating upon it.

11 6, *Enquire into the Effects of the Figure of the descending Body, in directing the Motion of Gravity.* Suppose of a figure broad and thin, cubical, oblong, round, pyramidal, &c. and how Bodies turn themselves whilst they remain in the same position as when first let go.

12 7. *Enquire into the Effects of the Continuation and Progression of the Fall, or Descent*, as to the acquiring a greater *impulse or velocity, and in what proportion to its length this velocity is increased*; for the Ancients, upon slender consideration, imagin'd, that this Motion being Natural, was always upon the increase.

13 (8) *Enquire into the Effect of Distance, or the near Approach of a Body going to the Earth, so as to fall swifter, slower, or not at all, supposing it come to be out of the Earth's sphere of activity, according to* Gilbert's *opinion, as to the Effects of plunging the falling Body deeper into the Earth, or placing it nearer the place*; for this also varies the Motion, as is manifest to those who work in Mines.

14 9, *Enquire into the Effects of the difference of Bodies, thro' which the Motion of Gravity is diffused and communicated, and whether 'tis equally communicated thro' rare porous Bodies, as thro' hard and solid ones.* Thus if the beam of a scale were one half of wood, and the other of silver, yet of the same weight, enquire whether this would not make an alteration in the scales; and again, whether metal laid upon wool, or a blown bladder, would weigh the same as in the naked scale.

15 (10, *Enquire into the Effects of the distance of a body from the point of suspension in the communication of the Motion of Gravity, that is, into the earlier or later rising in its inclination or depression;* as in scales, where one side of the beam is longer, tho' of the same weight with the other, whether this inclines the beam, or in syphons, where the longer leg will draw the water, tho' the shorter being made wider, contains a greater weight of water.

16 (11) *Enquire into the Effects of intermixing or coupling a light Body and a heavy one, for lessening the Gravity of Bodies*, as in the weight of creatures alive and dead.   17 (12)

the *Vis Inertiae* of Matter or its Indisposition to Motion or Rest; and hence the Gravitation of Matter, and the Insignificance of *Mathematical Centres* in the business of Attraction.

17 (12) *Enquire into the Ascents and Descents of the ligther and heavier parts of one entire Body whence curious separations are often made, as in the separation of wine and water, the rising of cream from milk*, &c.

18 (13.) *Enquire what is the Line and Direction of the Motion of Gravity, and how far it respects the Earth's centre, that is, the mass of the Earth , or the centre of its own Body, that is, the appetite of its parts* For these *centres* are properly supposed in Demonstrations , but are otherwise unserviceable in Nature.

19. (14) *Enquire into the Comparative Motion of Gravity, with other Motions, or to what Motions it yields, and what it exceeds* Thus in the Motion they call violent, the Motion of Gravity is with-held for a time , and so when a large weight of Iron is raised by a little Loadstone, the Motion of Gravity gives way to the Motion of Sympathy.

20. (15) *Enquire concerning the Motion of the Air, whether it rises upwards, or be as it were neutral*, which is not easy to be discovered without some accurate Experiments for the rising up of Air at the bottom of Water, rather proceeds from a resistance of the Water, than the Motion of the Air ; since the same also happens in Wood [a].   But Air mixed with Air makes no discovery , for Air in Air may seem as light, as Water in Water seems heavy but in Bubbles, which are Air surrounded with a thin pellicle of Water, it stands still for a time

21 (16) *Let the Bounds of Levity be enquired after* , for tho' Men make the Centre of the Earth the Centre of Gravity, they will perhaps hardly make the ultimate convexity of the Heavens the boundary of Levity , but rather, perhaps, as heavy bodies seem to be carried so far, that they rest, and grow as it were immoveable , light bodies are carried so far, that they begin a Rotation, or circular Motion

22 (17.) *Enquire the cause why Vapours and Effluvia are carried so high, as that called the middle region of the Air, since the matter of them is somewhat gross , and the rays of the Sun cease alternately by night.*

23 (18) *Enquire into the tendency of Flame upwards , which is the more abstruse, because Flame perishes every moment, unless perhaps in the midst of larger Flames for Flames broken from their continuity, are of small duration*

24. (19.) *Enquire into the motion and activity of Heat upwards* , as when Heat in ignited Iron sooner creeps upwards than downwards   And thus much by way of Example of our *particular Topical Enquiry* We must, for a Conclusion, admonish mankind, to alter their *particular Topicks* in such manner, as after some considerable progress made in the Enquiry, to raise *Topick* after *Topick* [b], if they desire to ascend to the Pinnacle of the *Sciences* For my own part, I attribute so much to these *particular Topicks*, that I design a particular Work upon their Use, in the more eminent and obscure subjects

[a] As when a Plate of Wood is press'd with the Hand against the bottom of a Pail of Water, for if the Hand be now taken away, the Wood is thrown up by the Water with great violence

[b] The Method of doing this, is particularly explained in the NOVUM ORGANUM.

c N for we are masters of questions, tho' not of things[a] And here we close the Subject of INVENTION

SECT. XIV.

Of the ART *of* JUDGMENT.

In the Art of Judgment by Induction there is little to remark

1 WE come now to the ART OF JUDGMENT, which treats of the *nature of Proof* or *Demonstration* This *Art*, as 'tis commonly received, concludes either by *Induction* or *Syllogism* for *Enthymemes* and *Examples* are only abridgments of these two[b] As to *Judgment by Induction*, we need not be large upon it, because what is sought, we both find and judge of, by the same operation of the Mind Nor is the matter here transacted by a medium, but directly, almost in the same manner as by the Sense: for Sense, in its primary objects, at once seizes the image of the object, and assents to the truth of it[c] 'Tis otherwise in *Syllogism*, whose proof is not direct, but mediate, and therefore the Invention of the *Medium*, is one thing, and Judgment, as to the consequence of an argument, another For the Mind first casts about, and afterwards acquiesces. But for the *corrupt Form of Induction*, we entirely drop it; and refer the *genuine one* to our *Method of interpreting Nature*[d] And thus much of *Judgment by Induction*

The Art of Judgment by Syllogism, its Origin

2 The other by *Syllogism* is worn by the File of many a subtile Genius, and reduced to numerous fragments, as having a great sympathy with the human Understanding for the Mind is wonderfully bent against fluctuating, and endeavours to find something fix'd and unmoveable, upon which, as a firm basis, to rest in its Enquiries And as *Aristotle* endeavours to prove, that in all motion of bodies, there is something still at rest, and elegantly explains the ancient Fable of *Atlas*, sustaining the Heavens on his shoulders, of the *Poles of the World*, about which the revolutions are performed: so men have a strong desire to retain within themselves an *Atlas*, or *Pole* for their Thoughts, in some measure to govern the fluctuations and revolutions of the Understanding, as otherwise fearing their *Heaven should tumble* And hence

it

---

[a] Tho' no express Work of the Author was published with this *Title*, yet all his *particular Enquiries* proceed in this Method, as the *History of Winds, Life and Death*, &c and the same is esteemed, followed by the *Royal Society*, for a considerable time, by drawing up *Heads of Enquiries* upon particular Subjects, sending them abroad, and publishing them in their *Philosophical Transactions* The same was likewise observed by Mr *Boyle*, and most other successful Enquirers into Nature, since the Lord *Bacon* See more to this purpose in the NOVUM ORGANUM, and Introductions to the THIRD AND FOURTH PARTS of the INSTAURATION

[b] An *Enthymeme* is no other than a *Syllogism* of two Propositions, the third being supplied by the Mind, as the word itself imports, and *Induction* is no more than a string of *Instances*, or *Examples* brought upon any Head

[c] As fast the Assent is given so quick, as scarce to be distinguished from the Sensation itself.

[d] Viz. the NOVUM ORGANUM.

2

it is, that they have been ever hasty in laying the *Principles of the Sciences*, about which all the variety of Disputes might turn without danger of falling, not at all regarding, that whoever too hastily catches at Certainties, shall end in Doubts, as he who seasonably with-holds his Judgment, shall arrive at Certainties.

3 'Tis therefore manifest that this ART OF JUDGING BY SYLLOGISM *Its Office* *is nothing more than a Reduction of Propositions to their Principles, by middle Terms* But *Principles* are supposed to be received by consent, and exempt from Question, whilst the *Invention of middle Terms* is freely permitted to the subtilty and investigation of the Wit This *Reduction* is of two kinds, *direct* and *inverse* 'Tis *direct*, when the *Proposition* itself is reduced to the *Principle*, and this is called *ostensive Proof* 'Tis *inverse*, when the Contradictory of the Proposition is reduced to the Contradictory of the *Principle*, which they call *Proof by absurdity* but the number or scale of the *middle Terms* is diminished, or increased, according to the remoteness of the *Proposition* from the *Principle*

4 Upon this foundation, we divide the ART OF JUDGMENT nearly *The Art of* as usual, into *Analyticks*, and the *Doctrine of Elenches*, or Confutations, the *Judgment di-* first whereof supplies *Direction*, and the other *Caution* for *Analyticks* di- *Analyticks*, rects the *true Forms of the consequences of Arguments*, from which if we vary, we *and the Doc-* make a wrong Conclusion. And this itself contains a kind of *Elench*, or redar- *trine of Con-* gution, for what is right, shews not only itself, but also what is wrong Yet *futations.* 'tis safest to employ *Elenches*, as Monitors, the easier to discover fallacies, which would otherwise ensnare the Judgment We find no *Deficiency* in *Analyticks*, for 'tis rather loaded with superfluities, than deficient[a]

5 We divide the *Doctrine of Confutations* into three parts, viz (1.) the *The Doctrine* *Confutation of Sophisms*, (2) the *Confutation of Interpretation*, and (3) the *of Confuta-* *Confutation of Images or Idols*. The *Doctrine of the* CONFUTATION OF SO- *tions divided* PHISMS, is extremely useful for altho' a gross kind of Fallacy is not im- *Confutation of* properly compared, by *Seneca*, to the Tricks of Jugglers, where we know *Sophisms* not by what means the things are perform'd, but are well assur'd they are not as they appear to be yet the more subtile *Sophisms* not only supply *Occasions of Answer*, but also in reality confound the Judgment This part concerning the *Confutation of Sophisms* is, in *Precept*, excellently treated by *Aristotle*, but still better by *Plato*, in *Example*, not only in the Persons of the ancient Sophists, *Gorgias*, *Hippias*, *Protagoras*, *Euthydemus*, &c but even in the person of *Socrates* himself, who, always professing to affirm nothing, but to confute what was produced by others, has ingeniously exprefs'd the *several Forms of Objections*, *Fallacies*, and *Redargutions* Therefore in this part we find no *Deficiency*, but only observe by the way, that tho' we place the *true and principal Use of this Doctrine in the redargution of Sophisms*, yet 'tis plain, that its degenerate and corrupt use tends to the raising of Cavils, and Contradictions, by means of those *Sophisms* themselves. which kind of Faculty is

S 2   highly

---

[a] Upon the Subject of *Analyticks*, see *Weigelius* in his *Analysis Aristotelica*, *ex Euclide restituta*, and *Morhof* in his *Polyhistor.* Tom. I. Lib. II. cap. 7 *de Methodis variis*

h ghl, esteemed, and has no small uses ᵃ Tho' 'tis a good distinction made between the *Orator* and the *Sophist*, that the former excels in swiftness, as t e *Gra, s u d*, the other in the turn, as the *Hare*

6 With regard to the CONFUTATIONS OF INTERPRETATION, we must here repeat what was formerly said of the transcendental and adventitious conditions of Beings, such as *Greater*, *Less*, *Whole*, *Parts*, *Motion*, *Rest*, &c For the different way of considering these things, which is either *Physically* or *Logically*, must be remember'd The *Physical Treatment* of them we have allotted to *primary Philosophy*, but their *Logical Treatment* is what we here call the *Confutation of Interpretation* And this we take for a sound and excellent part of Learning as general and common *Notions*, unless accurately and judiciously distinguished from their Origin, are apt to mix themselves in all Disputes, so as strangely to cloud and darken the Light of the Question ; and frequently occasion the Controversy to end in a quarrel about Words for Equivocations and wrong Acceptations of Words, especially of this kind, are the *Sophisms of Sophisms* wherefore 'tis better to treat of them separate, than either to receive them into *primary Philosophy* or *Metaphysicks*, or again to make them a part of *Analyticks*, as *Aristotle* has confusedly done. We give this *Doctrine* a name from its Use , because its true use is indeed *Redargution* and *Caution*, about the employing of Words So likewise that part concerning *Predicaments*, if rightly treated, as to the cautions against confounding or transposing the terms of *Definitions* and *Divisions*, is of principal use , and belongs to the present Article And thus much for the *Confutation of Interpretation*

7 As to the CONFUTATIONS OF IMAGES, or IDOLS, we observe that *Idols* are the deepest Fallacies of the human Mind, for they do not deceive in particulars, as the rest, by clouding and ensnaring the Judgment , but from a corrupt predisposition, or bad complexion of the Mind; which distorts and infects all the anticipations of the Understanding. For the Mind darkened by its Covering, the Body, is far from being a flat, equal and clear *Mirror*, that receives and reflects the rays without mixture , but rather a *Magical Glass*, full of *Superstitions* and *Apparitions* *Idols* are impos'd upon the Understanding, either (1) by *the general Nature of Mankind*, (2) *the Nature of each particular Man*, or (3) by *Words*, or *communicative Nature* The first kind we call IDOLS OF THE TRIBE , the second kind, IDOLS OF THE DEN , and the third kind, IDOLS OF THE MARKET ᵇ. There is also a fourth kind, which we call IDOLS OF THE THEATRE , being superinduced by *false Theories*, or *Philosophies*, and the *perverted Laws of Demonstration*. This last kind we are not at present concerned with , as it may be rejected and laid aside but the others seize the Mind strongly,

---

ᵃ For example, by giving occasion to farther Thought, Enquiry, and Dispute, which may end in some new Discovery, or the fuller clearing up and confirming some Truth

ᵇ The Reader should not be shocked at the use of these *new Terms*, since the DOCTRINE of IDOLS was itself new at the Time that this was wrote and being perhaps never touched upon before, the Author was obliged, for clearness and distinction sake, to give discriminating Names to the several Assortments of these *false Notions*, the *Doctrine* whereof is more fully explained and illustrated in the NOVUM ORGANUM.

ly, and cannot be totally eradicated.   Therefore no *Art of Analyticks* can be expected here, but the *Doctrine of the Confutation of Idols* is the *primary Doctrine of Idols*.   Nor indeed can the *Doctrine of Idols* be reduced to an *Art*, but can only be employ'd, by means of a certain *contemplative Prudence*, to prevent them

9 For IDOLS OF THE TRIBE[a], 'tis observable that the nature of the *(1) Into Idols* *Understanding* is more affected with *Affirmatives* and *Actives*, than with *Nega-* *of the* Tribe *tives* and *Privatives*, tho' in justness it should be equally affected with them both   *but if things fall out right, or keep their course, the Mind receives a stronger impression of this*, than of a much greater number of *Failures*, or contrary *Events*. which is the *Root* of all *Superstition* and *Credulity*   Hence *Diagoras*, being shewed in *Neptune*'s Temple, many *votive Pictures* of such as had escaped Shipwreck, and thereupon asked by his Guide, if he did not now acknowledge the *divine* Power? answered wisely, *But first shew me where those are painted that were shipwrecked, after having thus paid their vows*   And the case is the same, in the similar *Superstitions* of astrological Predictions, Dreams, Omens, &c   Again, *the Mind being of itself, an equal and uniform substance, presupposes a greater unanimity and uniformity in the nature of things, than there really is*, whence our thoughts are continually drawing parallels, and supposing relations in many things that are truly different, and singular.   Hence the *Chemists* have fantastically imagined their *four Principles* corresponding to the *Heavens*, *Air*, *Earth*, and *Water*, and the *Mathematicians* their circular Motions of the celestial bodies, &c   And again, *Men make themselves, as it were, the Mirror and Rule of Nature*   'Tis incredible what a number of *Idols* have been introduced into Philosophy, by the reduction of *Natural Operations to a correspondence with human Actions*, that is, by imagining Nature acts as Man does   which is not much better than the *Heresy of the Anthropomorphites*, that sprung up in the cells and solitude of ignorant monks, or the opinion of *Epicurus*, who attributed a *human figure to the Gods*   *Velleius*, the *Epicurean*, need not, therefore, have asked, *why God should have adorned the Heavens with Stars and Lights, as Master of the Works?* For if the *grand Architect* had acted a human Part, he would have ranged the Stars into some beautiful and elegant order, as we see in the vaulted roofs of Palaces, whereas, we scarce find among such an infinite multitude of Stars, any figure either square, triangular, or rectilinear   so great a difference is there betwixt the *Spirit of Man*, and the *Spirit of the Universe*

10 The IDOLS OF THE DEN have their Origin from the peculiar Na- *(2) The Idols* ture, both of *Mind* and *Body*, in each person, as also from Education, Cu- *of the* Den. stom, and the Accidents of particular persons   'Tis a beautiful *Emblem* that of *Plato*'s Den[b], for, to drop the exquisite subtilty of the parable, if any one should be educated from his infancy in a dark cave, till he were of full age,

---

[a] These might otherwise be called PARTIAL IDOLS, as being owing to the partiality or obliquity of the *Mind*, which has its particular bent, and admits of some things more readily than others, without a manifest Reason assign'd for it to the Understanding   However this be, they manifestly belong to the *Tribe of mankind*

[b] Whence the Author apparently took the Appellation, *Idols of the Den*.

 rge and fhould then of a fudden be brought into broad day-light, and behold its Apparatus of the Heavens and of Things , no doubt but many ftrange and abfurd fancies would arife in his Mind   and tho' men live indeed in the view of the Heavens, yet our Minds are confined in the caverns of our Bodies, whence of neceffity we receive infinite *Images of Errors and Falſhoods* , if the Mind does but feldom, and only for a fhort continuance, leave its Den, and not conftantly dwell in the *contemplation of Nature* , as it were in the open day-light   And with this *Emblem of Plato's Den* , agrees the foregoing doctrine, viz that *Men feek the Sciences in their own narrow Worlds* , and not in the great or common One.

11 But the IDOLS OF THE MARKET give the greateft difturbance , and from a certain agreement among mankind, with regard to the impofition of *Words* and *Names* , infinuate themfelves into the Underftanding, for *Words* are generally given according to vulgar conception , and divide things by fuch differences as the common people are capable of[a]   but when a more acute Underftanding, or a more careful Obfervation, would diftinguifh things better , Words murmur againft it   The remedy of this lies in *Definitions* , but thefe themfelves are in many refpects irremediable , as confifting of *Words* : for *Words g-nerate Words* , however men may imagine they have a command over Words , and can eafily fay *they will ſpeak with the Vulgar, and think with the Wiſe*   Terms of Art alfo, which prevail only among the Skilful, may feem to remedy the mifchief , and *Definitions* premifed to Arts in the prudent mathematical manner, to correct the wrong acceptation of Words yet all this is infufficient to prevent the feducing incantation of Names, in numerous refpects, their doing violence to the Underftanding, and recoiling upon it, from whence they proceeded   This evil therefore requires a new and a deeper *Remedy* , but thefe things we touch lightly at prefent , in the mean time, *noting this Doctrine of* GRAND CONFUTATIONS , *or the* DOCTRINE *of the* NATIVE AND ADVENTITIOUS IDOLS OF THE MIND, *for deficient* [b].

12 There is alfo wanting a confiderable *Appendix to the Art of Judgment.* *Ariſtotle* indeed marks out the thing, but has no where delivered the manner of effecting it   The defign is *to fhew what Demonſtrations fhould be applied to what Subjects* , fo that this Doctrine fhould contain the *Judging of Judgments*[c]   For *Ariſtotle* well obferves, that we fhould not require *Demonſtrations from Orators* , nor *Perſuaſion from Mathematicians* fo that if we err in the kind of proof, *Judgment* itfelf cannot be perfect.   And as there are four kinds of Demonftration, viz (1) by *immediate Conſent, and common Notions*, (2) by *Induction*, (3) by *Syllogiſm*, and (4) by *Congruity*, which *Ariſtotle* juftly calls *Demonſtration in Circle* , each of thefe *Demonſtrators* has its peculiar Subjects, and Parts of the *Sciences* , wherein they are of force , and others again from which they are excluded. for infifting upon

too

[a] Whence we have the Reafon of thefe Appellations, and in particular, the term *Idols of the Market*

[b] It is fuppied in the NOVUM ORGANUM

[c] What has been done towards fupplying this *Deficiency* , may be feen in *Morhof's Polyhiſtor,* Tom I Lib II cap 4 *de Studiis dirigendis Juaitu*

too ſtrict proofs in ſome Caſes, and ſtill more, the facility and remiſſneſs, in reſting upon ſlight proofs in others, is what has greatly prejudiced and obſtructed the *Sciences*.   And ſo much for the *Art of Judgment*.

SECT. XV.
Of the ART *of* MEMORY.

1. WE divide the ART OF MEMORY, or the KEEPING AND RETAIN- *The Art of* ING OF KNOWLEDGE, into *two Parts*, viz the *Doctrine of Helps* *Memory di-* for the *Memory*, and the *Doctrine of the Memory itſelf*   The Help for the *vided into the* Memory is *Writing*. and we muſt obſerve, that the *Memory*, without this *Helps for the* aſſiſtance, is unequal to things of Length and Accuracy ; and ought not other- *Memory,* wiſe to be truſted   And this holds particularly in *Inductive Philoſophy*, and in the *Interpretation of Nature*; for one might as well undertake to make an Almanack by the Memory, without writing, as to *interpret Nature* by bare Contemplation   Scarce any thing can be more uſeful in the *ancient and popular Sciences*, than a true and *ſolid Help for the Memory*, that is, a *juſt and learned Digeſt of Common-places*   Some, indeed, condemn this Method of *Common-placing* what one reads or learns, as prejudicial to Erudition, hindering the courſe of Reading, and rendring the Memory indolent , but as it is a wrong Procedure in the *Sciences* to be over-haſty and quick, we judge it of great ſervice in Studies, unleſs a Man be ſolid, and compleatly inſtructed, to beſtow Diligence and Labour in ſetting down *Common-places*, as it affords Matter to Invention, and collects and ſtrengthens the Judgment But among all the Methods and *Common-place Books* we have hitherto ſeen, there is not one of value[a], as favouring of the *School* rather than the *World*, and uſing rather vulgar and pedantical Diviſions, than ſuch as any way penetrate Things

2 And for the *Memory itſelf*, it ſeems hitherto to have been negligently *And the Doc-* and ſuperficially enquired into   There is indeed ſome Art of *Memory* extant *trine of the* but I know that much better *Precepts for confirming and enlarging the Memory* *Memory itſelf* may be had, than this *Art* contains , and that a better Practice of the *Art* itſelf may be form'd, than what is at preſent received   And I doubt not, if any one were diſpoſed to make an oſtentatious ſhew of this *Art*, that many ſurprizing things might be perform'd by it, and yet, as now managed, 'tis but barren and uſeleſs.   We do not, however, pretend that it ſpoils, or ſurcharges the *natural Memory*, which is the common Objection , but that 'tis not dextrouſly applied for aſſiſting the Memory in real Buſineſs, and ſe-

rious

---

[a] Upon the Subject of *Common-Place*, conſult *Morhof's Polyhiſtor*, Tom I Lib I Cap 21 *de Locorum Communium Scriptoribus*, and Mr *Locke's Common Place*, in his *Diſcourſe of the Conduct of the Underſtanding*

rious Affairs. But this turn, perhaps, I may receive from the *political Courfe of Life* I have led, never to value what has the appearance of Art, without any ufe For immediately to repeat a multitude of Names, or Words, once repeated before, or off-hand to compofe a great number of Verfes upon a Subject, or to touch any Matter that occafionally turns up with a fatyrical Comparifon, or to turn ferious things into jeft, or to elude any thing by Contradiction, or Cavil, &c of all which Faculties there is a great Fund in the Mind, and which may, by a proper Capacity and Exercife, be carried almoft to a miraculous height, yet I efteem all the things of this kind no more than Rope-dancing, Antick Poftures, and Feats of Activity And indeed they are nearly the fame things, the one being an abufe of the bodily, as the other is of the mental Powers and tho' they may caufe admiration, they cannot be highly efteemed

The Intentions of the Art of Memory, viz. Prænotion 3 This ART OF MEMORY has two *Intentions*, viz *Prænotion*, and *Emblem* By *Prænotion*, we underftand the breaking off of an endlefs Search, for when one endeavours to call any thing to mind, without fome previous Notion, or Perception of what is fought for, the Mind ftrives and exerts itfelf, endeavours and cafts about, in an endlefs manner But if it hath any certain Notion before-hand, the Infinity of the Search is prefently cut fhort, and the Mind hunts nearer home, as in an Inclofure. *Order, therefore, is a manifeft Help to Memory* For here there is a *previous Notion, that the things fought for muft be agreeable to Order* And thus *Verfe* is eafier remembred than *Profe*, becaufe if we ftick at any word in *Verfe*, we have a previous Notion, that 'tis fuch a word as muft ftand in the Verfe and this *Prænotion is the firft part of Artificial Memory* For in Artificial Memory, we have certain places digefted, and propofed beforehand but we make *Images* extemporary, as they are required, wherein we have a *previous Notion*, that the *Image* muft be fuch as may, in fome meafure, correfpond to its place, which thus ftimulates the Memory, and, as it were, ftrengthens it, to find out the thing fought for

And Emblem 4 But *Emblems* bring down intellectual to fenfible Things, for what is *fenfible*, always ftrikes the Memory ftronger, and fooner impreffes itfelf, than what is *intellectual* Thus the Memory of Brutes is excited by fenfible, but not by intellectual Things And therefore it is eafier to retain the *Image* of a Sportfman hunting the Hare, of an Apothecary ranging his Boxes, an Orator making a Speech, a Boy repeating Verfes, or a Player acting his Part, than the correfponding Notions of *Invention, Difpofition, Elocution, Memory*, and *Action* There are alfo other things that contribute to *affift the Memory*, but the *Art* at prefent in ufe, confifts of the two abovementioned[2] and to treat of the *particular Defects of Arts*, is foreign to our prefent purpofe[b]   SECT

---

[a] I fuppofe, that the *Art of Memory*, now commonly taught by *Memory Mafters*, is little more than a Lecture upon the Foundations here laid down, and perhaps their *Secret* is difclofed in Sir *Hugh Plat's Jewel Houfe of Art and Nature*, printed at *London*, in the year 1653 See p. 7——80 of that *Edition* Confult alfo, upon the *Means of improving the Memory, Morhof's Polyhiftor*, Tom I Lib II Cap 4 *de Subfidiis dirigendi Judicii*

[b] The *Author* intended a *Difcourfe upon the Helps of the intellectual Faculties*, and began the firft Draught of it, as we find in his Letter to Sir *Henry Saville* but the Defign was left uncompleated,

SECT. XVI.

Of the DOCTRINE *of* DELIVERY; *and first, of the* ELEMENTS *of* SPEECH.

1. WE next proceed to the *Art of delivering, uttering, and communi-* *cating such Things as are discover'd, judg'd of, and treasur'd up in the Memory·* and this we call by the general Name of TRADITIVE DOC- TRINE, which takes in all the *Arts* relating to *Words* and *Discourse* For altho' *Reason* be as the Soul of *Discourse*; yet they ought both to be treated separate, no less than the *Soul* and *Body* We divide this TRADITIVE DOCTRINE into *three Parts*, *viz* with regard (1) to the *Organ*, (2) the *Method*, and (3) the *Illustration, or Ornament, of Speech and Discourse* {.float-right}*Traditive Doctrine divided into Grammar, Method, and Ornament of Speech*

2 The *vulgar Doctrine of the Organ of Speech*, call'd GRAMMAR, is of two *kinds*, the one having relation to *Speaking*, the other to *Writing* For, as *Aristotle* well observed, *Words are the Marks of Thoughts, and Letters of Words* and we refer both of these to *Grammar* But before we proceed to its several Parts, 'tis necessary to say something, in general, of the *Organ of this Traditive Doctrine*, because it seems to have more Descendants besides *Words* and *Letters*. And here we observe, that *whatever may be split into differences, sufficiently numerous for explaining the variety of Notions, provided these differences are sensible, may be a means of conveying the Thoughts from Man to Man*[a]· for we find that Nations of different Languages, hold a Commerce, in some tolerable degree, by Gestures And from the Practice of some Persons born deaf and dumb, but otherwise ingenious, we see Con- versation may be held betwixt them, and such of their Friends as have learn'd their Gestures And 'tis now well known, that in *China*, and the more *Eastern Provinces*, they use at this day, certain *real*, not *nominal Characters*, to express, not *Letters* or *Words*, but *Things* and *Notions*, insomuch, that numerous Nations, tho' of quite different Languages, yet, agreeing in the use of these *Characters*, hold correspondence by *Writing*[b]. And thus a Book {.float-right}*Grammar, of two kinds, re- lative to Speaking and Writing*

completed, and little more done towards it, than the collecting of a few *Hints*, which shew that the Author design'd to consider the *ways of improving the Memory*, as well as the *Judg- ment*, and intended, principally, to recommend *Practice*, and the acquiring a *Habit*

[a] Hence, perhaps, several ways of communicating our Thoughts might be invented, besides those already in use, *viz* by applying, after a different manner, to the *Senses*, as by different *Colours, Sounds, Signs*, and *Touches*, differently changed and combined *Petr Montanus, Fabricius ab Aquapendente, Dr Wallis, Dr Holder, Bishop Wilkins, Mr Falconer*, and *Joh. Conrad Am- man*, have some things relating to this Subject

[b] See more to this purpose in *Spizelius de Re Literaria Chinensium*, Ed Lugd Bat 1660, *Webb's Historical Essay upon the Chinese Language*, printed at *London*, in 1669, Father *Besnier's Reunion des Langues*, Father *le Compte*, and other of the *Missionaries Letters*

VOL I.　　　　　　　　　　T　　　　　　　　　　　　wrote

wrote in such *Characters*, may be read and interpreted, by each Nation, in its own respective Language.

The Signs of Things divided into congruous and arbitrary, viz. 1) Hieroglyphicks and Gestures.   3 The Signs of Things, significative without the Help or Interposition of *Word* , are therefore of two kinds ~ the one *congruous*, the other *arbitrary*. Of the first kind, are *Hieroglyphicks* and *Gestures* , of the second, *real Characters*. The *use* of *Hieroglyphicks* is of great antiquity , being held in veneration, especially among that most ancient Nation the *Egyptians* , insomuch that this seems to have been an early kind of Writing , prior to the Invention of Letters, unless, perhaps, among the *Jews* [a]. And *Gestures* are a kind of *transitory Hieroglyphicks* for as *Words* are fleeting in the pronunciation, but permanent when wrote down , so *Hieroglyphicks*, express'd by Gesture, are momentary , but when painted, durable When *Periander*, being consulted how to preserve a Tyranny newly usurped, bid the Messenger report what he saw , and going into the Garden, cropt all the tallest Flowers ; he thus used as strong an *Hieroglyphick*, as if he had drawn it upon Paper.

(2) Real Characters.   4 Again, 'tis plain that HIEROGLYPHICKS and GESTURES, have always some similitude with the things signified , and are in reality *Emblems* whence we call them *congruous Marks of Things* but *real Characters* have nothing of the *Emblem* , as being no less mute than the elementary Letters themselves , and invented altogether at Discretion, tho' received by Custom, as by a tacit Agreement. Yet 'tis manifest, that a great number of them is required in writing for they must be as numerous as the radical Words. This *Doctrine*, therefore, *concerning the Organ of Speech*, that is, *the Marks of Things, we set down as wanting* For altho' it may seem a matter of little use, whilst Words and Writing with Letters are much more commodious Organs of Delivery , yet we think proper here to mention it, as no inconsiderable thing For whilst we are treating, as it were, of the *Coin of intellectual Matters* , 'tis not improper to observe, that as *Money* may be made of other Materials besides Gold and Silver ; so other Marks of Things may be invented, besides *Words* and *Letters* [b]

The Office and Use of Grammar.   5 GRAMMAR holds the place of a Conductor, in respect of the other *Sciences* , and tho' the Office be not noble, 'tis extremely necessary, especially as the *Sciences*, in our times, are chiefly derived from the *learned Languages* Nor should this Art be thought of small Dignity, since it acts as an Antidote against the Curse of *Babel* , *the Confusion of Tongues.* Indeed, human Industry strongly endeavours to recover those Enjoyments it lost through its own default Thus it guards against the *first general Curse*, the Sterility of the Earth, and the *eating our Bread in the Sweat of the Brow*, by all

---

[a] See *Caussinus's Polyhistor Symbolicus*, and *Symbolica Ægyptiorum Sapientia*, Ed Par 1618. And for other Writers upon this Subject, see *Morhof's Polyhistor*, Tom I. Lib IV Cap 2 *de variis Scripturæ modis*

[b] On this Foundation, Bishop *Wilkins* undertook his laborious Treatise of a *real Character*, or *Philosophical Language*, tho *Dalgarn* published a Treatise on the same Subject before him, viz. at *London*, in the Year 1661 In the same Year, *Becher* also published another to the same purpose at *Frankfort*, entitled, *Character pro Notitia Linguarum universali* See more upon this Subject in *Joachim Fritsch's Lingua Ludovicea*, *Kircher's Polygraphia*, *Paschius's Inventa Nova-Antiqua*, and *Morhof's Polyhistor*.

all the other Arts, as againſt the *ſecond*, the Confuſion of Languages, it calls in the aſſiſtance of *Grammar* Tho' this Art is of little uſe in any *maternal Language*, but more ſerviceable in learning the foreign ones, and moſt of all in the dead ones, which now ceaſe to be popular, and are only preſerved in Books

6. We divide GRAMMAR alſo, into two *Parts*, *Literary* and *Philoſophical*; the one employed ſimply about Tongues themſelves, in order to their being more expeditiouſly learned, or more correctly ſpoke, but the other is in ſome ſort ſubſervient to *Philoſophy* in which view *Cæſar* wrote his *Books of Analogy*, tho' we have ſome doubt whether they treated of the *Philoſophical Grammar* now under conſideration We ſuſpect, however, that they contained nothing very ſubtile or ſublime, but only deliver'd *Precepts of pure and correct Diſcourſe*, neither corrupted by any vulgar, depraved Phraſes, and Cuſtoms of Speech, nor vitiated by Affectation in which particular the Author himſelf excell'd [a] Admoniſh'd by this Procedure, I have form'd in my Thoughts, a *certain* GRAMMAR, not upon any *Analogy which Words bear to each other*, but ſuch as ſhould *diligently examine the Analogy or Relation betwixt* Words and Things, *yet without any of that Hermeneutical Doctrine, or Doctrine of Interpretation, which is ſubſervient to Logick.* 'Tis certain that Words are the Traces or Impreſſions of Reaſon, and Impreſſions afford ſome Indication of the Body that made them. I will therefore here give a ſmall Sketch of the Thing

7 And *firſt*, we cannot approve that curious Enquiry, which *Plato*, however gave into, about the *impoſition* and *original Etymology of Names*, as ſuppoſing them not given arbitrarily at firſt, but rationally and ſcientifically derived and deduced This indeed is an elegant, and, as it were, a waxen ſubject, which may handſomely be wrought and twiſted But becauſe it ſeems to ſearch the very Bowels of Antiquity, it has an awful appearance, tho' attended with but little Truth and Advantage [b] But it would be a noble kind of a *Grammar*, if any one, well vers'd in numerous *Languages*, both the *learned* and *vulgar*, ſhould treat of their various Properties, and ſhew wherein each of them excell'd, and fell ſhort for thus Languages might be enriched by mutual commerce, and one *beautiful Image of Speech*, or *one grand Model of Language, for juſtly expreſſing the Senſe of the Mind*, form'd, like the *Venus* of *Apelles*, from the excellencies of ſeveral And thus we ſhould, at the ſame time, have ſome conſiderable Marks of the Genius and Manners of People, and Nations, from their reſpective Languages *Cicero* agreeably remarks, that the *Greeks* had no word to expreſs the Latin INEPTUM [c]; becauſe, ſays he, the fault it denotes was ſo familiar among them, that they could not ſee it in themſelves. a *Cenſure* not unbecoming the *Roman Gravity*. And as the *Greeks* uſed ſo great a Licentiouſneſs in compounding of Words, which the *Romans* ſo religiouſly abſtained from, it may hence be collected,

Side notes:
Grammar divided into literary and philoſophical

A Philoſophical Grammar deficient

Directions for ſupplying it

T 2 that

---

[a] See the Account of *Cæſar's* Books *de Analogia*, given above in the PRELIMINARIES, *Sect* III 65.
[b] Thoſe who are curious to look into this Matter, may find it ſuccinctly treated in *Morhof's Polyhiſtor*, Tom I Lib IV Cap 3 *de Lingua univerſali & primæva*
[c] In *Engliſh*, unſuitable, childiſh, or trifling Behaviour

that the *Greeks* were better fitted for *Arts*, and the *Romans* for *Exploits* as variety of *Arts* makes compound Words in a manner necessary, whilst Civil Business, and the Affairs of Nations, require a greater simplicity of Expression The *Jews* were so averse to these Compositions, that they would rather strain a Metaphor than introduce them Nay, they used so few words and so unmix'd, that we may plainly perceive from their Language, they were a *Nazarene* People, and separate from other Nations 'Tis also worth observing, tho' it may seem a little ungrateful to modern Ears, that the *ancient Languages* are full of Declensions, Cases, Conjugations, Tenses, and the like, but the later Languages, being almost destitute of them, slothfully express many things by Prepositions and auxiliary Verbs For from hence it may easily be conjectured, that the Genius of former Ages, however we may flatter ourselves, was much more acute than our own And there are things enow of this kind to make a Volume It seems reasonable, therefore, to distinguish a *PHILOSOPHICAL* GRAMMAR from a simple *literary one*, and to set it down as follows [a]

In the things that belong to Grammar.
8 All the *Accidents of Words*, as *Sound*, *Measure*, *Accent*, likewise belong to Grammar But the primary Elements of simple Letters, or the Enquiry with what Percussion of the Tongue, Opening of the Mouth, Motion of the Lips, and Use of the Throat, the Sound of each Letter is produced, has no relation to Grammar, but is a part of the *Doctrine of Sounds*, to be treated under *Sight and Sub Optics* [b] The *Grammatical Sound* we speak of, regards only, *Sweet* and *Harsh* Some *harsh* and *sweet* Sounds are *general*, for there is no Language but in some degree avoids the Chasms of concurring Vowels, or the Roughness of concurring Consonants. There are others particular or respective, and *pleasing* or *displeasing* to the Ears of different Nations The *Greek Language* abounds in *Diphthongs*, which the *Roman* uses much more sparingly, and so of the rest

The Measure of Words the Original of Versification and Poetry.
9 But the *Measure of Words* has produced a large body of Art, viz *POETRY*, consider'd not with regard to its *Matter*, which was consider'd above [c], but its *Style*, and the Structure of Words, that is, *Versification* which tho' held as trivial, is honoured with great and numerous Examples Nor should this *Art*, which the *Grammarians* call *Prosodia*, be confined only to teaching the kinds of Verse and Measure, but *Precepts* also should be added, as to what kind of Verse is agreeable to every Subject The Ancients applied *Heroick Verse* to *Exploits*, *Elegy* to *Complaint*, *Iambick* to *Invective*, and *Lyrick* to *Odes* and *Hymns* and the same has been prudently observed by the modern Poets, each in his own Language only they deserve *Censure*

[a] Considerable Pains have been bestow'd upon this Subject by various Authors, an account whereof is given by *Morhof* in his *Polyhistor* See Tom I Lib IV Cap 3, 4, 5 or more particularly, *Abraham Mylii de Lingua Belgica cum aliis Linguis communitate*, *Henrici Schurii Diatribis rhetoricae de Origine Linguarum & quibusdam earum attributis*, *Thom Hayne de Linguis in genere & de variarum Linguarum Harmonia* in the *Appendix* to his *Grammatices Latinae Compendium*, and Dr *Wallis's Grammatica Linguae Anglicanae*

[b] This is the Subject which *Conrad Amman* has prosecuted with great diligence, in his *Surdus loquens*, and *Dissertatio de Loquela*, the first printed at *Amsterdam*, in 1692, and the Last printed

[c] Sect II of POETRY

in this, that some of them, thro' affectation of Antiquity, have endeavoured to set the modern Languages to *ancient Measure*, as *Sapphick*, *Elegiack*, &c which is both disagreeable to the Ear, and contrary to the structure of such *Languages* And in these cases, the *Judgment of the Sense is to be preferred to the Precepts of Art* Nor is this an *Art*, but the abuse of *Art*, as it does not perfect Nature, but corrupt her As to *Poetry*, both with regard to its *Fable* and its *Verse*, 'tis like a luxuriant Plant, sprouting not from a Seed, but by the mere vigour of the Soil whence it every where creeps up, and spreads itself so wide, that it were endless to be sollicitous about its *Defects* And as to the *Accents of Words*, there is no necessity for taking notice of so trivial a thing, only it may be proper to intimate, that these are observed with great exactness, whilst the ACCENTS OF SENTENCES are neglected tho' it is nearly common to all mankind, to sink the Voice at the end of a Period, to raise it in Interrogation, and the like [a] And so much for that *Part of Grammar* which regards *Speaking*

10 WRITING is practised either by means of the *common Alphabet*, now vulgarly received, or of a *secret and private one*, agreed upon betwixt particular persons, and called by the name of CYPHER But here a Question arises about the *common Orthography*, viz whether *Words should be wrote as they are pronounced, or after the common manner?* Certainly that *reformed kind of Writing*, according to the Pronunciation, is but an useless Speculation, because *Pronunciation* itself is continually changing, and the Derivations of Words, especially from the *foreign Languages*, are very obscure. And listly, as Writing in the received manner, no way obstructs the manner of Pronunciation, but leaves it free, an *Innovation* in it is to no purpose

Writing practised by Alphabet or Cypher

11 There are *several kinds* of CYPHERS, as the *simple*, those *mixt* with Non-significants, those consisting of two kinds of Characters, *Wheel-Cyphers*, *Key-Cyphers*, *Word-Cyphers*, &c There are three Properties required in *Cyphers*, viz (1) that they be easy to write and read, (2) that they be trusty and undecypherable, and (3) if possible, clear of suspicion For if a *Letter* should come into the hands of such as have a power over the Writer, or Receiver, tho' the *Cypher* itself be trusty, and impossible to *Decypher*, 'tis still subject to Examination and Question, unless there be no room to suspect or examine it

The Doctrine of Cyphers

12 There is a new and useful *Invention to elude the Examination of a Cypher*, viz to have *two Alphabets*, the one of significant, and the other of non-significant Letters, and folding up two Writings together, the one conveying the Secret, whilst the other is such as the Writer might probably send without danger. In case of a strict Examination about the *Cypher*, the Bearer is to produce the *non-significant Alphabet* for the *true*, and the *true* for the *non-significant*, by which means the *Examiner* would fall upon the

A Cypher to divert Examination.

out-

---

[a] The *Stage* having cultivated the *Accenting of Sentences* more than the *School*, the Rules of this Art might, perhaps, to advantage be borrow'd from thence, in order to form an early Habit of graceful Speaking

outward Writing , and finding it probable, suspect nothing of the inner [a].

13 But to prevent *all Suspicion,* we shall here annex a *Cypher* of our own, which has the highest perfection of a *Cypher,* that of signifying OMNIA PER OMNIA , *any thing by every thing* [b], provided only the matter included be five times less than that which includes it, without any other condition or limitation. The Invention is this , first *let all the Letters of the Alphabet be resolved into two only, by Repetition and Transposition* for a Transposition of *two Letters,* thro' *five places,* or different arrangements, will denote *two and thirty differences* , and consequently fewer, or *four and twenty,* the number of Letters in our Alphabet, as in the following EXAMPLE.

A BILITERAL ALPHABET, *consisting only of* a *and* b *changed through five Places, so as to represent all the Letters of the common* Alphabet.

A = aaaaa
B = aaaab
C = aaaba
D = aaabb
E = aabaa
F = aabab
G = aabba
H = aabbb
I = abaaa
K = abaab
L = ababa
M = ababb
N = abbaa
O = abbab
P = abbba
Q = abbbb
R = baaaa
S = baaab
T = baaba
V = baabb
W = babaa
X = babab
Y = babba
Z = babbb

{ Thus, in order to write an *A,* you write five *a's,* or aaaaa , and to write a *B,* you write four *a's,* and one *b,* or aaaab ; and so of the rest.

[a] The publishing of this *Secret* frustrates it's intention, for the *Examiner,* tho' he should find the *outward Letter probable,* would doubtless, when thus advertised, examine the *inner,* notwithstanding its *Alphabet* were deliver'd him for *Non-significants*
[b] For this *Cypher* is practicable in all things that are capable of two differences.

14 And here, by the way, we gain no small advantage , as this Contri- *And capable* vance shews a Method of expressing, and signifying one's Mind, to any di- *of being made* stance, by objects that are either *visible* or *audible*, provided only the ob- *general.* jects are but capable of two Differences , as Bells, Speaking-trumpets, Fire- works, Cannon, &c B it for *Writing*, let the *included Letter* be resolved into this *biliteral Alphabet*. suppose that *Letter* were the word F L Y , it is thus resolved .

F 　 L 　 Y.
aabab　ababa　babba[a].

15 Let there be also at hand *two other common Alphabets*, differing only *An Example* from each other in the make of their Letters , so that, as well the *Capital* as *of a double-* the *Small* be differently shaped, or cut, at every one's discretion　as thus *faced Alpha-* for Example, in *Roman* and *Italick* , each *Roman Letter* constantly represent- *bet.* ing A, and each *Italick Letter* B.

The *first*, or *Roman* ALPHABET.

A, a.
B, b.
C, c.
D, d
E, e
F, f
G, g.
H, h.
I, i.
K, k
L, l
M, m
N, n.
O, o
P, p.
Q, q.
R, r.
S, s
T, t.
V, v.
U, u.
W, w
X, x.
Y, y.
Z, z.

{ All the Letters of this *Roman Alphabet* are read, or decyphered, by translating them into the Letter A, only

The

[a] Compare these different Combinations of *a* and *b*, with the *Biliteral Alphabet* above; and you will find they correspond to the Letters F, L, Y, that is, denote the Word *Fly*.

The *second,* or *Italick* ALPHABET.

A,   *a*
B,   *c*
C,   *c*
D,   *d*
E,   *e*
F,   *f*
G,   *g*
H,   *b*
I,   *t*
K,   *k*
L,   *l*
M,   *m*
N,   *t*
O,   *o*
P,   *p*
Q,   *q*
R,   *r*
S,
T   *t*
V,   *v*
U,
W,
X
Y,
Z,   *z*

{ All the Letters of this *Italick Alphabet* are read by tranflating them into the Letter *B,* only

16 Now adjuft or fit any external *double-faced Writing,* letter by letter, to the internal *Writing,* firft made *biliterate,* and afterwards write it down for the *Letter,* or EPISTLE, to be fent. Suppofe the *external Writing* were STAY TILL I COME TO YOU , and the internal one were FLY then, as we faw above, the word *Fly,* refolved by means of the *Bilateral Alphabet,* is

    F   L   Y
aabab   ababa   babba.

whereto I fit, letter by letter, the *Words,* STAY TILL I COME TO YOU, obferving the ufe of my two *Alphabets of differently* fhaped *Letters* thus

    aabab   ababa   babba
    Stay *till* I co *me to you*

Having now adjufted my Writing, according to all my *Alphabets,* I fend it to my Correfpondent, who reads the fecret Meaning, by tranflating the *Roman Letters* into *a's,* and the *Italick ones* into *b's,* according to the *Roman* and *Italick*

Italick Alphabets, and comparing each combination of five of them with the *Biliteral Alphabet* [a]

17 This DOCTRINE OF CYPHERS has introduced another, relative to it, *viz.* the ART OF DECYPHERING, without the *Alphabet of the Cypher*, or knowing the Rules whereby it was form'd. This indeed is a Work of Labour and Ingenuity, devoted, as well as the former, to the secret service of Princes Yet by *a diligent Precaution it may be render'd useless*, tho', as matters now stand, 'tis highly serviceable For if the *Cyphers* in use were good and trusty, several of them would absolutely elude the Labour of the Decypherer, and yet remain commodious enough, so as to be readily wrote and read : But through the ignorance and unskilfulness of Secretaries and Clerks, in the Courts of Princes, the most important Affairs are generally committed to weak and *treacherous* CYPHERS [b] And thus much for the *Organ of Speech*.

The Art of decyphering may be eluded

SECT. XVII.

Of the METHOD *of* SPEECH.

1 THE DOCTRINE CONCERNING THE METHOD OF SPEECH, has been usually treated as a part of *Logick* it has also found a place in *Rhetorick*, under the name of *Disposition*, but the placing of it in the train of other *Arts*, has introduced a neglect of many useful things relating to it We therefore think proper to advance a *substantial* and *capital* Doctrine *of* METHOD under the *general Name* of TRADITIVE PRUDENCE [c]. But as the *kinds of Method* are various, we shall rather *enumerate* than *divide* them , but for one *only Method*, and perpetual splitting and subdividing,

The Method of Speech considered as the Doctrine of Traditive Prudence.

---

[a] The CYPHER here described, is of itself somewhat subtile, till it comes to be practised on *Paper*, but rendered much more difficult, by the inaccurate manner wherein it has been printed through all the Editions We hope however to have render'd the Invention intelligible, and to have express'd the Sense of the Author, tho' not directly as it stands in the Original Those who desire a fuller Explanation may consult Bishop *Wilkins's secret and swift Messenger*, or rather Mr *Falconer's Cryptomensis Patefacta*, or *Art of secret Information disclosed without a Key* The *trustiness* of this Cypher depends upon a dextrous use of two Hands, or two different kinds of Letters in the same Writing, which the skilful Decypherer, being thus advertised of, will be quicklighted enough to discern, and consequently be able to *decypher* tho' a *Foundation* seems here laid for several other *Cyphers*, that perhaps could neither be suspected nor decypher'd

[b] The Art of *Cyphering* is doubtless capable of great improvement 'Tis said that King *Charles* the first had a *Cypher* consisting only of a strait Line, differently inclined, and there are ways of Cyphering by the mere punctuation of a *Letter*, whilst the Words of the Letter shall be Non significants, or Sense, that leaves no room for Suspicion It may also be worth considering, whether the *Art of decyphering* could not be applied to *Languages*, so as to translate, for instance, a *Hebrew Book* without understanding *Hebrew* See *Morhof de variis Scripturæ Modis*, *Polyhist* Tom I Lib IV cap 2 and Mr *Falconer's Cryptomenysis Patefacta*

[c] *Method*, in general, may be defined the Order wherein the Mind proceeds from known Principles to make farther Discoveries, in all the *Sciences*

it scarce need be mention'd , as being no more than a *light Cloud of Doctr* that soon blows over tho' it also proves *destructive to the Sciences* , because the observers thereof , when they wrest Things by the Laws of their *Method* , and either omit all that do not justly fall under their *Divisions* , or bend them contrary to their own Nature , squeeze, as it were, the Grain out of the S   , and grasp nothing but the Chaff Whence *this kind of Method* produces   *Compendiums*, and loses the *solid Substance of the Sciences* [a]

2 Let the *first Difference* of METHOD be, therefore, betwixt the *Doctrinal and I   .* By this we do not mean, that the *initiative Method* should treat only of the *Entrance into the Sciences* , and the other their *entire D   * but, borrowing the word from *Religion,* we call that METHOD *   ,* which opens and reveals the *Mysteries of the Sciences* ; so that as the *Doctrinal* METHOD *teaches,* the *Initiative* METHOD should *intimate* the *Doctrinal Method* requiring a belief of what is deliver'd , but the *Initiative* rather that it should be examin'd The one deals out the *Sciences* to vulgar Learners , the other as to the children of Wisdom ∙ the one having for its End the Use of the Sciences, as they now stand ; and the other their Progress and further Advancement But this latter Method seems deserted For the Sciences have hitherto been deliver'd , as if both the *Teacher* and the *Learner* desired to receive Errors by consent the *Teacher* pursuing that *Method* which procures the greatest belief to his *Doctrine* , not that which most commodiously submits it to examination whilst the *Learner* desires present Satisfaction, without waiting for a *just Enquiry* , as if more concerned not to doubt, than not to mistake Hence the *Master,* thro' desire of Glory , never exposes the weakness of his own *Science* , and the *Scholar* thro' his aversion to Labour, trys not his own Strength Whereas *Knowledge*, which is deliver'd to others as a Web to be further wove, should, if possible be introduced into the Mind of another, in the manner it was first procured And this may be done by *Knowledge acquired by Induction* , but for that   [b] *Knowledge* we have at present, 'tis not easy for the Possessor to say by what road he came at it Yet in a greater or less degree, any one might review his Knowledge , trace back the steps of his own Thoughts , consent afresh , and thus transplant his Knowledge into the Mind of another, as it grew up in his own For 'tis in *Arts* as in Trees , if a Tree were to be used, no matter for the Root , but if it were to be transplanted, 'tis a surer way to take the Root, than the Slips So the Transplantation now practis'd of the *Sciences,* makes a great show, as it were of Branches, that , without the Roots, may be fit indeed for the *Builder,* but not for the *Planter* He who would promote the growth of the *Sciences,* should be less sollicitous about the Trunk or Body of them , and bend his care to preserve the Roots, and draw them out with some little Earth about them Of this kind of *Transplantation* there is some resemblance in the *Method of Mathematicians* [b], but in general we do not see that 'tis either
used

[a] This is spoke with particular regard to *Ramus* his *singular Method,* and *Dicotomies* , of which see more below § 8

[b] To this   see *Mosir's Brief Commentatio de Methodo Mathematica,* prefix'd to his *Elementa Matheseos Universæ,* as also his *Logicks* and *Metaphysicks.*

ufed or enquired after We therefore place it among the *Deficiencies*, under the name of the TRADITIVE LAMP, or, A METHOD FOR POSTERITY.[a]

3 There is another *difference of Method*, bearing fome relation to the for- *The concealed* mer Intention, tho' in reality almoft oppofite to it both of them have this *Method* in common, that they feparate the *vulgar Audience* from the *felect*, but herein they are oppofite, that the former introduces a more open, and the other a more fecret way of Inftruction, than the common. Hence let them be diftinguifhed, by terming the former *plain* or *open*, and the latter the *learned* or CONCEALED METHOD Thus transferring to the manner of Delivery the difference made ufe of by the Ancients, efpecially in publifhing their Books This *concealed*, or ENIGMATICAL METHOD, was itfelf alfo employed by the Ancients with prudence and judgment[b], but is of late difhonoured by many, who ufe it as a falfe light to fet off their counterfeit wares The Defign of it feems to have been, by the Veil of Tradition to keep the Vulgar from the *Secrets of the Sciences*, and to admit only fuch as had, by the help of a Mafter, attained to the interpretation of *dark Sayings*, or were able, by the ftrength of their own Genius, to enter within the Veil.

4. The next *difference of* METHOD is of great moment, with regard to *The Advan-* the *Sciences*, as thefe are delivered either in the way of *Aphorifm*, or *Metho-* *tages of* Apho- *dically* It highly deferves to be noted, that the general cuftom is, for *rifms over* men to raife, as it were, a formal and folemn *Art*, from a few *Axioms* and *Methods* *Obfervations* upon any fubject, fwelling it out with their own witty *Inventions*, illuftrating it by Examples, and binding the whole up into *Method*. But that other way of *Delivery*, *by Aphorifms*, has numerous Advantages over the Methodical And *firft*, it gives us a proof of the *Author's* Abilities, and fhews whether he hath entered deep into his *Subject* or not *Aphorifms* are ridiculous things, unlefs wrought from the central parts of the *Sciences*, and here all Illuftration, Excurfion, Variety of Examples, Deduction, Connexion, and particular Defcription, is cut off, fo that *nothing befides an ample ftock of Obfervations is left for the matter of Aphorifms* And, therefore, no Perfon is equal to the forming of *Aphorifms*, nor would ever think of them, if he did not find himfelf copioufly and folidly inftructed for writing upon a Subject. But in *Methods*, fo great a power have Order, Connexion, and Choice[c], that *methodical Productions* fometimes make a fhow of I know not what *fpecious Art*, which if they were taken to pieces, feparated and undrefs'd, would fall back again almoft to nothing *Secondly*, a *methodical Delivery* has

U 2   the

[a] Perhaps M *Tfchirnhaus's Medicina Mentis, five Tentamen genuinæ Logicæ, in qua differitur le Methodo detegendi incognitas Veritates*, may pave the way for fupplying this *Defideratum*; as proceeding upon a *Mathematical* and *Algebraical Foundation*, to raife a Method of Difcovering unknown Truths

[b] As by *Pythagoras*, who deliver'd the *Myfteries of the Sciences* in the way of *Numbers* and *Symbols*, or by a certain Notation inftead of Letters And fomewhat of this kind has long prevailed among the *Chinefe*, who by certain *figur'd Lines* exprefs not only their phyfical, but their moral and *political Doctrines* See Martini's *Hiftory of the Chinefe*, and Morhof's *Polyhift* Tom I Lib II cap 7 *de Methodis varius*, pag 394,395

[c] *Tantum feries juncturaque pollet,*
Tantum de medio fumptis accedit honoris.

the Power of enforcing Belief and Consent, but directs not much to *practical Indicators*, as carrying with it a kind of *Demonstration in Circle*, where the parts mutually enlighten each other, and so gratifies the Imagination the more. But as actions lie *scattered in common Life*, *scattered Instructions* suit them the best. *Lastly*, as *Aphorisms* exhibit only certain scraps and fragments of the *Sciences*, they carry with them an Invitation to others for adding and lending their Assistance; whereas *Methods* dress up the *Sciences* into Bodies, and make men imagine they have them compleat.

5 There is a farther *Difference of* METHOD, and that too very considerable. For as the *Sciences* are delivered either by *Assertions*, with their *Proofs*, or by *Questions*, with their *Answers*, if the latter METHOD be pursued too far, it retards the *Advancement of the Sciences*, no less than it would the march of an Army, to be sitting down against every little Fort in the way: whereas if the better of the Battle be gained, and the fortune of the War steadily pursued, such lesser places will surrender of themselves; tho' it must be allowed unsafe, to leave any large and fortified place at the back of the Army. In the same manner, Confutations are to be avoided, or sparingly used, in delivering the *Sciences*, so as only to conquer the greater Prejudices and Prepossessions of the Mind, without provoking and engaging the lesser Doubts and Scruples.

6 Another *Difference of* METHOD lies in suiting it to the *Subject*, for *Mathematics*, the most abstract and simple of the *Sciences*, is deliver'd *one* way, and *Physick* the more compound and perplexed, *another*. For an uniform *Method* cannot be commodiously observed, in a variety of Matter. And as we approve of *particular Topicks for Invention*, so we must, in some measure, allow of *particular Methods for Delivery*.

7 There is another *Difference of* METHOD to be used with judgment, in delivering the *Sciences*, and this is govern'd by the *Informations* and *Anticipations of the Science to be delivered*, that are before infused, and impressed upon the Mind of the Learner. For that *Science* which comes as an entire stranger to the mind, is to be delivered *one* way, and that which is familiarized by Opinions already imbibed and received, *another*. And therefore, *Aristotle*, when he thought to chastise, really commended *Democritus*, in saying, *that we should dispute in earnest, and not hunt after Comparisons*, &c. as if he would tax *Democritus* with being too full of *Comparisons*: whereas they whose *Intellects are already grounded in popular Opinion, have nothing left them but to dispute and prove*, whilst others have a double Task, whose Doctrines transcend the vulgar Opinions, *viz. first*, to render what they deliver intelligible, and *then* to prove it. Whence they must of necessity have recourse to Simily and Metaphor, the better to enter the human capacity. Hence we find in the more ignorant Ages, when Learning was in

---

* The *particular Topicks for Invention* were treated above Sect. XIII and for the particular *Method of Delivery* which the Author approves, he has given us Instances of it, in his *Novum Organum, History of Life and Death, Winds* &c.

† The Reader will along read in mind, that this was the situation of the Author in his time, and on that score approves of his *Figurative Style*; tho' it may not be altogether so, necessary at present, when we are more accustom'd to think Philosophically and Freely.

its infancy, and those Conceptions, which are now trite and vulgar, were new, and unheard of, every thing was full of *Parables* and *Similitudes*   otherwise the things then proposed would either have been passed over without due notice and attention, or else have been rejected as *Paradoxes*   For 'tis a *Rule in the Doctrine of Delivery*, that every *Science which comports not with Anticipations and Prejudices, must seek the assistance of Similies and Allusions.* And thus much for the *different kinds of* METHODS , which have not hitherto been observed   But for the others, as the *Analytic, Systatic, Diæretic, Cryptic, Homeric*, &c they are already justly discovered and ranged[a]

8 METHOD *has two parts*, one regarding the *Disposition of a whole Work*, or the Subject of a Book , and the *other*, the *Limitation of Propositions.* For *Architecture* not only regards the Fabrick of the whole Building , but also the Figure of the Columns, Arches, *&c* for *Method* is, as it were, *the Architecture of the Sciences*   And herein *Ramus* has deserved better, by reviving the ancient Rules of *Method*, than by obtruding his own *Dicotomies* But I know not by what fatality it happens, that, as the Poets often feign, the *most precious things* have the *most pernicius keepers*   Doubtless the endeavours of *Ramus* about the reduction of Propositions threw him upon his *Epitomes*, and the *Flats and Shallows of the Sciences*   For it must be a fortunate and well-directed Genius, that shall attempt to *make the Axioms of the Sciences convertible*, and not at the same time *render them circular*, that is, keep them from returning into themselves   And yet the Attempt of *Ramus* in this way has not been useless

9 There are still two other *Limitations of Propositions*, besides that for making them convertible , the *one for extending*, and the *other for producing* them   For if it be just that the Sciences have two other Dimensions, besides Depth, viz *Length* and *Breadth* their Depth bearing relation to their Truth and Reality, as these are what constitutes their Solidity, their Breadth may be computed from one Science to another , and their Length from the highest Degree to the lowest, in the same *Science* the one comprehends the Ends and true Boundaries of the *Sciences*, whence *Propositions* may be treated distinctly, and not promiscuously , and all Repetition, Excursion and Confusion avoided , the other prescribes a Rule how far, and to what particular Degree the *Propositions of the Sciences* are to be reduced   But no doubt something must here be left to Practice and Experience , for men ought to avoid the extreme of *Antoninus Pius*, and not mince *Cummin seed* in the *Sciences*, nor multiply divisions to the utmost   And 'tis here well worth the enquiry, how far we should check ourselves in this respect   For we see that *too extensive Generals*, unless they be reduced , afford little Information , but rather expose the *Sciences* to the ridicule of *practical Men* , as being no more fitted · for practice, than a general Map of the World to shew the road from *London* to *York.*   The best Rules may well be compared to a metalline Speculum, which represents the images of things; but not before 'tis polish'd . For so Rules and Precepts are useful, after having undergone the File of Experience.   But if these Rules could be made exact and clear from the first.

Method divided in respect of the whole, and the Limitation of Propositions

Three Limitations of Propositions

---

[a] See *Morhof's Polyhistor*, Tom I. Lib. II cap. 7. *de Methodis variis.*

firſt, it were better, becauſe they would then ſtand in leſs need of Experience [a]

Suꞁ... ...
M. ...

10 We muſt not omit that ſome men, rather oſtentatious than learned, have labour'd about a certain *Method*, not deſerving the name of a true Method, as being rather a kind of *Impoſture* which may neverthelefs be acceptable to ſome buſy minds   This Art ſo ſcatters the drops of the Sciences that any pretender may miſapply it for Oſtentation , with ſome appearance of Learning   Such was the *Art of Lully* [b], and ſuch the *Typocoſmia* cultivated by ſome for theſe are only a collection of *Terms of Art* heaped together, to the end that thoſe who have them in readineſs, may ſeem to underſtand the Arts whereto the Terms belong   Collections of this kind are like a *Pawn-broker's Shop*, where there are many Slips, but nothing of great value   And thus much for the Science which we call TRADITIVE PRUDENCE [c]

S E C T.   XVIII.

Of RHETORICK, *or* ORATORY.

Tra... ...
on... ...
com and E...
quence

1 WE next proceed to the *Doctrine of Ornament in Speech*, called by the name of RHETORICK or ORATORY   This, in itſelf, is certainly an excellent *Science* , and has been laudably cultivated by Writers. But to form a juſt Eſtimate, *Eloquence* is certainly inferior to *Wiſdom*   The great difference between them appears in the words of *God* to *Moſes*, upon his refuſing, for want of *Eloquence*, the Charge aſſign'd him   *Aaron ſhall be thy Speaker , and thou ſhalt be to him as God*   But for Advantage and popular Eſteem, *Wiſdom* gives place to *Eloquence*   *The wiſe in heart ſhall be called prudent , but the ſweet of tongue ſhall find greater things* ſays *Solomon*   clearly intimating, that *Wiſdom* procures a Name and Admiration , but that *Eloquence* is of greater efficacy in Buſineſs and civil Life

Transmiſſi-
... of Elo-
quence are car-
ried to a great
height

2 And for the cultivation of this *Art*, the emulation betwixt *Ariſtotle* and the *Rhetoricians* of his time, the earneſt ſtudy of *Cicero* , his long practice, and

---

[a] The Author, in this Section does not perhaps proceed altogether with his uſual Solidity and Diſtinctneſs, as having not yet thoroughly digeſted the Deſign of his *Novum Organum*, which may be conſidered as a Treatiſe upon Method, and a reduction of this more looſe *Doctrine*, to Rules

[b] Viz. the tranſcendental *Art* which taught a Method of treating all Subjects, in an oſtentatious or affected , learned manner

[c] The Doctrine of Method was diligently cultivated by *des Cartes*, in his Book *de Methodo* , who endeavour'd to reduce the whole Buſineſs of it to four Rules, which however are found in the Precepts of *Ariſtotle*   *Johan Beyer* undertook to write upon this Subject, in his *Filum Labyrinthi* according to the Deſign of the Lord *Bacon*, but appears not to have underſtood the Author, and has rather obſcured his Doctrine than improved it   But M *Tſchirnhaus* ſeems to have treated the Subject fully, to its merit, in his *Medicina Mentis*, mentioned above, in the Note of § 2   A great variety of Methods have been advanced by different *Authors*, an ample Catalogue whereof we have in *Morhof's Polyhiſt* Tom I Lib II cap 7 *de Methodis variis*

and utmoſt endeavour, every way to dignify Oratory, hath made theſe Authors even exceed themſelves, in their books upon the Subject. Again, the great *Examples* of Eloquence found in the *Orations of Demoſthenes* and *Cicero*, added to the perfection and exactneſs of their Precepts, have doubled its advancement   And therefore the *Deficiencies* we find in it, rather turn upon certain Collections belonging to its *Train*, than upon the *Doctrine* and *Uſe* of the Art itſelf

3. But, in our manner, to open and ſtir the Earth a little about the Roots *The Office and* of this *Science*, certainly *Rhetorick* is ſubſervient to the *Imagination*, as *Logick* *Uſe of Rheto-* is to the *Underſtanding*   And if the thing be well conſider'd, the Office and *rick* Uſe of this Art, is but to apply and recommend the *Dictates of Reaſon to the Imagination*, in order to excite the *Affections* and *Will*   For the Adminiſtration of Reaſon is diſturb'd three ways, *viz* (1) either by the Enſnaring of Sophiſtry, which belongs to *Logick*, (2) the Deluſion of Words, which belongs to *Rhetorick*, or (3) by the Violence of the Affections, which belongs to *Ethicks*. For as, in tranſacting buſineſs with others, Men are commonly over-reach'd, or drawn from their own Purpoſes, either by *Cunning*, *Importunity*, *or Vehemence*, ſo in the inward buſineſs we tranſact with ourſelves, we are either, (1) undermined by the *Fallacy of Arguments*, (2.) *diſquieted and ſolicit d* by the *Aſſiduity of Impreſſions* and *Obſervations*, or (3) *ſhaken and carried away by the Violence of the Paſſions*   Nor is the State of human Nature ſo unequal, that theſe *Arts* and *Faculties* ſhould have power to diſturb the *Reaſon*, and none to confirm and ſtrengthen it   for they do this in a much greater degree   The End of *Logick* is to teach the Form of Arguments, for defending, and not for enſnaring the *Underſtanding*   The End of *Ethicks* is ſo to compoſe the *Affections*, that they may co operate with *Reaſon*, and not inſult it   And laſtly, the End of *Rhetorick* is to fill the *Imagination* with ſuch Obſervations and Images, as may aſſiſt *Reaſon*, and not over-throw it   For the Abuſes of an Art come in obliquely only, and not for practice, but caution   It was therefore great injuſtice in *Plato*, tho' it proceeded from a juſt Contempt of the *Rhetoricians* of his time, to place *Rhetorick* among *the voluptuary Arts*, and reſemble it to *Cookery*, which corrupted wholeſome Meats, and, by variety of Sauces, made unwholeſome ones more palatable   For Speech is, doubtleſs, more employ'd to adorn Virtue, than to colour Vice   This Faculty is always ready, for *every Man ſpeaks more virtuouſly, than he either thinks or acts*   And 'tis excellently obſerved by *Thucydides*, that ſomething of this kind was uſually objected to *Cleon*, who, as he always defended the worſt ſide of a Cauſe, was ever inveighing againſt *Eloquence*, and the Grace of Speech, well knowing that no Man could ſpeak gracefully upon a baſe *Subject*, tho' every Man eaſily might upon an honourable one   For *Plato* elegantly obſerved, tho' the Expreſſion is now grown trite, that if *Virtue could be beheld, ſhe would have great Admirers*   But *Rhetorick*, by plainly painting Virtue and Goodneſs, renders them, as it were, conſpicuous   for as they cannot be ſeen by the corporeal Eye, the next degree is to have them ſet before us as lively as poſſible, by the ornament of Words, and the ſtrength of Imagination
The

The *Stoics*, therefore, were defervedly ridiculed by *Cicero*, for endeavouring to inculcate *Virtue* upon the Mind, by fhort and fubtile Sentences and Conclufions, which have little or no relation to the *Imagination*, and the *Will*

4. Again, if the *Affections* were orderly, and obedient to *Reafon*, there would be no great ufe of Perfuafion and Infinuation, to gain accefs to the Mind, it would then be fufficient, that Things themfelves were nakedly and fimply propofed and proved but, on the contrary, the Affections revolt fo often, and raife fuch Difturbances and Seditions, that *Reafon* would perfectly be led captive, did not the Perfuafion of *Eloquence* win over the *Imagination* from the fide of the Paffions, and promote an Alliance betwixt it and Reafon againft the *Affections* For we muft obferve, that the *Affections* themfelves always aim at an apparent Good, and, in this refpect, have fomething common with *Reafon* But here lies the difference, that the *Affections* principally regard a prefent Good, whilft *Reafon*, feeing far before it, chufes alfo the future and capital Good And, therefore, as prefent Things ftrike the *Imagination* ftrongeft, *Reafon* is generally fubdued But when *Eloquence*, and the *Power of Perfuafion*, raife up remote and future Objects, and fet them to view as if they were prefent, then *Imagination* goes over to the fide of *Reafon*, and renders it victorious Hence we conclude, that *Rhetorick* can no more be accufed of *colouring the worft Part*, than *Logick* of *teaching Sophiftry* For we know that the *Doctrines of Contraries* are the fame, tho' their Ufe be oppofite And *Logick* does not only differ from *Rhetorick*, according to the vulgar Notion, as the fift is like the Hand clench'd, and the other like the Hand open, but much more in this, that *Logick* confiders *Reafon* in its natural State, and *Rhetorick*, as it ftands in vulgar Opinion whence *Ariftotle* prudently places *Rhetorick* between *Logick* and *Ethicks*, along with *Politicks*, as partaking of them both For the *Proofs* and Demonftrations of *Logick*, are common to all Mankind, but the *Proof* and *Perfuafion* of *Rhetorick*, muft be varied according to the Audience, like a Mufician fuiting himfelf to different Ears And this *Application* and *Variation of Speech*, fhould, if we defire its Perfection, extend fo far, that if the fame things were to be deliver'd to different Perfons; yet a different Set of Words fhould be ufed to each Tho' 'tis certain that the greateft *Orators*, generally, have not this *particular* and *apt Eloquence* in private Difcourfe for whilft they endeavour at Ornament, and elegant Forms of Speech, they fall not upon that ready Application, and familiar Style of Difcourfe, which they might with more advantage ufe to Particulars And it were certainly proper to begin *a new Enquiry* into this *Subject* we therefore place it among the *Deficiencies*, under the title of PRUDENTIAL CONVERSATION[a], which the more attentively

a

---

[a] This Subject has not, that I find, been profecuted fuitably to its Merit The Author himfelf obferves upon it below, Sect XXIII of *Civil Doctrine*, as alfo in his *Effay on Difcourfe*, and in a note following but the *Art of Converfation*, founded upon juft Principles, and reduced to Rules feems fufficient The Foundations for this are in fome meafure laid by the learned *Morhof* in the Sketch of his *Hom Literate Erudita* See *Polybift* Tom I Lib I cap 15 See alfo *Jo Amer Bofii de Prudentia & Eloquentia Civili comparanda* Ed Jenæ, 1698, & *Prudentia confultatoria in usum aud orum Thomafiani, Ed Hal. Magdeburg 1721*

a Man confiders, the higher Value he will fet upon it: but whether this be placed under her *Rhetorick* or *Politicks*, is of no great fignificance

II 5 We have already obferved, that the *Defiderata* in this *Art*, are rather *Appendages* than *Parts of the Art* itfelf[a] and all of them belong to the *Repofitory* thereof, for the furnifhing of *Speech* and *Invention* To proceed in this View, *firft*, we find no Writer that hath carefully followed the prudent Example of *Ariftotle*, who began to *collect popular Marks*, or *Colours*, of *apparent* GOOD *and* EVIL, *as well fimple as comparative* Thefe, in reality, are but *Rhetorical Sophifms*, tho' of excellent ufe, efpecially in Bufinefs, and *private Difcourfe* But the Labour of *Ariftotle* about thefe *Colours*, has three Defects, for (1) tho' they are numerous, he recites but few, (2) he has not annexed their *Redargutions*, and (3) he feems not to have underftood their full ufe for they ferve as well to *affect* and *move*, as to *demonftrate* There are many *Forms of Speech*, which, tho' fignificative of the fame things, yet affect Men differently, as a fharp Inftrument penetrates more than a blunt one, fuppofing both of them urged with equal Force. There is nobody but would be more affected by hearing this Expreffion, *How your Enemies will triumph upon this*[b]? than if it were fimply faid, *This will injure your Affairs* therefore thefe *Stings* and *Goads of Speech* are not to be neglected And fince we propofe this as a *Defideratum*, we will, after our manner, give a Sketch of it, in the way of *Examples*, for *Precepts* will not fo well illuftrate the Thing

6 In *Deliberatives*, we *enquire* what is *Good*, what *Evil*; and of *Good*, which is the greater, and of *Evil*, which the lefs Whence the Perfuader's Task is to make things appear *good* or *evil*, and that in a higher or lower degree, which may be perform'd by true and folid Reafons, or reprefented by *Colours*, popular *Gloffes*, and *Circumftances*, of fuch force as to fway an ordinary Judgment, or even a wife Man, that does not fully and confiderately attend to the Subject But befides this Power to alter the nature of the Subject in appearance, and fo lead to Error, they are of ufe to quicken and ftrengthen fuch *Opinions* and *Perfuafions* as are true, for *Reafons* nakedly deliver'd, and always after one manner, enter but heavily, efpecially with delicate Minds whereas, when varied, and enliven'd by proper Forms and Infinuations, they caufe a ftronger Apprehenfion, and often fuddenly win the Mind to a Refolution Laftly, to make a true and fafe Judgment, nothing can be of greater Ufe, and Prefervation to the Mind, than the *Difcovery and Reprehenfion of thefe Colours*, fhewing in what cafes they hold, and in what not which cannot be done without a comprehenfive Knowledge of Things, but when perform'd, it clears the Judgment, and makes it lefs apt to flip into Error[c]

Marginal notes:
A Collection of Sophifms, or popular Colours of Good and Evil, deficient, as an Appendage to Rhetorick

Examples of the Method of fupplying this Deficiency

---

[a] See above, SECT XVIII 2

[b] *Hoc Ithacus velit, & magno mercentur Atridæ*

[c] This Paragraph is taken from the FRAGMENT OF THE COLOURS OF GOOD AND EVIL, ufually printed as an *Appendix* to the Author's *Effays* That *Fragment* was reconfider'd, better digefted, and finifhed by the Author, in order to fit it for this Place, in the DE AUGMENTIS SCIENTIARUM, to which himfelf affign'd it in the *Latin Edition* The reafon of its being called a *Fragment*, was, that the Author had made a large Collection of fuch kind of *Sophifms* in his youth, but could only find time in his riper years, to add the Fallacies and Confutations of the following twelve

SOPHISM I

Sophism 1

7 *What Men praise and celebrate, is* GOOD, *what they dispraise and censure,* EVIL

De. ...

THIS Soph'm deceives four ways, viz either thro' *Ignorance*, *Deceit*, *P...*, or the *natural Disposition of the Praiser or Dispraiser* (1) Thro' *Ignorance*, for what signifies the Judgment of the Rabble, in distinguishing Good and Evil? *Phocion* took it right, who being applauded by the Multitude, asked, *What he had done amiss?*[a] (2) Thro' *Deceit*, for those who praise or dispraise, commonly have their own Views in it, and speak not their real Sentiments[a] *'Tis naught, 'tis naught, says the Buyer, but when he 's gone, he boasteth* (3) Thro' *Party*, for Men immoderately extol those of their own, and depress those of the opposite Party (4) Thro' *Disposition* or *Temper*, for some Men are naturally form'd servile and fawning, and others captious and morose so that when such Persons praise or dispraise, they do but gratify their own Humour, without much regard to Truth

SOPHISM II.

Sophism 2

8 *What is commended, even by an Enemy, is a great Good, but what is censured, even by a Friend, a great Evil.*

I. F ...

THE *Fallacy* seems to lie here, that 'tis easily believ'd, the Force of Truth extorts from us what we speak against our Inclination

... De...

This *Colour* deceives thro' the Subtilty both of *Friends* and *Enemies* For Praises of Enemies are not always against their Will, nor forced from them by Truth, but they chuse to bestow them where they may create *Envy*, or *Danger*, to their Adversary Again, this *Colour* deceives, because Enemies sometimes use Praises, like *Prefaces*, that they may the more freely calumniate afterwards On the other side, it deceives by the *Craft of Friends*, who also sometimes acknowledge our Faults, and speak of them, not as compell'd thereto by any Force of Truth, but touch only such as may do little hurt, and make us, in every thing else, the best Men in the world And *last*, it deceives, because Friends also use their Reproofs, as Enemies do their Commendations, by way of *Preface*, that they may afterwards launch out more fully in our Praises

[a] *Laudat venales, qui vult extrudere, merces*

SOPHISM III

9 *To be deprived of a Good, is an Evil, and to be deprived of an* Sophism 3
Evil, a Good

THIS *Colour* deceives two ways, *viz* either by the comparison of *Good* Its *Fallacies*
and *Evil*, or by the Succession of *Good* to *Good*, or *Evil* to *Evil*
(1) By *Comparison* thus if it were Good for Mankind to be deprived of
Acorns, it follows not that such Food was bad, but that Acorns were
good, tho' Bread be better Nor, if it were an Evil for the People of *Sicily* to be deprived of *Dionysius* the elder, does it follow that the same *Dionysius* was a good Prince, but that he was less evil than *Dionysius* the younger
(2) By *Succession* for the Privation of a *Good* does not always give
place to an *Evil*, but sometimes to a *greater Good*, as when the *Blossom*
falls, the *Fruit* succeeds Nor does the Privation of an *Evil* always give
place to a *Good*, but sometimes to a *greater Evil*. For *Milo*, by the Death
of his Enemy *Clodius*, lost a fair Harvest of Glory.

SOPHISM IV.

10. *What approaches to Good, is Good, and what recedes from* Sophism 4
Good, is Evil.

'TIS almost universal, that *Things agreeing in Nature, agree also in Place*, Observation.
and that Things disagreeing in Nature, differ as widely in Situation for
all things have an Appetite of associating with what is agreeable; and of repelling what is disagreeable to them.
This *Colour* deceives three ways, *viz*. by *Depriving, Obscuring, and Pro-* Its *Fallacies*
tecting (1) By *Depriving* for the largest things, and most excellent in
their kind, attract all they can to themselves, and leave what is next them
destitute, thus the Under-wood growing near a large Tree, is the poorest
Wood of the Field; because the Tree deprives it of Sap, and Nourishment
Whence 'twas well said, that the Servants of the Rich are the greatest Slaves
And it was witty of him, who compared the inferior Attendants in the
Courts of Princes, to the *Vigils of Feast-days*, which, tho' nearest to *Feast-
days*, are themselves but *meagre* (2) By *Obscuring* for 'tis also the Nature of excellent things in their kind, tho' they do not impoverish the Substance of what lies near them, yet to *overshadow* and *obscure* it Whence
the Astrologers say, that tho' in all the *Planets*, Conjunction is the most perfect Amity, yet the *Sun*, tho' good in Aspect, is evil in Conjunction
(3) By *Protecting* for things come together, not only from a similitude
of Nature, but even what is evil, flies to that which is good, especially
in civil Society, for Concealment and Protection Thus *Hypocrisy draws
near to Religion for Shelter* [a] So *Sanctuary-Men*, who were commonly

X 2   Male-

---

[a] *Sæpe latet vitium proximitate boni*

Malefactors, used to be nearest the *Priests* and *Prelates* for the Majesty of good Things &c, for the Confines of them are Reverend On the other side God draws near to Evil, not for Society, but for Converstion and Reformation And hence Physicians visit the Sick more than the Sound and hence it was objected to our *Saviour*, that he conversed with *Publicans* and *Sinners*

SOPHISM V.

Sophism 5   11 *As all Parties challenge the first place, that, to which the rest unanimously give the second, seems the best Each taking the first place out of Affection to itself, but giving the second, where 'tis really due.*

Colour   THUS *Cicero* attempted to prove the *Academicks* to be the best *Sect*; for, faith he, ask a *Stoick* which Philosophy is best, and he will prefer his own then ask him, which is next best, and he will confess, the *Academick* Ask an *Epicurean* the same Question, who can scarce endure the *Stoick*, and as soon as he hath placed his own *Sect*, he places the *Academick* next him So if a *Prince* separately examined several Competitors for a Place, perhaps the ablest, and most deserving man would have most second Voices

Defect   This *Colour* deceives in respect of *Envy* ; for men are accustom'd next after themselves, and their own Faction, to prefer those that are *softest*, and most *plyable*, with intent to exclude such as would obstruct their Measures whence this *Colour of Majority* and *Preheminence*, becomes a *Sign of Enervation and Weakness*

SOPHISM VI.

Sophism 6   12 *That is absolutely best, the Excellence whereof is greatest.*

Defect   THIS *Colour* has these *Forms* let us not wander in Generals let us compare *Particular with Particular*, &c and tho' it seem strong, and rather *Logical* than *Rhetorical*, yet it is sometimes a *Fallacy* (1) because many things are exposed to great danger, but if they escape, prove more excellent than others whence their *Kind* is inferior, as being subject to Accident and Miscarriage, tho' more noble in the *Individual* Thus to instance in the *Blossoms of March*, one whereof, according to the *French Proverb*, is, if it escape Accidents, worth ten *Blossoms of May* [a], so that tho' in *general*, the Blossoms of *May* excel the Blossoms of *March*, yet in *Individuals* the best Blossoms of *March* may be prefer'd to the best of *May* (2) Because the Nature of things in some Kinds, or Species is more equal, and in others more unequal Thus warm Climates generally produce People of a sharper Genius than cold ones, yet the

extraor-

---

[a] *Bourgeon de Mars, Enfans de Paris, S'il ne s'echappe, vaut tant dix*

extraordinary Genius's of cold Countries usually excel the extraordinary Genius's of the warmer. So in the case of Armies, if the Cause were tried by single Combat, the Victory might often go on the one side, but if by a pitched Battle, on the other. for *Excellencies* and *Superiorities are rather accidental Things, whilst Kinds are governed by Nature, or Discipline.* (3) Lastly, *many Kinds have much Refuse*, which countervails what they have of excellent. and therefore tho' *Metal* be generally more precious than *Stone*, yet a *Diamond* is more precious than *Gold.*

Sophism VII

13 *What keeps a Matter safe and entire, is Good, but what leaves* Sophism 7. *no Retreat, is bad. for Inability to retire, is a kind of Impotency, but Power is a Good.*

THUS *Æsop* feign'd, that two Frogs consulting together, in a time of Illustration. Drought, what was to be done, the one proposed going down into a deep Well, because probably the Water would not fail there. but the other answer'd, if it should fail there too, how shall we get up again? And the Foundation of the *Colour* lies here, that human Actions are so uncertain, Foundation. and expos'd to Danger, that the best Condition seems to be that which has most *Outlets.* And this *Persuasion* turns upon such *Forms* as these. *You shall engage yourself. you shall not be your own Carver. you shall keep the matter in your own hands,* &c.

The Fallacy of the *Sophism* lies here, (1) Because Fortune presses so close Detection. upon human Affairs, that some Resolution is necessary. for *not to Resolve, is to Resolve.* so that Irresolution frequently entangles us in Necessities more than resolving. And this seems to be a Disease of the Mind, like to that of Covetousness, only transferred from the Desire of possessing Riches, to the Desire of possessing Free-will and Power: for as the covetous man enjoys no part of his Possessions, for fear of lessening them, so the unresolved Man executes nothing, that he may not abridge his Freedom, and Power of Acting. (2) Because Necessity, and the Fortune of the Throw, adds a Spur to the Mind, whence that Saying, *in other respects equal, but in necessity superior.*

Sophism VIII

14 *That Evil we bring upon ourselves, is Greater, and that pro-* Sophism 8. *ceeding from without us, Less.*

BEcause Remorse of Conscience doubles Adversity. as a Conciousness of Illustration. one's own Innocence is a great support in Affliction. Whence the Poets exaggerate those Sufferings most, and paint them leading to Despair, wherein the Person accuses and tortures himself[a]. On the other side, Persons lessen, and almost annihilate their Misfortunes, by reflecting upon their own Innocence.

[a] *Seque unam clamat causamque, caputque malorum.*

rocence and Merit Besides, when the *Evil* comes from without, it leaves
a Man to the full liberty of Complaint, whereby he spends his Grief, and
eases his Heart for we conceive indignation at human Injuries, and either me-
derate Revenge ourselves, or implore and expect it from the Divine Vengeance
Or if the Injury come from Fortune itself, yet this leaves us to an Expostula-
tion with the Divine Powers[a]   But if the *Evil* be derived from ourselves,
the Stings of Grief strike inwards, and stab and wound the Mind the deeper

This C. . . . deceives, (1) by *Hope*, which is the greatest Antidote of Evils
for 'tis commonly in our power to amend our *Faults*, but not our *Fortunes*
Whence D . . . . . . said frequently to the *Athenians*, " *What is worst for*
. . . . for the future, since it happens by Neglect and Misconduct, that
' *. . . Affairs are come to this low Ebb. Had you indeed acted your parts to the*
' *. . . , and . . . . Matters should have this gone backward, there would be no*
' *. . . . . of life . . . . . but as it has happened principally thro' your own Er-*
. . . , ... be corrected, all may be recovered" So *Epictetus*, speaking of
the degrees of the Mind's tranquillity, assigns the lowest place to such as accuse others higher, to those who accuse themselves, but the highest, to
those who neither accuse themselves nor others   (2) By *Pride*, which so
cleaves to the Mind, that it will scarce suffer men to acknowledge their
Errors And to avoid any such Acknowledgment, they are extremely
patient under those Misfortunes, which they bring upon themselves for as,
when a Fault is committed, and before it be known who did it, a great
stir and commotion is made, but if at length it appears to be done by a
Son, or a Wife, the bustle is all at an end and thus it happens when one
must take a Fault to one's self   And hence we frequently see that Women,
when they do any thing against their Friend's consent, whatever Misfortune follows, they seldom complain, but set a good face on it

SOPHISM IX

15 *The Degree of Privation seems greater than that of Diminu-*
tion, and the Degree of Inception greater than that of Increase

'TIS a Position in *Mathematicks*, that there is no proportion between
Something and Nothing, and therefore the degrees of *Nullity* and
Quidit; seem larger than the Degrees of *Increase* and *Decrease* as 'tis
more for a *Monoculus* to lose an Eye, than for a Man who has two So if
a Man has lost several Children, it gives him more grief to lose the last,
than all the rest, because this was the *Hopes of his Family* Therefore, the
Sybil, when she had burned two of her three Books, doubled her Price
upon the third, because the loss of this would only have been a degree of
Privation, and not of *Diminution*

This *Colour* deceives, (1) in things, whose use and service lie in a Sufficiency, Competency, or determinate Quantity Thus if a Man were to
pay a large Sum upon a Penalty, it might be harder upon him to want
twenty

---

[a] *A que Deos, a que Astra, no se crudelia, Mater*

twenty Shillings for this, than ten Pounds for another occasion   So in running through an *Estate*, the *first* step towards it, *viz* breaking in upon the Stock, is a higher degree of mischief than the *last*, *viz* spending the last Penny   And to this *Colour* belong those common Forms, *'tis too late to pinch at the bottom of the Purse, as good never a whit, as never the better*, &c   (2) It deceives from this Principle in Nature, *that the Corruption of one thing is the Generation of another*, whence the ultimate Degree of Privation itself, is often less felt, as it gives occasion, and a spur, to some new Course   So when *Demosthenes* rebuked the People, for hearkening to the dishonourable and unequal Conditions of King *Philip*, he called those Conditions the *Food of their Sloth and Indolence*, which they had better be without, because then their Industry would be excited to procure other Remedies   So a blunt *Physician*, whom I knew, when the delicate Ladies complained to him, *they were they could not tell how*, yet could not endure to take Physick, he would tell them, *their way was to be sick, for then they would be glad to take any thing*   (3) Nay, the Degree of Privation itself, or the extremest Indigence may be serviceable, not only to excite our Industry, but to command our Patience

The *second* part of this *Sophism* stands upon the same Foundation, or the Degrees betwixt *Something* and *Nothing*, whence the *Common-place of extolling the beginnings of every thing   well begun is half done*, &c   And hence the Superstition of the *Astrologers*, who judge the Disposition and Fortune of a Man, from the instant of his Nativity or Conception. *The second part of the Sophism illustrated*

This *Colour* deceives, (1) because many Beginnings are but imperfect Offers and Essays, which vanish and come to nothing, without Repetition and farther Advancement, so that here the second Degree seems more worthy and powerful than the first, as the *Body-horse* in a Team draws more than the *Fore horse*   whence 'tis not ill said, *the second Word makes the Quarrel*; for the *first* might perhaps have proved harmless, if it had not been retorted therefore the *first gives the occasion* indeed, but the *second* makes reconciliation more difficult   (2) This *Sophism* deceives by *Weariness*, which makes *Perseverance* of greater dignity than *Inception* for Chance or Nature may give a Beginning, but only settled Affection, and Judgment, can give Continuance   (3) It deceives in things, whose Nature and common Course carries them contrary to the first Attempt, which is therefore continually frustrated, and gets no ground, unless the force be redoubled.   Hence the *common Forms   not to go forwards, is to go backwards ; running up hill, rowing against the stream*, &c   But if it be with the stream, or with the hill, then the degree of Inception, has by much the advantage   (4) This *Colour* not only reaches to the degree of *Inception* from Power to Action, compared with the degree from Action to Increase, but also to the degree from Want of Power to Power, compared with the Degree from Power to Action : For the Degree from *want of Power to Power*, seems greater than that *from Power to Action* *And detected*

SOPHISM X

16 *What relates to Truth, is greater than what relates to Opi-*
nion but the meaſure and trial of what relates to Opinion, is
what a Man would not do, if he thought he were ſecret

SO the Epicureans pronounce of the *Stoical Felicity*, placed in *Virtue*, that
it is the *Felicity of a Player*, who, left by his Audience, would ſoon ſink
in his Spirit, whence they in ridicule call *Virtue a Theatrical Good* But 'tis
otherwiſe in Riches and Pleaſure, which are felt more inwardly

The Force of this Colour is ſomewhat ſubtile, tho' the Anſwer to the Example be eaſy as *Truth* is not choſen for the ſake of popular Fame, and as
every one ought principally to reverence himſelf ſo that a virtuous man will
be virtuous in a *Deſart*, as well as a *Theatre*, tho' perhaps *Virtue* is made ſomewhat more vigorous by Praiſe, as Heat by Reflection But this only denies the Suppoſition, and does not expoſe the Fallacy Allowing then, that
Truth, joined with *Labour*, would not be choſe, but for the Praiſe and
Fame which uſually attend it, yet it is no Conſequence, that *Virtue*
ſhould not be deſired principally for its own ſake, ſince Fame may be only
an *impulſe*, and not a *conſtituent* or *efficient* Cauſe   Thus, if when two Hor-
ſes are rode without the Spur, one of them performs better than the other,
but with the Spur the other far exceeds, this will be judged the better
Horſe And to ſay that his Mettle lies in the Spur, is not making a true
Judgment for ſince the Spur is a common Inſtrument in Horſemanſhip,
and no Impediment or Burden to the Horſe, he will not be eſteemed the
worſe Horſe that wants it, but the going well without it, is rather a point of
Delicacy than Perfection So Glory and Honour are the Spurs to Virtue,
which tho' it might languiſh without them, yet ſince they are always at
hand unſought, Virtue is not the leſs to be choſen for itſelf, becauſe it
needs the Spur of Fame and Reputation which clearly confutes the So-
phiſm

SOPHISM XI

17 *What is procured by our own Virtue and Induſtry, is a greater*
Good, and what by another's, or by the Gift of Fortune, a leſs

THE Reaſons are, (1) *Future Hope*, becauſe in the Favours of others, or
the Gifts of Fortune, there is no great certainty, but our own Virtue
and Abilities are always with us So that when they have purchaſed us one
Good, we have them as ready, and by uſe better edged, to procure us another (2) Becauſe, what we enjoy by the benefit of others, carries with it
an obligation to them for it, whereas what is derived from ourſelves, comes
                                                              without

2 *D huius meſſis, mihi plaudo*
—————————*Grata ſ o uno*
Gratia cum tremor ſil a ſimul a te pudorem

without clog or encumbrance   Nay, when the Divine Providence bestows Favours upon us, they require Acknowledgment, and a kind of Retribution to the Supreme Being, but in the other kind, *Men rejoice*, as the *Prophet* speaks, and *are glad*, *they offer to their Toils, and sacrifice to their Nets* (3) Because, what comes to us unprocured by our own Virtue, yields not that Praise and Reputation we affect, for Actions of great Felicity may produce much Wonder, but no Praise   So *Cicero* said to *Cæsar, we have enough to admire, but want somewhat to praise* [a]   (4) Because, the Purchases of our own Industry are commonly joined with Labour and Struggle, which have not only some Sweetness in themselves, but give an Edge and Relish to Enjoyment   *Venison is sweet to him that kills it* [b]

There are four Opposites or *Counter-Colours* to this *Sophism*, and may serve as *Confutations* to the four preceding Colours respectively. (1) Because Felicity seems to be a work of the Divine Favour, and accordingly begets Confidence and Alacrity in ourselves, as well as Respect and Reverence from others   And this Felicity extends to casual things, which human Virtue can hardly reach   So when *Cæsar* said to the Master of the Ship in a storm, *Thou carriest* Cæsar *and his Fortune*, if he should have said, *thou carriest* Cæsar *and his Virtue*, it had been but a small support against the danger   (2) Because those things which proceed from Virtue and Industry are imitable, and lie open to others, whereas Felicity is inimitable, and the Prerogative of a singular Person   Whence in general, Natural things are prefer'd to Artificial; because incapable of imitation   For whatever is imitable, seems common, and in every one's power   (3) The things that proceed from Felicity, seem free Gifts, unpurchased by Industry, but those acquired by Virtue, seem bought   whence *Plutarch* said elegantly of the *Successes of Timoleon*, (an extremely fortunate man) compared with those of his Contemporaries, *Agesilaus* and *Epaminondas, that they were like* Homer's *Verses, and besides their other Excellencies, ran peculiarly smooth, and natural.* (4) Because *what happens unexpectedly*, is more acceptable, and enters the Mind with greater pleasure   but this effect cannot be had in things procured by our own Industry.

Its Colour Colours and Confutation

SOPHISM XII

18. *What consists of many divisible Parts is greater, and more One than what consists of fewer. for all things when viewed in their Parts, seem greater, whence also a plurality of Parts shews bulky but a plurality of Parts has the stronger Effect, if they lie in no certain order, for thus they resemble Infinity, and prevent Comprehension.*

Sophism 12

THIS *Sophism* appears gross at first sight, for 'tis not plurality of Parts alone, without majority, that makes the Total greater   yet the Imagination is often carried away, and the Sense deceived with this *Colour*.   Thus to the Eye the Road upon a naked Plain may seem shorter, than where there are Trees, Buildings, or other Marks, by which to distinguish and divide the

Explanation.

[a] *Quæ miremur habemus, quæ laudemus expectamus*
[b] *Suavis cibus a venatu*

D...nce So w...en ... mo...ed Man d vi...es his Chests and B...gs, he ſeems
... ...ſ... re...r than he w...s, and therefore ... w...y to amplify any th...g,
... ... br...... ... into ſ...ver...l p...rts, an... ex...mine them ſ...pir...tely An... t...is
... ...es the gr...t...r ſh...w, ...f done w...thout Order, for Confuſion ſh...ws things
m...r... ...er...us th...n th...y ...re Bu... M...tters r...nged ...nd ſet in or...r, ...p-
pe...r more co...fi...e..., ...nd prove that no...hing is on...t...ed whilſt ſuch as are
re...... ... red ...n Confu...ion ...ot only appe...r more in number, but leave a ſuſ-
p...... ...n of m... n... more ....d

Th... C...... ...ecei...es, ... if the Mind entertain too great an opinion of
an... t...ng f...... ...en th... breaking of it will deſtroy th...t f...lſe Notion, and ſhew
the th...ng ....s it is, without Amplification Thus if a Man be ſick, or in
p...n t...... ...t...... ...eems longer without a Clock than with one for tho' the irk-
ſ...... ....o... P...in m...kes the t...me ſeem longer than it is, yet the meaſu...ing of
...t corr...cts th... Error, ...nd ſhe...s it ſhorter, th...n th...t falſe opinion had con-
c...... ...u ...   And ſo ... m...xed Plain, contrary to what was juſt before ob-
ſe...ve... th... ... .y, to the E...e, m...y ſeem ſhorter when undivided, yet
...... O...... h...n...e a...t...., that 'tis much ſhorter than it w...ll be fo...nd,
... ...r... ...n...on or th... ...d... Exp...r...at...on will afterw...rds cauſe it to appear
l...ng...r th...n ...n t...e Tr...th Therefore, if ... Man deſig...n to encour...ge the falſe
O...n...on or ...... ot...er, as to the greatneſs of ... thing, l...t him not divid..., and
f...t ...t ...... but ext...l it ...n th... gener...l This *Colour* deceives, (2) if the Matter be ....r... ...y ...c... ...nd di...perſed, as not all to appear at one view So
Flo...ers gro...ng in ...parate B...ds, ſhew more th...n if they grow in one Bed,
pro...i...ed ...ll the B...ds ...re in the ſ...me Plot, ſo as to be viewed at once, o-
th...r...i...e ...y ...pp...r more numerous when brought nearer, than when ſcatter...d ... ...r ...nd hence *...nd...d E...tes*, that lie contiguous, are uſually ac-
co...nted gr...ter th...n t...ey are for if they lie in different *Co...t...s*, they
co...l...no... ...o ...e l... li...... ...t...in Notice (3) This *So...h...ſm* deceives, thro' the excell...nce o... ....bo...e M...... ...de for all Compoſition is an infallible ſign
o... d...f...c... ...c... ...n ...rt...l...rs ... For if One would ſerve the turn, it were beſt,
but D...f...c... ....n...p...rf...ct...o...s r...quire to be pieced and helped out So
... ...b... ...g, w...s told that *O...e* was ſufficient And
....nvented the *Fable*, how the *Fox* br...gg'd to
... C , ... r of D...vices ...nd Stratagems he had to get from the
Lo...... ....n ...C... ... ...ſhe h...l b...t on..., ...nd that w...s to climb a
Tr...... .... than ...ll the S...ifts of *R...... ...rd* Whence
... .n ....es, ...d *f l...... ...... m...g...m* [b] And the Moral
o... .... r...l...ng upon ...n able and tr...ſty Fr...end in
... . th...... F...r...es a...d C...n...r...nces of one's own Wit

I... ...re ....o c...n...d...r ... l...rg... numb...r of this kind of *Soph...ſms*, whereto
....r .... w...re ann...xed, it might be a work of con-
f...d...r...... ....e, r...... ...n...ng into *Pr...m...r...y P...lo...o...h...*, and *Politicks*, as well
... R...... ....or the *popul...r m...ds*, or *Colours of apparent
C...... .... *comparative*

III

... ...t ... l... ... alia m...... [a]
... ... t ... ...t a cap...l one
... ...e ...e...h bore o...rds. (applying this *Deficiency*, is, perhaps, the
difficulty

III 19 A *second Collection* wanting to the *Apparatus of Rhetorick*, is that intimated by *Cicero*, when he directs a set 'of *Common-places*, suited to both sides of the Question, to be had in readiness But we extend this Precept farther, so as to include, not only *judicial*, but also *deliberative* and *demonstrative Forms* Our meaning is, that all the *Places of common use*, *whether for Proof, Confutation, Persuasion, Dissuasion, Praise, or Dispraise, should be ready studied, and either exaggerated, or degraded, with the utmost effort of Genius, or, as it were, perverse Resolution, beyond all measure of Truth*[a] And the best way of forming this *Collection*, both for Conciseness and Use, we judge to be that of contracting, and winding up these *Places* into certain acute, and short Sentences, as into so many *Clues*, which may occasionally be wound off into larger Discourses And something of this kind we find done by *Seneca*, but only in the way of *Suppositions* or *Cases*. The following *Examples* will more fully illustrate our Intention.

BEAUTY

For	*Against*
20 The Deformed endeavour, by Malice, to keep themselves from Contempt	Virtue, like a Diamond, is best plain set.
Deformed Persons are commonly revenged of Nature	As a good Dress to a deformed Person, so is Beauty to a vicious Man
Virtue is internal Beauty, and Beauty external Virtue	Those adorned with Beauty, and those affected by it, are generally shallow alike
Beauty makes Virtue shine, and Vice blush.	

Y 2

BOLDNESS.

difficulty that attends it Numerous *Sophisms*, of great influence, might indeed be collected from Books of *Morality Policy, Physicks, Chemistry*, and many other parts of Philosophy, as well as from common Converlation, but to shew wherein the Fallacy of such *Sophisms* lies, and clearly to confute them, may often require a penetrating Capacity, and a considerable Degree of Attention Whence a Work of this kind cannot be executed upon the Plan of the Author, but by men of general Knowledge, clear Discernment, Mathematical Sagacity, and strong Judgment But if such a Work were extant in its due latitude, it might afford an entertaining, as well as useful Picture of human Nature, and shew that nearly all the *Arguments* in common use are but a kind of *Sophisms* and thus defend the Mind against them

[a] Observe however, that these *Places* are still to be true and just, if taken in a *lower* or *higher Key*, otherwise they would be but mere Sophisms and Imposture Thus the two sides of the Question, may by moderation be made to comport, for instance,

FOR

Virtue, like a Diamond, is best plain set

AGAINST

Virtue, in a graceful Person, shews to greater advantage

These are Antithets, or Opposites, but reconcilable by relaxing, or softening the Rigour of each Position so that tho' *Virtue shews well, when plain set, yet it shews better, when accompanied with graceful Behaviour* But in *Pleading* and *Persuading*, more regard is had to Exaggeration and strong Expression than to Moderation and exact Truth. The part of the Judges to moderate, and balance, both sides of the Question.

I

BOLDNESS

For	*Against.*
21 A bashful Suitor shews the way to deny him	Boldness is the Verger to Folly
Boldness in a Politician is like Action to an Orator, the first, second, and third Qualification	Impudence is fit for nothing but Imposture
Love the Man, who confesses his Modesty, but hate him who accuses it.	Confidence is the Fool's Empress, and the Wife Man's Buffoon
A Confidence in carriage soonest unites Affections	Boldness is a kind of Dulness, join'd with a Perverseness.
Give me a reserved Countenance, and open Conversation.	

CEREMONIES

For	*Against*
22 A graceful Deportment is the true Ornament of Virtue	What can be more disagreeable than in common Life to copy the Stage?
If we follow the Vulgar in the use of Words, why not in Habit and Gesture?	Ingenuous Behaviour procures Esteem, but Affectation and Cunning, Hatred
He who observes not Decorums in smaller matters, may be a great Man, but is unwise at times	Better a painted Face and curled Hair, than a painted and curled Behaviour
Virtue and *Wisdom*, without all Respect and Ceremony, are, like foreign Languages, unintelligible to the Vulgar	He is incapable of great Matters, who breaks his Mind with trifling Observations
He, who knows not the Sense of the People, neither by Congruity, nor Observation, is senseless	Affectation is the glossy Corruption of Ingenuity
Ceremonies are the translation of Virtue into our own Language.	

CONSTANCY

For.	*Against*
23 Constancy is the Foundation of Virtue	Constancy, like a churlish Portress, turns away many useful Informations.
He is miserable who has no Notion of what he shall be	'Tis just that Constancy should endure Crosses, for it commonly brings them
If Human Judgment cannot be constant to things, let it at least be true to itself	The shortest Folly is the best
Even Vice is set off by Constancy	
Inconstancy	

Inconftancy of Fortune, with Inconftancy of Mind, makes a Dark Scene

Fortune, like *Proteus*, is brought
to herfelf by perfifting.

CRUELTY.

For.

24. No Virtue is fo often delinquent
as *Clemency*

Cruelty, proceeding from Revenge,
is Juftice, if from Danger, Prudence.

He who fhews Mercy to his Enemy, denies it to himfelf

Phlebotomy is as neceffary in the Body Politick, as in the Body Natural

Againft.

He who delights in Blood, is either
a wild Beaft, or a Fury.

To a good Man, Cruelty feems a
mere Tragical Fiction.

DELAY.

For.

25 Fortune fells many things to
the Hafty, which fhe gives to the
Slow

Hurrying to catch the Beginnings
of things, is grafping at Shadows

When things hang wavering, mark
them, and work, when they incline

Commit the beginning of Actions
to *Argus*, with his hundred Eyes,
the end to *Briareus*, with his hundred
Hands.

Againft

Opportunity offers the Handle of
the Bottle firft, then the Belly

Opportunity, like the *Sibyl*, dimi-
nifhes the Commodity, but enhances
the Price

Difpatch is *Pluto*'s Helmet.

Things undertaken fpeedily, are eafily performed.

DISSIMULATION

For

26 Diffimulation is a fhort Wifdom

We are not all to fay, tho' we all
intend, the fame Thing

Nakednefs, even in the Mind, is un-
comely

Diffimulation is both a Grace and
a Guard.

Diffimulation is the Bulwark of
Counfels.

Some fall a Prey to Fair-Dealing

The open Dealer deceives as well as
the Diffembler. for many either do
not underftand him, or not believe him

Open-dealing is a Weaknefs of
Mind.

Againft

If we cannot think juftly, at leaft
let us fpeak as we think

In fhallow Politicians, Diffimulation goes for Wifdom

The Diffembler lofes a principal Inftrument of Action, *Belief*

Diffimulation invites Diffimulation.

The Diffembler is a Slave

EMPIRE.

EMPIRE

For	*Against*
27 To enjoy Happiness, is a great Blessing, but to confer it a greater	'Tis a miserable State, to have few things to desire, and many to fear
Kings are more like Stars than Men, for they have an overful Influence	Princes, like the celestial Bodies, have much Veneration, but no Rest
To rule God's Vicegerents is to war against Heaven	Mortals are admitted to *Jupiter*'s Table, only for sport

ENVY

For	*Against.*
28 'Tis natural to hate those who reproach us	Envy has no Holidays.
Envy in a State is like a wholesome Severity	Death alone reconciles Envy to Virtue
	Envy puts Virtue to the trial, as *Juno* did *Hercules.*

EVIDENCE *against* ARGUMENTS.

For	*Against.*
29 To rely upon Arguments, is the part of a Pleader, not a Judge	If Evidence were to prevail against Arguments, a Judge would need no Sense but his Hearing
He who is sway'd more by Arguments than Testimony, trusts more to Wit than Sense	Arguments are an Antidote against the Poison of Testimonies.
Arguments might be trusted, if Men committed no Absurdities	Those Proofs are safest believed, which seldomest deceive.
Arguments against Testimonies, make the Case appear strange, but not true	

FACILITY

For	*Against*
30 Give me the Man who complies to another's Humour without Flattery	Facility is want of Judgment.
The Pexble Man comes nearest to the nature of Cold	The good Offices of easy Natures seem Debts, and their Denials, Injuries
	He thanks only himself, who prevails upon an easy Man
	All Difficulties oppress a yielding Nature, for he is engaged in all
	Easy Natures seldom come off with credit.

FLAT-

FLATTERY.

For.	*Against*
31 Flattery proceeds from Cuſtom, rather than ill Deſign	Flattery is the Style of a Slave
To convey Inſtruction with Praiſe, is a Form due to the Great	Flattery is the Varniſh of Vice.
	Flattery is fowling with a Bird-Call
	The Deformity of Flattery is Comedy, but the Injury, Tragedy.
	To convey good Counſel, is a hard Taſk.

FORTITUDE

For	*Against*
32 Nothing is terrible, but Fear itſelf	A ſtrange Virtue that, to deſire to deſtroy, to ſecure Deſtruction
Pleaſure and Virtue loſe their Nature, where Fear diſquiets.	A goodly Virtue truly, which even Drunkenneſs can cauſe
To view Danger, is looking out to avoid it	A Prodigal of his own Life, threatens the Lives of others
Other Virtues ſubdue Vice, but Fortitude even conquers Fortune	Fortitude is a Virtue of the Iron-Age

FORTUNE.

For.	*Againſt*
33 Publick Virtues procure Praiſe, but private ones, Fortune	The Folly of one Man, is the Fortune of another
Fortune, like the *Milk-Way*, is a Cluſter of ſmall, twinkling, nameleſs Virtues	This may be commended in Fortune, that if ſhe makes no Election, ſhe gives no Protection
Fortune is to be honour'd and reſpected, tho' it were but for her Daughters, Confidence and Authority	The Great, to decline Envy, worſhip *Fortune.*

FRIENDSHIP.

For	*Againſt*
34 Friendſhip does the ſame as Fortitude, but more agreeably	To contract Friendſhip, is to procure Fortune
Friendſhip gives the Reliſh to Happineſs	'Tis a weak Spirit, that divides Fortune with another
The worſt Solitude, is to want Friends	
'Tis juſt that the hollow-hearted ſhould not find Friendſhip.	

HEALTH

HEALTH

For	*Against*
55 The Care of Health subjects the Mind to the Body	Recovery from Sickness, is Rejuvenescency
An healthy Body is the Tabernacle but a sickly one, the Prison of th Soul	Pretence of Sickness, is a good Excuse for the Healthy
A sound Constitution forward Business, but a sickly one makes many Holidays	Health too strongly cements the Soul and Body
	The Couch has govern'd Empires, and the Litter, Armies.

HONOURS

For	*Against*
36 Honours are the Suffrages, not of Tyrants, but Divine Providence	To seek Honour, is to lose Liberty
Honours make both Virtue and Vice conspicuous	Honours give command where 'tis best not to will, and next, not to be able
Honour is the Touchstone of Virtue	The Steps of Honour are hard to climb, slippery a-top, and dangerous to go down
The Motion of Virtue is rapid to its place, but calm in it but the *Place* of Virtue is *Honour*	Men in great Place borrow others Opinions, to think themselves happy.

JESTS

For	*Against*
37 A Jest is the Orator's Altar	Hunters after Deformities and Comparisons, are despicable Creatures.
Humour in Conversation, preserves Freedom	To divert important Business with a Jest, is a base Trick
'Tis highly politick to pass smoothly from Jest to Earnest, and *vice versa*	Judge of a Jest, when the Laugh is over
Witty Conceits are Vehicles to Truths, that could not be otherwise agreeably convey'd	Wit commonly plays on the Surface of things, for Surface is the Seat of a Jest

INGRATITUDE

For	*Against*
38 Ingratitude is but perceiving the Cause of a Benefit	The Sin of Ingratitude is not made penal here, but left to the Furies
The desire of being grateful, neither does Justice to others, nor leaves one's self at liberty	The Obligations for Benefits, exceed the Obligations of Duties, whence Ingratitude is also unjust.

A

No

A Benefit of an uncertain Value, merits the lefs thanks. | No publick Fortune can exclude private Favour

INNOVATION.

For

39. Every Remedy is an Innovation

He who will not apply new Remedies, muft expect new Difeafes

Time is the greateft Innovator, and why may we not imitate Time?

Ancient Precedents are unfuitable, and late ones corrupt and degenerate

Let the Ignorant fquare their Actions by Example

As they who firft derive Honour to their Family, are commonly more worthy than thofe who fucceed them, fo Innovations generally excel Imitations

An obftinate adherence to Cuftoms, is as turbulent a thing as *Innovation.*

Since things of their own courfe change for the worfe, if they are not by prudence alter'd for the better, what End can there be of the Ill?

The Slaves of Cuftom are the Sport of Time.

Againft

New Births are deformed things

No Author is accepted, till time has authoriz'd him

All Novelty is Injury, for it defaces the prefent ftate of things

Things authoriz'd by Cuftom, if not excellent, are yet conformable; and fort well together

What Innovator follows the Example of Time, which infinuates new things fo quietly, as to be almoft imperceptible[a]?

Things that happen unexpected, are lefs agreeable to thofe they benefit, and more afflicting to thofe they injure.

JUSTICE.

For.

40 Power and Policy are but the Appendages of Juftice, for if Juftice could be otherwife executed, there were no need of them

'Tis owing to Juftice, that Man to Man is a God, not a Wolf

Tho' Juftice cannot extirpate Vice, it keeps it under.

Againft.

If Juftice confift in doing to another what we would have done to ourfelves; then Mercy is Juftice

If every one muft receive his due, then furely Mortals muft receive Pardon.

The common Juftice of a Nation, like a Philofopher at Court, renders Rulers aweful

---

[a] One can fcarce help anfwering to this Queftion, *the Lord Bacon* who has reformed the State of Learning fo quietly, that his Countrymen fcarce perceive how or by whom it was effected.

KNOWLEDGE *and* CONTEMPLATION

For	*Against.*
41 That Pleasure only is according to Nature, which never cloys.	A contemplative Life is but a specious Lazines
The sweetest Prospect is that below, into the Errors of others.	To think well is little better than to dream well.
'Tis best to have the Orbits of the Mind concentrick with those of the Universe	Divine Providence regards the World, but Man regards only his Country
All depraved Affections are false Valuations, but Goodness and Truth are ever the same	A political Man sows even his Thoughts

LAW.

For.	*Against.*
42 'Tis not expounding, but divining, to recede from the Letter of the Law	Generals are to be construed so as, to explain Particulars.
To leave the Letter of the Law, makes the Judge a Legislator.	The worst Tyranny is Law upon the rack

LEARNING.

For	*Against.*
43. To write Books upon minute Particulars, were to render Experience almost useless.	Men in Universities are taught to believe
Reading is conversing with the Wise, but acting is generally conversing with Fools	What Art ever taught the seasonable Use of Art?
Sciences of little significance in themselves, may sharpen the Wit, and marshal the Thoughts	To be wise by Precept, and wise by Experience, are contrary Habits, the one sorts not with the other.
	A vain use is made of Art, lest it should otherwise be unemploy'd.
	'Tis the way of Scholars to shew all they know; and oppose farther Information.

LIFE.

For	*Against.*
44. 'Tis absurd, to love the Accidents of Life above Life itself	The Philosophers, by their great Preparation for Death, have only render'd Death more terrible.
A long Course is better than a short one, even for Virtue.	Men fear Death thro' Ignorance, as Children fear the Dark.

With-   There

Without a Compaſs of Life, we can neither learn, nor repent, nor perfect.

There is no Paſſion ſo weak, but, if a little urged, will conquer the Fear of Death

A Man would wiſh to die, even thro' Wearineſs of doing the ſame things over and over again.

LOQUACITY.

For.

45. Silence argues a Man to ſuſpect either himſelf or others.

All Reſtraints are irkſome, but eſpecially that of the Tongue.

Silence is the Virtue of Fools.

Silence, like the Night, is fit for Treacheries

Thoughts, like Waters, are beſt in a running Stream

Silence is a kind of Solitude.

He who is ſilent, expoſes himſelf to Cenſure.

Againſt.

To ſpeak little, gives Grace and Authority to what is deliver'd.

Silence is like Sleep, it refreſhes Wiſdom

Silence is the Fermentation of the Thoughts.

Silence is the Style of Wiſdom; and the Candidate for Truth.

LOVE.

For.

46 Every Man ſeeks, but the Lover only finds, himſelf

The Mind is beſt regulated by the Predominancy of ſome powerful Affection

He who is wiſe, will purſue ſome one Deſire, for he that affects not one thing above another, finds all flat and diſtaſteful.

Why ſhould not one Man reſt in one Individual?

Againſt.

The Stage is more beholden to Love, than civil Life.

I like not ſuch Men as are wholly taken up with one thing.

Love is but a narrow Contemplation.

MAGNANIMITY.

For.

47. When the Mind propoſes honourable Ends, not only the Virtues, but the Deities are ready to aſſiſt.

Virtues proceeding from Habit, or Precept, are vulgar; but thoſe that proceed from the End, heroical.

Againſt.

Magnanimity is a poetical Virtue.

NATURE

For

48 Cuſtom goes in Arithmetical, but Nature in Geometrical Progreſſion [a]

As Laws are to Cuſtom in States, ſo is Nature to Cuſtom in particular Perſons

Cuſtom, againſt Nature, is a kind of Tyranny, but eaſily ſuppreſſed

Againſt

Men think according to Nature, ſpeak according to Precept, but act according to Cuſtom

Nature is a kind of a School-Maſter, Cuſtom, a Magiſtrate

NOBILITY

For

49 Where Virtue is deeply implanted from the Stock, there can be no Vice

Nobility is a Laurel confer'd by Time

If we reverence Antiquity in dead Monuments, we ſhould do it much more in living ones

If we deſpiſe Nobility in Families, what difference is there betwixt Men and Brutes?

Nobility ſhelters Virtue from Envy, and recommends it to Favour

Againſt

Nobility ſeldom ſprings from Virtue; and Virtue ſeldomer from Nobility

Nobles oftener plead their Anceſtors for Pardon, than Promotion

New riſing Men are ſo induſtrious, as to make Nobles ſeem like Statues.

Nobles, like bad Racers, look back too often in the Courſe.

POPULARITY

For

50 Uniformity commonly pleaſes wiſe Men, yet 'tis a Point of Wiſdom to humour the changeable Nature of Fools

To honour the People, is the way to be honour'd.

Men in place are uſually awed, not by one Man, but the Multitude.

Againſt.

He who ſuits with Fools, may himſelf be ſuſpected

He who pleaſes the Rabble, is commonly turbulent.

No moderate Counſels take with the Vulgar.

To fawn on the People, is the baſeſt Flattery.

PRAISE

For

51 Praiſe is the reflected Ray of Virtue.

Praiſe

Againſt

Fame makes a quick Meſſenger, but a raſh Judge.

What

[a] That is, *Cuſtom* gets ground ſlower than *Nature.*

Praife is the Honour obtain'd by free Voices

Many States confer Honours, but Praife always proceeds from Liberty.

The Voice of the People hath fomething of Divine, elfe how fhould fo many become of one mind?

No wonder if the Commonalty fpeak truer than the Nobility, becaufe they fpeak with lefs danger.

What has a good Man to do with the Breath of the Vulgar?

Fame, like a River, buoys up Things light and fwoln, but drowns thofe that are weighty

Low Virtues gain the Praife of the Vulgar, ordinary ones aftonifh them but of the higheft, they have no feeling

Praife is got by Bravery more than Merit, and given rather to the Vain and Empty, than to the Worthy and Subftantial

PREPARATION.

For.	*Againft.*
52. He who attempts great Matters with fmall Means, hopes for Opportunity, to keep him in Heart.	The firft Occafion is the beft Preparation.
Slender Provifion buys Wit, but not Fortune.	Fortune is not to be fetter'd in the Chains of Preparation
	The interchange of Preparation and Action, are politick, but the feparation of them oftentatious, and unfuccefsful.
	Great Preparation is a Prodigal, both of Time and Bufinefs.

PRIDE

For.	*Againft*
53. *Pride* is inconfiftent even with Vice and as Poyfon expels Poyfon, fo are many Vices expell'd by Pride	*Pride* is the Ivy of Virtue [a]
An eafy Nature is fubject to other Men's Vices, but a proud one only to it's own	Other Vices are only Oppofites to Virtues, but Pride is even contagious
Pride, if it rife from a contempt of others, to a contempt of itfelf, at length becomes *Philofophy*	*Pride* wants the beft Condition of Vice, Concealment.
	A proud man, while he defpifes others, neglects himfelf

READINESS.

For	*Againft.*
54 That is unfeafonable Wifdom, which is not ready.	That Knowledge is not deep fetch'd, which lies ready at hand.
He	Wif-

[a] *Viz* On account of creeping and twining about it

3

He who errs suddenly, suddenly reforms his Error

To be wise upon Deliberation, and not upon present Occasion, is no great Matter

Wisdom is like a Garment, lightest when readiest

They whose Counsels are not ripened by Deliberation, have not their Prudence ripened by Age

What is suddenly invented, suddenly vanishes

REVENGE.

For.	*Against*
55 Private Revenge is a kind of wild Justice	He who does the wrong, is the Aggressor, but he who returns it, the Protractor
He who returns Injury for Injury, violates the Law, not the Person	The more prone men are to Revenge, the more it should be weeded out
The fear of private Revenge is useful, for Laws are often asleep.	A revengeful Man may be slow in Time, tho' not in Will.

RICHES

For	*Against.*
56 They despise Riches, who despair of them	Great Riches are attended, either with Care, Trouble, or Fame; but no Use
Envy at Riches has made Virtue a Goddess	What an imaginary Value is set upon Stones, and other Curiosities, that Riches may seem to be of some Service?
Whilst Philosophers dispute whether all things should be referr'd to Virtue, or Pleasure, let us be collecting the Instruments of both	Many who imagine all things may be bought by their Riches, forget they have sold themselves
Riches turn Virtue into a common Good	Riches are the Baggage of Virtue, necessary, tho' cumbersome.
The Command of other Advantages are particular, but that of Riches universal	Riches are a good Servant, but a bad Master.

SUPERSTITION.

For.	*Against.*
57 They who err out of Zeal, tho' they are not to be approved, should yet be pitied	As an Ape appears the more deformed for his resemblance to Man; so the similitude of Superstition to Religion, makes it the more odious
Mediocrity belongs to Morality, Extremes to Divinity	What Affectation is in civil Matters, such is Superstition in divine.
A superstitious Man is a religious Formalist	It were better to have no Belief of a God, than such an one as dishonours him.
I should sooner believe all the Fables,	It

bles and Abfurdities of any Religion, than that the Univerfal Frame is without a Deity.

It was not the School of *Epicurus*, but the *Stoicks*, that difturbed the States of old.

The real Atheifts are Hypocrites; who deal continually in holy things without feeling.

SUSPICION.

For

58. Diftruft is the Sinew of Prudence, and Sufpicion a Strengthner of the Underftanding.

That Sincerity is juftly fufpected, which Sufpicion weakens.

Sufpicion breaks a frail Integrity, but confirms a ftrong one.

Againft

Sufpicion breaks the Bonds of Truft.

To be over-run with Sufpicion, is a kind of Political Madnefs.

TACITURNITY.

For.

59. Nothing is concealed from a filent Man; for all is fafely depofited with him.

He who eafily talks what he knows, will alfo talk what he knows not.

Myfteries are due to Secrets.

Againft

From a filent Man all things are concealed, becaufe he returns nothing, but Silence.

Change of Cuftoms keeps Men fecret.

Secrecy is the Virtue of a *Confeffor.*

A clofe Man is like a Man unknown.

TEMPERANCE.

For

60 To abftain and fuftain, are nearly the fame Virtue.

Uniformity, Concords, and the Meafure of Motions, are things Celeftial, and the Characters of Eternity.

Temperance, like wholefome Cold, collects and ftrengthens the Force of the Mind.

When the Senfes are too exquifite and wandring, they want Narcoticks, fo likewife do wandring Affections.

Againft.

I like not bare negative Virtues, they argue Innocence, not Merit.

The Mind languifhes, that is not fometimes fpirited up by excefs.

I like the Virtues, which produce the Vivacity of Action, not the Dulnefs of Paffion.

The Sayings, " *Not to ufe, that you* " *may not defire*," " *Not to defire, that* " *you may not fear*," &c. proceed from pufillanimous, and diftruftful Natures.

VAIN-

VAIN-GLORY

For	*Against*
61 He who seeks his own Praise, at the same time seeks the Advantage of others	The Vain-glorious are always Factious, False, Fickle, and upon the Extreme
He who is so strait-laced, as to regard nothing that belongs to others, will perhaps account publick Affairs impertinent	*Thraso* is *Gnatho*'s Prey
	'Tis shameful in a Lover, to court the Maid instead of the Mistress, but Praise is only Virtue's Hand-maid.
Such Dispositions as have a mixture of Levity, more easily undertake a publick Charge	

UNCHASTITY

For	*Against.*
62 'Tis Jealousy that makes Chastity a Virtue	Incontinency is one of *Circe*'s worst Transformations.
He must be a melancholy Mortal, that thinks *Venus* a grave Lady	The unchaste Liver has no reverence for himself, which is slackening the Bridle of Vice.
Why is a Part of Regimen, pretended Cleanness, and the Daughter of Pride, placed among the Virtues?	They who, with *Paris*, make Beauty their Wish, lose, as he did, Wisdom and Power
In Amours, as in Wild-fowl, there is no Property, but the Right is transferred with Possession	*Alexander* fell upon no popular Truth, when he said, that Sleep and Lust were the Earnest of Death

WATCHFULNESS

For	*Against*
63 More Dangers deceive by Fraud, than Force	He bids Danger advance, who buckles against it
'Tis easier to prevent a Danger, than to watch its approach	Even the Remedies of Dangers are dangerous.
Danger is no longer light, if it once seem light	'Tis better to use a few approved Remedies, than to venture upon many unexperienced Particulars.

WIFE AND CHILDREN

For	*Against*
64 Charity to the Common-wealth begins with private Families	He who hath Wife and Children, hath given Hostages to Fortune
Wife and Children are a kind of Discipline, but unmarried Men are morose and cruel	Generation and Issue, are human Acts, but Creation, and its Works, are divine.

A   Issue

A fingle Life, and a childlefs State fit men for nothing but Flight

He facrifices to Death, who begets no Children

The happy in other refpects are commonly unfortunate in their Children, left the human State fhould too nearly approach the divine

Iffue is the Eternity of Brutes, but Fame, Merit, and Inftitutions, the Eternity of Men

Private Regards generally prevail over publick

Some affect the Fortune of *Priam*, in furviving his Family

YOUTH.

For.

65 The firft Thoughts and Counfels of Youth, have fomewhat divine

Old Men are wife for themfelves, but lefs for others, and the publick Good.

If it were vifible, old Age deforms the Mind more than the Body

Old Men fear all things, but the Gods

Againft.

Youth is the Field of Repentance

Youth naturally defpifes the Authority of Age, that every one may grow wife at his peril

The Counfels whereat Time did not affift, are not ratified by him

Old Men commute *Venus* for the *Graces* [a].

66 The *Examples of Antithets*, here laid down, may not perhaps deferve the place affign'd them   but as they were collected in my youth, and are really *Seeds*, not *Flowers*, I was unwilling they fhould be loft   In this they plainly fhew a *juvenile Warmth*, that they abound in the *moral* and *demonftrative* kind, but touch fparingly upon the *deliberative* and *judicial*

IV 67   A third *Collection* wanting to the *Apparatus of Rhetorick*, is what we call *Leffer Forms*   And thefe are a kind of *Portals, Poftern-doors, Outer-Rooms*, *Back Rooms*, and *Paffages of Speech*, which may ferve indifferently for all Subjects fuch as *Prefaces, Conclufions, Digreffions, Tranfitions*, &c.   For as in Building, a good Diftribution of the Frontifpiece, Stair-cafes, Doors, Windows, Entries, Paffages, and the like, is not only agreeable, but ufeful. fo in Speech, if the Acceffories, and Under-parts, be decently and fkilfully contrived and placed, they are of great Ornament and Service to the whole Structure of the Difcourfe   Of thefe Forms, we will juft propofe one Ex-

A Collection of leffer Forms, wanting in Rhetorick

[a] The Reader will find confiderable Ufe made of this Collection by the *Author*, in his Essays, and other parts of his Works   It were eafy to continue fuch a Collection, in the way of an *Alphabetical Common place*   and the Ufefulnefs of the Thing might well recommend it, as in moft parts of Life, and both in writing and fpeaking, we have frequent Occafions for fhort and fententious Arguments, as well to defend ourfelves, as to prevail upon others   There is alfo a more capital Ufe of fuch a *Collection*, viz that of affifting the Underftanding, and enabling the Mind to form a true Judgment of Things, when both fides of the Queftion are thus pleaded for with the utmoft Strength   And fome Collections of this kind, we find in feveral *School Books*, ufed by the younger Scholars, as a Help in making their *Themes* or *Exercifes*   But the Thing in its full extent, according to the View of the Author, is perhaps ftill wanting

~mple or two[a]   For tho' they are Matters of no fmall ufe , yet becaufe
he~e we add nothing of our own, and only take naked Forms from *Demoftbe-*
~, C.~~, or other felect Authors , they may feem of too trivial a nature,
to fpend time therein

68.   EXAMPLES OF LESSER FORMS.

A CONCLUSION IN THE DELIBERATIVE.

So the paft Fault ma, be at once amended , and future Inconvenience prevented.

COROLLARY OF AN EXACT DIVISION.

That all ma, fee I would conceal nothing by Silence , nor cloud any thing by
Words

A TRANSITION, WITH A CAVEAT.

But let us leave this Subject for the prefent , ftill referving to ourfelves the
Liberty of a Retrofpection

A PREPOSSESSION AGAINST AN INVETERATE OPINION.

I will let you underftand to the full, what fprung from the thing itfelf , what
Error has tacked on it, and what Envy has raifed upon it

And thefe few Examples may ferve to fhew our meaning as to the *Leffer*
Form of Speech [b]

SECT.   XIX.

CRITICISM, *and* SCHOOL-LEARNING.

I THere remain two general APPENDAGES *to the* DOCTRINE OF DE-
LIVERY , the one relating to CRITICISM , the other to SCHOOL-
LEARNING   For as the principal part of *traditive Prudence* [c], turns upon the
writing,

[a] See ~~e Lo~d Shaftesbury, *advice to an Author*

[b] Tho ~~e An~~e~~s may fee~ o have perfected *Rhetorick* , yet the Moderns have given ~
~~~ ~ g~ Gerhard Voffius ~~~ow'd incredible Pains upon this Art, as appears by his Book
~~ ~~ ~~ C ~~~~~~~ *Rhetorices*, and ftill more by his *Inftitutiones Oratoria*   See alfo
~~~~ g Scheerfeur's *Apparatus Eloquentia*, *Tefmari Exercitationes Rhetorica, &c*   Seve~~
French Au~~ors have ~~ few fo cul~~ a~ed this Subject, particularly *Rapin*, in his *Reflexions fur*
l Eloquence, *Bro~~* , ~ his *Maniere de bien Penfer dans les Ouvrages de l Efprit*, and his *Pen-*
fees Ingenieufes, Father *Lamy*, in his *Art de Parler*   See alfo M *Caffander's French Tranflation*
of Ari~~c de s Rhetorick, ~~e anonymous Pieces, entitled, *l Art de Penfer*, and *l' Art de Perfuader*,
Le Clerc's Hiftoria Rhetorice in his *Ars Critica*, and *Stollius de Arte Rhetorica*, in his *Intro-*
duction ~~ Hiftoriam Literariam

[c] See above Sect XVII 1, 2 ~~

writing , fo its *relative* turns upon the *reading of Books* Now *Reading* is either regulated by the Affiftance of a *Mafter* , or left to every one's *private Induftry* but both depend upon Criticism and School-Learning

2 Criticism regards, *firft, the exaƈt correƈting and publifhing of approved Authors* , whereby the Honour of fuch *Authors* is preferved , and the neceffary Affiftance afforded to the *Reader* Yet the mifapplied Labours and Induftry of fome, have in this refpeƈt proved highly prejudicial to Learning for many *Criticks* have a way, when they fall upon any thing they do not underftand, of *immediately fuppofing a Fault in the Copy* Thus, in that Paffage of *Tacitus*, where a certain *Colony* pleads a Right of Proteƈtion in the Senate, *Tacitus* tells us, they were not favourably heard , fo that the Ambaffadors diftrufting their Caufe, endeavoured to procure the Favour of *Titus Vinius* by a Prefent, and fucceeded · upon which *Tacitus* has thefe Words , *Tvm dignitas & antiquitas Coloniæ valuit Then the Honour and Antiquity of the Colony had weight* , in allufion to the Sum receiv'd But a confiderable *Critick*, here expunges *Tvm*, and fubftitutes *Tantùm* , which quite corrupts the Senfe And from this ill praƈtice of the *Criticks*, it happens, that the *moft correƈted Copies are often the leaft correƈt* And to fay the truth, unlefs a *Critick* is well acquainted with the *Sciences* treated in the Books he publifhes, his Diligence will be attended with danger

3. A *fecond* thing belonging to Criticism, is the *Explanation* and *Illuftration of Authors* , by *Comments, Notes, Colleƈtions,* &c But here an ill cuftom has prevailed among the *Criticks*, of fkipping over the obfcure Paffages ; and expatiating upon fuch as are fufficiently clear : as if their Defign were not fo much to illuftrate their Author, as to take all occafions of fhewing their own Learning and Reading It were therefore to be wifhed, that every original Writer, who treats an obfcure or noble Subjeƈt, would add his own *Explanations* to his own Work , fo as to keep the Text continued and unbroken, by Digreffions or Illuftrations , and thus prevent any wrong Interpretation, by the Notes of others[a].

4 *Thirdly*, there belongs to *Criticifm* the thing from whence its Name is derived ; *viz a certain concife Judgment, or Cenfure of the Authors publifhed, and a Comparifon of them with other Writers, who have treated the fame Subjeƈt* Whence the Student may be direƈted in the choice of his Books , and come the better prepared to their perufal · and this feems to be the ultimate Office of the *Critick* , and has indeed been honour'd by fome greater Men in our Age, than *Criticks* are ufually thought [b]

Aa 2 5.

Criticifm divided as it regards (1) the correƈt publifhing of Authors

(2) The Illuftration of them by Notes, &c.

(3) A Cenfure of them,

---

[a] It were much to be wifhed, the Author had fet an Example of this in his own *Philofophical Works*, which might then have been currently underftood, and not have continued in a manner unknown, as they have done, except to a few But the Misfortune may lie here, that an Author cannot always forefee what Parts of his Works will be leaft intelligible to his Readers the whole being generally become clear and ftrong to himfelf, by repeated *Thought* or *Experience*

[b] The Author has given us an uncommon *Specimen* of this part of *Criticifm*, in his Cenfure of the *Works of the more eminent Philofophers* , which makes the Tenth Supplement to the *Augmentis Scientiarum* But the Subjeƈt of *Criticifm* itfelf has been confiderably changed, and improved, 'fince

For the DOCTRINE OF SCHOOL-LEARNING, it were the shorteſt way to refer to [...] who, in point of Uſefulneſs, have herein excell'd yet we [...], to ſome few Admonitions about it We highly approve the Education of Youth in *Colleges*, and not wholly in private Houſes, or *Schools*[a] For in Colleges, there is not only a greater Emulation of the Youth, among their Equals, but the Teachers have a venerable Aſpect and Gravity, which greatly conduces towards inſinuating a modeſt Behaviour, and the forming of tender Minds from the firſt, according to ſuch Examples and beſides theſe, there are many other Advantages of a *Collegiate Education*. But for the Order and Manner of Diſcipline, 'tis of capital Uſe to avoid too conciſe Methods, and too haſty an Opinion of Learning, which give a Pertneſs to the Mind, and rather make a ſhow of Improvement, than procure it But Exerciſes of Genius are to be ſomewhat favour'd, ſo that if a Scholar perform his uſual Exerciſes, he may be ſuffer'd to ſteal time for other things, whereto he is more inclin'd

6 It muſt alſo be carefully noted, tho' it has, perhaps, hitherto eſcaped Obſervation, that there are two correſpondent ways of enuring, exerciſing, and preparing the Genius the one, beginning with the eaſier, leads gradually on to more difficult things, and the other commanding and impoſing ſuch as are harder at firſt, ſo that when theſe are obtain'd, the eaſier may be more agreeably diſpatch'd For 'tis one Method to begin Swimming with Bladders, and another to begin Dancing with loaded Shoes Nor is it eaſy to ſee how much a prudent Intermixture of theſe two ways, contributes to improve the Faculties both of Body and Mind[b].

7 Again, the ſuiting of Studies to the Genius, is of ſingular Uſe which Maſters ſhould duly attend to, that the Parent may thence conſider what kind of Life the Child is fitteſt for And further, it muſt be carefully obſerved, not only that every one makes much greater Progreſs in thoſe things whereto he is naturally inclin'd, but alſo, that there are certain Remedies in a proper Choice of Studies, for particular Indiſpoſitions of Mind For example, Inattention, and a Volatility of Genius, may be remedied by Mathematicks wherein, if the Mind wander ever ſo little, the whole Demonſtration muſt be begun a new[c].

8.

face and time, inſomuch as to be reduced into the form of an *Art*, as particularly by the famed Mr le Clerc in his *Ars Critica*, who defines *Criticiſm* the *Art*, (1) of *Interpreting the ancient Writers, whether proſaical or poetical*, and (2) *diſtinguiſhing their genuine Writings from ſpurious* Thus making up a part omitted by the *Lord Bacon* To which might alſo be added the Diſcovery of Impoſition Interpolations, Prevarications, Pyracies, Mutilations, and Suppreſſions, &c both of the ancient and modern Authors, with the ways of rectifying, adjuſting and ſupplying the ſame In ſhort, Criticiſm, according to the later Acceptation, is the *Art of Judging of Hiſtorical Facts, Monuments, Books, and their Authors* And to take *Criticiſm* in this Light the Books that have been written upon it, in the laſt, and the preſent Age, might furniſh out a Library Many of them are enumerated by *Morhof, Struvius, Stollius*, and other Writers upon *Polymathy*, and *Literary Hiſtory*

  [a] See *Oſborn's* Advice to a *Son*
  [b] The Author intended a Diſcourſe upon this Subject, as appears by his Letter to Sir *Henry Savile* See SUPPLEMENT V
  [c] See the Author's Eſſay upon *Studies*, SUPPLEMENT XI

8 EXERCISES, alſo, are of great Efficacy in teaching but few have ob-ſerved, that theſe ſhould not only be prudently appointed, but prudently changed For, as *Cicero* well remarks, *Faults, as well as Faculties, are gene-rally exercis'd in Exerciſes*, whence a bad Habit is ſometimes acquired, and inſinuated together with a good one 'Tis therefore ſafer, that *Exerciſes* ſhould be intermitted, and now and then repeated, than always continued and follow'd Theſe things, indeed, may, at firſt ſight, appear light and trivial, yet they are highly effectual, and advantageous For as the great increaſe of the *Roman* Empire has been juſtly attributed to the Virtue and Prudence of thoſe ſix Rulers, who had, as it were, the Tuition of it in its Youth, ſo proper Diſcipline, in tender Years, has ſuch a Power, tho' latent and unobſerved, as neither Time, nor future Labour, can any way ſubdue in our riper Age

The proper Uſe of Academical Exercies

9 It alſo deſerves to be remarked, that even ordinary Talents in great Men, uſed on great Occaſions, may ſometimes produce remarkable Effects And of this we will give an eminent Inſtance, the rather becauſe the *Jeſuits* judiciouſly retain the Diſcipline among them And tho' the thing itſelf be diſreputable in the Profeſſion of it, yet it is excellent as a *Diſcipline* we mean the *Action of the Theatre*, which ſtrengthens the Memory, regulates the Tone of the Voice, and the Efficacy of Pronunciation, gracefully compoſes the Countenance and the Geſture, procures a becoming degree of Aſſurance, and laſtly, accuſtoms Youth to the Eye of Men The Example we borrow from *Tacitus*, of one *Vibulenus*, once a Player, but afterwards a Soldier in the *Panno-nian* Army This Fellow, upon the death of *Auguſtus*, raiſed a Mutiny, ſo that *Bleſus*, the Lieutenant, committed ſome of the Mutineers but the Sol-diers broke open the Priſon, and releaſed them Upon which, *Vibulenus* thus harangu'd the Army " *You*, ſays he, *have reſtored Light and Life to theſe* " *poor Innocents but who gives back Life to my Brother, or my Brother to me?* " *He was ſent to you, from the* German *Army, for a common Good, and that* " *Man murder'd him laſt Night, by the hands of his Gladiators, whom he al-* " *ways keeps ready to murder the Soldiers Anſwer*, Bleſus, *where haſt thou* " *thrown his Corpſe? Even Enemies refuſe not the right of Burial. When I* " *ſhall, with Tears and Embraces, have perform'd my Duty to him, command* " *me alſo to Death, but let our Fellow-Soldiers bury us, who are murder'd* " *only for our Love to the Legions*" With which Words, he rais'd ſuch a Storm of Conſternation and Revenge in the Army, that unleſs the thing had preſently appear'd to be all a Fiction and that the Fellow never had a Brother, the Soldiers might have murder'd their Leader but he acted the whole as a Part upon the Stage [a] And thus much for the LOGICAL SCIENCES [b]

The Action of the Stage re-commended as a part of Diſ-cipline

SECT

---

[a] This Example is evidently produced, not for *Imitation*, but only to ſhew the Force of *Action* and *Elocution*, and what conſiderable things they are capable of effecting

[b] The Subject of *Scholaſtick Diſcipline* is the more lightly touched by the *Author*, becauſe he refers us to the *Jeſuits*, who are certainly great Maſters in the Art of Education, but it does not appear that their Example is conſiderably follow'd in *England* particularly as to the *Thea-trical Exerciſes* here recommended 'Tis true, in ſeveral of our capital Schools, the Scholars annually act ſome ancient or modern Comedy, but this they uſually do after a childiſh manner; without

SECT. XX.

Of ETHICKS, *or* MORALITY.

WE next proceed to ETHICKS, which has the *human Will* for its Subject. *Reason* governs the *Will*, but *apparent Good* seduces it. Its Motives are the Affections, and its Ministers, the Organs and voluntary Motions 'Tis of this Doctrine that *Solomon* says, *Keep thy Heart with all diligence, for out of it are the Actions of Life* The Writers upon this *Science*, appear like *Writing-Masters*, who lay before their Scholars a number of beautiful Copies, but give them no Directions how to guide their Pen, or shape their Letters for so the Writers upon *Ethicks* have given us shining Draughts, Descriptions, and exact Images of Goodness, Virtue, Duties, Happiness, &c as the true Objects and Scope of the human Will and Desire, but for obtaining these excellent and well-described Ends, or by what means the Mind may be broke and fashion'd for obtaining them, they either touch this Subject not at all, or slightly[a] We may dispute as much as we please, that moral Virtues are in the human Mind, by Habit, not by Nature, that *generous Spirits are led by Reason, but low Herd by Reward and Punishment*, that *the Mind may be plied and bent*, like a crooked Staff, *by bending it the contrary way*, &c. But nothing of this kind of *Glance* and *Touch*, can in any way supply the want of the thing we are now in quest of[b]

2 The Cause of this Neglect I take to be, that latent Rock whereon so many of the Sciences have split, viz. the Aversion that Writers have to treat of trite and vulgar Matters, which are neither subtile enough for Dispute, nor eminent enough for Ornament[c] 'Tis not easy to see how great

---

[a] having been broke and form'd to an Audience, by a previous Course of *Exercises*, so as to give them the graceful Accent, the decent Deportment, and the ready Address, which recommend him to the Favour of the World, and fit him for Business But this is a Point which the Jesuits principally favour, and accordingly their Pupils commonly have a much more manly and bold Deportment, than other Pupils of equal standing, without that sheepish Modesty on the one side, and that pragmatical Assurance on the other so disadvantageous and disagreeable in civil Society See this farther more fully considerd by *Morhof* in his *Polyhistor, de Curriculo Studiosi, de Curriculo Aranuato, de Pedagogia regia, & de Exercitationibus* See also Mr *Locke of Education*

For the history of Ethicks, consult *Scheurlin s Bibliographia Moralis*, Ed 1686 *Placcius s Prodromus Philosophiae Moralis, Pasch is de variis Moralia tradendi modis formisque*, 1707 *Barbeyrac s Preface to his French Translation of Puffendorf de Jure Naturae & Gentium*, and *Stollii Introductio in Historiam Literariam* pag 692—752

[b] See The Continuation of Regulation, or the Mind, &c See below, 3

[c] This should be a general, or *fundamental Cause*, from whence naturally flow many particular ones, as Ignorance, Neglect, unruly Passions, &c which *Vincent Placcius* has drawn out into a Table, as imagining them omitted by the Author See *Commentarium de Morali Scientia neglecta*, of which, more in the subsequent Note[b]

a Misfortune hath proceeded hence, that Men, thro' natural Pride and Vain-glory, fhould chufe fuch Subjects and Methods of treating them, as may rather fhow their own Capacities, than be of ufe to the Reader. *Seneca* fays excellently, *Eloquence is hurtful to thofe it infpires with a defire of itfelf, and not of things* for Writings fhould make Men in love with the Subject, and not with the Writer. They, therefore, take the juft Courfe, who can fay of their Counfels as *Demofthenes* did, *If you put thefe things in execution, you fhall not only praife the Orator for the prefent, but yourfelves alfo foon after, when your Affairs are in a better pofture.* But in *Ethicks*, the Philofophers have culled out a certain fplendid Mafs of Matter, wherein they might prin-cipally fhow their Force of Genius, or Power of Eloquence but for other things, that chiefly conduce to Practice, as they could not be fo gracefully fet off, they have entirely dropt them. Yet fo many eminent Men, furely, ought not to have defpair'd of a like Succefs with *Virgil*, who procured as much Glory for Eloquence, Ingenuity, and Learning, by explaining the homely Obfervations of *Agriculture*, as in relating the heroick Acts of *Æneas*. And certainly if Men were bent, *not upon writing at leifure, what may be read at leifure*, but really to cultivate and improve active Life, the *Georgicks of the Mind* ought to be as highly valued, as thofe *heroical Portraits of Virtue, Goodnefs, and Happinefs*, wherein fo much pains have been taken.

3. We divide ETHICKS into two principal *Doctrines*, the one of the *Model* or *Image of Good*[a], the other of *the Regulation and Culture of the Mind*, which I commonly exprefs by the word *Georgicks*[b]. The firft defcribes the *Nature of Good*, and the other *prefcribes Rules for conforming the Mind to it.* The *Doctrine of the Image of Good*, in defcribing the nature of Good, con-fiders it either as fimple, or compounded, and either as to the kinds or de-grees thereof. In the latter of thefe, the *Chriftian Faith* has at length abolifh'd thofe infinite Difputes and Speculations, as to the fupreme degree of *Good*, call'd Happinefs, Bleffednefs, or the *Summum bonum*, which was a kind of heathen *Theology*. For, as *Ariftotle* faid, *Youths might be happy, tho' only in Hope*, fo, according to the Direction of Faith, we muft put ourfelves in the ftate of Minors, and think of no other Felicity, but that founded in Hope. Being therefore thus deliver'd from this oftentatious *Heaven* of the Heathens, we may, with lefs offence to Truth and Sobriety, receive much of what they deliver about the *Image of Good*. As for the *nature of pofitive and fimple Good*, they have certainly drawn it beautifully and according to the Life, in feveral Pieces, exactly reprefenting the Forms of Virtue and Duty, their Order, Kinds, Relations, Parts, Subjects, Provinces, Actions, and Difpen-fitions

Marginal notes:

Ethicks di-vided into the Doctrine of the Image of Good and the Geor-gicks of the Mind

The Heathen Summum bonum fu-perfeded by Chriftianity

The Heather Treatment of pofitive and fimple Good

---

[a] For the Reafon of this Appellation, fee Sect. XXI. 1

[b] This *Divifion of Ethicks* is though too general by *Vincent Placcius*, who has endeavour'd to improve the Author's *Doctrine of Morality*. The Title of the Work is *de Morali Scientia augenda Commentarium in Franc. Laconi*, &c. *de Dignitate & Augmentis Scientiarum Librum feptimum, Ethicæ Doctrinæ Originem, Incrementa, Decrementa, Fortunamque per varias gentes variam, ab Orbe condito hucufque fummatim exhibens*, &c. Francofurt 1677. The Divifion this Writer would eftablifh, is that hereafter intimated, Sect. XXII. 2. or the fame as in *Medicine*, whence he ufes the Terms *Phyfologia Moralis, Nofologia Moralis, Semiotica Moralis, Therapeu-tica Moralis*, and would introduce a kind of *Chirurgia Moralis*, thus making moral *Philofophers* the *Phyficians of the Mind.*   2

... ... all this they have recommended and infinuated to the Mind, ... Variety and Subtility of Argument, as well as Sweetnefs of Perfua... ... ... carefully guarding, as much as was poffible by Words, ... ed against popular Errors and Infults   And in deducing the na... ... ... they have not been wanting, but appointed three ... ... the compared contemplative, and active Life together, ... between Virtue with reluctance, and Virtue fecured and confirmed, ... the Cord betwixt Honour and Advantage, ball... ed the Fn... ... ... over-weigh'd, and the like   fo that this part of the ... ... is already nobly executed, and herein the Ancients have ... ... a wonderful Abilities   Yet the pious and ftrenuous Diligence of the Divines, ... in weighing and determining Studies, moral Virtues, Cafes of Confcience, ... fixing the Bounds of Sin, have greatly exceeded them   But if the Philo... ... before they defcended to the popular and received Notions of Virtue and Vice, Pain and Pleafure, &c   had dwelt longer upon difcovering the Roots and Fibres of Good and Evil, they would, doubtlefs, have thus gain'd great Light to their fubfequent Enquiries   efpecially if they had con... ulted the Nature of Things, as well as moral Axioms, they would have fhorten'd their Doctrine, and laid them deeper   But as they have entirely omitted this, or confufedly touch'd it, we will here briefly touch it over again, and endeavour to open and cleanfe the Springs of Morality, before we come to the GEORGICKS [a] OF THE MIND, which we fet down as deficient.

... ... All things are endued with an Appetite to two kinds of Good, the one, ... as the thing is a Whole in itfelf, the other, as 'tis a Part of fome greater ... ... Whole   and this latter is more worthy and more powerful than the other, as it tends to the Confervation of a more ample Form   The firft may be called the Good of Self-Good, and the latter, Good of Communion   Iron, by a particular Property, moves to the Loadftone, but if the Iron be heavy, it drops its Affection to the Loadftone, and tends to the Earth, which is the proper Region of fuch ponderous Bodies   Again, tho' denfe and heavy Bodies tend to the Earth, yet rather than Nature will fuffer a Separation in the Continuity of Things, and leave a Vacuum, as they fpeak, thefe heavy Bodies will be carried upwards, and forego their Affection to the Earth, to perform their Office to the World   And thus it generally happens, that the Confervation of the more general Form, regulates the leffer Appetites   But this Prerogative of the Good of Communion is more particularly imprefs'd upon Man, if he be not degenerate, according to that remarkable Saying of Pompey, who, being Governour of the City-Purveyance, at a time of Famine in Rome, and entreated by his Friends not to venture to Sea, whilft a violent Storm was impending, anfwer'd, My Going is neceffary, ... I ... ... to that the defire of Life, which is greateft in the Indivi... dual, doth ... ... in him outweigh his Affection and Fidelity to the State [b]   But

---

[a] For the meaning and Reafon of this Expreffion, fee above, 2 and hereafter, Sect XXII

... ... Moral ... ... feem wholly founded in the Laws of Nature   See Bifhop Cumber... ... De ... Philofophicæ de Legibus Naturæ, the Religion of Nature delineated, by Mr Wool... ... ... and Enquiry ... our Ideas of Beauty and Virtue, by Mr Hutchinfon

But no *Philosophy*, *Sect*, *Religion*, *Law*, or *Discipline*, in any Age, has so highly exalted the *Good of Communion*, and so far depreis'd the *Good of Individuals*, as the *Christian Faith*. Whence it may clearly appear, *that one and the same God gave those Laws of Nature to the Creatures, and the Christian Law to Men*. And hence we read, that some of the elect and holy Men, in an Extasy of Charity, and impatient Desire of the *Good of Communion*, rather wished their Names *blotted out of the Book of Life*, than that their Brethren should miss of Salvation.

5. This being once laid down, and firmly establish'd, will put an end to some of the soberest Controversies in *moral Philosophy*. And *first*, it determines that *Question about the preference of a contemplative to an active Life*, against the Opinion of *Aristotle*. As all the Reasons he produces for a *contemplative Life*, regard only *private Good*, and the Pleasure or Dignity of an *individual Person*, in which respects the *contemplative Life* is, doubtless, best, and like the Comparison made by *Pythagoras*, to assert the Honour and Reputation of Philosophy, when being ask'd by *Hiero*, who he was, he answer'd, " *I am a Looker-on, for as, at the Olympick Games, some come to try* " *for the Prize, others to sell, others to meet their Friends, and be merry,* " *but others again come merely as Spectators, I am one of the latter.*" But Men ought to know, that in the *Theatre of human Life*, 'tis only for *God* and *Angels* to be *Spectators*. Nor could any doubt about this matter have arisen in the *Church*, if a monastick Life had been *merely contemplative*, and unexercis'd in *ecclesiastical Duties*, as continual *Prayer*, the *Sacrifice of Vows, Oblations to* God, and the *writing of Theological Books*, for propagating the *Divine Law*, &c. But for a *mere contemplative Life*, which terminates in itself, and sends out no Rays either of Heat or Light into human Society, *Theology knows it not*.

6. It also determines the *Question*, that has been so vehemently controverted between the Schools of *Zeno* and *Socrates*, on the one side, who *placed Felicity in Virtue*, simple or adorn'd, and many other Sects and Schools on the other, as particularly the Schools of the *Cyrenaics* and *Epicureans*, who *placed Felicity in Pleasure*; thus making *Virtue* a mere Hand-maid, without which, *Pleasure* could not be well served. Of the same side is also that other School of *Epicurus*, as on the reformed Establishment, which declared *Felicity to be nothing but Tranquillity and Serenity of Mind*. With these also join'd the exploded School of *Pyrrho* and *Herillus*, who placed *Felicity in an absolute exemption from Scruples, and allowing of no fix'd and constant nature of Good and Evil*, but accounting all Actions *virtuous* or *vicious*, as they proceed from the Mind by a pure and undisturbed Motion, or with Aversion and Reluctance. But 'tis plain, that all things of this kind relate to *private* Tranquillity, and Complacency of Mind, and by no means to the *Good of Communion*.

7. Again, upon the Foundation above laid, we may confute the *Philosophy* of *Epictetus*, which rests upon supposing *Felicity placed in things within our power*, lest we should otherwise be *expos'd to Fortune and Contingence*; as if it were not much happier to fail of success in just and honourable De-

Several Questions in Morality determin'd upon the preceding Foundation, viz. (1) that an active, is preferable to a contemplative Life.

(2) Whether Felicity is placed in Virtue or Pleasure

(3) Whether Felicity be placed in Things within our power

Vol. I   Bb   signs,

... when that Failure makes for the publick Good, than to secure an un-
terrupted Enjoyment of those things, which make only for our private
... Thus *Gonzaga*, at the Head of his Army, pointing to *Naples*,
... professed, he had much rather, by advancing a step meet certain
D..th, than by retiring a step prolong his Life. And to this agrees the
... *King*, who pronounces *a good Conscience to be a continual Feast*, thereby
... the Consciousness of good Intentions, however unsuccessful,
... Joy more real, pure, and agreeable to Nature, than all the other
M... that can be furnished, either for obtaining one's Desires, or quieting
the Mind.

... It likewise censures that Abuse which prevail'd about the time of
... when Philosophy was turn'd into a certain Art, or *Profession of
L...*, as if its design were not to compose and quiet Troubles, but to avoid
... remove the Causes and Occasions thereof whence a *particular Regimen*
was to be enter'd into for obtaining this end, by introducing such a kind of
H... of the *Mind*, as was that of *Herodicus in the Body*, mention'd by
A..., whilst he did nothing all his life long, but take care of his Health,
and therefore abstain'd from numberless things, which almost deprived him
of the use of his Body whereas, if Men were determin'd to perform the
D...s of Society, that kind of bodily *Health* is most desirable, which is able
to suffer and support all sorts of Attacks and Alterations. In the same manner, that Mind is truly sound, and strong, which is able to break thro' numerous and great Temptations and Disorders whence *Diogenes* seems to
... justly commended the Habit which did not warily *abstain*, but
courageously *sustain*, which could check the Sallies of the Soul on the steepest
Precipice, and make it, like a well-broke Horse, stop and turn it the
shortest warning

9 *Lastly*, It reproves that Delicacy and unsociable Temper observed in
some of the most ancient Philosophers, of great repute, who too effeminate-
ly withdrew from civil Affairs, in order to prevent Indignities and Trouble
to themselves, and live the more free, and unspotted in their own Opinions
as to which point, the Resolution of a true Moralist should be such as *Gon-
...* requir'd of a Soldier, *viz. not to leave his Honour so fine, as for every
...ng to ... a dread* [a]

---

[a] It may be added, that the two seemingly opposite *Systems of Morality*, at present on foot,
... one ... ng upon the *Principle of Self Love*, the other upon the *Principle of Benevolence* are
easily adjusted upon the same Foundation The modern *Writers* upon this Subject of *Morality*,
are numerous an account of which may be found in *Struvius's Bibliotheca Philosophica*, Cap VI
de Scriptoribus Philosophiæ Practicæ, & sigillatim Ethicæ, pag 205—261 And again, in *Stollius's
Intr. difs in Bibliam Literariam*, de Disciplina Ethica, pag 798—823

SECT. XXI.

Of SELF-GOOD, and the GOOD OF COMMUNION.

I 1 WE divide INDIVIDUAL, or SELF-GOOD, into *active* and *passive* Self Good divided into active and passive This difference of *Good* is also found imprefs'd upon the Nature of all Things, but principally shews itself in two Appetites of the Creatures viz (1) that of *Self-Prefervation* and *Defence*, and (2.) that of *Multiplying* and *Propagating* The *latter*, which is *active*, seems stronger and more worthy than the *former*, which is *passive* For, throughout the Universe, the The active most predominant *celeftial Nature* is the principal Agent, and the *terreftrial*, the Patient. And in the Pleafures of Animals, that of Generation is greater than that of Feeding, and the Scripture says, '*tis more blessed to give, than to receive* And even in common life, no Man is so soft and effeminate, as not to prefer the performing and perfecting of any thing he had set his mind upon, before fenfual Pleafures The Preheminence of *active Good*, is also highly exalted from the confideration of the State of Mankind, which is mortal, and subject to Fortune For if Perpetuity and Certainty could be had in human Pleafures, this would greatly inhance them, but as the cafe now ftands, *when we count it a Happinefs to die late, when we cannot boaft of tomorrow, when we know not what a Day may bring forth*, no wonder if we earneftly endeavour after fuch things, as elude the Injuries of Time And thefe can be no other than our *Works*; accordingly in Scripture 'tis faid, *their Works follow them*

2 Another confiderable Preheminence of *active Good* is given it, and fupported, by that infeparable Affection of human Nature, the *Love of Novelty*, or *Variety* But this Affection is greatly limited in the *Pleafures of the Senfes*, which make the greateft part of *Paffive Good* To confider how often the fame things come over in Life, as Meals, Sleep, and Diverfion, it might make not only a refolute, a wretched, or a wife, but even a delicate Perfon wifh to die But in Actions, Enterprizes, and Defires, there is a remarkable Variety, which we perceive with great Pleafure, whilft we begin, advance, reft, go back to recruit, approach, obtain, &c Whence 'tis truly faid, that *Life without Purfuit is a vague and languid thing* and this holds true both of the wife and unwife indifferently So *Solomon* fays, *even a brainfick Man feeks to fatisfy his Defire, and meddles in every thing* And thus the moft potent Princes, who have all things at command, yet fometimes chufe to purfue low and empty Defires, which they prefer to the greateft affluence of fenfual Pleafures Thus *Nero* delighted in the *Harp*, *Commodus* in

Fencing,

F— —g, *Alterius* in *Racing*, &c   So much more pleasing is it to be active than in possession !

3   It must however be well observed, that *active, individual Good*, differs entirely from the *Good of Communion*, notwithstanding they may sometimes coincide   For altho' this *individual active Good* often produces Works of Beneficence, which is a *Virtue of Communion*, yet herein they differ, that these *Works* are perform'd by most Men, not with a design to assist or benefit others, but wholly for their own Gratification or Honour, as plainly appears, when a *five Good* falls upon any thing contrary to the *Good of Communion*   For that gigantick Passion, wherewith the great Disturbers of the World are carried away - as in the case of *Sylla*, and others, who would render all their Friends happy, and all their Enemies miserable, and endeavour to make the World carry their Image, which is really warring against Heaven   this Passion, I say, aspires to an *active, individual Good*, at least in Appearance, tho' it be infinitely different from the *Good of Communion*

4. We divide PASSIVE GOOD into *Conservative* and *Perfective*   for every thing has three kinds of Appetite, with regard to its own individual Good, the *first*, to preserve itself, the *second*, to perfect itself, and the *third*, to multiply or diffuse itself   The last relates to *active Good*, of which we have spoke already, and of the other two, the *Perfective* is the most excellent   For 'tis a less matter to preserve a thing in its State, and a greater to exalt it's Nature   But throughout the Universe are found some nobler Natures, to the Dignity and Excellence whereof inferior ones aspire, as to their Origins   whence the Poet said well of Mankind, that *they have an ethereal Vigour, and a celestial Origin* [a]   for the Perfection of the human *Form* consists in approaching the Divine or Angelick Nature   The corrupt and preposterous Imitation of this *perfective Good*, is the Pest of human Life, and the Storm that overturns and sweeps away all things   whilst Men, instead of a true and essential exaltation, fly, with blind Ambition, only to a local one   For as Men in sickness toss and roll from place to place, as if by change of situation they could get away from themselves, or fly from the Disease, so in Ambition, Men hurried away with a false Imagination of exalting their own Nature, obtain no more than change of Place, or eminence of Post

5   *Conservative Good* is the receiving and enjoying of things agreeable to our Nature   And this *Good*, tho' it be the most simple and natural, yet of all others it seems the lowest and most effeminate   'Tis also attended with a Difference, about which the Judgment of Mankind has been partly unsettled, and the Enquiry partly neglected   For the Dignity and Recommendation of the *Good of Fruition* or *Pleasure*, as 'tis commonly called, consists either in the *Real* or *Strength* thereof   the one being procured by *Uniformity*, and the other by *Variety*   The one has a less mixture of *Evil*, the other a stronger and more lively impression of *Good*   which of these is the best, is the *Question*   But whether human Nature be not capable of both at once   has not been examined

6.

---

[a] *Igneus est ollis vigor & coelestis origo*   See *Virgil* Æneid Lib vi v 730.

6 As for the *Question*, it began to be debated between *Socrates* and a *Sophist* *Socrates* afferted, that *Felicity lay in a conftant Peace and Tranquillity of Mind*, but the Sophift placed it in *great Appetite and great Fruition* From reafoning they fell to railing, when the *Sophift* faid, the Felicity of *Socrates* was the Felicity of a Stock or a Stone   *Socrates*, on the other hand, faid, the Felicity of the *Sophift* was the Felicity of one who is always itching, and always fcratching and both Opinions have their Supporters For the School even of *Epicurus*, which allowed that *Virtue greatly conduced to Felicity*, is on the fide of *Socrates*   And if this be the cafe, certainly Virtue is more ufeful in appeafing Diforders, than in obtaining Defires   The *Sophift's* Opinion is fomewhat favoured by the Affertion above mention'd, *viz* that *Perfective Good* is fuperior to *Confervative Good*, becaufe every obtaining of a Defire feems gradually to perfect *Nature* which tho' not ftrictly true, yet a circular motion has fome appearance of a progreffive one

7 As for the other point, *whether human Nature is not at the fame time capable both of Tranquillity and Fruition*, a juft determination of it will render the former Queftion unneceffary   And do we not often fee the Minds of Men fo framed and difpofed, as to be greatly affected with prefent Pleafures, and yet quietly fuffer the lofs of them? Whence that Philofophical Progreffion, *Ufe not, that you may not wifh*, *Wifh not, that you may not fear*, feems an Indication of a weak, diffident, and timorous Mind   And, indeed, moft Doctrines of the Philofophers appear to be too diftruftful; and to take more care of Mankind than the Nature of the thing requires   Thus they increafe the fears of Death, by the Remedies they bring againft it   For whilft they make the Life of Man little more than a Preparation and Difcipline for Death, 'tis impoffible but the Enemy muft appear terrible, when there is no end of the Defence to be made againft him   The Poet did better for a Heathen, who placed the End of Life among the Privileges of Nature[a]   Thus the Philofophers, in all cafes, endeavour to render the Mind too uniform, and harmonical, without inuring it to extreme and contrary Motions   And the Reafon feems to be, that they give themfelves up to a private Life, free from difquiet and fubjection to others   Whereas Men fhould rather imitate the Prudence of a Lapidary, who finding a Speck, or a Cloud, in a *Diamond*, that may be ground out without too much wafte, takes it away, or otherwife leaves it untouch'd and fo the Serenity of the Mind is to be confulted, without impairing its Greatnefs. And thus much for the Doctrine of SELF-GOOD [b]

II 8. The GOOD OF COMMUNION, which regards *Society*, ufually goes by the name of *Duty*, a word that feems more properly ufed of a Mind well-difpofed towards others whilft the Term *Virtue* is ufed of a Mind well formed and compofed within itfelf   *Duty*, indeed, feems at firft to be of political Confideration, but if thoroughly weighed, it truly relates to the rule

[a] *Qui fpatium vita extremum inter munera ponat Natura——*

[b] This Doctrine of *Self Good* feems to be now generally confidered under the Notion of *private*, and the *Good of Communion*, under that of *publick Virtue*   See the Lord *Shaftesbury's Characteriflicks*, and *the Enquiry into our Ideas of Beauty and Virtue*

rule and government of one's self, not others. And as in *Architecture*, 'tis one thing to fashion the Pillars, Rafters, and other Parts of the Building, and prepare them for the Work, and another, to fit and join them together. So the Doctrine of uniting Mankind in Society, differs from that which renders them conformable and well-affected to the Benefits of Society. This Part concerning *Duties*, is likewise divided into two, the one treating of the *Duties of Men in common*, and the other of *Respective Duties*, according to the *Place, Vocation, State, Person and Degree of Particulars* [a]. The first of these, we before observed [b], has been sufficiently cultivated, and explained, by the ancient and later Writers. The *other* also has been touched here and there, tho' not digested and reduced into any *Body of Science* [c]. We do not, however, except to its being treated piece-meal, as judging it the best way to write upon this Subject in separate parts. For who will pretend to consistently discourse, and define upon the peculiar and relative Duties of all Orders and Conditions of Men? But for Treatises upon this Subject, which have no tincture of Experience, and are only drawn from general and Scholastick Knowledge, they commonly prove empty and useless Performances. For tho' a By-stander may sometimes see what escaped the Player, and altho' it be a kind of Proverb, more bold than true with regard to Prince and People, that *a Spectator in the Valley takes the best view of a Mountain*, yet it were greatly to be wished, that none but the most experienced Men would write upon Subjects of this kind. For the Contemplations of *speculative Men* in *active Matters*, appear no better to those who have been conversant in Business, than the Dissertations of *Phormio* upon War appeared to *Hannibal*, who esteemed them but as Dreams and Dotage. One Fault, however, dwells with such as write upon things belonging to their own *Office* or *Art*, viz. that they hold no mean in recommending and extolling them.

The Doctrine of Fraud and Craft = §. 9 A. B. 5

9. To this Part of the *respective Duties of Vocations*, and particular *Professions*, belongs another, as a *Doctrine* relative, or opposite, to it, viz. the Doctrine of *Cautions, Frauds, Impostures, and their Vices*. For *Corruptions* and *Ills*, are opposite to Duties and Virtues; not but some mention is already made of them in Writings, tho' commonly but cursorily and satyrically, rather than seriously and gravely. For more Labour is bestowed in ridiculously reprehending many good and useful things in Arts, and exposing them to ridicule, than in separating what is corrupt and vicious therein, from what is sound and serviceable. *Solomon* says excellently, *a Scorner seeks Wisdom, and finds it not, but Knowledge is easy to him that understands*. For whoever comes to a *Science*, with an intent to deride and despise, will doubtless

[a] For the Modern Writers in this way, see *Morhof's Polyhistor* Tom III Lib I *de Philosophia morali & ejus tribus*, & *Stollii Introductio in Historiam Literariam de Philosophia generatim mo*rali in particular, consult *Pufendorf de Officio Hominis & Civis*.

[b] See above §. XX. 3.

[c] This seems to be attempted by *Grotius*, in his Book *de Jure Belli ac Pacis*, and by *Pufendorf in his de Jure Naturæ & Gentium*. See M. *Barbeyrac's* Translation of the latter into French.

[d] Many instances whereof, the Author has given us in his *Essays*, and the *Sapientia Veterum*.

lefs find things enow to cavil at , and few to improve by   But the ferious and prudent treatment of the *Subject* we fpeak of, may be reckoned among the ftrongeft Bulwarks of Virtue and Probity   For as 'tis fabulously related of the *Bafilisk*, that if he fees a Man firft, the Man prefently dies , but if the Man has the firft glance, he kills the *Bafilisk*   fo *Frauds*, *impo-ftures*, and *Tricks*, do no hurt, if firft difcovered , but if they ftrike firft, 'tis then they become dangerous, and not otherwife,   Hence we are beholden to *Machiavel*, and Writers of that kind, who openly and unmafked declare what Men do in fact , and not what they ought to do [a]   For 'tis impoffi-ble to join the *Wifdom of the Serpent*, *and the Innocence of the Dove* , with-out a previous knowledge of the Nature of Evil   as without this, Virtue lies expofed and unguarded   And farther, a *good* and *juft* Man cannot correct and amend the *Vicious* and the *Wicked*, unlefs he has firft fearched into all the Depths and Dungeons of Wickednefs   For Men of a corrupt and depraved Judgment, ever fuppofe that Honefty proceeds from Ignorance, or a certain fimplicity of Manners, and is rooted only in a Belief of our Tutors, In-ftructors, Books, Moral Precepts, and Vulgar Difcourfe   Whence unlefs they plainly perceive, that their perverfe Opinions, their corrupt and di-ftorted Principles, are throughly known to thofe who exhort and admonifh them, as well as to themfelves, they defpife all wholefome Advice , accord-ing to that admirable Saying of *Solomon*   *A Fool receives not the words of the Wife, unlefs thou fpeakeft the very things that are in his heart*   And *this part of* MORALITY, *concerning* CAUTIONS, *and* RESPECTIVE VICES, we fet down as *wanting* , under the Name of SOBER SATYR, *or the* INSIDES OF THINGS [b]

10   To the *Doctrine of* RESPECTIVE DUTIES,   belong alfo the *mutual Duties between Husband and Wife, Parent and Child, Mafter and Servant* , as alfo the *Laws of Friendfhip, Gratitude*, and the *Civil Obligations of Fra-ternities, Colleges, Neighbourhoods*, and the like , always underftanding that thefe things are to be treated, not as Parts of *Civil Society*, in which View they be-long to *Politicks*, but fo far as the Minds of Particulars ought to be in-ftructed, and difpofed to preferve thefe *Bonds of Society* [c]

The mutual Duties of Men belong to re-fpective Du-ties

11   The *Doctrine of the Good of Communion*, as well as of *Self-Good*, treats *Good* not only *fimply*, but *comparatively* , and thus regards the balancing of *Duty betwixt Man and Man, Cafe and Cafe, Private and Publick, Prefent and Future*, &c   So in the Difcourfe betwixt *Brutus, Caffius*, and others, as to the Confpiracy againft *Cæfar* , the Queftion was artfully introduced, *whether it were lawful to kill a Tyrant*   The Company divided in their Opi-nions

Compara-tive Good of Com-munion

---

[a] Perhaps the Treatife of *Hieron Cardan de Arcanis Prudentiæ Civilis*, is a capital Perfor-mance in this way, as expofing numerous Tricks, Frauds, and Stratagems of Government, fo as to prevent the honeft-minded from being impofed upon by them

[b] The *Author's* ESSAYS, in their *Latin Edition*, have the Title of *Sermones fidele , five Inte-riora Rerum* ; as if intended to fupply this DEFICIENCY , which in fome meafure they do   but the Defign has not, perhaps, been duly profecuted fince   See the ELEVENTH SUPPLEMENT, to the *de* AUGMENTIS SCIENTIARUM

[c] This appears to be the Scheme of the *Whole Duty of Man*, tho' the Author there proceeds upon the Footing of Revelation, as well as the *Law of Nature*

n.ons about it , some saying it was lawful, and that Slavery was the greatest
of Evils , others denying it, and asserting Tyranny to be less destructive
than *Civil War* , whilst a third kind, as if Followers of *Epicurus*, made it
an unworthy thing, that wise Men should endanger themselves for Fools.
But the Cases of *comparative Duties* are numerous, among which this Question frequently occurs , *Whether Justice may be strained for the safety of one's
Country, or the like considerable good in future ?* As to which, *Jason* the *Thes-
salian* used to say, *some Things must be done unjustly, that many more may
be done justly*   But the Answer is ready *present Justice is in our power ,
but of future Justice we have no security.* Let Men pursue those things
which are good and just at present , and leave Futurity to *divine Providence* [a]
And thus much for the DOCTRINE OF THE IMAGE OF GOOD

S E C T.   XXII.

Of the CULTIVATION *of the* MIND.

*The Doctrine
of the Cure of
the Mind de-
ficient*   1. WE next proceed to the CULTIVATION OF THE MIND, without which
the preceding Part of *Morality* is no more than an *Image* or beautiful
Statue, without Life or Motion   *Aristotle* expressly acknowledges as much
 "*'Tis therefore necessary*, says he, *to speak of Virtue , what it is, and whence
 *it proceeds for it were in a manner useless, to know Virtue, and yet be igno-
 "rant of the ways to acquire her* "   And tho' he has more than once repeated the same thing ; yet himself does not pursue it   And so *Cicero* gives
it as a high Commendation to *Cato*, that he embraced Philosophy, not for
the sake of disputing, as most do , but of living *Philosophically*   And tho'
at present few have any great regard to the *Cultivation and Discipline of the
Mind*, and a regular Course of Life , whence this part may appear superfluous , yet we cannot be persuaded to leave it untouched but rather conclude
with the Aphorism of *Hippocrates*, that *those who labour under a violent Disease,
yet seem insensible of their pain, are disordered in their Mind*   And Men in this
case want not only a Method of Cure, but a particular Remedy, to bring them
to their Senses If any one shall object, that the *Cure of the Mind* is the Office of
Divinity , we allow it yet nothing excludes Moral Philosophy from the train
of Theology, whereto it is as a prudent and faithful Hand-maid, attending and
administring to all its wants   But tho', as the *Psalmist* observes, *the Eyes of
the Maid are perpetually waiting on the Hands of the Mistress*, yet doubtless many things must be left to the Care and Judgment of the Servant So
Ethics, ought to be entirely subservient to *Theology*, and obedient to the
Precepts thereof, tho' it may still contain many wholesome and useful
Instructions,

[a] See the *Religion of Nature delineated*, by Mr *Woollaston*

Instructions, within its own limits   And therefore when we consider the excellence of this part of *Morality*, we cannot but greatly wonder 'tis not hitherto reduced to a *Body of Doctrine*   which we are oblig'd to note as deficient , and shall therefore give some Sketch for supplying it

2 And *first*, as in all case of Practice, we must here distinguish the Things in our power, and those that are not   for the one may be altered, whilst the other can only be applied   Thus the Farmer has no command over the Nature of the Soil, or the Seasons of the Year , nor the Physician over the Constitution of the Patient, or the Variety of Accidents   In the *Cultivation of the Mind*, and the *Cure of its Diseases*, there are three things to be considered , viz (1) the different *Dispositions*, (2) the *Affections*, and (3) the *Remedies* answering in Physick to the *Constitution*, the *Distemper*, and the *Medicines*. And of these three, only the last is in our power. Yet we ought as carefully to enquire into the things that are not in our power, as into those that are , because a clear and exact Knowledge thereof is to be made the Foundation of *the Doctrine of Remedies* , in order to their more commodious and successful Application   For Clothes cannot be made to fit, unless measure of the Body be first taken

The Things in our power to be distinguish ed with regard to that Cure

3 The first *Article therefore of the Culture of the Mind*, will regard the different *Natures* or *Dispositions* of Men   But here we speak not of the vulgar *Propensities to Virtues and Vices*, or Perturbations and Passions· but of such as are more internal and radical   And I cannot sometimes but wonder, that this Particular should be so generally neglected by the Writers both of *Morality* and *Politicks* , whereas it might afford great Light to both those Sciences   In *Astrological Traditions*, the *Natures* and *Dispositions* of Men are tolerably distinguished, according to the Influences of the Planets , whence some are said to be by Nature form'd for *Contemplation*, others for *Politicks*, others for *War*, &c   So likewise among the Poets of all kinds, we every where find Characters of Natures , tho' commonly drawn with excess, and bigger than the truth [a]   And this Subject of the different Characters of Dispositions, is one of those things wherein the common Discourse of Men is wiser than Books   a thing which seldom happens   But much the best Matter of all for such a Treatise, may be derived from the more prudent Historians , and not so well from Elogies or Panegyricks, which are usually wrote soon after the Death of an illustrious Person, but much rather from a whole *Body of History*, as often as such a Person appears   for such an interwoven Account gives a better Description than Panegyrick   And such Examples we have in *Livy*, of *Africanus* and *Cato* , in *Tacitus*, of *Tiberius*, *Claudius*, and *Nero* , in *Herodian*, of *Septimius Severus* , in *Philip de Comines*, of *Lewis the Eleventh* , in *Guicciardine*, of *Ferdinand of Spain*, the *Emperor Maximilian*, *Pope Leo*, and *Pope Clement*   For these Writers, having the Image of the Person to be described constantly before them, scarce ever mention any of their Acts, but at the same time introduce something of their Natures   So, likewise, some Relations which we have seen of the *Conclaves at*

A Work of the Characters, or Natures, of Persons deficient

---

[a] As particularly in *Homer*, the Characters of *Achilles, Hector, Briseis, Helen*, &c.

Rome, give very exact Characters of the *Cardinals* as the Letters of Ambassadors do of the Counsellors of Princes   Let, therefore, an accurate and full Treatise be wrote upon this fertile and copious Subject   But we do not mean, that these *Characters* should be received in *Ethicks*, as perfect civil Images, but rather as Out-lines, and first Draughts of the Images themselves   which being variously compounded and mixed one among another, afford all kinds of *Portraits*   So that an artificial and accurate Dissection may be made of Mens Minds and Natures, and the secret Disposition of each particular Man laid open, that from a knowlegde of the whole, the *Precepts* containing the Cure of the Mind, may be more rightly form'd.

4   And not only the *Characters* of *Dispositions impres'd by Nature*, should be received into this *Treatise*, but those also which are otherwise imposed upon the Mind by the *Sex*, *Age*, *Country*, *State of Health*, *Make of Body*, &c. And again, those which proceed from *Fortune*, as in *Princes*, *Nobles*, common *People*, the *Rich*, the *Poor*, *Magistrates*, *the Ignorant*, *the Happy*, the *Miserable*, &c   Thus we see *Plautus* makes it a kind of Miracle to find an old Man beneficent[a].   And St. *Paul* commanding a Severity of Discipline towards the *Cretans*, accuses the Temper of that Nation from the Poet   *The* Cretans are always Lyars, evil Beasts, and slow Bellies   *Sallust* notes it of the Temper of *Kings*, *that 'tis frequent with them to desire Contradictories*[c]. *Tacitus* observes, that *Honours and Dignities commonly change the Temper of Mankind for the worse*[d]   *Pindar* remarks, that *a sudden Flush of good Fortune generally enervates and slackens the Mind*[e]   The *Psalmist* intimates, that *'tis easier to hold a mean in the height, than in the increase of Fortune*[f]   'Tis true, *Aristotle*, in his *Rhetoricks*, cursorily mentions some such Observations; and so do others up and down in their Writings   but they were never yet incorporated into *moral Philosophy*, whereto they principally belong, as much as Treatises of the *difference of Soil and Glebe*, belong to *Agriculture*; or Discourses of the different Complexions or Habits of the Body, to Medicine   The thing must, therefore, be now procured, unless we would imitate the Rashness of *Empiricks*, who employ the same Remedies in all *Diseases* and Constitutions

The Doctrine of the Affections.   5   Next to this *Doctrine of Characters*, follows the DOCTRINE OF AFFECTIONS AND PERTURBATIONS, which, we observed above, are the *Diseases of the Mind*   For as the ancient Politicians said of *Democracies*, that the *People were to be the Sea*, and *the Orators like the Wind*, so it may be
truly

---

[a] Vid in tali view, consul *les Characteres des Passions, par M. de la Chambre*, Ed Amst 1658 [b] Clarum est de Characteribus latentibus Animi affectious, reprinted by *Conringius, Neuheusii Theatrum* ... *quo exteriora ju ac Hominum cognoscenda Indole & Animi Secretis*, 1633, M Evelyn's Digression concerning *Phisiognomy* in his *Discourse of Medals les Characteres de Theophraste*, *a ce dernier ... cours de ce Siecle, par M de la Bruyere*, 1700   See Stollii *Introductio in Historiam Literariam*, pag 823   See also more to this purpose above, Sect IV
[a] *Benigne as quidem hujus ... do ut adolescentulis est*
[c] *Plerumque Regia voluntate, ut vehementes sunt, sic mobiles, sæpeque ipsa sibi adversa.*
[d] *Status fœliciores ... multo is in melius*
[e] *Sunt qui magnam fœlicitatem concoquere non possunt*
[f] I Riches fly to thee, set not thy Heart upon them.

truly faid, that the nature of the Mind would be unruffled, and uniform, if the Affections, like the Winds, did not difturb it. And here again, we cannot but remember that *Ariftotle*, who wrote fo many Books of *Ethicks*, fhould never treat of the Affections, which are a principal Branch thereof, and yet has given them a place in his *Rhetoricks*, where they come to be but fecondarily confider'd for his *Difcourfes of Pleafure and Pain*, by no means anfwer the end of fuch a Treatife, no more than a *Difcourfe of Light, and Splendor*, would give the *Doctrine of particular Colours* For *Pleafure* and *Pain* are to *particular Affections*, as *Light* is to *Colours* The *Stoicks*, fo far as may be conjectured from what we have left of them, cultivated this Subject better, yet they rather dwelt upon fubtile *Definitions*, than gave any full and copious *Treatife* upon it. We alfo find a few fhort elegant Pieces upon fome of the *Affections*, as upon *Anger*, falfe *Modefty*, and two or three more But to fay the truth, the *Poets* and Hiftorians are the principal Teachers of this *Science*. for they commonly paint to the life in what particular manner the Affections are to be rais'd and inflamed, and how to be footh'd and laid how they are to be check'd and reftrained from breaking into Action, how they difcover themfelves, tho' fupprefs'd and fmother'd, what Operations they have, what turns they take, how they mutually intermix, and how they oppofe each other, &c Among which, the latter is of extenfive ufe in moral and civil Affairs I mean, how far one Paffion may regulate another, and how they employ each other's affiftance to conquer fome one, after the manner of *Hunters* and *Fowlers*, who take Beaft with Beaft, and Bird with Bird, which Man, perhaps, without fuch Affiftance, could not fo eafily do And upon this Foundation refts that excellent and univerfal Ufe of Rewards and Punifhments in civil Life. For thefe are the Supports of States, and fupprefs all the other *noxious Affections* by thofe two predominant ones, *Fear* and *Hope* And, as in *civil Government*, one Faction frequently bridles and governs another, the cafe is the fame in the internal *Government of the Mind*[a]

6. We come now to thofe Things which are within our own power, and work upon the Mind, and affect and govern the Will and the Appetite whence they have great Efficacy in altering the *Manners* And here Philofophers fhould diligently enquire into the *Powers and Energy of Cuftom, Exercife, Habit, Education, Example, Imitation, Emulation, Company, Friendfhip, Praife, Reproof, Exhortation, Reputation, Laws, Books, Studies*, &c for thefe are the things which reign in Mens Morals By thefe Agents, the Mind is form'd and fubdu'd, and of thefe Ingredients, *Remedies* are prepared, which, fo far as human Means can reach, conduce to the Prefervation and Recovery of the Health of the Mind

The things within our power that influence the Mind

Cc 2

7.

[a] Upon this Subject, confult *Lælius Peregrinus de nofcendis & emendandis Animi affectionibus*, Ed Lipha 1714 *Placcius de Typo Medicinæ moralis*, M *Perault de l'Ufage des Paffions*. 1668 *Johan Francifc Buddæus de Morbi mentis humanæ, de Sanitate mentis humanæ, & de Remediis morborum, quibus mens laborat*, in his *Elementa Philofophiæ Practicæ* Lib de Philofophia morali, Sect. III Cap 3, 4, 6. See *Stollii Introduct in Hiftoriam Literariam*, pag 813, 814.

To give an Instance or two in *Custom* and *Habit* , the Opinion of ——— seems narrow and careless, which asserts that *Custom has no power ———— ——— ———— are natural*, using this Example, that if a Stone be a ———— ———— thrown up into the Air, yet it will acquire no tendency to a spon- ———— ———— And again, *that by often seeing or hearing, we see and hear ———— ———* For tho' this may hold in some things, where Nature is ab- folute, yet 'tis otherwife in things where Nature admits *Intenfion* and *Re- ———* in a certain latitude   He might have feen, that a ftrait Glove, by being often drawn upon the Hand, will become eafy , that a Stick, by ufe and continuance, will acquire and retain a bend contrary to its natural one , that the Voice, by Exercife, becomes ftronger and more fonorous , that Heat and Cold grow more tolerable by Cuftom, &c   And thefe two laft Ex- amples come nearer to the point, than thofe he has produced   Be this as it will , the more certain he had found it that Virtues and Vices depended upon Habit, the more he fhould have endeavour'd to prefcribe Rules how fuch Habits were to be acquir'd, or left off fince numerous Precepts may be form'd, for the prudent directing of Exercifes, as well thofe of the Mind, as the Body   We will here mention a few of them

8 And the *firft* fhall be, that *from the beginning we beware of impofing ———— more upon it, and a more fuperficial Tasks than the thing requires*   For if too great a Burden be laid upon a middling Genius, it blunts the chear- ful Spirit of Hope , and if upon a confident one, it raifes an Opinion, from which he promifes himfelf more than he can perform , which leads to Indolence   and in both cafes the Experiment will not anfwer Ex- pectation   And this always dejects and confounds the Mind   But if the Tasks are too light, a great lofs is fuftain'd in the amount of the Progrefs

9 2) *To gain a Habit in the Exercife of any Faculty, let two Seafons be ———— ——— , the one when the Mind is beft, and the other when 'tis ———— ——— B ——* that by the former, the greater difpatch may be made , and by the latter, the Obftructions of the Mind may be wore down with a ftrenuous Application whence the intermediate times will flide away the more eafily and agreeably

10 (3) The third Example fhall be the Precept which *Ariftotle* tranfiently mentions, *——— to exert our utmoft againft that whereto we are ftrongly inclined by Nature*, thus, as it were, rowing againft the Stream, or bending a crooked Stick the contrary way, in order to bring it ftrait

11 (4) A fourth *Precept* may be founded on this fure Principle, that *the Mind is eafier, and more agreeably drawn on to thofe things which are not principally intended by the Operator, but conquer'd or obtain'd without preme- ditated Defign*, becaufe our Nature is fuch, as in a manner hates to be com- manded   There are many other ufeful *Precepts for the regulating of Cuftom ;* and if *Cuftom* be prudently and fkilfully introduced, it really becomes a *fecond Nature* but if unfkilfully and cafually treated, it will be but the Ape of Nature, and imitate nothing to the life , or aukwardly, and with de- formity.

         2

12. So, with regard to *Books, Studies,* and Influence over our Manners, there are numerous useful Rules and Directions. One of the Fathers, in great severity, call'd *Poetry* the *Devil's Wine*, as indeed it begets many Temptations, Desires, and vain Opinions. And 'tis a very prudent Saying of *Aristotle,* deserving to be well consider'd, that *young Men are improper Hearers of Moral Philosophy*, because the Heat of their Passions is not yet allay'd, and temper'd, by time and experience. And to say the truth, the reason why the excellent *Writings* and *moral Discourses* of the Ancients have so little effect upon our Lives and Manners, seems to be, that they are not usually read by Men of ripe Age and Judgment, but wholly left to unexperienced Youths and Children. And are not young Men much less fit for *Politicks* than for *Ethicks*; before they are well seasoned with Religion, and the Doctrines of Morality and Civility? For being, perhaps, depraved and corrupted in their Judgment, they are apt to think that moral Differences are not real and solid, but that all things are to be measured by Utility and Success. Thus the *Poet* said, *successful Villany is called Virtue* [a]. The Poets, indeed, speak in this manner satyrically, and thro' Indignation, but some Books of Politicks suppose the same positively, and in earnest. For *Machiavel* is pleased to say, " *if Cæsar had been conquer'd, he would have become more odious than Catiline* " as if there was no difference, except in point of Fortune, betwixt a Fury made up of Lust and Blood, and a noble Spirit, of all natural Men the most to be admired, but for his Ambition. And hence we see how necessary it is for Men to be fully instructed in moral Doctrines, and religious Duties, before they proceed to *Politicks.* For those bred up from their youth in the Courts of Princes, and the midst of Civil Affairs, can scarce ever obtain a sincere and internal Probity of Manners. Again, Caution also is to be used even in *moral Instructions,* or at least in some of them, left Men should thence become stubborn, arrogant, and unsociable. So *Cicero* says of *Cato, the divine and excellent Qualities we see in him are his own, but the things he sometimes fails in, are all derived, not from Nature, but his Instructors.* There are many other *Axioms* and *Directions,* concerning the things which Studies and Books beget in the Minds of Men, for 'tis true, that *Studies enter our Manners,* and so do Conversation, Reputation, the Laws, *&c*

13. But there is another *Cure of the Mind,* which seems still more accurate, and elaborate than the rest, depending upon this Foundation, that *the* *Minds of all Men are, at certain times, in a more perfect, and at others in a more depraved State.* The design of this Cure is therefore to improve the good times, and expunge the bad. There are two practical Methods of fixing the *good times*; viz. (1) *determined Resolutions*, and (2) *Observances* or *Exercises* which are not of so much significancy in themselves, as because they continually keep the Mind in its duty. There are also two ways of *expunging the bad times*, viz. by some kind of *Redemption,* or *Expiation* of what is past, and a new Regulation of Life for the future. But this

part

[a] *Prosperum & felix Scelus Virtus vocatur.*
And again,
Ille Crucem pretium sceleris tulit, hic Diadema.

part belongs to _Religion_, whereto _moral Philosophy_ is, as we said before, the genuine Hand-maid

Charity the
Perfection of
Virtue

12. We will, therefore, conclude these _Georgicks of the Mind_ with that Remedy, which of all others, is the shortest, noblest, and most effectual for forming the Mind to _Virtue_, and placing it near a state of Perfection, viz. that we would propose to ourselves just and virtuous Ends of our Lives and Actions, which we should acquire, in some degree, the Faculty of obtaining For if the Ends of our Actions are good and virtuous, and the Resolutions of our Mind for obtaining them fix'd and constant, the Mind will directly mould and form itself, at once, to all kinds of Virtue And this is certainly an Operation resembling the Works of Nature, whilst the others above-mention'd seem only manual Thus the Statuary finishes only that part of the Figure upon which his Hand is employ'd, without meddling with the others at that time, which are still but unfashion'd Marble Whereas Nature, on the contrary, when she works upon a Flower, or an Animal, forms the Rudiments of all the Parts at once. So when Virtues are acquir'd by Habit, whilst we endeavour at _Temperance_, we make but little advances towards _Fortitude_, or the other Virtues, but when we are once entirely devoted to just and honourable Ends, whatever the _Virtue_ be, which those Ends recommend and direct, we shall find ourselves ready dispos'd, and possess'd of some Propensity to obtain and express it And this may be that State of Mind which _Aristotle_ excellently describes, not as _virtuous_, but _divine_ So _Pliny_ proposes the Virtue of _Trajan_, not as an _Imitation_, but as an _Example_ of the Divine Virtue, when he says, _Men need make no other Prayers to the Gods, than that they would be but as good and propitious to Mortals, as_ Trajan _was_. But this favours of the prophane Arrogance of the Heathens, who grasp'd at Shadows larger than the Life The _Christian Religion_ comes to the point, by impressing _Charity_ upon the Minds of Men which is most appositely call'd the _Bond of Perfection_, because it ties up, and fastens all the Virtues together And it was elegantly said by _Menander_ of _sensual Love_, which is a bad Imitation of the _divine_, that _it was a better Tutor for human Life, than a left-handed Sophist_ intimating that the Grace of Carriage is better form'd by _Love_, than by an _awkward Preceptor_, whom he calls _left-handed_, as he cannot by all his operose Rules and Precepts, form a Man so dextrously and expeditiously, to value himself justly and behave gracefully, as _Love_ can do. So without doubt, if the Mind be possess'd with the Fervor of true _Charity_, he will rise to a higher degree of Perfection, than by all the _Doctrine of Ethicks_, which is but a Sophist compar'd to Charity And as _Xenophon_ well observed, whilst the other Passions, tho' they raise the Mind, yet distort and discompose it, by their Extacies and Excesses, whilst Love alone, at the same time composes and dilates it so all other human Endowments, which we admire, whilst they exalt and enlarge our Nature, are yet liable to Extravagance · but of _Charity_ alone, there is no Excess The Angels aspiring to be like God in power, transgress'd and fell, _I will ascend, and be like the most High_. and Man aspiring to be like God in _Knowledge_, transgress'd and fell, _ye shall be as Gods, knowing Good and Evil_ But in

aspiring

aſpiring to be like God in *Goodneſs* or *Charity*, neither Man nor Angel can, or ſhall tranſgreſs Nay, we are invited to an Imitation of it, *love your Enemies, do good to thoſe that hate you, pray for thoſe that deſpitefully uſe and perſecute you, that ye may be the Children of your Father, which is in Heaven · for he maketh his Sun to riſe upon the Good and upon the Evil, and ſends his Rain upon the Juſt and upon the Unjuſt* [a]   And thus we conclude this part of *Moral Doctrine*, relating to the *Georgicks of the Mind*

15 There might, however, be added, by way of APPENDIX, this Obſer- *Appendix to* vation, that *there is a certain Relation and Congruity found between the Good the Georgicks of the Mind, and the Good of the Body* For as the *Good of the Body* conſiſts *of the Mind.* in (1) Health, (2) Comelineſs, (3) Strength, and (4) Pleaſure ſo the *Good of the Mind*, conſider'd in a moral light, tends to render it (1) ſound and calm, (2) graceful, (3) ſtrong and agile for all the Offices of Life, and (4) poſſeſs'd of a conſtant quick Senſe of Pleaſure, and noble Satiſ-faction But as the four former Excellences are ſeldom found together in the Body, ſo are the four latter ſeldom found together in the Mind [b]. And thus we have finiſhed that principal Branch of *human Philoſophy*, which conſiders Man, out of *Society*, and as conſiſting of a *Body* and a *Soul*.

SECT. XXIII.

Of CIVIL DOCTRINE; *and firſt, of* CONVERSATION *and* DECORUM.

1 THere goes an old Tradition, that many *Grecian* Philoſophers had a *The Art of* ſolemn Meeting before the Ambaſſador of a foreign Prince; where *Silence* each endeavoured to ſhew his Parts, that the Ambaſſador might have ſome-what to relate of the *Grecian* Wiſdom but one among the number kept ſilence, ſo that the Ambaſſador turning to him, ask'd, *But what have you to ſay, that I may report it ?* he anſwered, *Tell your King, that you have found one among the* Greeks *who knew how to be ſilent* Indeed I had forgot in this
Compendium

[a] The Author, in making Morality terminate in the Chriſtian Doctrine of Charity, has been followed by many, and thus occaſion'd ſeveral Syſtems of *Chriſtian Ethicks*, among the princi-pal whereof, are the *Ethica Chriſtiana* of *Lambertus Danæus*, the *Ethica Sacra* of *Dandinus*, *Placcius de Fructu præcipuo Philoſophiæ moralis genuino*, *Joannis Cirelli Ethica Chriſtiana*, Dr *Henry More*, in his *Enchiridion Ethicum Henricus Erneſtii*, in his *Introductio ad veram Vitam*, and ſeveral more See *Struzius's Bibliotheca Philoſophica*, Cap 6 *de Scriptoribus Philoſophiæ Practica, & ſigillatim Ethicis*

[b] This *Doctrine of the Georgicks of the Mind* is expreſsly endeavoured to be ſupplied by Pro-feſſor *Weſenfeld*, in the Book he entitles *Arnoldt Weſenfeld Georgica Animi & Vitæ ſeu Patholo-gia practica, moralis nempe & civilis, ex phyſicis ubique ſontibus repetita* Francof 1695, & 1712. Some Account of this Work is given in the *Acta Eruditorum Menſ. Auguſt.* 1696. See alſo *Joan Franc Budæus de Cultura Ingeniorum*, Ed. Halæ 1699.

C... ... of Art, to insert the Art of Silence For as we shall now soon
to be led by the Course of the Work, to treat the Subject of Govern-
... we cannot have a better occasion for putting the Art of Silence in
... C... makes mention not only of an Art, but even of an Elo-
... to be found in Si..., and relates in an Epistle to Attie us, how once
in Conversation he made use of this Art O this it for, says he, I af-
... ... Ec.. ..., for If..., ...ing And P... d..., who pecu-
... ... the Man u expected, with some short surprizing Sentence,
... ... long ... ... rest, Tings ... ... a ...ta Effect than
... A... ... fore I ... ... determined either to be silent upon this Subject or ... ... next to it, very concise

T. D... ... 2 Ci... KNOWLEDGE turns upon a Subject of all others the most immersed
C... ... in Matter, and therefore very difficultly reduced to Axioms And yet
... ... there are some things that ese the Difficulty For (1) as Cato said, that
... ... the Re... ... re to So... easier to drive in the Flock than single, so in
this respect the Office of Ethics is, in some degree, more difficult than that
of P... ... (2) Again, Ethick endeavours to urge and furnish the Mind
with inward Goodness, while civil Doctrine requires no more than external
Carriage which is sufficient for So... ... Whence it often happens, that a
Re... man be good and the Times bad Thus we sometimes find in sacred
History, when mention is made of good, and pious Kings, that the People
had not ... Hearts to the Lord God of their Fathers And therefore in this respect also, Ethics has the harder task (3) States are moved
flowly, like great Machines, and with difficulty and consequently not soon
put out of order For, as in Egypt, the seven years of Plenty supplied the
seven years of Famine, so in Governments, the good Regulation of former
Times, will not presently suffer the Errors of the succeeding, to prove destructive But the Resolutions and Manners of particular Persons are more
sudden, ... and this, in the last place, bears hard upon Ethicks, but
favours Po... ...

C... ...   3 Ci... Knowledge has three Parts, suitable to the three principal Acts of
... ... Society, viz (1) Conversation, (2) Business, and (3) Government. For there
... ... are three Kinds of Good, that Men desire to procure by Civil Society, viz (1)
(1) ... ...   Refuge fr... ... ... (2) Assistance in the Affairs of Life, and (3) Protection
3 ...   against In... ... And thus there are three kinds of Prudence, very different,
C... ...   and frequently separated from each other, viz (1) PRUDENCE IN CONVER-
            SATION, (2) PRUDENCE IN BUSINESS, (3) PRUDENCE IN GOVERNMENT[d].

4

[a] The Author here makes a Compliment of his Silence to King James, as if he would not pretend to speak of the Art of Empire, to one who knew them so well, but the true Reason appears
to ... ... as though it was not proper to reveal the Mysteries of State See below Sect. XXV 1
[b] It is harder to make Man fingly virtuous, than conformable in Society, because as the Author observes contradicts it to a Principle in human Nature, to be more affected in publick than
in private and so informs the sentence, who has ever been a a Rehearsal, and a Play
[c] Hence ... the ... ... to be a due difference preserved between Ethicks and Politicks, tho many ... ... them together, and form a promiscuous Doctrine of the Law of Nature,
morality, Pol... ... and R... ... together, as particularly certain scriptural Casuists and political
D...
[d] From a ... ... of ... three parts of Civil Doctrine, there has of late been formed a new
kind

4. CONVERSATION, as it ought not to be over-affected, much lefs fhould *The Effect of* it be flighted fince a prudent Conduct therein, not only expreffes a certain *Decorum* Gracefulnefs in Men's Manners, but is alfo of great affiftance in the commodious Difpatch both of publick and private Bufinefs. For as *Action*, tho' an external Thing, is fo effential to an *Orator*, as to be preferred before the other weighty, and more internal parts of that Art, fo *Converfatior*, tho' it confift but of Externals, is, if not the principal, at leaft a capital Thing in the Man of Bufinefs, and the prudent management of Affairs What effect the Countenance may have, appears from the Precept of the Poet, *Contradict not your Words by your Looks* [a] For a Man may abfolutely cancel, and betray the Force of Speech, by his Countenance And fo may Actions themfelves, as well as Words, be deftroyed by the Look, according to *Cicero*, who, recommending Affability to his Brother towards the *Provencials*, tells him, it did not wholly confift in giving eafy accefs to them, unlefs he alfo received them with an obliging Carriage *'Tis doing nothing*, fays he, *to admit them with an open Door, and a lock'd up Countenance* [b]. But if the management of the Face alone, has fo great an Effect, how much greater is that of *familiar Converfation*, with all its Attendance? Indeed the whole of *Decorum* and *Elegance of Manners*, feems to reft in weighing and maintaining, with an even ballance, the dignity betwixt ourfelves and others, which is well expreffed by *Livy*, tho' upon a different occafion, in that Character of a Perfon, where he fays, that *I may neither feem arrogant nor obnoxious, that is, neither forget my own nor others Liberty*

5. On the other fide, a Devotion to *Urbanity*, and external Elegance, ter- *The Rules of* minates in an aukward and difagreeable Affectation For what is more pre- *Decency* pofterous than to copy *the Theatre in real Life?* And tho' we did not fall into this vicious Extreme, yet we fhould wafte time, and deprefs the Mind too much, by attending to fuch lighter matters Therefore, as in Univerfities, the Students, too fond of Company, are ufually told by their Tutors, that *Friends are the Thieves of Time*, fo the affiduous Application to the *Decorum of Converfation*, fteals from weightier Confiderations Again, they who ftand in the firft rank for *Urbanity*, and feem born, as it were, for this alone;

kind of Doctrine, which they call by the name of *Civil Prudence* This Doctrine has been principally cultivated among the *Germans*, tho' hitherto carried to no great length Yet *Hermannus Conringius* performed fomewhat confiderable in this way, in his Book *de Civile Prudentia*, publifhed in the year 1662, and *Chriftian Thomafius* has treated it excellently in the little Piece entitled, *Prima linea, de Jure confultorum Prudentia Confultatoria*, &c firft publifhed in the year 1705, but the third Edition, with Notes, in 1721 The Heads it confiders, are, (1) *de Prudentia in genere*, (2) *de Prudentia confultatoria*, (3) *de Prudentia Juris confultorum*, (4) *de Prudentia confulendi, intuitu actionum propriarum*, (5) *de Prudentia dirigendi actiones proprias in converfatione quotidiana*, (6) *de Prudentia in Converfatione felecta*, (7) *de Prudentia-intuitu Societatum domefticarum*, (8) *de Prudentia in Societate Civili*, and (9) *de Prudentia alios & aliis confulendi* The little Piece alfo of *Andr Bofius, de Prudentia Civili comparanda*, deferves the perufal A few more *German* Authors have treated this Subject, but generally in their own Language See *Morhof de Prudentia Civilis Scriptoribus, Struvii Bibliotheca Philofophica*, cap 7 and *Stollii Introductio in Hiftoriam Literariam, de Prudentia Politica*

[a] *Nec vultu deftrue verba tuo*
[b] *Nil intereft habere oftium apertum, vultum claufum*

feldom take pleasure in any thing elfe, and fcarce ever rife to the higher and more folid Virtues　On the contrary, the confcioufnefs of a defect in this particular, makes us feek a Grace from good Opinion, which renders all things elfe becoming　but where this is wanting, Men endeavour to fupply it by Good Breeding　And further, there is fcarce any greater or more frequent obftruction to Bufnefs, than an over-curious Obfervance of *external Decency*, with its attendant, too follicitous and fcrupulous a choice of Times and Opportunities　*Solomon* admirably fays, *he that regards the Winds, fhall not fow; and he that regards the Clouds, fhall not reap*　For we muft make Opportunities for our felves if we find them　In a word, *Urbanity* is like a Garment to the Mind, and therefore ought to have the Conditions of a Garment; that is, (1) it fhould be fafhionable, (2) not too delicate or coftly, (3). it fhould be fo made, as principally to fhew the reigning Virtue of the Mind, and to fupply or conceal Deformity　(4) and laftly, above all things, it muft not be too ftreight, fo as to cramp the Mind, and confine its Motion in Bufinefs　But this part of *Civil Doctrine*, relating to *Converfation*, is elegantly treated by fome Writers, and can by no means be reported as deficient [a]

SECT. XXIV.

The DOCTRINE *of* BUSINESS.

1　WE divide the DOCTRINE OF BUSINESS into the *Doctrine of various Occafions*, and the *Doctrine of Rifing in Life*　The firft includes all the poffible variety of Affairs, and is as the *Amanuenfis to common Life*　but the other collects, and fuggefts, fuch things only, as regard the improvement of a Man's private Fortune, and may, therefore, ferve each perfon as a *private Regifter* for his Affairs

2　No one hath hitherto treated the *Doctrine of Bufinefs* fuitably to its Merit, to the great Prejudice of the Character both of *Learning* and *Learned Men*, for from hence proceeds the Mifchief, which has fixed it as a Reproach upon

[a] It feems of late more cultivated among the *French* and *Germans*, than among the *Englifh*, as *Mora du Monde*, the *Models de Converfations*, the *Reflexions fur le Ridicule*, & *fur les bons de fociter*, *la Politeffe des Mœurs*, *l Art de Plaire dans la Converfation*, & *Frid Gentzkenius's De Prima de Decoro in his Syftema Philofophiæ*, may deferve the perufal　This laft Work, which is alfo publifhed in *Germany*, treat (1) of the nature of *Decorum*, and its Foundation, (2) of *Natural Decorum*, (3) of Human Decorum, (4.) the Decorum of Youth and Age, (5) the Decorum of Men and Women, (6) the Decorum of Hufband and Wife, (7) the Decorum of the Clergy, (8) the Decorum of Princes　and (9) the Decorum of the Nobility, and Men of Letters　See *Stollii Introductio in Hiftoriam Literariam, de Doctrina ejus quod Decorum pag* 795, 796

upon *Men of Letters*, that *Learning and Civil Prudence are seldom found together*. And if we rightly obferve thofe three kinds of *Prudence*, which we lately faid belong to *Civil Life* [a], that of *Converfation* is generally defpifed by *Men of Learning*, as a fervile thing, and an Enemy to Contemplation , and for the *Government of States*, tho' learned Men acquit themfelves well when advanced to the Helm, yet this promotion happens to few of them but for the prefent *Subject*, the *Prudence of Bufinefs*, upon which our Lives principally turn, there are no Books extant about it , except a few *Civil Admonitions*, collected into a little Volume or two, by no means adequate to the Copioufnefs of the Subject But if Books were written upon this Subject, as upon others , we doubt not that learned Men, furnifhed with *tolerable Experience*, would far excel the unlearned, furnifhed with much *greater Experience*, and outfhoot them in their own Bow [b]

3 Nor need we apprehend that the *Matter of this Science* is too various, to fall under Precept , for 'tis much lefs extenfive than the *Doctrine of Government*, which yet we find very well cultivated There feem to have been fome Profeffors of this kind of *Prudence* among the *Romans*, in their beft days. For *Cicero* declares it was the Cuftom, a little before his time, among the Senators moft famous for knowledge and experience, as *Coruncanius, Curius, Lælius*, &c to walk the *Forum* at certain hours, where they offered themfelves to be confulted by the People , not fo much upon Law, but upon Bufinefs of all kinds , as the *Marriage of a Daughter, the Education of a Son*, the purchafing of an Eftate, and other occafions of common Life Whence it appears, that there is a certain Prudence of advifing even in private Affairs ; and derivable from an univerfal Knowledge of Civil Bufinefs , Experience, and general Obfervations of fimilar Cafes So we find the Book which *Q. Cicero* wrote to his Brother, *de petitione Confulatus*, (the only Treatife, fo far as we know, extant upon any particular Bufinefs ,) tho' it regarded chiefly the giving of Advice upon that prefent Occafion ; yet contains many particular *Axioms of Politicks*, which were not only of temporary ufe, but prefcribe a certain permanent Rule for *popular Elections*. But in this kind, there is nothing found any way comparable to the *Aphorifms of Solomon*, of whom the Scripture bears Teftimony, that *his Heart was as the Sands of the Sea* For as the Sand of the Sea encompaffes the extremities of the whole Earth, fo his Wifdom comprehended all things, both human and divine. And in thofe *Aphorifms* are found many excellent Civil Precepts and Admonitions, befides things of a more theological Nature, flowing from the depth and innermoft Bofom of Wifdom ; and running out into a moft fpacious field of Variety. And as we place the *Doctrine of various Occafions* among the *Defiderata of the Sciences*, we will

This Doctrine reducible to Rule

D d 2 here

---

[a] See above *Sect* XXIII 3

[b] This may be extended to *Civil Knowledge* in general, fo as to comprehend not only *Politicks, Converfation*, and *Bufinefs*, but alfo *Commerce*, and the particular Arts of *Agriculture, Navigation, Architecture, War, Trades* &c For a Man of general Knowledge fuch as the Author, or Mr *Boyle* for inftance, muft needs be more capable of improving any particular Art or Science , than a perfon wholly bred up to, and employed about one Bufinefs only

here dwell upon it a little , and lay down an Example thereof, in the way of explaining some of these *Aphorisms,* or *Proverbs, of Solomon.*

A Specimen of the DOCTRINE OF VARIOUS OCCASIONS, *in the common Business of Life , by way of* Aphorism *and* Explanation.

APHORISM I.

4 *A soft Answer appeases Anger*

IF the Anger of a *Prince,* or *Superior,* be kindled against you , and it be now your turn to speak , *Solomon* directs, (1) that an Answer be made ; and (2) that it be soft. The first Rule contains three Precepts , viz. (1) To guard against a melancholy and stubborn silence · for this either turns the fault wholly upon you, as if you could make no Answer ; or secretly impeaches your Superior, as if his Ears were not open to a just Defence. (2) To beware of delaying the thing , and requiring a longer day for your Defence which either accuses your Superior of Passion , or signifies that you are preparing some artificial turn, or colour. So that 'tis always best directly to say something for the present, in your own excuse, as the occasion requires. And (3) To make a real Answer , an *Answer* not a mere *Confession,* or bare Submission , but a mixture of Apology and Excuse. For 'tis unsafe to do otherwise , unless with very generous and noble Spirits, which are extremely rare. Then follows the second Rule , that the *Answer be mild and soft,* not stiff and irritating [a]

APHORISM II.

5. *A prudent Servant shall rule over a foolish Son, and divide the Inheritance among the Brethren*

IN every jarring Family there constantly rises up some Servant, or humble Friend, of sway, who takes upon him to compose their Differences, at his own discretion , to whom, for that reason, the whole Family, even the Master himself, is subject. If this Man has a view to his own Ends, he foments and aggravates the Differences of the Family ; but if he prove just and upright, he is certainly very deserving. So that he may be reckoned even as one of the *Brethren* , or at least have the direction of the Inheritance, in trust

APHORISM

---

[a] How the Author put this Doctrine in practice, appears by his Answer to the House of Peers. See the Letter, towards the End of the FIFTH SUPPLEMENT to this *Work.*

Aphorism III.

6 If a wife Man contends with a Fool, whether he be in anger,
or in jeft, there is no quiet.

WE are frequently admonifhed to avoid unequal Conflicts, that is, not to *The Folly of* ftrive with the Stronger. But the admonition of *Solomon* is no lefs ufe- *contending* ful, that we fhould not ftrive with the Worthlefs. for here the Match is *with the obfti-* very unequal, where 'tis no Victory to conquer, and a great Difgrace to be *nate* conquer'd. Nor does it fignify if, in fuch a conteft, we fhould fometimes deal as in Jeft, and fometimes in the way of Difdain and Contempt. For what courfe foever we take, we are lofers, and can never come handfomely off. But the worft cafe of all is, if our Antagonift have fomething of the Fool in him, that is, if he be confident and headftrong.

Aphorism IV.

7. Liften not to all that is fpoke, left thou fhouldft hear thy Ser-
vant curfe thee

'TIS fcarce credible what Uneafinefs is created in Life, by an ufelefs Cu- *The Treachery* riofity, about the things that concern us. As when we pry into *of ufelefs Cu-* fuch Secrets, as being difcovered, give us diftafte, but afford no affiftance *riofity.* or relief. For (1) there follows Vexation and Difquiet of Mind, as all hu- man things are full of Perfidioufnefs and Ingratitude. So that tho' we could procure fome Magick-Glafs, wherein to view the Animofities, and all that Malice which is any way at work againft us, it were better for us to break it directly, than to ufe it. For thefe things are but as the ruftling of Leaves, foon over. (2) This Curiofity always loads the Mind with Sufpicion, which is a violent Enemy to Counfels, and renders them unfteady and perplexed. (3) It alfo frequently fixes the Evils themfelves, which would otherwife have blown over. For 'tis a dangerous thing to provoke the Confciences of Men, who fo long as they think themfelves concealed, are eafily changed for the better. but if they once find themfelves difcovered, drive out one Evil with another. It was therefore juftly efteemed the utmoft Prudence in *Pompey,* that he directly burnt all the Papers of *Sertorius,* unperufed by himfelf, or others.

Aphorism V.

8 Poverty comes as a Traveller, but Want as an armed Man

THIS Aphorifm elegantly defcribes how Prodigals, and fuch as take no *The way of fe-* care of their Affairs, make fhipwreck of their Fortunes. For Debt, *curing an* and Diminution of the Capital, at firft fteals on gradually, and almoft im- *Eftate.* perceptibly, like a *Traveller,* but foon after, *Want* invades, as an armed Man, that tr*t is, with a hand so ftrong and powerful, as can no longer be refifted ror 'tis uftly, find by the Ancien s, that Neceffity is of all things the ftronge*t. We muft, therefore, prevent the Traveller, and guard againft the armed M n

APHORISM VI

9 *He who inftructs a Scoffer, procures to himfelf reproach; and he who reproves a wicked Man, procures to himfelf a Stain.*

The assign of reproof to the wicked

THIS agrees with the Precept of our Saviour, not to throw Pearls before Swine. The Aphorifm diftinguifhes betwixt the Actions of *Precept* and *Reproof*, and again betwixt the Perfons of the *Scorner* and the *Wicked* and laftly, the Reward is diftinguifhed. In the former cafe, Precept is repaid by a lofs of Labour, and in the latter, of Reproof, 'tis repaid with a Stain alfo. For when any one inftructs and teaches a *Scorner*, he firft lofes his time, in the next place, others laugh at his Labour, as fruitlefs and mifapplied, and laftly, the *Scorner* himfelf difdains the Knowledge delivered. But there is more Danger in reproving a wicked Man, who not only lends no Ear, but turns again, and either directly rails at his Admonifher, who has now made himfelf odious to him, or at leaft, afterwards traduces him to others.

APHORISM VII

10 *A wife Son rejoices his Father, but a foolifh Son is a Sorrow to his Mother.*

The Joys and Griefs of Children diferently affect the Father from the Mother

THE Domeftick Joys and Griefs of Father and Mother from their Children, are here diftinguifhed. for a prudent and hopeful Son is a capital pleafure to the *Father*, who knows the value of Virtue better than the *Mother*, and therefore rejoices more at his Son's difpofition to Virtue. This Joy may alfo be heightened, perhaps, from feeing the good Effect of his own Management, in the Education of his Son, fo as to form good Morals in him by Precept and Example. On the other hand, the *Mother* fuffers and partakes the moft, in the Calamity of her *Son*, becaufe the maternal Affection is the more foft and tender. And again, perhaps, becaufe fhe is confcious that her Indulgence has fpoil'd, and depraved him.

APHORISM VIII

11. *The Memory of the Juft is bleffed, but the Name of the wicked fhall rot*

The diffrence between the Fame of good and bad Men after Death

WE have here that diftinction between the Character of good and evil Men, which ufually takes place after Death. For in the cafe of good Men, when Envy that purfues them whilft alive, is extinguifhed, their Name prefently flourifhes, and their Fame increafes every day. But the Fame of bad Men,

Men, tho' it may remain for a while, thro' the Favour of Friends and Faction, yet soon becomes odious, and at length degenerates into Infamy, and ends, as it were, in a loathsome odour.

Aphorism IX

12 *He who troubles his own House, shall inherit the Wind.*

THIS is a very useful Admonition, as to Domestick Jars and Differen- *The Folly of changing Conditions.* ces. For many promise themselves great matters from the separation of their Wives, the disinheriting of their Children, the frequent changing of Servants, &c as if they should thence procure greater Peace of Mind, or a more successful Administration of their Affairs. But such hopes commonly turn to Wind, these Changes being seldom for the better. And such Disturbers of their Families, often meet with various Crosses and Ingratitude, from those they afterwards adopt and chuse. They, by this means also, bring ill Reports, and ambiguous Rumours upon themselves. For as *Cicero* well observes, *all Men's Characters proceed from their Domesticks.* And both these Mischiefs *Solomon* elegantly expresses, by the *Possession of the Wind* for the frustration of Expectation, and the raising of Rumours, are justly compared to the Winds.

Aphorism X.

13. *The End of a Discourse is better than the Beginning*

THIS *Aphorism* corrects a common Error, prevailing not only among *The Conclu-* such as principally study Words, but also the more prudent, *viz* that *sions of Con-* Men are more sollicitous about the Beginnings and Entrances of their Dis- *versations to* courses, than about the Conclusions. and more exactly labour their Prefaces *be agreeable* and Introductions, than their Closes. Whereas they ought not to neglect the former, but should have the latter, as being Things of far the greater Consequence, ready prepared beforehand. casting about with themselves, as much as possible, what may be the last Issue of the Discourse, and how Business may be thence forwarded and ripened. They ought further, not only to consider the windings up of Discourses relating to Business, but to regard also such turns as may be advantageously and gracefully given upon departure, even tho' they should be quite foreign to the matter in hand. It was the constant practice of two great and prudent Privy Counsellors, on whom the weight of the Kingdom chiefly rested, as often as they discoursed with their Princes upon Matters of State, never to end the Conversation with what regarded the principal Subject, but always to go off with a Jest, or some pleasant Device, and as the *Proverb* runs, *washing off their salt-water Discourses with fresh, at the Conclusion.* And this was one of the principal Arts they had.

Aphorism.

APHORISM XI.

14 *As dead Flies cause the best Ointment to yield an ill Odour;*
so does a little Folly to a Man in Reputation for Wisdom and
Honour

THE Condition of Men eminent for Virtue, is, as this *Aphorism* excellently observes, exceeding hard and miserable, because their Errors, tho' ever so small, are not overlooked. But, as in a clear Diamond, every little grain, or speck, strikes the Eye disagreeably, tho' it would scarce be observed in a duller Stone, so in Men of eminent Virtue, their smallest Vices are readily spied, talk'd of, and severely censured, whilst in an ordinary Man, they would either have lain concealed, or been easily excused. Whence a little Folly in a very wise Man, a small Slip in a very good Man, and a little Indecency in a polite and elegant Man; greatly diminish their Characters and Reputations. It might, therefore, be no bad Policy, for Men of uncommon Excellencies, to intermix with their Actions a few Absurdities, that may be committed without Vice, in order to reserve a Liberty, and confound the Observation of little Defects.

APHORISM XII

15. *Scornful Men ensnare a City, but wise Men prevent Calamity*

IT may seem strange, that in the Description of Men, formed, as it were, by Nature, for the Destruction of States, *Solomon* should chuse the Character, not of a proud and haughty, not of a tyrannical and cruel, not of a rash and violent, not of a seditious and turbulent, not of a foolish or uncapable Man, but the Character of a Scorner. Yet this choice is becoming the Wisdom of that King, who well knew how Governments were subverted, and how preserved. For there is scarce such another destructive thing to Kingdoms, and Commonwealths, as that the Counsellors, or Senators, who sit at the Helm, should be naturally Scorners, who, to shew themselves courageous Advisers, are always extenuating the greatness of Dangers, insulting, as fearful Wretches, those who weigh them as they ought, and ridiculing the ripening Delays of Counsel and Debate, as tedious Matters of Oratory, unserviceable to the general Issue of Business. They despise Rumours, as the Breath of the Rabble, and things that will soon pass over, tho' the Counsels of Princes are to be chiefly directed from hence. They account the Power and Authority of Laws, but as Nets unfit to hold great Matters. They reject, as Dreams and melancholy Notions, those Counsels and Precautions, that regard Futurity at a distance. They satyrize and banter such Men as are really prudent and knowing in Affairs; or such as bear noble Minds, and are capable of advising. In short, they sap all the Foundations of *Political Government* at once: a thing which deserves the
greater

greater Attention, as 'tis not effected by open Attack, but by secret Undermining nor is it, by any means, so much suspected among mankind as it
deserves [a].

APHORISM XIII

16 *The Prince who willingly hearkens to Lyes, has all his Servants*
wicked.

WHEN a Prince is injudiciously disposed to lend a credulous Ear to *Credulity very*
Whisperers and Flatterers , pestilent Breath seems to proceed from *pernicious in*
him , corrupting and infecting all his Servants: and now some search into *Princes*
his Fears, and increase them with fictitious Rumours , some raise up in him
the Fury of Envy, especially against the most deserving , some, by accusing
of others, wash their own Stains away , some make room for the Preferment and Gratification of their Friends, by calumniating and traducing their
Competitors, &c. And these Agents are naturally the most vicious Servants of the Prince. Those again, of better Principles and Dispositions, after
finding little Security in their Innocence ; their Master not knowing how
to distinguish Truth from Falshood; drop their moral Honesty, go into the
eddy Winds of the Court, and servilely submit to be carried about with
them For as *Tacitus* says of *Claudius, There is no safety with that Prince, in-*
to whose Mind all things are infused and directed. And *Comines* well observes,
that 'tis *better being Servant to a Prince whose Suspicions are endless, tha whose*
Credulity is great.

APHORISM XIV.

17. *A just Man is merciful to the Life of his Beast, but the Mer-*
cies of the Wicked are cruel.

NAture has endowed Man with a noble and excellent *Principle of Com-* *Compassion to*
passion, which extends itself even to the Brutes, that by divine Appoint- *be limited.*
ment are made subject to him Whence this Compassion has some resemblance with that of a Prince towards his Subjects. And 'tis certain, that
the noblest Souls are most extensively merciful: For narrow and degenerate Spirits think Compassion belongs not to them ; but a great Soul,
the noblest part of the Creation, is ever compassionate. Thus under the
old Law there were numerous Precepts not merely ceremonial, as the or-
daining of Mercy, for example, the not eating of Flesh with the Blood
thereof , &c. So likewise the Sects of the *Essenes* and *Pythagoreans* totally
abstained from Flesh , as they do also to this day, with an inviolated Superstition, in some parts of the Empire of *Mogul* Nay the *Turks,* tho' a
cruel and bloody Nation, both in their Descent and Discipline, give Alms
to Brutes , and suffer them not to be tortured. But lest this Principle

---

[a] The Author, perhaps, had his Eye upon publick as well as private Assemblies

might seem to countenance all kinds of Compaſſion, *Solomon* wholeſomely
ſubjoins, *That the Mercies of the Wicked are cruel*, that is, when ſuch great
Offenders are ſpared, as ought to be cut off with the Sword of Juſtice For
this kind of Mercy is the greateſt of all Cruelties, as Cruelty affects but
particular Perſons, whilſt Impunity lets looſe the whole Army of Evil-
doers, and drives them upon the Innocent.

APHORISM XV.

18. *A Fool ſpeaks all his Mind, but a wiſe Man reſerves ſome-*
thing for hereafter

Erichon Diſ-
courſe preferr d
to continued
THIS *Aphoriſm* ſeems principally levell'd, not againſt the futility of light
 Perſons, who ſpeak what they ſhould conceal, nor againſt the pertneſs
with which they indiſcriminately, and injudiciouſly, fly out upon Men
and Things, nor againſt the talkative humour with which ſome Men
diſguſt their hearers, but againſt a more latent Failing, *viz* a very im-
prudent and impolitick management of Speech, when a Man in private
Converſation ſo directs his Diſcourſe, as, in a continued ſtring of Words, to
deliver all he can ſay, that any way relates to the Subject which is a great
prejudice to Buſineſs For, (1.) Diſcourſe interrupted and infuſed by parcels, enters deeper than if it were continued, and unbroke, in which caſe
the weight of things is not diſtinctly and particularly felt, as having not
time to fix themſelves, but one Reaſon drives out another, before it had taken root (2) Again, no one is ſo powerful or happy in Eloquence, as
at firſt ſetting out to leave the Hearer perfectly mute and ſilent, but he will
always have ſomething to anſwer, and perhaps to object, in his turn   And
here it happens, that thoſe things which were to be reſerved for Confutation,
or Reply, being now anticipated, loſe their Strength and Beauty (3) Laſtly, if a Perſon does not utter all his Mind at once, but ſpeaks by ſtarts,
firſt one thing, then another, he will perceive from the Countenance and
Anſwer of the Perſon ſpoke to, how each particular affects him, and in
what Senſe he takes it and thus be directed, more cautiouſly, to ſuppreſs
or employ the matter ſtill in reſerve

APHORISM XVI.

19 *If the Diſpleaſure of great Men riſe up againſt thee, forſake*
not thy Place for pliant Behaviour extenuates great Offences.

The Place of
...
Favourite...
...
THIS *Aphoriſm* ſhews how a Perſon ought to behave, when he has in-
 curred the Diſpleaſure of his *Prince*. The Precept hath two parts,
(1) that the Perſon quit not his Poſt, and (2) that he, with Diligence
and Caution, apply to the Cure, as of a dangerous Diſeaſe For when Men
ſee their Prince incenſed againſt them, what thro' Impatience of Diſgrace,
Fear of renewing their Wounds by ſight; and partly to let their Prince
behold

behold their Contrition and Humiliation, 'tis ufual with them to retire from their Office or Employ, and fometimes to refign their Places and Dignities into their Prince's hands But *Solomon* difapproves this Method, as pernicious. For, (1) it publifhes the Difgrace too much, whence both our Enemies and Enviers are more emboldened to hurt us, and our Friends the more intimidated from lending their affiftance   (2.) By this means the Anger of the Prince, which perhaps would have blown over of itfelf, had it not been made publick, becomes more fixed, and having now begun to difplace the Perfon, ends not but in his Downfall. (3.) This refigning carries fomething of Ill-will with it, and fhews a diflike of the Times; which adds the Evil of Indignation to that of Sufpicion   The following Remedies regard the Cure (1) Let him above all things beware how by any Infenfibility, or Elation of Mind, he feems regardlefs of his Prince's Difpleafure; or not affected as he ought. He fhould not compofe his Countenance to a ftubborn *Melancholly*, but to a grave and decent *Dejection* and fhew himfelf, in all his Actions, lefs brisk and chearful than ufual It may alfo be for his advantage to ufe the Affiftance and Mediation of a Friend with the Prince, feafonably to infinuate, with how great a Senfe of Grief the Perfon in difgrace is inwardly affected. (2) Let him carefully avoid even the leaft occafions of reviving the thing which caufed the Difpleafure, or of giving any handle to frefh Diftafte, and open Rebuke. (3) Let him diligently feek all occafions wherein his fervice may be acceptable to his Prince, that he may both fhew a ready Defire of retrieving his paft Offence, and his Prince perceive what a Servant he muft lofe if he quit him   (4) Either let him prudently transfer the Blame upon others, or infinuate that the Offence was committed with no ill defign, or fhew that their Malice, who accufed him to the Prince, aggravated the thing above meafure   (5) Laftly, let him in every refpect be watchful and intent upon the Cure

APHORISM XVII.

20. *The firft in his own Caufe, is juft · then comes the other Party, and enquires into him*

THE firft Information in any Caufe, if it dwell a little with the Judge, *How to con-* takes root, tinges and poffeffes him fo, as hardly to be removed again, *quer Prepof-* unlefs fome manifeft Falfity be found in the matter itfelf, or fome Artifice *feffion in a* be difcovered in delivering it. For a naked and fimple Defence, tho' juft and *Judge* prevalent, can fcarce balance the prejudice of a prior Information, or of itfelf reduce to an equilibrium the Scale of Juftice that has once inclined. It is, therefore, fafeft for the Judge to hear nothing as to the Merits of a Caufe, before both Parties are convened; and beft for the Defendant, if he perceive the Judge prepoffeffed, to endeavour, as far as ever the Cafe will allow, principally to detect fome Artifice, or Trick, made ufe of by the Plaintiff to abufe the Judge.

APHORISM

APHORISM XVIII.

21. He who brings up his Servant delicately, shall find him stubborn in the end.

PRinces and Masters are, by the Advice of *Solomon*, to observe Moderation in conferring Grace and Favour upon their Servants This Moderation consists in three things (1) In promoting them gradually, not by sudden starts (2) In accustoming them sometimes to Denial And, (3) as is well observed by *Machiavel*, in letting them always have something further to hope for And unless these particulars be observed, Princes in the end, will doubtless find from their Servants Disrespect and Obstinacy, instead of Gratitude and Duty For from sudden Promotion arises Insolence, from a perpetual obtaining one's Desires, impatience of Denial, and if there be nothing further to wish, there's an end of Alacrity and Industry.

APHORISM XIX.

22 A Man diligent in his Business shall stand before Kings; and not be ranked among the Vulgar.

OF all the Virtues which Kings chiefly regard and require, in the Choice of Servants, that of Expedition, and Resolution, in the dispatch of Business, is the most acceptable Men of depth are held suspected by Princes, as inspecting them too close, and being able by their strength of Capacity, as by a Machine, to turn and wind them, against their Will, and without their Knowledge Popular Men are hated, as standing in the light of Kings; and drawing the Eyes of the Multitude upon themselves. Men of Courage are generally esteemed turbulent, and too enterprizing Honest and just Men are accounted morose, and not compliable enough to the Will of their Masters Lastly, there is no Virtue but has its Shade, wherewith the Minds of Kings are offended, but Dispatch alone in executing their Commands, has nothing displeasing to them Besides, the Motions of the Minds of Kings are swift, and impatient of delay for they think themselves able to effect any thing, and imagine that nothing more is wanting, but to have it done instantly Whence Dispatch is to them the most grateful of all Things

APHORISM XX

23. I saw all the living which walk under the Sun, with the succeeding young Prince, that shall rise up in his stead.

THIS *Aphorism* points out the Vanity of those who flock about the next Successors of Princes The Root of this, is the Folly naturally implanted in the Minds of Men, *viz.* their being too fond of their own Hopes. For scarce any one but is more delighted with Hope than with Enjoyment.

Again,

Again, Novelty is pleasing, and greedily coveted by human Nature and these two things, *Hope* and *Novelty*, meet in the Succeſſor of a Prince The *Aphoriſm* hints the same that was formerly said by *Pompey* to *Sylla*, and again by *Tiberius* of *Macro*, that *the Sun has more Adorers riſing than ſetting.* Yet Rulers in poſſeſſion are not much affected with this, or eſteem it any great matter , as neither *Sylla* nor *Tiberius* did : but rather laugh at the Levity of Men , and encounter not with Dreams for *Hope*, as was well ſaid, is but a waking Dream.

APHORISM XXI.

24 *There was a little City, mann'd but by a few; and a mighty King drew his Army to it, erected Bulwarks againſt it, and entrenched it round : now there was found within the Walls a poor wiſe Man, and he by his Wiſdom delivered the City , but none remembred the ſame poor Man.*

THIS Parable deſcribes the corrupt and malevolent Nature of Men, *The Reward* who in Extremities and Difficulties generally fly to the Prudent and *of the more* the Courageous , tho' they before deſpiſed them : and as ſoon as the Storm *Deſerving* is over, they ſhew Ingratitude to their Preſervers. *Machiavel* had reaſon to put the Queſtion, " *Which is the more ungrateful towards the well deſerving, the Prince or the People?* tho' he accuſes both of Ingratitude. The thing does not proceed wholly from the Ingratitude either of Princes or People , but it is generally attended with the Envy of the Nobility , who ſecretly repine at the Event, tho' happy and proſperous , becauſe it was not procured by themſelves. Whence they leſſen the Merit of the Author, and bear him down.

APHORISM XXII.

25. *The Way of the Slothful is a Hedge of Thorns.*

THIS *Aphoriſm* elegantly ſhews, that Sloth is laborious in the end For *The advan-* diligent and cautious Preparation guards the foot from ſtumbling, and *tage of con-* ſmooths the way before 'tis trod , but he who is ſluggiſh, and defers all *triving Buſi-* things to the laſt Moment, muſt of neceſſity be at every ſtep treading as *neſs* upon Brambles and Thorns ; which frequently detain and hinder him · and the ſame may be obſerved in the Government of a Family · where if due Care and Forethought be uſed, all things go on calmly, and, as it were, ſpontaneouſly, without Noiſe and Buſtle: but if this Caution be neglected , when any great Occaſion ariſes, numerous Matters croud in to be done at once, the Servants are in confuſion , and the Houſe rings.

APHORISM XXIII.

26 *He who respects Persons in Judgment, does ill, and will for-*
sake the Truth, for a piece of Bread.

THIS *Aphorism* wisely observes, that Facility of Temper is more pernicious in a Judge than Bribery for Bribes are not offer'd by all, but
there is no Cause wherein something may not be found to sway the Mind
of the Judge, if he be a Respecter of Persons. Thus, one shall be respected
for his Country, another for his Riches; another for being recommended
by a Friend, &c So that Iniquity must abound where Respect of Persons
prevails, and Judgment be corrupted for a very trifling thing, as it were
for a Morsel of Bread.

APHORISM XXIV

27 *A poor Man, that by Extortion oppresses the Poor, is like a*
Land-flood that causes Famine

THIS *Parable* was anciently painted by the Fable of the *Leech*, *full*
and empty, for the Oppression of a poor and hungry Wretch is much
more grievous than the Oppression of one who is rich and full, as he
searches into all the Corners and Arts of Exaction, and Ways of raising Contributions The thing has been also usually resembled to a Sponge, which
sucks strongly when dry, but less when moist And it contains an useful Admonition o Princes, that they commit not the Government of
Provinces, or Places of Power, to indigent Men, or such as are in debt;
and again to the People, that they permit not their Kings to struggle with
Want

APHORISM XXV.

28 *A just Man falling before the Wicked, is a troubled Fountain,*
and a corrupted Spring.

THIS is a Caution to States, that they should have a Capital Regard
to the passing an unjust or infamous Sentence, in any great and weighty Cause, where not only the Guilty is acquitted, but the Innocent condemned To countenance private Injuries, indeed disturbs and pollutes the
clear Streams of Justice, as it were, in the Brook, but unjust and great
publick Sentences, which are afterwards drawn into Precedents, infect and
defile the very Fountain of Justice. For when once the Court goes on the
side of Injustice, the Law becomes a publick Robber, and one Man really a
Wolf to another

APHORISM

APHORISM XXVI.

29. *Contract no Friendship with an angry Man; nor walk with a furious one*

T HE more religiously the Laws of Friendship are to be observed amongst *The Caution* good Men, the more Caution should be used in making a prudent *required in* Choice of Friends.   The Nature and Humour of Friends, so far as concerns *contracting* ourselves alone, should be absolutely tolerated, but when they lay us un- *Friendships.* der a Necessity, as to the Character we should put on towards others, this becomes an exceeding hard and unreasonable Condition of Friendship   'Tis therefore of great moment to the Peace and Security of Life, according to the direction of *Solomon*, to have no Friendship with passionate Men, and such as easily stir up or enter into Debates and Quarrels   For such Friends will be perpetually entangling us in Strifes and Contentions, so that we must either break off with them, or have no regard to our own safety.

APHORISM XXVII

30. *He who conceals a Fault, seeks Friendship; but he who re-peats a Matter, separates Friends.*

T HERE are two ways of composing Differences, and reconciling the *The way of* Minds of Men, the one beginning with Oblivion and Forgiveness, *procuring Re-* the other with a Recollection of the Injuries, interweaving it with Apolo- *conciliation* gies and Excuses. I remember it the Opinion of a very wise Politician, " That he who treats of Peace without repeating the Conditions of the Dif- " ference, rather deceives the Mind with the sweetness of Reconciliation, " than equitably makes up the Matter." But *Solomon*, a still wiser Man, is of a contrary Opinion, and approves of forgetting, but forbids a repe-tition of the Difference, as being attended with these Inconveniencies : (1.) that it rakes into the old Sore, (2) that it may cause a new Difference; (3) and lastly, that it brings the Matter to end in Excuses   Whereas both sides had rather seem to forgive the Injury, than allow of an Excuse

APHORISM XXVIII.

31 *In every good Work, is Plenty, but where Words abound, there is commonly a Want*

S Olomon here distinguishes the Fruit of the Labour of the Tongue, and *The difference* that of the Labour of the Hand, as if from the one came Want, *betwixt an ef-* and from the other Abundance. For, it almost constantly happens, that *fective and a* they who speak much, boast much, and promise largely, are but bar- *verbose Per-* ren, and receive no Fruit from the things they talk of being seldom *son*

indu-

industrious or diligent in Works, but feed and satisfy themselves with Discourse alone, as with Wind whilst, as the Poet intimates, He who is conscious to himself, that he can really effect, feels the Satisfaction inwardly, and keeps silent [a] whereas, he who knows he grasps nothing but empty Air, is full of Talk and strange Stories

Aphorism XXIX
32 *Open Reproof is better than secret Affection*

The Reproof of Friends　THIS *Aphorism* reprehends the Indulgence of those who use not the Privilege of Friendship, freely and boldly to admonish their Friends, as well of their Errors as their Dangers. " What shall I do? says an easy " good-natured Friend, or what course shall I take? I love him as well as ' Man can do, and would willingly suffer any Misfortune in his stead ' " but I know his Nature, if I deal freely with him, I shall offend him ' at least chagreen him, and yet do him no Service Nay, I shall sooner ' alienate his Friendship from me, than win him over from those things he " has fixed his Mind upon " Such an effeminate and useless Friend as this, *Solomon* reprehends, and pronounces, that greater advantage may be received from an open Enemy· as a Man may chance to hear those things from an Enemy, by way of reproach, which a Friend, thro' too much Indulgence, will not speak out

Aphorism XXX.
33. *A prudent Man looks well to his Steps; but a Fool turns aside to Deceit*

The Honesty is true Policy　THERE are two kinds of Prudence, the one true and sound, the other degenerate and false the latter *Solomon* calls by the Name of Folly. The Candidate for the former has an eye to his Footings, looking out for Dangers, contriving Remedies, and by the Assistance of good Men defending himself against the bad: he is wary in entring upon Business, and not unprovided of a Retreat, watchful for Opportunities; powerful against Opposition, &c But the Follower of the other is wholly patch'd up of Fallacy and Cunning, placing all his hope in the circumventing of others, and forming them to his fancy. And this the Aphorism justly rejects, as a vicious, and even a weak kind of Prudence For, (1) 'Tis by no means a thing in our own power, nor depending upon any constant Rule. but is daily inventing of new Stratagems, as the old ones fail and grow useless. (2) He who has once the Character of a crafty, tricking Man, is entirely deprived of a principal Instrument of business, *Trust*, whence he will find nothing succeed to his wish. Lastly, however specious and pleasing these Arts may seem, yet they are often frustrated, as was well observed by *Tacitus*, when he said, that *crafty and bold Counsels, tho' pleasant in the Expectation, are hard to execute, and unhappy in the Event*

[a] *Qui silet est Firmus*

APHORISM

APHORISM XXXI.

34. *Be not over-righteous, nor make thyself over-wife, for why
shouldst thou suddenly be taken off?*

*T*HERE are times, says *Tacitus*, wherein great *Virtues* meet with certain
Ruin   And this happens to Men, eminent for Virtue and Justice,
sometimes suddenly, and sometimes after it was long forefeen But if Prudence be also joined, so as to make such Men cautious, and watchful of their
own safety, then they gain thus much, that their Ruin shall come suddenly, and entirely from secret and dark Councils   whence they may
escape Envy, and meet Destruction unexpected   But for that over-right-
teousness expressed in the *Aphorism*, 'tis not understood of Virtue itself, in
which there is no Excess, but of a vain and invidious Affectation, and
Shew thereof, like what *Tacitus* intimates of *Lepidus*, making it a kind of
Miracle, that he never gave any servile Opinion, and yet stood safe in severe times.

The danger of great Virtue in bad Times

APHORISM XXXII.

35. *Give occasion to a wise Man, and his Wisdom will be en-
creased*

*T*HIS *Aphorism* distinguishes between that Wisdom which has grown
up and ripened into a true Habit, and that which only floats in the
Brain, or is tost upon the Tongue, without having taken root   The former, when occasion offers, is presently rouzed, got ready, and distended,
so as to appear greater than itself, whereas the latter, which was pert before, stands amazed and confounded, when occasion calls for it · so that
the Person, who thought himself endowed with this Wisdom, begins to
question whether his Præconceptions about it, were not meer Dreams, and
empty Speculations.

*The difference betwixt shal-
low and found Knowledge*

APHORISM XXXIII.

36 *To praise one's Friend aloud, rising early, has the same effect
as curfing him.*

MOderate and seasonable Praises, dropt occasionally, are of great service
to the Reputation and Fortunes of Men, whilst immoderate, noisy and
fulsome Praises, do no good, but rather hurt, as the *Aphorism* expresses it
For (1) they plainly betray themselves to proceed from an excess of good-
will, or to be purposely designed, rather to gain Favour with the Person,
by false Encomiums, than to paint him justly   (2.) Sparing and modest
Praises generally invite the Company somewhat to improve them, but

*The Conduct to be observ-
ed in Praise*

profuse and immoderate ones, to detract, and take off from them (3) The principal thing is, that immoderate Praises procure envy to the Person praised, as all extravagant Commendations seem to reproach others that may be no less deserving

APHORISM XXXIV.

37. *As the Face shines in Water, so are Mens Hearts manifest to the Wise*

The auxiliary usage of Knowledge

THIS *Aphorism* distinguishes between the Minds of prudent Men, and those of others, by comparing the former to Water, or a Mirror, which receives the forms and images of things, whilst the latter are like Earth, or unpolished Stone, which reflects Nothing   And the Mind of a prudent Man is the more aptly compared to a Glass, because therein one's own Image may, at the same time, be viewed along with those of others, which could not be done by the Eye, without assistance   but if the Mind of a prudent Man be so capacious, as to observe and distinguish an infinite diversity of Natures and Manners in Men, it remains, that we endeavour to render it as various in the Application as 'tis in the Representation [a]

Farther Direction about the Method of treating the Subject

38   And so much by way of Example of the *Doctrine of various Occasions*.   For thus, it was not only usual among the Jews, but very common also among the wise Men of other ancient Nations, when they had, by observation, hit upon any thing useful in common Life, to reduce and contract it into some short Sentence, Parable, or Fable   Fables anciently supplied the defect of Examples, but now that times abound with variety of Histories, 'tis better, and more enlivening, to draw from real Life   But the method of writing best suited to so various and intricate a Subject, as the *different Occasions of Civil Business*, is that which *Machiavel* chose for treating Politicks, *viz* by Observation, or Discourse, upon Histories and Examples   For the Knowledge which is newly drawn, and, as it were, under our own Eye, from Particulars, best finds the way to Particulars again. And doubtless, 'tis much more conducive to Practice, that the Discourse follow the Example, than that the Example follow the Discourse   And this regards not only the Order, but the Thing itself, for when an Example is proposed as the Basis of a Discourse, 'tis usually proposed with its whole Apparatus of Circumstances, which may sometimes correct and supply it, whence it becomes as a Model for Imitation and Practice   whilst Examples, produced for the sake of the Treatise, are but succinctly and nakedly quoted, and, as Slaves, wholly attend the Call of the Discourse

The difference of Histories in this view

39   'Tis worth while to observe this difference, that as the Histories of Times afford the best matter for Discourses upon Politicks, such as those

I   of

[a] *Qui sapit, innumeris Moribus aptus erit*

of *Machiavel* [a], fo the Hiftories of Lives are moft advantageoufly ufed for inftructions of Bufinefs becaufe they contain all the poffible variety of Occafions and Affairs, as well great as fmall   Yet a more commodious Foundation may be had for the Precepts of Bufinefs, than either of thefe Hiftories , and that is, the difcourfing upon prudent and ferious Epiftles, fuch as thofe of *Cicero* to *Atticus*, &c   For Epiftles reprefent Bufinefs nearer and more to the Life, than either Annals or Lives [b]   And thus we have treated of the Matter and Form of the firft part of the *Doctrine of Bufinefs*, which regards *Variety of Occafions* , and place it among the *Defiderata* [c]

SECT. XXV.

Of SELF-POLICY; *or the* DOCTRINE *of* RISING IN LIFE.

I. 1. THERE is another part of the DOCTRINE OF BUSINESS, differing as much from the former, as the *being wife in the general,* and *being wife for one's felf.* The one feems to move, as from the Centre to the Circumference , and the other as from the Circumference to the Centre For there is a certain Prudence of *giving Counfel to others* , and another of *looking to one's own Affairs* both thefe indeed are fometimes found united, but ofteneft feparate   As many are prudent in the Management of their own private Concerns , and weak in publick Adminiftration, or the giving Advice like the Ant, which is a wife Creature for itfelf, but pernicious in a Garden   This Virtue of *Self-Wifdom* was not unknown even to the *Romans*, thofe great Lovers of their Country   Whence fays the Comedian, *the wife Man forms his own Fortune* [d], and they had it proverbial amongft them, *Every Man's Fortune lies in his own hand* [e].   So *Livy* gives this Character of the elder *Cato*, " *Such was his Force of Mind and Genius, that where-ever he had been born, he feem'd formed for making his own Fortune* "

2 But if any one publickly profefs'd, or made open fhow of this kind of Prudence, 'twas always accounted, not only impolitick, but ominous and unfortunate , as was obferved of *Timotheus* the *Athenian*, who after having

Private Policy different from publick

Is not to be profeffed

F f 2   performed

[a] Efpecially his *Princeps*, with the Notes of *Conringius*, Ed 1660
[b] See above of HISTORY, Sect I 36
[c] The Author's Effays, or *Sermones Fideles*, being fhort Difcourfes upon a variety of Moral, Political, and Oeconomical Subjects, may be efteemed a farth Attempt to fupply this Deficiency in the Doctrine of *Various Occafions*. See SUPPLEMENT XI. to this Piece *de Augmentis Scientiarum*
[d] *Nam pol fapiens fingit fortunam fibi.*
[e] *Faber quifque fortunæ propriæ*

performed many great Exploits, for the honour and advantage of his Country, and giving an account of his Conduct to the People, as the manner then was, he concluded the feveral Particulars thus, ' *And here Fortune had no* " *ſhare.* " after which time, nothing ever fucceeded in his hands. This was, indeed, too arrogant and haughty, like that of *Pharaoh* in *Ezekiel,* " Thou " *ſayſt the River is mine, and I made myſelf,*" or that of *Habakkuck,* " They " *rejoice, and ſacrifice to their Net,*" or again, that of *Mezentius* who cal-led *by His Hand and Jave'lin his God* [a], or liftly, that of *Julius Cæfar,* the on-ly time that we find him betraying his inward Sentiments: for when the Aruſpex related to him, that the Entrails were not profperous, he mutter'd foftly, " *They ſhall be better when I pleaſe,*" which was faid not long be-fore his unfortunate Death. And indeed this exceffive confidence, as it is a profane thing, ſo it is always unhappy. Whence great, and truly wife Men think proper to attribute all their Succeffes to their Felicity, and not to their Virtue and Induftry. So *Sylla* ftyled himfelf *happy,* not *great,* and *Cæſar,* at another time, more adviſedly, faid to the Pilot, " *Thou carrieſt Cæſar* " *a dhis Fortune.*"

3. But thefe Expreffions, " *Every one's Fortune is in his own hand, A wife* " *Man ſhall command the Stars, Every one is paſſable to Virtue,* &c." if un-derftood, and ufed, rather as Spurs to Induftry, than as Stirrups to Infolence, and rather to beget in Men a Conftancy and Firmnefs of Refolution, than Arrogance and Oftentation, they are defervedly efteemed found and whole-fome. And hence, doubtlefs, it is, that they find reception in the Breafts of great Men, and make it fometimes difficult for them to diffemble their Thoughts. So we find *Auguſtus Cæſar,* who was rather different from, than inferior to his Uncle, tho' doubtlefs a more moderate Man, required his Friends, as they ftood about his Death-bed, to give him their Applaufe at his Exit: as if conſcious to himfelf, that he had acted his part well upon the Stage of Life. And this part of Doctrine alfo is to be reckoned as *defiient:* not but that it has been much ufed and beaten in Practice, tho' not taken notice of in Books. Wherefore, according to our Cuftom, we fhall here fet down fome Heads upon the Subject, under the *Title* of the SELF-POLITICIAN, *or the* ART *of* RISING IN LIFE.

4. It may feem a new and odd kind of thing, to teach Men how to make their Fortunes. A Doctrine which every one would gladly learn, before he finds the Difficulties of it. For the things required to procure Fortune, are not fewer or lefs difficult than thofe to procure Virtue. It is as rigid and hard a thing to become a true *Politician,* as a true *Moraliſt.* Yet the treat-ing of this Subject nearly concerns the Credit, and Merit, of Learning. 'T is of great importance to the Honour of Learning, that Men of Bufinefs fhould know, Erudition is not like a Lark, which flies high, and delights in nothing but finging, but that 'tis rather like a Hawk, which foars aloft indeed, but can ftoop when fhe finds it convenient, and feize her Prey. Again, this alfo regards the Perfection of Learning, for the true Rule of a

perfect

[a] *Dextra mihi Deus, & Telum, quod miſſile libro,*
Nunc ad ſit——

perfect Enquiry, is, that *nothing can be found in the material Globe which has not its correspondent in the Cryftalline Globe, the Underftanding*, or, that there is Nothing found *in Practice*, which has not *its particular Doctrine and Theory* [b] But Learning efteems the Building of a *private Fortune*, as a Work of an inferior kind For no Man's *private Fortune* can be an End any way worthy of his Exiftence Nay, it frequenly happens, that Men of eminent Virtues renounce their Fortune, to purfue the Things of a fublimer Nature Yet even *private Fortune*, as it is the inftrument of Virtue, and doing good, is a *particular Doctrine*, worthy of Confideration

II 5 This *Doctrine* has its *Precepts*, fome whereof are *fummary* or *collective*, and others *fcattered* and *various* The *collective Precepts* are founded in a *juft Knowledge*, (1) of *ourfelves*, and (2) of *others* Let this, therefore, be the firft, whereon the Knowledge of the reft principally turns, *that we procure to ourfelves, as far as poffible, the Window once required by Momus* who feeing fo many Corners and Receffes in the Structure of the human Heart, found fault that it fhould want a Window, thro' which thofe dark and crooked turnings might be viewed This Window may be procured by diligently informing ourfelves of the particular Perfons we have to deal with, their Tempers, Defires, Views, Cuftoms, Habits, the Affiftances, Helps, and Affurances, whereon they principally rely, and whence they receive their Power, their Defects and Weakneffes, whereat they chiefly lie open, and are acceffible, their Friends, Factions, Patrons, Dependants, Enemies, Enviers, Rivals, their Times, and Manner of Accefs, their Principles, and the Rules they prefcribe themfelves, &c But our Information fhould not wholly reft in the *Perfons*, but alfo extend to the *particular Actions*, which from time to time come upon the Anvil, how they are conducted, with what Succefs; by whofe Affiftance promoted, by whom oppofed, of what Weight and Moment they are, what their Confequences, &c For a *Knowledge of prefent Actions*, is not only very advantageous in itfelf, but without it the *Knowledge of Perfons* will be very fallacious and uncertain For Men change along with their Actions, and are one thing whilft entangled and furrounded with Bufinefs, and another when they return to themfelves And thefe particular *Informations* with regard to *Perfons*, as well as *Actions*, are like the minor Propofitions in every active Syllogifm · for no Truth, nor excellence of Obfervations, or Axioms, whence the *major political Propofitions* are formed, can give a firm Conclufion, if there be an Error in the *minor Propofition* And that fuch a kind of Knowledge is procurable, *Solomon* affures us, who fays, that " *Counfel in the Heart of Man is like a deep Water, but a wife Man will draw it out* " for altho' the Knowledge itfelf does not fall under *Precept*, becaufe it regards Individuals, yet Inftructions may be given, of ufe for fetching it out

6. Men may be known fix different ways, viz. (1.) by their *Countenance*, (2) their *Words*, (3) their *Actions*, (4) their *Tempers*, (5) their *Ends*, and (6.) by the *Relation* of others. (1.) As to the *Countenance*, there is no great matter

Side notes: *Collective Precepts, viz be Information to be procured firft of other, next of ourfelves*

Six ways of knowing Men, (1) by the Countenance

[b] This is more fully explained and illuftrated in the *Novum Organum*, where *Theory* and *Practice* are treated together, as conftituting one infeparable *Doctrine*

p....er i..t.t o'd Proverb, *Fro..t..th'a fide* for altho' this may be faid, w..r.. fo..e..t..h of the external and general Compofure of the Countenance .nd Gefture, yet there lie conceal.d certa.. more fubtile Motions, and Actio..s of the E..es, Face, Looks and Behaviour, by which the Gate, as it were of the Mind, is unlocked and thrown open Who was more clofe th.n *T..o..* ? yet *Ta...*, on feveral occafions, obferves a Difference be-t..xt his Speech, and his inward S..ntiments. And indeed 'tis hard to find fo great, and mafterly a Diffembler, or a Countenance, fo well broke and commanded, as to carry on an artful and counterfeit Difcourfe, with-out fome w.. or other betraying it

7 '2, The *Word..* of Men are full of Deceit but this is well detected two ...s, t.. either when Words are fpoke on the *fudden*, or in *paffion* So *T..r..* being fuddenly furprized, and hurry'd beyond himfelf, with a fting-ing Speech from *Ag..p..a*, went a ftep out of his natural Diffimulation For, fays *Ta..t..*, fhe *t..is drew an u..commo.. Expreffion from his fecret Breaft, a..d..er ..t..er o..ve..g offe..d..d, becau..e fhe d..d ..ot rule* Whence the Poet not unjuftly calls thefe Perturbations, *Tortures*, Mankind being compell'd by them to betray their own Secrets[a] And Experience fhews, that there are very few fo true to their own Secrets, and of fo clofe a temper, as not fometime, thro' Anger, Oftentation, Love to a Friend, Impotence of Mind, or fome other Affection, to reveal their inward Thoughts But nothing fearches all the Corners of the Mind fo much, as *Diffimulation practifed againft Diffi-mulation*, according to the *Spanifh* Proverb, *tell a Lye, and find a Truth*[b].

8 (3) Even *Facts* themfelves, tho' the fureft Pledges of the human Mind, are not altogether to be trufted, unlefs firft attentively view'd and confider'd, as to their Magnitude and Propriety For 'tis certain, that Deceit gets it-felf a credit in fmall things, that it may practife to more advantage in larger And the *Italian* thinks himfelf *upon the Crofs with the Cryer*, or put up to fale, when, without manifeft caufe, he is treated better than ufual. For fmall Favours lull Mankind, and difarm them both of Caution and In-duftry; whence they are properly call'd by *Demofthenes*, the *Baits of Sloth*. Again, we may clearly fee the crafty and ambiguous nature of fome Actions, which pafs for Benefits, from that Trick practifed by *Mucianus* up-on *Antony* for after a pretended Reconciliation, he moft treacheroufly ad-vanced many of *Antony*'s Friends to *Lieutenancies, Tribunefhips*, &c and, by this Cunning, entirely difarm'd and defeated him, thus winning over *Antony*'s Friends to himfelf[c]

9 But the fureft Key for unlocking the Minds of others, turns upon fearching and fifting, either their *Tempers* and *Natures*, or their *Ends* and *Defigns* and the more weak and fimple, are beft judged by their *Temper*, but the more prudent and clofe, by their *Defigns*. It was prudently and wittily, tho', in my judgment, not fubftantially, advifed by the Pope's *Nuncio*, as to the choice of another to fucceed him, in his refidence at a foreign Court, that

a ——————*Vina tortus & ira*
b See the Author's *Effay* upon Simulation and Diffimulation, SUPPLEMENT XI
c See *Tacitus Hiftor* Lib. IV cap. 39.

that they fhould by no means fend one remarkably, but rather tolerably wife , becaufe a Man wifer than ordinary, could never imagine what the People of that Nation were likely to do   'Tis, doubtlefs, a common Error, particularly in prudent Men, to meafure others by the Model of their own Capacity   Whence they frequently over-fhoot the Mark , by fuppofing that Men project and form greater things to themfelves, and practife more fubtil Arts, than ever enter'd their Minds.   This is elegantly intimated by the *Italian* Proverb   *There is always lefs Mony, lefs Wifdom, and lefs Honefty, than People imagine.*   And therefore, in Men of fmall Capacities, who commit many Abfurdities , a Conjecture mult rather be form'd from the Propenfity of their Nature, than from their Ends in view   Whence Princes alfo, tho' for a quite different reafon, are beft judged by their Tempers , as private Perfons are by their Ends   For Princes, who are at the top of human Defires, have feldom any Ends to afpire after, with Ardor and Perfeverance , by the Situation and Diftance whereof, a Direction and Meafure might be taken of their other Actions   And this, among others, is a principal reafon why their *Hearts*, as the Scripture declares, are *unfearchable*   But every private Man is like a Traveller, who proceeds intently to the End of his Journey, where he fets up   Hence one may tolerably conjecture what a private Man will, or will not do , for if a thing be conducive to his Ends, 'tis probable he will do it , and *vice verfa*   And this Information, from the diverfity of the *Ends* and *Natures* of Men, may be taken comparatively, as well as fimply , fo as to difcover what Humour or Difpofition over-rules the reft   Thus *Tigellinus,* when he found himfelf outdone by *Turpilianus,* in adminiftring and fuggefting to *Nero*'s Pleafures, fearch'd, as *Tacitus* fays, into the Fears of *Nero* , and by this means got rid of his Rival [a]

10   As for that fecond-hand Knowledge of Mens Minds, which is had from the relation of others, it will be fufficient to obferve of it, that *Defects* and *Vices* are beft learnt from Enemies , *Virtues* and *Abilities*, from *Friends* , Manners and Times, from *Servants* , and Opinions and Thoughts, from *intimate Acquaintance*   for popular Fame is light, and the Judgment of Superiors uncertain , before whom Men walk more masked, and fecret   The truefi Character comes from *Domefticks*. *(6.) By the Relation of others*

11   But the fhorteft way to this whole Enquiry, refts upon three Particulars , *viz* (1) in procuring numerous Friendfhips, with fuch as have an extenfive and general Knowledge, both of Men and Things , or, at leaft, in fecuring a Set of particular Friends, who, according to the diverfity of Occafions, may be always ready to give a folid Information upon any point that fhall turn up   (2) In obferving a prudent Mean, and Moderation, between the freedom of Difcourfe and Silence , ufing *Franknefs* of *Speech* moft frequently   but when the thing requires it, *Taciturnity*. For opennefs of Speech invites and excites others to ufe the fame towards ourfelves, which brings many things to our knowledge   whilft Taciturnity procures Truft, and makes Men willing to depofite their Secrets with us, as in their own Bofom   (3) In gradually acquiring fuch a Habit of Watchfulnefs and Intentnefs *A fummary Reduction of the fix preceding Rules.*

[a] See *Tacitus Annal* Lib XVI Cap 18, 19

... is ... Difcourfe and Action, as at once to promote the bufinefs in hand, yet take notice of incidental matters For, as *Epictetus* would have a Philofopher fay to himfelf, in every Action, " *I will do this, yet keep to my* " *Rule.*" fo a Politician fhould refolve with himfelf in every Bufinefs, " *I ... difpatch Point, and yet learn fomewhat of future ufe.*" And therefore fuch Tempers as are wholly intent upon a prefent Bufinefs, without at all regarding what may intervene, which *Montaign* acknowledges was his own Defect, make excellent Minifters of State, but fail in advancing their private Fortunes A principal Caution muft alfo be had, to reftrain the Impetuofity, and too great Alacrity of the Mind, left much Knowledge fhould drive us on to meddle in many Matters for nothing is more unfortunate and rafh, than fuch a Procedure Therefore, the variety of Knowledge, to be here procured of Men and Things, comes but to this, that we make a judicious Choice both of the Matters we undertake, and of the Perfons whofe Affiftance we ufe, that we may thence know how to manage and difpofe all things with the greater Dexterity and Safety

The Know-
ledge of
ourfelf and
carefulnefs of
Self-Exam-
ination

III 12 Next to the Knowledge of others, comes the *Knowledge of our-* *felves* and it requires no lefs diligence, but rather more, to get a true and exact Information of ourfelves, than of others For that Oracle, *Know* *thy felf*, is not only a Rule of general Prudence, but has alfo a principal place in *Politics* And St *James* excellently obferves of Mankind, that " *he* " *who views his Face in a Glafs, inftantly forgets his Features*" Whence we had need be often looking And this alfo holds in Politicks But there is a difference in Glaffes The *divine one*, wherein we are to behold ourfelves, is the *Word of God*, but the *political Glafs* is no other, than the *State of Things* *and Times wherein we live* A Man, therefore, muft make a thorough Examination, not partially like a Self-Lover, into his own Faculties, Powers, and Abilities, and again, into his Defects, Inabilities, and Obftacles fumming up the account, fo as to make the latter conftantly appear greater, and the former rather lefs than they are And upon fuch an Examination, the following Particulars may come to be confider'd

(1) *Whether*
the Temper
fuits the
Time

13 Let the *firft Particular* be, *how far a Man's Manners and Temper* *fuit with the Time* for if they agree in all refpects, he may act more freely, and at large, and follow the bent of his Genius, but if there be any Contrariety, then he muft walk more cautioufly and covertly in the whole Scene of his Life, and appear lefs in publick as *Tiberius* did, who, being confcious that his Temper fuited not with the Age, never frequented the publick Shews, and for the laft twelve Years of his Life, came not to the Senate Whereas, *Auguftus* lived continually in open fight

(2) *Whether*
the feveral
kinds of Life
are agreeable

14 Let the *fecond Confideration* be, *how a Man can relifh the Profeffions,* *or Kinds of Life in ufe, and repute*, out of which he is to make a choice fo that if his Profeffion be not already enter'd upon, he may take that which is moft fuitable to his Genius But if he be already got into a kind of Life, for which he is unfit, that he may, upon the firft opportunity, quit it, and take to another. As *Valentine Borgia* did, who being educated by

his

his Father for the Priesthood, afterwards renounced it, follow'd his own Inclination, and appear'd in a military Character

15 Let a *third Confideration* be, *how a Man ftands, compared with his* (3) *Whether* *Equals and Rivals*, who may alfo probably be his Competitors in his Fortune *there be no*, and let him hold that Courfe of Life, in which there is the greateft *Rivals* want of eminent Men, and wherein 'tis moft likely that himfelf may rife the higheft as *Cæfar* did, who was firft an Orator, a Pleader, and fcarce any thing more than a Gown-man but when he found that *Cicero, Hortenfius*, and *Catulus* bore away the Prize of Eloquence, and that none had greatly fignaliz'd themfelves in War, except *Pompey*, he quitted the Gown, and taking a long farewell of Civil Power, went over to the Arts of the General and the Emperor, whereby he rofe to the top Pinnacle of Sovereignty

16 Let the *fourth Confideration* be, *to regard one's own Nature and Tem-*(4.) *To regard* *per, in the choice of Friends and Dependants* For different Men require dif-*one's own Tem-* ferent kinds of Friends fome, thofe that are grave and fecret others, fuch *per in the* as are bold and oftentatious, &c. 'Tis worth obferving, of what kind the *choice of* Friends of *Julius Cæfar* were, viz *Antony, Hirtius Balbus, Dolobella, Pollio*, &c who ufually fwore to *die, that he might live*[a], thereby expreffing an infinite Affection for *Cæfar*, but an Arrogance and Contempt towards every body elfe And they were all Men diligent in Bufinefs, but of no great Fame and Reputation.

17. Let a *fifth Confideration* be, *to beware of Examples*, *and not fondly*(5) *Not to* *fquare one's felf to the Imitation of others*, as if what was atchieved by them, *follow Exam-* muft needs be atchieved by us, without confidering the difference there may *ples too clofe.* be between our own Difpofition and Manners, compared with theirs we propofe to imitate *Pompey* manifeftly fell into this Error, who, as *Cicero* writes of him, had thefe Words often in his Mouth, *Sylla could do this, why* *fhall not I?* In which particular, he greatly impos'd upon himfelf For *Sylla*'s Temper and Method of acting, differ'd infinitely from his, the one's being fierce, violent, and preffing to the end, the other's compos'd, mindful of the Laws, and directing all to Majefty, and Reputation whence he was greatly curb'd, and reftrain'd, in executing his Defigns. And thefe Confiderations may ferve as a Specimen of the reft

18. But 'tis not enough for a Man to know himfelf, he muft alfo confider *That a Man* how he may moft commodioufly and prudently, (1) *fhew*, (2) *exprefs*, *muft learn* (3) *wind* and *fafhion* himfelf (1) As for *fhew*, we fee nothing more fre-*felf to ad-* quent in Life, than for the lefs capable Man to make the greater figure *vantage* 'Tis therefore no fmall excellence of *Prudence*, by means of a certain Art, and Grace, to reprefent one's beft fide to others; by fetting out our own Virtues, Merits, and Fortune, to advantage, which may be done, without Arrogance, or rendring one's felf difagreeable And, on the other fide, artificially concealing our Vices, Defects, Misfortunes, and Difgraces, dwelling upon the former, and turning them, as it were, to the light, but pal-

[a] *Ita vivente Cæfare moriar*

liating

l.ting the L.tt.., or effacing them by a well-adapted Construction, or Inter-
pr.t.t.o. Hence I...t.. says of *Muciarus,* the most prudent Man of
his Tim., and the most indefatigable in Business, that " *he had an Art of*
" *.....g .. f.. f.c.f whatever he spoke or acted* [a] " And certainly it
req res ..n.e Art, to prevent this Conduct from becoming fulsome, and
despic.ble yet Ostentation, tho' to the first degree of Vanity, is a Fault in
E..., r.ther than in *Po'...* For as 'tis usually said of Calumny, that
if l.d on bold.y, some of it will stick so it may be said of Ostentation,
unless perfectly monstrous and ridiculous, ' *paint yourself strongly, and some*
' *o.. ...ll 'q ?* " Doubtless it will dwell with the Croud, tho' the wiser sort
smile at it, so that the Reputation procured with the number, will abundantly reward the Contempt of a few But if this Ostentation be managed
with Decency and Discretion, it may greatly contribute to raise a Man's
Reputation, as particularly, if it carry the appearance of native Candour
and Ingenuity, or be used in times surrounded with Dangers, as among the
military Men in time of war, &c Or again, if our own Praises are let
fall, as it were by accident, and be not too seriously or largely insisted on ;
or if any one, in praising himself, at the same time mixes it with Censure and
Ridicule, or lastly, if he does it not spontaneously, but is provoked to it by
the Insolence and Reproach of others And there are many who, being by
Nature solid, and consequently wanting in this Art of spreading Canvas to
their own honour, find themselves punished for their Modesty, with some diminution of their Dignity

19 But, however Persons of weak Judgment, or too rigid Morals, may
disallow this *Ostentation of Virtue*, no one will deny, that we should endeavour to keep *Virtue from being undervalued thro' own neglect*, and less esteem'd
than it deserves This Diminution, in the Esteem of Virtue, happens three
ways, *viz* (1) when a Person presents, and thrusts himself, and his Service
into a Business unasked. for such Services are thought sufficiently rewarded
by accepting them (2) When a Man, at the beginning of a Business, over-
exerts himself, and performs that all at once, which should have been done
gradually tho' this, indeed, gains early Commendation, where Affairs succeed, but in the end it produces Satiety (3) When a Man is too quick,
and light, in receiving the Fruit of his Virtue, in Praise, Applause, and Favour, and pleases himself therewith against which, there is this prudent
Admonition, ' *beware lest thou seem unaccustom'd to great things, if such small*
" *o..... de'gl'ts..* '

20 A diligent *Concealment of Defects*, is no less important, than a prudent and artful Manifestation of Virtues *Defects* are principally conceal'd
and cover'd under three Cloaks, *viz* (1) *Caution,* (2) *Pretext,* and
(3) *Aff...ce* (1) We call that *Caution,* when a Man prudently keeps
from meddling in Matters, to which he is unequal, whilst, on the other
hand, daring and restless Spirits are injudiciously busying themselves in things
they are not acquainted with, and thereby publish and proclaim their own
Defects (2) We call that *Pretext,* when a Man, with Sagacity, and Prudence,

paves

* See *Tacit Histor* Lib II Cap 80.

paves and prepares himſelf a way, for ſecuring a favourable and commodious Interpretation of his *Vices* and *Defects*, as proceeding from different Principles, or having a different Tendency, than is generally thought For as to the *Concealment of Vices*, the Poet ſaid well, *that Vice often skulks in the Verge of Virtue* [a] Therefore, when we find any *Defect* in ourſelves, we muſt endeavour to borrow the Figure and *Pretext* of the neighbouring Virtue for a Shelter thus the Pretext of *Dulneſs* is Gravity, that of *Indolence*, Conſiderateneſs, &c And 'tis of ſervice to give out ſome probable Reaſon for not exerting our utmoſt Strength, and ſo make a *Neceſſity* appear a *Virtue* (3) *Aſſurance*, indeed, is a daring, but a very certain and effectual Remedy, whereby a Man profeſſes himſelf abſolutely to ſlight, and deſpiſe thoſe things he could not obtain, like crafty Merchants, who uſually raiſe the Price of their own Commodities, and ſink the Price of other Mens Tho' there is another kind of *Aſſurance*, more impudent than this, by which a Man brazens out his own *Defects*, and forces them upon others for *Excellencies*, and the better to ſecure this end, he will feign a diſtruſt of himſelf, in thoſe things wherein he really excels like Poets, who, if you except to any particular Verſe in their Compoſition, will preſently tell you, *that ſingle Line coſt them more pains than all the reſt*, and then produce you another, as ſuſpected by themſelves, for your Opinion, whilſt, of all the number, they know it to be the beſt, and leaſt liable to Exception But above all, nothing conduces more to the well repreſenting a Man's ſelf, and ſecuring his own Right, than not to diſarm one's ſelf by too much *Sweetneſs*, and *Good-nature*, which expoſes a Man to Injuries, and Reproaches, but rather, in all caſes, at times, to dart out ſome Spirks of a free and generous Mind, that have no leſs of the Sting than the Honey This guarded Behaviour, attended with a ready Diſpoſition to vindicate themſelves, ſome Men have from Accident and Neceſſity, by means of ſomewhat inherent in their Perſon or Fortune, as we find in the Deformed, Illegitimate, and Diſgraced, who, if they do not want Virtue, generally prove fortunate

21 (2) The *expreſſing*, or *declaring of a Man's ſelf*, is a very different thing from the *ſhewing himſelf*, as not relating to Virtue, but to the particular Actions of Life And here nothing is more politick, than to obſerve a prudent or ſound Moderation, or Medium, in diſcloſing or concealing one's Mind, as to particular Actions. For tho' profound Silence, the hiding of Counſels, and managing all things by blind and deaf Artifice, is an uſeful and extraordinary thing; yet, it often happens, that Diſſimulation produces Errors, which prove Snares And we ſee, that the Men of greateſt repute for Politicks, ſcruple not openly, and generouſly, to declare their Ends, without Diſſimulation thus *Sylla* openly declared, *he wiſh'd all Mortals happy, or unhappy, as they were his Friends, or Enemies* So *Cæſar*, upon his firſt Expedition into *Gaul*, profeſs'd *he had rather be the firſt Man in an obſcure Village, than the ſecond at* Rome And when the War was begun, he proved no Diſſembler, if *Cicero* ſays truly of him, *that he did not refuſe, but, in a manner, required to be called Tyrant, as he was*. So we find, in an

He muſt expreſs himſelf

Gg 2 Epiſtle

[a] *Sæpe latet vitium proximitate boni*

Epiftle of *Cicero* to *Atticus*, how little of a Diffembler *Augustus* was, who, at his firft entrance upon Affairs, whilft he remain'd the Delight of the Senate, ufed to fwear in this form, when he harangued the People, *ita Parentis Heros configui liceat* which was no lefs than Tyranny itfelf 'Tis true, to falve the matter a little, he would at thofe times ftretch his Hand towards the Statue of *Julius Cæfar*, erected in the place, whilft the Audience fmiled, applauded, admired, and cried out among themfelves, *What does he do therein?* &c but never fufpected him of any ill Defign, who thus candidly and ingenuoufly fpoke his mind   And yet all thefe we have named, were profperous Men   *Pompey*, on the other hand, who endeavour'd at the fame Ends, by more dark and concealed Methods, wholly bent himfelf, by numberlefs Stratagems, to cover his Defires and Ambition, whilft he brought the State to Confufion, that it might then of neceffity fubmit to him, and he thus procure the Sovereignty, to appearance againft his will   And when he thought he had gain'd his Point, as being made *fole Conful*, which no one ever was before him, he found himfelf never the nearer, becaufe thofe who would, doubtlefs, have affifted him, underftood not his Intentions   fo that at length he was obliged to go in the beaten Path, and under pretence of oppofing *Cæfar*, procured himfelf Arms, and an Army   fo flow, cafual, and generally unfuccefsful, are the Counfels cover'd with Diffimulation!   And *Tacitus* feems to have had the fame Sentiment, when he makes the *Art free of Diffimulation an inferior Prudence*, compared with *Policy*, attributing the former to *Tiberius*, and the latter to *Augustus* for fpeaking of *Livia*, &c. fays, *fhe was well temper'd with the Arts of her Husband, and Diffimulation of her Son*

The methods of leading and forming the Mind. 22 3 As for the *leading* and *forming of the Mind*, we fhould, doubtlefs, do our utmoft to render it pliable, and by no means ftiff and refractory, to Occafions and Opportunities, for *to continue the fame Men, when we ought to change, is to give up Opportunities of Bufinefs* can meet to that is, if Men remain as they did, and follow their own Nature after the Opportunities are changed. Whence *Livy*, introducing the elder *Cato* as a moft fkilful Architect of his own Fortune adds, that *he was of a pliant Temper* and hence it is, that grave, folid and unchangeable Natures generally meet with more Refpect than others.   This Defect fome Men have implanted in them by Nature, as being in themfelves ftiff, knotty and unfit for bending, but in others, 'tis acquir'd by Cuftom, which is a fecond Nature, or from an Opinion, which flily fteals into Mens Minds, that they fhould never change the method of acting, they had once found good and profperous   Thus *Machiavel* rightly obferves of *Fabius Maximus*, that *he would obftinately retain his moderate Cuftom of delaying and protracting the War, when now the times were changed, and required brisker Meafures*   In others again, the fame Defect proceeds from want of Judgment, when Men do not feafonably diftinguifh the Periods of Things and Actions, but alter too late, after the Opportunity is flipt   And fomething of this kind *Demosthenes* reprehended in the *Athenians*, when he faid, *they were like Rufticks in a Fencing-School, who always, after a Blow, guard the part that was hit, and not before*

fore And lastly, this *Defect* happens in others, because they are unwilling that the labour they have taken in the way once entered, should be lost, and know not how to found a Retreat but rather trust they shall conquer Occasions by Perseverance But this stickage and restiveness of the Mind, from whatever Root it proceeds, is highly prejudicial to Business, and Mens private Fortunes on the contrary, nothing is more politick, than to make the Wheels of the Mind concentrick with the Wheels of Fortune, and capable of turning together with them And thus much of the two *summary* or *collective Precepts, for advancing one's Fortune*

IV. 23 The *scatter'd Precepts for rising in Life*, are numerous · we shall single out a few by way of Example The *first* is, that the *Builder of his Fortune properly use and apply his Rule*, that is, accustom his Mind to measure and estimate the Price and Value of Things, as they conduce more or less to his particular Fortune and Ends and this with diligence, not by halves 'Tis surprizing, yet very true, that many have the *Logical Part of their Mind set right, and the Mathematical wrong*, and judge truly of the Consequences of things, but very unskilfully of their Value. Hence some Men are fond of Access to, and Familiarity with *Princes*, others, of popular Fame, and fancy these to be great Enjoyments whereas both of them are frequently full of Envy and Dangers Others, again, measure things according to their difficulty, and the labour bestowed in procuring them, imagining themselves must needs have advanced as far as they have moved So *Cæsar*, to describe how diligent and indefatigable the younger *Cato* was to little purpose, said in the way of *Irony, that he did all things with great labour* And hence it happens, that Men frequently deceive themselves, when having the assistance of some great or honourable Personage, they promise themselves all manner of Success whilst the truth is, they are not the *greatest*, but the *fittest Instruments that perform Business best and quickest* For improving the true *Mathematicks of the Mind*, it should be principally noted, what ought to come first, what second, &c in the raising and promoting a Man's Fortune And, in the first place, we set down the *Emendation of the Mind* for by removing the Obstacles, and levelling the Inequalities of the Mind, a way may be sooner open'd to Fortune, than the Impediments of the Mind be removed, with the assistance of Fortune. And, in the second place, we set down *Riches*, whereto most, perhaps, would have assign'd the first, as their use is so extensive But we condemn this Opinion, for a reason like that of *Machiavel*, in a similar case · for tho' it was an establish'd Notion, that *Money is the Sinews of War*, he said, more justly, that *War had no Sinews, but those of good Soldiers*. In the same manner it may be truly affirm'd, that the *Sinews of Fortune are not Money, but rather the Powers of the Mind*, Address, Courage, Resolution, Intrepidity, Perseverance, Moderation, Industry, &c In the *third place*, come *Fame* and *Reputation*, and this the rather, because they have certain Tides and Seasons, wherein, if they be not opportunely used, 'twill be difficult to recover them again For 'tis a hopeless Attempt, to recover a lost Reputation. In the last place, we set down *Honours*, which are easier acquir'd by any of the

[margin notes: Instances of miscellaneous Precepts for rising in Life, viz to estimate things justly. To amend the Mind To procure Wealth. Fame. Honours.]

the former thrice, much more by a Conjunction of them all, than any one of them can be procured by Honours But, as much depends upon obſerving the Order of Things, ſo likewiſe, in obſerving the Order of Time, in diſturbing of which, Men frequently err, and haſten to the End, when they ſhould only have conſulted the Beginning and ſuddenly flying at the greateſt things of all, raſhly ſkip over thoſe in the middle, thus neglecting the uſeful Precept, *Attend to what is immediately before you.*

24 Our ſecond Precept is, *to beware of being carried by Greatneſs, and Preſumption of Mind, to things too difficult, and thus of ſtriving againſt the ſtream* 'Tis a prudent Advice, in the raiſing of one's Fortune, to yield to Neceſſity [a] Let us look all round us, and obſerve where things lie open, where they are incloſed, and blocked up, where they ſtoop, and where they mount, and not miſemploy our Strength, where the way is impaſſable. In doing this, we ſhall prevent Repulſe, not ſtick too long in Particulars, win a Reputation of being moderate, give little offence, and laſtly, gain a certain ſort of Felicity whilſt the things that would probably have happen'd of themſelves, will be attributed to our own Induſtry

25 A third Precept, which ſeems ſomewhat to croſs the former, tho' not when well underſtood, is, *that we do not always wait for Opportunities, but ſometimes excite and lead them* This, *Demoſthenes* intimates in a high Strain, when he ſays " *that as 'tis a Maxim for the General to lead his Army, ſo a* " *wiſe Man ſhould lead things, make them execute his Will, and not himſelf* " *be obliged to follow Events*" And if we attend, we ſhall find two different kinds of Men, held equal to the management of Affairs for ſome know how to make an advantageous uſe of Opportunities, yet contrive or project nothing of themſelves, whilſt others are wholly intent upon forming Schemes, and neglect the laying hold of Opportunities, as they offer but either of theſe Faculties is quite lame, without the other

26 'Tis a *fourth Precept to undertake nothing that neceſſarily requires much time*, but conſtantly to remember, *Time is ever on the Wing* [b] And the only reaſon why thoſe who addict themſelves to toilſome Profeſſions, and Employs as Lawyers, Advoſer, &c are leſs verſed in making their Fortune, is the want of time from their other Studies, to gain a knowledge of Particulars, wait for Opportunities, and project their own Riſing We ſee in the Courts of Princes, the moſt effectual Men in making their own Fortunes, and invading the Fortunes of others, are ſuch as have no publick Employ, but are continually plotting their own Riſe and Advantage.

27. A *fifth Precept* is, that we, *in ſome meaſure, imitate Nature, which does nothing in vain* and this is not very difficult, if we ſkilfully mix and interlace our Affairs of all kinds For, in every Action, the Mind is to be ſo inſtructed and prepared, and our Intentions to be ſo dependant upon, and ſubordinate to each other, that if we cannot gain the higheſt Step, we may contentedly take up with the ſecond, or even the third But if we can fix on no part of our Proſpect, then we ſhould direct the pains we have been at to ſome other End ſo, as if we receive no benefit for the preſent, yet at leaſt, to

gain

[a] Fac ut accede, *Denique*
[b] Sed fugit interea, fugit irreparabile tempus

gain fomewhat of future advantage. But if we can obtain no folid Good from our Endeavours, neither in prefent nor in future, let us endeavour, at leaft, to gain a Reputation by it, or fome one thing or other; always computing with ourfelves, that, from every Action, we receive fome advantage more or lefs, and by no means fuffering the Mind to defpond, or be aftonifh'd, when we fail of our principal End. For there is nothing more contrary to *political Prudence*, than to be wholly intent upon any fingle thing: as he who is fo, muft lofe numberlefs Opportunities, which come fide-ways in Bufinefs, and which, perhaps, would be more favourable and conducive to the things that fhall turn up hereafter, than to thofe that were before purfued. Let Men, therefore, well underftand the Rule, " *thefe things fhould* " *be done,* but *thofe fhould not be omitted.*"

28. The *fixth Precept* is, that *we do not too peremptorily oblige ourfelves to* *any thing*, tho' it feem, at firft fight, not liable to contingency: but always referve a Window open to fly out, or fome fecret back-door for Retreat. *Not to be too ftrictly tied down to any thing*

29. A *feventh Precept* is, that old one of *Bias*, provided it be ufed not treacheroufly, but only by way of Caution and Moderation. " *Love as if* " *you were once to Hate, and Hate as if you were once to Love.*" For it furprizingly betrays and corrupts all forts of Utility, to plunge one's felf too far in unhappy Friendfhips, vexatious and turbulent Quarrels, or childifh and empty Emulations. And fo much, by way of Example, upon the *Doctrine, or Art, of Rifing in Life.* *Not to be too ftrongly attached to Perfons*

30. We are well aware, that good Fortune may be had upon eafier Conditions than are here laid down: for it falls almoft fpontaneoufly upon fome Men, whilft others procure it only by diligence and Affiduity, without much Art, tho' ftill with fome Caution. But as *Cicero*, when he draws the *perfect Orator*, does not mean that every *Pleader* either could or fhould be like him, and as in defcribing the *Prince*, or the *Politician*, which fome have undertaken, the Model is form'd to the perfect Rules of Art, and not according to common Life: the fame Method is obferved by us, in this *Sketch of the Self-Politican.* *Good Fortune fometimes comes eafy.*

31. It muft be obferved, that the *Precepts* we have laid down upon this Subject, are all of them lawful, and not fuch immoral Artifices, as *Machavel* fpeaks of, who directs Men to have little regard for Virtue itfelf, but only for the fhew, and publick reputation of it: " *becaufe,* fays he, *the* " *Credit and Opinion of Virtue, are a Help to a Man, but Virtue itfelf a Hin-* " *drance.*" He alfo directs his *Politician* to ground all his Prudence on this Suppofition, that *Men cannot be truly and fafely worked to his purpofe, but by Fear*, and therefore advifes him to endeavour, by all poffible means, to fubject them to Dangers and Difficulties. Whence his *Politician* may feem to be what the *Italians* call a *Sower of Thorns*. So *Cicero* cites this *Principle*, " *let our Friends fall, provided our Enemies perifh,*" upon which the *Triumvirs* acted, in purchafing the Death of their Enemies, by the Deftruction of their neareft Friends. So *Catiline* became a Difturber and Incendiary of the State, that he might the better fifh his Fortune in troubled *The preceding Precepts not immoral*

Waters;

Waters, declaring, that *if his Fortune was set on fire, he would quench it, not with Water, but Destruction* And so *Lysander* would say, that *Children were to be deceiv'd with Sweet-Meats, and Men by false Oaths* and there are numerous other corrupt and pernicious Maxims of the same kind, more indeed, as in all other cases, than of such as are just and sound   Now if any Man delights in this *corrupt* or *tainted Prudence*, we deny not but he may take a short cut to Fortune, as being thus disentangled, and set at large from all restraint of Laws, Good-nature and Virtue, and having no regard but to his own Promotion tho' 'tis in Life as in a Journey, where the shortest Road is the dirtiest, and yet the better, not much about

32 But if Men were themselves, and not carry'd away with the Tempest of Ambition, they would be so far from studying these wicked Arts, as rather to view them, not only in that general Map of the World, which shews all things to be Vanity and Vexation of Spirit, but also in that more particular one, which represents a Life separate from good Actions, as a Curse, that the more eminent this Life, the greater the Curse, that the noblest Reward of Virtue, is Virtue itself, that the extremest Punishment of Vice, is Vice itself and that, as *Virgil* excellently observes, good Actions are rewarded, as bad ones also are punished, by the Consciousness that attends them [a]   And, indeed, whilst Men are projecting, and every way racking their Thoughts, to provide and take care for their Fortunes, they ought, in the midst of all, to have an eye to the *Divine Providence*; which frequently over-turns, and brings to nought, the Machinations and deep Devices of the Wicked according to that of the Scripture, *he has conceived Iniquity, and shall bring forth Vanity* And altho' Men were not in this Pursuit to practise Injustice, and unlawful Arts, yet a continual, and restless search and striving after *Fortune*, takes up too much of their time, who have nobler things to regard   Even the Heathens observed, that Man was not made to keep his Mind always grovelling on the ground, and like the Serpent, eating the Dust [b]

33 Some, however, may flatter themselves, that by what sinister means soever their Fortune be procured, they are determined to use it well when obtained, whence it was said of *Augustus Cæsar*, and *Septimius Severus*, that " *they ought never to have been born, or never to have died* " so much Evil they committed in aspiring, and so much Good they did when seated   But let such Men know, that this recompensing of Evil with Good, tho' it may be approved after the Action, yet is justly condemned in the Design.

Lastly,

---

[a] *Quæ tibi, quæ digna viri, pro laudibus istis*
    Præmia posse rear solvi? Pulcherrima primum
    Dii moresque dabunt vestri———

This seems to be the Foundation of all *Morality, Virtue*, and true *Policy*, and well deserves to be fully explained, deduced, and applied in *Social, Civil*, and *Political Life*   See the Lord *Shaftsbury* upon *Virtue*, and our *Author* upon Ethicks, Sect XX, XXI and in his Essays *passim*

[b] *Atque affigit humo Divinæ particulam Auræ*
        Again,
    Os homini sublime dedit, cælumque tueri
    Jussit, & erectos ad sidera tollere vultus

Laſtly, it may not be amiſs, in this eager Purſuit of Fortune, for Men to cool themſelves a little with the Saying of *Charles the Fifth* to his Son, viz. " *Fortune is like the Ladies, who generally ſcorn and diſcard their over-* " *earneſt Admirers*" But this laſt Remedy belongs to ſuch, as have their Taſte vitiated by a Diſeaſe of the Mind. Let Mankind rather reſt upon the Corner-ſtone of *Divinity* and *Philoſophy*, both which nearly agree in the thing that ought firſt to be ſought For *Divinity* ſays, *Seek ye firſt the Kingdom of God, and all other things ſhall be added unto you* ſo *Philoſophy* directs us, firſt to ſeek the *Goods of the Mind*, and the reſt will either be ſupplied, or not much wanted. For altho' this Foundation, laid by human Hands, is ſometimes placed upon the *Sand*, as in the caſe of *Brutus*, who, at his death, cried out, " *O Virtue, I have reverenced thee as a* " *Being, but alas, thou art an empty Name!* yet the ſame Foundation is ever, by the Divine Hand, fixed upon a Rock. And here we conclude the *Doctrine of Riſing in Life*; and the general *Doctrine of Buſineſs*, together [a].

---

[a] The general *Doctrine of Buſineſs* has been but ſparingly touched, ſince the time of our Author The *Germans*, however, ſeem to have purſued it, in ſome tolerable degree, under the Title of *Oeconomical Prudence*, or the *Art of improving a private Fortune*. ſo as to bring it under a kind of Rules Thoſe who have applied themſelves to the Improvement of *mechanical Arts*, *Agriculture*, *Navigation*, *Trade*, *Commerce*, &c may alſo be reckoned in this number. Somewhat of the ſame kind ſeems to have been the original Deſign of the *Royal Society* and the Learned *Morhof* judges it expedient, that *Profeſſors* of this *Art* ſhould be appointed in Univerſities Doubtleſs, the Improvement and Introduction of uſeful and neceſſary *Arts*, is a ready and laudable way of advancing one's private Fortune; as by the diſcovery of *new Machines*, to eaſe the Labour of the Hand, the raiſing of Water by Fire; the ſawing of Timber by Windmills, the Invention of new Methods for ſhortening Works, the Cultivating and Tranſplanting of foreign Vegetables, the refining of Sugar, the making of Wines, the ſweetening of Sea-Water, &c according to the Deſign of the Author, in his *new Atlantis*, *Sylva Sylvarum*, and particular *Hiſtories* For the other Writers in this way, conſult *Morhof's Polyhiſtor Oeconomicus*, Tom. III. Lib. 3 *Struvius's Bibliotheca Philoſophica*, Cap 9 *de Scriptoribus Oeconomicis*, and *Stolla Introductio in Hiſtoriam Literariam, de Arte Oeconomica*.

SECT. XXVI.

The DOCTRINE *of* GOVERNMENT: *and first, of Extending the* BOUNDS *of* EMPIRE.

The Art of Empire

1 WE come now to the ART OF EMPIRE, or the *Doctrine of Governing a State*, which includes *Oeconomicks*[a], as a *City* includes a *Family*. But here, according to my former Resolution[b], I impose Silence upon myself, how well qualified foever I might feem to treat the Subject, from the conftant courfe of my Life, Studies, Employs, and the publick Pofts I have, for a long feries of Years, fuftained, even to the higheft in the Kingdom, which, thro' his Majefty's Favour, and no Merit of my own, I held for four years. And this I fpeak to Pofterity, not out of oftentation, but becaufe I judge it may fomewhat import the *Dignity of Learning*, to have a Man, born for Letters rather than any thing elfe, who fhould, by a certain Fatality, and againft the bent of his Genius, be compelled into active Life, and yet be raifed, by a prudent King, to the greateft Pofts of Honour, Truft, and Civil Employ[c]. And if I fhould hereafter have leifure to write upon *Government*, the Work will probably either be pofthumous or abortive[d]. But in the mean time, having now feated all the Sciences, each in its proper place, left fuch a high Chair as that of *Government*, fhould remain abfolutely vacant, we here obferve, that two parts of Civil Doctrine, tho' belonging not to the *Secrets of State*, but of a more open and vulgar Nature[e], are *deficient*, and fhall therefore, in our manner, give Specimens for fupplying them.

2

---

[a] The Art of Governing a Family.

[b] See above, Sect. XXIII. 1.

[c] That the Author's bent of Genius, was to Study and Contemplation, appears from feveral of his Letters to private Friends. See SUPPLEMENT V.

[d] It appears, by feveral Intimations, that the Author frequently revolved the Subject of Government in his Mind, as if he wanted, or expected to be called upon to treat it. See his LETTERS. And for a Specimen of his Abilities in this way, fee the *Political Mythology*, in his *Sapientia Veterum*, his *Political Essays*, the *Prudent Statesman*, and the *Difcourfe of a War with Spain*. But for any direct *Syftem*, or profeffed Difcourfe of Government, there was none publifhed before his Death or after, whatever he might have written, either in order to fupply the *Deficiency* of his *New Atlantis*, or the general *Deficiency* of mankind.

[e] Here again is plainly intimated the reafon why the Author does not treat the Subject of Government, as he has done the reft, viz. for fear of revealing what is not fit to be generally known. See above Sect. XXIII. 1. And yet an attentive Reader of his feveral Political Pieces, as that of *War*, the *Peace of the Church*, the *Prudent Statesman*, the *Political Mythology of the Ancients*, &c. will perhaps find abundantly more of this kind, than after fuch an Erafion could well be expected.

2 The *Art of Government* includes three *political Offices*, viz (1) the PRE- *Divided with*
SERVATION, (2.) the HAPPINESS, and (3.) the ENLARGEMENT *of a* *regard to* (1)
STATE. The two former have, in good measure, been excellently treated *the Prefervation*
by some[a], but there is nothing extant upon the laft which we therefore *Happinefs, and*
note as *deficient*, and propofe the following Sketch, by way of Example, for (3) *the En-*
fupplying it, under the Title of the MILITARY STATESMAN, or the *largement of*
DOCTRINE OF EXTENDING THE BOUNDS OF EMPIRE *States*

THE MILITARY STATESMAN

or,

A SPECIMEN OF THE DOCTRINE OF EN-LARGING THE BOUNDS OF EMPIRE

The Military
Statefman or
Doctrine of en-
larging Em-
pire, deficient

3 The Saying of *Themiftocles*, if applied to himfelf, was indecent and *The different*
haughty, but if meant in general, contains a very prudent Obfervation, *Talents of*
and as grave a Cenfure Being asked, at a Feaft, to touch a Lute; he an- *Governors*
fwered, "*He could not fiddle, but he could raife a fmall Village to a great City*"
Which Words, if taken in a *political Senfe*, excellently defcribe and diftinguifh two very different Faculties in thofe who are at the Helm of States
For upon an exact Survey, we fhall find fome, tho' but very few, that being raifed to the Council-board, the Senate, or other publick Office, can
enlarge a fmall State, or City, and yet have little Skill in Mufick but
many more, who having a good hand upon the Harp, or the Lute, that is,
at the Trifles of a *Court*, are fo far from enlarging a State, that they rather
feem defigned by Nature to overturn and ruin it, tho' ever fo happy and
flourifhing And indeed thofe bafe Arts, and Tricks, by which many
Counfellors, and Men of great place, procure the Favour of their Sovereign, and a popular Character, deferve no other name than a certain knack
of *Fiddling*, as being things more pleafing for the prefent, and more orna-
mental to the Practitioner, than ufeful, and fuited to enlarge the Bounds,
or increafe the Riches of the State, whereof they are Minifters Again,
there are, doubtlefs, Counfellors and Governours, who tho' equal to Bufinefs, and of no contemptible Abilities, may commodioufly manage Things
fo as to preferve them from manifeft Precipices and Inconveniences, tho'
they by no means have the creative Power of building and extending an Empire But whatever the Workmen be, let us regard the Work itfelf; viz.
what is to be deemed the true Extent of Kingdoms and Republicks, and
by what means this may be procured. a Subject well deferving to lie continually before *Princes*, for their diligent Meditation, left by over-rating
their own Strength, they fhould rafhly engage in too difficult and vain Enterprizes, or, thinking too meanly of their Power, fubmit to timorous and
effeminate Counfels

4.

[a] For an Account of thefe Writers, fee *Morhof's Polyhiftor*, Tom III *de Prudentia Civilis*
Scriptoribus, and *Stollii Introduct. in Hift Literar.* Cap. V *de Prudentia Politica.*

The difference of States

4. The Greatnefs of an *Empire*, in point of Bulk and Territory, is fubject to Menfuration, and for its Revenue, to Calculation   The number of Inhabitants may be known by Valuation or Tax, and the number and extent of Cities and Towns, by Survey and Maps   yet in all Civil Affairs, there is not a thing more liable to Error, than the making a true and intrinfick Eftimate of the Strength and Riches of a State   The Kingdom of Heaven is compared, not to an Acorn, or any large Nut ; but to a Grain of Muftard-feed, which tho' one of the leaft Grains, has in it a certain quick Property, and native Spirit, whereby it rifes foon, and fpreads itfelf wide : fo fome States of very large Compafs, are little fuited to extend their Limits, or procure a wider Command, whilft others of fmall Dimenfion, prove the Foundations of the greateft Monarchies.

The Greatnefs of States, how to be eftimated

5. Fortified Towns, well-ftored Arfenals, noble Breeds of War-Horfe, armed Chariots, Elephants, Engines, all kinds of Artillery, Arms, and the like, are nothing more than a Sheep in a Lion's Skin, unlefs the Nation it felf be, from its Origin and Temper, ftout and warlike.   Nor is number of Troops itfelf of any great fervice, where the Soldiers are weak and enervate   for, as *Virgil* well obferves, the Wolf cares not how large the Flock is. The *Perfian* Army in the Planes of *Arbela*, appeared to the Eyes of the *Macedonians*, as an immenfe Ocean of People, infomuch that *Alexander*'s Leaders being ftruck at the fight, counfell'd their General to fall upon them by night, but he replied, " *I will not fteal the Victory* " and 'twas found an eafier Conqueft than he expected   *Tigranes*, encamped upon a Hill, with an Army of four hundred thoufand Men, feeing the *Roman* Army, confifting but of fourteen thoufand, making up to him ; he jefted at it, and faid, " *Thofe Men are too many for an Embaffy, but much too few for a Battle* " yet before Sun-fet he found them enow to give him chafe, with infinite Slaughter.   And we have abundant Examples of the great inequality betwixt Number and Strength   This therefore may be *firft* fet down, as a fure and certain *Maxim*, and the capital of all the reft, with regard to the greatnefs of a State, that *the People be of a Military Race* ; or both by Origin and Difpofition warlike   The Sinews of War are not Money, if the Sinews of Men's Arms be wanting, as they are in a foft and effeminate Nation. 'Twas a juft Anfwer of *Solon* to *Crœfus*, who fhewed him all his Treafure : " *Yes, Sir, but if another fhou'd come with better Iron than you, he would be* " *Mafter of all this Gold* "   And therefore, all Princes whofe native Subjects are not hardy and military, fhould make a very modeft eftimate of their Power, as, on the other hand, thofe who rule a ftout and martial People, may well enough know their own Strength, if they be not otherwife wanting to themfelves   As to *hired Forces*, which is the ufual Remedy when *native Forces* are wanting, there are numerous Examples, which clearly fhew, that whatever State depends upon them, tho' it may perhaps for a time extend its Feathers beyond its Neft, yet they will mew foon after

A People op- preffed with Taxes cannot be ftrong

6 The Bleffing of *Judah* and *Iffachar* can never meet, fo that the fame Tribe, or Nation, fhould be both the *Lion's Whelp*, and the *Afs under the Burden*   nor can a People, overburdened with Taxes, ever be ftrong and warlike   'Tis true,

true, that Taxes levied by publick Consent, less dispirit, and sink the Minds of the Subject, than those imposed in absolute Governments, as clearly appears by what is called *Excise* in the *Netherlands*, and in some measure, by the Contributions called the *Subsidies* in *England* We are now speaking of the *Minds*, and not of the *Wealth* of the People for *Tributes by consent*, tho' the same thing with *Tributes imposed*, as to exhausting the Riches of a Kingdom, yet very differently affect the Minds of the Subject So that this also must be a Maxim of State, *that a People oppressed with Taxes is unfit to rule*

7. States and Kingdoms that aspire to Greatness, must be very careful *That the Nobles be few* that their Nobles and Gentry increase not too much, otherwise the common People will be dispirited, reduced to an abject State, and become little better than Slaves to the Nobility As we see in Coppices, if the Staddles are left too numerous, there will never be clean Under-wood, but the greatest part degenerates into Shrubs and Bushes. So in Nations, where the Nobility is too numerous, the Commonalty will be base and cowardly, and at length, not one Head in a hundred among them prove fit for a Helmet; especially with regard to the Infantry, which is generally the prime Strength of an Army Whence, tho' a Nation be full peopled, its Force may be small We need no clearer Proof of this, than by comparing *England* and *France* For tho' *England* be far inferior in extent, and number of Inhabitants, yet it has almost constantly got the better of *France* in War. for this reason, that the Rusticks, and lower sort of People in *England*, make better Soldiers than the Peasants of *France* And in this respect 'twas a very political and deep foresight of *Henry* the Seventh of *England*, to constitute lesser settled Farms, and Houses of Husbandry, with a certain fixed and inseparable Proportion of Land annexed, sufficient for a Life of Plenty so that the Proprietors themselves, or at least the Renters, and not Hirelings, might occupy them For thus a Nation may acquire that Character which *Virgil* gives of ancient *Italy*, " *a Country strong in Arms, and rich of Soil* [a] We must not here pass over a sort of People, almost peculiar to *England*, viz. the Servants of our Nobles and Gentry, as the lowest of this kind are no way inferior to the Yeomanry for Foot-service And 'tis certain that the hospitable Magnificence and Splendor, the Attendance and large Train, in use among the Nobility and Gentry of *England*, add much to our Military Strength as, on the other side, a close, retired Life among the Nobility, causes a want of Forces.

8. It must be earnestly endeavoured, that the *Tree of Monarchy*, like the *That the Natives be an over-match for the Foreigners* *Tree of Nebuchadnezzar*, have its Trunk sufficiently large and strong, to support its Branches and Leaves; or that the *Natives be enow to keep the foreign Subjects under* whence those States best consult their Greatness, which are liberal of Naturalization For it were vain to think a handful of Men, how excellent soever in Spirit, and Counsel, should hold large and spacious Countries under the yoke of Empire. This indeed might perhaps be done for a season; but it cannot be lasting. The *Spartans* were reserved and difficult

[a] *Terra potens Armis, atque ubere Gleba.*

fcult in receiving Foreigners among them, and therefore so long as they ruled within their own narrow Bounds, their Affairs stood firm and strong. But soon after they began to widen their Borders, and extend their Dominion farther than the Sword of Rome could well command the foreign Crowd, their Power sunk or broken. Never did Commonwealth receive new Citizens so profusively as the Rome, whence its Fortune was equal to so prudent a Conduct; and thus the Romans acquired the most extensive Empire of the Globe. It was their Custom to give a speedy Denization, and in the highest degree, that is, not only a Right of Commerce, of Marriage, and Inheritance, but also a Right of Vote, and of standing Candidate for Places and Honours. And this not only to particular Persons, but they conferred it upon whole Families, Cities, and sometimes whole Nations at once. Add to this, their Custom of settling Colonies, whereby Roman Roots were transplanted in foreign Soil. And to consider these two Practices together, it might be said, that the Romans did not spread themselves over the Globe, but that the Globe spread itself over the Romans, which is the securest Method of extending an Empire. I have often wondered how the Spanish Government could with so few Natives inclose and curb so many Kingdoms and Provinces. But Spain may be esteemed a sufficiently large Trunk, as it contains a much greater Tract of Country than either Rome or Sparta did at first. And altho' the Spaniards are very sparing of Naturalization, yet they do what comes next to it, promiscuously receive the Subjects of all Nations into their Army, and even their highest Military Office is often conferred upon foreign Leaders. Nay, it appears that Spain at length begins to feel their want of Natives, and are now endeavouring to supply it.

The German or German of Strangers

9 'Tis certain, that the sedentary Mechanick Arts, practis'd within doors, and the more curious Manufactures, which require the Finger rather than the Arm, are in their own nature opposite to a military Spirit. Men of the Sword, universally delight in exemption from Work, and dread Dangers less than Labour. And in this Temper they must be somewhat indulged, if we desire to keep their Minds in vigour. 'Twas, therefore, a great Advantage to Sparta, Athens, Rome, and other ancient Republicks, that they had the use, not of Freemen, but generally of Slaves, for this kind of domestick Arts. But after the Christian Religion gained ground, the use of Slaves was in great measure abolished. What comes nearest this Custom, is to leave such Arts chiefly to Strangers, who for that purpose should be invited to come in, or at least be easily admitted. The Native Vulgar should consist of three kinds, viz. Husbandmen, Free-servants, and Handycraftsmen, used to the strong masculine Arts, such as Smithery, Masonry, Carpentry, &c. without including the Soldiery.

10 But above all 'tis most conducive to the greatness of Empire, for a Nation to profess the Skill of Arms, as its principal Glory, and most honourable Employ. for the things hitherto spoke of, are but preparatory to the use of Arms, and to what end this Preparation, if the thing itself be not reduced to Action? Romulus, as the Story goes, left it in charge to his People at

his

his death, that of all things they should cultivate the Art of War, as that which would make their City the head of the World. The whole Frame and Structure of the *Spartan* Government, tended, with more Diligence indeed than Prudence, only to make its Inhabitants Warriors Such was also the Practice of the *Persians* and *Macedonians*, tho' not so constant and lasting The *Britons*, *Gauls*, *Germans*, *Goths*, *Saxons*, *Normans*, &c for some time also, principally cultivated Military Arts The *Turks* did the same ; being not a little excited thereto by their Law and still continue the Discipline, notwithstanding their Soldiery be now on its decline Of all *Christian Europe*, the only Nation that still retains and professes this Discipline, is the *Spanish* But it is so plain, that every one advances farthest in what he studies most, as to require no enforcing 'Tis sufficient to intimate, that unless a Nation professedly studies and practises Arms, and Military Discipline, so as to make them a principal Business, it must not expect that any remarkable Greatness of Empire will come of its own accord On the contrary, 'tis the most certain Oracle of Time, that those Nations which have longest continued in the Study and Profession of Arms, as the *Romans* and the *Turks* have principally done, make the most surprizing Progress, in enlarging the Bounds of Empire And again, those Nations which have flourished, tho' but for a single Age, in Military Glory, yet, during that time, have obtained such a greatness of Empire, as has remained with them long after, when their Martial Discipline was slackened

11 It bears some relation to the foregoing Precept, that *a State should have such Laws and Customs, as may readily administer just Causes, or at least Pretexts, of taking Arms* For there is such a natural Notion of Justice imprinted in Men's Minds, that they will not make War, which is attended with so many Calamities, unless for some weighty, or at least some specious Reason The *Turks* are never unprovided of a Cause of War, *viz* the Propagation of their Law and Religion The *Romans*, tho' it was a high Degree of Honour for their Emperors, to extend the Borders of their *Empire*, yet never undertook a War for that sole end Let it, therefore, be a Rule to all Nations that aim at Empire, to have a quick and lively sensibility of any Injury, done to their frontier Subjects, Merchants, or publick Ministers And let them not sit too long quiet, after the first Provocation Let them also be ready and chearful in sending *Auxiliaries* to their Friends and Allies which the *Romans* constantly observed, insomuch that if an Invasion were made upon any of their Allies, who also had a defensive League with others, and the former begg'd Assistance severally, the *Romans* would ever be the first to give it, and not suffer the Honour of the Benefit to be snatched from them by others As for the Wars anciently waged from a certain Conformity, or tacit Correspondence of States, I cannot see on what Law they stood Such were the Wars undertaken by the *Romans*, for restoring Liberty to *Greece*, such were those of the *Lacedemonians* and *Athenians*, for establishing or overturning *Democracies*, or *Oligarchies*, and such sometimes are those entered into by Republicks or Kingdoms, under pretext of protecting the Subjects of other Nations, or delivering

That the Laws and Customs should afford Occasions of War

I vering

vering them from Tyrann   It may suffice for the prefent purpofe, that no State expect any Greatnefs of Empire, unlefs it be immediately ready to feize an juft occafion of a *War*

12 No one Body, whether Natural or Political, can preferve its Health without Exercife, and *honourable War* is the wholefome Exercife of a *Kingdom or Commonwealth*   *Civil Wars* indeed are like the Heat of a Fever, but a War abroad is like the Heat of Motion, wholefome   for Men's Minds are enervated, and their Manners corrupted by fluggifh, and unactive Peace   And Ho vever it may be as to the Happinefs of a State, 'tis doubtlefs beft for its Greatnefs, to be, as it were, always in Arms   A *veteran Army*, indeed, kept conftantly ready for marching, is expenfive, yet it gives a State the difpofal of things among its Neighbours, or, at leaft, procures it a great Reputation in other refpects   as may be clearly feen in the *French*, who has now, for a long Succeffion of Years, kept a *ftanding army*, tho' not always in the fame part of the Country

13 The *Dominion of the Sea* is an *Epitome* of Monarchy   *Cicero*, in a Letter to *Atticus*, writing of *Pompey*'s Preparation againft *Cæfar*, says, the Defigns of *Pompey* are like thofe of *Themiftocles*, *for he thinks they who command the Sea, command the Empire*   And doubtlefs *Pompey* would have wearied *Cæfar* out, and brought him under, had he not, thro' a vain Confidence, dropt his Defign   'Tis plain, from many Examples, of how great confequence Sea-fights are   The Fight at *Actium* decided the Empire of the World · The Fight of *Lepanto* ftruck a Hook in the Nofe of the *Turk*   And it has frequently happened, that Victories, or Defeats at Sea have put a final end to the War, that is, when the whole Fortune of it has been committed to them   Doubtlefs the being *Mafter of the Sea*, leaves a Nation at great liberty to act, and to take as much, or as little of the War as it pleafes   whilft thofe who are fuperior in *Land Forces*, have yet numerous Difficulties to ftruggle with   And at prefent, amongft the *European* Nations, a *Naval Sovereign*, which is the Portion of *Great Britain*, is more than ever, of the greateft importance to *Sovereignty*, as well becaufe moft of the Kingdoms of *Europe* are not *Continents*, but in good meafure *furrounded by the Sea*, as becaufe the Treafures of both *Indies* feem but an Acceffory to the Dominion of the Seas

1_ The *Wars* of later times feem to have been waged in the dark, compared with the variety of Glory and Honour ufually reflected upon the military Men of former Ages   'Tis true, we have at this day, certain military Honours, defigned perhaps as Incentives to Courage, tho' common to Men of the Gown, as well as the Sword. we have alfo fome *Coats of Arms*, and publick Hofpitals, for Soldiers worn out, and difabled in the Service   but among the Ancients, when a Victory was obtained, there were Trophies, Funeral Orations, and magnificent Monuments, for fuch as died in the Wars   *Civick Crowns*, and *Military Garlands*, were beftowed upon all the Soldiers. The very name of Emperor was afterwards borrowed by the greateft Kings, from Leaders in the Wars   They had folemn Triumphs for their fuccefsful Generals   They had *Donatives* and great *Largeffes* for the Soldiers, when

the

the Army was disbanded. These are such great and dazzling Things in the eyes of Mortals, as to be capable of firing the most frozen Spirits, and enflaming them for War. In particular, the manner of Triumph among the *Romans* was not a thing of *Pageantry*, or empty Show, but deserving to be reckoned among the wisest and most noble of their Customs, as being attended with these three Particulars, viz. (1) the Glory and Honour of their Leaders, (2) the enriching of the Treasury with the Spoils, and (3) Donatives to the Army. But their triumphal Honours were, perhaps, unfit for Monarchies, unless in the Person of the King or his Son; which also obtained at *Rome* in the times of its *Emperors*, who reserved the honour of the Triumph, as peculiar to themselves, and their Sons, upon returning from the Wars, whereat they were present, and had brought to a Conclusion; only conferring their Vestments, and Triumphal Ensigns upon the other Leaders.

15. But to conclude, tho' no Man, as the *Scripture* testifies, can, by taking care, *add one Cubit to his Stature*, that is, in the little Model of the human body, yet in the vast Fabrick of Kingdoms and Commonwealths, 'tis in the power of *Kings* and *Rulers* to extend and enlarge the Bounds of Empire; for by prudently introducing such *Laws*, *Orders*, and *Customs* as those above mentioned, and the like, they might sow the Seeds of Greatness, for Posterity and future Ages. But these Counsels seldom reach the Ears of *Princes*, who generally commit the whole to the Direction and Disposal of Fortune [a]

That Empires may be enlarged by Prudence.

[a] Finding the *Doctrine of Government* more directly applied to *War*, in a Piece of the Author's, inscribed to *Prince Charles*, in the year 1624, on occasion of a War with *Spain*, it seems proper to make it Supplemental to this of the *Military Statesman*, under the Title of the TWELFTH SUPPLEMENT to this *general Work*. And observing also the general *Doctrine of Government*, farther extended, and enlarged by the Author, in his *Advice to Sir George Villiers*, it appeared suitable to the Design, that this likewise should be made Supplemental to the *Doctrine of Government*, as being a *Sketch* of the *Prudent Minister*, corresponding to the preceding one of the *Military Statesman*, tho' not indeed so well digested by the Author. See the THIRTEENTH SUPPLEMENT to this *general Work*.

SECT XXVII.

The DOCTRINE *of* UNIVERSAL JUSTICE: *or, the* FOUNTAINS *of* EQUITY.

1 THE other Doctrine we note in the *Art of Government*, is the DOCTRINE OF UNIVERSAL JUSTICE, or the *Fountains of Law*. They who have hitherto wrote upon Laws, write either as *Philosophers* or *Lawyers*. The *Philosophers* advance many things that appear beautiful in Discourse, but lie out of the road of Use, whilst the *Lawyers*, being bound and subject to the Decrees of the Laws prevailing in their several Countries, whether *Roman* or *Pontifical*, have not their Judgment free, but write as in Fetters. This *Doctrine*, doubtless, properly belongs to *Statesmen*, who best underſtand Civil Society, the Good of the People, Natural Equity, the Customs of Nations, and the different Forms of States. Whence they are able to judge of Laws by the Principles and Precepts, as well of natural Juſtice, as of Politicks. The preſent view, therefore, is to diſcover the Fountains or *Juſtice* and *Public Good*, and, in all the parts of Equity, to give a certain Character and Idea of what is juſt, according whereto, thoſe who deſire it, may examine the *Laws* of particular Kingdoms and States, and thence endeavour to amend them. And of this Doctrine, we ſhall, in our uſual way, give an Example aphoristically, in a ſingle *Title*.

A SPECIMEN OF THE METHOD OF TREATING UNIVERSAL JUSTICE
or,
THE FOUNTAINS OF EQUITY[a]

INTRODUCTION.

APHORISM I

2 Either *Law* or *Force* prevails in Civil Society. But there is ſome *Force* that reſembles *Law*, and ſome *Law* that reſembles *Force*, more than Juſtice. Whence there are three *Fountains of Injuſtice*, viz (1) mere *Force*, (2.) malicious Enſnaring, under colour of *Law*, and (3) the *Severity of the Law*.

APHORISM II.

3 The Ground of *private Right* is this. He who does an Injury, receives Profit or Pleaſure in the Action, and incurs Danger by the Example; whilſt others

---

[a] Whoever would continue, or improve the Work here begun, may conſult *Morhof's Polyhistor*, Tom II' Lib VI *de ſcriptoribus identia univerſalis Scriptoribus*, *Struvii Bibliothec Philoſoph* Cap 6,7 *et Scriptoribus Politicis*, and *Stollii Introductio in Hiſt. Liter* pag 753, &c *de Jure Naturali*

others partake not with him in that Profit or Pleafure, but think the Example concerns them   whence they eafily agree to defend themfelves by
Laws, left each Particular fhould be injured in his turn   But if it fhould
happen, from the Nature of the Times, and a Communion of Guilt, that
the greater or more powerful Part fhould be fubject to Danger, rather than
defended from it, by *Law*, Faction here difannuls the *Law*   and this cafe
frequently happens

APHORISM III

4   But *private Right* lies under the Protection of *publick Laws*   for Law
guards the People, and Magiftrates guard the Laws   But the Authority
of the Magiftrate is derived from the Majefty of the Government, the
Form of the Conftitution, and its fundamental Laws   Whence, if the political Conftitution be juft and right, the Laws will be of excellent ufe, but
if otherwife, of little Security

Private Right to be protected by publick Law

APHORISM IV.

5   *Publick Law* is not only the Preferver of *private Right*, fo as to keep
it unviolated, and prevent Injuries, but extends alfo to *Religion, Arms,
Difcipline, Ornaments, Wealth,* and all things that regard the Good of a
State.

Publick Laws extend to Religion, Arms, &c

APHORISM V

6   For the *End and Scope of Laws*, whereto all their Decrees and Sanctions ought to tend, is the *Happinefs of the People*   which is procurable,
(1) by rightly inftructing them in Piety, Religion, and the Duties of Morality, (2) fecuring them by Arms againft foreign Enemies, (3) guarding
them by Laws againft Faction, and private Injuries, (4) rendering them
obedient to the Government and Magiftracy, and (5) thus caufing them
to flourifh in Strength and Plenty   But Laws are the Inftruments and Sinews for procuring all this.

The End of Laws

APHORISM VI.

7   The *beft Laws*, indeed, fecure this good End: but many other Laws
fail of it   For Laws differ furprizingly from one another, infomuch, that
fome are, (1) excellent, others, (2) of a middle nature, and (3) others
again abfolutely corrupt   We fhall, therefore, here offer, according to the
beft of our Judgment, *certain Laws*, as it were, *of Laws*[a]   from whence an
Information may be derived, as to what is well, or what is ill laid down,
or eftablifhed by *particular Laws*.

The difference of Laws

Ii 2   APHO-

[a] As laying down the juft Foundations, and Rules of the Law, for the Law itfelf is go
vern'd by Reafon, Juftice, and good Senfe   But perhaps thefe Aphorifms of the Author follow the particular *Law of England* too clofe, to be allow'd, by other Nations, for the *Foundations
of univerfal Juftice*, which is a very extenfive Subject   See *Struvii Bibliothec Philofoph.* Cap. 8
de Scriptoribus Juris Natura & Gentium

APHORISM VII

8 But before we proceed to the Body of *particular Laws* [a], we will briefly touch upon the Excellencies and Dignities of *Laws in general* Now that may be esteemed a *good Law*, which is, (1) clear and certain in its Sense, (2) just in its Command, (3) commodious in the Execution, (4) agreeable to the Form of Government, and (5) productive of Virtue in the Subject [b]

TITLE I
OF THAT PRIMARY DIGNITY OF THE LAW, CERTAINTY

APHORISM VIII

9 *Certainty* is so essential to a *Law*, that a Law without it cannot be just For *if the Trumpet gives an uncertain Sound, who shall prepare himself to the Battle?* So if the Law has an uncertain Sense, who shall obey it? A *Law,* therefore ought to give warning before it strikes and 'tis a true Maxim, that *the best Law is that which leaves least to the Breast of the Judge*, which is effected by *Certainty*

APHORISM IX

10 *Laws* have two *Uncertainties*, the one where no *Law* is prescribed, the other when a *Law* is ambiguous and obscure wherefore we must first speak of *Cases omitted by the Law*, that in these also may be found some *Rules of Certainty*

APHORISM X

11 The narrowness of human Prudence cannot foresee all the *Cases* that Time may produce Whence *new Cases*, and *Cases omitted*, frequently turn up And for these there are three *Remedies*, or *Supplies*, viz (1) by proceeding upon *Analogy*, (2) by the use of *Precedents*, tho' not yet brought into a *Law*, and (3) by *Furies*, which decree according to *Conscience* and *Discretion*, whether in the *Courts of Equity*, or of *Common Law*

APHORISM XI

12 (1 In *Cases omitted*, the *Rule of Law* is to be deduced from *similar Cases*, but with Caution and Judgment And here the following Rules are to be observed Let *Reason be esteemed a fruitful, and Custom a barren thing; so as to breed no Cases* And therefore what is received against the Reason of a Law, or where its Reason is obscure, should not be drawn into Precedents

APHORISM XII

13 A *great publick Good, must draw to itself all Cases omitted*; and therefore when a Law remarkably, and in an extraordinary manner, regards and procures the *Good of the Publick*, let its Interpretation be full and extensive

APHO-

---

[a] See hereafter, Sect XXVII 98

[b] These are so many several *Titles*, or general *Heads*, laid down by the Author, as if he intended a full Treatise upon the Subject but he here only considers the first of them

APHORISM XIII

14. 'Tis a cruel thing to torture the Laws, that they may torture *The Laws not* Men   whence *penal Laws*, much lefs *capital Laws*, fhould not be extended *to be wrefted* to new Offences   But if the Offence be old, and known to the Law, and its Profecution fall upon a new Cafe, not provided for by Law, the Law muft rather be forfaken, than Offences go unpunifhed.

APHORISM XIV

15 *Statutes* that repeal the *Common Law*, efpecially in common and *Statutes of* *fettled Cafes*, fhould not be drawn by Analogy to *Cafes omitted*   For when *Repeal not to* the Republick has long been without an entire *Law*, and that in exprefs Cafes, *be extended to* there is little danger if *Cafes omitted* fhould wait their remedy, from a *Cafes omitted* new *Statute*

APHORISM XV

16 'Tis enough for fuch *Statutes* as were plainly *temporary Laws*, en-acted upon particular urgent Occafions of State, to contain themfelves within their proper Cafes, after thofe Occafions ceafe, for it were prepofterous to extend them, in any meafure, to *Cafes omitted*

APHORISM XVI

17 There is no Precedent of a Precedent, but Extenfion fhould reft *No Precedent* in immediate Cafes   otherwife it would gradually flide on to diffimilar Cafes, *of a Precedent* and fo the Wit of Men prevail over the *Authority* of *Laws*.

APHORISM XVII

18 In fuch *Laws* and *Statutes* as are concife, Extenfion may be more *Extenfion* freely allow'd, but in thofe which exprefs particular Cafes, it fhould be *more allow-* ufed more cautioufly.   For as Exception ftrengthens the Force of a *Law* in *able in fum-* unaccepted Cafes; fo Enumeration weakens it in Cafes not enumerated *mary Laws*

APHORISM XVIII

19 An *Explanatory Statute* ftops the Current of a precedent *Statute*, nor does either of them admit Extenfion afterwards   Neither fhould the Judge make a Super-Extenfion, where the Law has once begun one

APHORISM XIX

20. The *Solemnity* of *Forms* and *Acts*, admits not of *Extenfion* to fi- *Solemnity ad-* milar Cafes   for 'tis lofing the nature of Solemnity, to go from Cuftom to *mits not of* Opinion, and the Introduction of new things, takes from the Majefty of the *Extenfion.* old.

APHORISM XX

21. The *Extenfion of Law* is eafy to *After-Cafes*, which had no ex- *Extenfion to* iftence at the time when the Law was made   for where a Cafe could not *After Cafes* be defcribed, becaufe not then in being, a Cafe omitted is deem'd a Cafe *eafy* exprefled, if there be the fame reafon for it

APHO-

APHORISM XXI

22 (2) We come next to Precedents, from which Justice may be derived, where the Law is deficient but reserving Custom, which is a kind of Law, and the Precedents which, thro' frequent use, are passed into Custom, as into current Law we shall at present, speak only of such *Precedents* as happen but rarely, and have not acquired the Force of a *Law* with a view to shew how, and with what Caution, a *Rule* of *Justice* may be derived from them, when the *Law* is defective

APHORISM XXII

23 *Precedents* are to be derived from good and moderate Times, and not from such as are tyrannical, factious, or diffolute for this latter kind are a spurious Birth of Time, and prove more prejudicial than instructive.

APHORISM XXIII.

24 *Modern Examples* are to be held the safeft For why may not what was lately done, without any inconvenience, be safely done again? Yet recent Examples have the lefs Authority and, where things require a Reftoration, participate more of their own Times, than of right Reason

APHORISM XXIV

25 *Ancient Precedents* are to be received with Caution and Choice for the Courfe of Time alters many things, fo that what feems ancient, in time may, for Difturbance and Unfuitablenefs, be new at the prefent and therefore the *Precedents* of intermediate Times are the beft, or thofe of fuch Times as have moft agreement with the prefent, which ancient Times may happen to have, more than later

APHORISM XXV.

26 Let the Limits of a *Precedent* be obferved, and rather kept within than exceeded, for where there is no *Rule of Law*, every thing fhould be fufpected and therefore as this is a dark Road, we fhould not be hafty to follow.

APHORISM XXVI

27 Beware of *Fragments*, and *Epitomes of Examples*, and rather confider the whole of the Precedent, with all its Procefs for if it be abfurd to judge upon *part of a Law*, without underftanding the *whole*; this fhould be much rather obferved in *Precedent*, the ufe whereof is precarious, without an evident Correfpondence

APHORISM XXVII

28 Tis of great confequence thro' what hands the *Precedents* pafs, and by whom they have been allow'd For if they have obtain'd only among *Clerks* and *Secretaries*, by the *Courfe of the Court*, without any manifeft Knowledge of their Superiors, or have prevail'd among that Source of Errors, the Populace, they are to be rejected, or lightly efteem'd. But if they come before *Sena-*
tors,

tors, *Judges*, or *principal Courts*, so that of necessity they must have been strengthen'd, at least by the tacit Approval of proper Persons, their Dignity is the greater

APHORISM XXVIII

29 More Authority is to be allowed to those Examples, which, tho' less used, have been publish'd, and thoroughly canvas'd, but less to those that have lain buried, and forgotten, in the Closet, or Archives for *Examples*, like Waters, are wholesomest in the running Stream

APHORISM XXIX,

30 *Precedents in Law* should not be derived from History, but from publick Acts and accurate Traditions for 'tis a certain Infelicity, even among the best Historians, that they dwell not sufficiently upon *Laws*, and judicial Proceedings, or if they happen to have some regard thereto, yet their Accounts are far from being authentick

Precedents to be authentick

APHORISM XXX.

31 An *Example rejected* in the same, or next succeeding Age, should not easily be received again, when the same Case recurs for it makes not so much in its favour, that Men sometimes used it, as in its disfavour, that they dropt it upon Experience.

Should not easily be admitted, after once rejected

APHORISM XXXI

32 *Examples* are things of *Direction* and *Advice*, not Rules or Orders, and therefore should be so managed, as to bend the Authority of former times to the service of the present

Precedents are Matter of Direction, not Rule

APHORISM XXXII

33. (3) There should be both *Courts*, and *Juries*, to judge according to *Conscience* and *Discretion*, where the *Rule of the Law* is defective · for *Laws*, as we before observed, cannot provide against all Cases, but are suited only to such as frequently happen Time, the wisest of all things, daily introducing new Cases.

(3) Courts and Juries, under their Regulations

APHORISM XXXIII

34. But *new Cases* happen both in *criminal Matters*, which require Punishment, and in *civil Causes*, which require Relief The Courts that regard the former, we call *Censorial*, or *Courts of Justice*, and those that regard the latter, *Prætorial*, or *Courts of Equity*.

The Censorial and Prætorial Courts

APHORISM XXXIV

35 The *Courts of Justice* should have Jurisdiction and Power, not only to punish new Offences, but also to increase the Penalties appointed by the Laws for old ones, where the Cases are flagrant and notorious, yet not capital: for every enormous Crime may be esteemed as a new one.

Courts of Justice to have power of punishing new Offences

L   APHO-

APHORISM XXXV

C... *...* 36 In like manner, the *Courts of Equity* fhould have Power, as well of
E... *...* ...ng the Rigour of the Law, as of fupplying its Defects for if a Remedy
... be afforded to a Perfon neglected by the Law , much more to him who is
... hurt by the Law

APHORISM XXXVI

E... 37 Both the *Cenforial*, and *Prætorial Courts*, fhould abfolutely confine
... ...themfelves to enormous and extraordinary Cafes , without invading the or-
... dinary Jurifdiction   left otherwife the *Law* fhould rather be fupplanted,
than fuppli'd.

APHORISM XXXVII

... 38 Thefe *Senates* fhould refide only in *fupreme Courts* , and not be
... communicated to the lower for a power of fupplying, extending, or mo-
... derating the Laws, differs but little from a power of making them

APHORISM XXXVIII

Jurifdiction 39 Thefe *Courts of Jurifdiction* fhould not be committed to a fingle Per-
... of feveral fon , but confift of feveral and let not their Verdict be given in filence ,
but let the Judges produce the reafons of their Sentence openly, and in full
audience of the Court , fo that what is free in power, may yet be limited
by regard to Fame and Reputation

APHORISM XXXIX

... of 40 Let there be no *Records of Blood*, nor Sentence of capital Crimes
Life and Death paffed in any Court, but upon known and certain Laws *God* himfelf firft
... the end of pronounced, and afterwards inflicted Death   Nor fhould a Man lofe his
... ... Life, without firft knowing that he had forfeited it
L...

APHORISM XL

There fhould be 41 In the *Courts of Juftice*, let there be three *Returns of the Jury* , that
three Returns the Judges may not only lie under no neceffity of abfolving, or condemn-
of the Jury) ing , but alfo have a liberty of pronouncing the Cafe not clear   And let
there be, befides Penalty, a Note of Infamy, or Punifhment, by way of admonifhing others , and chaftifing Delinquents, as it were, by putting them to
the blufh, with Shame and Scandal

APHORISM XLI.

... are- 42 In *Courts of Juftice*, let the firft Overtures, and intermediate Parts of
... Parts of all great Offences, be punifh'd, tho' the End were not accomplifh'd   And
great Crimes this fhould be the principal ufe of fuch Courts for 'tis the part of Difci-
... punifh'd pline, to punifh the firft Buddings of Offences , and the part of Clemency,
to punifh the intermediate Actions, and prevent their taking effect

APHORISM XLII.

43 Great regard muft be had in *Courts of Equity*, not to afford Relief in thofe Cafes, which the Law has not fo much omitted, as defpifed for their Levity , or, for their Odioufnefs, judged unworthy of a Remedy

Cafes willingly omitted by the Laws, not to be relieved

APHORISM XLIII

44 But above all, 'tis of the greateft moment to the *Certainty of the Laws* we now fpeak of, that *Courts of Equity* keep from fwelling, and over-flowing , left, under pretence of mitigating the Rigour of the Law, they fhould cut its Sinews, and weaken its Strength, by wrefting all things to their own difpofal

The Courts of Equity to be kept within Bounds

APHORISM XLIV

45 No *Court of Equity* fhould have a right of decreeing againft a *Statute*, under any Pretext of Equity whatever   otherwife the Judge would be-come the Legiflator, and have all things dependent upon his Will.

No Equity-Court to de-cree againft a Statute

APHORISM XLV

46 Some conceive the *Jurifdiction* which decrees according to *Equity* and *Confcience*, and that which proceeds according to *ftrict Juftice*, fhould be de-puted to the fame *Courts* , whilft others would have them kept diftinct which feems much the better way   There will be no diftinction of Cafes, where there is a mixture of Jurifdictions. but *Arbitration* will, at length, fu-perfede the *Law*.

The Courts of Equity and Juftice to be kept diftinct

APHORISM XLVI

47 The ufe of the *Prætor's Table* ftood upon a good Foundation among the *Romans*, as that wherein he fet down, and publifhed, in what manner he would adminifter Juftice. According to which Example, the Judges in Courts of Equity, fhould propofe to themfelves fome certain Rules to go by, and fix them up to publick view   for as that Law is ever the beft, which leaves leaft to the breaft of the Judge , fo is that Judge the beft, who leaves leaft to himfelf [a]

The Judges in Equity to pub-lifh their own Rules

APHORISM XLVII.

48 There is alfo another way of fupplying *Cafes omitted* , viz   when one Law is made upon another, and brings the *Cafes omitted* along with it. This happens in thofe *Laws*, or *Statutes*, which, according to the common Phrafe, *look backwards*   But Laws of this kind are to be feldom ufed , and with great caution   for a *Janus-Face* is not to be admired in the *Law*

Retrofpective Laws to be ufed with dif-cretion

APHORISM XLVIII

49 He who captioufly and fraudulently eludes, and circumfcribes the Words or Intention of a Law, deferves to be hampered by a fubfequent

Are proper in fraudulent and evafive Cafes

[a] The Author made a Speech to this Effect, upon receiving the Seal, and taking his Place in Chancery   See SUPPLEMENT IV

Law   Whence, in fraudulent and evasive Cases, 'tis just for Laws to carry a Retrospection, and prove of mutual assistance to each other   so that he who invents Loop-holes, and plots the Subversion of *present Laws*, may, at least, be aved by *future*

Aphorism XLIX

50 Such Laws as strengthen and confirm the true Intentions of *Acts* and *Instruments*, against the Defects of *Forms* and *Solemnities*, very justly include past Actions   for the principal Fault of a *retrospective Law*, is, its causing disturbance, but these *confirming Laws* regard the Peace and Settlement of Transactions   Care, however, must be had, not to disturb things once adjudged

Aphorism L

51 It should be carefully observed, that not only such Laws as look back to what is past, invalidate former Transactions, but such also as prohibit and restrain things future, which are necessarily connected with things past   so, if, *e.g.* a *Law* should prohibit certain Artificers the Sale of their Wares in future, this Law, tho' it speaks for hereafter, yet operates upon times past, tho' such Artificers had then no other lawful means of subsisting

Aphorism LI

52 All *Declaratory Laws*, tho' they make no mention of time past, yet are, by the very Declaration itself, entirely to regard past Matters   for the Interpretation does not begin with the Declaration, but, as it were, is made contemporary with the Law itself   And therefore *Declaratory Laws* should not be enacted, except in Cases where the Law may be retrospected with Justice.   And so much for the *Uncertainty of Laws*, where the *Law* is extant   We proceed to the other part, where the *Laws*, tho' extant, are perplex'd and obscure

Aphorism LII.

53 The Obscurity of Laws has four Sources, viz (1) an *Accumulation of Laws*, especially such as are obsolete   (2) *An ambiguous Description, or an obscure and difficult Delivery*)   (3) *A Neglect, or Failure, in pointing out the Means of executing Justice*   (4) And lastly, *a Clashing and Uncertainty of Judgment*

Aphorism LIII

54 The Prophet says, "*It shall rain Snares upon them*" but there are no worse Snares than the *Snares of Laws*, especially the penal   which growing excessive in number, and useless thro' time, prove not a Lanthorn, but Nets, to the Feet

Aphorism LIV

55 There are two ways in use of making *new Statutes*, the one confirms and strengthens the former Statutes in the like Cases, at the same time adding or altering some Particulars   the other abrogates and cancels all that was en-
                                                                              acted

acted before, and inſtead thereof, ſubſtitutes a new uniform Law   And the latter Method is the beſt   For in the former, the Decrees become complicate and perplex'd, and tho' the Buſineſs be perform'd, yet the Body of Laws, in the mean time, becomes corrupt   but in the latter, greater Diligence muſt be uſed, when the *Law* itſelf comes to be weighed a-new, and what was before enacted, to be reconſider'd, antecedent to its paſſing   by which means the future Agreement, and Harmony of the Laws, is well conſulted.

APHORISM LV

56   It was in uſe among the *Athenians*, for ſix Perſons annually to examine the *contradictory Titles* of their Laws, and propoſe to the People ſuch of them as could not be reconciled, that ſome certain Reſolution might be taken about them   According to which Example, the Legiſlators of every State ſhould once in three, or five Years, as it ſhall ſeem proper, take a review of theſe *Contrarieties in Law*   but let them firſt be inſpected, and prepared, by Committees appointed for the Purpoſe, and then brought in, for the general Aſſembly to fix, and eſtabliſh, what ſhall be approved by Vote

The Contradictories in Law to be examined at proper Intervals

APHORISM LVI.

57   But let not an over-diligent and ſcrupulous Care be uſed in reconciling the *contradictory Titles of Laws*, by ſubtile and far-fetched Diſtinctions   for this is the weaving of the Wit   And whatever appearance it may have of Modeſty and Reverence, 'tis to be deem'd prejudicial, as rendering the whole Body of the Laws diſſimilar, and incoherent   It were therefore much better to ſuppreſs the worſt, and ſuffer the beſt to ſtand alone

APHORISM LVII

58   *Obſolete Laws*, that are grown into diſuſe, ſhould, in the ſame manner, be cancel'd   For as an *expreſs Statute* is not regularly abrogated by *diſuſe*, it happens that, from a Contempt of ſuch as are obſolete, the others alſo loſe part of their Authority.   Whence follows that Torture of *Mezentius*, whereby the living Laws are kill'd in the Embraces of the dead ones   But above all things, a Gangreen in the Laws is to be prevented

Obſolete Laws to be cancel'd

APHORISM LVIII

59   And let *Courts of Equity* have a right of decreeing contrary to *obſolete Laws, and Statutes* not newly enacted, for altho', as is well obſerved, no body ſhould be wiſer than the Laws, yet this ſhould be underſtood of the Laws when they are awake, and not when they ſleep   But let it be the Privilege, not of Judges in the Courts of Equity, but of Kings, ſolemn Counſels, and the higher Powers, to over-rule later Statutes found prejudicial to publick Juſtice, and to ſuſpend the Execution thereof by Edicts, or publick Acts, till thoſe Meetings are held which have the true power of repealing them, leſt, otherwiſe, the Safety of the People ſhould be endanger'd

Courts of Equity to have a right of decreeing contrary to obſolete Laws

APHORISM LIX

*New Digests
of Laws
deemed
heroical*

60 But if Laws, heap'd upon Laws, shall swell to such a vast Bulk, and labour under such Confusion, as renders it expedient to treat them a new, and reduce them into one sound and serviceable Corps, it becomes a Work of the utmost importance, deserving to be deem'd heroical and let the Authors of it be ranked among Legislators, and the Restorers of States and Empires[a].

APHORISM LX

And effected

61 Such an *Expurgation*, and *new Digest of Laws*, is to be effected by five Particulars , viz (1) by omitting all the *obsolete Laws*, which Justinian calls *antient Faces*, (2) by receiving the most approved Contradictories, and abolishing b..., (3) by expunging Laws of the same purport, and retaining only one, or the most perfect, (4) by throwing out such Laws as determine nothing, but propose Questions, and leave them undecided (5.) and lastly, by contracting and abridging those that are too verbose and prolix

APHORISM LXI

62 And it would be very useful in such a new *Digest*, separately to range and bring together all those Laws, received for *common Law*, which have a kind of immemorial Origin , and on the other side, the Statutes superadded from time to time because in numerous Particulars in the *Practice of the Law*, the Interpretation and Administration of the *common Law* differs from the *Statute Law* And this Method was observed by *Trebonianus*, in his *Digest* and *Code*

APHORISM LXII.

63 But in such a second Birth of the Law, and such a Recompilement of the ancient Books and Laws, the very Words and Text of the Law it self should be retained , and tho' it were necessary to collect them by Fragments, and small Portions, they may afterwards be regularly wove together For allowing it might perhaps be more commodious, and with regard to the true reason of the thing, better to do it by a new Text, than by such kind of Patch-work , yet in the *Law*, Style and Description are not so much to be regarded as Authority, and its Patron, *Antiquity* otherwise this might rather seem a Work of mere Scholar-ship and Method, than a *Corp of majestick Law*

APHORISM LXIII

64 'Twere adviseable in making this new *Digest*, not utterly to abolish the ancient Volumes, and give them up to Oblivion , but suffer them at least to remain in some Library, tho' with a Prohibition of their common use because in weighty cases it might be proper to consult and inspect the Revolutions

---

[a] Few will care to be concerned in so difficult and laborious an Undertaking , tho' a thing in itself of immense utility See *Tancred's Essay for a general Regulation of the Law.* Ed 2 172-

volutions and Series of ancient Laws   'Tis also a solemn thing to intermix Antiquity with things prefent. And fuch a *new Body of Laws*, ought to receive the Sanction of all thofe who have any Legiflative Power in the State, left under a pretence of digefting the old Laws, new ones fhould be fecretly obtruded.

APHORISM LXIV

65 'Twere to be wifhed, that fuch a *Recompilement of the Laws* might be undertaken in fuch times as excel the ancient, (whofe Acts and Works they model a-new) in point of Learning and univerfal Knowledge   the contrary whereof happened in the Work of *Juftinian*   For 'tis an unfortunate thing, to have the Works of the Ancients mangled, and fet together again, at the difcretion and choice of a lefs prudent, and lefs learned Age   But it often happens, that what is neceffary, is not beft

APHORISM LXV

66 Laws are *obfcurely defcribed* either (1) thro' their Loquacity and Superfluity of Words, (2) *through Over-Concifenefs*, or (3) *through their Preambles contradicting the Body of the Law*

A perplexed and obfcure Defcription of Laws.

APHORISM LXVI.

67 We at prefent treat of the *Obfcurity* which arifes from their ill Defcription, and approve not the Loquacity and Prolixity now ufed in drawing up the *Laws*, which in no degree obtains what is intended by it, but rather the contrary   for whilft it endeavours to comprehend and exprefs all particular Cafes in appofite and proper Diction, (as expecting greater certainty from thence,) it raifes numerous Queftions about Terms: which renders the true and real Defign of the Law more difficult to come at, thro' a huddle of Words

The Verbofity of the Law to be retrenched

APHORISM LXVII

68 Nor yet can we approve of a too concife and affected Brevity, ufed for the fake of Majefty and Authority, efpecially in this age, left the *Laws* fhould become like the *Lefbian Rule*[a]   A mediocrity therefore is to be obferved, and a well-defined generality of Words to be found, which tho' it does not accurately explain the Cafes it comprehends, yet clearly excludes thofe it does not comprehend

APHORISM LXVIII

69 Yet in the ordinary political *Laws* and *Edicts*, where Lawyers are feldom confulted, but the Politicians truft to their own Judgment, things ought to be largely explained, and pointed out to the Capacity of the Vulgar

APHO-

---

[a] The *Lefbians* are faid to have made their Rules from their Buildings, fo that if the Buildings were erroneous, the Rules they worked by became fo too, and thus propagated the Error   fo if the Laws were wrote concife, as if drawn up in perfect Times, or with an affectation of a fententious or majeftick Brevity, they might propagate Errors, inftead of correcting them.

APHORISM LXIX.

70 Nor do we approve of tedious *Preambles* at the head of Laws they were once only held impertinent, as introducing Laws in the way of *Dispute*, not in that of *Command* But as we do not suit ourselves to the Manners of the Ancients, these Prefaces are now generally used of Necessity, not only as Explanations, but as Persuasives to the passing of the Law in the Assembly of States, and likewise to satisfy the People yet, as much as possible let *Preambles* be avoided, and the *Law* begin with *commandings*

APHORISM LXX.

71 Tho' the Intent and Mind of the Law, may be sometimes drawn from these *Preambles*, yet its Latitude and Extent should by no means be derived from them for the *Preamble* frequently fixes upon a few of the more plausible and specious Particulars, by way of Example, whilst the Law embraces many more or, on the contrary, the Law restrains and limits many Things, the reason whereof it were not necessary to insert in the *Preamble* wherefore the extent of the Law is to be derived from the Body of the Law, the *Preamble* often exceeding, or falling short of this Extent

APHORISM LXXI

72 There is one very faulty Method of *drawing up the Laws*, viz when the Case is largely set forth in the *Preamble*, and then by the force of the word *which*, or some such relative, the Body of the Law is reflected back upon the *Preamble* and the *Preamble* inserted and incorporated in the *Body of the Law*, whence proceeds both Obscurity and Danger because the same Care is not usually employed in weighing and examining the Words of the *Preamble*, as the Words of the *Law itself*

APHORISM LXXII

73 There are five *Ways of interpreting the Law*, and making it clear, viz (1) By Reporting of Judgments, (2) By Instituting Authentick Writers, (3) By Auxiliary Books, (4) By Readings, and (5) By the Answers, or Consultations of learned Persons A due use of all these afford a great and ready Assistance in clearing the Laws of their Obscurity

APHORISM LXXIII

74 And above all, let the Judgments of the supreme and principal Courts be diligently and faithfully recorded, especially in weighty Causes, and particularly such as are doubtful, or attended with Difficulty or Novelty For Judgments are the Anchors of the Laws, as *Laws* are the Anchors of States

APHORISM LXXIV

75 And let this be the Method of taking them down. (1) Write the Case precisely, and the Judgments exactly, at length (2) Add the Reasons alleged by the Judges for their Judgment (3) Mix not the Authority

I   rity

rity of Cafes, brought by way of Example, with the principal Cafe   (4.)
And for the *Pleadings*, unlefs they contain any thing very extraordinary,
omit them

APHORISM LXXV

76 Let thofe who take down thefe *Judgments* be of the moft learned
Counfel in the Law, and have a liberal Stipend allowed them by the Publick   But let not the Judges meddle in thefe *Reports*, left favouring their
own Opinions too much, or relying upon their own Authority, they exceed the Bounds of a Recorder.

APHORISM LXXVI.

77 Let thefe *Judgments* be digefted in the *Order of Time*, and not in *Me-*
thod and *Titles*   For fuch Writings are a kind of Hiftories, or Narratives
of the Laws   and not only the Acts themfelves, but alfo their Times afford
Light to a prudent Judge

APHORISM LXXVII

78 Let a Body of Law be wholly compiled, (1) of the Laws that con- *Authentick*
ftitute the *common Law*, (2) of the Statutes, and (3) of the Judgments *Writers.*
on Record   and befides thefe, let nothing be deem'd authentick, or
elfe be fparingly received

APHORISM LXXVIII

79 Nothing conduces more to the Certainty of Laws, whereof we now
fpeak, than that the *authentick Writings* fhould be kept within moderate
Bounds, and that vaft multitude of Authors, and learned Men in the Law
excluded, which otherwife rend the Mind of the Laws, diftract the Judge,
make Law-fuits endlefs   and the Lawyer himfelf, finding it impoffible to
perufe and digeft fo many books, hence takes up with Compendiums   Perhaps fome good *Gloffary*, a few of the exacteft Writers, or rather a very few
Portions of a few Authors, might be ufefully received for Authentick. But
let the Books be ftill referved in Libraries, for the Judges and Counfel to
infpect occafionally   without permitting them to be cited, in pleading at the
Bar, or fuffering them to pafs into Authority

APHORISM LXXIX

80 But let not the Knowledge and Practice of the Law want its *auxiliary* *Auxiliary*
Books, which are of fix kinds   viz (1) *Inftitutes*, (2) *Explanations of Words*, *Books*
(3) the *Rules of Law*, (4) the *Antiquities of Law*, (5) *Summaries, or Abridg-*
ments, and (6) *Forms of Pleading*

APHORISM LXXX

81 Students are to be trained up to the Knowledge, and higher Parts of *viz Inftitutes.*
the Law, by *Inftitutes*, which fhould be wrote in a clear Method   Let the
whole of private Right, or the Laws of *Meum* and *Tuum*, be gone over in
                                                                    thefe

these *Elements* , not omitting some things, and dwelling too much upon others , but giving a little taste of all · that when the Student comes to peruse the *Corps* of *Law* , he may meet with nothing entirely new, or without having received some previous Notion thereof But the publick Law is not to be touched in these *Institutes* , this being to be drawn from the Fountains themselves [a]

Aphorism LXXXI

Explaining Terms 82 Let a *Comment* be made of *the* Terms of *the* Law , without endeavouring too curiously and laboriously to give their full Sense and Explanation the purport hereof being not to search the exact definitions of Terms, but to afford such Explanations only, as may open an easy way to reading the Books of the Law   And let not this *Treatise* be digested Alphabetically , rather leave that to the Index: but place all those Words together which relate to the same thing , so that one may help to the understanding of another

Aphorism LXXXII

Rules of the Law 83 It principally conduces to the *Certainty of Laws*, to have a just and exact *Treatise of the different Rules of Law* , a work deserving the diligence of the most ingenious and prudent Lawyers for we are not satisfied with what is already extant of this kind   Not only the known and *common Rules* are to be here collected , but others also, more subtile and latent, which may be drawn from the *Harmony of Laws*, and *adjudged Cases* such as are sometimes found in the best Records   And these *Rules,* or *Maxims,* are general Dictates of Reason, running thro' the different matters of *Law* , and make, as it were, its Ballast [b]

Aphorism LXXXIII

84 But let not the *Positions* or *Placits of Law* be taken for Rules, as they usually are very injudiciously ; for if this were received, there would be as many *Rules* as there are *Laws* a Law being no other than a commanding Rule   But let those be held for *Rule* , which cleave to the very Form of Justice   Whence, in general, the same *Rules* are found thro' the *Civil Law* of different States , unless they sometimes vary with regard to the Form of Government

Aphorism LXXXIV

85 After the *Rule* is laid down, in a short and solid expression, let Examples and clear Decisions of Cases be subjoined, by way of Explanation , Distinctions and Exceptions, by way of Limitation , and things of the same kind, by way of Amplification to the *Rule*

APHO-

---

[a] See above, *Aph.* I—V

[b] What the Author here commends we have a Specimen of in the Piece he entitles, *A Collection of some principal Rules and Maxims of the Common Law, with their Latitude and Extent* but as that Piece wholly regards the *Practice* and *Profession* of the *Law,* and is wrote in the direct *Law-manner,* we do not add it as a *Supplement* to this Work, tho' otherwise highly deserving

APHORISM LXXXV.

86 'Tis juftly directed not to take *Laws* from *Rules*, but to make the *Rules* from the *Laws* in being neither muft the Proof be derived from the Words of the Rule, as if that were the Text of the Law, for the Rule, like the magnetic Needle, does not make, but indicate the *Law*

APHORISM LXXXVI.

87 Befides the Body of the Law, 'tis proper to take a view of the *An-* *Antiquities of* *tiquities of Laws* , which tho' they have loft their Authority, ftill retain *Laws* their Reverence Thofe Writings upon Laws and Judgmenes, whether publifhed or unpublifhed, are to be held for *Antiquities of Law*, which preceded the Body of the Laws in point of time, for thefe *Antiquities* fhould not be loft , but the moft ufeful of them being collected, and fuch as are frivolous and impertinent rejected, they fhould be brought into one Volume, without mixing *ancient Fables*, as *Trebonianus* calls them, with the *Laws* themfelves

APHORISM LXXXVII.

88 But for Practice, 'tis highly proper to have the *whole Law or-* *Abridgments.* *derly digefted under Heads and Titles*, whereto any one may occafionally turn on a fudden, as to a Store-houfe furnifhed for prefent ufe Thefe *Summaries* bring into order what lay difperfed , and abridge what was diffufive and prolix in the Law. But care muft be had, left thefe *Abridgments* fhould make men ready for practice, and indolent in the Science itfelf: for their Office is to ferve but as Remembrancers, and not as perfect Teachers of the Law And they are to be made with great Diligence, Fidelity and Judgment, that they may fairly reprefent, and not fteal from the Laws.

APHORISM LXXXVIII

89. Let *different Forms of Pleading* be collected in every kind; for this *Pleadings* tends to Practice and doubtlefs they lay open the *Oracles* and *Myfteries* of the Law , which conceals many fuch And thefe are better, and more fully difplayed in *Forms of Pleading*, than otherwife , as the Hand is better feen when opened

APHORISM LXXXIX

90. Some method ought to be taken for folving, and putting an end to *Anfwers and* *particular Doubts*, which arife from time to time for 'tis a hard thing, if *Confultations.* they who defire to keep clear of Error, fhould find no one to fet them right ; but that their Actions muft be ftill endangered, without any means of knowing the Law, before the Cafe is determined

APHORISM XC

91 But we approve not that the Anfwers of prudent Men, whether Counfellors, or Profeffors of Law, given to fuch as ask their Advice, fhould

have so great Authority, as that the Judge might not lawfully depart from their Opinion. Let Points of Law be taken from sworn Judges.

Aphorism XCI.

92 We approve not that Judgments should be tried by feigned Causes and Persons, with a View to predetermine what will be the *Rule of Law* for this dishonours the Majesty of Laws, and should be judged as a Prevarication. Besides, 'tis monstrous for *Judgments* to copy the Stage.

Aphorism XCII

93 Therefore let as well Judgments as Answers and Advice proceed from none but the Judges, the former in Suits depending, and the latter in the way of Opinion upon difficult Points of Law. But these Notices, whether in private or publick Affairs, are not to be expected from the Judges themselves, for that were to make the Judge a Pleader, but from the Prince or State and let them recommend it to the Judges; who, invested with such Authority, are to hear the Arguments on both sides, and the Pleadings of the Counsel, employed either by those whom it concerns, or appointed by the Judges themselves, if necessary, and after the matter is weigh'd, let the Judges declare the Law, and give their Opinion· and such kind of Opinions should be recorded, and published among judged Cases, and be reckoned of equal Authority with them

Aphorism XCIII.

Readings to be directed so as to terminate Disputes.   94 Let the *Readings* upon the Law, and the Exercises of such as study it, be so instituted and order'd, that all things may tend to the resolving and putting an end, and not to the raising and maintaining of Questions and Controversies in the Law. But at present a School seems every where opened for multiplying Disputes, Wranglings, and Altercations, about the Laws; in the way of shewing the Wit of the Disputants· Tho' this is also an ancient Evil, for it was esteemed a piece of Glory of old to support numerous Questions of Law, as it were by Sects and Factions, rather than to end them. But this ought to be prevented

Aphorism XCIV.

The Uncertainties of Judgments in their Reversal.   95 *Judgments prove uncertain,* either (1) thro' an untimely and hasty passing of Sentence, (2) the Emulation of Courts, (3) a wrong and unskilful recording of Judgments, or, (4) thro' a too easy and ready way opened for their Reversion. Therefore let Care be taken, (1) that Judgments proceed upon mature deliberation, (2) that Courts preserve a due Reverence for each other; (3) that Judgments be faithfully and prudently recorded, and (4) that the Way for Reversing of Judgments be made narrow, craggy and thorny.

APHORISM XCV

96 If Judgment be given upon a Cafe, in any principal Court, and a *Decrees to be reverfed with Solemnity* like Cafe come into another Court , proceed not to Judgment before a Con-fultation be held in fome confiderable Affembly of the Judges. For if De-crees are of neceffity to be cut off, at leaft let them be honourably in-terred.

APHORISM XCVI

97 For Courts to quarrel and contend about Jurifdiction, is a piece of *The Courts to maintain Peace with one another* human Frailty , and the more, becaufe of a childifh Opinion, that 'tis the Duty of a good and able Judge to enlarge the Jurifdiction of his Court whence this Diforder is increafed, and the Spur made ufe of, inftead of the Bridle   But that Courts, thro' this heat of Contention, fhould, on all fides uncontrollably reverfe each other's Decrees, which belong not to Jurif-diction, is an intolerable Evil, and by all means to be fuppref'd by Kings, the Senate, or Government   For 'tis a moft pernicious Example that Courts, which make Peace among the Subjects, fhould quarrel among themfelves

APHORISM XCVII

98. Let not too eafy a Paffage be opened for the *Repealing of Sentence,* by Appeal, Writ of Error, Re-hearing, &c.   Some are of Opinion, that a Caufe fhould be removed to a higher Court, as a new Caufe ; and the Judgment given upon it, in the lower, be entirely laid afide, and fufpend-ed whilft others again would have the Judgment remain in its force, and only the Execution to be ftopt   We approve of neither; unlefs the Court, where the Sentence pafs'd, were of a very inferior nature : but would rather have both the Judgment ftand, and its Execution proceed; provided a Caveat be put in by the Defendant, for Cofts and Damages, if the Sentence fhould be reverfed.

99. Let this TITLE, *of the Certainty of Laws,* ferve for a *Specimen of that Digeft* we propofe and have in hand [a].   And thus we conclude the Head of *Civil Doctrine,* and with it *Human Philofophy ,* as with *Human Philofophy, Philofophy in general.*

100 And now ftanding ftill to breathe, and look back upon the Way we *A general Re-trofpection* have paffed, we feem all along to have been but turning and trying the In-ftruments of the *Mufes ,* for a Confort to be play'd upon them by other hands or to have been grating Mens ears, that they may have the better

L l 2

Mufick

[a] The Scheme of this *Digeft,* offer'd to Queen *Elizabeth,* and afterwards to King *James the Firft,* we place as the FOURTEENTH SUPPLEMENT to this *general Work,* tho' the Defign itfelf was not executed by the Author   Some Progrefs however was made in the *Hiftory of the Nature, Ufe, and Proceedings of the Laws of England,* which make the FIFTEENTH SUPPLEMENT to the pre-fent Work

Musick hereafter[a]   And indeed, when I set before me the present State of the Times, wherein Learning makes her third Visit to mankind[b], and carefully reflect how well she finds us prepared, and furnished with all kinds of Helps, the Sublimity and Penetration of many Genius's of the Age, those excellent Monuments of the ancient Writings, which shine as so many great Lights before us, the Art of Printing, which largely supplies Men of all Fortunes with Books, the open Traffick of the Globe, both by Sea and Land whence we receive numerous Experiments, unknown to former Ages, and a large Accession to the mass of *Natural History*, the leisure which the greatest Minds in the Kingdoms and Provinces of *Europe* every where enjoy, as being less immersed in Business than the ancient *Greek*, by reason of their populous States, or the *Romans*, thro' the extensiveness of their Empire, the Peace at present spread over *Britain, Spain, Italy, France*, and many other Countries, the exhaustion of all that can be invented or said in Religious Controversies[c], which have so long diverted many of the best Genius's from the Study of other Arts, the uncommon Learning of his present *Britannic Majesty*[d], about whom, as about a Phœnix, the fine Genius's flock, from all quarters, and lastly, the inseparable Property of Time, which is daily to disclose Truth   When all these things, I say, are considered by us, we cannot but be raised into a Persuasion, that this *third Period* of Learning may far exceed the two former of the *Greeks* and *Romans*, provided only that Men would well and prudently understand their own Powers, and the Defects thereof, receive from each other the *Lamps of Invention*, and not the *Firebrands of Contradiction*, and esteem the search after Truth, as a certain noble Enterprize, not a thing of Delight or Ornament, and bestow their Wealth and Magnificence upon matters of real Worth and Excellence, not upon such as are vulgar and obvious[e]   As to my own Labours, if any one shall please himself, or others, in reprehending them, let him do it to the full, provided he but weigh and consider what he says[f]   And certainly the Appeal is just, tho' the thing perhaps may not require it, from Mens first Thoughts to their second, and from the present Age to Posterity[g]

101.

---

[a] Observe, that all hitherto done, is but in order to regulate and conduct *Enquiries* in future

[b] Alluding only to the two famous ones, among the *Greeks* and *Romans*

[c] This is spoke like one who was versed in *Ecclesiastical History*, and *polemical Divinity*, for scarce any Religious Dispute can be raised, that has not been upon the Carpet before but many have found the Art, by heat and warmth, to revive old Doctrines, Opinions, and Heresies, and pass them upon the Crowd for new, as if *Religious Controversies* were to be entailed upon Mankind, and descend from one Generation to another

[d] *viz.* King *James* I

[e] See the way of doing this pointed out in the Author's *New* ATLANTIS

[f] *Verbera sed audi*

[g] This Appeal of the Author from Mens first Thoughts, to their second, or from thence again to Posterity, may well deserve our Attention   as it appears, by numerous Instances, that he does no give us his own first crude immature Thoughts, upon any Subject he treats, but offers the Result of his Enquiries after long Experience, Meditation, and frequent Rejections of superficial and popular Notions   so that if he errs, it is rather his Unhappiness than

his

101 We come, laftly, to that *Science,* which the two former Periods of Time were not bleffed with , *viz* *facred* and *infpired* Theology . the Sabbath of all our Labours and Peregrinations

---

S E C T. XXVIII.

The Doctrine *of* Inspired Theology, *or* Divinity.

1 **H**Aving now, with our fmall Bark of Knowledge, failed over, and fur-*The Divifion* rounded the Globe of the *Sciences,* as well the old World as the new, *and Cultiva-* (let Pofterity judge with what Succefs ,) we fhould pay our Vows and con-*tion of Divi-* clude , did there not ftill remain another part to be viewed , *viz facred* *nity left to D.-* or *infpired Theolog*y But if we were difpofed to furvey it, we muft quit the *vines* fmall Veffel of *human Reafon,* and put ourfelves on board the *Ship of the Church,* which alone poffeffes the *Divine Needle* for juftly fhaping the *Courfe* Nor will the Stars of Philofophy, that have hitherto principally lent their Light, be of farther fervice to us and therefore 'twere not improper to be filent alfo upon this Subject, as well as upon that of *Government* For which reafon, we will omit the juft diftributions of it, and only contribute, according to our flender Ability, a few Particulars in the way of *good Wifhes.* And this we do the rather, becaufe we find no Tract in the whole Region of Divinity, that is abfolutely deferted or uncultivated fo great has the Diligence of Men been, in fowing either *Wheat* or *Tares* We fhall therefore only propofe three *Appendages of Theology* , treating not of the Matter already form'd, or to be form'd by *Divinity,* but only of the *Manner of forming it* Neither will we here, as we have hitherto practifed, give any Sketches, annex any Specimens, or lay down any Precepts for thefe Treatifes , but leave all this to *Divines* [a].

2 The Prerogative of God extends over the whole Man, and reaches *The Preroga-* both to his *Will* and his *Reafon* , fo that Man muft abfolutely renounce *tive of Reve-* himfelf, and fubmit to God and therefore, as we are obliged to *obey the* *lation over the* *divine Law,* tho' our Will murmur againft it, fo are we obliged to *believe* *Light of Na-* *the Word of God,* tho' our Reafon be fhock'd at it. For if we fhould be-*ture.* lieve only fuch things as are agreeable to our *Reafon,* we affent to the *Matter*

ter

his Fault, and would not have his Reader err along with him   This Conduct in an Author, doubtlefs requires, that the Reader fhould not be hafty, or judge off-hand, but duly weigh and confider, before he paffes Cenfure

  [a] The Addrefs and Conduct of the Author, in this, and the fucceeding Paragraph, will be manifeft to thofe who are converfant in *Ecclefiaftical Hiftory,* and apprized of the Mifchiefs of *Infidelity*

te), and not to the *Author* which is no more than we do to a suspected Witness But the *Faith imputed to* Abraham *for Righteousness*, consisted in a Particular, laugh'd at by *Sarah.* who, in that respect, was an Image of the *natural Reason* And therefore, *the more absurd and incredible any divine Mystery is, the greater honour we do to God in believing it*, and *so much the more noble the Victory of Faith* [a] As Sinners, the more they are oppress'd in Conscience, yet relying upon the Mercy of God for Salvation, honour him the more, for all Despair is a kind of reproaching the Deity. And, if well consider'd, *Belief is more worthy than Knowledge*, such Knowledge, I mean, as we have at present for in *Knowledge*, the human Mind is acted upon by Sense, which results from material things but in *Faith, the Spirit is affected by Spirit*, which is the more worthy Agent 'Tis otherwise in the *State of Glory* for then *Faith shall cease, and we shall know as we are known* Let us therefore conclude, that *sacred Theology* must be drawn from the *Word* and *Oracles of God*, not from the *Light of Nature*, or the Dictates of Reason 'Tis written, that *the Heavens declare the Glory of God* but we no where find it, that *the Heavens declare the Will of God*, which is pronounced *a Law and a Testimony, that Men should do according to it*, &c Nor does this hold only in the great Mysteries of the Godhead, of *the Creation*, and of the *Redemption*, but belongs also to the true *Interpretation of the moral Law Love your Enemies, do good to them that hate you*, &c *that ye may be the Children of your heavenly Father, who sends his Rain upon the Just and the Unjust* Which Words are *more than human*, and go beyond the *Light of Nature*. So the heathen Poets, especially when they speak pathetically, frequently expostulate with *Laws* and *moral Doctrines*, (tho' these are far more easy and indulgent than Divine Laws,) as if they had a kind of malignant Opposition to the freedom of Nature [b] according to the Expression of *Dendamis*, the *Indian*, to the Messengers of *Alexander*, " viz that *he had heard indeed some-* " *what of* Pythagoras, *and the other wise Men of* Greece, *and believed them* " *to have been great Men, but that they held a certain fantastical thing, which* " *they called Law and Morality, in too great veneration and esteem*" We cannot doubt, therefore, that a large part of the Moral Law is too sublime to be attained by the Light of Nature tho' 'tis still certain, that Men, even from the Light and Law of Nature, have some Notions of Virtue, Vice, Justice, Wrong, Good, and Evil

Two Significa-tions of the Light of Na-ture 3 We must observe, that the *Light of Nature* has two Significations, (1) as it arises from Sense, Induction, Reason and Argument, according to the Laws of Heaven and Earth and (2) as it shines in the human Mind, by internal Instinct, according to the Law of Conscience which is a certain Spark, and, as it were, a Relique of our primitive Purity And in this latter sense chiefly, the Soul receives some Light, for beholding and discerning the

[a] On the Foundation here laid down, it cannot appear incredible, that the Author should write the *Characteristicks of a believing Christian in Paradoxes, and seeming Contradictions*, which makes the SIXTEENTH SUPPLEMENT to this *general Work*, for he is here express that *Reason and Faith* are Opposites and if this Position be allow'd, *Revelation* will then, perhaps, stand on its just *Foundation*

[b] ———— *Et quod natura remittit Invida jura negant.* ————

the Perfection of the moral Law, tho' this Light be not *perfectly clear*, but of such a nature, as rather to reprehend Vice, than give a full Information of Duty   whence *Religion*, both with regard to *Mysteries* and *Morality*, depends upon *divine Revelation* [a].

4   Yet the *Use of human Reason* in spiritual things, is various, and very extensive   for Religion is justly called a *reasonable Service*   The Types and Ceremonies of the *old Law*, were rational and significative, differing widely from the Ceremonies of Idolatry and Magick   which are a kind of deaf and dumb Shew ; and generally uninstructive, even by *innuendo*.   But the *Christian Faith*, as in all things else, excels in this, that it preserves the golden Mean in the use of Reason, and Dispute, the Child of Reason, between the Laws of the *Heathens*, and of *Mahomet*, which go into extremes   for the heathen Religion had no *constant Belief*, or Confession, and the *Mahometan* forbids all *Disputes in Religion*   whence one appears with the face of manifold Error, the other as a crafty and subtile Imposture   whilst the *sacred Christian Faith*, both receives and rejects the use of Reason and Dispute, under due limitation

The Use of human Reason allowable in Religion

5. The *Use of human Reason in Matters of Religion*, is of two kinds, the one consisting in the *Explanation of Mysteries*, the *other* in the *Deductions* from them   As to the *Explanation of Mysteries*, we find that God himself condescends to the Weakness of our Capacity, and opens his Mysteries, so as they may be best understood by us, inoculating, as it were, his Revelations into the Notions and Comprehensions of our Reason· and accommodating his Inspirations to the opening of our Understanding, as a Key is fitted to open the Lock   Tho', in this respect, we should not be wanting to ourselves for as God makes use of our Reason in his Illuminations, so ought we likewise to exercise it every way ; in order to become more capable of receiving and imbibing Mysteries   provided the Mind be enlarged, according to its Capacity, to the Greatness of the Mysteries; and not the Mysteries contracted to the Narrowness of the Mind.

This Use of Reason is of two Kinds, regarding, (1.) the Explanation of Mysteries

6   With regard to *Inferences*, we must know, that we have a certain secondary and respective, not a primitive and absolute, use of Reason, and Arguing, left us about Mysteries   For after the Articles and Principles of *Religion* are so seated, as to be entirely removed from the Examination of Reason, we are then permitted to draw Inferences from them, agreeable to their Analogy   But this holds not in natural things, where *Principles* themselves are subject to Examination by *Induction*, tho' not by *Syllogism*   and have, besides, no repugnancy to Reason, so that both the first and middle Propositions, are derivable from the same Fountain. 'Tis otherwise in *Religion*, where the first Propositions are self-existent, and subsist of themselves, uncontrolled by that Reason which deduces the subsequent Propositions. Nor is this the case in *Religion* alone, but likewise in other Sciences, as well the serious as the light, where the *primary Propositions* are postulated, as things wherein the use of Reason cannot be absolute.   Thus in *Chess*, or other

And (2) Inferences from them.

---

[a] Hence Divines have justly applied themselves to the Proof and Demonstration of a *Revelation*, which being once established, the Doctrines it delivers are incontestable

other Games of the like nature, the first Rules and Laws of the Play, are merely positive Postulates, which ought to be entirely received, not disputed but the skilful playing of the Game, is a Matter of Art and Reason So in human Laws, there are numerous Maxims, or mere *Placits of Law* received, which depend more upon Authority than Reason, and come not into dispute But then for the Enquiry, what is not absolutely, but relatively most *just* herein, *viz* in conformity with those Maxims. this, indeed, is a point of Reason, and affords a large Field for Dispute. Such, therefore, *is that human Reason* which has place in sacred Theology, and is founded upon the good-pleasure of God

The Uses of human Reason 7 And as the use of human Reason, in things divine, is of two kinds, so is it attended with two Excesses (1) the one, when it too curiously enquires into the manner of a Mystery, (2) the other, when it attributes an equal Authority to the Inference, as to the Principles For he may seem a Disciple of *Nicodemus*, who shall obstinately enquire, *How can a Man be born when he is old?* But he can be esteemed no Disciple of St *Paul*, who does not sometimes insert in his Doctrine, *I, not the Lord*, or, *according to my Judgment*, which is the Stile that generally suits with Inferences Whence it seems a thing of capital Use and Benefit, to have a sober and diligent TREATISE wrote, *concerning the proper Use of human Reason in Divinity*, by way of a DIVINE LOGICK For this would be like an Opiate in Medicine, and not only lay asleep those empty Speculations which sometimes disturb the Schools, but also allay that Fury of Controversy which raises such Tumults in the Church This TREATISE, therefore, we place among the things that are wanted under the Name of THE MODERATOR, or the TRUE USE OF HUMAN REASON IN THEOLOGY [a]

The first Appendage to Theology namely, The Moderator

A Desire of the Decree of Unity among Christians desired 8 'Tis of the utmost importance to the *Peace of the Church*, to have the *Covenant of Christians*, prescribed by our Saviour in two particulars, that seem somewhat contradictory, well and clearly explained the one whereof runs thus, *he who is not with us, is against us*, and the other thus, *he who is not against us, is for us* whence it plainly appears, that there are some Points wherein he who differs is to be excluded the *Covenant*, and others again, wherein Christians may differ, and yet keep Terms The *Bonds of the Christian Communion* are *one Faith, one Baptism*, &c not one Ceremony, one Opinion, &c Our Saviour's Coat was seamless, but the Garment of the Church of many Colours The Chaff must be separated from the Wheat, but the Tares in the Field are not to be hastily plucked up from the Corn *Moses*, when he saw the *Egyptian* contending with the *Israelite*, did not say, *Why strive ye?* but drew his Sword, and kill'd the *Egyptian* but when he saw two *Israelites* fighting together, tho' the Cause of one of them might have been unjust; yet he says to them, *Ye are Brethren, why strive ye?* All which being

---

[a] Many of the modern *rational Divines* have treated this Subject, particularly Dr *Tillotson*, Dr *Clarke*, Mr *Whiston*, &c or if more unexceptionable Writers are required, see Mr *Boyle's Christian Virtuoso*, and *Things above Reason consider'd*, and Mr *Locke* on the *Reasonableness of Christianity* But the Point does not appear settled to general Satisfaction, nor Divines agreed upon it among themselves

being well confider'd, it feems a thing of great ufe and moment, to define *what, and of how great Latitude thofe Matters are, which totally cut off Men from the Body of the Church, and exclude them the Communion of the Faithful.* And if any one fhall imagine this done already, we advife him ferioufly to reflect, with what Juftice and Moderation But 'tis highly probable, that whoever fpeaks of *Peace*, will meet with that Anfwer of *Jehu* to the Meffenger; *What has Peace to do with* Jehu? *What haft thou to do with Peace? Turn, and follow me* For the Hearts of moft Men are not fet upon *Peace*, but *Party* And yet we think proper to place among the things wanting, A Discourse upon the Degrees of Unity in the City of God, as a wholefome and ufeful Undertaking [a]

The fecond Appendage to Divinity wanting, a Difcourfe of Unity

9 The holy *Scriptures* having fo great a fhare in the Conftitution of Theology, a principal regard muft be had to their Interpretation We fpeak not of the Authority of interpreting, eftablifh'd by the *Confent of the Church*, but of the *manner of interpreting* which is either *methodical*, or *loofe*. For the pure Waters of Divinity are drawn, and employ'd, nearly in the fame manner as the *natural Waters* of Springs, *viz.* (1.) either received in Cifterns, and thence derived thro' different Pipes, for the more commodious Ufe of Men, or (2) immediately poured into Veffels for prefent Occafions The former *methodical way* has produced the *fcholaftick Divinity*; whereby the *Doctrine of Theology* is collected into an Art, as in a Ciftern, and thence diftributed around, by the conveyance of *Axioms* and *Pofitions*

Two ways of interpreting Scripture; viz. the methodical, and the loofe

10. But the *loofe way of interpreting* has two Exceffes, the one fuppofes fuch a Perfection in the *Scriptures*, that all *Philofophy* fhould be derived from their Fountains, as if every other Philofophy were a profane and heathenifh thing And this Diftemper principally reigned in the School of *Paracelfus*, and fome others tho' originally derived from the *Rabbies* and *Cabbalifts* But thefe Men fail of their End, for they do not, by this means, *honour the Scriptures*, as they imagine, but rather debafe and pollute them. For they who feek a *material Heaven*, and a *material Earth*, in the Word of God, abfurdly feek for *tranfitory things* among *eternal* To look for *Theology* in *Philofophy*, is looking for the living among the dead, and to look for *Philofophy* in *Theology*, is to look for the dead among the living.

The loofe way fubject to two Exceffes.

11 The other *Excefs, in the manner of Interpretation*, appears, at firft fight, juft and fober, yet greatly difhonours the Scriptures, and greatly injures the Church, by *explaining the infpired Writings in the fame manner as human Writings are explained* For we muft remember, that to God, the Author of the Scriptures, thofe two things lie open which are concealed from Men; the *Secrets of the Heart*, and the *Succeffions of Time* Therefore, as the Dictates of Scripture are directed to the Heart, and include the Viciffitudes of all Ages, along with an eternal and certain Foreknowledge of all Herefies, Contradictions, and the mutable States of the Church, as well in general, as

---

[a] This *Defideratum* the Author himfelf has endeavour'd to fupply, in his Difcourfe of the *Peace of the Church*, which makes the Seventeenth and laft Supplement to this *General Arrangement of Knowledge, and Method of improving the Sciences.*

n particulars, thefe Scriptures are not to be *interpreted barely according to* ... *of the P* ... *or with regard to the Occafion upon which the* ... *or* ... *by the Context, or the principal Scope of the Paſſge,* ... *a knowledge of their containing, not only in groſs or collectively,* ... *in particular Words and Claufes, numberless Rivulets and* ... *of Doctrine, for watering all the parts of the Church, and all the Minds of the* ... For 'tis excellently obferved, that the Anfwers of our *Saviour* are not fuited to many of the Queftions propofed to him, but appear, in a manner, impertinent and this for two Reafons, (1.) becaufe, as he knew the Thoughts of thofe who put the Queftion; not from their Words, as Men know them, but immediately and of himfelf, he anfwer'd to their Thoughts, and not to their Words and (2) becaufe he fpoke not to thofe alone who were prefent, but to us alfo now living, and to the Men of every Age and Place, where the Gofpel fhall be preached And this Obfervation holds in other parts of *Scripture* [a]

12 We find, among *Theological Writings*, too many *Books of Controverſies and Diverſe*, a vaft Mafs of that we call *pofitive Theology*, *Common-Places*, *particular Treatiſes*, *Cafes of Confcience*, *Sermons*, *Homilies*, and numerous prolix *Comments* upon the feveral Books of the Scriptures But the thing we want and propofe, as our third *Appendix to Theology*, is, A SHORT, SOUND, AND JUDICIOUS COLLECTION OF NOTES, AND OBSERVATIONS, UPON PARTICULAR TEXTS OF SCRIPTURE, without running into Common-place, purfuing Controverfies, or reducing thefe Notes to artificial Method, but leaving them quite loofe, and native a thing we find fometimes done in the more learned kind of *Sermons*, which are feldom of long duration tho' it has not hitherto prevail'd in Books, defign'd for Pofterity But certainly, as thofe Wines which flow from the firft treading of the Grape, are fweeter and better, than thofe forced out by the Prefs, which gives them the Roughnefs of the Husk and the Stone, fo are thofe Doctrines beft and wholefomeft, which flow from a gentle Crufh of the Scripture, and are not wrung into *Controverfies* and *Common-place* And this *Treatife* we fet down as wanting, under the Title of the FIRST FLOWINGS OF THE SCRIPTURES

13 And now we have finifhed our *fmall* GLOBE *of the intellectual World*, with all the Exactnefs we could, marking out and defcribing thofe parts of it, which we find either not conftantly inhabited, or not fufficiently cultivated. And if, thro' the Courfe of the Work, we fhould any where feem to depart from the Opinion of the Ancients, we would have it remembred, that this is not done for the fake of Novelty, or ftriking into different Paths from them, but with a defire of improving For we could neither act confiftently with ourfelves, nor the Defign, without refolving to add all we could to the Inventions of others at the fame time wifhing that our own Difcoveries may be exceeded by thofe of Pofterity. And how fairly we
have

---

[a] Hence thofe appear not to act injudicioufly, who feek for an allegorical, and fpiritual Meaning in the Scripture, after the Example of *Origen*, and other learned Fathers of the Church Tho' it not prefent warmly difputed, whether the Scriptures are to be *literally* or *fpiritually* ... ed

have dealt in this matter, may appear from hence ; that our Opinions are every where proposed naked and undefended ; without endeavouring to bribe the Liberty of others by Confutations For where the things advanced prove juft, we hope, that if any Scruple or Objection arife in the firft reading, an Anfwer will of itfelf be made in the fecond. And wherever we have erred, we are certain to have done no Violence to the Truth by litigious Arguments, the effect whereof, is the procuring Authority to Error, and detracting from what is well invented for *Error receives Honour, and Truth a Repulfe from Contention*

14 And here I cannot but reflect, how appofitely that Anfwer of *Themiftocles* may be applied to myfelf, which he made to the Deputy of a fmall Village, haranguing upon great things, " *Friend, thy Words require a City.*" For fo it may be faid of my *Views*, that they *require an Age*, perhaps a *whole Age* to prove[a], and *numerous Ages to execute.* But as THE GREATEST THINGS ARE OWING TO THEIR BEGINNINGS, 'twill be enough for me to have *fown for Pofterity*, and the Honour of the *immortal Being*, whom I humbly entreat, thro' his Son, our Saviour, favourably to accept thefe, and the like *Sacrifices of the human Underftanding*, feafon'd with Religion, and offer'd up to his Glory !

SECT. XXIX.

The COAST *of the* NEW INTELLECTUAL WORLD: *or, a* RECAPITULATION *of the* DEFICIENCIES *of* KNOWLEDGE; *pointed out in the preceding* WORK, *to be fupplied by* POSTERITY.

1. THE HISTORY OF MONSTERS; or irregular Productions of Nature, in all the three Kingdoms, Vegetable, Animal, and Mineral.

2 *The* HISTORY OF ARTS, or *Nature* form'd and wrought by human Induftry

3. A *well-purged* HISTORY OF NATURE in her extent, or the *Phænomena of the Univerfe.*

4.

---

[a] The Age is now paft, and in what ftate do we find ourfelves? Certainly fomewhat the more advanced in Knowledge by thefe Labours of the Author tho' we ftill come far fhort of Perfection The learned *Morhof* undertakes to fhew, that all the modern Improvements made by our own Nation, in *Philofophy*, are owing to the Lord *Bacon*, who, as that Writer expreffes it, *every where abounds with the Seeds of Things*, many whereof, we may add, were fown fo deep, as not yet to have fprouted See *Morhof's Polyhiftor paffim*

4 INDUCTIVE HISTORY, or *Historical Matters* consequentially deduced from Phænomena, Facts, Observations, Experiments, Arts, and the active Sciences

5 An UNIVERSAL LITERARY HISTORY, or the Affairs relating to *Learning* and *Knowledge*, in all Ages and Countries of the World

6 BIOGRAPHY, or the Lives of all eminent Persons

7 The HISTORY OF PROPHECY, or the *Accomplishment of divine Prediction*, to serve as a Guide in the *Interpretation of Prophecies.*

8 The PHILOSOPHY OF THE ANCIENT FABLES, or a just Interpretation of the *Mythology of the Ancients*

9. PRIMARY PHILOSOPHY, or a Collection of *general Axioms*, subfervient to all the *Sciences*

10 PHYSICAL ASTRONOMY, or a *Philosophical History of the Heavens*

11 A JUST ASTROLOGY, or the *real Effects of the Celestial Bodies upon the Terrestrial*

12 A CALENDAR OF DOUBTS, or *Natural Problems*, to be continued thro' all Ages, along with a *Calendar of vulgar Errors*

13. A COLLECTION OF THE OPINIONS OF THE ANCIENT PHILOSOPHERS.

14. An *Enquiry* into the SIMPLE FORMS OF THINGS, or that which constitutes their Essences, and Differences

15. NATURAL MAGICK, relative to the *Doctrine of Forms.*

16 An INVENTORY OF KNOWLEDGE, or an *Account of the Stock of Learning among Mankind*

17 A CALENDAR OF LEADING EXPERIMENTS, for the better Interpretation of Nature

18. SHORT AND COMMODIOUS METHODS OF CALCULATION, in Business, Astronomy, &c

19 The DOCTRINE OF GESTURE, or the Motions of the Body with a View to their Interpretation

20. COMPARATIVE ANATOMY, BETWIXT DIFFERENT HUMAN BODIES

21 *A Work upon* INCURABLE DISEASES, to lessen their Number, and fix a true Notion of INCURABLE in Medicine

22 The LAUDABLE MEANS OF PROCURING EASY DEATHS

23 A SET OF APPROVED AND EFFECTUAL REMEDIES, *for Diseases*

24 The WAYS OF IMITATING NATURAL SPRINGS, AND BATH-WATERS

25. The FILUM MEDICINALE, or PHYSICIANS CLUE, in Prescription.

26 A NATURAL PHILOSOPHY, fundamental to Physick

27 The WAYS OF PROLONGING LIFE

28 An ENQUIRY INTO THE NATURE AND SUBSTANCE OF THE SENSITIVE SOUL.

29 The DOCTRINE OF MUSCULAR MOTION, or the Efficacy of the Spirits in moving the Body.

30 The DOCTRINE OF SENSE AND SENSIBILITY, or the Difference betwixt *Perception and Sense.*

31 An ENQUIRY INTO THE ORIGIN AND FORM OF LIGHT , or *the Foundation of Opticks*

32 The ART OF INVENTING ARTS

33 The TRUE USE OF INDUCTION in *Philosophy.*

34 The ART OF INDICATION, or DIRECTION, in *Philosophy*

35 A LEARNED OR SAGACIOUS KIND OF EXPERIENCE , different from the Vulgar, and leading to the direct Improvement of Arts

36 A PARTICULAR TOPICAL INVENTION , directed by the Light of leading *Questions,* or proper Heads of Enquiry

37 The DOCTRINE OF IDOLS , or a Detection and Confutation of the *Prejudices, false Conceptions,* and *Errors of the Mind*

38 A NEW ENGINE , or Helps *for the Mind corresponding to those of the Hand*

39 An APPENDIX TO THE ART OF JUDGMENT , assigning the Kinds of Demonstration proper to every Subject.

40 An INTERPRETATION of the *Marks, Signatures, or Impressions of Things*

41 A PHILOSOPHICAL GRAMMAR , or an Account of the *various Properties of different Languages, in order to form one perfect Pattern of Speech*

42. The TRADITIVE LAMP , or *the proper Method of delivering down the Sciences to Posterity*

43 The DOCTRINE OF PRUDENCE IN PRIVATE DISCOURSE; or *Colours of Good and Ill*

44 A COLLECTION OF SOPHISMS , with their *Confutations*

45 A COLLECTION OF STUDIED ANTITHETS , or *short and strong Sentences, on both sides of the Question , in a variety of Subjects.*

46 A COLLECTION OF LESSER FORMS OF SPEECH , *for all the Occasions of Writing and Speaking*

47 SOBER SATYR , or the INSIDES OF THINGS.

48 The GEORGICKS OF THE MIND , or the Means of *procuring the true moral Habit of Virtue*

49. An ACCOUNT OF THE CHARACTERS OF NATURES OF PERSONS.

50 The DOCTRINE OF THE AFFECTIONS, PASSIONS, OR PERTURBATIONS OF THE MIND

51. The SECRETARY TO THE USES OF LIFE , or *the Doctrine of various Occasions.*

52. The DOCTRINE OF BUSINESS , or *Books upon all Kinds of Civil Employments, Arts, Trades, &c*

53 SELF-POLICY, *the Doctrine of Rising in Life;* or the Means of advancing a Man's private Fortune.

54 The MILITARY STATESMAN ; or *the Political Doctrine of enlarging the Bounds of Empire*

55 The DOCTRINE OF UNIVERSAL JUSTICE; or *the Fountains of Equity*

56 The MODERATOR IN DIVINITY , or the true Use of human *Reason* in the Business of *Revelation.*

27 The Degrees of Unity in Religion, *adjusted*, with a View to preserve the Peace of the Church.

28 The First Readings of the Scripture, or a Set of short, found, and judicious Notes upon particular Texts, tending to Use and Practice [a]

[a] When these *Desiderata of Knowledge* shall be duly supplied, may we not reasonably expect a more perfect *Philosophy* and a happier *World* than what we at present enjoy? The Misfortune is here, that there is an almost *universal Indolence* in Mankind, with regard to those Things that have never yet been effected. And 'till the Intellect be thoroughly convinced of the Use and Practicality of these Things, and the Affections be won over to the side of Reason, there is no room to expect any very great Improvements, or Enlargements, in the present form and superficial Set of *Arts* and *Sciences*. This were a large Field to enter upon, but the Author has contracted the whole, and brought it to a fixed Point of View, in his Novum Organum or a new Machine for the Mind, to which we therefore refer. See, in particular, Part I Sect VI of that Work.

END OF THE

DE AUGMENTIS SCIENTIARUM.

29 MR C4

A GENERAL

SUPPLEMENT

TO THE

DE AUGMENTIS SCIENTIARUM:

OR, THE

Several PIECES of the AUTHOR,

Tending to Supply the

DEFICIENCIES of KNOWLEDGE,

Pointed out in that WORK.

PREFACE.

THE Defiderata of *Knowledge, pointed out in the* de Augmentis Scientiarum, *may require all the Affiftance that can any way be procured to fupply them. We, therefore, here range together the feveral* leffer *Works of the Author, that have a Tendency to this End, and place them in the Order they ftand indicated by that general and leading Performance · which the Author appofitely fuppofes a kind of* Globe of the Intellectual World, *where the Sum of Knowledge in his Time, is branched, and laid down from juft Obfervation and Experience, under the feveral Sciences, or capital Heads of* Learning; *together with the Coafts and Roads that lead to the hitherto undifcovered Parts of Philofophy. Some of thefe Parts are brought to a nearer View, by the following* Supplemental Pieces, *which alfo afford particular Directions and Examples for enlarging or extending the Empire of Man over the Works of Nature. And tho' the whole of this* Supplemental Part *may appear confiderably large, yet it falls infinitely fhort of executing the feveral* Plans *laid down in the* de Augmentis Scientiarum *and poffibly all the modern Improvements and Difcoveries, however numerous they may be thought, would not go far in filling them up. The Defigns of that Work are fo vaft, that perhaps many Ages are ftill required to execute them If the prefent Sum of Knowledge were to be taken, in the Aphoriftical Manner, that is, be nakedly fet down, without Opinions, Incertainties, and foreign Ornaments; how much more bulky a Volume would it make than the* de Augmentis Scientiarum? *It is not, however, the* Quantity, *but the* Quality

lity of the Materials, that chiefly imports the Advancement of Philosophy But let any Man soberly consider, whether the thing we commonly call by the name of Learning, *be much more than the* Husk *or* Foliage *of solid, serviceable and effective Philosophy, whose entire Plants are* Aphorisms *, and whose Seeds are* Axioms, *pregnant with Works To set this Truth in its proper Light, is the Author's principal Design, in most of the following Attempts*

29 MR 64

SUPPLEMENT I.

THE

NEW ATLANTIS:

OR, A

PLAN of a SOCIETY

FOR THE

Promotion of KNOWLEDGE.

PREFACE.

THE *present* Piece *has, perhaps, been esteemed a greater* Fiction *than it is·* *The* Form *of the* History *is purely imaginary , but the* Things *mentioned in it seem purely Philosophical ; and, if Men would exert themselves, probably practical. But whilst our Minds labour under a kind of* Despondency *and* Dejection, *with regard to* operative Philosophy *, and refuse to put forth their strength, the* Wings of Hope *are clipped And, in this Situation, the Mind seems scarce accessible but by* Fiction. *For plain Reason will here prove dull and languid , and even* Works *themselves rather stupefy than rouze and inform Whence the prudent and seasonable use of* Invention *and* Imagery, *is a great Secret for winning over the Affections to Philosophy We have here, as in miniature, a Summary of* Universal Knowledge ; *Examples, Precepts and Models for improving the Mind in* History, Geography, Chronology, Military Discipline, Civil Conversation, Morality, Policy, Physicks, &c *whence it appears like a kind of Epitome, and farther Improvement of the Scheme of the* de Augmentis Scientiarum *The dignity and utility of the* Design *may appear from hence; that not only Mr* Cowley *endeavoured to imitate it, in his* Plan of a Philosophical Society ; *but even the* Royal Society of London, *and the* Royal Academy of Paris, *have, from their first Institution, employed themselves, and still continue employed, in its execution.*

The

The NEW ATLANTIS[a]: *or a Plan of a* Society *for the Promotion of* KNOWLEDGE.

Delivered in the Way of Fiction.

SECT I.

A first long Voyage, intimating the Discovery of a new Country

1. AFter a twelvemonth's stay at *Peru*[b], we sailed from thence for *China* and *Japan*, by the *South-Sea*, and had fair Winds from the East, tho' soft and gentle, for above five Months. then the Wind changed and settled in the West, for several days, so that we made little way, and sometimes purposed to sail back. But now there arose strong Winds from the South, one point to the East, which carried us to the North. by which time our Provisions failed us. And being thus amidst the greatest wilderness of Waters in the World, we gave ourselves for lost. Yet lifting up our hearts to God, who *sheweth his wonders in the Deep*, we besought him, that as in the beginning he disclosed the face of the Deep, and made dry Land appear, so we might now discover Land, and not perish. The next day about Evening, we saw before us, towards the North, the appearance of thick Clouds, which gave us some hopes. for as that part of the *South-Sea* was utterly unknown, we judged it might have *Islands* or *Continents*, hitherto undiscovered. We, therefore, shaped our Course towards them, and in the dawn of the next day plainly discerned Land.

The Ships arrival to an unknown Port Tarr i amiable Birth, r

2. After sailing an hour longer, we entered the Port of a fair City, not large, but well built, and affording an agreeable Prospect from the Sea. Upon offering to go on shore, we saw People with Wands in their hands, as it were forbidding us, yet without any Cry or Fierceness, but only warning us off by Signs. Whereupon we advised among ourselves what to do. when a small Boat presently made out to us, with about eight Persons in it, one whereof held in his hand a short, yellow Cane, tipped at both ends with blue, who made on board our Ship, without any shew of distrust. And seeing one of our number present himself somewhat at the head of the rest, he drew out, and delivered to him, a little Scroll of yellow polish'd Parch-

---

[a] The Title is evidently taken from *Plato's* Account of the *Atlantis*, which some will have a Fable, and others a real History. And either way, the thing has somewhat of the marvellous, see *Plato's Timæus*. See also hereafter § 26

[b] The Narration may be supposed delivered by a Philosophical *Spaniard*, the capital Person of the Ship's Company. See hereafter, § 3, 11 &c

3.

Parchment [a], wherein were, written in ancient *Hebrew*, ancient *Greek*, *Latin* of the *School*, and in *Spanish*, these Words   *Land ye not, and provide to be gone within sixteen days, except ye have farther time given you but if ye want fresh Water, Provision, Help for your Sick, or Repair for your Ship, write down your Wants, and ye shall have what belongs to Mercy*   The Scroll was sealed with Cherubims Wings, and a Cross

3   This being deliver'd, the Officer return'd, and left only a Servant to *The Officers take no Fees* receive our Answer   Our Answer was, in *Spanish*, That our Ship wanted no Repair, for we had rather met with Calms and contrary Winds, than Tempests   but our Sick were many, so that if not permitted to land, their Lives were in danger   Our other Wants we set down in particular, adding, that we had some little store of Merchandize, which, if they pleased to traffick for, might supply our Wants, without being burdensome to them. We offered Money to the Servant, and a Piece of Crimson Velvet to be presented the Officer.   but the Servant took them not, and would scarce look upon them: so left us, and return'd in another little Boat that was sent for him

4   About three Hours after our Answer was dispatch'd, there came to us *A superior Officer examines them* a Person of Figure   He had on a Gown with wide Sleeves, a kind of Water-Camblet, of an excellent and bright Azure [b], his under Garment was green, so was his Hat, being in the form of a Turban, curiously made, his Hair hanging below the Brims of it.   He came in a Boat, some part of it gilt, along with four other Persons, and was follow'd by another Boat, wherein were twenty. When he was come within Bow-shot of our Ship, Signals were made to us, that we should send out our Boat to meet him, which we presently did, manned with the principal Person amongst us but one, and four of our number with him.   When we came within six Yards of their Boat, they bid us approach no farther   we obeyed, and thereupon the Person of Figure, before described, stood up, and, with a loud Voice, in *Spanish*, asked, *Are ye Christians?*   We answered, yes, fearing the less, because of the Cross we had seen in the Signet   At which Answer, the said Person lift up his right Hand towards Heaven, and drew it softly to his Mouth, a Gesture they use when they thank God, and then said, *If ye will swear by the Merits of the Saviour, that ye are no Pirates, nor have shed Blood, lawfully or unlawfully, within forty Days past, ye have Licence to come on shore*   We said, we were all ready to take the Oath   Whereupon, one of those that were with him, being, as it appear'd, a *Notary*, made an entry of this Act   Which done, another of the Attendants in the same Boat, after his Lord had spoke to him, said aloud, *My Lord would have ye know, that it is not out of Pride, or Greatness, that he does not come on board your Ship, but as in your Answer, you declare you have many sick among you, he was warned by the* CITY-CONSERVATOR OF HEALTH *to keep at a distance.*   We bowed ourselves, and answered, we accounted what was already done a great Honour,

and

---

[a] They have a Paper of this kind in the *East Indies*

[b] Observe, that this was a Colour, till of late, wanting in *Europe*, particularly in the Art of *Callico Printing*, and staining of *Linen*

and singular Humanity, but hoped, that the Sickness of our Men was not infectious Then he returned

A N -ry
c me ce -d
ter
5 A while after came the *Notary* on board our Ship, holding in his hand a Fruit of that Country, like an Orange, but of a Colour between Orange tawny and Scarlet, and of an excellent Odour This he used as a Preservative against Infection He gave us our Oath, by the name of *Jesus*, and his Merits and told us, that the next day, by six in the Morning, we should be brought to the HOUSE OF STRANGERS; so he call'd it, and be there accommodated At his leaving us, we offer'd him a Present, but he smiling, said, he must not be twice paid for one Labour. meaning, that he had a Salary sufficient from the State for his Service For, as we found afterwards, they call an Officer who takes Rewards, *twice paid*.

First of their
Number 50 c?
first
6 Next Morning early, we were visited by the same Officer as at first, with his Cane, who said, he came to conduct us to the HOUSE OF STRANGERS. and that he had prevented the Hour, to allow us the whole Day for our Business For, said he, if you will follow my advice, there shall first go with me some few of you, to view the Place, that it may be made convenient for you, and then you may send for your Sick, and the rest of your number intended to come on shore We thanked him, and answer'd, that this care he took of desolate Strangers, God would reward So six of us went with him and when we came to land, he walk'd before, first turning to us, and saying he was but our Servant, and our Guide. He led us thro' three fair Streets, and all the way we went, were gather'd People on both sides, standing in a row, but in so civil a manner, as if it had been, not to wonder at, but to welcome us and many of them, as we passed by, spread their Arms a little, which is their Gesture, when they bid welcome [a].

A Description
of the House
of Strangers
7 The HOUSE OF STRANGERS is fair and spacious, built of Brick, of a bluer Colour than our Brick [b], with curious Windows, some of Glass, some of oiled Cambrick [c] He brought us first into a fair Parlour, above stairs, then asked us, what number of Persons we were? And how many sick? We answered, we were in all fifty one, whereof our Sick were seventeen He desired us to have patience, and stay till he returned, as he did about an hour after, then led us to see the Chambers, provided for us, which were nineteen in number so contrived, that four better than the rest, might receive four principal Men of our Company, and lodge them separate, and the other fifteen, lodge two and two together. The Chambers were handsome, chearful, and decently furnished. Then he led us to a long Gallery, where he shew'd us on one side seventeen neat Cells, with Partitions of Cedar These Cells, being in all forty, were design'd as

an

---

[a] The Good breeding conspicuous in this Fable, is no less than its Morality, Civil Policy and Philosophy, which renders it an excellent Lesson, that might have its use in *Universities* and *Schools* With which view perhaps it was that the Author seems to have intended a *Latin* Edition of it, as may be supposed from Dr *Rawley's Preface* and 'tis pity but a more elegant *Latin* Version were given of it than that which usually goes along with the Author's *Latin* Works

[b] Blue Bricks might prove a Curiosity in Building, and seem no difficult to make If earth that turns blue in burning, cannot be procured, the *blue Glazing* is common.

[c] Which makes excellent Blinds

an INFIRMARY He told us also, that as any of our Sick recovered, they might be removed from the Cells to the Chambers: for which purpose there were appointed ten spare Chambers, besides those already mentioned

8 He then brought us back to the Parlour, and lifting up his Cane a *The Strangers* little, as they do when they give any Charge, or Command, said to us, *Ye* *not to go a* *are to know, the Custom of the Country requires, that after this day and to-* *broad for three* *morrow, which we give you for removing your People from your Ship, ye are to* *Days* *keep within doors for three Days But let it not trouble you, nor think yourselves* *restrain'd, but rather left to your rest and ease You shall want nothing, and* *there are six of our People appointed to attend you, for any Business you may have* *abroad* We gave him thanks, with due Affection, and Respect, and said, God surely is manifested in this Land We also offer'd him a considerable Present; but he smil'd, and only said, What? *twice paid!* And so he left us

9. Soon after this, our Dinner was served in; which we thought better *Their Meats* than any collegiate Diet we had known in *Europe* We had also Liquors *and Drinks de-* of three sorts, all wholesome and excellent, *viz* Wine of the Grape, Drink of*scribed* Grain, or a Liquor like Ale with us, but finer[a], and a kind of Cyder, made of a Fruit of that Country, an extremely pleasant and refreshing Liquor[b]

10 There were also brought us, for our Sick, plenty of those scarlet *Their Medi-* Oranges[c], which, they said, were an assured Remedy for Sickness taken at *cines intima* Sea[d] They gave us likewise certain small grey, or whitish Pills, whereof*ted.* they desired our Sick would take one every Night, before sleep, which Medicine, they said, would hasten their Recovery[e]

11 The next Day, after the trouble of removing our Men, and Goods, *The Speech of* from the Ship, was somewhat over, I called our Company together, and *the Leader to* said to them, *My dear Friends, let us know ourselves, and how it stands with* *the rest of the* *us. We are Men cast on Land, as* Jonas *was, out of the Whale's Belly, when* *Strangers* *we were as buried in the deep and now we are on shore, we seem to be but between Death and Life, for we are beyond both the old World and the new and whether we shall ever see* Europe *again, God only knows A kind of Miracle has brought us hither, and it must be little less that shall bring us hence. Therefore, in regard of our Deliverance past, and our Danger present, and to come, let us look up to God, and every Man reform his own ways Besides, we are here come among a Christian People, full of Piety and Humanity let us not bring such confusion of face upon ourselves, as to shew our Vices, or Unworthiness, before them There is still more for they have by Command, tho' in form of Curtesy, cloyster'd*

---

[a] See the Author's *Sylva Sylvarum*, under the *Articles* DRINKS, FOODS, CLARIFICATION, and MATURATION

[b] The Improvements that may still be made in *potable Liquors*, are very considerable This also is touched upon in several Parts of the *Sylva Sylvarum* See in particular the *Article* SUGAR

[c] See above, § 5

[d] 'Tis usual in *France*, and other Countries, to hold a Lemmon in the hand, and frequently apply it to the Nose when Persons visit disagreeable or infectious Places

[e] Those who would know the simple kind of Medicine here intimated, may, perhaps, be enabl'd to conjecture it from the Author's *History of Life and Death*.

within the Wall, for three Days. Who knows whether it be not to make some trial of our Manner? And if they find them bad, to banish us directly, if good, agree us farther time. For the Men they have appointed to attend us, may be rather Spies than Men. Therefore, let us so bear ourselves, that we may be at peace with God, and find favour in the eyes of this People.

12. Our Company, with one Voice, thanked me for my Admonition, and promis'd me to live foberly and decently, without giving any the least occasion of offence. So we fpent our three Days agreeably, and at eafe, in expectation of what fhould follow.

13. During this time, we had fresh Joy every hour from the Recovery of our Sick, who thought themfelves caft into fome *divine Pool of Healing*, they mended fo favourably, and fo faft.[a]

14. After our three Days were expired, there came to us a Perfon we had not feen before, cloathed in blue, as the former, only his Turban was white, with a fmall red Crofs on the top. He had alfo a Tippet of fine Linen. At his coming in, he bended to us a little, and fpread his Arms. We faluted him in a very fubmiffive manner, as expecting from him Sentence of Life or Death. He defired to fpeak with fome few of us; whereupon fix only ftay'd, and the reft quitted the Room. He faid, *I am, by Office, Governour of this Houfe of Strangers, by Vocation, a Chriftian Prieft, and come to offer you my Service as Strangers, but chiefly as Chriftians. The State has given you leave to ftay a Week or more. and let it not trouble you, if your Occafions fhould require farther time, for the Law, in this particular, is not ftrict; and I myfelf hope to obtain more time for you, if it be convenient. The Houfe of Strangers is at this time rich, for it has flood un-Revenue thefe thirty-feven Years, it being fo long fince any Stranger arrived in this part; therefore take ye no care, the State will defray your Expence during your Continuance; nor fhall you ftay one Day the lefs for that. As for any Merchandize ye have brought, ye fhall be fairly dealt with, and have our return either in Merchandize, or in Gold and Silver; for to us it is all the fame. And if you have any other Requeft to make, conceal it not. For ye fhall not make your Countenance fall by our Anfwer. Only this I tell you, that none of you muft go above a Karan, that is, a Mile and an half, from the Wall of the City, without fpecial Leave.*

15. We anfwered, after looking a while upon one another, admiring this Civility, that we could not well tell what to fay, as wanting Words to exprefs our Thanks, and that his generous Offers left us nothing to afk. That we feem'd to have before us a Picture of our Salvation, as we, who were but lately within the Jaws of Death, were now brought to a place, where we found nothing but Confolations. For the Command laid upon us, that we would not fail to obey it, tho' it was impoffible but our Hearts fhould defire to tread farther upon this happy Ground. We added, that our Tongues fhould firft cleave to the Roofs of our Mouths, e'er we fhould forget, either his reverend Perfon, or this whole Nation, in our Prayers. We alfo humbly befought him to accept of us as his true Servants, by as juft a right as ever Men on Earth were bound, laying and prefenting both our Perfons, and all we

[a] When fhall this be the happy State of Phyfick in *Europe?* See the Author's *Hiftory of Life and Death.*

we had, at his feet He faid he was a Prieft, and looked for a Prieft's Reward, which was our brotherly Love, and the Good of our Souls and Bodies[a] So he went from us, not without Tears of Tendernefs in his Eyes, and left us alfo confufed with Joy, faying among ourfelves, that we were come into a Land of Angels, who appeared to us daily, and prevented us with Bleffings which we thought not of, much lefs expected

16 Next day, about ten, the Governour came to us again, and, after Salutations, told us familiarly, he was come to vifit us, and calling for a Chair, fat him down, and about ten of us, the reft being either of the meaner fort, or gone abroad[b], fat down with him, when he began thus *We of this Ifland of Benfalem, (fo they call it in their Language,) have this advantage, by means of our folitary Situation, the Laws of Secrecy enacted for our Travellers, and our feldom admitting of Strangers; that we know moft Parts of the habitable World, yet remain ourfelves unknown Therefore, becaufe he who knows leaft is the fitteft to ask Queftions, it feems more reafonable, that ye ask me, than that I ask you* _{The Company revifited by the Governour, who entertains them with an account of the Ifland}

17 We humbly thanked him for giving us the leave, as conceiving, by the tafte we had already, there was no worldly thing more worthy to be known, than the State of their happy Country But above all, fince we were met from feveral ends of the Earth, and hoped affuredly to meet one day in Heaven, we defired to know who was the Apoftle of that Nation, and how it was converted to the *Faith?* He feem'd to be well-pleafed at the Queftion, and faid, *Ye knit my Heart to you, by asking this firft, for it fhews, that you firft feek the Kingdom of Heaven and I fhall gladly fatisfy you.* _{Its Converfion to Chriftianity}

18 *About twenty Years after the Afcenfion of our Saviour, there was feen in the night, by the People of Renfufa, (a City upon the Eaftern Coaft of our Ifland,) in appearance fome Miles off at Sea, a great Pillar of Light, not conical, but in the form of a Cylinder[c], rifing from the Sea, a great height towards Heaven on the top of it was a large Crofs of Light, more refplendent than the Body of the Pillar At this ftrange Sight, the People of the City flocked together upon the Sands, then put themfelves into a number of fmall Boats, in order to approach it nearer But when the Boats were come within fome fmall diftance of the Pillar, they could row no farther Now, there was in one of the Boats a wife Man of* SOLOMON'S COLLEGE[d], *which is the very Eye of this Kingdom, who having a while attentively view'd, and devoutly contemplated this Pillar and Crofs, fell upon his face, then raifing himfelf upon his knees, and lifting up his hands to Heaven, he prayed in this manner* _{The Miracle whereby it was wrought}

19. *Lord God of Heaven and Earth, thou haft vouchfafed of thy Grace to thofe of our Order, to know thy Works of Creation, and the Secrets thereof, and to difcern between divine Miracles, the Works of Nature, the Works of Art, and* _{The Prayer of a Fellow of Solomon's College at the fight of the Miracle}

[a] Is it not in the nature of Things, that Men might imitate this Example?
[b] Having now leave, fee above, § 14
[c] Obferve here the true nature of a Miracle all Flame naturally rifes pyramidal from the Earth, on account of the preffure of the Atmofphere, fo that a Cylindrical Pillar of Light is, upon Earth, fupernatural See below, § 19
[d] See more of this *College* hereafter, *Sect* II

Im-

Impoſtures and Illuſions of all ſorts [a] I do here acknowledge, before this People, that the thing we now ſee is thy Finger, and a true MIRACLE And, for as much as we Learn in our Books, that thou never workeſt Miracles, but to a divine and excellent end, the Laws of Nature being thy own Laws, which thou exceedeſt not but upon great occaſions, we moſt humbly beſeech thee to proſper this great Sign, to give us the INTERPRETATION, and Uſe thereof, in mercy, which thou doſt, in part, ſecretly, promiſe by ſending it to us.

The Proceſs of the Miracle, and a Conjecture, whereby the Canon was known, as to the Books of the Old and New Teſtament

20 His Prayer being thus ended, he preſently found the Boat he was in moveable again, whilſt the reſt remained ſtill faſt and taking that for an aſſurance of leave to approach, he cauſed the Boat to be GENTLY, AND WITH SILENCE, rowed towards the Pillar [b] But before he came up to it, the Pillar, with the Croſs of Light, burſt, and diffuſed itſelf abroad, as it were into a Firmament of Stars, which alſo vaniſhed ſoon after and there was nothing left but a ſmall Cheſt of Cedar, not at all wet, though it floated [c] In the fore part of it, which was next him, there grew a ſmall green Branch of Palm When the wiſe Man had taken it, with all reverence, into his Boat, it opened of itſelf, and there were found in it a Book and a LETTER, both written on fine Parchment, and wrapped in fine Linen. The Book contained all the *Canonical Books of the Old and New Teſtament*, as you have them, (for we know what your Churches receive,) with the *Apocalypſe* itſelf, and ſome other Books of the New Teſtament, which were not at that time written [d] and for the *Letter*, it was in theſe Words.

The Epiſtle of St Bartholomew

21 I Bartholomew, *a Servant of the Higheſt, and Apoſtle of* JESUS CHRIST, *was warned by an Angel in a Viſion of Glory, that I ſhould commit this Ark to the Sea Therefore I teſtify and declare, unto that People, where God ſhall ordain this Ark to come, that in the ſame day comes unto them Salvation, and Peace, and Good-will, from the Father, and the Lord* JESUS

A further Miracle wrought both in Book and Letter

22 There was alſo a great Miracle wrought both in the *Book* and the *Letter*, conformable to that in the *Gift of Tongues* For not only the Natives, but the *Hebrews*, *Perſians*, and *Indians*, at that time in the Iſland, read every one the *Book* and *Letter*, as if wrote in his own Language And thus was this Land ſaved from *Infidelity*, by an Ark, through the apoſtolical and miraculous annunciation of St *Bartholomew* Here he pauſed, and a Meſſenger called him from us

The Converſation with the Governor renewed

23 Next day he came to us again, ſoon after Dinner, and excuſed himſelf, that he was called from us ſo abruptly, but now propoſed to make amends, if we held his Company agreeable We anſwer'd, that we held it ſo pleaſing, as to forget both Dangers paſt, and Fears to come, whilſt we heard him, and that an Hour ſpent with him, was worth Years of our former Life.

---

[a] The Diſtinctions here made, cannot, perhaps, be too exactly obſerved by Philoſophers.

[b] Obſerve now Divine MYSTERIES are to be approached

[c] The Miracle ſeems all of a piece, not Patch work, which is a Characteriſtick of *falſe Miracles*

[d] St *Clemens's Epiſtle* ſuppoſe thoſe of St *Ignatius*, *Polycarp*, and ſome Parts of the *Conſtitutions* By this were a ſurprizing Addition to the Miracle, and an inconteſtible Proof of its being Divine, that Books ſhould be ſo inſpired, and received before they were written, or the human Authors of them, perhaps, in being See the *de Augmentis Scientiarum*, Sect XXVIII of the Defect of I and Theology, or Divinity

Life   He bowed, and after we were feated again, he faid, Well, the Queftions are on your part

24. One of our number, after a fhort Paufe, obferved, there was a matter we were no lefs defirous to know, than afraid to afk, left we fhould prefume too far   but, encouraged by his Humanity, we would venture to propofe it, befeeching him, if he thought not fit to anfwer, yet to pardon and reject it   We faid, we well obferved, what he was pleafed to relate, that this happy *Ifland*, tho' known to few, yet was itfelf acquainted with moft Nations of the World, which we found true, confidering they had the Languages of *Europe*, and a knowledge of our State and Affairs, whilft we in *Europe* never had any glimpfe of this Ifland   The Governour here returned a gracious Smile, and faid, we did well to poftulate pardon for a Queftion, which might imply we thought this a Country of Magicians, that fent out Spirits into all parts, to bring them Intelligence of other Countries   We anfwered with all poffible Humility, yet with an air of certainty[a], that we knew he fpoke this only in the way of pleafantry, that we were apt enough to think there was fomething fupernatural in the Ifland, but rather *angelical* than *magical*   yet to let his Lordfhip truly know, what made us tender in afking the Queftion, it was no fuch opinion, but only becaufe he had before intimated, that this Country had certain *Laws of Secrecy*, with regard to Strangers[b]   He anfwered, you remember right, and therefore, in refpect of what I fhall now fay, I muft referve fome Particulars, which are not lawful for me to reveal, but there will enough be left to give you fatisfaction

The Queftion put, how this Ifland became acquainted with all the World, whilft itfelf remain'd unknown

25. About three thoufand Years ago, the Navigation of the World, for remote Voyages, was greater than at this day[c]   nor are we ignorant, how much it is of late increafed with you   But whether the Example of the Ark, that faved the Remnant of Men from the univerfal Deluge, gave them Courage to venture upon the Deep, or what it was, fuch is the Truth.   The *Phœnicians*, and efpecially the *Tyrians*, had great Fleets   The *Carthaginians* had their Colony, which is ftill farther Weft   Towards the Eaft, the Shipping of *Ægypt*, and of *Paleftine*, was likewife great.   *China* alfo, and the great *Atlantis*, which you call *America*, tho' they have now only Junks and Canoes, abounded then with tall Ships   This *Ifland*, as appears by faithful Regifters, had, at that time, fifteen hundred ftout Ships of Burthen   There is little Hiftory of all this with you, but we have ample knowledge of it[d].

The Governour's Anfwer

The ancient Shipping

26   At that time, this Country was frequented by the Ships of all the Nations above-mentioned, and frequently brought hither Men of other Countries,

Benfalem, anciently much reforted to by all Nations

---

[a] Here is a great Secret in *Civil Converfation* exemplified

[b] See above, § 14

[c] There feem to be fome obfcure Intimations of this in *Hiftory*   and the Particulars hereafter deliver'd, may deferve the Confideration of thofe that are beft verfed in ancient *Hiftory*, *Geography*, and *Chronology*   Fo a more particular Knowledge of the hiftorical Facts here intimated, confult the *Univerfal Hiftory, from the earlieft Accounts of Time, to the prefent*   fome confiderable Parts whereof are already publifhed

[d] There are many 'hiftorical Paffages in the *Turkifh Spy*, rarely to be met with in other Authors, that may give fome light to feveral of thefe Intimations, which are not fo far fabulous, as to be deftitute of all Authority, or a confiderable degree of Probability   L.

tres, there no Navigators, viz *Persians*, *Chaldeans*, and *Arabians*, so that nearly all the Nations of Fame reforted to us and of thefe we have fome Remains, and little Tribes to this day And for our own Ships, they made many Voyages, as well to your *Straights*, which you call the *Pillars of Hercules*, as to other parts of the *Mediterranean* and *Atlantick*, viz *Peguin*, or *Cambalu* and *Quiz*, up the *Eaft Seas*, as far as the Borders of *Eaft-Tartary*

The great Atlantis, fome of ame 26 At the fame time, and for an age after, the People of the great *Atlantis* flourifhed For tho' the Defcription made of it by a great Man with you[a], as if the Defcendants of *Neptune* fettled there, be all poetical and fabulous, yet fo much is true, that the great *Atlant*, as well *Peru*, then called *Coya*, as *Mexico*, then called *Tirombol*, were potent Kingdoms, in Arms, Shipping, and Riches fo that nearly at the fame time, they both made two great Expeditions, the *Mexicans* thro' the *Atlantick* to the *Mediterranean*, and the *Peruvians* thro' the *South-Sea* upon this our Ifland And for the former Expedition, which was into *Europe*, the fame Author amongft you, feems to have had fome relation of it from the *Ægyptian* Prieft he introduces for fuch a thing there affuredly was But whether the ancient *Athenians* had the Glory of repelling, and deftroying thofe Forces, I can fay nothing but certain it is, there never returned Ship, or Man, from that Voyage[b] Nor would the *Mexican Expedition*, upon ourfelves, have proved more fuccefsful, if they had not met with Enemies of greater Clemency For the King of this Ifland, by name *Altabin*, a wife Man, and a great Warrior, knowing both his own Strength, and that of his Enemies, cut off their Land-Forces from their Ships, befet their Navy, and their Camp, with a greater Force than theirs, and compell'd them to furrender, without ftriking ftroke and after they were at his mercy, contented himfelf with their Oath only, that they would no more bear Arms againft him, and difmifs'd them in fafety[c]

Fatal deftruction, Inundation, or Deluge 27 But the Divine Vengeance foon over-took thefe afpiring Enterprizes For within lefs than an hundred Years, the great *Atlantis* was utterly loft and deftroy'd not by an Earthquake, as fome imagined, for that whole Tract is little fubject to Earthquakes, but by a particular *Deluge*, or *Inundation*, thofe Countries having, at this day, much greater Rivers, and higher Mountains to pour down Waters, than any part of the old World It is true, this Inundation was not deep, nor above forty foot in moft places, fo that, tho' it deftroy'd Man and Beaft in general, yet fome few wild Inhabitants of the Woods efcaped Birds alfo were faved, by flying to the high Trees

2.8

---

[a] The great Man here meant I fuppofe, is *Plato*, who, in his *Timæus*, introduces a Difcourfe betwixt Solon and an *Ægyptian* Prieft, giving *Solon* an account of the *Grecian* Antiquities, of which the *Greeks* themfelves had no Tradition And among the reft, relates the Particulars of the great *Atlantis*, their *Kings, Forces, Inundations*, &c which here feem confiderably improved by our Author See *Plato's Timæus*

[b] The feveral Parts of the following Relation, being taken together, feem to give a jufter, or more rational Account of the ignorant and barbarous State of *America*, at its firft Difcovery by the *Europeans*, than we generally meet with in Hiftories

[c] Here is an eminent Example of *military Prudence*, mixed with *Chriftian Compaffion*

28 As for the Inhabitants, tho' they had Buildings in many places higher *The Confe-* than the Waters, yet the Inundation continued so long in the Vales, that *quences there-* those who were not drown'd, perish'd for want of Food and Necessaries *of upon the Inhabitants* Whence, no wonder that *America* should be thin peopled, and the Inhabitants rude and ignorant, as being *younger by a thousand Years, than the rest of the World*, the distance between the universal Deluge, and their particular Inundation [a] For the poor Remnant of Men left in the Mountains, peopled the Country again but slowly, and being simple and savage, (not like *Noah* and his Sons, the chief Family of the Earth,) they were unable to leave *Letters*, *Arts*, and *Civility* to their Posterity and having likewise, in their mountainous Habitations, been used to clothe themselves with the Skins of Beasts, when they afterwards came down into the Valleys, and found the Heats intolerable, and knowing no lighter Apparel, they were obliged to go naked Only they greatly delighted in the Feathers of Birds, a Custom they also received from their Ancestors of the Mountains invited to it by the infinite Flights of Birds, that came up to the high Grounds, while the Waters remain'd below And by this great accident of time, we lost our Traffick with the *Americans*, among whom, as lying nearest to us, we had most Commerce [b]

29. For the other Parts of the World, it is manifest, that in the succeed- *The Decay of* ing Ages, Navigation every where decay'd; especially remote Voyages were *Navigation in* wholly dropp'd Whence People of other Nations came not to us, unless *succeeding Ages* by accident, as you have done. But yet as our Shipping, for Number, Strength, Mariners, Pilots, *&c* is as great as ever, you will wonder why we should sit indolent at home whence I am now led to answer your principal *Question*

30 About nineteen hundred Years ago, there reign'd in this Island a King, *Why the Inha-* whose Memory, of all others, we most adore, not superstitiously, but as *bitants of Ben-* being a divine Instrument, tho' a mortal Man His Name was *Solomona*, *salem remain* and we esteem him the *Law-Giver* of our Nation This King had a large *at home* Heart, *inscrutable for Goodness*, and was wholly bent upon making his King- *An account of* dom flourishing, and his People happy [c] Taking it therefore into considera- *their King* tion, (1) how sufficient his Country was to maintain itself, without any fo- *Solomona* reign assistance [d], being five thousand six hundred Miles in Circuit, and of great Fertility (2) finding also that his Shipping might be advantigeously employ'd in Fishing, Transportation, and trading to certain small Islands near us, and under our own Laws and (3) weighing the then flourishing Con-

[a] We have here a Specimen of the Author's Sagacity, in *interpreting* the Works of Nature from *Phænomena* and where only Conjecture can be had, it might be proper to deliver it in the way of Fiction, so as to preserve *certain Philosophy* distinct from *conjectural* which have too often been disadvantageously mixed together

[b] Does not this Account of *America* seem, in some respects, confirm'd by the *Periplus*, or Circumnavigation of *Hanno*? See Dr Hook's *Discourse of Earthquakes*, pag 373—375

[c] This carries an oblique Instruction to King *James the First*, whom the Author frequently stiles the *English Solomon*, and counselled to become the Law-Giver of his Country, by undertaking a *just Recompilement of the Laws* of England, and many other noble Acts of Beneficence, Glory, and Perpetuity

[d] See the *Thirteenth* SUPPLEMENT to the *de Augmentis Scientiarum*

Condition of his Country, which might be a thousand ways altered for the worse, but scarce any one way for the better he judged nothing wanting to his noble and heroical Intentions, but to give perpetuity to what in his time was so happily established[a]

31 Amongst his other fundamental Laws, he made the Prohibitions we have against the entrance of Strangers; at that time, tho' after the Calamity of divers, frequent, in order to prevent Innovations, and mixtures of Manners Indeed the like Law, against the admission of Strangers, without Licence, is ancient in *China*, and still continues[b], but it is there a trivial thing our *Law-Giver* made his Act of another temper For, *first*, he has preserved all the Points of Humanity, in providing for the Relief of Strangers distressed *Here we all rose up and bowed He went on.* Our King also still desiring to join *Humanity* and *Policy* together[c], and thinking it contrary to *Humanity*, that Strangers should be detained against their wills, and contrary to *Policy*, that they should return, and discover their knowledge of our State, he ordain'd, that of the Strangers permitted to land, as many might, at all times, depart as desired it but then those who were willing to stay, should have fair Conditions, and the means of living afforded them by the State In which Particular his Fore sight reached so far, that now, so many Ages since, we have no Records of any one Ship that ever returned, and out of thirteen Persons only, at several times, who chose to return in our own Bottoms What these few may have reported abroad, I know not: but you must think, whatever they have said, could be taken for no other than a *Dream*[a]

32 With regard to our own visiting of foreign Countries, our *Law-Giver* thought fit wholly to restrain it But it is not so among the *Chinese*, who sail where-ever they can which shews that their *Law for keeping out Strangers*, is a Law of Pusillanimity and Fear But this Restraint of ours, has only one Exception, which is admirable, as preserving the Good arising from a Communication with Strangers, and avoiding the Inconvenience I will open it to you, tho' I shall seem a little to digress, but you will soon find it pertinent

33 Among the excellent Acts of our King, that which holds the prehemimence, was the Institution of an *Order*, or SOCIETY, which we call SOLOMON's-HOUSE, the noblest *Foundation* upon Earth, and the Luminary of this Kingdom[e] It is dedicated to the Contemplation of the Works and
Creatures

---

[a] What this was will soon appear

[b] The *Jesuits* have found means to enter, chiefly under the Characters of *Physicians*, *Astronomers*, *Mathematicians*, &c

[c] We have here an admirable Lesson for *Princes*

[d] One cannot forbear reflecting how easy it is for a Man of Genius, to give the most improbable Thing an air of Truth, and at the same time, cut off all the means of Detection Whence Fiction is a dangerous thing in Philosophy, unless it be used *profeffedly* If it had been thus used by certain Philosophers, Travellers, &c *Common Sense* might have been a more *common* Thing, than we find it in this day

[e] The whole Fact appears to have been principally invented for the sake of the following Plan of a *Philosophical Society*, the *Designation* whereof shews a most penetrating and comprehensive Genius See hereafter, Sect II

Creatures of God   Some think it bears the Founder's Name, a little corrupted, as if it should be called *Solomona*'s *House*.   But our Records write it as it is spoken   whence it seems to denote the wise King of the *Hebrews*, who is famous with you, and no stranger to us, for we have some parts of his Works which you have not, particularly the *Natural History* he wrote of all the Plants, from the Cedar to the Moss, and of all things that have Life and Motion   This leads me to think, that our King, finding himself, in many respects, like that wise King of the *Hebrews*, honoured him with the Title of this Foundation   And I the rather incline to this Opinion, because I find, in ancient Records, this *Order*, or *Society*, is sometimes called by the name of SOLOMON's HOUSE, and sometimes the COLLEGE OF THE SIX DAYS WORKS   whence I am satisfied, that our excellent King had learned from the *Hebrews*, that God created the World, and all that therein is, in the space of six Days, and therefore instituting this House for discovering the true Natures of all things, he gave it also that second Name.   But now to our purpose

34   When the King forbid his People to sail to any part, not under his *The Missions of* own Dominion, he ordained, that every twelve Years two Ships should be *the Fellows of* sent on different Voyages, each Ship having on board a *Mission* of three *this Society* Fellows of *Solomon's House*, whose sole Office it should be to bring back accounts of the Affairs and State of those Countries to which they were appointed, with a more immediate regard to the *Sciences*, *Arts*, *Manufactures*, and *Inventions* of the World   and also to procure for us *Books*, *Instruments*, and *Models* in every kind   These Ships, after they had landed the Fellows, were to return, and the Mission to continue abroad till the new one was sent [a]. These Ships, besides the necessary Provision, are only freighted with Treasure, to remain with the Fellows for purchasing such Things, and rewarding such Persons, as they think proper   To say how the ordinary Sailors are kept undiscovered at land, how they conceal themselves under the Names of different Nations, to what places these Voyages have been designed, the Rendezvous appointed for the new Missions, &c. is forbid me   But thus, you see, we maintain a Traffick, not for Gold, Silver, Jewels, Silks, or Spices, but for God's first Creature LIGHT, that is, to procure Light, as to the Growth and Improvement of all Parts of the World [b].   *And when he had said this, he was silent   so were we all*, being indeed astonished to hear such strange things related with such probability.   And he perceiving that we were willing to say somewhat, but had it not ready, courteously prevented us, by Questions about our Voyage, and Successes, and in the end concluded, that we might do well to consider what time of stay to require, desiring us not to

[a] Is not something of this kind practised by the *Jesuits*?   And can Philosophy thrive in all its Branches, unless the same Course be taken by Philosophical Countries?   See the *Preliminaries* to the *De Augmentis Scientiarum*, Sect IV

[b] Here lies, perhaps, the greatest Obstacle to the Advancement of Knowledge, the predominant Passion of Gain   to be serious upon which Head, is almost sufficient to render a Man's Sense suspected   And yet, till Gain shall become only a secondary Consideration, there is reason to believe that the greatest Advantages of Philosophy will remain unreaped.   See the Fable of *Atalanta* explained in the *Sapientia Veterum*.

ftint ourfelves, for that he would procure as much as we wifhed Upon which we all rofe up, and prefented ourfelves to kifs the Skirt of his Tippet, but he would not permit us, fo took his leave

35 Our People being now informed, that the State ufed to offer Conditions to fuch Strangers as would continue among them, we could fcarce get any of the Company to look after the Ship, or prevent them from going directly to the Governour to crave Conditions But, with much difficulty, we reftrained them, till we might agree among ourfelves what Courfe to take

---

SECT. II.

1 WE now took ourfelves to be free, apprehending no danger, and paffed the time delightfully, viewing what was to be feen in the City, and Places adjacent, and making acquaintance with many of the better fort, in whom we found fuch Humanity, Freedom, and Affection to Strangers, as might have made us forget all that was dear to us in our own Countries. We continually met with Things worthy of Obfervation and indeed, if there be a Mirror in the world to detain Mens Eyes, it is that Country, which, by all the accounts we received, is not to be equalled for its *Laws*, *Cuftoms*, *Policy*, *Morality*, and *Philofophy* [a]

2 One thing very extraordinary happen'd whilft we continued there, viz one of the *Fathers of* SOLOMON'S HOUSE, for fome fecret Reafon, vifited the City, a thing that had not been feen among them for twelve Years before He entred with a decent and folemn Pomp and Ceremony, and in three days after, fent us word he would admit all our Company into his Prefence; and hold a private Conference with one of us The time being fix'd, we were introduced, and found him richly and gravely clothed, feated upon a low Throne, with a Cloth of State over his Head, of blue Sattin, embroider'd attended only by two Pages of Honour, richly dreffed, in white [b] At our entrance we bowed low, as we were inftructed to do, and as we approached his Chair, he ftood up, and held out his naked Hand in a Pofture of Bleffing Each of us ftooped, and kiffed the Hem of his Tippet This being over, the reft departed, and I remain'd, as was intended [c] then ordering

---

[a] Poffibly the Author intended to have enriched this Fable, not only with a *Body of Laws*, but a Set of *Cuftoms* and moral *Doctrines*, all tending to render a Nation happy, and politically philofophical 'Tis fufficiently evident, that the whole Defign is not executed Perhaps feveral Particulars here wanting might be fupplied from Sir *Thomas More's Utopia* With regard to a *Body of Laws* for this purpofe, fee *A Continuation of the New Atlantis*, printed at *London*, in 1660

[b] Obferve, that the Author all along makes a grave and decent Ufe of Wealth, to be an Attendant upon Knowledge, in whofe power it certainly is, to obtain not only Riches, but every other human Bleffing

[c] By thus making the reft of the Company depart, the Author intimates, that the following Account is not fuited to vulgar Ears

dering the Pages out of the Room, he caufed me to fit down by him, and thus fpoke to me in *Spanifh*

3. God blefs thee, my Son   I will give thee the greateft Jewel I have, and *The Father's* impart to thee, for the Love of God and Men, an account of SOLOMON's *Difcourfe to* HOUSE   I will relate, (1) the End of our *Inftitution*, (2) the Apparatus and *the chief Man* Inftruments for our Works, (3) the Functions and Employments of our *of the Com-* Fellows, and (4) the Rites and Ordinances we obferve *pany*

4 The End of our Foundation is the KNOWLEDGE OF CAUSES, the fecret *The End of the* Motions of Things, and the Enlargement of the Empire of Man, by the *Inftitution of* effecting of all Things poffible[a]. *Solomon's College*

5 Our Apparatus and Inftruments are thefe   *Large Caves*, of different *Its Apparatus* depths   fome of them fix hundred Fathom, and others running under great *of Caves* Hills and Mountains, three Miles together.   For we find that the Height of a Hill, and the Depth of a Cave from the Flat, is the fame thing, both being defended alike from the Sun, and the open Air.   Thefe Caves we call the *Lower Region*, and we ufe them for all forts of *Coagulations, Indurations, Refrigerations*, and *Confervations* of Bodies   We employ them likewife for imitating *natural Mines*, and producing new artificial Metals, by Compofitions, and certain Materials, which we fuffer to lie in them for many Years. Sometimes alfo we ufe them for *curing Difeafes*, and *prolonging Life* in certain Hermits, who voluntarily chufe to live in them, where they are well accommodated with all things neceffary   and thus they not only lengthen their Days, but give us Informations of many confiderable Particulars[b].

6 We practife *Burials* in different kind of *Earths*, where we lay up feve-*Burials* ral *Cements*, as the *Chinefe* do their Porcellane[c]   But we have them in greater variety than they, and fome that are much finer   We have alfo a great variety of *Compofts*, and *Soils*, for making the Earth fruitful[d]

7 We have *tall Towers*, the higheft about half a Mile tall   fome likewife *Towers and* ftand upon very high Mountains, fo as to reach three Miles perpendicular *Obfervatories* from the Earth's Surface   And thefe Places we call the UPPER REGION; accounting the Air between the high Places and the low, as a MIDDLE
                        Pp 2   REGION

[a] Let this, and all that fucceeds, be well compared with the Author's Doctrine laid down in the *Novum Organum*, whereby not only the bare Poffibility, but the Practicability of the whole Scheme will, in great meafure, appear   And for a further proof hereof, fee the *De Augmentis Scientiarum*, the *Sylva Sylvarum*, the *Scala Intellectus*   and remember that all thefe were the Works of one Man, whofe whole Life was taken up with civil Bufinefs, except the five laft Years

[b] Is not fomething of this kind, tho inferior in its Defign, practifed in the Salt-Mines of *Wilizca*, in Poland, where a whole People continue to live under-ground?   But the Intimations here given by the Author, go beyond the *common Philofophy*, and tend to eftablifh another of a much nobler and more ferviceable kind   The Cave at the Royal Obfervatory at *Paris* may, in fome meafure, fhew the nature of this Defign

[c] See the Article *Burials* in the *Sylva Sylvarum*

[d] Every Article here is fo pregnant with *grand philofophical Views*, and *Directions for farther Difcoveries*, that a large *Comment* were requifite to unfold and draw them out for popular Ufe   As they here lie clofe wedged, in the *aphoriftical*, or *axiomatical manner*, they will probably affect only the firft rate Philofophers   It feems a juft Obfervation, that the generality of Readers, like the generality of Game, are only to be caught by Nets wide fpread, *viz* by the *Afiatick Style*, rather than the *Laconic*   And on this account, concife Hints and Intimations are always moft acceptable to the Intelligent, as larger Difcourfes, and full Explanations, are to the lefs knowing

REGION We use thefe *Towers*, according to their feveral Heights and Situations, for *Infolation, Refrigeration, Confervation*, and the *Obfervation* of *Meteors*, as *Winds, Rain, Snow, Hail*, and fome of the *fiery Meteors* Upon
feveral of thefe *Towers* are Dwelling-places for *Hermits*, whom we fometimes
vifit, and inftruct what to obferve [a]

Lakes 8 We have great *Lakes*, both falt and frefh, for Fifh and Fowl [b] We
ufe them alfo for the Burials of fome natural Bodies for we find a difference
betwixt things buried in *Earth*, or in Air below the Earth, and thofe that

And Pc are buried in Water. We have alfo *Pools*, fome whereof ftrain frefh Water
out of Salt, and others, by Art, turn frefh Water into falt [c]

R k 9 We have likewife *Rocks* in the midft of the Sea, and certain *Bays* upon the Shore, for particular Works, which require the Air and Sea-Vapour [d].

Cataracts 10 Again, we have violent Streams and Cataracts, which ferve us for nu-
for Me. and merous Motions and likewife *Engines* for multiplying and increafing the
Wind Engines force of Winds, to fet various Machines in motion [e]

Artificial 11 We have many *artificial Springs* and Fountains, made in imitation of
Springs the natural Sources and Baths, impregnated with different Minerals [f]

Wells for In- 12 We have *little Wells*, for making Infufions of many Things, where the
fusions Waters take the Virtue quicker, and better, than in Veffels or Bafins [g]. And
amongft the reft, we have a Water, which we call the WATER OF PARA-
DISE, being, by fomething we do to it, made fovereign for Health, and the
prolongation of Life [h]

Meteor-Houfes 13 We have *fpacious Houfes*, where we imitate, and exhibit *Meteors*, as
Snow, Hail. Rain, certain artificial Rains, of other Bodies befides Water [i],
Thunders, Lightenings, &c as alfo various Generations of Bodies in Air, as
Frogs, Flies, &c.

Chambers of 14 We have certain Chambers, which we call CHAMBERS OF HEALTH,
Health where we qualify the Air, as we judge proper, for the Cure of many Difeafes,
and the Prefervation of Health [k]

15.

---

[a] This were ufing the Humour of the ancient *Hermits, Stylites*, &c to fome good purpofe
The modern Obfervatories feem in a confiderable degree, to execute this part of the Author's Defign
[b] See the *Sylva Sylvarum*, under the Article *Fifh*
[c] See the *Sylva Sylvarum*, under the Article *Percolation*
[d] As in the making of *Bay-Salt*, for example, and other more curious Purpofes, in the way
of *Congelation Irfpiffation Exhalation, Impregnation*, &c
[e] See the Author's *Hiftory of Winds*
[f] To this purpofe, fee *New Experiments and Obfervations upon Mineral Waters*, by Dr. *Hoffman*,
printed at *London*, 1731
[g] See the Article *Infufion*, in the *Sylva Sylvarum*
[h] See the Author's *Hiftory of Life and Death*, and his *Methufalem Water*, in the *Sylva Sylvarum*, under the Article *Medicine*
[i] Of which there have been many Inftances in Nature, viz Showers of Mud, Fifh, &c
See Mr *Boyle's Works*, and the *Philofophical Tranfactions*
[k] This is a noble Intimation for Phyficians, if they were bent upon improving their Art
The Air is a general Menftruum, capable of receiving, and being impregnated with the *Effluvia,
Fumes*, and *Exhalations* of all kinds of Drugs, or Simples, and of thus conveying them in Refpiration into the Lungs and Blood, perhaps to better advantage than any other way And thus
Death and Sicknefs are frequently convey'd, by the fame way that Health and long Life poffibly
might be But what Society is fet a part for making Experiments of this kind? Or what has
all *Europe* done, for thefe hundred Years, towards executing the entire Scheme of *Solomon's
College*?

15 We have alſo large and elegant Baths, of ſeveral Mixtures, for the *Artificial* Cure of Diſeaſes, or reſtoring the Body from Dryneſs occaſion'd by Age and *Baths* others for confirming it, in its vital Parts, and recruiting it in its Strength, Juices, and Subſtance [a]

16 We have many large *Orchards* and *Gardens*, wherein we do not ſo much re- *Orchards and* gard Beauty, as variety of Ground and Soil, proper for different Trees and Plants *Gardens for* Some of theſe Places are very extenſive, and planted with Vines, Fruit-Trees, *Experiments* and Shrubs, that bear Berries for making ſeveral kinds of Drinks, beſides Wine *upon Vegeta-* Here alſo we try Experiments of grafting and inoculating, as well of Wild- *tion* Trees as Fruit-Trees, which produce many Effects [b]. Here likewiſe, by Art, we make Trees, and Flowers, to come earlier or later than their Seaſons, and to ſhoot and bear abundantly out of their natural Courſes. By Art we alſo render them larger, and their Fruit bigger, ſweeter, and more different in Taſte, Smell, Colour, and Figure, than Nature alone produces them. And others we ſo order, that they become of ſingular medicinal Uſe [c]

17 We have alſo Methods of making *Plants riſe by Mixtures of Earths,* *Plants grow-* without Seeds [d], and likewiſe of making new Plants, differing from the vul- *ing without* gar, and of converting one Plant into another [e]. *Seeds*

18 We have *Parks* and *Encloſures* for all ſorts of *Beaſts* and *Birds*, which *Parks and En-* we keep not only for Curioſity and Entertainment, but for Diſſections and *cloſures, for* Experiments, with a view to diſcover what may be wrought upon the human *Animals, and* Body. And by theſe means we become Maſters of many ſtrange Effects *the Production* ſuch as the continuing of Life, tho' ſeveral Parts, which you account vital, be *of new Species.* periſhed, and cut away, the recovering of ſome Creatures after they ſeem dead, and the like [f] We alſo try Poiſons, and other Medicines upon them; as well with regard to *Chirurgery*, as *Phyſick* [g] By Art, likewiſe, we make Animals larger, or taller, than their kind, and contrariwiſe ſtint their Growth [h]. We alſo make them more fruitful, than their kind, and again barren, or not generative. We likewiſe make them differ ſeveral ways, in Colour, Shape, and Activity We have Methods of making Commixtures, and Copulations of different ſorts, which produce many new kinds, and thoſe not barren, con-

trary

[a] See the Article *Baths*, in the *Sylva Sylvarum* ſee alſo the *Hiſtory of Life and Death*

[b] See the *Sylva Sylvarum*, under the Articles *Vegetables* and *Vegetation*

[c] Tho' Gardening, and the Subject of Vegetation, in general, has received conſiderable Improvements of late, yet there ſeems to be wanting a ſkilful Sagacity in this Art, to direct the proper Experiments both of Light and Profit This Sagacity might, in good meaſure, be learnt from a due Knowledge and Proſecution of the Author's *Doctrine of Learned Experience* See *De Augmentis Scientiarum* Sect XII

[d] This Particular may appear ſtrange, but it is countenanced by the *Growth of Muſhrooms*, and ſeveral other Experiments in the *French Memoirs*, &c tending to ſhew, that the Seeds of all material Things, are every where diffuſed in the Earth, and Atmoſphere

[e] Many Experiments of this kind ſtill remain to be tried See the *Sylva Sylvarum*, under the Article *Vegetables* and *Vegetation*

[f] This kind of *Anatomy* has certainly not been proſecuted as it deſerves

[g] Here is a rational, and almoſt unexceptionable Method chalked out for diſcovering the Cures of certain Diſeaſes, vulgarly accounted incurable See the *Sylva Sylvarum*, under the Articles *Medicine, Plague*, &c

[h] See the *Sylva Sylvarum*, under the Articles *Animals, Growth*, &c.

try, to our general Opinion[a] We produce numberless kinds of Serpents, Worms, Flies, and Fishes, by means of *Putrefaction*, some whereof advance to be perfect Creatures like Beasts or Birds, and propagate Neither is this the Effect of Chance, but we know before-hand, from what Matter and Commixture, and of what kind these Creatures will arise[b]

Ponds for Experimenting upon Fish

19 We have particular Ponds, where we make Trials upon Fishes, after the same manner as I said of Beasts and Birds[c]

Breeding Places for several Insects

20 We have Breeding-Places for those kinds of Worms, and Flies, which are of particular use, such as your *Silk-worms*, and *Bees*[d]

Particular Brew-houses, Bake-houses, &c

21 I will not detain you by recounting our *Brew-Houses*, *Bake-Houses*, and *Kitchens*, where we make different kinds of *Drinks*, *Breads*, and *Meats* of extraordinary Virtues Here we make, not only Wines of the Grape, but Drinks of other Juices of Fruits, Grains and Roots, and with Mixtures of

Drinks of various kinds

Honey, Sugar, Manna, and Fruits dry'd and preserved, as also of the Tears or Tappings of Trees, and of the Pulp of Canes[e] And these Drinks are of several Ages, some forty Years old We also brew Drinks with several Herbs Roots, and Spices, and again, with several kinds of Flesh and White-Meats and some of these Drinks are, in effect, both *Meat* and *Drink*, so that many, especially the aged, desire to live upon them, with little or no use of Meat or Bread[f] And above all, we endeavour to prepare Drinks of extremely thin and fluid Parts, that they may insinuate into the Body ; yet without all sharpness or fretting for some of them being laid upon the back of the Hand, will soon pass thro' to the Palm, yet taste mild in the Mouth[g] We have also *Waters*, which we ripen so, that they become nourishing, and prove such excellent Drink, that many will use no other

Bread of several kinds

22 We have also *Breads* of several Grains, Roots, and Kernels, some of dried Flesh and Fish, with different kinds of Seasonings Some of these Breads greatly provoke the Appetite, and others nourish so that many will live upon them, without any other Meat

23.

---

[a] Experiments of this kind have been extremely rare in *Europe* on account, perhaps, of the prevalence of the vulgar Opinion here mentioned

[b] Here is a pitch of Perfection to which, in the general Opinion, *Natural Philosophy* will never arrive But this, perhaps, is a greater Argument of our Indolence, than of our Knowledge

[c] See the Article *Fish Flesh* &c in the *Sylva Sylvarum*

[d] See the *Sylva Sylvarum*, under the Articles Caterpillars, *Insects*, *Putrefaction* &c

[e] These are very useful Intimations. See the *Sylva Sylvarum*, under the Articles *Clarification*, *Drinks*, *Manna*, *Percolation*, *Sugar*, and *Wines*

[f] See the *History of Life and Death* and the *Sylva Sylvarum*, under the Article *Foods*

[g] This will doubtless seem incredible, yet there are *Instances* that might serve to render it probable We see the same thing done in Metals, where a Liquor will pass thro' the Substance of them without corroding their Parts, as Oil will do into Iron And so some Medicines are extremely penetrating, and active in the Body, yet innocent, and without any corrosive Virtue But for a *fermented Liquor* so subtle and penetrating as that here intimated, perhaps it has not yet been made, nor indeed, can it well be expected, till Men shall become better acquainted with the Nature and Management of *Fermentation*, and the ways of applying it to *fermentable Matters* less gross than the common It is worth enquiring, *whether a fermented Liquor or Wine can be prepared, which, instead of shooting Tartar, shall strike a neutral, or alkaline Salt to one Side of the containing Vessel* An active penetrating Wine of this kind, might possibly, by continued use dissolve the Stone in the Bladder

2

23 For *Meats*, we have some that are made so soft and tender, and yet *Meats of va-*
without any Corruption, that a weak Stomach may convert them into good *rious kinds*
Juices, as well as a strong one would Meats otherwise prepared   We have
also certain *Foods*, and likewise *Breads*, and *Drinks*, which enable Men to
fast long after using them, and others that make the Flesh of the Body
more hard and tough, and the Strength far greater than natural [a]

24 We have *Dispensaries*, or *Shops of Medicines*, wherein, as our variety *Shops of Me-*
of Plants and Animals is much greater than with you in *Europe*, so our *dicines*
variety of Simples, Drugs, and medicinal Ingredients, must consequently be
greater   and these we have of different Ages, and long Fermentations [b] And,
for our Preparations, we have not only all manner of exquisite *Distillations*, and
Separations, especially those by gentle Heats, and Percolations thro' different Strainers, and gross Substances, but also Exact Forms of Composition, whereby the Ingredients incorporate almost as if they were natural
Simples [c]

25 We have many *mechanic Arts*, which you have not, and a variety of *Manufactures*
Stuffs made by their Means; such as *Papers*, *Linens*, *Silks*, *Tissues*, Works in
Feathers, of great Beauty and Lustre, excellent Dyes [d], &c   We have likewise
Shops, as well for such Manufactures and Productions as are not brought
into vulgar use amongst us, as for those that are. For you must know, that
tho' many of the Things before enumerated are grown into common use
throughout the Kingdom, yet, when they were of our own *Invention*, we constantly retain not only Samples, Models, or Patterns thereof, but also *Prin-
cipals*

26 We have *Furnaces* of great diversity, and for different Heats, as *Furnaces and*
fierce and quick, strong and constant, soft and mild, blown, quiet, dry, *chemical Ap-*
moist, and the like   But above all, we have Heats in imitation of the Sun's *paratus.*
Heat, that operate with several Inequalities, and, as it were, periodically, by
way of progress and return, whereby we produce extraordinary Effects [e].
Besides these, we have *digesting Heats*, by means of Dunghills, the Bellies, Stomachs, Blood, and Bodies of living Creatures, and again, of Hay, and
Herbs laid up moist, of Quick-Lime, &c   We have likewise Instruments
that generate Heat by Motion, Places for strong Insolations, and others
under the Earth, which yield us Heats either by Nature, or Art.   All these
different Heats we use, as the Nature of our Operations require [f].   27.

[a] Certainly these things are not altogether impracticable, even with the slender degree of Knowledge we have at present, but Men are so enamour'd with the talkative Philosophy, that the
active one finds few Votaries

[b] By means, suppose, of particular Methods of preserving them from the Air, and other Injuries

[c] The Rule here intimated seems to have been little consider'd in *Pharmacy*, where the numerous Mixtures made, are generally slight, gross, and imperfect

[d] See the Catalogue of *particular Histories* required for the Interpretation of *Nature*   Introduction to the *Sylva Sylvarum*, Sect II

[e] This Direction for imitating the Sun's periodical Heat in chemical Operations, is more fully
insisted on by the Author in other places   See the *Novum Organum*, Part II Sect I *& alibi*
passim   See also the *Sylva Sylvarum*, under the Articles *Flame* and *Heat*

[f] Here are excellent Intimations for the Improvement of *Chemistry*, which has hitherto been
confined to a small variety of Heats   Whoever would imitate Nature in her various Productions,

o   27 We have *Optick-Houses*, where we make Experiments upon Light and Colours, and out of things, in themſelves uncoloured and tranſparent, repreſent diverſities of Colours, not barely by Refractions, or in the way of Rainbows, as by means of Gems and Priſms of Glaſs, but ſingly and ſimply [a]. We likewiſe repreſent all kinds of Multiplications of Light, which we convey to great diſtances, and thus become able to diſcern extremely ſmall Points and Lines   Here we exhibit the various kinds of Light, Deluſions, and Deceptions of the Sight, in Figures, Magnitudes, Motions, Colours, and the Phænomen of Shadows   We have alſo ſeveral ways, yet unknown to you, of producing Light, originally from various Bodies [b].   We are able to ſee Objects diſtinctly at an immenſe Diſtance, both in the Heavens, and upon the Earth, and can repreſent all things near us, as if they were far off; and things afar off, as if they were near; thus making imaginary Diſtances.   We have alſo *Helps for the Sight*, greatly exceeding the Spectacles and Reading Glaſſes in uſe with you [c]   We have means of ſeeing extremely minute Bodies, with great diſtinctneſs, as the ſmalleſt Flies, Mites, &c. the Grains and Flaws in Gems, &c which could not otherwiſe be diſcovered   and thus we are enabled to make certain Obſervations upon Urine, Blood, &c that were not practicable without this aſſiſtance [d]   We have artificial Rainbows, Halo's, and Circles about Lights   We exhibit all manner of Reflections, Refractions, and Multiplications of the Rays of Light [e]

Collections of Gems and Fossil.   28. We have *Precious Stones* of all kinds, many of great Beauty, and to you unknown, Cryſtals likewiſe, and Glaſſes of different ſorts, and among the reſt, ſome of vitrified Metals, and other Materials, beſides thoſe of which you make your Glaſs in *Europe*   We have likewiſe great numbers of *Foſſils*, and imperfect Minerals, which you have not   We have Load-ſtones of prodigious Virtues, and other ſcarce and valuable Stones, both natural and artificial [f]

Sound Houses.   29. We have alſo *Sound-Houſes*, where we practiſe and produce all kinds of *Sounds*   We have *Harmonies*, unknown to you, of *quarter Sounds*, and leſſer *Slides of Sounds*   We have many different *Muſical Inſtruments*, ſome of them ſweeter than any of yours, and alſo curious Bells, and Sets or Rings thereof

tions, ſhould, as near as poſſible, uſe the ſame kind of Heats and Proceſſes, as ſhe employs   See the Article *Heat* in the *Sylva Sylvarum*

[a] Here are ſome Intimations for farther Diſcoveries in Opticks, than any hitherto made, how much ſoever this Subject may have been cultivated

[b] As Glaſs ſuppoſe, by Friction, Quickſilver by Agitation, &c

[c] This may perhaps, be thought a thing ſpoke at random   but certainly the beſt Methods of helping the Sight are not hitherto generally practiſed   By the beſt Methods I mean ſuch as improve and ſtrengthen the Organ, and enable the Eye at length to perform its Office, without aſſiſtance   And in this view, let full Trial, and due Improvement, be made of *ſhort Tubes*, without Glaſſes, after the manner recommended in the *Philoſophical Tranſactions*, N° 37

[d] We have here a general Direction to the Microſcope, but ſomething farther is ſtill wanted in Philoſophy

[e] If this *Fable* had been wrote ſince the time of Mr *Boyle*, Dr *Hook*, and Sir *Iſaac Newton*, its phyſical Part would, doubtleſs, have appeared as if taken from them

[f] Perhaps the Foundation of that excellent Collection of *Foſſils*, and other natural and artificial Curioſities, belonging to the *Royal Society* of *London*, was laid in this Paragraph.

I

thereof. We can reprefent *fmall Sounds*, as great and *deep*, and loud ones, as little and weak We make many different Tremblings and Warblings of Sounds, which are entire in their Origin We reprefent and imitate all articulate Sounds, Letters, and the Voices and Notes of Beafts and Bird's We have certain Helps, which, applied to the Ear, greatly improve the Hearing We have many ftrange and artificial Echoes, that reflect the Voice a great number of times, and, as it were, tofs it from one part to another. and fome that give back the Voice louder than it came, fome fhriller, and fome deeper, and fome again that render the Voice different in the Letters, or articulate Sounds, from what they receive it We alfo practife certain ways of conveying Sounds by Trunks, and Pipes, in a ftrange variety of Lines, to furprizing Diftances[a].

30 We have *Perfume-Houfes*, wherein we alfo purfue the Bufinefs of *Tafte* We multiply Smells, which may feem ftrange[b] We imitate Odours, and make them breathe out of other Mixtures than thofe that naturally yield them We make many Imitations of *Taftes*, fo as to deceive any Man And in this Houfe we have alfo a *Confectionary*, where we make all kinds of Sweet-Meats, dry and moift, feveral pleafant Wines, Milks, Broths, and Sallads, in far greater variety than you have them[c].

[margin: Perfume-Houfes, and a Confectionary]

31 We have *Engine-Houfes*, where we make Engines and Inftruments for all forts of Motions Here we employ much more violent Powers than any you have, and make, and multiply them more eafily, and with fmall Force, by the means of Wheels, and other Contrivances fo as to exceed the Force of your largeft Cannon[d] We here exhibit Ordnance, the Inftruments of War, and Engines of all kinds. Here we try and preferve our new Mixtures and Compofitions of Gun-Powder, unquenchable Fires, and Fire-Works of infinite variety, both for Pleafure and Ufe[e] We here alfo imitate the Flights of Birds We practife fome degree of flying in the Air[f] We have Ships and Boats for going under Water[g], and living at Sea, as alfo Swimming-Girdles, and Supporters We have divers Clocks, and other Machines of

[margin: Engine-Houfes]

[a] The Author has, with confiderable Diligence, profecuted this whole Enquiry, in his *Sylva Sylvarum* See the Article *Sounds* But to bring it to the degree of Perfection here intimated, may require a confiderable number of Hands, and a length of Time And if due Application were ufed, I conceive that no one Particular here intimated is impracticable

[b] Suppofe by Reflexion, or rather by the Condenfation of Air, which is the Medium or Vehicle of Odours, as well as Sounds

[c] The Particulars intimated in this Paragraph, have been but little purfued in the way of pure philofophical Enquiry, tho' capable of adding greatly to the innocent Pleafures of Life, and the laudable Gratification of the Senfe and Appetite

[d] The Author here feems to intimate certain Combinations of the mechanical Powers, as the Lever, the Wedge, the Pulley, and the Screw, but then the Effect will be flow Perhaps he alfo had in view certain *deftructive Explofions*, of which we have fome Examples in Chemiftry

[e] This Direction feems not to have been follow'd fo far as it might, both in the way of Entertainment, and Service in Life Perhaps it were practicable to imitate the Phænomena of the Sun and Day-light, and of the Moon and Stars, at any time, in a fpacious Room, fo as to require no other Illumination

[f] See the Article *Flying*, in the *Sylva Sylvarum*

[g] *Cornelius Drebbel* is faid to have made a Veffel of this kind, and to have experienced it in the River *Thames*

return ; and some kinds of *perpetual Motions*[a]   We imitate the Motions of Animals, in Images of Men, Beasts, Birds, Fishes and Serpents   We have also great numbers of other different Motions, surprizing for their Fineness, Subtilty, and Uniformity [b]

A Mathe-matical House

32 We have a *Mathematical House*, where we exhibit all kinds of Instruments, exquisirely made , as well for the service of Geometry, as Astronomy.

Houses of De-ception

33. We have *Deception-Houses*, for imposing upon the Senses, where we exhibit all the Feats of Juggling, false Apparitions, Impositions, Illusions, and their Fallacies   And you will easily believe, that we who have so many things truly natural, which raise the Admiration, could, in abundance of particulars, deceive the Senses , if we were disposed to disguise those natural Things, and endeavour to make them appear more miraculous.   But we abominate Imposture and Falshood , insomuch, that all our Fellows are strictly forbid, under pain of Ignominy and Fines, to shew any natural Work, or Thing, adorned and pompous, or otherwise than pure and simple, as it is in itself, without the least Affectation of Wonder and Strangeness[c].   These are, my Son, the Riches of *Solomon's House*

The Em-ployments O-fices, and Fellows

34 For the several Employments and Offices of our *Fellows* ; we have twelve , who sail into foreign Countries, under the Names of other Nations ;

Twelve Mer-chants of Light

and bring us the Books, Abstracts, and Models of Experiments of all other Parts of the World   These we call MERCHANTS OF LIGHT[d]

Three Depre-dators

35 We have three who collect the *Experiments* contained in Books.   These we call DEPREDATORS

Three Mystery-Men

36 We have three that collect the Experiments of all mechanical Arts, liberal Sciences, and Practices not yet brought into Arts   These we call MYSTERY MEN[e].

Three Miners

37 We have three that try new Experiments, such as themselves think proper   These we call PIONEERS, or MINERS[f].

Three Com-pilers

38 We have three that draw the Experiments of the former Sets into Tables and Tables, to give the better light for the deduction of OBSERVATIONS and AXIOMS from them [g]   These we call COMPILERS.

39

---

[a] Imperfect ones suppose, as a Piece of Clock-Work, for instance, that might be wound up by the *Spring Tide*, &c   But for a perfectly self moving Engine, the Author gives no Intimation about it

[b] The Doctrine of Mechanicks has been considerably cultivated of late, but still comes short of Perfection

[c] This Injunction is of the utmost Importance, for guarding the Understanding, and preserving common Sense   For want of a Check of this kind, many Authors, instead of delivering plain natural Truths, have utter'd strange Doctrines, in the way of Miracle, and thus sometimes infatuated whole Nations   Doubtless, if it were practicable, it should be made penal, thus to corrupt Mens Minds, and ruin common Sense, by imposing false Notions, and propagating Superstition and Delusion thro a People

[d] The great Sagacity and Justness, shewn in directing the following Particulars, and their vast Utility will scarce be discerned, unless the Reader has a tolerable Knowledge of the Scheme and Tendency of the Author's *Novum Organum*

[e] See the *De Augmentis Scientiarum*, Sect IV

[f] See the *De Augmentis Scientiarum*, Sect III 8

[g] See the *Novum Organum*, Part II Sect I

39. We have three that look into the Experiments of their Fellows, and *Three Bene-*
cast about, how to draw out of them Things of practical Ufe for Knowledge *factors*
and the fervice of Life , that is, as well for *Works*, as for the *plain Demonftra-*
tion of Caufes, the means of *natural Divinations*, and the eafy and clear difcovery of the Virtues and Powers of Bodies Thefe we call DOWRY-MEN, or
BENEFACTORS

40 Then, after divers *Meetings* and *Confultations* of our whole Number, *Three Lamps*
to confider of the former Labours and Collections, we have three, whofe
Care and Bufinefs it is, to direct from the whole *New Experiments of a fub-*
limer kind, that penetrate farther into Nature than the former   Thefe
we call LAMPS

41. We have three others that perform the *Experiments* fo directed; and *Three Inocula-*
report them.   Thefe we call INOCULATORS *tors*

42 We have three that raife the former Difcoveries, by Experiments, into *Three Inter-*
larger *Obfervations*, *Aphorifms*, and *Axioms*   Thefe we call INTERPRETERS *preters of Na-*
OF NATURE [a]. *ture*

43. We have alfo, as you will eafily imagine, Pupils and Learners, that *Pupils and*
the Succeffion may not fail [b], befides a great number of Servants and Atten- *Servants*
dants, both Men and Women

44 We likewife hold *Confultations*, as to which of our new *Inventions* and *Confultations*
Experiments fhould be publifhed, and which not , and all take an Oath of
Secrecy, for concealing of thofe we think proper to keep fecret : tho' part of
thefe we fometimes reveal to the State, and fometimes not [c].

45 For our *Rites* and *Ordinances*, we have two very long and beautiful *Their Rites*
Galleries, in one whereof we place Samples and Models of all the more ex- *and Ordinan-*
cellent Inventions , in the other, the *Statues* of all *principal Inventors*   Here *ces, in pre-*
we have the Statue of *Columbus*, who difcovered the *Weft-Indies*, that of the *ferving Models*
Inventor of Ships, your *Monk that invented Ordnance* and *Gun-Powder* , the *of Inventions,*
Inventor of Mufick, the *Inventor of Letters*, the *Inventor of Printing*, the *of Inventors*
Inventor of Aftronomical Obfervations, the *Inventor of Works in Metal*, the
Inventor of Glafs, the *Inventor of S.lk*, the *Inventor of Wine*, the *Inventor of*
Corn and Bread, the *Inventor of Sugars* and all thefe by more certain Tra-
dition than you have them   We have likewife the Statues of many Inventors among ourfelves, who difcover'd excellent Works, which, fince you
have not feen, it were too tedious to defcribe them befides, you might eafily
err in the underftanding of my Defcriptions.   In fhort, upon every *Invention*

Qq 2

of

[a] We have here a moft ferviceable Leffon in Philofophy, fhewing the way wherein Knowledge is to be gather'd, like Honey, from feveral Flowers, and treafured up for ufe Without
a Metaphor, the whole Procefs of the Mind, in philofophical Enquiries, is here exactly defcribed

[b] Thus the penfionary Members of the *Royal Academy of Sciences* at *Paris* have their *Eleves*

[c] Perhaps this Referve of a Power of with holding certain Difcoveries from the State, tho'
a thing in itfelf ex remely wife and prudent, (becaufe Governours are not always good moral
Philofophers,) may be the greateft Objection againft the founding of fuch a College as is here
model'd out   Certainly, as the Author intimates above, it requires a Prince of a large Heart,
and a Philofophical People, to execute this Plan in all its Parts   It has, however, been executed
to advantage, in fome of its Parts witnefs the *Royal Society* of *London*, and the *Royal Academy*
of *Paris*, and poffibly may in more hereafter

of Value, we erect a *Statue to the Inventor*; and give him a liberal and honourable Reward[a]　Thefe Statues are fome of Brafs, fome of Marble,
fome of Cedar gilt, other and curious gilt Woods, fome of Iron, fome of
Silver, fome of Gold

Their Religious Ceremonies　46. We have certain Hymns and Services, which we daily repeat, of Praife
and Thanks to God for his marvellous Works　and Forms of Prayers,
imploring his Aid and Blefling for the Illumination of our Labours, and the
turning of them to good and pious Ufes

In Progress　47 Laftly, we have our Progreffes, or Vifitations, to feveral principal
Cities of the Kingdom, where we publifh fuch new profitable Inventions, as we
think proper　We alfo give out *natural Divinations* of Difeafes, Plagues,
Swarms of hurtful Creatures, Scarcity, Tempefts, Earthquakes, Inundations,
Comets, the Temperature of the Year, &c and add our Advice to the People upon thefe Occafions, directing them as to what they fhall do, either by
way of Prevention, or Remedy[b]

Conclusion　48 When he had faid this, he ftood up　and I, as I had been taught,
kneel'd down, then he laid his right Hand upon my Head, and faid, *God
ble*ſ *thee, my Son; and God blefs this Relation which I have made　I give thee
leave to publifh it for the good of other Nations, being ourfelves a happy People,
in a Land unknown.*　Here he left me　but affign'd a noble Bounty to our
whole Ship's Company.　For they are extremely liberal where ever they
come[c]

　　[a] Perhaps there cou'd be no greater Spur to Inventions of all kinds, than thus to have the
Inventor honoured and rewarded　This Subject is touched by the Author on feveral other Occafions

　　[b] Natural Philofophy muft be confiderably improv'd, beyond what it is at prefent, before any
fuch Prediction can be made, and fuch Directions given　See the Article *Divination*, in the
Sylva Sylvarum

　　[c] Here again we have a fufficient Intimation, that Wealth might eafily be made the Attendant of *Knowledge*, and practical Philofophy　The Author appears to have propofed a Scheme
of this kind to King *James the Firft*, fhewing him a way of becoming immenfely rich, without being burdenfome to his Subjects　This way was, fo far as I can difcover, by making great Improvements in Mineral Works, and the Draining of Lands and Mines　But no great ftrefs can be
laid upon Mr *Bufhel's Account* of this Matter　For tho that Gentleman was long a Domeftick
to the Author, and probably knew many of his Lord's Defigns, yet, when he wrote the *Abridgment of the Lord Chancellor Bacon's Philofophical Theory in Mineral Profecutions*, he appears not
to have had the perfect ufe of his Reafon, perhaps on account of his Misfortunes in Life

SUPPLEMENT II.

A

SPECIMEN

OF THE

HISTORY

OF

GREAT BRITAIN.

THE

Beginning of a HISTORY

OF

GREAT BRITAIN[a].

1 BY the deceafe of Queen *Elizabeth*, the Iffue of King *Henry* VIII failed, being fpent in one Generation, and three Succeffions. For that King, tho' one of the goodlieft Perfons of his time, yet left by his fix Wives but three Children, who reigning fucceffively, and dying childlefs, made place for the Line of *Margaret*, his eldeft Sifter, married to *James* IV of *Scotland* There fucceeded, therefore, to the Kingdom of *England*, *James* VI then King of *Scotland*, defcended of the fame *Margaret*, both by Father and Mother fo that by an extraordinary Event in the Pedigree of Kings, it feemed as if the Divine Providence, to extinguifh all Envy, and Note of a Stranger, had doubled upon his Perfon, within the Circle of one Age, the Royal Blood of *England* by both Parents *The Succeffion of the Crown of England devolves upon James VI of Scotland.*

2 This Succeffion drew the Eyes of all Men towards it, being one of the moft memorable Accidents that had appear'd for a long time in the Chriftian World For the Kingdom of *France* having been reunited the Age before, in all the Provinces thereof, which were formerly difmembred, and the Kingdom of *Spain*, being of later date united, and made entire, by the annexing of *Portugal*, in the Perfon of *Philip* II there remained but this third and laft Union for balancing the Power of thefe three great Monarchies, and difpofing of the Affairs of *Europe* to a more affured and univerfal Peace *The Effect of this Succeffion, as to the Peace of Europe.*

3 This Event was the more admired, becaufe the Ifland of *Great Britain*, divided from the reft of the World, was never before united in itfelf under one *England and Scotland never united under one King before.*

[a] The Defign of the following *Specimen*, or *Beginning* of the Hiftory of *Great Britain*, may be learnt from the Author s Letters to the Lord Chancellor, and the King himfelf, on this Subject See SUPPLEMENT V Sect I See alfo *De Augment Scientiar* Sect I 26.

one King, notwithstanding the People are of one Language, and not separated by Mountains, or great Waters. and notwithstanding also, that the uniting of them had been in former times industriously attempted, both by War and Treaty

A Free and Pr... ... an... c...nt ... ... g ... ... tr... Pr... s... fie... s

4 It therefore seem'd a manifest Work of Providence, reserved for these Times, insomuch that the Vulgar conceived there was now an end to superstitious Prophecies, (the Belief of Fools, but the Talk sometimes of wise Men,) and to an ancient tacit Expectation, which had by tradition been strongly infused into Mens Minds [a]. But as *the best Divinations, and Predictions, are the probable and political Conjectures, and Foresight of wise Men*, so the Foresight of King *Henry* VII was now in all Mens mouths, who, being one of the deepest, and most prudent Princes in the world, had, upon the Deliberation concerning the Marriage of his eldest Daughter into *Scotland* [b], shewed himself, by his Discourse, sensible, and almost prescient of this Event

The Reputa- tion of his Succession aug- mented by many extra ordinary Cir- cumstac es

5 A concurrence likewise of several uncommon, external Circumstances, gave great Reputation to this Succession. A King in the strength of his Years, supported with great Alliances abroad, established with royal Issue at home, at peace with all the World, and practised in the Government of such a Kingdom, as might rather afford variety of Accidents to a King, than corrupt him with Affluence, or Vain-Glory, and one who, besides his universal Capacity and Judgment, was thoroughly versed in Matters of Religion, and the Church, which in these times, by the confused use of both Swords, are become so intermixed with Considerations of State, that most Councils of sovereign Princes, or Republicks, depend upon them

The Unanimi- ty and Tranquility at the King's en- trance

6. But nothing fill'd foreign Nations more with admiration, and expectation of this Succession, than the wonderful and unexpected Consent of all the Subjects of *England*, to receive the King without the least Scruple, Pause, or Question. For it had been generally dispersed by the Fugitives beyond the Seas, that after Queen *Elizabeth*'s decease, there must follow in *England* nothing but Confusions, Interreigns, and Perturbations of State, greater than the ancient Calamities of the *Civil Wars* between the Houses of *Lancaster* and *York*, as the Dissensions were likely to be more mortal and bloody, when foreign Competition should be added to domestick, and Divisions in Religion, to Matters of Title to the Crown

The seditious Book of Par- sons the Je- suit.

7 And in particular, *Parsons* the Jesuit, under a disguised Name, had, not long before, published an express Treatise, wherein, whether his Malice made him believe his own Fancies, or whether he thought it the fittest way to move Sedition, (like evil Spirits, which seem to foretel the Tempest they mean to raise) he laboured to display and colour all the vain Pretences and Dreams of Succession he could devise and had thus possess'd many abroad, who knew not the Affairs at home, with his Vanities.

8.

---

[a] The Prophecy here meant, seems to be this. When HEMPE is spun, England's done. See the Author's *Essay on Prophecies*, SUPPLEMENT XI

[b] See above, § 1

8 There were alſo within the Kingdom divers Perſons, both wiſe and *All Diſcourſe* well-affected, who, tho' they queſtion'd not the Right, yet ſetting before *of a Succeſſor* themſelves the Waves of Peoples Hearts, guided no leſs by ſudden and *prohibited by* temporary Winds, than by the natural Courſe and Motion of the Waters, *Q Elizabeth* dreaded the Event. For Queen *Elizabeth* being a Princeſs of extreme Cau- tion, and yet one who loved Admiration above Safety, and knowing the Declaration of a Succeſſor might, in point of Safety, be diſputable, but in point of Admiration and Reſpect, aſſuredly to her diſadvantage, had from the beginning ſet it down for a Maxim of State, to impoſe a ſilence as to the Succeſſion [a] Nay, it was not only reſerved as a Secret of State, but reſtrain'd by ſevere Laws, that no Perſon ſhould preſume to give opinion, or argue about the ſame ſo that tho' the evidence of the Right drew all the Subjects of the Land to think one thing, yet the fear of the Law, made no Man privy to others Thoughts It therefore rejoiced all Men to ſee ſo fair a Morning of a Kingdom, and to be thoroughly ſecured againſt former Ap- prehenſions, as when a Man wakes out of a frightful Dream

9. And thus not only the Conſent, but the Applauſe and Joy was infinite, *The great and* and inexpreſſible, throughout the Kingdom, upon this Succeſſion. The Con- *univerſal Joy* ſent may be truly aſcribed to the clearneſs of the Right, but the general *at this Succeſ-* Joy, Alacrity, and Gratulation, were the Effects of differing Cauſes For *ſion* Queen *Elizabeth*, altho' ſhe had many Virtues, and uſed many Demon- ſtrations, that might draw and knit the Hearts of her People to her; yet carrying a cloſe hand in Gifts, and a high one in points of Prerogative, did not fully content either her Servants or Subjects, eſpecially in her later days, when the continuance of her Reign, which extended to five and forty Years, might diſcover in People their natural deſire and inclination to change ſo that a new Court, and a new Reign, were not unwelcome to many. Num- bers rejoiced, and eſpecially thoſe of ſettled Eſtates and Fortunes, that their Fears and Uncertainties were blown over. Others, who had made their way with the King, or offered their ſervice in the Reign of the Queen, thought now the time was come for which they had prepared and generally all ſuch as had any dependance upon the late Earl of *Eſſex*, (who had mixed the Service of his own Ends, with the popular pretence of advancing the King's Title,) thought their Cauſe better'd

10 Again, ſuch as might ſuſpect they had given the King any occaſion *The Behaviour* of diſtaſte, endeavour'd by their Forwardneſs and Confidence, to ſhew it was *of thoſe at-* but their Firmneſs to the former Government, and that thoſe Affections *tached to the* ended with the Time The Papiſts fed their Hopes, by comparing the Caſe *former Go-* of the Papiſts in *England*, under Queen *Elizabeth*, with that of the Papiſts *The Papiſts* in *Scotland*, under the King; conſtruing their Condition in *Scotland* the leſs grievous, and forming Conjectures of the King's Government here according- ly beſides the Comfort they miniſtred to themſelves, from the Memory of the Queen his Mother The Miniſters, and thoſe who ſtood for the Preſ- *The Presby-* bytery, thought their Cauſe ſympathized more with the Diſcipline of Scot- *tery.*

---

[a] See the Character of this Queen, SUPPLEMENT III.

Ind, than with the Hierarchy of *England*, and so took themselves to be a degree nearer their Desires   Thus all Conditions of Persons promis'd themselves some future Advantage, which they might, perhaps, over-rate, according to the nature of Hope, yet not without some probable ground of Conjecture

The King's Book publish'd at his Entrance   11 At this time also came forth in print the King's Book, entitled *Βασιλικὸν Δῶρον*, containing Matter of Instruction to the Prince his Son, as to the *Office of a King*, which Book falling into every Man's hand, fill'd the whole Kingdom as with a good Perfume, or Incense, before the King's coming in for being excellently written, and having nothing of Affectation, it not only satisfied better than particular Reports of the King's Disposition, but far exceeded any formal or curious Edict, or Declaration, which could have been devised, of that nature wherewith Princes, in the beginning of their Reigns, usually grace themselves, or at least, express themselves gracious in the eyes of their People[a]   And thus much for the general State and Constitution of Mens Minds upon this Change the Actions themselves passed in the following manner[b]

[a] The Author seems to have wrote this *Specimen* to oblige the King, to whom it was presented

[b] For the continuation of the History here begun, see *Burnet, Herbert, Thuanus, Larrey, &c*

29 MR 64

SUPPLEMENT III.

Containing the

LIVES,

O R,

CIVIL CHARACTERS

O F

JULIUS CÆSAR.

AUGUSTUS CÆSAR.

King HENRY VII. and,

Queen ELIZABETH.

PREFACE.

THE *Four following Pieces, are all that the Author appears to have wrote in the way of* Character *or* Biography. *The Advantages of this kind of* Writing *are shewn, and the Practice of it recommended, in the* de Augmentis Scientiarum [a] *It is a Practice that now seems to obtain pretty generally in* Europe; *and affords us the Lives of many eminent Persons, both publick and private. Whether the Author had any particular View in drawing the Civil Characters of* Julius *and* Augustus Cæsar, *or whether he intended to have gone through with the Twelve* Cæsars *in the same manner, does not appear*

The Character of King Henry *the Seventh is taken from the Recapitulation of the* English History *of that Prince; collated with the Author's* Latin *Version and the rest are new translated from the* Latin Originals.

[a] See Sect I 27 of that Piece

I

A Civil Character of JULIUS CÆSAR.

The general Fortune and Temper of Cæsar

1 *J*Ulius *Cæsar*, at the first encountered a rugged Fortune; which turned to his advantage · for this curbed his Pride, and spurr'd his ` dustry He was a Man of unruly Passions, and Desires, but extremely clear and settled in his Judgment and Understanding as appears by his ready Address, to extricate himself both in Action and Discourse, for no Man ever resolved quicker, or spoke clearer But his Will and Appetite were restless, and ever launched out beyond his Acquisitions, yet the Transitions of his Actions were not rash, but well concerted for he always brought his Undertakings to compleat and perfect Periods Thus, after having obtained numerous Victories, and procured a great degree of Security in *Spain*, he did not slight the Remains of the Civil War in that Country, but having, in Person, seen all things fully composed and settled there, he immediately went upon his Expedition against the *Parthians*

His Tems per

2 He was, without dispute, a Man of a great and noble Soul, tho' rather bent upon procuring his own private advantage, than good to the Publick for he referred all things to himself, and was the truest Centre of his own Actions Whence flowed his great and almost perpetual Felicity and Success for neither his Country, nor Religion, neither good Offices, Relations, nor Friends, could check or moderate his Designs Again, he was not greatly bent upon preserving his Memory, for he neither established a State of things, built lasting Monuments, nor enacted Laws of perpetuity, but worked entirely for his own present and private Ends, thus confining his Thoughts within the Limits of his own Times 'Tis true, he endeavoured after Fame and Reputation, as he judged they might be of service to his Designs, but certainly, in his Heart, he rather aimed at Power, than Dignity, and courted Reputation and Honours only as they were Instruments of Power and Grandeur. So that he was led, not by any laudable Course of Discipline, but by a kind of natural Impulse, to the Sovereignty, which he rather affected to seize, than appear to deserve.

3. This

3 This Procedure ingratiated him with the People, who had no Digni- *Favoured by* ty to lose, but, among the Nobility and Gentry, who desired to retain *the People, but* their Honours, it gained him the Character of a bold, aspiring Man And *for his haugh-* certainly they judged right, for he was naturally very audacious, and never *tiness* put on the Appearance of Modesty, but to serve a turn Yet this daring Spirit of his was so tempered, that it neither subjected him to the Censure of Rashness, or intolerable Haughtiness, nor rendered his Nature suspected but was taken to proceed from a certain Simplicity, and Freedom of Beha- viour, joined with the Nobility of his Birth And in all other respects he had the Reputation, not of a cunning and designing, but of an open and sin- cere Man. And tho' he was a perfect Master of Dissimulation, and wholly made up of Art, without leaving any thing to Nature but what Art had approved, yet nothing of Design or Affectation appeared in his Carriage · so that he was thought to follow his own natural Disposition He did not, however, stoop to any mean Artifices, which Men unpractised in the World, who depend not upon their own Strength, but the Abilities of others, em- ploy to support their Authority · for he was perfectly skilled in all the ways of Men, and transacted every thing of consequence in his own Person, with- out the Interposition of others

4 He had the perfect Secret of extinguishing Envy, and thought it pro- *His Thirst of* per in his Proceedings to secure this Effect, tho' with some diminution of *Power.* his Dignity For being wholly bent upon real Power, he almost constant- ly declined, and contentedly postponed all the empty Show, and gaudy Ap- pearance of Greatness, till at length, whether satiated with Enjoyment, or corrupted by Flattery, he affected even the Ensigns of Royalty, the Style and Diadem of a King which proved his ruin He entertained the thought *The means* of Dominion from his very youth and this was easily suggested to him by *whereby he* the Example of *Sylla*, the Affinity of *Marius*, the Emulation of *Pompey*, *obtained it* and the Corruption and Troubles of the Times But he paved his way to it in a wonderful manner · first, by a popular and seditious, and afterwards by a military and imperial Force For at the entrance he was to break thro' the Power and Authority of the Senate, which remaining entire, there was no passage to an immoderate and extraordinary Sovereignty. Next, the Power of *Crassus* and *Pompey* was to be subdued, which could not be but by Arms. And therefore, like a skilful Architect of his own Fortune, he be- gun and carried on his first Structure by Largesses, by corrupting the Courts of Justice, by renewing the Memory of *Caius Marius*, and his Party ; whilst most of the Senators and Nobility were of *Sylla*'s Faction by the *Agrarian* Laws ; by seditious Tribunes, whom he instigated, by the Fury of *Catiline*, and his Conspirators, whom he secretly favoured, by the Ba- nishment of *Cicero*, upon whom the Authority of the Senate turned, and other the like Artifices : but what finished the Affair, was the Alliance of *Crassus* and *Pompey*, joined with himself

5 Having thus secured all Matters on this side, he directly turned to *Works on both* the other, he was now made Proconsul of *Gaul* for five years, and after- *sides, dissem-* wards continued for five more, he was furnished with Arms, Legions, and *bles and* *throws the* *blame on* commanded *others*

comm̃anded a warlike Province, adjacent to *Italy* For he knew, that after he had ſtrengthened himſelf with Arms, and a military Power, neither *Craſſus* nor *Pompey* could make head againſt him, the one truſting to his Riches, the other to his Fame and Reputation, the one decaying in Age, the other in Authority, and neither of them reſting upon true and ſolid Foundations And all this ſucceeded to his Wiſh, eſpecially as he had bound, and obliged all the Senators, Magiſtrates, and thoſe who had any Power, ſo firmly to himſelf, by private Benefits, that he feared no Conſpiracy, or Combination againſt his Deſigns, till he had openly invaded the State And tho' this was ever his Scheme, and at laſt put in execution, yet he did not unmaſk, but what by the reaſonableneſs of his Demands, his Pretences of Peace, and moderating his Succeſſes, he turned the whole load of Envy upon the oppoſite Party, and appeared to take Arms of neceſſity, for his own Preſervation and Safety The Emptineſs of this Pretence manifeſtly appeared, when the Civil Wars were ended, all his Rivals, that might give him any diſturbance, ſlain, and he poſſeſſed of the Regal Power for now he never once thought of reſtoring the Republick; nor ſo much as pretended it Which plainly ſhewed, as the Event confirmed, that his Deſigns were all along upon the Sovereignty, and accordingly he never ſeized Occaſions as they happened, but rais'd and worked them out himſelf

His great Talent in Military Affairs 6 His principal Talent lay in military Matters, wherein he ſo excell'd, that he cou'd not only lead, but mould an Army to his Mind. For he was as ſkilful in governing Men's Paſſions, as in conducting Affairs and this he did not by any ordinary Diſcipline, that taught his Soldiers Obedience, ſtung them with Shame, or awed them by Severity, but in ſuch a manner, as raiſed a ſurprizing Ardour and Alacrity in them, and made them confident of Victory and Succeſs, thus endearing the Soldiery to him, more than was convenient for a free State And as he was well verſed in War of all kinds, and as he joined Civil and Military Arts together, nothing could come ſo ſuddenly upon him, but he had an Expedient ready for it, nothing ſo adverſe, but he drew ſome advantage from it

His Conduct 7 He had a due regard to his Perſon, for in great Battles he would ſit in his Pavilion, and manage all by Adjutants Whence he received a double advantage, as thus coming the ſeldomer in Danger, and in caſe of an unfortunate turn, could animate and renew the Fight, by his own Preſence, as by a freſh Supply In all his Military Preparations he did not ſquare himſelf to Precedents only, but ever with exquiſite Judgment, took new Meaſures, according to the preſent Exigence

His Friendſhips 8 He was conſtant, ſingularly beneficent, and indulgent in his Friendſhips but made ſuch choice of Friends, as eaſily ſhewed that he ſought for thoſe who might forward, and not obſtruct his Deſigns And as he was both by Nature and Habit led, not to be eminent among great Men, but to command among Inferiors, he made Friends of mean and induſtrious Perſons, to whom he alone gave Law As for the Nobility, and his equals, he contracted Friendſhip with them juſt as they might ſerve his turn; and admitted none to his Intimacies, but ſuch whoſe whole Expectations centered upon him

9. He

9 He was tolerably learned , but chiefly in what related to Civil Policy *His Learning* For he was well versed in History , and perfectly understood both the Edge and Weight of Words ' and because he attributed much to his good Stars, he affected to be thought skilful in Astronomy. His Eloquence was natural to him, and pure

10 He was given to Pleasures, and profuse in them , which served at *His Pleasures* his first setting out as a Cloak to his Ambition for no Danger was apprehended from one of this cast Yet he so governed his Pleasures, that they were no prejudice to himself, nor business , but rather whet than blunted the Vigour of his Mind He was temperate in Diet ; not delicate in his Amours , and pleasant and magnificent at publick Shews.

11 This being his Character, the same thing at last was the means of *His End.* his Fall, which at first was a step to his Rise , *viz* his Affectation of Popularity for nothing is more popular than to forgive our Enemies [b]. Thro' which virtue, or cunning, he lost his Life.

II

A Civil Character of AUGUSTUS CÆSAR.

IF ever Mortal had a great, serene, well-regulated Mind, it was *Augustus Cæsar* as appears by the heroical Actions of his early Youth. For men of a turbulent nature commonly pass their youth in various Errors , and in their middle age, first begin to shew themselves but those of a sedate and calm Disposition may shine even in the bud And as the perfection of the Mind, like that of the Body, consists in Health, Gracefulness, and Strength , in the latter he was inferior to his Uncle *Julius* , but in Beauty and Health of Mind superior. For *Julius Cæsar* being of a restless, discomposed Spirit, as those generally prove who are troubled with the falling-sickness, yet cleared the way to his own Ends, with the utmost Address and Prudence His Error was the not rightly fixing his Ends , but with an insatiable and unnatural Appetite still pursuing farther Views Whereas *Augustus*, sober and mindful of his Mortality, seemed to have thoroughly weigh'd his Ends , and laid them down in admirable order For first he desired to have the Sovereign Rule , next he endeavoured to appear worthy of it , then thought it but reasonable, as a Man, to enjoy his exalted Fortune , and lastly, he turned his Thoughts to such Actions, as might perpetuate his Name, and transmit some Image and Effect of his Government to Futurity Hence in his Youth he affected Power , in his middle Age, Dignity , in his Decline of Life, Pleasure , and in his old Age, Fame, and the Good of Posterity

[a] See some of his Sayings in SUPPLEMENT VI under the Article *Cæsar.* See also the *de Augmentis Scientiarum* Prelim Sect III 65
[b] See the Author's *Essay on Charity* SUPPLEMENT XI Sect I.

III

A Civil Character of King HENRY VII.

His Virtue and Fortune

1 THIS King was that kind of Miracle, which affects wife Men, but does not strike the ignorant   There are numerous Particulars, both in his Virtues and his Fortune, not so fit for Common place, as for grave and prudent Observation

His Zeal of Religion

2 He was certainly religious, both in his Temper and Behaviour   And as he could see clearly, for those times, into Superstition, so he would be blinded now and then thro' Policy   He promoted Ecclesiasticks, and was tender in the Privilege of Sanctuaries, tho' they caused him so much mischief   He built and endowed many Religious Houses, besides his memorable Hospital of the *Savoy*, yet he was a great Alms giver in secret, which shews, that his Works in publick, were dedicated to God's Glory, not his own

His Love of Peace

3 He always professed to love and seek Peace, and it was his usual Preface in his Treaties, *That when Christ came into the World, Peace was sung ; and when he went out of it, Peace was bequeathed*   This could not be imputed to fear or softness in him, being a martial and active Man, but was doubtless a truly Christian and Moral Virtue   Yet he knew the way to Peace was not to seem too desirous of it   and therefore he would frequently raise Reports, and feign Preparations for War, till he had mended the Conditions of Peace

His great Success in War

4 It was also remarkable, that being so great a lover of Peace, he should be so successful in War   For both his foreign and domestick Wars were so fortunate, that he never knew a Disaster   The War at his coming in, and the Rebellions of the Earl of *Lincoln*, and the Lord *Awdley*, he terminated by Victory,   the Wars of *France* and *Spain* by Peace, sought at his hands the War of *Britain*, by the accidental Death of the Duke   the Insurrection of the Lord *Lovel*, and that of *Perkin* at *Exeter*, and in *Kent*, by the Flight of the Rebels, before they came to blows   so that his Felicity in Arms was still peculiar and inviolate, perhaps chiefly because in suppressing Rebellions he ever appeared in person.   The First of the Battle he would sometimes leave to his Lieutenants, reserving himself to second the Onset   but he was ever in some part of the Action   Yet this proceeded not from Warmth or Bravery in him, but partly from a Distrust of others.

His regard to the Laws

5 He always greatly countenanced the Laws of the Kingdom, and would seem to maintain them by his own Authority ; tho' this he did, without any way falling short of his Ends   for he held the Reins of the Laws so commodiously, as to lose no part either of his Revenue or Prerogative.   And yet, as he would sometimes wind up the Laws to his Prerogative, so he would, at others, purposely lower his Prerogative to his Parliament.   For tho' the Regulation
lation

lation of the Mint, Treaties of Peace, and the Affairs of the Army, are matters of abfolute Right, yet he would often refer thefe to Parliament

6 Juftice was well adminiftred in his Time; except where the King was Party, and excepting alfo, that the Privy-Council intermeddled too much in Cafes of *Meum* and *Tuum* For the Council was then a mere Court of Juftice, efpecially in the beginning of his Reign But in that part of Juftice and Policy, which is durable, and carved, as it were, in Brafs, and Marble, *viz The making of good Laws*, he greatly excelled *The Admini ftration of Ju ftice in his Time*

7 His Juftice alfo was mixed with Mercy, for in his Reign but three of the Nobility fuffered capitally, *viz* the Earl of *Warwick*, the Lord Chamberlain, and the Lord *Audley* Tho' the two former were as numbers, in refpect to the Violence and Hatred of the People But never were fuch great Rebellions known to be expiated with fo little Blood, fhed by the Sword of Juftice, as the two extraordinary ones of *Exeter* and *Blackheath* His general Pardons to the Rebels ever went both before and after his Sword But then he had a ftrange method of interchanging ample, and unexpected, Pardons with fevere Executions Which, confidering his Wifdom, could not be attributed to any Inconftancy, or Wavering, but either to fome fecret Reafon, or to a certain Rule he had prefcribed himfelf, *to try both Corrofives and Lenitives, by turns* *His Mercy*

8. But the lefs Blood he drew, the more Treafure he ufually took, and, as fome malicioufly conftrued it, he was fparing in the one, that he might fqueeze the more in the other for to have taken both, would indeed have been intolerable Doubtlefs he was naturally inclined to hoarding, and admired Riches too much for one in fo high a fphere. And indeed he was touched with Remorfe at his death, for having oppreffed his People, and extorted Money, by ways of all kinds This Excefs of his had, at that time, many Interpretations Some were of opinion, that the perpetual Rebellions wherewith he had been harafs'd, drove him to hate his People, fome, that it tended to abate the Fiercenefs of his Subjects, by keeping them low, others, that he intended to leave a *Golden Fleece* to his Son, and others, in fine, that he had fome fecret defign of a foreign War But thofe, perhaps, come neareft the Truth, who impute it to Nature, Years, Peace, and a Mind taken up with no other Ambition, or Purfuit Whereto may be added, that having frequent occafion to obferve the Neceffities and Shifts which other Princes were drove to for Money, this ftrongly fhewed him the Felicity that attends full Coffers *His Covetouf nefs and Op preffions.*

9 In expending of Treafure, he kept this Rule, never to fpare any Charge his Affairs required In his Buildings he was magnificent; in his Rewards clofe-handed fo that his Liberality extended rather to what regarded himfelf, and his own Memory, than to the rewarding of Merit *His Expences*

10 He was of a high and exalted Mind, a lover of his own Opinion, and his own Way, as one that revered himfelf, and would reign alone Had he been a private Man, doubtlefs he would have been termed proud But in a wife Prince, it was no more than keeping a juft and due diftance between himfelf and his Subjects, which he conftantly did towards all, not admitting any one a near Approach, either to his Authority, or Secrets. For he was *His Temper and moral Character*

governed

governed by none about him. His Consort, the Queen, who had blessed him with several Children, and with a Crown also, tho' he would not acknowledge it, could do little with him. His Mother he indeed reverenced much, but seldom admitted her to a share of his Counsels. He had no Person agreeable to him for Conversation, unless we should account for such, Bishop *Fox* and *B* and *Empson*, because they were frequently with him. but it was as the Tool is with the Workman. He had as little Vainglory as any other Prince, tho' without any diminution of State and Majesty, which he ever kept up to the height, being sensible, that the Reverence of Majesty holds the People in Obedience whilst Vain-glory, if rightly considered, prostitutes Princes to popular Breath.

He was just and constant to his Confederates, but close and cautious. He searched into them so much, yet kept himself so close, and reserved, that they stood as it were in the Light to him, and he in the Dark to them. But this was carried without any appearance of Secrecy, and rather with the shew of Frankness and Familiarity, as one who communicated his own Affairs to others, and at the same time enquired into theirs.

12 As for the little Envies and Emulations, which usually pass between Princes, to the detriment of their Affairs, he had nothing of them, but went earnestly and substantially about transacting his Business. His Reputation, tho' great at home, was still greater abroad. For Foreigners, who could not see the Conduct, and particular Passages of his Affairs, but only the Conclusions and general Issues of them, observed that he was ever in strife, and ever superior. It was partly occasioned also by the Letters and Relations of foreign Ambassadors, who attended his Court in great numbers, for these he not only pleased by Courtesy, Reward, and familiar Conversation, but also raised their Admiration, by discovering an universal Knowledge of the Affairs of *Europe*. Which, tho' he had chiefly drawn from the Ambassadors themselves, and their Informations, yet what he had gathered from them all, seemed extraordinary to every particular. So that they always wrote to their Superiors in high Terms, of his Wisdom, and Policy. Nay, when returned to their several Countries, they frequently gave him Intelligence by Letter, of all Occurrences that happen'd worthy of note, such a Talent he had, at ingratiating himself with foreign Ministers.

13 He was sollicitous to procure, by all Methods, Intelligence from every quarter, for which end, he not only used the Industry of foreign Ministers, residing here, and of his own Pensioners, which he kept at the Court of *Rome*, and the Courts of other Princes, but the Vigilance likewise of his own Ambassadors abroad. And with this view, his Instructions were exact, even to Curiosity, and orderly digested into Articles, more of which generally regarded Enquiry than Negotiation, and required distinct and particular Answers.

14 As for his Emissaries, which he secretly employed both at home and abroad, to discover what Practices and Conspiracies were on foot against him, they seem, in his case, to have been exceedingly necessary. he had so many Moles, as it were, perpetually at work, to undermine him. Neither

can

can this be accounted unlawful. For if Spies are approved in War, against lawful Enemies, much more against Conspirators and Traitors. His Industry, in thus employing Emissaries, had this good Effect, that as many Conspiracies were detected by their means, so the Fame and Suspicion of his Spies, doubtless kept many others from being attempted

15 He was no uxorious Husband, nor indulgent, yet complaisant, companionable, and free from Jealousy He was affectionate to his Children, and careful of their Education, for he aspired to procure their Advancement he was careful also, that all the Honour and Respect becoming their Quality, should be paid them, but not greatly desirous, to have them exalted in the eyes of the People   *His Domestick Character*

16 He referred most of his Business to his Privy-Council, and often presided among them in person, well knowing this to be the right and solid way both to strengthen his Authority, and inform his Judgment To which end also he was patient of their Liberty, as well in advising, as voting, till he had declared his own Opinion, which he usually reserved to the end of the Debates   *His Conduct in the Council.*

17 He kept a strict hand upon the Nobility, and chose rather to advance to his Service such Clergymen and Lawyers, who were more obsequious to him, and less gracious with the People, which made for his Authority, but not for his Safety insomuch that I am fully persuaded, this Method of his was a principal cause of the frequent Commotions that happened in his Reign, because the Nobility, tho' loyal and obedient, did not chearfully co-operate with him, but left his Designs rather to take their Chance, than urged their Accomplishment.   *Promoted the Clergy and Lawyers, to the neglect of the Nobility*

—

18 He was never afraid of his Servants and Ministers, tho' Men of the brightest Parts and greatest Abilities, as *Lewis* XI was. But on the contrary, made use of the most eminent of his time otherwise his Affairs could not have prospered as they did. Neither did he care how crafty and subtile they were, for he thought himself even here their superior   *His choice of able Ministers*

19 And as he shewed great Judgment in the choice of his Ministers, he was as constant in protecting those he had once chose It is strange, that tho' he was a dark, close Prince, excessively suspicious, his Reign turbulent, and full of Conspiracies, yet in twenty four Years, he never displaced, or discomposed Counsellor, or near Servant, except *Stanley*, the Lord-Chamberlain   *His Constancy in protecting his Servants*

20 For the Disposition of his Subjects towards him, as there are three Affections, which naturally tye the Hearts of the People to their Soveraign, *viz Love, Fear,* and *Reverence* ; he had their Reverence in a high degree, much of their Fear, but so little of their Love, as to be beholden to the other two, for his security   *How respected by his Subjects*

21 He was a sober, serious, thoughtful Prince, full of Cares and secret Observations, and had Notes and Memorandums always ready by him, written with his own hand, particularly relating to the choice of Persons for employ, those he designed to reward, enquire about, or beware of,   *His exact and scrupulous Diligence in taking Notes, &c*

I

those

those who were nearly link'd together, either by Faction, or good Offices; those who had formed into Parties, and the like, thus keeping a kind of Diary of his own Thoughts. There goes a pleasant Story, that his Monkey, provoked to it, as was imagined, by one of the Bed-chamber, once tore his principal Note-book to pieces, as it lay somewhat carelessly exposed whereat the Court, which liked not that scrupulous Diligence, were ready to burst with Laughter

22. But tho' he abounded in Apprehensions and Suspicions, yet as he easily took them up, he as easily laid them down, and made them submit to his Judgment Whence they were rather troublesome to himself, than dangerous to others Yet it must be acknowledged, that his Thoughts were so numerous, and so complicated, that they could not often consist together, but that which was of service one way, proved hurtful another Neither was it possible for him to be wise, or happy, so much beyond the Condition of Mortals, as always to weigh things truly, in their exact Proportions Certain, the rumour that raised him so many, and so great Troubles, — That the Duke of *York* was saved, and still alive, did, at the beginning, get strength and credit from himself, being desirous of having it believed, in hopes of softening the Imputation of reigning in his own Right, and not in the Right of his Wife

23. He was affable, and soothingly eloquent, so as to use strange Sweetness and Insinuation in his Speech, where he would persuade, or effect any thing that he earnestly desired

24. He was rather studious than learned, reading, for the most part, Books wrote in *French* Yet he understood *Latin*, as appears from hence, that Cardinal *Hadrian*, and others who were well acquainted with *French*, yet always wrote to him in *Latin*

25. For his Pleasures, there is no mention found of them Yet by his Instructions to *Marchmont* and *Styles*, with regard to the Queen of *Naples*, it appears he could very skilfully interrogate upon Beauty, and the Parts thereof He did by Pleasures, as great Princes do by Banquets of Sweet-meats, look upon them a little, and go away For never was Prince more immersed in his own Affairs, being wholly taken up with them, and himself wholly in them insomuch, that at Justs, Tournaments, or other Mock-fights, Masks, and the like publick Assemblies, he seemed to be rather a princely and grave Spectator, than much delighted

26. Doubtless, as in all other Men, and particularly in Kings, his Fortune influenced his Nature, and his Nature again influenced his Fortune He ascended to the Throne, not only from a private Fortune, which might teach him Moderation, but also from the Fortune of an exil'd Man, which had given him the Spurs of Industry and Sagacity And his Government being rather prosperous than calm, had raised his Confidence by Success, but in the mean time almost corrupted his Nature by perpetual Vexations This Practice, by his frequent Escapes from Dangers (which had taught him to rely upon extempore Remedies) was turned rather into a Dexterity at extricating himself from Misfortunes, when they pressed him, than into

2   a

a Forefight to prevent and remove them at a diftance   Thus, the Eyes of his Mind were not unlike the corporeal Eyes of thofe who fee ftrong near at hand, but weak at a diftance   For his Prudence was fuddenly rouzed by the occafion , and the more, if the occafion were fharpened by Danger

27 Thefe Influences his Fortune had upon his Nature , nor were there *How his Na-* wanting, on the other hand, certain Influences, which his Nature had upon *ture influen-* his Fortune   For whether it were the Shortnefs of his Forefight, or the Ob- *ced his Fortune* ftinacy of his Will, or the dazzling of his Sufpicions, or what , certain it is, that the perpetual Troubles in his Fortune, could not have arifen with-out fome great Defects in his Nature, and rivetted Errors in the radical Conftitution of his Mind   which he was obliged to falve and correct by a thou-fand little Induftries, and Arts , all which beft appear in the *Hiftory* itfelf

28 But to take him with all his defects, and compare him with the *Compared* Kings of *France* and *Spain*, his Contemporaries, we fhall find him more *with his Con-* politick than *Lewis* XII of *France* ; and more faithful and fincere than *Fer- the Kings of* *dinando* of *Spain*   But to change *Lewis* XII. for *Lewis* XI who reigned a *France and* little before, the Comparifons will be more fuitable, and the Parallels *Spain* more exact   For thefe three, *Lewis* XI *Henry*, and *Ferdinando*, may be efteemed as the three *Magi* among the Kings of that Age   To conclude, if this King did no greater matters, it was his own fault , for what he undertook, he compaffed

29 He was comely in Perfon , a little above the juft Stature , well and *His Perfon* ftrait limbed , but flender   His Countenance ftruck a Reverence, fomewhat refembling that of an Ecclefiaftick   And as it was not gloomy or fuper-cilious, fo neither was it winning or pleafing , but like the Face of one compofed and fedate in Mind   tho' this was not happy for the Painter , as being beft when he fpoke

30 He had the Fortune of a true Chriftian, as well as of a great King , *His Death* in living exercifed, and dying penitent   So that he triumphed victoriously, as well in Spirituals as Temporals   and fucceeded in both Conflicts, that of *Sin*, and that of the *Crofs.*

31 He was born at *Pembroke* Caftle , and buried at *Weftminfter*, in one *And Funeral* of the nobleft Monuments of *Europe*, both for the Chapel, and the Se-pulchre   So that he dwells more richly dead, in the Monument of his Tomb, than when alive, either at *Richmond*, or any other of his Palaces. I could wifh he might do the like in this *Monument* of his *Fame* [a].

* For a fuller Account of this extraordinary Prince, confult the Author's *Hiftory of his Reign.*

Some

IV.

Some ACCOUNT *of the* FELICITIES *attending the* LIFE *and* REIGN *of Queen* ELIZABETH a.

BOTH Nature and Fortune confpired to render Queen *Elizabeth* the Glory of her Sex, and an Ornament to Crown'd Heads This is not a Subject for the Pen of a Monk, or any such cloifter'd Writer For fuch Men in their own Style, are attach'd to their Party, and tranfmit things of this nature unfaithfully to Pofterity Certainly this is a Province for Men of the firft Rank, or fuch as have fate at the Helm of States, and been acquainted with the Depths and Secrets of Civil Affairs

I. For all Ages have efteemed a Female Government a Rarity, if profperous, a Wonder, and if both long and profperous, almoft a Miracle But this Lady reign'd forty four Years compleat, yet did not out-live her *Felicity* Of this I purpofe to fay fomewhat, without running into Praifes To Praife is the Tribute of Men, but *Felicit*, the Gift of God

3 And firft, I account it a part of her *Felicity*, that fhe was advanced to the Throne, from a private Fortune For it is implanted in the Nature of Men, to efteem an unexpected Succefs an additional *Felicity* But what I mean, is that the Princes educated in Courts, as the undoubted Heirs of a Crown, are corrupted by Indulgence, and thence generally render'd lefs capable, and lefs moderate in the management of Affairs And therefore we find thofe the beft Rulers, who are difciplin'd by both Fortunes Such was, with us, King *Henry* VII and with the *French*, *Lewis* XII who both of them came to the Crown almoft at the fame time, not only from a private, but alfo from an adverfe and rugged Fortune and the former proved famous for his Prudence, the other for his Juftice In the fame manner this Princefs alfo had the dawn of her Fortune chequered, but in her Reign it proved unufually conftant and fteady From her Birth fhe was entitled to the Succeffion, but afterwards difinherited, and then poftpon'd In the Reign of her Brother, her Fortune was more favourable and ferene, but in the Reign of her Sifter, more hazardous and tempeftuous Nor was fhe advanced on a fudden, from a Prifon to the Throne, which might have made her haughty and vindictive, but being reftored to her liberty, and ftill growing in hopes, at laft in a happy Calm, fhe obtain'd the Crown without Oppofition or Competitor And this I mention to fhew, that Divine Providence intending an excellent Princefs prepared and advanced her by fuch degrees of Difcipline

4 Nor ought the Misfortunes of her Mother to fully the Glory of her Birth, efpecially becaufe 'tis evident that King *Henry* VIII was engaged in a new Amour before his Rage kindled againft Queen *Anne*, and becaufe the Temper of that King is cenfured by Pofterity, as exceedingly prone both to Amours and Jealoufies, and violent in both, even to the effufion of Blood Add to this, that fhe was cut off thro' an Accufation manifeftly improbable,

a For the Occafion and Defign of this Piece, fee the Author's Letter to Sir *George Carey*, &c. Sect I

improbable, and built upon flight Conjectures, as was then fecretly whifper'd, and Queen *Anne* herfelf protefted her innocence, with an undaunted greatnefs of mind, at the time of her death For by a faithful and generous Meffenger, as fhe fuppofed, fhe, juft before her Execution, fent this Meffage to the King, *That his Majefty conftantly held on in his purpofe of heaping new Honours upon her, for that firft he had raifed her from a private Gentlewoman, to the Honour of a Marchionefs, next advanced her into a Partnerfhip of his Bed, and Kingdom, and when now there remain'd no higher earthly Honour, he defign'd to promote her an Innocent to the Crown of Martyrdom.* But the Meffenger durft not carry this to the King, now plunged in a new Amour, tho' Fame, the Afferter of Truth, has tranfmitted it to Pofterity

5 Again, 'tis no inconfiderable part of Queen *Elizabeth*'s Felicity, that the courfe of her Reign was not only long, but fell within that Seafon of her Life, which is fitteft for governing. Thus fhe begun her Reign at twenty-five; and continued it to the feventieth Year of her Age. So that fhe neither felt the Harfhnefs of a Minority, the Checks of a Governour's Power, nor the Inconveniencies of extreme old Age, which is attended with Miferies enough in private Men, but in Crown'd Heads, befides the ordinary Miferies, it ufually occafions a decay of the Government, and ends with an inglorious *Exit* For fcarce any King has lived to extreme old Age, without fuffering fome Diminution in Empire and Efteem Of this we have an eminent Inftance in *Philip* the Second, King of *Spain*, a potent Prince, and admirably verfed in the Arts of Government, who, in the decline of Life, was throughly fenfible of this Misfortune. and therefore wifely fubmitted to the neceffity of things, voluntarily quitted his Acquifitions in *France*, eftablifh'd a firm Peace with that Kingdom, and attempted the like with others, that fo he might leave all quiet and compofed to his Succeffor. Queen *Elizabeth*'s Fortune, on the contrary, was fo conftant and fix'd, that no declenfion of Affairs follow'd her lively, tho' declining Age nay, for an affured Monument of her *Felicity*, fhe died not till the Rebellion of *Ireland* ended in a Victory, left her Glory fhould otherwife have appeared any way ruffled or incompleat

Her Reign extended to the full Prime of her Life

6 It fhould likewife be confider'd over what kind of People fhe reign'd For had her Empire fallen among the *Palmyremans*, or in foft unwarlike *Afia*, it had been a lefs wonder, fince a Female in the Throne would have fuited an effeminate People but in *England*, a hardy military Nation, for all things to be directed and govern'd by a Woman, is a matter of the higheft Admiration

Her ruling a hardy warlike People

7 Yet this Temper of her People, eager for War, and impatient of Peace, did not prevent her from maintaining it all her Reign. And this peaceable Difpofition of hers, join'd with Succefs, I reckon one of her chiefeft Praifes as being happy for her People, becoming of her Sex, and a Satisfaction to her Confcience Indeed about the tenth Year of her Reign, there rofe a fmall Commotion in the North of her Kingdom, but it was prefently fuppreffed The reft of her Reign paffed in a fecure and profound Peace And

Her Enjoyment of Peace

I judge it a glorious Peace, for two reasons, which, tho' they make nothing to its Merit, yet contribute much to its Honour The one, that it was rendered more conspicuous and illustrious, by the Calamities of our Neighbours, as by so many Flames about us   The other, that the Blessings of Peace were not unattended with the Glory of Arms, since she not only preserved, but advanced the honour of the *English* Name for martial Greatness For what by the Supplies she sent into the *Netherlands*, *France*, and *Scotland*, the Expeditions by Sea to the *Indies*, and some of them round the World, the Fleets sent to infest *Portugal*, and the Coasts of *Spain*, and what by the frequent Conquests and Reductions of the *Irish* Rebels, we suffered no decay in the ancient military Fame and Virtue of our Nation

8 It is likewise a just addition to her Glory, that neighbouring Princes were supported in their Thrones by her timely Aids, and that suppliant States, which, thro' the Misconduct of their Kings, were abandoned, devoted to the Cruelty of their Ministers, the Fury of the Multitude, and all manner of Desolations, were relieved by her.

9 Nor were her Counsels less beneficent than her Supplies, as having so often interceded with the King of *Spain*, to reconcile him to his Subjects in the *Netherlands*, and reduce them to obedience, upon some tolerable Conditions   And she with great Sincerity importun'd the Kings of *France*, by repeated Admonitions, to observe their own Edicts, that promised Peace to their Subjects. 'Tis true, her Advice proved ineffectual for the common Interest of *Europe* would not allow the first, lest the Ambition of *Spain* being uncurbed, should fly out, as Affairs then stood, to the prejudice of the Kingdoms and States of *Christendom* and the latter was prevented by the Massacre of so many innocent Men, who, with their Wives and Children, were butchered in their own Houses, by the Scum of the People, arm'd and let loose, like so many Beasts of Prey, upon them by publick Authority This Blood-shed cry'd aloud for Vengeance, that the Kingdom stain'd by so horrible an Impiety, might be expiated by intestine Slaughter   However, by interposing, she perform'd the part of a faithful, prudent, and generous Ally

10 There is also another reason for admiring this peaceful Reign, so much endeavour'd and maintain'd by the Queen; viz that it did not proceed from any Disposition of the Times, but from her own prudent and discreet Conduct For as she struggled with Faction at home, upon account of Religion, and as the Strength and Protection of this Kingdom was a kind of Bulwark to all *Europe*, against the extravagant Ambition and formidable Power of *Spain*, there wanted no occasions of War yet with her Force and Policy, she surmounted these Difficulties This appeared by the most memorable Event, in point of *Felicity*, that ever happen'd thro' the whole course of Affairs in our time For when the *Spanish Armada* enter'd our Seas, to the Terror of all *Europe*, and with such assurance of Victory, they took not a single Boat of ours, nor burnt the least Cottage, nor touched our Shore, but were defeated in the Engagement, dispersed by a miserable

Flight,

Flight, and frequent Wrecks, and so left us at home in the enjoyment of an undisturbed Peace [a]

11. Nor was she less happy in disappointing Conspiracies, than in subduing the Forces of her open Enemies. For several Plots against her Life were fortunately discovered, and defeated And yet upon this account, she was not the more fearful or anxious of her Person, for she neither doubled her Guards, nor confined herself to her Palace, but appeared in publick as usual, remembering her Deliverance, but forgetting her Danger
Her Success in discovering and defeating Conspiracies

12. The nature of the Times wherein she flourished, must also be consider'd For some Ages are so barbarous and ignorant, that Men may be as easily govern'd as Sheep But this Princess lived in a learned and polite Age, when it was impossible to be eminent without great Parts, and a singular Habit of Virtue
Ruled in a learned Age, over a knowing People

13. Again, Female Reigns are usually eclipsed by Marriage, and all the Praises thus transfer'd upon the Husband · whilst those who live single, appropriate the whole Glory to themselves. And this is more peculiarly the case of Queen *Elizabeth*, because she had no Supporters of her Government, but those of her own making · she had no Brother, no Uncle, nor any other of the Royal Family to partake her Cares, and share in her Administration And for those she advanced to Places of Trust, she kept such a tight Rein upon them, and so distributed her Favours, that she laid each of them under the greatest Obligation and Concern to please her, whilst she always remain'd Mistress of herself
Ruled without Consort

14. She was indeed childless, and left no Issue behind her which has been the case of many fortunate Princes, as of *Alexander the Great*, *Julius Cæsar*, *Trajan*, &c and is a disputed point, some taking it for a diminution of *Felicity*, as if Men could not be compleatly happy, unless bless'd both in their own Persons, and in their Children, and others accounting it the Perfection of *Felicity*, which then alone seems to be compleat, when Fortune has no more power over it · which, if Children are left behind, can never be the case
Left no Children

15. She had likewise her outward Embelishments, a tall Stature, a graceful Shape and Make, a most majestick Aspect, mixed with Sweetness, and a happy State of Health Besides all this, she was strong and vigorous to the last, never experienced a reverse of Fortune, nor felt the Miseries of old Age, and obtain'd that complacency in Death, which *Augustus Cæsar* so passionately desired, by a gentle and easy *Exit* This is also recorded of that excellent Emperor *Antoninus Pius*, whose Death resembled a sweet and gentle Slumber So likewise in the Distemper of the Queen, there was nothing shocking, nothing presaging, nothing unbecoming of human Nature. She was not desirous of Life, nor impatient under Sickness, nor racked with Pain She had no dire or disagreeable Symptom, but all things were of that kind, as argued rather the Frailty, than the Corruption or Disgrace of Nature Being emaciated by an extreme dryness of Body, and the Cares that attend a Crown, and never refresh'd with Wine, or with a full and
Her Person graceful, and her Death easy

Tt 2   plenti-

[a] For a more particular Account of this memorable Event, see SUPPLEMENT XII

plentiful Diet, she was, a few Days before her Death, struck with a Dead-Palsy, yet, what is unusual in that Distemper, retain'd, in some degree, her Speech, Memory, and Motion. In this condition she continued but a little while, so that it did not seem the *last Act* of her *Life*, but the *first Step* to her *Death*. For to live long after our Faculties are impair'd, is accounted miserable; but for Death to hasten on with a gradual loss of the Senses, is a gentle, a pleasing, and easy Dissolution.

16 To fill up the measure of her *Felicity*, she was exceeding happy, not only in her own Person, but also in the Abilities and Virtues of her Ministers of State. For she had the fortune to meet with such, as perhaps this Island never before produced at one Time. But God, when he favours Princes, raises up, and adorns the Spirits of their Ministers also.

17 There remain two *posthumous Felicities*, which may seem more noble and august, than those that attended her living; the one is that of her *Successor*, and the other of her *Memory*. For she had such a Successor, who, tho' he may exceed and eclipse her Greatness, by his masculine Virtues, his Issue, and a new Accession of Empire, yet is zealous of her Name and Glory, and gives a kind of Perpetuity to her Acts, having made little change either in the choice of Ministers, or the method of Government: so that a Son rarely succeeds a Father with less Alteration or Disturbance.

18 As for her *Memory*, 'tis so much in the mouths, and so fresh in the minds of Men, that Envy being extinguish'd, and her Fame light up by Death, the *Felicity* of her Memory seems to vie with the *Felicity* of her Life. For if thro' Party-Zeal, or difference in Religion, a factious Report be spread abroad, it is neither true, nor can be long-lived. And for this reason in particular, I have made the present *Collection* of her *Felicities*, and the Marks of the Divine Favour towards her, that no malicious Person might dare to curse, where God has so highly blessed.

19 If it should be here objected, as *Cicero* objected to *Cæsar*, *we have matter enough to admire, but would gladly see something to praise*, I answer, that true Admiration is a superlative degree of Praise. Nor could that *Felicity* above-described be the Portion of any, but such as are remarkably supported and indulged by the Divine Favour, and, in some measure, worked it out by their own Morals and Virtues. I shall, however, add a word or two as to the Morals of the Queen, but only in such Particulars, as have occasion'd some malicious Tongues to traduce her.

20 As to her *Religion*, she was pious, moderate, constant, and an Enemy to Novelty. And for her Piety, tho' the Marks of it are most conspicuous in her Acts and Administrations, yet there were visible Marks of it, both in the course of her Life, and her ordinary Conversation. She was seldom absent from divine Service, and other Duties of Religion, either in her Chapel, or Closet. She was very conversant in the Scriptures, and Writings of the Fathers, especially St *Augustine*. Herself composed certain Prayers upon some emergent Occasions. When she mention'd the name of God, tho' in ordinary Discourse, she generally added the Title of *Creator*, and composed
both

both her Eyes and Countenance to some sort of Humility and Reverence ; which I have myself often observed

21 As to what some have given out, that she was altogether unmindful *Not regardless of Mortality, so as not to bear the mention of Old-Age or Death, it is ab-*of Mortality* solutely false for several Years before her Death, she would often face- tiously call herself *the old Woman*, and discourse about what kind of Epi- taph she liked adding, that she was no lover of pompous Titles, but on- ly desired her Name might be recorded in a Line or two, which should briefly express *her Name, her Virginity, the Time of her Reign, the Reforma- tion of Religion under it, and her Preservation of Peace* 'Tis true, in the Flower of her Age, being importuned to declare her Successor, she answer- ed, *That she could by no means endure a Shroud to be held before her Eyes, while she was living.* And yet some Years before her Death, at a time when she was thoughtful, and probably meditating upon her Mortality, one of her Familiars mentioning in Conversation, that several great Offices and Places in the State were kept vacant too long, she rose up and said, with more than ordinary Warmth, *That she was sure her Place would not be long vacant*

22 As to her Moderation in Religion, it may require some pause, be-*Whether she cause of the severity of the Laws, made against her Subjects of the *Ro-*were moderate mish* Persuasion but I will mention such things as were well known, and *in Religion* carefully observed by myself. 'Tis certain, she was, in her Sentiments, a- verse to the forcing of Consciences yet, on the other hand, she would not suffer the State to be endangered, under the pretence of Conscience and Religion Hence she concluded, that to allow a Liberty and Toleration of two Religions, by publick Authority, in a military, and high-mettled Nation, that might easily fall from Difference in Judgment to Blows, would be certain Destruction Thus in the beginning of her Reign, when all things look'd suspicious, she kept some of the Prelates, who were of a more tur- bulent and factious Spirit, Prisoners at large, tho' not without the warrant of the Law but to the rest of both Orders, she used no severe Inquisition, but protected them, by a generous Connivance And this was the Po- sture of Affairs at first. Nor did she abate much of this Clemency, tho' provoked by the Excommunication of Pope *Pius Quintus*, which might have raised her Indignation, and driven her to new Measures ; but still she re- tained her own generous Temper For this prudent and couragious Lady was not moved with the Noise of those terrible Threats, being secure of the Fidelity and Affection of her Subjects, and of the Inability of the *Popish* Faction within the Kingdom to hurt her, unless seconded by a foreign Enemy.

23 But about the three and twentieth year of her Reign, the Face of*The Altera- Affairs changed This Difference of the Times is not artfully feigned, to *tion of her serve a turn, but stands expressed in the Publick Records, and engraven, *Measures upon as it were, in Leaves of Brass For before that year, none of her Subjects, *Invasion.* of the *Romish* Religion, had been punished, with any Severity, by the Laws formerly enacted But now the ambitious and monstrous Designs of *Spain*, to conquer this Kingdom, began by degrees, to open themselves

A

A principal part of which was, by all publick Ways and Means, to raise a Faction, in the Heart of the Kingdom, of such as were disaffected, and desirous of Innovation, in order to join the Enemy upon the Invasion. Their Hopes of effecting this, were grounded upon the Difference there was amongst us in Religion, whence they resolved to labour this Point effectually. And the Seminaries at that time budding, Priests were sent into *England*, to sow and raise up an Affection for the *Romish* Religion, to teach and inculcate the Validity of the Pope's Excommunication, in releasing Subjects from their Allegiance, and to awaken and prepare Mens Minds to an Expectation of a Change in the Government.

24. About the same time *Ireland* was attempted by an Invasion, and the Name and Government of Queen *Elizabeth* vilified and traduced by scandalous Libels. In short, there was an unusual swelling in the State, the Prognostick of a greater Commotion. Yet I will not affirm, that all the Priests were concerned in the Plot, or privy to the Designs then carrying on but only that they were corrupt Instruments of other Men's Malice. 'Tis however attested by the Confession of many, that almost all the Priests sent into this Kingdom, from the Year abovementioned, to the thirtieth Year of the Queen, wherein the Design of *Spain*, and the Pope, was put in execution by the *Armada*, had it in their Instructions, among other Parts of their Function, to insinuate, *That Affairs could not possibly continue long as they were, that they would soon put on a new face, that the Pope and the Catholick Priests would take care for the* English *State, provided the* English *were not their own Lawrance.* Again, some of the Priests had manifestly engaged themselves in Plots and Contrivances, which tended to the undermining and subverting of the Government: and what was the strongest Proof, the whole Train of the Plot was discovered by Letters intercepted from several Parts, wherein it was expressly mentioned, *That the Vigilancy of the Queen and her Council in respect of the Catholicks, would be baffled, because the Queen only settled, that no Nobleman, or Person of Distinction, should rise to head the Catholick Faction: whereas the Design they laid was, that all things should be disposed and prepared by private Men, of an inferior Rank, without their conspiring or consulting together, but wholly in the secret way of Confession.* And these were the Artifices then practised, which are so familiar and customary to that Order of Men.

25. In such an impending Storm of Dangers, the Queen was obliged, by the Law of Necessity, to restrain such of her Subjects as were disaffected, and rendred incurable by these Poisons, and who in the mean time began to grow rich by Retirement, and Exemption from publick Offices: and accordingly some severer Laws were enacted. But the Evil daily increasing, and the Origin thereof being charged upon the *Seminary Priests*, bred in Foreign Parts, and supported by the Bounty and Benevolence of Foreign Princes, the professed Enemies of this Kingdom, which Priests had lived in Places, where the Name of Queen *Elizabeth* was always tacked to the Titles of *Heretick, Excommunicated, and Accursed*, and who, tho' they themselves were not engaged in the treasonable Practices, yet were known to be the intimate Friends of those that had set their hands to Villanies of that kind, and who, by their Artful and poisonous Insinuations, had infected the whole Body of the Catho-

Catholicks, which before was lefs malignant, there could no other Remedy be found, but the forbidding fuch Perfons all entrance into this Kingdom, upon pain of Death which at laft, in the twenty feventh Year of her Reign, was accordingly enacted

26 Yet the Event itfelf, which followed foon after, when fo violent a Storm fell upon this Kingdom, with all its Weight, did not, in the leaft, abate the Envy and Hatred of thefe Men, but rather increafed it, as if they had divefted themfelves of all Affection to their Country And afterwards, indeed, tho' our Fears of *Spain*, the occafion of this Severity, were abated, yet becaufe the Memory of the former times was deeply imprinted in Mens Minds, and becaufe it would have looked like Inconftancy, to have abrogated the Laws already made, or Remiffnefs to have neglected them, the very Conftitution and Nature of Affairs fuggefted to the Queen, that fhe could not with fafety return to the State of Things, that obtained before the three and twentieth Year of her Reign

This Law why continued

27. To this may be added, the Induftry of fome to increafe the Revenues of the *Exchequer*, and the Earneftnefs of the Minifters of Juftice, who ufually regard no other Safety of their Country, but what confifts in the Laws, both which called loudly for the Laws to be put in execution However, the Queen, as a Specimen of her Good-nature, fo far took off the Edge of the Law, that but a few Priefts, in proportion, were put to death. And this, we fay, not by way of Defence, for the Cafe needs none, as the Safety of the Kingdom turned upon it, and as the Meafure of all this Severity came far fhort of thofe bloody Maffacres, that are fcarce fit to be named among Chriftians, and have proceeded, rather from Arrogance and Malice, than from Neceffity, in the Catholick Countries. And thus we think, we have made it appear, that the Queen was moderate in the Point of Religion, and that the Change which enfued, was not owing to her Nature, but to the Neceffity of the Times

Farther Reafons of it

28 The greateft Proof of her Conftancy in Religion, and Religious Worfhip, is, that notwithftanding Popery, which in her Sifter's Reign had been ftrenuoufly eftablifhed by publick Authority, and the utmoft Diligence, began now to take deep root, and was confirmed by the Confent and Zeal of all thofe in Office, and Places of Truft, yet becaufe it was not agreeable to the Word of God, nor to the primitive Purity, nor to her own Confcience, fhe, with much Courage, and with very few Helps, extirpated and abolifhed it Nor did fhe do this precipitantly, or in a heat, but prudently and feafonably as may appear from many Particulars; and among the reft, from a certain Anfwer fhe occafionally made For upon her firft Acceffion to the Throne, when the Prifoners, according to Cuftom, were releafed, as fhe went to Chappel, a Courtier, who took a more than ordinary freedom, whether of his own Motion, or fet on by a wifer Head, delivered a petition into her Hand, and in a great Concourfe of People, faid aloud, "That there were ftill four or five Prifoners unjuftly detained, that " he came to petition for their Liberty as well as the reft, and thefe were " the four Evangelifts, and the Apoftle St *Paul*, who had been long im- " prifoned in an unknown Tongue, and not fuffered to converfe with the

Proofs of her fettled Affection for Religion

" People "

" People " The Queen anſwered, with great Prudence, *That it was beſt to conſult them firſt, whether they were willing to be releaſed or no* And by thus ſtriking a ſurprizing Queſtion, with a wary, doubtful Anſwer, ſhe reſerved the whole Matter entirely in her own Breaſt

The Prudence ſhewn in bringing about the Re formation

29 Nor yet did ſhe introduce this Alteration timorouſly, and by Fits and Starts, but orderly, gravely and maturely, after a Conference betwixt the Parties, and calling a Parliament and thus at length, within the Compaſs of one Year, ſhe ſo ordered, and eſtabliſhed all things belonging to the Church, as not to ſuffer the leaſt Alteration afterwards, during her Reign Nay, almoſt every Seſſion of Parliament, her publick Admonition was, that no Innovation might be made in the Diſcipline or Rites of the Church And thus much for her *Religion*

Her Levities

30 Some of the graver ſort may perhaps aggravate her Levities, in loving to be admired and courted, nay, and to have Love-Poems made on her, and continuing this Humour longer than was decent for her Years yet to take even theſe Matters in a milder Senſe, they claim a due Admiration, being often found in fabulous Narrations, as that of " a certain Queen in the for-
" tunate Iſlands, in whoſe Court Love was allowed, but Luſt baniſhed."
Or if a harſher Conſtruction can be put upon them, they are ſtill to be highly admired, as theſe Gaities did not much eclipſe her Fame, nor in the leaſt obſcure her Grandeur, nor injure her Government, nor hinder the Adminiſtration of her Affairs for things of this ſort are rarely ſo well tempered and regulated in Princes

Her moral character

31 This Queen was certainly good and moral, and as ſuch ſhe deſired to appear She hated Vice, and ſtudied to grow famous by honourable Courſes Thus, for example, having once ordered an Expreſs to be written to her Ambaſſador, containing certain Inſtructions, which he was privately to impart to the Queen-Mother of *France*, her Secretary inſerted a Clauſe for the Ambaſſador to uſe, importing, " That they were two Queens,
' from whoſe Experience, and Arts of Government, no leſs was expected
' than from the greateſt Kings " She could not bear the Compariſon, but ordered it to be ſtruck out, ſaying, " She uſed quite different Arts
" and Methods of Government, from the Queen-Mother "

Her deſire of acquiring eſteem, tho' ſhe had lived in a private ſtate

32 She was alſo not a little pleaſed, if any one by chance had dropt ſuch an Expreſſion as this, " That tho' ſhe had lived in a private Station, her
" Excellencies could not have paſſed unobſerved by the Eye of the World "
So unwilling was ſhe, that any of her Virtue, or Praiſe, ſhould be owing to the height of her Fortune

Her great Talents for Government

33 But if I ſhould enter upon her Praiſes, whether moral or political, I muſt either fall into a Common-place of Virtues, which would be unworthy of ſo extraordinary a Princeſs, or if I would give them their proper Grace and Luſtre, I muſt enter into a *Hiſtory of her Life*, which requires more Leiſure, and a richer Vein than mine To ſpeak the Truth, the only proper Encomiaſt of this Lady is *Time*, which, for ſo many Ages as it has run, never produced any thing like her, of the ſame Sex, for the Government of a Kingdom

S U P-

SUPPLEMENT IV.

SELECT

SPEECHES

ON

Particular Occasions;

CIVIL, JUDICIAL, and MORAL[a].

PREFACE.

THE Author's Character as a Speaker, is no less extraordinary, than as a Writer His Contemporary Mr Johnson, the celebrated Poet, tells us, " His Hearers could not cough, or look aside from him without loss; that " he commanded where he spoke , and had his Judges angry and pleased at his " devotion , that the Fear of every Man, who heard him was, lest he should " make an end, &c [a] " A late learned Prelate, thought it no strained Complement to say, " That it was well for Cicero, and the Honour of his Orations, " that the Lord Bacon composed his in another Language [b]." And other eminent Men have declared as much [c] To speak moderately of these Speeches, they are studied full, strong and definitive ; no way sophistical ; but as honest and hearty, as they are learned and political.

The Number he left behind him, including his Charges, is considerable. They were published by Dr Rawley, after the Author's death. We have here selected the more capital, ranged them in some Order , and left them nearly in their old English Dress , which seems to suit them better than a new one.

[a] See Mr Johnson's Discoveries, pag 101
[b] See Archbishop Tennison's Account of all the Lord Bacon's Works, pag 62
[c] See Tatler, N° 267 and Spectator N° 554

SECT.

SECT I

SPEECHES ON CIVIL OCCASIONS.

SPEECH I.

Upon presenting a Petition of the House of Commons, to his Majesty, for regulating the Purveyors[a].

'T IS well known to your Majesty, that the Emperors of *Rome*, for their better Glory and Ornament, used in their Titles the additions of the Countries and Nations where they had obtained Victories as *Germanicu., Britannicus*, and the like But after all those Names, followed, as in the higher place, the Name of *Pater Patriæ*, as the greatest Title of all human Honour, immediately preceding the Name of *Augustus*, whereby they meant to express some affinity they had, in respect of their Office, with divine Honour Your Majesty might, with good reason, assume many of those other Names, as *Germanicus, Saxonicus, Br tannicus, Francicus, Daricus*, and others, as appertaining to you, not by Bloodshed, as they bore them, but by Blood your Majesty's Royal Person being a noble confluence of Streams and Veins, wherein the Royal Blood of many Kingdoms of *Europe* are met, and united. But no Name is more worthy of you, nor may more truly be ascribed to you, than that of *Father of your People*, which you may bear and express, not in the formality of your Style, but in the real Course of your Government We ought not to say to you, as was said to *Ju' is Cæsar, That we have already for what to admire you, and that now we up for somewhat for which to commend you* for we may justly acknowledge, that we have found in your Majesty, great cause both of Admiration and Commendation For great is the Admiration wherewith you have possessed us since this Parliament began, in those two Cases, wherein we have had access to you, that of the return of Sir *Francis Goodwin*, and that of the *Union* whereby it seems to us, that one of these being so subtile a Question of Law, and the other so high a Cause of State, that, as the Scripture says of the wisest of Kings, *His Heart was as the Sands of the Sea*, which

tho'

[a] The Speech was made, and the Petition presented, the first Session of Parliament in the Reign of King *James* I

tho' it be one of the largeft Bodies, yet confifts of the fmalleft Portions; fo in thofe two Examples, it appears to us, that God has given your Majefty a rare fufficiency, both to compafs and fathom the greateft Matters, and to difcern the leaft   And for matter of Praife and Commendation, which chiefly belongs to Goodnefs, we cannot but with great thankfulnefs profefs, that your Majefty, within the Circle of one year of your Reign, has endeavoured to unite your Church, which was divided, to fupply your Nobility, which was diminifhed, and to eafe your People, where they were burdened and oppreffed

Under the laft of thefe, *viz* the eafe and comfort of your People, falls the Meffage I now bring to your Majefty, concerning the great Grievance arifing by the manifold abufes of *Purveyors*, differing, in fome degree, from moft of the things wherein we deal and confult   For 'tis true, the Knights, Citizens, and Burgeffes, in Parliament affembled, are a reprefentative Body of your Commons, and third State, and in many Matters, altho' we apply ourfelves to perform the Truft of thofe that choofe us, yet it may be, we fpeak much out of our own Senfe and Difcourfe. But in this Grievance, being of that nature whereto the poor People is moft expofed, and Men of Quality lefs, we moft humbly defire your Majefty to conceive, that you do not hear our Opinions or Senfes, but the very Groans and Complaints themfelves of your Commons, more truly and lively than by Reprefentation. For there is no Grievance in your Kingdom fo general, fo continual, fo fenfible, and fo bitter to the common Subject, as this whereof we now fpeak, wherein it may pleafe your Majefty to vouchfafe me leave, *firft*, to fet forth to you the dutiful and refpectful carriage of our Proceeding, *next*, the Subftance of our Petition, and *thirdly*, fome Reafons and Motives, which in all humblenefs we offer to your Majefty's Royal Confideration, affuring ourfelves, that never King reigned who had better Notions of Head, and Motions of Heart, for the Good and Comfort of his loving Subjects   For the *firft*, in the Courfe of Remedy which we defire, we intend not in any fort, to derogate from your Majefty's Prerogative, nor to touch, diminifh, or queftion any of your Majefty's Regalities or Rights   For we feek nothing but the Reformation of Abufes, and the Execution of former Laws, whereto we are born   And altho' it be no ftrange thing in Parliament, for new Abufes to crave new Remedies, yet in thofe Abufes we content ourfelves with the old Laws   only defire a Confirmation, and quickening of them in their Execution, fo far are we from any Humour of Innovation or Encroachment

As to the *Court of the Green Cloth*, ordained for the provifion of your Majefty's moft honourable Houfhold, we hold it ancient and reverend. Other Courts refpect your political Perfon, but that refpects your natural Perfon   Yet, to ufe that Freedom, which to Subjects that pour out their Griefs before fo gracious a King, is allowable, we may very well alledge, a Comparifon ufed by one of the Fathers in another Matter, and not unfitly reprefenting our Cafe, in this Point   *viz.* that of the Leaves and Roots of Nettles, the Leaves are venomous and ftinging, where they touch, the

Root

Root not fo, but without Venom or Malignity. and yet 'tis the Root
that bears and supports all the Leaves

As to the Subftance of our Petition, 'tis no other, than by the Benefit
of your Majesty's Laws to be relieved of the Abuses of Purveyors which
Abufes naturally divide themfelves into three forts the *firft*, they take in
kind what they ought not to take, the *fecond*, they take in quantity a far
great r Proportion then comes to your Majefty's ufe, the *third*, they take
in an unlawful manner, directly and exprefly prohibited by divers Laws
For the firft of thefe I am a little to alter their Name, for inftead of *Ta-*
kers, they become *Takers*, inftead of taking Provifion for your Majefty's
Service, they tax your People, *ad redimendam vexationem* impofing upon the, and extorting from them Sums of Money, fometimes in grofs,
fometimes in the nature of Stipends annually paid, *ne vocentur*, to be
freed and eafed of their Oppreffion. Again, they take *Trees*, which by
Law they cannot do, Timber-trees, which are the Beauty, Countenance,
and Shelter of Men's Houfes, that Men have long fpared from their own
Purfe and Profit, that Men efteem, for their Ufe and Delight, above ten
times the Value, that are a lofs, which Men cannot repair or recover.
Thefe they take, to the defacing and fpoiling of your Subjects Manfions and
Dwellings, except they may be compounded with to their own Appetites
And if a Gentleman be too hard for them, while he is at home, they will
watch their time, when there is but a Bailiff or a Servant remaining, and
put the Ax to the Root of the Tree, before the Mafter can ftop it Again,
they ufe a ftrange and moft unjuft Exaction, in caufing the Subjects to pay
a Poundage of their own Debts, due from your Majefty to them fo that
a poor Man, when he has had his Hay, or his Wood, or his Poultry,
which perhaps he was loth to part with, and referved for the Provifion of his
own Family, taken from him, and that not at a juft Price, but under the
Value and comes to receive his Money, he fhall have after the rate of Twelve
Pence in the Pound abated, for Poundage, of his due Payment, upon fo
hard Conditions Nay further, they are grown to that Extremity, as to
take double Poundage, once when the Debenture is made, and again when
the Money is paid

As to the *fecond Point*, viz that the *quantity* they take is far above
what anfwers to your Majefty's ufe, they are the greateft Multiplyers in
the world For 'tis affirmed to me, by Gentlemen of good Report, and
Experience in thefe Caufes, as a Matter which I may fafely avouch before
your Majefty, that there is no Pound Profit which redounds to your Majefty in this Courfe, but induces three Pound Damage upon your Subjects,
befides the Difcontent And to the end they may make their Spoil more
fecurely, whereas divers Statutes ftrictly provide, that whatfoever they take,
fhall be regiftred and attefted, that by making a Comparifon of what is
taken from the Country, and what is anfwered above, their Deceits might
appear, they, to obfcure their Deceit, utterly omit the Obfervation of this,
which the Law prefcribes.

The

The *third* Abuse, viz the unlawful manner of their taking, is so manifold, as rather requires an enumeration of some of the Particulars, than a Prosecution of all   For the Price, by Law, they ought to take as they can agree with the Subject, but by Abuse they take at an imposed and enforced Price· by Law they ought to make but one Appraisement, by Neighbours in the Country, by Abuse they make a second Appraisement at the Court-Gate, and when the Subjects Cattle come up many Miles, lean, and out of plight, by reason of their Travel, then they rate them anew at an abated Price By Law they ought to take between Sun and Sun; by Abuse they take in the Twilight, and in the Night-time, a time well chosen for Malefactors by Law they ought not to take in the Highways, a Place by your Majesty's high Prerogative protected, and by Statute in special Words excepted, by Abuse they take in the Ways, in contempt of your Majesty's Prerogative and Laws by Law they ought to shew their Commission, and the Form of Commission is by Law set down the Commissions they bring, are against the Law, and because they know so much, they will not shew them. A number of other Particulars there are, whereof I have given your Majesty a taste, and the chief of them, upon deliberate Advice, are set down in Writing, by the Labour of certain Committees, and Approbation of the whole House, more particularly and lively than I can express them, myself having them at the second hand, by reason of my abode in *London.* But this Writing is a Collection of theirs who dwell among the Abuses of these Offenders, and Complaints of the People, and such must needs have a more perfect understanding of all Circumstances of them

It remains only that I use a few Words, the rather to move your Majesty in this Cause and a very few will suffice, for such great Enormities neither require any aggravating, nor so great Grace as uses of itself to flow from your Majesty's Princely Goodness, any artificial Persuading   There are two things only, which I think proper to set before your Majesty, the one the Example of your most noble Progenitors, Kings of this Realm, who from the first King that endowed this Kingdom with the great Charters of their Liberties until the last, have ordained most of them in their several Reigns, some Laws or Law against this kind of Offenders, and especially the Example of one of them, that King, who for his Greatness, Wisdom, Glory, and Union of several Kingdoms, resembles your Majesty most, both in Virtue and Fortune, King *Edward* III who in his time only, made Ten several Laws against this Mischief

The second is the Example of God himself, who said and pronounced, *That he will not hold them guiltless that take his Name in vain* For all those great Misdemeanors are committed in and under your Majesty's Name, and therefore we hope your Majesty will hold them twice guilty, that commit these Offences, once for oppressing the People, and again for doing it under the Colour and Abuse of your Majesty's most dreaded, and beloved Name. So that I will conclude with the Saying of *Pindar, optima res Aqua;* not for the excellency, but the common use of it, and so contrariwise the

2   Matter

Matter of Abuse in the Purveyance, if not the most heinous Abuse, yet certainly is the most common and general Abuse of all others in this Kingdom.

It remains, that according to the command laid upon me, I do in all humility present this Writing to your Majesty's royal hands, with most humble Petition, on behalf of the Commons, that as your Majesty has been pleased to vouchsafe your gracious Ear to hear me, so you would be pleased to enlarge your Patience to hear this Writing read, which is more material

SPEECH II.

Upon the general NATURALIZATION *of the* SCOTISH NATION[a].

Mr SPEAKER,

MY Design is to answer the Inconveniencies alledged, if we should give way to this Naturalization, which I suppose you will not find so great as they are made, but that much Dross is put into the Balance to help the Weight

1 *The first Inconvenience is, that there may ensue from this Naturalization, a Surcharge of People upon* England, *which is supposed to have already its full Charge.*

A grave Objection, Mr *Speaker*, and dutiful, for it proceeds not from any Unkindness to the *Scotish* Nation, but from a Natural Fastness to our selves for that Answer of the Virgins, *ne forte non sufficiat vobis & nobis*, proceeds not out of any Envy, but out of Providence, and the original Charity which begins with ourselves

To this so weighty and so principal Objection, I shall offer three several Answers, every one of them being, to my Understanding, of itself sufficient

(1) The *first* is, that the Opinion of the Number of the *Scotish* Nation, likely to plant themselves among us, will be found a thing rather in Conceit than Event, for, you will find, those plausible Similitudes of a Tree thriving better, if removed into the more fruitful Soil, and of Sheep or Cattle finding a Passage open, will leave the more barren Pasture, and get into a better, to be but superficial Arguments, that have no sound Resemblance with the transplanting or transferring of Families · for the Tree we know, by Nature, as soon as 'tis set in a better Ground, can fasten upon it, and take Nutriment from it, and a Sheep, as soon as he gets into a better Pasture, will feed   But there belongs more to a Family, or particular Person, that shall remove from one Nation to another   for if they have not Stock, Means, Acquaintance, Customs, Habitations, Trades, Countenance, and the like,

[a] This *Speech* was made in the *House of Commons*, the fifth *Year* of King *James* I

like, they will ftarve in the midft of the rich Pafture, and are far from gra-
zing at their pleafure therefore in this point, which is conjectural, Experience is the beft Guide for the time paft, and a Pattern of the time to
come I think no Man doubts, but his Majefty's firft coming in, was
the greateft Spring-Tide for the Confluence and Entrance of that Nation.
Now I would fain know, in thefe four Years, and the Fulnefs and Strength
of the Court and Tide, how many Families of *Scotfmen* are planted in the
Cities, Boroughs, and Towns of this Kingdom, for I affure myfelf, that
more than fome Perfons of Quality, about his Majefty's Perfon here at
Court, and in *London*, and fome other inferior Perfons, that have a dependance upon them, the Return and Certificate, if fuch a Survey fhould be
made, would be of a number extremely fmall I appeal to all your private Knowledges of the Places you inhabit Now, Mr *Speaker*, I am fure,
there will be no more fuch Spring-tides

But you will tell me of a multitude of Families of the *Scotifh* Nation in
Polonia, and if they multiply in a Country fo far off, how much more at
hand? So that you muft of neceffity impute it to fome fpecial accident of
Time and Place, that draws them thither For you fee plainly, before
your Eyes, that in *Germany*, which is much nearer, and in *France*, where
they are invited with Privileges, and with this very Privilege of Naturalization, yet no fuch Number can be found, fo that neither Nearnefs of
Place, nor Privilege of Perfon, can be the Caufe. But to fpeak what I
think, of all Places in the World, they will never take that Courfe of Life
in this Kingdom, which they content themfelves with in *Poland*, for the
Nature of all Men is rather to difcover Poverty abroad, than at home
No Gentleman, who has over-reached himfelf in Expences, and muft therefore abate his Countenance, but will rather travel, and do it abroad, than
at home, and we know they have good high Stomachs, and have ever
ftood in fome Terms of Emulation with us and therefore they will never
live here, except they can live in good Fafhion. So that I affure you, Mr.
Speaker, I am of opinion, that the fear we now have to admit them,
will prove like that Contention between the Nobility and People of
Rome, for admitting of a *Plebeian* Conful, which in paffing was very vehement, and mightily ftood upon, but when the People had obtained the
Point, they never made any *Plebeian* Conful for fixty Years after and fo
will this be for many Years, as I am perfuaded, rather a Matter in Opinion and Reputation, than in Ufe or Effect And this is my firft Anfwer
to this main Inconvenience, pretended from a Surcharge of People.

(2) My *fecond* Anfwer to the Objection is this I muft have leave to
doubt, that *England* is not yet peopled to the full, for certainly the Territories of *France*, *Italy*, *Flanders*, and fome great part of *Germany*, do in
equal fpace of Ground bear and contain a far greater quantity of People,
if they were muftered by the Poll Neither can I fee, that this Kingdom is
fo much inferior to thofe in Fruitfulnefs, as 'tis in Population which makes
me conceive we have not our full Charge. Befides, I fee manifeftly among
us, the Badges and Tokens rather of a Scarcity, than of a Prefs of People,

as drowned Lands, Commons, Wastes, and the like, which is a plain Demonstration, that however there may be an over-swelling of People hereabout *London*, which is most in our Eye, yet the Body of the Kingdom is but thin sown with them and whoever shall compare our Ruins and Decays of ancient Towns, with the Erections and Augmentations of new, cannot but judge that *England* has been far better peopled in former Times . it may be in the *Heptarchy*, or otherwise for generally it holds a Rule, the smaller the State, the greater the Population *pro rata* And whether this be true or no, we need but to remember how many of us serve in this House for desolate and decayed Boroughs

Again Mr *Speaker*, whoever looks into the Principles of *State*, must hold, that they are the *Mediterranean* Countries, and not the Maritime, which need to fear Surcharge of People, for all Sea-Provinces, and especially Islands, have another Element besides the Earth and Soil, for their Sustenance And what an infinite Number of People are, and may be sustained, by Fishing, Carriage by Sea, and Merchandizing ? Wherein I again discover, that we are not at all pinched by the multitude of People, otherwise it were impossible we should relinquish and resign such an infinite Benefit of Fishing to the *Fleming*, as 'tis well known we do And therefore I see we have Wastes by Sea, as well as by Land, which still is an infallible Argument that our Industry is not awakened to seek Maintenance by any over-great Charge or Press of People And lastly, Mr *Speaker*, there was never any Kingdom, in the Ages of the World had, I think, so fair and happy means to issue and discharge the multitude of their People, if it were too great, as this Kingdom, in regard of that desolate and wasted Kingdom of *Ireland*, which being a Country blessed with almost all the Dowries of Nature, as Rivers, Havens, Woods, Quarries, good Soil, a temperate Climate, and now at last blest also under his Majesty with Obedience, does, as it were, continually call to us for our Colonies and Plantations And thus I conclude my second Answer to this pretended Inconvenience of Surcharge of People

(^) My third Answer is this I demand, Mr *Speaker*, what is the worst Effect that can follow from a Surcharge of People? Look into History, and you shall find it no other than some honourable War, for the enlargement of their present Borders which Inconvenience in a valiant and warlike Nation, I know not whether I should term it an Inconvenience, for the Saying is most true, tho' in another Sense, *omne solum forti patria* It was spoken indeed of the Patience of an exiled Man, but is no less true of the Valour of a warlike Nation And certainly if we held ourselves worthy, whenever a just Cause should be given, either to recover our antient Rights, or to revenge our late Wrongs, or to attain the Honour of our Ancestors, or to enlarge the Patrimony of our Posterity, we would never in this manner forget the Considerations of Amplitude and Greatness, and fall at variance about Profit and Reckonings, fitter much for private Persons, than for Parliaments and Kingdoms And thus, Mr. *Speaker*, I leave this first Objection to its three Answers

                                        2. *The*

2 *The* second Objection *is, that the fundamental Laws of* England *and* Scotland *are yet different and several, nay, that 'tis declared they shall continue so, and that there is no intent in his Majesty to make an Innovation in them, and therefore that it would not be seasonable to proceed with this Naturalization, and endow them with our Rights and Privileges, except they should likewise receive and submit themselves to our Laws* And this Objection likewise, I allow to be a weighty Objection, and worthy to be well answered and discussed

The Answer I offer is, that for my part, Mr *Speaker,* I wish the *Scotish* Nation governed by our Laws, for I hold our Laws with some reducements worthy to govern, tho' it were the World but this is what I say, and therein desire your Attention, that according to true Reason of State, Naturalization is first in Order, and precedent to Union of Laws, in degree a less matter than Union of Laws, and in Nature separable, not inseparable from Union of Laws for Naturalization only takes out the Marks of a Foreigner, but Union of Laws makes them entirely as our selves Naturalization takes away Separation, but Union of Laws takes away Distinction Do we not see, Mr *Speaker,* that in the Administration of the World, under the great Monarch God himself, that his Laws are diverse, one Law in Spirits, another in Bodies, one Law in Regions celestial, another in elementary and yet the Creatures are all one Mass or Lump, without any *Vacuum* or Separation Do we not likewise see in the State of the Church, that among People of all Languages and Lineages, there is one Communion of Saints, and that we are Fellow-Citizens, and naturalized of the heavenly *Jerusalem*, and yet there are divers and several Ecclesiastical Laws, Policies, and Hierarchies, according to the saying of that worthy Father, *in veste varietas fit, scissura non fit?* Therefore certainly, Mr. *Speaker,* the Bond of Law is the more special and private Bond, and the Bond of Naturalization the more common and general, for the Laws are rather *figura reipublicæ* than *forma*, and rather Bonds of Perfection than Bonds of Entireness So we see in the Experience of our own Government, that in the Kingdom of *Ireland* all our *Statute Laws,* since *Poyning's* Law, are not in force, yet we deny them not the Benefit of Naturalization In *Guernsey* and *Jersey,* and the Isle of *Man,* our common Laws are not in force, and yet they have the benefit of Naturalization Neither need any Man doubt but that our Laws and Customs must in small time gather, and win upon theirs, for here is the Seat of the Kingdom, whence come the supreme Directions of State here is the King's Person and Example, of which the Verse says, *Regis ad exemplum totus componitur Orbis* And therefore 'tis impossible, altho' not by solemn and formal Act of States, yet by the secret Operation of no long time, but they must come under the Yoke of our Laws, and so *dulcis tractus pari jugo* And this is the Answer I give to the *second Objection*

3. *The* third Objection, *is some Inequality of the Fortunes of* England *and* Scotland, *by the Commixture whereof there may ensue Advantage to them, and Loss to us.*

And

...nd here, Mr *Speak* r, 'tis well that this Difference or Disparity consists but in the external Goods of Fortune, for indeed it must be confessed, that for the Goods of the Mind, and the Body, they are *alteri nos*, second selves for to do them right, we know in their Capacities and Understandings, they are a People ingenious, in Labour industrious, in Courage valiant, in Body hard, active and comely. More might be said, but in commending them we do but in effect commend ourselves, for they are of one Piece and Continent with us, and the truth is, we participate both of their Virtues and Vices. For if they have been noted to be a People not so tractable in Government, we cannot, without self-flattery, free ourselves altogether from that Fault, being indeed a thing incident to all martial People, who, as we see it evident by the Example of the *Romans* and others, are like fierce Horses, which tho' better for Service than others, yet are harder to break and manage.

But this Objection I propose to answer not by the Authority of Scriptures, which say, 'tis more blessed to give than to receive, but by an Authority formed and derived from the Judgment of ourselves, and our Ancestors in the same Case, as to this Point. For, Mr *Speaker*, in all the Line of our own Kings, none carries a greater Commendation, than his Majesty's noble Progeny of King *Edward* I. And among his other Commendations, both of War and Policy, none is more celebrated than his Enterprize for the Conquest of *Scotland*, as not bending his Designs to glorious Acquisitions abroad, but to solid Strength at home, which if it had succeeded, could not but have brought in all those Inconveniencies, of the Commixture of a more opulent Kingdom with a less, that are now alledged. For 'tis not the Yoke either of our Laws or Arms, that can alter the Nature of the Climate, or of the Soil, neither is it the Manner of the Commixture that can alter the Matter of Commixture: and therefore if it were good for us then, 'tis good for us now, and not to be prized the less, because we paid not so dear for it.

The second Objection, Mr *Speaker*, is rather a Pre-occupation of an Objection on the other side, for it may be very pertinently asked, about what do we contend? The Benefit of Naturalization is by the Law already settled and invested, in as many as have been, or shall be born, since his Majesty's coming to the Crown. There needs no more therefore, but to bring the *ante-nati* into the Degree of the *Post-nati*, that men grown may be in no worse Case than Children, and elder Brothers in no worse Case than younger: so that we stand but upon a little Difference in the time of one Generation from another. To this, Mr *Speaker*, it is said by some, that the Law is not so; but that the *Post-nati* are Aliens as well as the rest. A Point that I mean not much to argue, because I desire in this place to speak rather of Convenience than of Law: only I must acknowledge, to me the Opinion seems contrary to the Reason of the Law, contrary to the Form of Pleading in the Law, and contrary to Authority and Experience of Law. For Reason of Law, methinks the Wisdom of the common Laws of *England* is admirable, in the Distribution of the Benefit and Protection of the Laws, according to the four several Conditions of

Persons,

Perfons, in an excellent Proportion.   The Degrees are four, two of Aliens, and two of Subjects

(1) The *first Degree* is of an Alien born under a King or State, that is an Enemy   If fuch an one come into this Kingdom without fafe-conduct, 'tis at his peril   the Law gives him no protection, neither for Body, Lands, nor Goods , fo that if he be flain, there is no remedy by any Appeal at the Party's Suit , altho' the Wife were an *Englifh* Woman   but at the King's Suit the Cafe may be otherwife, in regard of the offence to the Peace and Crown

(2.) The *fecond Degree* is of an Alien born under the Faith and Allegiance of a King or State, that is a Friend   To fuch a perfon the Law imparts a greater benefit and protection , that is, concerning things perfonal, tranfitory, and moveable , as Goods and Chattels, Contracts, and the like , but not concerning Freehold and Inheritance   The reafon is, becaufe he may be an Enemy, tho' he is not , for the State, under the obeifance of which he is, may enter into a quarrel and hoftility   and therefore as the Law has but a tranfitory Affurance of him , fo it rewards him but with tranfitory Benefits.

(3) The *third Degree* is of a Subject who, having been an Alien, is made free by Charter and Denization.   To fuch an one the Law imparts yet a more ample benefit , for it gives him power to purchafe Freehold and Inheritance to his own ufe , and likewife enables the Children born after his Denization to inherit   yet he cannot make Title, or convey Pedegree from any Anceftor paramount , for the Law thinks it not proper to make him in the fame degree with a Subject born, becaufe he was once an Alien; and fo might once have been an Enemy   and Mens Affections cannot be fo fettled by any Benefit, as when from their Nativity they are inbred and inherent

(4) And the *fourth*, which is the perfect *Degree*, is of fuch a perfon as neither is an Enemy, nor could have been an Enemy in time paft, nor can be an Enemy in time to come , and therefore the Law gives him the full benefit, Naturalization

Now, Mr *Speaker*, if thefe are the true Steps and Paces of the *Law*, no man can deny, but whoever is born under the King's Obedience, never could be an Enemy , a Rebel he might, but no Enemy   and therefore, in Reafon of Law, is naturalized   Nay, contrariwife, he is bound *jure naturitatis* to defend the Kingdom of *England* against all Invaders or Rebels   and therefore as he is obliged to the Protection of Arms, and that perpetually and univerfally , fo he is to have the perpetual and univerfal Benefit and Protection of Law, which is Naturalization

For *Form of pleading*, 'tis certain, that if a Man would plead another to be an Alien, he muft not only fet forth negatively, and privatively, that he was born out of the Obedience of our fovereign Lord the King; but affirmatively, under the Obedience of a foreign King, or State in particular   which can never be done in this Cafe

As for Authority, I will not prefs it; you all know what has been publifhed by the King's Proclamation.   And for Experience of Law, we fee it in the Subjects of *Ireland* , in the Subjects of *Guernfey*, and *Jerfey*, Parcels of the Dutchy of *Normandy* , and in the Subjects of *Calais*, when it was *Englifh*.

But

But to drop all Argument of Law, and keep to Point of Convenience, I hold all *Poi-s an* naturalized *in so jure*, yet am far from Opinion, that it should be a thing superfluous, to have done it by Parliament, chiefly in respect of that true Principle o State, *Principum actiones præcipue ad famam sunt componendæ* It will lift up a Sign, to all the World, of our Love towards them, and a good Agreement with them

And these are, Mr *Speaker*, the material Objections, which have been made on the other side, whereto you have heard my Answers weigh them in your Wisdoms And so I conclude the general Part

II Now, Mr *Speaker*, I must fill the other Ballance, in expressing the conveniences we shall incur, if we do not proceed to this Naturalization And here, the Inconvenience which above all others exceedingly moves me, and may move you, is a Position of State, collected out of the Records of Time, viz That wherever several Kingdoms, or States, have united in Sovereignty, if that Union has not been fortified, and bound in with a further Union, that of Naturalization, it has followed, that at one time or other, they have broke again, being, upon all Occasions, apt to relapse, and revolt to the former Separation

Of this Assertion the first Example I shall set before you, is of that memorable Union between the *Romans* and the *Latins*, which continued from the Battle at the Lake of *Regilla*, for many Years, to the Consulships of C *Plautius*, and L *Æmilius Mamercus* At which time, there began, about this very point of Naturalization, a War call'd *Bellum Sociale*, being the most bloody, and pernicious, that ever the *Roman* State endured wherein, after numbers of Battles, and infinite Sieges, and Surprizes of Towns, the *Romans*, in the end, prevailed, and mastered the *Latins* but as soon as ever they had the Honour of the War, looking back to what Perdition and Confusion they were near being brought, they presently naturalized them all

Again, let me set before you the Example of *Sparta*, and the rest of the *Peloponnesus*, their Associates The State of *Sparta* was a nice and jealous State, in this point of imparting Naturalization to their Confederates But what was the issue of it? After they had held them in a kind of Society, and Amity, for several Years, upon the first Occasion given, which was no more than the Surprizal of the Castle of *Thebes*, by certain Conspirators, there immediately ensued a general Revolt, and Defection of their Associates, which was the ruin of their State, never afterwards to be recovered

In later Times, behold the like Events in the Kingdom of *Aragon*, which Kingdom was united with *Castile*, and the rest of *Spain*, in the Persons of *Ferdinando* and *Isabella*, and so continued many years tho' it yet stood a Kingdom, sever'd and divided from the rest of the Body of *Spain* in Privileges, and directly in this point of Naturalization, or Capacity of Inheritance What came of this? Thus much, that now, of fresh memory, not above twelve years since, only upon the Voice of a condemned Man, out of the Grate of a Prison towards the Street, who cried, *Fueros Libertad, Libertad*, (which is as much as, Liberties or Privileges,) there was raised a dangerous Rebellion, which was suppressed, with great difficulty, by an Army Royal After which Victory, nevertheless, to avoid farther Inconvenience,

their

their Privileges were difannull'd, and they incorporated with *Caftile*, and the reft of *Spain*. Upon fo fmall a Spark, notwithstanding fo long a Continuance, were they ready to break, and fever again!

The like may be faid of the States of *Florence*, and *Pifa*, which City of *Pifa* being united to *Florence*, but not endued with the Benefit of Naturalization, upon the firft fight of foreign Affiftance, by the Expedition of *Charles* VIII of *France* into *Italy*, revolted, tho' it be fince again reunited and incorporated, and obtained the aforefaid Benefit

The fame Effect we fee in the moft barbarous Governments; which fhews it rather to be an Effect of Nature for it was thought a fit Policy, by the Council of *Conftantinople*, to retain the three Provinces of *Tranfylvania*, *Wallachia*, and *Moldavia*, which were as the very Nurfes of *Conftantinople*, in refpect of their Provifions, that they might be the lefs wafted, only under Waywods, as Vaffals and Homagers, and not under Bafhaws, as Provinces of the *Turkifh* Empire which Policy, we fee by late experience, proved unfortunate, as appear'd by the Revolt of the fame three Provinces, under the Arms and Conduct of *Sigifmond*, Prince of *Tranfylvania*, a Leader very famous for a time and this Revolt is not yet fully recovered Whereas we feldom or never hear of Revolts of Provinces incorporate with the *Turkifh* Empire.

On the other fide, Mr. *Speaker*, we fhall find, that wherever Kingdoms and States have been united, and that Union incorporated by the Bond of Naturalization mutually, they never afterwards, upon any occafion of trouble, or otherwife, are found to break, and fever again as we fee moft evidently before our eyes, in divers Provinces of *France*, that is to fay, *Guienne*, *Provence*, *Normandy*, *Britain*, which, notwithstanding the infinite Troubles of that Kingdom, never offered to break again We fee the like Effect in all the Kingdoms of *Spain*, which are mutually naturalized, as *Leon*, *Caftile*, *Valentia*, *Andaluzia*, *Granada*, *Murcia*, *Toledo*, *Catalonia*, and the reft except *Aragon*, which held the contrary Courfe, and therefore had the contrary fuccefs, and *Portugal*, of which there is not yet fufficient Trial

And laftly, we fee the like Effect in our own Nation, which never rent afunder, after it was once united, fo that we now fcarce know whether the *Heptarchy* were a true Story, or a Fable Therefore, Mr *Speaker*, when I revolve thefe Examples and others, fo lively expreffing the neceffity of a Naturalization, to avoid a Relapfe into a Separation, I greatly apprehend, that unlefs we proceed with this Naturalization, tho' not perhaps in his Majefty's Time, who has fuch Intereft in both Nations, yet, in the Time of his Defcendants, thefe Realms will be in continual danger to divide and break again.

Now if any Man be of that carelefs Mind, *maneat noftros ea cura nepotes*, or of that hard Mind, as to leave things to be tried by the fharpeft fword fure I am, he is not of St *Paul*'s Opinion, who affirms, *that whofoever ufes not Forefight, and Provifion for his Family, is worfe than an Infidel*, much more, if we fhall not ufe Forefight for thefe two Kingdoms, that comprehend, in them, fo many Families, but leave things open to the Dangers of future Divifions And thus I have expreffed to you the Inconvenience, which, of all others, finks deepeft with me, as the moft weighty.

Neither

Neither do there want other Inconveniences, Mr *Speaker*, the Effects and Influences whereof, I fear, will not be adjourned to so long a day as this I have spoke of for I leave it to your Wisdom to consider, whether, if by the denial of this Naturalization, any Pique, Alienation, or Unkindness, should be, or but be thought to be, or noised to be, between these two Nations, whether it will not quicken and excite all the concealed envious and malicious Humours against us, either foreign or at home, and so open the way to Practices, and other Engines, and Machinations, to the disturbance of this State? As for that other Inconvenience of his Majesty's Engagement in this Action, 'tis too binding and too pressing to be spoke of, and may do better a great deal in your Mind's than in my Mouth, or in the Mouth of any Man else, because it presses our Liberty too far

III I come now to the third general Part of my Division, concerning the Benefits which we shall purchase, by knitting this Knot surer and stricter between these two Kingdoms, in the Communicating of Naturalization

The Benefits may appear to be two, *Safety* and *Greatness* As to *Safety*, Mr *Speaker*, it was well said by *Titus Quintus* of the State of *Peloponnesus*, that the *Tortoises are safe in their Shell*, but if any Parts lie open, they endanger all the rest We know well, that altho' the State at this time enjoys a happy Peace, yet for the time past its more ancient Enemy has been the *French*, and a more late the *Spaniard*, and both these had as it were their several Postern Gates, whereby they might have approach and entrance to annoy us *France* had *Scotland*, and *Spain* had *Ireland*, for these were the two accesses which encouraged both these Enemies to assail and trouble us We see that of *Scotland* is cut off by the Union of these two Kingdoms, if it shall be now made constant and permanent, and that of *Ireland* is cut off likewise by the convenient Situation of the West of *Scotland* towards the North of *Ireland*, where the Sore was, which being suddenly closed, was continued closed by means of this Salve so that now there are no parts of this State exposed to Danger, as a Temptation to the Ambition of Foreigners, but their Approaches and Avenues are taken away And doubtless, Foreigners, who had so little Success with these Advantages, will have much less Hopes now they are taken from them And so much for *Safety*

For *Greatness*, Mr *Speaker*, I think a Man may speak it soberly and without Bravery, that this Kingdom of *England*, having *Scotland* united, *Ireland* reduced, the Sea-Provinces of the Low Countries contracted, and Shipping maintained, is one of the greatest Monarchies, in Forces, truly esteemed, that has been in the World For certainly the Kingdoms here on Earth have a resemblance with the Kingdom of Heaven, which our Saviour compares not to any great Kernel or Nut, but to a very small Grain, yet such an one, as is apt to grow and spread and such do I take the Constitution of this Kingdom to be, if we shall bend our Counsels to Greatness and Power, and not quench them too much with the Consideration of Utility and Wealth For, Mr *Speaker*, was it not a true Answer that *Solon* of *Greece* made to the rich King *Crœsus* of *Lydia*, shewing him a great quantity of Gold, which he had amassed together in Ostentation of his Greatness and Might?

But

But *Solon* faid to him, contrary to his Expectation, why, Sir, if another come that has better Iron than you, he will be Lord of all your Gold. Neither is the Authority of *Machiavel* to be defpifed, who fcorns that Proverb of State, taken firft from a Speech of *Mucianus*, *that Monies are the Sinews of War*, and faid, *There are no true Sinews of War, but the Sinews of the Arms of valiant Men.*

Nay more, Mr *Speaker*, whoever fhall look into the Seminaries and Beginnings of the Monarchies of the World, will find them founded in Poverty *Perfia* was a Country barren and poor, in refpect of *Media*, which they fubdued *Macedon* was a Kingdom ignoble and mercenary, till the time of *Philip*, the Son of *Amyntas* *Rome* had poor and paftoral Beginnings. The *Turks*, a Band of *Sarmathian Scythes*, that in a vagabond manner made Incurfion upon that part of *Afia*, yet called *Turcomania*, out of which, after much variety of Fortune, fprung the *Ottoman* Family, now the Terror of the World. So we know, the *Goths*, *Vandals*, *Alans*, *Huns*, *Lombards*, *Normans*, and the reft of the Northern People, in one Age of the World made their Defcent upon the *Roman* Empire, and came not as Rovers, to carry away a Prey and be gone again, but planted themfelves in a number of rich and fruitful Provinces, where not only their Generations, but their Names remain to this day, witnefs *Lombardy*, *Catalonia*, a Name compounded of *Goth* and *Alan*, *Andalufia*, (a Name corrupted from *Vandalitia*,) *Hungaria*, *Normandy*, &c

Nay, the late Fortune of the *Switzers*, a People bred in a barren and mountainous Country, is not to be forgot, who firft ruined the Duke of *Burgundy*, who had almoft ruined the Kingdom of *France* when after the Battle near *Granfon*, the rich Jewel of *Burgundy*, prized at many thoufands, was fold for a few Pence, by a common *Swifs*, that knew no more what a Jewel meant than *Æfop*'s Cock. And again, the fame Nation, in revenge of a Scorn, was the ruin of the *French* King's Affairs in *Italy*, *Lewis* XII. For this King, when he preffed fomewhat rudely, by an Agent of the *Switzers*, to raife their Penfions, broke into Words of Choler, *What*, fays he, *will thofe Villains of the Mountains put a Tax upon me ?* Which Words loft him his Dutchy of *Milan*, and chafed him out of *Italy*

All thefe Examples, Mr *Speaker*, well prove *Solon*'s Opinion of the Authority and Maftery, that Iron has over Gold. And therefore to fpeak my Heart, methinks we fhould a little difdain that *Spain*, (which however of late it has begun to rule, yet of ancient time ferved many Ages, firft under *Carthage*, then under *Rome*, after under the *Saracens*, *Goths*, and others,) fhould of late Years take the Spirit to dream of a Monarchy in the Weft, according to that Device, *video Solem Orientem in Occidente*, only becaufe they have ravifhed from fome wild and unarmed People, Mines, and Store of Gold, and on the other fide, that this Ifland of *Britain*, feated and manned as it is, and that has, I make no queftion, the beft Iron in the World, that is, the beft Soldiers of the World, fhall think of nothing, but Accounts and Audits, and *Meum & Tuum*, and I cannot tell what.

Mr *Speaker*, I have gone thro' the Parts I proposed to myself ; wherein if any Man shall think I have sung a *Placebo*, for my own particular, I would have him know, that I discern it were much alike for my private Fortune, to rest a *Tacebo*, as to sing a *Placebo* in this Business: but I have spoke out of the Fountain of my Heart, *I believed, therefore I spoke*, so that my Duty is performed the Judgment is yours, God direct it for the best

SPEECH III.

Upon a Motion for Uniting the Laws of ENGLAND and SCOTLAND.

Mr SPEAKER,

WERE it now a time to wish, as 'tis to advise, no Man should be more forward, or more earnest than myself in this Wish, that his Majesty's Subjects of *England* and *Scotland* were governed by one Law, and that for many Reasons

First, because it will be an infallible Assurance, that there shall never be a Relapse in succeeding Ages to a Separation

Second'y, because 'tis best drawing upon an equal foot ; but if the Draught lie most upon us, and the Yoke lie least on them, or contrariwise, 'tis not equal

Th rdly, the Qualities of their Laws and ours are such as promise an excellent Temperature in the compounded Body   for if the Prerogative here be too indefinite, it may be the Liberty there is too unbounded if our Laws and Proceedings are too prolix and formal, it may be theirs are too summary and unformal

Fourthly, I discern no great Difficulty in this Work , for their Laws, compared with ours, are like their Language compared with ours . for as their Language has the same Roots with ours, but a little more mixture of *Latin* and *French* , so their Laws and Customs have the like Grounds as ours, with a little more mixture of the Civil Law, and *French* Customs.

Lastly, the Means to this Work seem no less excellent than the Work itself for if both Laws shall be united, 'tis necessary for a Preparation and Inducement thereto, that our own Laws may be reviewed and recompiled , which I think such a Work, that his Majesty cannot, in these his times of Peace, undertake one that is more Politick, more Honourable, or more Beneficial to his Subjects, for all Ages . for this continual heaping up of Laws, without digesting them, makes but a Chaos and Confusion, and often turns the Laws into Snares to the People, as 'tis said in Scripture ; *it shall rain Snares upon them* and the Snares of the Law are the worst of Snares. And therefore this Work, I esteem to be indeed an heroical Work , and what if I might live to see, I would not desire to live after. So that for this good

Wish of the Union of the Laws, I consent to the full and I think you may perceive by what I have said, that I come not in this, to the Opinion of others, but that I was long ago settled in it myself. Nevertheless as this is moved out of Zeal, so I take it to be moved out of time, as commonly all zealous Motions are, while Men move so fast on to the End, that they give no attention to the Means for if it be time to talk of this now, 'tis either (1) Because the Bufiness in hand cannot proceed without it, or (2) Because in Time and Order this Matter should proceed, or (3) Because we shall lose some Advantage towards this Effect, so much defired, if we go on in the Course we are about But not one of these three is in my Judgment true, and therefore the Motion is unfeafonable

(1) For *First*, that there may not be a Naturalization without an Union in Laws, cannot be maintained Look into the Example of the Church, and the Union thereof, you shall fee the Original Bonds to be one Faith, one Baptifm, and not one Policy, one Cuftom And fo in the Civil State, the main Bonds are one Allegiance, one Birth-right or Naturality; and not one Law, or one Adminiftration of Law and therefore one of the Fathers made an excellent Obfervation upon the two Myfteries, the one that in the Gofpel, where the Garment of Chrift is faid to have been without Seam, the other that in the Pfalm, the Garment of the Qneen reprefenting the Church is faid to have been of divers Colours, whereupon he concludes well, *in Vefte varietas fit, fciffura non fit* allowing divers Forms of Ecclefiaftical Laws and Ufages, fo as there be no Schifm or Separation. And in this Cafe, Mr. *Speaker*, we are now about to make this Monarchy of one Piece, and not of one Colour Look again into the Examples of Foreign Countries, and take that next us of *France*, and there you shall find they have this Diftribution, *Pais du droit eferit*, and *Pais du droit Couftumier* For *Gafcoigne, Languedoc, Provence,* and *Dauphiny*, are Countries governed by the Letter, or Text of the Civil Law but the Ifle of *France, Tourain, Berry, Anjou,* and the reft, and moft of *Britain* and *Normandy*, are governed by Cuftoms, which amount to a municipal Law; and ufe the Civil Law only for Grounds, and the Decifion of new and extraordinary Cafes, yet Naturalization paffes thro' all

(2) *Secondly*, that this Union of Laws should precede the Naturalization, or that it should go hand in hand therewith, I fuppofe likewife can hardly be maintained, but the contrary, that Naturalization should precede, and that not in the precedence of an Inftant, but in diftance of Time. For the Union of Laws will ask length of Time to perfect, both for the compiling and paffing of them during all which, if this Mark of Strangers should not be taken away, I fear it may induce fuch a Habit of Strangenefs, as would rather be an impediment than a Preparation to farther Proceeding; for he was a wife Man who faid, *When things go fmoothly, they prove favourable to grand Attempts* [a], and in thefe Cafes, *Not to advance, is to run back* [b]. And as in a Table-Book, you muft put out the former Writing

[a] *Opportuni magnis conatibus tranfitus rerum*
[b] *Non progredi eft regredi*

before you can put in new ; and again, that which you write down, you write Letter by Letter, but that which you put out, you put out at once so we have now to deal with the Tables of Men's Hearts, wherein 'tis in vain to think of entring the willing acceptance of our Laws and Customs, except you first rub out all Marks of Hostility or foreign Condition , and these are to be rubbed off at once, without Gradations , whereas the other Points are to be imprinted and engraven distinctly by degrees

(3) *Thirdly*, whereas 'tis conceived by some, that the Communication of our Benefits and Privileges is a good hold we have over them, to draw them to submit themselves to our Laws, 'tis an Argument of some Probability, but yet to be answered many ways   For first, the Intent is mistaken, which is not, as I conceive it, to draw them wholly to a Subjection to our Laws, but to draw both Nations to one Uniformity of Law

Again, to think that there should be a kind of articulate and indented Contract, that they should receive our Laws to obtain our Privileges, 'tis a Matter, in reason of State, not to be expected , being that which scarcely a private Man will acknowledge, if it come to what *Seneca* speaks of, *Beneficium accipere est libertatem vendere.* No, but Courses of State describe and delineate another way, which is to win them either by Benefit or by Custom, for we see in all Creatures, that Men feed them first, and reclaim them after so in the first Institution of Kingdoms, Kings first won People by many Benefits and Protections, before they prest any Yoke And for Custom, which the Poet calls *imponere morem*, who doubts but the Seat of the Kingdom, and the Example of the King resting here with us, that our Manners will quickly be there, to make all things ready for our Laws? And lastly, the Naturalization, which is now proposed, is qualified with such Restrictions, that there will be enough kept back to be used at all times, for an adamant of drawing them further on towards our Desires   And therefore, to conclude, I hold this Motion of the *Union of Laws* very worthy, and arising from very good Minds; but yet not proper for this Time

SPEECH

SPEECH IV.

For perfuading the Houfe of Commons to receive the King's Meffages, by their Speaker, and from the Body of the Council, as well as from the King himfelf [a].

'TIS my Defire, that if any of the King's Bufinefs, either of Honour or Profit, fhall pafs the Houfe, it may be not only with external prevailing, but with Satisfaction of the inward Man   For in confent, where Tongue-ftrings, not Heart-ftrings, make the Mufick, the Harmony may end in Difcord.   To this I fhall always bend my Endeavours.

The King's Sovereignty, and the Liberty of Parliament, are as the two Elements, and Principles of this State, which, tho' the one be more active, the other more paffive, yet they do not crofs, or deftroy, but ftrengthen, and maintain one another   Take away Liberty of Parliament, and the Griefs of the Subject will bleed inwards.   Sharp and eager Humours will not evaporate, and then they muft exulcerate, and fo may endanger the Sovereignty itfelf   On the other fide, if the King's Sovereignty receive Diminution, or any degree of Contempt with us, who are born under an hereditary Monarchy, fo that the Motions of our State cannot work in any other Frame or Engine, it muft follow, that we fhall be a *Meteor*, or Body, imperfectly mix'd · which kind of Bodies come fpeedily to Confufion, and Diffolution.

And herein 'tis our Happinefs, to make the fame Judgment of the King, as *Tacitus* made of *Nerva   Nerva tempered things, that before were thought incompatible, Sovereignty and Liberty* [b].   And 'tis not amifs, in a great Council, and a great Caufe, to put the other part of the Difference, which was fignificantly expreffed by the Judgment that *Apollonius* made of *Nero*, when *Vefpafian* came out of *Judea* towards *Italy*, to receive the Empire. as he paffed by *Alexandria*, he fpoke with *Apollonius*, a Man much admired, and afked him what was *Nero*'s Fall, or Overthrow?   *Apollonius* anfwered, *Nero could tune the Harp well; but in Government, he always either wound up the Pins too high, or let them down too low.*   Here we fee the difference between a regular and an able, and an irregular and incapable Prince, *Nerva*, and *Nero*   The one wifely tempers, and mingles the Sovereignty with the Liberty of the Subject, and the other interchanges it, and varies it unequally, and abfurdly   Since therefore we have a Prince of fuch excellent Wifdom and Moderation, of whofe Authority we ought to be tender, as he is likewife of our Liberty, let us enter into a true and indifferent Confideration, how far the Cafe in queftion may touch his Authority, and how far our Liberty   and to fpeak clearly,

---

[a] This *Speech* was made when the Author was *Sollicitor General*, in the Seventh Year of King *James* I

[b] *Divus Nerva Res olim diffociabiles mifcuit, Imperium & Libertatem.*

..., ... Opinion, it concerns his Authority much, and our Liberty
...

The Questions are two the one, whether our *Speaker* be exempted from
delivering a Message from the King without Licence? The *other*, if it be not
the same, if he receive it from the Body of the Council, as immediately from
the King. And I will speak of the last first, because it is the circumstance
of the present Case.

First then, let us see how it concerns the King, and next, how it concerns
us. For the King, certainly if you may not receive his Pleasure by his representative Body, which is his Council of State, you both straiten his Majesty, in point of convenience, and weaken the Reputation of his Council.
All Kings, tho' they are *Gods on Earth*, yet they are *Gods of Earth* they
may be of extreme Age, they may be indisposed in Health, they may be
absent. In these Cases, if their Council may not supply their Persons, to
what infinite Accidents do you expose them? Nay more, sometimes in Policy, Kings will not be seen, but cover themselves with their Council, and if
this be taken from them, great part of their Safety is taken away.

For the other point, of weakening the Council, you know they are nothing
without the King they are no Body Politick they have no Commission
under Seal. So that if you begin to distinguish and disjoin them from the
King *...* *... ... ...*, for they have *lumen de lumine* and by distinguishing you extinguish the principal Engine of the State. For 'tis
truly affirmed, that *consilium non habet potestatem delegatam, sed inhæren-
... ... and 'tis but *Rex in Cathedra* the King in his Chair or Consistory,
where His Will and Decrees, which in Privacy are more changeable, become settled and fix'd.

Now to what concerns ourselves. *First*, for Dignity, no Man must
think this a Disparagement to us for the greatest Kings in *Europe*, by their
Ambassadors, receive Answers and Directions from the Council in the
King's absence, and if that Negotiation be fit for the Fraternity and
Party of Kings, it may much less be excepted to by Subjects.

For Use or Benefit, no Man can be so raw and unacquainted in the Affairs of the World, as to conceive there should be any Disadvantage in it,
as if such Answers were less firm and certain. For it cannot be supposed,
that Men of so great Caution, as Counsellors of State commonly are, will
err, or adventure so far as to exceed their Warrant. And therefore I
conclude, that in this Point there can be to us neither Disgrace nor
Disadvantage.

For the Point of the Speaker, *First*, on the King's part, it may have
a shrewd Illation for it has a Shew, as if there could be a stronger Duty,
than the Duty of a Subject to a King. We see the Degrees and Differences of Duties in Families between Father and Son, Master and Servant,
in Bodies corporate, between Communities and their Officers, Recorders,
Stewards and the like, yet all these give place to the King's Commands.
The Bonds are more special, but not so forcible. On our part, it concerns us nothing. For first, 'tis but of the Channel, how the King's Mes-

sage

fage ſhall be conveyed to us, and not of the Matter   Neither has the Speaker any ſuch Dominion, as that by coming out of his Mouth, it ſhould preſs us more than out of a Privy Counſellor's   Nay, it ſeems to be a great Truſt of the King towards the Houſe, when he doubts not to put his Meſſage into their Mouth, as if he ſhould ſpeak to the City by the Recorder   therefore methinks we ſhould not entertain this unneceſſary Scruple   It is one Uſe of Wit to make clear things doubtful, but 'tis a much better Uſe of it, to make doubtful things clear, and to that I would have Men bend themſelves.

SPEECH V.

Upon Occaſion of the Undertakers, or certain Perſons who were ſaid to have undertaken, that the King's Buſineſs ſhould paſs in the Houſe of Commons, to his Majeſty's Wiſh [a].

Mr SPEAKER,

I Have been hitherto ſilent in this Matter of *Undertaking*, wherein, as I perceive, the Houſe is much enwrapped   *Firſt*, becauſe to be plain with you, I did not underſtand well what it meant, or what it was: and I love not to offer at what I do not thoroughly conceive   That private Men ſhould *undertake* for the Commons of *England*, Why! a Man might as well undertake for the four Elements   'Tis a thing ſo giddy, and ſo vaſt, as cannot enter into the Brain of a ſober Man   and eſpecially in a New Parliament, when it was impoſſible to know who ſhould be of the Parliament   and when all who know ever ſo little of the Conſtitution of this Houſe, know it to be ſo open to Reaſon, that men do not know, when they enter theſe Doors, what Mind themſelves will be of, till they hear things argued and debated   Much leſs can any Man make a *Policy of Aſſurance*, what Ship ſhall come ſafe home to the Harbour in theſe Seas

I have heard of Undertaking in ſeveral kinds   There were Undertakers for the Plantations of *Derry* and *Colerain* in *Ireland*, the better to command and bridle thoſe Parts.   There were not long ago ſome Undertakers for the North-Weſt Paſſage, and now there are ſome Undertakers for the Project of dyed and dreſſed Cloths, and in ſhort, every Novelty uſes to be ſtrengthened and made good by a kind of Undertaking · but for the ancient Parliament of *England*, which moves in a certain Manner and Sphere, to be undertaken, it paſſes my reach to conceive what it ſhould mean.   Muſt we be all dyed and dreſſed, and no pure Whites amongſt us? Or muſt
there

[a] This *Speech* was made when the Author was *Attorney General*, in the Twelfth Year of King *James.*

there be a new Paſſage found for the King's Buſineſs, by a Point of the Compaſs that was never failed before? Or muſt there be ſome Forts built in this Houſe, that may command the reſt? Mr *Speaker*, I know but of two Forts in this Houſe which the King ever has, the Fort of Affection, and the Fort of Reaſon the one commands the Hearts, and the other the Heads, others I know none I think *Æſop* was a wiſe Man, who deſcribed the Fly ſitting upon the Spoke of the Chariot Wheel, and ſaying to herſelf, *What a Duſt do I raiſe?* So, for my part, I think that all this Duſt is raiſed by light Rumours and Buzzes, and not upon any ſolid Ground.

The *Second Reaſon* that made me ſilent was, becauſe this Suſpicion and Rumour of *Undertaking*, ſettles upon no certain Perſon It is like the Birds of *Paradiſe* in the *Indies*, that have no Feet, and therefore they never light upon any Place, but the Wind carries them away, and ſuch a thing I take this Rumour to be

And *laſtly*, when the King had in his two ſeveral Speeches freed us from the main of our Fears, by affirming directly, that there was no Undertaking to him, and that he would hold it no leſs a Derogation to his own Majeſty, than to our Merits, to have the Acts of his People transferred to particular Perſons, it quieted me thus far, that theſe Vapours were not gone up to the Head, however they might glow and heat in the Body

Nevertheleſs, ſince I perceive, that this Cloud hangs over the Houſe, and that it may do us hurt, as well in Fame abroad, as in the King's Ear, I reſolved with myſelf, to do the part of an honeſt Voice in the Houſe, and counſel you what I think for the beſt Wherein, *Firſt*, I will ſpeak plainly of the pernicious Effects of the Accidents of this Bruit, and Opinion of *Undertaking* towards Particulars, towards the Houſe, towards the King, and towards the People

Secondly, I will tell you, in my Opinion, what Undertaking is tolerable, and how far it may be juſtified with a good Mind, and on the other ſide, this ſame ripping up of the Queſtion of Undertakers, how far it may proceed from a good Mind, and in what kind it may be thought malicious and dangerous

Thirdly, I will ſhew you my poor Advice, what means there are to put an end to this Queſtion of Undertaking, not falling for the preſent upon a preciſe Opinion, but breaking it, how many ways there are, by which you may get out of it, and leaving the Choice of them to a Debate at the Committee

And laſtly, I will adviſe you how things are to be managed at the Committee, to avoid Diſtraction, and Loſs of Time

For the firſt of theſe, I can ſay to you but as the Scripture ſays, *ſi invicem mordetis, ab invicem conſumemini*, if you fret and gall one another's Reputation, the end will be, that every Man ſhall go hence, like Coin cried down, of leſs Price than he came hither. If ſome ſhall be thought to fawn upon the King's Buſineſs openly, and others to croſs it ſecretly, ſome ſhall be thought Practiſers that would pack the Cards, and others be thought Papiſts that would ſhuffle the Cards what a Miſery is this, that we ſhould come together to fool one another, inſtead of procuring the Publick Good?

And

And this ends not in Particulars, but will make the whole House contemptible for now I hear Men fay, that the Queftion of Undertaking is the predominant Matter of the House   So that we are now, according to the Parable of *Jotham*, in the Cafe of the Trees of the Foreft, that when the Queftion was, whether the Vine fhould reign over them, that might not be, and whether the Olive fhould reign over them, that might not be   but we have accepted the Bramble to reign over us   For it feems that the good Vine of the King's Graces is not fo much in efteem, and the good Oil, whereby we fhould falve and relieve the Wants of the State and Crown, is laid afide too   and this Bramble of Contention and Emulation, this *Abimelech*, which muft reign and rule amongft us

Then for the King, nothing can be more directly oppofite to his Ends and Hopes than this   for you have heard him profefs like a King, and like a gracious King, that he does not fo much refpect his prefent Supply, as this Demonftration, that the Peoples Hearts are more knit to him than before.   Now then if the Iffue fhall be this, that whatfoever be done for him, fhall be thought done but by a number of Perfons laboured and packed, this will rather be a fign of Diffidence and Alienation, than of a natural Benevolence and Affection in his People at home, and rather Matter of Difrepute, than of Honour abroad   So that, to fpeak plainly, the King had better call for new Cards, than play with thefe if they are packed

And then for the People, 'tis my manner ever to look as well beyond a Parliament, as upon a Parliament   and if they without fhall think themfelves betrayed by thofe that are their Deputies, and Attorneys here, 'tis true we may bind them, and conclude them, but it will be with fuch a Murmur and Diffatisfaction as I would be loth to fee.   Thefe things might be diffembled, and fo Matters left to bleed inwards, but that is not the way to cure them.   And therefore I have fearched the Sore, in hopes that you will endeavour the Medicine.   But to do this more thoroughly, I muft proceed to my fecond part, and tell you clearly and diftinctly, what is to be fet on the right hand, and what on the left, in this Bufinefs

Firft, if any Man has done good Offices, and advifed the King to call a Parliament, to increafe the good Affection and Confidence of his Majefty towards his People, I fay that fuch a Perfon rather Merits well than commits any Error   Nay further, if any Man has, out of his own good Mind, given any Opinion of the Minds of the Parliament in general, how 'tis probable, they will be found; and that they will have a due feeling of the King's Wants, and not deal dryly, or illiberally with him, this Man who thinks of other Men's Minds, as he finds his own, is not to be blamed   And ftill farther, if any Man has coupled this with good Wifhes and Propofitions, that the King comforts the Hearts of his People, and teftifies his own Love to them, by filing off the harfhnefs of his Prerogative, retaining the Subftance and Strength, and to that purpofe, like the good Houfholder in the Scripture, who brought forth old Store and new, has revolved the Petitions and Propofitions of the laft Parliament, and added new, I fay this Man has fown good Seed, and he who fhall draw him into Envy for it, fows Tares.   Thus much on the right hand

But on the other fide, if any fhall mediately or immediately infufe into his Majefty, that the Parliament is, as *Cato* faid of the *Romans*, like Sheep, which a Man had better drive a Flock of than one, and that tho' they may be wife Men feverally, yet in this Affembly they are guided by fome few, which if made and affured, the reft will eafily follow this is a plain robbing the King of Honour, and his Subjects of Thanks, and 'tis to make the Parliament vile and fervile in the Eyes of their Sovereign and I account it no better than a fupplanting of the King and Kingdom Again, if a Man fhould make this Impreffion, that it would be enough for the King to fend us fome things of Shew, that may ferve for Colours, and let fome eloquent Talks be told of them, and that will ferve *ad faciendum populum*, any fuch Perfon will find, that this Houfe well underftands falfe Lights, and that it is no wooing Tokens, but the true Love already planted in the Breafts of the Subjects, that will make them do for the King And this is my Opinion, as to thofe who may have perfuaded a Parliament.

There is on the other fide, for I mean in all things to deal plainly if any Man has been confident about the Call of a Parliament, thinking that the beft means were firft for the King to make his utmoft Trial to fubfift of himfelf, and his own Means, I fay an honeft and faithful Heart might confer to that Opinion and the Event it feems does not greatly difcredit it hitherto Again if any Man fhall have been of opinion, that 'tis not a particular Party that can bind the Houfe, or that it is not Shews or Colours can pleafe the Houfe, I fay that Man, tho' his Speech tend to Difcouragement, yet 'tis coupled with Providence But by your leave, if any Man, fince the Parliament was called, or when it was in Speech, fhall have laid Plots, to crofs the good Will of the Parliament to the King, by poffeffing them, that a few fhall have the Thanks, and that they are, as it were, bought and fold, and betray'd, and what the King offers them are but Baits prepared by particular Perfons, or have raifed Rumours that 'tis a packed Parliament, to the end nothing may be done, but that the Parliament may be diffolved, as Gamefters call for new Cards, when they fufpect a Pack I fay thefe are Engines and Devices, naught, malign, and feditious.

Now for the Remedy, I fhall rather break the Matter, as I faid in the beginning, than advife pofitively. I know but three ways (1) Some Meffage or Declaration to the King, (2) Some Entry or Proteftation among ourfelves. Or (3) fome ftrict and punctual Examination As for the laft of thefe I affure you, I am not againft it, if I could tell you where to begin, or where to end For certainly I have often feen it, that things when they are in fmother, trouble more than when they break out Smoke blinds the Eyes, but when it blazes forth into Flame, it gives light to the Eyes But then if you fall to an Examination, fome Perfon muft be charged, fome Matter muft be charged, and the Manner of that Matter muft likewife be charged for it may be in a good Fafhion, and it may be in a bad, in as much Difference as between black and white and then how far Men will ingenuoufly confefs, how far they will politically deny, and what we

can

can make out upon their Confeffion, and how we fhall prove againft their Denial   it is an endlefs piece of work, and I doubt that we fhall grow weary of it

A Meffage to the King, is the Courfe I beft like, provided it be carefully and confiderately handled   for if we fhall reprefent to the King, the Nature of this Body as it is, without the Veils or Shadows that have been caft upon it, I think we fhall do him Honour, and ourfelves Right

For any thing that is to be done amongft ourfelves, I do not fee much gained by it, becaufe it goes no farther than ourfelves, yet if any thing can be wifely conceived to that end, I fhall not be againft it   but I think the purpofe of it is fitteft to be, rather that the Houfe conceives all this to be but Mifunderftanding, than to take Knowledge that there is indeed a juft Ground, and then to feek by Proteftation to give it a Remedy. For Proteftations, and Profeffions, and Apologies, I never found them very fortunate   but that they rather increafe Sufpicion than clear it

Why then, the laft part is, that thefe things be handled at the Committee, ferioufly and temperately, wherein I wifh, that thefe four Degrees of Queftions were canvaffed in order

Firft, whether we fhall do any thing at all in it ; or pafs it by, and let it fleep

Secondly, whether we fhall enter into a particular Examination of it

Thirdly, whether we fhall content ourfelves with fome Entry or Proteftation amongft ourfelves

And *Fourthly*, whether we fhall proceed to a Meffage to the King ; and what

Thus, I have told you my Opinion. I know it were more fafe and politick to have been filent, but it is, perhaps, more honeft and loving to fpeak   The old Verfe is, *Nam nulli tacuiffe nocet, nocet effe locutum*   but *David* fays, *filui a bonis, & dolor meus renovatus eft*   When a Man fpeaks he may be wounded by others, but if he hold his peace from good things, he wounds himfelf   So I have done my part, and leave it for you to do what you fhall judge to be beft.

SPEECH VI.

Made in the STAR-CHAMBER, *before the Summer Circuit;
the King being in* Scotland[a].

THE King, by his perfect Declaration, published in this Place, concerning Judges and Justices, has made the Speech of his Chancellor, accustomed before the Circuits, rather of Ceremony than of Use. For as in his Book to his Son he has set forth a true Character and Platform of a King, so in this Speech he has done the like of a Judge and Justice which shews, that as his Majesty is excellently able to govern in chief, so he is likewise well seen and skilful in the inferior Offices and Stages of Justice and Government, which is a thing very rare in Kings. Yet, somewhat must be said, to fulfil an old Observance, but upon the King's Grounds, and very briefly: for as *Solomon* says, in another Case, *in such thing, who is he that can come after the King?*

First, you that are the Judges of Circuits, are, as it were, the Planets of the Kingdom, and no doubt you have a great share in the Frame of this Government, as the other have in the great Frame of the World. Do, therefore, as they do, move always, and be carried with the Motion of your first Mover, which is your Sovereign. A popular Judge is a deformed thing: and *Plaudits* are fitter for Players than for Magistrates. Do good to the People, love them, and give them Justice, but let it be as the *Psalm* says, *looking for nothing*, neither Praise nor Profit. Yet my meaning is not, when I advise you to beware of Popularity, that you should be imperious and strange to Gentlemen of the Country. You are above them in Power, but your Rank is not much unequal: and learn this, that Power is ever of greatest Strength, when it is civilly carried.

Second, you must remember, that besides your ordinary Administration of Justice, you carry the two Mirrors of State: for it is your Duty in these your Visitations, to represent to the People, the Graces and Care of the King, and again, upon your return, to present to the King, the Distastes and Griefs of the People.

Mark what the King says in his Book, procure Reverence to the King and the Law, inform my People truly of me, how zealous I am for Religion, how I desire Law may be maintained, and flourish, that every Court should have its Jurisdiction, that every Subject should submit himself to the Law. And of this you have lately had no small occasion of Notice, by the great and strict Charge that the King has given me,

as

---

[a] This Speech was made when the Author was *Lord Chancellor. Ann.* 1617.

as Keeper of his Seal, for governing of the *Chancery*, without Tumour or Excefs

As for the other Glafs, of reprefenting to the King the Griefs of his People, without doubt 'tis properly your part , for the King ought to be informed of any thing amifs in the State of nis Countries, from Obfervations and Relations of the Judges, (who indeed know the Pulfe of the Country) rather than from Difcourfe   But for this Glafs, I gladly hear from you all, that there was never greater Peace, Obedience, and Content in the Country , tho' the beft Governments are always like the faireft Cryftals, wherein every Ificle or Grain is feen, which in a fouler Stone is not perceived

Now to fome few Particulars , of all others I muft begin with the Caufe of Religion, and efpecially the hollow Church-Papift   St *Auftin* has a good Comparifon as to fuch Men, affirming them like the Roots of Nettles, which themfelves fting not, yet bear all the ftinging Leaves · let me know of fuch Roots, and I will root them out of the Country

Next, for the Matter of Religion , in the principal place I recommend both to you, and to the Juftices, the countenancing of pious and zealous Preachers.   I mean not Sectaries, or Novelifts, but thofe who are found, and conform, and are yet devout and reverend . for there will be a perpetual Defection, except you keep Men in by Preaching, as well as the Law does by punifhing , and commonly Spiritual Difeafes are not cured but by Spiritual Remedies

Next, let me recommend to you the repreffing of Faction in the Countries , whence enfue infinite Inconveniencies and Perturbations of all good Order, and the croffing of all good Service in Court and Country   *Cicero*, when he was Conful, devifed a fine Remedy, being both mild and effectual , for he fays, *eos qui otium perturbant, reddam otiofos*   Thofe that trouble others quiet, I will give them quiet , they fhall have nothing to do, nor no Authority fhall be put into their hands   If I may know from you, of any in the Country that are Heads or Hands of Faction, or Men of turbulent Spirits, I fhall give them *Cicero*'s Reward, as much as in me lies.

And you, the *Juftices of Peace* in particular, let me fay this to you, that never King of this Kingdom did you fo much Honour as the King has done you in his Speech, by being your immediate Director, and by forting you and your Service with the Service of Ambaffadors, and of his neareft Attendants.

Nay more, it feems his Majefty is willing to do the State of *Juftice of Peace* Honour actively alfo , by bringing in, with Time, the like Form of Commiffion into the Government of *Scotland*, as the glorious King *Edward* III planted this *Commiffion* here in this Kingdom   And therefore you are not fit to be Copies, unlefs you be fair written, without Blots, or any thing unworthy of your Authority.

SPEECH VII.

Made to the Speaker's Excuse and Oration[2].

Mr SERJEANT RICHARDSON,

THE King has observed your grave and decent Speech, tending to excuse and disable yourself for the Place of Speaker. In answer whereof his Majesty commands me to say, that he in no sort admits of the same.

First, because if the Party's own Judgment should be admitted, in case of Elections, in respect of himself, it would follow that the most confident and conceited Persons would be received, and the most considerate Men, and those who understand themselves best, be rejected.

Secondly, his Majesty so much relies upon the Wisdom and Discretion of the House of Commons, that have chosen you with an unanimous Consent, that his Majesty thinks not proper to swerve from their Opinion in that wherein themselves are principally interested.

Thirdly, you have disabled your self so well, that the Manner of your Speech has destroyed the Matter of it.

And therefore the King allows of the Election, and admits you for Speaker.

To the SPEAKER's ORATION.

Mr SPEAKER,

THE King has attended to your eloquent Discourse, containing much good Matter, and much good Will, whereto you must expect from me such an Answer only, as is pertinent to the Occasion, and limited in respect of Time.

I may divide what you have said into four parts. (1) The first was a Commendation of Monarchy. (2) The second was a large Field, containing a thankful Acknowledgment of his Majesty's Benefits and Acts of Government. (3) The third contained some Passages as to the Institution and Use of Parliaments. (4) The fourth and last, consisted of certain Petitions to his Majesty, on the behalf of the House and yourself.

1) For your Commendation of Monarchy, and preferring it to other States, it requires no Answer; the Schools may dispute it, but time has tried it, and we find it the best. Other States have curious Frames, soon put out of order; and those made fit to last are not commonly fit to grow or spread; contrariwise, those made fit to spread and enlarge, are unfit to continue and endure. But Monarchy is like a Work of Nature, well composed, both to grow and continue.

(2) For

---

[2] This Speech was made by the Author as *Lord Chancellor.*

(2) For the second Part of your Speech, wherein with no less Truth than Affection, you acknowledge the great Felicity we enjoy by his Majesty's Government, his Majesty commands me to say to you, that Praises and Thanksgivings he knows to be the true Oblations of Hearts, and loving Affections but that which you offer him, he will join with you in offering to God But for my part, I must say to you, as the *Grecian* Orator said in the like Case, *Solus dignus harum rerum laudator tempus*, time is the only Encomiast worthy of his Majesty and his Government For thro' the Revolution of so many Ages as have passed over this Kingdom, many noble and excellent Effects were never produced till his Majesty's Days, but have been reserved, as proper, and peculiar to them And because this is no part of a Panegyrick, but mere History, and because they are so many Articles of Honour fit to be recorded, I will mention them and they are eight

First, his Majesty is the first that has laid the Corner-Stone of these two mighty Kingdoms of *England* and *Scotland*, and taken away the Wall of Separation whereby his Majesty is become the Monarch of the most puissant and military Nations of the World and if one of the ancient Witch en was not deceived, Iron commands Gold

Secondly, the Plantation and Reduction of *Ireland* to Civility, did by God's Providence wait for his Majesty's Times, being a Work resembling indeed the Works of the ancient Heroes There is no new Piece of that kind in modern times.

Thirdly, this Kingdom now first in his Majesty's Times has attained a later Portion in the new World, by the Plantation of *Virginia* and the *Summer Islands*. And certainly it is with the Kingdoms on Earth, as in the Kingdom of Heaven, sometimes a Grain of Mustard-seed proves a great Tree Who can tell?

Fourthly, his Majesty has made that True, which was before Titular, and verified the Style of Defender of the Faith wherein his Majesty's Pen has been so happy, as tho' the deaf Adder will not hear, yet he is charmed that he does not hiss I mean, in the graver sort of those that have answered his Majesty's Writings

Fifthly, 'tis certain, that since the Conquest, one cannot assign twenty Years, which is the time that his Majesty's Reign now draws to, of inward and outward Peace. Insomuch, that the Time of Queen *Elizabeth*, of happy Memory, and always magnified for a peaceable Reign, was nevertheless interrupted the first twenty Years with a Rebellion in *England*, and both the first and last twenty Years with Rebellions in *Ireland* Yet I know, that his Majesty will make good both his Words, as well that of *Nemo me impune lacessit*, as the other of *Beati pacifici*

Sixthly, that true and primitive Office of Kings, which is to sit in the Gate, and judge the People, was never performed in like Perfection, by any of the King's Progenitors whereby his Majesty has shewn himself to be *Lex loquens*, and to sit upon the Throne, not as a dumb Statue, but as a speaking Oracle.

Seventhly,

S....'*ly*., for his Majesty's Mercy, shew me a time, wherein a King of this Realm has reigned almost twenty Years, in his white Robes, without the Blood of any Peer of this Kingdom the Ax turn'd once or twice towards a Peer, but never struck

Lastly, the flourishing of Arts and Sciences, refreshed by his Majesty's Countenance and Bounty, was never in such height, especially that Art of Arts, Divinity for we may truly confess, that since the primitive Times, there were never so many Stars in that Firmament

These things, Mr *Speaker*, I have partly chosen out of your Heap, and are so far from being vulgar, that they are in effect singular, and proper to his Majesty, and his Times So that I have made good my first Assertion ; that the only worthy Commender of his Majesty is Time, which has so set off his Majesty's Merit, by the Shadows of Comparison, that it surpasses the Lustre, or Commendation of Words

(3) As to the third point concerning Parliaments, I need say little for there was never that Honour done to the Institution of a Parliament, which his Majesty did it, in his last Speech, making it, in effect, the Perfection of Monarchy for altho' Monarchy be the more ancient, and independent, yet by the Advice and Assistance of Parliament, it is the stronger, and surer built And you, Mr *Speaker*, well observed, that when the King sits in Parliament, and his Prelates, Peers, and Commons attend him, he is in the Exaltation of his Orb I wish things may be so carried, that he may be then in the greatest Serenity and Benignity of Aspect, shining upon his People both in Glory and Grace Now you know, that the shining of the Sun, whereby all things exhilarate and fructify, is either hindered by Clouds above, or Mists below, perhaps by Brambles and Briars, that grow upon the ground itself All which I hope, at this time, will be dispelled and removed

(4) I come now to the last Part of your Speech, concerning the Petitions but before I deliver his Majesty's Answer in particular, I must speak somewhat in the general And what can be here pertinently said, must either regard, (1) the Subject or Matter of Parliament Business, (2) the Manner and Carriage of the same, or (3) the Time, and the husbanding and marshalling thereof (1) The Matters to be handled in Parliament are either, (1) of Church, (2) of State, (3) of Laws, or (4) of Grievances

For the two first, Church and State, ye have heard the King himself speak, and as the Scripture says, *Who is he that in such things shall come after the King ?* For the other two, I shall say somewhat, but briefly.

Laws are things proper for your own Element and therein you are rather to lead than be led Only 'tis not amiss to put you in mind of two things the one that you do not multiply or accumulate Laws more than need There is a wise and learned Civilian, who applies the Curse of the Prophet, *Pluet super eos laqueos*, to multiplicity of Laws for they do but ensnare and entangle the People I wish rather, that you would either revive good Laws that are discontinued, or provide against the slack Execution of Laws already

already

already in force, or prevent the subtile Evasions from Laws, which Time and Craft have undermined, than to make *novas creaturas Legum*, Laws upon a new Mould

The other Point relating to Laws is, that ye busy not yourselves too much in private Bills, except it be in Cases wherein the Help and Arm of ordinary Justice is too short

For Grievances, his Majesty has with great Grace opened himself. Nevertheless the Limitations, which may make up your Grievances, not to beat the Air only, but meet a desired Effect, are principally two. The one, that ye do not hunt after Grievances, such as may seem rather stirred here, when ye are met, than to have sprung from the Desires of the Country ye are to represent the People, ye are not to personate them

The other, that you do not heap up Grievances, as if Number should make a Shew, where the Weight is small, or as if all things amiss, like *Plato*'s Common wealth, should be remedied at once   It is certain, that the best Governments, yea, and the best of Men, are like the best precious Stones, wherein every Flaw or Speck is seen and noted, more than in those that are generally foul and corrupted

Therefore contain yourselves within that Moderation, as may tend rather to the effectual Ease of the People, than to a discursive Envy or Scandal upon the State

As for the manner of carrying Parliament Business, ye must know, that ye deal with a King, who has been longer King, than any of you have been Parliament Men, and a King that is no less sensible of Forms, than of Matter, and as far from induring diminution of Majesty, as from regarding Flattery, or Vain-glory, and a King that understands as well the Pulse of the Peoples Hearts, as his own Orb   Therefore, let your Grievances have a decent and reverend Form and Style, and be *tanquam gemitus columbæ*, without Pique or Harshness   and on the other side, in what you do for the King, let it have a Mark of Unity, Alacrity, and Affection ; which will be of this force, that whatever you do in Substance, will be doubled in Reputation abroad

For the Time, if ever Parliament was to be measured by the Hourglass, it is this, in regard of the instant Occasion flying away irrecoverably   Therefore, let your Speeches in the House be the Speeches of Counsellors, and not of Orators   let your Committees tend to dispatch, not to dispute, and so marshal the Times, that the publick Business, especially the proper Business of the Parliament, be put first, and the private Bills be put last, as Time shall give leave, or within the Spaces of the publick

For the four Petitions, his Majesty is pleased to grant them all, as liberally, as the ancient and true Custom of Parliament warrants, and with the Cautions that have ever gone with them, *viz* that the Privilege be not used for defrauding of Creditors, and defeating of ordinary Justice · that Liberty of Speech turn not into Licence, but be joined with that Gra-

...ity and Difcretion, as may favour of Duty and Love to your Sovereign, Reverence to your own Affembly, and Refpect to the Matters ye handle. that your Accefs be at fuch fit times, as may ftand beft with his Majefty's Pleafure and Occafions, and that Miftakings and Mifunderftandings, be rather avoided and prevented, than folved or cleared

SECT

SECT. II.

SPEECHES in JUDICIAL PROCEEDINGS.

SPEECH I.

The CHARGE *againſt the Lord* Sanquhar *for Murther*[a].

MY Lord *Sanquhar*, your Fault is great ; it cannot be extenuated , and it need not be aggravated and you have made ſo full an Anatomy of it, from your own feeling, as cannot be matched by myſelf, or any Man elſe in my Opinion

This Chriſtian and Penitent Courſe of yours draws me to agree, that even in extreme Evils there are Degrees , ſo that your Offence is not of the higheſt Strain for if you had thought to take away a Man's Life for his Vineyard, as *Abab* did , or for Envy, as *Cain* did , ſurely the Offence had been more odious. Your Temptation was Revenge , which the more natural 'tis in Man, the more have Laws, both human and divine, ſought to repreſs it. But in one thing you and I ſhall never agree , *viz*, that generous Spirits are hard to forgive no, contrariwiſe, generous and magnanimous Minds are readieſt to forgive , and 'tis a weakneſs and impotency of Mind to be unable to forgive

But though Murther may ariſe from ſeveral Motives, more or leſs odious , yet the Law, both of God and Man, involves them in one Degree , and therefore in *Joab*'s Caſe, which was a Murther upon Revenge, and correſponding to yours, he for a dear Brother, and you for a dear part of your own Blood, yet there was a ſevere Charge given, that it ſhould not paſs unpuniſhed

A a 2   And

---

[a] The Lord *Sanquhar*, a *Scotch* Nobleman, having, in private Revenge, ſuborned *Robert Carliſe* to murther *John Turner*, Maſter of Defence, thought by his Greatneſs to have born it out, but the King would not ſuffer Nobility to ſhelter Villany, and according to Law, on the 29th of *June* 1612, the ſaid Lord *Sanquhar*, having been arraigned and condemned by the Name of *Robert Creighton* Eſq was executed before *Weſtminſter* hall gate. At whoſe Arraignment the Lord *Bacon*, then *Attorney General*, made this Speech

And certainly the Circumstance of Time is heavy upon you, it is now five years since this unfortunate Man *Turner*, be it upon Accident or Despight, gave the Provocation, which was the Seed of your Malice. All Passions are assuaged with Time, Love, Hatred, Grief, &c. all Fire, burns out with Fire, if no new Fewel be added to it; but for you to have the Gall of Bitterness so long, and to have been in a restless Case for his Blood, is a strange Example. And I must tell you plainly, that I conceive you have rather suck'd those Affections of dwelling in Malice, out of *Italy*, and outlandish Manners, where you have conversed, than out of any part of this Island of *England* or *Scotland.*

But farther, my Lord, I would have you look a little upon this Offence in the Glass of God's Judgment, that God may have the Glory. You have Friends and Entertainment in Foreign Parts; it had been an easy thing for you to have sent *Carisle*, or some other Blood-hound to *York*, when your Person had been beyond the Seas, and so this News might have come to you in a Pacquet, and you might have looked on, and seen how the Storm would pass; but God bereft you of this Providence, and bound you here under the hand of a King, tho' abundant in Clemency, yet no less zealous of Justice.

Again, when you came in at *Lambeth*, you might have persisted in the denial of the Procurement of the Fact, *Carisle*, a resolute Man, might have cleared you; for they that are resolute in Mischief, are commonly obstinate in concealing their Procurers, and so nothing would have been against you but Presumption. But then God, to take away Obstruction of Justice, gave you the Grace to make a clear Confession, which ought indeed to move true Comfort to you, more than any Evasion, or Device whereby you might have escaped. There were many other Impediments, which might have interrupted this Day's Justice, had not God, in his Providence, removed them.

But now, that I have given God the honour, let me give it where 'tis next due, that is, to the King. This Murther was no sooner committed, and brought to his Majesty's Ears, but his just Indignation cast itself presently into a deal of Care and Providence, to have Justice done.

First came forth his Proclamation, somewhat of a rare Form, and devised, and in effect directed to his Majesty himself, signifying that he prosecuted the Offenders, as it were with the Breath and Blasts of his Mouth. Then did his Majesty stretch forth his long Arms, for Kings you know have long Arms, one of them to the Sea, where he took hold of *Gray*, shipped for *Sweden*, who gave the first light of Testimony, the other Arm to *Scotland*, and there he took hold of *Carisle*, e'er he was warm in his House, and brought him the length of this Kingdom, under such a safe Watch and Custody, as he could have no means to escape or mischief himself, nor learn any Lesson to stand mute, in which Cases perhaps this day's Justice might have received a Stop: so that I conclude his Majesty has shewed himself God's true Lieutenant, and that he is no Respecter of Persons, but *English*, *Scots*, Noblemen, Fencer, are to him alike, in respect of Justice.

Nay, I muft farther fay, that his Majefty has had in this Matter a kind of Prophetical Spirit· for from that time *Carlifle* and *Grey*, and you, my Lord, were fled, no Man knew whither, to the four Winds, the King ever fpoke in a confident and undertaking manner, that where-ever the Offenders were in *Europe*, he would produce them to Juftice

Laftly, to return to you, my Lord, tho' your Offence has been great, your Confeffion has been free, and your Behaviour and Speech full of Difcretion, and this fhews, that altho' you could not refift the Temptation, yet you bear a generous and Chriftian Mind, anfwerable to the noble Family of which you are defcended. This I commend to you, and take it for an affured Teftimony of God's Mercy and Favour, in refpect whereof all worldly things are but Trafh, and fo 'tis fit for you, as your State now is, to account them

SPEECH II.

The CHARGE *againft* William Talbot, *Counfellor at Law, upon an Information in the Star-Chamber, for a Writing under his Hand; whereby, when being demanded whether the Doctrine of* Suarez, *as to the depofing and killing of Kings excommunicated, were true or no? he anfwered, That he referred himfelf to what the Church of* Rome *fhould determine thereof* [a].

My LORDS,

WHAT I am now to fpeak to, is one of the greateft Caufes of the Chriftian World, the Conflict betwixt the lawful Authority of Sovereign Princes, which is God's Ordinance for the Comfort of Human Society, and the fwelling Pride and Ufurpation of the See of *Rome*, in Temporals, tending entirely to Anarchy and Confufion. And if this Pretence of the Pope of *Rome*, by Challenges to make Kings as Banditti, profcribe their Lives, and expofe their Kingdoms to Prey, and if all Perfons who fubmit themfelves to this Power of the Pope, be not, by all poffible Severity repreffed and punifhed, the State of Chriftian Kings will be like the ancient Torment defcribed by the Poets, in the Hell of the Heathens, of a Man fitting richly robed, folemnly attended, delicious Fare, &c with a Sword over his Head, hanging by a fmall Thread, ready every Moment to be cut by an accurfing and accurfed Hand   Surely thefe are the Prerogatives of God alone   *I will loofen the Girdles of Kings*, or again, *he poureth Contempt*

[a] This was delivered by the Author in quality of *Attorney-General*, in the Eleventh Year of King *James*

... ... Pr... , or I will give a King to my Wrath, and take him away
... in Di... sure, and the like   but if such are the Claims of a mortal Man, certainly they are the Mysteries of the Person who *exalts himself
*... ... ... is called God, not above God, but *above all that is called God*;
that is, I of Kings and Magistrates.

The Offence wherewith I charge the Prisoner at the Bar, is this that
he is maintained, and maintains under his Hand, a Power in the Pope to
depose and murther Kings   In what sort he does this, I will deliver in his
own Words, without pressing or straining.

But I cannot proceed to the particular Charge so coldly, as not to express the extreme and imminent Danger, wherein our dread Sovereign
is, and in him all of us , nay, and all Princes of both Religions stand
at this day by the spreading of this furious and pernicious Opinion of
the Pope's Temporal Power , which tho' the modest sort would blanch
with the Distinction of *in ordine ad spiritualia*, yet that is but an
elusion, for he who makes the Distinction, will also make the Case.
This Danger, tho' it be notorious, yet because there is a kind
of Dulness, and almost a Lethargy in the present Age, give me
leave to set before you two Glasses, such as certainly never met in
one Age, that of *France*, and that of *England*   In that of *France*,
the Tragedies acted and executed in two immediate Kings, in the
Glass of *England*, the same, or more horrible, attempted likewise in
a Queen and King immediate , but ending in a happy deliverance   In
France, *Henry* III in the face of his Army, before the Walls of *Paris*, stab'd
by a wretched Jacobin Fryar   *Henry* IV a Prince whom the *French* sur-
name the Great, one that had been a Saviour and Redeemer of his Country from infinite Calamities, and a Restorer of that Monarchy to the ancient State and Splendor, and a Prince almost heroical , at the time when
he was at the point of mounting his Horse to command the greatest Forces that of a long time had been levied in *France*, this King likewise stil-
letto'd by a rascal Votary, who had been enchanted and conjured for that
purpose

In *England*, Queen *Elizabeth* of blessed Memory, a Queen to be ranked
with the greatest Kings, often attempted by like Votaries , *Sommervile*,
Parry, Stage, and others , but still protected by the *Watchman that slum-
bers not*   Again, our excellent Sovereign King *James*, the Clemency of
whose Nature was enough to quench all Malignity , and a King shielded
and supported by Posterity , yet this King, in the Chair of Majesty, his
Vine and Olive-Branches about him, attended by his Nobles and third
State in Parliament, ready, in the twinkling of an Eye, to have been
blown to Ashes, and dispersed to the four Winds   My Lord Chief Justice, I observed, when speaking of this *Powder Treason*, laboured for
Words, and tho' they came from him with great Efficacy, yet he truly
confessed, and so must all Men, that this Treason is above the Charge
and Report of Words

Now,

Now, my Lords, in thefe Glaffes, befides the Facts themfelves, and the Danger, I muft fhew you two things, the one the Ways of God, which turn the Sword of *Rome* upon the Kings that are the Vaffals of *Rome*, but protect thofe Kings which have not accepted the Yoke of this Tyranny the other, that this is a common Caufe of Princes, and involves Kings of both Religions and therefore his Majefty did moft worthily and prudently ring out the Alarm-Bell, to awaken all Princes to think of it ferioufly, and in time

But this is a miferable Cafe, that while thefe *Roman* Soldiers either thruft the Spear into the Side of God's Anointed, or at leaft crown them with Thorns, or piercing and pricking Cares and Fears, they can never be fecure of their Lives or States   And as this Danger is common to Princes of both Religions, fo Princes of both Religions have been likewife equally fenfible of every Injury that touched their Temporals

Thuanus reports in his Hiftory, that when the Kingdom of *France* was interdicted by the violent Proceedings of Pope *Julius* the Second, King *Lewis* the Twelfth, otherwife noted for a moderate Prince, caufed Coins of Gold to be ftamped with his own Image, and this Superfcription, *Perdam nomen Babylonis è terra*   And *Thuanus* fays, himfelf has feen divers Pieces thereof   Whence this Catholick King was fo much incenfed at that time, in refpect of the Pope's Ufurpation, that he preceded *Luther*, in applying *Babylon* to *Rome*   The Emperor *Charles* the Fifth, who was accounted one of the Pope's beft Sons, yet in temporal Affairs proceeded with ftrange Rigour towards Pope *Clement*, never regarding the Pontificality, but kept him eighteen Months in a peftilent Prifon, and was hardly diffuaded by his Council from having fent him Captive into *Spain*, and made fport with the Threats of *Frosberg* the *German*, who wore a filk Rope under his Caffock, which he would fhew in all Companies, telling them, that he carried it to ftrangle the Pope with his own hands   As for *Philip* the Fair, 'tis well known how he brought Pope *Boniface* the Eighth to an ignominious End, that of dying mad and enraged, and how he ftyled his Refcript to the Pope's Bull, whereby he challenged his Temporals, *Sciat Fatuitas veftra*, not your *Beatitude*, but your *Stultitude*, a Style worthy to be continued in like Cafes for certainly that claim is mere Folly and Fury   And for domeftick Examples, never did any Kings keep up the Partition-wall between Temporal and Spiritual, better than ours, in times of greateft Superftition   I inftance only in King *Edward* I. who fet up fo many Croffes, and yet oppofed that part of the Pope's Jurifdiction, no Man more ftrongly

Now to the particular Charge of this Man, I muft inform your Lordfhips the Occafion and Nature of his Offence   There has been lately publifhed a Work of *Suarez*, a *Portugueze*, and a Profeffor in the Univerfity of *Coimbra*, a confident and daring Writer, fuch an one as *Tully* defcribes, in derifion, *nihil tam verens, quam ne dubitare, aliqua de re, videretur* who fears nothing fo much as that *he fhould feem to doubt of any thing* A Fellow, who thinks with his Magifteriality and Goofe quill, to give Laws and

Menages

Men gave to Crowns and Scepters In this Man's Writing, the Doctrine of deposing and murdering Kings rises to a higher Pitch, and is more artful, and positively expressed than heretofore I here find three Assertions, which are not in the Vulgar Track, but are such as Men's Ears are not much acquainted with The first is, *That the Pope has a Superiority over Kings and Emperors, to depose them, not only for spiritual Crimes, as Heresy, and Schism, but for Faults of a temporal nature* since a tyrannical Government ever tends to the Destruction of Souls So that by this Position, Kings of either Religion are alike comprehended, and none exempted The *second* is, that after a Sentence given by the Pope, this Writer defines of a series, or succession of Hangmen, or *Sbirri*, lest an Executioner should fail His Assertion is, That when a King is sentenced by the Pope to deprivation or death the Executioner first in place, is he to whom the Pope shall commit the Authority, which may be a foreign Prince, it may be a particular Subject, it may be, in general, to the first Undertaker But if there be no Direction or Assignation in the Sentence, special nor general, then *de jure*, it appertains to the next Successor so that the Successor be apparent, and a Catholick, but if he be doubtful, or no Catholick, then it devolves to the Commonalty of the Kingdom so that he will be sure to have it done by one Minister or other In the *third*, he distinguishes two kinds of Tyrants, a Tyrant in Title, and a Tyrant in Government, the Tyrant in Government cannot be resisted or killed, without a precedent Sentence by the Pope, but a Tyrant in Title may be killed by any private Man whatsoever By which Doctrine he puts the Judgment of Kings Titles, (which are never so clear, but some vain exception may be made to them,) upon the Fancy of every private Man, and also couples the Judgment and Execution together, that he may judge by a Blow, without any other Sentence Your Lordships see what monstrous Opinions these are, and how both the Beast with seven Heads, and the Beast with many Heads, Pope and People, are at once let in upon the sacred Persons of Kings

To proceed with the Narrative ; there was an extract of certain Sentences and Portions of this Book, to the Effect of those above mentioned, made by a great Prelate and Counsellor upon a just occasion , and there being some Hollowness and Hesitation in these Matters discovered and perceived in *Talbot*, he was asked his Opinion concerning them, in presence of his Majesty and afterwards they were delivered to him, that upon Advice, he might sedately declare himself whereupon, under his Hand, he subscribes thus " Concerning this Doctrine of *Svarez*, I perceive by what I have read in " his Book, that the same concerns Matter of Faith, the Controversy " growing upon Exposition of Scriptures and Councils , wherein being un- " studied, I cannot take upon me to judge , but I submit my Opinion " therein to the Judgment of the Roman Catholick Church, as in all Points ' concerning Faith I do "

Upon these words, my Lords, I charge *William Talbot* to have committed a great Offence , and such, as if he had entered into a voluntary and malicious Publication of the like Writing, would have been too great an

Offence

Offence for the Capacity of this Court. But becaufe it grew from a queftion asked by a Council of State, and fo rather feems, in a favourable Con-
ftruction, to proceed from a kind of Submiffion to anfwer, than from any
malicious or infolent Will, it was fit, according to the Clemency of thefe
Times, to proceed in this manner before your Lordfhips And let the
Hearers take thefe things right, for certainly if a Man be required by the
Lords of the Council, to deliver his Opinion, whether King *James* be King
or no? and he delivers his Opinion that he is not, this is High Treafon
but I do not fay that thefe Words amount to that, and therefore let me
open them truly, and therein open alfo the Eyes of the Offender himfelf

My Lords, a Man's Allegiance muft be independent, not provifional
and conditional *Elizabeth Barton*, called the holy Maid of *Kent*, affirmed,
that if King *Henry* VIII did not take *Katherine* of *Spain* again to his Wife,
within a Twelve Month, he fhould be no King and this was judged Treafon For tho' this Act be contingent and future, yet Treafon of compaffing and imagining the King's Deftruction is prefent.

In like manner if a Man fhould voluntarily publifh or maintain, that
whenfoever a Bull or Deprivation fhall come forth againft the King, that from
thence he is no longer King, this is of like nature but with this I do not
charge the Offender neither The true Latitude of his Words is, that if
the Doctrine, as to the killing of Kings, be matter of Faith, he fubmits
himfelf to the Judgment of the *Roman* Catholick Church fo that his allegiance
depends not fimply upon the Pope's Sentence of Deprivation againft the
King, but upon another Point alfo, *viz* if thefe Doctrines are already, or
fhall be declared Matter of Faith But little is gained by this for altho' it
may make fome difference as to the Guilt of the Party, yet little as to the
Danger of the King For the fame Pope of *Rome* may, with the fame
Breath, declare both So that ftill upon the Matter, the King is made
but Tenant at Will, of his Life and Kingdoms, and the Allegiance of his
Subjects is pinn'd upon the Pope's Act And certainly 'tis time to ftop
the current of this Opinion of acknowledging of the Pope's Power in
Temporals, or elfe it will fupplant the Seat of Kings And let it not
be miftaken that Mr *Talbot's* Offence fhould be no more than the refu-
fing the Oath of Allegiance For 'tis one thing to be filent, and another
thing to affirm As for the Point of Matter of Faith, or not Faith, to
tell your Lordfhips plain, it would aftonifh a Man to fee the Gulf of this
implicit Belief If a Man fhould ask Mr *Talbot* whether he condemns
Murder or Adultery, or the Doctrine of *Mahomet*, or of *Arius*, inftead of
Suarez, muft he anfwer with this Exception, that if the Queftion concern
Matter of Faith, (as it does, for the moral Law is matter of Faith) that
therein he fubmits himfelf to what the Church fhall determine? And, no
doubt, the Murder of Princes is more than fimple Murder.

But to conclude, *Talbot*, I will do you this right, to declare that you came afterwards to a better Mind, wherein, if you had been conftant, the King, out of his great Goodnefs, was refolved not to have proceeded with you in this Courfe of Juftice: but then again you ftarted afide like a broken Bow. So that by your Variety and Vacillation you loft the acceptable time of the firft Grace, which was not to have convened you.

Nay, I will go farther, your laft Submiffion I conceive to be fatisfactory and complete, but then it was too late, the King's Honour was upon it, it was publifhed, and a day appointed for hearing, yet what Preparation that may be to the fecond Grace of Pardon I know not, but I know my Lords out of their accuftomed favour, will admit you, not only to your Defence concerning what has been charged, but to extenuate your Fault by any Submiffion that God fhall now put into your Mind to make.

SPEECH III.

The CHARGE *againft* Owen, *indicted for High Treafon, in the* King's Bench[a].

THE Treafon wherewith this Man ftands charged, is for the kind and nature of it ancient, as ancient as there is any Law of *England*, but in the particular, late and upftart: and again, in the manner and boldnefs of it, new and unheard of till this Man. Of what mind he is now, I know not, but I take him as he was, and as he ftands charged. For High Treafon is not written in Ice, that when the Body relents, the Impreffion fhould go away. I fhall by way of Declaration open five things. The *firft* is the Clemency of the King, becaufe 'tis a kind of Rarity to have a Proceeding in this place upon Treafon: and perhaps it may be wondered at by fome, why after fo long an Intermiffion, it fhould light upon this Fellow, being a Perfon but contemptible, and a kind of venomous Fly of the Seminaries.

The *Second* is, the Nature of this Treafon concerning the Fact, which of all kinds of compaffing the King's Death, I hold to be the moft dangerous, and as different from other Confpiracies, as the lifting up of a thoufand hands againft the King differs from lifting up one.

The *Third Point* that I will fpeak to, is the Doctrine or Ground of this Treafon, wherein I fhall not argue like a Divine or Scholar, but as a Man bred in Civil Life: and to fpeak plainly, I hold the Opinion to be fuch as deferves rather Deteftation than Conteft.

The *Fourth Point* is the Degree of this Man's Offence, which is more prefumptuous than I have known any other to have fallen into of this kind, and has a greater Overflow of Malice and Treafon.

And

[a] Bought by the Author as *Attorney General*.

And *Fifthly*, I will remove somewhat that may seem to extenuate this Man's Offence, as he has not affirmed simply, that 'tis lawful to kill the King, but conditionally, that if the King be excommunicate, 'tis lawful to kill him, which makes little difference either in Law or Danger.

For the King's Clemency, I speak it with comfort, that I have now served his Majesty as Sollicitor and Attorney, eight years, yet this is the first time that ever I gave in Evidence against a Traytor, at this Bar, or any other. There has not wanted Matter, in that Party of the Subjects, whence this kind of Offence flows, to irritate the King: he was irritated by the Powder Treason, which might have turned Judgment into Fury. He has been irritated by monstrous and wicked Libels, irritated by a general Insolency and Presumption in the Papists throughout the Land, and yet his Majesty keeps *Cæsar's* Rule   *Nil malo, quam eos esse similes sui, & me met*   He leaves them to be like themselves; whilst he remains like himself, and strives to overcome Evil with Good   A strange thing; bloody Opinions, bloody Doctrines, bloody Examples, and yet the Government still unstained with Blood.   As for this *Owen*, tho' his Person be, in his Condition, contemptible, yet we see by miserable Examples, that these Wretches, which are but the Scum of the Earth, have been able to stir Earthquakes, by murdering of Princes   and if it were in case of Contagion (as this is a Contagion of the Heart and Soul) a Beggar may bring a Plague into the City as well as a great Man   so that 'tis not the Person but the Matter which is to be considered.

For the Treason itself, which is the *Second Point*, my Desire is to open it in the Depth thereof, if it were possible, but 'tis bottomless: and so the Civil Law says, *Conjurationes omnium proditionum odiosissimæ & perniciosissimæ*.   Kings can arm against hostile Invasions, and the Adherence of Subjects to Enemies, Rebellions must go over the Bodies of many good Subjects before they can hurt the King   but Conspiracies against the Persons of Kings are like Thunder Bolts, that strike on a sudden, and are hardly to be avoided.   *Major metus a singulis quam ab universis*   There is no Preparation against them   and that Preparation, which may be of guard or custody, is a perpetual Misery.   And therefore they who have written of the Privileges of Ambassadors, and of the Amplitude of Safe-Conducts, define that if an Ambassador, or Man who comes in upon the highest Safe-Conduct, practise a Matter of Sedition in a State, yet by the Law of Nations he ought to be remanded, but if he conspire against the Life of a Prince, by Violence or Poison, he is to be tried   *Quia odium est omni Privilegio majus*   Nay, even among Enemies, and in the most deadly Wars, Conspiracy, and the Assassination of Princes, has been accounted villanous and execrable.

The Manners of conspiring and compassing the King's Death are many but 'tis most apparent, that among all the rest this surmounts   *First*, because 'tis grounded upon pretended Religion, which is a Trumpet that inflames the Heart and Powers of a Man with Daring and Resolution, more than any thing else.   *Secondly*, 'tis the hardest to be avoided   for when a

particular

particular Conspiracy, is plotted or attempted against a King by some one or some few Conspirators, it meets with a Number of Impediments Commonly he that has the Head to devise it, has not the Heart to undertake it and the Person that is used, sometimes fails in Courage, sometimes fails in Opportunity, sometimes is touched with Remorse But to publish and maintain, that it may be lawful for any Man living to attempt the Life of a King, this Doctrine is a venomous Sop, or as a Legion of malign Spirits, or an universal Temptation that enters at once into the Hearts of all who are any way prepared, or have any predisposition to be Traytors so that what fails in any one, is supplied in many If one Man faint, another will dare it one Man has not the Opportunity, another has it one Man relent, another will be desperate. And *thirdly*, particular Conspiracies have their Periods of Time, within which if they be not taken, they vanish, but this is endless, and imports perpetuity of springing Conspiracies And so much concerning the Nature of the Fact

For the third Point, which is the Doctrine, that upon Excommunication of the Pope, with Sentence of Deposing, a King may be slaughtered by any Son of *Adam*, and that 'tis Justice and no Murder, that their Subjects are absolved of their Allegiance, and the Kings themselves exposed to Spoil and Prey I said before, that I would not argue the Subtilty of the Question 'tis rather to be spoken to by way of Accusation of the Opinion as impious, then by way of dispute as doubtful Nay, I say, it deserves rather some Holy War, or League among all Christian Princes of either Religion, for the extirpating and razing of the Opinion, and the Authors thereof, from the Face of the Earth, than the Style of Pen or Speech Therefore in this kind I will speak to it in a few Words, and not otherwise And, I protest, if I were a Papist I should say as much. nay, I should speak it perhaps with more Indignation and Feeling For this horrible Opinion is our Advantage, but 'tis their Reproach, and will be their Ruin

This Monster of Opinion is to be accused of three most evident and most miserable Slanders

First, of the Slander it brings to the Christian Faith, being a plain Plantation of Irreligion and Atheism

Secondly, the Subversion which it introduces of all Policy and Government

Thirdly, the great Calamity it brings upon Papists themselves, of which the more moderate sort, as Men misled, are to be pitied [a]

For the *first*, if a Man visits the foul and polluted Opinions, Customs, or Practices of Heathenism, Mahometism, and Heresy, he will find they come not to this height. Take the Examples of damnable Memory among the Heathen The Proscriptions in *Rome* of *Sylla*, and afterwards of the Triumvirs, were but of a finite number of Persons, and those not many, that were exposed to any Man's Sword, but what is that to the proscribing of

---

[a] The Speech is imperfect, and breaks off abruptly, before the second Article is gone through

of a King, and all that fhall take his part? And what was the Reward of a Soldier that among them killed one of the profcribed? A fmall Piece of Money. But what is now the Reward of one that fhall kill a King? The Kingdom of Heaven. The moft fcandalous Cuftom among the Heathen was, that fometimes the Prieft facrificed Men, but we do not read of any Priefthood that facrificed Kings.

The Mahometans make it a part of their Religion to propagate their Sect by the Sword, yet by honourable Wars, never by Villanies and fecret Murders. Nay, I find that the *Saracen* Prince, from whom the Name of Affaffin is derived, who had divers Votaries at command, which he fent and employed for the killing of feveral Princes in the Eaft, (by one of whom *Amurcth* the firft was flain, and *Edward* the firft of *England* wounded,) was put down, and rooted out by the common Confent of the *Mahometan* Princes.

The Anabaptifts, 'tis true, come neareft. For they profefs the pulling down of Magiftrates, and they can chaunt the Pfalm, *To bind their Kings in Chains, and their Nobles in Links of Iron.* This is the Glory of the Saints, much like the temporal Authority which the Pope challenges over Princes. But here lies the difference, that theirs is a fanatical Fury, and the Pope's a grave and folemn Mifchief. *he imagines Mifchief as a Law*, a Law-like Mifchief.

As for the Defence which they make, it aggravates the Sin, and turns it from a Cruelty towards Men, to a Blafphemy towards God. For to fay that all this is *in ordine ad fpirituale*, to a good end, and for the Salvation of Souls, is directly to make God the Author of Evil, or to draw him into the Likenefs of the Prince of Darknefs, and to fay with thofe that Saint *Paul* fpeaks of, *Let us do Evil that Good may come of it.* Of whom the Apoftle fays definitively, *That their Damnation is juft.*

For the deftroying of Government univerfally, 'tis moft evident, that this is not the Cafe of Proteftant Princes only, but of Catholick Princes likewife. Nay, 'tis not the Cafe of Princes only, but of all Subjects and private Perfons. For as to Princes, let Hiftory be perufed, to fhew what has been the Caufe of Excommunication, and this Tumour of it, the depofing of Kings. it has not been for Herefy and Schifm alone, but for Collation and Inveftitures of Bifhopricks and Benefices, intruding upon Ecclefiaftical Poffeffions, or violating of any ecclefiaftical Perfon or Liberty. Nay, generally they maintain, that it may be for any Sin. So that the Difference between their Doctors, fome holding that the Pope has his temporal Power immediately, and others only *in ordine ad fpirituale*, is but Delufion, and an Abufe. For all comes to one. What is there that may not be made fpiritual by Confequence, efpecially when he who gives the Sentence may make the Cafe? And the miferable Experience has followed accordingly. For this murdering of Kings has been put in practife, as well againft Papift Kings as Proteftant, fave that it has pleafed God fo to guide it by his admirable Providence, as the Attempts upon Papift

Princes

have been executed. and the Attempts upon Proteftant Princes
are difcovered except in the Cafe of the Prince of *Orange* and not here neither,
and he was joined too faft with the Duke of *Anjou*, and the Papifts.

Speech IV.

The Charge against M. L. S. W. H. J. *for Scandal, and
traducing the King's Juftice, in the Proceedings against*
Wefton *in the* Star-Chamber[a].

THE Offence wherewith I charge the three Prifoners at the Bar, is a
Mifdemeanor of a high nature , tending to the defacing and fcandal of
Juftice in a great Caufe capital   The particular Charge is this.   The
King, among other his princely Virtues, is known to excel in that proper
one of the imperial Throne, Juftice   'Tis a Royal Virtue, which employs
the other three Cardinal Virtues in her Service   Wifdom to difcover, and
difcern the Guilty and Innocent   Fortitude to profecute and execute   Temperance, fo to carry Juftice as it be not paffionate in the purfuit , nor confufed in involving Perfons upon light Sufpicion, nor precipitate in time.
For this his Majefty's Virtue of Juftice, God has of late raifed an occafion,
and erected as it were a Stage, or Theatre, for him to fhew, and act it, in the
purfuit of the untimely Death of Sir *Thomas Overbury*, and therein clean-
fing the Land from Blood   For, my Lords, if Blood fpilt pure, cries to
Heaven in God's Ears, much more Blood defiled with Poifon.

This great Work of his Majefty's Juftice, the more excellent it is, your
Lordfhips will foon conclude, the greater the Offence of any that have fought
to affront or traduce it   And therefore, before I defcend to the Charge of
thefe Offenders, I will fet before your Lordfhips the Weight of what they
have fought to impeach , fpeaking fomewhat of the general Crime of
impoifoning , and then, of the particular Circumftances of this Fact upon
Overbury , and thirdly, of the King's great and worthy Care and Carriage in
the Bufinefs

This Offence of Impoifonment is truly figured in the Defcription made
of the Nature of one of the *Roman* Tyrants, *viz* that he was *Lutum fanguine
maceratum*, *More drench'd and tempered with Blood* for as 'tis one of the
higheft Offences in Guilt, fo 'tis the bafeft of all others in the Mind of
the Offenders   Treafons, *magnum aliquid fpectant* they aim at great things ;
but this is vile and bafe.

I tell your Lordfhips what I have noted, that in the Books of the Old
and New Teftament, I find Examples of all other Offences and Offenders in the World , but not one of an impoifonment or an impoifoner   I
find a fear of cafual Impoifonment , when the wild Vine being fhred into the
Pot, they came complaining in a fearful manner , Mafter, *mors in olla*

And

[a] Exhibited by the Author as *Attorney-General, Anno* 1615

And I find mention of Poifons of Beafts and Serpents, *the Poifon of Afps is under their Lips* but I find no Example in Scripture of Impoifonment I have fometimes thought of the Words in the Pfalm, *Let their Table be a Snare*; which certainly is true of Impoifonment for herein the Table, the daily Bread for which we pray, is turned to a deadly Snare but I think rather this was meant of the Treachery of Friends, that partook of the fame Table

Impoifonment is an Offence, my Lords, that has the two Spurs of offending, *fpes perficiendi*, & *fpes celandi* 'tis eafily committed, and eafily concealed 'Tis an Offence like the Arrow that flies by Night It difcerns not whom it hits for many times the Poifon is laid for one, and another takes it as in *Sanders*'s Cafe, where the poifoned Apple was laid for the Mother, and was taken up by the Child, and kill'd the Child and fo in that notorious Cafe, whereupon the Statute of 22 *Henry* VIII cap 9 was made, where the Intent being to poifon but one or two, Poifon was put into a little Veffel of Yeaft, that ftood in the Bifhop of *Rochefter*'s Kitchen, with which Yeaft, Pottage was made, wherewith feventeen of the Bifhop's Family were poifoned Nay, divers of the Poor that came to the Bifhop's Gate, and had the broken Pottage in Alms, were likewife poifoned And therefore if any Man fhould comfort himfelf by thinking thus, here is a great talk of Impoifonment, I hope I am fafe, for I have no Enemies, nor have nothing that any Perfon fhould long for Why? 'tis all one, for he may fit at Table by another for whom the Poifon is prepared, and have a Drench of his Cup, or of his Pottage And fo, as the Poet fays, *concidit infelix alieno vulnere*, he may die the death defigned for another It was therefore moft gravely, judicioufly, and properly provided by the Statute abovementioned, that Impoifonment fhould be High Treafon; becaufe whatever Offence tends to the utter Subverfion and Diffolution of human Society, is in the Nature of High Treafon.

Laftly, 'tis an Offence which I may truly fay is not *noftri generis, nec fanguinis.* 'Tis rare in the Ifle of *Britain* 'tis neither of our Country, nor of our Church you may find it in *Rome* or *Italy* There is a Region, or perhaps a Religion for it and if it fhould come among us, certainly it were better living in a Wildernefs than in a Court.

For the particular Fact upon *Overbury*, I knew the Gentleman. 'Tis true his Mind was great, but it moved not in any good Order, yet certainly it commonly flew at good things, and the greateft Fault that ever I heard of him, was, that he made his Friend his Idol But I leave him as Sir *Thomas Overbury*, and take him as he was the King's Prifoner in the Tower, and then fee how the Cafe ftands

In that place the State is, as it were, anfwerable to make good the Body of a Prifoner And if any thing happen to him there, it may, tho' not in this Cafe, yet in fome others, caft an Afperfion and Reflexion upon the State it felf For the Perfon is utterly out of his own defence his own Care and Providence can ferve him in no ftead He is in Cuftody and Prefervation of the Law, and we have a Maxim in our Law, that when a State is in Prefervation of the Law, nothing can deftroy or hurt it And God

                                                                    forbid

forc̓d but the like fhould be for the Perfons of thofe that are in Cuftody of the Law, and therefore this was a Circumftance of great Aggravation

Laftly, to have a Man chafed to Death in fuch a maner, as appears now upon Record, by Poifon after Poifon, firft *Rofaker*, then *Arfenick*, then *Mercury Sublimate*, then *Sublimate* again, is a thing would aftonifh a Man's Nature to hear of The Poets feign, that the Furies had Whips, corded with poifonous Snakes, and one would think this were the very Cafe, to have a Man tied to a Poft, and be fcourged to death with Snakes for fo diverfity of Poifons may truly be termed

I will now come to what is the Principal, *viz* his Majefty's princely and facred Proceeding in this Cafe Wherein I will firft fpeak of the Temper of his Juftice, and then of the Strength thereof

Firft it pleafed my Lord Chief Juftice to let me know the Charge his Majefty gave to himfelf firft, and afterwards to the Commiffioners in this Cafe, worthy certainly to be written in Letters of Gold wherein his Majefty made it his prime Direction, that it fhould be carried without Touch to any that was innocent, nay more, not only without Impeachment, but without Afperfion which was a moft noble and princely Caution, for Men's Reputations are tender things, and ought to be like Chrift's Coat, without Seam And it was the more to be refpected in this Cafe, becaufe it met with two great Perfons a Nobleman that his Majefty had favoured and advanced, and a Lady, being of a great and honourable Houfe tho' I take it true, what the Writers fay, *There is no Pomgranate fo fair or fo found, but bears a perifh'd Kernel* Nay, I fee plainly in thofe excellent Papers of his Majefty's own hand-writing, being as fo many Beams of Juftice, ifluing from the Virtue that fhines in him, that it was fo evenly carried without Prejudice, as fhewed, that his Majefty's Judgment was *tanquam tabula rafa*, as a fair Table-Book, and his Ear *tanquam janua aperta*, as a Gate, not fet open, but wide open to Truth, as it fhould be by degrees difcovered Nay, I fee plainly, that in the beginning, till further Light appeared his Majefty was little moved with the firft Tale, which he vouchfafes not fo much as the name of a Tale, but calls it a Rumour, which is a needlefs Tale

For the Strength or Refolution of his Majefty's Juftice, I muft tell your Lordfhips plainly, I do not wonder to fee Kings thunder out Juftice in Cafes of Treafon, when they are touched themfelves, and that they are *Cafe & dolore propri* but that a King fhould *pro amore juftitiæ* only, contrary to the Tide of his own Affection, for the Prefervation of his People take fuch care of a Caufe of Juftice, this is rare and worthy to be celebrated far and near For, I think, I may truly affirm, there was never in this Kingdom, nor in any other, the Blood of a private Gentleman vindicated *in tam a to no regni*, or to fay better *cum tanto plaufu regni* If it had concerned the King or Prince, there could not have been greater nor better Commiffioners to examine it The Term has been almoft turned into a *Juftitia* or Vacation, the People themfelves being more willing to

look

look on in this Bufinefs than to follow their own   There has been no Care of Difcovery omitted, no Moment of Time loft   And therefore I will conclude this part with the faying of *Solomon, Gloria Dei celare rem, & gloria Regis fcrutare rem*

Now I will come to the particular Charge of thefe Gentlemen, whofe Qualities and Perfons I refpect and love, for they are all my particular Friends but now I can only do this Duty of a Friend to them, make them know their Fault to the full   And therefore I will, by way of Narrative, declare to your Lordfhips the Fact, with the Occafion of it

That wretched Man *Wefton*, the Actor, or mechanical Party in this Impoifonment, being indicted by a very fubftantial Jury of felected Citizens, to the number of Nineteen, who found *Billa vera*, yet he at firft ftood mute: but after fome days intermiffion, it pleafed God to caft out the dumb Devil, and that he put himfelf upon his Trial, and was by a Jury alfo of great Value, upon his Confeffion, and other Teftimonies, found guilty · fo that thirty one fufficient Jurors have paffed upon him   Whereupon Judgment and Execution was awarded againft him

After this, being in preparation for another World, he fent for Sir *Thomas Overbury*'s Father, and falling upon his Knees, with great Remorfe and Compunction, asked him forgivenefs.   Afterwards, again, of his own Motion, he defired to have his like Prayer of forgivenefs recommended to Sir *Thomas*'s Mother, who was abfent   and at both times, out of the abundance of his Heart, confeffed that he was to die juftly   And, again, at his Execution, which is a kind of fealing-time of Confeffions, even at the point of Death, he again publickly confirmed, that his Examinations were true, and that he had been juftly and honourably dealt with   Here is the Narrative which induces the Charge   The Charge itfelf is this.

The Offence of *M L* ftands fingle, but that of the other two is in confort, yet all three meet in their Center, which was to interrupt or deface this excellent Piece of Juftice   *M I* I fay, between *Wefton*'s ftanding mute and his Trial, takes upon him to make a moft falfe, odious, and libellous Relation, containing as many Untruths as Lines, and fets it down in Writing with his own hand, and delivers it to Mr. *Henry Gibb*, of the Bedchamber, to be put into the King's hand   in which Writing he falfifies and perverts all that was done the firft day at the Arraignment of *Wefton*, turning the Edge and Point of his Imputations principally upon my Lord Chief Juftice of *England*, whofe Name thus occurring I cannot pafs by, and yet I cannot defcend to flatter   but this I will fay of him, and I would fay as much to Ages, if I fhould write a Hiftory, that never Man's Perfon, and his Place, were better met in a Bufinefs, than my Lord *Coke*, and my Lord Chief Juftice, in the Caufe of *Overbury*

Now, my Lords, in this Offence of *M L.* for the particulars of thefe flanderous Articles, I will obferve them when the Writings and Examinations are read, for I do not love to fet the Glofs before the Text.   But in general I note to your Lordfhips, *firft*, the Perfon of *M. L*   I know he is a *Scots* Gentleman, and therefore more ignorant of our Laws and Forms:

but I cannot tell whether this extenuates his Fault in respect of Ignorance, or aggravates it in respect of Presumption, that he should meddle in what he understood not: but I doubt, it comes not out of his Quiver, some other Man's Cunning wrought upon this Man's Boldness.

Second, I may note the greatness of the Cause, wherein he, being a private, mean Gentleman, presumed to deal. *M L* could not but know to what great and grave Commissioners the King had committed this Cause; and that his Majesty, in his Wisdom, would expect a return of all things from them, to whose Trust he had committed this Business. For 'tis the part of Commissioners, as well to report the Business, as to manage the Business, and then his Majesty might be sure to have had all things well weighed, and to have been truly informed: and therefore it should have been far from *M L* to have presumed to put forth his Hand to so high and tender a Business, which was not to be touched but by the Hands employed.

Thirdly, I note, that this Infusion of a Slander into a King's Ears, is of all Forms of Libels and Slanders, the worst. 'Tis true, that Kings may keep secret their Information, and then no Man ought to enquire after them, while they are shrin'd in their Breast. But where a King is pleased that a Man shall answer for his false Information, there, the false Information to a King exceeds in Offence the false Information of any other kind, being a kind of Impoisonment of a King's Ear. And thus much for the Offence of *M L.*

The Offence of *S W* and *H J.* was this. At the time and place of the Execution of *Weston*, to supplant his Christian Resolution, and to scandalize the Justice already past, and perhaps to cut off the Thread of that which is to come, these Gentlemen, with others, came mounted on horseback, and in a ruffling and facing manner, put themselves forward to re-examine *Weston*, upon Questions directly cross to what had been tried and judged, for the Point tried was, that *Weston* had poisoned *Overbury*. And *S W*'s Question was, whether *Weston* did poison *Overbury* or no. A Contradictory directly. *Weston* answered only, that he did him wrong, and turning to the Sheriff, said, you promised me that I should not be troubled at this time. Nevertheless he press'd him to answer, saying, he desired to know it, that he might pray with him. I know not that *S W* is an Ecclesiastick, that he should cut any Man from the Communion of Prayer. And yet for all this vexing the Spirit of the poor Man, now in the Gates of Death, *Weston* nevertheless stood constant, and said, I die not unworthily. My Lord Chief Justice has my Mind under my Hand, and he is an honourable and just Judge. This is *S W* his Offence.

For *H J* he was not so much a Questionist, but wrought upon the others Questions, and like a kind of Confessor, wished him to discharge his Conscience, and to satisfy the World. What World? I marvel! It was sure the World at *Tyburn*. For the World at *Guild-hall*, and the World at *London*, was satisfied before, witness the Bells that rung. But Men have got a fashion now-a-days, that two or three Busy-bodies will take upon

them

them the Name of the World, and broach their own Conceit, as *if it were* a general Opinion. Well, when they could not work upon *Weston*, H J in Indignation turned about his Horfe, when the other was turning off the Ladder, and faid he was forry for fuch a Conclufion, that was to have the State honoured or juftified.

The Offence of *H. J* had another Appendix, before this in time, which was, that at the day of the Verdict given by the Jury, he alfo muft needs give his Verdict, faying openly, that if he were of the Jury, he fhould doubt what to do   But, he fays, he cannot well tell whether he fpoke this before the Jury had given their Verdict, or after, wherein there is little gained   For whether *H. J* were a Pre-juror or a Poft-juror, the one was as to prejudge the Jury, the other as to taint them.

Of the Offence of thefe two Gentlemen in general, your Lordfhips muft give me leave to fay, that 'tis an Offence greater and more dangerous than is conceived   I know well, that as we have no *Spanifh* Inquifitions, nor Juftice in a Corner, fo we have no gagging of Men's Mouths at their Death, but that they may fpeak freely at the laft hour   but then it muft come from the free Motion of the Party, not by the temptation of Queftions. And then thefe Queftions asked, ought to tend to the farther Revealing of their own or others Guilt, but to ufe a Queftion in the nature of a falfe In-terrogatory, to falfify that which is *res judicata*, is intolerable. for that were to erect a Court or Commiffion of Review at *Tyburn*, againft the *King's-Bench* at *Weftminfter*   And befides, 'tis a vain and idle thing · for if they anfwer according to the Judgment paft, it adds no Credit, or if it be contrary, it derogates nothing   but yet it fubjects the Majefty of Ju-ftice to popular and vulgar Talk and Opinion.

My Lords, thefe are great and dangerous Offences, for if we do not maintain Juftice, Juftice will not maintain us.

Speech V.

The Charge *against* Frances *Countess of* Somerset, *upon the poisoning of Sir* Thomas Overbury [a].

May it please your Grace, my Lord High Steward of England, and you my Lords the Peers

I Am very glad to hear this unfortunate Lady takes this course, to confess fully and freely, and thereby to give Glory to God, and to Justice 'Tis the Nobleness of an Offender to confess ; and therefore those meaner Persons upon whom Justice passed before, confessed not, she does. I know your Lordships cannot behold her without Compassion many things may move you; her Youth, her Person, her Sex, her Noble Family, nay her Provocations, if I should enter the Cause itself, and Furies about her, but chiefly her Penitence and Confession. But Justice is the Work of this day, the Mercy-Seat was in the inner part of the Temple, the Throne is publick

But since this Lady has, by her Confession, prevented my Evidence, and your Verdict, and that this day's Labour is eased, there remains in the legal Proceeding, only for me to pray that her Confession may be recorded, and Judgment thereupon But because your Lordships are met, and that this day and to-morrow are the days that crown all the former Justice, and that in these great Causes it has been ever the manner to regard Honour and Satisfaction, as well as the ordinary Parts and Forms of Justice, the Occasion itself admonishes me to give your Lordships, and the Hearers, the Satisfaction of declaring the Proceedings of this excellent Work of the King's Justice, from beginning to end.

This is now the second time, within the compass of thirteen Years Reign of our happy Sovereign, that this high Tribunal Seat for the Trial of Peers, has been opened and erected, and that with a rare Event, supplied and exercised by one and the same Person, which is a great Honour to you my *Lord High Steward*

In all this time the King has reigned in his white Robe, not sprinkled with one drop of Blood of any of his Nobles of this Kingdom Nay, such have been the Depths of his Mercy, that even those Noblemens Bloods *Cobham* and *Grey*, were attainted and corrupted, but not spilt or taken away, so that they remained rather Spectacles of Justice in their continual Imprisonment, than Monuments of Justice in the Memory of their Suffering

'Tis true, that the Objects of his Justice then and now were very different for then it was the Revenge of an Offence against his own Person and Crown, and upon Persons that were Malecontents, and Contraries to the State and Government, but now 'tis the Revenge of the
Blood

[a] Exhibited by the Author, in quality of *Attorney General*, before the Lord *High Steward*, and the House of Peers, *Anno* 1616

Blood and Death of a particular Subject, and the Cry of a Prisoner • 'tis upon
Persons that were highly in his favour, whereby his Majesty, to his great
honour, has shewed to the World, as if it were written in a Sun-beam, that
he is truly the Lieutenant of him with whom there is no respect of Persons;
that his Affections royal are above his Affections private, that his Favours
and Nearness about him are not like Popish Sanctuaries, to privilege Malefactors, and that his being the best Master, does not hinder him from being
the best King in the world His People, on the other side, may say to
themselves, I will lay me down in Peace, for God, the King, and the Law
protect me against great and small. It may be a Discipline also to great
Men, especially such as are swoln in their Fortunes from small Beginnings,
that the King is as well able to level Mountains, as to fill Valleys, if such be
their Desert.

But to the present Case The great Frame of Justice, my Lords, in this
Action has a *Vault* and a *Stage*, a Vault wherein these Works of darkness
were contrived, and a Stage with Steps, by which it was brought to light.
For the former of these, I will not lead your Lordships into it, because I
will aggravate nothing against a Penitent, neither will I open any thing a-
gainst him that is absent The one I will give to the Laws of Humanity,
and the other to the Laws of Justice. I will therefore reserve that till to-
morrow, and hold myself to what I called the *Stage* or *Theatre*, whereto
indeed it may be fitly compared, since things were first contained within the invisible Judgments of God, as within a Curtain, but afterwards came
forth, and were acted most worthily by the King, and his Ministers.

Sir *Thomas Overbury* was murdered by Poison, *September* 15. 1613. This
foul and cruel Murder did for a time cry secretly in the ears of God; but
God gave no answer to it, otherwise than by that Voice he sometimes uses,
which is *Vox Populi*, the Speech of the People • for there went then a murmur that *Overbury* was poisoned, and yet the same submiss and low Voice
of God, the Speech of the Vulgar, was not without a Counter-tenor, or
Counter-blast of the Devil, who is the common Author both of Murder and
Slander, for it was given out that *Overbury* was dead of a foul Disease, and
his Body, which they had made a *Corpus Judaicum* with their Poisons, so that
it had no whole part, must be said to be leprosed with Vice, and thus his
Name poisoned as well as his Body For as to Dissoluteness, I have not
heard the Gentleman charged with it his Faults were Insolency, Turbulency,
and the like of that kind

Mean time there was some Industry used to lull asleep those that were
the Revengers of the Blood, the Father and the Brother of the Murdered And thus things stood for the space of two years, during which
time God so blinded the two great Procurers, and dazzled them with
their Greatness, and nailed fast the Actors and Instruments with Security upon their Protection, that neither the one looked about, nor the
other stirred or fled, or were conveyed away, but remained here still, as
under a privy Arrest of God's Judgment, insomuch, that *Franklin*, who
should have been sent over to the *Palsgrave* with store of Money was by God's
Providence, and the Accident of a Marriage of his diverted and stay'd

But

But about the beginning of the laſt Summer, God's Judgments began to come out of their depths; and as the revealing of Murder is commonly ſuch as appears to be *God's Work, and marvellous in our Eyes*; ſo in this particular it was moſt wonderful, for it came forth firſt by a Complement, a matter of Courteſy. My Lord of *Shrewsbury* recommended the late Lieutenant *Helwiſſe* to a Counſellor of State, only for Acquaintance, as an honeſt worthy Gentleman. The Counſellor of State anſwered civilly, that my Lord did him a Favour, that he ſhould embrace it willingly, but muſt let his Lordſhip know, that there lay a heavy Imputation upon that Gentleman *Helwiſſe*, as Sir *Thomas Overbury*, his Priſoner, was thought to have died a violent and untimely Death. When this Speech was reported back by my Lord of *Shrewsbury* to *Helwiſſe*, *percuſſit illico animum*, he was ſtruck with it: and being a politick Man, and probably ſuſpecting that the Matter would break out at one time or other, and that others might get the ſtart of him, and thinking to make his own Caſe by his own Tale, reſolved with himſelf, on this Occaſion, to diſcover to my Lord of *Shrewsbury*, and that Counſellor of State, that there was an Attempt, whereto he was privy, to have poiſoned *Overbury*, by the hands of his Under-keeper *Weſton*, but that he checked it, put it by, and diſſuaded it: But then he left it thus, that it was but as an Attempt, or an untimely Birth, never executed, and as if his own Fault had been no more, but that he was honeſt in forbidding it, but fearful of revealing, and impeaching, or accuſing, great Perſons: and ſo with this fine Point he thought to ſave himſelf.

But that Counſellor of State wiſely conſidering, from the Lieutenant's own Tale, that it could not be ſimply a Permiſſion or Weakneſs, becauſe *Weſton* was never diſplaced by the Lieutenant, notwithſtanding that Attempt, and comparing the ſequel with the beginning, thought it a fit Matter to be brought before his Majeſty, by whoſe appointment *Helwiſſe* ſet down the like Declaration in Writing.

Upon this ground the King played *Solomon*'s part, *Gloria Dei celare rem, & gloria Regis inveſtigare rem*, and ſets down certain Papers of his own hand, which I might term *Keys of Juſtice*, and may ſerve both as a Precedent for Princes to imitate, and a Direction for Judges to follow. And his Majeſty carried the Balance with a conſtant and ſteady hand, evenly, and without prejudice, whether it were a true Accuſation of the one part, or a Practice and factious Scandal of the other.

This excellent Foundation of Juſtice, being laid by his Majeſty's own hand, was referred to ſome Counſellors to examine further, who gained ſome degrees of Light from *Weſton*, but yet imperfect. It was afterwards referred to Sir *Edward Coke*, Chief Juſtice of the *King's Bench*, as a Perſon beſt practiſed in legal Examinations, who took indefatigable pains in it without intermiſſion, having, as I have heard him ſay, taken at leaſt three hundred Examinations in this Buſineſs.

But theſe things were not done in a Corner, I need not ſpeak of them. 'Tis true that my Lord Chief Juſtice, in the dawning of the Light, finding the Matter touched upon theſe great Perſons, very diſcreetly became ſuitor to the King, to have greater Perfons than his own Rank joined with him , whereupon your Lordfhips, my Lord High Steward of *England,* my Lord Steward of the King's Houfe, and my Lord *Zouch,* were joined with him

Neither wanted there this while Practice to fupprefs Teftimony, deface Writings, weaken the King's Refolution, flander the Juftices, and the like Nay, when it came to the firft folemn Act of Juftice, which was the Arraignment of *Wefton,* he had his Leffon to ftand mute , which had arrefted the whole Wheel of Juftice, but that this dumb Devil, by the means of fome difcreet Divines, and the potent Charm of Juftice together, was caft out , fo that this poifonous Adder ftopt not his Ear to thefe Charms, but relented, and yielded to his Trial

Then followed the other Proceedings of Juftice againft the other Offenders, *Turner, Helwiffe,* and *Franklin* But all thefe being only the Organs and Inftruments of this Fact, the Actors, and not the Authors, Juftice could not have been crowned without this laft Act againft thefe great Perfons, elfe *Wefton's* Cenfure, or Prediction, might have been verified, when he faid he hoped the fmall Flies fhould not be caught, and the greater efcape Wherein the King, being in great Straits, between the defacing of his Honour, and of his Creature, has chofen the better part , referving always Mercy to himfelf.

The time alfo of Juftice has had its true Motions The time till this Lady's Deliverance was due to Honour, Chriftianity and Humility, in refpect of her Pregnancy The time fince was due to another kind of Deliverance too, which was, that fome Caufes of State that were in the Womb, might likewife be brought forth , not for Matter of Juftice, but for Reafon of State Likewife this procraftination of days had the like weighty Grounds and Caufes

Frances, Countefs of *Somerfet,* has been indicted and arraigned, as Acceffary before the Fact , for the Murder and Impoifonment of Sir *Thomas Overbury,* and has pleaded guilty, and confeffes the Indictment · I pray Judgment againft the Prifoner.

SPEECH VI.

The CHARGE *against* Robert *Earl of* Somerset, *concerning the poisoning of Sir* Thomas Overbury.

May it please your Grace, my Lord High Steward of England, and you my Lords the Peers

YOU have here before you *Robert* Earl of *Somerset*, to be tried for his Life, concerning the procuring and consenting to the Impoisonment of Sir *Thomas Overbury*, then the King's Prisoner in the Tower of *London*, as an Accessary before the Fact

I know your Lordships cannot behold this Nobleman, but you must remember his great Favour with the King, and the great Place he has held and born, and must be sensible that he is yet of your number and body, a Peer as you are, so that you cannot cut him from your Body but with Grief and therefore that you will expect from us, who give in the King's Evidence, found and sufficient Matter of Proof, to satisfy your Honours and Consciences

And for the manner of the Evidence also, the King our Master commanded us not to expatiate, nor make Invectives, but materially to pursue the Evidence, as it conduces to the Point in question, a Matter, that tho' we are glad of so good a Warrant, yet we should have done of ourselves, for far be it from us, by any strains of Wit or Art to seek to play Prizes, or to blazon our Names in Blood, or to proceed otherwise than upon just Grounds   We shall carry the Lanthorn of Justice, which is the Evidence, before your Eyes upright, and be able to save it from being put out by any Winds of Evasions, or vain Defences   this is our part, not doubting, but that this Evidence, in itself, will carry that Force, as it shall little need Advantages or Aggravations

My Lords, the Course I shall hold in delivering what I have to say is this   *First*, I will speak somewhat of the nature and greatness of the Offence now to be tried, and that the King, however he might use this Gentleman heretofore, as the Signet upon his Finger, *to borrow the Scripture-Phrase*, yet in this Case could not but put him off; and deliver him into the hands of Justice

Secondly, I will speak to the Nature of the Proofs, which in such a Case are competent

Thirdly, I will state the Proofs

And *lastly*, I will produce the Proofs, either out of the Examinations and Matters in Writing, or Witnesses *viva voce*.

2   The

The Offence it self is of all Crimes, next to High-Treason, the greateft, being the fouleft of Felonies   And take this Offence with the Circumftances, it has three Degrees, *viz*   (1) Murder; (2) Murder by Impoifonment; And (3) Murder committed upon the King's Prifoner in the *Tower*   I might add, that 'tis a Murder under the colour of Friendfhip, but that is a moral Circumftance, which I leave to the Evidence it felf

For Murder, my Lords, the firft Record of Juftice in the World was a Judgment upon it in the Perfon of *Cain*, and tho' it were not punifhed by Death, but with Banifhment, and a Mark of Ignominy, in refpect of the Primogeniture, or Population of the World, or other Points of God's fecret Will, yet it was adjudged, and is the firft Record of Juftice   So it likewife appears in Scripture, that the Murder of *Abner* by *Joab*, tho' it were by *David* refpited in refpect of great Services paft, or Reafon of State, yet it was not forgot   But of this I will fay no more   It was ever admitted, and fo ranked in God's own Tables, that Murder is of Offences between Man and Man, next to Treafon, and Difobedience of Authority, the greateft.

For Impoifonment, I am forry it fhould be heard of in this Kingdom. 'tis not the growth of our own Country, 'tis an *Italian* Crime, fit for the Court of *Rome*, where the Perfon that intoxicates the Kings of the Earth, with his Cup of Poifon, in heretical Doctrine, is often really and materially intoxicated and impoifoned himfelf.

But it has three Circumftances, which make it grievous beyond other Murders   whereof the *firft* is, that it takes a Man in full Peace, in God's and the King's Peace, he thinks no harm, but is comforting Nature with Refection and Food · fo that, as the Scripture fays, *his Table is made a fnare to him*

The *fecond* is, that it is eafily committed and eafily concealed, and, on the other fide, hardly prevented, and hardly difcovered. for Murder by Violence Princes have Guards, and private Men have Houfes, Attendants, and Arms. neither can fuch Murders be committed but *cum fonitu*, and with fome overt and apparent Act that may difcover and trace the Offender   But for Poifon, the Cup it felf of Princes will fcarce ferve, in regard of many Poifons that neither difcolour nor diftafte, and fo pafs without Noife or Obfervation

And the *laft* is, becaufe it contains, not only the deftruction of the maliced Man, but of any other, *Quis modo tutus erit?*   For many times the Poifon is prepared for one, and is taken by another, fo that Men die the Death defigned for others   *concidit infelix alieno vulnere*   and it is as the *Pfalm* calls it, *the Arrow that flies by Night*, it has no aim or certainty

The third Degree of this particular offence is, that it was committed upon the King's Prifoner, who was out of his own Defence, and merely in the King's Protection, and for whom the King and State was a kind of Refpondent · this is a thing that aggravates the Fault much   For certainly, my Lord of *Somerfet*, let me tell you, that Sir *Thomas Overbury* is the firft Man that was murdered in the *Tower* of *London*, fince the Murder of the two young Princes

For the nature of the Proofs, your Lordships muft confider, that Impoifonment of all Offences is the moft fecret, fo fecret, that if in all Cafes
of Impoifonment you fhou'd require Teftimony, you were as good proclaim
Impunity I will put Book-Examples Who cou'd have impeached *Livia*
by Teftimony, of impoifoning the Figs upon the Tree, which her Husband
ufed for his pleafure to gather with his own Hands? Who cou'd have impeach'd *Parifatis* for poifoning one fide of the Knife that fhe carved with,
and keeping the other fide clean, fo that herfelf eat of the fame Piece of
Meat with the Lady fhe poifoned? The Cafes are infinite, and indeed not
fit to be mentioned, of the Secrecy of Impoifonments, but wife Triers muft
take upon them, in thefe fecret Cafes, *Solomon*'s Spirit, that where there
cou'd be no Witneffes, collected the Act by the Affection But we are not now
to come to that Cafe for what your Lordships are to try, is not the Act of
Impoifonment, this being done to your hand, all the World by Law is concluded to fay, that *Overbury* was poifoned by *Wefton* But the Queftion before you is of the procurement only, and of the abetting, as the Law terms it,
as acceffary before the Fact · which abetting is no more than to do or ufe any
act or means, which may aid or conduce to the Impoifonment. So that
'tis not the buying or making of the Poifon, or the preparing, or confecting
or commixing of it, or the giving or fending or laying the Poifon, that are the
only Acts which amount to abetment. But if there be any other act or
means done or ufed to give the opportunity of Impoifonment, or to facilitate
the execution of it, or to ftop or divert any impediment that might hinder it;
and this be with an intention to accomplifh and atchieve the Impoifonment;
all thefe are abetments, and acceffaries before the Fact I will put you a familiar Example. Allow there be a Confpiracy to murder a Man on the Road,
and it be one Man's part to draw him to that Journey by Invitation, or by
colour of fome Bufinefs, and another takes upon him to diffuade fome Friend
of his, whom he had purpofed to take in Company, that he be not too
ftrong to make his Defence, and another goes along with him, and holds
him in talk till the firft blow be given · all thefe, my Lords, without fcruple
are abettors of the Murder, tho' none of them give the blow, nor affift to
give the blow My Lords, he is not the Hunter alone that lets flip the
Dog upon the Deer, but he that lodges the Deer, or raifes him, or puts
him out, or he who fets a Toil that he cannot efcape, or the like But
this, my Lords, is little wanting in the prefent Cafe, where there is fuch a
Chain of Acts of Impoifonment as has been feldom feen, and could hardly
have been expected, but that greatnefs of Fortune commonly makes grof-
nefs in offending.

For the Proofs themfelves, I fhall hold this Courfe.

Firft, Make a Narrative or Declaration of the Fact it felf.

Secondly, I will break and diftribute the Proofs, as they concern the Prifoner

And *Thirdly,* According to that Diftribution, I will produce, and read,
or ufe them

So that there is nothing, I fhall fay, but you, my Lord of *Somerfet,* fhall
have three means to anfwer it. *Firft,* When I open it, you may take your

Aim,

Aim *Secondly*, When I diftribute it, you may prepare your Anfwers without Confufion And *Laftly*, when I produce the Witneffes or Examinations themfelves, you may again ruminate and re-advife how to make your Defence And this I do the rather, becaufe your Memory may not be oppreffed with Length of Evidence, or with Confufion of Order. Nay more, when your Lordfhip fhall make your Anfwer in your turn, I will put you in mind, when caufe fhall be, of your Omiffions.

Firft, therefore, for the fimple Narrative of the Fact Sir *Thomas Overbury*, for a time was known to have had great Intereft and Friendfhip with my Lord of *Somerfet*, both in his meaner Fortunes, and after infomuch, that he was a kind of Oracle of Direction to him, and if you will believe his own Vaunts, (being of an infolent *Thrafonical* Difpofition,) he took upon him, that the Fortune, Reputation, and Underftanding of this Gentleman, who is well known to have had a better Teacher, proceeded from his Company and Counfel

And this Friendfhip refted not only in Converfation and Bufinefs of Court, but likewife in Communication of Secrets of State For my Lord of *Somerfet*, at that time exercifing the Office of Secretary provifionally, acquainted *Overbury* with the King's Pacquets of Difpatches from all Parts, *Spain*, *France*, the *Low-Countries*, &c And this not by glimpfes, or now and then, whifpering in the Ear for Favour, but in a fettled manner Pacquets were fent, fometimes open'd by my Lord, fometimes unbroken to *Overbury*, who perufed, copied, regiftred them, made Tables of them as he thought good. fo that I will undertake, the time was when *Overbury* knew more of the Secrets of State than the Council-Table. Nay, they were grown to fuch an inwardnefs, that they made a play of all the World befides themfelves, and had Cyphers and Jargons for the King, the Queen, and all the great Men, things feldom ufed, but either by Princes and their Embaffadors, and Minifters, or by fuch as work and practife againft, or at leaft upon Princes But underftand me, my Lord, I fhall not charge you this day with any Difloyalty ; only I fay this, for a Foundation, that there was a great Communication of Secrets between you and *Overbury* ; and that it had relation to Matters of State, and the greateft Caufes of this Kingdom.

But, my Lords, as it is a Principle in Nature, that the beft things are in their Corruption the worft, and that the fweeteft Wine makes the fharpeft Vinegar, fo it fell out with them, that this excefs of Friendfhip, as I may fo term it, ended in mortal hatred on my Lord *Somerfet*'s part. For it fell out, about a Year before *Overbury*'s Imprifonment in the *Tower*, that my Lord of *Somerfet* was entred into unlawful Love towards his unfortunate Lady, then Countefs of *Effex*, which went fo far, that it was then fecretly projected, chiefly between my Lord Privy-Seal, and my Lord of *Somerfet*, to effect a nullity in the Marriage with my Lord of *Effex*, and fo proceed to a Marriage with *Somerfet*.

This Marriage and Purpofe *Overbury* ftrongly oppofed, under pretence of doing the true part of a Friend, as accounting her an unworthy Woman ; but the truth was, that *Overbury*, who, to fpeak plainly, had little that was folid

for

for Religion, or Moral Virtue, but as a Man possess'd with Ambition and Vain-glory, was loth to have any Partners in the Favour of my Lord Somer-ſ, and especially not the House of the *Howards*, against whom he had always profess'd Hatred and Opposition   So that all was but miserable Bargains of Ambition

And, my Lords, that this is no sinister Construction will well appear, when you shall hear that *Overbury* made his Brags to my Lord of *Somerset*, that he had won him the Love of the Lady by his Letters and Industry, so far was he from Cases of Conscience in this Matter And certainly, my Lords, however the Tragical Misery of that poor Gentleman *Overbury* ought some-what to obliterate his Faults, yet because we are not now upon point of Civility, but to discover the Face of Truth to the Face of Justice, and that 'tis material to the true Understanding of the State of this Cause, *Overbury* was naught and corrupt, the *Ballads* must be mended in that Point

But when *Overbury* saw he was here likely to be dispossessed of my Lord whom he had possess'd so long, and by whose Greatness he had promised himself to do Wonders, and being a Man of an unbounded and impetuous Spirit, he began not only to dissuade, but to deter him from that Love and Marriage, and finding him fix'd, thought to try stronger Remedies, supposing that he had my Lord's Head under his Girdle, in respect of Communication of Secrets of State, or, as himself calls them in his Letters, Secrets of all natures, and therefore dealt violently with him, to make him desist, with Menaces of discovery of Secrets, and the like

Hence grew two Streams of Hatred upon *Overbury*; the one from the Lady, in respect that he crossed her Love, and abused her Name, which are Furies to Women, the other of a deeper and more mineral nature, from my Lord of *Somerset* himself; who was afraid of *Overbury*'s Temper, and that if he did break from him and fly out, he would mine into him, and trouble his whole Fortunes

I might add a third Stream from the Earl of *Northampton*'s Ambition, who desired to be first in Favour with my Lord of *Somerset*, and knowing *Overbury*'s Malice to himself and House, thought that Man must be removed and cut off   So it was resolved and decreed amongst them, that *Overbury* should die

Hereupon, they had variety of Devices. To send him beyond Sea, upon occasion of Employment, that was too weak, and they were so far from giving way to it, that they crost it   There rested but two ways, Assault and Poison For that of Assault, after some Proposition and Attempt, they desisted, it was a Thing too open, and subject to more variety of Chances That of Poison was likewise a hazardous Thing, and subject to many Preventions and Cautions, especially to such a jealous and working Brain as *Overbury* had, except he were first fast in their hands

The way, therefore, was first to get him into a Trap, and lay him up, and then they cou'd not miss the Mark. Therefore, in Execution of this Plot, it was devised, that *Overbury* should be designed to some honourable Employment in Foreign Parts, and shou'd under-hand by the Lord of *Somerset* be

encouraged

encouraged to refufe it, and fo upon that Contempt be laid Prifoner in the *Tower*, and then they wou'd look he fhou'd be clofe enough, and Death fhou'd be his Bail

Yet were they not at their end   For they confidered, that if there was not a fit Lieutenant of the *Tower* for their Purpofe, and likewife a fit Under-keeper of *Overbury*   *Firft*, They fhou'd meet with many Impediments in ex-hibiting the Poifon. *Secondly*, They fhou'd be expos'd to Obfervation, that might difcover them   And *Thirdly*, *Overbury*, in the mean time might write clamorous Letters to his Friends, and fo all might be difappointed Therefore the next Link of the Chain was to difplace the then Lieutenant *Waade*, and to place *Helwiffe*, a principal Abettor in the Impoifonment Again to difplace *Cary*, who was the Under-keeper in *Waade*'s time, and to place *Wefton*, who was the principal Actor in the Impoifonment· And this was done with fuch expedition, that there were but fifteen days between the Commitment of *Overbury*, the difplacing of *Waade*, the placing of *Hel-wiffe*, the difplacing of *Cary* the Under keeper, the placing of *Wefton*, and the firft Poifon given two days after

Now when they had this poor Gentleman clofe Prifoner in the *Tower*, where he cou'd not efcape nor ftir, where he cou'd not feed but by their Hands, where he cou'd not fpeak nor write but thro' their Trunks, then was their Time to execute the laft Act of this Tragedy   Then muft *Franklin* be Purveyor of the Poifons, and procure five, fix, feven, feveral Potions, to be fure to hit his Complection   Then muft Mrs *Turner* be the Say-Miftrefs of the Poifons, to try upon Beafts, what's prefent, and what works at diftance of Time   Then muft *Wefton* be the Tormentor, and chafe him with Poifon after Poifon, Poifon in Salts, Poifon in Meats, Poifon in Sweetmeats, Poifon in Medicines and Vomits, till at laft his Body was al-moft come, by the ufe of Poifons, to the State that *Mithridates*'s Body was by the ufe of Prefervatives, that the force of the poifons was blunted upon him, *Wefton* confeffing, when he was chid for not difpatching him, that he had given him enough to poifon twenty Men *Laftly*, Becaufe all this asked time, courfes were taken by *Somerfet*, both to divert all means of *Overbury*'s Deli-very, and to entertain him by continual Letters, partly of Hopes and Pro-jects for his Delivery, and partly of other Fables and Negotiations, fome-what like a kind of Perfons, who keep Men in talk of Fortune-telling, when they have a felonious Intention   And this is, in fhort, the true Narra-tive of this Act of Impoifonment

For the Diftribution of the Proofs, there are four Heads of them to prove you guilty, my Lord of *Somerfet*, of this Impoifonment, whereof two are precedent to the Impoifonment, the third is prefent, and the fourth is fub-fequent   For 'tis in Proofs, as 'tis in Lights, there is a direct Light, and there is a Reflection of Light, or Back-light

The *firft* Head, or Proof is, that there was a root of Bitternefs, a mortal Malice or Hatred, mix'd with deep and bottomlefs Fears, that you had to-wards Sir *Thomas Overbury*.

The

The *third* is, that you were the principal Actor, and had your hand in all those Acts, which conduced to the Impoisonment, and which gave opportunity and means to effect it, and without which, the Impoisonment could never have been, and which could serve or tend to no other end but the Impoisonment

The *wrath*, that your Hand was in the very Impoisonment it self, which is more than needs to be proved, and that you directed Poison, that you delivered Poison, that you continually hearkened to the success of the Impoisonment, and that you spurred it on, and called for dispatch when you thought it lingred

And *lastly*, That you did all the things after the Impoisonment, which may detect a guilty Conscience, for the smothering of it, and avoiding punishment for it, which can be but of three kinds viz (1) That you suppressed, as much as in you was, Testimony (2.) That you defaced and destroyed, and clipt and misdated all Writings that might give light to the Impoisonment And (3) that you flew to the Altar of Guilt, which is a Pardon, and a Pardon of Murder, and a Pardon for your self, and not for your Lady

In this, my Lord. I direct my Speech to you, because I would have you attend the Points of your Charge, and so of your Defence the better. And two of these heads I have taken to my self, and left the other two to the King's two Serjeants

For the *first* main part, which is the mortal Hatred coupled with Fear, that was in my Lord of *Somerset* towards *Overbury*, altho' he palliated it with a great deal of Hypocrisy and Dissimulation, even to the end, I shall prove it manifestly, my Lords, by matter both of Oath and Writing. The Root of this hatred was, what has cost many a Man's Life, that is, Fear of discovering Secrets Secrets, I say, of a high and dangerous nature Wherein the course that I will hold shall be this. *First*, I will shew, that such a Breach and Malice was between my Lord and *Overbury*, and that it burst out into violent menaces and threats on both sides

Secondly, That these Secrets were not light, but of a high nature, for I will give you the elevation of the Pole They were such as my Lord of *Somerset*, for his part, had made a Vow, that *Overbury* should neither live in Court nor Country That he had likewise opened himself and his own Fears so far, that if *Overbury* ever came out of the *Tower*, either *Overbury* or himself must die for it And on *Overbury*'s part, he had threatned my Lord, that whether he lived or died, my Lord's Shame should never die, but he would leave him the most odious Man of the World And farther, that my Lord was likely enough to repent it, in the place where *Overbury* wrote, which was the *Tower* of *London*. He was a true Prophet in that, so here is the height of the Secrets

Thirdly, I will shew you, that all the King's Business was, by my Lord, put into *Overbury*'s Hand so that there is work enough for Secrets, whatever they were. And like Princes Confederates, they had their Cyphers and Jargons

Fourthly,

Fourthly, I will shew you it is but a Toy to say, that the Malice was only in respect he spoke dishonourably of the Lady, or for fear of breaking the Marriage, because *Overbury* was a Coadjutor to that Love, and the Lord of *Somerset* was as deep in speaking ill of the Lady, as *Overbury* And again, it was too late for that matter, for the Match was then made and past And if it had been no more than to remove *Overbury* from disturbing of the Match, it had been an easy matter to have banded him beyond Seas, for which they had a fair way, but that would not serve their turn

And *lastly, periculum periculo vincitur*, to go so far as an Impoisonment, but must have a deeper Malice than Flashes. for the Cause must bear a proportion to the Effect

For the next general Head of Proofs, which consist in Acts preparatory to the middle Acts, they are in eight several Points of the Compass, as I may term it

First, That there were Devices and Projects to dispatch *Overbury*, or to overthrow him, plotted between the Countess of *Somerset*, the Earl of *Somerset*, and the Earl of *Northampton*, before they fell upon the Impoisonment: for always before Men fix upon a course of Mischief, there are some Rejections, but die he must, one way or other.

Secondly, That my Lord of *Somerset* was a principal Practiser, I must speak it, in a most perfidious manner, to set a train for *Overbury* to get him into the *Tower*, without which, they never durst have attempted the Impoisonment

Thirdly, That the placing of Lieutenant *Helwisse* one of the Impoisoners, and the displacing of *Waade*, was by the means of my Lord of *Somerset*

Fourthly, That the placing of *Weston*, the Under-Keeper, who was the principal Impoisoner, and the displacing of *Cary*, and the doing of all this within fifteen days after *Overbury's* Commitment, was by the means and countenance of my Lord of *Somerset*. And these two were the active instruments of the Impoisonment · and this was a Business that the Lady's Power could not reach to

Fifthly, That because there must be a time for the Tragedy to be acted, and chiefly, because they would not have the Poisons work on the sudden, and because the strength of *Overbury's* Nature, or the very Custom of receiving Poison into his Body, overcame the Poison, that they wrought not so fast, therefore *Overbury* must be held in the *Tower* And as my Lord of *Somerset* got him into the Trap, so he kept him in, and abused him with continual hopes of Liberty, and diverted all the true and effectual means of his Release, and made light of his Sickness and Extremities

Sixthly, That not only the Plot of getting *Overbury* into the *Tower*, and the Devices to keep him there, but the strange manner of his close keeping, being in but for a Contempt, was by the Device and Means of my Lord of *Somerset*, who denied his Father to see him, denied his Servants that offered to be shut up close Prisoners with him, and, in effect, managed it so, that he was close Prisoner to all his Friends, and open and exposed to all his Enemies.

Seventhly,

Sixtly, That the Advices which my Lady received, time after time, from the Lieutenant, or *Weston*, as to *Overbury*'s State of Body, were ever sent up to the Court, tho' it were in progress, and that, from my Lady such a thirst and listening this Lord had to hear he was dispatched

Lastly, There was a continual Negotiation to set *Overbury*'s Head on work, that he should make some recognition to clear the Honour of the Lady, and that he should become a good Instrument towards her and her Friends all which was but Entertainment For your Lordships shall plainly see divers of my Lord of *Northampton*'s Letters, whose Hand was deep in this Business, written in dark Words and Clauses, that there was one thing pretended, and another intended, that there was a real Charge, and somewhat not real, a main Drift and a Dissimulation Nay, farther, there are some Passages, which the Peers in their Wisdom will discern to point directly at the Impoisonment.

After this followed the Evidence it self.

SECT.

SECT. III.

SPEECHES on MORAL OCCASIONS.

SPEECH I.

Againſt DUELLING [a].

My LORDS,

I Thought it fit for my Place, and theſe Times, to bring before your Lordſhips the Caſe of private Duels, to ſee if this Court can reclaim ſo unbridled an Evil It may therefore be proper to conſider the Nature, the Cauſes, and the Remedies of Duelling, which the Laws of *England* provided in this reſpect

When Revenge is extorted out of the Magiſtrate's hand, and every Man ſhall bear the Sword, not to defend, but to aſſault, and private Men give Law to themſelves, and pretend to right their own Wrongs; no Mortal can foreſee the Dangers and Inconveniencies, that may ariſe and multiply thereon

It may cauſe ſudden Storms in Court, to the diſturbance of the King, and danger of his Perſon: it may grow from private Quarrels to Tumult and Commotion, from particular Perſons to Diſſenſions of Families and Alliances, and even to national Quarrels, according to the infinite variety of Accidents, which fall not under foreſight ſo that the State by this means is like a diſtempered and imperfect Body, continually ſubject to Inflammations and Convulſions

Beſides, both in Divinity and in Policy, Offences of Preſumption are the greateſt Other Offences yield to the Law, not daring to juſtify themſelves; but this Offence expreſsly affronts the Law, as if there were two Laws; one a kind of Gown Law, and the other a Law of Reputation, as they

---

[a] Delivered in the way of Charge, as Attorney-General, upon an Information in the *Star-Chamber*, againſt *Prieſt* and *Wright*.

term it so that the Pulpit and the Courts of Justice muſt give place to the Law of Tavern-Tables, and ſuch reverend Aſſemblies, and the Year-Books and Statute-Books give place to certain French and Italian Pamphlets upon the Doctrine of Duels.

Again, 'tis a miſerable Effect when hopeful young Men, ſuch as the Poets call *Sons of the Morning*, on whom the Expectation and Comfort of their Friends depends ſhall be caſt away in ſuch a vain manner, but much more 'tis to be deplored, when ſo much noble and genteel Blood ſhall be ſpilt upon ſuch Follies, when if it ventured in the Field, in Service of King and Country, it might turn the Fortune of a Day, and ſway the Fate of a Kingdom. So that this Spirit of Duelling diſturbs Peace, disfurniſhes War, brings Calamity upon private Men, Danger upon the State, and Contempt upon the Law.

As to the Cauſes of Duels, the firſt Motive no doubt is a falſe and erroneous Notion of Honour and Reputation, whence they are properly call'd *base brave Duels*. For to judge truly, 'tis no better than a Sorcery that enchants the Spirits of young Men, bearing great Minds, with a falſe Show, and a kind of ſatanical Illuſion and Apparition of Honour, againſt Religion, againſt Law, againſt moral Virtue, and againſt the Precedents and Examples of the beſt and moſt valiant Nations.

This being the Seed of the Miſchief, 'tis nouriſh'd by vain Diſcourſes, raw and unripe Conceits, which have nevertheleſs ſo prevail'd, that tho' a Man were ſtaid and ſober-minded, and rightly conceived the Vanity and Unlawfulneſs of theſe Duels, yet the Stream of vulgar Opinion impoſes a Neceſſity upon Men of Worth and Merit to conform themſelves, or elſe there is no living or looking upon Mens Faces. whence we have not to do, in this Caſe, ſo much with particular Perſons, as with unſound and depraved Opinions, like the Dominations and Spirits of the Air, which the Scripture ſpeaks of.

We may add, that Men have almoſt loſt the true Notion of Fortitude and Valour. For Fortitude diſtinguiſhes the Grounds of Quarrels, whether they be juſt and worthy, and ſets a better Price upon Mens Lives, than to beſtow them idly. And indeed 'tis a Weakneſs and Diſeſteem of a Man's ſelf, to put one's Life upon ſuch childiſh Performances. A Man's Life is not to be trifled away, 'tis to be offered up and ſacrificed to honourable Services, publick Merit, good Cauſes, and noble Adventures. 'Tis in Expence of Blood, as 'tis in Expence of Money, to make a Profuſion upon every vain and idle Occaſion, is no Liberality; nor is it Fortitude to make Effuſion of Blood, unleſs the Cauſe be worthy.

There are four Things that ſeem very effectual for repreſſing this depraved Cuſtom of particular Combats.

The *firſt* is that there appear, and be declared, a conſtant and ſettled Reſolution in the State to aboliſh it. For this is a thing that muſt go down at once, or not at all, when every particular Man will think himſelf acquitted in his Reputation, finding that the State takes it as an Inſult againſt the King's Power and Authority, and thereupon has abſolutely reſolved to ſuppreſs it. So it was delivered in expreſs Words, in the Edict of *Charles* IX. of *France*, con-

cerning

cerning Duels, that the King took upon himself the Honour of all that thought themselves grieved or interested for not having fought the Duel And thus must the State do in this Business, and trust them, not a Man of a reasonable and sober Disposition, be he ever so valiant, but will be glad of it, when he shall see the Law and Rule of State take off his hands a vain and unnecessary Hazard.

Secondly, Care must be taken that this Evil be not pampered, nor its Humour fed. The publick compounding of Quarrels, which is otherwise in use by private Noblemen, and Gentlemen, appears so punctual and formal, and has such Respect and Relation to the received Opinions, what's before-hand, and what's behind hand, as without all question, it in a manner countenances and authorizes this Practice of Duels, as if it had in it somewhat of Law and Right

Thirdly, As the Offence is grounded upon a false Notion of Honour, it should be punished in the same kind. The Fountain of Honour is the King and his Countenance the Access to his Person continues Honour in Life, and to be banish'd his Presence, is one of the greatest possible Eclipses of Honour Now if the King should be pleased, when any of these Offences are committed by Persons of eminent Quality, to banish or exclude them his Court for certain Years, I think there is no Man of good Blood will commit an Act that shall cast him into the Darkness of not beholding his Sovereign's Face

Lastly, The Root of this Offence is stubborn: for it despises Death, the utmost of Punishments, and it were a just, but a miserable Severity, to execute the Law without all Remission or Mercy, where the Cause proves capital Yet the late Severity of *France* was greater, where, by a kind of martial Law, establish'd by the King and Parliament, the Person, who had slain another, was presently had to the Gibbet, in so much that Gentlemen of great Quality were hanged with their Wounds bleeding; left a natural Death should prevent the Example of Justice. But the Course we propose is of greater Lenity, tho' of no less Efficacy, which is to punish all the middle Acts and Proceedings that tend to the Duel, and so to hew and vex the Root in the Branches which no doubt in the end will kill the Root, and yet prevent the Extremity of the Law

The Law of *England* is excepted to, as deficient in two Points with regard to Duels.

The *one*, that it should make no difference between an insidious and foul Murder, and the killing of a Man upon fair Terms, as they now call it.

The *other*, that it has provided no sufficient Punishment, and Reparation for contumelious Words, as the Lye, and the like.

But these are no better than childish Novelties, against the divine Law, against all Laws in effect, and against the Examples of all the bravest and most virtuous Nations of the World

In the Law of God, there is no Difference found, but between Homicide voluntary and involuntary. And in the Case of Man-slaughter, or accidental Murder, there were Cities of Refuge, so that the Offender was put to his Flight, and that Flight was subject to Accident; whether the Revenge of Blood should overtake him before he had got Sanctuary or no 'Tis true, our Law has made a more subtile Distinction between the Will inflamed, and the Will advised, between Manslaughter in Heat, and Murder upon Malice prepense, or cold Blood, as the Soldiers call it, an Indulgence suited to the Temper and nature of the Nation, for *Rage is a short Fury, and a Man in P* . . .

This Privilege of Passion the ancient *Roman* Law restrain'd to the Case of the Husband's taking the Adulterer in the Fact, to that Rage and Provocation only it admitted Homicide as justifiable. But for a Difference in the case of killing and destroying a Man, upon a forethought Purpose, between foul and fair, 'tis a monstrous Child of this latter Age, and without all' Shadow in any Law divine or human. Only we find in Scripture, that *Cain* inticed his Brother into the Field, and slew him treacherously, but *Lamech* vaunted of his Manhood, that he would kill a young Man, tho' it were to his hurt. so that I find no difference between an insidious and a braving or presumptuous Murder, but the Difference between *Cain* and *Lamech*

All History allows that *Greece* and *Rome* were the most valiant and generous Nations of the World, and what is more to be noted, they were Free States, and not under a Monarchy. Whence one would think it much more reasonable, that particular Persons should have righted themselves ; and yet they had not this Practice of Duels, nor any thing like it. and surely they would have had it, if there had been any Virtue in it. 'Tis memorable, that there was a Combat of this kind between two Persons of Quality among the *Turks*, when one of them being slain, the other was convened before the Council of *Bashaws*, and the Manner of the Reprehension was this. " How " durst you fight? Are there not Christians enough to kill! Did you not know " that whoever was slain, the loss would be the Grand Seignior's?" So that the most warlike Nations, whether generous or barbarous, have ever despised this Manner of Duelling, wherein Men now glory

'Tis true, two Kinds of Combats seem authorized. The one, when upon the Approach of Armies, in the Face of one another, particular Persons have made Challenges for a Trial of Valour in the Field, upon a publick Quarrel. This the *Romans* call'd *Pugna per provocationem*, and was never, but between the Generals themselves, who were absolute, or between Particulars by Licence of the Generals, and not upon private Authority. So *David* asked leave when he fought with *Goliah*; and *Joab*, when the Armies were met, gave leave, and said, *Let the young Men play before us.* And of this kind was that famous Example in the Wars of *Naples*, between twelve *Spaniards* and twelve *Italians*, where the *Italians* bore away the Victory ; besides other infinite the like Examples worthy and laudable, sometimes by single Persons, and sometimes by Numbers

The *second* Kind of Combat is a judicial Trial of Right, when the Right is obscure, introduced by the *Goths* and the *Northern* Nations, but more anciently entertain'd in *Spain*, and this yet remains in some Cases as a divine Lot of Battle, tho' controverted by Divines, as to the Lawfulness of it. so that, as a wise Writer says, " They who engage in this manner, seem to tempt

" God,

" God, as expecting he should shew and work a Miracle, and make him
" victorious whose Cause is the justest , whereas the contrary often happens "
But however it be, this Kind of Combat has its Warrant from Law   Nay,
the *French* themselves, whence this folly seems chiefly to have arisen, never
had it but in Practice and Toleration, not authorized by Law , and yet of
late they have been obliged to purge this Folly with extreme Rigour , infomuch that many Gentlemen, left between Death and Life in the Duels, were
hurried to the Gibbets with their Wounds bleeding   For the State found
it had been neglected so long, that nothing could be thought Cruelty, which
tended to suppress it.

The second Defect pretended in our Law, that it has provided no Remedy
for Lyes and Fillips, may receive the like Answer.   It would have been
thought Madness amongst the ancient Law-givers, to assign a Punishment
upon the Lye given , which in effect is but a Word of Denial, a Negative of
another's Saying   Any Law-giver, if he asked the Question, would have
made *Solon*'s Answer , that he had ordain'd no Punishment for it, because he
never imagined the World would have been so fantastical as to take it so
heinously   The *Civilians* dispute whether any Action of Injury lie for it ,
and rather resolve the contrary.   And *Francis* the First of *France,* who originally stamped this Disgrace so deep, is taxed in the Judgment of all wise
Writers, for beginning the Vanity , as it was he, who having himself given
the Lye and Defy to the Emperor, to make it current in the World, said in a
solemn Assembly,   that no honest Man would bear the Lye   which was the
Fountain of this new Learning

As for Words of Reproach and Contumely, whereof the Lye was never
esteem'd any, it were incredible, but that the Orations themselves are extant,
what extreme and exquisite Reproaches were tossed up and down in the Senate
of *Rome*, the Places of Assembly, and the like in *Greece,* and yet no Man took
himself fouled by them, but held them for Breath, and the Style of an
Enemy , and either despised them or returned them   but no Blood was spilt
upon the Occasion

So every Touch or light Blow of the Person, are not in themselves considerable , only they have got upon them the Stamp of a Disgrace, which
makes such trifling Things pass for great Matters   The Law of *England,*
and all Laws, hold these Degrees of Injury to the Person, Slander, Battery,
Maim, and Death ; and if there be extraordinary Circumstances of Spight
and Contumely, as in case of Libels, Bastinadoes, and the like, the Law
punishes them exemplarily   But for this Apprehension of a Disgrace, that
a Fillip should be a mortal Wound to the Reputation , Men should hearken
to the saying of *Gonsalvo,* the great Commander, who always said, a Gentleman's Honour should be of a good strong Warp or Web, that every little
thing should not catch in it   whereas now they seem Cob-web Lawn, which certainly is Weakness, and not true Greatness of Mind, but like a sick Man's
Body, so tender as to feel every thing   And so much to shew the Wisdom
and Justice of the Law of the Land, in this Particular.

For

For the Capacity of this Court, I take it for certain, that wherever an Offence is Capital, or Matter of Felony, tho' it be not acted, the Combination or Practice tending to that Offence, is punifhable in this Court, as a high Mifdemeanour. Now every Appointment of the Field, however fpecioufly they may gild it, is but a Combination and plotting of Murder. Nor fhall I ever account it otherwife, in a Place of Juftice. Whence it follows, that the Cafe of Duelling is a Cafe fit for the Cenfure of this Court. And of this there are Precedents in the very Point of Challenge.

Therefore, to come to the Part that regards my felf, I fay, that by the Favour of the King and the Court, I will profecute in this Court, in the following Cafes.

(1) If any Man appoint the Field, tho' the Fight be not performed. (2) If any Man fend a Challenge in Writing, or any Meffage of Challenge. (3) If any Man carry or deliver a Writing, or Meffage of Challenge. (4) If any Man fhall accept or return a Challenge. (5) If any Man fhall accept to be a Second in a Challenge, on either Side. (6) If any Man fhall depart the Realm, with Intention and Agreement to fight beyond the Seas. And, (7) If any Man fhall revive a Quarrel by fcandalous Reports or Writings, contrary to a Proclamation publifhed in that Behalf. And this Method of nipping Duels in the Bud, is certainly fuller of Clemency and Mercy, than fuffering them to go on; and hanging Men with their Wounds bleeding, as they did in *France*. And for the Support of Juftice, true Honour, Religion, and the Law, againft this empty Difguife or Puppet-fhow of Honour, I entreat your Lordfhip's Countenance and Affiftance in my Profecutions of this Kind.

Laftly, I have a Petition to the Nobility and Gentry of *England*, that they would efteem themfelves at a juft Price, *Non hos quæfitum munus in ufus*, their Blood is not to be fpilt like Water; and that they would perfuade themfelves there can be no Form of Honour, but upon a worthy Subject.

SPEECH II.

Made by the Author upon taking of his Place in Chancery, as LORD-KEEPER *of the* GREAT-SEAL *of* ENGLAND, *in performance of the* CHARGE *His* MAJESTY *gave him, when he received the Seal, in the Year* 1617.

BEFORE I enter into the Bufinefs of this Court, I fhall take the advantage of fo many honourable Witneffes, to publifh and make known fummarily, what Charge the King's moft excellent Majefty gave me, when I received the Seal, and what Orders and Refolutions I my felf have taken in Conformity to that Charge, that the King may have the Honour of Direction, and I the Part of Obedience: whereby your Lordfhips, and the reft

of the Prefence, fhall fee the whole time of my fitting in Chancery contracted into one Hour   And this I do for three Caufes,

Firft, to give an account to the King of his Command

Secondly, that I may be a Guard and Cuftody to my felf, and my own
Doings, that I do not fwerve or recede from any thing that I have profeffed
in fo noble a Company

And *thirdly*, that all Men who have to do with the Chancery, or the Seal,
may know what they fhall expect, and both fet their Hearts and my Ears
at reft, not moving me to any thing againft thefe Rules, knowing that an
Anfwer is now turn'd from a *nolumus*, into a *non poffumus*   It is no more I
will not, but I cannot, after this Declaration.

And this I do alfo under three Cautions

The *firft* is, that there are fome things of a more fecret and council-like
nature, which are rather to be acted than publifhed   But the Things which
I fhall fpeak of to-day, are of a more publick nature.

The *fecond* is, that I will not trouble this Prefence with every Particular,
which would be too long, but felect thofe Things which are of greateft
Efficacy, and conduce moft *ad fummas rerum*   leaving many other Particulars to be fet down in a publick Table, according to the good Example of
my laft Predeceffor, in his beginning

And *laftly*, that thefe Imperatives, which I have made but to my felf,
and my times, be without prejudice to the Authority of the Court, or
wifer Men that may fucceed me, and chiefly that they are wholly fubmitted
to the great Wifdom of my Sovereign, the abfoluteft Prince in Judicature
that has been in the Chriftian World   for if any of thefe things which I intend to be fubordinate to his Directions, fhall be thought by his Majefty to
be inordinate, I fhall be moft ready to reform them.   Thefe Things are but
tanquam Album Prætoris, for fo did the *Roman Prætors*, (which have the
greateft Affinity with the Jurifdiction of the Chancellor here,) who fet
down at their Entrance, how they would ufe their Jurifdiction   And this
I fhall do, my Lords, in *verbis mafculis*, no flourifhing or painted Words,
but fuch as are fit to go before Deeds.

The King's Charge, which is my Lanthorn, refted upon four Heads

The *firft* was, that I fhould contain the Jurifdiction of the Court within
its true and due Limits, without Swelling or Excefs

The *fecond*, that I fhould think the putting of the great Seal to Letters
Patents, was not a Matter of Courfe, after precedent Warrants, but that I
fhould take it to be the Maturity and Fulnefs of the King's Intentions.
And therefore, that it was one of the greateft Parts of my Truft, if I faw
any Scruple or Caufe of Stay, that I fhould acquaint him, concluding with a
quod dubites ne feceri

The *third* was, that I fhould retrench all unneceffary Delays, that the
Subject might find he enjoy'd the fame Remedy againft the fainting of
the Seal, and againft the Confumption of the Means and Eftate; which was
fpeedy Juftice, *bis dat, qui cito dat.*

The

The *fourth* was, that Justice might pass with as easy a Charge as might be, and that these same Brambles that grow about Justice, of needless Charge and Expence, and all Manner of Exactions, might be rooted out so far as possible.

These Commands, my Lords, are righteous, and, as I may term them, sacred, and therefore to use a sacred Form, I pray God bless the King for his great Care over the Justice of the Land, and give me his poor Servant Grace and Power to observe his Precepts.

Now for a beginning towards it, I have set down and applied particular Orders to every one of these four general Heads.

For the Excess or Tumour of this Court of Chancery, I shall divide it into five Natures.

The *first* is, when the Court embraces or retains Causes, both in Matter and Circumstance, merely determinable, and fit for the common Law for, my Lords, the Chancery is ordain'd to supply the Law, and not to subvert the Law. Now to describe to you, or delineate what those Causes are, and upon what Differences, that are fit for the Court, were too long a Lecture. But I will tell you what Remedy I have prepared. I will keep the Keys of the Court my self, and I will never refer any Demurrer or Plea, tending to discharge or dismiss the Court of the Cause, to any Master of the Chancery, but judge of it my self, or at least the Master of the Rolls. Nay farther, I will appoint regularly, on *Tuesday* weekly, which is the Day of Orders, first to hear all Motions of that nature before any other, that the Subject may have his *Vale* at first, without farther attending, and that the Court do not keep and accumulate a Miscellany and Confusion of Causes of all natures.

The second Point concerns the time of Complaint, and the late Comers into Chancery, which stay till a Judgment be passed against them at the common Law, and then complain, wherein your Lordships may have heard a great Rattle and a Noise of a *præmunire*, and I cannot tell what. But that Question the King has settled, according to the ancient Precedents in all times continued. And this I will say, that the Opinion not to relieve any Case after Judgment, would be a guilty Opinion, guilty of the Ruin, and Naufrage, and perishing of infinite Subjects and as the King found it well out, why should a Man fly into the Chancery, before he be hurt? *The Worst need't the Physician, but the Sick.* But, my Lords, the Power would be preserved, but then the Practice would be moderate. My Rule shall be therefore, that in case of Complaints after Judgment, (except the Judgments be upon *nihil dicit*, which are but Disguises of Judgment, obtain'd in Contempt of a preceding Order of this Court,) yea, and after the Verdicts also, I will have the Party complainant enter into good Bond to prove his Suggestion, so that if he will be relieved against a Judgment at common Law, upon Matter of Equity, he shall do it, *tanquam in vinculis*, at his peril.

The third Point of Excess may be the over-frequent and facile granting of Injunction, for the staying of the common Laws, as the altering Possessions, wherein these shall be my Rules.

I

I will grant no Injunction merely upon Priority of Suit, that is to say, because this Court was first possess'd — a thing that was well reform'd in the late Lord Chancellor's time: but when Chancellor *Bromley*'s time, I remember that Mr. *Davy* the Council at the Law, put a Reply upon the Court in nature of a Bill, to file it was no more but, my 'Lord, the Bill came in on *Monday*, and the Arrest at common Law was on '*Tuesday*, I pray the Injunction upon Priority of Suit.' He caused the Court that had a lewd Desire, to prefer a Bill in Chancery before the Bond due to him was forfeited, to dash an Order that he might have his Money at the day, because he would be sure to be defeat at the other. I do not mean upon such a Matter of an Horserace, on posting who shall be first in Chancery or in Courts of Law.

Neither will I grant an Injunction upon Matter contain'd in the Bill only, be it never so probable and prevalent, but upon Matter confessed in the Defendant's Answer, or Matter pregnant in Writing or of Record, or upon Contempt of the Defendant in not appearing, or not answering, or trifling with the Court by insufficient answering. For then it may be thought the Defendant stands out on purpose to get the Start at the common Law; and so to take advantage of his own Contempt, which must not be suffered.

As for Injunctions for Possession, I will maintain Possessions as they were at the time of the Bill exhibited; and for the space of a Year before, except the Possession were gotten by Force, or by any Trick.

Neither will I alter Possession upon interlocutory Orders, until a Decree, except upon Matter plainly confessed in the Defendant's Answer, joined with a plain Disability and Insolvency of the Defendants to answer the Profits.

As for taking the Possession away in respect of Contempts, I will have all the Proceedings of the Court spent first, and a Sequestration of the Profits before I come to an Injunction.

The fourth Part of Excess in concerning the communicating of the Authority of the Court, or too far, and making upon the Matter too many Chancellors, by relying too much upon the Reports of the Masters of the Chancery is confident. I know my Lords the Masters of Chancery are reverend Men, and the great Mass of Business of the Court cannot be forwarded without them; and 'tis a thing the Chancellor may soon fall into for his own Ease, to rely too much upon them. But the Course that I will take generally shall be this, that I will make no binding Order upon any Report of the Masters, without giving a Seven-night's Day at the least, to shew Cause against the Report; which nevertheless I will have done modestly, and with due reverence towards them. And again, I must utterly discontinue the making of any hypothetical or conditional Orders, that if a Master of the Chancery do certify thus, that then it is ordered without further Motion; for this is a Surprize, and gives no time for Contradiction.

The last Point of Excess is, if a Chancellor shall be so full of himself, as to neglect the Assistance of reverend Judges in Cases of Difficulty, especially if they touch upon Law; or calling them, shall do it, but *pro forma t-n' m,* and give no due Respect to their Opinions here, my Lords, (preserving the Dignity and Majesty of the Court, which I count rather increased than diminished by grave and due Assistance,) I shall never be found so sovereign or abundant in my own Sense, but I shall both desire and make a true use of Assistants. Nay, I assure your Lordships, if I should find any main Diversity of Opinion in my Assistants from my own, tho' I know well the Judicature wholly resides in my self, yet, I think, I should have recourse to the Oracle of the King's own Judgment, before I should pronounce. And so much for the temperate use of the Authority of this Court, wherein the Health of the Court greatly consists, as that of the Body consists in Temperance.

For the second Command of his Majesty, as to the staying of Grants at the Great Seal, there may be just cause of stay, either in the matter of the Grant, or in the manner of passing the same. Out of both, I extract these six principal Cases, which I will now make known. and which, nevertheless, I understand to be wholly submitted to his Majesty's Will and Pleasure, after by me he shall have been informed, for if *iteratum mandatum* come, Obedience is better than Sacrifice.

The *first* Case is, where any Matter of Revenue, or Treasure, or Profit, passes from his Majesty, my first Duty shall be to examine, whether the Grant has passed in the due and natural course by the great Officers of the Revenue, the Lord Treasurer and Chancellor of the Exchequer, and with their privity. which if I find it not to be, I must presume it to have passed in the dark, and by a kind of Surreption, and I will stop it 'till his Majesty's pleasure shall be farther known.

Secondly, If it be a Grant that is not merely vulgar, and has not of course passed at the Signet by a *fac-simile*, but needs Science, my Duty shall be to examine whether it has passed by the learned Counsel, and had their Dockets, which is that which his Majesty reads, and that leads him. And if I find it otherwise, altho' the matter were not in itself inconvenient, yet I hold it just cause of stay, for Precedent's sake, to keep Men in the right way.

Thirdly, If it be a Grant, which I conceive, out of my little Knowledge, to be against the Law, of which nature *Theodosius* was wont to say, when he was pressed, "I said it, but I granted it not, if it be unlawful." I will call the learned Counsel to it, as well him that drew the Book, as the rest, or some of them, and if we find cause, I will inform his Majesty of our Opinion, either by myself or some of them. As for the Judges, they are Judges of Grants past, but not of Grants to come, except the King call them.

Fourthly, If the Grants be against the King's Book of Bounty, I am expressly commanded to stay them, until the King either revise his Book in general, or give direction in particular.

Fifthly, If as a Counsellor of State, I foresee Inconvenience to ensue by the Grant, in reason of State, in respect of the King's Honour, or Discontents or Murmur of the People, I will not truft my own Judgment, but I will either acquaint his Majefty with it, or the Council-Table, or fome fuch of my Lords as I fhall think fit

Laftly, For matter of Pardons, if it be of Treafon, Mifprifion of Treafon, Murder, either expreffed or involute, by a *non obftante*, or of a Piracy, or *Præmunire*, or of Fines, or exemplary Punifhment in the Star-Chamber, or of fome other natures, I fhall ftay them 'till his Majefty confiders how far Grace fhall abound, or fuperabound

And if it be of Perfons attainted and convicted of Robbery, Burglary, &c then I will examine whether the Pardons paffed the Hand of any Juftice of Affize, or other Commiffioners, before whom the Trial was made, and if not, I think it my duty alfo to ftay them

Thus your Lordfhips fee in this matter of the Seal, agreeable to the Command I have received, I mean to walk in the Light, fo that Men may know where to find me   and this publifhing thereof plainly, I hope will fave the King from a great deal of Abufe, and me from a great deal of Envy, when Men fhall fee that no particular turn or end leads me, but a general Rule

For the third general head of his Majefty's Precepts concerning fpeedy Juftice, I am refolved that my Decree fhall come fpeedily, if not inftantly, after the Hearing, and my figned Decree pronounced   For it has been a manner much ufed of late, in my laft Lord's time, (of whom I learn much to imitate, and with due Reverence to his Memory let me fpeak it, much to avoid,) that upon the folemn and full Hearing of a Caufe nothing is pronounced in Court, but Breviates are required to be made   which I do not diflike in itfelf in perplexed Caufes   For I confefs I have fomewhat of the Cunctative, and I am of opinion, that whofoever is not wifer upon advice than upon the fudden, is no wifer at fifty Years old than he was at thirty   And it was my Father's ordinary Word, *You muft give me Time*   But yet, I find, that when fuch Breviates were taken, the Caufe was fometimes forgotten a Term or two, and then fet down for a new Hearing, or a Rehearing three or four Terms after   Of which kind of Intermiffion I fee no ufe, and therefore I will promife regularly to pronounce my Decree within few days after my Hearing, and to fign my Decree at leaft in the Vacation after the pronouncing   For frefh Juftice is the fweeteft. And befides, Juftice ought not to be delay'd, and it will alfo avoid all means-making or labouring· for there ought to be no labouring in Caufes, but the labouring of the Counfel at the Bar

Again, becaufe Juftice is a facred Thing, and for which end I am called to this Place, I fhall add the afternoon to the forenoon, and fome fourth Night of the Vacation to the Term, for expediting and clearing of the Caufes of the Court, only the depth of the three long Vacations I would referve in fome meafure free for Bufinefs of State, and for Studies of Arts and Sciences, to which in my nature I am moft inclined.

There is another point of true Expedition, which refts much in my-felf, and that is in the manner of giving Orders. For I have feen an Af-

fectation

fectation of Difpatch turn utterly to delay and length : for the manner of it is to take the tale out of the mouth of the Counfellor at the bar, and to give a curfory Order, nothing tending or conducing to the end of the Bufinefs. It makes me remember what I heard one fay of a Judge that fat in the Chancery, that he would make eighty Orders in a Morning out of the way, and it was fort of few vanced, for it was nothing to the end of the Bufinefs. And this is the work, as fixty, eighty, a hundred Orders in a Caufe, to and fro, begetting one another, and, like *Penelope*'s Web, doing and undoing. But I mean not to purchafe the Praife of expeditive in that kind, but as one that have a feeling of my Duty, and of the cafe of others, my endeavour fhall be to hear patiently, and to caft my order into fuch a Mould, as may fooneft bring the Subject to the end of his Journey.

As for fuch Delays as may concern others, the great abufe is, that if the Plaintiff have got an Injunction to ftay Suits at common Law, then he will fpin on his Caufe at length. But by the Grace of God, I will make Injunctions an hard Pillow to fleep on ; for if I find that he profecutes not with effect, he may, chance, when he is awake, to find not only his Injunction diffolved, but his Caufe difmiffed.

There are other particular Orders, I mean to take for Non-profecution, or faint Profecution, wherewith I will not trouble you now, becaufe *fumma fequar faftigia Rerum.* And fo much for matter of Expedition.

Now for the fourth and laft point of the King's Command, for the cutting off of unneceffary Charge to the Subject, a great part of it is fulfilled in the preceding Article, touching Expedition, for it is the length of Suits that multiplies Charge chiefly, but yet there are fome other Remedies that conduce thereto.

Firft, therefore, I fhall maintain ftrictly, and with feverity, the former Orders which I find made by my Lord Chancellor for the immoderate and needlefs Prolixity, and length of Bills and Anfwers, and fo forth, as well in punifhing the Party, as fining the Counfel, whofe Hand I fhall find at fuch Bills, Anfwers, &c.

Secondl., For all the Examinations taken in the Court, I give charge to the Examiners (upon peril of their Places) that they do not ufe idle Repetitions, or needlefs Circumftances, in fetting down the Depofitions taken by them ; and I wifh I could help it likewife in Commiffions in the Country, but that is almoft impoffible.

Thirdl,, I fhall take a diligent Survey of the Copies in Chancery, that they have their juft Number of Lines, and without open and waftful Writing.

Fourthl,, I fhall be careful that there be no Exaction of any new Fees, but according as they have been heretofore fet and tabled.

As for Lawyers Fees, I muft leave that to the Confcience and Merit of the Lawyer, and the Eftimation and Gratitude of the Client ; but yet this I can do, I know there have ufed to attend this Bar a number of Lawyers, that have not been heard fometimes, fcarce once or twice in a Term, and that make the Client apply to great Counfel and Favourites (as they call them, a term fitter for Kings than Judges) and that for every Order that a

mean

mean Lawyer might difpatch, and as well   Therefore to help the generality of Lawyers, and therein to eafe the Client, I will conftantly obferve
that every *Tuefday*, and other Days of Orders, after nine a-clock, I will
hear the Bar until eleven, or half an hour after ten at the leaft   And
fince we are upon the point whom I will hear, your Lordfhips will give me
leave to tell you a fancy   It falls out, that there are three of us the King's
Servants in great place, that are Lawyers by defcent, Mr Attorney Son of a
Judge, Mr Sollicitor likewife Son of a Judge, and my felf a Chancellor's Son

Now becaufe the Law roots fo well in my time, I will water it at the
Root thus far, as befides thefe great ones, I will hear any Judge's Son before a Serjeant, and any Serjeant's Son before a Reader

Laftly, For the better eafe of the Subjects, and the bridling of contentious Suits, I fhall give better (that is, greater) Cofts where the Suggeftions
are not proved, than hath been hitherto ufed

There are divers other Orders for the better Regulation of this Court;
for granting of Writs, and for granting of Benefices and other things which
I fhall fet down in a Table.   But I will deal with no other to-day, but fuch
as have a proper relation to his Majefty's Command; it being my comfort that I ferve fuch a Mafter, that I fhall need to be but a Conduit for
the conveying only of his Goodnefs to his People   And it is true, that I
affect and afpire to make good that Saying, *optimus Magiftratus præftat
optimæ legi*, which is true in his Majefty   But for my felf, I doubt I fhall
not attain it   But yet I have a domeftic Example to follow   My Lords,
I have no more to fay, but will now go on to the Bufinefs of the Court.

SPEECH III.

Made in the Exchequer by the Author, as LORD-KEEPER,
to Sir JOHN DENHAM, *call'd to be one of the Barons
of the Exchequer.*

Sir JOHN DENHAM,

THE King of his gracious Favour has made choice of you for one of
the Barons of the Exchequer, to fucceed one of the graveft and moft
reverend Judges of this Kingdom, for fo I hold Baron *Altham* was   The
King takes you not upon credit, but upon proof, and great proof of your
former Service, and that in both the kinds wherein you are now to ferve:
for as you have fhew'd yourfelf a good Judge between Party and Party,
fo you have fhewed yourfelf a good Minifter of the Revenue; both when you
was Chief Baron, and fince as Counfellor of State in *Ireland*, where the
Counfel in great meafure manage and meffuage the Revenue.

And

And to both these parts I will apply some Admonitions, not vulgar or discursive, but apt for the Times, and in few Words, for they are best remembred

First, Therefore, above all, you ought to maintain the King's Prerogative, and to set down with your self, that the King's Prerogative and the Law are not two things, but the King's Prerogative is Law, and the principal Part of the Law, the first born or *Pars prima* of the Law and therefore in conserving or maintaining that, you conserve and maintain the Law There is not in the Body of Man one Law of the Head, and another of the Trunk, but all is one entire Law

The next point I would advise you, is, that you acquaint yourself diligently with the Revenue, and also with the ancient Records and Precedents of this Court When the famous Case of the Copper-Mines was argued in this Court, and judged for the King, it was not upon the fine Reasons of Wit, as that the King's Prerogative drew to it the chief *in quaque specie* the Lion is the chief of Beasts, the Eagle the chief of Birds, the Whale the chief of Fishes, and so Copper the chief of Minerals, for these are but Dalliances of Law, and Ornaments but it was the grave Records and Precedents that grounded the Judgment of that Cause, and therefore I would have you born guide and arm yourself with them against these Vapours and Fumes of Law, which are extracted out of Men's Inventions and Conceits

The third Advice I will give you, has a large Extent, it is, that you do your endeavour in your place so to manage the King's Justice and Revenue, that the King may have most Profit, and the Subject least Vexation. For when there is much vexation to the Subject, and little Benefit to the King, the Exchequer is sick and when there is much Benefit to the King, with less Trouble and Vexation to the Subject, then the Exchequer is sound For example, if there shall be much racking for the King's old Debts, and the fresher and later Debts shall be either more negligently called in, or over easily discharged, or over-indulgently stalled, or if the number of Informations be many, and the King's Part or Fines for Compositions a trifle, or if there be much ado to get the King new Land upon Concealments, and that which he has already be not known and survey'd, nor the Woods preserved, this falls within what I term the sick State of the Exchequer, and makes every Man ready with his Undertakings and Projects, to disturb the ancient Frame of the Exchequer this being the burden of the Song, that much goes out of the Subject's Purse, and little comes to the King's Therefore give them not that advantage Sure I am, that besides your own Associates, the Barons, you serve with two superior great Officers, that have honourable and true Ends, and desire to serve the King, and right the Subject

SPEECH IV.

Made in the COMMON PLEAS *to* Justice HUTTON, *called to be one of the Judges of the* COMMON PLEAS.

Mr. Serjeant HUTTON,

THE King being duly informed of your Learning, Integrity, Discretion, Experience, Means, and Reputation in your Country, has thought fit not to leave you these Talents to be employ'd upon your self only, but to call you to serve Him and his People in the place of one of his Justices of the Court of Common Pleas

This Court, where you are to serve, is the local center and heart of the Laws of this Kingdom here the Subject has his Assurance by Fines and Recoveries, here he has his fixed and invariable Remedies by *Præcipes* and Writs of Right, here Justice opens not by a by gate of Privilege, but by the great gate of the King's original Writs out of the Chancery

Here issues Process of Out-lawry, if Men will not answer Law in this Center of the Law, they shall be cast out. And therefore 'tis proper for you, by all means, with your Wisdom and Fortitude, to maintain the Laws of the Realm. Wherein neverthelefs I would not have you head-strong, but heart-strong, and to weigh and remember that the twelve Judges of the Kingdom are as twelve Lions under *Solomon*'s Throne they must shew their stoutness in elevating and bearing up the Throne To represent the Portraiture of a good Judge, (1) You should draw your Learning out of your Books, not out of your Brain; (2) You should mix well the Freedom of your own Opinion with the Reverence of the Opinion of your Fellows, (3) You should continue the studying of your Books, and not spend on, upon the old Stock, (4) You should fear no Man's Face, and yet not turn Stoutness into Bravery, (5) You should be truly impartial, and not so as that Men may see Affection through fine Carriage, (6) You should be a Light to Jurors, to open their Eyes, and not to lead them by the Nofes, (7) You should not affect the Opinion of Pregnancy and Expedition by an impatient and catching hearing of the Counsellors of the Bar, (8) Your Speech should be with Gravity, as one of the Sages of the Law, and not talkative, nor with impertinent flying out, to shew Learning, (9) Your Hands, and the Hands of your Hands, those about you, should be clean, and uncorrupt from Gifts, meddling in Titles, and from serving of turns, be they of great ones or small ones, (10) You should contain the Jurisdiction of the Court within the ancient mere-stones, without removing the Mark; (11) And *lastly*, you should carry such a hand over your Ministers and Clerks, as that they may rather be in awe of you, than presume upon you [a]

Thefe

a See Vol II pag 73—76

These and the like points of the Duty of a Judge, I forbear to enlarge upon as knowing that you come so furnished and prepared with these good Virtues, that whatever I could say cannot be new to you

S P E E C H V.

Made to Sir WILLIAM JONES, *call'd to be Lord Chief Justice of* Ireland [a].

Sir WILLIAM JONES,

THE King being duly inform'd of your Sufficiency every way, has call'd you to the state and degree of a Serjeant at Law, tho' not to stay here, but to serve him as Chief Justice of his Bench in *Ireland.* And therefore what I shall say to you, must be applied not to your Serjeant's place, which you take only in passage, but to that great place where you are to settle And not to the delay of the business of the Court, I will lead you the short Journey by Examples, and not the long one by Precepts

The place you shall now serve in, has been fortunate to be well served in four Successions before you Do but take the Constancy and Integrity of Sir R b t Gardier, the Gravity, Temper, and Direction of Sir *James Lea*, the Quickness, Industry, and Dispatch of Sir *Humphry Winch*; the Care and Affection to the Commonwealth, with the prudent and politick Administration of Sir *John Denham*, and you shall need no other Lessons They were all *Lincoln's-Inn* Men, as you are, you have known them as well in their Beginnings, as in their Advancement

But because you are there to be not only Chief Justice, but a Counsellor of State, I will put you in mind of the great Work now in hand, that you may frame your Thoughts according to it *Ireland* is the last of the Sons of *Europe*, which has in many Parts been reclaimed from Desolation and a Desert, to Population and Plantation, and from savage and barbarous Customs to Humanity and Civility This is the King's work in chief it is his Garland of heroical Virtue and Felicity, denied to his Progenitors, and reserved to his Times

The Work is not yet conducted to Perfection, but is in a fair Advance, and this I will confidently say, that if God bless this Kingdom with Peace and Justice, no Usurer is so sure in seventeen Years to double his Principal with Interest, and Interest upon Interest, as that Kingdom is within the same time to double the Stock both of Wealth and People So that the Kingdom, which within these twenty Years, wise Men doubted whether they should with a Pool, is now likely to become almost a Garden, and younger Sister to *Great-Britain* And therefore you must set down with yourself to

be

a By the Author as Lord Keeper, *anno* 1617

be not only a juft Governour, and a good Chief-Juftice, as it were in *England* ; but under the King and the Deputy you are to be a Mafter-Builder, a Mafter-Planter, and a Reducer of *Ireland*.   To which end, I will trouble you at this time but with three Directions

The *Firft* is, That you have a fpecial care of the three Plantations.   That of the North, which is in part effected , that of *Wexford*, which is now in Diftribution ;   and that of *Longford* and *Letrim*, which is now in Survey. And take this from me, That the Bane of a Plantation is, when the Undertakers or Planters make fuch hafte to a little mechanical, prefent Profit, as difturbs the whole Frame and Noblenefs of the Work for times to come. Therefore hold them to their Covenants, and the ftrict Ordinances of Plantation.

The *Second* is, That you be careful of the King's Revenues , and by little and little conftitute him a good Demefne, if poffible, which hitherto is little or none   for the King's Cafe is hard, when every Man's Land fhall be improved in value, with manifold increafe, and the King fhall be tied to his dry Rent.

My *Laft* Direction, tho' firft in weight, is, That you do all good endeavours to proceed refolutely and conftantly, and yet with due Temperance and Equality, in Matters of Religion , left *Ireland* civil become more dangerous to us than *Ireland* favage.

SUPPLEMENT V.

SELECT

LETTERS

UPON

VARIOUS OCCASIONS:

Relating to the

AUTHOR'S LIFE and WRITINGS.

PREFACE.

THE following Letters are not all that the Author wrote; but selected from a larger number, as containing somewhat remarkable either with regard to his Life or Writings According to this distinction, they are here divided into two Sections, the first whereof contains some Account of his active, as the other does of his contemplative Life.

They are severally ranged as near the Order of Time, as could well be discover'd by their Dates or otherwise The Stile of those originally wrote in English is seldom alter'd, or only where a Word or Expression was obsolete, that their native simplicity might be the better preserv'd. And where any illustration is wanting, the Notes occasionally supply it chiefly from Mr. Stephens's excellent Edition of the Lord Bacon's Letters.

SECT. I.

Letters relating to the AUTHOR'S LIFE.

I.

To the Lord Treaſurer BURGHLEY; *upon determining his Courſe of Life.*

WITH as much confidence as my own honeſt and faithful devotion to your Service, and your honourable Aſſiſtance to me, can breed in a Man, I commend my ſelf to your Lordſhip I now methinks grow ſomewhat ancient, *one and thirty Years* is a great deal of Sand in the Hour-glaſs. My Health, I thank God, I find confirm'd, and I do not fear that Action will impair it, becauſe I eſteem my ordinary Courſe of Study and Meditation to be more laborious than moſt parts of Action. I ever bore a mind to ſerve her Majeſty in ſome middle Place, that I could diſcharge, not as a Man born under *Sol*, that loves Honour, nor under *Jupiter*, that loves Buſineſs, (for the contemplative Planet carries me away wholly,) but as a Man born under an excellent Sovereign, that deſerves the Dedication of all Men's Abilities Beſides, I do not find in my ſelf ſo much Self love, but that the greater part of my Thoughts are to deſerve well, if I were able, of my Friends, and particularly of your Lordſhip, who, being the *Atlas* of this Common-wealth, the Honour of my Houſe, and the ſecond Founder of my poor Eſtate, I am tied by all Duties, both of a good Patriot, of an unworthy Kinſman, and of an obliged Servant, to employ whatever I can, to do you ſervice. Again, the Meanneſs of my Eſtate ſomewhat moves me, for tho' I cannot accuſe my ſelf, that I am either prodigal or ſlothful, yet my Health is not to ſpend, nor my Courſe to get. Laſtly, I confeſs, that I have as vaſt contemplative Ends, as I have moderate civil Ends · for I have taken all Knowledge to be my Province; and if I could purge it of two ſorts of Rovers, whereof the one with frivolous Diſputes, Confutations and Verboſities, the other with blind Experiments, and

auricular

auricular Traditions and Impostures, has committed so many Spoils, I hope I should bring in industrious Observations, grounded Conclusions, and profitable Inventions and Discoveries, the best State of that Province. This, whether it be Curiosity, or Vain-glory, or Nature, or, if one take it favourably, the Love of Mankind, is so fix'd in my Mind, that it cannot be removed ᵃ And I easily see, that a Place of any reasonable countenance, brings Command of more Wits than of a Man's own, which is the thing I greatly affect And for your Lordship, perhaps you shall not find more Strength and less Encounter in any other And if you find now, or at any time, that I seek or affect a Place, whereto any who are nearer to your Lordship shall lay claim, say then I am a dishonest Man And if your Lordship will not carry me on, I will not do as *Anaxagoras* did, who reduced himself, with Contemplation, to voluntary Poverty but this I will do, I will sell the Inheritance I have, and purchase a less of quicker Revenue, or some Office of Gain, that shall be executed by a Deputy, and so give over all care of Service, and become some sorry Author, or a true Pioneer in that Mine of Truth, which (he said) lay so deep What I now write to your Lordship are rather Thoughts than Words, being set down without Art, Disguise or Reserve wherein I have done honour both to your Lordship's Wisdom, in judging that will be best believed of you which is truest, and to your Good-Nature, in keeping nothing from you. And thus I wish your Lordship all Happiness, and for my self Means and Occasion, to my faithful Desire, to do you service

Gross-Inn, Ann 1591

II.

To the Lord Treasurer BURGHLEY; *offering Service.*

I Know I may commit an Error in writing this Letter, both at a time of great and weighty Business, and also when I am not induced thereto by any new particular Occasion; and therefore your Lordship may accuse me either of Levity, or Ignorance of Duty But I have ever noted it as a Part of your Lordship's Wisdom, not to exclude inferior Matters among the Cares of great ones and I thought it would better manifest what I desire to express, if I wrote out of a deep and settled Consideration of my own Duty, rather than upon the Spur of a particular Occasion And therefore, my singular good Lord, *ex abundantia cordis*, I must acknowledge how greatly and diversly your Lordship has vouchsafed to tie me to you by many Benefits The Reversion of the Office which your Lordship procured me, and carried thro' great and vehement Opposition, tho' it bear no Fruit, yet is one of the fairest Flowers of my poor Estate Your Lordship's constant and serious
Endeavours

ᵃ See the Letter to Father *Fulgentio*, Sect II *ad finem.*

Endeavours to have me Sollicitor, your late honourable Wishes for the Place of the *Wards*, together with your Lordship's Attempt to give me way by the Remove of Mr *Sollicitor*, these are Matters of singular Obligation besides many other Favours, as well by your Lordship's Grants from your self, as by your Commendation to others, which I have had for my help, and may justly persuade my self, out of the few Denials I have received, that fewer might have been, if my own industry and good-fortune had been answerable to your Lordship's Goodness But on the other side, I must humbly beg your pardon, if I speak it, the Time is yet to come that your Lordship is to use, command or employ me, in my Profession, upon any Service or Occasion of your own, or relating to your Lordship: which has made me fear sometimes, that you rather honourably affect me, than thoroughly discern of my most humble and dutiful Affection to your Lordship again, which if it were not in me, I know not whether I were unnatural, unthankful, or unwise This causes me most humbly to pray you would believe, that your Lordship is, upon just Title, a principal Owner and Proprietor of that, I cannot call Talent, but Mite, which God has given me, which I ever do, and shall devote to your Service. And in like humble manner, I pray your Lordship to pardon my Errors, and not to impute to me the Errors of any other, but to conceive of me to be a Man that daily profits in Duty 'Tis true, I do in part comfort myself, supposing 'tis my Weakness and Insufficiency that moves your Lordship, who has so general a Command, to use others more able But however that be, for Duty and Homage, I will undertake, that Nature and true Thankfulness shall never give place to political Dependance Lastly, I most humbly desire you, to continue to me that good Favour, Countenance and Encouragement, in the Course of my poor Labours, whereof I have had some Taste and Experience; for which I return your Lordship my very humble Thanks And thus again, craving your pardon for so long a Letter, that carries so empty an Offer of so mean a Service, tho' a true and unfeigned Signification of an honest and avowed Duty, I remain, &c

III.

To the Lord Treasurer Burghley; *excusing a Speech in Parliament.*

I Was sorry to find, by your Lordship yesterday, that my last Speech in Parliament, delivered in discharge of my Conscience, and Duty to God, her Majesty, and my Country, was offensive. If it were mis-reported, I would be glad to attend your Lordship, to disavow any thing I said not; if it were mis-construed, I would be glad to explain my self, to exclude any Sense I meant not. If my Heart be mis-judged by Imputation of Po-

popularity

pularity or Oppofition, by any envious or officious Informer, I have great wrong, and the greater, becaufe the manner of my *Speech* evidently fhew'd that I fpoke fimply, and only to fatisfy my Confcience, and not with any advantage or policy to fway the Caufe, and my Terms carry'd all fignification of duty and zeal towards her Majefty and her fervice 'Tis true, that from the beginning, whatever was above a double *Subfidy*[a], I wifh'd might (for precedent fake) appear to be extraordinary, and (for difcontent's fake) not have been levied upon the poorer fort, tho' I otherwife wifh'd it as rifing as I think this will prove, and more This was my mind, I confefs it, and therefore I moft humbly pray your Lordfhip, firft to continue me in your good Opinion, and then to perform the part of an honourable Friend towards your poor Servant and Ally, in drawing her Majefty to accept of the fincerity and fimplicity of my Heart, and to bear with the reft, and reftore me to her Majefty's good favour, which is to me dearer than Life.

IV.

To the Lord Treafurer BURGHLEY; *craving his affiftance.*

I Give you humble Thanks for your favourable Opinion, which, by Mr Secretary's Report, I find you conceive of me, for the obtaining of a good Place, which fome of my honourable Friends have wifh'd to me, *nec opinanti* I will ufe no reafon to procure your Lordfhip's mediation, but that your Lordfhip and my other Friends fhall in this beg my Life of the Queen, for I fee well the Bar will be my Bier; as I muft and will ufe it, rather than my poor Eftate or Reputation fhall decay But I ftand indifferent, whether God call me or her Majefty. Had I that in poffeffion, which by your Lordfhip's only means, againft the greateft Oppofition, her Majefty granted me, I wou'd never trouble her Majefty, but ferve her ftill a Volunteer, without pay Neither do I in this more than obey the advice of my Friends, as one that wou'd not be wholly wanting to my felf. Your Lordfhip's good opinion fomewhat confirms me, as that I take comfort in above all others, affuring your Lordfhip, that I never thought fo well of my felf for any one thing, as that I have found a fitnefs, to my thinking, in my felf, to obferve and revere your Virtues, &c

[a] See the Author's Speech upon the Motion of *Subfidy*, in Mr *Blackbourne's* Edition, *Vol.* IV pag 300

V.

V.

To the Lord Treasurer BURGHLEY ; *recommending his first Suit for the Sollicitor's Place.*

THO' I know, by late experience, how, mindful your Lordship vouchsafes to be of me and my poor Fortunes, since it pleased you, during your Indisposition, when her Majesty came to visit your Lordship, to make mention of me for my Employment and Preferment, yet, being now in the Country, I presume your Lordship, who of your self had so honourable a care of the matter, will not think it a trouble to be follicited therein. My hope is, that whereas your Lordship told me her Majesty was somewhat gravelled, upon the offence she took at my *Speech* in Parliament, your Lordship's favourable word (as you assur'd me, that for your own part you judg'd I spoke to the best) will be as a good Tide to remove her from that Shelf. And 'tis not unknown to your Lordship, that I was the first of the ordinary sort, in the lower House of Parliament, that spoke for the *Subsidy* and what I said afterwards in difference, was but in circumstance of Time and Manner ; which methinks shou'd be no greater matter, since there is a variety allow'd in Counsel, as a Discord in Musick, to make it more perfect. But I may justly doubt, not so much her Majesty's impression upon this particular, as her opinion otherwise of my Insufficiency, which tho' I acknowledge to be great, yet it will be the less, because I purpose not to divide my self between her Majesty and the Causes of other Men, but to attend her business only, hoping that a whole Man of mean abilities, may do as well as half a Man better able. And if her Majesty think she shall make an adventure in using one who is rather a Man of study, than of practice and experience, surely I may remember to have heard that my Father was made *Sollicitor of the Augmentation*, (a Court of much business) when he had never practised, and was but seven and twenty years old, and Mr *Brograve* was, in my time, call'd to be *Attorney of the Dutchy*, when he had practised little or nothing, and yet discharged his Place with great sufficiency. But these things, and the like, are as her Majesty shall be made capable of them. wherein, knowing what Authority your Lordship's Commendation has with her Majesty, I conclude that the Substance of Strength, which I may receive, will be from your Lordship. 'Tis true, my Life has been so private, that I have had no means to do your Lordship service, but yet, you know, I have made offer of such as I could yield. for as God has given me a Mind to love the Publick, so, incidently, I have ever had your Lordship in singular admiration, whose happy Ability her Majesty has so long used, to her great honour and yours. Besides, that amendment of state or countenance, which I have receiv'd, has been from you. And therefore if your Lordship shall stand a good Friend to your poor Ally, you fhall but *tueri Onus proprium*, which you have begun   And your Lordfhip fhall beftow your benefit upon one that has more fenfe of obligation than of felf-love

Jun the 7th, 1595

VI.

To Sir ROBERT CECIL; *intimating Sufpicion of unfair Practices.*

I Forbear not to write as much as I thought to have faid to your Honour to-day, if I cou'd have ftaid, knowing that if you fhou'd make other ufe of it, than is due to good meaning, and than I am perfuaded you will, yet to Perfons of judgment, and that know me otherwife, it will rather appear (as it is) a precife honefty. and *fuum cuique tribuere*, than any hollownefs 'Tis my luck ftill to be a-kin to fuch things as I neither like in nature, nor wou'd willingly meet with in my courfe, yet cannot avoid, without fhew of bafe timorousnefs, or elfe of unkind or fufpicious ftrangenefs. I am of one Spirit ftill, I ever lik'd the *Galenifts* that deal with good Compofitions, and not the *Paracelfifts* that deal with fine Separations   And in Mufick, I ever loved eafy Airs, that go full, all the parts together, and not thofe ftrange points of Accord and Difcord. This I write not, I affure your Honour, officioufly, except it be according to *Tully*'s Offices, that is, honeftly and morally   For tho', I thank God, I reckon upon the proceeding in the Queen's fervice, or not proceeding, both ways, and therefore neither mean to fawn nor retire, yet I naturally defire the good opinion of any Perfon, who for fortune or fpirit is to be regarded, much more with a Secretary of the Queen, and a Coufin-german, and one, with whom I ever thought my felf to have fome fympathy of nature, tho' accidents have not fuffer'd it to appear. Thus not doubting of your honourable interpretation, and ufage of what I have written, I commend you to the divine prefervation.

Grays-Inn

VII.

To Sir ROBERT CECIL; *expoftulating upon his Conduct towards the Author.*

YOUR Honour knows, my manner is, tho' it be not the wifeft way, yet taking it for the honefteft, to do as *Alexander* did by his Phyfician, in drinking the Medicine, and delivering the advertifement of fufpicion, fo I truft on, and yet do not fmother what I hear. I affure you, Sir, that by a wife Friend of mine, and not factious toward you, I was told with affeve-

ration,

ration, that your Honour was bought by Mr. *Coventry* for two thousand Angels, and that you wrought in a contrary spirit to my Lord your Father.
And he said farther, that from your Servants, from your Lady, from some
Counsellors that have observ'd you in my business, he knew you wrought
underhand against me the truth of which Tale I do not believe. You know
the event will shew, and God will right But as I reject this report, (tho'
the strangeness of my case might make me credulous) so I admit an Opinion, that the last Messenger my Lord and your self used, dealt ill with
your Honours, and that the word *Speculation,* which was in the Queen's
mouth, rebounded from him, as a Commendation, for I am not ignorant
of those little Arts [a] Therefore, I pray, trust him not again in my matter.
This was much to write, but I think my Fortune will set me at liberty,
who am weary of subjecting my self to every Man's Charity.

VIII.

To the Earl of ESSEX; *reminding him of his Suit.*

I May perceive, by my Lord Keeper, that your Lordship, as the time
serv'd, signify'd to him an intention to confer with his Lordship at better opportunity, which in regard of your several and weighty occasions, I
have thought good to put you in remembrance of, that now at his coming
to Court it may be executed, desiring your Lordship, nevertheless, not to
conceive, out of my diligence in solliciting this matter, that I am either much
in Appetite or much in Hope. As for Appetite, the Waters of *Parnassus* are
not like the Waters of the *Spaw,* that give a stomach, but rather quench desires And for Hope, how can he hope much, that can alledge no other
reason than that of a bad Debtor, who wou'd perswade his Creditor to lend
him new Sums, and enter further with him, to make him satisfy the old:
and to her Majesty, no other reason than that of a Waterman, I am her
first Man of those who serve in Counsel of Law?

IX.

To the Earl of ESSEX; *upon the Queen's refusal of the Author's Service.*

I Pray God her Majesty's weighing be not like the Weight of a Ballance,
Gravia deorsum, Levia sursum But I am as far from being alter'd in Devotion towards her, as I from distrust that she will be alter'd in Opinion
towards me, when she knows me better. For my self, I have lost some

H h h 2

Opinion,

---

[a] It shou'd seem that the Author had been represented to the Queen, as a Man of *Speculation* and *Study,* with a view to hinder his Preferment an Artifice often practised against Men
of Learning See above, Letter V

Opinion, some Time, and some Means this is my account But then for O-
pinion 'tis a blast that goes and comes , for Time, 'tis true, it goes and comes
not , but yet I have learn'd that it may be redeem'd , for Means, I value
that most, and he rather, because I am purposed, not to follow the practice
of the Law and no reason is only, because it drinks too much Time, which
I have dedicated to better purposes And even for the point of estate and
means, I partly incline to *T...Is*'s Opinion, that a Philosopher may be rich
if he will Thus your Lordship sees how I comfort my self , to the increase
whereof, I wou'd fain please my self to believe that to be true which my
Lord Treasurer writes, viz *That 'tis more than a Philosopher can morally di-
ge.* But without any such high conceit, I esteem it like the pulling out of
an aching Tooth, which I remember, when I was a Child, and had little
Philosophy, I was glad of when 'twas done For your Lordship, I think
my self more beholden to you than to any Man, and I say I reckon my
self as a *Common,* and as much as is lawful to be inclosed of a *Common,* so
much your Lordship hath been sure to have

X

To the Earl of ESSEX *, about his Lordship's Conduct with the Queen*

I Will no longer defer part of what I meant to have said to your Lordship at B...., from the Introduction I then made , only I humbly
desire your Lordship before you hear my poor advice, to consider, *first,*
whether I have not reason to think that your Fortune comprehends mine , *next,*
whether I shift my Counsel, and do not *constare mihi* , for I am persuaded,
there are some wou'd give you the same Counsel as I shall, but for deroga-
ting from what they have said heretofore *thirdly,* whether you have receiv'd
injury by my advice, for altho' you once told me that having submitted
upon my vehement Motion at N... h, (the Place where you renew'd
a Treaty with her Majesty of obsequious kindness,) she had taken advantage
of it , yet I suppose you do since believe, that it did greatly attemper a
cold malignant Humour then growing upon her, towards you , and has done
you good in the consequence And for my being lately against your estran-
ging your self, tho' I give place to none in true gratulation, yet I do not
repent of those Counsels nor judge of the Play by the first Act But whether
I advise you the best or for the best, Duty binds me to offer to you my
wishes

I said to your Lordship the last time, *Martha, Martha, attendis ad pluri-
ma,* *unum sufficit,* was the Queen if this be not the beginning, I see no end
of another course I will not now speak of favour of affection, but of other
correspondence and agreeableness, which, whenever it shall be join'd with
the other of Affection, I durst wager my Life (let them make what *Prosopo-*
pœia's

pœia's they will of her Majesty's nature,) that in you she will come to the Question of, *Quid fiet homini, quem Rex vult honorare?* But how is it now? *A Man of a nature not to be ruled, that has the advantage of my Affection, and knows it, of an Estate not grounded to his Greatness, of a Popular Reputation, of a Military Dependence* I demand whether there can be a more dangerous Image than this, represented to any Monarch living, much more to a Lady, and of her Majesty's apprehension? And is it not evident, that whilst this impression continues in her Majesty's Breast, you can find no other condition than inventions to keep your Estate bare and low, crossing and disgracing your Actions, extenuating and blasting your Merit, carping with contempt at your nature and fashions, breeding, nourishing, and fortifying such Instruments as are most factious against you, repulses and scorns of your Friends and Dependents, that are true and stedfast, winning and inveigling away from you such as are flexible and wavering, thrusting you into odious Employments and Offices, to supplant your Reputation, abusing you, and feeding you with dalliances and demonstrations, to divert you from descending into the serious consideration of your own case, and perhaps venturing you in dangerous and desperate Enterprises Herein it may please your Lordship to understand me, for I mean nothing less, than that these things shou'd be plotted and intended, as in her Majesty's royal Mind towards you I know the excellency of her nature too well But I say, whereever the above-mention'd impression is taken in any King's Breast towards a Subject, the recited Inconveniences must necessarily follow, of political consequence, in respect of such Instruments as are never failing about Princes: which spy into their humours and designs, and not only second them, but in seconding increase them, yes and often, without their knowledge, pursue them farther than themselves wou'd Your Lordship will ask the Question, wherewith the *Athenians* used to interrupt their Orators, when they exaggerated their dangers, *Quid igitur agendum est?* I will tell your Lordship, *Quæ mihi nunc in mentem veniunt,* supposing nevertheless, that your self, out of your own wisdom upon the Case, with this plainness and liberty represented to you, will find out better expedients and remedies I wish a cure apply'd to each of the five above-mention'd Impressions, which I will take not in order, but as I think they are of weight

And first, for removing that Impression of your Nature to be *opiniatre,* and not manageable, above all things I wish, that all matters past, which cannot be revoked, your Lordship wou'd turn altogether upon dissatisfaction, and not upon your Nature or proper Disposition. This String you cannot, upon every apt occasion, harp upon too much *Next,* whereas I have noted you to fly and avoid the resemblance or imitation of my Lord of *Leicester,* and Lord Chancellor *Hatton,* yet I am perfuaded it will do you much good, between the Queen and you, to alledge them (as oft as you find occasion) for Authors and Patterns, for I know no readier means to make her Majesty think you are in your right way *Thirdly,* when at any time your Lordship happens in Speeches to do her Majesty right, (for there is no such thing as Flattery amongst you all) I fear you handle it, *magis in speciem,*

c m, a'o i i's verti, quom ut f atire vid aris So that a Man may read
Formality in your Countenance, whereas your Lordship fhou'd do it fami-
li rly, *& ora ore fid* Fourthly, you fhou'd never be without fome Parti-
cul rs on foot, which you fhou'd feem to purfue with earneftnefs and affection, and then let them fall, upon taking knowledge of her Majefty's
oppofition and diflike Of which, the weigntieft fort may be, if your
Lordship offer to labour in behalf of fuch as you favour, for fome of the
Places now void, chaſing thofe Subjects you think her Majefty is likely to
oppofe and if you fay this is *conjunctum cum abena agitia*, I will not anfwer, *bec on alter conftab irt*, but I fay, commendation from fo good a
Mouth does not hurt a Man, tho' you prevail not A lefs weighty fort of
Particulars may be the pretence of fome Journeys, which, at her Majefty's
requeſt, your Lordship might relinquiſh, as if you wou'd pretend a Journey
to fee your Eſtate towards *Wales*, or the like · for as to great foreign Journeys of employ and ſervice, it ſtands not with your gravity to play or ſtrata-
gem with them And the lighteſt fort of particulars, tho' not to be neglected, are in your Habit, Apparel, Geſtures, and the like.

The ſecond Impreſſion of greateſt prejudice, is that of a Military Dependence, wherein I cannot ſufficiently wonder at your procedure You fay
War is your occupation, and go on in that courſe, whereas, if I might have
adviſed your Lordship, you ſhou'd have left that character at *Plymouth*, any
more than when in Council, or in recommending fit Perſons for military
Service, where it was ſeaſonable And here, my Lord, I pray miſtake me
not, I am not now to play the part of a Gown-Man, that wou'd frame you
beſt to my own turn I know what I owe you I am infinitely glad of
this laſt Journey, now 'tis paſt, the rather, becauſe you may make fo honourable a full Point for a time You have Property good enough in that
greatneſs there is none can, for many years, afcend near you in competition.
Beſides, the diſpoſing of the Places and Affairs, both concerning the Wars,
(while you increaſe in other greatneſs) will of themſelves flow to you,
which will preſerve that Dependence in full meaſure 'Tis a thing of all o-
thers I wou'd have you retain, the Times conſider'd, and the neceſſity of
the Service, for other reaſon I know none yet I fay, keep it in ſubſtance,
but aboliſh it in ſhew to the Queen, for her Majefty loves Peace *Next*, fhe
loves not Charge *Th rdl*, that kind of Dependence makes a ſuſpected greatneſs Therefore, *quod in fat agimus* Let that be a ſleeping Honour a while,
and cure the Queen's Mind in that point

    Therefore again, as I heard your Lordship deſigning to your ſelf the Earl
Marſhal's Place, or the Place of Maſter of the Ordnance, I did not fo well
like of either, becauſe of their affinity with a martial Greatneſs But for
the Places now vacant, in my judgment, I wou'd name you to the Place of
Lord Privy-Seal For 'tis the third Perſon of the great Officers of the
Crown. Next, it has a kind of ſuperintendence over the Secretary. It has
alſo an affinity with the *Court of Wards*, in regard of the Fees from the Li-
veries, and 'tis a great Honour, a quiet Place, and worth a thouſand Pounds
a Year my Lord Admiral's Father had it, who was a martial Man, and

it fits a Favourite to carry her Majesty's Image in Seal, who bears it best expressed in Heart   But my chief reason is, that which I first alledg'd, to divert her Majesty from this Impression of martial Greatness   In concurrence whereof, if your Lordship shall not remit any thing of your former Diligence at the *Star-Chamber*, if you shall continue such Intelligences as are worth the cherishing, if you shall pretend to be as bookish and contemplative as ever, all these Courses have both their Advantages and Uses in themselves otherwise, and serve exceeding aptly to this Purpose   Whereto I add one Expedient more, stronger than all the rest, and for my own confident Opinion, void of any Prejudice or Danger of Diminution to your Greatness, and that is, the bringing of some martial Man to be of the *Council*, dealing directly with her Majesty in it, as for her Service, and your better Assistance   chusing, nevertheless, some Person that may be known not to come in against you by any former Division   I judge the fittest to be my Lord *Mountjoy*, or my Lord *Willoughby*   And if your Lordship see deeper into it than I do, that you wou'd not have it done in effect, yet in my Opinion, you may serve your turn by the pretence of it, and stay it nevertheless

The *third* Impression is of a Popular Reputation, which, because 'tis a thing good in itself, being obtained as your Lordship obtains it, that is, *bonis artibus*, and because, well governed, 'tis one of the Flowers of your Greatness, both present and to come, it should be handled tenderly   The only way is to quench it *verbis*, not *rebus*   and therefore to take all occasions with the Queen, to speak against Popularity and popular Courses vehemently, and to tax it in all others, but, nevertheless, to go on in your honourable common-wealth Courses as you do   And therefore I will not advise you to cure this, by dealing in Monopolies, or any Oppressions, only, if in Parliament your Lordship be forward for Treasure, in respect of the Wars, it becomes your Person well   and if her Majesty object Popularity to you at any time, I would say to her, a *Parliament will shew that*, and so feed her with Expectation

The *fourth* Impression, that of the Inequality between your Estate of Means and your Greatness of Respects, is not to be neglected.   For believe it, my Lord, till her Majesty find you careful of your Estate, she will not only think you more likely to continue chargeable to her, but suppose you have higher Imaginations   The Remedies are, first, to profess it in all speeches to her   next, in such Suits wherein both Honour, Gift and Profit may be taken, to communicate freely with her Majesty, by way of inducing her to grant that it will be this benefit to you   Lastly, to be plain with your Lordship, nothing can make the Queen or the World think so much that you are come to a provident care of your Estate, as the altering of some of your Officers; who, tho' they are as true to you as one hand to the other; yet *opinio veritate major*   but if, in respect of the Bonds they may be entered into for your Lordship, you cannot so well dismiss them; this cannot be done but with Time.

For the *fifth* and last, which is of the Advantage of a Favourite; as, sever'd from the rest, it cannot hurt, so, join'd with them, it makes her Majesty more

fearful

fearful and apprehenſive, as not knowing her own Strength. The only Remedy for this is, to give way to ſome other Favourite, as in particular you ſhall find her Maieſty inclined, ſo that the Subject has no dangerous aſpect towards yourſelf For otherwiſe, whoſoever ſhall tell me, that you may not have ſingular uſe of a Favourite at your devotion, I will ſay he underſtands not the Queen's Affection, nor your Lordſhip's Condition.

October 4. 1596

XI.

To the Earl of ESSEX; *deſiring he would excuſe the Author's Deſign to the Queen, of going abroad, after his Refuſal.*

I Am ſorry her Majeſty ſhould take my motion of Travelling in offence But ſurely, under her Majeſty's royal Correction, 'tis ſuch an Offence as it would be to the Sun, when a Man, to avoid the ſcorching Heat thereof, flies into the Shade And your Lordſhip may eaſily think, that having now, theſe twenty Years 'for ſo long 'tis ſince I went with Sir *Amyas Paulet* into *France*[a], from her Majeſty's royal Hand) made her Service the Scope of my Life, I ſhall never find a greater grief than this, *relinquere amorem primum* But ſince p... a ... tantum in noſtra poteſtate, I hope her Majeſty of her Clemency, and Juſtice, will pardon me, and not force me to pine here with melancholy For, tho' my Heart be good, yet my Eyes will be ſore, ſo that I ſhall have no pleaſure to look abroad And if I ſhould otherwiſe be affected, her Majeſty, in her Wiſdom, will but think me an impudent Man, that would face out a Diſgrace. Therefore, as I have ever found you my good Lord and true Friend, I pray ſo open the matter to her Majeſty, as ſhe may diſcern the Neceſſity of it, without adding hard Thoughts to her Rejection, of which, I am ſure, the latter I never deſerved.

An. 1598

XII.

To the Earl of ESSEX; *upon the Earl's Expedition into* Ireland.

YOUR late Obſervance of my Silence, in your Occaſions, makes me ſet down a few wandring Lines, as one that would ſay ſomewhat, and can ſay nothing, upon your Lordſhip's intended Charge for *Ireland*. My Endeavour I know you will accept graciouſly and well, whether you
take

---

[a] The Author being then about eighteen

take it by the handle of the Occasion, minister'd from your self, or of the Affection from whence it proceeds,

Your Lordship is designed to a Service of great Merit and Danger and as the Greatness of the Danger must needs include a like proportion of Merit, so the Greatness of the Merit may include no small consequence of Danger, if it be not temperately governed For all immoderate Success extinguishes Merit, and stirs up Distaste and Envy, the assured Fore-runners of whole Charges or Danger But I am at the last Point first, some good Spirit leading my Pen to presage Success to your Lordship wherein, 'tis true, I am not without my Oracles and Divinations, none of them superstitious, and yet not all natural For first, looking into the Course of God's Providence, in things now depending, and calling to mind, how great things God has done by her Majesty and for her, I collect he has disposed of this great Defection in *Ireland*, thereby to give an urgent occasion to the Reduction of that whole Kingdom, as upon the Rebellion of *Desmond* there ensued the Reduction of that whole Province

Secondly, Your Lordship goes against three of the unluckiest Vices of all others, Disloyalty, Ingratitude and Insolence, which three Offences, in all Examples, have seldom their Doom adjourn'd to the next World

Lastly, He that shall have had the honour to know your Lordship inwardly, as I have had, shall find *bona Exta*, whereby he may better ground a Divination of Good, than upon the Dissection of a Sacrifice. But that part I leave, as 'tis fit for others to be confident upon you, and you to be confident upon the Cause, the Goodness and Justice whereof is such, as can hardly be matched in any Example it being no ambitious War against Foreigners, but a Recovery of Subjects, and that after Lenity of Conditions often tried ; and a Recovery of them not only to Obedience, but to Humanity and Policy from more than *Indian* Barbarism

There is yet another kind of Divination, familiar to matters of State, being that which *Demosthenes* so often relied upon, when he said, what for the Time past is worst of all, is for the Time to come the best which is, that things go ill, not by Accident, but by Errors, wherein, if your Lordship has been heretofore an awaking Censor, yet you must look for no other now, but *Medice, cura te ipsum* And tho' you shall not be the happy Physician that comes in the Decline of the Disease, yet you embrace that condition which many noble Spirits have accepted for Advantage, which is, that you go upon the greater danger of your Fortune, and the less of your Reputation; and so the Honour countervails the Adventure of which Honour your Lordship is in no small possession, when her Majesty (known to be one of the most judicious Princes in discerning of Spirits that ever governed) has made choice of you, merely out of her royal Judgment, (her Affection inclining rather to continue your Attendance,) into whose Hand and Trust to put the Command and Conduct of so great Forces, the gathering the Fruit of so great Charge, the Execution of so many Counsels, the redeeming of the Defaults of so many former Governors, and the clearing of the Glory of her so many happy Years Reign, only in this part eclipsed Nay more, how far the Danger of the State is interlaced with the Danger of *England*, and therefore how great the Honour is, to keep and defend the Approaches or Avenues of this Kingdom, I hear many discourse, and there is a great difference, whether the Tortoise gathers herself within her Shell hurt or unhurt

And if any Man be of opinion, that the Nature of the Enemy extenuates the Honour of the Service, being but a Rebel and a Savage, I differ from him for I see the justest Triumphs that the *Romans* in their Greatness obtain'd, and those from whence the Emperors in their Titles received Addition and Denomination, were of such an Enemy as this, that is, People barbarous, and not reduced to Civility, magnifying a kind of lawless Liberty, and prodigal of Life, harden'd in Body, fortified in Woods and Bogs, and placing both Justice and Felicity in the Sharpness of their Swords such were the *Germans*, ancient *Britons*, and divers others Upon which kind of People, whether the Victory were a Conquest or a Re-conquest, upon a Rebellion or a Revolt, it made no difference in Honour, and therefore 'tis not the enriching predatory War that gives the Pre-eminence in Honour, else would it be more honour to bring in a Carack of rich Burden, than one of the twelve *Spanish* Apostles [a]. But then this Nature of the People yields a higher Point of Honour, considered in Truth and Substance, than any War can yield, which should be atchieved against a civil Enemy, if the end may be, *pacisque imponere morem*, to replant and refound the Policy of that Nation, to which nothing is wanting, but a just and civil Government which Design, as it descends to you from your noble Father, who lost his Life in that Action, (tho' he paid tribute to Nature and not to Fortune,, so I hope your Lordship shall be as fatal a Captain to this War, as *Africanus* was to the War of *Carthage*, after both his Uncle and Father had lost their Lives in *Spain*, in the same War. Now tho' all this be not much to the purpose of Advice, yet 'tis what I have left me, being no military Man, and ignorant in the Particulars of State For a Man may, by the Eye, set up the White in the midst of the Butt, tho' he be no Archer

Therefore I will only add this Wish, according to the *English* Phrase, which terms a well-meant Advice, a Wish, that your Lordship in the whole Action, looking forward, would set it down, that Merit is worthier than Fame, and looking back hither, remember, *That Obedience is better than Sacrifice* For endeavouring at Fame and Glory, may make your Lordship, in the Adventure of your Person, to be valiant as a private Soldier, rather than as a General it may make you in your Commands rather to be gracious than disciplinary, it may make you press action rather hastily than seasonably and safely, it may make you seek rather to atchieve the War by force, than by intermixture of Practice, it may make you, if God shall send prosperous Beginnings, rather seek the Fruition of that Honour, than the Perfection of the Work in hand And for the other Point, that is, the proceeding like a good Protestant, upon express Warrant, and not upon good Intention, your Lordship in your Wisdom knows, that as 'tis most fit for

you

[a] Alluding to the *Spanish Armada*, wherein were twelve Ships, called by the Names of the twelve Apostles

you to defire convenient liberty of Inftructions, fo 'tis no lefs fit for you to obferve the due limits of them, remembring that the exceeding of them may not only procure, in cafe of adverfe accidents, a dangerous difavow, but alfo, (in cafe of profperous fuccefs) be fubject to interpretation, as if all were not referred to the right end

Thus I have prefum'd to write to your Lordfhip, *in methodo ignorantiæ*, which is, when a Man fpeaks of any Subject, not according to its merits, but according to the model of his own Knowledge and moft humbly defire that the weaknefs thereof may be fupply'd in your Lordfhip, by a kind reception, as 'tis in me by my beft wifhes.

In 1599

XIII.

To the Lord HENRY HOWARD; *clearing himfelf of Afperfion in the Cafe of the Earl of* ESSEX.

THERE are very few befides your felf, to whom I wou'd perform this refpect, for I contemn *Mendacia Famæ*, as it walks among inferiors, tho' I neglect it not, as it may have entrance into fome Ears. For your Lordfhip's love, rooted upon good Opinion, I efteem it highly, becaufe I have tafted the Fruits of it, and we have both tafted of the beft Waters, in my account, to knit Minds together. There is fhaped a tale in *London*'s Forge, which beats apace at this time, that I fhou'd deliver Opinion to the Queen, in my Lord of *Effex*'s Caufe, firft, that 'twas *Præmunire*; and now laft, that twas High Treafon, and this Opinion to be in oppofition and encounter of the Lord Chief Juftice's Opinion, and the Attorney-General's. My Lord, I thank God, my Wit ferves me not to deliver any Opinion to the Queen, which my Heart ferves me not to maintain, one and the fame Confcience of Duty guiding and fortifying me But the untruth of this Fable, God and my Sovereign can witnefs, and there I leave it knowing no more remedy againft Lyes, than others do againft Libels

The Root, no queftion, of it is, partly, fome light-headed Envy at my Acceffes to her Majefty, which being begun and continu'd fince my Childhood, as long as her Majefty fhall think me worthy of them, I fcorn thofe that fhall think the contrary And another reafon is, the afperfion of this Tale, and the Envy thereof, upon fome greater Man, in regard of my nearnefs And therefore, my Lord, I pray you anfwer for me, to any Perfon that you think worthy your own Reply, and my Defence As for my Lord of *Effex*, I am not fervile to him; having regard to my Superior's Duty. I have been much obliged to him. And, on the other fide, I have fpent more Time, and more Thoughts, about his well doing, than ever I did about my own I pray God that you, his Friends amongft you, be in the right *Nulla remedia tam faciunt dolorem, quam quæ funt falutaria.* For my part, I

have

have deserv'd better, than to have my Name objected to Envy; or my Life to a Ruffian's violence [a] But I have the Privy-Coat of a good Conscience I am sure these Courses and Rumours hurt my Lord more than all So having open'd my self to your Lordship, I desire exceedingly to be prefer'd in your good Opinion and Love

XIV.

To Sir FULKE GREVILLE[b]; *complaining of his disappointment in Preferment.*

I Understand of your pains to have visited me, for which I thank you My matter is an endless question I assure you I had said, *requiesce anima mea* but now I am otherwise put to my Psalter, *nolite confidere* I dare go no farther Her Majesty had, by set Speech, more than once assured me of her intent on to call me to her Service, which I cou'd not understand but of the Place I had been named to And now, whether *invid is homo hoc fert*, or whether my matter must be an Appendix to my Lord of *Essex*'s Suit, or whether her Majesty, pretending to prove my Ability, means but to take advantage of some Errors, which, like enough, at one time or other I may commit, or what it is, but her Majesty is not ready to dispatch it And what tho' the *Master of the Rolls*, and my Lord of *Essex*, your self and others, think my Case certain, yet in the mean time, I have a hard condition to stand so, that whatever Service I do to her Majesty, it shall be thought to be but *Servitium ufeatum*, Lime-twigs, and Fetches to place my self and so I shall have Envy, not Thanks This is a Course to quench all good Spirits, and to corrupt every Man's Nature, which will, I fear, much hurt her Majesty's Service in the end I have been like a Piece of Stuff bespoken in the Shop, and if her Majesty will not take me, perhaps the selling by Parcels will be more gainful For to be, as I told you, like a Child following a Bird, which when he is nearest flies away, and lights a little before, and then the Child after it again, and so on *in infinitum*, I am weary of it as also of wearying my good Friends, of whom, nevertheless, I hope in one Course or other gratefully to deserve And so not forgetting your Business, I cease to trouble you farther with this *justa & moderata Querimonia* for indeed, I confess, *primus amor* will not be easily cast off.

XV

---

[a] To the same purpose, the Author writes another Letter, to Sir *Robert Cecil*, in the year 1600 concluding thus "As to any Violence to be offer'd me, wherewith my Friends tell me, " with no small Terror, I am threaten'd, I thank God I have the Privy Coat of a good Con " science and have long since put off any fearful care of Life, or the accidents of Life "
[b] Afterwards Lord *Brooke*, and Chancellor of the Exchequer to King *James*

XV.

To the Queen; *upon his keeping from Court.*

I Moft humbly intreat your Majefty, not to impute my abfence to any Weaknefs of Mind or Unworthinefs But I affure your Majefty, I find Envy beating fo ftrongly upon me, that it were not ftrength of Mind, but ftupidity, if I fhou'd not decline the occafions, except I cou'd do your Majefty more fervice than I can any ways difcern I am able to do My Courfe towards your Majefty, (God is my witnefs) has been pure, and unleavened. and never poor Gentleman, I am perfuaded, had a deeper and truer defire and care of your Glory, your Safety, your Repofe of Mind, your Service; wherein, if I have exceeded my outward Vocation, I moft humbly crave your Majefty's pardon for my prefumption On the other fide, if I have come fhort of my inward Vocation, I moft humbly crave God's pardon for quenching the Spirit But in this mind I find much folitude, and want of comfort, which I judge to be, becaufe I take Duty too exactly, and not according to the Dregs of this Age, wherein the old Anthem might never be more truly fung, *totus mundus in maligno pofitus eft* My Life has been threatened, and my Name libelled, which I count an honour. But thefe are the Practices of thofe whofe Defpairs are dangerous, yet not fo dangerous as their Hopes, or elfe the Devices of fome, that wou'd put out all your Majefty's Lights, and fall to reckoning how many years you have reign'd. which I befeech our bleffed Saviour may be doubled, and that I may never live to fee any eclipfe of your Glory, interruption of Safety, or indifpofition of your Perfon, which I recommend to the divine Majefty

An 1600.

XVI.

To the Earl of Northumberland; *tendring Service.*

AS the Time of fowing the Seed is known, but the Time of its coming up and difclofing, is cafual, or according to the Seafon fo, I am a witnefs to my felf, that there has been long cover'd in my Mind, a Seed of Affection and Zeal towards your Lordfhip, fown by the efteem of your Virtues, and your particular honours and favours to my Brother deceafed, and my felf, which Seed ftill fpringing, now burfts forth into this Profeffion And to be plain with your Lordfhip, 'tis very true, (and no Wind of Civil Matters can blow this out of my Head or Heart,) that your great capacity, and love towards Studies and Contemplations of a higher and

worthier

worthier Nature than popular, (a Nature rare in the World, and in a Person of your Lordship's quality almost singular,) is to me a great and chief motive to draw my Affection, and Admiration, towards you And therefore, my Lord, if I may be of any use to your Lordship, by my Head, Tongue or Pen Means or Friends, I humbly pray you to hold me your own, and herewithal, not to do so much wrong to my good intention, nor partly to your own worth, as to conceive that this recommendation of my Service proceeds out of any straits of my Occasions, but merely out of an Election, and indeed the Fulness of my Heart

A 1603

XVII.

To the Earl of DEVONSHIRE, *Lord Lieutenant of* Ireland; *apologizing for his Conduct, with relation to the Earl of* ESSEX

I Cannot be ignorant, and ought to be sensible of the Wrong I sustain in common Discourse, as if I had been false or ungrateful to the noble, but unfortunate Earl of *Essex*. For satisfying the vulgar sort, I do not so much regard it tho' I love a good Name, 'tis yet but as a Handmaid, and Attendant of Honesty and Virtue For I am of his opinion who said pleasantly, it was a shame that a Suitor to the Mistress shou'd make love to the Maid, and therefore to court common Fame, otherwise than it follows on honest Courses, I find my self no way fit or disposed On the other side, there is no worldly thing that concerns my self, which I hold more dear, than the good Opinion of certain Persons, amongst whom, there is none I wou'd more willingly satisfy than your Lordship First, because you loved my Lord of *Essex*, and therefore will not be partial to me, which is part of what I desire Next, because it has ever pleased you to shew your self to me an honourable Friend, and so no baseness in me to endeavour to satisfy you And lastly, because I know your Lordship is excellently grounded in the true rules and habits of Duties and Moralities, which are what must decide this matter And here my defence needs be but simple and brief, for whatever I did in that action and proceeding, was done in my Duty and Service to the Queen and the State, in which I wou'd not shew my self false-hearted, nor faint-hearted, for any Man's sake living For every honest Man that has his Heart well planted, will forsake his King rather than forsake God, and forsake his Friend rather than forsake his King, and yet will forsake any earthly Commodity, yea, and his own Life in some cases, rather than forsake his Friend I hope the World has not forgot these degrees, else the Heathen saying, *Amicus usque ad aras*, *A Friend as far as Conscience will reach*, shall judge them.

And

And if any Man shall say, I did officiously intrude my self into that Business, because I had no ordinary Place, the like may be said, in effect, of all the Business that passed the Hands of the learned Counsel, either of State or Revenues these many years, wherein I was continually used For, the Queen knew her strength so well, that she expected her Word shou'd be a Warrant, and after the manner of the best Princes before her, did not always tye her Trust to Place, but sometimes divided private Favour from Office And for my part, tho' I was not so unpractised in the World, but I knew the Condition was subject to Envy and Danger yet because I knew again she was constant in her Favours, and made an end where she began, and especially because she upheld me with extraordinary Access, and other Demonstrations of Confidence and Grace, I resolved to endure it in expectation of better

But my Scope and Desire is, that your Lordship would have patience to know the truth, with some particularity, of all that has passed in this Cause, wherein I had any part, that you may perceive how honest a Heart I ever bore to my Sovereign, to my Country, and to that Nobleman, who had so well deserved of me, and so well accepted of my deservings, and whose fortune I cannot remember without much Grief But for any action of mine towards him, there is nothing that passed me in my Life, that comes to my remembrance with more clearness, and less check of Conscience for it will appear, that I was not only not opposite to my Lord of *Essex*, but that I employed the utmost of my Wits, and adventur'd my Fortune with the Queen, to have re-instated him, and so continued faithfully and industriously, till his last fatal Impatience after which day, there was no time to work for him, tho' the same Affection in me, when it could not work on the proper Subject, went to the next, with no ill effect towards some others, who, I think, do rather not know it, than not acknowledge it And this I will assure your Lordship, I shall leave nothing untold, that is Truth, for any enemy that I have, to add and on the other side, I must reserve much that makes for me, in many respects of Duty, which I esteem above my Credit and what I have here set down, I protest, as I hope to have any part in God's favour, is true.

'Tis well known, how I, many years since dedicated my Labours and Studies to the Use and Service of my Lord of *Essex*; which I protest I did not, as making choice of him for the likeliest means of my own Advancement, but out of the humour of a Man that ever, from the time I had any use of Reason, whether it were from reading good Books, or the example of a good Father, or by Nature, loved his Country more than was answerable to his Fortune And I held, at that time, my Lord to be the fittest instrument of doing good to the State, and therefore applied myself to him in a manner which I think rarely happens among Men for I did not only labour carefully and industriously in what he set me about, whether matter of advice or otherwise, but neglecting the Queen's Service, my own Fortune, and in a sort my Vocation, I did nothing but advise and ruminate with my self, to the best of my Understanding, Proposals and Memorials of any thing that might concern his Lordship's Honour, Fortune or Service. And when, not long after I enter'd into this course, my Brother, Mr. *Anthony Bacon*, came from beyond the

Seas,

Seas, being a Gentleman whole Abilities the World takes notice of for matters of State, especially foreign, I likewise knit his Service to my Lord's disposing And on the other side, I must and will ever acknowledge my Lord's Love, Trust, and Favour, towards me, and last of all, his Liberality having possessed me of Land, to the value of eighteen hundred Pounds, and this at such a time, and with so kind and noble Circumstances, that the Manner was as much as the Matter And the Manner of it was this After the Queen had denied me the Sollicitor's Place, for which his Lordship had been a long and earnest suitor on my behalf, it pleased him to come to me from *Richmond* to *Twicknam-Park* and say, "Mr *Bacon*, the Queen has denied me the Place "for you, and has placed another I know you are the least part of your 'own matter, but you fare ill because you have chosen me for your Mean "and Dependence you have spent your time and thoughts in my matters, "I die, (those were his very Words,) if I do not somewhat towards your "Fortune, you shall not deny to accept a piece of Land, which I will bestow "upon you" I answered, that for my Fortune it was no great matter but that his Lordship's offer made me call to mind what used to be said, when I was in *France*, of the Duke of *Guise*, that he was the greatest Usurer in *France*, because he had turned all his Estate into Obligations, meaning, that he had left himself nothing, but only had bound numbers of Persons to him Now, my Lord, said I, I would not have you imitate his Course, nor turn your Estate thus, by great Gifts, into Obligations, for you will find many bad Debtors He bid me take no care for that, and pressed it whereupon I said, my Lord, I see I must be your Homager, and hold Land of your Gift, but do you know the manner of doing homage in Law? 'Tis always with a saving of his Faith to the King, and his other Lords, and therefore, my Lord, said I, I can be no more yours than I was, and it must be with the ancient Savings, and if I grow to be a rich Man, you will allow me to give it back again, to some of your unrewarded Followers

But to return, sure I am, that while I had most credit with him, his Fortune went on best and yet in two main points we always directly and contradictorily differed, which I will mention, because it gives light to all that followed The one was, I ever set this down, that the only course to be held with the Queen, was by Obsequiousness and Observance and I remember I would usually engage confidently, that if he would take that course constantly, and with choice of good particulars to express it, the Queen would be brought in time to *Absalom*'s Question, *What should be done to the Man that the King would honour?* Meaning that her Goodness was without limit, where there was a true Concurrence, which I knew in her Nature to be true My Lord, on the other side, had a settled Opinion, that the Queen could be brought to nothing but by a kind of Necessity and Authority, and I well remember, when by violent courses at any time he had got his will, he would ask me, Now, Sir, whose Principles are true? And I would again say to him, my Lord, these courses are like hot Waters, they will help at a pinch, but if you use them, you will spoil the Stomach, and be obliged still to make them stronger and stronger, and yet in the
end

end they will leſſen their operation, with much other variety, wherewith I uſed to touch that ſtring

Another point was, that I always vehemently diſſuaded him from ſeeking Greatneſs by a military, or popular Dependence, as what would breed Jealouſy in the Queen, Preſumption in himſelf, and Perturbation in the State and I uſually compared theſe two Dependencies to *Icarus's* two Wings, which were join'd on with Wax, and would make him venture to ſoar too high, then fail him at the height And I would farther ſay to him, My Lord, ſtand upon two Feet, and fly not upon two Wings The two Feet are the two kinds of Juſtice, commutative and diſtributive uſe your Greatneſs for the advancing of Merit and Virtue, and relieving Wrongs and Burdens, you ſhall need no other Art or *Fineſſe* But he would tell me, that Opinion came not from my Mind, but from my Robe

It is very true, that I, who never meant to enthral my ſelf to my Lord of *Eſſex*, nor any other Man, more than ſtood with the Publick Good, did, tho' I cou'd prevail little, divert him by all means poſſible from Courſes of the Wars and Popularity for I ſaw plainly the Queen muſt either live or die, if ſhe lived, the Times would be as in the Decline of an old Prince, if ſhe died, the Times would be as in the Beginning of a new one, and that if his Lordſhip roſe too faſt in theſe Courſes, the Times muſt be dangerous for him, and he for them. Nay, I remember, I was thus plain with him upon his Voyage to the Iſlands, when I ſaw every Spring put forth ſuch actions of Charge and Provocation, and told him, My Lord, when I came firſt to you, I took you for a Phyſician, that deſired to cure the Diſeaſes of the State, but now I doubt you will be like thoſe Phyſicians who can be content to keep their Patients low, becauſe themſelves would always be in requeſt. Which plainneſs he, nevertheleſs, took very well, as he had an excellent Ear, and was *patientiſſimus veri*, and aſſured me, the caſe of the Realm requir'd it: and I think this Speech of mine, and the like renewed afterwards, pricked him to write that Apology which is in many Men's hands

But this difference in two points, ſo capital, and ſo material, bred in proceſs of time a diſcontinuance of Privacy, (as the manner of Men is ſeldom to communicate where they think their Courſes not approved,) between his Lordſhip and my ſelf; ſo that I was not, as before, call'd nor adviſed with, for a Year and a half before his going into *Ireland* yet as to his going, it pleaſed him expreſsly, and in a ſet manner, to deſire my Opinion and Counſel At which time, I did not only diſſuade, but proteſt againſt his going, telling him, with as much Vehemence and Aſſeveration as I could, that Abſence in that kind would exulcerate the Queen's Mind, whereby it would not be poſſible for him to carry himſelf ſo, as to give her ſufficient Content, nor for her to carry herſelf ſo, as to give him ſufficient Countenance: which would be ill for her, ill for him, and ill for the State And becauſe I would omit no Argument, I remember I ſtood alſo upon the Difficulty of the Action, ſetting before him out of Hiſtory, that the *Iriſh* was ſuch an Enemy as the ancient *Gauls*, or *Britons*, or *Germans* were and that we ſaw how the *Romans*, who had ſuch Diſcipline to govern their Soldiers, and ſuch Donatives to encourage them, and the whole World in a manner to levy them;

yet when they came to deal with Enemies, that placed their Felicity only in Liberty, and the Sharpness of their Sword, and had the natural elemental Advantages of Woods and Bogs, and Hardness of Bodies, they ever found they had their hands full of them, and therefore concluded, that going over with such expectation as he did, and the churlishness of the Enterprize not likely to answer it, would mightily diminish his Reputation And many other Reasons I used, so that I never, in my life-time, dealt with him so earnestly both by Speech, by Writing, and all the means I could devise For, I did, as plainly see his overthrow chain'd, as it were by Destiny, to that Journey, as 'tis possible for any Man to ground a Judgment upon future Contingents But however his Ear was open, yet his Heart and Resolution were shut against that Advice, whereby his Ruin might have been prevented *

After my Lord's going, I saw how true a Prophet I was, in regard of the evident Alteration that naturally succeeded in the Queen's Mind, and thereupon I was still in watch, to find the best occasion that I cou'd either take or minister, to pluck him out of the fire, if it had been possible And not long after, methought I saw some Overture thereof, which I apprehended readily, a Particular known to very few And I the rather relate it, because I hear it is said, that while my Lord was in *Ireland*, I revealed some things against him, or I cannot tell what, which if it were not a mere Slander, as the rest is, but had any, tho' ever so little colour, was surely upon this occasion

The Queen, one day at *Nonsuch*, (a little before *Cuffe's* coming over,) where I attended her, shew'd a passionate distaste of my Lord's proceedings in *Ireland*, as if they were unfortunate, rash, contemptuous, and not without some private End of his own, and all that might be, and was pleased, as she spoke of it to many whom she trusted least, so to fall into the like Discourse with me whereupon I, who was still awake, and true to my grounds, which I thought surest for my Lord's good, said to this effect "Madam, I know " not the Particulars of State, but I know this, that Prince's Actions " must have no abrupt Periods or Conclusions, otherwise I should think, " that if you had my Lord of *Essex* here, with a white Staff in his hand, as " my Lord of *Leicester* had, and continued him still about you, for Society " to your self, and for an Honour and Ornament to your Attendance and " Court, in the Eyes of your People, and in the Eyes of foreign Ambassa- " dors, then were he in his proper Element, for to discontent him as you " do, and yet to put Arms and Power in his hands, may be a kind of Temp- " tation to make him prove cumbersome and unruly And, therefore, if you " would *imporere bonam clausulam*, and send for him, and satisfy him with " Honour here near you, if your Affairs, which I am not acquainted with, " will permit it, I think were the best way " Which Course, your Lordship knows, if it had been taken, all had been well, and no Contempt in my Lord's coming over, nor continuance of these Jealousies, which that Employment of *Ireland* bred, and my Lord here in his former Greatness

The next news I heard was, that my Lord was come over, and committed to his Chamber, for leaving *Ireland* without the Queen's Licence This was

at

* If *Letter* XII preceding, does not appear to answer this Character fully, we must consider it wrote, as it was, immediately before the *Earl's* Departure, for *Ireland*, when the Expedition was resolved upon

at *Nonſuch*, where I came to his Lordſhip, and talked with him privately about a quarter of an hour and he aſked my opinion of the courſe that was taken with him I told him, " My Lord, *Nubecula eſt, cito tranſib.t*, it is " but a Miſt But I ſhall tell your Lordſhip, it is as Miſts are, if it go " upwards, it may perhaps cauſe a ſhower, if downwards, it will clear up. " And therefore, my good Lord, carry it ſo, as to take away, by all means, " all Umbrage and Diſtaſte from the Queen, and eſpecially, if I were wor- " thy to adviſe you, obſerve three Points *Firſt*, make not this Ceſſation or " Peace, concluded with *Tyrone*, as a Service wherein you glory, but as a " ſhuffling up of a Proſecution which was not very fortunate *Next*, repreſent " not to the Queen any neceſſity of State, whereby, as by a Coercion or " Wrench, ſhe ſhould think herſelf enforced to ſend you back into *Ireland* ; " but leave it to her *Thirdly*, ſeek acceſs *importunè, opportunè*, ſeriouſly, ' ſportingly, every way." I remember my Lord was willing to hear me, but ſpoke little, and ſhook his Head ſometimes, as if he had thought I was in the wrong, but ſure I am, he did juſt contrary in every one of theſe three points.

After this, during the time my Lord was committed to the Lord-Keeper's, I often came to the Queen, as I uſed to do about Cauſes of her Revenue and Law-Buſineſs, as is well known, by reaſon of which Acceſs, according to the ordinary Charities of Court, it was given out, that I was one of them that incenſed the Queen againſt my Lord of *Eſſex*. I will not think that theſe Speeches grew any way from her Majeſty's own Speeches, whoſe Me- mory I ſhall ever honour, if they did, ſhe is with God : and *Miſerum eſt ab illis lædi, de quibus non poſſis quæri* But I muſt give this Teſtimony to my Lord *Cecil*, that once, in his Houſe at the *Savoy*, he dealt with me directly, and ſaid to me, " Couſin, I hear it, but I believe it not, that you ſhould do " ſome ill office to my Lord of *Eſſex* for my part I am merely paſſive, and " not active in this Action, I follow the Queen, and that heavily, for I lead " her not. My Lord of *Eſſex* is one that in Nature I could conſent with, as well " as with any one living, the Queen indeed is my Sovereign, and I am " her Creature I may not loſe her · and the ſame courſe I would wiſh you " to take" Whereupon I ſatisfied him how far I was from any ſuch mind.

And as ſometimes it happens, that Men's Inclinations are open'd more in a Toy, than in a ſerious matter, a little before, about the middle of *Michael- mas* Term, her Majeſty propoſed to dine at my Lodge, at *Twicknam Park*, againſt which I had prepared a *Sonnet*, directly tending to draw on her Ma- jeſty's Reconcilement to my Lord, which I alſo ſhewed to a great Perſon, and one of my Lord's neareſt Friends, who commended it. This, tho' it be but a Toy, yet plainly ſhewed in what Spirit I proceeded, and that I was ready, not only to do my Lord good Offices, but to publiſh and declare myſelf for him.

And never was I ſo ambitious of any thing in my life, as to have carried ſome Token or Favour from her Majeſty to my Lord, uſing all the Art I had, both to procure her Majeſty to ſend, and myſelf to be the Meſſenger For I feared not to alledge, that this Proceeding towards my Lord, was a thing in the People's eyes very ungracious, and therefore wiſh'd her Majeſty, whatever ſhe did, to diſcharge herſelf of it, and lay it upon others, and therefore, that she should intermix her Proceedings with some immediate Graces from herself, that the World might take knowledge of her princely Nature and Goodness, lest it should alienate the Hearts of her People from her which I stood upon, knowing well, that if she once relented, to send or visit, those Demonstrations would prove matter of substance for my Lord's Good And to draw that Employment upon myself, I advised her Majesty, that whenever God should move her to turn the light of her Favours towards my Lord, to make signification to him thereof, that her Majesty, if she did it not in Person, would at least use some such means, as might not entitle themselves to any part of the Thanks, as Persons that were thought powerful with her to work her, or to bring her about, but to use one that could not be thought more than a mere Conduit of her own Goodness But I could never prevail with her, tho' I am persuaded she saw plainly whereat I levelled, and held me in jealousy, that I was not hers entirely, but still had inward and deep Respects towards my Lord, more than then stood with her Will and Pleasure

About the same time, I remember an Answer of mine in a matter that had some affinity with my Lord's Cause, and tho' it grew from me, yet went about in other's Names For her Majesty was highly incensed with a Book, dedicated to my Lord of *Essex*, being a History of the first Year of King *Henry* IV as thinking it a seditious Prelude, to put Boldness and Faction into the People's head, and said, she had an opinion, there was Treason in it, and asked me, if I could find no Passages in it that might be drawn within the Case of Treason Whereto I answered, for Treason I found none, but for Felony very much And when her Majesty hastily asked me wherein, I told her, the Author had committed very apparent Theft, for he had taken most of the Sentences of *Tacitus*, translated them into *English*, and put them into his Text And another time, when the Queen would not be persuaded, that it was his writing whose Name was to it, but that it had some more mischievous Author, and said, with great indignation, that she would have him racked to produce his Author I replied, Nay, Madam, he is a Doctor, never rack his Person, but rack his Style, let him have Pen, Ink, Paper, and help of Books, and be enjoined to continue the History where it breaks off, and I will undertake, by collating the Styles, to judge whether he were the Author or no

But for the main Matter, sure I am, when the Queen at any time asked my Opinion of my Lord's Case, I ever in one tenor said to her, that they were Faults which the Law might term Contempts; because they were the Transgression of her particular Directions and Instructions but then, what defence might be made for them, in regard of the great Interest the Person had in her Majesty's Favour, in regard of the Greatness of his Place, and the Largeness of his Commission, in regard of the Nature of the Business, being Action of War, which in common Cases cannot be tied to Strictness of Instructions; in regard to distance of the Place, having also a Sea between, that his Demands and her Commands must be subject to Wind and Weather, in regard of a Council of State in *Ireland*, which he had at his Back to avow his Actions upon, and lastly, in regard of a good Intention, that he would

alledge

alledge for himself, which I told her in some Religions was held a sufficient Dispensation for God's Commandments, much more for Princes. In all these regards, I besought her Majesty to be advised again and again, how she brought the Cause into any publick Question.

Nay, I went farther, for I told her, my Lord was an eloquent and well-spoken Man, and besides his Eloquence of Nature or Art, he had an Eloquence of Accident, that surpassed them both, which was the Pity and Benevolence of his Hearers. And therefore, that when he should come to answer for himself, I believed his Words would have such unequal Passage above theirs that should charge him, as would not be for her Majesty's Honour, and therefore wished the Conclusion might be, to wrap it up privately between themselves, and that she would restore my Lord to his former Attendance, with some addition of Honour, to take away discontent.

But this I will never deny, that I shew'd no Approbation generally of his being sent back into *Ireland*, both because it would have carried a Repugnancy to my former Discourse, and because I was, in my own Heart, fully persuaded, it was not good either for the Queen, for the State, or for himself and yet I did not dissuade it, but left it ever as *Locus lubricus*. For this particular, I well remember, that after your Lordship was named for the Place in *Ireland*, and not long before your going, it pleased her Majesty at *Whitehall* to speak to me of that Nomination at which time I said to her, " Surely, Madam, if " you mean not to employ my Lord of *Essex* thither again, your Majesty can- " not make a better choice " and was going on to shew some reason, but her Majesty interrupted me with great Passion " *Essex*! said she; whenever " I send *Essex* back again into *Ireland*, I will marry you, claim it of me " Whereto I said, " Well, Madam, I will release that Contract, if his going " be for the good of your State "

Immediately after, the Queen thought of a Course to have Somewhat published in the *Star-Chamber*, for the satisfaction of the World, about my Lord of *Essex* his Restraint, and my Lord not to be called to it, but the occasion to be taken by reason of some Libels then dispersed Which when her Majesty proposed to me, I was utterly against it; and told her plainly, that the People would say, my Lord was wounded in his Back, and that Justice had her Ballance taken from her, which ever consisted of an Accusation and Defence; with many other quick and significant Terms to that purpose· insomuch, that I remember I said, my Lord *in Foro Famæ* was too hard for her, and therefore I wished her, as I had done before, to wrap it up privately. And certainly I offended her at that time, which was rare with me for I call to mind, that both the *Christmas, Lent*, and *Easter* Term following, tho' I came divers times to her, upon Law Business, yet methought her Face and Manner was not so clear and open to me as at the first And she directly charged me, that I was absent that day at the *Star-Chamber*, which was very true but I alledged some Indisposition of Body to excuse it: and during all the time aforesaid, there was *altum Silentium* from her to me, as to my Lord of *Essex's* Causes.

But

But towards the end of *Easter* Term, her Majesty told me, that she had found my Words true, for the Proceeding in the *Star-Chamber* had done no good, but rather kindled factious Bruits, as she term'd them, than quenched them, and therefore that she was determined now, for the Satisfaction of the World, to proceed against my Lord in the *Star-Chamber*, by an Information *Ore tenus*, and to have my Lord brought to his Answer However, she said, she would assure me, that whatever she did should be towards my Lord *ad castigationem, & non ad destructionem*, as indeed she had often repeated the same Phrase before Whereto I said, utterly to divert her, " Madam, if you will have " me speak to you in this Argument, I must speak to you as Friar *Bacon*'s ' Head spoke, that said first, *Time is*, and then, *Time was*, and *Time will* " *not be* for certainly 'tis now too late, the Matter is cold, and has taken " too much Wind " Whereat she seem'd again offended, and rose from me, and that resolution for a while continued and after, in the Beginning of *Mid-summer* Term, I attending her, and finding her settled in that Resolution, she falling upon the like Speech; 'tis true, that seeing no other Remedy, I said to her slightly, " Why, Madam, if you will needs have a Proceeding, " you were best have it in some such sort as *Ovid* spoke of his Mistress, " *est aliquid Luce patente minus*, to make a Council-table Matter of it; and " there an end " Which again she seem'd to take ill but yet I think it did good at that time, and help'd to divert the Course of Proceeding by Information in the *Star-Chamber*

Nevertheless, it pleased her to make a more solemn matter of the Proceeding; and a few days after, Order was given that the Cause should be heard at *York-house*, before an Assembly of Counsellors, Peers, and Judges, and some Audience of Men of Quality to be admitted . and then did some principal Counsellors send for us of the *learned Counsel*, and notified her Majesty's Pleasure to us, only it was said to me openly, by one of them, that her Majesty was not yet resolved, whether she would have me forborn in the Business or not And hereupon might arise that other sinister and untrue Report, that I hear is raised of me, that I was a Suitor to be used against my Lord of *Essex* at that time for 'tis very true, that I who knew well what had passed between the Queen and me ; and what occasion I had given her both of Distaste and Distrust, in crossing her Disposition, by standing stedfast for my Lord of *Essex*, and suspecting it also to be a Stratagem, arising from some particular Emulation, I writ to her two or three Words of Complement, signifying to her Majesty, that if she would be pleased to spare me in my Lord of *Essex*'s Cause, out of the Consideration she took of my Obligation towards him, I should esteem it one of her greatest Favours but otherwise, desiring her Majesty to think that I knew the degrees of Duties, and that no particular Obligation whatever, to any Subject, could supplant or weaken that Entireness of Duty that I owed, and bore, to her and her Service And this was the goodly Suit I made, being a respect that no Man in his Wits could have omitted. But nevertheless, I had a farther reach in it, for I judged that day's work would be a full Period of any Bitterness or Harshness, between the Queen and my Lord and therefore, if I declared myself fully, according to her Mind at that time, which could not do my Lord any manner of prejudice, I should keep my credit with her for ever after, whereby to do my Lord service Hereupon, the next news that I heard, was, that we were all sent for again, and that her Majesty's Pleasure was, we all should have parts in the Business and the Lords falling into Distribution of our Parts, it was allotted me, that I should set forth some undutiful Carriage in my Lord, in giving occasion and countenance to a *seditious Pamphlet*, as it was term'd, which was dedicated to him, this being the Book before mentioned of King *Henry* IV. Whereupon, I replied to their Lordships, that it was an old Matter, and had no manner of Coherence with the rest of the Charge, being Matters of *Ireland*, and therefore that I having been wronged by Bruits before, this would expose me the more to them and it would be said I gave in my own Tales in evidence It was answered again, with good shew, that considering how I stood tied to my Lord of *Essex*, that part was thought fittest for me, which did him least hurt for whereas all the rest was Matter of Charge and Accusation, this only was Matter of Caveat and Admonition Wherewith, tho' I was in my own Mind little satisfied, because I knew well a Man were better to be charged with some Faults, than admonished of others, yet the Conclusion binding upon the Queen's Pleasure directly, I could not avoid the Part laid upon me And if in the Delivery I did not handle this Part tenderly, (tho' no Man before me, in so clear terms, freed my Lord of all Disloyalty,) that must be ascribed to the superior Duty I owed to the Queen's Fame and Honour, in a publick Proceeding; and partly to the Intention I had of upholding myself in credit and strength with the Queen, the better to do my Lord good Offices afterwards.

For as soon as this day was past, I lost no time, but directly attended her Majesty, fully resolved to try and use my utmost endeavours to bring my Lord again speedily into Court and Favour And knowing how the Queen was to be used, I thought, that to make her conceive the Matter went well then, was the way to make her leave off there: and I remember, I said to her, " You have now, Madam, obtain'd victory over two things, which the " greatest Princes in the World cannot at their Wills subdue, the one is over " Fame, the other is over a great Mind for surely the World is now reason- " ably well satisfied and for my Lord, he shewed such Humiliation towards " your Majesty, that I am persuaded he was never in his Life more fit for " your Majesty's Favour than now therefore, if your Majesty will not spoil " it by lingring, but give over at the best, and, when you have made so good " a full-point, receive him again with Tenderness, I shall then think that all " past is for the best." Whereat, I remember, she took exceeding great content; and often repeated and put me in mind, that she had ever said, her Proceedings should be *ad reparationem*, and not *ad ruinam*, as intimating that now was the time I should well perceive, that saying of hers should prove true And farther, she ordered me to set down in writing all that past that day I obey'd her Command, and within a few days after, brought her again the Narration, which I read to her in two several Afternoons. And when I came to the Part that set forth my Lord's own Answer, which
was

was my principal Care, I well remember she was extraordinarily moved with it, in kindness and relenting towards my Lord, and told me afterwards, speaking how well I had expressed my Lord's Part, that she perceived old Love would not easily be forgot; whereto I answered suddenly, that she meant that of her self. In conclusion I advised her, that now she had taken a Representation of the Matter to her self, she would let it go no farther, for, Madam, said I, the Fire blazes well already, why should you stir it? And besides, it may please you to keep a Convenience with your self in this case; for since your express Direction was, there should be no Register nor Clerk to take this Sentence, nor no Record or Memorial made of the Proceeding, why should you now do that popularly, which you would not admit to be done judicially? Whereupon she agreed, that Writing should be suppressed, and I think there were not five Persons that ever saw it.

But from this time, during the whole latter end of that Summer, while the Court was at *Nonsuch* and *Oatlands*, I made it my Task and Scope to take and give occasion for my Lord's Re-instatement in his Fortunes; which Intention I also signified to my Lord, as soon as ever he was at his liberty, so that I might without danger of the Queen's Indignation, write to him. And having received from his Lordship, a courteous and loving Acceptation of my Good-will and Endeavours, I applied it in all my accesses to the Queen, which were very many at that time, and purposely sought and wrought upon other variable Pretences, but only and chiefly for that purpose. On the other side, I did not forbear to give my Lord, from time to time, the faithful notice of what I found, and what I wished. And I drew for him, by his Appointment, some Letters to her Majesty, which tho' I knew well his Lordship's Gift and Style was better than my own, yet, because he required it, alledging, that by his long restraint he was grown almost a Stranger to the Queen's present Conceits, I was ready to perform it. And sure I am, that for the space of six Weeeks, or two Months, it prospered so well, that I expected continually his being restored to his Attendance. And I was never more welcome to the Queen, nor more made of, than when I spoke fullest and boldest for him, in which kind the particulars were exceeding many whereof, for an Example, I will relate one or two. Her Majesty once speaking of a Fellow that undertook to cure, or ease my Brother of his Gout, she asked me how it went forward. I told her Majesty, that at the first he received good by it, but after, in the course of his Cure, he found himself rather worse. The Queen said again, " I will tell you, *Bacon*, the Error of
" it the manner of these Physicians, and especially these Empiricks, is to
' continue one kind of Medicine, which at first is proper, being to draw
" out the ill humour, but after they have not the discretion to change their
" Medicine, but still apply drawing Medicines, when they should rather in
" tend to cure and corroborate the Parts." " Good Lord, Madam, said I,
" how wisely and aptly you can speak, and discern, of Physick minister'd to
' the Body, and consider not that there is the like occasion of Physick mi-
" nister'd to the Mind as now in the Case of my Lord of *Essex*, your
                                                                " princely

" Princely Word ever was, that you intended to reform his Mind, and not to
" ruin his Fortune I know well you cannot but think, you have drawn the
" Humour sufficiently , and therefore it is more than time, if it were
" but for fear of mortifying, or exulcerating, that you apply'd and mi-
" nister'd Strength and Comfort to him , for these Gradations of yours are
" fitter to corrupt than correct any Mind of greatness." Another time I
remember she told me for News, that my Lord had wrote her some very
dutiful Letters, and that she had been mov'd by them , and when she took
it to be the abundance of his Heart, she found it to be but a preparative to
a Suit for renewing his Farm of sweet Wines Whereto I reply'd, " O
" Madam, how your Majesty construes these things! as if these two
" cou'd not well stand together , which indeed Nature has planted in all
" Creatures ! For there are but two Sympathies, the one towards Perfection,
" the other towards Preservation , that to Perfection, as the Iron tends to
" the Loadstone , that to Preservation, as the Vine creeps towards a Stake
" or Prop that stands by it not for any love to the Stake, but to uphold it
" self.   And therefore, Madam, you may distinguish my Lord's desire to do
" you service is as to his Perfection , and that which he thinks himself born
" for whereas his desire to obtain this thing of you, is but for a Sustenta-
" tion "

And not to trouble your Lordship with many other particulars like these,
it was at the same time that I drew, with my Lord's privity, and by his appointment, two Letters , the one written as from my Brother , the other as
an Answer return'd from my Lord , both to be by me, in secret, shew'd to
the Queen which it pleased my Lord very strangely to mention at the Bar
The scope of them was but to represent and picture to her Majesty, my
Lord's mind to be such, as I knew her Majesty wou'd most have had it.
Which Letters, whoever shall see, (for they cannot now be retracted or alter'd, being by reason of my Brother's, or his Lordship's Servants delivery,
long since come into several hands ,) let him judge, especially if he knew
the Queen, and remember those Times, whether they were not the labours
of one that sought to bring the Queen about, for my Lord of *Essex* his
good

I he truth is, the issue of all his dealing grew to this, that the Queen had
by some sickness of my Lord's, as I imagine, lik'd him worse and worse , and
grew more incensed towards him   Then she remembring, probably, the continual, incessant, and confident Speeches and Courses, that I had held on my
Lord's side, became utterly alienated from me , and for the space of three
months, which was between *Michaelmas* and *New-year's tide* following, wou'd
not so much as look on me, but turned away from me, with express and purposed Discountenance, wherever she saw me , and at such time as I desired
to speak with her about Law-business, ever sent me very slight refusals insomuch that immediately after *New year's tide*, I desir'd to speak with her ,
and being admitted to her, I dealt plainly with her, and said, " Madam,
" I see you withdraw your Favour from me , and now I have lost many
" Friends for your sake, I shall lose you too , you have put me, like one of

" thofe the *French* call *Enfans perdus*, that ferve on foot before the Horfe;
" fo have you put me into matters of Envy without Place, or without
" Strength, and I know at Chefs a Pawn before the King is ever much
" plaid upon. A great many love me not, becaufe they think I have been a-
" gainft my Lord of *Effex*, and you love me not, becaufe you know I have
" been for him; yet it will never repent me, that I have dealt in fimplicity
" of Heart towards you both, without refpect of Cautions to my felf, and
" therefore *vivit, & devfque pereo* If I do break my Neck, I fhall do it as
" *Derington* did, who walked on the Battlements of the Church many days,
" and took a view and furvey where he fhou'd fall and fo, Madam, I am
" not fo fimple, but that I have a profpect of my Overthrow, only I
" thought I wou'd tell you fo much, that you may know it was Faith, and not
" Folly, that brought me to it, and fo I will pray for you" Upon which
Speech of mine, uttered with fome paffion, her Majefty was exceedingly
moved, and accumulated a number of kind and gracious Words upon me,
and will'd me to reft upon this, *gratia mea fufficit*, and a number of other
fenfible and tender Words and Demonftrations, fuch as greater cou'd not be
but as to my Lord of *Effex*, *ne verbum quidem* Whereupon I departed,
refting then determin'd to meddle no more in the matter, as what I faw
wou'd overthrow me, and not do him any good And thus I then made
my own Peace, with my own Confidence

And this was the laft time I faw her Majefty, before the eighth of *February*, the day of my Lord of *Effex*'s misfortune, after which, what I perform'd
at the Bar, in my publick Service, your Lordfhip knows, by the rules of
Duty, I was to do it honeftly, and without prevarication but for putting
my felf into it, I proteft before God, I never mov'd either the Queen, or
any Perfon living, concerning my being ufed in the Service, either of Evi
dence or Examination, but it was merely laid upon me, with the reft of
my Fellows And for the time that paffed between the Arraignment and
my Lord's fuffering, I well remember I was but once with the Queen, when,
tho' I durft not deal directly for my Lord as things then ftood, yet generally
I both commended her Majefty's Mercy, terming it to her as an excellent
Balm, that continually diftill'd from her fovereign Hands, and made an excellent Odour in the Senfes of her People and not only fo, but I took the
hardinefs to extenuate, not the Fact, for that I durft not, but the Danger,
telling her, that if fome bafe or cruel-minded Perfons had enter'd into fuch an
Action, it might have caufed much Blood and Combuftion but it well appear'd, they were fuch as knew not how to play the Malefactors, and fome
other Words, which I now omit

And for the reft of my carriage in that Service, I have honourable Witneffes, who can tell, that the next day after my Lord's Arraignment, by my
diligence and information, touching the Quality and Nature of the Offenders,
fix of nine were ftaid, which otherwife had been attainted, I bringing
their Lordfhip's Letter for their ftay, after the Jury was fworn to pafs upon them, fo near it went and how careful I was, and made it my part,
that whofoever was in trouble about that matter, as foon as ever his Cafe

was

was sufficiently known and defined of, might not continue in restraint, but be set at liberty, and many other Parts, which, I am well assur'd of, stood with the Duty of an honest Man

But for the Case of Sir *Thomas Smith*, I will not deny that the Queen demanding my Opinion of it, I told her, I thought it was as hard as many of the rest, but what was the reason? Because at that time I had seen only his Accusation, and had never been present at any Examination of his, and the matter so standing, I had been very untrue to my Service, if I had not deliver'd that Opinion But afterwards, upon Re-examination of some that charged him, and weaken'd their own Testimony, and especially hearing himself *viva voce*, I went instantly to the Queen, out of the soundness of my Conscience, not regarding what Opinion I had formerly deliver'd, and told her Majesty, I was satisfy'd and resolv'd in my Conscience, that, for the reputation of the Action, the Plot was to countenance the Action farther by him, in respect of his Place, than they had indeed any interest or intelligence with him

It is very true also, about that time her Majesty taking a liking to my Pen, upon what I had formerly done concerning the Proceeding at *York-House*, and likewise upon some other Declarations, which in former times by her appointment I put in writing, commanded me to write that Book, which was published, for the better satisfaction of the World which I did, but so, as never Secretary had more particular and express Directions and Instructions, in every Point, how to guide my Hand in it. And not only this, but after I had made a first draught thereof, and proposed it to certain principal Counsellors, by her Majesty's appointment, it was perused, weighed, censured, and made almost a new Writing, according to their Lordships better consideration, wherein their Lordships and my self were as religious and curious of Truth, as desirous of Satisfaction · and my self indeed gave only words, and form of style, in pursuing their direction And after it had passed their allowance, it was again exactly perused by the Queen her self, and some alterations made again by her appointment: nay, and after it was sent to the Press, the Queen, who, as she was excellent in great matters, so she was exquisite in small, noted that I could not forget my ancient respect to my Lord of *Essex*, in terming him ever my Lord of *Essex*, almost in every Page of the Book, which she thought not fit, but would have it made *Essex*, or the late Earl of *Essex*, whereupon it was printed *de novo*, and the first Copies suppressed by her peremptory command

And this, my Lord, to my best remembrance, is all that passed wherein I had a part, which I have set down, as near as I could, in the very Words and Speeches that were used, not because they are worthy the repetition, I mean, those of my own, but to the end your Lordship may lively and plainly discern between the Face of Truth, and a smooth Tale: and the rather also, because in things that passed a good while since, the very Words and Phrases did sometimes bring to my remembrance the Matters, wherein I appeal to your honourable Judgment, whether you do not see the traces of

an

an honeft Man and had I been as well believed either by the Queen or by
my Lord, as I was well heard by them, both my Lord had been fortunate,
and fo had my felf, in his fortune

To conclude therefore, I humbly pray your Lordfhip to hold me in your
good opinion, till you know I have deferved, or find that I fhall deferve
the contrary

XVIII.

To Mr ROBERT KEMPE, *upon the Death of the Queen.*

THIS alteration is fo great, that you might juftly conceive fome coldnefs
of my Affection towards you, if you fhou'd hear nothing from me, I
living in this place   'Tis in vain to tell you with what a wonderful ftill,
and calm this Wheel is turn'd round, which, whether it be a *Remnant* of
her *Felicit,* [a] that is gone, or a Fruit of his *Reputation* that is coming, I
will not determine   For I cannot but divide my felf between her *Memory*
and his *Name* Yet we account it but a fair Morn, before Sun-rifing, till his
Majefty's prefence, tho' for my part I fee not whence any Weather fhould
arife   The Papifts are contained with Fear enough, and Hope too much
The *French* is thought to turn his Practice upon procuring fome difturbance
in *Scotland*, where Crowns may do wonders   But this Day is fo welcome to
the Nation, and the time fo fhort, that I do not fear the Effect.   There is
a continual pofting by Men of good quality towards the King; the rather,
I think, becaufe this Spring-time 'tis but a kind of fport   'Tis hoped that
as the State here has performed the part of good Attorneys, to deliver the
King quiet poffeffion of his Kingdoms, fo the King will redeliver them quiet
poffeffion of their Places, rather filling Places void, than removing Men
placed

'   1603

XIX.

To Sir THOMAS CHALONER[b], *in* Scotland, *before the King's Entrance; defiring recommendation to his Majefty.*

FOR our Money-matters, I am affured you received no diffatisfaction,
for you know my Mind, and you know my Means, which now the
opennefs of the time, caufed by this bleffed Confent, and Peace, will increafe, and fo our Agreement, according to your time, be obferved   For
the prefent, according to the *Roman* Adage, that *one Clufter of Grapes ripens
beft befide another*, I know you hold me not unworthy, whofe mutual
friendfhip

[a] See the Author's Account of her *Felicity* Vol I *Supplement* III
[b] Preceptor to Prince Henry, and the firft Difcoverer of Alum-Mines in *England*

friendship you should cherish and I, for my part, conceive good hope, that you are likely to become an acceptable Servant to the King our Master not so much for any Way made heretofore, (which, in my judgment, will make no great difference) as for the Stuff and Sufficiency which I know to be in you, and whereof, I know, his Majesty may reap great service And therefore, my general request is, that according to that industrious Vivacity, which you use towards your Friends, you will further his Majesty's good Opinion and Inclination towards me, to whom Words cannot make me known, neither my own, nor others, but Time will, to no disadvantage of any that shall fore-run his Majesty's experience, by their Testimony and Commendation And tho' occasion give you the precedence of doing me this special good Office, yet I hope shortly to have means of requiting your Favour More particularly, having thought good to make oblation of my most humble Service to his Majesty by a few Lines, I desire your loving care, and help, by your self, or such means as I refer to your discretion, to deliver and present the same to his Majesty's hands Of which Letter I send you a Copy, that you may know what you carry, and may receive of Mr. *Matthews* the Letter it self, if you be pleased to undertake the delivery. Lastly, I commend to your self, and such your Courtesies, as occasion may require, this Gentleman Mr. *Matthews*, eldest Son to my Lord Bishop of *Durham*, and my very good Friend, assuring you, that any Courtesy you shall use towards him, you shall use to a very worthy young Gentleman, and one, I know, whose acquaintance you will much esteem

An. 1603.

XX.

To the King; *offering Service upon his Majesty's coming in.*

'TIS observed by some, upon a place in the *Canticles*, *ego sum flos campi, & lilium convallium*, that, *à dispari*, 'tis not said, *ego sum flos horti & lilium montium*, because the Majesty of that Person is not inclosed for a few, nor appropriated to the great And yet, notwithstanding this royal virtue of Access, which both Nature and Judgment have planted in your Majesty's Mind, as the Portal of all the rest, could not alone, my Imperfections considered, have animated me to make oblation of my self immediately to your Majesty, had it not been join'd with a habit of the like Liberty, which I enjoy'd with my late dear sovereign Mistress, a Princess happy in all things, but most happy in such a Successor And yet farther, and more nearly, I was not a little encouraged upon a supposal, that to your Majesty's sacred Ear, there might perhaps have come some notice of the good Memory of my Father [a], so long a principal Counsellor in this your King-

[a] *Viz.* Sir *Nicholas Bacon*, Lord Keeper of the Great-Seal for twenty Years, under Queen *Elizabeth*

Kingdom, as also a more particular knowledge of the infinite Devotion and incessant Endeavours, beyond the Strength of his Body, and the Nature of the Times, which appeared in my good Brother, Mr *Anthony Bacon*, towards your Majesty's Service, and were, on your Majesty's part, thro' your singular Benignity, by many most gracious and lively Significations and Favours, accepted and acknowledged, beyond the merit of any thing he could effect which Endeavours and Duties, for the most part, were common to myself with him, tho' by design, as between Brethren, dissembled And therefore, most high and mighty King, my most dear and dread sovereign Lord, since now the Corner-stone is laid of the mightiest Monarchy in *Europe*, and that God above who has ever a hand in bridling the Floods and Motions both of the Seas, and of People's Hearts, has, by the miraculous and universal Consent, in your coming in, given a sign and token of great Happiness, by the Continuance of your Reign, I think there is no Subject of your Majesty's, who loves this Island, and is not hollow or unworthy, whose Heart is not set on fire, not only to bring you Peace-offerings, to make you propitious, but to sacrifice himself a Burnt-offering to your Majesty's Service amongst which number, no Man's fire shall be more pure and fervent than mine; but how far it shall blaze out, rests in your Majesty's Pleasure So thirsting after the Happiness of kissing your royal Hand, I continue ever, &c

An 1603

XXI.

To the Earl of NORTHUMBERLAND; *recommending a Proclamation to be made by the King at his Entrance.*

I Hold it a thing formal and necessary, for the King to forerun his coming, (be it ever so speedy,) with some gracious Declaration, for the cherishing, entertaining, and preparing of Men's Affections For which purpose, I have conceived a Draught, it being a thing familiar in my Mistress's Times, to have my Pen used in publick Writings of Satisfaction. The use of this may be in two sorts First, properly, if your Lordship think it convenient to shew the King any such Draught, because the Veins and Pulses of this State cannot but be best known here which, if your Lordship should do, then I would desire you to withdraw my Name, and only signify, that you gave some Heads of Direction, of such a Matter to one, of whose Style and Pen you had some opinion The other is collateral, that tho' your Lordship make no other use of it, yet 'tis a kind of Portraiture of that, which I think worthy to be advised, by your Lordship, to the King, and perhaps more compendious and significant, than if I had set them down in Articles [a]

An 1603　　　　　　　　　　　　　　　　　　　　　　　　XXII.

[a] This Proclamation was superseded by the Publication of the King's Book *de Officio Regis* See Vol. I Suppl'em II

XXII.

To the Earl of NORTHUMBERLAND; *giving some Character of the King at his Arrival.*

I Would not have loft this Journey, and yet I have not what I went for. for I have had no private Conference, to purpofe, with the King   No more has almoft any other *Englifh*   for the Speech his Majefty admits with fome Noblemen, is rather Matter of Grace than Bufinefs.   He fpoke with the Attorney, urged by the Treafurer of *Scotland*, but no more than needs muft   After I had received his Majefty's firft Welcome, I was promifed private Accefs, yet not knowing what Matter of Service your Lordfhip's Letter carried, and well knowing, that Primenefs in advertifement is much ; I chofe rather to deliver it to Sir *Tho Heskins*, than to cool it in my own hands, upon expectation of Accefs   Your Lordfhip fhall find a Prince the fartheft from Vain-glory that may be, and rather like a Prince of the ancient form, than of the later time   His Speech is fwift and curfory, and in the full Dialect of his Country, in Speech of Bufinefs, fhort, in Speech of Difcourfe, large   He affects Popularity, by gracing fuch as he has heard to be popular, and not by any fafhions of his own   He is thought fomewhat general in his Favours, and his Virtue of Accefs is rather, becaufe he is much abroad and in prefs, than that he gives eafy audience   He haftens to a Mixture of both Kingdoms and Occafions, fafter, perhaps, than Policy will well bear. I told your Lordfhip once before, that his Majefty rather feemed to afk counfel of the time paft, than of the time to come   but 'tis yet early to ground any fettled opinion   The Particulars I refer to Conference ; having in thefe Generals gone farther in fo tender an Argument, than I would have done, were not the Bearer hereof fo affured

An. 1603.

XXIII.

To Mr. MATTHEWS; *fignifying the Proceedings of the King, at his firft Entrance.*

MY aim was right in my Addrefs of Letters to thofe Perfons in the Court of *Scotland*, who were likelieft to be ufed for the Affairs of *England*   but the pace they held was too fwift, for the Men were come away before my Letters could reach them.   With the firft I have renewed Acquaintance,

tance and 'twas like a *Bill of Revivor*, by way of Cross-suits, for he was as ready to have begun with me. The second arrived this day, and grew acquainted with me instantly in the Council-chamber, and was willing to entertain me with farther Demonstrations of Confidence, than I was willing, at that time, to admit. But I have had no serious Speech with him, nor do I yet know whether any of the Duplicates of my Letter have been delivered to the King. It may, perhaps, have proved your luck to be the first.

Things are here in good Quiet. The King acts excellently well, for he puts in Claules of Reserve to every Proviso. He says, he would be sorry to have just cause to remove any. He says, he will displace none, who have served the Queen and State sincerely, &c. The truth is, here are two extremes; some few would have no Change, no not Reformation, and many would have much Change even with Perturbation. God, I hope, will direct this wise King to hold a mean between Reputation enough, and no Terrors. In my particular, I have many Comforts and Assurances, but in my own Opinion the chief is, that the canvassing World is gone, and the deserving World is come. And withal, I find myself as one awaked out of sleep, which I have not been this long time, nor could, I think, have been now, without such a great noise as this, which yet is *in aura leni*. I write this to you in haste, my End being no more, than to make you know, that I will ever continue the same, and still be sure to wish you as heartily well as to myself.

A. 1603

XXIV.

To the Earl of SALISBURY; *suing for the Sollicitor's Place.*

I Am not privy to myself of any such ill deserving towards your Lordship, as that I should think it an impudent thing to be a Suitor for your favour in a reasonable matter, your Lordship being to me as you cannot cease to be; but rather it were a simple and arrogant part in me to forbear it.

'Tis thought Mr *Attorney* shall be Chief-Justice of the Common-Pleas, and in case Mr *Sollicitor* rise, I would be glad, now at last, to be *Sollicitor*, chiefly because I think it will increase my Practice, wherein, God blessing me a few Years, I may mend my Estate, and so after fall to my Studies and Ease, whereof one is requisite for my Body, and the other for my Mind; wherein, if I shall find your Lordship's favour, I shall be more happy than I have been, which may make me also more wise. I have small store of means about the King, and to sue myself, 'tis not fit, and therefore I shall leave it to God, his Majesty, and your Lordship, for I must still be next the door. I thank God, in these transitory things I am well resolved. So beseeching your Lordship not to think this Letter the less humble, because 'tis plain, I rest, &c.

XXV.

XXV.

To the Earl of Salisbury; *again suing for the Sollicitor's Place.*

I Am not ignorant how mean a thing I stand for, in desiring to come into the *Sollicitor's* Place for I know well 'tis not the thing it has been, time having wrought an alteration both in the Profession, and in that particular Place Yet because, I think, it will increase my Practice, and satisfy my Friends; and because I have been voiced to it, I would be glad it were done Wherein I may say to your Lordship, in the confidence of your poor Kinsman, and of a Man by you advanced, *tu idem fer opem, qui spem dedisti* for, I am sure, 'twas not possible for a Man living to have received from another, more significant and comfortable Words of Hope, your Lordship being pleased to tell me, during the Course of my last Service, that you would rule me, and that, when you had resolved to raise a Man, you were more careful of him than himself; and that what you had done for me in my Marriage, was a benefit to me, but of no use to your Lordship, and therefore I might assure myself, you would not leave me there with many like Speeches, which, I know my Duty too well, to take any other hold of, than the hold of a thankful Remembrance And I acknowledge, that all the World knows, your Lordship is no dealer of holy Water, but noble and real, and on my part, I am, of a sure ground, that I have committed nothing that may deserve alteration And therefore my hope is, your Lordship will finish a good work, and consider, that time grows precious with me, and that I am now in *vergentibus Annis* And altho' I know that your Fortune is not to need an hundred such as I am, yet I shall be ever ready to give you my first and best Fruits, and to supply, as much as in me lies, Worthiness by Thankfulness

XXVI.

To the Lord Chancellor; *suing for the Sollicitor's Place.*

A S I conceived it to be a resolution, both with his Majesty, and among your Lordships of his Council, that I should be placed Sollicitor, and the Sollicitor be removed to be the King's Serjeant, so I most thankfully acknowledge your furtherance therein, your Lordship being the Man,

who firſt deviſed the Means   Wherefore my humble requeſt to your Lordſhip is, that you would ſet in with ſome ſtrength to finiſh this Work, which
I aſſure your Lordſhip, I deſire the rather, becauſe, when placed, I hope,
for many favours, at laſt to be able to do you ſome better ſervice   For as I
am, your Lordſhip cannot uſe me, nor ſcarcely, indeed, know me   Not
that I vainly think, I ſhall be able to do any great matters, but certainly
it will frame me to uſe a more induſtrious Obſervance, and Application to
ſuch as I honour ſo much as I do your Lordſhip, and not, I hope, without
ſome good offices, which may, now and then, deſerve your thanks   And
herewithal, I humbly pray your Lordſhip to conſider, that time grows precious with me, and that a married Man is ſeven Years older in his Thoughts
the firſt day   And therefore, what an uncomfortable thing is it for me to
be unſettled ſtill? Certainly, were it not, that I think my ſelf born to do my
Sovereign ſervice, and therefore in that Station I will live and die, otherwiſe,
for my own private Comfort, 'twere better for me, that the King ſhould blot
me out of his Book, or that I ſhould turn my Courſe to ſerve in ſome other
kind, than for me to ſtand thus at a ſtop, and to have that little Reputation,
which, by my Induſtry, I gather, to be ſcatter'd and taken away by continual Diſgraces, every new Man coming above me   Sure I am, I ſhall
never have fairer Promiſes and Words from all your Lordſhips   For I know
not what my Services are, ſaving that your Lordſhips told me they were good,
and I would believe you in a much greater matter   Were it nothing elſe, I
hope the Modeſty of my Suit deſerves ſomewhat, for I know well, the Sollicitor's Place is not as your Lordſhip left it, time working alteration, ſomewhat in the Profeſſion, much more in that particular Place   And were it
not to ſatisfy my Wife's Friends, and to get myſelf out of being a common
Gaze and a Speech, I proteſt, before God, I would never ſpeak a word of
it   But, to conclude, as my honourable Lady, your Wife, was ſome means
to make me change the Name of another, ſo if it pleaſe you to help me to
change my own Name, I can be but more and more bound to you   and
I am much deceived, if your Lordſhip find the King not well inclined, and
my Lord of *Saliſbury* forward and affectionate

XXVII.

To the KING; *petitioning for the Sollicitor's Place.*

HOW honeſtly ready I have been, to do your Majeſty humble ſervice,
to the beſt of my power, and in a manner beyond my power, as I
now ſtand, I am not ſo unfortunate, but your Majeſty knows   For both in
the *Commiſſion of Union* (the labour whereof, for Men of my Profeſſion, reſted
moſt upon my hand,) and this laſt Parliament, in the Bill of the *Subſidy*,
both Body and Preamble; in the Bill of Attainders, in the Matter of Purveyance, in the Eccleſiaſtical Petitions, in the Grievances, and the like;

as I was ever careful, fometimes to put forward that which was good , fome-times to keep back that which was not fo good , fo your Majefty was pleafed, kindly to accept of my Services, and to fay to me, fuch Conflicts were the Wars of Peace , and fuch Victories the Victories of Peace and therefore fuch Servants as obtained them, were by Kings, that reign in Peace, no lefs to be efteemed, than Services of Commanders in the Wars In all which, neverthelefs, I can challenge to myfelf no Sufficiency , but that I was diligent, and reafonably happy, to execute thofe Directions, which I received immediately, either from your royal Mouth, or from my Lord of *Salisbury* At which time, it pleafed vour Majefty alfo, to promife and affure me, that upon the Remove of the then Attorney, I fhould not be forgotten , but brought into ordinary Place This was after confirm'd to me, by many of my Lords, and towards the End of the laft Term, the manner alfo in particular was fpoke of , *viz.* that Mr *Sollicitor* fhould be made your Majefty's Serjeant, and I Sollicitor fo 'twas thought beft to fort with both our Gifts and Faculties, for the good of your Service And of this Refolution both Court and Country took notice. Neither was this any Invention or Project of my own , but moved from my Lords , and I think firft from my Lord Chancellor whereupon refting, your Majefty well knows I never open'd my mouth for the greater Place , tho', I am fure, I had two Circumftances, which Mr Attorney, that now is, could not alledge the one, nine Years Service of the Crown , the other, the being Coufin-german to the Lord of *Salisbury*, whom your Majefty efteems and trufts fo much. But for the lefs Place, I conceiv'd 'twas meant me But after Mr Attorney *Hobart* was placed, I heard no more of my Preferment , and it feem'd to be at a ftop, to my great difgrace and difcouragement. For, gracious Sovereign, if ftill, when the Waters are ftirred, another fhall be put in before me , your Majefty had need work a Miracle, or elfe I fhall be ftill a lame Man, to do your Majefty fervice And, therefore, my moft humble Suit to your Majefty, is , that this, which feemed to me in-tended, may fpeedily be performed And, I hope, my former Service fhall be but as Beginnings to better, when I am better ftrengthened For fure I am, no Man's Heart is fuller of Love and Duty towards your Majefty and your Children , as, I hope, time will manifeft, againft Envy and Detraction, if any be To conclude, I moft humbly crave pardon for my Boldnefs, and reft, *&c.*

XXVIII.

To Sir EDWARD COKE; *expoftulating upon Sir* Edward's *Behaviour.*

I Thought beft, once for all, to let you know in Plainnefs what I find of you, and what you fhall find of me You take to yourfelf a liberty of difgracing and difabling my Law, my Experience, my Difcretion. what it

pleafes

pleafes you, I pray think of me. I am one that know my own wants, and other Mens, and it may be, perhaps, that mine mend, when others ftand at a ftay. And furely I fhall not endure, in publick, to be wronged, without repelling the fame, to right myfelf. You are great, and therefore have the more Enviers who would be glad to have you paid at another's coft. Since the time I mifs'd the Sollicitor's Place, the rather, I think, by your means, I cannot expect that you and I fhall ever ferve as Attorney and Sollicitor together but either to ferve with another, upon your Remove, or to ftep into fome other Courfe. fo that I am more free than ever from any occafion of unworthy conforming myfelf to you, more than general good-manners, or your particular good ufage fhall require. And if you had not been fhort-fighted in your own fortune, I think you might have had more ufe of me. But that Tide is paft. I write not this to fhew my Friends what a brave Letter I have fent to Mr Attorney, I have none of thofe humours but what I have written, is to a good end, the more decent carriage of my Mafter's Service, and our particular better underftanding of one another. This Letter, if anfwered by you in Deed, and not in Word, I fuppofe it will not be worfe for us both, elfe 'tis but a few Lines loft, which, for a much fmaller matter, I would have adventured. So this being to your felf, I for my part reft, &c.

XXIX.

To the KING; *upon occafion of Mr.* SUTTON's *Eftate* [a].

I Find it a pofitive Precept of the old Law, that there fhould be no Sacrifice without Salt. the Moral whereof may be, that God is not pleafed with a good Intention, unlefs feafoned with fuch Judgment and Difcretion, as may render it not eafily fubject to corrupt, for Salt, in the Scripture, is an Emblem both of Wifdom and Duration. But many charitable Defigns, are Sacrifices without Salt, having indeed the Materials of a good Intention, but not feafon'd with fuch Conduct and Regulations, as may preferve them found and ufeful. For tho' the choice of Directors and Managers, may for the prefent be excellent, yet they cannot long furvive. and the very nature of large Acts of Charity and Beneficence, being apt to provoke a mifemployment, no diligence of theirs can well prevent it from running the fame way, as great Donations of the like kind have done. And to defign a Building fit for a Prince's Palace, to the ufes of an Hofpital, is all one as to give an embroidered Cloak to a Beggar. And certainly 'tis eafy to forefee, that if fuch an Edifice, with a very liberal Endowment, be erected into one Hofpital, it muft foon degenerate, and become a Place of Preferment for fome great Perfon, to be its Mafter, and he to take all the Sweet,

and

---

[a] Left for founding the *Charter-Houfe.* This Advice was given the King whilft the Author was Sollicitor General.

and the poor Penſioners be ſtinted, and receive but the Crumbs. which is the caſe of many Hoſpitals in this Kingdom, that have only the Names of Hoſpitals, and really are rich Poſts in reſpect of the Maſterſhip, whilſt the Poor, which is the *tropter quid*, are little relieved. And many Charities of the *Romiſh* Religion, in their great Foundations, have ſhared the ſame Fate which being begun in Oſtentation, and Vain-glory, have ended in Corruption and Abuſe.

But if this Foundation of Mr *Sutton*'s, ſuch as it is, be perfect and good in Law. I am too well acquainted with your Majeſty's Diſpoſition, to adviſe any Courſe of Power, or Profit, not grounded upon a Right. Nay farther, if the Defects be ſuch as a Court of Equity may remedy, I wiſh that as St *Peter*'s Shadow cured Diſeaſes, ſo the very Shadow of a good Intention may cure Defects of that nature. But if there be a Right, and Birth-right planted in the Heir, and not remediable by Courts of Equity, and that Right be ſubmitted to your Majeſty, whereby 'tis both in your Power and Grace, what to do: then I wiſh that this rude Maſs and Chaos of a good Deed, were directed rather to a ſolid Merit, and durable Charity, than to a Blaze of Glory, that will but crackle a little in Talk, and quickly be extinguiſhed. And this may be done, ſtill obſerving the Nature of Mr *Sutton*'s Intent, tho' varying *in individuo* for it appears he had in Notion a triple good, an Hoſpital, a School, and maintaining of a Preacher which Individuals refer to theſe three general Heads, Relief of the Poor, Advancement of Learning, and the Propagation of Religion. Now then, if I ſhall ſet before your Majeſty, in every of theſe three kinds, what is moſt wanting in your Kingdom, and what is likely to be the moſt fruitful, and effectual Uſe of ſuch a Beneficence, and leaſt likely to be perverted, this I think will be no ill ſcope, how meanly ſoever performed for out of Variety repreſented, Choice may be beſt grounded.

As to the Relief of the Poor, I judge that ſome Number of Hoſpitals, with competent Endowments, will do far more good than one Hoſpital of an exorbitant greatneſs for tho' the one will be more ſeen, yet the other will be the more felt. For if your Majeſty erect many, beſides obſerving the ordinary Maxim, *Bonum quo communices, eo melius*, Choice may be made of thoſe Towns and Places where there is moſt need, and ſo the Remedy may be diſtributed as the Diſeaſe is diſperſed. Again, greatneſs of Relief accumulated in one Place, rather invites a Swarm, and a Surcharge of Poor, than relieves thoſe naturally bred in the Places; like ill-tempered Medicines, that draw more Humour to the Part, than they evacuate from it. But chiefly, I rely upon this Reaſon, that in great Hoſpitals the Revenues will draw the Uſe, and not the Uſe the Revenues, and ſo thro' the Maſs of the Wealth, they will ſwiftly tumble down to a Miſ-employment. And if any Man ſay, that in the two Hoſpitals of *London*, there is a Precedent of Greatneſs concurring with good Employment, let him conſider, that thoſe Hoſpitals have annual Governors, that they are under the ſuperior Care and Policy of ſuch a State, as the City of *London*, and chiefly, that their Revenues conſiſt not upon Certainties, but upon Caſualties, and free Gifts which Gifts wou'd be withheld, if they appeared once to be perverted, ſo that it keeps them in a continual good Behaviour, and how, to employ them aright none of which Points do match with the present Cafe.

The next Confideration may be, whether this intended Hofpital, as it has a more ample Endowment than others, fhou'd not likewife work upon a better Subject, or be converted to the Relief of maim'd Soldiers, decay'd Merchants, aged Houf-keepers, deftitute Church-men, and the like, whofe Condition being of a better Sort, than loofe People, and Beggars, deferves both a more liberal Stipend, and fome proper Place of Relief, not intermixed with the bitter Sort of Poor. which Project, tho' fpecious, yet, in my judgment, will not anfwer the Defign in thefe times. For certainly, few Men in any Vocation, who have been fome-body, and bear a Mind fomewhat according to the Confcience and Remembrance of what they have been, will ever defcend to that Condition, as to profefs to live upon Alms, and become a Corporation of decl-red Beggars, but will rather chufe to live obfcurely, and, as it were, hide themfelves with fome private Friends whence the end of fuch an Inftitution will be, to make the Place a Receptacle of the vileft, idleft, and moft diffolute Perfons of every Profeffion, and to become a Cell of Loiterers, caft Serving-men and Drunkards, with Scandal rather than Fruit to the Common wealth. And of this kind I can find but one Example with ufe, v.z. the Alms Knights of *Windfor* which particular wou'd give a Man fmall Encouragement, to follow that Precedent.

Therefore the beft effect of Hofpitals, is to make the Kingdom, if it were poffible capable of that Law, that there fhou'd be no Beggar in *Ifrael* for 'tis fuch People that are a Burden, an Eye fore, a Scandal, and a Seed of Danger and Tumult in the State. But chiefly 'twere to be wifh'd, that fuch Beneficence towards the Relief of the Poor, were fo beftowed, as that not only the mere and naked Poor fhou'd be fuftained, but alfo, that the honeft Perfon, which has hard means to live, and upon whom the Poor are now charged, fhou'd be in fome fort eafed for that were a work generally acceptable to the Kingdom, if the publick hand of Alms might fpare the private hand of Tax. And therefore, of all other Employments of that kind, I moft commend Houfes of Relief, and Correction, which are mix'd Hofpitals, where the impotent Perfon is relieved, the fturdy Beggar buckled to work, and the unable Perfon alfo not maintain'd to be idle, but is fuited with fuch Work, as he can manage and perform and where the Ufes are not diftinguifh'd, as in other Hofpitals, whereof fome are for aged and impotent, and fome for Children, and fome for Correction of Vagabonds, but are general and promifcuous fo that they may take off Poor of every fort from the Country, as the Country breeds them and thus the Poor themfelves fhall find the Provifion, and other People the fweetnefs of the Abatement of the Tax. Now if it be objected, that Houfes of Correction, in all Places, have not done the Good expected, tho' it cannot be denied, that in moft Places they have done much it muft be remembred, there is a great difference between what is done, by the diftracted Government of Juftices of Peace, and what may be done by a fettled Ordinance, fubject to a regular Vifitation, as this may be. And

besides,

brfides, the want in Houfes of Correction, has been commonly of a competent and certain ftock, for the Materials of the Labour which in this cafe
may likewife be fupplied.

As to the Advancement of Learning; I fubfcribe to the Opinion, that
for Grammar-Schools, there are already too many, and therefore no Providence to add where there is Excefs for the great number of Schools in the
Realm, caufes a Want, and an Overflow, both of them inconvenient, and one
of them dangerous For by means thereof they find want, in the Country
Towns, both of Servants for Hufbandry, and Apprentices for Trade and
on the other fide, there being more Scholars bred, than the State can prefer
and employ, and the active part of that Life not bearing a proportion to the
preparative, it muft needs fall out, that many Perfons will be bred unfit for
other Vocations, and unprofitable for that wherein they are brought up:
which fills the Kingdom with indigent, idle, and wanton People.

In this Point therefore, I wifh Mr *Sutton*'s Intention were exalted a degree;
that what he meant for Teachers of Children, your Majefty would make for
Teachers of Men, wherein it has been my ancient Opinion and Obfervation,
that in the Univerfities of this Realm, there is nothing more wanting, towards the flourifhing State of Learning, than honourable and plentiful Salaries of Readers in Arts and Profeffions In which Points, as your Majefty's
Bounty has already made a Beginning, fo this occafion is offered of God to
make a Proceeding Surely, Readers in the Chair are as the Parents in Sciences,
and deferve to enjoy a Condition not inferior to their Children, who embrace
the practical part, elfe no Man will fit longer in the Chair, than till he can
walk to a better Preferment. For if the principal Readers, thro' the Meannefs of their Entertainment, be but Men of fuperficial Learning, and
fhall take their place but in paffage, it will make the Mafs of Sciences
want the chief and folid Dimenfion, which is Depth, and to become but petty
and compendious Habits of Practice. Therefore I could wifh, that in both
the Univerfities, the Lectures as well of the three Profeffions, Divinity, Law, and
Phyfick, as of the three Heads of Science, Philofophy, Oratory, and the Mathematicks, were raifed in their Penfions to a hundred Pounds *per Annum* each:
which, tho' not near fo great as they are in fome other Places, where the
high Reward whiftles for the ableft Men, out of all foreign Parts, to fupply
the Chair, yet it may be a Portion to content a worthy and able Man, if
he be likewife contemplative in Nature, as thofe Spirits are that are fitteft
for Lectures

As to the Propagation of Religion, I fhall fet before your Majefty three
Propofals, none of them Devices of my own, otherwife, than that I ever
approved them The *Firft* is, a *College for Controverfies*, whereby we fhall
not ftill proceed fingle, but fhall, as it were, double our Files which certainly will be found in the Encounter

The *Second* is, a *Receptacle for Converts to the Reformed Religion*; either of
Youth or otherwife for I doubt not but there are in *Spain, Italy*, and other
Countries of the Papifts, many whofe Hearts are touched with a Senfe of
thofe Corruptions, and an Acknowledgement of a better Way, which Grace

is many times fmother'd and choaked, thro' a worldly Confideration of Neceffity and Want, Men not knowing where to have Succour and Refuge This, likewife, I hold a Work of great Piety, and a Work of great Confequence, that we alfo may be wife in our Generation, and that the watchful and filent Night may be ufed as well for fowing of good Seed, as of Tares

The Third is, the Imitation of a memorable and religious Act of Queen Elizabeth, who finding a part of Lancafhire to be extremely backward in Religion, and the Benefices fwallowed up in Impropriations, did, by decree, in the Dutchy, erect four Stipends, of a hundred Pounds *per Annum* each, for Preachers well chofen, to help the Harveft, who have done a great deal of good, in the parts where they have laboured Neither do there want other Corners in the Realm, that would require, for a time, the like extraordinary help

Thus I have briefly delivered to your Majefty my Opinion, as to the Employment of this Charity, whereby that Mafs of Wealth, which was, in the Owner, little better than a Heap of Muck, may be fpread over your Kingdom, to many fruitful Purpofes, your Majefty planting and watering, and God giving the increafe

XXX.

To the King, *petitioning for Promife of the Attorney's Place.*

YOUR great and princely Favours towards me, in advancing me to a Place, and, what is more to me, your Majefty's kind and gracious Acceptance, from time to time, of my poor Services, much above their merit and value, has almoft perfuaded me, that I may fooner be wanting to myfelf in not afking, than find your Majefty's Goodnefs wanting to me, in any reafonable and modeft Defires Therefore, perceiving at this time, how Preferments of Law fly about my ears, to fome above me, and to fome below me, I conceived your Majefty might rather think it a kind of Dulnefs, or want of Faith, than Modefty, if I fhould not come with my Pitcher to Jacob's Well, as others do Wherein I fhall propofe to your Majefty, what tends more to the fettling of my Mind, than the raifing of my Fortune, being fometimes attacked with this Thought, that by reafon of my flownefs to apprehend fudden Occafions, keeping on in one plain courfe of painful fervice, I may, *in fine dierum*, be in danger to be neglected and forgotten and if that fhould be, then were it much better for me, now, while I ftand in your Majefty's good Opinion, and have fome little Reputation in the World, to give over the courfe I am in, and try to do you fome honour by my Pen, either by writing fome faithful Narrative of your happy Times, or by recompiling your Laws, which, I perceive your Majefty labours with, or fome other the like Work, than to fpend my time in the laborious Place where I now ferve, if it fhall be deprived of thofe outward Ornaments it

ufed

ufed to have, in refpect of an affured Succeffion, to fome Place of more Dignity and Reft, which now feems a Hope altogether cafual, if not wholly intercepted Wherefore my humble Suit to your Majefty is, that I may obtain your royal Promife of the *Attorney*'s Place, when it fhall be vacant, it being but the natural and immediate Step and Rife, which the Place I now hold has ever claim'd, and almoft never fail'd of In this Suit I make no Friends, but to your Majefty; rely upon no other Motive but your Grace, nor any other Affurance but your Word whereof I had good Experience, when I came to the Sollicitor's Place, that it was like to the two great Lights, which in their motions are never retrograde.

XXXI.

To the KING; *petitioning for the Place of Attorney-General.*

I Underftand, by fome of my good Friends, to my great Comfort, that your Majefty has in mind your royal Promife, which is to me *Anchora Spei*, as to the Attorney's Place. I hope Mr Attorney fhall do well. I thank God, I wifh no Man's Death, nor much my own Life, more than to do your Majefty fervice For I account my Life the Accident, and my Duty the Subftance But this I will be bold to fay, if it pleafe God that ever I ferve your Majefty in the *Attorney*'s Place, I have known an Attorney *Coke*, and an Attorney *Hobart*, both worthy Men, and far above myfelf. but if I fhould not find a middle way, between their two Difpofitions and Carriages, I fhould not fatisfy myfelf. But thefe things are far or near, as it fhall pleafe God. Mean while, I moft humbly pray your Majefty to accept my Sacrifice of Thankfgiving, for your gracious Favour.

XXXII.

To the KING; *upon the Lord Chancellor's Sicknefs.*

I Am glad to underftand, by *Murray*, that your Majefty accepts of my poor Endeavours, in opening to you the Paffages of your Service, that Bufinefs may come the more prepared to your royal Judgment the Perfection whereof, as I cannot expect they fhould fatisfy in every Particular, yet I hope, thro' my Affiduity, there may refult a good Total.

My Lord Chancellor's Sicknefs falls out *duro tempore* I have always known him a wife Man, and of juft Elevation for Monarchy but your Majefty's Service muft not be mortal. And if you lofe him, as your Majefty has now of late purchafed many Hearts by depreffing the Wicked, fo God minifter to you a Counterpart, to do the like, by raifing the Honeft.

Feb 9. 1615.

XXXIII.

To the KING; *relating to the Chancellor's Place.*

YOUR worthy Chancellor [a], I fear, goes his laft day God has hitherto ufed to weed out fuch Servants as grew unfit for your Majefty, but now he has gather'd to himfelf one of the choicer Plants, a true Sage, out of your Garden but your Majefty's Service muft not be mortal

Upon this heavy accident, I pray your Majefty, in all humblenefs and fincerity, to give me leave to ufe a few Words I muft never forget, when I moved your Majefty for the Attorney's Place, that 'twas your own fole Act, and not my Lord of *Somerfet*'s, who, when he knew your Majefty had refolved it, thruft himfelf into the bufinefs to gain thanks and therefore I have no reafon to pray to Saints

I fhall now again make oblation to your Majefty, firft of my Heart; then of my Service, thirdly, of my Place of Attorney, which, I think, is honeftly worth 6000*l per Annum* and fourthly, of my Place in the Star-chamber, which is worth 1600*l per Annum*, and with the Favour and Countenance of a Chancellor, much more I hope I may be acquitted of Prefumption, if I think of it, both becaufe my Father had the Place, which is fome civil Inducement to my defire, and chiefly, becaufe the Chancellor's Place, after it went to the Law, was ever conferred upon fome of the learned Counfel, and never upon a Judge For *Audeley* was raifed from King's Serjeant, my Father from Attorney of the *Wards*, *Bromley* from Sollicitor; *Puckering* from Queen's Serjeant, and *Egerton* from Mafter of the Rolls, having newly left the Attorney's Place. Now, I befeech your Majefty, let me put to you the prefent Cafe truly. If you take my Lord *Coke*, this will follow, firft, your Majefty fhall put an over-ruling Nature, into an over ruling Place, which may breed an extreme; next, you fhall blunt his Induftry in matter of Finances, which feems to aim at another Place, and laftly, popular Men are no fure Mounters for your Majefty's Saddle If you take my Lord *Hobart*, you fhall have a Judge at the upper end of your Council-board, and another at the lower end, whereby your Majefty will find your Prerogative pent. for tho' there fhould be Emulation between them, yet, as Legifts, they will agree in magnifying that wherein they are beft He is no Statefman, but an Oeconomift, wholly for himfelf, fo that your Majefty will find little help in him for the Bufinefs If you take my Lord o'*Canterbury*, I will fay no more, but that the Chancellor's Place requires a whole Man and to have both Jurifdictions, fpiritual and temporal, in that height, is fit but for a King For my felf, I can only prefent your Majefty with *Gloria in obfequio*, yet I dare promife, that if I fit in that Place, your Bufinefs fhall not make fuch fhort turns upon you, as it does, but when a
Direction

[a] Chancellor *Egerton*.

Direction is once given, it shall be pursued and performed, and your Majesty shall only be troubled with the true Care of a King, which is, to think what you would have done in Chief, and not how it should be effected

I presume also, in respect of my Father's Memory, and having been always gracious in the Lower House, I have interest in the Gentlemen of *England*, and shall be able to do some good, in rectifying that Body of Parliament-men, which is *Cai do reium* For let me tell your Majesty, that Part of the Chancellor's Place, which is to judge in Equity, between Party and Party, that same *Regnum judiciale*, which, since my Father's time, is but too much enlarged, concerns your Majesty least, farther than the acquitting of your Conscience for Justice but 'tis the other Parts of a Moderator among your Council, of an Overseer over your Judges, of a Planter of fit Justices and Governors in the Country, that imports your Affairs, and these Times most

I will add also, that I hope, by my Care, the inventive part of your Council will be strengthened, who now commonly exercise rather their Judgments, than their Inventions, and the inventive part comes from Projectors, and private Men, which cannot be so well in which kind, my Lord *Salisbury* had a good Method, if his Ends had been upright

To conclude, if I were the Man I would be, I should hope, that as your Majesty has of late won Hearts by depressing, you should in this lose no Hearts by advancing for I see your People can better skill of *Concretum* than *Abstractum*, and that the Waves of their Affections flow rather after Persons than Things so that Acts of this nature, (if this were one) do more good than twenty Bills of Grace If God call my Lord Chancellor; the Warrants and Commissions requisite for taking off the Seal, the working with it, and for reviving of Warrants under his hand, which die with him, and the like, shall be in readiness And in this, Time presses more, because 'tis the End of a Term, and almost the Beginning of the Circuits, so that the Seal cannot stand still but this may be done as heretofore, by Commission, till your Majesty has resolved on an Officer

Feb. 12 1615.

XXXIV.

To Sir GEORGE VILLIERS; *solliciting to be sworn of the Privy-Council.*

I Humbly pray you, not to think me over-hasty, or much in appetite, if I put you in remembrance of my motion, of strengthening me with the Oath and Trust of a Privy-Counsellor; not for my own Strength, but for the Strength of my Service The Times I submit to you, who know them best. But sure I am, never Times more required a King's Attorney to be well armed, and

to wear a Gauntlet, not a Glove. The Arraignments when they proceed ,
the Contention between the Chancery and King's-Bench , the great Cause
of the *Rege inconfulto*, which is fo precious to the King's Prerogative , and
divers other Services that concern the King's Revenue, and the Repair of his
Eftate. Befides, it pleafes his Majefty to accept well of my Relations, as to
his Bufinefs, which may feem a kind of interloping for one, that is no Privy-
Counfellor but I leave all to you, thinking myfelf infinitely bound to you
for your great favours, the Beams whereof, I fee plainly, reflect upon me,
even from others fo that now I have no greater Ambition than this, that
as the King fhews himfelf to you the beft Mafter, fo I might be found
your beft Servant

Feb. 27 1616.

XXXV.

To Sir GEORGE VILLIERS; *upon accepting a Place in Council.*

THE King gives me a noble Choice and you are the Man my Heart
ever told me you were Ambition would draw me to the latter
part of the Choice , but in refpect of my hearty Wifhes, that my Lord
Chancellor may live long , and the fmall hopes I have that I fhall live long
my felf , and above all, becaufe I fee his Majefty's Service daily and inftantly
bleeds, towards which, I perfuade myfelf, that I fhall give, when I am of
the Table, fome effectual furtherance ; I accept of the former , to be
Counfellor for the prefent, and to give over pleading at the Bar · let the other
matter reft upon my Proof, and his Majefty's Pleafure, and the Accidents
of Time For, to fpeak plainly, I fhould be loth that my Lord Chancellor,
to whom I owe moft, after the King and yourfelf, fhould be locked to his
Succeffor, for any advancement, or gracing of me.

June 3 1616

XXXVI.

To the KING; *propofing to regulate his Majefty's Finances.*

I Often, with gladnefs, and for a remedy of my other Labours, revolve in
my Mind the great Happinefs which God has accumulated upon your
Majefty, every way , and how compleat the fame would be, if the State of
your Means were once rectified, and well ordered , your People military
and obedient, fit for War, ufed to Peace . your Church enlightened with
good Preachers, as an Heaven of Stars , your Judges learned, and learning
from

from you ; juft, and juft by your Example· your Nobility in a right diftance between Crown and People , no Oppreffors of the People , no Over-fhadowers of the Crown your Council full of the Tributes of Care, Faith, and Freedom, your Gentlemen, and Juftices of the Peace, willing to apply your royal Mandates to the Nature of their feveral Counties , but ready to obey your Servants in awe of your Wifdom, in hope of your Goodnefs the Fields growing every day, by the Improvement and Recovery of Grounds, from the Defart to the Garden, the City grown from Wood to Brick, your Sea-walls, or *Pomærium* of your Ifland, furveyed, and improving, your Merchants embracing the whole Compaſs of the World, Eaft, Weft, North and South, the Times give you Peace , and yet offer you Opportunities of Action abroad and laftly, your excellent royal Iffue entails thefe Bleffings of God to all Pofterity. It remains therefore, God having done fo great things for your Majefty, and you for others , that you would do fo much for your felf, as to go thro' with the rectifying and fettling of your Eftate and Means which only is wanting ; *hoc rebus defuit unum* I therefore, whom only Love and Duty to your Majefty, and your royal Line, has made a *Financier*, intend to prefent your Majefty a perfect Book of your Eftate, like a Perfpective-Glafs, to draw your Eftate nearer to your Sight , befeeching your Majefty to conceive, that if I have not attain'd to what I would do, in that which is not proper for me , in my Element, I fhall make your Majefty amends in fome other thing, in which I am better verfed.

Jan. 2. 1618.

XXXVII.

To Mr. MATTHEWS ; *believing his Danger lefs than he found it.*

I Say to you, upon the occafion you gave me in your laft, *modicæ Fidei, quare dubitafti?* I would not have my Friends too apprehenfive either of me, or for me ; for, I thank God, my Ways are found and good and I hope God will blefs me in them. When once my Mafter, and afterwards my felf, were in extremity of Sicknefs, (which was no time to diffemble) I never had fo great Pledges and Certainties of his Love and Favour : and what I knew then , fuch as took a little poor advantage of thefe later times, know fince. As for the Nobleman who paffed that way by you, I think he is faln out with me for his pleafure ; or elfe, perhaps, to make good fome of his own miftakings. For he cannot, in his heart, but think worthily of my Affection, and Well-deferving towards him ; and as for me, I am very fure that I love his Nature and Parts.

XXXVIII.

XXXVIII.

To Mr. MATTHEWS; *intimating his Apprehension of some Danger.*

'TIS not for nothing, that I have deferred my Essay *De amicitia* [a], whereby it has expected the Proof of your great Friendship towards me Whatsoever the Event be, (wherein I depend upon God, who ordains the Effects, the Instrument, all,) yet your incessant thinking of me, without loss of a Moment of Time, or a Hint of Occasion, or a Circumstance of Endeavour, or the Stroke of a Pulse, in Demonstration of your Affection to me, infinitely ties me to you Secrecy I need not recommend, otherwise than that you may recommend it over to your Friend, both because it prevents Opposition, and because 'tis the King's and my Lord Marquis's nature, to do things unexpected

XXXIX.

To Mr MATTHEWS.

THE Report of this Act, which I hope will prove the last of this Business, will probably, by the Weight it carries, fall and seize on me And, therefore, not now at will, but upon necessity, it becomes me to call to mind what passed, and (my Head being then wholly employed about Invention) I may the worse put things, upon account of my own Memory I shall take Physick to-day upon this change of Weather, and advantage of Leisure, and I pray you not to allow your self so much Business, but that you may have time to bring me your friendly Aid before Night, &c.

XL.

To the Right Honourable the Lords Spiritual and Temporal, in the Upper House *of Parliament assembled* [b].

I Humbly pray your Lordships all, to make a favourable and true Construction of my Absence 'Tis no feigning or fainting, but Sickness both of my Heart and of my Back, tho' join'd with that Comfort of Mind, which persuades me, I am not far from Heaven, whereof I feel the first Fruits.

And

[a] See the Author's Essay on Friendship, Vol II Pag. 70.
[b] Taken from the Journal of the House of Lords

And becaufe, whether I live or die, I wou'd be glad to preferve my Honour and Fame, fo far as I am worthy, hearing that fome Complaints of bafe Bribery are coming before your Lordfhips, my Requefts unto your Lordfhips are

Firft, That you will maintain me in your good Opinion, without Prejudice, until my Caufe be heard

Secondly, That in regard I have fequeftred my Mind at this time, in great part, from worldly matters, thinking of my Account and Anfwers in a higher Court, your Lordfhips will give me convenient time, according to the Courfe of other Courts, to advife with my Counfel, and to make my Anfwer; wherein, neverthelefs, my Counfel's part will be the leaft for I fhall not, by the Grace of God, trick up an Innocency with Cavils, but plainly and ingenuoufly (as your Lordfhips know my manner is) declare what I know or remember

Thirdly, That according to the Courfe of Juftice, I may be allowed to except to the Witneffes brought againft me, and to move Queftions to your Lordfhips for their crofs Examinations, and likewife to produce my own Witneffes, for the Difcovery of the Truth

And laftly, That if there be any more Petitions of the like nature, that your Lordfhips wou'd be pleafed, not to take any Prejudice or Apprehenfion of any number or mufter of them, efpecially againft a Judge that makes 2000 Orders and Decrees in a Year not to fpeak of the courfes that have been taken for hunting out Complaints againft me; but that I may anfwer them, according to the Rules of Juftice, feverally and refpectively

Thefe Requefts, I hope, appear to your Lordfhips no other than juft. And fo thinking myfelf happy, to have fuch noble Peers, and reverend Prelates, to difcern of my Caufe, and defiring no privilege of Greatnefs, for fubterfuge of Guilt; but meaning to deal fairly and plainly with your Lordfhips, and to put myfelf upon your Honours and Favours, I pray God to blefs your Counfels and Perfons.

March 19. 1620

XLI.

To the KING; *imploring Remittance of his Sentence.*

IT has pleas'd God, for thefe three Days, to vifit me with fuch extremity of Head-ach, upon the hinder part of my Head, fixed in one place, that I thought verily it had been fome Impoftumation. And then the little Phyfick I have, told me, that either it muft grow to a Congelation, and fo to a Lethargy, or break, and fo to a mortal Fever and fudden Death. which Apprehenfion, and chiefly the Anguifh of the Pain,

made

made me unable to think of any Bufinefs But now the Pain itfelf is affuaged, I refume the Care of my Bufinefs; and therein proftrate myfelf again, by my Letter, at your Majefty's Feet

Your Majefty can bear me witnefs, that at my laft fo comfortable accefs, I did not fo much as move your Majefty, by your abfolute Power of Pardon, or otherwife, to take my Caufe into your hands, and to interpofe between tne Sentence of the Houfe: and, according to my own defire, your Majefty left it to the Sentence of the Houfe, and it was reported by my Lord Treafurer

But now, if not *per omnitotentiam*, as the Divines fpeak, but *per poteſtatem ſuaviter aſtonertem*, your Majefty will gracioufly fave me from a Sentence, with tne good liking of the Houfe, and that the Cup may pafs from me, is the utmoft of my defires

This I move with the more belief, becaufe I affure my felf, that if it be Reformation which is fought, the very taking away of the Seal, upon my general Submiffion, will be as much in example, for thefe four hundred years, as any farther Severities.

The means of this, I moft humbly leave to your Majefty But furely, I conceive, that your Majefty opening your felf in this kind to the Lords Counfellors, and a Motion from the Prince, after my fubmiffion, and my Lord Marquis ufing his intereft with his Friends in the Houfe, may effect the fparing of a Sentence, I making my humble Suit to the Houfe for that purpofe, join'd with the Delivery of the Seal into your Majefty's hands.

This is the laft Suit I fhall make to your Majefty in this Bufinefs, pro ftrating my felf at your Mercy-feat, after fifteen Years Service, wherein I have ferved your Majefty, in my poor Endeavours, with an entire Heart, and as I prefumed to fay to your Majefty, am ftill a Virgin, for Matters which concern your Perfon or Crown: and now only craving, that after eight fteps of Honour, I be not precipitated all at once But becaufe he that has taken Bribes, is apt to give them, I will go farther, and prefent your Majefty with a Bribe For if your Majefty give me Peace and Leifure, and God give me Life, I will prefent your Majefty with a good Hiftory of *England*, and a better Digeft of your Laws.

March 21. 1621

XLII.

To the KING; *imploring Favour.*

TIME has been, when I have brought you *Gemitum Columbæ* from others, now I bring it from my felf I fly to your Majefty with the Wings of a Dove, which once within thefe feven days I thought would have carried me a higher flight [a] When I enter into my felf, I find not the Materials of fuch a Tempeft as is come upon me· I have been, as

your

[a] See the preceding Letter

your Majesty knows best, never Author of any immoderate Counsel, but always desired to have things carried *suavibus modis*. I have been no avaricious Oppressor of the People I have been no haughty, intolerable, or hateful Man, in my Conversation or Carriage I have inherited no Hatred from my Father, but am a good Patriot born. Whence should this be? For these are the things that use to raise dislikes abroad

For the House of Commons, I began my credit there, and now it must be the Place of the Sepulture thereof and yet in this Parliament, upon the Message touching Religion, the old Love revived, and they said, I was the same Man still, only Honesty was turned into Honour

For the Upper-House, even within these days, before these Troubles, they seem'd as to take me into their Arms, finding in me Ingenuity, which they took to be the true strait Line of Nobleness, without any Crooks or Angles

And for the Briberies and Gifts, wherewith I am charged, when the Books of Hearts shall be opened, I hope I shall not be found to have the troubled Fountain of a corrupt Heart, in a depraved Habit of taking Rewards to pervert Justice · however, I may be frail, and partake of the Abuses of the Times

Therefore, I am resolved, when I come to my Answer, not to trick up my Innocence by Cavils or Voidances, but to speak to them the Language that my Heart speaks to me, in excusing, extenuating, or ingenuously confessing, praying to God to give me Grace to see the bottom of my Faults, and that no Hardness of Heart may steal upon me, under shew of more Neatness of Conscience, than is cause But not to trouble your Majesty any longer, craving pardon for this long mourning Letter, what I thirst after, as the Hart after the Streams, is, that I may know, by my matchless Friend that presents you this Letter [a], your Majesty's Heart, (which is an *Abyss* of Goodness, as I am an *Abyss* of Misery) towards me I have been ever your Man, and counted my self but an Usufructuary of myself, the Property being yours And now make my self an Oblation, to do with me as may best conduce to the Honour of your Justice, the Honour of your Mercy, and the Use of your Service, resting as Clay in your Majesty's gracious Hands.

March 25, 1621

XLIII.

To the Right Honourable the Lords of Parliament, in the Upper-House assembled; the humble Submission and Supplication of the Lord Chancellor [b].

I Humbly crave, at your Lordships hands, a benign Interpretation of what I now write for Words that come from wasted Spirits, and an oppressed Mind, are safer deposited in a noble Construction, than circled with any reserved Caution

VOL. I   O o o   This

[a] Viz The Marquis of *Buckingham*
[b] From the Journal of the House of Lords.

This being moved, and, as I hope, obtain'd, in the nature of a Protection for all that I shall say, I make into the rest of that, wherewith I shall at this time trouble your Lordships, a very strange Entrance! for in the midst of a State of as great Affliction as I think a mortal Man can endure; (Honour being above Life) I begin with the professing of Gladness in some Particular.

The *First* is, That hereafter the Greatness of a Judge or Magistrate, shall be no Sanctuary or Protection of Guilt, which, in few words, is the Beginning of a golden World.

The *next*, That after this Example, perhaps, Judges will fly from every thing like Corruption, tho' it were at a great distance, as from a Serpent, which tends to the purging of the Courts of Justice, and the reducing them to their true Honour and Splendor.

And in these two Points, God is my Witness, that tho' it be my Fortune to be the Anvil whereon those good Effects are beaten and wrought, I take no small comfort.

But to pass from the Motions of my Heart, whereof God only is Judge, to the Merits of my Cause, whereof your Lordships are Judges, under God, and his Lieutenant, I understand there has been heretofore expected from me some Justification and therefore I have chosen one only Justification instead of all others, out of the Justification of *Job* For after the clear Submission, and Confession, which I shall now make to your Lordships, I hope I may say, and justify, with *Job* in these Words, *I have not hid my Sin, as Adam, nor concealed my Faults in my Bosom* This is the only Justification which I will use.

It remains therefore, that, without Fig-leaves, I ingenuously confess and acknowledge, that having understood the Particulars of this Charge, not formally from the House, but enough to inform my Conscience and Memory, I find Matters sufficient and full, both to move me to desert my Defence, and to move your Lordships to condemn and censure me.

Neither will I trouble your Lordships by singling those Particulars which I think might fall off *Quid te exempta juvat spinis de pluribus una?* Neither will I prompt your Lordships to observe upon the Proofs, where they come not home, or the Scruple touching the Credit of the Witnesses. Neither will I represent to your Lordships, how far a Defence in divers things might extenuate the Offence, in respect of the Time and Manner of the Gift, or the like Circumstances But only leave these things to spring out of your own noble Thoughts, and Observations, of the Evidence and Examinations themselves, and charitably to wind about the Particulars of the Charge, here and there as God shall put into your Minds, and so submit my self wholly to your Piety and Grace.

And now I have spoken to your Lordships as Judges, I shall say a few Words to you as Peers and Prelates, humbly commending my Cause to your noble Minds and magnanimous Affections.

Your Lordships are not simply Judges, but Parliamentary Judges, you have a farther extent of arbitrary Power than other Courts and if your Lord-

ships

ships be not tied by ordinary Courses of Courts, or Precedents, in Point of Strictness and Severity; much more in Points of Mercy and Mitigation

And yet, if anything I shall move shou'd be contrary to your worthy Ends of introducing a Reformation, I would not seek it, but herein I beseech your Lordships leave to tell you a Piece of History. *Titus Manlius* took his Son's Life for giving battle against the Prohibition of his General: not many Years after, the like Severity was pursued by *Papirius Cursor*, the Dictator, against *Quintus Maximus*, who being upon the point to be sentenced; by the Intercession of some principal Persons of the Senate, was spared: whereupon *Livy* makes this grave and gracious Observation, *Neque minus firmata est disciplina militaris Periculo Quinti Maximi, quam miserabili Supplicio Titi Manlii*, the Discipline of War was no less established by the questioning of *Quintus Maximus*, than by the punishing of *Titus Manlius* And there is the same reason in the Reformation of Justice, for the questioning of Men of eminent Places has the same Terror, tho' not of the same Rigor with the Punishment.

But my Case stands not there, for my humble Desire is, that his Majesty would take the Seal into his hands which is a great Downfal, and may serve, I hope, in itself for an Expiation of my Faults.

Therefore, if Mercy and Mitigation be in your power, and do no way cross your noble Ends, why should not I hope for your Lordships Favour and Commiseration?

Your Lordships will be pleased to behold your chief Pattern, the King, our Sovereign, a King of incomparable Clemency, and whose Heart is inscrutable for Wisdom and Goodness Your Lordships will remember, that there sat not these hundred Years before, a Prince in your House, and never such a Prince, whose Presence deserves to be made memorable by Records and Acts mixed of Mercy and Justice Your Lordships are either Nobles, (and Compassion ever beats in the Veins of noble Blood,) or reverend Prelates, who are the Servants of him, *that would not break the bruised Reed, nor quench the smoking Flax.* You all sit upon one high Stage, and therefore cannot but be more sensible of the Changes of the World, and of the Fall of any of high Place.

Neither will your Lordships forget, that there are *Vitia Temporis*, as well as *Vitia Hominis*, and that the Beginning of Reformations has the contrary Power to the Pool of *Bethesda*, which had Strength to cure him only that was first cast in, whereas this has commonly Strength to hurt him only that is first cast in. And for my part, I wish it may stay there, and go no farther [a]

Lastly, I assure my self, your Lordships have a noble feeling of me, as a Member of your own Body, and one, that, in this very Session, had some taste of your loving Affections, which, I hope, was not a Lightning before the Death of them, but rather a Spark of that Grace, which now, in the conclusion, will more appear.

Therefore, my humble Suit to your Lordships is, that my penitent Submission may be my Sentence, and the Loss of the Seal my Punishment, and that

[a] It is plain, that the Author looked upon himself as a kind of *Sacrifice*, and in Speech to the King wished, that as he was the *first*, so he might be the *last* Sacrifice in that Reign See the *Account of his Life*, prefixed to this *Volume*.

your

your Lordships will spare any farther Sentence, but recommend me to his Majesty's Grace and Pardon for all that is past God's holy Spirit be among you

A r. 22 1621.

XLIV.

To the KING; *imploring Assistance.*

IN the midst of my Misery, which is rather assuaged by Remembrance, than by Hope . my chiefest worldly Comfort is, to think, that since the time I had the first Voice of the Commons House of Parliament, for Commissioner of the Union, to the time I was this last Parliament chosen, by both Houses, their Messenger to your Majesty in the Petition of Religion, (which two were my first and last Services,) I was evermore so happy, as to have my poor Services graciously accepted by your Majesty, and likewise not to have had any of them miscarry in my hands Neither of which Points I can any way take to my self, but ascribe the former to your Majesty's Goodness, and the latter to your prudent Directions, which I was ever careful to have and keep For, as I have often said to your Majesty, I was towards you but as a Bucket and Cistern, to draw forth and conserve, whilst your self was the Fountain. To this Comfort of nineteen Years Prosperity, there succeeded a Comfort in my greatest Adversity, somewhat of the same nature, which is, that in those Offences wherewith I was charged, there was not one that had special relation to your Majesty, or any of your particular Commands For as towards Almighty God, there are Offences against the first and second Table, and yet all against God, so with the Servants of Kings, there are Offences more immediate against the Sovereign, tho' all Offences against Law, are also against the King To which Comfort there is added this Circumstance, that as my Faults were not against your Majesty, otherwise than as all Faults are, so my Fall was not your Majesty's Act, otherwise than as all Acts of Justice are yours This I write not to insinuate with your Majesty, but as a most humble Appeal to your Majesty's gracious Remembrance, how honest and direct you have ever found me in your Service whereby I have an assured Belief, that there is in your Majesty's own princely Thoughts, a great deal of Serenity and Clearness towards me, your Majesty's now prostrate and cast down Servant Neither, my most gracious Sovereign, do I by this mention of my Services lay claim to your princely Grace and Bounty, tho' the Privilege of Calamity doth bear that Form of Petition I know well, had they been much more, they had been but my bounden Duty Nay, I must also confess, they were, from time to time, far above my Merit over and super-rewarded by your Majesty's Benefits heaped upon me Your Majesty was, and is that Master to me, who raised and advanced me nine times, thrice in Dignity, and six times in Office The Places indeed were the painfullest of all your Services, but then they had both Honour and Profits And the then Profits might have maintain'd my now Honour, if I had been wise Neither was your Majesty's immediate Liberality wanting towards me in some Gifts, if I may hold them All this I do most thankfully acknowledge, and herewith conclude, that for any thing arising from my self to move your Eye of Pity

towards

towards me, there is much more in my prefent Mifery, than in my paft Services, fave that the fame, your Majefty's Goodnefs, which may give relief to the one, may give value to the other

And indeed, if it may pleafe your Majefty, this Theme of my Mifery is fo plentiful, as it need not be coupled with any thing elfe I have been fome Body, by your Majefty's fingular and undeferved Favour, even the prime Officer of your Kingdom your Majefty's Arm has been often laid over mine in Council, when you prefided at the Table fo near I was I have born your Majefty's Image in Metal, much more in Heart I was never, in nine-teen Years Service, chidden by your Majefty, but contrarywife, often over-joyed, when your Majefty would fometimes fay, I was a good Hufband for you, tho' none for my felf fometimes, that I had a way to deal in Bufinefs, *fuavibus modis*, which was the way moft according to your own Heart and other moft gracious Speeches of Affection and Truft, which I feed on to this day But why fhould I fpeak of thefe things, which are now vanifh'd, only the better to exprefs the Downfal?

For now 'tis thus with me, I am a Year and a half old in Mifery, tho', I muft ever acknowledge, not without fome Mixture of your Majefty's Grace and Mercy for I do not think it poffible, that any one whom you once loved, fhould be totally miferable My own Means, thro' my own Impro-vidence, are poor and weak, little better than my Father left me The poor things that I have had from your Majefty, are either in queftion or at cour-tefy My Dignities remain Marks of your paft Favour, but Burdens of my prefent Fortune The poor Remnants I had of my former Fortunes, in Plate or Jewels, I have fpread upon poor Men, to whom I owed, fcarce leaving my felf a convenient Subfiftence So that, to conclude, I muft pour out my Mifery before your Majefty, and fay, *fi deferis tu, perimus*

But as I can offer to your Majefty's Compaffion little arifing from my felf to move you, except it be my extreme Mifery, which I have truly laid open, fo looking up to your Majefty's own felf, I fhould think I committed *Cain's* Fault, if I fhould defpair. Your Majefty is a King, whofe Heart is as infcrutable for fecret Motions of Goodnefs, as for Depth of Wifdom You are Creator-like, factive, and not deftructive You are the Prince, in whom has ever been noted an Averfion to any thing that favoured of a hard Heart; as, on the other fide, your princely Eye was wont to meet with any Motion that was made on the relieving part Therefore, as one that had the happinefs to know your Majefty near hand, I have, moft gracious Sovereign, Faith enough for a Miracle, and much more for a Grace, that your Majefty will not fuffer your poor Creature to be utterly defaced; nor blot that Name quite out of your Book, upon which your facred Hand has been fo oft, for the giving him new Ornaments and Additions.

To this degree of Compaffion, I hope God will difpofe your princely Heart, already prepared to all Piety. And why fhould I not think, but that the thrice noble Prince, who would have pull'd me out of the Fire of a Sentence, will help to pull me out of an abject and fordid Condition in my laft Days? And that excellent Favourite of yours, the Goodnefs of whofe Nature contends

tends w th the Greatness of his Fortune, will kiss your hands with Joy for any work of Piety you shall do for me And as all commiserable Persons, especially such as find their Hearts void of all Malice, are apt to think all Men play them, so I assure myself, that the Lords of your Council, who, out of their Wisdom and Nobleness, cannot but be sensible of human Events, will, in th s way which I go, for the relief of my Estate, further and advance your Majesty's Goodness towards me For there is, as I conceive, a kind of Fraternity between great Men that are, and those that have been, being but the several Tenses of one Verb Nay, I further presume, that both Houses of Parliament will love their Justice the better, if it end not in my ruin for I have been often told, by many of my Lords, as it were in the way of ex cusing the Severity of the Sentence, that they knew they left me in good hands And your Majesty knows well, I have been all my Life long acceptable to those Assemblies, not by Flattery, but by Moderation, and by the honest expressing of a desire to have all things go fairly and well

But if it may please your Majesty (for Saints, I shall give them Reverence, but no Adoration, my Address is to your Majesty, the Fountain of Goodness,) your Majesty shall, by the Grace of God, not feel that in Gift, which I shall extremely feel in Help for my Desires are moderate; and my Courses mea sured to a Life orderly and reserved, hoping still to do your Majesty honour in my way Only I most humbly beseech your Majesty to give me leave to conclude with those Words which Necessity speaks · Help me, dear Sovereign Lord and Master, and pity me so far, as that I, who have born a Bag, be not now in my Age, forced in effect, to bear a Wallet, nor that I, who desire to live to study, may not be driven to study to live I most humbly crave par don for a long Letter, after a long silence God of Heaven ever bless, pre serve, and prosper your Majesty

An 1622

XLV.

To the Marquis of BUCKINGHAM, *recommending* Mr. Matthews.

THO' I have troubled your Lordship with many Letters, oftener than I think I should, save that Affection keeps no account, yet upon the repair of Mr *Matthews*, a Gentleman so much your Lordship's Servan, and to me another self, as your Lordship best knows, you would not have thought me a Man alive, except I had put a Letter into his hand, and withal by so faithful and approved a mean, commended my Fortunes afresh to your Lordship

To speak my Heart to your Lordship, I never felt my Misfortunes so much as now not for that part which may concern my self, who profit both in Patience, and settling my own Courses, but when I look abroad, and see the Times so stirring, so much Dissimulation and Falshood, Baseness and Envy in the World, and so many idle Clocks going in Men's Heads, then it grieves me much, that I am not sometimes at your Lordship's Elbow, that I might give you some of the Fruits of the careful Advice, modest Liberty, and true Information of a Friend, that loves your Lordship as I do for tho' your Lordship's Fortunes be above the Thunders and Storms of inferior Regions, nevertheless, to hear the Wind, and not to feel it, will make one sleep the Letter.

My good Lord, somewhat I have been, and much have I read, so that few things, which concern States, or Greatness, are new Cases to me and therefore, I hope, I may be no unprofitable Servant to your Lordship I remember, the King used to make a Character of me, far above my worth, that I was not made for small matters and your Lordship would sometimes bring me from his Majesty, that *Latin* Sentence, *De minimis non curat Lex* And it has so fallen out, that since my retiring, Times have been fuller of great matters than before, wherein, perhaps, if I had continued near his Majesty, he might have found more use of my Service, if my Gift lay that way But that is but a vain Imagination of mine True it is, that as I do not aspire to use my Talent in the King's great Affairs, yet for what may concern your Lordship, and your Fortune, no Man living shall give you a better account of Faith, Industry and Affection, than I shall I must conclude with that which gave me the occasion of this Letter, which is, Mr *Matthews*'s Employment, to your Lordship, in those parts wherein I am verily persuaded your Lordship will find him a wise and able Gentleman, and one that will bend his Knowledge of the World, to serve his Majesty and the Prince, and especially your Lordship

Grays-Inn, Apr. 18. 1623.

XLVI.

To the King; *petitioning for a total Remission of his Sentence.*

BEFORE I make my Petition to your Majesty, I make my Prayers to God above, *pectore ab imo*, that if I have held any thing so dear as your Majesty's Service, nay, your Heart's Ease, and your Honour's, I may be repulsed with a Denial but if that has been the Principal with me, then that God, who knows my Heart, would move your Majesty's royal Heart to take Compassion of me, and to grant my desire

I prostrate my self at your Majesty's Feet, I, your ancient Servant, now sixtyfour Years old in Age, and three Years five Months old in Misery I desire not from your Majesty, Means, nor Place, nor Employment, but only after so long a time of Expiation, a compleat, and total Remission of the Sentence of the Upper-House, to the end, that Blot of Ignominy may be removed from me;

me , and from my Memory with Posterity , that I die not a condemned Man, but may be to your Majesty, as I am to God, *nova Creatura.* Your Majesty has pardoned the like to Sir *John Bennet* [a], between whose Case and mine, not being partial to my self, but speaking out of the general Opinion, there was as much difference, I will not say, as between black and white, but as between black and grey Look therefore down, dear Sovereign, upon me also in pity I know your Majesty's Heart is inscrutable for Goodness , and my Lord of *Buckingham* used to tell me, you were the best-natured Man in the World and its God's Property, that those he has loved, he loves to the end Let your Majesty's Grace, in this my Desire, stream down upon me, and let it be out of the Fountain and Spring-head, and *ex mero motu* , that living or dying, the Print of the Goodness of King *James* may be in my Heart, and his Praises in my Mouth This, my most humble request, granted, may make me live a Year or two happily , and denied, will kill me quickly But yet the last thing that will die in me, will be the Heart and Affection of, &c

Feb. 30. 1624

XLVII.

To the Earl of ARUNDEL *and* SURREY.

I Was likely to have the Fortune of the Elder *Pliny*, who lost his Life by trying an Experiment about the burning of the Mount *Vesuvius* , for I was also desirous to try an Experiment or two, upon the Conservation and Induration of Bodies For the Experiment itself, it succeeded excellently, but in the Journey between *London* and *Highgate*, I was taken with such a Fit of Vomiting, as I knew not whether 'twere the Stone, or some Surfeit, or Cold , or indeed a touch of them all three But when I came to your Lordship's House, I was not able to go back, and therefore was forced to take up my Lodging here, where your House-keeper is very careful and diligent about me, which, I assure my self, your Lordship will not only pardon towards him, but think the better of him for it. For indeed your Lordship's House was happy to me , and I kiss your noble Hands for the Welcome, which, I am sure, you give me to it, &c

I know how unfit it is for me to write to your Lordship with any other Hand than my own, but my Fingers are so dis-jointed with this Fit of Sickness, that I cannot steadily hold a Pen [b]

An. 1626.

[a] Sir *John Bennet*, Judge of the Prerogative Court, was in the Year 1621, accused, convicted, and censured in Parliament, for taking Bribes, and committing several Misdemeanors relating to his Office

[b] The Author died a few Days after this Letter was wrote.

SECT. II.

Letters relating to the AUTHOR'S *Writings.*

I.

To his Brother, Mr. ANTHONY BACON [a]; *dedicating the first Edition of his* Essays *to him.*

I Now act like one that has an Orchard ill-neighboured, and gathers his Fruit, before 'tis ripe, to prevent stealing These Fragments of my Conceits were going to the Press · to endeavour their stay had been troublesome, and subject to interpretation , to let them pass, had been to venture the wrong they might receive by untrue Copies, or some garnishment, which it might please any one to bestow upon them. I therefore held it best to publish them myself, as they pass'd long ago, from my Pen, without any farther disgrace than the weakness of the Author And as I ever thought there might be as great a vanity in with-holding men's Conceits from the World, as in obtruding them , so in these Particulars I have play'd my self the Inquisitor; and find nothing, to my understanding, in them, contrary or infectious to the state of Religion, or Manners ; but rather medicinal Only I disliked now to publish them, because they will be like the late new half-pence ; which tho' the Silver were good, yet the Pieces were small But since they would not stay with their Master, but would needs go abroad, I have preferr'd them to you, who are next my self; dedicating them, such as they are, to our love , in the depth whereof, I sometimes wish your [b] Infirmities translated upon my self, that her Majesty might have the service of so active and able a Mind , and I might be, with excuse, confin'd to these Contemplations and Studies, for which I am fittest.

Gray's-Inn, Jan 30. 1597

II.

[a] Elder and only Brother to the Author, said to have been his equal in Genius , but inferior in Learning and Knowledge

[b] The Gentleman was lame in his Feet, and troubled with the Gout.

II.

To the Earl of NORTHAMPTON [a]; *desiring him to present the* Advancement of Learning *to the* KING.

HAving finish'd a work upon the *Advancement of Learning*, and dedicated it to his Majesty, whom I dare avouch, if the Records of Time err not, to be the most learned King that has reign'd; I was desirous, in a kind of congruity, to present it by the most learned Counsellor in this Kingdom, to the end that so good an Argument, lighting upon so bad an Author, might receive some reputation by the hands into which, and by which, it should be delivered And, therefore, I make it my humble Suit to your Lordship, to present this mean, but well-meant Writing to his Majesty; and with it my humble and zealous Duty: and also, my like humble Request of pardon, if I have too often taken his name in vain; not only in the Dedication, but also in vouching the authority of his Speeches and Writings

Ann 1605.

III.

To Sir THOMAS BODLEY [b]; *upon presenting him the* Advancement of Learning.

I Think no man may more truly say with the Psalm, *multum incola fuit anima mea*, than my self; for I confess, since I was of any understanding, my Mind has, in effect, been absent from what I have done: and in absence are many Errors, which I willingly acknowledge, and among the rest, this great one, which led the rest; that knowing my self, by inward calling, to be fitter to hold a Book than to play a Part, I have led my life in civil Causes, for which I was not very fit by Nature, and more unfit by the preoccupation of my Mind. Therefore calling my self home, I have now, for a time, enjoy'd my self; whereof likewise I desire to make the World partaker My Labours, (if I may so term that, which was the comfort of my other Labours) I have dedicated to the King; desirous, if there be any good in them, it may be as the Fat of a Sacrifice, incensed to his honour And the second Copy I have sent to you, not only in good Affection, but in a kind

---

[a] Author of a Book *against the Poison of supposed Prophecies*, dedicated to Sir *Francis Walsingham* Ann 1583

[b] The Founder of the *Bodleia* Library at *Oxford*.

kind of Congruity, in regard of your great and rare Defert of Learning. For Books are the Shrines where the Saint is, or is believed to be. And you having built an Ark to fave Learning from Deluge, deferve propriety in a new Inftrument or Engine, whereby Learning fhould be improved or advanced.

Ann. 1605.

IV.

To the Earl of Salisbury [a] ; *upon prefenting him the* Advancement of Learning.

I Prefent your Lordfhip with a Work of my vacant time, which if it had been more, the Work had been better. It appertains to your Lordfhip, (befides my particular refpects) in fome propriety ; in regard you are a great Governor in a Province of Learning. And, what is more, you have added to your place Affection towards Learning, and to your Affection, Judgment: the latter whereof, I could be content were lefs for the time , that you might the lefs exquifitely cenfure what I offer you But fure I am, the Argument is good, if it had lighted upon a good Author. But I fhall content my felf to awake better Spirits, like a Bell-ringer, who is firft up to call others to Church. So with my humble defire of your Lordfhip's good acceptation, I remain, &c.

Ann. 1605.

V.

To the Univerfity of Cambridge; *upon prefenting his* Advancement of Learning *to their Public* Library.

I Would, to my ability, hereby difcharge the Duties of a Son ; and exhort you all to purfue the fame method ; and, with a becoming Moderation, yet a freedom of the Underftanding, in earneft, endeavour the *Advancement of the Sciences* not burying in a napkin the Talent lent you by the Ancients. Queftionlefs the divine Light will favour and fhine upon you, if you do but humble and fubmit Philofophy to Religion, dextroufly make a right ufe of the Keys of the Senfes ; and, dropping all eagernefs of oppofition, each of you calmly difpute with his fellow, as it were with himfelf.

Ppp 2

VI.

[a] *Viz.* Sir *Robert Cecil*, Son to the Lord *Burghley*, he was long Secretary of State, and for fome years Lord Treafurer, and Chancellor, of the Univerfity of *Cambridge*.

I

VI.

To TRINITY-COLLEGE, CAMBRIDGE; *upon presenting them the* Advancement of Learning.

THE state and progress of all things is owing to their Origins; and therefore as I drew the Origins of the *Sciences* from your Fountains, I judge it proper to return you their increase. I have also hopes that these Plants of mine may thrive and flourish with you, as in their native Soil. Let me therefore exhort you to promote the growth of the *Sciences*, so far as may consist with Discretion, and the Respect due to the Ancients and next after the sacred Volume of God's *Word*, the Scriptures, to study diligently that great Volume of his *Works*, to which all other Books serve but as Comments.

VII.

To the University of OXFORD; *upon presenting them the* Advancement of Learning.

AS I have wrote to the *University of Cambridge*, whose Pupil I am, I should be wanting in my Duty, not to present her *Sister* the same token of my Affection And as I have exhorted them, so likewise I exhort you. strenuously to endeavour the *Advancement of the Sciences*; not esteeming the Labours of the Ancients as nothing, nor as every thing but discreetly considering your own proper strength, sometimes to prove and try it. No doubt of a happy issue, if you do not take arms against one another, but, with united force, make your attack upon the *Nature of Things* which alone will afford sufficient matter of Victory and Glory.

VIII.

To Mr. MATTHEWS [a]; *with the* Advancement of Learning.

I Perceive you have some time when you can be content to think of your Friends, from whom, since you have borrow'd yourself, you do well, not paying the Principal, to send the Interest, at six month's day.

I

- Son to Dr T^by Matthews, Bishop of Durham, and afterwards of York He wrote an ...n' g. on the Duke of Florence's Felicity See Sect I. Letter 19 *ad finem.*

I have now at laſt taught that Child to go, at the ſwadling whereof you were My Work upon the Proficiency and Advancement of Learning, I have put into two Books , whereof the former [a], which you ſaw, I can't but account as a Page to the latter [b] I have now publiſh'd them both , whereof I thought it a ſmall Adventure to ſend you a Copy, who have more right to it than any Man, except Biſhop *Andrews*, who was my Inquiſitor

I write this, in anſwer to your good Wiſhes , which I return, not as Flowers of *Florence*, but as you mean them · whom, I conceive, Place can't alter, no more than Time ſhall me, except it be for the better.

Ann 16●5.

IX.

To the Lord Chancellor EGERTON [c]; *preſenting him the* Advancement of Learning.

I Humbly preſent your Lordſhip with a Work, wherein, as you have much Command over the Author , ſo you have great Intereſt in the Argument · for, to ſpeak without flattery, few have ſuch Uſe of Learning, or ſuch Judgment in Learning, as I have obſerved in your Lordſhip.   And, again, your Lordſhip has been a great Planter of Learning, not only in thoſe places in the Church, which have been in your own Gift , but alſo in your commendatory Vote, no Man has more conſtantly held, *detur dignior.* And therefore, both your Lordſhip is beholden to Learning, and Learning to your Lordſhip which makes me preſume that you will accept of theſe my Labours , the rather, becauſe your Lordſhip, in private Speech, has often begun to me in expreſſing your admiration of his Majeſty's Learning, to whom I have dedicated this Work , and whoſe Virtue and Perfection in that kind, chiefly moved me to a Work of this nature.

Ann 1605

X.

To the Lord Treaſurer BUCKHURST [d]; *upon preſenting him the* Advancement of Learning.

I Have finiſhed a Work upon the *Advancement or ſetting forward of Learning*, which I have dedicated to his Majeſty, the moſt learned of a Sovereign, or Temporal Prince, that Time has known , and upon reaſon,

not

---

[a] *De Dignitate Scientiarum*
[b] *De Augmentis Scientiarum*
[c] Lord *Elleſmere*
[d] Chancellor of the Univerſity of *Oxford*, Lord Treaſurer, and Earl of *Dorſet*, celebrated as a Poet, an Orator, and a Writer.

rot unlike, I humbly prefent one of the Books to your Lordfhip, not only, as a Chancellor of an *Univerfity*, but as one that was excellently bred in all Learning, which I have ever noted to fhine in all your Speeches and Behaviour and therefore your Lordfhip will yield a gracious afpect to your firft Love, and take pleafure in the adorning of that wherewith your felf are fo much adorned. And fo humbly defiring your favourable acceptance thereof, I remain, *&c*.

Ann. 1605

XI.

To Dr. PLAYFER [1]; *defiring him to tranflate the* Advancement *into* Latin.

A Great Defire will take a fmall occafion to hope, and put in tryal, that which is defired. It pleafed you, a good while fince, to exprefs to me the liking you conceived of my Book of the *Advancement of Learning*, and that more fignificantly, as it feem'd to me, than out of Courtefy or civil Refpect As I then took content in your Approbation thereof, fo I fhould efteem and acknowledge, not only my Content increafed, but my Labours advanced, if I might obtain your good Help in that nature which I defire. wherein, before I fet down in plain terms my Requeft, I will open my felf, what 'twas I chiefly fought, and propofed in that Work, that you may perceive what I now defire, to be purfuant thereupon If I do not much err (for any Judgment that a Man makes of his own doings, had need be fpoken with a *fi nunquam fallat imago*,) I have this Opinion, that if I had fought my own Reputation, it had been a much fitter Courfe for me to have done as Gardeners ufe to do, by taking their Seed and Slips, and rearing them firft into Plants, and fo uttering them in Pots, when they are in Flower, and in their beft State But as my end was Merit of the State of Learning, and not Glory, and as my Purpofe was rather to excite other Mens Wits, than to magnify my own, I was defirous to prevent the uncertainty of my own Life and Times, by uttering rather Seeds than Plants nay, and farther, as the Proverb is, by fowing with the Bafket, rather than with the Hand Wherefore, fince I have only taken upon me to ring a Bell, to call other Wits together, which is the meaneft Office, it cannot but be agreeable to my defire, to have that Bell heard as far as poffible And fince they are but as Sparks which can work only upon Matter prepared, I have the more reafon to wifh, that thofe Sparks may fly abroad, that they may the better find and light upon fuch Minds and Spirits as are apt to be kindled And therefore the Privacy of the Language confidered, wherein it is written, exclu-

ding

[1] Profeffor of Divinity in the Univerfity of *Cambridge*.

ding fo many Readers , as, on the other fide, the obfcurity of the Argument, in many parts of it, excludes many others , I muft account it a fecond Birth of that Work, if it might be tranflated into *Latin* , without manifeft lofs of the Senfe and Matter For this purpofe, I could not reprefent to my felf any Man, into whofe hands I do more earneftly defire that Work fhould fall, than your felf , for by what I have heard and read, I know no Man a greater Mafter in commanding Words to ferve Matter. Neverthelefs, I am not ignorant of the Worth of your Labours , whether fuch as your Place and Profeffion impofes, or fuch as your own Virtue may, upon your voluntary Election, take in hand But I can lay before you no other perfuafions, than either the Work it felf may affect you with ; or the Honour of his Majefty to whom 'tis dedicated ; or your particular Inclination to my felf: who, as I never took fuch comfort in any Labours of my own, fo I fhall never acknowledge my felf more obliged in any thing to the Labours of another, than in that which fhall affift it . which your Labour, if I can, by my Place, Profeffion, Means, Friends, Travel, Work, Deed, requite to you, I fhall efteem my felf fo ftrictly bound thereto, as I fhall be ever moft ready both to take and feek occafion of thankfulnefs. So leaving it neverthelefs, *falva amicitia,* as reafon is, to your good liking, I remain, *&c* [a].

XII.

To the King; with the Difcourfe of the Plantation of Ireland.

I Know not better how to exprefs my good Wifhes of a new Year to your Majefty, than by this little Book, which in all humblenefs I fend you. The Stile is a Stile of Bufinefs, rather than curious or elaborate And herein I was encouraged by my Experience of your Majefty's former Grace, in accepting of the like poor Field-fruits upon the *Union*. And certainly I reckon this Action as a fecond Brother to the Union For I affure my felf, that *England, Scotland* and *Ireland* well united, is fuch a Trefoil, as no Prince, except your felf, wears in his Crown , *fi potentia reducatur in actum* I well know, that for me to beat my Brains about thefe things, is, *Majora quam pro fortuna*; but yet, *Minora quam pro ftudio ac voluntate* For as I ftill bear an extreme Zeal to the Memory of my old Miftrefs, Queen *Elizabeth* , to whom I was rather bound for her Truft, than her Favour, fo I muft acknowledge my felf more bound to your Majefty,

[a] The Doctor eagerly embraced the Propofal, and returned a Specimen of a Tranflation, the *Latinity* whereof was found too exquifite, fo that the Author, who required ftrong and mafculine Expreffion, did not encourage him to proceed. See *Bacon's Remains,* by *Tennifon,* Pag 26

jefty, both for Truft and Favour whereof I will never deceive the one, as I can never deferve the other.

Ann. 1606.

Of the PLANTATION *of* IRELAND.

IT feems God has referved to your Majefty's times *two Works*, which among the Works of Kings have the fupreme Preheminence, *viz.* the *uniting*, and *planting* of Kingdoms. For tho' it be great fortune for a King to deliver his Kingdom from long Calamities; yet in the Judgment of thofe who have diftinguifh'd the Degrees of Sovereign Honour, to be a Founder of States excels all the reft For as in Arts and Sciences, to be the firft Inventor, is more than to illuftrate or amplify, as in the Works of God, the Creation is greater than the Prefervation, and as in the Works of Nature, the Birth and Nativity is more than the Continuance. fo in Kingdoms, the firft Foundation, or Plantation, is of nobler Dignity and Merit than all that follows Thefe Foundations are but of two kinds, the firft, that which makes one of more, and the fecond, that which makes one of none, the latter refembling the Creation of the World *out of nothing*, and the former the Edification of the Church to *Simplicity and Unity* And it has pleafed the divine Providence to put both thefe Foundations into your hands, the one, in the *Union of Britain*, the other, in the Plantation of great parts of *Ireland* Which Enterprizes being once happily accomplifhed, you may juftly be faid to have given new Birth to *Britain* and *Ireland* For Unions and Plantations are the very Nativities or Birth-days of Kingdoms And herein likewife your Majefty has yet a Fortune extraordinary, and differing from former Examples in the fame kind. For moft Unions and Plantations of Kingdoms have been founded in the effufion of Blood, but your Majefty builds *in folo puro, & in area pura*, that needs no expiatory Sacrifice for Blood, and therefore, no doubt, this is under a higher and more affured Bleffing

I fhall firft fpeak of the Excellency of the Work; and then of the Means to compafs and effect it For the Excellence of the Work, I will divide it into four noble and worthy Confequences, that will follow thereupon

The *firt* is *Honour*, whereof I have faid enough already, were it not that the Harp of *Ireland* reminds me of that glorious Emblem, or Allegory, wherein the Wifdom of Antiquity fhadowed out Works of this nature For the Poets feigned, that *Orpheus*, by the virtue and fweetnefs of his Harp, affembled the Beafts and Birds, of their nature wild and favage, to ftand about him, as in a Theatre, forgetting their Affections of Fiercenefs, of Luft, and of Prey, and liftening to the Tunes and Harmonies of the Harp and foon after, called likewife the Stones and the Woods to remove, and

ftand

stand in order about him   Which Fable was anciently interpreted of the reducing and planting of Kingdoms, when People of barbarous Manners are brought to give over their Customs of Revenge and Blood, and of dissolute Life, Theft, and Rapine, and to give ear to the Wisdom of Laws and Governments   whereupon immediately follows the calling of Stones for Building and Habitation, and of Trees, for the Seats of Houses, Orchards, Enclosures, and the like.   This Work therefore, of all others, the most memorable and honourable, your Majesty has now in hand, and may the better effect, by joining the Harp of *David*, in casting out the evil Spirit of Superstition, with the Harp of *Orpheus*, in the casting out Desolation and Barbarism.

The *second* Consequence of this Enterprize, is the *avoiding of an Inconvenience*, which commonly attends upon happy Times, and is a bad effect of a good Cause.   The present Age seems generally inclined to Peace in these Parts, and your Majesty's most Christian Temper promises the same, more especially to these your Kingdoms   But the effect of Peace in a fruitful Kingdom, where the Stock of People, receiving no diminution by War, must continually multiply and increase, will in the end be a Surcharge or Overflow of People, more than the Territory can well maintain, which often insinuating a general Necessity and want of Means into States, turns external Peace into internal Troubles and Seditions.   Now, what an excellent Diversion of this Inconvenience is ministred to your Majesty in this Plantation of *Ireland?*   Wherein so many Families may receive Sustenance and Fortunes   and the Discharge of them also out of *England* and *Scotland*, may prevent many Seeds of future Perturbations.   So that, the Issue will be, as if a Man were at a loss to discharge a Flood of Waters from the place where he has built his House, and should afterwards turn them into fair Ponds or Streams, for Pleasure, Provision, or Use.   For thus your Majesty will have a double Convenience, in discharging of People here, and in making use of them there.

The *third* Consequence is, the great Safety likely to ensue to your Majesty's State, in general, by this Act, in discomfiting all hostile Attempts of Foreigners, which the Weakness of that Kingdom has heretofore invited   A general Reason is, because, as one of the *Romans* said of *Peloponnesus, The Tortoise is safe within her Shell* [a], but if she put forth any part of her Body, it endangers, not only the part so put forth, but all the rest: and in the human Body, if there be any weak or affected Part, this is sufficient to draw Rheums or Humours to it, to the disturbance of the Health of the whole-Body   And for Particulars, the example is too fresh, that the Indisposition of that Kingdom has been a continual Attractive of Troubles and Infestations upon this State.   and tho' your Majesty's Greatness in some measure discharges this Fear, yet without your increase of Power, Envy must likewise increase

The *fourth* and last *Consequence* is, the great Profit and Strength likely to redound to your Crown, by working upon this unpolished part thereof

---

[a] *Testudo intra tegumen tuta est*

whence your Majesty, being in the Prime of Life, is likely to receive more upon the First-Fruits, and your Posterity, a growing and springing Vein of Riches and Power. For this Island being another *Britain*, as *Britain* was said to be another World, has so many Dowries of Nature, the Fruitfulness of the Soil, the Ports, the Rivers, the Fishing, the Quarries, the Woods, and especially its Race of valiant, hardy, and active Men, that it is not easy, even upon the Continent, to find such a Conflux of Commodities, if the hand of Men did but join with the hand of Nature. And so much for the Excellence of the Work, in point of Honour, Policy, Safety, and Utility.

For the Means to effect this Work, your Majesty will not want the Information of expert and industrious Persons, who have served you there, and know the Country, nor the Advice of a grave and prudent Council here, which knows the Pulses of the Hearts of People, and the ways and passages of conducting great Actions besides that Fountain of Wisdom and Universality, which is in your self. Yet in a thing of so publick a nature, it is not amiss for your Majesty to hear variety of Opinions for as *Demosthenes* says well, " the good Fortune of a Prince or State, sometimes puts a good " Motion into a Fool's mouth."

I think, therefore, the Means of accomplishing this Work, consists of two principal Parts The *first*, the Invitation and Encouragement of Undertakers the *second*, the Order and Policy of the Project it self For as in all Engines of the Hand, there is somewhat that gives the Motion and Force and the rest serves to guide and govern it, the Case is the same in these Enterprizes or Engines of State For the former, no doubt, but next to the Providence and Finger of God, which writes these excellent Desires in the Tables of your Majesty's Heart, your Authority and your Affection is the first Mover in this Cause and therefore, the more strongly and fully your Majesty shall declare your self in it, the more shall you quicken and animate the whole Proceeding For this is an Action, which, as its worthiness supports it, so its Nature requires it to be carried in some height of Reputation and 'tis fit, in my Opinion, for Pulpits and Parliaments, and all Places to ring and resound of it. For what may seem Vanity, in some things, I mean matter of Fame, is of great efficacy in this

But now to descend to the inferior Spheres, and speak of what Co operation in the Subjects or Undertakers may be raised, and by what means And to take plain Grounds, which are the surest; all Men are drawn into Actions by three things, *viz* (1) *Pleasure*, (2) *Honour*, and (3) *Profit* But before I pursue these three Motives, it is fit to interlace a word or two, as to the quality of the Undertakers, wherein my Opinion is simply this, that if your Majesty shall make these Portions of Land to be planted, but as Rewards, or as Suits, or as Fortunes for those in want, and are likeliest to seek most after them, they will not be able to go through with the Charge of good substantial Plantations, but will, *deficere in Opere medio*, and then this Work will succeed, as *Tacitus* says, *acribus Initiis Fine incurioso* So that, this must rather be an Adventure for such as are full, than a set-

ting

ting up of those that are low of Means   for such Men are fit to perform these Undertakings, as are fit to purchase dry Reversions after Lives or Years, or such as are fit to put out Money upon long Returns   So that the Undertakers themselves should be Men of Estates and Plenty

(1.) To come now to the Motives   *First*, for Pleasure. In this tract of Soil, there are no warm Winters, nor Orange-Trees, nor strange Beasts, nor Birds, or other Points of Curiosity and Diversion, as there are in the *Indies*, and the like   so that there can be no Foundation made upon matter of Pleasure, otherwise, than that the very desire of Novelty and Experiment in some stirring Natures may work somewhat, and therefore, 'tis the other two Points of Honour and Profit, whereon we are wholly to rest

(2) For *Honour* or *Countenance*, if I mention to your Majesty, whether in Wisdom you shall think convenient, the better to express your Affection to the Enterprize, and for a Pledge thereof, to add the Earldom of *Ulster* to the Prince's Titles, I shall but learn it out of the Practice of King *Edward* I who used the like Course, as a means the better to restrain the Country of *Wales*   And I take it, the Prince of *Spain* has the addition of a Province in the Kingdom of *Naples*, and other Precedents, I think there are   and 'tis likely to put more Life and Encouragement in the Undertakers.

Again, considering the large Territories to be planted, it is not improbable your Majesty will think of raising some Nobility there, which if done, merely upon new Titles of Dignity, without any reference to the old, and if done, also, without putting too many Portions into one hand, and lastly, without any great Franchises or Commands, I do not see any Danger can ensue   as, on the other side, it may draw some Persons of great Estate and Means into the Action, to the great furtherance and supply of the Charges thereof

And for Knighthood, to such Persons as have not attained it, or otherwise Knighthood, with some new Difference and Precedence, may no doubt work with many   And if any Man think that these things are *aliquid nimis*, for the Proportion of this Action, I confess, plainly, that if your Majesty will have it really and effectually performed, my Opinion is, you cannot bestow too much Sun-shine upon it.   For *Lunæ radiis non maturescit botrus*   Thus much for Honour.

(3) For *Profit*, it will consist in three Parts, *viz* *First*, the easy Rates that your Majesty shall be pleased to give the Undertakers of the Land, they receive

Secondly, The Liberties you may be pleased to confer upon them   I mean not Liberties of Jurisdiction, as Counties Palatine, or the like; which has been the Error of the ancient Donations and Plantations in that Country   but only Liberties tending to Convenience, as of transporting any of the Commodities growing upon the Country new planted, or importing from hence all things appertaining to their necessary use, Custom-free, and liberty of taking Timber, or other Materials, in your Majesty's Woods there, and the like.

The

The turd Part is, Eafe of Charges, that the whole mafs of the Charge co not reft upon the private Purfe of the Undertakers

The two former of thefe Parts, I pafs over, becaufe in that Project, which with good diligence and providence has been prefented to your Majefty, by your Minifters of that Kingdom, they are, in my opinion, well handled

For the third, I defpair not, but that the Parliament of *England*, if it perceive, that this Action is not a flafh, but a folid and fettled Purfut, will give aid to a Work fo Religious, fo Politick, and fo Profitable And the contribution of the Charge falls naturally into three kinds, each whereof refpectively ought to have its proper Fountain and Iffue For as there proceeds from your Majefty's Royal Bounty, and Munificence, the Gift of the Land, and other Materials, together with the Endowment of Liberties, and as the Charge, which is private, *viz* the building of Houfes, ftocking of Grounds, Provifions, &c is to reft upon the particular Undertakers fo whatever is publick, as the building of Churches, walling of Towns Town houfes, Bridges, Caufe-ways, or High-ways, and the like, ought not properly to be upon particular Perfons, but to come from the publick State of this Kingdom, to which the Work is likely to return fo great an addition of Glory, Strength, and Commodity

Of the Project it felf, I fhall need to fpeak the lefs, in regard 'tis fo confiderably digefted already for the County of *Tyrone* and therefore my Labour fhall be but in thofe things, wherein I fhall either add to, or diffent from what is fet down, which will include five Points or Articles.

And Firft, They mention a Commiffion for this Plantation, which of all things is moft neceffary, both to direct and appeafe Controverfies, and the like

To this I add two Propofals the *one*, that the Commiffioners fhould, for certain time, refide and abide in fome habitable Town of *Ireland*, near the new-planted Country, to the end, that they may be more at hand, for the Execution of the Parts of their Commiffion And probably, by drawing a concourfe of People and Tradefmen to fuch Towns, it will be fome Help and Commodity to the Undertakers, for the things they fhall ftand in need of And likewife, it will be a more fafe Place of Receipt and Store, wherein to unlade and depofite fuch Provifions, as are afterwards to be employ'd

The *fecond* is, that your Majefty would make a Correfpondence between the Commiffion there, and a *Council of Plantation* here, according to the Precedent of the like *Council of Plantation* for *Virginia* an Enterprize, in my opinion, differing as much from this, as *Amadis de Gaul* differs from *Cæfar*'s Commentaries By a Council of Plantation, I mean fome Perfons chofen by way of Reference, upon whom the Labour may reft, to prepare and report things to the Council of State here, concerning that Bufinefs. For altho' your Majefty has a grave and fufficient Council in *Ireland*, from whom, and upon whom, the Commiffioners are to have Affiftance and Dependance, yet that anfwers not the purpofe I intend For as, upon

I

the

the Advice both of Commissioners, and the Council of *Ireland* itself, there will be many Occasions to crave Directions from your Majesty, and your Privy Council here, which are busied with a world of Affairs ; it cannot but give a greater Expedition, and better Perfection to some Directions and Resolutions, if the matters may be considered of before-hand, by such, as may have a continual Care of the Cause   And it will be likewise a Comfort and Satisfaction to some principal Undertakers, if they may be admitted of that Council

Secondly, There is a Clause, wherein the Undertakers are restrain'd, that they shall execute the Plantation in Person , from which I must dissent, upon the Grounds I have already taken   For 'tis not probable that Men of great Means and plentiful Estates will endure the Fatigue, Disorders, and Adventures of going thither in Person , but rather, I suppose, many will undertake Portions, as an Advancement for their younger Children or Relations; or for the *Sweetness of the Expectation* of a great *Purchase in the end*   And therefore, 'tis likely, they will employ Sons, Kinsfolks, Servants, or Tenants , and yet be glad to have the Estate in themselves   And perhaps some again will join their Purses together, and make, as it were, a Partnership, or Joint-Adventure, and yet send some one Person by Consent, for executing the *Plantation*

Thirdly, There is a main Point, wherein I fear the Project form'd has too much of the Line and Compass, and will not be so natural and easy to execute , nor yet so political and convenient *viz.* that the Buildings should be scatter'd upon every Portion , and the Castle or principal House draw the Tenements and Farms about it, as it were, into Villages and Hamlets , and that there should be four *corporate Towns*, for the Artificers and Tradesmen

My Opinion is, that the Building be altogether in Towns, to be composed as well of Husbandries as of Arts   My Reasons are, *First*, when Men come into a Country waste, and void of all things necessary for the use of Man , if they set up together in a place, one of them will better supply the wants of the other. Workmen of all sorts will be the more continually at work, without loss of time , when, if Work fail in one place, they may have it near hand   The Ways will be more passable for Carriage to those Seats or Towns, than they can be to a number of dispersed solitary Places   and infinite other Helps and Easements, scarcely to be comprehended in Thought, will ensue from a Vicinity and Society of People. Whereas, if they build scattered, every Man must have a *Cornu-Copia* in himself, for all things he shall use ; which cannot but cause much Difficulty and Waste   *Secondly*, It will draw Provisions and Necessaries out of the inhabited Country, because they will be sure of vent , whereas in dispersed Habitations, every Man must reckon only upon what he brings with him, as they do in the storing of Ships   *Thirdly*, The Charge of *Bawnes*, as they call them, to be made about every Castle or House, may be spared , when the Habitations shall be congregated only into Towns   And *lastly*, it will be a means to secure the Country against future Dangers , in case of any Revolt and Defection for by a slight Fortification of no great charge, the Danger of any Attempts

of

of Arts and Sciences may be prevented the Omission of which Point, in the last Plantation of Munster, made the Work of Years to be but the Spoil of Days And if any Man think it will draw People too far off from the Grounds they are to labour , 'tis to be understood, that the number of the Towns be increased accordingly , and likewise, that the Situation of them be s in a Center, with respect to the Portions assigned them for in the champaign Countries of England, where the Habitation is in Towns, and not dispersed, 'tis no new thing to go two Miles to plough part of their Grounds , and two Miles compass will take up a good deal of Country

The second Point, is a Point wherein I shall differ from the Project, rather in Quantity and Proportion, than in Matter It is allowed the Undertaker, within the five Years of Restraint, to alien a third part in Fee-Farm, and to demise another for forty Years , which I fear will mangle the Portions, and be but a shift to make Money of two Parts· whereas I am of Opinion, the more the first Undertaker is forced to keep in his own hands, the more the Work is likely to prosper For, *First*, the Person liable to the State here to perform the Plantation, is the immediate Undertaker Secondly, The more his Profit depends upon the annual and springing Commodity, the more sweetness he will find in putting forward the husbanding of Grounds , and therefore is likely to take more care of it *Thirdly*, Since the Natives are excluded, I do not see that any Persons are likely to be drawn over of that condition, as to give Fines, and undertake the Charge of Building for I am persuaded, that the People transported will consist of Gentlemen and their Servants, and of Labourers and Hinds , and not of wealthy Yeomen and therefore the charge of building, as well of the Tenements and Farms, as of the capital Houses themselves, will probably rest upon the Undertakers, which may be recompensed in the end to the full, if they make no long Estates or Leases and therefore this Article is to receive some Qualification *Fifthly*, I think it requisite that Men of Experience in that Kingdom, should enter into some particular Consideration of the Charges and Provisions, of all kinds, that will be incident to the Plantations. that thereupon some Advice may be taken for the furnishing and accommodating them most conveniently thus assisting private Industry, with publick Care and Order

XIII.

To Sir THOMAS BODLEY; *desiring him to return the* Author's Cogitata & Visa.

AS I am going to my House in the Country, I shall want my Papers, which I beg you, therefore, to return You are, I bear you witness, Slothful and you help me nothing, so that I am half in conceit you affect not the Argument for my self, I know well you love and affect I can say no more to you, but *Non canimus furdis, respondent omnia Sylvæ* If you be not *of the Lodgings chalked up*, whereof I speak in my *Preface* [a], I am but to pass by your Door But if I had you a fortnight at *Gorhambury*, I wou'd make you tell me another tale, or elfe I wou'd add a *Cogitation* against Libraries, and be revenged on you that way

XIV

[a] There is no Preface of the Author to the *Cogitata & Vifa*, as publifhed by *Gruter*, and that whole Piece appears no more than a very imperfect Sketch of the firft Part of the *Novum Organum*, and never intended to be publifhed Yet as the Sentiments, fo far as they go, are generally the fame with thofe of the *Novum Organum*, it may not be amifs to know the Opinion entertain'd of them, by that very learned Gentleman Sir *Thomas Bodley* We will, therefore, here annex his Letter in Anfwer, as it fhould feem, to the Author upon that Subject

" I think you know I have read your *Cogitata & Vifa*, which I proteft I have done with
" great defire, reputing it a Token of your fingular Love, that you joined me with thofe of
" your chiefeft Friends, to whom you would commend the firft perufal of your Draught for
" which I pray give me leave to fay but this to you
" *Firft* That if the Depth of my Affection to your Perfon and Spirit, to your Work and
" your Words, and to all your Abilities, were as highly to be valued as your Affection is to
" me, it might walk with yours arm in arm, and claim your Love by juft Defert But there
" can be no comparifon, where our States are fo uneven, and our Means to demonftrate our
" Affections fo different infomuch that for my own, I muft leave it to be prized in the Na-
" ture that it is, and you fhall ever find it moft addicted to your worth
" As touching the Subject of your Book, you have fet on foot fo many rare and noble Spe-
" culations, as I cannot chufe but wonder (and I fhall wonder at it ever) that, your Expence
" of time confidered, in your publick Profeffion, which hath, in a manner, no acquaintance
" with Scholarfhip or Learning, you fhould have culled out the Quinteffence, and fucked up
" the Sap of the chiefeft kind of Learning
" For however, in fome Points, you vary altogether from that which is, and has been ever,
" the received Doctrine of our Schools, and was always by the wifeft, as ftill they have been
" deemed, of all Nations and Ages, adjudged the trueft yet it is apparent, that in thofe very
" Points, and in all your Propofals and Plots in that Book, you fhew yourfelf a Mafter Work-
" man
" For my felf, I muft confefs, and I fpeak it *ingenuè*, that for the matter of Learning, I
" am not worthy to be reckoned in the number of Smatterers And yet becaufe it may feem,
" that being willing to communicate your Treatife with your Friends, you are likewife wil-
" ling to liften to whatever I, or others can, except againft it I muft deliver to you, for my
" private opinion, that I am one of the Crew, that fay there is, and we profefs, a far greater
" Hold faft of Certainty in the Sciences, than you by your Difcourfe will feem to acknowledge
" For whereas, *firft*, you object the ill Succefs and Errors of Practitioners in Phyfick, you
" know as well they proceed from the Patient's Unrulinefs for not one of a hundred obeys
" his Phyfician, in obferving his Cautions, or by Mifinformations of their own Indifpofitions,
" for few are able in this kind to explain themfelves, or becaufe their Difeafes are by Nature
" incurable, which is incident, you know, to many forts of Maladies, or for fome other hid-
" den caufe, which cannot be difcovered by Courfe of Conjecture tho' I am full of this Be-
" lief, that as Phyfick is adminiftred now-a-days by Phyficians, it is much to be afcribed to
" their Negligence, or Ignorance, or other touch of Imperfection, that they fucceed no bet-
" ter in their Practice for few are found of that Profeffion, fo well inftructed in their Art,
" as they might be, by the Precepts which their Art affords which tho' it be defective in re-
" gard of fuch Perfection, yet for certain it flourifhes with admirable Remedies, fuch as tract
" of time has taught by experimental Events, and are the open Highway to that principal
" Knowledge you recommend
" As for Alchymy and Magick, fome Conclufions they have that are worthy the preferving,
" but all their Skill is fo accompanied with Subtleties and Guiles, as both the Crafts and Craft-
" mafters are not only defpifed, but named with Derifion whereupon, to make good your
" principal Affertion, methinks you fhould have drawn your Examples from that, which is
" taught in the liberal Sciences, not by picking out Cafes, that happen very feldom, and may
" by

XIV.

To the Bishop of ELY [a]; *along with the* Cogitata & Visa

NOW your Lordship has been so long in the Church and Palace, disputing between Kings and Popes [b], methinks you should take pleasure to look into the Field, and refresh your Mind, with some matter of Philosophy tho' that Science be now, thro' Age, grown a Child again,

" by all Confession be subject to Reproof, but by controlling the Generals and Grounds, and
" eminent Positions, and Aphorisms, which the greatest Artists and Philosophers have from
" time to time defended For it goes for current among Men of Learning, that those kind of
" Arts, which the Ancients term'd *Quadriviales*, confirm their Propositions by infallible De-
' monstrations

And likewise in the *Triviales*, such Lessons and Directions are delivered us, as will effect
" very near, or as much altogether, as every Faculty promises Now in case we should con
' cur to do as you advise, which is to renounce our common Notions, and cancel all our
' Theorems, Axioms Rules and Tenets, and so to come Babes *ad Regnum Naturæ*, as we are
" will'd by Scriptures to come *ad Regnum Cœlorum*, there is nothing more certain, in my
' Understanding, than that it would instantly bring us to Barbarism, and after many thousand
' Years, leave us more unprovided of theorical Furniture than we are at this present for that
" were indeed to become very Babes, or *Tabula rasa*, when we shall leave no Impression of
" any former Principles, but be driven to begin the World again, and to travel by trials of
" Axioms and Sense (which are your Proofs by Particulars) what to place *in Intellectu*, for our
" general Conceptions, it being a Maxim of all Men's approving, *in Intellectu nihil esse quod non
" prius fuit in Sensu* and so in appearance, it would befall us, that 'till *Plato's* Year be come
" about, our Insight in Learning would be of less Reckoning than now it is accounted

" As for that which you inculcate, of a Knowledge more excellent than now is among us,
" which Experience might produce, if we would but essay to extract it out of Nature by
" particular Probations it is no more, upon the matter, but to incite us unto that, which,
' without Instigation, by a natural Instinct, Men will practise of themselves For it cannot in
" reason be otherwise thought, but that there are infinite Numbers in all parts of the World,
" (for we may not in this Case confine our *Cogitations* within the Bounds of *Europe*,) which
' embrace the course that you propose, with all the Diligence and Care, that Ability can perform
" for every Man is born with an Appetite of Knowledge, wherewith he cannot be so glutted,
" but still, as in a Dropsy, thirst after more But yet why they should hearken to any such
" Persuasions, as wholly to abolish these settled Opinions and general Theorems, to which they
" attained by their own and their Ancestor's Experience, I see nothing yet alledged, to induce
" me to think it

" Moreover, I may speak, as I should suppose, with good Probability, that if we should
" make a mental Survey, what is likely to be effected all the World over, those five or six In
" ventions, which you have selected *, and imagine to be but of modern standing would make
' but a slender shew amongst so many hundreds of all kinds, and which are daily brought to
" light by the Enforcement of Wit, or casual Events, and may be compared, or partly pre
" ferred, above those that you have named

Bur were it so here, that all were admitted that you can require, for the Augmentation of
" our Knowledge, and that all our Theorems and general Positions were utterly extinguished
" with

* Suppose Printing, the Sea-Compass, Gunpowder, Ordnance, Silk, Sugar, Paper, &c

[a] Viz Dr *Andrews*, afterwards Bishop of *Winchester*
[b] He was concerned in the Dispute betwixt King *James*, *Bellarmine*, and *Baronius*

again, and left to Boys and young Men   And becaufe you uf d to make me believe you took a liking to my Writings, I fend you fome of this Vacation's Fruits, and thus much more of my Mind and Purpofe   I haften not to publifh, perifhing I would prevent, and I am forced to refpect, as well my times, as the matter.   For with me, 'tis thus, and I think, with all Men in my Cafe: if I bind my felf to an Argument, it loads my Mind,

but

" with a new Subftitution of others in their places, what hope may we have of any Benefit
" of Learning by this Alteration?

" Affuredly as foon as the new are brought, with their Additions, to Perfection, by the In-
" ventors and their Followers, by an interchangeable Courfe of natural things, they will fall by
" degrees to be buried in oblivion and fo on Continuance to perifh out-right, and that per-
" chance upon the like to your prefent Pretences, by propofal of fome means to advance our
" Knowledge to an higher pitch of Perfection . for ftill the fame Defects, that Antiquity found,
" will refide in Mankind   And therefore, other Iffues of their Actions, Devices, and Studies,
" are not to be expected, than, is apparent by Records, were in former times obferved

" I remember here a Note, which *Paterculus* made of the incomparable Wits of the *Greci-
" ans* and *Romans* in their flourifhing State, that there might be this Reafon of their notable
" Downfal in their Iffue that came after, becaufe by Nature, *Quod fummo ftudio petitum eft
" afcendit in fummum, difficilifque in perfecto mora eft*, infomuch that Men, perceiving
" they could go no further; being come to the top; they turned back again of their own ac-
" cord; forfaking thofe Studies that are moft in Requeft, and betaking themfelves to new En-
" deavours, as if the thing that they fought had been by prevention furprized by others

" So it fared in particular with the Eloquence of that Age, when their Succeffors found,
" they could hardly equal, by no means excel their Predeceffors, they began to neglect the
" Study thereof; and both to write and fpeak for many hundred Years in a ruftical Manner,
" till this later Revolution brought the Wheel about again, by inflaming gallant Spirits to give
" the Onfet afrefh, with ftraining and ftriving to climb to the top and height of Perfection,
" not in that Gift only, but in every other Skill in any part of Learning

" For I do not hold it an erroneous Conceit to think of every Science, that as now they
" are profeffed, fo they have been before in all precedent Ages, tho' not alike in all places,
" nor at all times alike in one and the fame place; but according to the Changings and Twi-
" nings of Times, with a more exact and plain, or with a more rude and obfcure kind of
" teaching   And if the Queftion fhould be asked, what proof I have of it, I have the Doc-
" trine of *Ariftotle*, and of moft of the learned Men, of whom we have any Means to take
" any notice, that as there is of other things, fo there is of Sciences, *ortus & interitus*, which
" is alfo the Meaning, if I fhould expound it, of *nihil novum fub Sole* and it is as we'l to be ap-
" plied *ad facta*, as *ad dicta, ut nihil neque dictum, neque factum, quod non fit dictum & fac-
" tum prius*   I have farther for my Warrant, that famous Complaint of *Solomon* to his Son,
" againft the infinite making of Books in his time, of which in all Congruity, it muft needs
" be underftood, that a great part were Obfervations and Inftructions in all kind of Literature,
" and of thofe there is not now fo much as one petty Pamphlet, only fome part of the Bible
" excepted, remaining to Pofterity

" As then there was not, in like manner, any footing to be found of millions of Authors, that
" were long before *Solomon*, and yet we muft give credit to what he affirmed that
" whatfoever was then, or had been before, it could never be truly pronounced of it, *Behold
" this is new*

" Whereupon I muft, for my final Conclufion, infer, feeing all the Endeavours, Study, and
" Knowledge of Mankind, in whatfoever Art or Science, have ever been the fame, as they are
" at this prefent, tho' full of Mutabilities according to the Changes and accidental Occafions
" of Ages and Countries, and learned Men s Difpofitions, which can never but be fubject to
" Intention and Remiffion, both in their Devices and Practices of their Knowledge, if now we
" fhould accord in Opinion with you   Firft, To condemn our prefent Knowledge of Doubts
" and Incertitudes which you confirm but by Averment, without other force of Argument,
" and then to difclaim all our Axioms and Maxims, and general Affertions, that are left by

2

but if I rid my Mind of the present Thought, 'tis rather a Recreation This has put me upon these *Miscellanies* [a], which I purpose to suppress, if God give me leave to write a just and perfect Volume of Philosophy [b] which I go on with, tho' slowly. I send not your Lordship too much, lest it should glut you. Now let me tell you what my desire is. If your Lordship be still so good, as when you were the good Dean of *Westminster*; my request is, that not by Points, but by Notes, you would mark to me whatever shall seem, either not current in the Stile, harsh to Credit and Opinion, or inconvenient for the Person of the Writer, for no Man can be Judge and Party: and when our Minds judge by Reflexion on our selves, they are more subject to Error. And tho', for the matter it self, my

Judgment

' Tradition from our Elders to us, which (for so it is to be pretended) have passed all Probations ' of the largest Wits that ever were. And *lastly*, to imagine, being now become again, as ' it were, *an secundum*, by the frequent spelling of Particulars, to come to the notice of the ' true Generals, and so at last to create new Principles of Sciences, the end of all would be, ' that when we shall be possessed of the Learning, which we have, all our consequent Tra- ' ditions will but help us in a Circle, to conduct us to the Place from whence we set forward, ' and bring us to the Happiness to be restored *in integrum* which will require as many Ages ' as have marched before us to be atchieved

" And this I write with no Dislike of increasing our Knowledge with new-found Devices; " which is undoubtedly a Practice of high Commendation, in regard of the Benefit they will " yield for the present, that the World has ever been, and will assuredly for ever continue, full " of such Devices, whose Industry has been very obstinate and eminent that Way, and has " produced strange Effects above the reach, and the hope of Men's common Capacities, and " yet our Notions and Theorems have always kept in Grace, both with them, and with the " rarest that ever were named among the Learned

" By this you see to what Boldness I am brought by your Kindness, that if I seem to be " too free in this Contradiction, it is the Opinion that I hold of your noble Disposition, and " of the Freedom in these Cases that you will afford your special Friend, that hath induced me " to do it. And although I my self, like a Carrier's Horse, cannot balk the beaten Way, in " which I have been trained, yet such is my Censure of your *Cogitata*, that I must tell you, ' to be plain, you have very much wronged your self and the World to smother such a Trea- ' sure so long in your Coffer, for though I stand well assured, for the tenor and subject of ' your main Discourse, you are not able to impannel a substantial Jury in any *University*, that " will give a Verdict to acquit you of Error yet it cannot be gain-said, but all your Treatise " abounds overabound with choice Conceits of the present State of Learning, and with so worthy ' Contemplations of the Means to procure it, as may persuade any Student to look more nar- " rowly to his Business, not only by aspiring to the greatest Perfection of that, which is now- " a days divulged in the Sciences, but by diving yet deeper into (as it were) the Bowels and ' Secrets of Nature, and by enforcing of the Powers of his Judgment and Wit, to learn of ' St. *Paul cujusdam meliora Dona* which Course, would to God (to whom I wish so much in your ' Ear, you had followed at the first, when you fell into the study of such a Study, as was " not worthy such a Student. Nevertheless, being so as it is, that you are therein so led, and ' our Country soundly served, I cannot but wish, with all my Heart, as I do very often, that ' you may gain a fit Reward to the full of your Deserts which I hope will come with heaps " of Happiness and Honour ∗

Fulham, Feb 19 1607

∗ *For Answer to the Doctrinal Points of this Letter, See* Nov Organ Part I Aph 92—115

Judgment be in some things fixed, and not accessible by any Man's Judgment that goes not my way, yet even in those things, the Admonition of a Friend may make me express my self differently [a]

XV.

To Sir GEORGE CAREW [b]; *presenting him the Memoir* in felicem Memoriam Elizabethæ.

BEing asked a Question by this Bearer, an old Servant of my Brother *Anthony Bacon's*, whether I would command him any thing into *France*, and being at better leisure than I would, in regard of Sickness; I began to remember, that neither your Business nor mine, tho' great and continual, can be, upon an exact Account, any just Occasion, why so much good-will as has passed between us, should be so much discontinued as it has been And therefore, because one must begin, I thought to provoke your Remembrance of me, by a Letter: and thinking to fill it with somewhat besides Salutations; it came to my mind, that this last Summer's Vacation, upon occasion of a factious Book, that endeavoured to verify, *Misera Fæmina*, (the Addition of the *Pope's Bull*,) upon Queen *Elizabeth*; I wrote a few Lines in her *Memorial* [c], which I thought you would be pleased to read; both for the Argument, and because you used to bear Affection to my Pen. *Verum, ut aliud ex alio*, if it came handsomely to pass, I would be glad the *President de Thou*, who has wrote a History of that Fame and Diligence, saw it, chiefly because it may perhaps serve him for some use in his History; wherein I should be glad he did right to the Truth, and to the Memory of that Lady, as I perceive, by what he has already written, he is well inclined to do. I should be glad also, it were some Occasion, such as Absence may permit, of some Acquaintance, or mutual Notice between us. For tho' he has many ways the precedence, yet this is common to us both, that we serve our Sovereigns in eminent places of Law, and not our selves only, but that our Fathers did so before us. And lastly, that both of us love Learning, and the liberal Sciences, which was ever a Bond of Friendship in the greatest distance of Places But of this I make no farther Request, than your own Occasions and Respects may advance or limit, my principal purpose being to salute you and send you this Token

XVI.

---

[a] The Author appears to have taken deliberate Advice concerning his *Novum Organum*, and has endeavoured to remove all the considerable Objections he could any way learn were made to it See *Part* I Sect IV V VI *&c* of that Work

[b] Sent Embassador to *Poland*, in the Year 1597, and Embassador to *France*, in the Year 1606

[c] See Pag 320, of the present Volume.

I

XVI.

To Mr. MATTHEWS; *along with a part of the* Instauration [a].

I Plainly perceive by your affectionate Writing, as to my Work, that one and the same thing affects us both; *viz* the good end whereto 'tis dedicated. for as to any Ability of mine, it cannot merit that Degree of Approbation As for your Caution about Church-men, and Church-Matters, for any impediment it might be to the Reputation of my Work; it moves me not, but as it may hinder the Fruit and Good which might come of a quiet and calm Paſſage to the good Port whereto 'tis bound, I hold it a juſt Reſpect, provided, that to fetch a fair Wind, I go not too far about. But the truth is, that I have no occaſion to meet them in my way, unleſs, as they will needs confederate themſelves with *Ariſtotle*, who, you know, is intemperately magnified by the School-men, and is alſo allied, as I take it, to the Jeſuits, by *Faber*, who was a Companion of *Loyola*, and a great *Ariſtotelian*. I ſend you at this time the only part which has any harſhneſs [b], and yet I framed to my ſelf an Opinion, that whoſoever allowed well of that *Preface* [c] you ſo much commend, will not diſlike, or at leaſt ought not to diſlike this other Speech of Preparation, for 'tis written out of the ſame Spirit, and out of the ſame Neceſſity nay, it does more fully lay open, that the Queſtion between me and the Antients, is not of the Virtue of the Race, but as to the Rightneſs of the Way. And to ſpeak truth, 'tis to the other but as *palma* to *pugnus*, part of the ſame thing, more at large You conceive right, that in this, and the other, you have Commiſſion to impart and communicate them to others, according to your Diſcretion Other Matters I write not of. For my ſelf, I am like the Miller of *Grantcheſter*, who uſed to pray for Peace among the Willows; for while the Winds blew, the Wind-Mills wrought, and the Water-Mill was leſs cuſtomed So I ſee that Controverſies of Religion muſt hinder the Advancement of the *Sciences* Let me conclude, with my perpetual Wiſh towards your ſelf, that the Approbation of your ſelf, by your diſcreet and temperate Carriage, may reſtore you to your Country, and your Fiends to your Society [d]

Grays-Inn, Octob 10 1609.

XVII.

---

[a] *Viz* the *Novum Organum*, or rather, perhaps, the *Cogitata & Viſa*; which was the Foundation of the *Novum Organum*

[b] See *Novum Organum* Part I Sect 2, 3, 4, &c

[c] See the Introduction to the *Nov Organ.* which probably is of the ſame Tenour with the unpubliſhed Preface to the *Cogitata & Viſa*

[d] This perhaps relates to Mr *Matthews's* having turned Papiſt.

XVII.

To the Lord Chancellor; with a Proposal for a compleat British History.

SOME late Act of his Majesty, referred to some former Discourse I have heard from your Lordship, bred in me a great Desire, and the strength of a Desire, a Boldness to make an humble Proposal to your Lordship, such as in me can be no better than a Wish, but which if your Lordship should apprehend it, may take some good and worthy Effect The Act I speak of, is the Order given by his Majesty for erecting a Monument for our late Sovereign Queen *Elizabeth* wherein I observe, that as her Majesty did always right to his Majesty's Hopes, so he does in all things right to her Memory a very just and princely Retribution But from this Occasion, by a very easy Ascent, I have passed farther, from the Representative of her Person, to the more true and feeling Representation of her Life and Government: for as Statues and Pictures are dumb Histories, so Histories are speaking Pictures; wherein, if my Affection be not too great, or my Reading too small, I am of opinion, that if *Plutarch* were alive to write Lives by Parallels, it would gravel him, both for Virtue and Fortune, to find her Parallel among Women And tho' she was of the passive Sex, yet her Government was so active, as, in my simple Opinion, it made more Impression upon the several States of *Europe*, than it received from thence But I confess to your Lordship, I could not stay here, but went a little farther into the Consideration of Times, which have passed since King *Henry* VIII, wherein I find the strangest Variety, that in so little number of Successions of any Hereditary Monarchy, has ever been known. The Reign of a Child; the Offer of an Usurpation, tho' it were but as a quotidian Ague, the Reign of a Lady married to a Foreigner; and the Reign of a Lady solitary and unmarried. so that, as it comes to pass in massy Bodies, that they have certain trepidations and waverings before they fix and settle, it seems, that by the Providence of God, this Monarchy, before 'twas to settle in his Majesty, and his Generations, has had its prelusive Changes in these barren Princes. Neither could I contain my self here; but calling to remembrance the Unworthiness of the History of *England* [a], in the grand Continuance thereof, and the Partiality and Obliquity of that of *Scotland*, in the latest and largest Author that I have seen; I conceived it would be Honour for his Majesty, and a Work very memorable, if this Island of *Great Britain*, as 'tis now join'd in Monarchy for the Ages to come; so it were join'd in History for the Times past, and that one just and compleat History were compiled of both Nations. And if any.

---

[a] See Pag. 50, and 52, of this *Volume.*

... In case I think, it may refresh the Memory of former Discords, he ... ... with this Verse, *o ... bæc meminisse juvabit* for the Case being not altered, 'tis a Matter of Comfort and Gratulation to remember other Troubles. Thus much, if it may please your Lordship, is in the optative Mood, and 'tis time that I look'd a little into the Potential, wherein the hope I conceived was grounded upon three Observations. *First*, The nature of these times, flourishing in Learning, both of Art and Language, which gives hope, not only that it may be done, but that it may be well done. *Second*, I see that which all the World sees in his Majesty, both a wonderful Judgment in Learning, and a singular Affection towards Learning, and Works which are of the Mind, more than of the Hand. For there cannot be the like Honour sought and found, in building of Galleries, and planting of Elms along Highways, and in such outward Ornaments, wherein *France* is now so busy, as there is in the uniting of States, settling of Controversies, nourishing and augmenting of Learning and Arts, and the particular Actions appertaining to these, of which kind *Cicero* judged truly, when he said to *Cæsar, quantum operibus tuis detrahet vetustas, tantum addet laudibus*. And *Third*, I call to mind, that your Lordship, at some times, has express'd to me a great desire, that something of this nature should be perform'd, answerable indeed to your other noble and worthy Courses and Actions, joining and adding to the great Services towards his Majesty, other great Deservings, both of the Church, Commonwealth, and particular Men. So that the opinion of so great and wise a Man, seems to me a good Warrant, both of the Possibility and Worth of this matter. But all this while, I assure my self, I cannot be so far mistaken by your Lordship, as if I sought an Office or Employment for my self: for no Man knows better than your Lordship, that if there were in me any Faculty thereto, yet neither my Course of Life, nor Profession, would permit it. But as there are so many good Painters, both for Hand and Colours, it needs only Encouragement and Instructions to give life to it. Thus in all Humbleness I conclude, presenting to your Lordship this Wish, which, if it perish, 'tis but a loss of that which is not

XVIII.

To the KING; *relating to the History of his Majesty's Times.*

HEaring your Majesty is at leisure to peruse History, a desire took me to make an experiment what I cou'd do in your Majesty's Times; which being but a leaf or two, I beg your pardon, if I send it for your Recreation; considering that Love must creep, where it cannot go. But to this I add these Petitions. *First*, That if your Majesty dislike any thing, you wou'd conceive I can amend it upon the least beck. *Next*, That if I have

not

not fpoken of your Majefty encomiaftically, you would be pleas'd only to afcribe it to the Law of a Hiftory, which does not clutter together Praifes upon the firft mention of a Name, but rather difperfes, and weaves them through the whole Narrative. And as for the proper place of Commemoration, which is in the Period of Life, I pray God I may not live to write it *Thirdly,* That the reafon why I prefum'd to think of this Oblation, was becaufe, whatever my inability be, yet I fhall have that advantage, which almoft no Writer of Hiftory has had; for I fhall write of Times, not only fince I cou'd remember, but fince I cou'd obferve And *laftly,* that 'tis only for your Majefty's reading [a]

XIX.

To the Univerfity of CAMBRIDGE; *upon prefenting them his Book* De Sapientia Veterum.

AS I would not wifh to live without the Helps and Comforts of Philofophy, I muft have the higheft value for the place that derived them to me. And as, on this account, I profefs both my felf, and all that is mine, owing to you, 'tis the lefs wonder if I reftore you what is your own; that it may return, by a natural motion, to its Origin. And yet I know not how, there are but few things return'd to you, tho' numberlefs have proceeded from you

It may not, perhaps, be too affuming if I fhould hope, that by a moderate Converfation with things, which my Courfe and Manner of Life has neceffarily brought along with it, I have made fome addition to the Difcoveries of learned Men I am well perfuaded that Contemplations, transferr'd to active Life, acquire fomewhat of new Grace and Vigour and perhaps where a plentiful ftock of matter is fupplied, they take deeper root, or at leaft grow taller and more leafy. Neither, poffibly, may you yourfelves be aware, how extenfive your own Learning is, or to how many things it may be applied. 'Tis however but juftice to attribute the whole to you, as all increafe is principally owing to the firft Beginnings From a Man of full employ you will not expect any thing finifh'd, or a prodigy of time and leifure· but attribute it to my affection for you, that among the Thorns of civil Bufinefs, thefe Seeds have not quite been choak'd, but that your own has been prefei v'd for you [b].

XX.

[a] See the Sketch here mention d, pag 303 of this Volume
[b] See *Supplement* VII

XX.

To the Earl of SALISBURY[a]; *presenting him the Book* De Sapientia Veterum.

WHatever is dedicated to the University of *Cambridge*, belongs to you of course, by your right of Chancellorship, but all, that I can give, is due to you in your own particular. The thing moft to be confidered is, whether what I here present, as your due, be worthy of you. and if the leaft thing therein, the Genius of the Author, prove, through your good opinion of me, no Obftacle; the reft will be no Difhonour to you. For if the Time be weigh'd, primitive Antiquity has the higheft Veneration, if the Form of teaching, *Parable* is like the Ark, wherein the richeft Treafures of the Sciences are preferved; if the Matter of the Work, 'tis *Philofophy*, the fecond Ornament of Life, and of the human Soul. For altho' Philofo phy, now as in its old Age, growing childifh again, is with us given up to young Men and Children; yet, next to Religion, I judge it of all things the moft momentous, and moft worthy of human Nature. Nay, civil Policy, in which you are fo great a Mafter, flows from this Fountain, and makes no fmall part of it.

But if any one fhall think the matters here treated are trite and vulgar, I do not take upon me to judge of my own Performance, but have endeavoured to go deeper than firft Appearances, beaten Paths, or the Roads of Com- mon-Place, and to produce fomewhat towards the higher parts of Life, and the Secrets of the Sciences. The Fables may indeed be vulgar things to vulgar Capacities, but they perhaps require, and I hope will find, fub- limer Underftandings to fathom them. But whilft I endeavour to r flect fome Dignity upon the Work, becaufe 'tis dedicated to you, I run the rifque of paffing the Bounds of Modefty, as I am the Author. Be it as it will, I defire you wou'd receive it as a Token of the Affection, and high Reverence I bear you, and afford it the fhelter of your Name.

XXI.

To Mr. MATTHEWS; *along with the Book* De Sapientia Veterum.

IHeartily thank you for your Letter, of the 24th of *Auguft*, from *Sala- manca*, and, in recompence, fend you a little Work of mine, that has begun to pafs the World. They tell me my *Latin* is turned into Silver,

and

---

[a] Lord High Treafurer of *England*, and Chancellor of the Univerfity of *Cambridge*.

and become current. Had you been here, you shou'd have been my Inquisitor, before it came forth. but I think the greatest Inquisitor in *Spain* will allow it. One thing you must pardon me, if I make no haste to believe, that the World should be grown to such an Ecstasy, as to reject Truth in Philosophy, because the Author dissents in Religion; no more than they do by *Aristotle* or *Averroes*. My great Work goes forward, and after my manner, I always alter when I add· So that nothing is finish'd 'till all is finish'd. This I have wrote in the midst of a Term and Parliament, thinking no time so possess'd, but that I should talk of these Matters with so good and dear a Friend

    Gray's-Inn, Feb. 27, 1610.

XXII.

To his Brother, Sir JOHN CONSTABLE; *dedicating a new Edition of his* Essays.

MY last *Essays* I dedicated to my dear Brother, Mr *Anthony Bacon*[a], who is with God. Looking amongst my Papers this Vacation, I found others of the same Nature which, if I my self shall not suffer to be lost, it seems the World will not, by the often printing of the former Missing my Brother, I have found you next, in respect of Bond, both of near Alliance, and of strict Friendship and Society; and particularly of Communication in Studies wherein I must acknowledge my self beholden to you. For as my Business found rest in my Contemplations, so my Contemplations ever found rest in your loving Conference and Judgment.

    1612.

XXIII.

To Mr. MATTHEWS; *upon the Subject of his Writings.*

I Heartily thank you for your Letter, of the tenth of *February*; and I am glad to receive from you Matter of Encouragement and Advertisement about my Writings. For my part, I wish, that since there is no *Lumen siccum* in the World, but all *madidum*, and *maceratum*, infused in Affections, and Bloods or Humours, that these Things of mine had such Separations as might make them more acceptable· provided they claim'd not so much acquaintance with the present Times, as to be thereby less apt to last And to shew you that I purpose to new mould them, I send you a Leaf or two of the Preface, carrying some Figure of the whole Work; wherein I propose to

take

[a] See above *Letter* I

take what I count real and effectual of both Writings ᵃ And chiefly, to add a Pledge, if not Payment, to my Promises, I send you also a Memorial of Queen *Elizabeth* ᵇ, to requite your Eulogy of the late Duke of *Florence*'s Felicity Of this, when you were here, I shew'd you a Model, when I thought, you seem'd more willing to hear *Julius Cæsar* commended than Queen *Elizabeth* But this I now send you is more full, and has more of the Narrative and besides has one part which, I think, will not be disagreeable either to you, or that place, being the true Tract of her Proceedings towards the Catholicks which are infinitely mistaken And tho' I do not imagine they will pass there, yet they will gain upon excuse I find Mr. *le Zure* to use you well I mean his Tongue of you, which shews you either honest, or wise but this I speak merrily For in truth, I conceive hope, you will so govern yourself, that we may take you as assuredly for a good Subject and Patriot, as you take yourself for a good Christian, and so we again enjoy your Company, and you your Conscience, if it may no otherways be. For my part, assure yourself, as we say in the Law, *mutatis mutandis*, my Love and good Wishes to you are not diminish'd ᶜ.

XXIV.

To Mr. MATTHEWS; *upon the Memorial of the Felicities of Queen* Elizabeth, *and the* Instauration.

I Thank you for your last ; and beg you would believe, that your liberty in giving opinion of those Writings I sent you, is what I sought, expected, and take in exceeding good part so that it makes me continue my hearty Wishes for your Company here, to use the same liberty upon my Actions, as you now exercise upon my Writings For that of Queen *Elizabeth*, your Judgment, of the Temper and Truth of the Part which concerns some of her foreign Proceedings, concurs fully with the Judgment of some others, and as Things go, I suppose they are likely to be more and more justified and allowed And, as you say, for another Part, that it opens a broad Way to a Field of Contradiction ; on the other side, 'tis written me from the Leiger at *Paris*, and some others, that it *carries a manifest Impression of Truth, and ever convinces as it goes* These are their very Words, which I write not for my own Glory, but to shew what variety of opinion rises from the disposition of several Readers. And I must confess my desire to be, that my Writings should not court the present Time, or some few Places, so as to make them either less general, or less permanent in future Ages
For

ᵃ I conceive this relates to the Author's *Cogitata & Visa*, whereof there were several Copies, in different Forms, and at length the whole was published by the Author, in the form of the first or preliminary Part of his *Novum Organum*
ᵇ See pag 320, of the present Volume.
ᶜ See above Letter XIII

For the *Instauration*[a]; I read your full Approbation thereof, with much Pleasure, as my Heart is much more upon it, and as I less expected your Concurrence in a Matter so obscure Of this I can assure you, that though many Things of great hope decay with Youth, and tho' Multiplicity of Civil Business uses to diminish the price of Contemplations; yet the proceeding in that Work gains upon my Affection and Desire, both by Years and Business. And therefore I hope, even by this, that 'tis well-pleasing to God, from whom, and to whom, all Good moves[b].

XXV.

To Sir HENRY SAVILLE[c]; *concerning a* Discourse *upon the* INTELLECTUAL POWERS.

REturning from your Invitation at *Eaton*, where I had refresh'd my self with Company I loved, I fell into a Consideration of that part of Policy, whereof Philosophy speaks too much, and Laws too little, *viz the Education of Youth* Whereupon fixing my Mind a while, I soon found and noted in the Discourses of Philosophers, which are so large on this Subject, a strange Silence concerning one principal Part, as to the framing and seasoning of Youth to moral Virtues They handle it indeed, but as to the Improvement and Help of the intellectual Powers, for instance the Imagination, Memory, and Judgment, they say nothing whether they thought it a matter, wherein Nature only prevail'd, or referred it to the several Arts, which teach the use of Reason and Speech. But for the former, however they distinguish betwixt Habits and Powers, it is manifest by Experience, that the Motions and Faculties of the Wit and Memory may not only be governed and guided, but also confirm'd and enlarged by Custom, and Practice duly applied, as a Man, by the practice of shooting, will not only learn to come nearer the Mark, but also to draw a stronger Bow And for comprehending these Precepts within the Arts of *Logick* and *Rhetorick*, if it be rightly considered, their Office is altogether distinct from this point for 'tis no part of the Doctrine of the use of an Instrument, to teach how to whet or grind it, how to quench it, or give it a stronger Temper Wherefore, finding this part of Knowledge not broken, I have, but *tanquam aliud agens*, entered into it, and salute you with it. dedicating it, after the ancient manner, first to a dear Friend, and next to a proper Person, as you have both Place to practise it, and Judgment and Leisure to look deeper into it Herein I must call you to mind, Ἄριϛον μεν ὕδωρ. For though the Argument be not of great Depth and Dignity, 'tis of great and universal use Nor do I see why, to consider it rightly, that shou'd not be a Learning of Dignity, which

S ſſ 2

teaches

---

[a] *Viz* The *Novum Organum*

[b] See the Letter to Father *Fulgentio*, at the end of this Section

[c] The Founder of a Geometry and Astronomy Professorship at *Oxford*, and the Editor of St *Chrysostom's* Works, *&c*

teaches to raise and ennoble the highest and worthiest part of the Mind. But however that be, if the World receives any Benefit from this Writing, let the Thanks be to the good Friendship and Acquaintance between us.

The first Draught of a Discourse upon Helps for the INTELLECTUAL POWERS [a].

I Ever held it for an infolent and unlucky Saying, *Faber quifque Fortunæ fuæ*, except it be meant only as a Hortative, or Spur, to correct Sloth otherwise, if it be taken as it founds, and a Man enters into a high Imagination, that he can compafs and fathom all Accidents, and afcribes all Succeffes to his Drifts and Reaches, and the contrary, to his Slips and Errors · 'tis commonly feen, that the evening Fortune of that Man is not fo profperous, as of him, who, without flacking his Induftry, attributes much to Felicity and Providence above him But if the Sentence run thus, *Faber quifque Ingenii fui*, it were fomewhat true, and much more profitable Becaufe it would teach Men to bend themfelves, to reform those Imperfections they now feek but to cover, and to attain those Virtues, which they now feek to have only in appearance and fhew. Yet every Man attempts to be of the *firft* Trade of Carpenters, and few bind themfelves to the *fecond* · tho' the rifing in Fortune feldom mends the Mind. On the other hand, the removing of the Stands and Impediments of the Mind, often clears the Paffage and Current to a Man's Fortune But 'tis certain, that as the moft excellent of Metals, Gold, is of all others the fofteft, and moft ductile; fo the perfecteft of breathing Subftances, Man, is the moft fufceptible of Help, Improvement, Impreffion, and Alteration, not only in his Body, but in his Mind and Spirit · and there again, not only in his Appetite and Affections, but in his Faculties of Wit and Reafon

As to the human Body, we find many ftrange Inftances, how Nature is mafter'd by Cuftom, even in Actions that feem of the greateft Difficulty, and leaft Poffibility Thus in the Improvement of voluntary Motions, what furprifing things are effected by the Application and Practice of Tumblers and Rope-dancers, as to feats of Activity and Agility ? And again in fuffering Pain, which is thought fo contrary to the Nature of Man, there are many Examples of Penances, in ftrict Orders of Superftitions, that may well verify the Report of the *Spartan* Boys, fcourged upon the Altar fo cruelly that they fometimes died thereof; and yet were never heard to complain And, for those Faculties, reckoned more involuntary, as Fafting, and Abftinence, Voracity, great Drinking, living without Drink, enduring vehement Cold, &c there are various Examples of ftrange Victories over the Body.

Nay, as to Refpiration, fome by the continual Ufe of Diving and Working under the Water, have brought themfelves to hold their Breath an incredible while, and others been able, without Suffocation, to endure the ftifling Breath

of

---

[a] Both the preceding *Letter*, and the following *Draught*, feem put down rather in the way of——, for farther Correction, Improvement, and Enlargement, than as any thing finished, —— for the Prefs

of an Oven or Furnace. Some Impoftors and Counterfeits, likewife, have been able to wreath and turn their Bodies into ftrange Forms and Poftures; and others to bring themfelves into Trances, &c all which demonftrate how varioufly, and to what a high pitch, the Body of Man may be moulded and wrought.

If it be objected that it is fome fecret Property of Nature in thefe Perfons, whereby they have attain'd to thofe Points, and that 'tis not for every Man to do the like, tho' he had been put to it, whence fuch things come but rarely to pafs 'Tis true, fome Perfons are apter than others, but tho' the greater Aptnefs caufes Perfection, yet the lefs does not difable fo that the more apt Child, taken to be made a Rope-dancer, will prove more excellent, but the lefs apt will be a Rope-dancer too, tho' of the fecond Rank And doubt-lefs thefe Abilities wou'd have been more common, and others of the fame kind have been likewife brought upon the Stage, but for two Reafons the one, becaufe of Men's diffidence in prejudging them as Impoffibilities, for it holds in thefe things, as the Poet fays, *poffunt quia poffe videntur*; for no Man will know how much may be done, unlefs he believe that a great deal may be done The other Reafon is, becaufe they are Practices ignoble and inglorious, of no great ufe, and therefore excluded from the Reward of Value and, on the other fide, they are painful; fo that the Recompence balances not the Labour.

And for the Will of Man, this is of all things moft manageable and obedient, or admits many Medicines to cure and alter it. The moft fovereign of all is *Religion*, which proves able to change and transform the Will in the deepeft and moft inward Inclinations and Motions *Next* to this is *Opinion* and *Apprehenfion*, whether infufed by Tradition and Teaching, or wrought in by Difpute and Perfuafion. The *third* is *Example*, which transforms the Will into the Similitude of what is moft familiar to it. The *fourth* is, when one Affection heals and corrects another; as when Cowardice is cured by Shame and Difhonour, or Sluggifhnefs and Backwardnefs, by Indignation and Emulation, and fo of the like. And *laftly*, when all thefe Means, or any of them, have new formed the human Will, then Cuftom and Habit corroborates and confirms the reft No wonder, therefore, if this Faculty of the Will, which inclines the Affection and Appetite, as being but the Beginnings and Rudiments of the Will, may befo well managed, fince it admits accefs to fuch various Remedies. The Effects hereof are fo numerous, and fo well known, as to require no Enumeration, but generally they proceed as Medicines - which are of two kinds, Curative and Palliative · for either the intention is really and truly to reform the Affections, reftrain them if too violent, and raife them if too foft and weak; or elfe to cover them, or, if occafion be, to act and reprefent them. Of the former fort, Examples are plentiful in the Schools of Philofophers, and all other Inftitutions of moral Virtue, and of the other fort, Examples are more plentiful in the Courts of Princes, and all political Traffick where 'tis ordinary to find, not only deep Diffimulations, which fo fuffocate the Affections, that no Mark appears of them

QUE-

outwardly , but also lively Simulations and Affectations, carrying the tokens of Passions which are not real , as Laughter, Tears, &c [a].

XXVI.

To Mr. MATTHEWS; *entreating Judgment upon his Writings.*

BEcause you should not lose your Labour this Afternoon, which I must needs spend with my Lord *Chancellor* [b], I desire you will not leave the Writing, I left you last, with any Man, so long, as that he may take a Copy of it , because, first, it must be censured by you, and then considered again by me.   The thing I most expect from you is, that you would read it carefully over by your self, and make some little Note in Writing, where you think, that I do, perhaps *indormiscere* , or where I do *indulgere Genio* , or where, in fine, I give any manner of Disadvantage to my self   This, *super totam materiam*, you must not fail to note , besides, all such Words and Phrases as you cannot like   for you know in how high Esteem I have your Judgment

XXVII.

Dedication of the NOVUM ORGANUM *to King* James.

YOUR Majesty may perhaps accuse me of Theft , in stealing from your Affairs so much Time, as is necessary for a Work of this nature [c] I have no Excuse to plead   for there is no making a Restitution of Time , unless, possibly, if the Things I here offer, shou'd prove of value , the Time, that was taken from your Business, may be paid back to the Memory of your Name, and the Honour of your Reign   This I may say of them, they are every way new, tho' copied from a very old Original , the World itself, and the Nature of the Mind and of Things   And to declare my Thoughts freely , I usually esteem this Work more as the Birth of Time than of Genius   The only strange part is, how the Seeds of the Matter, and such strong Suspicions of the Weakness of the Things that have so long prevail'd,could come into any one's Mind · for all the rest will easily follow

And, without dispute, there is somewhat fortuitous, or casual, in the Thoughts of Men, as well as in their Actions and Discourse   But for this
Calu-

---

[a] This Piece was left very imperfect and only a few loose Hints farther added, in order to [...] beingcontinued   See *de Augm Scient* Pag 195,—197, &c
[b] This seem pleasantly meant of himself, being perhaps at this time Chancellor , and the Letter regarding some part of the *Novum Organum*
[c] This Piece was publish'd whilst the Author was Chancellor

Cafualty ; if there be any Good in what is here produced, I owe it, *first*, to the boundlefs Mercy and Goodnefs of God , and *next*, to the Felicity of your Times that as, whilft living, I have ferved your Majefty with the finceref Affection, I may perhaps, when I am dead, hold out a Light to Pofterity, by this new *Touch*, fet up in the Obfcurity of *Philofophy*[a]. And doubtlefs, the Reftoration and new Building up of the Sciences, is a Work well befitting the Times of the wifeft and moft learned of our Kings.

And here I have a Petition to offer, no way unworthy of your Majefty , but of the utmoft importance to the Work in view 'Tis this , that fince in many Inftances you refemble *Solomon* , as in your difcerning Judgment , the Peace of your Kingdom , the Largenefs of your Heart , and the noble Variety of the Books you have compofed , you would go on to imitate that King , and, after his Example, procure fuch a juft and fcrupulous *Natural and Experimental Hiftory* to be collected, as may fupply Materials for a found and ferviceable Philofophy[b] that at laft, after fo many Ages of the World are run, *Philofophy* and the *Sciences* may no longer remain pendant and airy; but be fettled upon the folid Foundations of an univerfal and thoroughly weighed Experience. I have fupplied the *Crane*[c] , but the *Materials* for the Building muft be fetched from Things themfelves.

XXVIII.

To the Univerfity of Cambridge; *upon prefenting the* Novum Organum *to their Public Library.*

AS I am your Son and Pupil, it will be a Pleafure for me to give into your Bofom, the Birth I am lately delivered of , and fhould otherwife efteem as a Child expofed. Be not concerned, that the Way I tread is new; for fuch Things muft neceffarily happen thro' the Revolutions of Times and of Ages. The Ancients are ftill left in poffeffion of their Glory , the Glory of Genius and fine Parts · but for *Faith* , that is only due to the *Word of God*, and to *Experience* To bring the *Sciences* back to *Experience* is impoffible, but to build them up a-new from Experience, tho' it be a Work of difficulty, is ftill practicable

York-Houfe, *Octob* 3. 1620

XXIX

---

[a] The Author feems once to have defigned *Novum Lumen Scientiarum*, for his Title, inftead of *Novum Organum*

[b] See the Method of compiling this Hiftory, Vol III pag 8,—16

[c] *Organum præbui* This may fhew that the Tte *Novum Organum*, has a Metaphorical Senfe. See the Author's Introduction to the Piece Vol II pag 338

XXIX.

To the King, presenting the History of HENRY VII. *and a Proposal for a new Digest of the Laws of* England.

I Acknowledge my self, in all humility, infinitely obliged to your Majesty's Grace and Goodness, for that, at the Intercession of my noble and constant Friend, my Lord *Marquis*, your Majesty has been pleased to grant me, that which the Civilians say is *res inæstimabilis*, my Liberty So that now, whenever God calls me, I shall not die a Prisoner Nay, farther, your Majesty has vouchsafed to cast a second and iterate Aspect of your Eye of Compassion upon me; in referring the Consideration of my broken Estate to my good Lord the Treasurer: which, as it is a singular Bounty in your Majesty, so I have yet so much left of a late Commissioner of your Treasury, that I would be sorry to sue for any thing, that might seem immodest These your Majesty's great Benefits, *in casting your Bread upon the Waters*, because my Thanks cannot any ways be sufficient to attain; I have raised your Progenitor, of famous Memory, and now, I hope, of more famous Memory than before, King *Henry* VII. to give your Majesty thanks for me. which Work, most humbly kissing your Majesty's Hands, I do present And because in the beginning of my Trouble, when in the midst of the Tempest, I had a kenning of the Harbour, which I hope now by your Majesty's Favour I am entring into, I made a tender to your Majesty of two Works, a History of *England*, and a *Digest of your Laws* as I have performed a Part of the one, so I have herewith sent your Majesty, by way of an Epistle, a new Offer of the other [a] But my desire is farther, if it stand with your Majesty's good Pleasure, since now my Study is my Exchange, and my Pen my Factor, for the use of my Talent, that your Majesty, who is a great Master in these things, would be pleased to appoint me some Task to write, and that I shall take for an Oracle. And because my *Instauration*, which I esteem my great Work, and do still go on with in silence, was dedicated to your Majesty; and this History of King *Henry* VII. to your lively and excellent Image, the Prince if now your Majesty will be pleased to give me a Theme, to dedicate to my Lord of *Buckingham*, whom I have so much reason to honour, I should with more Alacrity embrace your Majesty's Direction than my own Choice. Your Majesty will pardon me for troubling you thus long.

Gorhambury, *March* 20 1621

XXX.

[a] See Supplement XIV

XXX.

DEDICATION *of the* HISTORY OF WINDS *to Prince*
CHARLES.

THE First-Fruit of my *Natural History* [a], is here most humbly offered to your Highness and tho' it be a thing very small in bulk,
like a Grain of Mustard-Seed, 'tis still an *Earnest* of what, God willing,
shall follow For I have obliged my self, as it were by a Vow, every
Month of my Life, to publish one or more Parts thereof, according as
the Subject shall prove more or less difficult or copious And, perhaps,
others may, by my Example, be stirred up to the like Industry, especially
after they shall thoroughly understand the Nature of the Business on foot.
for in a just and well-appointed *Natural History*, are lodged the Keys both
of the Sciences, and of Works

XXXI.

To the Duke of BUCKINGHAM, *Lord High Admiral of*
ENGLAND; *dedicating the last Edition of his Essays.*

SOlomon says, *a good Name is as precious Ointment*; and I assure my self,
such will your Grace's Name be with Posterity. For your Fortune
and Merit have both been eminent, and you have planted Things that are
likely to last I now publish my *Essays*, which of all my Works have
been most current because, as it seems, they come home to Mens Business
and Bosoms I have enlarged them, both in Number and Weight, so that
they are, indeed, a new Work I thought it, therefore, agreeable to my Affection and Obligation to your Grace, to prefix your Name to them, both
in *English* and *Latin* for I conceive, that the *Latin* Volume of them, being
in the universal Language, may last as long as Books last. My *Instaura-*
tion [b] I have dedicated to the King, my History of *Henry* the Seventh, and
my Portions of Natural History, to the Prince, and these I dedicate to
your Grace, being the best Fruits, that, by the good increase which God
gives to my Pen and Labours, I could yield

[a] See Vol III pag 8 —16
[b] Viz The *Novum Organum*

XXXII.

To the Bishop of WINCHESTER[2]; *concerning the Author's published and intended Writings.*

REprefenting to one's felf like Examples of Calamity in others, is no fmall Confolation For Examples have a quicker Impreffion than Arguments, and at the fame time certify us, *that no new Thing has happened to us* This they do the better, the more the Examples are alike in Circumftances to our own, efpecially, if they happen in Perfons greater and worthier than our felves For as it favours of Vanity, to match our felves highly in our own Conceit, 'tis, on the other hand, a found Conclufion, that if our Betters have felt the like Misfortunes, we have the lefs caufe to be grieved

In this kind of Confolation, I have not been wanting to my felf tho' as a Chriftian, I have tafted, thro' God's Goodnefs, of higher Remedies. Having therefore, thro' the Variety of my Reading, fet before me many Examples, both of ancient and later times, my thoughts have chiefly refted upon three Particulars, as the moft eminent and the moft refembling All three were Perfons that had held high place of Authority in their Countries, all three ruined, not by War, or other Difafter, but by Juftice and Sentence, as Delinquents and Criminals, all three famous Writers, infomuch that the remembrance of their Calamities is now to Pofterity, but as a little Picture of Night-work, remaining among the fair and excellent Tables of their Acts and Works and all three fit Examples to quench any Man's Ambition of rifing again, for they were every one of them reftored with great Glory, only to their farther Ruin and Deftruction, ending in a violent Death The Men were *Demofthenes, Cicero,* and *Seneca,* Perfons that I durft not claim affinity with, if the fimilitude of our Fortunes had not contracted it When I had confidered thefe Examples, I was carried on farther to obferve, how they bore their Fortunes, and principally how they employ'd their Time, when banifhed, and difabled for publick Bufinefs that I might learn by them ; and they be as well my Counfellors as my Comforters. And here I noted how differently their Fortunes wrought upon them, efpecially as to employing their Time and Pen *Cicero,* during his Banifhment, which lafted almoft two Years, was fo foftened and dejected, that he wrote nothing but a few womanifh Epiftles. Yet, in my opinion, he had leaft reafon of the three to be difcouraged for altho' it was judged by the higheft kind of Judgment, in form of a Statute, or Law, that he fhould be banifhed, his whole Eftate confifcated and

seized,

feized, his Houfes pulled down, and that it fhould be highly penal for any Man to propofe a Repeal, yet his Cafe, even then, had no great blot of Ignominy, for it was thought but a Tempeft of Popularity that overthrew him *Demoſthenes*, on the contrary, tho' his Cafe was black, being condemned for Bribery, and not fimple Bribery, but Bribery in the nature of Treafon, and Difloyalty, yet took fo little notice of his Fortune, that during his Banifhment, he intermeddled confiderably with political Matters, and took upon him to counfel the State, as if he had been ftill at the Helm, as appears from fome Epiftles of his, which are extant *Seneca*, indeed, who was condemned for many Corruptions and Crimes, and banifhed into a folitary Ifland, kept a mean, and tho' his Pen did not freeze, yet he abftained from intruding into Matters of Bufinefs, but fpent his time in writing upon excellent Subjects, of ufe for all Ages.

These Examples confirmed me in my Refolution, whereto I was otherwife inclined, of employing my time wholly in Writing, and to put that Talent, or Half-Talent, that God has given me, not as before, to particular Exchanges, but to Banks or Mounts of Perpetuity, which will not break Therefore, having lately publifhed a part of my *Inftauration*, which is the Work, that in my own Judgment I moft efteem [a], I think to proceed in fome new Parts thereof And tho' I have received from many places abroad, fuch Teftimonies, with relation to that Work, as I could not expect at firft, in fo abftrufe an Argument, yet I have juft caufe to doubt, that it flies too high over Mens Heads I therefore purpofe, tho' I break the Order of Time, to draw it down to the Senfe, by fome Examples of Natural Hiftory and Enquiry.

And as my Book of the *Advancement of Learning*, may be fome Preparative, or Key, for the better opening of the *Inftauration*, becaufe it exhibits a Mixture of new and old Thoughts, whereas the *Novum Organum* gives the new unmixed, otherwife than with fome little fprinkling of the old for the Tafte's fake, I have thought proper to procure a Tranflation of that Book into the general Language, with great and ample Additions and Enrichments, efpecially in the fecond Part, which treats of the Divifion of the Sciences, infomuch, as to ferve for the firft part of the *Inftauration*, and acquit my promife in that part

Again, becaufe I cannot altogether defert the civil Character I have born, which if I fhould forget, enow would remember, I have alfo entered into a *Work of Laws*, propofing a Character of Juftice in a middle Term, between the fpeculative and grave Difcourfes of Philofophers, and the Writings of Lawyers, which are tied and obnoxious to their particular Laws [b] And altho' I purpofed to make a particular Digeft, or Recomplement of the Laws of my own Nation, yet, as 'tis a Work of Affiftance, and what I cannot mafter by my own Forces and Pen, I have laid it afide

Now

---

[a] The *Novum Organum*
[b] See Vol 1 Pag 242—261

Now having in the Work of my *Instauration* had a View to the general good of Men, in their very Being, and the Dowries of Nature, and in my Work of Laws, to the general Good of Men in Society, and the Dowries of Government, I thought that in Duty I owed somewhat to my own Country, which I ever loved insomuch, that altho' my Place has been far above my Desert, yet my Thoughts and Cares concerning the Good thereof, were beyond, and over and above my Place So now being, as I am, no more able to do my Country Service, it remains that I do it Honour which I have endeavoured in my Work of the Reign of King *Henry* the Seventh.

As for my *Essay*, and some other Particulars of that nature, I count them but as the Recreations of my other Studies, and in that manner purpose to continue them tho' I am not ignorant that those kind of Writings would, with less pains and assiduity, perhaps, yield more Lustre and Reputation to my Name, than the others I have in hand. But I judge the use a Man should seek in publishing his Writings before his Death, to be but an untimely Anticipation of that which is proper to follow, and not to go along with him

An. 1622

XXXIII.

To Dr. WILLIAMS, *Bishop of* Lincoln; *concerning the Author's* Letters *and* Speeches.

I Find that the Antients, as *Cicero*, *Demosthenes*, the younger *Pliny*, and others, have preserved both their *Orations* and *Epistles* In imitation of whom, I have done the like by my own; which nevertheless I will not publish while I live but I have been bold to bequeath them to your Lordship, and Mr Chancellor of the Dutchy My *Speeches*, perhaps, you will think fit to publish. the *Letters*, many of them, touch too much upon late Matters of State, to be published, yet I was willing they should not be lost I have also, by my Will, erected two Lectures in Perpetuity, in each University one, with an Endowment of 200 *l per Annum* severally. They are to be for *Natural Philosophy*, and the *Sciences* thereupon depending which Foundations I have required my Executors to order, by the Advice and Direction of your Lordship, and my Lord Bishop of *Coventry* and *Litchfield* These are my present Thoughts [a]

XXXIV

[a] See the Life of the Author

XXXIV.

To Father FULGENTIO[a]; *giving some Account of his Views and Designs in his Writings.*

I Acknowledge my self a Letter in your debt: but my Excuse is too just ; being no other than a severe Illness, from which I am not yet recovered

'Tis my desire you should know the Views I have in the Works whereon my Thoughts are bent, not with any Hopes of perfecting, but thro' a Spirit of attempting, and serving After-Ages, which may be riper for these Matters

I judge it best to have them all in *Latin* [b], and to divide them into Volumes, the first whereof to consist of the Books *de Augmentis Scientiarum*, which are already perfected and published, as the first part of my *Instauration*

The *Novum Organum* should immediately follow, but my *Moral* and *Political Writings* step in between, as being more finished   These are the History of King *Henry* the Seventh, and the small Book which in your Language you have called *Saggi Morali*; but I give it a graver Title, that of *Sermones Fideles* [c], or *Interiora Rerum* [d]   And these Essays will not only be enlarged in Number, but still more in Substance [e]   Along with them goes also the little Piece *de Sapientia Veterum*   But this Volume, as I said, comes in between, not in the order of the *Instauration* [f]

Then shall follow the *Novum Organum*, whereto a second Part is still to be added, tho' I have already conceived, and measured it out in my Mind [g]. And thus the *second* Part of the *Instauration* will be perfected

As to the *third* Part, viz *The History of Nature*, 'tis a Work worthy of some King, or Pope, College, or Order, and can never be laboured, as it requires, by a private Hand   And for those Parts of it already published, viz of *Winds*, and of *Life and Death*, they are not purely Historical, because of the *Axioms* and larger Observations interspersed, but a mix'd kind of Writing, consisting of *Natural History*, and a rude imperfect Machinery of the Understanding [h], designed for the *fourth* Part of the

---

[a] A Learned Jesuit at *Venice*, who wrote the Life of Father *Paul*
[b] The Author in putting his Works into *Latin*, seems to have considerably improved them
[c] Faithful Counsels
[d] Inside of Things
[e] The Author appears to have wrote several Essays originally in *Latin* which were not formerly printed along with the *English*
[f] The *Latin* Edition seems to observe this intended Order
[g] But this *Second Part* was never published, tho' the Heads for it are laid down in the *Novum Organum*, Part II Aph 21
[h] See the *Novum Organum*, Part II Sect I and II See also Vol I pag 15

the *Instauration* Which *fourth* Part is therefore to follow; and will contain numerous Examples of our new Machine [a], more exactly suited to the Rules of Induction [b]

In the *fifth* place is to come the Book I call the *Introduction to Secondary Philosophy*, containing my Discoveries about *New Axioms* raised from Experiments, so as to set up the Pillars of the Fabrick, which before lay at length And this we make a *fifth* Part of the *Instauration*

In the *sixth* and last place comes the *Secondary Philosophy* it self, which I absolutely despair of, but perhaps it may grow up with Posterity : as there are some considerable Foundations laid for it, in such of our Preliminaries, as reach almost to the Universalities of Nature [c]

Thus you see, my Weakness is attempting great Things, with this only Hope, that they seem to proceed from the Providence and abundant Goodness of God, because the Constancy of my Mind, has hitherto neither slackened in the Design, nor my Ardor cool'd after all this time. For 'tis now forty Years since I wrote a Juvenile Treatise upon the very same Subject, and with great Assurance gave it the pompous Title of *Temporis Partus max.* [d] And another Reason is, that, for its extreme Utility, this my Labour seems already blessed with the *Divine Earnest* of future Success [e]

[a] *Viz.* The *Novum Organum*
[b] See Pag. 15 Vol I
[c] This seems to require the utmost Attention of Philosophers, and all the Assistance they can give to them
[d] The Great Birth of Time
[e] See also Letter XXXII pag. 5—

29 MR 64

SUP-

SUPPLEMENT VI.

A

COLLECTION

OF

APOPHTHEGMS:

Serving as a HELP to DISCOURSE[*].

[*] See the *de Augment. Scientiar.* pag 56

The Author's Preface.

Julius Cæsar wrote a Collection of Apophthegms, as appears by an Epistle to Cicero, so did Macrobius, a consular Man 'Tis pity Cæsar' Book should be lost, for I imagine it was collected with Judgment whereas those of Plutarch, Stobæus, and especially the Moderns, draw much of the Dregs Certainly, Apophthegms are of excellent use They are pointed Speeches the Words of the Wise are as Goads, says Solomon. Cicero prettily calls them Salt-pits, out of which you may take Salt, and sprinkle it where you please They serve to interlace in continued Discourse, they serve to recite upon occasion, of themselves and they may serve, if you take out their Kernel, at your own I have, for my Recreation, amidst more serious Studies, collected a few, not neglecting the common ones; many of that kind being excellent, and added some new ones, which might otherwise have been lost [a]

[a] This Collection of *Apophthegms* is no way perfect, or such as had passed the Judgment of the Author We have therefore rejected many of the less considerable sort, and thrown the rest into Alphabetical Order, that Additions and Improvements may the more readily be made to them Several of those omitted turned either upon Pun, or a particular kind of Pleasantry, which has been censured, as unbecoming the Gravity of the Author Indeed they do not appear to have been put to the Press by himself It should rather seem that some of his Domesticks published them, for we find several of his own Sayings among them, delivered as of a second Person, under his name What Dr *Tennison* thought of them, may appear from his *Account of the Author's Works*, Pag 59

A

COLLECTION

OF

APOPHTHEGMS.

1. *A* GATHOCLES, after taking *Syracufe*, the Inhabitants where- Agathocles, of, during the Siege, had fpoke all manner of ill of him, fold them for Slaves, and then faid to them, *Now, if you ufe fuch Words again, I will tell your Mafters of you.*

2 *Alcibiades* vifiting *Pericles*, ftay'd a while before he was admitted. When Alcibiades, he came in, *Pericles* civilly excufed it, and faid, I was ftudying how to give my Account But *Alcibiades* replied, if you will be ruled by me, *ftudy rather how to give no Account*

3. *Cæfar Borgia*, after a long Divifion between him and the Lords of *Ro-* Alexander, *magna*, came to agree with them. In this Agreement, there was an Ar- *the Pope.* ticle, that he fhould not at any time call them all together in Perfon. The meaning was, that knowing his dangerous Nature, if he meant them Trea- fon, he might have an opportunity to opprefs them all at once. Yet he ufed fuch a fine Art, and fair Carriage, that he won their Confidence to meet all together in Council at *Cinigaglia*, where he murdered them all. This Act, when related to Pope *Alexander*, his Father, by a Cardinal, as a happy thing, but very perfidious, the Pope faid, *it was they that broke their Covenant firft, by coming together.*

4. It being reprefented to *Alexander*, to the advantage of *Antipater*, a ftern Alexander the and imperious Man, that he only of all his Lieutenants wore no Purple, Great. but kept the *Macedonian* Habit of Black, *Alexander* faid, *Yes, but Antipater is all Purple within.*

5 Alexander used to say, of his two Friends, *Craterus* and *Hephæstion*, that *Hephæstion* loved *Alexander*, and *Craterus* loved the King

6 *Alexander*, after the Battle of *Granicum*, had very great offers made him by *Darius*, but consulting with his Captains concerning them, *Parmenio* said, Sure I would accept of these Offers, if I were *Alexander*. *Alexander* answered, *So would I if I were* Parmenio.

7 *Alexander*, used to say, he knew himself to be mortal, chiefly by two things, Lust, and Sleep

8 When *Alexander* passed into *Asia*, he gave large Donatives to his Captains, and other principal Men of Virtue, insomuch, that *Parmenio* asked him, Sir, what do you keep for your self? He answered, *Hope*

9 *Alexander*, when his Father wished him to run for the Prize, at the *Olympick* Games, for he was very swift, answered, he would, if he might run with Kings

Accius 10 *Accius* of *Arazer* used to say, in commendation of Age, that Age appeared best in four things old Wood best to burn, old Wine to drink; old Friends to trust, and old Authors to read.

11 *Alexis Castle* being informed, by his Steward, that his Income would not hold way with his Expence the Bishop asked him, whence it chiefly arose? The Steward told him, from the Multitude of his Servants The Bishop bid him make a List of such as were necessary, and such as might be spared which he did; and the Bishop taking occasion to read it before most of his Servants, said to his Steward, Well, let these remain, because I have need of them, and these also, because they have need of me

Antisthenes 12 *Antisthenes* would say, concerning the popular States of *Greece*, that he wondered how, at *Athens*, wise Men proposed, and Fools disposed.

Anaxagoras 13 When it was told *Anaxagoras*, that the *Athenians* had condemned him to die, he said again, *And Nature them*

Ann Bullen 14 Queen *Ann Bullen*, as she was led to the Block, call'd one of the King's Privy Chamber, and said to him; Commend me to the King, and tell him, he has been ever constant in his course of advancing me from a private Gentlewoman, he made me a Marchioness, from a Marchioness, a Queen, and now having left me no higher Degree of earthly Honour, he crowns my Innocence with Martyrdom

Anonymous 15 A *French* Gentleman, discoursing with an *English* one, of the Salique Law, that excludes Women from inheriting the Crown of *France*, the *English* Gentleman said, that it was meant of Women themselves; not of such Males as claim'd by Women. The *French* Gentleman asked, where do you find that Gloss? The *English* one, replied, Sir, look on the backside of the Salique Law, and there you will find it indorsed, implying, that the Salique Law is but a mere Fiction.

16 A Nobleman, upon the complaint of his Servant, laid a Citizen by the heels, thinking to bend him to his Servant's bow; but the Fellow being stubborn, the Servant came to his Lord, and told him, Your Lordship I know has gone as far as you well may, but it works not, for the Fellow is

more

more perverfe than before. Said my Lord, *Let's forget him a while, and then he will remember himfelf.*

17 One came to a Cardinal in *Rome*, and told him, he had brought his Eminence a curious white Palfry , but that he fell lame by the way. Says the Cardinal to him, I'll tell thee what thou fhalt do , go to fuch a Cardinal, and fuch a Cardinal, naming him half a dozen of Cardinals, and tell them as much , and thus, tho' by thy Horfe, if he had been found, thou coud'ft have obliged but one , with thy lame Horfe thou may'ft pleafe half a dozen.

18 A Captain being fent upon an Enterprize, by his General, with Forces unlikely to atchieve it , the Captain faid to him, Sir, appoint but half fo many. Why, fays the General ? The Captain anfwered , *becaufe 'tis better that few die than many*

19 A parcel of Scholars going a Rabbit-hunting, carried a Scholar with them, who had not much more Wit than he was born with , and gave him in charge, that if he faw any, he fhould be filent, for fear of fcaring them ; but he no fooner efpied Rabbits before the reft, but he cried aloud, *Ecce multi cuniculi!* which he had no fooner faid, but the Rabbits fled to their Burrows and he being rebuked by them for it, cry'd, who the Devil would have thought, that Rabbits underftood *Latin* ?

20. It was faid of *Auguftus*, and afterwards of *Septimius Severus*, both doing infinite Mifchief in their beginnings, and infinite good towards their end ; that they fhould either never have been born, or never died.

21 A great Officer in *France* was in danger of lofing his Place, but his Wife, by her fuit, made his Peace , whereupon a pleafant Fellow faid, the Officer had been crufh'd, but that he faved himfelf upon his Horns.

22 There was a Conference in Parliament, between the Lords and Commons, about a Bill of Accountants, which came down from the Lords, praying, that the Lands of Accountants, whereof they were feized, when they entred upon their Office, might be liable for their Arrears to the Queen The Commons defired, that the Bill might not look back to former Accountants, but extend only to the future Upon this, the Lord Treafurer faid , Why, if you had loft your Purfe by the way, would you look forwards for it, or backwards ? *The Queen has loft her Purfe*

23. The Deputies of the Reformed Religion, after the Maffacre at *Paris* upon St. *Bartholomew*'s Day, treating with the King and Queen-Mother for a Peace , both fides agreed upon the Articles · the Queftion was, about Security for the Performance After fome particulars propofed and rejected, the Queen-Mother faid, Why is not the Word of a King fufficient ? One of the Deputies anfwered, No, by St. *Bartholomew*, Madam.

24. A Friar of *France*, in earneft difpute about the Salique Law, would needs prove it by Scripture ; citing that Verfe of the Gofpel, *The Lillies of the Field do neither labour, nor fpin·* applying it thus ; that the *Flower-de-Luces* of *France* cannot defcend, neither to the Diftaff, nor to the Spade ; that is, neither to Women, nor to Peafants.

25. A Minister being deprived for Nonconformity, said to some People, ... some who understood this, as to his being a turbulent Fellow, that would have moved Sedition, complained of him, whereupon being examined, he said, his meaning was, *that he would* ...

26. Many Men, especially such as affect Gravity, have a manner after other Men's Speech to shake their Heads. A great Officer of this Country would say, it was as Men shake a Bottle, to see if there be any Wit in their Heads or no.

27. A Man being very jealous of his Wife, insomuch, that which way soever she went, he would be prying at her heels, and she being offended thereat, told him in plain Terms, that if he did not leave off his Proceedings, in that nature, she would graft such a pair of Horns upon his Head, as should hinder him from coming out of any Door in the House.

28. A Lady of the West Country gave great Entertainment to most of the polite Gentlemen thereabouts, and amongst others, Sir *Walter Raleigh* was one. This Lady, tho' otherwise a stately Dame, was a notable Housewife, and in the Morning early, she called to one of her Maids, and asked, Are the Pigs served? Sir *Walter Raleigh*'s Chamber joined to the Lady's, so that he heard her; a little before Dinner, the Lady coming down in great State into a Room full of Gentlemen, as soon as Sir *Walter Raleigh* set eyes upon her, Madam, said he, are the Pigs served? The Lady answered, *you know best, whether you have had your Breakfast.*

29. A Master of Requests to Queen *Elizabeth*, had often moved for Audience, and been put off, at last he came to the Queen in Progress, and had a new Pair of Boots on. The Queen, who hated the smell of new Leather, said to him, Fie, Sloven, thy new Boots stink. Madam, said he, *'tis not my new Boots that stink, but the stale Bills I have kept so long.*

30. A King of *Hungary* took a Bishop in Battle, and kept him Prisoner: whereupon the Pope writ a Monitory to him, as having broke the Privilege of Holy Church, and taken his Son. The King sent an Embassy to him, and withal the Armour wherein the Bishop was taken, with this Inscription, *Vide num hæc sit vestis filii tui!* see now whether this be thy Son's Coat!

31. A Merchant dying greatly in debt, his Goods were set to Sale, a Stranger would needs buy a Pillow there, saying, this Pillow sure is good to sleep on, since he could sleep upon it, who owed so much Money.

32. A Lover met his Lady in a close Chair, she thinking to have gone unknown, he came and spoke to her; she asked him, how did you know me? He said, because my *Wounds bleed at the approach of my Murdress.*

33. A Gentleman brought Musick to his Lady's Window. She hated him, and had warned him often away, and when he would not desist, she threw Stones at him: whereupon, one in Company, said to him, What greater Honour can your Musick have, than that Stones come about you, as they did about *Orpheus?*

34. A Painter turning Physician, one said to him, You have done well ∙ for before, the Faults of your Work were seen, but now they are hid.

35 There was a Gentleman came to the Tilt, all in Orange-Tawny, and ran very ill. The next Day, he came again, all in Green, and ran worse. One of the Lookers-on asked another, the Reason why this Gentleman changed his Colours The other answered, surely, because it may be reported, that he in Green, ran worse than he in the Orange-Tawny

36 It was said, amongst some of the grave Prelates of the Council of *Trent,* where the School-Divines bore the sway, that the School Men were like the Astronomers, who, to solve the *Phænomena,* supposed Eccentricks, and Epicycles, and a wonderful Engine of Orbs, tho' no such Things existed: so they, to solve the practice of the Church, had devised a great number of strange Positions

37 They said of *Henry* Duke of *Guise,* that he was the greatest Usurer of *France,* because he had turned all his Estate into Obligations meaning, that he had sold and mortgaged all his Patrimony, to give large Donatives to other Men.

38. A Philosopher disputing with *Adrian* the Emperor, did it but weakly; one of his Friends that stood by, afterwards said to him, methinks you were not like your self yesterday, in Argument with the Emperor, I could have answered better my self. Why, said the Philosopher, would you have me contend with a Man that commands thirty Legions?

39 *Nerva* the Emperor succeeded *Domitian,* who had been tyrannical; and in his time many noble Houses were over-thrown by false Accusations, the Instruments whereof were chiefly, *Marcellus* and *Regulus.* *Nerva* one night supped privately with six or seven; amongst whom, there was one, a dangerous Man, who began to take the like courses as *Marcellus* and *Regulus* had done The Emperor fell into discourse of the Injustice and Tyranny of the former time, and particularly of the two Accusers, and said, what should we do with them, if we had them now? One of them that was at Supper, and a free-spoken Senator, said, Marry, they should sup with us

40. One having found a great Treasure hid under ground, in his Grandfather's House, being somewhat doubtful of the Case, signified his Discovery to the Emperor. The Emperor made a Rescript thus, *Use it.* He writ back again, that the Sum was greater than his Condition could use. The Emperor writ a new Rescript thus, *Abuse it.*

41 At a Banquet, where those call'd the seven Wise Men of *Greece,* were invited by the Embassador of a Foreign King, the Embassador related, that there was a Neighbour mightier than his Master, picked Quarrels with him, by making impossible Demands, otherwise threatning War, and now at present demanded of him, to drink up the Sea. To which one of the wise Men said, I would have him undertake it. Why, saith the Embassador, how shall he come off? Thus said the Sage, Let the King first stop the Rivers which run into the Sea, and are no part of the Bargain; and then your Master will perform it. 2

42 At the same Banquet, the Embassador desired the seven, and some other wise Men, to deliver each some Sentence, or Parable, that he might Report to his King the Wisdom of *Greece*. This they did, only one was silent which the Embassador perceiving, said to him, Sir, why do not you say somewhat, that I may report? He answered, report to your Lord, that *there are some of the* Grecians *who can hold their tongue*

43 One of the Philosophers was asked, how a Wise Man differed from a Fool? He answered, send them both naked to a Stranger, and you will see.

44 An *Epicurean* vaunted, that many other Sects of Philosophers turned *Epicureans*, but never any *Epicureans* turned of another Sect whereupon a Philosopher of another Sect, said, the Reason was plain, for Cocks might be made Capons, but Capons could never be made Cocks.

45 The *Turks* made an Expedition into *Persia*; and because of the strait Jaws of the Mountains of *Armenia*, the Bashaws consulted which way they should get in One who heard the debate, said, here's a deal to do how you should get in, but no care is taken how you should get out

46 P , King of *Macedon*, maintaining an Argument with a Musician, in points of his Art, somewhat peremptorily, the Musician said to him, *God forbid, Sir, your Fortune were so hard, that you should know these things better than me*

47 There was a Conspiracy against the Emperor *Claudius*, by *Scribonianus*, examined in the Senate, where *Claudius* sat in his Chair, and one of his freed Servants stood at the back of it In the Examination, that freed Servant, who had much power with *Claudius*, very saucily had almost all the Words, and amongst other things, asked in scorn, one of the examined, who was also a freed Servant of *Scribonianus*, I pray, if *Scribonianus* had been Emperor, what would you have done? He answered, I would have stood behind his Chair, and held my peace

48 One was saying, that his Great-Grandfather, and Grandfather, and Father died at Sea Quoth another, who heard him, If I were you, I would never go to Sea Why, said the other, where did your Great-Grandfather, and Grandfather, and Father die? He answered, in their Beds? Then said the first, And if I were you, I would never go to Bed

49 One of the Fathers said, there is but this difference, between the death of old Men, and young ones; that old Men go to Death, and Death comes to young Men

50 The Ambassadors of *Asia Minor* came to *Antonius*, after he had imposed a double Tax upon them, and said plainly to him, that if he would have two Tributes in one Year, he must give them two Seed-times, and two Harvests

51 A Nobleman said to a great Counsellor, that he would have made the worst Farrier in the World, because he never shod a Horse, but he pricked him: for he never commended any Man to the King, but he would come in the end with a *But*, and drive a Nail to his disadvantage.

52. A Gentleman fell sick, and a Friend of his said to him, Surely, you are in danger, pray send for a Physician. The sick Man answered, *'tis no matter for if I die, I will die at leisure*

53. One of the Seven ufed to fay, that Laws were like Cobwebs, which catched the fmall Flies, but let the great ones break through

54 A cowardly *Spanifh* Soldier, in a Defeat given by the *Moors*, ran away with the foremoft afterwards, when the Army in general fled, this Soldier was miffing, whereupon, it was faid by fome, that he was flain No fure, fays another, he is alive; for the *Moors* eat no Hare's Flefh.

55 A Gentleman, who was punctual of his Word, and loved the fame in others, when he heard, that two Perfons had agreed upon a meeting about ferious Affairs, at a certain time and place, and that the one failed in the performance, or neglected his Hour, would ufually fay of him, *be is a young Man then*

56 *Philip*, *Alexander*'s Father, gave Sentence againft a Prifoner, at a time he was drowfy, and feemed to give little Attention. The Prifoner, after Sentence was pronounced, faid, *I appeal* The King fomewhat moved, faid, to whom do you appeal? The Prifoner anfwered, from *Philip*, when he gave no ear, to *Philip*, when he fhall give ear

57. *Antachidas*, when an *Athenian* faid to him, the *Spartans* are unlearned, Antachidas faid again, true, *for we have learned no Vice of you.*

58. *Antigonus*, being told that the Enemy had fuch Volleys of Arrows, Antigonus that they hid the Sun, faid, it falls out well, for 'tis warm Weather, and fo we fhall fight in the Shade

59. *Antigonus* ufed often to go difguifed, and to liften at the Tents of his Soldiers, and at one time heard fome fpeak very ill of him Whereupon he opened the Tent a little, and faid to them, *if you would fpeak ill of me, you fhould go farther off*

60 *Demades* the Orator, in his old Age was talkative, and would eat Antipater hard. *Antipater* would fay of him, that he was like a Sacrifice, whereof nothing was left, but the Tongue and the Paunch

61 *Antifthenes* being asked, what Learning was moft neceffary in human Antifthenes. Life, anfwered, to unlearn that which is bad.

62 *Vefpafian* asked *Apollonius*, what was the Caufe of *Nero*'s Ruin? He Apollonius anfwered, *Nero* could tune the Harp well, but in Government, he always wound up the Strings too high, or let them down too low.

63 *Ariftippus* was an earneft Suitor for fome Grant to *Dionyfius*, who giving Ariftippus no ear to his Suit, *Ariftippus* fell at his Feet, and then *Dionyfius* granted it. One who ftood by, faid afterwards to *Ariftippus*; You a Philofopher, and fo bafe as to throw your felf at a Tyrant's Feet to obtain a Favour! *Ariftippus* anfwered; the Fault is not mine, but *Dionyfius*'s, that carries his Ears in his Feet.

64 One faid to *Ariftippus*; 'Tis a ftrange thing, that Men fhould rather give to the Poor, than to Philofophers. he anfwered, 'Tis becaufe they think themfelves may fooner come to be poor, than to be Philofophers

65 *Ariftippus* being reproached of Luxury, by one that was not rich, for giving fix Crowns for a fmall Fifh, anfwered, Why, what would you have given? The other faid, twelve Pence. *Ariftippus* replied, and fix Crowns is no more with me.

66.

66. *Aristippus* failing in a Tempest, shewed signs of Fear One of the Seamen said to him, in an insulting manner, We Plebeians are under no concern, but you, a Philosopher, are afraid. *Aristippus* answered; It is not an equal Wager, whether you should perish or me

67 There was an Orator, who defended a Cause of *Aristippus*, and prevailed afterwards he asked *Aristippus*, Now, in your Distress, what good did *Socrates* do you? *Aristippus* answered, in making what you said of me, to be true

68 *Aristippus* said, those who studied particular Sciences, and neglected Philosophy, were like *Penelope*'s Suitors, that made love to the Waiting-Woman.

69 Queen *Elizabeth*, in her Progress. coming to the House of Sir *Nicholas Bacon*, then Keeper of the Great-Seal, said to him, my Lord, what a little House you have got? He answered, Madam, *my House is well enough, only you have made me too great for it*

70 Sir *Nicholas Bacon* being appointed a Judge for the Northern Circuit, and coming to pass Sentence on the Malefactors, one of them mightily importuned him to save his Life, but when nothing he said could avail, he at length desired his Mercy on account of Kindred Prithee, said my Lord, how came that in? Why, if it please you, my Lord, your Name is *Bacon*, and mine is *Hog*, and in all Ages *Hog* and *Bacon* have been a kin. Nay, but replied the Judge, you and I cannot be kindred, unless you be hanged, for a *Hog* is not *Bacon* until it be hanged.

71. Sir *Nicholas Bacon*, when a certain nimble-witted Counsellor at the Bar, interrupted him often, replied, there is a great difference betwixt you and me *a ratio to me to speak, and a turn to you to hold your tongue.*

72 Sir *Nicholas Bacon*, upon Bills exhibited to discover where Lands lay, upon proof, that they had a certain quantity of Land, but could not set it forth, used to say, *and if you cannot find your Land in the Country, how will you be like to find it in the Chancery?*

73 When Sir *Nicholas Bacon*, the Lord-Keeper, lived, every Room in *Gorhambury* was served with a Pipe of Water from the Ponds, distant about a Mile off In the Life-time of Mr *Anthony Bacon*, the Water ceased after whose death his Lordship coming to the Inheritance, could not recover the Water without infinite Charge When he was Lord-Chancellor, he built *Verulam* House, close by the Pond-yard, for a place of Privacy, when called upon to dispatch any urgent Business And being asked, why he built that House there, his Lordship answered, that since he could not carry the Water to his House, he would carry his House to the Water

74 When my Lord-President of the Council came first to be Lord-Treasurer, he complained to my Lord-Chancellor of the troublesomness of the Place, because the Exchequer was empty The Lord Chancellor answered, my Lord, be of good cheer, *for now you shall see the bottom of your Business at first*

75 A Lady walking with Mr. *Bacon* [a] in *Grays-Inn* Walks, asked him, whose was that Piece of Ground that lay next under the Walls? He answered, theirs

Then

[a] *Viz* The Author as the *Apophthegms* above were those of his Father See the Note to the Preface of this Piece

Then she asked him, if those Fields beyond the Walks were theirs too? He answered, Yes, Madam, as you are ours, to look on, and no more

76 One day, Queen *Elizabeth* told Mr *Bacon*, that my Lord of *Essex*, after a great Protestation of Penitence and Affection, fell in the end only upon the suit of renewing his Farm of sweet Wines he answered, I read that in Nature, there are two kinds of sympathetic Motions or Appetites, the one, as of Iron, to the Load-stone, for Perfection, the other, as of the young Vine to the Stake, for Support, and, that her Majesty was the one, and the Earl's Suit the other.

77 The Book of deposing King *Richard* the Second, and the coming in of King *Henry* the Fourth, supposed to be written by Dr *Hayward*, who was committed to the *Tower* for it, having much incensed Queen *Elizabeth*, she asked Mr *Bacon*, then of her learned Counsel, whether there were any Treason contained in it? Who intending to take off the Queen's Bitterness, answered, No Madam, for Treason I cannot say there is any, but very much Felony The Queen apprehending it gladly, asked, how? and wherein? Mr *Bacon* answered, because he had stolen many things out of *Tacitus*.

78 There were Fishermen drawing the River at *Chelsea* Mr *Bacon* came thither by chance in the Afternoon, and offered to buy their Draught they were willing for thirty Shillings Mr *Bacon* offered ten They refused it. Why then, says Mr. *Bacon*, I will be only a Looker-on They drew, and catched nothing Says Mr *Bacon*, are not you mad Fellows now, that might have had an Angel in your Purse, to have made merry withal, and now you must go home with nothing? Ay but, say the Fishermen, we had hope to make a better gain of it. Says Mr. *Bacon*, Well then, I'll tell you, *Hope is a good Breakfast, but a bad Supper*

79 Mr *Bacon*, having been vehement in Parliament against Depopulation and Inclosures, the Queen soon after told him, she had referred the hearing of Mr. *Mills*'s Cause to certain Counsellors and Judges, and asking him how he liked it, he answered, Oh Madam! my Mind is known, I am against all Inclosures, and especially against inclosed Justice

80 Sir *Francis Bacon*, newly made Lord Keeper, being in *Gray's-Inn* Walks, with Sir *Walter Raleigh*, one came and told him, that the Earl of *Exeter* was above He continued, upon the occasion, still walking a good while. At last, when he came up, my Lord of *Exeter* met him, and said, My Lord, I have made a great venture, to come up so high Stairs, being a gouty Man. His Lordship answered, Pardon me, my Lord, I have made the greatest venture of all, for I have ventured upon your Patience

81 When Sir *Francis Bacon* was made the King's Attorney, Sir *Edward Coke* was advanced from Lord Chief Justice of the *Common-Pleas*, to Lord Chief Justice of the *King's-Bench*, which is a Place of greater Honour, but less Profit, and withal was made Privy Counsellor. A few days after, the Lord *Coke* meeting the King's Attorney, said to him, Mr Attorney, this is all your doing 'Tis you that have made this stir Mr Attorney answered, Ah, my Lord! Your Lordship all this while has grown in breadth, you must now grow in height, or else you would be a Monster.

82 In Eighty-eight, when the Queen went from *Temple-Bar* along *Fleet-...*, the Lawyers were rank'd on one Side, and the Companies of the City on the other. ... Mr *B...* to a Lawyer who stood next him. Now observe the Courtiers, if they bow first to the Citizens, they are in Debt, °if first to us, they are in L...

83 When Mr *A... C...*, in the Exchequer, gave high Words to Sir *Fra... B...* ... stood much upon his higher Place, Sir *Francis* said to him Mr *Attorney*, the less you speak of your Greatness, the more I shall ... of it, and the more, the less.

84 Sir *F... B...* used to say of an angry Man who suppress'd his Passion, to be thought worse than he spoke, and of an angry Man who would ... that he spoke worse than he thought.

85 He used to say, that Power in an ill Man, was like the Power of a black Witch, that did hurt, but no good. He would add, that the Magicians could turn Water into Blood, but could not turn the Blood again to Water.

86 Sir *Francis Bacon* coming into the Earl of *Arundel's* Garden, where there were a great Number of antient Statues of naked Men and Women, made a Stand, and as astonish'd, cried out, The Resurrection!

87 Sir *Francis Bacon*, who was always for moderate Counsels, when one was speaking for such a Reformation of the Church of *England*, as would in effect make it no Church, said thus to him, Sir, the Subject we now talk of is the Eye of *England*, and if there be a Speck or two in the Eye, we endeavour to take them off, but he were a strange Oculist, who would put out the Eye.

88 Sir *Francis Bacon* used to say, that those who left useful Studies for scholastic Speculations were like the Olympic Gamesters, who abstain'd from necessary Labours, that they might be fit for such as were unnecessary.

89 He also frequently used this Comparison, the Empirical Philosophers are like Ants, they only lay up and use their Store, the Rationalists are like Spiders, that spin all out of their own Bowels. But give me a Philosopher, who, like the Bee, has a middle Faculty, gathering from abroad, but digesting what is gathered by his own Virtue.

90 The Lord *Bacon* used to commend the Advice of a plain old Man at *Buxton*, who sold Brooms. A proud lazy young Fellow came to him for a Broom upon trust, to whom the old Man said, Friend, *hast thou no Money?* ... *Bird, and borrow of thy Belly, they'll ne'er ask thee again, I ... every day.*

91 The Lord St. *Albans*, who was not over-hasty to raise Theories, but proceeded softly by Experiments, used to say to some Philosophers who would not go his pace, Gentlemen, Nature is a Labyrinth, in which the very haste you move with, will make you lose your Way.

92 The same Lord speaking of the *Dutch*, used to say, that we could not ... them, for our Safety, nor keep them, to our Profit, and sometimes express'd that Sense by saying, We hold the *Belgic* Lion by the Ears.

93

93 The fame Lord, when a Gentleman feemed not much to approve of his Liberality to his Retinue, faid to him, Sir, I am all of a piece, if the Head be lifted up, the inferior Parts of the Body muft rife too

94 Mr *Bettenham*, Reader of *Grays-Inn*, ufed to fay, That Riches were like *Bettenham* Muck, which when it lay in a Heap, gave but an ill Odour, but when fpread upon the Ground, it was the Caufe of much Fruit

95 Mr *Bettenham* faid, virtuous Men were like fome Herbs and Spices, that give not out their fweet Smell till they are broken or crufh'd.

96 *Bias* gives in Precept, Love as if you fhould hereafter hate, and hate as if *Bias* you fhould hereafter love

97. *Bion*, an Atheift, being fhewed at a Port-City, in a Temple of *Neptune*, *Bion* many Pictures of fuch as had in Tempeft made their Vows to *Neptune*, and efcaped Shipwreck, was ask'd, how fay you now? Do you not acknowledge the Power of the Gods? Nay, but fays he, where are they painted who were drowned after their Vows?

98 *Bion* ask'd an envious Man, who was very fad, What harm had befallen him, or what Good had befallen another?

99 *Bion* was failing, and there happen'd a great Tempeft, when the Mariners, that were wicked and diffolute Fellows, call'd upon the Gods, but *Bion* faid to them, *Peace, let them not know you are here.*

100 *Brefquet*, Jefter to *Francis* the Firft of *France*, kept a Calendar of Fools, *Brefquet* wherein he ufed to make the King fport, telling him always the Reafon why he put any one into his Calendar. When the Emperor *Charles* the Fifth, upon Confidence of the noble Nature of *Francis*, pafs'd thro' *France*, for appeafing the Rebellion of *Gaunt* ; *Brefquet* put him into his Calendar. The King asked him the Caufe, he anfwer'd, Becaufe you having fuffer'd from *Charles* the greateft Bitternefs that ever one Prince did from another, he would neverthelefs truft his Perfon in your hands. Why, *Brefquet*, cries the King, what wilt thou fay, to fee him pafs back in as great fafety as if he marched through the midft of *Spain*? Says *Brefquet*, Why then I will put him out, and put you in.

101 Sir *Edward Dyer*, a grave and wife Gentleman, believed in *Kelley* the *Brown* Alchemift, that he did indeed the Work, and made Gold, infomuch that he went into *Germany*, where *Kelley* then was, to inform himfelf fully thereof. After his Return, he dined with my Lord of *Canterbury*, when Dr *Brown* the Phyfician was at Table. They fell in talk of *Kelley*. Sir *Edward Dyer* turning to the Archbifhop, faid, I do affure your Grace that what I fhall tell you is truth, I am an Eye-witnefs thereof, and if I had not feen it, I fhould not have believed it. I faw Mr *Kelley* put of the bafe Metal into the Crucible, and after it was fet a little upon the Fire, and a very fmall quantity of the Medicine put in, and ftirred with a Stick, it came forth in great proportion perfect Gold, to the Touch, to the Hammer, and to the Teft. My Lord Archbifhop faid, You had need take care what you fay, Sir *Edward*, for here is an Infidel at the Board. Sir *Edward Dyer* replied pleafantly, I fhould have looked for an Infidel fooner in any Place than at your Grace's Table. What fay you, Dr *Brown*, cried the Archbifhop? Dr

Brown anſwer'd, after his blunt and huddling manner, The Gentleman has ſpoken enough for me Why, ſays the Archbiſhop, what has he ſaid? Marry, quoth Dr *Brown*, he ſaid he would not have believed it, except he had ſeen it, no more will I

102 Queen *Elizabeth* was naturally dilatory in Suits, and the LordTreaſurer *Brough* being a wiſe Man, and willing to feed her humour, wou'd ſay to her, Madam, you do well to let Suitors wait for, *bis dat, qui cito dat*, if you grant them ſpeedily, they will come again the ſooner.

103 The *Roman*, when they ſpoke to the People, uſed to ſtyle them ye *Romans* But when Commanders in War ſpoke to their Army, they ſtyled them my Soldiers There was a Mutiny in *Cæfar's* Army, for ſomewhat the Soldiers wou'd have, yet did not declare themſelves in it, but only demanded Diſcharge, tho' with no intent it ſhould begranted but knowing *Cæfar* had now great need of their Service, thought by that means to bring him to their Views, whereupon with one Cry they asked Diſmiſſion *Cæfar*, after Silence made, ſaid, For my part, *ye Romans*, which Title actually ſpoke them diſmiſſed, when immediately they mutinied again, and would not ſuffer him to go on with his Speech, till he had called them by the Name of his *Soldiers* and ſo with one Word he appeas'd the Sedition.

104 There was a Soldier who vaunted before *Julius Cæfar*, of the hurts he had received in his Face *Julius Cæfar* knowing him to be but a Coward, told him, you had beſt take heed the next time you run away, how you look back.

105 *Julius Cæfar* as he paſſed by, was by acclamation of ſome that ſtood in the way termed King, to try how the People would take it. The People ſhew'd great Diſtaſte at it *Cæfar* finding where the Wind ſtood, ſlighted it, and ſaid, I am not King, but *Cæfar*, as if they had miſtaken his Name. For *Rex* was a Sirname amongſt the *Romans*, as *King* is with us

106 *Cæfar* when he firſt got poſſeſſion of *Rome*, after *Pompey's* flight, offered to enter the ſacred Treaſury to ſeize the Money But *Metellus*, Tribune of the People, forbid him, and when *Metellus* was violent in it, and would not deſiſt, *Cæfar* turn'd to him and ſaid, Preſume no further, or I will lay you dead And when *Metellus* with thoſe Words was ſomewhat aſtoniſh'd, *Cæfar* added, Young Man, it had been eaſier for me to do it, than to ſpeak it

107 *Auguſtus Cæfar* would ſay, He wonder'd *Alexander* ſhould fear to wan Work, having no more Worlds to conquer, as if it were not as hard to keep, as to conquer

108 *Cæfar*, in the Book he wrote againſt *Cato*, (which is loſt) to ſhew the force of Opinion and Reverence of a Man that had once obtain'd a popular Reputation, ſays, That ſome Perſons finding *Cato* drunk, were aſhamed inſtead of *Cato*

109 *Auguſtus Cæfar*, out of great Indignation againſt his two Daughters, and *Poſthumus Agrippa*, his Grand-child, whereof the two firſt were infamous, and the laſt otherwiſe unworthy, would ſay, That they were not his Seed, but ſome Impoſthumes that had broke from him.

110 *Francis Carvajal*, the great Captain of the Rebels of *Peru*, had often Carvajal given chafe to *Diego Centeno*, a principal Commander of the Emperor's Party   He was afterwards taken by the Emperor's Lieutenant *Gasca*, and committed to the Cuftody of *Diego Centeno*, who ufed him with all poffible Courtefy, infomuch that *Carvajal* asked him, I pray Sir, who are you that ufe me with this Courtefy? *Centeno* faid, Do you not know *Diego Centeno*? *Carvajal* anfwer'd, Truly Sir, I have been fo ufed to fee your Back, that I know not your Face   .

111 *Caffius*, after the Defeat of *Craffus* by the *Parthians*, whofe Weapons Caffius were chiefly Arrows, fled to the City of *Charras*, where he durft not ftay any time, fearing to be purfued and befieged   He had with him an Aftrologer, who faid to him, Sir, I would not have you go hence while the Moon is in *Scorpio*. *Caffius* anfwered, I am more afraid of *Sagittarius*

112. The elder *Cato* ufed to fay, The *Romans* were like Sheep, a Man could Cato. better drive a Flock of them than one

113 The elder *Cato* buried his Wife, and married a young Woman in his old Age · His Son came to him and faid, Sir, wherein have I offended, that you have brought a Step mother into your Houfe? The old Man anfwer'd, Nay, Son, thou pleafeft me fo well, that I would be glad to have more fuch.

114. *Cato* would fay, That wife Men learn'd more by Fools, than Fools by wife Men.

115 *Cato* at a time that many of the *Romans* had Statues erected to their honour, was asked by one in a kind of wonder, why he had none? He anfwer'd, He had much rather that Men fhould wonder why he had no Statue, than why he had

116. *Clodius* was acquitted by a corrupt Jury, that had palpably taken Catulus. Money, before they gave their Verdict, but asked of the Senate a Guard, that they might go according to their Confciences, becaufe *Clodius* was a feditious young Nobleman. Whereupon, all the World gave him for condemned ; but he was acquitted. *Catulus* the next day feeing fome of them together that had acquitted him, faid to them, What made you ask us for a Guard? Were you afraid your Money fhould have been taken from you?

117 *Charles*, King of *Sweden*, a great Enemy to the Jefuits, when he took Charles any of their Colleges, would hang the old Jefuits, and fend the young ones to his Mines, faying, Since they wrought fo hard above ground, he would try how they could work under ground

118 *Chilon* would fay, That Gold was try'd by the Touch-ftone, and Men Chilon by Gold

119 *Cineas*, an excellent Orator, Statefman, and principal Friend to *Pyrrhus*, Cineas falling into intimate Difcourfe with that King, difcern'd his endlefs Ambition, and when *Pyrrhus* told him in confidence, how he intended firft a War upon *Italy*, and hoped to fucceed, *Cineas* asked, What will you do then? Then fays he, We will attempt *Sicily*. *Cineas* replies, Well Sir, what then? Said *Pyrrhus*, if the Gods favour us, we may conquer *Africa* and *Carthage*. What then, Sir, fays *Cineas*? Why then, fays *Pyrrhus*, we may

... ... our R... ... ...ifice and feaſt every day, and make merry
... our T... s. A'.., S..., ſaid *Cineas*, we may do that now, without all
... ...

120 C... ...rg... ...ce upon O...th, and the Jury, which conſiſted of fif
... ..., na... ... ...g... ...ſt it, when after in the Senate *Cicero* and
C... ...ing in h... ..., C... upbraided him and ſaid, the Jury gave him no
c... C... ...d, F... and twenty gave me credit, but there were
t... ...t... ...g ... ...one for they had their Money before-hand

12... C... ...at ...nner where...n antient Lady ſpoke of ner Years, and
...d S...e was but forty One who ſat by *Cicero*, whiſper'd him in the
ear, and ſaid, She talks of old, but ſhe muſt be much more. *Cicero*
anſwer'd ...im again, I muſt believe her, for I have heard her ſay ſo any time
theſe ten Years

122 There was a Law made by the *Romans*, againſt the Bribery and Extortion of the Governors of Provinces, whereupon *Cicero* ſaid in a Speech to the
People, That he thought the Provinces would petition the State of *Rome*,
to have that Law repealed. For, ſaid he, the Governours bribed and extorted before, as much as was ſufficient for themſelves, but now they bribe
and extort not only for themſelves, but for the Judges, and Jurors, and Magiſtrates

123 After the Defeat of the younger *Cyrus*, *Falinus* was ſent by the King to
the Gr...k, who had rather the Victory than otherwiſe, to command them
to yield their Arms, which being denied, *Falinus* ſaid to *Clearchus*, Well
then, the King lets you know, that if you remove from the Place where
you are now encamped, 'tis War, if you ſtay, a Truce. Which ſhall I
ſay you will do? *Clearchus* anſwer'd, It pleaſes us as it pleaſes the King
How is that, ſaid *Falinus*? *Clearchus* anſwer'd, If we remove, 'tis War, if
we ſtay, a Truce. and ſo would not diſcloſe his Purpoſe

124 *Michael Angelo*, painting in the Pope's Chapel, a Piece of Hell and the
damned Souls, made one of the damned Souls ſo like a Cardinal who was
his Enemy, that every body at firſt ſight knew him, whereupon the Cardinal complained to Pope *Clement*. humbly praying it might be defaced
The Pope ſaid to him, Why 'tis true, I have power to deliver a Soul out
of Purgatory, but not out of Hell

125 *Craſſus* the Orator had a Fiſh, by the *Romans* called *Muraena*, which
he made very tame, and fond of him. The Fiſh died, and *Craſſus* wept for
it One day falling in a Contention with *Domitius* in the Senate, *Domitius*
ſaid, Fooliſh *Craſſus*, you wept for your *Muraena* *Craſſus* replied, That's
more than you did for both your Wives.

126 *Demoſthenes* fled from Battle, being afterwards reproached with it, ſaid,
He that ſlies, may fight again

127 An Orator at *Athens* ſaid to *Demoſthenes*, The *Athenians* will kill you if
they grow mad *Demoſthenes* replied, And they will kill you, if they are in
their Senſes

128 *Dogenes* begging, as many Philoſophers then uſed, begg'd more of a
prodigal Man than of the reſt who were preſent: whereupon one ſaid to
him,

him, See your Baseness, that when you find a liberal Mind, you take most of him   No, said *Diogenes* , for I mean to beg of the rest again

129 *Diogenes*, when Mice came about him as he was eating, said, I see that even *Diogenes* feeds Parasites

130 *Diogenes* call'd an ill Physician, Cock , Why so, says he ? *Diogenes* answer'd, Because when you crow, Men rise

131. *Diogenes* having seen the Kingdom of *Macedon*, which before was contemptible and low, begin to rise aloft before he died , and being asked how he would be buried ? He answer'd, With my Face downwards for within a while the World will be turn'd upside down , and then I shall lie right

132 *Dionysius* the Tyrant, after he was deposed and brought to *Corinth*, Dionysiu. kept a School, where many used to visit him , and amongst others, one, who when he came in, open'd his Mantle, and shook his Clothes, thinking to give *Dionysius* a gentle Scorn , because it was the manner to do so at coming in to see him while he was Tyrant   But *Dionysius* said to him, I prithee do so rather when thou goest out ; that we may see thou stealest nothing

133. When King *Edward* the Second was among his Torturers, who hurri- K. Edward. ed him to and fro, that no Man should know where he was, they once set him down upon a Bank , and the more to disguise his Face, shaved him, and washed him with cold Water out of the Ditch   The King said, Well, yet I will have warm Water for my Beard , and so shed tears in abundance

134 It being the Custom to release Prisoners at the Inauguration of a Q Elizabeth Prince , as Queen *Elizabeth* went to the Chapel, the day after her Coronation, a Courtier, well known to her, either of his own head, or by the instigation of a wiser Man, presented her a Petition , and before a great Audience, besought her with a loud Voice, that now this good Time there might be four or five principal Prisoners more released , which were the four Evangelists and the Apostle *Paul*, who had been long shut up in an unknown Tongue   The Queen answer'd gravely, It were best to enquire of them first, whether they would be released or no

135 The Lord of *Essex*, at the Succour of *Roan*, made twenty four Knights , a great Number for that Time   And several of them being Gentlemen of small Fortunes, Queen *Elizabeth* said upon it, that my Lord might have done well to have built his Alms-houses, before he made his Knights

136 Queen *Elizabeth* seeing Sir *Edward* —— in her Garden, look'd out at her Window, and asked him , What does a Man think of, when he thinks of nothing ? Sir *Edward*, who had not felt the Effects of some of the Queen's Grants so soon as he hoped, answer'd , Madam, he thinks of a Woman's Promise.   The Queen shrunk in her Head, but was heard to say , Well, Sir *Edward*, I must not confute you   Anger makes dull Men witty, but it keeps them poor

137 When any great Officer, ecclesiastical or civil, was to be made, Queen *Elizabeth* would enquire after the Piety, Integrity, and Learning of the Man , and when satisfied in these Qualifications, she considered of his Personage · And upon such an Occasion, she was once pleased to say to me ,
Bacon,

Been, How can the Magiftrate maintain his Authority, when the Man is defpifed?

138 My Lord Chancellor *Elefmere*, when he had read a Petition which he difliked, would fay, What, you would have my Hand to this now? And the Party anfwering, yes, he would fay farther, Well, fo you fhall nay, you fhall have both my Hands to it, and fo would tear it to pieces.

139 The *Lacedemonians* had a Cuftom of fpeaking very fhort, which being in Empire, they might do at pleafure. But after their Defeat at *Leuctra*, in an Affembly of the *Grecians*, they made a long Invective againft *Epaminondas*, who ftood up and faid no more than this, *I am glad we have brought you to your Speech*.

140 *Epictetus* ufed to fay; that the Vulgar, in any ill that befell them, blame others, Novices in Philofophy blame themfelves, but Philofophers blame neither themfelves nor others.

141 *Ethelwold*, Bifhop of *Winchefter*, in a Famine, fold all the rich Veffels and Ornaments of the Church, to relieve the Poor with Bread, and faid, there was no reafon that the dead Temples of God fhould be fumptuoufly furnifhed, and the living Temples fuffer want.

142 *Stephen Gardiner*, Bifhop of *Winchefter*, a great Champion for the Popifh Religion, ufed to fay of the Proteftants who ground upon the Scripture, that they were like Pofts, who bring Truth in their Letters, and Lyes in their Mouths.

143 When his Lordfhip [1] was newly advanced to the great Seal, *Gondomar* came to vifit him. My Lord faid, he was to thank God and the King for that Honour, but yet, fo he might be rid of the Burthen, he could very willingly forego the Honour. And that he formerly defired, and the fame continued with him ftill, to lead a private Life. *Gondomar* anfwered, he would tell him a Tale of an old Rat, that would needs leave the World, and acquainted the young Rats that he would retire into his Hole, and fpend his Days folitary, and enjoy no more Comfort, and commanded them upon his high Difpleafure, not to offer to come to him. They forbore two or three Days. At laft, one more hardy than the reft, incited fome of his Fellows to go along with him, and he would venture to fee how his Father did, for he might be dead. They went in, and found the old Rat fitting in the midft of a rich *Parmezan* Cheefe.

144 *Goralto* would fay, The Honour of a Soldier ought to be of a ftrong Web, meaning, it fhould not be fo fine and curious, that every little Difgrace fhould catch and ftick in it.

145 Sir *Fulk Grevil*, afterwards Lord *Brook*, in Parliament, when the Houfe Commons, in a great Bufinefs, ftood much upon Precedents, faid to them, Why do you ftand fo much upon Precedents? The Times hereafter will be good or bad. If good, Precedents will do harm, if bad, Power will make a way where it finds none.

146 *Hannibal* faid of *Fabius Maximus*, and of *Marcellus*, the former whereof waited upon him, fo as he could make no Progrefs, and the latter had many

sharp

[1] See the Preface.

sharp fights with him, that he feared *Fabius* like a Tutor, and *Marcellus* like an Enemy.

147 *Fabius Maximus* being resolved to spin out the War, still waited upon *Hannibal's* Progress to curb him, and for that purpose encamped upon the high Ground but *Terentius*, his Colleague, fought with *Hannibal*, and was in great danger of an over-throw, but then *Fabius* came down from the high Grounds, and won the day Whereupon *Hannibal* said, he always thought the Cloud which hung upon the Hills, would at one time or other cause a Tempest

148 *Hanno* the *Carthaginian*, was sent Commissioner by the State, after the second *Carthaginian* War, to supplicate for Peace, and in the end obtained it but one of the sharper Senators said, As you have often broke the Peace, whereto you had sworn, pray by what God will you now swear? *Hanno* answered, By the same Gods that have so severely punished us for forswearing our selves.

149 In Chancery, once when the Counsel of the Parties set forth the Boundaries of the Land in question, by the Plot, and the Counsel of one part said, we lie on this side, my Lord, and the Counsel of the other part said, we lie on this side the Lord Chancellor *Hatton* stood up, and said, If you lie on both sides, whom will you have me to believe?

150 *Heraclitus* the obscure said, the dry Light is the best Soul meaning, when the intellectual Faculties are in vigour, not drenched, or as it were, blooded by the Affections.

151. Mr *Howland*, arguing a Case, with a young Student, happened to say, I would ask you but this Question The Student presently interrupted him, to give him an Answer whereupon, Mr *Howland* gravely said, Nay, tho' I ask you a Question, I did not design you should answer me, I mean to answer my self.

152 King *James*, having made a full Declaration to his Parliament, concluded thus, I have now given you a Mirror of my Mind, use it therefore like a Mirror, and beware how you let it fall, or soil it with your Breath

153 His Majesty said to his Parliament another time, finding some causeless Jealousies among them; that the King and his People, were as Husband and Wife, and therefore, of all things, Jealousy between them was most pernicious

154 His Majesty, if he apprehended his Council might think he varied in Business, tho' he remained constant, would say, that the Sun often shines watery, but that this is not owing to the Sun, but to some Cloud, which being dissipated, the Sun receives its usual brightness

155 Cardinal *Evereux*, having, in a grave subject of Divinity, sprinkled many witty Ornaments of Learning, his Majesty said, they were like the blue, and yellow, and red Flowers in Corn, which make a pleasant shew, but hurt the Corn

156. His Majesty used to be very earnest with the Country Gentlemen to go from *London* to their Seats and sometimes he would say thus to them, Gentlemen, at *London* you are like Ships in the Sea which shew like nothing,

out in your own Country Villages, you are like Ships in a River, which look like great things

157 Soon after the Death of a great Officer, who was judged no Advancer of the King's Matters, the King said to his Sollicitor *Bacon*, Now tell me truly, what say you of your Cousin that is gone? Mr *Bacon* answered, Sir, since your Majesty charges me, I'll e'en deal plainly with you, and give you such a Character of him, as if I were to write his History I do think he was no fit Counsellor to make your Affairs better, but yet he was fit to have kept them from growing worse The King said, On my So'l, Man, in the first place, thou speakest like a true Man, and in the latter, like a Kinsman

158 His Majesty, as he was a Prince of Judgment, so he was a Prince of a pleasant Humour As he was going thro' *Lewisham* to *Greenwich*, he asked what Town it was? They said *Lewisham*. He asked a good while after, what Town is this we are now in? They said still it was *Lewisham*. On my So'l, said the King I will be King of *Lewisham*.

159 In some other of his Progresses, he asked how far 'twas to a certain Town, they said, six Miles Half an hour after, he asked again One said, six Miles and an half The King alighted out of his Coach, and crept under the Shoulder of his led Horse. And when some asked his Majesty what he meant? I must stalk, said he, for yonder Town is shy, and flies me

160 *Fabius*, the *Thessalus*, used to say; some things must be done unjustly, and many others may be done justly.

161 D- *Johnson* said, that in Sickness there were three things material; the Physician, the Disease, and the Patient and if any two of these joined, then they get the Victory If the Physician and the Patient join, down goes the Disease, if the Physician and the Disease join, down goes the Patient, but if the Patient and the Disease join, then down goes the Physician

162 Queen *Isabella*, of *Spain*, used to say, Whoever has a good Presence, and a good Address, carries continual Letters of Recommendation

163 *Prior Fideus* says, that the Sense is like the Sun, for the Sun seals up the Globe of Heaven, and opens the Globe of Earth. so the Sense obscures Heavenly Things, and reveals the Earthly.

164. Bishop *Latimer* said, in a Sermon at Court, that he heard great Speech how the King was poor, and many ways were propounded to make him rich for his part, he thought of one way, which was, that they should help the King to some good Office, for all his Officers were rich

165 *Lewis* the Eleventh of *France*, having much abated the greatness and power of the Peers, Nobility, and Court of Parliament, would say, that he had brought the Crown out of Ward.

166 As *Livia* went abroad in *Rome*, there met her naked young Men sporting in the Streets, whom *Augustus* going about to punish severely *Livia* spoke for them, and said, 'twas no more to chaste Women, than so many Statues.

188 Mr *Popham*, afterwards Lord Chief Justice *Popham*, when he was Speak- Popham
er, and the House of Commons had sate long, and done in effect nothing,
coming one day to Queen *Elizabeth*, she said to him, Now Mr Speaker,
what has pass'd in the House of Commons? He answer'd, if it please your
Majesty, seven Weeks

189 *Hiero* being visited by *Pythagoras*, ask'd him, of what Condition he Pythagoras
was? *Pythagoras* answered, Sir, you have been at the *Olympian* Games Yes,
said *Hiero* Thither, said *Pythagoras*, some come to win Prizes, some
to sell their Merchandize, some to meet their Friends, and to make merry,
and others only to look on I am one of the Lookers on; meaning it of
Philosophy, and a contemplative Life

190. *Titus Quinctius* was in the Council of the *Achaians*, when they delibe- Quinctius
rated, whether in the ensuing War, between the *Romans* and King *Antiochus*,
they should confederate with the *Romans* or with King *Antiochus* In that Council the *Ætolians*, who incited the *Achaians* against the *Romans*, to disable their
Forces, gave great Words, as if the late Victory which the *Romans* had obtained
against *Philip* King of *Macedon*, had been chiefly by the Strength and Forces of
the *Ætolians* themselves And on the other side, the Embassador of *Antiochus*
extol'd the Forces of his Master, sounding what an innumerable Company he
had brought in his Army, and gave the Nations strange Names, as *Elymæans*,
Caducians, and others After both their Harangues, *Titus Quinctius* rose up
and said, 'twas an easy matter to perceive what had join'd *Antiochus* and the
Ætolians together, viz the reciprocal lying of each as to the other's Forces

191. When *Rabelais*, the great Jester of *France*, lay on his Death-bed, they Rabelais
gave him the extreme Unction, and a familiar Friend of his coming to
him afterwards, asked him how he did *Rabelais* answered, just going my
Journey, they have greas'd my Boots already

192 *Rabelais* tells a Tale of one who was very fortunate in compounding
Differences His Son undertook the said Course, but could never compound
any. Whereupon he came to his Father, and asked him, what Art he
had to reconcile Differences? He answered, he had no other but this,
to watch when the two Parties were wearied, and their Hearts too great to
seek Reconcilement at each other's hands, then to mediate betwixt them
and upon no other Terms. After which, the Son went home, and prospered in the same Undertaking

193 A cowardly Fellow in *Oxford* who was a very good Archer, being Raleigh
grossly abused by another, applied to Sir *Walter Raleigh*, then a Scholar, and
asked what he should do to repair the Wrong he had suffered? *Raleigh*
answered, why challenge him at a match of Shooting

194 Sir *Henry Savil* being asked his Opinion of the Poets, by my Lord Savil
Essex, he answer'd, that he thought them the best Writers, next to those that
wrote Prose

195 Pope *Adrian* was talking with the Duke of *Sesa*, that *Pasquin* gave great Sesa
Scandal, and that he would have him thrown into the River But *Sesa*
answered, do it not, holy Father, for then he will turn Frog, and whereas
now he chants but by day, he will then chant both day and night

I 196.

196 Simonides being afked by _Hiero_, what he thought of God? afked a Week's time to confider of it, and at the Week's end he afked a Fortnight's time, at the Fortnight's end, a Month. At which _Hiero_ wondering _Simonides_ anfwered, that the longer he thought upon the matter, the more difficult he found it.

197 Pope _Sixt_ the fifth, who was a very poor Man's Son, and his Father's Houfe ill thatched, fo that the Sun fhone through it in many Places, would fport with his Ignobility, and fay, he was _Nato di Cafa illuftre_, Son of an illuftrious Houfe.

198 They feign a Tale of _Sixtus Quintus_, whom they called Size-Ace, that after his Death he went to Hell, and the Porter of Hell faid to him, You have fome reafon to offer your felf here, becaufe you were a wicked Man, yet becaufe you were a Pope, I have Orders not to receive you. But there is your own Place, Purgatory, you may go thither. So he went and fought about a great while for Purgatory, but could find no fuch Place. Upon that he took heart, and went to Heaven and knocked. Saint _Peter_ afked who was there? He anfwered, Pope _Sixtus_. _Peter_ faid, why do you knock? you have the Keys. _Sixtus_ anfwered, 'tis true, but 'tis fo long fince they were given, that I doubt the Wards of the Lock are altered.

199 _Socrates_ was pronounced by the Oracle of _Delphos_ to be the wifeft Man of _Greece_, which he would evade ironically, faying, there could be nothing in him to verify the Oracle but this, that he was unwife, and knew it, and others unwife, and knew it not.

200 _Socrates_ being fhewed the Book of _Heraclitus_ the obfcure, and afked his Opinion of it, anfwered, thofe Things which I underftood of it are excellent, fo I imagine are the reft, but they require a _Delian Diver_.

201 _Solon_ compared the People to the Sea, and Orators and Counfellors to the Winds, becaufe the Sea would be calm and quiet, if the Winds did not trouble it.

202 _Solon_, when he wept for his Son's Death, and one faid to him; weeping will do no good, anfwer'd, 'tis therefore I weep.

203 _Solon_ being afked, whether he had given the _Athenians_ the beft Laws, anfwered, the beft of thofe they will receive.

204 When _Crœfus_, out of his Glory, fhewed _Solon_ his great Treafures of Gold, _Solon_ faid to him, if another King come that has better Iron than you, he will be Mafter of all this Gold.

205 A Croud gathering about _Stilpho_ the Philofopher, one faid to him, the People come wondering about you, as to fee fome ftrange Beaft, no, fays he, 'tis to fee a Man, which _Diogenes_ fought with his Lanthorn at Noon-day.

206 _Eneas Sylvius_, who was Pope _Pius Secundus_, ufed to fay, that the former Popes did wifely to fet Lawyers to debate, whether the Donation of _Conftantine_ the Great to _Sylvefter_, of St _Peter's_ Patrimony, were good in Law or no; the better to flip over the Matter of Fact, whether there was ever any fuch Thing or no.

207 *Themistocles*, when an Ambassador from a mean State spoke great Themis- Matters, said to him , Friend, thy Words would require a City tocles

208 *Theodosius*, when he was pressed by a Suitor, and denied him, the Theodosius Suitor said , Why Sir, you promis'd it. He answer'd, I said it , but I did not promise it, if it be unjust.

209 *Trajan* would say of the vain Jealousy of Princes, who seek to make Trajan away such as aspire to the Succession , that there never was a King who put his Successor to death

210 A Suitor to *Vespasian*, to lay his Suit the fairer, said, 'twas for his Bro- Vespasian ther , tho' indeed 'twas for a Piece of Money The Emperor was informed of the false Pretence, sent for the Party interested, and asked him , whether his Agent was his Brother or no ? He durst not tell the Emperor an untruth, and confess'd 'twas not his Brother Whereupon the Emperor said, fetch me the Money, and you shall have your Suit dispatched , which he did The Courtier, who was Agent, sollicited *Vespasian* soon after about this Suit Why, said *Vespasian*, I gave it t'other day to a Brother of mine.

211 *Vespasian* set a Tax upon Urine , *Titus* his Son undertook to speak of it to his Father, and represented it as a sordid thing *Vespasian* said nothing for that time ; but a while after, when 'twas forgotten, sent for a Piece of Silver out of the Money so raised, and calling his Son, bid him smell to it , and asked him whether he found any Offence ? who said, no. Yet, says *Vespasian*, this comes out of Urine

212 When *Vespasian* passed from *Jewry* to take upon him the Empire, he went by *Alexandria*, where were two famous Philosophers, *Apollonius* and *Euphrates* The Emperor heard their Discourse, as to Matter of State, in the presence of many , and when he was weary of them, he broke off, and in a secret Derision, finding their Discourses but speculative, and not to be put in practice, said , Oh that I might govern wise Men , and wise Men govern me !

213 *Jack Weeks* said of a great Man, just then dead, who pretended to some Weeks. Religion, but was none of the best Livers , *Well, I hope he is in Heaven Every Man thinks as he wishes , but if he be in Heaven, 'twere pity it should be known*

214 A *Welchman* being at the Sessions-house, and seeing the Prisoners hold Welchman up their Hands at the Bar, said to some of his Acquaintance there , that the Judges were excellent Fortune tellers for if they did but look upon a Man's Hand, they would certainly tell whether he should live or die

215 *Whitehead*, a grave Divine, of a blunt stoical Nature, was much esteem- Whitehead. ed by Queen *Elizabeth* , but not preferred, because he was against Episcopal Government He came one day to the Queen, and the Queen happen'd to say to him, I like thee better, *Whitehead*, because thou livest unmarried He answered, in troth I like you the worse, for the same Reason Wotton

216 Sir *Henry Wotton* used to say that Criticks were like the Brushers of Noblemen's Clothes

217 Colonel V___, upon a Muster taken against the *Moors*, was desired by a Servant of his to stand a little out of the smoak of the Fire-Arms but he did again, that was his Incense

218 Z___ was the first of the *Ottomans* that shaved his Beard, whereas his Predecessors wore it long One of his Bashaws asked him, why he altered the Custom of his Predecessors? He answered, because you Bashaws shall not lead me by the Beard, as you did them

219 The Lord *Bacon* said of Apophthegms, he is no wise Man who will lose his Friend for his Wit, but he is less wise, who will lose his Friend for another Man's Wit

APPENDIX.

Containing short Sentences, and certain Rules for Discourse.

1 A Gamester, the greater Master he is of his Art, the worse Man

2 Much bending, breaks the Bow, much unbending, the Mind

3 He conquers twice, who upon Victory overcomes himself

4 If Vices were profitable upon the whole, the virtuous Man would be a Sinner

5 He sleeps well, who feels not that he sleeps ill.

6. To deliberate upon useful Things, is the safest Delay.

7 Grief decreases, when it can swell no higher.

8. Pain makes even the innocent Men Lyars

9 In Desire, Expedition it self is Delay.

10 The smallest Hair has its Shadow

11 He who has lost his Faith, what has he left to live on?

12 Fortune makes her Favourites Fools

13 Fortune is not content to do a Man but one ill Turn

14 'Tis invisible Fortune that makes a Man happy, and unenvied.

15 A beautiful Face is a silent Commendation.

16 'Tis a miserable Thing to be injured by one 'tis in vain to complain of.

17 A Man dies as often as he loses his Friends.

18 The Tears of an Heir are Laughter under a Vizard.

19 Nothing is pleasant without a mixture of Variety

20 He bears Envy best, who is either couragious or happy

21 None but a virtuous Man can hope well in bad Circumstances.

22 In taking Revenge, Haste is criminal

23 When Men are in Calamity, 'tis offensive even to laugh

24 He accuses *Neptune* unjustly, who has been twice ship-wreck'd

25 He who injures one, threatens an hundred

26 All Delay is ungrateful, but we are not wise without it

27 Happy is he who dies before he calls for Death

28 A bad Man, when he pretends to be a Saint, is then the worst of all.

29 Lock and Key will scarce secure what pleases every body

30 They live ill, who think of living always

31 That Sick Man is unwise, who makes his Physician his Heir.

32 He of whom many are afraid, has himself many to fear.

33 There's no Fortune so good, but it bates an Ace

34. 'Tis part of the Gift to deny genteelly

35 The Coward calls himself cautious And the Miser calls himself frugal

36. Life is an Age to the Miserable, but to the Happy a Moment

Short Rules for Conversation.

1. TO deceive Men's Expectations, generally argues a settled Mind, and unexpected Constancy, as in matter of Fear, Anger, sudden Joy, Grief, and all Things that may affect or alter the Mind, on publick or sudden Accidents

2 'Tis necessary to use a stedfast Countenance, not wavering with Action, as in moving the Head or Hand too much, which shews a fantastical, light, and fickle Operation of the Mind It is sufficient, with leisure, to use a modest Action of either

3. In all kinds of Speech, 'tis proper to speak leisurely, and rather drawingly, than hastily, because hasty Speech confounds the Memory, and often drives a Man to a *Non-plus*, or an unseemly stammering whereas slow Speech confirms the Memory, and begets an Opinion of Wisdom in the Hearers

4 To desire in Discourse to hold all Arguments, is ridiculous, and a want of true Judgment, for no Man can be exquisite in all Things.

5 To have common-Places of Discourse, and to want variety, is odious to the Hearers, and shews a Shallowness of Thought 'tis therefore good to vary, and suit Speeches to the present occasion, as also to hold a Moderation in all Discourse, especially of Religion, the State, great Persons, important Business, Poverty, or any thing deserving Pity

6 A long continued Discourse, without a good Speech of Interlocution, shews Slowness and a good Reply, without a good Set of Speech, shews Shallowness and Weakness

7 To use many Circumstances, before you come to the Matter, is wearisome, and to use none at all, is blunt

8 Bashfulness is a great hindrance to a Man, both in uttering his Sentiments, and understanding what is propos'd to him, 'tis therefore good to press forwards, with Discretion, both in Discourse and Company of the better Sort

SUPPLEMENT VII.

De Sapientia Veterum:

THE

MYTHOLOGY

OR

CONCEALED KNOWLEDGE

OF THE

ANCIENTS,

DECYPHERED and EXPLAINED;

In *Natural Philosophy, Morality* and *Civil Policy*[a].

Zzz 2

[a] See the *de Augment. Scientiar.* pag 58.

PREFACE.

THE present Piece appears like a rich Cabinet of Antiques, *opened and set to View. The happy Talent, which the Author, in his Physical Works, employs to interpret* Nature; *is here employed to interpret the dark Oracles of Men. And to say the Truth, he seems to have used the like Artifice in both; proceeding according to the* Inductive Method, *delivered in the second Part of the* Novum Organum· *without which, or something of the kind, it would not be easy to derive such Depths of Knowledge from the* Ænigma's, *or dark Parables of Antiquity. For Example, he first culls out his* Fable, *with Choice and Judgment; then trims or prunes it; rejecting what is superfluous or spurious, next turns and views it in different Lights, and at length finds out the* Key for Decyphering *it, in the most natural and advantageous Manner· and thus having got the right End of the Thread, the* Interpretation *follows as it were spontaneously. Tho' the whole still remains to be coolly sate upon and revised, in order to discover, if the* Imagination *has not been too busy in working off the* Interpretation, *or if no Levity, misbecoming the Ancient Sages, has crept in. And as the Author certainly bestowed this, or perhaps much greater, Diligence and Application, in trimming these ancient* Fables, *and fitting them with suitable* Interpretations; *it seems*

but

but a piece of Justice in the Reader, that he be not over-hasty to pronounce upon the Performance This is mentioned the rather, because some have thought, that the Author here employed his Imagination *more than his* Judgment *But the Appeal from Men's first Thoughts to their second, is the Privilege of every careful Writer*

THE

THE

MYTHOLOGY

OR

CONCEALED KNOWLEDGE

OF THE

ANCIENTS,

DECYPHERED and EXPLAINED.

INTRODUCTION:

Containing a short Critique *upon the* MYTHOLOGY *of the Ancients.*

1. THE earlieft Antiquity lies buried in Silence and Obli- *Mythology earlier than our prefent Hiftory* vion, excepting the Remains we have of it in facred *Writ.* This Silence was fucceeded by *Poetical Fables*; and thefe, at length, by the Writings we now enjoy. fo that the concealed and fecret Learning of the Ancients, feems feparated from the Hiftory and Knowledge of the following Ages, by a *Veil*, or *Partition-Wall of Fables*, interpofing between the Things that are loft, and thofe that remain [a].

2. Many may imagine that I am here entring upon a Work of Fancy, *Has been wrefted and abufed* or Amufement; and defign to ufe a Poetical Liberty, in explaining Poetical Fables 'Tis true, Fables in general are compofed of ductile Matter, that may be drawn into great Variety, by a witty Talent, or an inventive Genius, and be delivered of plaufible Meanings which they never contain'd But this Procedure has already been carried to excefs and great numbers, to procure the Sanction of Antiquity to their own Notions and Inventions, have miferably wrefted and abufed the *Fables* of the Ancients.

3 Nor is this only a late or unfrequent Practice, but of ancient *But not therefore to be rejected* date, and common, even to this day. Thus *Chryfippus*, like an Interpreter of Dreams, attributed the Opinions of the *Stoicks* to the Poets of old · and the Chemifts, at prefent, more childifhly apply the *Poetical Transformations* to their Experiments of the Furnace.

---

[a] *Varro* diftributes the Ages of the World into three Periods, *viz* the *Unknown*, the *Fabulous*, and the *Hiftorical* Of the former we have no Accounts but in *Scripture*, for the fecond, we muft confult the Ancient *Poets*, fuch as *Hefiod*, *Homer*, or thofe who wrote ftill earlier, and then again come back to *Ovid*, who in his *Metamorphofes*, feems in imitation, perhaps, of fome ancient *Greek* Poet, to have intended a compleat Collection, or a kind of continued and connected *Hiftory* of the fabulous Age, efpecially with regard to *Changes*, *Revolutions*, or *Transformations*

And tho' I have well weighed and considered all this; and throughly seen into the Levity which the Mind indulges for Allegories and Allusions, yet I cannot but retain a high Value for the *ancient Mythology*. And certainly, it were very injudicious to suffer the fondness and licentiousness of a few, to detract from the honour of Allegory and Parable in general. This would be rash, and almost prophane: for, since *Religion* delights in such Shadows and Disguises, to abolish them were, in a manner, to prohibit all Intercourse betwixt Things divine and human.

4. Upon deliberate Consideration, my Judgment is, that *a concealed Instruction and Allegory was originally intended in many of the ancient Fables*. This Opinion may, in some respect, be owing to the Veneration I have for Antiquity; but more to observing, that some *Fables* discover a great and evident Similitude, Relation and Connection with the Thing they signify, as well in the structure of the Fable, as in the propriety of the Names, whereby the Persons or Actors are characterized: insomuch, that no one could positively deny a Sense and Meaning, to be from the first intended, and purposely shadowed out in them. For who can hear, that *Fame after the Giants were destroyed, sprung up as their posthumous Sister*, and not apply it to the Clamour of Parties, and the seditious Rumours which commonly fly about for a time, upon the quelling of Insurrections [a]? Or who can read, how *the Giant Typhon cut out and carried away* Jupiter's *Sinews, which* Mercury afterwards stole, and again *restored to* Jupiter, and not presently observe, that this Allegory denotes strong and powerful Rebellions, which cut away from Kings their Sinews, both of Money and Authority: and that the way to have them restored, is by Lenity, Affability, and prudent Edicts, which soon reconcile, and as it were steal upon the Affections of the Subject [b]? Or who, upon hearing that memorable *Expedition of the Gods against the Giants, when the Braying of* Silenus's *Ass greatly contributed in putting the Giants to flight*, does not clearly conceive, that this directly points at the monstrous Enterprizes of rebellious Subjects, which are frequently frustrated and disappointed by vain Fears and empty Rumours?

5. Again, the Conformity and Purport of the *Names*, is frequently manifest, and self-evident. Thus *Metis*, the Wife of *Jupiter*, plainly signifies *Counsel*; *Typhon*, Swelling; *Pan*, Universality; *Nemesis*, Revenge, &c. Nor is it a wonder, if sometimes

a

[a] See hereafter, Sect III. Fab.

[b] See hereafter, Sect III. Fab. 6.

a piece of Hiſtory, or other things are introduced, by way of Ornament; or if the Times of the Action are confounded, or if part of
one *Fable* be tacked to another, or if the Allegory be new turned
for all this muſt neceſſarily happen, as the *Fables* were the Inventions of Men who lived in different Ages, and had different Views,
ſome of them being ancient, others more modern; ſome having an
Eye to *Natural Philoſophy* [a], and others, to *Morality*, or *Civil
Policy*

6 It may paſs for a farther Indication of a concealed and ſecret *The Abſurdity*
Meaning, that ſome of theſe *Fables* are ſo abſurd, and idle, in *of ſome Fables*
their Narration, as to ſhew and proclaim an Allegory, even afar off *the r ve ng*
A *Fable* that carries probability with it, may be ſuppoſed invented *Allegorical*
for pleaſure, or in imitation of Hiſtory, but thoſe that could never
be conceived, or related in this way, muſt ſurely have a different
uſe For example, what a monſtrous Fiction is this, that Jupiter
ſhould take Metis *to Wife, and as ſoon as he found her pregnant,
eat her up, whereby he alſo conceived, and out of his Head brought
forth* Pallas *armed?* Certainly no Mortal could, but for the ſake
of the Moral it couches, invent ſuch an abſurd Dream as this,
ſo much out of the Road of Thought [1]

7. But the Argument of moſt weight with me is this, that many *The Fables*
of theſe *Fables*, by no means appear to have been invented by the *earlier than*
Perſons who relate and divulge them, whether *Homer, Heſiod,* or *the Relators*
others for if I were aſſured they firſt flowed from thoſe later
Times and Authors that tranſmit them to us, I ſhould never expect
any Thing ſingularly great or noble from ſuch an Origin. But
whoever attentively conſiders the Thing, will find that theſe *Fables*
are delivered down, and related by thoſe Writers, not as Matters then
firſt invented and propoſed, but as Things received and embraced
in earlier Ages Beſides, as they are differently related by Writers
nearly of the ſame Ages, 'tis eaſily perceived, that the Relators
drew from the common Stock of ancient Tradition, and varied but
in point of Embelliſhment, which is their own And this principally raiſes my Eſteem of theſe *Fables*, which I receive, not as
the Product of the Age, or Invention, of the Poets, but as ſacred
Reliques, gentle Whiſpers, and the Breath of better Times; that
from the Traditions of more ancient Nations came, at length, into
the Flutes and Trumpets of the *Greeks*. But, if any one ſhall, notwithſtanding this, contend that Allegories are always adventitious, or

---

[a] See with regard to *Natural Hiſtory* and *Phyſicks*, Dr *Hook's* Diſcourſe of *Earthquakes*

2

impofed upon the ancient Fables, and no way native, or genuinely contained in them, we might here leave him undisturbed in that gravity of Judgment he affects, (tho' we cannot help accounting it for what dull and phlegmatic) and if it were worth the trouble, proceed to another kind of Argument.

8 Men have proposed to answer two different, and contrary Ends, by the use of Parable; for Parables serve, as well to instruct or illustrate, as to wrap up and envelope so that tho', for the prefent, we drop the concealed use, and suppose the ancient *Fables* to be vague, undeterminate Things, formed for Amusement, still the other use must remain, and can never be given up And every Man, of any Learning, must readily allow, that this Method of instructing is grave, sober, or exceedingly useful, and sometimes neceffary in the Sciences as it opens an easy and familiar Passage to the human Underftanding, in all new Discoveries that are abstrufe, and out of the road of vulgar Opinions Hence, in the first Ages, when fuch Inventions and Conclusions of the human Reason, as are now trite and common, were new and little known; all things abounded with Fables, Parables, Similes, Comparisons, and Allusions, which were not intended to conceal, but to inform and teach whilst the Minds of Men continued rude and unpractised in Matters of Subtilty and Speculation, or even impatient, and in a manner uncapable of receiving fuch things as did not directly fall under and strike the Senfes For as *Hieroglyphicks were in ufe before Writing, fo were Parables in ufe before Arguments* And even, to this day, if any Man would let new Light in upon the human Underftanding, and conquer Prejudice, without raising Contefts, Animofities, Oppofition, or Difturbance, he muft still go in the fame Path, and have recourfe to the like Method of Allegory, Metaphor, and Allufion [a]

9 To conclude, the Knowledge of the early Ages was either *great* or *happy*, great, if they by Defign made this ufe of Trope and Figure, happy, if whilst they had other Views, they afforded Matter and Occafion to fuch noble Contemplations. Let either be the Cafe, our Pains, perhaps, will not be mifemploy'd, whether we illuftrate Antiquity, or Things themfelves

10.

[a] What ufe the Author has made of his Art, will appear to a careful Reader of his *de Augmentis Scientiarum* and *Novum Organum* And tho' fome are of Opinion that Knowledge is fo far improved of late, and Mens Minds fo opened and prepared, that new Difcoveries and the naked Truth will be beft received, when delivered in plain and fimple Language, without foreign Art or Colour, yet he, who acts upon fuch a Suppofition, will perhaps find it erroneous even tho' the Subject be but of a Phyfical, and not of a Moral, Political, or Religious Nature

10. The like indeed has been attempted by others ; but to ſpeak in-
genuouſly, their great and voluminous Labours have almoſt de- ſtroy'd the Energy, the Efficacy and Grace of the Thing, whilſt be- ing unſkilled in Nature, and their Learning no more than that of Common-Place, they have applied the Senſe of the Parables to certain general and vulgar Matters, without reaching to their real Purport, genuine Interpretation, and full Depth For my ſelf, there- fore, I expect to appear new in theſe common Things, becauſe, leaving untouched ſuch as are ſufficiently plain, and open, I ſhall drive only at thoſe that are either deep or rich [a]

[a] In effect, the Author appears to have judiciouſly choſe his *Fables*, as they were pregnant with uſeful Matter, yet not of the eaſieſt kind to interpret thus, in his uſual Way, ſetting others an Example for proſecuting the Thing farther, as not having himſelf exhauſted this fruitful Subject See *de Augment Scientiar* pag 56—69

SECT.

SECT. I.

The concealed Physical Knowledge of the Ancients decyphered.

I.

The Fable *of* Cœlum, *explained of the* Creation, *or* Origin *of all* Things.

The FABLE.

Cœlum, &c. Cœlum Father

1 THE *Poets relate, that* Cœlum (*a*) *was the most ancient of all the Gods, that his Parts of Generation were cut off by his Son* Saturn, *that* Saturn (*b*) *had a numerous Offspring,*

Jup. usurps the Kingdom

but devoured all his Sons, as soon as they were born (*c*), *that* Jupiter, *at length, escaped the common Fate, and when grown up, drove his Father* Saturn *into* Tartarus, *usurped the Kingdom, cut off his Father's Genitals, with the same Knife wherewith* Saturn *had dismembred* Cœlum *d*), *and throwing them into the Sea, thence sprung* Venus (*e*)

Two Wars on Jupiter

2 *Before* Jupiter *was well established in his Empire, two memorable Wars were made upon him, the first by the* Titans, *in subduing of whom* Sol, *the only one of the* Titans *who favoured* Jupiter, *performed him singular Service The second by the* Giants, *who being destroyed and subdued by the Thunder and Arms of* Jupiter, *he now reigned secure* (*f*).

The EXPLANATION.

The Fable a physical Account of the Origin of the World

3 THIS *Fable* appears to be an enigmatical Account of the *Origin of all Thing*, not greatly differing from the Philosophy afterwards embraced by *Democritus,* who expresly asserts the Eternity of Matter, but denies

denies the Eternity of the World   thereby approaching to the Truth of
ſacred Writ, which makes *Chaos*, or un-informed Matter to exiſt before
the ſix Days Works

4   The meaning of the Fable ſeems to be this   (*a*) *Cœlum* denotes the con- *Cœlum diſ-*
cave Space, or vaulted Roof that incloſes all Matter, and (*b*) *Saturn* the *membred*
Matter it ſelf; which cuts off all Power of Generation from his Father
as one and the ſame quantity of Matter remains invariable in Nature,
without Addition or Diminution [a]   (*c*) But the Agitations and ſtruggling *Saturn de*
Motions of Matter, firſt produced certain imperfect and ill-join'd Compo- *vouring his*
ſitions of Things, as it were ſo many firſt Rudiments, or Eſſays of Worlds; *Children*
till, in proceſs of Time, there aroſe a Fabrick capable of preſerving its
Form and Structure. (*d*) Whence the firſt *Age* was ſhadowed out by the
Reign of *Saturn*, who, on account of the frequent Diſſolutions, and ſhort *The Reign of*
Durations of Things, was ſaid to *devour his Children*   And the ſecond *Age Saturn*
was denoted by the Reign of *Jupiter*, who thruſt, or drove thoſe frequent and *The Reign of*
tranſitory Changes into *Tartarus*, a place expreſſive of Diſorder   This *Jupiter*
Place ſeems to be the middle Space, between the lower Heavens, and the
internal Parts of the Earth, wherein Diſorder, Imperfection, Mutation,
Mortality, Deſtruction, and Corruption are principally found

5   (*e*) *Venus* was not born during the former Generation of Things, under *The Birth of*
the Reign of *Saturn*   for whilſt Diſcord and Jar had the upper hand of *Venus.*
Concord and Uniformity in the Matter of the Univerſe, a change of the
entire Structure was neceſſary   And in this manner, *Things* were generated
and deſtroy'd, before *Saturn* was diſmembered. But when this manner of
Generation ceaſed [b], there immediately followed another, brought about
by *Venus*, or a perfect and eſtabliſhed Harmony of Things, whereby
Changes were wrought in the Parts, whilſt the univerſal Fabrick remained
entire and undiſturbed   *Saturn*, however, is ſaid to be thruſt out and de- *Saturn, why*
throned, not killed, and become extinct, becauſe agreeably to the Opi- *not killed*
nion of *Democritus*, the World might relapſe into its old Confuſion and
Diſorder   which *Lucretius* hoped would not happen in his Time [c]

6   (*f*) But now, when the World was compact, and held together by its *Sol aſſiſting*
own bulk and energy, yet there was no Reſt from the beginning   for firſt, *Jupiter*
there followed conſiderable Motions and Diſturbances in the Celeſtial Regions, tho' ſo regulated and moderated by the Power of the *Sun*, prevailing
over the Heavenly Bodies, as to continue the World in its State   Afterwards
there followed the like in the lower Parts, by *Inundations, Storms, Winds,*
general *Earthquakes, &c*   which, however, being ſubdued and kept under,
there enſued a more peaceable and laſting Harmony and Conſent of
Things.

7 It

[a] See the *Introduction* to the Author's Hiſtory of *Rarefaction* and *Condenſation*, Vol III   The
original Quantity of Matter remaining invariably the ſame, explains that Circumſtance in the
Fable, of the ſame Knife being uſed for the diſmembring of *Saturn*, as had before been uſed
for the diſmembring of *Cœlum*

[b] *Viz* When *Jupiter* poſſeſſed the Throne, or after a durable World was formed   Let the
figurative or perſonifying Manner of Expreſſion, uſual among the Poets, be all along conſider'd.

[c] *Quod procul à nobis flectat Fortuna gubernans,*
  Et Ratio potius, quam Res perſuadeat ipſa.

The Fable : ? *7* It may be faid of this *Fable*, that it includes *Philofophy*; and again, that *Philofophy* includes the *Fable* for we know, by Faith, that all thefe Things are but the *Oracles of Senfe*, long fince ceafed and decayed, both the Matter and Fabrick of the World being juftly attributed to a Creator [a].

II.

The Fable of PROMETHEUS; *explained of an over-ruling Providence, and of Human Nature.*

The FABLE.

Prometheus creates Man and fteals Fire from Heaven 1 THE Ancients relate that Man was the Work of Prometheus, and formed of Clay (a), only the Artificer mixed in with the Mafs, Particles taken from different Animals (b) And being defirous to improve his Workmanfhip, and endow as well as create the Human Race; he ftole up to Heaven with a bundle of Birch Rods; and kindling them at the Chariot of the Sun, thence brought down Fire to the Earth, for the Service of Men (c)

A difpleafure to God 2 They add, that for this meritorious Act, Prometheus was repay'd with ingratitude by Mankind, fo that, forming a Confpiracy, they accufed both him and his Invention to Jupiter. But the matter was otherwife received, than they imagined for the Accufation proved extremely grateful to Jupiter, and the Gods, *Perpetual Youth beftowed on Men* infomuch, that delighted with the Action (d), they not only indulged Mankind the ufe of Fire, but moreover conferred upon them a moft acceptable and defirable Prefent, viz Perpetual Youth (e).

The Care for it loft by Men 3 But Men, foolifhly overjoyed hereat, laid this Prefent of the Gods upon an Afs, who, in returning back with it, being extremely thirfty, and coming to a Fountain; the Serpent, who was Guardian thereof, would not fuffer him to drink, but upon Condition of receiving the Burden he carried, whatever it fhould be. The filly *And transferred to Serpents* Afs complied, and thus the perpetual Renewal of Youth was, for a Sup of Water, transferred from Men to the Race of Serpents (f).

4 Prometheus, not defifting from his unwarrantable Practices, *Prometheus offers a Mock Sacrifice* tho' now reconcil'd to Mankind, after they were thus tricked of their Prefent (g), but ftill continuing inveterate againft Jupiter, had the boldnefs to attempt Deceit, even in a Sacrifice, and is

said

---

[a] Next fhould follow the *Fable* of Pan, explained in the *de Augmentis Scientiarum*, for that *Fable* feems naturally to fucceed the prefent as the *Phænomena* of the Univerfe, come to be confidered immediate after its Origin See *de Augment Scientiar* pag 59, &c

said to have once offered up two Bulls to Jupiter; *but so, as in the Hide of one of them, to wrap all the Flesh and Fat of both, and stuffing out the other Hide only with the Bones, then in a religious and devout Manner, gave* Jupiter *his choice of the two   Jupiter detesting this sly Fraud and Hypocrisy, but having thus an opportunity of punishing the Offender, purposely chose the Mock-Bull* (h).

5. *And now giving way to Revenge, but finding he could not* Pandora equipped with her Box *chastise the insolence of* Prometheus, *without afflicting the human Race, (in the Production whereof,* Prometheus *had strangely and insufferably prided himself;) he commanded* Vulcan *to form a beautiful and graceful Woman, to whom every God presented a certain Gift, whence she was called* Pandora ᵃ. *They put into her Hands an elegant Box, containing all sorts of Miseries and Misfortunes; but Hope was placed at the bottom of it   With this Box she first goes to* Prometheus, *to try if she could prevail upon him to receive and open it; but he being upon his Guard, warily refused the offer. Upon this refusal, she comes to his Brother* Epimetheus, *a Man of a* The Box opened *very different Temper, who rashly and inconsiderately opens the Box.* (i) *When finding all kinds of Miseries and Misfortunes issued out of it, he grew Wise too late; and with great hurry and struggle endeavoured to clap the Cover on again · but with all his Endeavour, could scarce keep in* Hope, *which lay at the Bottom* (k).

6 *Lastly,* Jupiter *arraigned* Prometheus *of many heinous Crimes* › Prometheus arraigned by Jupiter. *as that he formerly stole Fire from Heaven, that he contemptuously, and deceitfully mocked him by a Sacrifice of Bones, that he despised his Present* ᵇ; *adding withal a new Crime, that he attempted to ravish* Pallas *for all which he was sentenced to be bound* Condemned *in Chains, and doomed to perpetual Torments.   Accordingly, by* Jupiter's *Command, he was brought to Mount* Caucasus, *and there* Fastened to Caucasus *fastned to a Pillar, so firmly, that he could no way stir.   A Vulture, or Eagle stood by him, which in the day-time gnawed and consumed his Liver, but in the night the wasted Parts were supplied again   whence Matter for his Pain was never wanting* (l).

7 *They relate, however, that his Punishment had an End; for* Released Hercules *sailing the Ocean, in a Cup, or Pitcher, presented him by the* Sun, *came at length to* Caucasus, *shot the Eagle with his Arrows; and set* Prometheus *free* (m).   *In certain Nations also there were instituted particular* Games of the Torch, *to the honour of* Prometheus, *in which they, who run for the Prize, carried* lighted The Promethean Games *Torches, and as any one of these Torches happened to go out, the*

ᵇ As if it were *All Gift*   ᵇ *Viz* that by *Pandora.*

VOL. I.   Bbbb   *Bearer*

Bearer withdrew himself, and gave way to the next; and that Perſon was allowed to win the Prize, who firſt brought in his lighted Torch to the Goal (n).

The EXPLANATION.

Prometheus Providence

8 (a) THIS *Fable* contains and enforces many juſt and ſerious Confiderations, ſome whereof have been, long ſince, well obſerved, but ſome again remain perfectly untouched *Prometheus* clearly and expreſsly ſignifies *Providence*, for of all the Things in Nature, the formation and endowment of Man was ſingled out by the Ancients, and eſteemed the peculiar Work of Providence The Reaſon hereof ſeems, (1.) That the Nature of Man includes a Mind and Underſtanding, which is the Seat of Providence, (2) That it is harſh and incredible, to ſuppoſe Reaſon and Mind ſhould be raiſed, and drawn out of ſenſeleſs and irrational Principles, whence it becomes almoſt inevitable, that Providence is implanted in the human Mind, in Conformity with, and by the Direction and the Deſign of the greater over-ruling Providence But, (3) The principal Cauſe is this, that Man ſeems to be the Thing, in which the whole World centers, with reſpect to *final Cauſes*, ſo that if he were away, all other Things would ſtray and fluctuate, without End or Intention, or become perfectly diſjointed, and out of frame. For all Things are made ſubſervient to Man, and he receives uſe and benefit from them all Thus the Revolutions, Places, and Periods of the celeſtial Bodies, ſerve him for diſtinguiſhing Times and Seaſons, and for dividing the World into different Regions the Meteors afford him Prognoſtications of the Weather, the Winds fail our Ships, drive our Mills, and move other Machines, and the Vegetables and Animals of all kinds, either afford us Matter for Houſes and Habitations, Cloathing, Food, Phyſick, or tend to eaſe, or delight, ſupport, or refreſh us ſo that every Thing in Nature ſeems not made for it ſelf, but for Man

9 (b) And 'tis not without Reaſon added, that the Maſs of Matter, whereof Man was formed, ſhould be mixed up with Particles taken from different Animals, and wrought in with the Clay, becauſe, 'tis certain, that of all Things in the Univerſe, Man is the moſt compounded, and recompounded Body, ſo that the Ancients not improperly ſtyled him a *Microcoſm*, or little World within himſelf For altho' the Chemiſts have abſurdly, and too literally, wreſted and perverted the Elegance of the Term *Microcoſm*, whilſt they pretend to find all kind of mineral and vegetable Matters, or ſomething correſponding to them, in Man, yet it remains firm and unſhaken, that the human Body is of all Subſtances the moſt mixed, and organical whence it has ſurprizing Powers and Faculties For the Powers of ſimple Bodies are but few, tho' certain and quick, as being little broken, or weakened, and not counterballanced by Mixture But Excellence, and Quantity of Energies lie in Mixture and Compoſition [a]   10.

[a] The Inſtances of this Poſition deſerve to be collected Conſider of the Mechanical Powers, Medicine, Poiſons, Plants, Companies, Governments, Arts, the advancement of Philoſophy, &c.

10 Man, however, in his first Origin, seems to be a defenceless, naked *The Invention* Creature, slow in assisting himself, and standing in need of numerous Things *of Fire* Prometheus, therefore, hastened to the Invention of Fire, which supplies and administers to nearly all human Uses and Necessities, insomuch, that if the Soul may be called the *Form of Forms*, if the Hand may be called the *Instrument of Instruments*, Fire may, as properly, be called the *Assistant of Assistants*, or the *Helper of Helps* For hence proceed numberless Operations, hence all the *Mechanic Arts*, and hence infinite Assistances are afforded to the Sciences themselves.

11. (c) The manner wherein *Prometheus* stole this Fire, is properly described *How stole by* from the Nature of the Thing, he being said to have done it by applying a *Prometheus* Rod of Birch, to the Chariot of the Sun. for Birch is used in striking and beating, which clearly denotes the Generation of Fire to be from the violent Percussions, and Collisions of Bodies, whereby the Matters struck are subtilized, rarified, put into Motion, and so prepared to receive the Heat of the Celestial Bodies, whence they, in a clandestine and secret manner, collect and snatch Fire, as it were by stealth, from the Chariot of the Sun [a].

12 (d) The next is a remarkable part of the *Fable*, which represents, that *Jupiter pleas'd* Men, instead of Gratitude and Thanks, fell into Indignation and Expostula- *with the apparent Ingra-* tion, accusing both *Prometheus* and his Fire to *Jupiter*. and yet the Ac- *titude of Men* cusation proved highly pleasing to *Jupiter*, so that he, for this Reason, *to Prome-* crowned these Benefits of Mankind, with a new Bounty. Here it may seem *theus.* strange, that the Sin of Ingratitude to a Creator and Benefactor, a Sin so heinous as to include almost all others; should meet with Approbation and Reward. But the Allegory has another View, and denotes, that the Accusation *Explained of* and Arraignment both of *human Nature*, and *human Art*, among Mankind, *calling Men* proceeds from a most noble and laudable Temper of the Mind; and tends *and Nature* to a very good purpose whereas the contrary Temper is odious to the *to account* Gods; and unbeneficial in it self For they who break into extravagant Praises of *human Nature*, and the Arts in vogue, lay themselves out in admiring the Things they already possess, and will needs have the *Sciences* cultivated among them, to be thought absolutely perfect and compleat; in the *first* place, show little Regard to the *Divine Nature* · whilst they extol their own Inventions, almost as high as his Perfection In the *next* place, Men of this Temper are unserviceable and prejudicial in Life, whilst they imagine themselves already got to the Top of Things, and there rest, without farther Enquiry On the contrary, they who arraign and accuse both Nature and Arts, and are always full of Complaints against them, not only preserve a more just and modest Sense of Mind, but are also perpetually stirred up to fresh Industry, and new Discoveries. Is not then the Ignorance and Fatality of Mankind to be extremely pitied, whilst they remain Slaves to the Arrogance of a few of their own Fellows, and are doatingly fond of that Scrap of *Grecian* Knowledge, the *Peripatetic* Philo-

Bbbb 2   sophy;

[a] See the Author's Example of an Enquiry into the *Form of Heat*, in the *Novum Organum* Part II Sect I See also the Chapter of *Fire* in *Boerhaave's Chemistry*

sophy, and this to such a Degree, as not only to think all Accusation or Arraignment thereof useless, but even hold it suspect and dangerous? Certainly, the Proceoure of *Empedocles*, tho' furious, but especially that of *Democritus* (who with great Modesty complained, that all Things were abstruse, that we know nothing, that Truth lies hid in deep Pits, that Falshood is strangely joined and twisted along with Truth, &c) is to be preferred before the confident, assuming and dogmatical School of *Aristotle* [a] Mankind are, therefore, to be admonished, that the Arraignment of Nature and of Art, is pleasing to the Gods, and that a sharp and vehement Accusation of *Prometheus*, tho' a Creator, a Founder, and a Master, obtained new Blessings and Presents from the Divine Bounty, and proved more sound and serviceable than a diffusive Harangue of Praise and Gratulation And let Men be assured, that a *fond Opinion they have already acquired enough, is a principal Reason why they have acquired so little* [b]

Prometheus' Tour or returning Accusing Prometheus

13 [c] That the perpetual Flower of Youth should be the Present which Mankind received as a Reward for their Accusation, carries this Moral; that the Ancients seem not to have despaired of discovering Methods, and Remedies, for retarding old Age, and prolonging the Period of Human Life, but rather reckoned it among those things which, thro' sloth and want of diligent Enquiry, perish and come to nothing, after having been once undertaken, than among such as are absolutely impossible, or not placed within the reach of the human Power For they signify, and intimate, from the true use of Fire, and the just and strenuous Accusation, and Conviction of the Errors of Art, that the divine Bounty is not wanting to Men in such kind of Presents, but that Men indeed are wanting to themselves, and lay such an inestimable Gift upon the back of a *slow-paced Ass* that is, upon the back of the heavy, dull, lingring Thing, Experience; from whose sluggish and tortoise Pace proceeds that ancient Complaint of the shortness of Life, and the slow advancement of Arts [c]. And certainly it may well seem, that the two Faculties of *Reasoning* and *Experience*, are not hitherto properly joined, and coupled together; but to be still new Gifts of the Gods, separately laid, the one upon the back of a light Bird, or *abstract Philosophy*, and the other upon an Ass, or slow-paced Practice and Trial. And yet good Hopes might be conceived of this Ass; if it were not for his Thirst, and the Accidents of the Way. For we judge, that if any one
                                                                        would

[a] The Address of the Author may here deserve to be observed What he is forced on many occasions to stifle, or at most to speak only by halves, for fear of offending, he here openly avouches, in a manner that is scarce liable to exception Indeed, he appears to have chose the present Subject, the rather because the Course and Nature of *deciphering the Mythology* of the *Ancients*, would give him an opportunity of freely, or less offensively expressing his Sentiments, for the improvement of Arts and Sciences, and the general Advantage of Mankind

[b] Certainly, few appear sensible what a number of great Things are still wanting in Philosophy, for the Accommodation of Human Life, or even to prevent dreadful Calamities, such as happen by Fire, Water, Storms, &c Things wherein Men seem either quite regardless or confounded, as if they had no Faculties for procuring a Command over Nature in these Particulars And to examine it closely, we shall perhaps find the *moral* and *political World* subject to their Calamities, no less than the *physical* See Vol II pag 61.

[c] See the Introduction to the *History of Life and Death* Vol III p 335

would conftantly proceed, by a certain Law and Method, in the Road of Experience, and not by the way, thirft after fuch Experiments as make for *Profit* or *Oftentation* [a], nor exchange his Burden, or quit the original Defign, for the fake of thofe [b]; he might be an ufeful Bearer of a new and accumulated divine Bounty to Mankind [c]

14 (*f*) That this Gift of perpetual Youth fhould pafs from Men to Serpents, feems added by way of Ornament, and Illuftration to the *Fable* [d], perhaps intimating, at the fame time, the fhame it is for Men, that they, with their *Fire*, and numerous *Arts*, cannot procure to themfelves thofe Things which Nature has beftowed upon many other Creatures [e]

The Gift of perpetual Youth transferred to Serpents

15. (*g*) The fudden Reconciliation of *Prometheus* to Mankind, after being difappointed of their Hopes, contains a prudent and ufeful Admonition. It points out the Levity and Temerity of Men in new Experiments, which, not prefently fucceeding, or anfwering to Expectation, Men precipitantly quit their new Undertakings, hurry back to their old ones, and grow reconciled thereto [f].

The Reconciliation of Prometheus to Men.

16 (*h*) After the *Fable* has defcribed the State of Man, with regard to *Arts* and *intellectual Matters*, it paffes on to *Religion*· for after the inventing and fettling of Arts, follows the eftablifhment of divine Worfhip; which Hypocrify prefently enters into, and corrupts. So that by the two Sacrifices we have elegantly painted the Perfon of a Man truly Religious, and of an Hypocrite One of thefe Sacrifices contained the Fat, or the *Portion of God*, ufed for burning and incenfing, thereby denoting Affection and Zeal, incenfed up to his Glory It likewife contained the Bowels, which are expreffive of Charity; along with the good and ufeful Flefh But the other contained nothing more than dry Bones, which neverthelefs ftuffed out the Hide, fo as to make it refemble a fair, beautiful, and magnificent Sacrifice, hereby finely denoting the external and empty Rites and barren Ceremonies, wherewith Men burden and ftuff out the divine Worfhip Things rather intended for Show and Oftentation, than conducing to Piety Nor are Mankind fimply content with this Mock Worfhip of God, but alfo impofe and father it upon him, as if he had chofe and ordained it. Certainly the Prophet, in the Perfon of God, has a fine Expoftulation, as to this Matter of Choice *Is this the fafting which I have chofen, that a Man fhould afflict his Soul for a Day, and bow down his Head like a Bulrufh?*

The Mock Sacrifice

17 (*i*) After thus touching the State of Religion, the Fable next turns to *Manners*, and the Conditions of human Life And tho' it be a very common, yet is it a juft Interpretation, that *Pandora* denotes the Pleafures and Licentioufnefs, which the Cultivation and Luxury of the Arts of civil Life introduce, as it were, by the inftrumental Efficacy of *Fire* whence the Works of the voluptuary Arts are properly attributed to *Vulcan*, the God of

Vulcan forming Pandora

---

[a] See the *Fable* of *Atalanta*, Fab. V below
[b] As a moft the whole Body of Mankind, both Philofophers and others, feem to have done.
[c] See the Author's Method of *Learned Experience*, *de Augment Scientiar*. Sect XII.
[d] See *Introduction*, § 5 &c
[e] See the Author's *Hiftory of Life and Death*
[f] Which is one principal Reafon of the flow Advancement of *Arts*.

of Fire   And hence infinite Miseries and Calamities have proceeded to the Minds, the Bodies, and the Fortunes of Men, together with a late Repentance; and this not only in each Man's particular, but also in Kingdoms and States   for Wars and Tumults, and Tyrannies, have all arisen from this same Fountain, or Box of *Pandora*

The Behaviour of Epimetheus to Pandora

18 (*k*) 'Tis worth observing how beautifully, and elegantly, the *Fable* has drawn two reigning Characters in human Life; and given two Examples, or Tablatures of them, under the Persons of *Prometheus* and *Epimetheus*   The Followers of *Epimetheus* are improvident, see not far before them, and prefer such Things as are agreeable for the present; whence they are oppressed with numerous Straits, Difficulties, and Calamities, with which they almost continually struggle   but in the mean time gratify their own Temper, and, for want of a better Knowledge of Things, feed their Minds with many vain Hopes   and as with so many pleasing Dreams, delight themselves, and sweeten the Miseries of Life

That of Prometheus

19 (*l*) But the Followers of *Prometheus* are the prudent, wary Men, that look into Futurity, and cautiously guard against, prevent, and undermine many Calamities and Misfortunes.   But this watchful, provident Temper is attended with a deprivation of numerous Pleasures, and the loss of various Delights, whilst such Men debar themselves the use even of innocent Things· and what is still worse, rack and torture themselves with Cares, Fears, and Disquiets, being bound fast to the Pillar of Necessity, and tormented with numberless Thoughts (which for their swiftness are well compared to an Eagle) that continually wound, tear, and gnaw their Liver, or Mind, unless, perhaps they find some small Remission by Intervals, or as it were at Nights: but then new Anxieties, Dreads, and Fears, soon return again, as it were in the Morning   And therefore, very few Men, of either Temper, have secured to themselves the Advantages of Providence, and kept clear of Disquiets, Troubles, and Misfortunes

Assisted by Hercules

20 (*m*) Nor indeed can any Man obtain this End, without the Assistance of *Hercules*, that is, of such Fortitude and Constancy of Mind, as stands prepared against every Event, and remains indifferent to every Change, looking forward without being daunted, enjoying the Good without disdain, and enduring the Bad without impatience   And it must be observed, that even *Prometheus* had not the Power to free himself, but owed his Deliverance to another   for no natural, inbred Force and Fortitude could prove equal to such a Task.   The Power of releasing him came from the utmost Confines of the *Ocean*, and from the *Sun*; that is, from *Apollo*, or *Knowledge*   and again, from a due Consideration of the uncertainty, instability, and fluctuating State of human Life, which is aptly represented by sailing the *Ocean*   Accordingly *Virgil* has prudently joined these two together, accounting him happy who *knows the Causes of* Things, and has conquered all his *Fears, Apprehensions,* and *Superstitions* [*].

21

* *Felix qui potuit rerum cognoscere Causas,*
   Quique metus omnes & inexorabile Fatum
   Subjecit pedibus, strepitumque Acherontis avari

21 'Tis added, with great Elegance, for supporting and confirming the human Mind, that the great *Hero* who thus delivered him, fail'd the *Ocean* in a Cup or Pitcher , to prevent the Fear, or Complaint, as if, through the Narrownefs of our Nature, or a too great Fragility thereof, we were abfolutely incapable of that Fortitude and Conftancy, to which *Seneca* finely alludes, when he fays, *'Tis a noble Thing, at once to participate the Frailty of Man, and the Security of a God.* _{Hercules croffing the Ocean in a Pitcher}

22. We have hitherto, that we might not break the connexion of Things, defignedly omitted the laft Crime of *Prometheus*, that of attempting the Chaftity of *Minerva* , which heinous Offence, it doubtlefs was, that caufed the Punifhment of having his Liver gnaw'd by the *Vulture*. The Meaning feems to be this , that when Men are puffed up with Arts and Knowledge, they often try to fubdue even the divine Wifdom , and bring it under the Dominion of Senfe and Reafon whence inevitably follows a perpetual, and reftlefs rending and tearing of the Mind A fober and humble Diftinction muft, therefore, be made betwixt *divine* and *human* Things , and betwixt the Oracles of Senfe and Faith , unlefs Mankind had rather chufe an *heretical Religion*, and a *fictitious* and *romantic Philofophy* [a]. _{Prometheus attempting Pallas.}

23. (*n*) The laft Particular in the Fable is the *Games of the Torch*, inftituted to *Prometheus* , which again relates to *Arts* and *Sciences*, as well as the Invention of Fire, for the Commemoration and Celebration whereof, thefe Games were held And here we have an extremely prudent Admonition, directing us to expect the *Perfection of the Sciences from Succeffion* , and not from the Swiftnefs and Abilities of any fingle Perfon· for he who is fleeteft and ftrongeft in the Courfe, may perhaps be lefs fit to keep his Torch alight, fince there is danger of its going out from too rapid, as well as from too flow a motion [b]. But this kind of conteft with the Torch feems to have been long dropt, and neglected , the Sciences appearing to have flourifhed principally in their firft Authors, as *Ariftotle*, *Galen*, *Euclid*, *Ptolemy*, &c whilft their Succeffors have done very little, or fcarce made any attempts. But it were highly to be wifhed, that thefe *Games* might be renewed, to the honour of *Prometheus*, or human Nature , and that they might excite Conteft, Emulation and laudable Endeavours , and the Defign meet with fuch Succefs, as not to hang tottering, tremulous, and hazarded upon the Torch of any fingle Perfon [c]. Mankind, therefore, fhould be admonifhed to rouze themfelves, and try and exert their own Strength and Chance , and not place all their Dependance upon a few Men, whofe Abilities and Capacities, perhaps, are not greater than their own. _{The Games of the Torch}

24. Thefe are the Particulars which appear to us fhadowed out by this trite and vulgar *Fable* , tho' without denying that there may be contained in it feveral Intimations that have a furprizing Correfpondence with the *Chriftian Myfteries*. _{The Fable may allude to Chriftianity}

I

[a] See the *De Augment Scientiar* Sect XXVIII and *Supplem* XV
[b] This Matter is abundantly explained in the *de Augmentis*, and *Novum Organum*
[c] The Author here feems to have had himfelf in view , as being the only Reftorer or Promoter of thefe Games, in his Time See the Doctrine of the *Traditive Lamp*, in the *de Augment Scientiar* Vol I pag 146, 147

Mysteries. In particular, the Voyage of *Hercules*, made in a Pitcher, to re-lease *Prometheus*, bears an allusion to the *Word* of *God*, coming in the frail Vessel of the Flesh to redeem Mankind. But we indulge our selves no such Liberties as these, for fear of using *strange Fire* at the *Altar of the Lord*[a].

III.

The FABLE *of* ORPHEUS *explained; of* NATURAL *and* MORAL PHILOSOPHY.

INTRODUCTION.

The Fable of Orpheus explained

1 THE *Fable of Orpheus*, tho' trite and common, has never been well interpreted ; and seems to hold out a Picture of *universal Philosophy* : for to this Sense may be easily transferr'd what is said of his being a wonderful and perfectly divine Person, skill'd in all kinds of Harmony, subduing and drawing all Things after him by sweet and gentle Methods and Modulations. For the Labours of *Orpheus* exceed the Labours of *Hercules*, both in power and dignity , as the Works of *Knowledge* exceed the Works of *Strength*

The FABLE.

Eurydice recovered

2. ORpheus *having his beloved Wife snatched from him by sudden Death, resolved upon descending to the Infernal Regions , to try, if by the Power of his Harp he could re-obtain her And in effect, he so appeased and soothed the Infernal Powers by the Melody and Sweetness of his Harp and Voice, that they indulged him the Liberty of taking her back ; on condition that she should follow him behind, and he not turn to look upon her 'till they came into open Day* (a) · *But he, thro' the impatience of his Care and Affection, and thinking himself almost past danger, at*

And lost again

length looked behind him ; whereby the Condition was violated, and she again precipitated to Pluto's Regions From this time
Orpheus

---

a This Fable, and its Explanation may deserve to be read again and again, as a little System of Physics, Morality Religion, and all kinds of Learning And perhaps the full Interpretation and Elegence of the whole can scarce be perceived, without having frequent Recourse from the Parts of the Explanation to the corresponding Parts of the *Fable*

Orpheus *grew penſive and ſad, a Hater of the Sex, and went into Solitude* (b)*; where by the ſame Sweetneſs of his Harp and Voice he firſt drew the wild Beaſts of all ſorts about him, ſo that, forgetting their Natures, they were neither actuated by Revenge, Cruelty, Luſt, Hunger, or the Deſire of Prey, but ſtood gazing about him, in a tame and gentle manner, liſtening attentively to his Muſic　Nay, ſo great was the Power and Efficacy of his Harmony, that it even cauſed the Trees and Stones to remove, and place themſelves, in a regular Manner, about him. When he had for a time, and with great admiration, continued to do this, at length the* Thracian *Women, raiſed by the Inſtigation of* Bacchus, *firſt blew a deep and hoarſe-ſounding Horn, in ſuch an outrageous manner, that it quite drowned the Muſic of* Orpheus. *And thus the Power, which, as the Link of their Society, held all Things in order, being diſſolved, Diſturbance reign'd anew, each Creature returned to its own Nature, and purſued and prey'd upon its Fellow, as before　The Rocks and Woods alſo ſtarted back to their former Places; and even* Orpheus *himſelf was at laſt torn to pieces by theſe female Furies, and his Limbs ſcattered all over the Deſart. But, in Sorrow and Revenge for his Death, the River* Helicon, *ſacred to the Muſes, hid its Waters under Ground, and roſe again in other Places* (c).

margin notes:
Orpheus in his Muſic moves the Beaſts
The Trees and Stones
His Muſic drowned
Things return to their own Natures
Orpheus torn to pieces
Helicon ſinks and riſes again

The EXPLANATION.

3 (a) THE *Fable* receives this Explanation　The *Muſic of Orpheus* is of two kinds, one that appeaſes the *infernal Powers*, and the other that draws together the wild Beaſts and Trees　The former properly relates to *natural*, and the latter to *moral Philoſophy*, or civil Society. The Re-inſtatement and Reſtoration of corruptible Things, is the nobleſt Work of *natural Philoſophy*, and, in a leſs degree, the Preſervation of Bodies in their own State, or a prevention of their Diſſolution and Corruption　And if this be poſſible, it can certainly be effected no other way than by proper and exquiſite Attemperations of Nature; as it were by the Harmony and fine touching of the Harp [a]. But as this is a Thing of exceeding great Difficulty, the End is ſeldom obtained, and that, probably, for

margin notes:
Orpheus's Muſic of two kinds
Regarding Morals and Phyſics

[a] Without an Allegory, by diſcovering and acting according to the Laws of Nature, as thoſe of *Attraction, Gravitation, Motion, Separation, Mixture, Preſervation, Putrefaction, Regeneration,* &c. See the *Sylva Sylvarum paſſim,* and the *Hiſtory of Life and Death*

ro reafon more than a curious and unfeafonable Impatience and Sollicitude [a]

b) And therefore Philofophy being almoft unequal to the Tafk, has caufe to grow fad, and hence betakes it felf to *human Affairs*, infinuating into Men's minds the love of Virtue, Equity and Peace, by means of Eloquence and Perfuafion thus forming Men into Societies, bringing them under Laws and Regulations, and making them forget their unbridled Paffions and Affections, fo long as they hearken to Precepts, and fubmit to Difcipline. And thus they foon after build themfelves Habitations, form Cities, cultivate Lands, plant Orchards, Gardens, &c. So that they may not improperly be faid to remove and call the Trees and Stones together

5 And this regard to *Civil Affairs*, is juftly and regularly placed after the Death is diligent Trial made for reftoring the *mortal Body* [b], the Attempt being fruftrated in the end: becaufe the unavoidable Neceffity of Death, thus evidently laid before Mankind, animates them to feek a kind of Eternity by Works of Perpetuity, Character and Fame

6 'Tis alfo prudently added, that *Orpheus* was afterwards averfe to Women and Wedlock; becaufe the Indulgence of a married State, and the natural Affections which Men have for their Children, often prevent them from entring upon any grand, noble, or meritorious Enterprize for the public Good [c], as thinking it fufficient to obtain Immortality by their Defcendants, without endeavouring at great Actions.

7 (*c*) And even the Works of Knowledge, tho' the moft excellent among human Things, have their Periods for after Kingdoms and Commonwealths have flourifhed for a time, Difturbances, Seditions and Wars often arife in the Din whereof, firft the Laws are filent, and not heard [d], and then Men return to their own depraved Natures whence cultivated Lands and Cities foon become defolate and wafte And if this Diforder continues, Learning and Philofophy is infallibly torn to pieces, fo that only fome fcattered Fragments thereof can afterwards be found up and down, in a few places like Planks after a Shipwreck And barbarous Times fucceeding, the River *Helicon* dips under Ground, that is, Letters are buried, till Things having undergone their due Courfe of Changes, Learning rifes again, and fhews its Head, tho' feldom in the fame Place, but in fome other Nation [e]

I V.

[a] Men being eager to fee the end of *natural Philofophy*, without having Patience to purfue the means for the Laws of Nature are not eafily found, efpecially in that prepofterous and artful manner, by Reafoning and *Speculation*, without proper *Tryals*, and *Experimental Enquiry*.

[b] See above § 3

[c] See the Effay on Marriage and Single Life Vol II pag 102

[d] Here lies the Allegory of the *deep founding Horn*, mentioned in the *Fable*

[e] Thus we fee that
Orpheus denotes Learning,
Eurydice, Things, or the Subject of Learning,
Bacchus and } Men's ungovern'd Paffions and Appetites, &c
the Thracian Women }
And in the fame manner, thefe *Fables* might be familiarly illuftrated. and brought down to the Capacities of Children, who ufually learn them in an unfcientifical manner at School.

V.

The FABLE *of* ATALANTA *and* HIPPOMĒNES;
explained of the Conteſt betwixt ART *and* NATURE.

The FABLE.

1. ATalanta, *who was exceeding fleet, contended with* Hippo-menes *in the Courſe, on condition, that if* Hippomenes *won, he ſhould eſpouſe her; or forfeit his Life, if he loſt. The Match was very unequal, for* Atalanta *had conquered Numbers, to their deſtruction.* Hippomenes, *therefore, had recourſe to Stratagem. He procured three golden Apples, and purpoſely carried them with him they ſtarted,* Atalanta *out-ſtripped him ſoon, then* Hippomenes *bowled one of his Apples before her, a croſs the Courſe, in order, not only to make her ſtoop, but to draw her out of the Path. She, prompted by female Curioſity, and the Beauty of the golden Fruit, ſtarts from the Courſe to take up the Apple* Hippomenes, *in the mean time, holds on his way, and ſteps before her, but ſhe, by her natural Swiftneſs, ſoon fetches up her loſt Ground; and leaves him again behind* Hippomenes *however, by rightly timing his ſecond and third Throw, at length, won the Race; not by his Swiftneſs, but his Cunning.*

Atalanta conquered by Stratagem.

The EXPLANATION.

2. THis Fable ſeems to contain a noble Allegory of the Conteſt betwixt *Art* and *Nature.* For *Art,* here denoted by *Atalanta,* is much ſwifter, or more expeditious, in its Operations than *Nature,* when all Obſtacles and Impediments are removed, and ſooner arrives at its End This appears almoſt in every Inſtance Thus Fruit comes ſlowly from the Kernel, but ſoon by Inoculation or Inſition Clay, left to it ſelf, is a long time in acquiring a ſtony Hardneſs, but is preſently burnt by Fire into Brick [a] So again in human Life, Nature is a long while in alleviating and aboliſhing the remembrance of Pain, and aſſuaging the Troubles of the Mind, but moral Philoſophy, which is the Art of living, performs it preſently.

Atalanta denotes Nature

And Hippomenes Art

Cccc2   Yet

---

[a] A proper Collection of theſe *Inſtances* ſhould be made for the Encouragement of Men in their Endeavours to advance Arts, and produce conſiderable Effects

Yet this Prerogative and singular Efficacy of Art, is stopt and retarded, to the infinite detriment of human Life, by *certain golden Apples* for there is no one Science, or Art, that constantly holds on its true and proper Course to the end , but they are all continually stopping short, forsaking the track, and turning aside to Profit and Convenience , exactly like *Atalanta*. Whence, 'tis no wonder that *Art* gets not the Victory over *Nature* , nor, according to the Condition of the Contest, brings her under Subjection but, on the contrary, remains subject to her, as a Wife to a Husband [a]

VI.

The F A B L E *of* E R I C T H O N I U S ; *explained of the improper Use of Force in* N A T U R A L   P H I L O S O P H Y.

The F A B L E.

T H E *Poets feign that* Vulcan *attempted the Chastity of* Minerva ; *and impatient of Refusal, had recourse to Force but in the Struggle, his* Semen *fell upon the Ground, and produced* Erichonius , *whose Body from the Middle upwards was comely, and well proportioned, but his Thighs and Legs, small, shrunk, and deformed, like an Eel Conscious of this Defect, he became the Inventor of Chariots , so as to shew the graceful, but conceal the deformed Part of his Body.*

The E X P L A N A T I O N.

T His strange and monstrous Fable seems to carry this Meaning. *Art* is here represented under the Person of *Vulcan* ; by reason of the various Uses it makes of Fire and *Nature* under the Person of *Minerva* , by reason of the Industry employed in her Works. Art, therefore, whenever it

[a] The Author in all his physical Works proceeds upon this Foundation, that it is possible, and practicable, for Art to obtain the Victory over Nature , that is, for human Industry and Power to procure, by the means of proper Knowledge, such things as are necessary to render Life as happy and commodious as its mortal State will allow For instance, that it is possible to lengthen the present Period of human Life , bring the Winds more under Command, and every way extend and enlarge the Dominion, or Empire, of Man over the Works of Nature. And let no one fearfully apprehend, that there is danger in thus endeavouring to take the Reins of Government out of Nature's hands, and putting them into the weak hands of Men for the Distinction betwixt Men and Nature, is imaginary, and only made to help the Understanding, Man himself being necessarily subject to the *Laws of Nature* tho' within the Compass of these Laws he has a very extensive Power, that will always be commensurate to Knowledge

it offers violence to Nature, in order to conquer, subdue, and bend her to its Purpose, by Tortures and Force of all kinds ; seldom obtains the End proposed [a]   Yet upon great Struggle and Application, there proceed certain imperfect Births , or lame abortive Works , specious in appearance, but weak and unstable in use   which are, nevertheless, with great Pomp, and deceitful Appearances, triumphantly carried about, and shewn by Impostors   A Procedure very familiar, and remarkable, in *chemical Productions*, and new *mechanical Inventions* , especially when the Inventors rather hug their Errors, than improve upon them , and go on *struggling with Nature*, not *courting her*, in the proper obsequious manner, for an intimate Embrace [b]

VII.

The FABLE *of* ICARUS, *and that of* SCYLLA *and* CHARYBDIS; *explained of Mediocrity in* NATURAL *and* MORAL PHILOSOPHY

The FABLE.

1. MEdiocrity, *or the holding of a middle Course, has been highly extolled in Morality ; but little in matters of Science , tho' no less useful and proper here   whilst in* Politicks *'tis held suspected, or to be employ'd with Judgment. The Ancients described* Mediocrity *in Manners, by the Course prescribed to* Icarus; *and in matters of the Understanding, by the Steering betwixt* Scylla *and* Charybdis *, on account of the great difficulty and danger in passing those Streights.*

   Mediocrity useful in the Sciences

2. Icarus, *being to fly cross the Sea, was ordered by his Father neither to soar too high, nor fly too low , for as his Wings were fastened together with Wax, there was danger of its melting by the Sun's heat in too high a flight ; and of its becoming less tenacious by the moisture, if he kept too near the vapour of the Sea   But he, with a juvenile Confidence, soars aloft , and fell down headlong*

   Icarus's Flight and Fall

                                                              The

---

[a] See below, *Fable* VIII.

[b] 'Tis a fundamental Position with the Author, that *Nature*, like the Ladies, can only be won by Submission   See the *Novum Organum* passim

The EXPLANATION.

*The De-
r e tæ xt
ænd and
D.*

3 THE *Fable* is vulgar, and eafily interpreted , for the Path of Virtue lies ſtrait, between Exceſs on the one fide, and Defect on the
other And no wonder that Exceſs ſhould prove the bane of *Icarus*, exult-
ing in juvenile Strength and Vigour for Exceſs is the natural Vice of Youth ,
as Defect is that of old Age And if a Man muſt periſh by either, *Icarus*
choſe the better of the two , for all Defects are juſtly eſteemed more depraved than Exceſſes There is ſome Magnanimity in Exceſs, that, like a Bird,
claims kindred with the Heavens but Defect is a Reptile, that baſely crawls
upon the Earth 'Twas excellently ſaid by *Heraclitus* , *a dry Light makes
the beſt Soul* for if the Soul contracts moiſture from the Earth, it perfectly
degenerates and ſinks On the other hand, Moderation muſt be obſerved,
to prevent this fine Light from burning, by its too great Subtilty and
Dryneſs But theſe Obſervations are common

*The Allegory
of Scylla and
Charybdis*

4 In Matters of the Underſtanding it requires great Skill, and a particular Felicity, to ſteer clear of *Scylla* and *Charybdis* If the Ship ſtrikes upon
Scylla, 'tis daſhed in pieces againſt the Rocks if upon *Charybdis*, it is ſwal-
lowed outright This Allegory is pregnant with matter , but we ſhall only
obſerve the Force of it lies here, that a Mean be obſerved in every Doctrine
and Science, and in the Rules and Axioms thereof, between the Rocks of
Diſtinctions, and the Whirl-pools of *Univerſalities* for theſe two are the Bane
and Shipwreck of fine Genius's and Arts [a].

VIII.

The FABLE *of* PROTEUS; *explained of Matter and its Changes.*

The FABLE.

*Proteus, Nep-
tunes Herdf-
man and a
Prophet.*

1 PRoteus, *according to the Poets, was* Neptune's *Herdſman ;
an old Man* (a), *and a moſt extraordinary Prophet ; who underſtood Things paſt and preſent as well as future , ſo that beſides
the*

[a] For Arts are founded on Particulars, as we ſee in the Arts of Paper, Sugar, Gunpowder,
&c ſo that General Arts ſlip thro them and ſubtile Diſtinctions and Diviſions ſplit and
grind Nature ſo far, as to render the Objects unfit for the Hand, the Senſe, or even the
Underſtanding to work with, to advantage Hence thoſe fruitleſs and barren Speculations of
the Schoolmen, the infinite Diviſibility of Matter, and mathematical Notions, and metaphyſical
Powers introduced into Phyſics

the *bufinefs of Divination, he was the Revealer and Interpreter of all Antiquity, and Secrets of every kind   He lived in a vaft Cave, where his Cuftom was to tell over his Herd of Sea-Calves at Noon, and then to fleep (b).   Whoever confulted him, had no other way of obtaining an Anfwer, but by binding him with Mana-cles and Fetters , when he, endeavouring to free himfelf, would change into all kinds of Shapes and miraculous Forms , as of Fire, Water, wild Beafts, &c. 'till at length he refumed his own Shape again (c).*

His Tranf-formations

The EXPLANATION.

2 (*a*) THis Fable feems to point at the Secrets of Nature , and the States of Matter.   For the Perfon of *Proteus* denotes *Matter*, the oldeft of all Things, after God himfelf [a], that refides, as in a Cave, under the vaft Concavity of the Heavens   He is reprefented as the Servant of *Neptune* , becaufe the various Operations and Modifications of Matter, are principally wrought in a fluid State.   The Herd, or Flock of *Proteus*, feems to be no other than the feveral kinds of Animals, Plants and Mine-rals, in which Matter appears to diffufe and fpend it felf , fo that after having formed thefe feveral Species, and as it were finifhed its Task, it feems to fleep and repofe ; without otherwife attempting to produce any new ones.   And this is the Moral of *Proteus's* counting his Herd, then going to fleep

Proteus de-notes Matter

His Herd, what

3 (*b*) This is faid to be done at Noon, not in the Morning or Evening, by which is meant the Time beft fitted and difpofed for the Production of Species, from a Matter duly prepared, and made ready before-hand , and now lying in a middle State, between its firft Rudiments and Decline   which, we learn from facred Hiftory, was the Cafe at the time of the Creation , when, by the efficacy of the divine Command, Matter directly came together, without any transformation or intermediate Changes, which it affects ; in-ftantly obeyed the Order , and appeared in the form of Creatures.

Counting them at Noon

4 (*c*) And thus far the Fable reaches of *Proteus*, and his Flock, at liber-ty and unreftrained.   For the Univerfe, with the common Structures and Fabricks of the Creatures, is the Face of Matter, not under conftraint, or as the Flock wrought upon, and tortured, by human means   But if any skill-ful *Minifter of Nature* fhall apply Force to Matter , and by defign torture and vex it, in order to its Annihilation , it, on the contrary, being brought under this Neceffity, changes and transforms it felf into a ftrange Variety of Shapes and Appearances , for nothing but the Power of the Creator can annihilate, or truly deftroy it · fo that at length, running thro' the whole Circle of Transformations, and compleating its Period, it in fome de-gree

Proteus bound.

[a] *Proteus properly fignifies primary, oldeft, or firft*

gree reftores it felf, if the Force be continued And that Method of binding, torturing, or detaining, will prove the moft effectual and expeditious,
which makes ufe of *Manacles* and *Fetters*, that is, lays hold and works upon
Matter in the extremeft Degrees [a]

   5 The addition in the Fable that makes *Proteus* a Prophet, who had the
Knowledge of Things paft, prefent and future, excellently agrees with the
nature of Matter ; as he who knows the Properties, the Changes, and the
Procefses of Matter, muft, of neceffity, underftand the Effects and Sum of
what it does, has done, or can do , tho' his Knowledge extends not to all
the Parts and Particulars thereof [b]

IX.

The FABLE *of* CUPID, *explained of the Corpufcular*
Philofophy.

The FABLE.

1. **T**HE *Particulars related by the Poets of* Cupid, *or* LOVE,
do not properly agree to the fame Perfon, yet they differ
only fo far, that if the Confufion of Perfons be rejected, the Cor-
refpondence may hold They fay, that Love *was the moft ancient*
of all the Gods, and exifted before every thing elfe, except Chaos,
which is held coeval therewith (a) *But for* Chaos, *the Ancients*
never paid divine Honours, nor gave the Title of a God thereto.
Love *is reprefented abfolutely without Progenitor* (b) ; *except-*
ing only that he is faid to have proceeded from the Egg of Nox ,
but that himfelf begot the Gods, and all Things elfe, on Chaos (c)
His Attributes are four , viz. 1. Perpetual Infancy (d), 2. Blindnefs (e), 3 Nakednefs (f), *and* 4 Archery (g)

2 *There was alfo another* Cupid, *or* Love, *the youngeft Son of*
the Gods, born of Venus , *and upon him the Attributes of the elder*
are transferred, with fome degree of Correfpondence (h)

                                      The

---

[a] The Author has propofed a certain Method of working in this manner, by means of a new
Engine or particular Digeftor applied to the Fire See *Sylva Sylvarum*, pag 93 and the *Hi-*
ftory of Rarity and Denfity, Sect V 7, 8, 9

[b] See above *Fable* V *ad finem* See alfo the *Nov Organ*. Part II Aph 1, 2, 3, 4, 5, &c

The EXPLANATION.

3. (*a*) THis *Fable* points at, and enters, the Cradle of Nature. *Love* feems The moving to be the *Appetite*, or *Incentive*, of the primitive Matter, or, to Principle of fpeak more diftinctly, the *natural Motion*, or *moving Principle*, of the origi-Matter the nal Corpufcles, or Atoms this being the moft ancient, and only Power that Egg of Nox made and wrought all Things out of Matter (*b*) 'Tis abfolutely without Parent, that is, without *Caufe*, for *Caufes* are as Parents to *Effects* but this Power or Efficacy could have no *natural Caufe*, for, excepting God, nothing was before it. and therefore it could have no Efficient in Nature And as nothing is more inward with Nature, it can neither be a *Genus* nor a *Form*, and therefore, whatever it is, it muft be fomewhat pofitive, tho' inexpreffi-ble (*c*) And if it were poffible to conceive its *Modus* and *Procefs*, yet it could not be known from its *Caufe*; as being, next to God, the *Caufe of Caufes*, and it felf without a Caufe And perhaps we are not to hope that the *Modus* of it fhould fall, or be comprehended, under human Enquiry. Whence 'tis properly feigned to be the Egg of *Nox*, or laid in the dark ᵃ

4 The divine Philofopher declares, that *God has made every Thing beautiful* Confirmed *in its Seafon, and has given over the World to our Difputes and Enquiries* · *but* from Solo-*that Man cannot find out the Work which God has wrought, from its Beginning* mon. *up to its End.* Thus the fummary or collective Law of Nature, or the *Prin-ciple of Love*, impreffed by God upon the original Particles of all Things, fo as to make them attract each other and come together; by the repetition and multiplication whereof, all the variety in the Univerfe is produced, can fcarce poffibly find full admittance into the Thoughts of Men, tho' fome faint Notion may be had thereof The *Greek* Philofophy is fubtile, and bufied in difcovering the *material Principles of Things*, but negligent and languid in difcovering the *Principles of Motion*, in which the Energy and Effi-cacy of every Operation confifts And here the *Greek* Philofophers feem The Greek perfectly blind and childifh for the Opinion of the *Peripateticks*, as to Philofophers. the *Stimulus* of Matter, by *Privation*, is little more than Words, or rather Sound than Signification. And they who refer it to God, tho' they do well therein, yet they do it by a Start, and not by proper Degrees of Af-fent: for doubtlefs *there is one fummary* or *capital Law* in which Nature meets, *fubordinate to God*; viz the Law mentioned in the Paffage above quoted from *Solomon*; or *the Work which God has wrought from its Begin-ning up to its End* ᵇ.

5 *Democritus*, who farther confidered this Subject, having firft fuppofed Democritus an Atom, or Corpufcle, of fome dimenfion or figure, attributed thereto

ᵃ Let it be examined what Approximations have been made by the modern Philofophers to the Inveftigation of this Principle, in their *Doctrines*, *Calculations*, and *Attempts* to affign the Caufe of *Gravity*
ᵇ *Viz* The Chain of Caufes and Effects, traced gradually up to its laft Link, where Philo-fophy ends but not before it has difcovered *every intermediate Link*

one Appetite, Defire, or firft Motion fimply , and another comparatively : imagining that all Things properly tended to the Centre of the World , thofe containing more Matter falling fafter to the Center, and thereby removing, and in the Shock driving away, fuch as held lefs   But this is a flender Conceit, and regards too few Particulars , for neither the Revolutions of the celeftial Bodies, nor the Contractions and Expanfions of Things, can be reduced to this Principle   And for the Opinion of *Epicurus*, as to the *cafual* and *fortuitous agitation of Atoms* ; this only brings the Matter back again to a Trifle, and wraps it up in Ignorance and *Night* [a]

6 (*d*) *Cupid* is elegantly drawn a perpetual *Child* · for Compounds are larger Things, and have their Periods of Age , but the firft Seeds or Atoms of Bodies are fmall, and remain in a perpetual infant State [b].

7 (*e*) He is again juftly reprefented *naked* , as all Compounds may properly be faid to be dreffed and cloathed, or to affume a Perfonage , whence nothing remains truely naked, but the original Particles of Things

8 (*f*) The Blindnefs of *Cupid* contains a deep Allegory , for this fame *Cupid, Love*, or Appetite of the World. feems to have very little Forefight, but directs his Steps and Motions conformably to what he finds next him , as blind Men do when they feel out their way · which renders the divine and over-ruling Providence and Forefight the more furprizing , as by a certain fteady *Law*, it brings fuch a beautiful Order, and Regularity, of Things out of what feems extremely cafual, void of Defign, and as it were really blind

9 (*g*) The laft Attribute of *Cupid* is *Archery* , viz a Virtue or Power operating at a diftance   for every thing that operates at a diftance , may feem, as it were, to dart, or fhoot with Arrows   And whoever allows of Atoms and Vacuity, neceffarily fuppofes that the Virtue of Atoms operates at a diftance , for without this Operation, no Motion could be excited, on account of the *Vacuum* interpofing , but all Things would remain fluggifh and unmoved

10 (*h*) As to the other *Cupid*, he is properly faid to be the youngeft Son of the Gods , as his Power could not take place before the formation of Species, or particular Bodies   The Defcription given us of him transfers the Allegory to Morality , tho' he ftill retains fome refemblance with the ancient *Cupid*   for as *Venus* univerfally excites the Affection of Affociation, and the defire of Procreation , her Son *Cupid* applies the Affection to Individuals   fo that the general Difpofition proceeds from *Venus*, but the more clofe Sympathy from *Cupid*   The former depends upon a near Approximation of Caufes , but the latter upon deeper, more neceffitating and uncontroulable Principles , as if they proceeded from the antient *Cupid*, on whom all exquifite Sympathies depend [c]

X *The*

---

[a] See above § 3
[b] See Sir *Ifaac Newton* of the *Original Particles of Matter*, in the Queries at the End of his *Opticks*
[c] See this *Fable* farther illuftrated at the Beginning of the *fifth Part* of the Author's *Inftauration* Vol III

X.

The FABLE *of* DEUCALION; *explained of an useful Hint in Natural Philosophy.*

The FABLE.

1. THE *Poets tell us, that the Inhabitants of the old World being* The Oracle of *totally destroyed by the universal Deluge, excepting* Deuca- Deucalion lion *and* Pyrrha; *these two, desiring with zealous and fervent* and Pyrrha. *Devotion, to restore Mankind, received this* Oracle *for Answer; that* they should succeed by throwing their Mother's Bones behind them. *This at first cast them into great sorrow and despair, because, as all Things were levelled by the Deluge, it was in vain to seek their Mother's Tomb · but at length, they understood the Expression of the* Oracle *to signify the* Stones of the Earth, *which is esteemed the Mother of all Things.*

The EXPLANATION.

2. THis Fable seems to reveal a Secret of Nature, and correct an Error Reveals familiar to the Mind, for Men's Ignorance leads them to expect a Secret of the Renovation or Restauration of Things, from their Corruption and Re- Nature mains, as the Phœnix is said to be restored out of its Ashes which is a very improper Procedure; because such kind of Materials have finished their Course, and are become absolutely unfit to supply the first Rudiments of the same Things again · whence, in Cases of Renovation, recourse should be had to more common Principles [a].

  [a] See the *Sylva Sylvarum,* and the History of Life and Death, *passim.*

XI.

XI.

The FABLE *of* SPHINX; *explained of the Sciences.*

The FABLE.

Sphinx de-
scrib'd

1. T*Hey relate that Sphinx was a Monster, variously formed, having the Face and Voice of a Virgin* (a)*, the Wings of a Bird* (b)*, and the Talons of a Gryphin* (c)*. She resided on the Top of a Mountain, near the City* Thebes (d) *, and also beset the Highways* (e) *Her manner was to lie in ambush, and seize on Travellers, and having them in her power, proposed to them certain dark and perplexed Riddles* (f)*, which it was thought she received from the Muses* (g) *And if her wretched Captives could not solve, and interpret, these Riddles, she with great Cruelty fell upon them, in their Hesitation and Confusion, and tore them to pieces* (h) *This Plague having reigned a long time, the* Thebans *at length offered their Kingdom to the Man who could interpret her Riddles, there being no other way to subdue her* (i)*.* Oedipus*, a penetrating and prudent Man, tho' lame in his Feet, excited by so great a Reward, accepted the Condition* (k)*; and with a good Assurance of Mind, chearfully presented himself before the Monster, who di-*

Her Riddle

rectly asked him, What Creature that was, which being born four-footed, afterwards became two-footed, then three-footed, and lastly four footed again? Oedipus*, with a presence of mind, replied it*

Solv'd by
Oedipus

was Man; *who, upon his first birth, and infant State, crawl'd upon all four, in endeavouring to walk; but not long after that, went upright upon his two natural Feet, again, in old Age walked three-footed, with a Stick, and at last growing decrepid, lay four-footed confined to his Bed And having by this exact Solution obtained the Victory, he slew the Monster; and laying the Carcass upon an Ass* (l)*, led her away as in triumph. And upon this he was, according to the Agreement, made King of* Thebes.

The

The EXPLANATION.

2. (a) THIS is an elegant, inſtructive Fable, and ſeems invented to repre- *Sphinx is*
ſent *Science*, eſpecially as join'd with *Practice*   For *Science* may, *Science*
without abſurdity, be called a *Monſter*, being ſtrangely gazed at, and *A Monſter*
admired, by the ignorant and unſkilful   Her Figure and Form is various, *Her various*
by reaſon of the vaſt variety of Subjects that Science conſiders.   Her Voice *Form*
and Countenance are repreſented female, by reaſon of her gay Appearance *Her female*
and Volubility of Speech [a]   (b) Wings are added, becauſe the Sciences and *Face and Voice*
their Inventions run, and fly about, in a moment, for Knowledge, like *Wings*
Light communicated from one Torch to another, is preſently catch'd, and
copiouſly diffuſed.   (c) Sharp and hooked Talons are elegantly attributed to *Talons*
her, becauſe the Axioms and Arguments of Science enter the Mind, lay
hold of it, fix it down, and keep it from moving or ſlipping away.   This
the ſacred Philoſopher obſerved, when he ſaid, *The Words of the Wiſe are*
like Goads, or Nails, driven far in   (d) Again, all Science ſeems placed
on high, as it were on the tops of Mountains, that are hard to climb *Reſiding on*
for Science is juſtly imagined a ſublime and lofty Thing, looking down *high*
upon Ignorance from an Eminence, and at the ſame time taking an extenſive View on all ſides, as is uſual on the Tops of Mountains   (e) Science *Beſetting*
is ſaid to beſet the Highways, becauſe thro' all the Journey and Peregri- *the Highways*
nation of human Life, there is Matter and Occaſion offered of Contemplation

3 (f) *Sphinx* is ſaid to propoſe various difficult Queſtions, and Riddles, *Propoſing*
to Men, which ſhe received from the *Muſes*, and theſe Queſtions, ſo long *Riddles*
as they remain with the *Muſes*, may very well be unaccompanied with Severity.   for while there is no other End of Contemplation and Enquiry but
that of Knowledge alone, the Underſtanding is not oppreſſed, or driven to
Straits and Difficulties, but expatiates and ranges at large, and even receives a degree of Pleaſure from Doubt and Variety. (g) But after the Muſes have given over their Riddles to *Sphinx*, that is, to *Practice* (b), which
urges and impels to Action, Choice and Determination, then it is that they
become torturing, ſevere, and trying· and unleſs ſolved and interpreted,
ſtrangely perplex and haraſs the human Mind, rend it every way, and perfectly tear it to pieces [b]   All the Riddles of *Sphinx*, therefore, have two
Conditions

---

[a] For Science or Philoſophy has, in the general, rather been a ſhewy and talkative Thing,
than ſolid, ſerviceable, and effective

[b] To gain the clearer Notion of this we need only conſider the Neceſſities and Inconveniences, under which the Inhabitants, even of civilized Countries, frequently labour, from Inundations, Conflagrations, Dearths, Storms, Lightning, Wars, Devaſtations, Tyrannical Governments, blind and furious Zeal, Superſtition, want of Commerce and certain Commodities, all which Particulars, when they come to be practically conſidered, in order to
their being remedied, removed or prevented, diſtract and perplex the Mind, eſpecially when
the Cauſes of theſe Effects remain unknown, ſo as not to be governable by human Means

Conditions annexed, viz. *Destruction* to those who do not solve them, and *Empire* to those that do. For he who understands the Thing proposed, obtains his End; and every Artificer rules over his Work [a].

4. The *Sphinx* has no more than two kinds of Riddles, one relating to the Nature of Things, the other to the Nature of Man; and correspondent to these, the Prizes of the Solution are two kinds of *Empire*, the *Empire over Nature*, and the *Empire over Man*. For the true and ultimate End of *natural Philosophy* is Dominion over natural Things, natural Bodies, Remedies, Machines, and numberless other Particulars; tho' the Schools, contented with what spontaneously offers, and swollen with their own Discourses, neglect, and in a manner despise, both Things and Works [b].

5. (*k*) But the Riddle proposed to *Oedipus*, the Solution whereof acquired him the *Theban* Kingdom, regarded the Nature of Man; for he who has thoroughly looked into and examined human Nature, may, in a manner, command his own Fortune; and seems born to acquire Dominion and Rule [c]. Accordingly, *Virgil* properly makes the Arts of Government to be the Arts of the *Romans* [d]. It was, therefore, extremely apposite in *Augustus Cæsar*, to use the Image of *Sphinx* in his Signet, whether this happened by accident or by design; for he of all Men was deeply versed in *Politics*, and through the course of his Life very happily solved abundance of new Riddles, with regard to the Nature of Man; and unless he had done this with great Dexterity and ready Address, he would frequently have been involved in imminent Danger, if not Destruction.

6. 'Tis, with the utmost elegance, added in the *Fable*, that when *Sphinx* was conquered, her Carcass was laid upon an Ass; for there is nothing so subtile and abstruse, but after being once made plain, intelligible and common, it may be received by the slowest Capacity.

7. (*m*) We must not omit, that *Sphinx* was conquered by a lame Man, and impotent in his Feet; for Men usually make too much haste to the Solution of *Sphinx*'s Riddles; whence it happens, that she prevailing, their Minds are rather racked and torn by Disputes, than an Empire gained by Works and Effects.

XII.

---

[a] This is what the Author so frequently inculcates in his *Novum Organum*, viz. that Knowledge and Power are reciprocal, so that to improve in Knowledge, is to improve in the Power of Commanding Nature, by introducing new Arts, and producing Works and Effects.

[b] This is largely prosecuted in the *Novum Organum*.

[c] See the *de Augment. Scientiar.* Sect. XXV of *Self Policy, or the Doctrine of Rising in Life*.

[d] *Tu regere Imperio Populos, Romane, memento*
    Hæ tibi erunt Artes.

[e] See the first Part of the *Novum Organum*, passim.

XII.

The FABLE *of* PROSERPINE; *explained of the* SPIRIT *included in natural Bodies.*

The FABLE.

1. THey *tell us,* Pluto *having, upon that memorable Division of Empire among the Gods, received the infernal Regions for his Share, despaired of winning any one of the Goddesses in Marriage, by an obsequious Courtship, and therefore, through Necessity, resolved upon a Rape* (a) *And watching his Opportunity, he suddenly seizes upon* Proserpine, *a most beautiful Virgin, the Daughter of* Ceres, *as she was gathering* Narcissus *Flowers* (b) *in the Meads of* Sicily, *and hurrying her to his Chariot, carried her with him to the subterraneal Regions, where she was treated with the highest Reverence, and styled the Lady of* Dis (c) *But* Ceres *missing her only Daughter, whom she extremely loved, grew pensive and anxious, beyond measure* (d), *and taking a lighted Torch* (e) *in her Hand, wandered the World over in quest of her Daughter, but all to no purpose, 'till suspecting she might be carried to the infernal Regions, she with great lamentation, and abundance of tears, importuned* Jupiter *to restore her, and with much ado prevailed, so far as to recover and bring her away, if she had tasted nothing there This proved a hard Condition upon the Mother, for* Proserpine *was found to have eaten three Kernels of a Pomgranate* (f). Ceres, *however, desisted not, but fell to her entreaties and lamentations afresh, insomuch that, at last, it was indulged her, that* Proserpine *should divide the Year betwixt her Husband and her Mother; and live six Months with the one, and as many with the other* (g) *After this,* Theseus *and* Perithous, *with uncommon audacity, attempted to force* Proserpine *away from* Pluto's *Bed, but happening to grow tired in their Journey, and resting themselves upon a Stone, in the Realms below, they could never rise from it again, but remain sitting there for ever* (h) Proserpine, *therefore, still continued Queen of the lower Regions; in honour of whom there was also added this grand Privilege, that tho' it had never*

Pluto carries away Proserpine,

Gathering Narcissus.

Ceres goes out to seek her

Recovers her, upon Condition

Theseus and Perithous attempt to force Proserpine from Pluto

Proserpine divides the Year betwixt her Mother and Husband.

never been permitted any one to return, after having once defcended thither, a particular exception was made, that he who brought a golden Bough, as a Prefent to Proferpine, *might on that condition defcend and return   This was an only Bough, that grew in a large dark Grove, not from a Tree of its own, but, like the* Mifletoe, *from another ; and when plucked away, a frefh one always fhot out in its ftead (i).*

The EXPLANATION.

2 (a) THIS *Fable* feems to regard *natural Philofophy*, and fearches deep into that rich and fruitful Virtue and Supply, in fubterraneous Bodies, from whence all the Things upon the Earth's Surface fpring, and into which they again refolve and return   By *Proferpine* the Ancients denoted that *Ætherial Spirit* fhut up and detained within the *Earth*, here reprefented by *Pluto*, the Spirit being feparated from the fuperior Globe, according to the Expreffion of the Poet [a]   This Spirit is conceived as ravifhed, or fnatched up by the *Earth*, becaufe it can no way be detained, when it has time and opportunity to fly off , but is only wrought together and fixed by fudden Intermixture and Comminution, in the fame manner as if one fhould endeavour to mix Air with Water , which cannot otherwife be done, than by a quick and rapid agitation, that joins them together in Froth , whilft the Air is thus catched up by the Water (b)   And it is elegantly added, that *Proferpine* was ravifhed whilft fhe gathered *Narciffus* Flowers , which have their Name from Numbednefs or Stupefaction , for the Spirit we fpeak of, is in the fitteft difpofition to be catched up by terreftrial Matter, when it begins to coagulate, or grow torpid, as it were

3 (c) 'Tis an Honour juftly attributed to *Proferpine*, and not to any other Wife of the Gods, that of being the Lady, or Miftrefs, of her Hufband , becaufe this *Spirit* performs all the Operations in the fubterraneal Regions , whilft *Pluto*, or the Earth, remains ftupid, or as it were ignorant of them [b]

4. (d) The Æther, or the Efficacy of the heavenly Bodies, denoted by *Ceres*, endeavours with infinite diligence, to force out this Spirit, and reftore it to its priftine State (e)   And by the Torch in the Hand of *Ceres*, or the Æther, is doubtlefs meant the *Sun*, which difperfes Light over the whole Globe of the Earth , and if the Thing were poffible, muft have the greateft fhare

[a] *Sive recens Tellus, feductaque nuper ab alto*
Æthere cognati retinebat femina Cæli
[b] See the *Sylva Sylvarum*, under the Articles *Imagination, Nature, Spirit and Sympathy* . See alfo the *Axioms* at the End of the *Hiftory of Life and Death*

share in recovering *Proserpine*, or re-instating the *subterraneal Spirit*. (*f*) Yet *Proserpine* still continues and dwells below, after the manner excellently described in the Condition betwixt *Jupiter* and *Ceres* For first, 'tis certain that there are two ways of detaining the Spirit, in solid and terrestrial Matter, the one by *Condensation* or *Obstruction*, which is mere violence and Imprisonment the other, by *administring a proper Aliment*, which is spontaneous and free. For after the included Spirit begins to feed and nourish it self, 'tis not in a hurry to fly off, but remains as it were fixed in its own Earth. And this is the Moral of *Proserpine's* tasting the Pomgranate and were it not for this, she must long ago have been carried up by *Ceres* who with her Torch wandered the World over ; and so the Earth have been left without its Spirit. For tho' the Spirit, in Metals and Minerals, may perhaps be, after a particular manner, wrought in by the Solidity of the Mass , yet the Spirit of Vegetables and Animals has open Passages to escape at ; unless it be willingly detained, in the way of sipping and tasting them [a]. *[margin: Tasting the Pomgranate]*

5. (*g*) The second Article of Agreement, that of *Proserpine's* remaining six Months with her Mother, and six with her Husband, is an elegant Description of the division of the Year for the Spirit diffused thro' the Earth, lives above Ground in the vegetable World, during the Summer Months ; but in the Winter returns under Ground again. *[margin: Living six Months with her Husband, and six with her Mother]*

6 (*h*) The Attempt of *Theseus* and *Perithous* to bring *Proserpine* away, denotes that the more subtile Spirits, which descend in many Bodies to the Earth, may frequently be unable to drink in, unite with themselves, and carry off the subterraneous Spirit ; but, on the contrary, be coagulated by it, and rise no more ; so as to increase the Inhabitants, and add to the Dominion of *Proserpine* [b]. *[margin: The Attempt of Theseus and Perithous]*

7. (*i*) The Alchemists will be apt to fall in with our Interpretation of the golden Bough, whether we will or no ; because they promise golden Mountains, and the Restoration of natural Bodies from their *Stone* , as from the Gates of *Pluto* but we are well assured, that their Theory has no just Foundation , and suspect they have no very encouraging practical Proofs of its Soundness Leaving, therefore, their Conceits to themselves , we shall freely declare our own Sentiments upon this last Part of the *Fable* We are certain from numerous Figures and Expressions of the Ancients, that they judged the *[margin: The golden Bough.]*

---

[a] This Point is largely explained in the *Author's History of Life and Death*, but still deserves to be set in a more full and general Light, by new Instances and Enforcements, as a Particular, which, tho' neglected, or almost overlooked, infinitely regards the Improvement of natural Philosophy See the *Sylva Sylvarum*, under the Articles *Imagination, Nature, Spirits, Sympathy,* &c

[b] Many Philosophers have certain Speculations to this Purpose Sir *Isaac Newton*, in particular, suspects that the Earth receives its vivifying Spirit from the Comets And the Philosophical *Chemists* and *Astrologers* have spun the Thought into many phantastical Distinctions and Varieties See *Newton Princip* Lib III p 473, &c. See also *Sylva Sylvarum*, p 222, &c.

the Confervation, and in fome degree, the Renovation of natural Bodies, to be ro defperate or impoffible Thing, but rather abftrufe, and out of the common Road, than wholly impracticable[a] And this feems to be their Opinion in the prefent Cafe, as they have placed this *Bough* among an infinite number of Shrubs, in a fpacious and thick Wood They fuppofed it of Gold, becaufe Gold is the Emblem of Duration They feign'd it adventitious, not native, becaufe fuch an effect is to be expected from Art; and not from any Medicine, or any fimple or mere natural Way of working[b].

[a] See above, pag 557 § 12.
[b] The Author's *Hiftory of Life and Death* is a Comment upon this Text.

SECT.

S E C T. II.

The concealed Moral Philosophy of the Ancients.

I.

The FABLE *of* MEMNON; *explained of the fatal Precipitancy of* YOUTH.

The FABLE.

1. THE *Poets make* Memnon *the Son of* Aurora; *and bring* Memnon's *him to the* Trojan *War in beautiful Armour, and flushed* Fate *with popular Praise, where, thirsting after farther Glory, and rashly hurrying on to the greatest Enterprizes, he engages the bravest Warrior of all the* Greeks, Achilles; *and falls by his Hand, in single Combat.* Jupiter, *in commiseration of his Death, sent Birds to grace his Funeral, that perpetually chanted certain mournful and bewailing Dirges. 'Tis also reported, that the Rays of the rising Sun striking his Statue, used to give a lamenting Sound*

The EXPLANATION.

2 THis *Fable* regards the unfortunate End of those promising Youths, who, The Son of the like Sons *of the Morning,* elate with empty Hopes and glittering Morning Outsides, attempt things beyond their strength, challenge the bravest Heroes provoke them to the Combat, and proving unequal, die in their high Attempts.

3. The

Dis b said 3 The Death of such Youths seldom fails to meet with infinite Pity; as no mortal Calamity is more moving and afflicting, than to see the Flower of Virtue cropt before its time [a]   Nay, the Prime of Life enjoyed to the full, or even to a degree of Envy, does not assuage or moderate the Grief occasioned by the untimely Death of such hopeful Youths. But Lamentations and Bewailings fly, like mournful Birds, about their Tombs, for a long while after especially upon all fresh Occasions, new Commotions, and the beginning of great Actions, the passionate Desire of them is renewed, as *by the Sun's Morning Ray*.

II.

The FABLE *of* TYTHONUS; *explained of predominant Passions.*

The FABLE.

Tythonus made immortal 1 'TIS *elegantly fabled of* Tythonus, *that being exceedingly beloved by* Aurora, *she petitioned* Jupiter *that he might prove immortal, thereby to secure herself the everlasting Enjoyment of his Company but through Female Inadvertence she forgot to add, that he might never grow old: so, that though he proved immor-* *At length turned to a Grashopper* *tal, he became miserably worn and consumed with Age, insomuch, that* Jupiter, *out of pity, at length transformed him to a Grashopper.*

The EXPLANATION.

Desires Pleasure 2 THis *Fable* seems to contain an ingenious Description of Pleasure; which at first, as it were in the *Morning of the Day*, is so welcome, that Men pray to have it everlasting . but forget that *Satiety* and *Weariness* of it will, like old Age, overtake them , tho' they think not of it: so that at length, when their Appetite for pleasurable Actions is gone, their *And Satiety* Desires and Affections often continue whence we commonly find that aged Persons delight themselves with the Discourse and Remembrance of the things agreeable to them in their better days   This is very remarkable in Men of a loose, and Men of a military Life · the former whereof *In old Age* are always talking over their Amours , and the latter the Exploits of their Youth , like Grashoppers, that show their Vigour only by their chirping [b]

III. *The*

[a] See the Author's *Speech against Duelling* Vol I pag 393
[b] See the *History of Life and Death*, Vol III pag 416, 417

III.

The FABLE *of* NARCISSUS; *explained of* SELF-LOVE.

The FABLE.

1. **N**Arciſſus *is ſaid to have been extremely beautiful and comely,* Narciſſus *but intolerably proud and diſdainful, ſo that, pleaſed with*graced by Nature *himſelf, and ſcorning the World, he led a ſolitary Life in the Woods; hunting only with a few Followers, who were his profeſs'd Admirers. and amongſt the reſt, the Nymph* Echo *was his conſtant Attendant   In this Method of Life 'twas once his fate to approach a clear Fountain, where he laid himſelf down to reſt, in the noon-day Heat, when, beholding his Image in the Water, he fell into ſuch a* A Self-Admirer *Rapture and Admiration of himſelf, that he could by no means be got away, but remain'd continually fixed and gazing; till at length he was turn'd into a Flower, of his own Name, which appears early* And turned into a Flower *in the Spring, and is conſecrated to the infernal Deities,* Pluto, Proſerpine *and the* Furies.

The EXPLANATION.

2. **T**His *Fable* ſeems to paint the Behaviour and Fortune of thoſe, who, Repreſents for their Beauty, or other Endowments, wherewith Nature, (with-Self-Lovers out any Induſtry of their own,) has graced and adorned them, are extravagantly fond of themſelves. For Men of ſuch a Diſpoſition generally affect retirement, and abſence from publick Affairs, as a Life of Buſineſs muſt neceſſarily ſubject them to many Neglects and Contempts, which might diſturb and ruffle their Minds   whence ſuch Perſons commonly lead a ſolitary, private and ſhadowy Life, ſee little Company, and thoſe only ſuch as highly admire and reverence them, or, like an Echo, aſſent to all they ſay.

3 And they who are depraved, and rendered ſtill fonder of themſelves by Who prove this Cuſtom, grow ſtrangely indolent, unactive, and perfectly ſtupid. The indolent *Narciſſus*, a Spring-flower, is an elegant Emblem of this Temper, which at firſt flouriſhes, and is talked of, but when ripe, fruſtrates the Expectation conceived of it

4 And that this Flower ſhould be ſacred to the *infernal Powers*, carries on And become the Alluſion ſtill farther, becauſe Men of this humour are perfectly uſe-as Flowers of leſs little value

in all refpects for whatever yields no Fruit, but paſſes, and is no more, like the Way of a Ship in the Sea, was by the Ancients confecrated to the infernal Shades and Powers.

IV.

The FABLE *of* JUNO'S COURTSHIP; *explained of Submiffion, and Abjection.*

The FABLE.

1. THE *Poets tell us, that* Jupiter, *to carry on his Love-Intrigues, affumed many different Shapes; as of a Bull, an Eagle, a Swan, a Golden Shower,* &c *but when he attempted* Juno, *he turned himſelf into the moſt ignoble and ridiculous Creature; even that of a* wretched, wet, weather-beaten, affrighted, trembling, and half-ſtarved Cuckow.

The EXPLANATION.

2 THis is a wife *Fable*, and drawn from the very Entrails of Morality. The *Moral* is, that Men ſhould not be *conceited of themſelves*, and imagine that a Diſcovery of their Excellencies will always render them acceptable for this *can only ſucceed according to the Nature and Manners of the Perſon they court, or ſolicit*, who, if he be a Man not of the ſame Gifts and Endowments, but altogether of a *haughty and contemptuous Behaviour*, here repreſented by the Perſon of *Juno*, they muſt entirely drop the Character that *carries the leaſt Show of Worth, or Gracefulneſs If they proceed upon any other footing, 'tis downright Folly*. Nor is it ſufficient to act the *Deformity of Obſequiouſneſs*, unleſs they really change themſelves, and become abject and contemptible in their Perſons [a]

V. The

---

[a] Thoſe, who, upon a ſuperficial reading of the Author's ſubmiſſive *Letters* to King *James*, have been forward to cenſure them, as indecently *mean, ſordid* and *begging*, may here be taught to correct their Judgment.

V.

The FABLE *of* CASSANDRA; *explained of too free and* UNSEASONABLE ADVICE.

The FABLE.

1. THE *Poets relate, that Apollo falling in Love with Caf-* Caffandra de-*fandra, was ftill deluded and put off by her; yet fed with* ceives Apollo. *Hopes, till fhe had got from him the Gift of Prophecy and having now obtain'd her End, fhe flatly rejected his Suit. Apollo, unable to recall his rafh Gift, yet enraged to be out-witted by a Girl, an-nex'd this Penalty to it, that though fhe fhou'd always prophefy true, fhe fhou'd never be believed. whence her Divinations were always flighted, even when fhe again and again predicted the Ruin of her Country.*

The EXPLANATION.

2. THis *Fable* feems invented to exprefs the Infignificance of unfeafon- *The Moral* able Advice   For they who are conceited, ftubborn, or intractable, and liften not to the Inftructions of *Apollo*, the God of Harmony, fo as to learn and obferve the Modulations and Meafures of Affairs, the Sharps and Flats of Difcourfe, the difference betwixt judicious and vulgar Ears, and the proper Times of Speech and Silence, let them be ever fo intelligent, and ever fo frank of their Advice, or their Counfels ever fo good and juft, yet all their Endeavours, either of Perfuafion or Force, are of little fignificance, and rather haften the Ruin of thofe they advife   But at laft, when the calami-tous event has made the Sufferers feel the effect of their neglect, they too late reverence their Advifers, as deep, forefeeing and faithful Prophets.

3. Of this we have a remarkable Inftance in *Cato* of *Utica*, who difcovered *Illuftration* afar off, and long foretold, the approaching Ruin of his Country, both in the firft Confpiracy, and as it was profecuted in the civil War between *Cæfar* and *Pompey*, yet did no good the while, but rather hurt the Commonwealth, and hurried on its deftruction   which *Cicero* wifely obferved in thefe Words. "*Cato,* " *indeed, judges excellently, but prejudices the State   for he fpeaks as in the Com-* " *mon-wealth of* Plato, *and not as in the Dregs of* Romulus [a]."

VI *The*

[a] The Fable of *Dionyfus*, or *Bacchus*, explained of the human Paffions, fhou'd have come next after this   fo as immediately to precede the *Fable* of the *Sirens*, had it not been already made ufe of by way of *Example*, in the *de Augmentis Scientiarum*   See Vol 1 pag 66.

VI.

The FABLE *of the* SIRENS; *explained of Mens Passion for Pleasures.*

INTRODUCTION.

1. THE *Fable* of the *Sirens* is, in a vulgar Sense, justly enough explained of the pernicious Incentives to Pleasure. but the *Ancient Mythology* seems to us like a Vintage ill press'd and trod. for though something has been drawn from it, yet all the more excellent Parts remain behind, in the Grapes that are untouched.

The FABLE.

The Sirens

2. THE Sirens *are said to be the Daughters of* Achelous, *and* Terpsichore *one of the* Muses (a) *In their early days they had Wings, but lost them upon being conquered by the Muses, with whom they rashly contended (b)   And with the Feathers of these Wings, the Muses made themselves* Crowns; *so that from this time the Muses wore Wings on their Heads, excepting only the Mother to the Sirens (c)*

Their Place of Residence

3. *These* Sirens *resided in certain pleasant Islands, and when, from their Watch-tower, they saw any Ship approaching; they first detained the Sailors by their Music; then inticing them to Shore, destroyed them (d)*

Their Music

4. *Their Singing was not of one and the same kind, but they adapted their Tunes exactly to the Nature of each Person; in order to captivate and secure him   And so destructive had they been, that these Islands of the* Sirens *appeared, to a very great distance, white with the Bones of their unburied Captives (e).*

Remedies against their deluding Power

5 *Two different Remedies were invented to protect Persons against them; the one by* Ulysses, *the other by* Orpheus. U-*lysses commanded his Associates to stop their Ears close with Wax. and he determining to make the Trial; and yet avoid*

I   *the*

the Danger; ordered himself to be tied fast to a Mast of the Ship; giving a strict Charge not to be unbound, even tho' himself shou'd entreat it (f). But Orpheus, without any binding at all, escaped the Danger, by loudly chanting to his Harp the Praises of the Gods; whereby he drowned the Voices of the Sirens (g)

The EXPLANATION.

6. (a) THis *Fable* is of the moral kind, and appears no less elegant, *The Sirens, or* than easy to intrepret For *Pleasures* proceed from *Plenty* and *Pleasures, an-* *Affluence*, attended with Activity or Exultation of the Mind [1]. Anciently, *ciently wing'd* their first Incentives were quick, and seiz'd upon Men, as if they had been winged: but Learning and Philosophy afterwards prevailing, had, at least, the Power to lay the Mind under some restraint, and make it consider the Issue of Things, and thus deprived *Pleasures* of their Wings

7 (b) This Conquest redounded greatly to the Honour and Ornament of *The loss of the* the Muses, for after it appeared, by the Example of a few, that Philosophy *Sirens Wings* cou'd introduce a Contempt of *Pleasures*, it immediately seem'd to be a *an Honour to* *the Muses* sublime Thing that cou'd raise and elevate the Soul, fix'd in a manner down to Earth, and thus render Men's Thoughts, which reside in the Head, winged as it were, or sublime

8 (c) Only the Mother of the *Sirens* was not thus plumed on the Head *Terpsichore* which doubtless denotes *superficial Learning*, invented and used for Delight, *not plumed on* *the Head* and Levity An eminent Example whereof we have in *Petronius*, who, after receiving Sentence of Death, still continued his gay frothy Humour, and, as *Tacitus* observes, used his Learning to solace or divert himself, and instead of such Discourses as give a firmness and constancy of Mind, read nothing but loose Poems and Verses [b] Such Learning as this seems to pluck the Crowns again from the Muses Heads, and restore them to the *Sirens*

9 (d) The *Sirens* are said to inhabit certain Islands, because Pleasures ge- *The Sirens in-* nerally seek Retirement, and often shun Society. And for their Songs, *habit Islands* with the manifold Artifice and Destructiveness thereof, this is too obvious, and common, to need any Explanation (e) But that particular, of the *White with* Bones stretching like white Clifts, along the Shores, and appearing afar off, *the Bones of* contains a more subtile Allegory; and denotes, that the Examples of others *their Cap-* *tives.*

---

[a] The one denoted by the River *Achelous*, and the other by *Terpsichore*, the Muse that in-vented the *Cithara*, and delighted in *Dancing*

[b] *Vivamus, mea Lesbia atque amemus,*
Rumoresque Senum severiorum
Omnes unius æstimemus Assis
　　　　　　And again
Jura Senes norint, & quod sit Fasque Nefasque
Inquirant tristes, Legumque examina servent

Calamity and Misfortunes, tho' ever fo manifeft and apparent, have yet but little force to deter the corrupt Nature of Man from Pleafures

The Remedies againft the Sirens

10 (f) The Allegory of the Remedies againft the *Sirens* is not difficult, but very wife and noble It propofes, in effect, three Remedies, as well againft fubtile as violent Mifchiefs, two drawn from Philofophy, and one from Religion

The firft Remedy

11 (1) The firft means of efcaping, is to refift the earlieft Temptation in the beginning, and diligently avoid and cut off all occafions that may follicit or fway the Mind, and this is well reprefented, by ftopping of the Ears a kind of Remedy to be neceffarily ufed with mean and vulgar Minds, fuch as the Retinue of *Ulyffes*

The fecond

12 (2) But nobler Spirits may converfe, even in the midft of Pleafures, if the Mind be well guarded with Conftancy and Refolution And thus fome delight to make a fevere Trial of their own Virtue; and thoroughly acquaint themfelves with the folly and madnefs of Pleafures, without complying, or being wholly given up to them · which is what *Solomon* profeffes of himfelf, when he clofes the account of all the numerous Pleafures he gave a loofe to, with this Expreffion, *but Wifdom ftill continued with me.* Such Heroes in Virtue may, therefore, remain unmov'd by the greateft Incentives to Pleafure, and ftop themfelves on the very precipice of Danger, or, according to the Example of *Ulyffes*, they interdict themfelves all pernicious Counfel, and Obfequioufnefs of their Friends and Companions, which have the greateft power to fhake and unfettle the Mind

The third

13 (g) (3) But the moft excellent Remedy, in every Temptation, is that of *Orpheus* who, by loudly chanting and refounding the Praifes of the Gods, confounded the Voices, and kept himfelf from hearing the Mufick of the *Sirens* for *divine Contemplations* exceed the Pleafures of Senfe, not only in Power, but alfo in Sweetnefs

VIII.

The FABLE *of* DIOMED; *explained of* Perfecution, *or* Zeal *for* Religion.

The FABLE.

Diomed wounds Venus

1. **D**iomed *acquired great Glory and Honour, at the* Trojan *War; and was highly favoured by* Pallas, *who encouraged and excited him, by no means to fpare* Venus, *if he fhould cafually meet her in Fight He followed the Advice with too much Eagernefs and Intrepidity, and accordingly wounded that Goddefs in her Hand,*

Hand (a). This presumptuous Action remained unpunished for a time; and when the War was ended, he returned, with great glory and renown, to his own Country; where finding himself embroiled with domestick Affairs, he retired into Italy. *Here also, at first he was well received, and nobly entertained by King* Daunus; *who,* 〔*Is honourably received by* Daunus〕 *besides other Gifts and Honours, erected Statues for him over all his Dominions. But upon the first Calamity that afflicted the People after the Stranger's Arrival,* Daunus *immediately reflected, that he entertained a devoted Person in his Palace, an Enemy to the Gods, and one who had sacrilegiously wounded a Goddess with his Sword, whom it was impious but to touch. To expiate, there-fore, his Country's Guilt; he without regard to the Laws of Hos-* 〔*And mur-dered*〕 *pitality, which were less regarded by him than the Law of Re-ligion, directly slew his Guest; and commanded his Statues, and all his Honours to be rased and abolished (b). Nor was it safe for others to commiserate, or bewail, so cruel a Destiny; but even his Companions* 〔*His Compa-nions forbid to lament his Death*〕 *in Arms, whilst they lamented the Death of their Leader, and filled all Places with their complaints, were turned into a kind of Swans, which are said, at the approach of their own Death, to chaunt sweet melancholy Dirges (c).*

The EXPLANATION.

2. (a) **T**HIS *Fable* intimates an extraordinary and almost singular 〔*Displays the Fate of a Zealot for Religion.*〕 Thing. For no *Hero*, besides *Diomed*, is recorded to have wounded any of the Gods. Doubtless, we have here described the Nature and Fate of a Man, who professedly makes any divine Worship, or Sect of Religion, tho' in it self vain and light, the only scope of his Actions, and resolves to propagate it by Fire and Sword. For although the bloody Dissentions and Differences about Religion were unknown to the Ancients; yet so copious and diffusive was their Knowledge, that what they knew not by *Experience*, they comprehended in Thought and Representation. Those, therefore, who endeavour to reform, or establish, any Sect of Religion, tho' vain, corrupt, and infamous, (which is here denoted under the Person of *Venus*) not by the force of Reason, Learning, Sanctity of Manners, the weight of Arguments, and Examples, but would spread or extirpate it by Persecution, Pains, Penalties, Tortures, Fire and Sword, may, perhaps, be instigated hereto by *Pallas*, that is, by a certain rigid, prudential Conside-ration, and a Severity of Judgment, by the Vigour and Efficacy whereof, they see throughly into the Fallacies and Fictions of the Delusions of this kind: and thro' aversion to depravity and a well-meant Zeal, these Men usual-ly, for a time, acquire great Fame and Glory, and are, by the Vulgar, to whom no moderate Measures can be acceptable, extolled, and almost adored.

adored, as the only Patrons and Protectors of Truth and Religion, Men of any other Disposition seeming, in comparison with these, to be lukewarm, mean-spirited, and cowardly. This Fame and Felicity, however, seldom endures to the end, but all Violence, unless it escape the Reverses and Changes of Things by untimely Death, is commonly unprosperous in the issue. And if a change of Affairs happens, and that Sect of Religion, which was persecuted and oppress'd, gains strength, and rises again, then the Zeal and warm Endeavours of this sort of Men are condemned, their very name becomes odious, and all their Honours terminate in Disgrace.

Domestical Treachery and Entertainment.
3 (*b*) As to the point that Diomed should be slain by his hospitable Entertainer, this denotes that religious Dissentions may cause Treachery, bloody Animosities and Deceit, even between the nearest Friends.

4 (*c*) That Complaining or Bewailing should not, in so enormous a Case, be permitted to Friends affected by the Catastrophe, without Punishment, includes this prudent Admonition, that almost in all kinds of Wickedness and Depravity, Men have still room left for Commiseration, so that they who hate the Crime, may yet pity the Person, and bewail his Calamity, from a Principle of Humanity and Good-Nature and to forbid the Overflowings and Intercourses of Pity upon such occasions, were the extremest of Evils yet in the *Cause of Religion and Impiety*, the very Commiserations of Men are noted and suspected. On the other hand, the Lamentations and Complainings of the Followers and Attendants of Diomed, that is, of Men of the same Sect, or Persuasion, are usually very sweet, agreeable, and moving, like the dying Notes of Swans, or the Birds of Diomed. This also is a noble and remarkable part of the Allegory, denoting, that the last Words of those who suffer for the sake of Religion, strongly affect and sway Mens Minds, and leave a lasting Impression upon the Sense and Memory [a].

[a] See the *de augment. Scientiæ* Vol. I Sect. XXVIII. pag. 261. and Vol. II pag. 161.

SECT.

SECT. III.
The secret Political Knowledge of the Ancients.

I.

The FABLES *of* ACTEON *and* PENTHEUS; *explained of Curiosity, or Prying into the Secrets of Princes, and Divine Mysteries.*

The FABLE.

1. THE *Ancients afford us two Examples, for suppressing the impertinent* Curiosity *of Mankind, in diving into Secrets; and imprudently longing and endeavouring to discover them The one of these, is in the Person of* Acteon, *and the other, in that of* Pentheus. Acteon *undesignedly chancing to see* Diana *naked, was* Acteon's *turned into a Stag; and torn to pieces by his own Hounds* (a). Crime *And* Pentheus *desiring to pry into the hidden Mysteries of* Bacchus's *Sacrifice; and climbing a Tree for that purpose, was struck with a* That of Pen- *Phrenzy. This Phrenzy of* Pentheus *caused him to see Things* theus *double; particularly the Sun, and his own City* Thebes, *so that running homewards, and immediately espying another* Thebes, *he runs towards that, and thus continues incessantly tending first to the one, and then to the other, without coming at either* (b)

The

The EXPLANATION.

Actæon &c.
L... &c.
&c ... &c.
Secrets of
Princes.

THE first of these *Fables* may relate to the *Secrets of Princes*; and the second to *divine Mysteries* For they who are not intimate with a Prince, yet against his will have a Knowledge of his Secrets, inevitably incur his Displeasure. and therefore, being aware that they are singled out, and all opportunities watched against them, they lead the Life of a Stag, full of Fears and Suspicions It likewise frequently happens, that their Servants and Domesticks accuse them, and plot their Overthrow; in order to procure Favour with the Prince for whenever the King manifests his Displeasure, the Person it falls upon must expect his Servants to betray him, and worry him down, as *Actæon* was worried by his own Dogs.

... of Pen-
theus to Di-
vine Myste-
ries.

3 (*b*) The Punishment of *Pentheus* is of another kind · for they who, unmindful of their mortal State, rashly aspire to *divine Mysteries*, by climbing the Heights of Nature and Philosophy, here represented by climbing a Tree, their Fate is perpetual Inconstancy, Perplexity and Instability of Judgment For as there is one Light of Nature, and another Light that is divine, they see, as it were, *two Suns*. And as the Actions of Life, and the Determinations of the Will, depend upon the Understanding, they are distracted as much in Opinion, as in Will· and therefore judge very inconsistently, or contradictorily, and see as it were *Thebes* double for *Thebes* being the Refuge and Habitation of *Pentheus*, here denotes the *Ends of Actions*: whence they know not what course to take; but remaining undetermined and unresolved in their Views and Designs, they are merely driven about by every sudden Gust, and Impulse of the Mind[a]

II.

The FABLE *of the* GODS *swearing by the* RIVER STYX; *explained* of Necessity, *in the* Oaths *or* solemn Leagues *of* Princes.

The FABLE.

The Oath of
Styx

I. THE only solemn Oath, by which the Gods irrevocably obliged themselves, is a well-known Thing, and makes a part of many ancient Fables To this Oath they did not invoke any
celestial

---

[a] See the *de Augment Scientiar* Sect XXVIII

celeftial Divinity, or divine Attribute , but only called to witnefs the River Styx, which, with many Meanders, furrounds the infernal Court of Dis For this Form alone, and none but this, was held inviolable and obligatory · and the Punifhment of falfifying it was, that dreaded one of being excluded, for a certain number of Years, the Table of the Gods. *The Punifhment of its Violation*

The EXPLANATION.

2 THIS Fable feems invented to fhew the Nature of the Compacts and Confederacies of Princes , which, tho' ever fo folemnly and religioufly fworn to, prove but little the more binding for it fo that Oaths in this Cafe feem ufed, rather for Decorum, Reputation, and Ceremony , than for Fidelity, Security, and Effectuating And tho' thefe Oaths were ftrengthened with the Bonds of Affinity, which are the Links and Ties of Nature , and again, by mutual Services and good Offices, yet we fee all this will generally give way to Ambition, Convenience, and the Thirft of Power · the rather, becaufe 'tis eafy for Princes, under various, fpecious Pretences, to defend, difguife, and conceal their ambitious Defires, and Infincerity , having no Judge to call them to account.   There is, however, one true and proper *Confirmation of their Faith*, tho' no celeftial Divinity , but, that great Divinity of Princes, *Neceffity*, or, the *Danger of the State* , and the *Securing* of *Advantage* *This Oath fhews the Nature of Princes Confederacies*

3 This *Neceffity* is elegantly reprefented by *Styx*, the *fatal River*, that can never be croffed back.   And this Deity it was, which *Iphicrates*, the *Athenian*, invoked in making a League and becaufe he roundly and openly avows what moft others ftudioufly conceal, it may be proper to give his own Words Obferving, that the *Lacedemonians* were inventing and propofing a variety of Securities, Sanctions and Bonds of Alliance , he interrupted them thus: *There may indeed, my Friends, be one Bond and Means of Security between us , and that is, for you to demonftrate you have delivered into our hands, fuch things as that if you had the greateft defire to hurt us, you could not be able.*   Therefore, if the Power of offending be taken away , or if by a Breach of Compact there be danger of Deftruction or Diminution to the State, or Tribute, then it is that Covenants will be ratified, and confirmed, as it were by the *Stygian Oath* , whilft there remains an impending Danger of being prohibited and excluded the *Banquet of the Gods* by which Expreffion the Ancients denoted the Rights and Prerogatives, the Affluence and the Felicities of Empire and Dominion [a]. *Neceffity the ftrongeft Security of Princes Oaths*

[a] See *de Augment Scientiar.* pag 234, &c.

III.

III.

The FABLE *of* JUPITER *and* METIS; *explained of Princes and their Council.*

The FABLE.

Jupiter took Metis his Wife, 1. THE *ancient Poets relate that* Jupiter *took* Metis *to Wife, whose name plainly denotes Counsel, and that she being pregnant by him, and he perceiving it, would by no means wait the time of her Delivery, but directly devoured her whence himself also became pregnant, and was delivered in a wonderful* *And brings for b Pallas* *manner; for he, from his Head or Brain, brought forth* Pallas *armed*

The EXPLANATION.

S. Kings marry their Council 2. THIS Fable, which in its literal Sense appears monstrously absurd, seems to contain a *State Secret*, and shews with what Art Kings usually carry themselves towards their Council, in order to preserve their own Authority and Majesty, not only inviolate, but so as to have it magnified and heightened among the People For Kings commonly link themselves, as it were in a nuptial Bond, to their Council, and deliberate and communicate with them after a prudent and laudable Custom, upon Matters of the greatest importance, at the same time, justly conceiving this no diminution of their Majesty but when the Matter once ripens to a Decree *And Decree,* or *Order*, which is a kind of Birth, the King then suffers the Council to go on no further, lest the Act should seem to depend upon their Pleasure. Now therefore, the King usually assumes to himself whatever was wrought, elaborated, or formed, as it were, in the Womb of the Council, (unless it be a Matter of an invidious nature, which he is sure to put from him) so that the Decree and the Execution shall seem to flow from himself And as this Decree, or Execution, proceeds with Prudence, and Power, so as to imply Necessity, 'tis elegantly wrapt up under the Figure of *Pallas armed*

As from them-selves 3. Nor are Kings content to have this seem the effect of their own Authority, Free-Will, and uncontrolable Choice, unless they also take the whole Honour to themselves, and make the People imagine that all good and wholesome Decrees proceed entirely from their own *Head*, that is, their own sole Prudence and Judgment [a]

[a] See the Essay on State Counsel, Vol II pag 137

IV. *The*

IV.

The FABLE *of* ENDYMION; *explained of* COURT-FAVOURITES.

The FABLE.

1. *THE Goddess* Luna *is said to have fallen in Love with the Shepherd* Endymion, *and to have carried on her Amours with him, in a new and singular manner: it being her Custom, whilst he lay reposing in a native* Cave, *under Mount* Latmus, *to descend frequently from her Sphere, enjoy his Company whilst he slept; and then go up to Heaven again And all this while,* Endymion's *Fortune was no way prejudiced by his unactive and sleepy Life, the Goddess causing his Flocks to thrive, and grow so exceeding numerous, that none of the other Shepherds could compare with him* {Luna's Amour with Endymion sleeping,} {Turns to his Advantage}

The EXPLANATION.

2. THIS Fable seems to describe the Tempers and Dispositions of Princes, who being thoughtful and suspicious, do not easily admit to their Privacies such Men as are prying, curious, and vigilant, or as it were *sleepless*, but rather such as are of an easy, obliging Nature; and indulge them in their Pleasures, without seeking any thing farther but seeming ignorant, insensible, or as it were lulled asleep before them Princes usually treat such Persons familiarly, and quitting their Throne like *Luna*, think they may with safety unbosom to them This Temper was very remarkable in *Tiberius*, a Prince exceeding difficult to please, and who had no Favourit s but those that perfectly understood his Ways, and at the same time, obstinately dissembled their Knowledge, almost to a degree of Stupidity {So Kings make choice of sleeping Favourites}

3 The *Cave* is not improperly mentioned in the *Fable*; it being a common thing for the Favourites of a Prince to have their pleasant Retreats; whither to invite him, by way of Relaxation, tho' without Prejudice to their own Fortunes these Favourites usually making a good Provision for themselves. For tho' their Prince should not, perhaps, promote them to Dig- {Endymion's Cave.}

nities, yet out of real Affection, and not only for Convenience, they generally feel the enriching Influence of his Bounty.

V.

The FABLE of NEMESIS; explained of the Reverses of FORTUNE.

The FABLE.

Nemesis the Daughter of Nox and Oceanus

Her Enfigns

1 NEmesis *is represented as a Goddess venerated by all; but feared by the Powerful and the Fortunate* (a). *She is said to be the Daughter of* Nox *and* Oceanus (b). *She is drawn with Wings* (c), *and a Crown* (d); *a Javelin of Ash in her right Hand* (e), *a Glass containing* Ethiopians *in her left* (f); *and riding upon a Stag* (g).

The EXPLANATION.

Nemesis denotes Retribution

2 (a) THE *Fable* receives this Explanation. The word *Nemesis* manifestly signifies Revenge, or Retribution for the Office of this Goddess consisted in interposing, like the *Roman* Tribunes, with an *I forbid it*, in all Courses of constant and perpetual Felicity so as not only to chastise Haughtiness, but also to repay, even innocent and moderate Happiness with Adversity as if it were decreed, that none of human Race should be admitted to the *Banquet of the Gods*, but for Sport [a]. And, indeed, to read over that Chapter of *Pliny*, wherein he has collected the Miseries and Misfortunes of *Augustus Cæsar*, whom of all Mankind one would judge most fortunate, as he had a certain Art of using and enjoying Prosperity, with a Mind no way tumid, light, effeminate, confused, or melancholic; one cannot but think this a very great and powerful Goddess, who could bring such a Victim to her Altar [b].

her Parents

3 (b) The Parents of this Goddess were *Oceanus* and *Nox*; that is, the fluctuating Change of Things, and the obscure and secret divine Decrees. The Changes of Things are aptly represented by the *Ocean*, on account of its perpetual ebbing and flowing; and secret Providence is justly expressed by

[a] See above, pag 591 § 3.
[b] As she also brought the Author himself. For the Character of *Augustus*, see pag 313. of the present Volume.

by *Night*   Even the *Heathens* have obferved this *Secret* Nemefis *of the Night*; or the difference betwixt divine and human Judgment [a]

4. (c) Wings are given to *Nemefis*, becaufe of the fudden and unforefeen *Her Wings.* changes of things, for, from the earlieft Account of Time, it has been common for great and prudent Men to fall by the Dangers they moft defpifed   Thus *Cicero*, when admonifhed by *Brutus* of the Infidelity and Rancour of *Octavius*, coolly wrote back, " I cannot, however, but be ob- " liged to you, *Brutus*, as I ought, for informing me, tho' of fuch a " trifle "

5. (d) *Nemefis* alfo has her Crown, by reafon of the invidious and malig- *Her Crown.* nant Nature of the Vulgar, who generally rejoice, triumph, and crown her, at the fall of the Fortunate, and the Powerful   (e) And for the Javelin *Javelin.* in her right Hand, it has regard to thofe whom fhe has actually ftruck and transfixed   (f) But whoever efcapes her Stroke, or feels not actual Calamity or Misfortune, fhe affrights with a black and difmal Sight in her left Hand: for doubtlefs, Mortals on the higheft Pinacle of Felicity, have a profpect of Death, Difeafes, Calamities, perfidious Friends, under- mining Enemies, Reverfes of Fortune, &c. reprefented by the *Ethiopians Bottle of* in her Glafs. Thus *Virgil*, with great Elegance, defcribing the Battle of *Ethiopians* *Actium*, fays of *Cleopatra*, that *fhe did not yet perceive the two Afps behind her* [b], but foon after, which way foever fhe turned, fhe faw whole Troops of *Ethiopians* ftill before her

6 (g) Laftly, 'tis fignificantly added, that *Nemefis* rides upon a Stag, *Riding upon a* which is a very long-lived Creature, for tho', perhaps, fome by an untimely *Stag.* Death in Youth, may prevent or efcape this Goddefs, yet they who enjoy a long flow of Happinefs and Power, doubtlefs, become fubject to her at length, and are brought to yield.

VI.

The FABLE *of the* CYCLOPS DEATH; *explained of bafe* COURT-OFFICERS.

The FABLE.

1. 'TIS related that the Cyclops, *for their Savagenefs and The Cyclops Cruelty, were by Jupiter firft thrown into* Tartarus, *and imprifoned, there condemned to perpetual Imprifonment* (a). *but that after-*

[a] ——Cadit Ripheus, juftiffimus unus
  Qui fuit ex Teucris, & feruantiffimus æqui
  Diis aliter vifum
[b] Regina in mediis patrio vocat Agmina fiftro,
  Necdum etiam geminos à tergo refpicit angues.

wards Tellus *perfuaded* Jupiter *it would be for his Service to re-*
leafe them, and employ them in forging Thunder-bolts. (b) *This he*
accordingly did, and they, with unwearied Pains and Diligence,
hammered out his Bolts, and other Inftruments of Terror, with
a frightful and continual Din of the Anvil (c)

2. *It happened long after, that* Jupiter *was difpleafed with*
Æfculapius, *the Son of* Apollo, *for having, by the Art of Medi-*
cine, reftored a dead Man to Life (d) *but concealing his Indig-*
nation, becaufe the Action in it felf was pious and illuftrious;
he fecretly incenfed the Cyclops *againft him, who, without re-*
morfe, prefently flew him with their Thunder-bolts in Revenge
whereof, Apollo, *with* Jupiter's *connivance, fhot them all dead with*
his Arrows (e)

The EXPLANATION.

3 (a) THIS Fable feems to point at the Behaviour of Princes; who
having cruel, bloody, and oppreffive Minifters, firft punifh and
difplace them but afterwards, by the Advice of *Tellus* (b), that is, fome
earthly-minded and ignoble Perfon, employ them again, to ferve a turn,
when there is occafion for Cruelty in Execution, or Severity in Exaction.
(c) but thefe Minifters being bafe in their Nature, whet by their former Difgrace, and well aware of what is expected from them, ufe double Diligence
in their Office, till proceeding unwarily, and over-eager to gain Favour, they
fometimes (d) from the private Nods, and ambiguous Orders of their Prince,
perform fome odious or execrable Action (e) When Princes, to decline the
Envy themfelves, and knowing they fhall never want fuch Tools at their beck,
drop them, and give them up to the Friends and Followers of the injured
Perfon, thus expofing them, as Sacrifices to revenge and popular Odium
whence with great Applaufe, Acclamations, and good Wifhes to the Prince,
thefe Mifcreants at laft meet with their defert.

VII. *The*

VII.

The FABLE *of the* GIANTS *Sister; explained of*
Publick Detraction.

The FABLE.

1. THE *Poets relate, that the* Giants, *produced from the* The Giants
Earth (*a*), *made War upon* Jupiter, *and the other Gods* (*b*); Earth-born.
but were repulsed and conquered by Thunder (*c*): *whereat the*
Earth, *provoked, brought forth* Fame (*d*), *the youngest* Sister *of the*
Giants, *in Revenge for the Death of her* Sons (*e*).

The EXPLANATION.

2. THE Meaning of the *Fable* seems to be this. (*a*) The *Earth* denotes Denote the
the Nature of the Vulgar, who are always swelling, and rising Vulgar, apt
against their Rulers, and endeavouring at Changes (*b*) This Disposition to rebel
getting a fit opportunity, breeds Rebels and Traitors, who, with impetuous
Rage, threaten and contrive the overthrow and destruction of Princes

3 (*c*) And when brought under and subdued, the same vile and restless And spread
Nature of the People, impatient of Peace, (*d*) produces Rumours, De-Rumours and
tractions, Slanders, Libels, &c to blacken those in Authority. (*e*) so that Defamations.
rebellious Actions, and *seditious Rumours* differ not in Origin and Stock, but
only as it were in *Sex*, *Treasons*, and *Rebellions*, being the *Brothers*, and
Scandal, or *Detraction*, the *Sister* ª.

VIII. *The*

ª See the *Essay* upon Seditions and Troubles, Vol II pag 156

VIII.

The FABLE *of* TYPHON; *explained of* REBELLION.

The FABLE.

Juno enraged at Jupiter 1   THE Fable *runs, that* Juno, *enraged at* Jupiter's *bringing forth* Pallas *without her Assistance, incessantly sollicited all the Gods and Goddesses, that she might produce without* Jupiter · *and having by violence and importunity obtained the Grant, she struck the Earth, and thence immediately sprung up* Typhon; *a huge and dreadful Monster, whom she committed to the nursing of a Serpent As soon as he was grown up, this Monster waged War* Typhon takes *on* Jupiter, *and taking him Prisoner in the Battel, carried him* Jupiter Prisoner *away on his Shoulders, into a remote and obscure Quarter and there cutting out the Sinews of his Hands and Feet, he bore them off; leaving* Jupiter *behind miserably maimed and mangled* (a)

Steal his Sinews   2 *But* Mercury *afterwards stole these Sinews from* Typhon; *and restored them to* Jupiter *Hence, recovering his Strength,* Jupi- *The Sinews restored.* ter *again pursues the Monster, first wounds him with a Stroke of his Thunder, when Serpents arose from the Blood of the Wound and* *And Typhon subdued* now *the Monster being dismay'd, and taking to flight,* Jupiter *next darted Mount* Ætna *upon him; and crushed him with the Weight* (b).

The EXPLANATION.

To describe the Fate of Kings 3 (a)   THIS Fable *seems designed to express the various Fates of* Kings, and the turns that Rebellions sometimes take, in Kingdoms. For Princes may be justly esteemed married to their States, as *Jupiter* to *Juno* but it sometimes happens, that being depraved by long wielding of the Scepter; and growing tyrannical, they would engross all to themselves; and slighting the Counsel of their Senators and Nobles, conceive by themselves, that is, govern according to their own arbitrary Will and Pleasure. *And the Rebellion of their Subjects* This inflames the People, and makes them endeavour to create and set up some Head of their own Such Designs are generally set on foot by the secret Motion and Instigation of the Peers and Nobles, under whose connivance the common sort are prepared for rising whence proceeds a *Swell*

III

in the State, which is appositely denoted by the nursing of *Typhon*. This growing Posture of Affairs is fed by the natural Pravity, and malignant Disposition of the Vulgar, which to Kings is an envenomed Serpent. And now the Disaffected uniting their Force, at length break out into open Rebellion; which, producing infinite Mischiefs, both to Prince and People, is represented by the horrid and multiplied Deformity of *Typhon*, with his hundred Heads, denoting the divided Powers, his flaming Mouths, denoting Fire and Devastation, his Girdles of Snakes denoting Sieges and Destruction; his Iron Hands, Slaughter and Cruelty, his Eagles Talons, Rapine and Plunder, his plumed Body, perpetual Rumours, contradictory Accounts, &c. And sometimes these Rebellions grow so high, that Kings are obliged, as if carried on the backs of the Rebels, to quit the Throne; and retire to some remote and obscure part of their Dominions; with the loss of their *Sinews*, both of Money and Majesty.

4. (*b*) But if now they prudently bear this Reverse of Fortune, they may, in a short time, by the assistance of *Mercury*, recover their *Sinews* again, that is, by becoming moderate and affable; reconciling the Minds and Affections of the People to them, by *gracious Speeches*, and *prudent Proclamations*, which will win over the Subject chearfully to afford new Aids and Supplies; and add fresh Vigour to Authority But prudent and wary Princes here seldom incline to try their Fortune by a War; yet do their utmost, by some grand Exploit, to crush the Reputation of the Rebels: and if the Attempt succeeds, the Rebels, conscious of the Wound received, and distrustful of their Cause, first betake themselves to broken and empty Threats, like the *hissings of Serpents*, and next, when matters are grown desperate, to flight. And now, when they thus begin to shrink, 'tis safe and seasonable for Kings to pursue them with their Forces, and the whole Strength of the Kingdom, thus effectually quashing and suppressing them, as it were by the weight of a Mountain [a]

How allay'd and suppressed.

IX.

The FABLE *of* ACHELOUS; *explained of* WAR, *by Invasion.*

The FABLE.

1. THE *Ancients relate, that* Hercules *and* Achelous *being Rivals in the Courtship of* Deianira; *the Matter was contested by single Combat · when* Achelous *having transformed himself,*

The Combat of Hercules and Achelous.

[a] See *Essays*, Vol. II. pag 155—160.

ſelf, as he had Power to do, into various Shapes, by way of Trial, at length, in the form of a fierce wild Bull, prepares himſelf for the Fight (a)   But Hercules ſtill retains his human Shape, engages ſharply with him, and in the iſſue broke off one of the Bull's Horns; and now Achelous in great Pain and Fright, to redeem his Horn, preſents Hercules with the Cornu-copia (b).

The EXPLANATION.

Reſiſting's War in Defenſe,   2 (a) **T**HIS Fable relates to military Expeditions and Preparations for the Preparation of War on the defenſive ſide, here denoted by *Achelous,* appears in various Shapes, whilſt the invading ſide has but one ſimple Form, conſiſting either in an Army, or perhaps a Fleet   But the Country that expects the Invaſion, is employed infinite ways, in fortifying Towns, blockading Paſſes, Rivers, and Ports, raiſing Soldiers, diſpoſing Garriſons, building and breaking down Bridges, procuring Aids; ſecuring Proviſions, Arms, Ammunition, &c   So that there appears a new face of things every day, and at length when the Country is ſufficiently fortified and prepared, it repreſents to the Life, the Form, and Threats of a fierce, fighting Bull

And Offenſive   3 (b) On the other ſide, the Invader preſſes on to the Fight, fearing to be diſtreſſed in an Enemy's Country   And if after the Battel he remains Maſter of the Field, and has now broke, as it were, *the Horn of his Enemy,* the Beſieged, of courſe, retire inglorious, affrighted, and diſmay'd, to their Strong-holds, there endeavouring to ſecure themſelves, and repair their Strength, leaving at the ſame time their Country a Prey to the Conqueror which is well expreſſed by the *Amalthean Horn,* or *Cornu-copia* [a].

29 MR 64

X. *The*

---

[a] The Fable of *Perſeus, explained of War,* ſhould immediately follow this of *Achelous,* but that is already inſerted in the *de Augmentis Scientiarum,* pag 64.

X.

The FABLE *of* DÆDALUS; *explained of Arts and Artists;
in* KINGDOMS *and* STATES.

The FABLE.

1. THE *Ancients have left us a Description of mecha-* Dædalus mur-
nical Skill, Industry, and curious Arts converted to ders his Brother Artist
ill Uses, in the Person of Dædalus, *a most ingenious but exe-*
crable Artist. This Dædalus *was banished for the Murder of his*
brother Artist, and Rival (a), *yet found a kind Reception in*
his Banishment, from the Kings and States where he came (b). Is banished
He raised many incomparable Edifices to the Honour of the Gods,
and invented many new Contrivances for the beautifying and
ennobling of Cities and publick Places; but still he was most
famous for wicked Inventions. Among the rest he contrived the Invents many
Engine for satisfying the monstrous Lust of Pasiphae *with a Bull* , mechanical
Structures.
wherein, by his abominable Industry and destructive Genius, he af-
fisted to the fatal and infamous Production of the Monster Minotaur;
that devourer of promising Youths (c) *And then, to cover one Mif-* His Labyrinth
chief with another, and provide for the Security of this Monster, he in- and the Clue
vented and built a Labyrinth, a Work infamous for its End and De-
sign, but admirable and prodigious for Art and Workmanship (d). *Af-*
ter this, that he might not only be celebrated for wicked Inventions;
but be sought after, as well for Prevention as for Instruments of Mif-
chief; he formed that ingenious Device of his Clue, which led
directly thro' all the windings of the Labyrinth (e). *This* Dæda- Persecuted by
lus *was persecuted by* Minos, *with the utmost Severity, Diligence,* Minos
and Enquiry, but he always found Refuge and means of esca-
ping (f). *Lastly, endeavouring to teach his Son* Icarus *the Art* Teaches Icarus
of flying; the Novice trusting too much to his Wings, fell from to fly.
his towering flight and was drowned in the Sea (g).

The EXPLANATION.

THE Senfe of the Fable runs thus. (a) It firft denotes Envy; which is continually upon the watch, and ftrangely prevails among excellent Artificers, for no kind of People are obferved to be more implacably and deftructively envious to one another than thefe

(b) In the next place, it obferves an impolitick and improvident kind of Punifhment inflicted upon *Dædalus*, that of *Banifhment*, for good Workmen are gladly received every where. fo that Banifhment to an excellent Artificer, is fcarce any Punifhment at all, whereas other Conditions of Life cannot eafily flourifh from home For the admiration of Artifts is propagated and increafed among Foreigners and Strangers; it being a Principle in the Minds of Men, to flight and defpife the mechanical Operators of their own Nation

(c) The fucceeding Part of the Fable is plain, concerning the ufe of mechanick Arts, whereto human Life ftands greatly indebted; as receiving from this Treafury numerous Particulars for the Service of Religion, the Ornament of civil Society, and the whole Provifion and Apparatus of Life: but then the fame Magazine fupplies Inftruments of Luft, Cruelty, and Death For, not to mention the Arts of Luxury and Debauchery, we plainly fee how far the Bufinefs of exquifite Poifons, Guns, Engines of War, and fuch kind of deftructive Inventions, exceeds the Cruelty and Barbarity of the *Minotaur* himfelf

(d) The Addition of the Labyrinth contains a beautiful Allegory, reprefenting the nature of mechanick Arts in general for all ingenious and accurate mechanical Inventions may be conceived as a Labyrinth, which, by reafon of their fubtilty, intricacy, croffing, and interfering with one another, and the apparent refemblances they have among themfelves, fcarce any Power of the Judgment can unravel and diftinguifh, fo that they are only to be underftood and traced by the Clue of Experience ᵃ

(e) 'Tis no lefs prudently added, that he who invented the windings of the Labyrinth, fhould alfo fhew the Ufe and Management of the *Clue* for mechanical Arts have an ambiguous or double Ufe, and ferve as well to produce as to prevent Mifchief and Deftruction, fo that their Virtue almoft deftroys or unwinds it felf

(f) Unlawful Arts, and indeed frequently Arts themfelves, are perfecuted by *Minos*, that is, by Laws, which prohibit and forbid their Ufe among the People but notwithftanding this, they are hid, concealed, retained, and every where find reception and fculking-places, a thing well obferved by

---

ᵃ In this light we are to confider all the Furniture and Apparatus of Shops, Warehoufes and Magazines.

by *Tacitus* of the *Astrologers* and *Fortune-tellers* of his Time. These, says he, *are a kind of Men that will always be prohibited, and yet will always be retained in our City*

8 (g) But lastly, all unlawful and vain Arts, of what kind soever, lose *Unlawful or* their Reputation in tract of time ; grow contemptible and perish, thro' their *vain Arts,* over-confidence, like *Icarus* , being commonly unable to perform what *how best sup-* they boasted   And to say the truth, such Arts are better suppressed by *pressed* their own vain Pretensions, than checked or restrained by the bridle of Laws [a].

   [a] The Author's *Essays* are Writings nearly of the same kind with the present, tho' more reserved, and guarded   Indeed, he scarce seems any where to speak his Sentiments with so great Freedom and Perspicuity, as under the *Pretext*, or *Intention*, of exp'aining these *ancient Fables* For which Reason, this Piece may deserve to be the more read, by such as desire to understand the rest of his Works.

The End of the First Volume.

Lightning Source UK Ltd.
Milton Keynes UK
UKOW05f1910050915

258084UK00014B/903/P